Brown and Blue and Greek

A history of fraternities, sororities, and early student organizations at Tufts University

Charles J. Trantanella

Outside front cover: Members of the Tufts Commons Club pose in front of their house at 890 Broadway Avenue, Somerville, May 29, 1922. Tufts University Archives, Melville S. Munro papers, MS036.001.007.00001

Inside front cover: Chi Omega members pose at the bottom of the hill in front of Ballou Hall, April 6, 1924. Tufts University Archives, Melville S. Munro papers, MS036.001.005.00001

Back cover, top: Studio portrait of the women of Alpha Kappa Gamma during the 1903–04 school year. Tufts University Archives, Historical materials collection, 1819-07-03-2012, Loose prints, 1819-07-03-2009-04-09, UA136.002.DO.03975.

Back cover, bottom: Sigma Nu fraternity house, 92 Professors Row, winter of 1989. Author's photograph.

Publisher's Cataloging-in-Publication data

Names: Trantanella, Charles J., author.
Title: Brown and blue and Greek : a history of fraternities, sororities, and early student organizations at Tufts University / Charles J. Trantanella.
Description: Includes bibliographical references and index. | Charles J. Trantanella: Westford, MA, 2017.
Identifiers: ISBN 978-0-9986013-0-4
Subjects: LCSH Tufts University–Greek letter societies. | Tufts University–History. | BISAC HISTORY / Social History
Classification: LCC LD5393 .T73 2017 | DDC 378.7444–dc23

Printed on acid free paper in the United States of America by Walch Printing, Portland, Maine 04103

All inquiries, omissions, and errata should be sent care of the author at tranti@comcast.net

To my wife Valerie, my children Emily and Ben,

and to the memory of three outstanding gentlemen I might never have known, had it not been for Sigma Nu:

Lionell Dozier, ZH472

Adam Metry, ZH474

Jim Gyuro, EA1216

Contents

Illustrations

PREFACE

To begin, I'd like to repeat a phrase I heard so many times throughout this project, one that is wholly true for me. I never thought I'd join a fraternity. After all, my knowledge of such organizations had been shaped poorly at a young age, ironically by a very influential fraternity man: my sixth grade teacher, Mr. DeBrisco. The year, so long removed, was 1978. Mr. DeBrisco was a twenty-something rookie teacher with a six-foot frame that induced a real fear among us kids that first day of school. But soon we all adored him, for he was a brilliant teacher. His enthusiasm rang loudest during story time, when he either read from a favorite book or told a personal anecdote. The story I remember most vividly involved his college fraternity. Thanks to the publicity surrounding the movie *Animal House*, I had at least heard the word "fraternity," but the concept was mostly foreign to me, so I didn't really understand what he was talking about. Then, he began describing "hell week." My ears perked up, for it wasn't every day that my teacher said a bad word in class. This week-long event, he told us, was the last barrier he and his fellow pledges had to cross before initiation, and it was anything but pleasant. The rite of passage culminated with the eating of a sandwich made from various deli meats, multiple slices of bread, conflicting condiments, and, to top everything off, goldfish. Only these were not the fun little crackers. No, these were shiny, wiggling goldfish, the kind so often confined to clear glass bowls and then, sadly, the toilet. Mr. DeBrisco wasn't a fan of this seafood delicacy, and he watched in horror as each pledge before him choked down a few of the critters in absolute disgust. However, the wait gave him time to foment a plan. When his turn arrived, he carefully let each fish slither into his mouth, then feigned choking for a few seconds until told to spit the doomed guppy into the trash. His ruse worked. Shortly thereafter he was accepted into his fraternity as a brother, despite never swallowing a goldfish. Regardless, I was horrified.

My fear of fraternities only grew stronger a few years later when I saw the movie *Fraternity Row*. I stumbled onto this cinematic classic one Saturday afternoon, and as I watched, I immediately made the connection between the pledge experiences depicted on the screen, and Mr. DeBrisco's goldfish story. So of course, it was upsetting to watch when, at the end of the movie (spoiler alert), the main character chokes to death while trying to swallow some unsavory food. I sensed an awful pattern here in fraternities and decided such organizations were not for me. Then, I came to Tufts. From day one the fraternities and their houses were hard to miss, as were their reputations: Delta Upsilon was the football house, Delta Tau Delta was the rich house, 123 (Theta Delta Chi) was the party house, Zeta Psi was the rugby house, and so on. None seemed all that appealing to me in terms of joining, but, like most freshmen, all seemed interesting from a social life perspective. In other words, I wanted to go to a fraternity party and see what the hype was all about. Somehow one of my friends garnered some invitations to a Theta Chi event a few weeks into the semester, so one Saturday night I tagged along with my posse and headed inside. The party was hot, loud, and crowded – pretty much everything I expected. But, I did manage to have some fun that night, even if my attempts at playing beer pong resulted in nothing but laughter from the Theta Chi brothers. In the weeks that followed, I went to a few more fraternity parties, and while overall they were enjoyable, I still wasn't sure I wanted to join one of the chapters on campus.

Everything changed when I went home for semester break. Among my high school friends, more than a few were wearing pledge pins, while others still had become full-fledged fraternity brothers or sorority sisters. All seemed to be generally excited about their involvement in Greek life, and many asked if I, too, was thinking of joining one. One friend in particular at Washington & Lee University told me how he'd joined Sigma Nu. Sigma Nu? "Hey, they have a chapter at Tufts," I told him, "though I haven't been to their house yet, and I don't know any of the brothers." "You should check it out," he replied. "Sigma Nu's a strong national, especially in the South and West. Their headquarters are just down the street from my chapter house." Hmmm.

A few weeks later, I went back to school for the spring semester and began to think, seriously, about this fraternity idea. Recruitment season was ramping up, with advertisements for rush parties appearing all over campus, and to be honest, the events looked like a lot of fun – Mexican food night, international beer tasting, semi-formal cocktail party, beach luau – a veritable cornucopia of social options, all free. I was not the only one intrigued by such possibilities. Many of my fellow freshmen were interested in joining a fraternity, as enthusiasm for Greek life was on a definite upswing. Then one night, some guys in my dorm asked one of my roommates if he wanted to come to a Sigma Nu rush party. He said "yes," and then quickly roped me into going with him, since he didn't want to arrive solo. We walked the quarter mile from our dorm to the Sigma Nu house and stepped through the front door for the first time. Greeting us were a bunch of brothers who shook our hands, bade us welcome to Sigma Nu, and then offered us a beer. With little self-confidence, backed by a huge fear of walking into the unknown, I had visions of being shunted into a side room just like Pinto and Flounder in the opening scene of *Animal House*, where I would be summarily ignored until I got the message and left. But that didn't happen. Instead, Sigma Nu brothers came up to my roommate and me, asking where we were from, our course of study, hobbies, all the normal get-to-know-you stuff. Within ten minutes, I'd left my roommate behind and was heavily involved in a conversation with one Sigma Nu brother, Curt, about cross-country running, as I was on the Tufts team, and he'd run competitively in high school. As the conversation progressed, he told me quite a bit about Sigma Nu as a national organization, and how it had been founded just after the Civil War as a protest against hazing. "We take our history very seriously," Curt told me, "and we don't haze here." This impressed me, for many of my friends who'd joined other fraternities had, indeed, been put through some rough hazing, and I didn't see the point of such madness. Then, Curt mentioned he was the president, or Commander, of the chapter. "Really?" I said, my freshman insecurities shining through. "Why, does that surprise you?" he answered, wondering if I was insulting him with my remark. "Oh no!" I said. "I just figured a fraternity president would be too important to talk to a freshman. I didn't expect you to be so cool!" Curt laughed, and invited me to come back a second night to another rush party. I accepted without hesitation, for I was starting to realize a fraternity was nothing like I'd seen in the movies. Instead, it was something I could accept.

I proceeded to become a constant fixture in the Sigma Nu house during rush week, meeting and talking to as many brothers as I could each night. All were truly remarkable people. I met poets, pre-meds, musicians, athletes, intellectuals, partiers, comedians, slackers, dreamers, and a host of other descriptors, all guys I likely never would have met otherwise. Those in the chapter fit not a single stereotype. But together, they were Sigma Nu. And at the end of rush week, they offered me a bid to join their brotherhood. The ensuing conversation with my parents was a bit awkward, as they were worried I'd be subject to all sorts of hazing and demeaning behavior should I accept (if memory serves me correctly, I had watched *Fraternity Row* with my father). I assured them I would not. A few days later, they let me make the final call. I accepted my bid to join Sigma Nu.

The pledging ceremony took place shortly thereafter. Myself and three other "bid acceptors" were told to arrive at the house at seven o'clock in coat and tie, knock once, and then enter one at a time when called by name. Soon enough came my turn. The door opened, and standing first in the hallway to greet me was Dylan, a brother I'd talked with quite a bit during rush week. So of course, upon seeing him, I smiled and said "hello." The ultra-stern look on his face told me he wanted nothing of my pleasantries. Here come the goldfish, I thought. But nothing of the sort happened. Instead, he told me there would be no hazing, but that I and my fellow bid acceptors would be put through a ritual pledging ceremony, one we should take seriously, for what we were about to go through was considered secret. The ensuing ceremony was fascinating; I had never experienced anything like it. Then, when it ended, I was pinned as a pledge of Sigma Nu.

I spent the next few months getting to know all of the brothers in the chapter. I ate dinner at the chapter house every night, wore my pledge pin (almost) without fail, washed dishes, cleaned every corner of the abode, played endless games of foosball, and went to parties big and small on the weekends (if not an occasional weeknight). I also met, once a week, with my fellow pledges and our Pledge Marshal, Mike, a senior in charge of getting us through the program and fully initiated. Our course of study began by memorizing the Greek alphabet and the locations of all other Sigma Nu chapters in New England, if not the rest of the country. We also discussed the history of fraternities in general, starting with Phi Beta Kappa, the Union Triad, the Miami Triad, Sigma Nu, and then our own Zeta Eta chapter, which had been first organized some thirty-five years earlier. I also met alumni, especially at the annual White Rose Formal in downtown Boston, and got to put faces to the legendary names I'd heard about. But most importantly, as the days and weeks went by, I came to see the Sigma Nu chapter house as my home, a place I could walk into any time, day or night, and be among friends. Opening the front door might lead me to a group of guys studying in the chapter room, or others playing foosball, or some watching reruns of *Family Ties* on television, or a few getting out their guitars to jam, or a bunch planning a late night trip into Chinatown for some cheap food. Life at Sigma Nu was nothing I had expected. Instead, it was better than I could have imagined.

I became an official Sigma Nu the day classes ended in the spring semester of 1986. The initiation ceremony was even more intricate than the pledging one, and I was enthralled by the words and idyllic symbolism of the ritual, created by the founders of Sigma Nu over a century earlier. From there, I became an enthusiastic member of my fraternity, remaining active throughout the rest of my undergraduate career. After finishing at Tufts, I headed to the University of Arizona for graduate school and affiliated with my fraternity's Epsilon Alpha chapter, for I wanted to continue the experience. My two chapters were quite different in many respects, with Arizona being much larger in terms of the size of the brotherhood and the chapter house. But both chapters were filled with men I was proud to call my friends, my brothers. Years later I became a chapter advisor to the group at Tufts, where again, I got to know some remarkable undergraduates. These days, I don't see enough of any of my brothers on a regular basis, but I cherish the time we've spent together and hope for more.

OF COURSE, THAT'S ONLY HALF THE STORY of how I arrived at this book, for thousands of Tufts men and women have had similar experiences, yet only a miniscule few have put pen to paper on the topic. Just over a decade ago, when my daughter was a toddler, she would often direct me to draw chalk figures in our driveway of her favorite characters from the animated series *Arthur*. I am not much of an artist, but luckily my depictions of Arthur, D.W., Binky,

Buster, and the rest of the crew were good enough to capture her imagination. After drawing the same figures each afternoon, though, I began to look for ways to make things more interesting for me. So one day, just for fun, I drew some Greek letters on Arthur's shirt, as if to suggest he was in a fraternity. My daughter liked the funny-shaped letters, so I kept drawing them on Arthur and his buddies, sometimes using combinations of actual national organizations like Sigma Nu and Gamma Phi Beta, other times using random letters that looked interesting together like Psi Delta Phi. Repeating this ritual each day got me thinking back on my own fraternity experiences as an undergraduate, and how much I had enjoyed learning the history of my own and other national organizations. Eventually I channeled this interest into a late night research project. I obtained a list of all the national fraternities from the North American Interfraternity Conference website, and set about documenting when and where they were first founded, how many active chapters they currently had on their rosters, and any other interesting facts I might find, such as if they had ever merged with another organization. I worked on this project for about a year with no real goal other than personal enjoyment. Then, I put it aside and went on to other things.

Years later, in the summer of 2010, I stumbled across the Tufts website and noticed the archivists had started digitizing many of the school's records, especially old photographs of the campus. I was immediately drawn to the century-old pictures of Professors Row, which showed these glorious, Victorian houses amidst a strikingly barren backdrop, certainly not the urban landscape we know as Medford and Somerville today. I loved the pictures of my old chapter house at 92 Professors Row, a house that generally looks the same as it did in the late 1800s. But other houses were just as fascinating. For weeks I poured through these pictures, looking earnestly through every corner of the digital archives lest I miss even one. Then, one day, I stumbled across a photo of the Phi Sigma Kappa house at Tufts from the late 1950s. Phi Sigma Kappa? I knew of the organization from my earlier research, but I never knew the fraternity had placed a chapter at Tufts. Soon enough, I found a few more "unknowns" (at least to me) – Sigma Tau Alpha, Beta Tau, Delta Zeta, Sigma Kappa – all now dormant, with only small, tantalizing bits of their digital history to examine. My curiosity got the best of me, so I kept digging, wondering if I could learn more details about these long lost fraternities and sororities. I found Professor Miller's book from the 1950s, *Light on the Hill*, and Alaric Start's book from the 1890s, *History of Tufts College*, and while these books had some great information on many of the Greek-letter organizations at Tufts, they were woefully short in documenting all. So, one night while reflecting on my unsatisfied curiosity, I made what I considered (at the time) to be a calm, rational decision. I vowed to gather all the information I could about these organizations and write my own book, one that told a succinct story of each and every fraternity and sorority that had ever been at Tufts. I'd focus my research on the quantifiable, such as the date each chapter started, where they had a house on campus, how many members they'd had, and the years they were active. Additionally, I'd look to gather a few tidbits about the goals and aims of each organization, maybe even some old composite photographs or pictures of the insignia. I envisioned putting all of this in an oversized coffee-table type book, one printed with glossy paper and made to be work of art. And best of all, I figured this project would take no longer than nine months to complete. Oh, the folly of inexperience! Alas, here I am, seven years later, finally finished.

I have no one to blame for the timeframe but myself. No deadlines, coupled with an obsessive desire to learn as much as I could, left me the freedom to pursue stories well beyond their logical conclusion, in hopes I would find another. I so often did. The tales I gathered about Greek life at Tufts College and Tufts University led me to change my focus, from the merely quantifiable to the all-important human element. I became particularly interested in why the various organizations came together and why they went away, for those that indeed have gone dormant. In addition, I was fascinated by the turning points within each organization, those moments throughout the years that had a profound impact on the life of the chapter or the greater Tufts campus, for better or worse. As for scope, I wanted to understand all Greek organizations that have ever had a Tufts undergraduate among their active membership. Early on, though, I did set some research limits. I decided to exclude the Greek-letter honor societies such as Phi Beta Kappa (though its original history as a social fraternity is discussed), since these groups are not social in nature and tend to have little history beyond lists of honorees. I also decided to exclude the professional fraternities at the Tufts Medical and Dental schools such as Phi Delta Epsilon, as these organizations are outside my own experience; no doubt these groups have a wonderful history, but I wanted to focus on undergraduate student life.

Once I'd set the basic framework and had gathered significant research material, I started writing, and soon realized I needed to focus my words. Originally I intended some level of discussion on the routine – each and every chapter holds meetings, recruits new members, organizes social events big and small, participates in philanthropy and community service, interacts with the Tufts administration, and ultimately looks to continue for another year. Writing about such normalcy for every organization, though, soon became deathly boring for me, so I assumed it would be even worse for you, the reader. As a result, I decided to focus words, where appropriate, on the exception and the extraordinary within each chapter, and leave the reader to assume there is the every day in every organization that runs continuously in the background. I break this rule at times, especially when discussing the older organizations, since chapter life, if not student life in general, has certainly changed over the years, and looking back at the way things used to be has been a lot of fun. In taking this overall approach, I believe I tell a story not just of Greek life at Tufts, but of student life in general, in a manner and scope unlike any other.

SO WHAT IS A FRATERNITY OR SORORITY? Simply put (at least in my opinion), a group of friends who wish to be something more. Helping to strengthen this bond is the literal, a constitution to define and a set of by-laws to govern the organization. But just as crucial is the symbolic, accomplished through the use of identifying symbols (most often Greek letters) and, most importantly, a ritual. The ceremonial words within the ritual, considered secret in nearly every organization (Delta Upsilon being a noted exception), and often crafted by the original founders, are repeatedly spoken together in meetings and initiations, to remind all members of their core values, and that they should be working to better themselves, and those around them, through their participation. Also in this message is a mandate to come together, to share with each other the social experience that is collegiate undergraduate life. But of course, the symbolic is fraught with reality. There are bills to pay and chapter houses to run and university rules to follow and activities to plan and problems to solve. There is also a need to work as a group and come to a consensus on issues, even when faced with a wide range of opinions that make compromise painfully difficult, if not impossible. But, in these instances of conflict there are unique chances to learn and grow, both as an individual and as a group.

OUR STORY STARTS with a brief introduction of how Tufts College came to be, followed in Chapter 1 by a broad history of fraternities and sororities in the United States. Next, Chapter 2 presents a discussion of some of the earliest student organizations at Tufts. While technically not fraternities, these groups were vital to the development of Tufts as a college campus. They were experiments in many ways, as students searched for organized social interaction outside the classroom. That these organizations died out, while the Greek-letter fraternities did not, is an interesting phenomenon. Next comes the heart of the book. Chapters 3 and 4 deal with the social fraternities and sororities, respectively, where "social" refers to those organizations most familiar to college students. These are the ones with houses on campus that tend to provide a social outlet for students. Chapter 5 presents the stories of the historically black, Latino, and multicultural Greek-letter organizations, some of which have been in operation for more than a century. While not as visible to the average student walking around campus due to their lack of a chapter house, these organizations are just as important to their members and the greater Tufts community. Chapter 6 deals with four stories that speak of larger issues within the Greek community, stories that transcended time and place. Some of these are controversial; all are interesting. Finally, Chapter 7 presents some general thoughts on the current state and future of Greek life at Tufts.

To close, I will say this about my work: there is no unifying thesis built into these words. I am not trying to prove any point or argue any hypothesis. Instead, this is a documentary of what has happened, put through the filter of my own experiences, intellect, and writing style. I am undoubtedly a supporter of Greek-letter organizations, for my own experience was overwhelmingly positive. I also know they are far from perfect, and in their past mistakes (many of which are discussed) there is certainly enough fodder for those who argue against their continuance. Perhaps what I've written could be considered fair and balanced, perhaps not. Either way, I feel this is an honest record of Greek life at Tufts University.

ACKNOWLEDGEMENTS

The summer after my freshman year of college (when I was a newly minted Sigma Nu brother), I worked for Sono Record and Book Exchange in downtown Norwalk, Connecticut, a retail store filled with an eclectic assortment of media to read, watch, and listen. Don't look for it now, the store (as well as the used record industry) went out of business decades ago. But back in the day, Sono Record and Book was a fun place to snoop around for old vinyl treasures. One of the perks of the job was looking through the albums people brought to trade or sell before our customers could get their hands on them. Thoughts of finding a rare Beatles record with the coveted apple pressing always filled my mind each time I thumbed through a new stack of vinyl. Of course, I never did find anything worth real money, as most people's collections contained only poor excuses for sonic masterpieces. However, I did find something else. One day someone brought in an album by the 60s psychedelic artist Donovan, and though I don't remember the specific words per se, I do remember the gist of the liner notes: "I have no one to thank for this album but myself. I wrote all the songs, played all the instruments, and recorded all the parts. This album is entirely my creation." I am still struck by the arrogance of this statement, because so little in this world is accomplished at the hands of just one person. This book is a prime example. I did not create this on my own. Instead, I have a lot of people to thank, for without them, this story would never have been written.

FIRST AND FOREMOST, I would like to thank the archivists and librarians who provided so much help with my research. Topping the list are the folks in the Tufts University Digital Collections and Archives. I am forever grateful to Susanne Belovari, Erin Faulder, Molly Bruce, Sarah Gustafson, Morgan VanClief, Dan Santamaria, Pam Hopkins, Rose Oliveira, and the entire staff for providing access to a world of material. From scanning old photographs, to hauling out materials from deep within the archives on numerous occasions, to pointing me in directions I never knew existed, I have enjoyed our interactions immensely. It has been a pleasure and a privilege to work with these keepers of history. Next, I am indebted to the archivists at the University of Illinois at Urbana-Champaign, including Denise Rayman, Lindy Smith, Lisa Renee Kemplin, Rory Grennan, Linda Stahnke, Angela Jordan, Leanna Barcelona, Anna Trammell, and Megan Toups. Over the years, these archivists have answered every question, tracked down every obscure article, and uncovered more history than I could have imagined. Additionally, I would like to thank Jason Tomberlin and Samantha Crisp from the University of North Carolina-Chapel Hill, and Bernadette Siddiqi from New York University, for their help with questions on the founders of the Zeta Psi fraternity. For assistance with research into Heth Aleph Res, I would like to thank Eric Biddy from the Meadville Theological School. To Dina Kellams and Bradley Cook at Indiana University, I am thankful for their help understanding a controversial football game that Tufts played nearly a century ago. At the University of Massachusetts-Amherst, Anne L. Moore provided a wealth of information regarding the educational path of Jester Hairston. Finally, I would like to thank Heather Halliday and the archivists at the American Jewish Historical Society in New York City for photocopying hundreds of pages related to the Phi Epsilon Pi fraternity.

Next on the list are the alumni of Tufts University. When I first started, I never intended to interview alumni, as I was not sure their voices would add substantially to the work. Even more so, I had never conducted a personal interview in my life, and the thought of doing so was terrifying. However, early on I hit a number of dead ends in my research, so I reached out to two alumni in particular to help fill some voids. The first was Jack Erickson (ΨΥ), a friend and fellow baseball coach here in Westford, Massachusetts. The second was Tony Bove (ΦΣΚ/25 Whitfield), an alumnus I found through the power of Google. Both told me stories of their experiences that made me realize there was more to history than what was captured in newspaper articles and old yearbooks. There was the human side that offered context and understanding. Soon after speaking with Jack and Tony, I decided to reach out to at least a few alumni from each organization, especially those who were active at the time of a turning point, and just listen. About two-thirds of those I asked did not respond, and I can hardly blame them. After all, my introductory email came out of nowhere, and I knew I was asking questions some might not want to discuss. However, to those who did respond, I am forever grateful for their help, encouragement, and information.

In order of organization, I'd like to thank: Alan Sugarman, Alanna Tuller, Kevin Lowther, Phil Primack, Robert Hayden, Tom Hart, Jayne Kraft Haymon (Alethea), Benjamin Cohen (ΑΕΠ), Tom Fantini (ΑΕΠ/Nichols House), Fred Fierst (ΑΕΠ), Michael Gitten (ΑΕΠ), Michael Leven (ΑΕΠ), Miles Rubin (ΑΕΠ/Nichols House), Lowell Thomas (ΑΕΠ/Nichols House), Sarah Shrewsbury (Nichols House), Saundria Chase Gray (ΑΚΑ), Robin Scott-Hawkins (ΑΚΑ), Jean Lawler Cohen (ΑΟΠ), Meredith Kaplan Stoma (ΑΟΠ), Ellen Sullivan Gaudiano (ΑΦ), Sheri O'Boyle Montgomery (ΑΦ), Nancy Shalowitz (ΑΦ), Daniel Darlington (ΑΦΑ), Namsoo Dunbar (ΑΦΑ), Mark Wasielewski (ΑΦΔ), Valerie Avila (ΑΡΛ), John Budris (ΑΣΦ), Bill Gehling (ΑΣΦ), Jeffrey Kleeger (ΑΣΦ), George Haug (ΑΤΩ), Robert McLaughlin, Sr. (ΑΤΩ), Bill Mintz (ΑΤΩ), Jack Obadia (ΑΤΩ), Linford Stiles (ΑΤΩ), Norma Pereira Atkinson (ΑΞΔ/Alethea), Nadine Ullmann Brozan (ΑΞΔ/Alethea), Nancy Potter (ΑΞΔ), Kevin Callahan (ATO of Massachusetts), Amy Friedlander (ATO of Massachusetts), David Lindstedt (ATO of Massachusetts), Maurene Golden (ΧΩ), Christina Rush (ΧΩ), Susan Mosny Steed (ΧΩ), Lisa Romeo Thompson (ΧΩ), Pam Mosny Veasy (ΧΩ), Gael McTammany Casner (Delta Tau Delta little sister), Allan Clemow (ΔΤΔ), John Kubisch (ΔΤΔ), Thomas O'Brien (ΔΤΔ), Bill Anderson (ΛΥ), Paula Rivituso Itaya (ΔΖ), Greg Matthews (Kippie House), Leo 'Chip' Roche (Kippie House), and Glenn Garcia (ΛΥΛ).

Continuing: Christopher Bennett (ΩΨΦ), David Carl (ΩΨΦ), Harry Lightfoot (ΩΨΦ), Eric Walker (ΦΒΣ), Tom Baer (ΦΕΠ), Dennis Burnham (ΦΕΠ), Brooks Johnson (ΦΕΠ), Richard Levine (ΦΕΠ), Neil Peck (ΦΕΠ), Chet Webster (ΦΕΠ), Steve Trinward (ΦΣΚ), Kristina Brown Brunelle (ΦΣΣ), Gayle Pitman (ΦΣΣ), Mark McGillivray (ΨΥ), Tom Snarsky (ΨΥ), Daniel Walsh (ΨΥ), Terrie Williams Schachter (Thalia), Audrey Saperstein Shapiro (ΣΚ/Thalia), Cindy Vide (ΣΚ), Vanessa Salazar (ΣΛΥ), John Harrington (ΣΝ), DeWitt Peterson (ΣΝ), Ted Snowe (ΣΝ), Robert Stern (ΣΝ), Stephen Viegas (ΣΝ), Daniel Walter (ΣΝ), Pablo Carbonell (ΣΦΕ), Ken Languedoc (ΣΦΕ), Burt Grossman (ΤΕΦ), Lewis Smoler (ΤΕΦ), Musawwir Martin Spiegel (ΤΕΦ), Earle Yaffa (ΤΕΦ), Barbara Haroian Solakian (Thalia), Ed Farley (ΒΧ/ΘΧ), Ron Grant (ΒΧ/ΘΧ), Leo Greenberg (ΘΧ), Warren 'Biff' Manhard (ΒΧ/ΘΧ), John Reid (ΒΧ/ΘΧ), Tom Rockett (ΒΧ/ΘΧ), David Lincoln (ΘΔΧ), Bill Cummings (ΘΔΘ/ΦΣΚ), Bruce Gordon (ΘΔΘ), Corey Ackerman (ΖΒΤ), Hugh Bassewitz (ΖΒΤ), David Lickstein (ΖΒΤ), and Eric Shapiro (ΖΒΤ). Finally, I would also like to recognize a few alumni who provided information but asked to remain anonymous.

Not to be outdone were the faculty and administrators of Tufts University, who were generous with their time and their encouragement. In this regard, I would like to thank Tufts President Anthony Monaco; Professor Sol Gittleman, with whom I've had numerous discussions on the history of Tufts, all of which have been informative and educational. I only wish I'd taken one of his classes while an undergraduate; Dean of Students Bruce Reitman, who spoke with me for hours on two occasions and provided one of the best quotes of the entire project (see the section on Delta Zeta Delta); Director of Fraternity and Sorority Life Su McGlone; Professor Stephen Bailey, who offered insight into his committee's efforts to reform the Greek system in the early 1990s; Bruce Ketchen, the long time manager of Walnut Hill Properties, which owns many of the fraternity houses; Joe Golia, Director of Student Activities and a classmate of mine from high school; David Brittan, former editor of *Tufts* magazine, who published a story I wrote on the Heth Aleph Res fraternity; John Wolfson, current editor of *Tufts* magazine, who published a story on the 1916 football team; and Mini Jaikumar, Daniel Coleman, Sondra Szymczak, Alexandra Dunk, and the rest of the Traditions committee of the Tufts Alumni office, who invited me on numerous occasions to present my research to the Traditions committee.

I am also indebted to many within the national fraternity and sorority community for graciously searching their archives for small pieces of obscure information, such as articles from the late 1800s or initiate dates of long lost members. In order of organization, and with their respective names and positions when we spoke, I'd like to thank:

ΑΕΠ: Ann Atkinson, Director of Communications; and James Fleischer, Chief Operating Officer.

ΑΟΠ: Mariellen Sasseen, Editor of *To Dragma,* who provided some wonderful information on the earliest history of the Alpha Delta Sigma sorority.

ΑΦ: Jenny Thompson, Archivist.

ΑΣΦ: Robert W. Kutz, Grand Historian.

ΑΤΩ: Matt DeWolfe, Director of Marketing and Communications; and Wynn Smiley, Chief Executive Officer. I am especially grateful to Mr. Smiley for allowing me access to archival materials related to Gamma Beta's operations in the early 1970s.

ΑΞΔ: Lauren Blankenbaker Felts, Director of Communications and Marketing, who provided me with a copy of the 1906 petition from Tau Epsilon Sigma, the oldest petition I was able to examine.

ΒΘΠ: Martin Cobb, Director of Communication; and Tim Herrmann, Associate Editor, *The Beta Theta Pi.*

ΧΩ: Whitney Heckathorne, Director of Communications.

ΔΤΔ: Brook Pritchett, Director of Communications.

ΦΔΘ: Laurie Rosenberger, Assistant to the Executive Vice President.

ΦΓΔ: Towner Blackstock.

ΠΒΦ: Eily Cummings, Director of Marketing and Communications; and Juli Holmes Willeman, Executive Director.

ΠΛΦ: Andy Golbert; and Ian Lowe, Director of Chapter Operations.

ΣΝ: Barbara Hunter; Jon Sprenger, Associate Vice President; and Brad Beacham, Executive Director.

ΣΦΕ: Gay-Lynn Carpenter, Communications Director.

ΣΣΣ: Carol Gregory Swango, Archivist.

ΘΧ: Kelly Jones, Assistant Editor of *The Rattle*; and Bart Zino, Director of Communication.

ΘΔΧ: William A. McClung, Executive Director; and Adam McCready, who provided a wealth of archival material and old photographs of Kappa charge.

ΖΨ: David Hunter, Executive Director.

I also relied on the expertise and help from a number of folks outside the collegiate world of Greek letter organizations. A big thank you to: Barbara Vitale, my friend and fellow Deacon at First Parish Church, for providing the Latin translations quoted within the text; Jennifer Gravley and author Michael Shay, for fielding questions on General Edwards and his honorary induction into the Beta Tau fraternity; Edward Gordon, who wrote a short history on some early fraternity houses in Somerville; Rabbi Shoshana Perry and her colleagues for their help in attempting to decode the secret meaning of Heth Aleph Res. We were not successful in this venture, but the discussions were a whole lot of fun; author Marianne Sanua, for her help in understanding the Jewish fraternity and sorority movement; Shira Kohn, for the numerous discussions we had on the Alpha Epsilon Phi organization; Angela Harkness, my friend and lawyer who helped untangle some legal issues surrounding the take over of 106 Professors Row by the Tufts administration; Sarah and Jason Snow, two researchers who uncovered the story of Jan Rosenbach, the refugee student who fled Nazi Europe for Tufts and the Phi Epsilon Pi house in 1941; and Howard Mumm, who provided a wealth of information on 2LT Bob Atlas, a Tufts graduate and AEPi member who was killed in World War II.

I owe a mountain of gratitude and praise to the reviewers of the manuscript. First up is Professor Emeritus Douglas Hodgkin of Bates College, who provided me with a great framework early on in this project and offered numerous suggestions in the years that followed, all of which only made my work better. Professor Hodgkin is a renowned political scientist, teacher, author, mentor, Maine historian, and my father-in-law. Next is Fran Becque, the Historian and Archivist of the Pi Beta Phi fraternity. Fran is a long time advocate of fraternity history, and runs the blog "Focus on Fraternity History & More." She was kind enough to publish a short article I wrote on the history of the Heth Aleph Res fraternity a few years ago, the first words from this book I let out to the world. Then, Bob McCully, the Grand Historian of Sigma Nu, who also sent along a wealth of material relating to the establishment of my own Zeta Eta chapter at Tufts. Our conversations relating to Sigma Nu history in general have been wonderful as well. Last but not least is Bill Briscoe, Historian of Delta Upsilon, who also provided some wonderful information on the earliest days of the fraternity's Tufts chapter, including photographs of the first chapter house in all of its Victorian glory.

Finally, I would like to thank my family. To my wife Valerie, and my children Emily and Ben, thank you for all those discussions we had about "my Baird's project" over dinner, and supporting me every step of the way. I also owe much of the book design to Emily and Ben, whose artistic talents far outweigh mine. To my parents, Sheilagh Trantanella and the late Charles Trantanella, Jr., thank you for trusting in me to make my own decision about pledging Sigma Nu. As far as my love of history, I believe I owe this to my mom. Her life-long fascination with the human side of the Civil War in particular taught me there is more to history than names, places, and dates. History is about people and what they choose to do with the time they are given. Last but not least, to my brothers in the Zeta Eta and Epsilon Alpha chapters of Sigma Nu, thank you for helping shape an experience I never could have imagined, but one for which I am eternally grateful.

Brown and Blue and Greek

INTRODUCTION

"What, Charles, do you intend to do with that bleak hill over in Medford?"

The hill was a small piece of farmland in Medford that Charles Tufts, a prominent businessman from nearby Charlestown, had acquired through inheritance, and the question was one posed by his relatives. Originally called Walnut Tree Hill due to a preponderance of a certain type of flora, the hill by the early 1800s had been clear-cut for farmland and pasture. From its top, one had great views of Boston, Cambridge and Harvard, the Bunker Hill monument, numerous church spires, and varied landscapes from rivers to marshes to the ocean. With such an inspiring panorama, the hill's description as being "bleak" must have referred to some other aspect of the property that, over time, had given the Tufts family great pause. Perhaps the hill was not the best for farming, or perhaps it looked rather unsightly from their family home. Either way, Charles Tufts could see a potential in the space. As legend has it, he answered his family's blunt question with the immortal response, "I will put a light on it." As for what that light would be, no one was really sure, but opportunity eventually came knocking. In 1840, prominent members of the Universalist church in Massachusetts began working to establish a new seminary to train "young men for the gospel ministry." Universalism as a religious movement was nearing the high point of its popularity in America, but as an institution it lagged other mainline Protestant religions for it did not have a presence in the world of higher education. Now, the Universalists were ready to make the leap. Charles Tufts, a prominent member of the First Universalist Society in Charlestown, quickly donated his bleak hill for the cause, and the establishment of the Walnut Hill Evangelical Seminary was underway. But ultimately, the school was not to be. The Universalists were unable to build such an enterprise in Medford, at least not yet.[1]

In the meantime, Charles Tufts began adding to his real estate portfolio by acquiring more property around Walnut Tree Hill. Then, in the late 1840s, the Universalists were ready to try again in their quest to open a school. Only this time, they wanted to establish not a seminary, but a college of letters, where

Universalists could send their sons to educate their minds. And once again, Charles Tufts agreed to help the cause by donating more of his land on Walnut Tree Hill to the effort. However, he was not the only Universalist benefactor with land to donate, so now the trustees of the soon-to-be-established college had a decision to make: should they pick the bleak hill in Medford, or should they pick the other space offered to them in Franklin, Massachusetts, some twenty miles south of Boston? In the end, they chose the hill, and in deference to the man who gave the land, Tufts College was born. Then came the hard part of actually building the school. When chartered by the Massachusetts legislature in 1852, Tufts College was still nothing more than a barren, clear-cut hill. No trees, no buildings, no quad, no nothing – just an empty hill. Everything would have to be built from scratch.[2]

Starting a year later, the trustees of Tufts College did just that. They began by erecting one grand structure, affectionately called College Hall at the time, but eventually titled Ballou Hall, in honor of the school's first president, Hosea Ballou 2d. The cornerstone to the three-storied brick masterpiece was laid at the top of Walnut Tree Hill in the hot summer sun of July 19, 1853. Among the attendees at the ceremony was Charles Tufts himself, no doubt delighted his light was starting to shine on "the Hill," as the campus would come to be known. By the fall of 1854, College Hall was complete, thus allowing the four professors and seven students to move in and begin their work. The Hill, though, was hardly a sight to admire. Even with the grand building on its top, it was still quite bleak:

> To one approaching the College, the prospect was uninviting. Dilapidated walls stretched in all directions over the hill on which the college is located. Boulders were scattered over the campus. No trees offered their inviting shade. The east end of the [College] Hall was partially hidden behind a lofty pile of old lumber, while the ground was overgrown with weeds and strewn with rubble, so that it was a matter of some difficulty to gain access to the building…[3]

As for what Charles Tufts thought of the mess when school opened, his words were not recorded, but he must not have been too discouraged, for he eventually gave the college even more of his land. Nine years later, though, the look of the campus had hardly improved. As H. M. Knowlton of the class of 1867 described in his article for the school magazine, *Tuftonian*,

> College Hill in 1863, when I first saw it, had scarcely lost its former name of Walnut Hill. Although the college had been there nine years, the grounds were still in a very crude condition. The Hill… was practically still a farm, in which the new and scattered college buildings looked quite

out of harmony with the surroundings. The main building over in the meadow of the farm always appeared to us to face the wrong way. There was not even the slightest attempt at a lawn anywhere, not even in front of the halls. There were but few gravel paths.[4]

And yet, out of the emptiness and weeds and pile of dilapidated lumber grew one of the finest universities in the world, one that survived numerous economic hardships, multiple world wars, and the ever-changing needs of higher education. No doubt the founders of Tufts College would be surprised, possibly even perplexed, by the curriculum of today's university; after all, majoring in chemical engineering or taking a class in rock climbing have little to do with becoming a better Universalist, which was, in many ways, the primary reason for the founding of the college. Times have certainly changed. Now, over one hundred-sixty years later, here we are.[5]

Not surprisingly, the transformation of The Hill over the past century and a half is a great story. Numerous authors have detailed this history at various points along the way, including Alaric Start in 1896 (which he compiled while an undergraduate student, no less), Professor Russell Miller in the 1950s and 1980s, and Professor Sol Gittleman in 2004. However, many of these histories deal with the elders of the college, notably its trustees, presidents, faculty, benefactors, and generous alumni. These people are certainly important to the story of Tufts College and Tufts University, and they deserve a fair amount of credit for what the school has come to be since that cornerstone of College Hall was laid. But they are not the whole story. To make it whole, one has to consider the students, the mass of faces that arrive each fall in relative anonymity, to succeed or fail as they look for their own light on the hill. Little has been written about these students or what they have done with their years on campus. They might not have erected the buildings or planned the quadrangle, but they did help build the school, right from the very beginning. Indeed, it took those first seven undergraduates only a matter of days after arriving on campus to create the first organization Tufts College would see, the Mathetican literary society. The students who followed have not stopped since. This is the story of some of the organizations they created, most notably the fraternities and sororities.[6]

1 IN THE BEGINNING

The birth of fraternities and sororities

If there is one aspect of collegiate life that remains as controversial today as it did nearly two hundred fifty years ago, it is the existence of fraternities and sororities. Since their founding amidst the American Revolution, Greek-letter organizations have been praised, mocked, driven underground, expelled, welcomed, banned, and reborn on campuses across the country numerous times over. To many outsiders, the college Greek system is and always has been filled with spoiled rich kids who care more about having a good time than studying, and they can't imagine why anyone would want to join such a group. To many insiders, joining their particular organization was one of the best decisions they made in college, and they can't imagine why others are so against fraternities and sororities as a whole. This debate will likely go on indefinitely, but often lost in the conversation is that fraternities and sororities were not mandated onto college campuses by some outside authority, nor were they dreamed up by college administrators. Instead, they were created by students, for students. This is how they began.

THE FIRST FRATERNITY – PHI BETA KAPPA

Colleges and universities are a ubiquitous part of modern-day America, with dozens if not hundreds of accredited institutions in each state and commonwealth. Of course, such a plethora of educational opportunities beyond secondary school has not always been available. When the thirteen colonies declared their independence from Great Britain on July 4, 1776, there was a grand total of nine colleges spread throughout eight of those colonies, and to say student life on those campuses was different than today would be a gross understatement. College in the earliest years of America was extremely regimented, and the course of study was (by today's standards) extremely dull. All students took the same courses, as they were all studying primarily to be ministers or teachers. Classes consisted of lectures, with professors talking and students listening. Rote memorization was the norm. Independent thought in the classroom was almost non-existent, as that sort of thinking was highly frowned upon. Discipline and study were the true marks of a scholar, at least in the minds of the older faculty members. Beyond the rigid curriculum, though, the college also exerted a heavy influence on the lives of its students, with the faculty acting as surrogate parents. Students, who were typically much younger than today's collegians, were expected to abide by preset schedules including mandatory chapel attendance every day. Free time existed, but even then students had to follow a set of arcane rules, such as not leaving campus without permission of the faculty. Order, obedience, and conformity defined normal student life. Transgression brought punishment, physical or otherwise, pure and simple.[1]

But many students had other thoughts and other ideas, so naturally they created outlets to express themselves freely and appropriately. One such outlet was the literary society. These groups were essentially the book clubs of their day, where students would come together to read and discuss various texts including fiction (not normally part of a college curriculum), write essays, give lectures, and debate issues, all outside of the classroom, all away from the watchful eyes of the faculty. Literary societies sprung up on nearly every American college campus in the eighteenth and nineteenth centuries, with important-sounding names such as "Linonia" at Yale and "Cliosophic Society" at Princeton. They were by far the most popular of extra-curricular activities up through the mid 1800s, as the modern-day college sports craze was decades away from taking hold. All students were encouraged, if not expected, to join a literary society upon entering college, though it was truly their choice, since admission was open to all. It was in these literary groups where students learned to speak in public, to debate their side of the story, and to express themselves in a manner not afforded in the classroom. It was here where students learned.[2]

One school where the early literary societies operated somewhat differently was the College of William and Mary (W&M) in Williamsburg, Virginia. In 1750, a group of students organized a society called "F.H.C.," and while it was scholarly in its pursuits (at least in the beginning), it was noticeably different from its counterparts at other schools. For one, membership in F.H.C. was not open to everyone, but only those chosen. One had to be deemed worthy enough by the society for admission, not the other way around. Second, the members were bound together by secrecy, with rituals and symbols only intended to be heard and understood by those in the group. The outside world may have known the group as F.H.C. (which led to its nickname, the "Flat Hat Club"), but only its members knew the official meaning of those three letters, which supposedly stood for the Latin phrase, "Fraternitas, Hilaritas, Cognitioque" – friendship, conviviality, and knowledge. Other organizations, most notably the Freemasons (who were quite active in Colonial America), utilized secrets to bind their members into a cohesive group well before F.H.C. was established. However, F.H.C. was one of the first organizations to bring secrecy to college students on a college campus. As for a reason, the use of secrecy was surely a form of protest against the overbearing nature of college faculty, who exerted near total influence over the lives of those colonial students. By using secrets, the students displayed a level of independence from the faculty. They knew things their teachers did not.[3]

After its founding, though, it appears F.H.C. eventually became known more for its social activities than its literary work, at least according to the recollections of President Thomas Jefferson, a member of F.H.C. in the 1760s. Still, F.H.C. carried on until about 1772, when it apparently disappeared from campus for reasons unknown. In its vacuum, students at W&M created a new select, secret organization called "P.D.A." around 1773, which was very similar in form to F.H.C. Many referred to this new group by its nickname, "Please Don't Ask," since the meaning of the initials was a closely held secret. As for its scholarly pursuits, P.D.A. apparently started as a serious literary organization, but it soon devolved into a rowdy social club with a reputation for heavy drinking. The idea may have been noble, but clearly the execution was not.[4]

A changing attitude, though, was soon to come. In 1776, a fifteen-year old student at W&M named John Heath looked to make his name on campus. Known to be quite adept in the study of ancient Greece, John was also popular among his peers. At some point that year, the story goes, John became intrigued with the P.D.A. Society, but was eventually passed over for membership for reasons lost to history. This was just as well – the more he learned about P.D.A., the less he thought of the organization, for he wanted no part of their debauchery. However, John was clearly intrigued by the ideas behind the group and, more importantly, thought he could do better. So, on the early winter's night of December 5, 1776, John and four other men – Thomas Smith, Richard Booker, Armistead Smith, and John Jones – gathered in the Apollo Room of the Raleigh Tavern in Williamsburg, Virginia, to form a new organization, an honorable organization they called Phi Beta Kappa. The use of Greek letters for the society's name reflected John Heath's deference to Greek history and his status as the recognized leader of the group. But there was more to Phi Beta Kappa than just a Greek name. These five men wanted an experience different from that offered by societies such as P.D.A., so they came together through the promise of literary pursuit, friendship, and the desire to become better men. Phi Beta Kappa would be their outlet to debate and discuss and grow as individuals, while also enhancing their friendship through social interaction. Conviviality was a major part of Phi Beta Kappa, even from its beginning. Indeed, the members often retired after their meetings to the common area of Raleigh Tavern to enjoy the atmosphere, but not too much. Excessive drunkenness was highly frowned upon, lest the group devolve into a society like P.D.A.[5]

Phi Beta Kappa, though, did share two key attributes with both P.D.A. and F.H.C., and not by coincidence. First and foremost, Phi Beta Kappa was not for everyone. The society was highly selective in its membership, opting only for the best students who had to be voted in. Second, the Greek letters were more than just a name, they were the secret shorthand for the society's motto, "Philosophia Biou Kybernetes," which translates as "Philosophy, the Guide of Life." Secrecy did not stop with the motto, as it eventually came to include rituals, oaths, handshakes, and hidden meanings in the badge publicly displayed by its members. New initiates were sworn to treat these secrets with the utmost reverence, as evidenced by a portion of the initiation ritual:

> I, (state your name), do swear on the holy Evangelists of Almighty God, or otherwise, as calling the Supreme Being to attest this my oath, declaring that I will, with all my possible efforts, endeavour [sic] to prove true, just, and deeply attached to this our growing fraternity; in keeping, holding, and preserving all secrets that pertain to my duty, and for the promotion and advancement of its internal welfare.

As a result, Phi Beta Kappa was not just a literary society, it was a Greek-letter fraternity, the first recognized organization of its kind.[6]

After its forming, Phi Beta Kappa enjoyed a spirited existence at W&M for a number of years, meeting every few weeks and months where its members debated topics, enjoyed each other's company, and initiated a few worthy men every so often. But within short order, the fraternity began to practice a radical idea for the time, and that was expansion of their organization to other places and institutions. Nearly every other literary society of the day was confined to one particular campus, with almost no formal interaction between like groups at different colleges. Literary societies were, in practice, local and independent. But Phi Beta Kappa felt itself more than just a literary society, so it looked to establish other "meetings" of the fraternity (or "chapters" as they came to be known) to bring worthy men outside of W&M into its fold. As for why Phi Beta Kappa took this route, historians point to a connection between the fraternity and freemasonry. Some of the early members of Phi Beta Kappa were known to be active in the Masonic order in Williamsburg, and as Masons they would have been quite familiar with the idea of expansion. Indeed, at a meeting of Phi Beta Kappa on May 4, 1779, one of those Masons, Samuel Hardy, proposed a method for establishing new chapters of his fraternity in Virginia, if not eventually all of the states. The legacy of this action cannot be understated. By establishing other chapters of the fraternity, chapters that all used the same symbols, rituals, and secrets, Phi Beta Kappa became one of the earliest national collegiate organizations, if not the very first. Many of the secrets within the society, especially the handshake or "grip," were designed so that members could identify themselves to others they did not personally know. In a further act of foresight, Phi Beta Kappa also developed a naming system based upon the Greek alphabet to distinguish between the different chapters. Such a system would allow the various groups to communicate with each other in an official manner. As originally envisioned, the first chapter at W&M was called the Alpha chapter (also referred to as the Mother chapter), and then the next established chapter would take the subsequent letter, Beta, followed by Gamma, Delta, etc., with the name of each chapter indicating its founding date relative to the others. Records show that Phi Beta Kappa did charter a number of other chapters from Beta to Theta between 1779 and 1780. However, almost all of these chapters were based in nearby towns as opposed to other college campuses. This, too, was radically different, since until then collegiate societies had only been meant for undergraduates. Almost from its beginning, Phi Beta Kappa looked to bridge the gap between collegians, graduates, and professionals.[7]

While expansion was a welcomed idea among the members in Williamsburg, it would soon prove fruitless. It appears none of the town-wide chapters ever became viable organizations, in part because the Revolutionary War began displacing normal life in Virginia at every turn. But ultimately, Phi Beta Kappa would survive the conflict due to the efforts of one man, Elisha Parmele. Having studied at Yale and graduated from Harvard in 1778, Elisha then headed to Williamsburg, as his poor health demanded he relocate to a warmer climate. Within a year of his arrival, Elisha had been initiated into Phi Beta Kappa at W&M, where apparently he became enthralled with the fraternity and looked to help expand its influence to other colleges. His chance came in early December 1779, when he was granted the authority to establish two other chapters at schools he knew intimately, Yale and Harvard. So, he packed up and headed back north. By the summer of 1781, Elisha had succeeded in both of these efforts, and not a moment too soon. Both the College of William and Mary and the mother chapter of Phi Beta Kappa were no more. British forces under their notorious traitor of a leader, Benedict Arnold, had closed in on Williamsburg in early January of that year, forcing the school to close and the residents to flee.[8]

The establishment of chapters at Yale and Harvard, though, led to a minor change in the naming convention. As originally envisioned, the Harvard chapter was to be named Epsilon and the Yale chapter Zeta, in deference to the order in which their charters had been granted. However, it appears the members of Phi Beta Kappa at Harvard and Yale were not comfortable with this arrangement, for they both felt that since they were the first in their respective states, they had a right to the "Alpha" designation as well. So, both chapters simply changed their name. Yale became known as the Alpha of Connecticut, and Harvard the Alpha of Massachusetts. The original Alpha chapter at W&M was in no position to object since it was no longer active. Thus, the Yale and Harvard chapters were on their own to run Phi Beta Kappa as they saw fit, and they did, especially when it came to further expansion. In this regard, though, they were in no hurry. By 1825, some forty years after arriving in New England, Phi Beta Kappa's active roll totaled a mere five chapters.[9]

Though its extent was limited, Phi Beta Kappa was very well received on the campuses where it started, and soon became an elite organization within the ranks of collegiate life. However, the fraternity did have to deal with a certain amount of paranoia from the general population in the early 1800s because of its secret nature. To put it simply, secrecy scared most people. Religious leaders often preached that secrecy was immoral if not worse, and propaganda peddled by many alluded to the control of America through outside entities cloaked in secret schemes. The paranoia culminated in 1826 in what would later be called "The Morgan Affair." William Morgan, by most accounts, was a perennial failure as well as a drunkard. He was also a Mason, but apparently not a great fan of the organization, for he wrote a book exposing the group's secrets, complete with the grandiose title, *Illustrations of Masonry by One of the Fraternity Who has devoted Thirty Years to the subject: 'God said, Let There Be Light, and there was light'*. But before he could publish the book, he was arrested for larceny and thrown into debtor's prison. Someone paid off his debts, which led to his release, followed promptly by his disappearance. He was never seen alive again. Rumors put the blame for his abduction and supposed murder squarely on the Masons, for obvious reasons. However, a year after Mr. Morgan's disappearance, his book was published anyway. Then came the backlash. The general public, wary enough over secrecy in general, was much disturbed by the fate of Mr. Morgan. Indeed, this event was the catalyst for a fervent but short-lived political movement in the United States known as the Anti-Masonic Party. Secret organizations were now under a microscope.[10]

The lens turned to Phi Beta Kappa just a few years later. In 1831, a supposed member of Phi Beta Kappa from Harvard named Avery Allyn followed in Mr. Morgan's footsteps by publishing his own expose, entitled, *Ritual of Freemasonry, Illustrated by Numerous Engravings, to which is added a Key to the Phi Beta Kappa, the Orange, and Odd Fellows Societies, with Notes and Remarks.* This book was both a harsh critique of the fraternity as well as a disclosure of its secrets. It was not, however, seen as controversial as Mr. Morgan's work, at least to the members of Phi Beta Kappa. For years, many within the fraternity had been debating the use of secrecy, with some chapters openly advocating for the end of such practices. Now, with this publication and the general backlash against secret societies, the various chapters of Phi Beta Kappa all eventually acquiesced and gave up their secrets. Phi Beta Kappa, as a secret fraternity, was no more. Instead it became an honor society, one looking to recognize the very best students at a particular college or university. Admission into Phi Beta Kappa was (and still is) seen as an achievement, but now it was different. So, while Phi Beta Kappa is considered the first fraternity, it did not become the ultimate model for the modern Greek-letter organizations on college campuses today. That effort would take something else. Phi Beta Kappa's influence on this movement, though, is undeniable.[11]

THE "ALMOSTS"
KUKLOS ADELPHON AND CHI DELTA THETA

When Elisha Parmele headed north to continue the work of Phi Beta Kappa, he left behind his fraternity's five fledging town-based chapters in Virginia, and these groups did not enjoy the success of their counterparts at Harvard and Yale. However, it appears those chapters did not go gently into that good night. Rather, by 1812, there is strong evidence to suggest those seemingly defunct chapters in Virginia had morphed into a brand new society at the University of North Carolina (UNC) called Kuklos Adelphon. Also known by such other names as the Circle of Brotherhood, K A, and the Alpha Society, Kuklos Adelphon was most commonly referred to as Kappa Alpha. In practice it was a secret, select fraternity, for it operated in much the same way as Phi Beta Kappa, and this was no coincidence – the rituals, symbols, and secrets of Kappa Alpha were almost exactly the same as those of Phi Beta Kappa, thus giving credence to its derivation from this earlier organization. Over the years, Kappa Alpha established a number of chapters at colleges in the south as well as town-based chapters in various communities, thus becoming a national organization. However, as a whole it was quite de-centralized. It may technically have been a national fraternity, but there was little contact between the chapters, and each was allowed to modify both their constitution and ritual as they saw fit. In a sense, the chapters acted more as independent, local fraternities, with a weak link back to the mother chapter at UNC. Using this model, Kappa Alpha persevered well into the 1850s, taking its place alongside other national Greek-letter fraternities that were rapidly expanding in the South. But ultimately, this incarnation of Kappa Alpha would stumble.[12]

A strong allure for fraternities since their inception has been their secrecy. From rituals to passwords to special handshakes, the secrets of a particular organization are, in strong manner, their essence. Being privilege to the meaning behind the letters, symbols, and mottos of an organization indicated one had been fully accepted as a member, while all others remained on the outside. Of course, it is in their secrecy where such organizations are at their most vulnerable. At no time was this more true than the mid-1800s, when it was not uncommon for one fraternity to attempt a raid on the repository of another, so they could steal their secret documents and humiliate them in public. And it was in the exposing of secrets where Kappa Alpha met its doom, though it would not be via theft, but outright betrayal. In 1855, the members of Kappa Alpha at the University of Alabama were deeply divided along the political lines of secession or union. A majority of the chapter was in strong favor of Alabama remaining in the United States, while a minority was fervently for secession. One member of the minority faction, so fed up with the discourse, decided to blow the cover on his whole organization. In an act of treason, he disclosed Kappa Alpha's secrets to a rival fraternity, which then published and distributed them among the greater fraternity world. Then, as the story goes, the Kappa Alpha traitor got on a boat and left the country for many years, only to return to America just before he died.[13]

The aftermath of the betrayal was staggering. With its secrets now exposed, Kappa Alpha as an organization fell apart almost instantly. Many chapters quickly joined other national fraternities (whose secrets were still intact), including most members of the mother chapter at UNC going to Chi Psi, and the majority faction at Alabama going to Phi Gamma Delta. A few years later, in 1858, the former Kappa Alpha chapter at the University of South Carolina reformed as a brand new fraternity called Phi Mu Omicron, and quickly reclaimed old Kappa Alpha chapters at six other schools. Indeed, the badge of Phi Mu Omicron contained the date "A.D. 1812," in homage to the original Kuklos Adelphon at UNC. Phi Mu Omicron kept many of the secret symbols of its predecessor, but added others as it looked to re-establish itself among the ranks of national organizations. However noble the intentions of Phi Mu Omicron's founders, though, they could not stop the forces of the Civil War. The fraternity as a whole fast became a victim, closing down forever during the conflict.[14]

Still, Kappa Alpha in its original form was not completely gone. In 1858, the same year as Phi Mu Omicron started, a few Kappa Alpha men revived their fraternity at UNC, evidently hoping the passage of three years would render unknown the previous divulgence of their fraternity's secrets. As it turned out, the chapter did thrive for a number of years after this revival, and was one of only three fraternities at UNC to survive the Civil War (the other two were Chi Phi and Zeta Psi). However, in 1866, another disloyal member once again exposed the secrets of Kappa Alpha to the outside world. This time it really was too much. The group disbanded for good that year, thereby relegating Kappa Alpha to the collegiate history books. Among its alumni was James K. Polk, President of the United State of America and UNC graduate from the class of 1818.[15]

MEANWHILE, as Kappa Alpha worked to establish itself in the South in the early 1800s, another collegiate Greek-letter organization looked to assert its influence on campus life up north. For many years, Phi Beta Kappa was the premier literary organization for seniors at Yale University, with membership restricted to only the very best of the fourth-year students. It operated without a rival until 1821, when Professor James L. Kingsley started a similar literary society called Chi Delta Theta, to "compliment [sic] and encourage literary as distinguished from scholastic ability." Chi Delta Theta was meant for the writers at Yale, not just the debaters and orators who made up the bulk of Phi Beta Kappa. Chi Delta Theta was also a secret organization, with its own rituals and symbols, though it was a little more selective than its rival. During the early 1800s, about a third of the seniors were admitted into Phi Beta Kappa, but only about a fourth were chosen for membership in Chi Delta Theta (including all of the known good writers). But the two organizations were also complimentary, as many students belonged to both. Such was a mark of prestige on campus, for wearing the two badges of Phi Beta Kappa and Chi Delta Theta was so much better than wearing one.[16]

Chi Delta Theta existed as a local organization at Yale until the summer of 1830, when eight members of the junior class at Amherst College petitioned the society for a charter, which was granted. Chi Delta Theta was not the first literary society at Amherst College, but it was the first national organization, beating out Phi Beta Kappa to campus by some twenty-three years. Like the chapter at Yale, Chi Delta Theta at Amherst was a select, prestigious organization whose members spent time reciting original poetry, translating ancient texts, and debating one another on topics in literature. However, unlike the chapter at Yale, the Amherst group admitted members of both the junior and senior class. Faculty members usually reigned as president of Chi Delta Theta, where they hosted meetings and, at the end of each discussion, offered a critique of the student's work, whether they wanted it or not.[17]

Both chapters of Chi Delta Theta remained quite active for many years, though it appears the organization did not expand any further. All seemed to be going quite well for the organization until the mid 1840s when both shut down. The culprit was the emergence of other groups and activities on campus, which captured the attention of the students and pulled them in other directions. Both schools were still quite small by today's standards, so each could only support a reasonable number of organizations. As newer groups emerged, the older literary societies were often pushed aside. Chi Delta Theta did see a revival at Yale in 1868, but this incarnation was solely focused on publishing the Yale Literary Magazine. The organization under this mission continued on for many years, and there is evidence it merged with the Manuscript Society in the 1950s, an organization that is still active today.[18]

So, while Phi Beta Kappa, Kuklos Adelphon, and Chi Delta Theta have earned their place as some of the earliest national collegiate organizations in America, they did not come to define the modern Greek-letter fraternity system that people know today. Instead, it would take a different society (albeit with a familiar name) on a campus tucked away in upstate New York to start the idea that finally took hold.

THE MODERN FRATERNITY MOVEMENT BEGINS

In the fall of 1825, five seniors at Union College in Schenectady, New York – John Hart Hunter, Isaac W. Jackson, Thomas Hun, Charles Clark Young, and

Andrew E. B. Knox – found themselves wondering what to do next. They had all been part of a military company on campus for a number of years, where they drilled in precision and bonded as friends. However, their esteemed leader, Captain Edward Bayard, had graduated the previous semester, leaving their military company without a commander. A new leader appeared at the start of the school year, but he failed to rally the men to his cause, and soon thereafter the company disbanded, leaving the five aforementioned men with "an aching void." These five were partially connected together through other organizations – three were in the Philomathean literary society, two in the Adelphic, and all but Andrew were in Phi Beta Kappa – but these societies did not bring them together with the same fervor as their military company. So, the men decided to rectify the situation. On the night of November 26, 1825, they met in a dormitory room and formed a new society, one that would cement their friendship not just for the remainder of their time at Union but for years to come, one that would bind them together through secrets. That day those five men formed a fraternity they called Kappa Alpha.[19]

The purpose of Kappa Alpha, these men stated, was both literary and social, with somewhat equal emphasis on both aspects. In many ways, this new fraternity was very similar to Phi Beta Kappa. Both had a literary aspect to their meetings. Both were select. Both had a similar symbol, as the key of Kappa Alpha was clearly patterned on the key of Phi Beta Kappa. However, there were a few subtle changes between the two organizations. Although Phi Beta Kappa was selective in its membership, Kappa Alpha was even more selective; while Phi Beta Kappa allowed graduate students and people from the surrounding community into its society, Kappa Alpha was for Union College students only; and while Phi Beta Kappa was run by its graduates, Kappa Alpha would be run solely by the undergraduates.[20]

The concept of combining a literary and social group into a secret Greek-letter organization only for undergraduates proved to be very popular at Union College. By 1827, just two years after Kappa Alpha's founding, two new fraternities had emerged at Union as rivals: Delta Phi and Sigma Phi. These three fraternities, commonly referred to as the Union Triad, remained local to the school until 1831, when Sigma Phi established a chapter at Hamilton College, thus making Sigma Phi the first national, social fraternity. From there, fraternities rapidly appeared on numerous campuses. Many of these fraternities remained local to one particular college, but a significant number established other chapters at campuses across the country. Union College, in fact, would see the birth of six national fraternities that are still active today, thus earning its nickname as the "Mother of all fraternities." Miami University in Oxford, Ohio, though, also lays claim to this title, as the school saw the birth of six national fraternal organizations as well between 1839 and 1914, and a few of these today are some of the largest in terms of established chapters.[21]

Thus began the modern social fraternity movement that exists today, with the national organizations founded in this model collectively referred to as the "traditionally white" fraternities – minority representation was essentially non-existent when the bulk of these organizations started their operations, as we shall see. Aside from the racial make-up, nearly all of the national fraternities founded before 1900 had three common characteristics: they were selective in membership, they were secret (with a noted exception in Delta Upsilon), and they were only for men. The prohibition against women was not an issue in the earliest years, as most colleges did not admit women until the later 1800s. Still, some women were initiated into otherwise all-male fraternities during this time, such as Miss Lucy Pattie into the Kentucky Chi chapter of Sigma Alpha Epsilon at the Kentucky Military Institute. When the members of that chapter all left to fight in the Civil War, they entrusted the chapter's records and secrets to Miss Pattie. She kept them safe throughout the war and only relinquished them when a former member of the chapter gave her the secret grip, which she had been taught. In honor of her dedication, the Kentucky Chi chapter made Miss Pattie a member of Sigma Alpha Epsilon. She may not have attended any meetings or held any positions in the chapter, but she was revered by the men of Kentucky Chi, and she so loved Sigma Alpha Epsilon that she was buried wearing her fraternity pin. Other national fraternities, including Beta Theta Pi, are also known to have initiated female members around this same time. However, the practice of admitting women was hardly widespread, and by the late 1800s, nearly all of the national fraternities had adopted a formal policy of excluding women. But as more women went off to college and saw the benefits fraternities brought to campus life, the more they wanted in on the game.[22]

WOMEN'S FRATERNITIES

The opening of Harvard College in 1636 brought higher education to the residents and natives of the newest of British colonies. Harvard, though, was not for everyone, especially women. In fact, for just about the next two hundred years, all colleges and universities that opened their doors in America opened them only to men. Women, the general feeling went, had no real need of higher education, as they were expected to marry and raise children, hardly a calling that required proficiency in Latin or mastery of trigonometry. This general exclusion of women changed forever in 1837 when two significant events occurred nearly six hundred miles apart. At one end of this revolution were four women who enrolled at Oberlin College in Ohio, the first time a college allowed such a mixing of the sexes in the classroom. Co-education had finally come to America, and in the decades that followed, many schools in the Midwest especially opened their campuses to both men and women. At the other end of the revolution was Mary Lyon, an elementary school teacher from Massachusetts who, like many of her day, disliked the idea of co-education. After teaching for over fifteen years, she came to feel that women were underserved by education in general, and needed a higher-level school all for themselves. So, in 1837, the same year Oberlin admitted women, Ms. Lyon opened the Mount Holyoke Female Seminary (now Mount Holyoke College), one of the first schools to offer higher education exclusively to women. Both Oberlin and Mount Holyoke, while fully prepared to educate women, were not as prepared to occupy their time outside of the classroom. For that, the female students would need to create everything for themselves. But, neither of these two aforementioned schools can claim credit as the birthplace of the first women's fraternity, or sorority as more commonly known. That honor belongs to another school, a world away (in many aspects) from either Ohio or Massachusetts.[23]

THE TOWN OF MACON, GEORGIA, was nothing more than a forest grove near the Ocmulgee River when surveyors began marking off streets and lots in 1823. A year later the town was incorporated, and soon thereafter the residents of Macon built their first permanent house of worship, a Methodist church. The men and women of Macon then soon took hold of a radical thought, one that was decidedly frowned upon by generations past. They embraced the idea that women should be afforded the opportunities of a college education, so they could "contribute to the valuable store of literature, philosophy, and religion." The townspeople of Macon rightly sensed a woman's place in the world was changing, and they wanted to be at this forefront. That such a liberal, progressive idea took hold in a small town in the deep South, where the enslavement of nearly an entire race of people was given not a second thought, seems somewhat out-of-place in retrospect. It took the folks of Macon nearly ten years to pull their plan together, but in 1836, and with the help of the Methodist church, they finally obtained a charter for their new school, which they named the Georgia Female College. Over the next three years, the trustees and benefactors worked to erect a building, hire a president, adopt a curriculum, and find professors to carry out their education plan. By January of 1839, everything was in place and the school opened to the public. Ninety young women enrolled that first semester over all four classes, certainly a great start for such a new school. But a few years later, the college was essentially bankrupt, unable to pay even ten cents on the dollar towards its debts. Luckily a number of benefactors stepped in to save the day, and by the 1850s the school was back on sound financial ground with a new name: Wesleyan Female College.[24]

The school may have had a new name, and its finances may have been sorted out, but student life at Wesleyan in 1850 was hardly posh and cozy. Instead, it was downright Spartan, with the women living in cold dormitories heated only by damp firewood left at their doors each morning. The Wesleyan professors controlled the women's daily routines to the minutiae, and if one dared utter a word against the overbearing authority, she usually faced a harsh punishment and was "sorry she spoke." Free, unadulterated time outside of the classroom was rare, but in those few moments the women gathered as best they could and became friends. By the spring of 1851, one student in particular, Eugenia Tucker, felt she and her classmates needed something more outside the classroom, something that could help them develop a sense of culture and refinement not possible through the curriculum. Eugenia soon found fifteen other women who felt much the same way, and together that spring they formed a secret literary society. With so much of their daily lives controlled by their professors, these women probably turned to secrecy as a form of rebellion, much as the founders of Phi Beta Kappa had done nearly eighty years earlier. And while they may not have been aware of Phi Beta Kappa, the women were certainly aware of secret organizations, as the town of Macon had been home to a Masonic lodge almost since its founding, and no doubt many of their fathers were members. But the women had higher aspirations than just pure rebellion. They created their society, as they stated, for "the avowed purpose of bettering one another and themselves morally, mentally, and socially." For a motto, they chose, "We live for one another," emphasizing the closeness of their friendship. All they needed now was a name, and for that they turned to a well-liked professor, Edward Meyers, who suggested they call themselves the Adelphean Society. The first secret society for women in the United States had just been born. It would hardly be the last.[25]

The Adelphean Society soon proved a popular addition to the Wesleyan campus, so much that within a year, a rival organization called the Philomathean Society appeared on campus, ready to challenge the Adelphean for prestige. Membership in the Philomathean Society, like the Adelphean, was secret and exclusive, and both societies were very popular on the Wesleyan campus into the early 1900s, until secret societies were abolished at the school. Elsewhere in the country, other women were also creating new organizations for themselves on their own campuses. In 1856, at the Troy Female Seminary in New York, a few women were very familiar with the Theta Delta Chi fraternity at nearby Rensselaer Polytechnic Institute, as some of their relatives were active members. The more these women learned about Theta Delta Chi, the more they wanted to be a part of such an organization. With the help of the fraternity men, the women started a new society called Chi Theta Delta on their campus, in obvious deference to the fraternity of their relatives. Indeed, the badge of Chi Theta Delta was nearly identical to the fraternity's design, and the two organizations shared the same secret grip. The year 1856 also saw the birth of a society for women on the campus of Elmira College, an all-female school in New York opened just a year earlier. Named Callisophia, the organization was a literary society that offered its members the opportunity to engage in debates and di course. The group also started its own library for use by the general camp subscribed to many newspapers and magazines, and organized lectures of outside professionals, thereby offering all women at Elmira a breadth of knowledge outside of the classroom. Ten years later, Callisophia gained a rival when the Philomathea Society (no relation to the Philomathean society at Wesleyan Female College) started its operations and offered many of the same opportunities to the campus as Callisophia.[26]

These five organizations spread over three campuses, being some of the first for women students, all shared one trait that limited their influence across the nation: they all stayed local to their respective campus throughout the 1800s. Indeed, regular contact between colleges in America was almost non-existent at the time, save for some fragmented knowledge spread by an occasional transfer student. For example, at Elmira College, the women did not begin exchanging student publications with other schools in the northeast until 1875, some twenty years after Callisophia was first organized. With little knowledge of their operations reaching the general college population, it was no wonder these societies remained hidden outposts of inspiration that were unable to spark a national movement. It did not help, too, that these early societies existed solely at all-female schools, which, except for Chi Theta Delta, had no model to follow of a national student organization. As a result, the modern women's fraternity movement we know today would actually start someplace else.[27]

BY THE MID 1800s, educational opportunities for women at the collegiate level had begun spreading rapidly across the Midwest United States. As new territories were settled, public land-grant universities and private, religious-backed colleges sprung up faster than ever before, with many of them admitting both women and men right from the beginning. These colleges and universities soon grew in size and prestige, especially after the Civil War, when young folks were no longer required for the war effort. It wasn't too long before the national Greek-letter fraternities came to these newer schools looking for good men to start new chapters. One such campus was Monmouth College in Illinois, a private co-educational college founded in 1853 by leaders of the local Presbyterian Church. Monmouth gained its first two fraternities some twelve years later with the establishment of Beta Theta Pi and Delta Tau Delta. Within short order the women of Monmouth saw what the fraternities meant to the men on campus – a sense of close friendship, a bond in secrecy, and a desire to be better. So, in the spring of 1867, five female students at Monmouth came together one night to talk about these new fraternities. Eventually one of the women, Emma Brownlee, summarized their discussion into a simple question: "Why cannot we college girls also have a fraternity?" It was the question that sparked a movement. On April 28, 1867, this group of now eleven women at Monmouth met in secret to plan their new organization, and a week later they adopted the constitution of their new fraternity, I. C. Sorosis. All that was left was to announce their organization to the campus. Nearly two weeks later, they did so in dramatic fashion when they all paraded into the chapel proudly wearing their emblem, a golden arrow, for all to see. Although they were somewhat nervous about how they would be received on campus, their fears were soon put aside when the male students, who recognized the meaning of the act, immediately rose to their feet and cheered loudly. Acceptance had just been earned.[28]

What made I. C. Sorosis different from those earlier societies such as Adelphean at Wesleyan Female College or Chi Theta Delta at Troy Female Seminary is what it did next. From the beginning, I. C. Sorosis looked to emulate the expansion practices of the national male fraternities. I. C. Sorosis may have been founded at Monmouth College, but it was not going to stay there. In the summer of 1868, just a year after starting, the women of I. C. Sorosis felt they were ready to bring their organization to another campus. All they needed was a volunteer – expansion, they figured, was best accomplished by sending one of their own to another campus. Taking this leap of faith was Libbie Brook, who voluntarily transferred to Iowa Wesleyan University in Mount Pleasant, Iowa, in the fall of 1868. Once on campus, Libbie found a suitable group of women and established the second chapter of I. C. Sorosis, thus marking the first time a women's collegiate organization had ever gone national. From there, I. C. Sorosis began expanding to other colleges in the Midwest, having either transfer students or relatives of members to set up new chapters. Expansion in this regard was slow but steady, and within ten years of its founding the fraternity had established five chapters in three Midwestern states. Within twenty years, the chapter roll stood at eleven.[29]

In the meantime, as I. C. Sorosis began spreading across the Midwest, a number of other women's fraternities came into existence, and they, too began to expand slowly across the same geographical area. It did not take long for I. C. Sorosis to cross paths with these newer organizations, where the competition for new members began in earnest. However, these organizations were a little different than I. C. Sorosis in that they used Greek letters to identify themselves to the world. These newer organizations, including Kappa Alpha Theta, Kappa Kappa Gamma, Gamma Phi Beta, and Alpha Phi, stood in stark contrast to I. C. Sorosis, one of the only fraternities with a Latin-based moniker. By the early 1880s, this difference had become a real issue, as members of I. C. Sorosis were struggling at times in the recruitment battle simply because their organization was not readily associated with Greek letters. Their rivals played on their name as a sign of inferiority, telling rushees "the I. C.'s were only Latins or something," and therefore not a true fraternity. Although the argument was somewhat absurd, it was causing much consternation within I. C. Sorosis, and was even cited as one cause in the loss of their chapters at Indiana Asbury University (now DePauw University) and State Institute in Bloomington, Indiana. The debate over this problem went on within the organization for years, with the natural line drawn between those who favored old traditions, and those who appreciated new realities. Finally, after years of editorials and letters and countless discussions amongst the members, the delegates at the 1888 convention put the issue to a vote. In unanimous fashion, they dropped their Latin name in favor of a Greek one. As for what that name would be, there was no debate. They chose the three letters that had previously comprised their secret motto, Pi Beta Phi. The transformation was complete, and soon enough the fraternity was growing once again.[30]

THUS BEGAN the modern Greek-letter fraternity movement for women. But as nearly any modern college student would tell you, the term "women's fraternity" is hardly used today (if at all) to describe organizations such as Pi Beta Phi or Kappa Alpha Theta. Instead, women's fraternities all across the country are collectively referred to as "sororities," a term that has been in use for over one hundred years. This descriptor, however, was not available when I. C. Sorosis, Kappa Alpha Theta, and other early women's fraternities were founded, because it had yet to be invented. In 1874, a group of four women at Syracuse University started a secret fraternity they called the Gamma Phi Beta. Eight years later, some members of Gamma Phi Beta happened across Professor Frank Smalley, a member of the school's Latin department, and started up a conversation. It did not take Professor Smalley long to express his displeasure over their use of "fraternity" to describe their organization. He knew all too well the Latin roots of "fraternity" suggested brotherhood, which he thought awkward for the women of Gamma Phi Beta. So, he constructed a new word to describe their organization, "sorority," with its roots meaning "sisterhood." The word quickly caught on at Syracuse and beyond, and by the early 1900s was in widespread use around the country. But not all were happy about this. Many women's fraternities openly revolted against this new word and its derivations such as "sororial" (an awkward equivalent of "fraternal"), opting to avoid the descriptor whenever possible. Even today, many of the national women's fraternities do not describe themselves as a sorority, as they instead use "fraternity" in their official name.[31]

THE JEWISH FRATERNITY MOVEMENT

No country in modern times has been built so strongly by immigration as America. Various times in the country's history have seen an influx of one particular ethnicity over another, starting first with Europeans but eventually including many other nations and cultures. In the late 1800s and early 1900s, it was the Jewish immigrants who began arriving in America in large number from central Europe, driven from their homes by a rise in anti-Semitic feelings on the continent. A vast majority of these immigrants settled in New York City and its surrounding areas. And once they settled, they realized a good future could be had with a college education. So off to college these first- and second-generation Jewish immigrants went, highly motivated not just to succeed, but also to exceed all expectations. Once on campus, these Jewish students noticed student life outside of the classroom, most notably the Greek-letter organizations, which were growing rapidly at the dawn of the twentieth century. Many were intrigued by the idea of the fraternities and sororities, but soon enough they realized the problem. Jews, for the most part, were simply not allowed into these organizations. With a firm basis in Christianity, many national fraternities and sororities could not contemplate how a Jewish person could accept their ideals, their rituals, or their secrets, so they were summarily excluded. Jews were certainly not the only group of students to be excluded – Catholics, Asians, African-Americans, Muslims, nearly anyone not white and Protestant was usually denied membership from the outset. Of these denied groups, however, the Jews were by far the largest, and each year their enrollment in colleges across the country only grew. It was only a matter of time before their exclusion from the Greek-letter organizations would lead them to form their own.[32]

Yale University in New Haven, Connecticut was where they tried first. In the early spring of 1895, Frederick Werner, Louis Levy, and Henry Fisher found themselves intrigued by the idea of a fraternity, but also excluded from those on the Yale campus because of their religion. Instead of walking away as many had before, though, they sensed a way forward. They felt the membership restrictions as practiced by the fraternities were in actuality only hindering them. Exclusion, they reasoned, would not allow their members to grow as individuals or realize "the true purpose and aim of fraternity." So, that spring they decided to create a new organization, one that would be non-sectarian in all aspects, admitting men based on merit, not religion. They called their fraternity Pi Lambda Phi. Not content to stay just at Yale, the fraternity quickly expanded to a number of campuses over the next few years, including Columbia, the City College of New York, Cornell, M.I.T., the University of Chicago, the University of Pennsylvania, Harvard, New York University (NYU), and Union College. The first national fraternity open to Jews was off to a blazing start.[33]

It was also in serious danger of burning out. From the beginning, Pi Lambda Phi ran into major logistical problems. Correspondence between the various chapters was poor at best, with the fraternity seemingly ill prepared to operate effectively as a national organization. At Columbia, for example, the Yale founders of Pi Lambda Phi were forced to remove two "undesirables" by revoking the group's charter and then re-issuing a new one to the chapter, minus the two aforementioned men. What, exactly, was undesirable about these two was not recorded, but this incident was probably a big distraction for the Columbia chapter as it looked to establish itself on campus. And then, just like that, the chapters of Pi Lambda Phi began to shut down. With no strong national leader and no real support between the chapters, interest soon waned and men dropped out. The mother chapter at Yale lasted but three years, closing in 1898. Many of the remaining chapters were gone by 1899; the last two at Columbia and NYU closed down by 1901. Pi Lambda Phi was now completely defunct, a mere six years after starting. Jewish men would have to look elsewhere.[34]

IN 1898, the same year the mother chapter of Pi Lambda Phi closed down, a Professor of Semantic Languages at Columbia University, Richard Gottheil, faced what he considered a serious problem. He and his father, Rabbi Dr. Gottheil, had long been interested in the Zionist movement to establish a Jewish state in Palestine. However, at the time many young Jewish men did not share the same interest or enthusiasm in this cause. Indeed, these younger men seemed to be pulling away from the old traditions and customs of their elders as they settled into American life, which only added to the consternation of Professor Gottheil. So, he decided to bring the young men back into the fold. That year he gathered a group of fourteen students from the Jewish Theological Seminary in New York City and formed an organization he hoped would generate renewed interest not just in the Zionist movement, but also in Judaism. As for the name of this organization, his colleague, the Rev. Dr. Bernard Drachman, suggested three letters, "Z. B. T.," representing Hebrew words from Isaiah 1:27, "Zion shall be redeemed by justice." The organization, being one of only few in New York City open to Jewish male students, soon drew students from nearby colleges and universities, and while the group's emphasis on Zionism soon gave way to the more general promotion of Judaism, its members also spent time at their meetings having fun. They smoked pipes, drank beer, ate food, and even sang songs, not unlike the practice of many Greek-letter fraternities of the day. So, by the turn of the twentieth century, many within Z. B. T. came to view the organization as their fraternity. Then, they made it official. In 1903, the organization absorbed a local Greek-letter fraternity at the City College of New York (CCNY), Omicron Epsilon Phi, and turned it into the CCNY Chapter of the Z. B. T. Fraternity. Other chapters were soon established at schools in New York City, and then in 1906, the organization voted to change its name to the Zeta Beta Tau Fraternity (ZBT), a full-fledged Greek letter organization for collegiate men. Expansion across the country soon followed. All the while, ZBT was, and would remain for some time, a fraternity for Jews only.[35]

THUS BEGAN THE START of the Jewish fraternity movement in America, at least for the men. The women were not far behind. In the early 1900s, women living in and around New York City who wished to become elementary school teachers often enrolled at the New York Normal School (now Hunter College) for their training. Although hardly prestigious as compared to other schools in New York City, New York Normal College educated many women for what was seen as a noble, if not a working-class profession. One such woman studying there during the 1902–03 school year was Frances Zellermayer, who just happened to be a sister of a founding member of the Z.B.T. organization. In March 1903, Frances and six of her friends decided they wanted to form an organization to study the plight of women in the Bible as well as modern Jewish literature, two topics not normally a part of their educational experience. They also wanted to have fun. The seven called their organization J.A.P. (pronounced jay-ay-peez), where the letters supposedly stood for "Just A Plain" sorority, a reflection of their modest backgrounds. J.A.P. stayed local to New York Normal School until 1913, when it established its second chapter at the Brooklyn Law School. At this time, the organization also decided to follow in the footsteps of Z.B.T. by changing its name to Greek letters, being known henceforth as the Iota Alpha Pi (IAPi) sorority, the first for Jewish women.[36]

In the years following the start of ZBT and IAPi, New York City in particular saw an explosion of new Jewish Greek-letter fraternities and sororities. Dozens came to life, and many soon went national by expanding to the Midwest, particularly, where quotas limiting Jewish enrollment were not as prevalent as in the Northeast. Many of these organizations limited membership to Jews only through their constitutions and by-laws, but a few fraternities such as Phi Epsilon Pi and Delta Sigma Phi, and a few sororities such as Phi Sigma Sigma, embraced religious diversity as they looked to bring together different religions under one fraternal banner, lest they practice the discrimination they'd known all too well. These non-sectarian organizations, though, often struggled to maintain religious inclusion. Many saw their membership become mostly if not wholly Jewish after their founding, especially when they expanded in earnest through the 1920s. Such outcome was inevitable in retrospect. These non-sectarian groups were often the first fraternal organizations on campus that allowed Jewish men and women to join. With but one social outlet, Jews often filled the membership ranks of these organizations, which quickly gave them a reputation as a "Jewish" fraternity or sorority, whether they liked it or not. In at least one case, though, non-sectarianism officially went awry. In 1909, the Delta Sigma Phi fraternity, which had been founded by Christians and Jews, faced a challenge when eight Jewish students looked to join the chapter at Columbia University. By this time, ZBT claimed most of the Jewish fraternity men at Columbia, leaving the Delta Sigma Phi chapter predominantly Christian in membership. When these eight were subsequently denied entry into Delta Sigma Phi due to their religion, they formed their own fraternity, which they called Phi Sigma Delta, partially to emphasize their feeling the group who turned them away was backwards in their thinking. A few years later, Delta Sigma Phi made it official when they changed their constitution so that only Christians could be members. Non-sectarianism, though wonderful in theory, proved very hard to implement in the early 1900s.[37]

Although most Jewish fraternities and sororities had been formed in response to religious discrimination, many continued, somewhat ironically, to practice their own form of exclusion. For some of these organizations, being Jewish simply wasn't enough – one had to be of the right Jewish heritage. The older, established Jews from Germany in particular (who were often well represented in Jewish fraternities) looked down upon the newcomers from Eastern Europe or Russia. As a result, many Jews interested in joining a fraternity or sorority were asked about their heritage, such as the birthplace of their parents. Background checks were routine before one could be initiated, and certainly many were disregarded or "blackballed" for a lack of social status, or living in the wrong neighborhood, or even having poor manners. Still, Jewish fraternities and sororities remained popular well into the 1950s, until the Civil Rights movement led to major changes in the American fraternity system. Before then, discriminatory clauses and membership practices were the norm for nearly all Greek-letter organizations, especially the traditionally white, Christian fraternities and sororities. However, as the move for Civil Rights spread, these organizations came under fire for their discriminatory practices, and starting in the 1950s they began removing their official barriers for membership based on race and creed. Now, as Jewish men and women looked to join a Greek-letter organization, they had a much wider variety of choices. And while Jewish fraternities and sororities also removed their membership restrictions, it was Jews who moved to the formerly white, Christian organizations in much larger numbers than the reverse. Many historically Jewish organizations thus closed or merged as this trend continued into the 1960s. Today, there are but a handful of historically Jewish organizations still in existence as compared to a century ago, and nearly all of them no longer emphasize the Jewish religion as they had in their past. The two exceptions are the Alpha Epsilon Pi Fraternity, which calls itself a "Jewish fraternity" that has a goal of "developing leadership for the Jewish community," and the Alpha Epsilon Phi Sorority, which identifies itself as a Jewish sorority that seeks members who "appreciate our Jewish heritage and are comfortable in a culturally Jewish environment." Both of these organizations, though, have no official restrictions for membership based on religion.[38]

BLACK GREEK–LETTER ORGANIZATIONS

Students heading off to college often arrive on campus relatively alone, without many friends or acquaintances, and are often filled with nervous anticipation over how they will adapt to campus life. Such anxiety is usually tempered within a few days and weeks as they begin interacting with one another and start forming associations, through classes, sports teams, or other activities. In the late 1800s and early 1900s, though, one particular group of students struggled in this type of assimilation. When African-Americans went off to a college with a predominantly Caucasian populace (which described the vast majority of colleges and universities at the time), they, too, arrived alone, but that is also how they tended to stay. They may have been tolerated at these institutions, but they were certainly not welcomed. Instead, they were surrounded by white students and white teachers who at best felt a difference in race meant a difference in thought, ability, and character, and at worst despised their presence. Those few African-American college students needed outside support and encouragement to succeed, yet they found very little. So, they turned to themselves. But all too often there were just too few African-Americans at any one school to form any type of support network. Isolated and alone, many gave up on college after weeks or months and simply went home.[39]

One such institution where this pattern had been repeated was Indiana University, in Bloomington, Indiana. Students of color had been attending the university since just after the Civil War, but their presence was hardly greeted with enthusiasm over time. For example, by 1872, the Ku Klux Klan had established a strong identity on campus, in part to ensure African-Americans would not flock to the school in number. However, at the start of the 1903–04 school year, ten African-American men enrolled at Indiana University, one of the largest blocs ever to do so until that time. These ten men were naturally drawn to one another, and as they sought solace in companionship, they decided that school year to form a Greek-letter fraternity they called Alpha Kappa Nu. Fraternities had existed at Indiana University for over half a century, but by 1903 they were decidedly closed to men of color. The details behind the founding of Alpha Kappa Nu have unfortunately been lost to history, but we can assume these ten men looked to emulate in their organization the fraternal spirit and sense of brotherhood they must have seen in the white fraternities. They also recognized the collective power to be had from drawing other African-Americans into their group, for within a few weeks of starting at Indiana, the men of Alpha Kappa Nu announced plans to establish a second chapter at Wilberforce University, a historically black school in Wilberforce, Ohio.[40]

The birth of this new fraternity was first announced sometime in late 1903 or early 1904 by a Chicago-area newspaper. The small article was then reprinted throughout 1904 in the quarterly journals of many established national white fraternities and sororities. Most of these organizations were seemingly curious about Alpha Kappa Nu and its plans for national expansion. Others, though, were downright dismissive, mocking the new fraternity with racial epithets and outright ridicule. However, despite this initial attention (both good and bad), it appears that Alpha Kappa Nu was unable to establish a strong presence at Indiana University, and there is no evidence the fraternity ever expanded to Wilberforce University or anywhere else. Many of those initial members left Indiana University before graduation, thereby preventing the organization from establishing any foothold on the campus. The efforts of those ten to create

Alpha Kappa Nu, incomplete as they may have been, were not completely in vain, though, for within ten years, another group of African-American men at Indiana University used the memory of Alpha Kappa Nu as a basis for their new fraternal organization. This time they would succeed.[41]

Meanwhile, around the time the Alpha Kappa Nu fraternity appeared at Indiana, an African-American student at the Jefferson Medical College in Philadelphia named Henry Minton felt spurned. When he enrolled at the school in 1902, he was already well accomplished, having previously earned the Ph.G. degree from the Philadelphia College of Pharmacy, which he used to open a drug store, the first African-American to do so in Philadelphia. Now he wanted to be a medical doctor. On his journey through education and entrepreneurship, Mr. Minton met many men who were members of collegiate and professional fraternities, and he was intrigued by these organizations and their ideals. However, his attempts to join such an organization over the years never came to fruition, as the Greek-letter fraternities on the campuses where he had enrolled were all closed to men of his race. The denials did nothing, though, to temper his desire for such an association, especially one that could bring other well educated and accomplished African-American men together. So, while studying at Jefferson Medical College, he decided to start his own fraternity. As for inspiration, Mr. Minton looked to create an organization that would combine "the tenets of Skull and Bones at Yale and Phi Beta Kappa." Or, in other words, an organization both for fellowship and congeniality, as well as scholarship and achievement. With such an organization, Mr. Minton felt the members of this fraternity could then look to serve the African-American community, by helping fellow citizens overcome the socio-economic disadvantage they faced due to segregation. So, on May 15, 1904, Mr. Minton gathered three other doctors in Philadelphia to discuss this grand idea for a new fraternity, and the four came away from the meeting eager to put it into practice. At their second meeting, which now included two other men, the group formalized their plans and created the Sigma Pi Phi fraternity, also known as Boulé. From its outset, Sigma Pi Phi was a highly selective and elite organization, reserving admission for only the best. And elite it was, as membership during those first few years numbered less than twenty, with the men more concerned about strengthening their ties to one another than bringing in new members.[42]

Unlike Alpha Kappa Nu, Sigma Pi Phi was able to set its roots down in Philadelphia and become, slowly, the organization its founders had intended. The fraternity became a national organization a few years later when it established its second, or Beta Boulé in Chicago, followed by other Boulés in Baltimore, Memphis, Washington D.C., and New York City. But, unlike collegiate Greek-letter fraternities, Sigma Pi Phi soon restricted its membership to college graduates, for the fraternity only wanted men who were already accomplished in their communities. Despite this restriction, Sigma Pi Phi continued to grow throughout the twentieth century, and indeed has been continuously active since 1904, thus making it the oldest active Greek-letter fraternity founded by African-Americans. Sigma Pi Phi is still considered a very elite and selective organization, and it is also somewhat mysterious – it was essentially unknown to those outside the organization until the 1980s.[43]

However, with Sigma Pi Phi eschewing college undergraduates for members, its influence on the greater fraternity movement for African-Americans is essentially non-existent. Instead, it would be the students who created their own fraternal organizations. After Indiana University, one school where this happened with some success was Wilberforce University, previously mentioned in the story of Alpha Kappa Nu. As one of the few colleges dedicated to the education of African-Americans, Wilberforce offered a far different experience for its students than predominantly white schools. Student life was, in a sense, very normal for those at Wilberforce, with men and women having many opportunities to associate outside the classroom in various clubs and organizations. By 1907, the men of Wilberforce had established two Greek-letter fraternities, Beta Kappa Sigma and Gamma Phi. Of these, Gamma Phi would go on to exist at Wilberforce for nearly three decades, and there is some evidence the fraternity expanded to other schools, thus making it one of the first national collegiate organizations for African-American men. However, Beta Kappa Sigma and Gamma Phi are mere footnotes to the black Greek-letter fraternity movement, preliminary ideas that add to the collective history but do not define it as a whole, because they were unable to break out into the mainstream. For that, it would take a group of men at Cornell University to start the modern day experience known as black Greek-letter organizations (BGLOs).[44]

IF ONE HAD TO PICK a college in the early twentieth century where the African-American fraternity movement would finally take hold, Cornell University in Ithaca, New York, would be an unlikely candidate. Although open to students of all races since its founding in 1865, Cornell University was historically filled with white students, men mostly, similar to just about every college and university in the Northeast United States. Indeed, prior to 1905, only about fifteen African-Americans had graduated Cornell University, and most of these graduates had been women. But in the fall of 1905, Cornell experienced a boom in the enrollment of African-Americans, when a number of men and even a few women came to Ithaca for their college education. These students, though, also arrived with something to prove. They realized others at Cornell, as well as the general public around Ithaca, would be watching to see how they handled themselves both in and out of the classroom. Would they follow the historical norm and struggle as a group, possibly graduating one or two while the rest dropped out or were sent away for poor scholarship? Or, would they reverse the trend and prove to everyone they belonged at Cornell? They were determined to do the latter, but recognized success could only happen if they stuck together. So, in the fall of 1905, a group of about ten men and a few women formed a literary society to help them achieve this goal. Called the Social Study Club, its main organizer and first president was Charles C. Poindexter, the only graduate student in the mix. The club often met in Charles' off-campus apartment, where they helped each other with schoolwork and discussed pressing issues of the day, such as education reform and the lack of opportunities afforded to African-Americans. However, the women of the group, who were noticeably outnumbered, soon dropped out, leaving just the men to continue.[45]

As the 1905–06 school year progressed, the men of the Social Study Club became close friends, and soon they realized they had a special bond to each other, not unlike the camaraderie they saw in the fraternities on campus. Many of the men in the Social Study Club worked as cooks and janitors in Cornell's fraternity houses, so they were acutely aware of how those organizations operated. And the more they saw, the more they realized their group should make the obvious change to a Greek-letter fraternity. But this change would take some time. By the spring of 1906, the group had changed its name to Alpha Phi Alpha, but still operated as a literary society, with its main goal being the advancement of scholarship. The debate over the future of the organization went on into the fall semester of 1906, with many members advocating for fraternity. Most vocal in opposition to this was Charles Poindexter, who remained adamant that the club remains a literary society. He was driven to this opinion by his belief that men of all races needed to build bridges to one another and interact in positive ways. Exclusive fraternities, he felt, went against this ideal, as they limited interactions between men, especially those of different races. The debate over the future direction of Alpha Phi Alpha culminated on December 4, 1906, in a vote on one question: remain as a literary society, or become a full-fledged Greek-letter social fraternity? In the end, the arguments for inclusion so eloquently proposed by Charles failed. Only he and one other member voted to remain a society, while seven others voted to become a fraternity. With majority rule the Alpha Phi Alpha Fraternity was born. The two dissenters resigned from the organization, leaving seven as the recognized founders, or "Jewels" as they are known: Henry A. Callis, Charles S. Chapman, Robert H. Ogle, Vertner W. Tandy, Nathaniel A. Murray, Eugene K. Jones, and George B. Kelly.[46]

After becoming a fraternity, the men of Alpha Phi Alpha almost immediately decided to expand their organization beyond Cornell, as they recognized their fraternity could be a positive force in the lives of other African-American college students. As for which schools to consider for expansion, they quickly focused only on those with high standards for academic excellence. They wasted little time in this endeavor, and within a year they established their second chapter at Howard University, followed by their third and fourth chapters at Virginia Union University in 1907, and the University of Toronto in 1908. Expansion hardly stopped with those schools, especially after the fraternity became incorporated in the State of New York in 1908. Within ten years, eighteen total chapters had been established across the Midwest and eastern portions of the United States, a phenomenal growth rate for such a young organization. Today, Alpha Phi Alpha is the largest Greek-letter fraternity in the world, with nearly eight hundred active undergraduate and alumni chapters in seven countries.[47]

Thus began the BGLO movement that exists today. Of all the schools that Alpha Phi Alpha entered early in its history, though, it was at Howard University where the BGLOSs exploded onto the American college scene. Between 1908 and 1920, five national black Greek-letter organizations started at Howard: Omega Psi Phi and Phi Beta Sigma for men, and Alpha Kappa Alpha, Delta Sigma Theta, and Zeta Phi Beta for women. All five of these organizations soon expanded to the rest of the nation, and today are all some of the largest in the world in terms of the number of active chapters. Unlike many of the traditionally social fraternities, all of the BGLOs count numerous alumni chapters on their active roles. Indeed, significant alumni involvement is a hallmark of BGLOs today, as they bridge the gap between collegian and professional.[48]

MULTICULTURAL FRATERNITIES AND SORORITIES

A recent phenomenon in national Greek-letter societies is the emergence of multicultural fraternities and sororities. Such organizations are similar in form to BGLOs, as they are often based around a particular ethnicity, religion, or lifestyle, and their aims are typically more focused on community service than social activities (though this statement is by no means universal). Chapters are typically smaller in size as compared to the historically white fraternities, and few occupy houses on or close to campus. And yet, they are not as new as it would appear, for the multicultural movement can trace its roots back over one hundred years ago, similar in time to the formation of the BGLOs. This is no coincidence. In the early 1900s, as members of different ethnic groups began attending American colleges and universities in larger numbers, they were often marginalized away from the predominantly white student population, especially when it came to student housing, just like African-Americans. Naturally, these various groups tended to band together for support, and when they looked around for a model of how to strengthen their association, they saw the Greek-letter organizations. It did not take them long to start their own.[49]

One school where this first happened for Asian students was the University of California at Berkeley (UC Berkeley). Chartered in 1868 soon after California became a state (as well as a haven for gold prospectors), UC Berkeley quickly rose in prominence among American universities, and by the dawn of the 20th century had become a popular destination for Asian students as well. One country well represented in this movement was China. In the fall of 1901, around ten Chinese men from Tientsin University enrolled at UC Berkeley, and once on campus they noticed much about student life, including the eighteen or so Greek-letter fraternities and sororities, many of which occupied chapter houses. But, membership in these organizations was closed to the men, as many national Greek-letter fraternities had policies at the time barring non-white, non-Christian members. Undaunted by this exclusion, but obviously interested in fraternity life, these ten men decided that fall to start their own fraternity. Very little is known about this organization (including its name), but one member of Sigma Alpha Epsilon fraternity at UC Berkeley remarked, in a letter to his brothers across the nation, that these men represented the first Chinese fraternity to be established in America. However, for all intents and purposes, this fraternity soon vanished from campus without leaving much of a history.[50]

The next attempt to form a Chinese fraternity came about ten years later on the opposite side of the country from Berkeley, and this one met a much different fate. In 1910, nearly two dozen Chinese students from colleges and universities in the Northeast met at Trinity College in Hartford, Connecticut, as part of the Eastern Chinese Student Alliance Conference. This group had been formed as a support network for Chinese students who were struggling with assimilation into the American culture. During the conference, the men recognized one way to ease this struggle would be through the fellowship they saw in Greek-letter fraternities on their respective campuses. So, twenty-one delegates at the conference decided to form their own fraternity for Chinese men, which they called F. F. Within ten years of its founding, F. F. had placed another chapter in China, thus making it an international organization. Today, after more than one hundred years of existence, F. F. is still an active fraternity with chapters around the world, although it has morphed over time from a collegiate organization to a highly exclusive brotherhood for Chinese professionals who have studied in either the United States or Europe. In many ways, F. F. is similar in mission to the Sigma Pi Phi fraternity for African-Americans.[51]

Following the formation of F. F., numerous other Chinese fraternities began appearing on college campuses and in cities. One of the first was the Rho Psi fraternity, which began at Cornell University in 1916. This fraternity eventually became an international organization with chapters in the United States and China and then, in 1976, expanded its focus by admitting women. This group, now known as the Rho Psi Society, is still active today on a few college campuses. Following Rho Psi, numerous other fraternities and sororities specifically for Asians and Asian-Americans were established as the twentieth century moved on, such as Pi Alpha Pi for men at UC Berkeley in 1926, and Chi Alpha Delta for women at UCLA in 1928. Many of these organizations, though, failed to gain much traction on college campuses, and World War II put nearly all of them out of existence. The tide started turning back in the 1960s with first and second-generation Asian Americans (as opposed to foreign born Asians) enrolling in ever increasing numbers. Many of these students sought out common ground among their peers, and with the rise in popularity of fraternities and sororities in the 1980s, they began forming their own, especially on the West Coast, with UC Berkeley the birthplace for many. Today there are over fifty active national Greek-letter organizations that focus on Asian culture, making this the largest subset of fraternities and sororities after the traditionally white organizations. Some are specific to one particular Asian heritage, while many others were established as Pan-Asian groups looking to bring different cultures into one group. Most of these organizations are but twenty to thirty years old, so in many ways their history and legacy is still being written.[52]

AFTER FRATERNITIES AND SORORITIES founded for Asians and Asian-Americans, the next largest ethnic group represented by Greek-letter organizations is the Latino community. And once again, it was near the turn of the twentieth century when these organizations made their first appearance, as students from Latin America and the newly acquired Commonwealth of Puerto Rico began enrolling in American colleges and universities in significant numbers. These students, like most minorities at the time, were often ridiculed with derogatory remarks and subject to discrimination, as the general populace reacted poorly to the changing landscape not only on college campuses, but within America as well. In this atmosphere, Hispanic students began coming together in groups both to support one another, and to help change the public's perception of their ethnicity. One of the first such groups to be established was the Union Hispano-Americana (UHA), founded in 1898 by a group of Latin American men at Rensselaer Polytechnic Institute (RPI) in Troy, New York. The UHA, though, was more than just a support group for students from Latin America and Spain at RPI; it was also a secret organization that placed emphasis on intellect and culture. A few years later and a thousand miles apart, some Latin American male students at Louisiana State University (LSU) in Baton Rouge, Louisiana, started a similar organization called Sociedad Hispano-Americana (SHA). First appearing in 1904, SHA eventually became the Greek-letter fraternity Sigma Iota in 1911. However, unlike the UHA which stayed local to RPI, Sigma Iota went on to establish about a dozen chapters in the United States as well as Belgium, Switzerland, and Guatemala City, thus making it a truly international organization. Within a few years, other local Greek-letter fraternities for Latin American men appeared, including Pi Delta Phi at the Massachusetts Institute of Technology in 1916, and Phi Lambda Alpha at UC Berkeley in 1919. These organizations soon began communicating with one another, and by the early 1930s, those that remained active had merged into a single organization known as Phi Iota Alpha fraternity.[53]

For the next forty years or so following the merger, Phi Iota Alpha was essentially the only Latino fraternity in America, with about ten active chapters across the country. But, by the early 1970s, Phi Iota Alpha as a national organization was in dire straits, with nearly all of its chapters closed. The end came in 1976 with the graduation of the last active member of its last active chapter at LSU. Still, the Latino fraternity movement was not over, as around the same time, other organizations with a mission similar to Phi Iota Alpha began appearing on other campuses, including Lambda Theta Phi at Kean College of New Jersey in 1975 and Lambda Sigma Upsilon at Rutgers University in 1979. Then, starting in the 1980s, as Hispanics began attending college in numbers much greater than the past, the Latino movement exploded onto the collegiate scene, with the formation of over a dozen new national fraternities. Kean College was also the home of the first Latina sorority, Lambda Theta Alpha, which began operations in 1975. For Latina women, though, the sorority movement did not significantly expand until the late 1980s, when about twenty national sororities formed in a ten-year period. Today, there are nearly thirty-five Latino/a active national Greek-letter organizations, including at least one co-ed fraternity. Included in this active group is Phi Iota Alpha, which was revived at RPI in 1984 and now counts fifty-two active chapters and twenty-five colonies.[54]

The last thirty years have also seen the emergence of numerous other national fraternities and sororities dedicated to different ethnicities, religions, and sexual orientations. These organizations, which now number in the dozens, represent some of the newest Greek-letter societies with a national presence, and in many ways they are still defining themselves and their impact on campus life. To paraphrase the musician Sammy Hagar, only time will tell if these organizations stand the test of time. If history repeats itself, and history tells us that it often does, the multicultural movement should eventually consolidate, with some organizations merging and others simply expiring; such was the case in the late 1800s and early 1900s when the historically white fraternities and sororities expanded in large number. But such fate is not for certain, and is probably best left for historians to discuss and summarize a hundred years from now.[55]

AT TUFTS UNIVERSITY, fraternities and sororities from all of these genres – traditional, Jewish, BGLO, and multicultural organizations – have been active on campus at one time or another since 1855. And by all accounts, these organizations have coexisted peacefully on campus with one another, which is not a claim that can be made by all schools with similar organizations. But of course they have not all been perfect, or have acted with the utmost integrity at all times, or been free of mistakes including overt acts of racism and discrimination. It is in these stories of triumph and failure, and recovery or not, where one finds history. It is not just of the fraternities, sororities, and other organizations, but ultimately a part of the collective story known as Tufts University.[56]

2

EARLY SOCIETIES AT TUFTS

The first student organizations, from literary groups to drinking clubs

A student entering Tufts University today is greeted with an amazing set of options, including where to live on campus, what courses to take, which extra-curricular activities to join, and which sports to play. In many ways, it is easy for today's student to take all of these choices for granted, as if they have always existed. But of course that is not the case; student life at Tufts was created over time. It all started in the fall of 1854 when seven students arrived on campus to find three professors in an unfinished building, and almost nothing more. Tufts College was certainly more about possibilities than reality that fall, as the classrooms had no blackboards, the library had no books, the laboratory had no equipment, and the college had no leader – President Ballou was still traveling around Europe when the students first arrived, and would not return to campus until a few weeks into the semester. Still, the seven students had each other, and they would get to know one another well, as they were all living together and taking the same classes in that one unfinished building, known then as College Hall. Their mornings began in the chapel, with a reading from Scriptures and a prayer. Then, off to lectures – Latin, Greek, Mathematics (Algebra), History, and Rhetoric comprised their course of study, with no other options. After classes, the seven were confined to the town of Medford and needed permission from the faculty to go elsewhere, including Somerville, even though that town's border was a few hundred feet away from College Hall. The students, by design, were never far from the faculty's reach.[1]

While such a prescribed regimen was common throughout other American colleges and universities in the mid 1800s, it was, in retrospect, not all that inspiring and probably very boring. But, that was all there was. The college had not provided anything else for the seven men to do while on campus, except eat, sleep, and study. Those seven students, though, were not about to sit around and wait for someone else to break their boredom. No, they were pioneers, men in their late teens and early twenties who chose to enroll in a brand new school and help create a college experience. As it turned out, it took them just about a week to put their first stamp on campus life. On the night of October 4, 1854, all seven met in the dormitory room shared by Benjamin Hathaway and

Nathaniel Faunce and created the very first student organization at Tufts College. It wasn't the football team or the Amalgamates or the Society of Women Engineers. It was a literary society, the Mathetican.[2]

MATHETICAN SOCIETY

(Local society, 1854 – 1878, 1883 – 1885, 1886, 1892 – 1896)

That the seven men decided to create a literary society was certainly normal for the day, as nearly every college and university at the time had at least one such organization. But it appears the decision was theirs, and theirs alone, as opposed to some mandate by the faculty. At their first meeting, five of the seven men committed to creating the constitution and structure of their new society from the ground up. It took them just two weeks to get their affairs in order, and on October 18, 1854, the seven met for a second time and voted unanimously to adopt the constitution they had written. The Mathetican Society was officially born, with the following charter members:

Harvey Hersey (1857)
Thomas Harris Angell (1858)
Benjamin Allen Hathaway (1858)
Herman Joseph Smith (1858)
Henry Bowers Walton (1858)
Edward K. Sampson
Nathaniel B. Faunce

Thomas Angell is credited with naming the society as The Mathetican, a title he probably derived from the word "mathetic," meaning "of or relating to science or learning."[3]

The first scholarly activity of the Mathetican took place a couple of weeks later. On Saturday, November 4, the seven met in Benjamin and Nathaniel's dormitory room and held a debate. As for a topic, they chose a current event: "The secret society the Know Nothing Society in our country has a greater tendency to evil than good." Henry and Herman argued for the affirmative, while Edward and Thomas took the negative. The Know Nothing Society, also known as the American Party, was a short lived anti-immigrant, anti-Catholic political organization that would sweep into power in Massachusetts eight days after this debate, only to burn out as a movement just a couple of years later. While unfortunately the winner of the debate was not recorded, the contest did set the tone for the society. Soon enough, they were meeting weekly to engage in a "regular literary programme [sic] ... consisting of a debate, a declamation, and an essay or short talk." Current events were especially popular topics of discussion, though occasionally historical events were also considered.[4]

Over the next few years, the Mathetican Society grew into a very active and popular organization, which isn't surprising since there were almost no other extra-curricular activities to occupy the men's time (and it was only men – Tufts was all male for its first forty years). Within a couple of years, most likely after the first dormitory was completed in 1856, the Mathetican Society was given exclusive control of the northeast corner room on the third floor of College Hall, and operated out of this home for many years. By its constitution, the Mathetican was open to all students at Tufts, though before one could become a full member he had to be voted in and pay the required dues of $1.00. The vote, however, was considered a "rather useless formality," as no one was ever denied membership. The faculty continued to leave the group alone, thereby allowing the members the freedom to express themselves openly amongst their peers. The students did not take this freedom lightly. Even more so, they turned the Mathetican into a bona fide addition to the liberal arts curriculum. Starting in the 1870s, the society held a major social event each year, either on Commencement day or on the anniversary of its founding, October 18. These programs featured poetry, music, a prayer, and an oration, sometimes given by a celebrity of the day. For example, Walt Whitman wrote one of the poems for the celebration in 1874, and Ralph Waldo Emerson delivered an oration around the same time. Finally, many of its members went on to become Tufts professors after graduation, including one of its first, Heman Dearborn. Such continuity further endeared the society to the college.[5]

WALNUT HILL FRATERNITY (Local society, 1857 – 1858)
ZETAGATHEAN (Local society, 1871 – 1883)

But with the Mathetican's prominence came competition, eventually from three different entities. The first challenger to the Mathetican Society appeared just a few years after its founding. During the spring of 1857, a number of freshmen (including the future third president of Tufts College, Elmer Hewitt Capen) became disillusioned with the way the Mathetican Society ran its affairs. What exactly bothered these men is not known, but it must have been irreconcilable, for rather than working through the issue, they instead formed a rival society called the Walnut Hill Fraternity. This name, though, is somewhat misleading, as the organization was not a true fraternity, but rather a literary society – similar to the Mathetican Society, it had an open membership policy and did not use any secret rituals or rites. Soon after its founding, the Walnut Hill Fraternity moved into College Hall and occupied a room in the northwest corner of the third floor, directly across from the Mathetican Society. So much for separating the two rivals, but with space on campus at a premium, there were likely no other options. The Walnut Hill Fraternity got off to a strong start, as all but two from the Class of 1860 and then few from the Class of 1861 snubbed the Mathetican and joined the new organization. However, the enthusiasm espoused by founders was hard to maintain, and there is strong evidence the group merged with the Mathetican Society by the start of the 1858 fall semester. As for the demise of the Walnut Hill Fraternity, it appears the college was too small at the time to support two literary societies with open membership, so the younger and less established society became the obvious casualty.[6]

The second challenge to the Mathetican Society came from the Divinity School, although this challenge was one welcomed with open arms. Opened in the fall of 1869, the Divinity School at Tufts College was meant to be a separate educational entity, with its students wholly segregated from the undergraduates. However, logistical realities meant the Divinity students often shared buildings, dormitories, and classes with their liberal arts peers. As a means of forging their own identity, the Divinity School students formed their own literary society in the fall of 1871, which they called the Zetagathean Society. This organization was nearly identical in purpose and structure to the Mathetican society, with one noted exception – only divinity students were allowed to join. A friendly rivalry between the two societies quickly ensued, since they were not in competition for members. One outcome of this rivalry was a public debate on January 13, 1873, the first such debate the entire campus was allowed to witness (previous debates within the Mathetican were closed to outsiders). The topic of the debate was a surprisingly divisive issue of the day: "Resolved, that it is inexpedient for the American government to admit Catholics to the rights of full citizenship." The Mathetican Society chose to argue in the negative, but in the end the Zetagathean Society won the debate. In other words, the future ministers-to-be successfully argued that Catholics who had immigrated to America should not be considered full citizens. Plans for a second debate were discussed in 1878, but soon thereafter the Mathetican Society ceased to exist, so the debate never occurred. The Zetagathean Society continued for a few more years on its own, with its signature event being an anniversary celebration at the end of each school year. However, following commencement in 1883, the Zetagathean ceased operations.[7]

The third challenge to the Mathetican Society would prove to be a lot more formidable than the first two, and eventually lead to its downfall. Within two years of the Mathetican's founding, two Greek-letter fraternities, Zeta Psi and Theta Delta Chi, had established chapters on campus. These fraternities were social in nature, although both also had a literary side to them at the time, thus duplicating many of the ideas of the Mathetican Society. But the biggest difference lay in their membership practices. The fraternities were selective in their membership, whereas the Mathetican Society was open to any student. As a result, a natural rivalry developed between the fraternity men (or "society" men, as they were called at the time) and the non-fraternity (or "non-society") men, with each group claiming to be stronger and more important than the other on campus. The Mathetican Society, which aimed to bring all students together, suffered greatly when the growing student body began segregating itself into smaller factions. Also, as more students enrolled at Tufts, they started other organizations such as the Chess Club and the Amateur Radio Club, and these groups further competed against the Mathetican Society for both members and time. At one point, the Mathetican lost the use of its room in College Hall when the administration requisitioned the space for a classroom. They were given a new room on campus, but this one was no longer considered "home" by the members, so many began skipping the meetings. The situation proved fatal on its twenty-fourth anniversary, October 18, 1878, when the Mathetican Society held its last meeting – a victim, if you will, of progress.[8]

After the downfall of the Mathetican Society, various groups of students attempted a few revivals, but these efforts failed to hold the interest of the campus for very long. In the fall of 1883, a group of incoming freshmen formed a literary society which they first called the "Tufts Literary Association," but then changed the name a year later to the "Mathetican Society of Tufts College," in tribute to the original society. This second incarnation lasted until April 15, 1885, when indifference and apathy again took its toll. In the fall of 1886, a group of non-society men organized themselves under the banner of the Mathetican Society, but within a few months they became the Tufts Chapter of the Delta Upsilon fraternity and lost the Mathetican moniker altogether. Indeed, the goal of this group all along was to obtain a charter from Delta Upsilon, not to re-establish the old literary society, and they only used the name to add credence to their fraternity petition. A third revival came about in 1892, but despite the initial enthusiasm among the students and the faculty, the Mathetican Society was declared dormant once again on January 24, 1896. With this closing, the society voted to transfer the remaining monies in its treasury (a mere $9.95) to the newly formed Tufts Debating Union, and deposit its records in the library. The Mathetican Society was now a part of Tufts history.[9]

IN THE FINAL ANALYSIS, it appears the Mathetican Society worked very well when the few students could easily be drawn into one cohesive group, especially when there weren't many other things to do on campus. However, as the student population grew, so too did their range of interests, not to mention the breadth and depth of the courses offered by the college. This outward growth hampered the inclusive spirit of the Mathetican Society, thus making it obsolete. In attempting to cater to everyone, it eventually served no one. And yet, the ideas and events that came out of the Mathetican Society can still be found today, from prominent speakers at graduation, to campus debates on issues big and small, to numerous courses covering all types of literature, especially those away from mainstream thinking. The Mathetican Society may be gone for good, but it was a great first step in developing what is now Tufts University.[10]

Other Early Student Organizations

One common trait between the Mathetican Society, the Walnut Hill Fraternity, and the Zetagathean Society is they were all meant as serious, academic organizations. While undoubtedly the members of those groups had fun during their meetings and activities, the goal of these societies was to produce scholarly work. But these early students were not only interested in academics. They were young men, often away from home for the first time, and like all young men they could not live solely by strict rules and set schedules. They were social and wanted to have fun, maybe even push the limits at times just to see what they could get away with. One outlet they pursued was the establishment of select societies, including chapters of national Greek-letter fraternities and local organizations that only ever existed at Tufts College. The missions of these different organizations ranged from the serious to the downright silly, concrete proof these early students had a great sense of humor. Admission into nearly all of these groups was limited, either by course of study or by a vote of the active membership, and many employed secrecy to distinguish between those on the inside, and those not. Still, most were not long for this world. Nearly all of them lived but a very short existence, with none, except the chapters of the national Greek-letter fraternities, surviving until the present day. Nonetheless, they tell a great story of the Tufts College community in the mid to late 1800s. After all, these students were trying to figure out campus life without a map. The journey was bound to be interesting.

ORDER OF THE COFFEE POT (Local society, 1858 – 1869)
ORDER OF THE ROUND TABLE (Local society, 1864 – 1871)

Providing adequate student housing is a challenge faced by every residential college and university throughout history. Although the seven students who enrolled at Tufts in the fall of 1854 were able to room in College Hall their first year, the trustees knew from the beginning such an arrangement could only temporary. Tufts College needed a place for students to live separate from the academic building, the sooner the better. So, before that first school year was finished, the trustees voted to erect a dormitory on campus. By the fall of 1856, the building now known as Packard Hall was complete and ready to house up to twenty-six students. Additionally, the basement of the dormitory was a boarding facility, the first campus dining hall in essence, and was run by a Mr. Tower, who lived with his family alongside the students in the dormitory. The meal plan cost a mere $2.00 per week, a bargain even when adjusted by inflation to today's prices. However, the meals prepared by Mr. Tower, while adequate in nature, were not always appetizing and failed to satiate some of the men at times, especially as the hour grew late. With few options for late-night snacking (Espressos Pizza and Hee Kar Lau were not open for business just yet), the students were forced to improvise in order to satisfy their cravings. The college pantry, which was housed in the front-side of the basement of Packard Hall, was an obvious target, but it was protected from unauthorized entry by horizontal iron bars across the window, the high tech security system of the day. These bars may have looked secure, but as the students soon found out, they had one glaring weakness: they could easily be breeched with a long-handled flat shovel, thus giving the men access to the contents of the room. Soon enough, the students were using the shovel to procure all sorts of foodstuff including cakes and pies. They supplemented this bounty by requisitioning eggs from Mr. Tower's henhouse behind Packard Hall. Many nights, after the more studious men had gone off to bed, this crew of late-night snackers would enjoy each other's company with a second supper of coffee and their ill-gotten treats.[11]

By 1858, with the operations of this group well honed, the men decided to formalize their association by calling themselves the Order of the Coffee Pot. As suggested by the name, this society was very social in nature, and the chief activity of the group appears to have been the late-night suppers. Such revelry is clearly indicated in the society's motto, "Quum nobis placeat, cujus refert," which loosely translates as, "Since it pleases us, whose business it is." Membership in the Order was limited to upper classmen, and it appears to have been somewhat selective since the total number of actives at any one time was rather small. However, the Order did count members of both the Zeta Psi and Theta Delta Chi fraternities among its rolls, so the group was in complement to and not in competition with the Greek-letter organizations. Members identified themselves with a silver badge (called a fob) engraved with a coffee pot on one side and the club's motto on the other. The fob was proudly worn at all meetings.[12]

The Order of the Coffee Pot existed without a rival until July of 1864, when a group of students organized a similar society called the Order of the Round Table. In keeping with the non-serious nature of the club, the motto of the Order of the Round Table was "Utilitas Pariterque Delectatio," which translates as "Usefulness and at the same time delight." Very little is known about this society, though it appears to have been a selective club for students other than freshman as it counted sophomores, juniors, and seniors on its roll throughout its existence. Like the Order of the Coffee Pot, the Order of the Round Table had members who were also in either Zeta Psi or Theta Delta Chi, so the Round Table was not in competition with the Greek-letter fraternities. In a stroke of irony, the symbol of the Order of the Round Table was actually an octagonal silver plate, not a round one as would be suggested by its name.[13]

Both the Order of the Coffee Pot and the Order of the Round Table each lasted for about ten years or so, with the Order of the Coffee Pot graduating its last active members in June of 1869, and the Round Table staying active until the spring of 1871. In the end, only forty students were ever members of the Order of the Coffee Pot, while twenty-three were members of the Order of the Round Table. But the Order of the Coffee Pot in particular would show up again on the Tufts campus some eighty years later, at least in spirit. One of the first members of the Order of the Coffee Pot was Sheldon Conner, class of 1859. After graduating Tufts, Mr. Conner rose to the rank of Brigadier General during the Civil War and then became the Governor of Maine from 1876–78. Throughout that time, General Conner kept possession of his fob, which he passed down to his daughter. By the fall of 1950, this fob had migrated from his daughter to some of her friends, and these friends contacted the Tufts administration wondering about the history of the group and the significance of the medallion. President Leonard Carmichael, aware of the historical value of the item, immediately asked the owners if he could take possession of the medallion for a while in order to study it. Although he was able to keep the medallion in his office for a semester, he was unable to convince its owners to donate the artifact to the Tufts archives, so he was forced, reluctantly, to send it back, where it apparently disappeared into history. In a letter to the owners of the fob, President Carmichael stated he was thinking of restarting the order, but in the end his efforts at a revival did not succeed.[14]

EPSILON PI KAPPA CHI (Local society, 1863 – 1865)
OLD GIMLET FRATERNITY (Local society, 1864 – 1866)
PENTAGON (Local society, 1865 – 1866)
S.F. (Local society, 1869 – 1872)
MATERIAL POINTS (Local Society, circa 1873)
KAI GAI (Local society, circa 1878 – 1879)

In the years during and immediately following the Civil War, the number of organizations on campus continued to grow as small groups of students banded together around a common cause. One of the first was a society called Epsilon Pi Kappa Chi, founded in 1863. Although its name seemed to imply this group was a Greek-letter fraternity, its membership was mainly comprised of members of both Zeta Psi and Theta Delta Chi, so it was probably more of an informal social club than a serious fraternal organization. However, nothing regarding its operations has survived to this day. By November 1864, Epsilon Pi Kappa Chi counted ten members in its ranks including two graduates and eight undergraduates from the sophomore, junior, and senior classes. This was the first and last listing of the society in the *Tuftonian*.[15]

In 1864, another local secret society called Old Gimlet Fraternity made its appearance on campus. This group appears to have been very tongue-in-cheek in disposition, as all members were given silly titles such as “Ye High Mug Wamp,” “Great Magoffigin,” “Gorilla,” and “Grand Putty Gumpus” for the officers, with "Master Borer," "A Little Bit," and "A Big Bore" for the rank-and-file (collectively known as the Augers). This group also included members of Zeta Psi and Theta Delta Chi, so it, too, was not in competition with the fraternities. The Old Gimlet Fraternity lasted but two school years before fading into history; perhaps its members found it a bore.[16]

A short-lived secret society of math students called Pentagon sprang up during the 1865–66 school year. This group counted but five students on its rolls, including members of Zeta Psi and Theta Delta Chi. Apparently, fraternity members had plenty of free time to join other organizations. The society's motto was "Infinitely Small Quantities May Be Neglected," and indeed after a year, Pentagon vanished to nothing.[17]

In 1869, a society known only by the initials S. F. appeared on campus. For its first year, S. F. appears to have existed sub rosa, since it did not publish its membership list or its seal until November, 1870. S. F. appears to have been an exclusive society, as its members do not show up on the rolls of Theta Delta Chi or Zeta Psi. In all likelihood, then, S. F. was a fraternity meant to compete with the other two Greek-letter organizations on campus. However, S. F. was unable to establish itself as a viable entity, as it only initiated eight men over three school years before going dormant at the end of the 1871–72 school year.[18]

Not to be outdone by the math majors, eight civil engineering students in 1873 formed a society called Material Points, with the motto "Vivre Les Ingenieurs," or "Long Live the Engineers." Of its eight members, one was also in Zeta Psi and one was also in Theta Delta Chi, so Material Points was not in competition with the fraternities. Unfortunately, the scope and mission of this organization has been lost to history, but it very well may have been the first for engineering students at Tufts College.[19]

Finally, another tongue-in-cheek secret society known as the Tough(ts) [sic] Chapter of Kai Gai made its appearance on campus during the 1878–79 school year. The society, which listed its members by initials and not by name in the 1879 *Brown and Blue* yearbook, had as part of its organization a "Committee on Derangement" and a "Vote Snatcher." These titles suggest the organization was probably meant for fun if not mischief, but nothing is really known about Kai Gai or its operations. However, by May of 1879, it appears Kai Gai had gained the use of a meeting hall somewhere on or close to campus, so perhaps there was a serious mission to the group.[20]

OF COURSE, these were not the only organizations started by students during the 1800s, as there were dozens of other clubs and groups offering the students a variety of extra-curricular outlets. However, one aspect of the societies mentioned above is worth noting. Professor Miller, in his book on the history of Tufts College, *Light on the Hill*, claims many of these organizations such as the Order of the Coffee Pot and the Old Gimlet Fraternity were founded as alternatives to the Zeta Psi and Theta Delta Chi, with membership intended only for those not in either fraternity. Aside from S. F., though, there was quite a bit of overlap in membership between the two national Greek-letter fraternities and these local organizations as mentioned, so it appears there was more camaraderie between the fraternity and non-fraternity men than as first reported.[21]

KAPPA GAMMA RHO (Alpha chapter, circa 1887)
RHO KAPPA TAU (Local society, circa 1895 – 1899)

From the moment colleges were founded in America in the seventeenth century, until midway through the twentieth century, freshmen arriving on campus could almost always be assured of one thing: a "welcoming" by the sophomore class. This greeting usually manifested itself in various forms of hazing, including the forced memorization of school songs, the wearing of beanies, the kidnapping and subsequent drop miles away from campus, the smoking out of rooms (where smoke was blown through a keyhole until the room was filled, thus forcing the freshman to exit and, in all likelihood, be subjected to more hazing), and even tarring and feathering some of the more "lucky" ones. While hazing of the freshman by the sophomores does not appear to have been as widespread (or as demeaning) at Tufts College, it most certainly occurred, and was in general tolerated, to a certain degree, by the administration. By the early 1880s, however, the roughest aspects of hazing had gone out of fashion at Tufts, mainly because the incoming classes fought back against many of the more barbaric practices. Still, even after the so-called death of hazing at Tufts College in 1882, the sophomores continued to have some fun at the expense of the new students, mostly in the form of visitations, where they would stop by the dorm rooms of freshman and pull a prank of some sort. Such actions, though, paled in comparison to years past.[22]

The situation remained relatively low-key until 1887, when the sophomores looked to re-start a formal indoctrination of freshman through a new mythical hazing society they called Kappa Gamma Rho. According to rumors on campus, this society would be "entirely different from that of any other known college organization," and by their own admission they hoped to be "the most secret and mysterious society in existence." The group even called itself the "Alpha" chapter, implying the society planned to take the national collegiate world by storm. In reality, though, Kappa Gamma Rho never really got off the ground, despite its bold statements as printed in the 1888 edition of the *Brown and Blue* yearbook. As a result, the grand, mythical hazing society folded soon thereafter before inflicting any lasting harm on the incoming freshmen at any college, Tufts or otherwise.[23]

A few years later, though, some sophomores started another hazing society as a successor to Kappa Gamma Rho, which they called Rho Kappa Tau. The members of this society once again took charge of the freshman visitations, which included a return of smoking out the students and forcing them to create song-and-dance programs to entertain sophomores. And while Rho Kappa Tau appears to have been somewhat more active than its predecessor Kappa Gamma Rho, its activities never seemed to capture the imagination or the backing of the students. The editors of the *Tuftonian* were especially harsh in their criticism of Rho Kappa Tau, as time and again they openly called for the group simply to go away.[24]

The end of Rho Kappa Tau, though, appears to have come not from the scathing editorials, but from the wrath of the administration. By 1896, the hazing of freshman outside the control of Rho Kappa Tau had come to include activities known as chapel rushes. At the time, students were still required to attend chapel services every morning. Following the conclusion of the morning prayers, the classes would file out in order, with the freshmen going first. Naturally a bottleneck occurred at the exit, so often times the sophomores would "rush" or harass the freshman as they tried to leave, and then keep on them once outside. Pushing, shoving, and taunting of the freshmen were common, but that was not all. More often than not the rush became an excuse to grapple, with many individual wrestling matches and fist fights breaking out both inside and outside the sanctuary. In 1897, the college administration banned such hazing practices by threatening to revoke the scholarship of any student involved in the rush. But in the fall of 1898, with a new group of freshmen on campus, the sophomores were still engaging in chapel rushes. So, President Capen brought the hammer down. He told the students that engaging in a chapel rush was a felony crime, and he would not tolerate criminals on his campus. Chapel rushing was over. A byproduct of this decree was the demise of Rho Kappa Tau, as it, too, faded into history shortly thereafter.[25]

THE FULL MOON CLUB (Local society, 1901 – 1904)

Although technically not an early student organization, the Full Moon Club is worth mentioning for it was a unique group, the likes of which have not been seen since. By the fall of 1901, Tufts College was home to two class societies whose membership was restricted to a particular graduation year: Tower Cross for the seniors, and the Ivy Society for the juniors. The mission of these two societies was generally to promote class spirit through various social and scholarly activities, as well as perform pertinent campus duties such as gathering photographs of sports teams, running underclass elections, and overseeing fraternity rush week. Membership was quite selective, and the students viewed election into either society as quite an honor. In the fall of 1901, the college began making plans to start a sophomore honorary society called Sword and Shield, which would act in the same vein as Tower Cross and the Ivy Society.

However, for a group of twelve sophomore men, this new organization held little interest. Instead, they decided to form their own class society called the Full Moon Club, but with a twist. As they stated in the 1904 edition of the *Brown and Blue* yearbook, the goal of the Full Moon Club was "the promotion of good fellowship among its members, and by keeping it a society of the Class of 1904, and not making it a sophomore society, its good fellowship is assured, not for three years of college life, but for all time." However grandiose this description, though, the real purpose of the Full Moon Club was to get together and get drunk, plain and simple. The time and location of all of its meetings were kept secret, though the student body could often tell when the meetings ended "for every one of the members of the club returned home in a questionable state." The members of the club were exclusively fraternity men, with each of the five active fraternities represented by at least one Full Mooner, as they were called. And since the Full Mooners were never interested in bringing new members, their organization died out after the 1904 graduation class departed campus.[26]

The Full Moon Club's homage to itself from the 1904 edition of the Brown & Blue yearbook. Most of the letters appear to be initials of the members, but any meaning behind "S.A.A.B.F." and "L.F.H." has been lost to history.

THE SOCIAL FRATERNITIES

3

Building a campus community from the ground up

The history of Greek life at Tufts University begins with those organizations commonly referred to as "social" fraternities. This descriptor is chosen solely out of convenience, since these groups have generally been the most visible on campus given their occupancy of chapter houses, and their propensity to host social events on weekends. Their stories, however, go much further.

ZETA PSI (Kappa Chapter, 1855 – present)
THETA DELTA CHI (Kappa Charge, 1856 – present)

In the beginning, there was Zeta Psi. And but a year later, there was Theta Delta Chi. These two organizations, the first Greek-letter fraternities ever established at Tufts, brought life, energy, and a host of ideas to a very young campus. They were rivals, without a doubt, but throughout most of their history, they practiced a true, sincere cooperation and shared many a similar experience. Both have the Kappa moniker to signify their place in their national hierarchy. Both were nearly kicked out of their respective organizations a number of times in their early years. But through determination and good political skills, they not only kept their charters, they rose to a position of prominence in the nascent fraternity world. In the 1860s, both saw nearly all of their members leave campus to fight the Civil War. Still, neither closed down. Theta Delta Chi built the first fraternity house on campus in the summer of 1893, and five years later, Zeta Psi became their neighbor when they purchased a house from Professor William R. Shipman; their houses are still just a hundred feet apart today. Combined, the two chapters count thousands of alumni including six college and university presidents, four who served their alma mater, Tufts College. They have both managed to keep their charters continuously for over one hundred sixty years, though each has come close to dormancy in modern times. Their stories are distinct and their legacies are unique, but their history is best told together.[1]

It almost never was

In the fall of 1845, a teenager named John Bradt Yates Sommers enrolled at the University of the City of New York (now New York University, or NYU), ready to begin his education. John, the son of a preacher, was born and raised in New York City and, like many urban college students of his day, commuted to school from his home, a row house at 82 Madison Street. His classmates described him as being of a "quiet, refined nature," but also a charismatic leader "who naturally drew men toward him." So, it was no real surprise to all who knew John when, that fall, he received a bid from each of the three fraternities on campus: Delta Phi, Sigma Phi, and Psi Upsilon. Of these bids, John supposedly took a great interest in Psi Upsilon, which was considered the strongest of the three at the time. But, he had a slight problem with Psi Upsilon. As it turned out, the fraternity had recently expelled his good friend, and he felt the expulsion was rather unwarranted. So John walked away from Psi Upsilon, a fateful decision if there ever was one.[2]

Despite this setback, John remained intrigued by the operations of the fraternities, and over time his interest only grew. By the early part of 1847, he began working with his long-time friend, William Henry Dayton, and a fellow classmate, John Moon Skillman (who was even younger than John), to plan a new fraternal organization. They met often at John's row house, where they discussed their fraternity and outlined all it would become. However, by this time William's health was in serious decline due to tuberculosis. On the advice of his doctors, William made plans to head south to the University of North Carolina (UNC) and its more temperate climate. The impending separation, though, soon gave the men a grand idea. Instead of just starting one chapter of their fraternity at NYU, they would also organize a second at UNC. Finally, on June 1, 1847, after months of work, the three men signed the document proclaiming their pledge of loyalty to each other and their fraternity, Zeta Psi. On that day, John Sommers was seventeen years of age, John Skillman a mere sixteen, and William, the elder of the group, was twenty.[3]

Unfortunately, Zeta Psi's plan for immediate expansion fell apart due to tragedy just a month later. William's health continued to deteriorate during the summer, and as he made his way to UNC in August of 1847, he succumbed to tuberculosis. With heavy hearts, John Sommers and John Skillman carried on with their fraternity at NYU when the fall semester of 1847 resumed, working quickly to initiate men and build Zeta Psi into an organization of prominence on campus. Expanding to other schools, though, was never far from their minds. By the spring of 1848, less than a year after the official beginning of the fraternity, the members of Zeta Psi established a second chapter at Williams College, followed by a third at Rutgers College. The year 1852 was especially good in terms of expansion, as Zeta Psi increased its roll of chapters from six to nine, including the establishment of Rho chapter at Harvard University. For Tufts College, the birth of Rho chapter would prove to be fateful.[4]

The sixth child

In the 1840s, a student wishing to attend the most progressive, most prestigious, and most prominent college in America didn't necessarily look to Harvard or Yale or Princeton. Instead, he often turned to Union College in Schenectady, New York. At the time, Union drew men from all over the country who were eager to learn from the school's highly esteemed faculty, especially its president, Reverend Eliphalet Nott. Such was the environment when, in the spring of 1847, six sophomores – Abel Beach, Theodore Brown, Andrew Green, William Hyslop, William Akin, and Samuel Wile – gathered in the West College building to discuss an idea. The men were good friends who enjoyed each other's company, and that day they talked about forming their own literary society as a means of solidifying their relationship. During the next few weeks and months, though, while contemplating the goals of their new society, the men soon gravitated towards a slightly different idea. They would start a new secret fraternity, one that would be both social and literary in nature. Union College was no stranger to fraternities. By 1847, six other national organizations were represented on campus, including five that had started there. Over the next year, the six men refined their idea, wrote their constitution and ritual, and created their insignia. Finally, on the night of June 5, 1848, the six original founders and six additional men gathered together at an off campus house and unanimously resolved to start a secret association called Theta Delta Chi. Union College had just seen the birth of its sixth Greek-letter fraternity.[5]

Within one year of its official founding, Theta Delta Chi became a national organization by expanding to the nearby Ballston Law School in Ballston, New York. In a departure from other national fraternities, Theta Delta Chi identified its branches as "charges" rather than chapters, so the group at Ballston Law School became known as Beta Charge, while the one at Union became the Alpha Charge. Unfortunately, Beta Charge lived but one year, as the school moved to another location and the members were absorbed by Alpha. Within a few years, though, Theta Delta Chi had expanded in earnest to the University of Vermont (1852), Rensselaer Polytechnic Institute (1853), the College of William and Mary (1853), and Brown University (1853). For Tufts College, the establishment of the Zeta Charge at Brown University would prove to be fateful.[6]

Zeta Psi comes to Tufts

In the summer of 1853, Harvard University was over two hundred years old and had a prestige among American colleges that few schools could match

(Union College excluded, of course). Meanwhile, two and a half miles from Harvard, construction began on a new building in Medford to house the recently chartered Tufts College. As work progressed during the 1853–54 school year, though, Tufts remained but a college on paper. It had no reputation, no history, and no students. Its leadership included a reluctant president who spent considerable time that year traveling around Europe instead of overseeing the construction. And yet, to members of the Rho chapter of Zeta Psi at Harvard, this new school was more than just a slowly forming brick building on a barren hill; it was an opportunity. Tufts College, they decided, would be a great campus for a chapter of their fraternity. So, in August of 1854, the men of Rho chapter headed to Zeta Psi's national convention in Springfield, Massachusetts, seeking permission to organize a chapter at Tufts College. Not a single student had yet walked through the doors of the soon-to-be-completed College Hall, but somehow those Harvard students convinced the fraternity's leadership of their idea. By the end of the convention, Rho chapter had been authorized to start a new chapter at Tufts College.[7]

The job was eventually entrusted to two men from Rho chapter, Robert M. Morse and John L. Flagg. For an entire school year, however, the two men did nothing substantive in this regard. Perhaps they were disappointed when, just a few weeks after their fraternity's convention, only seven students enrolled at Tufts to begin their education. Or perhaps they wanted to learn more about Tufts as an institution, to make sure the school was indeed worthy of a chapter. Either way, in the weeks before Tufts College opened for its second year in the fall of 1855, the two men of Rho chapter decided, finally, the time was right. They turned to one Tufts student in particular, Benjamin A. Hathaway, who was returning for his second year. They could not have picked a more able leader. Not only had Benjamin survived that first year of Tufts College, he had also helped create the Mathetican literary society. So, Robert and John authorized Benjamin to organize a Zeta Psi chapter, picking only the best from among the other twenty students. Benjamin chose five. Then, on October 22, 1855, these six were initiated into Zeta Psi by Rho chapter on the campus of Harvard. The new chapter at Tufts was called Kappa, with the following charter members:

Benjamin Allen Hathaway (1858)
Hermon Joseph Smith (1858)
Henry Bacon Brown (1859)
William Henry Hobbs (1859)
John Collins Redman
John F. Wood

Of this group, only Hermon had been on campus with Benjamin the previous year, meaning in all likelihood Benjamin had only known the other four men for a few weeks before choosing them to be part of the fraternity. A seventh man, Thomas S. Bridgham, was initiated into the chapter at the second meeting.[8]

Almost immediately, though, Kappa chapter had a serious problem. On October 17, 1855, just a few days before Kappa came into existence, the Grand Officers of Zeta Psi met in an emergency meeting in New York City to discuss rumors that the Harvard men were working to start a new chapter at Tufts. Apparently there was a misunderstanding regarding the authority granted to Rho chapter during the convention in 1854, because now, just a year later, the Grand Officers felt much differently. In no uncertain terms, they demanded Rho chapter cease and desist all efforts with the current group of Tufts men and start over, this time following the proper laws of the fraternity. "Resolved," they wrote, "That the said so-called chapter at Tufts College is not and cannot as it now exists constitute a branch or chapter of the Zeta Psi fraternity… [but that] after prior necessary and regular proceedings have been had, [we] will grant a charter to such new chapter as may regularly be established in Tufts College." Copies of the resolutions were then sent to each of the active chapters of Zeta Psi, including Rho, although the document arrived after the initiation. The men of Harvard must have been dumbfounded when they read these words, for they had clearly obtained authorization in 1854 to start a chapter at Tufts. And yet now they were being told to start over from the beginning. In the face of this injustice, the men of Rho decided to fight for their brothers in Kappa chapter. Their first chance came at a special national meeting of Zeta Psi in early May of 1856. Just as the meeting was about to recess, the delegates from Harvard, along with their newly acquired allies from Delta chapter at Rutgers University, announced they would not abide by the resolution against Kappa chapter. Such an act of open defiance was not well received by others, and soon a motion was offered to support the Grand Officers and the action they were taking. In their haste to quell the dissent, the leaders of Zeta Psi then called for a quick vote on the motion, even thought the delegates were tired after a long day's work and many didn't completely understand the facts of the situation. But, the leaders must have thought, the men in the room would certainly respect their authority and vote favorably on the motion. They did not. The delegates, by a majority of eight votes, rebutted the actions of the Grand Officers and made it clear they wanted Kappa chapter in its current form to remain a part of Zeta Psi. Two national leaders resigned immediately in protest. Clearly, the matter was a delicate one within the fraternity.[9]

It was also far from settled. The fight over Kappa began anew a few months later at the regularly scheduled convention in New Brunswick, New Jersey (home of the Delta chapter at Rutgers), which opened on July 3, 1856. The first order of business was the reinstatement of the two officers who had resigned back in May, thereby setting the stage for renewed confrontation. Then came a motion to remove any reference to the Tufts affair from the meeting held back in May; if passed, it would have meant that the original resolution of October 1855, banning Rho from organizing a new chapter at Tufts, would be in effect without controversy, and Kappa would be gone. The delegates from Rho countered by moving to strike the original resolution altogether; if passed, it would have meant Rho had indeed been granted the authority at the 1854 convention to start a chapter at Tufts as they saw fit, so Kappa could continue in its present form. With two competing motions, and tempers flaring on both sides, one question was finally put to a vote of the delegates: "Shall the minutes of the Grand Officers [from October 1855] be accepted?" Voting "yea" meant Kappa chapter was null and void, while voting "nay" meant Kappa remained. By this point, the delegates from Rho had built a healthy coalition of supporters looking to defeat this motion, but as each chapter stood to vote, the outcome seemed no clearer. Phi votes three for Yea! Delta votes three for Nay! And so it went. But when the final votes were counted the "yeas" had prevailed over the "nays" by a majority of one. The minutes of the Grand Officer were accepted, and Kappa was no more.[10]

Well, not quite. It appears the fight over Kappa was never about the men at Tufts, but was instead about Zeta Psi's official procedure for establishing a new chapter, and how Rho had apparently overstepped its authority. Now it was over, but the controversy had left behind an almost evenly divided fraternity, one that was in danger of breaking apart. Recognizing the situation, the Grand Officers quickly worked out a compromise. They put forth a new resolution, stating that Rho's original authority to start a chapter at Tufts was null and void, but that Rho had worked in good faith to expand Zeta Psi to Tufts College, and if they presented the petition from the Tufts men to the Grand Officers for the establishment of Kappa chapter, the petition would be given a vote. So Rho chapter did just that, and without any recorded controversy, the petition was accepted. Kappa at Tufts College was now an official chapter of the Zeta Psi fraternity, with all those initiated since its unofficial beginning considered members of the fraternity.[11]

While this ordeal played out far from campus, the members of Kappa continued to meet on a regular basis in the dormitory room of Henry Brown and John Redman, where they carried on with their operations and initiated more men. Working out of a dormitory room, though, was somewhat peculiar, as fraternities at that time normally based their operations out of rented chapter rooms near campus. Such an arrangement gave the fraternity not only a private space to perform their secret rituals, but also a place to congregate and socialize. The members of Kappa chapter were no different in this need. By December 1856, they had rented a room "in a wooden story-and-a-half structure just east of the bridge at Medford" for their meetings. However, it appears the men did not get along too well with the landlord of this building, known only as "Angel," for he often acted otherwise when the chapter was even a little late on rent payments. So, Zeta Psi moved to another space on Main Street in Medford. This home also proved to short-lived, as a fire in 1860 destroyed the building and all early records of the chapter. And then, in April of 1861, shots were fired at Fort Sumter off the coast of South Carolina. The Civil War had just begun, a conflict that nearly destroyed Kappa altogether.[12]

Do I have to go?

With the months of 1854 passing by ever so quickly, Augustus Scott of Milford, Massachusetts, found himself in a bind. He would be leaving for college that fall to begin his freshman year; that was a given. The problem was where. As a dutiful son, he was expected to follow the will of his parents, who were early adopters of the Universalist faith, and head off to the brand new Mecca of Universalism that was Tufts College. Augustus, though, wasn't so sure. Tufts College had yet to be officially dedicated, and while it would open for students in the fall of 1854, those who enrolled were told to expect an annoyance or two during the year while everything settled into place. That wasn't exactly the college experience Augustus was looking to enjoy firsthand. In addition, he didn't know any of the men who were thinking of going to Tufts, so there was nothing positive to draw him to the new school. Instead, he wanted to head south to Brown University, a school he knew quite well given his geographical proximity to the campus. After some persuasion, he convinced his parents he'd be better off at Brown. So, in September of 1854, Augustus packed his bags and headed to the college of his choice.[13]

Once on campus, Augustus quickly attracted the attention of the Zeta Charge of Theta Delta Chi, one of six active fraternities at the time. This Charge had only been established at Brown a year earlier, thus making it the youngest fraternity on campus. Nonetheless, Augustus was soon initiated into Theta Delta Chi, where he became an enthusiastic member of his fraternity. By the end of his freshman year, Augusts was well settled into life at Brown University, and given the choice, would probably have stayed there to finish his degree. His parents, though, had continued to watch the progress of Tufts College during the 1854–55 school year, and when it became clear the school would officially open the following fall, they implored their son to transfer. Brown University was, after all, a Baptist school led by a Baptist minister, hardly the right influence for a young Universalist. Reluctantly, Augustus agreed, and in the fall of 1855, he arrived on the Medford campus to begin his sophomore year.[14]

Augustus transitioned quickly to life at Tufts College during those first few weeks. He became friends with most of the other men and seemed to fit in quite well on campus. However, he clearly longed for a closer association with some of them, similar to the one he'd experienced in his fraternity at Brown. To make matters worse, within a few weeks some of his new friends were touting their new allegiance to Zeta Psi, thus leaving Augustus on the outside. But joining them was not an option, for he was a Theta Delta Chi. So, he began thinking seriously about placing a charge of his beloved fraternity at Tufts College. Then, he acted. Throughout the 1855–56 school year, he talked of this idea with a few men not involved in Zeta Psi, and eventually persuaded Winsor B. French and William E. Gibbs, along with a few others, to join him in the endeavor. Later in the school year, Augustus sent a petition to Alpha Charge at Union College, asking for permission to bring Theta Delta Chi to the Medford campus. His wish was granted. Tufts College was now primed for its second fraternity.[15]

When Augustus returned for his junior year with charter in hand, he immediately looked over the incoming freshman class for a few more good men. A number of freshmen fit this description, including "one young fellow, tall and slim, rather awkward in manner, but with a cheery smile and a clear eye that would always look you in the face." That young fellow was Elmer Hewitt Capen, who would eventually become an integral part of Tufts College history. But on August 29, 1856, Elmer was just a brand-new freshman when he and a group of others gathered for their initiation into Theta Delta Chi. Augustus, along with George W. Carr from the Zeta Charge at Brown and men from the newly organized Iota Charge at Harvard ran the initiation ceremony, and once it was finished, the Kappa Charge of Theta Delta Chi had been born. The charter members were:[16]

Augustus Elwin Scott (1858)
William Erastus Gibbs (1859)
Winsor Brown French (1859)
Obed Chester Turner (1859)
Elam Porter (1860)
Elmer Hewitt Capen (1860)
Benjamin Kimball Russ (1860)
Horatio McIntire
Oscar Gerard Sawyer

The initiation was a perilous affair. Augustus had secured the use of a loft in a Medford volunteer firehouse just north of campus for the ceremony, and one of the firemen assured Augustus his group would not be disturbed. But, while the ceremony was on going, some other firemen noticed the lights in the normally dark building and wandered in to see what was going on. Augustus and the men were able to keep the onlookers at bay, but clearly the loft was not as private as they were led to believe. Nonetheless, the fire engine house served as the first meeting place of the fraternity for a number of months.[17]

The earliest meetings of Theta Delta Chi were devoted to initiating more members, electing officers including Winsor French as the first president, and engaging in scholarly activities. Debates were especially popular those first few weeks, with the members of the Charge tackling issues such as the powers of government, celibacy, and temperance (all were very much against the drinking of alcohol in excess). Members also read essays and declamations, while others championed the organization of a library. However, these literary and scholarly activities began to fade over time as the Charge focused more on social activities. The firehouse was well equipped to serve meals, so the fraternity soon took advantage of this set-up. As charter member William Gibbs described, "Lady nicotine and poor cigars became rather prominent in the Charge, and oyster suppers were of great delight to the brothers." Finances, too, proved to be somewhat of a challenge that first year. In March of 1857, for example, the Charge secretary was denied permission to purchase an inkwell for the keeping of minutes, which resulted in very brief records. The financial situation only got worse that following summer when two members attended the annual national convention of Theta Delta Chi. On top of the expenses associated with the trip, the two were also charged $6.65 for thirty copies of poems written by members of the Epsilon Charge at the College of William and Mary. They hadn't asked for the copies, but they sure were expected to pay for them. Unfortunately, these poems have not survived to this day.[18]

In 1858, Kappa moved its operations from the firehouse to rooms in Usher Hall near Medford Square, and these rooms were apparently more to the Charge's liking, as they stayed there for many years. However, during the 1858–59 school year, a serious situation arose with respect to Kappa's charter. At the time, the Alpha Charge at Union held almost all of the power over the national organization, and it seemed they were now having regrets about expanding to New England, especially Harvard and Tufts. So, Alpha gathered a coalition of like-minded charges at the twelfth convention of Theta Delta Chi in the summer of 1859, and began to push for Kappa's removal. Their task would not be easy. Representing Kappa were Elmer Capen and Winsor French, two men who were not going down without a fight. So eloquent were the two that after they presented their arguments to the entire convention, not one person stood up against them. Then, in a stroke of irony (or perhaps because of his earlier speech), Winsor was pressed into service to deliver the poem at the banquet when the original speaker did not show up. By all accounts he performed well, for as Elmer remarked, "we [Kappa Charge] saved the occasion from a disastrous failure." Kappa Charge had passed its first test. It would not be the last.[19]

Brother against brother

In the aftermath of the Fort Sumter attack in April 1861, the students at Tufts College must have felt not only their nation, but their personal lives were falling apart. Blood had been shed, states had seceded from the Union, war had been declared, and these men knew without a doubt they would soon be in the conflict. War, after all, is fought by the young. As for allegiance, the campus was Union, since all students hailed from northern states including a majority from New England. That made for a common enemy in the Confederacy, and the thought of engaging the Rebels in battle soon became a powerful draw to both students and alumni (who were all relatively young as well). So off they went to fight, in droves. Over the course of the war, approximately 30 percent of all Tufts College undergraduates and alumni enlisted in various units of the Union Army. Many joined front-line infantry and cavalry regiments based in their home states, units that fought numerous battles both small and large, famous and not. Many were fraternity men.[20]

Horatio Bisbee holds the honor of being the first Tufts student to enlist. Born in Canton, Maine, in 1839, Horatio entered Tufts in the fall of 1858 as a freshman. A year later, he joined the Kappa chapter of Zeta Psi, one of nine men to be initiated that year. But in the spring of 1861 his life changed forever. Three days after the surrender of Fort Sumter, he answered to his sense of duty by dropping out of Tufts and enlisting in the Union Army, where he landed as a private in the 5th Regiment, Massachusetts Volunteer Infantry. His stay in the 5th Massachusetts, though, was not long – a few months later, he was discharged and sent back to civilian life. But Horatio was not interested in this path. So, he returned to his home state of Maine and helped organize the new 9th Regiment of the Maine Volunteer Infantry. Along with his enlistment in the 9th Maine came a promotion, first to Captain of Company F, and then eventually to Colonel of the regiment. His leadership capabilities were tested over the year and a half he served with the 9th Maine, as he dealt with awful field accommodations, rampant disease, low morale, the near mutiny of his troops, and then combat in a number of campaigns. Despite these obstacles he led the men exceptionally well. In March 1863, he was honorably discharged from service once again, retaining his rank of Colonel. This time, though, Horatio had seen enough of war. He pursued a different direction, eventually becoming a lawyer and a United States congressman from the state of Florida.[21]

Horatio Bisbee's enlistment in 1861 sparked a fire among Zeta Psi members and alumni in particular, for before the war was over, nearly half of the chapter's membership joined the fight, including three of the six charter members. One Zeta Psi alumnus, Sheldon Connor, rose to the rank of Brigadier General in the Union Army. The chapter had two gold stars, one being Captain Oliver Lowell, who was wounded at the Battle of Gettysburg, taken prisoner by the Confederate Army, and then died the following day. The other was Lieutenant Henry Walton, killed in the Battle of Cedar Creek, Virginia, on October 19, 1864.[22]

Rienzi Loud was one particular member of Zeta Psi who had quite an odyssey as a Union soldier. Originally hailing from Rockland, Massachusetts, he enrolled at Tufts in the fall of 1859, and shortly thereafter was initiated into

Zeta Psi. However, after his first semester, he headed to Dowagiac, Michigan, to become a teacher. At the time, it was quite common for college students to teach during school breaks, and indeed administrators encouraged this practice since it allowed the men to keep up with their studies while earning money for tuition. Rienzi, however, did not return to Tufts the following semester, opting instead to continue teaching in Michigan. Then came the war. He answered the call by joining the 1st Michigan Cavalry Regiment. But, after some time in the 1st Michigan Cavalry, Rienzi left the regiment and headed back to Massachusetts, where he was commissioned in early 1864 as a Second Lieutenant in a brand new regiment, the 5th Massachusetts Colored Cavalry. As its name suggests, this unit consisted of colored enlisted men who were led by white officers. Together Lt. Loud and his men fought their first battle at Petersburg, Virginia. From there, the regiment participated in the siege of Richmond, Virginia, and following the city's surrender in March, 1865, Lt. Loud and his troops were some of the first to enter the city. He survived the war and eventually moved back to Michigan where, like Horatio Bisbee, he became a prominent lawyer.[23]

As it turned out, Rienzi Loud was not the only member of Zeta Psi to serve in a colored unit. Hermon Smith, a founding member of the Kappa chapter, graduated from Tufts in 1858 and then began his medical training in a highly unorthodox manner (at least by today's standards) – he worked alongside a doctor in Vermont as an apprentice of sorts, and also sat in on some medical lectures at Harvard University, Dartmouth College, and the College of Physicians and Surgeons of New York. Though most of this training appears to be rather informal and certainly not complete, Hermon felt compelled to put his skills to work towards the war effort. In 1864, he took and passed the medical exams for the Union army, thus earning himself a commission as an assistant surgeon in the 5th United States Colored Cavalry. This regiment, which would eventually be comprised of freed slaves from Kentucky, fought a number of battles late in the Civil War. Hermon served in the regiment until his discharge in 1866, when he then returned to Dartmouth College and earned his medical degree in earnest a year later.[24]

Theta Delta Chi sent nearly as many men as Zeta Psi to fight the war. Six undergraduate members were the first from Kappa Charge to leave in 1862, followed by fifteen undergraduates and alumni in later years. One such alumnus was Winsor French, a charter member of Kappa Charge, who graduated in 1859 and became a lawyer in Saratoga Springs, New York. When the war erupted, Winsor began gathering a number of local men with the goal of forming a volunteer company. Such was the way many volunteer units came about during the civil war, via door-to-door recruitment of friends and neighbors. By 1862, Winsor's group had become Company D of the 77th New York Infantry Regiment, and the men of the company looked to install him as their captain since he had been so instrumental in its formation. However, the commander of the entire 77th New York, Colonel McKean, recognized an important leadership quality in Captain French, so he promoted him to the regimental level and made him his adjutant (assistant). During the next year, Capt. French participated in many battles, and for his performance on the field he was promoted to Colonel in 1863, then given command of the 77th New York a few months later. Col. French and his regiment eventually found themselves fighting in the Battle of Cedar Creek, Virginia. Early in the battle, an incoming shell violently knocked General Bidwell off his horse, and unfortunately the general succumbed to his injuries just few hours later. In his place, Col. French assumed command of the entire brigade, which was considerably larger in scope than a regiment. Ultimately, Col. French and his brigade re-captured territory that had been lost to the Confederates at the Battle of Bull Run over four years earlier. Finally, in March of 1865, Col. French was promoted to Brigadier General in recognition of his service. As a result, both Zeta Psi and Theta Delta Chi each have a Brigadier General from the Civil War among their alumni.[25]

Theta Delta Chi's only gold star of the war was Lewis E. Munro. Hailing from Roxbury, Massachusetts, Lewis graduated from Tufts College in 1863. A few months later, Lewis received a commission as a First Lieutenant in the brand new 59th Massachusetts Volunteer Infantry Regiment. By the late spring of 1864, the 59th Massachusetts prepared for the assault on Petersburg, Virginia, with now Captain Munroe leading his troops into battle. The assault, however, soon bogged down into trench warfare, with the Union soldiers unable to breech the defenses of the Confederates. In an attempt to break the stalemate, some miners from the 48th Pennsylvania had the idea to tunnel under the Confederate lines, fill the chamber with black powder, and detonate it. After days and weeks of digging, the miners were finally ready for their surprise. At 4:40 a.m. in the morning of July 30, 1864, the Union troops detonated the buried four tons of gunpowder, which set off a huge explosion that destroyed fortifications, equipment, and men in one fell swoop, while also creating a giant crater. Union troops, including Capt. Munroe and his men of the 59th Massachusetts, swarmed through the crater as planned. However, while Capt. Munroe was standing on the rim of the crater directing his troops, a Confederate sharpshooter got him in the forehead, killing him instantly. Ultimately the assault failed that day, as did many other assaults in the months that followed. Indeed, the city of Petersburg didn't surrender until April 3, 1865, nearly a year after the siege began. Captain Munroe, in some of his last words before he left for war, told his fraternity brothers to "Keep bright the lights of Theta Delta Chi."[26]

Meanwhile, on the home front

While the fraternity men at Tufts were leaving campus and joining the war effort, the operations of their respective chapters were being left to an ever-decreasing number of students. Of the two, though, it was Zeta Psi who suffered the most in this regard. After graduation in July 1862, Kappa chapter was left with only two active members, Benjamin Kinsman and Horace Makechnie. These men had only been initiated a year earlier, but now they were left to carry on the tradition. The national officers of Zeta Psi realized this situation probably meant the chapter was doomed, so at their convention in Boston on December 30, 1862, they suspended Kappa's charter for the duration of the war, and instructed the two men to send all materials to Epsilon chapter at Brown University for safe-keeping. Still, Benjamin and Horace did not give up. They continued to meet on a semi-regular basis over the next two years, either in their dormitory room or in the vestry of the Universalist church in Medford, to discuss the ways and means of reforming their chapter. Despite their efforts to remain active, though, they did not initiate a single other member into Zeta Psi for two years. Finally, just after they began their senior year, the two were able to rebuild the chapter. A group of nine men had recently formed a new local society at Tufts College, most likely with the intention of bringing another national fraternity to campus, but Benjamin and Horace convinced them instead to join Kappa chapter of Zeta Psi en masse. From there, the fraternity continued to grow in members and was never again left with so few, at least until another war came calling.[27]

Kappa Charge of Theta Delta Chi, on the other hand, never reached such low numbers of men as Zeta Psi, and indeed the Charge had at least one member graduate every year throughout the 1860s. But the war was never far from their minds. In keeping with their literary traditions, the members of Kappa Charge often spent their meetings debating the war policies. They also kept a watchful eye on their rival, Zeta Psi, which seemed to be faltering as each semester passed. At one point in the fall of 1864, members of Kappa Charge celebrated the presumed demise of Zeta Psi, but the celebration quickly ended when Zeta Psi was reborn with those nine new members. To make matters worse for Theta Delta Chi, Zeta Psi soon moved to chapter rooms in Usher Hall, the same building they called home. But, during that school year, the two fraternities began to cooperate in ways that made a lasting impact on life at Tufts College. In November of 1864, they jointly published the first-ever campus magazine, *The Tuftonian*, at ten cents a copy. Before 1864, no one at Tufts had published any student-centric tome such as a yearbook or a school newspaper. The only regular publication was a yearly *Catalogue of Tufts College*, with useful information such as the names and addresses of each student, a listing of the faculty, the course of study, the school calendar, and the admission requirements. But the *Catalogue* did not offer a real glimpse of student life; it contained information for the students, not about them. So, Zeta Psi and Theta Delta Chi decided to tell the story of their classmates in *The Tuftonian*, initially published once a year in November. On its pages were a listing of all active student organizations (of which there were many, for such a small school) as well as information about campus life and the alumni. Today, these words offer the best if not only source of information regarding the early years of Tufts College. And for this, we have only the students to thank – it appears the administration played no role in this publication, leaving the distribution and finances solely to the members of Zeta Psi and Theta Delta Chi.[28]

The two fraternities continued their joint publication until a falling out in 1872, when they could not resolve their differences regarding what to publish in *The Tuftonian.* In the wake of the spilt, Zeta Psi alone continued to publish *The Tuftonian* much in the style of its past, focusing on information about campus life. Theta Delta Chi, on the other hand, started its own alternative magazine called *The Budget*, which was similar in many ways to *The Tuftonian*, but also offered poetry and philosophical essays, thereby earning the distinction as being the first undergraduate literary publication at Tufts College. Professor Charles Fay, a Tufts graduate and member of Theta Delta Chi, is credited with naming this new periodical, since its publication was always under dire financial stress. Indeed, the fraternity only published two issues in 1874 and 1875 before closing it down. Meanwhile, by the spring of 1874, the students at Tufts felt the college could use an additional publication, one that was more frequent than *The Tuftonian.* So, in April of that year, a group of students formed the Tufts College Publishing Association, and two months later they issued their first journal, *The Tufts Collegian.* This publication focused on essays and editorials first, local campus news second, and soon became very popular among the students. By 1878, the two fraternities had reconciled their literary differences and joined with the Tufts Collegiate Publishing Association to produce a monthly magazine using an old name, *The Tuftonian.* In addition, starting in 1878, Zeta Psi and Theta Delta Chi also jointly published the first yearbook at Tufts, aptly named the *Brown and Blue* after the newly chosen school colors. The fraternities eventually gave up complete control of both publications, but still maintained a heavy influence over their content, especially *The Tuftonian*, by placing numerous members in editorial and staff positions within the Tufts College Publishing Association each year. This influence would go unchecked for nearly a decade, until the non-fraternity men finally decided to challenge this dominance.[29]

Meanwhile, the students at Tufts in the 1860s were also branching out into other areas, most notably collegiate sports. Before the Civil War, athletics at Tufts College was an informal affair, with no organized teams or competitions. That all changed in September 1863, when the sophomore class ('66) challenged the freshman class ('67) to a game of "New York ball," the first time such a competition had been held. The only problem was, almost no one at Tufts had ever heard of this game, except for three sophomores from New York who had learned to play while at the Clinton Liberal Institute. But the freshman were up for a challenge, and quickly learned that New York ball was better known as "base ball," similar in many ways to the game they knew called "rounders." The competition was on! After the three innings the freshmen were ahead 10 to none, in what was probably an example of beginner's luck. This did not last. When the game ended a few hours later, the sophomores had triumphed 90 to 30. Nonetheless, baseball (to use the modern name) soon became a very popular sport on campus, with informal games breaking out nearly every day.[30]

Baseball would not stay an informal sport for very long. By 1864, the students had organized two official baseball teams, the All-Nine of Tufts (considered the better of the two) and the Ballou Club. Credit to organizing the All-Nine is given to Henry W. Cory, a member of Theta Delta Chi and the first captain of the team. These two clubs contained twenty-three student athletes and eight student managers, or about half the undergraduates in the college. Of the two fraternities, Theta Delta Chi had more of its members on the two teams, including nearly all of the players on the Ballou Club. Both squads played games against other colleges such as Dartmouth and Brown, as well as amateur club teams such as the Lowells and the Tri-mountains. These games often featured plenty of offense, with final scores such as 82 to 26 against, and 113 to 37 for Tufts. One reason for so much offense is that no one used baseball gloves (they hadn't been introduced to the sport yet), so fielding errors were quite common. As for a uniform, the men wore their normal clothes along with a special belt, emblazoned with the word "Tufts" (which was not provided by the school, but purchased by the men).[31]

While the early incarnation of baseball was primarily a Theta Delta Chi affair, the two fraternities do share a legacy of cooperation on another athletic field, more specifically the Mystic River. In the fall of 1864, the members of Theta Delta Chi decided they would not limit themselves to just baseball, but would instead try another sport: rowing. So, they purchased a forty-five foot, six-oared lapstreak boat, hauled it down to the Mystic River, and began regular training. They soon realized they'd be better served by storing their boat near the river, so they secured a boathouse about a half-mile from campus and set up the "Theta Boat Club." The only thing they lacked was a competitive rival. Not to worry, Zeta Psi eagerly stepped in to fill this void, as they soon purchased a similar six-oared boat for their own crew team. In addition, Zeta Psi also erected a boathouse near Theta Delta Chi's structure, thereby adding to the rivalry. The Zeta Psi crew called themselves the "Undine Boat Club," named after the mystical water nymph of lore. The two competitors were then off to the races. Although it appears no formal competition occurred between the two boat clubs, they did stage many friendly races in "English fashion" with one boat behind the other in a staggered start, since the width of the river did not permit the two boats to race side-by-side. On one occasion that first year, the Theta boat rowed all the way into Boston Harbor, where they were soon intercepted by a Russian war ship stationed in the area. But the Theta boat club would only last for just over one year. By 1866, the crew from Theta Delta Chi had tired of the long walk from campus to their boathouse, so they sold their craft and went back to baseball. Zeta Psi's Undine Boat Club remained active until the 1871–72 school year, although it is unclear if they competed officially against other teams. Nonetheless, the crew races between Theta and Undine boat clubs between 1864 and 1866 represent the first interfraternity competitions at Tufts.[32]

Ups and downs

After the Civil War ended in the spring of 1865, and the campus returned to a normal college routine, the two fraternities were seen as bright spots within each of their national organizations. The war had forced the closure of many chapters of both Zeta Psi and Theta Delta Chi, but not at Tufts. Now it was up to the Tufts men to help rebuild their respective national organizations. The Kappa chapter of Zeta Psi started first in this regard, by re-forming the Rho chapter at Harvard in 1865. But in a case of history repeating itself, the members of Kappa undertook this revival of Rho under their own initiative and without proper authorization from the Grand Officers of Zeta Psi. As a result, the Grand Officers were once again faced with a constitutional problem involving the Harvard and Tufts chapters. The situation resulted in an animated discussion at the convention that year, but by the end the delegates decided to recognize this re-establishment of Rho chapter.[33]

For the Kappa Charge of Theta Delta Chi, the rebuilding first began at home. By 1867, the Charge was down to just three active members and was in serious debt over its expenses. The situation seemed so dire that the newly organized Grand Lodge of Theta Delta Chi, which now controlled the national organization, looked to revoke Kappa's charter and start over. The members of Kappa Charge, though, did not give up. Instead, they recruited new members and paid off their debts. By 1870, they were back on solid ground and making their presence known. For example, in 1869, Kappa Charge initiated Charles Ransom Miller, who then went to Dartmouth College and established the Omicron Deuteron Charge on that campus. In 1872, members of Kappa Charge were directly responsible for reviving the defunct Eta Charge at Bowdoin College, and in the years that followed Kappa helped establish new charges at Boston University (Lambda, in 1877) and Amherst College (Mu Deuteron, in 1884), and helped revive the Iota Charge at Harvard (1882). There is also good reason to believe Kappa was instrumental in the founding of the Theta Deuteron Charge at MIT in 1890. All told, six charges in New England owe their start or revival in the late 1800s to Kappa at Tufts College.[34]

It was in 1875, though, when Kappa Charge gained a distinction never before achieved in Theta Delta Chi. That year, Kappa Charge was the first in its national organization to see one of its own rise to the educational precipice, when Elmer Hewitt Capen became the third President of Tufts College. Throughout his thirty-year tenure, President Capen was immensely popular with the students, faculty, and trustees, and he helped bring the school into the twentieth century. He oversaw the construction of many buildings including Goddard Chapel, Goddard Gymnasium, Barnum Museum, Dean Hall, Miner Hall, Paige Hall, the Bromfield-Pearson building, Curtis Hall (then known as Commons Hall), and Metcalf Hall. He was a big proponent of coeducation and one of the main reasons Tufts College opened its doors to women in 1892. He made admission into the college much more difficult, increased the number of elective courses, and added the electrical and mechanical engineering departments to the school. His influence, though, was felt especially within Kappa Charge, as the undergraduate members held themselves to the utmost of standards, lest they embarrass their president and fellow fraternity brother with bad behavior or poor judgment. And Kappa Charge's contribution to the school's leadership did not stop there. To date, the Charge has contributed three presidents and one acting president to Tufts College including Leonard Carmichael, who guided Tufts College through World War II.[35]

In the 1880s, Kappa Charge made one more contribution to the literary world, only this one was at the national level. By this time, most national fraternities were circulating semi-regular magazines to their active members, alumni, and other national Greek-letter organizations. Such publications were the main form of communication between the various chapters, but they had a higher purpose as well, for they were viewed as a symbol of prestige within the greater fraternity world. You simply could not be the best without one. But by the early 1880s, Theta Delta Chi's magazine, *The Shield*, had long been defunct, and its absence was certainly noted among the other national fraternities. Many within Theta Delta Chi wanted to resume publication, but no one took the lead, so all attempts at its revival went nowhere. That all changed in 1883, when Edwin Start of Kappa Charge decided to step forward and bring *The Shield* back into circulation. The leaders of the Grand Lodge of Theta Delta Chi were all for the idea, but they didn't give Edwin much of a chance due to the large expense of producing a national magazine. Despite this lack of confidence from his superiors, Edwin forged ahead and enlisted an alumnus of Kappa Charge, E. W. Powers, to help with the business aspect. A few months later, in January 1884, *The Shield* was back in circulation. The members of Kappa Charge continued to publish new editions for just over a year, until the Grand Lodge (which no longer feared failure) took over the operation. Soon the magazine was known throughout the inter-fraternity world as one of the better journals, thus helping Theta Delta Chi enhance its prestige at the national level.[36]

Theta Delta Chi members pose for a studio portrait, June, 1885.

MEANWHILE, the members of Zeta Psi weren't exactly resting on their laurels. Throughout the 1870s and 1880s, the chapter maintained a strong position on campus, one that would be enviable even today. Among its membership were the captain of the football team in 1875, the valedictorians and salutatorians in 1876, and nearly one-third of all students elected to Phi Beta Kappa before 1900. However, by 1880 the Grand Officers of Zeta Psi had developed some serious misgivings about Kappa chapter. Tufts College was, in their mind, an institution seemingly headed down in prestige, not up. By extension, so too was Kappa chapter, a situation that could only hurt the reputation of Zeta Psi. A resolution passed at the convention that year to investigate the chapter more closely, and from then on Kappa had a black mark upon its name within the national organization. Over the next three years, that black mark showed up in the minutes of the conventions as a condition against the chapter. No action was ever taken with regards to the resolution, but no action was ever taken to revoke the mark either, so there it remained for all in Zeta Psi to notice. However, at the national convention of 1883, Frederick Snow from Kappa chapter decided he'd finally had enough. He was tired of seeing his chapter singled out each year in the convention minutes without any justification. So, he brought the issue to the convention floor and demanded those who had a problem with

Kappa step forth and speak. But only silence ensued, until someone else moved to remove the stigma against Kappa chapter. Without dissent, this new motion passed with ease. The black mark against Kappa was gone.[37]

Well, not quite. The fight may have ended in 1883, but the battle did not. Some eight years later, just before the convention of 1891 was to take place, yet another resolution was proposed, this one asking Kappa chapter to give up their charter for the next three years. The resolution was put forth by Walter G. Eliot of Alpha chapter, who once again feared the future of Tufts College was in doubt and therefore not worthy of hosting a chapter of his fraternity. As a peace offering, Walter also proposed that the existing chapter at Tufts be combined with Lambda chapter at Bowdoin, and that Lambda members be given the ability to initiate new Tufts men they felt were worthy. As was customary, the central office of Zeta Psi circulated this and other resolutions to the chapters of Zeta Psi prior to the convention, so the delegates knew what was coming. Of course, the central office at the time was but one man, Israel Pierson, and he was not in support of this resolution. So, he used his powers as national secretary to do something about this injustice. While he did circulate Walter's resolution, he also included a letter of rebuttal from Willard S. Martin of Kappa chapter (an undergraduate at the time), and his own personal comment, presented below:

> It would be an insult to your intelligence to attempt to show that the proposed scheme is unconstitutional, and to your sense of right and of obligation to Zeta Psi to make any comment upon the proposition. Two facts stand out prominently: The record of the KAPPA CHAPTER [his emphasis] is an honorable one, and the Chapter has had a continuous existence since its organization, thirty-five years ago.

At the convention, all chapters threw their support behind Kappa chapter, and the resolution failed by a unanimous vote. Kappa chapter would never again be challenged by another within Zeta Psi.[38]

Home sweet home

In the early spring of 1846, a freshman named David E. James at the University of Michigan faced a serious problem. A semester earlier, he had helped establish the Alpha Epsilon chapter of the Chi Psi fraternity at Michigan, the very first fraternity on campus. But soon thereafter, David and the rest of his chapter discovered a hard truth. Simply put, the faculty was very much opposed to secret societies, and if they discovered the existence of Chi Psi, they would likely expel the chapter, if not all of its members. The fraternity had taken steps to remain inconspicuous, mainly by holding its meetings and initiations away from campus at a local hotel. However, by that spring, David felt the chapter needed a safer place to meet, one that was farther away from the prying eyes of the faculty, so he started to look for a new home. Soon enough he found it. East of campus was a stretch of woods known as the "Black Forest." It was remote, virtually uninhabited, and private; a perfect spot if there ever was one. So in April of that year, David hired some men to venture into the woods about a mile and a half, clear a small field, and build a log cabin out of the felled lumber. The resulting structure was certainly modest – a single room, twenty feet wide by twenty-four feet long, heated only by a fireplace at one end. But to the chapter it was perfect. A month later the construction was complete, and the chapter started gathering at their lodge in the woods for meetings and initiations. The first fraternity house in America had just been built.[39]

Ultimately it would take decades for Chi Psi's lodge in the woods to morph into the fraternity houses prevalent today on many college campuses, places where members live together, eat together, and socialize. This transformation began in earnest around the 1880s, though it was more than just creating functional living spaces. Fraternity houses quickly became symbols of status as well. At Tufts College, it was Theta Delta Chi who acted first. In the early 1880s, members of the Charge began having informal discussions about such a project, and by February 1882, those informal discussions culminated in a call for action. "Dear Brother," the letter from the new housing committee began, "it is impossible to obtain rooms suitable for the use of the Society within a convenient distance from the college." To solve this problem, the housing committee proposed a grand idea. They would build a house for Kappa Charge, the very first the Tufts campus had ever seen. But, as the letter made perfectly clear, they needed the alumni's money – the undergraduates could not finance the project all by themselves, which was estimated at $5,000 in total. Then, the committee awaited the responses. Many alumni wrote back, pledging money as they were able, while others could only offer moral support. Just over a year later, with momentum for the project still pushing forward, the alumni formally established Kappa Charge of Theta Delta Chi Fraternity, Incorporated, to take over the project. But in the end, the corporation held no other meeting after this first one, and the idea of building a chapter house went silent.[40]

And silent the idea would stay until the spring of 1892, when a newly revived alumni corporation decided to try once again. That semester, the corporation petitioned the trustees of Tufts for the right to purchase a lot near the intersection of Curtis Street and Professors Row for their house. The trustees agreed to sell the land on the same terms they had sold other lots to professors, a mere ten cents per square foot. Still, this is about as far as the corporation went, as they did nothing more on the matter. Then, in the fall of 1892, everything changed. The local Hebrew-letter fraternity Heth Aleph Res established the first ever chapter house at Tufts College that October, when two members rented rooms at 31 George Street in Medford and started a boarding plan for the entire chapter in the residence. About six months later, the Delta Tau Delta (DTD) chapter followed suit, when they rented the former residence of Professor Hooper at 12 Conwell Avenue in West Somerville, and three members moved in. To celebrate the opening of their chapter house, DTD held a reception for the campus, and in attendance were delegates from the other fraternities. To the Theta Delta Chi men in particular, the event was transformative. DTD had clearly thrown down the gauntlet by saying this is how a fraternity should be, living together and socializing in a house on campus. Never again would Theta Delta Chi's off-campus rooms be seen as adequate accommodation. Now, they needed a home.[41]

Within a few months after the DTD reception, the alumni corporation sprang back into action, and this time they were determined to see the project through. Only now, they wanted to be closer to the heart of campus. So, they asked the trustees if they could purchase a different lot from the college, this one right behind Professor Shipman's house. The trustees agreed, and by the end of the school year, the alumni corporation bought the lot at 123 Packard Avenue for $1,000, contracted the design, and broke ground. As for an architect, the fraternity turned to Mr. J. P. Rinn, who some years earlier had designed the ever-impressive Goddard Chapel. The total cost of the project was now estimated at $7,000, and with about $500 in the coffers, the alumni corporation borrowed $5,000 from the West Somerville Co-operative Bank and then began soliciting its alumni again to pay for the rest. Construction began over the summer of 1893, and by November, the wooden house was complete and ready for occupancy. The structure,

> was a square frame building of three floors and dormer windows in a steep roof. The kitchen and dining room were in the basement; a large living room, a billiard room, cloak room, and lavatory were on the first floor. Three suites and bath occupied the second floor, and provided living accommodations for six brothers. The Charge room and a small sleeping apartment were on the top floor.

The construction of 123 Packard Avenue sparked a mini housing boom on campus, with two more fraternities building their own homes a year later on Sawyer Avenue, just a block away. By the middle 1890s, almost all of the six active fraternities were operating out of houses on or very close to campus, either ones they owned or rented. The lone exception was Zeta Psi.[42]

Playing catch-up

By 1892, Zeta Psi had been in its rooms in Usher Hall for some thirty-seven years, and had even renovated the space twice. Apparently the chapter was very

The original Theta Delta Chi house at 123 Packard Avenue as built in 1893.

content in these accommodations, for when the other fraternities began setting up houses on campus, Zeta Psi did not seem all that interested in following suit. The chapter frequently talked about moving from Usher Hall, but rather than considering spaces closer to campus, they actually looked farther away, towards Boston. In addition, they also began dreaming up their ideal meeting place, which they envisioned as a stone castle in a medieval motif. In 1893, the chapter began soliciting funds from the alumni to build their castle, but after securing around $1500 (which was no small feat, given the poor economic climate of the day), the project languished. In 1894, the chapter did move its operations from Medford to rooms in the Odd Fellows Hall of North Cambridge. These rooms were about a mile from campus, and members often traveled there and back by horse drawn coach or even a barge on the Mystic River. Zeta Psi was now clearly the exception at Tufts, as the other five fraternities operated out of houses and rooms on or adjacent to campus. As the 1890s went on, more and more members of Zeta Psi began worrying about this discrepancy by calling for a permanent home on campus. But by then none was to be had. The situation must have been very frustrating to the chapter, especially when Delta Upsilon was essentially given land in 1894 just a block off campus for their new house, even before they had raised sufficient funds for the project. Zeta Psi, on the other hand, had a sizeable bank account ready to be spent, but a year earlier had passed on the opportunity to buy that same lot for reasons unknown, and the trustees didn't seem interested in giving them another. Perhaps, they must have thought, they had missed their chance.[43]

All was not lost, though, because Zeta Psi did have another card to play, and that was an inside track to a campus resident who wanted to move. Professor

William R. Shipman, an 1859 graduate of Middlebury College and member of the Delta Kappa Epsilon fraternity, came to Tufts College in 1864 as a professor of English literature, rhetoric, and logic. A few years later, in 1868, he built his house at 80 Professors Row, employing ship carpenters from the nearby Mystic River shipyards. As the years went on he married and had a son, Albert, who grew up on the campus of Tufts College. So, it was no surprise when, in the fall of 1893, Albert Shipman enrolled as a freshman at Tufts. He soon caught the eye of Zeta Psi, and a few months later he was initiated into Kappa chapter. But then, Professor Shipman's life got smaller. His wife passed away in 1894, and Alfred left school in 1895 to become a traveling salesman. His house, which was once filled with his family and a few boarding students, was now nearly empty. By the summer of 1898, then, Professor Shipman was ready to downsize. After all, he also owned a second, smaller house on campus at 101 Talbot Avenue, just behind his current residence, and that space was much more accommodating to his present situation. So, one day that summer, as he was talking with a young colleague, Professor Lewis (who was also an alumnus of Kappa chapter of Zeta Psi), he casually remarked, "Why don't the Zetes buy my house for a Fraternity house?"[44]

For Kappa chapter of Zeta Psi, this offer must have seemed a godsend, even if the house at 80 Professors Row was a mere hundred feet away from their biggest rival, Theta Delta Chi. In the summer of 1898, then, seven alumni formed the Kappa Chapter of Zeta Psi Corporation, and within weeks the corporation's directors had authorized the purchase of Professor Shipman's house and lot, so long as the price did not exceed $7500. In addition, they also voted to lay new floors in the house, buy some furniture, and upgrade the property with the most recent of amenities, electricity. Soon the two parties agreed on a price, and just before the start of the 1898–99 school year the fraternity moved in. And while Professor Shipman's house was not the stone castle as originally envisioned by the chapter, it held a prominent position on Professors Row, offered six members the opportunity to live together, and allowed the chapter to eat, meet, and socialize together. It had taken forty-three years, but Zeta Psi finally had a home.[45]

Don't wait up

When the calendar rolled over to a new century in the year 1900, both Kappa chapter of Zeta Psi and Kappa Charge of Theta Delta Chi were closing in on fifty years of continuous activity, nearly synonymous with the age of the college itself. Naturally, celebrations were in order. The Kappa Charge of Theta Delta Chi held its fiftieth anniversary gathering over the weekend of November 1–3, 1906. The celebration started with an elaborate banquet at Young's Hotel in Boston, and no detail was too small. "The dining hall was draped with the Stars and Stripes, the College Brown and Blue and the fraternity banners. The tables were handsomely decorated with carnations and small silk fraternity flags. At each place were a streamer marked with the occasion, the dinner card… and the Semi-Centennial song." The program for the evening featured many speakers, including Augustus Scott, the founder of the Charge, and Frederick Hamilton, the newly elected president of Tufts College, who'd taken over after the unexpected death of President Capen. While most of the speeches were quite remarkable in their form and content, it was President Hamilton who had arguably the best opening line of the evening:

> I stand before you as a miserable specimen of broken faith. When I left my house, I solemnly promised Madam, the Presidentress, that I would come out on the 11:25 train. I am not going to do anything of the sort, because the Kappa Charge never will have another fiftieth anniversary, and I propose to make my speech if it takes all summer.

President Hamilton then went on to talk about the similarities between members of Kappa Charge throughout those fifty years, as he looked to dispel the idea that the older alumni were somehow not as boisterous back in their day as the current undergraduates. He also offered praise to President Capen, whom he credited as being the only college administrator in New England to promote and encourage fraternities during the 1870s, while other presidents at nearby institutions looked to suppress the fraternity movement, or, in the case of Harvard, shut it down completely. Nearly one hundred twenty years later, President Jean Mayer of Tufts University would take roughly the same position on fraternities as President Capen, while his peers, especially at New England colleges and universities, looked to end Greek life once and for all.[46]

Over there, over there

The advent of The Great War in the summer of 1914 had little impact on the life of Tufts College, at least for a couple of years. However, by the fall of 1916, with the war grinding on, the students could begin to sense the United States would soon be in the conflict, one way or another. As a result, undergraduate men started dropping out of school to enlist, and by the late spring of 1917, the number of dropouts had reached one hundred or so, nearly a quarter of all enrolled men that year. A significant number of these (about forty) joined the Naval Coast Defense Reserve, which, as the name suggests, had the men stationed along the coastline to protect the United States from hostile navies. However, for Herbert D. Miller of Theta Delta Chi, volunteering for a reserve defense unit, or joining the Army and remaining in the United States to train for war, was not how he wanted to serve. Instead, he wanted to get directly involved as soon as possible. So, he took one of the only routes offered to Americans in 1917 who wanted in on the action – he became a medic, of sorts. Specifically, he helped organize the all-volunteer Tufts College Ambulance Unit, with the mission of traveling to the battlefields of France and transporting wounded soldiers from the front lines to aid stations. Similar units were also being organized on college campuses across the country, including Dartmouth, Yale, Harvard, the University of California, and Marietta College in Ohio. All the Tufts group needed was at least twenty men and an ambulance (which they had to buy), and they'd be ready to go. It took Herbert and others just a few months to accomplish both of those goals. So, with patriotism abounding in the air, the college gave the twenty-two men a send-off in Goddard Chapel on May 30, 1917, and a few days later the unit began its journey to France. For many, the trip was probably the first time they'd been on the open ocean, let alone out of the country. Morale was high, the cause was noble, and the men were anxious to get to work.[47]

They arrived in France with their ambulance a few weeks later and immediately learned a harsh reality of war. The French Army, as it turned out, had plenty of ambulances thanks to other American college groups that had arrived in previous months. However, they were dreadfully short of ammunition carriers in the transportation corps. By the summer of 1917, the French Army had been fighting for three long years, and the older men who had comprised the bulk of the transportation corps were needed back home to work their farms and rebuild French industry. So, after being briefed on the situation, the Tufts College Ambulance Unit willfully traded medicine for supply, signed up for a six-month stint with the French artillery, and became the bulk of Section H, Transport Matériel 184 (TM 184). Along with this assignment, though, came a change in clothing. Since the men were now supporting combat elements of the French Army, they put on French Army uniforms.[48]

The Tufts men of TM 184 spent the summer and fall of 1917 hauling artillery shells and other necessities of war from major supply depots to smaller ones just behind the front line. The unit sometimes came under fire during these re-supply operations, and indeed suffered a few casualties during its time of service. But unlike the native French soldiers, the Americans were strictly limited to a service term of six months, so TM 184 was pulled off the line by early December 1917 and the men were sent back home. Many of these veterans, upon arriving back to America, volunteered for the Army and other military units. But not Herbert Miller. He had seen enough of war. So, he returned to Tufts College in January of 1918 to restart his studies. However, he was hardly fit for the task. His classmates described him as being "shell-shocked, with dysentery and nerve strain." He had started his service with so much enthusiasm nearly a year earlier, but now he was a tired phantom of his former self. To add to the strain, his beloved fraternity, Kappa Charge of Theta Delta Chi, was just as shell-shocked. During that previous school year, nearly every member of the fraternity had left college to join the war effort. But rather than giving up, Herbert saw a chance for redemption. He had gone to war wearing a small Theta Delta Chi flag over his heart, and now his fraternity needed him. So, he gathered the few remaining active members of the Charge and held regular meetings throughout that spring semester, or at least he tried to; sometimes he was the only one present. Nonetheless, Herbert kept Kappa Charge active, while the fog of war continued to engulf the campus.[49]

Everything then changed for the worse in the fall of 1918. The United States was now officially at war, and Tufts College was no longer just a school, but a Student Army Training Corps, or S.A.T.C. (as the program was commonly known around the country). The transition from college to S.A.T.C. was unmistakable. The men were all in uniform, the activities were all military, and the fraternity houses were all closed. Some of these houses were taken over by the Army for official use, others were used as dormitories, and some such as Theta Delta Chi at 123 Packard Avenue and Zeta Psi at 80 Professors Row where simply shuttered and locked. To make matters worse, under the rules of the S.A.T.C., the men were soldiers first, students second, and participating in fraternity operations, even regular meetings, was against orders, akin to being absent without leave. Nonetheless, the Kappa Charge of Theta Delta Chi, under the leadership of its president Frank Lincoln, continued to hold semi-regular meetings every couple of weeks that semester, often in Herb Miller's room, even though such activities were against the rules. The members of Zeta Psi also flaunted this no-meeting rule, as did nearly every other fraternity chapter with members still on campus.[50]

These changes and rules were all short-lived, though, as the war ended about a month into the school year, with the signing of the Armistice on November 11, 1918. The S.A.T.C. remained on campus through the rest of that fall semester, but by January 1919, Tufts College was once again an institute of higher learning. Almost immediately the fraternities began returning to normal operations, including Zeta Psi and Theta Delta Chi, who were able to re-occupy their houses. And certainly, with the war to end all wars now in the past, the members of both fraternities must have felt they would never again be so disrupted by conflict. All that was left, it seemed, was to honor the twenty-one students and alumni from Tufts who had earned a gold star.[51]

When the old just won't do

Throughout the early 1900s, the operations of Zeta Psi and Theta Delta Chi were certainly the envy of the other fraternities since they owned their houses, while the others did not. However, ownership had its headaches, as both Zeta Psi and Theta Delta Chi struggled to pay off their mortgages and maintain their houses with regular upkeep. By 1905, the financial challenges of Zeta Psi in particular became apparent to the trustees of Tufts College. As it turned out, when Professor Shipman sold his house to Zeta Psi, he still had a mortgage on the property from the Universalist Publishing House. The fraternity agreed to pay off this mortgage over time, but by that fall the chapter had fallen woefully short on its obligations. The trustees then stepped in and acquired the mortgage with the expectation the fraternity would then repay the college. Again the chapter laid out a payment plan, but during the next five years the payments were sporadic at best, especially with regards to the mortgage interest. By 1918, the trustees could take no more shenanigans. They took over possession of the property, and rumor had it they would use the house for the future residence of the college president.[52]

With the immediate likelihood of losing their house, one they had waited so many years to occupy, the alumni of the chapter sounded the alarm and began raising money in earnest. They soon negotiated a new repayment plan and, more importantly, stuck to it, even with the war disrupting life both on campus and off. On September 29, 1919, the alumni-run housing corporation made its last mortgage payment to Tufts, and the title to the house was finally theirs. The only caveat was a clause added to the title by the trustees, which gave the college the right to acquire the property at any time in the future, provided they offered a fair price and gave ample notice to the house corporation. "After all," the trustees felt, "the Fraternity exists by reason of the College." It seems the trustees were practicing some foresight here, for years later this clause would come back to haunt the chapter when the structure at 80 Professors Row found itself in the way of progress.[53]

But the Zeta Psi house, though it was now completely owned by the house corporation, was hardly a palace. As noted by one alumnus at the time, "When the heater wasn't out of commission the gas stove was and when the roof didn't leak the bathroom did." It was clear to the house corporation the chapter needed a newer, more modern home. By the 1920s, the Grand Chapter of Zeta Psi was routinely funding the building of large chapter houses across the country, and the alumni considered borrowing money from the national organization for such a bold project. However, they instead listened to their conservative New England mind-set and held off from implementing this idea, lest the debt of a new house crush them as it almost did in 1918. So, the house corporation continued to fix and repair and carry on with the old house at 80 Professors Row.[54]

Meanwhile, right next door to Zeta Psi, the Charge house for Theta Delta Chi at 123 Packard Avenue was also showing its age. Although this house wasn't nearly as old as Zeta Psi's, it also wasn't built by ship carpenters, and the lack of quality in the construction was all too apparent. By the 1920s, for example, the porch on the side of the house had a noticeable and permanent list to it, and

Zeta Psi members and their cook pose on the steps of their house at 80 Professors Row, May 25, 1926. Those wearing a "T" are varsity athletes.

the pipes often froze in the winter. So, in 1922, the house corporation of Theta Delta Chi voted to start a new building fund, with the idea they'd either build or buy a new house in five years. The effort was slow to get moving, but by 1925 funds from alumni started coming in earnest. The corporation made its first attempt at purchasing a new house in the summer of 1928, when Clarence "Pop" Houston, a graduate of the Class of 1914 and member of Theta Delta Chi, wrote to President Cousens, saying the Charge was interested in buying Professor McCollister's house at 48 Professors Row, should it become available in the near future. The problem here, it seemed, was that Theta Delta Chi was misinformed about Professor McCollister's plans, as he had no intention of moving anytime soon. Instead, President Cousens suggested the Charge stay where it was and renovate its current house.[55]

This was not the answer the house corporation wanted, since the structure was in terrible shape and only getting worse. So, a few months later, in November 1928, they took a bold step and voted to raze the current house, replacing it with a newer, more modern structure to be ready by the fall of 1929. Apparently this schedule was a little too aggressive, though, for years went by without any activity. By the early spring of 1930, the housing corporation had finally solidified plans for the new house, which was estimated to cost around $45,000. After securing a mortgage from the Trustees of Tufts College, the house corporation brought in the wrecking crew and the old house was soon razed. In its place would be a vastly different structure – brick instead of wood, Georgian colonial instead of English Victorian, large instead of small. As for specifics, rooms would accommodate twenty-two men, while the basement kitchen could comfortably feed fifty at every meal. The first floor was to be the centerpiece of the structure, as it contained a living room that covered the entire south side of the house and a lounge that was planned as a library. Construction took a number of months, but by September 1930, the three-story house was complete and the brotherhood moved in. Theta Delta Chi had just built the first modern brick fraternity house the Tufts campus had ever seen. Every other fraternity could only stare, and wonder how they'd catch up.[56]

For Zeta Psi, seeing their oldest rival build the first modern brick fraternity palace must have been somewhat disconcerting, if not a little depressing. In many ways, this was their own fault – they could have been the first to build such a house back in the 1920s, but they had abandoned the idea. Then, they abandoned the idea a second time. In February 1930, perhaps sensing that Theta Delta Chi's plan for a new residence was about to come to fruition, Zeta Psi's housing corporation started developing plans for a new, two-story brick fraternity house in place of their current structure, one large enough to house twenty-two men and provide two guest rooms, one for alumni and one for ladies. The corporation estimated $60,000 would be needed for the project, and so they began the arduous task of fundraising. But apparently the onset of the Depression was too much; the project languished, and was soon forgotten all together, leaving the old house at 80 Professors Row to grow even older. Meanwhile, the new home for Theta Delta Chi was proving to be a great boon for the Charge. Pledge classes were larger than ever, old debts were paid off, and the Charge came to dominate the various inter-fraternity sports competitions. To the other fraternities on campus, the future became clear. They, too, needed larger and newer houses, if they were going to compete against Theta Delta Chi for the unofficial title of "best" fraternity on campus.[57]

It took Zeta Psi a few years, but in the summer of 1936, they finally embarked on a long awaited and much needed upgrade to their housing. Once again, though, their house corporation abandoned the idea of a new structure and instead looked to renovate their aging structure built by ship carpenters. One reason for this decision was probably practical. After all, the Depression was still dominating the national economy, so renovation was much more viable than new construction. That summer a new wing was added to the back of the house, containing a kitchen and an updated dining room. The first floor was remodeled to contain two suites for three men each, a music room (presumably for a grand piano), and an expanded lounge area. The rooms on second and third floors were also expanded so that a total of seventeen men could now live in the house, almost triple the number that had lived there before. When construction was complete, theirs was certainly not the largest house on campus, but it was comparable in size to Theta Delta Chi's house, thereby putting both fraternities on the same level as far as accommodations were concerned. As it turned out, Zeta Psi was not the only fraternity that upgraded their house over that summer, but it was the only one to work within its existing structure – the Delta Tau Delta and Alpha Tau Omega fraternities razed their aged Victorian houses and built large, Georgian-style brick houses, similar to Theta Delta Chi's home. Within two years, two other fraternities on Professors Row also tore down their antiquated houses for modern brick structures. With imitation being the sincerest form of flattery, Theta Delta Chi must have been smiling with each brick laid.[58]

Put on your uniform

Of all the historical events witnessed by the students and faculty of Tufts College, none have been as dramatic as World War II. Following the attack on Pearl Harbor and America's subsequent entry into the war, college life at Tufts in general, and within the fraternities in particular, was anything but usual. Both Zeta Psi and Theta Delta Chi continued their normal existence during the 1941–42 school year of rushing new members, holding regular meetings, and planning social gatherings, but even these operations were all about transition. Students began leaving school to enlist, others were drafted, and society prepared for war. The situation only intensified in the spring of 1943, when a significant change came to the Tufts College academic calendar. By a vote of the faculty, the school switched from a two-term system to a year-round schedule of three terms, each sixteen weeks in length, with almost no vacation in between. The impetus for this change was the anticipated choice of Tufts College as a training center for the U.S. Navy, and such a designation would require year-round instruction. Soon enough, the Navy did set up a branch of its training regimen known as the V-12 program at Tufts, which would start on July 1, 1943. And when the Navy did arrive, so, too did lots and lots of sailors-to-be. Naturally, all of these sailors needed a place to live.[59]

The men's dormitories were an obvious choice, but they could not house enough, so the Navy also took over all of the women's dormitories, thereby displacing the female students to private boarding houses. In the mean time, the fraternities were struggling. Although the chapters were adding new members each year, few of them (including Zeta Psi and Theta Delta Chi) could muster enough men to support the operations of a chapter house. But taxes and mortgages had to be paid, and if the fraternity members could not fill the houses, then perhaps someone else could. So, starting in July of 1943, the fraternities became part of the war effort. For Zeta Psi, their house became a dormitory for women, whereas for Theta Delta Chi, their house became a Naval infirmary, which was put to good use by men injured during their physical training.

Meanwhile, the members of these two fraternities continued on as best they could. They held meetings on a semi-regular basis, with Zeta Psi often gathering in the Barnum Room, and Theta Delta Chi congregating at Professor Houston's house. The two fraternities also held social events for their members and alumni each school year, though certainly not with the consistency of pre-war times. And, most importantly, they continued to initiate new members, mostly men in the V-12 program. The initiations, though, could barely keep up with the student turnover, as the V-12 men were not on campus for years at a time but only months. Indeed, by the summer of 1945, Theta Delta Chi counted but eight members on its active roll, all Navy men.[60]

When peace was declared in late summer of 1945 and the V-12 program was disbanded, Tufts College began its transition back to a normal school of higher education. By the fall of 1946, both Zeta Psi and Theta Delta Chi were back in possession of their houses, and with veterans especially streaming back to campus, both fraternities were soon growing their memberships for the first time in years. And while casualties of war were felt in nearly every corner of America, it was Theta Delta Chi that paid an especially high price in the Tufts community, at least in terms of gold stars. Seven members of Kappa Charge gave their life during the war. These men were honored with a ceremony at 123 Packard Avenue on January 19, 1947.[61]

As the 1940s turned into the 1950s and then the 1960s, both Zeta Psi and Theta Delta Chi continued to maintain a strong presence on campus, with many members standing out in areas such as athletics and scholarship. The two fraternities also survived the turmoil of the late 1960s that engulfed the campus over the Vietnam War. Neither closed down, even while almost half of the other fraternity chapters went out of existence between 1969 and 1974. The late 1970s saw the beginnings of a resurgence in Tufts fraternities, but by now the emphasis was clearly on the social aspects of Greek life. Kappa Charge of Theta Delta Chi in particular embraced this new role as social host. One could argue perhaps they embraced this too much, as their enthusiasm for a good time nearly led to their demise.[62]

Have a drink on me

In the spring of 1970, when offered a chance to describe their fraternity to the Tufts community, the members of Kappa Charge of Theta Delta Chi wrote, "[we are] almost totally social. We just want to have this place as a place to let off steam with a party." Such a description, which surely would have horrified the original founders of the Charge were they alive to hear it, came during a time of immense change on campus, when nearly all of the fraternities were questioning their reason for existence in the shadow of the Vietnam War. The administration, with much bigger issues to deal with, hardly interfered with the fraternities at all. So, Theta Delta Chi in particular continued with its mission of being a social outlet, and though the practice seemed to be destroying the house from within, on went the parties. As one alumnus described it, the Charge at this time was a "chaotic, disenchanted, and destructive organization." The low point for the Charge was the fall of 1978, when membership stood at just seven brothers, and the prospect of closing down seemed a likely outcome. However, the Charge rallied over the next year and increased membership back to a sustainable level. The larger question was, had the attitude within the brotherhood changed?[63]

By 1980, the answer to that question would be painfully clear. Campus life had certainly evolved over the past decade, as the legal drinking age in Massachusetts had been raised and a new president of Tufts had been inaugurated, one who looked to hold the students to a higher standard when it came to social activities. Theta Delta Chi, however, had not evolved in similar fashion, so it was only a matter of time before trouble struck. It did that fall. On the night of October 18–19, 1980, Theta Delta Chi held a campus-wide party at its house that was supposed to end at 12:45 a.m. So, in the early morning, the Tufts police came by the Charge house to enforce the shutdown rule and end the party. Lo and behold, the fraternity was not all that interested in stopping. A classic standoff thus ensued, only to be exacerbated around 1:00 a.m. when additional officers came to the house and, in a show of force, ended the party. While walking around the house and clearing the guests, the officers noted a number of safety violations including blocked fire exits, overcrowding, the lack of identifying patrons who were of legal drinking age, and the distribution of a controlled substance (nitrous oxide). As a result of these violations, the Student Activities Office prohibited Theta Delta Chi from having any more campus-wide parties for five months. The age of liability, though in its infancy, had begun to dominate social policy, and by placing Theta Delta Chi on probation, the administration hoped to begin effecting a change in behavior.[64]

These hopes were soon dashed. Five months later, just a few days after their probation had ended, and one night after holding a sanctioned party without incident, Theta Delta Chi held a second, unsanctioned party. And this one was a doozy. As the party progressed into early Sunday morning, the Tufts police received a complaint about a disturbance at 123 Packard Avenue. When they arrived, they found over one hundred patrons in the house who were having fun and, once again, not necessarily in the mood to leave. Approximately thirty Somerville police officers were then called to the house to help disperse the crowd, and by the end of the incident seven people, including five members of Theta Delta Chi, were spending the rest of the night in jail. Unfortunately, the problems did not end here. As the semesters marched on each school year, the complaints continued to pile up for Theta Delta Chi: continued fire code violations in the house, reprimands for showing pornography to rushees, the holding of an unauthorized party during a hurricane when the school was shut down, situations of alcohol poisonings at a mid-week informal gathering, a fight and subsequent arrest of a non-Tufts student, and a general lack of upkeep of the physical property at 123 Packard Avenue. The administration was fast growing tired of Theta Delta Chi. "By and large the last ten years it has been the same fraternity that has been a problem all along," said President Mayer in the spring of 1987, referring to Theta Delta Chi.[65]

During this time of scrutiny, though, the members of Theta Delta Chi seemed to relish in their reputation as a house that knew how to party in spite of the rules. They also placed much less emphasis on their Greek-letter name, preferring instead their long-time nickname of "123," a reference to their address on Packard Avenue. While members of other fraternities at Tufts often wore shirts displaying their letters, the members of Theta Delta Chi generally did not. Instead, they were more often seen with shirts using the "123" moniker – for example, one t-shirt read, "Here come the jesters, 1 2 3." A similar lack of insignia occurred with pledge pins. While pledges of nearly all other fraternities could be seen wearing their official pledge pins for the full six to twelve week process, pledges of Theta Delta Chi did not. Instead, they generally displayed no insignia until initiation week, and even then it was not a pin, but rather a trench coat and orange winter knit hat emblazoned with the numbers "1 2 3" across the front. To those outside the organization, Theta Delta Chi seemed more of an independent group than a chapter of an international fraternity. The fraternity also portrayed a sense of invulnerability since their alumni corporation owned both the house and the land. In addition, the Kappa Charge had supplied Tufts with four presidents over the years and still had many powerful friends among the Trustees. With little to fear, why worry about rules or consequences?[66]

Meanwhile, the Tufts administration was taking substantive steps to rein in such behavior, not just with Theta Delta Chi, but with all of the fraternities in general. At the core of this effort was a formal relationship statement between each fraternity and the administration that, in a nutshell, promised better behavior and an adherence to campus rules in exchange for official support and continued existence. Theta Delta Chi's relationship went a little further, as the Trustees of Tufts College also entered into an agreement with the alumni house corporation, whereby the administration had the sole right to acquire the house and property for a fair price if the house corporation decided to sell, and, at any time, if they needed the property for "University purposes" – eminent domain at its finest. Such clauses were typical of the agreements between the administration and other fraternity house corporations, and this was probably not the first such agreement between the two entities over the years. But the agreement also contained another clause. If the house corporation rented 123 Packard Avenue to a group other than the Kappa Charge of Theta Delta Chi for more than five years, then Tufts could purchase the property without restriction. In other words, if Kappa Charge lost its charter with Theta Delta Chi, it could be in serious danger of losing its house, even if a group continued to operate there as a local organization. With this agreement, it appears, the administration was warning the fraternity to improve its operations, or else Kappa Charge and its house could be gone forever.[67]

A year after signing the agreement with the trustees, Kappa Charge was hardly in a better place. In early November 1989, the fraternity was placed on warning status related to a number of small infractions. The biggest complaints seemed to be a lack of upkeep of the house and grounds, and a failure to comply with the new social policy governing fraternity parties. The membership disputed many of the complaints while also arguing they had been working to improve their operations that semester. In conjunction with this turnaround, they began to receive numerous instances of praise for their philanthropic work with local charities, something they had noticeably lacked in years prior. A few weeks later, though, it all came crashing down. Fraternity rush for the spring semester of 1990 began at the end of January with one new policy firmly in place: all rush activities must be dry, without the presence of alcohol. Even two years earlier, unfettered alcohol during rush week was a given in nearly every fraternity house, as recruitment events had traditionally centered on drinking and parties. But times had changed and the fraternities in general had accepted the rule without complaint. As for enforcement, the student-run Inter-Greek Council (IGC) sent monitors to each rush event to observe and report the presence of any alcohol. On the night of January 30, 1990, a spotter for the IGC went to 123 Packard Avenue and witnessed a member of Theta Delta Chi drinking from an open beer can on two separate occasions. Apparently the member was just enjoying a beer on his own, not related to the rush event. The circumstance, though, had little bearing on the situation. Beer was not allowed anywhere near the event. And yet there it was.[68]

The IGC investigated the incident, and a few weeks later ruled that Theta Delta Chi had indeed violated the dry rush policy on two accounts. All that was left was the punishment. On its own, the violation was not considered overly severe, since alcohol was not provided to any of the rushees, and indeed the IGC could have rendered no punishment at all. However, given the history of problems involving Theta Delta Chi, doing nothing was not an option. So, a few days later the IGC issued its ruling, and it was the harshest punishment they could dole out. Theta Delta Chi was no longer a recognized fraternity at Tufts University, at least for the next three years. They could no longer hold rush events or parties or use University property in any official manner, and they had to vacate their house by May 31, 1990. In making its ruling, the judicial board of the IGC cited a "blatant failure to meet the spirit and letter of the Relationship Statement... during a crucial time in the existence of the Greek system at Tufts." By 1990, the faculty was in the early stages of a long and detailed evaluation of the entire Greek system, one that seemed skewed towards ending fraternities and sororities at Tufts. Now was not the time, in the eyes of many trying to save the Greek system, to be a rebel. A day after the IGC ruling, the international officers of Theta Delta Chi suspended the charter of Kappa Charge, which they were required to do of any charge that lost its campus recognition. For over one hundred thirty-four years, Kappa Charge had been continuously active at Tufts, initiating new members each and every school year, even when the nation was at war. Now, it was all on hold, possibly over for good.[69]

Do not mess with me

Almost immediately, the members of Kappa Charge announced their plan to appeal the decision of the IGC to the Committee on Student Life (or CSL, a faculty-run organization that oversaw the IGC at the time), as was their right. But a month later the appeal failed. The CSL upheld the suspension, citing the multiple problems of Theta Delta Chi over the years, in conjunction with the rush violation, as being more than enough to merit the suspension. "Theta Delta Chi had been given every opportunity to reform itself [over the years] and had failed to heed those repeated warnings," said Professor Edelmen, the head of the CSL. Both the IGC and the CSL stated, however, that Kappa Charge was welcome back to campus after its three-year probation, and if it came back it would be able to re-occupy its house at 123 Packard Avenue. Such sentiment was hardly consoling to the current members of Theta Delta Chi, but that was the best they could do. The appeals process was over and all Kappa Charge could do was wait.[70]

Well, not exactly. For all its faults and shortcomings and problems, Theta Delta Chi still had many friends in high places within the Tufts administration, and these people were not going to take the suspension lying down. Within days of the denial of the appeal, prominent alumni began contacting the Tufts administration looking for answers and, more importantly, a way off suspension. Warren Carley, a 1932 graduate of Tufts, a former member of the Board of Trustees of Tufts College from 1964 to 1981, and an ardent supporter of his fraternity, Kappa Charge of Theta Delta Chi, was one such alumnus up for a fight. In his letter to Provost Sol Gittleman, the number two administrator behind President Jean Mayer, Mr. Carley pleaded for the lifting of the suspension and the immediate return of Kappa Charge to campus, as he felt the punishment was undeserved. Provost Gittleman's response to Mr. Carley could be summarized as follows: stay out of this. In his letter, Provost Gittleman emphasized that Tufts University was at a critical junction with regards to all of its fraternities, as Medford had expelled all chapter houses from its borders and Somerville was close to doing the same. Only through substantial actions of the administration had the Greek system been able to remain on campus, Provost Gittleman wrote, and while all other fraternities had accepted the new rules and regulations, Theta Delta Chi had not. Provost Gittleman ended his letter by saying,

> I only want to ensure you that in this house [Theta Delta Chi] perhaps more than any other on campus, there is a need for a break with the past, with a total and complete cleansing of values and traditions, so that in three years a new, unsullied, and fresh group of young man[sic] can appear in that house and start anew. That is the hope and desire of everyone thus far involved in this case. The alternative is the end of Greek life at Tufts. Take your choice.[71]

While the alumni continued to fight the suspension behind closed doors, the housing corporation was left to worry about their property at 123 Packard Avenue. Once the Charge moved out in May 1990, there would no longer be any tenants paying rent, but taxes still had to be paid and the property still had to be maintained. So, rather than shutter the house for three years, or do something more drastic such as sell the property to Tufts, the housing corporation decided to rent their house to students. The faculty-led Committee on Social Fraternities and Sororities (CFS) was given the power to choose the tenants, so they voted to let the student-led IGC pick a Greek-letter organization to live in the house. There was certainly some irony here, as the IGC had suspended the fraternity in the first place, but the IGC was the logical choice – as a group, they had developed an impartial system to award houses to fraternities and sororities based on a wide set of criteria. A number of organizations applied to move into 123 Packard Ave, and in the end, the IGC picked the Alpha Omicron Pi (AOII) sorority as the tenant. AOII, which could trace its roots back at Tufts to 1895, had never occupied a chapter house on campus throughout its history, and since its re-chartering in 1987, had been operating out of various off-campus apartments and university-owned co-ops. In the fall of 1990, then, AOII moved into the old Theta Delta Chi house with a new address, 125 Packard Avenue. Although no official reason was given for the address change, it appears that while the alumni corporation would allow a temporary lease of the property to another organization, they were not about to let anyone else use the "123" nickname.[72]

Meanwhile, the alumni of Kappa Charge were hardly taking the suspension lying down. Mr. Carley and others continued to correspond with the Tufts administration, looking for any way to reduce the suspension of Kappa Charge and get them back on campus sooner. These alumni, many of whom were also tied in with current and former trustees of Tufts College, argued relentlessly that the punishment seemed grossly out of proportion to the offense. But the administration was unwavering. "We are fighting two battles: one against those who want the Greeks gone; and another against the Thetas and their alumni who won't accept the disciplinary actions. If you let us alone, we'll have your kids back in three years, no doubt…" wrote Provost Gittleman in one such reply to an alumnus. The alumni as a group, however, would not leave it alone. So, in the late spring 1991, just over a year into the suspension, the alumni took the only action left at their disposal. They, along with the undergraduate members of the fraternity, sued Tufts University.[73]

Like I said, do not mess with me

Actually, they sued more than just the university. Also named in the lawsuit were six individual students who were either members of the IGC Judiciary board or officers in the IGC back in 1990 when the suspension was handed down. As for the basis of the lawsuit, the fraternity argued that although the IGC had only suspended the fraternity, they had in reality killed off Kappa Charge of Theta Delta Chi, since no undergraduate members would be left when the suspension ended in the spring of 1993. The older alumni, in particular, were galled by the thought of a one hundred thirty-five year tradition ending due to the presence of one beer at a rush party. As for the individual students named in the lawsuit, some were members of AOII who had been on the IGC when the suspension was handed down. The fraternity argued these members of AOII had an ulterior motive for voting to suspend Kappa Charge, as it allowed their previously un-housed sorority to occupy the property. This particular claim did not sit well with the Tufts administration, since the decision to allow AOII into the house came months after the suspension, and that process was hardly straightforward; after all, the decision went through the fraternity's alumni housing corporation, to the faculty-led CFS, and then to the student-run IGC. To say the members of AOII on the IGC had control of such decisions following the suspension was preposterous. But now it was official, and by suing Tufts and some of its students, the fraternity had gained a seat once again at the bargaining table.[74]

Leading the negotiations for the Tufts administration was President Jean Mayer, who was adamantly opposed to changing or reducing the suspension. Supporting President Mayer were many in the Tufts community, including Provost Gittleman, Dean Bruce Reitman, and members of the IGC. President Mayer sincerely felt the IGC and CFS had done a very good job at handling the suspension, and he did not like that Mr. Carley and other former trustees were continuing to interfere with a disciplinary action of this nature. But these men held considerable power and they, like the lawsuit, could not be ignored. So, President Mayer acquiesced, and over the next few months he negotiated a settlement with the fraternity. By late January 1992, the details were ready.

Theta Delta Chi could return to campus later that spring, one year early, and rush new members subject to certain conditions, including oversight by alumni of the fraternity and the Dean of Students office. Assuming all went well, Theta Delta Chi would regain recognition in September 1992, and could also move back into their house that fall, thus displacing AOII. The six undergraduate members named in the lawsuit were freed from any responsibility, and the settlement included no provisions for monetary damages for or against either party. President Mayer and Theta Delta Chi made the settlement official by issuing a joint press release in early February, stating the suspension has served its purpose. Behind the scenes, President Mayer was hardly happy with the outcome, but at least it was all over. Well, not quite. Instead of showing some humility by keeping quiet, the remaining undergraduate members of Theta Delta Chi made yet another mistake. They decided to brag.[75]

SOMETIMES A VICTORY LAP is warranted. In this case, no. Two days after the settlement was announced to the Tufts Community, *The Tufts Daily* ran a front-page article entitled, "Theta Delta Chi sees settlement as victory; Members saw Tufts' case as weak." Featuring interviews only of undergraduate Theta Delta Chi members and not university officials, the article was a poke-in-the-eye at the President Mayer's administration, with quotes such as, "Tufts finally gave in because their whole case was weak, and they did not want to go to court over the issue." In addition, the article implied that the remaining members of the fraternity would have substantial influence in choosing the new members when rush started in a few days, a fact which galled the IGC in particular, as a major reason they issued the three-year suspension was to purge the fraternity of its old membership and let a new group start over. Now, the small group of current Theta Delta Chi members was in a position to influence the fraternity once again. And while nearly all of these current members would graduate in just a few months, one in particular would not. His name was Mr. B., an undergraduate member of Theta Delta Chi who was supposed to be a senior in the spring of 1992, but had taken some time off from school so he was only a junior that semester. As a result, when the fraternity reclaimed its house in the fall, Mr. B. would be living there along with the newest members of the Charge, and as the eldest member of the fraternity, he would undoubtedly have considerable influence over the group. But in the irony of all ironies, it was Mr. B. who had been caught drinking the beer during rush week back in 1990, the event that resulted in the suspension of Theta Delta Chi in the first place.[76]

As could be expected, two groups within the Tufts community became very upset over this situation. One was the IGC, as they had been led to believe the current members of Theta Delta Chi would have no part in the upcoming rush, and they certainly did not think Mr. B. would be able to live in the Charge house the following fall semester. Such revelations made the whole suspension seem somewhat moot, and threatened to diminish the power of the IGC as it looked to regulate Greek life at Tufts. Their anger, though, was a distant second to President Mayer's. He was, without a doubt, furious. He had tried to do the right thing, to appease the alumni while maintaining the integrity of the student-run IGC, but it had all gone wrong. So, he exercised the only option he could. In a show of force, he tore up the settlement with Theta Delta Chi. The two groups would have to start over with their negotiations. In the mean time, the rush events were immediately suspended. The current members of Theta Delta Chi, who had been boastful a week earlier, were now silent.[77]

A new settlement was reached just a few days later, and while it was substantially the same as the original one, it did explicitly disempower the small group of current Theta Delta Chi undergraduate members. Rush week would start up again soon, but the process would be run solely by alumni who had graduated prior to 1986, and the current undergraduates would have no say in choosing the new members. In addition, no member who was active when the Charge was suspended in 1990 would be allowed to live in the house in the fall. While this clause only applied to Mr. B., the message was clear. Theta Delta Chi would be a new fraternity starting in the fall of 1992. And indeed that is what happened. A month later, Kappa Charge secured thirty-eight new pledges, and the legacy of Theta Delta Chi continued on.[78]

All that was left now for President Mayer was some reflection on the whole incident. In February 1992, as the settlement was coming to a close, President Mayer began a personal correspondence with trustee emeritus Robert Meserve. A graduate of Tufts College in 1931 and trustee from 1955 until 1979, including a five-year stint as the chairman, Mr. Meserve had served his alma mater long and well. Back in 1976, Mr. Meserve had been one of the trustees to advocate for the hiring of President Mayer when others on the search committee were not as enthusiastic. As for Theta Delta Chi, Mr. Meserve had actually been a member of another fraternity (Sigma Tau Alpha) while an undergraduate, but for this matter he was clearly on the side of his longtime friend, Mr. Carley. In his letters to Mr. Meserve, President Mayer lambasted the efforts of Theta Delta Chi alumni, especially Mr. Carley, to interfere with the original suspension as handed down by the IGC. He was afraid other fraternities, if they faced suspension in the future, would turn to similar tactics to override the checks and balances the administration had set up to regulate the Greek system. "This has been a bad chapter in the history of the University," President Mayer wrote in one response. Mr. Meserve, though, was not impressed with any of this diatribe. His responses, which included both friendly banter and personal castigation, displayed an arrogant sense of dismissal towards President Mayer. After all, Jean Mayer was an outsider. He had not graduated from Tufts, nor had he been a member of a fraternity, and he had been passed over for president twice before being hired in 1976. Mr. Meserve had great respect for President Mayer, he admitted, but he failed to see the impact this incident had on the university. Instead, Mr. Meserve was more concerned with the effect it had on his long time friend, Mr. Carley. It appears these letters were the last correspondence between President Mayer and Mr. Meserve, and they did not end on a friendly note. A few months later, the trustees removed President Mayer from office, relegating him to the newly created position of Chancellor of Tufts. However, before he could start in this new position, President Mayer passed away on New Year's Day in 1993.[79]

SINCE THE RE-FORMING OF KAPPA CHARGE in 1992, the fraternity has been able to keep its troubles in the past, thanks in part to greater oversight by the alumni and the national organization. The biggest challenge to the fraternity came in the fall of 2003, when the national organization and the alumni put the membership through a re-evaluation, as they looked to institute a new pledge process that reduced the potential for hazing. About one-third of the active membership declined to participate in this review, so they were removed as active members of the fraternity. The remaining members carried on quite successfully, and in the spring of 2006, the Charge celebrated its 150th anniversary over commencement weekend. As part of the celebration, Warren Carley was honored by the undergraduate members of Theta Delta Chi with the Guy C. Pierce Service Award, in recognition of his contributions to the Charge in particular and the Tufts community in general. Guy Pierce had been instrumental in building the Charge house in 1930. Warren Carley, of course, had been instrumental in getting it back.[80]

Meanwhile, over at the Zeta Psi house…

Throughout the 1980s, while Theta Delta Chi was accruing violations and suspensions that appeared often on the front pages of *The Tufts Daily*, Zeta Psi had its own disciplinary issues that were also front page news. From an incident involving racial insensitivity towards residents of the Asian House, to a violation of the school's firearms policy by storing weapons and ammunition in the chapter house, Zeta Psi was not immune to official inquiry into its actions, or sanctions aimed at correcting its behavior. For the most part, though, these transgressions were isolated incidents and never resulted in a multi-year suspension or the loss of the charter. Instead, as the end of the 20th century approached, Zeta Psi faced a more serious problem from an unlikely source: music.[81]

Music has long been a part of the Tufts community, both as a course of instruction and as entertainment for students and faculty alike. The first campus quartet appeared in 1856, while the Music Department started offering formal instruction in 1867. Cohen Auditorium, built in 1955, and the Aidekman Arts Center, built in 1991, have both been the centerpieces of the music program at

Tufts, as the buildings offer a performance arena, practice space, and classrooms for music education. By the late 1990s, though, it was clear to many in the Tufts administration that the facilities dedicated to the music department were inadequate, and there was a distinct lack of space for smaller, more intimate concerts, where sound quality could be optimized. But hope for a new space was all the administration could do, until one day in early 1999 an anonymous donor stepped forward and gave $4 million to the music department for such a facility. With the donation, though, came a catch: the new music center must be built near the center of campus. As it turned out, such a restriction was hardly an issue, since there was no practical place for a music facility outside the land-locked Medford campus. So, the administration looked inside for a space, and soon had a design for a 33,000 square foot building that would bring music at Tufts into the next century. Then, they found the perfect location right in the heart of campus, where Packard Avenue meets Professors Row. Of course, standing in the way of this plan were two houses, Dearborn House at 72 Professors Row (the Academic Resource Center), and Zeta Psi at 80 Professors Row. But, the solution was simple. Tufts would tear both houses down.[82]

The problem with this plan, of course, was that while Dearborn House as an academic building could easily be commandeered, the Zeta Psi house could not. Since 1919, the chapter's housing corporation had owned the title to the property, and in all likelihood they would not sell without some major concessions. Tufts did have an edge in the negotiations, though, as back in 1918, the housing corporation agreed to a provision whereby Tufts could purchase the house at any time, so long as they gave a six-month notice and paid a fair price. Starting in the fall of 1999, then, the university began these negotiations, but from the start they did not go smoothly. Many within Zeta Psi were not happy their home for over one hundred years, in one of the oldest buildings on campus, was about to be pulled out from under them. Also, the housing corporation balked at the idea that a clause added to the deed in 1918 could still be valid in 1999. In a show of good faith, though, the administration offered to tear down 128 Professors Row, the financial aid office at the time, and build Zeta Psi a new fraternity house at that address, using the proceeds from the sale of 80 Professors Row as funding. Not all within Zeta Psi were happy with this plan, but at least it did allow the fraternity to set up a block away with a new, modern house.[83]

However, as the year 2000 progressed into 2001, the project ran into some problems. The estimated cost of the music building continued to rise as the details of the building were further developed, and this put enormous pressure on subsequent fundraising. Initially, the $4 million donation covered half the costs, but now the price tag had risen to $12 million, and would probably go higher. The only bright spot seemed to be in the negotiations with Zeta Psi's housing corporation. Although they had hit a standstill for a while, by the fall of 2001 the corporation had agreed to sell their house and land, provided the administration built them a new fraternity house at 128 Professors Row before razing the old one. Many in Zeta Psi were openly skeptical this plan would go forward, but the administration projected confidence that construction would begin shortly after the 2002 commencement.[84]

By the fall of 2002, though, the project had not started. Meanwhile, the cost of the music building had now eclipsed $25 million, and fundraising still had not raised enough money to cover the first phase of the construction. In addition, another campus project, this one to build a new dormitory near the campus center on Talbot Avenue, was well underway. To create adequate space for the dormitory, a fourth house at 20 Professors Row would also be razed. However, when this was all announced to the campus in early October 2002, one person in particular decided to speak up. Her letter to *The Tufts Daily* was simply titled "Save Ballou's House." Written by Anne Sauer, an alumna of the class of 1991 and former assistant archivist at Tufts, the article talked about the fallout of the proposed new dormitory and music center in terms of what would be lost. The razing of 20 Professors Row in particular was heartbreaking to Ms. Sauer, since this house just happened to be the second building ever constructed on campus in 1854, and had served as the residence for Hosea Ballou 2d, the first president of Tufts. Ending her letter she wrote, "More than just an address, this house is a part of the history of Tufts. Can it be saved?" Most assumed it could not.[85]

But then something happened, something unexpected. In developing the plans for the new dormitory and music building, the Tufts administration had supposedly gained permission from the city of Somerville to tear down those four old houses. However, the initial approval was apparently given before the razing of 20 Professors Row was detailed, and when this fact came to light, Somerville stepped in and said "no." By May 2003, the Somerville Historic Preservation Committee (SHPC) formally objected to razing not only 20 Professors Row, but also the other three houses at 72, 80, and 128 Professors Row. Those houses, the SPHC determined, were a part of Somerville's history as well, so they could not be destroyed. And without the approval of the SHPC, Somerville would not issue a building permit. The administration was now in a terrible bind. Construction was scheduled to begin in just a few weeks, as all that was left was the expected approval from the trustees. Now, both the new dormitory and the new music building were once again on hold.[86]

The fight between Tufts and the SHPC would go on for over another year, and in the end, the SHPC won. None of the aforementioned four houses, including Zeta Psi's at 80 Professors Row, could ever be torn down. In the end, Tufts decided to move the location of the new music building to a parking lot adjacent to the Aidekman Arts Center, a change that resulted in a complete redesign of the facility. The new dormitory, Sophia Gordon Hall, was also redesigned so that it did not require the destruction of 20 Professors Row. For proponents of the music building, especially, it had been a long six years before their dream of a new facility was realized. For Zeta Psi, the outcome was certainly what a majority in the fraternity had always wanted. But they, too, had been on a journey. It just happened to be one that nobody wanted.[87]

The lights are on, but no one's home

The problem began in February 2003, when a Zeta Psi pledge, returning to his dorm one Thursday night after drinking at the fraternity house, had an accident that resulted in a head injury. The accident was severe enough to land the individual in the intensive care unit, and while the details of the events preceding the accident were somewhat murky, the aftermath was not. Two months later, the fraternity faced charges from the faculty-led CFS including hazing, distribution of alcohol to minors, and endangerment of others. In May 2003, the verdict came in as guilty. As for punishment, the fraternity faced a two-year social probation where no alcohol would be allowed in the house until the fall of 2005, and they had to shutter the house for two summers, thereby placing a financial burden on the chapter due to lost rental income. The house corporation decided to appeal the punishment, and since they were free to choose which two summers the house would be closed, they decided to rent out rooms to all comers during the summer of 2003 while the appeal went forward.[88]

With university operations over the summer much curtailed from the regular school year, the appeal remained pending for a few weeks. But then in late July, the situation went from bad to worse. One night, a Tufts University police officer walked by the Zeta Psi house and heard a commotion on the roof. He went inside to investigate, and when he stepped out onto the roof deck, he found about twenty-five partygoers standing next to a portable pool and drinking beer from a keg. The officer asked the guests to produce identification, but rather than comply, many vanished into the night. Eventually the officer found a resident who was also a member of Zeta Psi, and asked him what was going on. The Zeta Psi member, who was studying at the time, told the officer the person who organized the party and bought the keg was a summer resident, but was not a member of the fraternity. Nonetheless, the evidence was clear. There was a keg out in the open, and kegs had been banned from all fraternity houses years earlier. In the eyes of the administration, there was no excuse for this transgression. The members of Zeta Psi and the summer residents had been warned not to break the rules, and yet they did. So, a few days after the incident, everything came crashing down. The appeal was denied, meaning the Zeta Psi house was now subject to the original punishment as handed down back in May. In addition, the fraternity faced new charges relating to the presence of the keg, which, in light of previous incidents, was not going to be taken lightly.[89]

The house corporation of Zeta Psi sensed the facts were not in their favor, so rather than go through a lengthy investigation process they would most likely lose, they proposed a settlement. They would close the house for the 2003–04 school year, the first time the house had been completely shuttered since World War I. The settlement took effect shortly after students had arrived back on campus. All residents of Zeta Psi had to move out by midnight on September 1, 2003. In addition, the alumni offered to suspend the operations of the fraternity for the school year. No meetings, no rush events, no pledging, nothing. Anything related to the fraternity was essentially banned for the year, and failure to comply could mean the end of Kappa chapter. In general it had been a terrible six months for Greek life at Tufts, with Delta Upsilon and Alpha Phi also facing temporary house closures, so Zeta Psi was not the only organization in the crosshairs. All they could do, then, was wait to restart once again in the fall of 2004.[90]

Déjà vu, all over again…

And wait they did. When the fall of 2004 rolled around, Zeta Psi moved back into its house, though it still had one more year of probation to work through and one more summer closure to enact. The school year seemed to be going well enough for the chapter, as the fraternity was able to restart its operations and return to a sense of normalcy. But the spring of 2005 was not a good semester for fraternities at Tufts. Over at the Delta Tau Delta house, a pledge nearly died one night due to alcohol poisoning, and also implicated in the scandal was the Chi Omega sorority. And then, in April 2005, Zeta Psi got caught yet again with a keg in its house, even though the chapter was still on probation and was not supposed to have alcohol in its house. On the surface this seemed a blatant violation, one that could lead to even more severe sanctions, if not the closing of the chapter. Yet that is not what happened. Miraculously, the discovery of the keg did not lead to any additional punishment against the fraternity. A semester later, Zeta Psi was off probation and back to normal operations. All the transgressions, it seemed, were finally behind the fraternity. And since then, the chapter has maintained its presence on campus and continued its legacy without significant controversy.[91]

FOR OVER ONE HUNDRED SIXTY YEARS AND COUNTING, both the Kappa chapter of Zeta Psi and the Kappa Charge of Theta Delta Chi have been part of the Tufts community. They have not always been perfect, but they have always managed to recover. Back in 1905, when Kappa Charge held its fiftieth anniversary, an alumnus of the fraternity, Arthur Peirce, gave a speech entitled "Duty to Future." In his speech, Mr. Peirce wondered what Kappa Charge might look like fifty years later – in 1956 – when surely few of those seated would still be alive. His words echo the true nature of fraternities in general, and so they are worth repeating:

> Take good men and be bound to make them better. Inspire them with the highest ideals of fraternity life and we shall have no need to fear that there shall be any break in the organized life of this Charge for another half century; but we shall look forward with high hopes to a better day that is to come, feeling sure that, proud as we are of the fifty years gone by, under your efforts and by God's blessing, the best is yet to be.[92]

DELTA UPSILON (Tufts Chapter, 1886 – present)

The year was 1834, and for many students on the campus of Williams College that fall, the situation was unacceptable. During the previous school year, the Kappa Alpha Society (KA) fraternity had come to campus, the first national organization to arrive at Williams. A few months later another national fraternity, Sigma Phi, also started a chapter on campus, and that's when the problems really began. At the time, Williams College was known for preparing men for the ministry, with the principles of fairness and openness especially popular among the students and the faculty. Campus honors, most students felt, should go to those who are most deserving, while officers in the literary societies, most agreed, should be elected from the most qualified. But KA and Sigma Phi saw those two areas as ripe for their influence. Together they conspired to take control of these domains, which then elevated the fraternities as the major political force on campus. By pooling votes, they alone could decide who obtained honors and who ran the literary societies – and more often than not, these accolades went to fraternity men, whether these men deserved them or not. In addition, the two fraternities could hide their machinations behind secret meetings and rituals, with the rest of the student body unaware of their intentions or methods until it was too late. Secrecy had long been a concern for the faculty of Williams College, with many feeling the practice was inherently against the Christian ideals at the heart of the school. The power grab displayed by the fraternities during the 1833–34 school year had only intensified the disdain between those in, and those out.[93]

KA and Sigma Phi, though, had a problem of their own. Combined, the two fraternities represented only a small percentage of the undergraduates, and if the non-society men ever organized themselves into a cohesive unit, the fraternities would be vastly outnumbered. In the fall of 1834, twenty men from the sophomore and junior classes did just that. They gathered ten more from the newly arrived freshman class whom they felt were the best, and together formed an anti-secret society called The Social Fraternity. This group's mission was to challenge the political control of the two secret societies and provide a social and intellectual outlet for the students, one that was based on openness, not secrecy. Within short time, The Social Fraternity broke the political hold of the two secret fraternities at Williams, and soon came to dominate life on campus, counting more than half the students as members. And the anti-secrecy movement didn't stop there. A few years later, similar organizations began appearing on other college campuses in the Northeast including Union College, the birthplace of the modern fraternity movement. Eventually, most of these organizations united under the banner of the Anti-Secret Confederation, with a motto in Greek of *Ouden Adelon*, or "Nothing Secret." Then, in 1864, the Anti-Secret Confederation adopted a new name for its fraternity, Delta Upsilon (DU). Further refinement to the society came in 1879 when DU dropped its anti-secret stance in favor of non-secrecy, vowing to work with the other national Greek letter fraternities (all of which were secret organizations) while celebrating its own philosophy of having nothing to hide. DU then began a rapid period of growth across the country as it looked to champion its ideals and grow its influence among college students. Soon enough, Tufts College came calling.[94]

Déjà vu all over again

Some fifty-three years after the founding of DU, a number of Tufts students found themselves just as dismayed about campus affairs as those men at Williams College had been so many years earlier. To say the two fraternities at Tufts dominated student life in the spring of 1886 would be an understatement. Combined, Zeta Psi and Theta Delta Chi counted only one-third of the students as their members, and yet they ran much of the social activities on campus, printed class yearbooks and literary magazines, and contributed a disproportionate number of men to the athletic teams and student leadership positions. In essence, the fraternity men were a very powerful force on campus, a position they had held for many years prior and, seemingly, would hold for many years to come, much to the dismay of the rest. Although the non-society men were larger in number than the fraternity men and thus could have been the major political and social presence on campus, they just could not come together – infighting, distrust, and poor leadership had plagued them for years and was not about to abate anytime soon. Just about the only unifying force among these men was their disdain for secret organizations, but even this feeling was not strong enough to bring about any real action. So, they floundered, while the two fraternities ruled. But around this time, a student in the Tufts Divinity School named Irving Tomlinson could sense there were some natural leaders in this group of non-society men. Over the course of a few months in early 1886, Irving began talking to these men about forming a new chapter of his fraternity, Phi Delta Theta. He had joined Phi Delta Theta while an undergraduate at Buchtel College in Ohio (now the University of Akron), and he hoped to grow his fraternity by establishing a chapter at Tufts College. Apparently, Irving was even encouraged by Zeta Psi and Theta Delta Chi in his quest to bring Phi Delta Theta to campus, perhaps because the two fraternities felt another secret society would only add to their collective power over the student body. All he needed was a few good men.[95]

As it turned out, Irving's efforts were galvanizing, but in a different direction. One student he'd tried to recruit for his plan, a junior named Wilson L. Fairbanks, held the strong opinion that Tufts did not need another secret society on campus – the two already controlled too much of campus life as it was. Yet here was Irving, looking to add to this injustice. So, in late May of 1886, Wilson gathered five other men who shared his opinion, men he had been talking with informally that entire semester, and together they discussed a course of action to reset the balance of campus life. As it turned out, Irving had also spoken to many in this group about forming a chapter of Phi Delta Theta, but to a man they quickly decided they'd have nothing to do with this idea. Instead, they coalesced around Wilson and the idea of bringing a new national fraternity to Tufts, one built upon the principles of non-secrecy and openness. That fraternity was Delta Upsilon. Wilson's group then spent the next few weeks investigating DU, mainly by communicating with members of the Harvard chapter and reading past issues of the fraternity's national magazine, *The Delta Upsilon Quarterly*. These actions only strengthed the group's decision to pursue DU. As a result, on June 15, 1886, Wilson and twelve other men (the group was growing fast) signed a formal petition for a charter and sent it off to DU's national headquarters. However, the school year ended some three days later, which left the national office too little time to investigate the petition or consult other chapters for their opinion, two necessary steps before they could consider the granting of a charter. Alas, the Tufts men were just a little too late, and would have to try again.[96]

So that is exactly what they did. When classes resumed in the fall of 1886, Wilson and his group of twelve picked up right where they'd left off. First, they felt that their prospects for a charter would improve if they became an official group at Tufts, so they became the Mathetican Society, a name previously used by the literary society nearly as old as the college itself, though that group had waned in recent years. Second, they sent further correspondence to DU's national headquarters about their desire for a charter, which resulted in the sending of Robert K. Bickford from the Harvard chapter to investigate. Such was the power other chapters and their members once held in determining if a school was worthy of a chapter – if Robert said "no," the whole idea would have died right there. Luckily for the Tufts men, the opposite occurred. Robert was so impressed with the group that he invited them to meet the entire DU chapter at Harvard. This meeting also went very well, and soon thereafter the Harvard chapter voted unanimously to recommend the Tufts group for a charter at the next national convention, scheduled for late October of that year. With recommendation in hand, the Mathetician Society, now at seventeen members, sent a second formal petition to DU's national offices.[97]

Letters and formal recommendations were one thing, but before a charter could be granted, the delegates at the national convention wanted to hear directly from the Tufts petitioners themselves. So, in a hastily arranged trip, Wilson and his classmate Frank Melcher proceeded to the Delta Upsilon convention in Hamilton, New York, where, on October 29, 1886, they presented their case to the delegates of the assembly. Wilson and Frank were actually breaking new ground here, as the Tufts group was the first to petition DU directly for a charter; all previous chapters had been organized either by the national organization, or by an existing chapter of the fraternity. One can imagine the range of emotions these two men must have felt as they addressed the delegates, but some of the only words recorded about the event were, "After some debate the delegates voted to admit this group." Immediately afterwards, Wilson and Frank telegraphed the good news back to the Tufts campus. All that was left was the installation ceremony, which took place on December 4, 1886, at Quincy House in Boston. The eighteen founding members, including one additional member who was added between the petition and the granting of the charter, were as follows:[98]

Wilson Lincoln Fairbanks (1887)
Henry Wilde Hayes (1887)
Frank Otis Melcher (1887)
Alva Edson Snow (1887)
Clemente Valdes (1887)
True Worthy White (1887)
Lewis Dwight Coburn (1888)
Clarence Augustus Crooks (1888)
Frank Williams Durkee (1888)
Charles Henry Murdock (1888)
George Frederick Murdock (1888)
Frederick Howard Swift (1888)
William Best Eddy (1889)
Clarence Freeman French (1889)
John Stevens Lamson (1889)
Burdett Henry Loomis (1889)
Herbert Olin Maxham (1889)
Frederick Theodore Nelson (1890)

Although one might have expected the other Tufts fraternities, Zeta Psi and Theta Delta Chi, to be skeptical if not dismissive of DU's arrival on campus, they actually felt quite the opposite. "We are glad to welcome to the college a third Greek letter fraternity," they wrote in *The Tuftonian* shortly before DU's installation ceremony, and hoped the group would be successful. Their feeling might have been different, though, had they foreseen the speed with which the new fraternity rose to the forefront. Over the next few months and years, DU members took up leadership roles all over campus, including positions on the editorial staff of *The Tuftonian* magazine and the annual *Brown and Blue* yearbook, thus breaking up the domination of Zeta Psi and Theta Delta Chi. Other members became key participants of sports teams, while numerous musicians in the chapter joined the banjo/mandolin club, the glee club, and the orchestra. Most importantly, though, the general feeling among the brotherhood was that their arrival had finally eradicated the "strong factional feeling that was so rampant in college affairs [at Tufts] a year ago…" Wilson and his group had succeeded in bringing a new campus order, much as they had hoped when they first got together in May of 1886, much like the founders of DU had hoped when they first gathered at Williams College back in 1834.[99]

Why can't we be friends?

There was one group, however, that was not too pleased with the establishment of DU at Tufts, or at least the way it was described to the world, and that was Irving's fraternity, Phi Delta Theta. In January of 1887, Wilson published a short history of his chapter's founding in *The Delta Upsilon Quarterly*, the national magazine of his fraternity. By the late 1800s, many national fraternities produced semi-annual magazines, which they sent not only to their members, but also to the national offices of other fraternities. Such magazines constituted a main form of communication between different organizations at the time, and while the articles were generally informative, they were not above bragging on many occasions. In his article, Wilson discussed at length how his group had rejected Phi Delta Theta early on in the process, deciding instead to pursue DU. It didn't take long for the national office of Phi Delta Theta to discover this apparent slander of its fraternity, and then realize every other national fraternity knew of the slander as well. Phi Delta Theta had a different story to tell about the birth of DU at Tufts, and through their national magazine, *The Scroll of Phi Delta Theta*, they did just that.[100]

The blunt response to DU came in June of 1887, just a few months after Wilson published his story. In the editorial section of its magazine, Phi Delta Theta emphatically insisted it was <u>they</u> who had first rejected Wilson and his group, and not the other way around as had been published in the *Quarterly*. With a written eloquence befitting of the time, Phi Delta Theta also referred to Wilson's group as "the barbarian of Tufts," harsh words that conveyed the anger felt by Phi Delta Theta at having its reputation soiled through a poor accounting of history. Two years later, Phi Delta Theta published another insult of the national DU organization, by writing, "perhaps we shall soon see some of our friends claiming to have stolen the sweet morsel from us, just as Delta Upsilon did in the case of the applicants she accepted after our refusal at Tufts." To add insult to injury, the editors ended their article by mocking DU for never responding to their original account of the situation.[101]

The outrageousness of this second article finally brought an official response from the Tufts chapter. In a letter published in the May 1889 edition of *The Delta Upsilon Quarterly*, Wilson addressed the blasphemy of Phi Delta Theta in exquisite detail, where he again stated that it was his group who rejected Phi Delta Theta first, and this time gave circumstantial proof to back up his claim, including details he'd left out of his earlier article. He concluded his rebuttal by writing, "The *Tufts* Chapter of Delta Upsilon has, then, an honorable excuse for being." Apparently the arguments in this letter were strong enough to end the controversy, as neither side spoke of the incident again in print. However, the episode speaks volumes about how inter-fraternal affairs were handled at the time, through eloquently written letters that often met with long delays, conveying sentiments not soon forgotten.[102]

THE PERSON RESPONSIBLE for the cavalcade of harsh words between Phi Delta Theta and DU is undoubtedly Irving Tomlinson. In the early spring of 1886, Phi Delta Theta, it appears, was well aware Irving was trying to start a chapter at Tufts. However, the President of the Alpha province of Phi Delta Theta (a region that covered existing and potential chapters in Massachusetts), made it very clear to Irving that "he could not favor such a project [of establishing a chapter at Tufts]." Reasons were not given, but perhaps Phi Delta Theta thought Tufts College was not large enough or prestigious enough a school to host a chapter. Irving ignored this decision, however, and instead spent the spring of 1886 trying to convince some of Wilson's group to choose Phi Delta Theta, perhaps hoping that a formal petition might change the mind of his fraternity's national officers and thus lead to a chapter at Tufts. But this was not to be. In the final analysis, it appears that both Phi Delta Theta and the Tufts men of DU rejected each other, though neither group knew of the other's rejection until those articles began appearing in print a year later.[103]

Irving would go on to graduate from the Tufts Divinity School in 1888, and in the following decade he began a long association with Mary Baker Eddy and the Christian Science Church. Wilson, after graduating from Tufts in 1887, went on to a storied career in journalism, eventually becoming the telegraph editor of *The New York Times*. It is unknown if the two men ever encountered one another again following their time at Tufts, but that certainly would have been an interesting conversation.[104]

Home sweet home

Although DU may have started in opposition to Zeta Psi and Theta Delta Chi, they quickly emulated one practice of their rivals during their first year, and that was the establishment of chapter rooms. The only difference was location. Whereas Zeta Psi and Theta Delta Chi both had rooms north of campus,

DU set up its accommodations to the south, in Davis Square. Every Tuesday night, the members of DU made the "ten minutes' walk from the College" to their chapter rooms for their weekly meetings. Fraternity business was always on the agenda, but so, too, were literary discussions (mainly of American novels), debates, musical interludes by the chapter orchestra, and even a good old-fashioned spelling bee. Occasionally the chapter hosted larger parties on weekends, where music and whist competitions entertained their guests. And so DU operated happily for many years, until the rules changed.[105]

That change, of course, came about when Theta Delta Chi built the first fraternity house at Tufts in the summer of 1893. Even in years prior, though, the members of DU began to realize their future as an organization lay in occupying a house near campus, not rooms off campus. The late 1880s and early 1890s saw fraternity houses coming into vogue across the country, and articles in *The Delta Upsilon Quarterly* frequently discussed chapter homes in all their grandeur. No doubt the Tufts members read these articles with some amount of envy, especially when photographs of these stately, Victorian-style chapter houses filled the pages. But the chapter never acted on their desire for a house, probably because no one at Tufts had yet to do so. Then Theta Delta Chi built their palace, and it was up to the remaining four fraternities on campus to follow, or fall behind. Of these four, DU built first. However, while Theta Delta Chi's housing effort was primarily alumni driven, DU's was not. Instead, it was the undergraduate members who took on all aspects of the task at hand. First they became a bona fide Massachusetts corporation, filing the proper paperwork on May 11, 1894, with the stated purpose of building and maintaining a chapter house. Then, a mere five days later, they completed their negotiations with the Trustees of Tufts College for a plot of land, and here they hit the jackpot. For a mere $1 they bought a parcel on the newly constructed Sawyer Avenue, just a stone's throw away from the Theta Delta Chi house. Over the next few months, the corporation secured mortgages from Tufts College and a local bank, and then construction began. And with each beam nailed into place, the members of Theta Delta Chi in particular must have gasped, for DU's house was casting a larger and larger shadow over 123 Packard Avenue.[106]

By the fall of 1894, construction was complete and the chapter moved in to its brand new home at 13 Sawyer Avenue. DU was not the only fraternity to build a house that summer, as the local Heth Aleph Res fraternity of the Divinity School also built a house just down the street. But DU's, as described in *The Tuftonian*, was by far the grandest:

> Every one admires the Delta Upsilon Chapter House built on Sawyer Avenue during the summer. The house is a large, three story, shingled building, with a broad piazza in front, and at present is painted a dark olive, with white trimmings. The interior of the building is finished in southern

pine, cypress, and white wood. On the first floor are the society parlors and culinary department; the two upper stories furnish fourteen men with rooms, in the shape of seven suites, and there is a spacious billiard and card room in the basement.

DU had made a bold statement. Their house was twice the size of Theta Delta Chi's and looked four times as impressive, to say the least. The future must have seemed especially bright to the men when they arrived that fall and moved in.[107]

That brightness, however, soon faded. Unfortunately for DU, they had decided to build while America was in the midst of a severe economic depression, and those arms of financial despair soon engulfed the chapter. By February of 1895, not even a year after construction had finished, the chapter was unable to keep up with the mortgage payments. With few options, DU turned to the college trustees for financial help, hoping they could take the house off their hands. The answer was "no." The trustees were not interested in purchasing the property, as they felt the appraised value was too high. However, one trustee, Albert Metcalf, made sure the board kept negotiating with DU, as he was keenly interested in Tufts buying the property. He had already financed the building of the first women's dormitory, Metcalf Hall, but with more women enrolling in Tufts College each year, he recognized another dormitory was sorely needed, and this house would be perfect. So, discussions between DU and the trustees continued on for almost a year, albeit with no resolution. In the mean time, the fraternity fell further and further behind on its mortgage payments. Finally, in March of 1896, the trustees had to act, lest the house go into foreclosure. For $8,000, they purchased the deed to the house, and after paying off the expenses and mortgages, left the chapter with about $1,000. This was certainly enough money for the fraternity to alleviate their near-term financial problems, but now they had a bigger one. Where would they live?[108]

As an obvious answer, the chapter figured they would simply rent 13 Sawyer Avenue back from the trustees, and carry on as usual. However, within a month after buying the house, the trustees had already decided to rename the property as Blake House and convert it into a women's dormitory. DU was out of luck, and this news couldn't have come at a worse time. In a few months, the chapter would be one of the hosts for DU's annual convention when it came to Boston, and the chapter had planned to show off their stately home to the fraternity at large. Now, they were in a bind. Apart from being embarrassed over the situation, the chapter knew the prestige they had built up within the national organization would likely evaporate when they could not offer their home to the convention delegates and their guests. But rather than give up and accept this fate, the members and alumni began lobbying the trustees in earnest, looking for any way to get back into their house. For weeks they tried, offering numerous proposals and arguments to the trustees, each of which was either turned aside or tabled until a later meeting. They were getting nowhere. Then, in the summer of 1896, the trustees had a sudden change of heart. They decided not to open a new women's dormitory, but instead allow DU to rent their former house for just one single year, at $560. Then, they'd have to move out. It wasn't much of a deal, but it was the best the trustees would offer.[109]

With no other options, the men accepted, and when the convention came to Boston in October 1896, they were able to hold their head high and show off their house with pride to the national DU organization. By all accounts the convention was a rousing success, with the Tufts chapter garnering two official resolutions of praise from the national organization, thus assuring their prestige and honor remained intact. Still, the problem remained of where the chapter would go after their lease ran out. Many of the trustees continued to push for the conversion of the house into a women's dormitory, but the feeling was not unanimous. So, when DU asked for an extension of the lease in 1897, the trustees agreed, but only for one more year. And so it went each spring when the fraternity returned to the negotiating table. Throughout the rest of the 1890s and well into the 1900s, DU stayed at 13 Sawyer Avenue, but they could never secure a long-term rental agreement. The trustees would only rent the house one year at a time, while always threatening to convert the property into a women's dormitory. At least, though, the trustees didn't raise the rent with each new lease. The rent stayed at $560 per year for quite a long time.[110]

The only upside to this living space uncertainty was a new and sustained effort by the members to buy another house. Starting in 1899, the house corporation began the arduous task of raising money for this effort, and they used the lack of a long-term lease as the main selling point. As for money, the amount being asked from each alumnus was rather modest – $2 a year for the first ten years after graduation, though larger donations were also accepted. Even then, many alumni were unable to contribute due to pressing financial needs of their own. Over the years, though, money did flow into the corporation, and by 1911 the fraternity was ready to make its first attempt at buying a new house. Rumor had it that Professor Bray at 98 Professors Row was selling his house that year, so the fraternity jumped at the chance. But this rumor proved to be completely false, so DU kept renting and raising money and hoping another house would come on the market. They would wait many more years, but in the end it was worth it.[111]

The 25th Anniversary

Formal anniversary celebrations within fraternities at Tufts were common throughout the early 1900s, with grand banquets held in Boston hotels, or smaller events at the chapter house. For DU, the twenty-fifth anniversary party on December 4, 1911, was a combination of both. The event began at their chapter house in the afternoon with a "smoker" and live music performed by the undergraduates, followed by a banquet at the Riverbank Court in Cambridge, where some of the chapter's founders, along with Tufts President Hamilton, gave speeches and toasts. However, a few weeks later the event was overshadowed by sadness. While life in the early 1900s was not always easy, and death at an early age much more common than today, one particular founder of the chapter suffered a truly tragic fate. Frank Melcher, who had accompanied Wilson Fairbanks to the national convention in 1886 to help petition for the Tufts charter, became a very successful railroad man after his graduation. By 1911, he'd become the second vice-president of the Rock Island Railroad Company, a very prominent and important position in its day, as it put him in full charge of the company's operations. On January 21, 1912, Frank was asleep in his parked, private railroad car when an express train plowed into it, killing him instantly. Frank had planned to attend the twenty-fifth anniversary of the chapter's founding in Boston a month earlier, where he would have been reunited with Wilson, but had cancelled at the last moment.[112]

Brothers in Arms

The entry of the United States into the Great War in April of 1917 had a profound effect on life at Tufts, as students either dropped out to enlist, or were drafted in droves over the next three semesters. When classes did resume in October 1918, after being delayed a few weeks due to the influenza epidemic, Tufts College was no longer just an institute of higher learning, but also a quasi-military base due to its participation in the Student Army Training Corps program, otherwise known as the S.A.T.C. This program claimed nearly all of the male students on campus, and its impact on DU was immediate. Although the chapter still had six active members on campus, all were in the S.A.T.C. and therefore could not hold chapter meetings of any sort, for such gatherings were against Army regulations. To make matters worse, their house was commandeered and turned into a women's dormitory. DU's worst nightmare had just come true. For over twenty years, the chapter had remained in 13 Sawyer Avenue despite the yearly threats by the trustees to turn it into a dormitory. Now that transformation had occurred, leaving the actives and alumni of DU to wonder if they'd ever get the house back.[113]

First, though, they had a war to fight. By October 1918, every single active member of DU was involved in the war effort, with a fair number fighting overseas. One member hoping to join that fight was Albert J. Briggs, a mechanical engineering student who was supposed to have graduated in June 1918. Some three months prior to this milestone, though, while finishing his degree and teaching gas engine work in the mechanical engineering department, Albert found himself unable to resist the call to service any longer. As for what he

Delta Upsilon house party, 13 Sawyer Avenue, November 3, 1917.

wanted to do, there was no doubt: he wanted to be a pilot in the U.S. Army. So, he dropped out of Tufts that month and enlisted in the Aviation section, only to be told he was underweight and therefore could not fly. The closest he could get was a job with the Curtis Aeroplane Company in their engine department, where his training as a mechanical engineer allowed him to excel in this arena. But still, he wanted to fly. A few months later, he enlisted again in the Aviation section, and this time he was accepted. He graduated from the Princeton School of Aeronautics in early September 1918, and was then ordered to Camp Dick in Dallas, Texas, for further training. However, on the way to Camp Dick, Albert came down with influenza, like so many others did that fall. He was hospitalized briefly, but the illness was too much to overcome. He died at Camp Dick on October 7, 1918. His eulogy as printed in *The Delta Upsilon Quarterly*, tells of a young man who would be missed:

> Brother Briggs, known to his many friends here as "Stan," was a loyal and devoted worker in the chapter. His cheerful disposition made him one of the most congenial and companionable of fellows. Straight, clean, loyal and upright, he was a man of whom Delta U is proud. He was very prominent in the Tufts College Musical Clubs and was College Cheer Leader during his last year at college.

Albert was one of three gold stars for the chapter. The other two were William H. Stiles, class of 1919, who died of influenza while stationed at Camp

Devens, Massachusetts, and Lieutenant David E. Henry, class of 1913, who also died of influenza, but in a hospital in St. Nazaire, France, some three months after the fighting ended. Lt. Henry had presumably seen combat with his unit, the 301st Infantry Regiment of the 76th Division.[114]

The armistice on November 11, 1918 marked the beginning of the end for the S.A.T.C. program at Tufts, with the men rapidly mustering out of the military and returning to civilian and collegiate life. Among the few DU members living through this transition in late 1918 was John MacAfee, and as the transformation from Army base to school unfolded around him, he could sense men would be coming back in droves, especially among his fraternity brothers. So, with amazing foresight, he approached the Tufts administration and asked if his fraternity could re-occupy 13 Sawyer Avenue once the normal college program resumed in January 1919. Much to his surprise, the administration said yes. The house was now back in DU's hands, at least for another year. As for a reason, it seems the administration was worried too few students would enroll in January, so they looked to avoid the possibility of being stuck with a dormitory they could not fill. As for another reason, it seems the Tufts community as a whole wanted to return to a regular college experience, one that put the war behind them, as soon as possible. Restarting campus traditions, especially the fraternities, was seen as a vital piece of reclaiming the normalcy, and the best way to ensure this was to put the chapters back into their houses.[115]

As it turned out, the leaders of Tufts should not have been worried about low enrollment. With the S.A.T.C. program now closed, and the active Army instituting a rapid reduction of force across the country, the campus was filled that January with ex-S.A.T.C. men and veterans alike, all eager to get back to school. Soon DU counted sixteen members on campus, more than enough to fill their house and restart their fraternity. Things began in earnest when fraternity rush season opened a few weeks later. With so much renewed enthusiasm for college life, and with the chapter house firmly in hand, DU recruited ten new members, bringing their ranks up to twenty-six. Tufts as a whole was coming back to life in rapid succession, with the administration restarting athletic teams and competitions, and the students organizing cherished class activities such as banquets. The members of DU were especially involved in this effort. Many took prominent positions in these revitalized sports teams, musical clubs, and class governing councils, just as they had done before the war. By the end of the semester, the active roll of DU had grown even more, to thirty-one men. Life in the fraternity was good once again.[116]

I'll take that one, please

In the years following The Great War, DU's main nemesis continued to be the one-year lease of its house. The fraternity just could not get the administration to agree to longer terms, and the threat of losing their home to a women's dormitory always hung over their heads. Members of the housing corporation knew they had to end this uncertainty, but as the 1920s progressed, they were unable to find an appropriate alternative space. The rapid growth in the number of fraternities at Tufts following the end of the Great War put great pressure on the local housing market, since all of these organizations began renting or buying houses of their own. So, with few viable options, the housing corporation decided to undo, or at least try, what they had done nearly thirty years earlier. In 1925, they approached the trustees with a deal. They offered to buy back their house at 13 Sawyer Avenue for $8,000 (the sale price in 1896), plus an additional 5 percent annual interest, minus the rent payments they'd made over the years. The trustees, upon hearing this offer, essentially laughed them out of the room. They knew the house was worth well over $20,000 at this point, so the amount of money being offered by DU was woefully short. Also, the trustees felt the fraternity was already getting a great deal, as they should have been charging $1500 a year rent, not the $400 as specified by the current lease. No sale. The house would remain Tufts property, and the chapter would remain its tenants, one year at a time.[117]

And so they did until the mid 1930s, when a rapid change in fraternity housing swirled around DU once again, thus forcing them to take a serious look at their living situation. Theta Delta Chi had set a new standard a few years earlier when they knocked down their antiquated wooden structure and built a grand, brick fraternity house. Whereas once DU's house cast a larger shadow over Theta Delta Chi's, now the shadow had been reversed. Additionally, word around campus said the other fraternities on Professors Row would soon tear down their old, wooden structures and build new brick houses, also in the grand Georgian architecture style. The shadow over DU, it appeared, was poised to grow even larger. And they could do nothing except watch. As renters, they could not follow this trend of tear down and rebuild, even though their house desperately needed major work. Quite simply, 13 Sawyer Avenue by then was a deteriorating firetrap, its grand design betrayed by poor construction that had not aged well, and the Tufts administration as owners had no immediate plans of modernizing the structure. If DU was going to survive as a chapter and compete on the new campus landscape, the men had to get out of that house and into a better place.[118]

The efforts to find a new house reached a fever pitch in the spring of 1936, when the housing corporation made a bold prediction in its alumni newsletter. On or before the chapter's upcoming fiftieth anniversary (December 4, 1936), the housing corporation said, they would lay the cornerstone of a brand new house. As to where that house would be on campus, no one really knew, but negotiations for a new plot of land had at least started with the administration. In reality, though, this prediction was a total bust. The fiftieth anniversary came and went that December without any cornerstone, since the plot of land never materialized. So, all DU could do was wait until an opportunity came. One finally did just a few months later, in early 1937. Sitting at 114 Professors Row that spring was an old Victorian home, known as both Sawyer House and then Knight House after its former faculty residents. Now, it was a women's dormitory, a role it had played for the previous twenty years. In a stroke of good fortune, the trustees decided to sell the house to DU in April of that year. At first glance the house hardly seemed to be worth any price to the fraternity. It was nearly twenty years older than their current one and was much smaller in terms of living area. But that did not matter, for it had a great location on Professors Row, and DU could own it outright, no more yearly leases. They were also never going to live there. They would raze it, immediately. In its place, they planned to build a new brick fraternity house, the largest the campus had ever seen. DU's shadow would once again fall on others.[119]

The deal for the house was completed by the summer of 1937, and while construction took a little longer than anticipated, by January 1938, the chapter was ready to move into their new home. It had most definitely been worth the wait. As described in the *Tufts Weekly*,

> The house is of an architecture typical of the Salem – Newburyport area, is well built with plans to meet the highest requirements, and has available accommodations for 23 men.
>
> Among the outstanding points of the new house are the large recreation room in the basement paneled in knotty pine, the murals in the library, the large living room, and the attractively furnished dining room.
>
> Other features are the complete furnishings throughout the house; the built-in closets, the draperies and curtains in the entire house, the clever electrical fixtures, and a complete alumni room.

It was certainly a stroke of irony that the chapter displaced a women's dormitory in acquiring their new house, especially concerning what happened next. The house at 13 Sawyer Avenue immediately became another fraternity's problem – when DU moved out, the Tufts administration re-rented the antiquated firetrap to another fraternity, Phi Mu Delta, which was currently occupying an off-campus chapter house. For years Phi Mu Delta had wanted a house closer to the heart of campus, so despite the physical condition of the building, they moved in.[120]

Wars, both far and near

The first few years for DU in the new house were certainly good ones, as membership flourished and the men continued to hold prominent campus positions such as captain of the football team, editor of the *Tufts Weekly*, and president of the Inter-Fraternity Council. However, life at college changed after December 7, 1941, when war once again turned the campus upside down. The largest change came in the summer of 1943, when Tufts instituted a year-round school calendar and transitioned from a college into a training base for Naval officers known as the V-12 program. Soon, Naval officers were streaming to campus for intensive course work prior to deployment. These men needed to be housed, and with dormitories crammed to the maximum, the Navy claimed DU's house for additional living space. Although designed to sleep twenty-three, the house soon had fifty-three Navy men calling it "home," with bunk bed after bunk bed crammed into every available corner. The chapter still had about twenty-five active members on campus that year, with a majority enrolled in the V-12 program, and these men looked to continue their fraternity as best they could despite not having their house. They planned parties and formals and meetings, as did the other organizations, but as such the effort was a losing battle. The V-12 program cycled men through campus at an alarming pace, and while the chapter did initiate some new men throughout the war (this time around, Navy men were allowed to join fraternities), by 1945, DU, along with all fraternities at Tufts, was essentially defunct.[121]

The end of hostilities in Europe and Asia caused men to flood back to campus in the fall of 1945 and spring of 1946. One member of DU who would not be coming back, unfortunately, was Ensign Richard J. S. Taylor. On June 6, 1944, Ensign Taylor was aboard the USS LCT-30, with the mission of delivering men and equipment of the 467th Antiaircraft Artillery, Automatic Weapons Battalion to Omaha Beach in Normandy, France, at 8:30 a.m., some two hours after the invasion of Europe had begun. After unloading its troops and cargo, LCT-30 began backing away from shore when a German artillery shell penetrated the deck and exploded in the engine room. Ensign Taylor and a co-worker were killed, the only two casualties of the incident.[122]

BY SEPTEMBER 1946, the V-12 program was long gone from Tufts, and so, too, were the Navy men living in DU's house. In rapid succession, the campus transitioned back to a college, much as it did after the end of World War I. DU took back possession of their house that semester and immediately began rebuilding their membership. For the first time since 1942, all of the Tufts fraternities held a formal, coordinated rush period that semester, and here DU did especially well. They pledged thirty-four men, the second highest number on campus and only one pledge behind the top spot. Soon enough, the fraternity was back to a normal routine of new member recruitment, social activities, and community outreach, putting the war in the past and the future in front. Life continued as such well into the 1950s and 1960s, with the chapter cementing its reputation as a fraternity for athletes, most notably football and baseball players. DU avoided the controversy surrounding restrictive membership clauses during this time, since the national organization, from its founding, did not restrict membership based on race, color, or creed. One of the only major negatives for the chapter during this time was the death of its chief founding member, Wilson Fairbanks, who passed away in 1953, a day shy of his 88th birthday. Wilson had long been a supporter of both the Tufts chapter and the national organization.[123]

About that house...

The late 1960s and early 1970s were by far the most tumultuous in terms of Greek life at Tufts, echoing the general state of society. During this time numerous chapters either folded (including all of the sororities) or resigned from their national organization to become co-operative, if not also co-educational, living groups. One fraternity where such upheaval had minimal impact was DU. While other chapters on campus saw their numbers plummet into the single digits, DU did not. Certainly DU's long history of having athletes among its membership insulated the chapter from the widespread rejection of traditions by many of the students. Those who joined the football team, for example, were generally looking for a more traditional college experience, and many of them saw that in DU as well. Also, it probably helped that DU did not have any secret rituals or rites. Such practices were especially unpopular with students in the early 1970s, so here DU had a slight advantage over the other organizations. Still, all was not perfect in the chapter. Issues such as the controversy over the continued Reserved Officers' Training Corps (ROTC) program at Tufts divided the brotherhood along lines of support, or not. By 1970, such disagreements had caused membership to fall to one-third its normal size. Also, in the fall of 1971, student protests greeted the chapter after it was discovered they had hired a stripper to perform during a recruitment event. Such negative publicity, as it turned out, did not have much of a long-term impact on DU, but it did add to the general discontent for fraternities among the students.[124]

Sill, as the 1970s progressed, DU more often than not held the title of the largest fraternity on campus, and continued to be a haven for athletes. They rode the wave of renewed popularity later that decade when the movie *Animal House* became a hit, and soon enough at Tufts, DU became most associated with this movie, for better or worse. One reason for this association was an article in the Tufts alumni magazine, *Criterion*, which included details about some alleged pledge activities within DU, such as swallowing goldfish, assigning nicknames, and building snow sculptures on their lawn that were not entirely appropriate (much in line with some scenes in the movie). The attention, however, had no lasting negative impact on DU, as the fraternity continued to support a large and active brotherhood. Instead, life in DU continued on, with just an occasional bump in the road. A confrontation with Chi Omega in the spring of 1985 resulted in the chapter losing the right to host parties or have pledges for the entire upcoming school year, the first time DU had faced such serious punishment in its then ninety-nine year history. Then, unfortunately, over the next thirty years, DU found itself on probation for a semester or longer a number of times, more so than almost every other fraternity on campus, mostly for incidents involving hazing. The "Animal House" image, it seems, has been difficult to erase.[125]

Aside from probation, the chapter has seen a larger problem in recent years, and that is the deteriorating physical condition of its house. After seventy-plus years of occupancy, the grand Georgian-style brick structure still looks stately on the outside, but the inside is a different story. Maintenance over the years has waxed and waned, which is certainly not unique to DU. However, in the spring of 2010, following a minor flood on campus, health inspectors toured a number of buildings on campus to assess damage, and when they came to 114 Professors Row, they found serious problems with "mold, water damage, and damaged doors." In response, the inspectors closed down 114 Professors Row and evicted the residents, who were then forced to find other accommodations for the remainder of the semester. Unfortunately, a year later the physical state of the house was still far from perfect. The City of Somerville inspected the house again in July 2011, only to find more problems. Simply put, the house was a mess. Water damage in the basement was still ongoing, and major systems such as heat and electricity were in need of serious repairs and upgrades. In response, the inspectors exercised their only viable option – they revoked the lodging license for the house and declared the structure unsafe for occupancy. The members of DU knew their house needed serious repairs, but now they were forced to make them on an accelerated time schedule, and at a much higher cost than anticipated. A few months and much hard work later, and well after the start of classes in the fall of 2011, the renovations were complete and the chapter regained its lodging license. Since then, life has continued on normally within DU. It is unknown, though, if the chapter still plays host to spelling bees.[126]

DELTA TAU DELTA (Beta Mu chapter, 1889 – 2005, 2010 – present)

If you were a member of the Universalist church in the late 1880s and wished to be educated at a college founded in your faith, you had but five options: Tufts College in Massachusetts, St. Lawrence University in New York, Westbrook Seminary and Female College in Maine, Lombard College in Illinois, and Buchtel College in Ohio. If you wanted to become a Universalist minister, however, your options were reduced to three, since neither Buchtel College nor Westbrook Seminary had a divinity school. As a result, graduates of these two schools often ventured to one of the other three to complete their ministerial training. One such Buchtel graduate taking this journey was Elmer Felt, who came to the Divinity School of Tufts College in the fall of 1888. Elmer, though, was more than just a graduate of Buchtel who wanted to become a minister. He was also a member of the Delta Tau Delta fraternity, and he had an idea.[127]

Riders on the storm

In 1858, trouble was brewing on the campus of Bethany College in what is now West Virginia. For a number of years prior, members of the Neotrophian Literary Society, an organization nearly as old as the school itself, awarded a prize to the best orator in the group. Such an honor was highly coveted, since it was an acknowledgement by one's peers of superior scholarly achievement – the winner was definitely the big man on campus. However, the vote for the award in 1858 left some in the society feeling rather miffed. That year, a subset of members conspired to award the prize to someone many considered a less deserving candidate. What had once been a true democratic vote based on principles had now been compromised for the sake of politics and popularity. Soon enough eight men stood up against this injustice and took action. These eight formed a secret fraternity, the first ever established on the Bethany campus, with the goal of wrestling control of the Neotrophian away from the conspirators and returning it to the members at large, which they did. These eight men called their fraternity Delta Tau Delta.[128]

As originally envisioned, Delta Tau Delta (DTD) had no intentions of expanding beyond Bethany College. After all, it had been formed in response to a specific injustice on that campus. But like all good ideas, the fraternity soon embraced a larger purpose and spread to nearby schools such as Washington and Jefferson College in 1861, Ohio University in 1862, and Allegheny College in 1863. The Civil War, though, proved disastrous for DTD, as almost every college with a chapter closed down for some time, including Bethany in 1863. The one exception was Washington and Jefferson College, which took control of the fraternity's affairs when Bethany closed. Legend has it that this first transfer of power required two men to ride horseback over treacherous roads during a winter storm in order to keep the fraternity alive. Following the war, old chapters were revived and new ones established, but as a national entity DTD was hardly stable. Control stayed with Washington and Jefferson for but a short time, until it passed to a number of schools every few years, sometimes by choice, other times by necessity when the governing chapter closed down. During this time of uncertainty, though, DTD established its Eta chapter at Buchtel College in 1873, the very chapter Elmer Felt would join years later. Stability finally took hold when DTD established true national governance through the creation of its Arch Chapter in 1883. Then, DTD began a rapid expansion across most of the country, even absorbing the southern-based W. W. W. Society (also known as the Rainbow Fraternity) in late 1884. However, there was still one area of the country without a DTD chapter, the Northeast. That would soon change.[129]

Congratulations, it's twins!

When Elmer walked onto the Tufts College campus in the fall of 1888, it appears he was certain of two things: he wanted to be a minister, and he wanted to start a new chapter of his fraternity. Ministerial training would take three years by design; establishing his fraternity would go considerably quicker. During his first few weeks and months on campus, Elmer began looking around for men he wanted as fraternity brothers. Not only did he consider fellow Divinity School students, he also pondered the undergraduate class of men. Although separated from these men by course of study, Elmer lived in the East Hall dormitory alongside liberal arts and engineering undergraduates, so he was surely familiar with all on campus. By early 1889, he'd identified six men he wanted as brothers, three from the Divinity School and three enrolled in the Engineering course, all from the class of 1891. Then, in late February of that year, he sent along a petition to the Arch Chapter asking for the right to establish a new chapter at Tufts College. As it turned out, a second group of men from Boston University also sent a petition to the Arch Chapter around the same time. These two petitions represented the first from schools in the Northeast, and while some within the Arch Chapter wondered if expansion into a new area of the country was a good idea, others were enthusiastic about the petitions. The debate lasted for months, but on April 18, 1889, the Arch Chapter voted yes to both. The chapter at Tufts would be called Beta Mu, whereas the group at Boston University would be called Beta Sigma, in deference to the name of the petitioning local society. The formal installation occurred a few weeks later on May 9, 1889, at a joint ceremony in the Quincy House, Boston. The six founding members of Beta Mu chapter were:[130]

Charles Byrd Moore (1891 – Divinity)
Warren Herbert Fiske (1891 – Engineering)
William Courtney Pottle (1891 – Engineering)
Henry Reuben Rose (1891 – Divinity)
Benjamin Franklin Thompson (1891 – Engineering)
William Shaw White (1891 – Divinity)

The installation of two DTD chapters in one night did not go unnoticed in the fraternity world. A few weeks after the ceremony, the editors of *The Delta Upsilon Quarterly* commented on this action by writing, "Delta Tau Delta, we believe, enjoys the distinction of being the first fraternity to give birth to twins." As it turned out, there would soon be a third chapter in New England, as a group at the Massachusetts Institute of Technology (MIT) submitted their petition just a few days before those from Tufts College and Boston University were approved. Had this group from MIT turned in their petition a few weeks earlier, the outcome would have been triplets![131]

The editors of *The Tuftonian* were very enthusiastic about the arrival of DTD, saying, "the new fraternity has begun life at Tufts under the most favorable auspices and… Delta Tau Delta will stand for what is best in our social life, and be found true to the highest interests of the college." Such a feeling of welcome was not, in all likelihood, universal on campus. Just a few years earlier, a number of editorials appeared in *The Tuftonian* in opposition to secret societies, and such sentiment probably still existed among some students. Outwardly, however, the founding of DTD evoked no controversy. DTD wasted no time growing its organization both in terms of membership and prestige. The chapter soon counted the quarterback of the "foot ball eleven" among its members, along with two editors of *The Tuftonian*, positions considered to be the bellwether of status on campus. By the end of the spring semester in 1890, membership had grown to thirteen men, and the chapter had moved into its first "home" – five furnished rooms in a house near the college railroad station. Not a bad start for the newest Tufts fraternity.[132]

There were, of course, a few minor hiccups along the way. Elmer Felt, the founder and spiritual leader of the chapter, withdrew from the Divinity School before graduating when he was called as a minister. Additionally, DTD ran into some controversy with the Tufts chapter of Delta Upsilon, which they wrote about in their national magazine, *The Rainbow of Delta Tau Delta*, for all within the greater fraternity world to read:

> We suppose we ought to say in this letter, that the Delta Upsilon chapter here induced one of our pledged men to break his pledge to us and unite with them. We wonder if this is fraternity tactics? Delta Upsilon has a good reputation elsewhere, but this recent action has lowered her in the estimation of all the fraternities on College Hill, and has put us on our guard so that we will know how to act next fall.

Although this was undoubtedly not the first time a Tufts fraternity enticed the pledge of another to switch allegiance, the incident seemed to catch DTD off guard. But, it did serve to show that within a year of its founding, DTD was considered an equal to the other fraternities on campus – otherwise, Delta Upsilon would never had pilfered one of their pledges. The chapter recovered soon enough, and then did something the other fraternities did not expect. They pulled ahead of everyone else.[133]

Homeward bound

Although DTD set up its chapter rooms near the Tufts train station relatively quickly, they also knew their future lay in a more permanent place of residence. With the growing popularity of chapter homes, described so eloquently in words and pictures within *The Rainbow of Delta Tau Delta*, the men of Beta Mu chapter most certainly looked at their DTD peers with some envy, and wondered how they could establish a home of their own. As a first step, in early 1890 the undergraduates formed a corporation, Beta Mu Chapter of Delta Tau Delta Fraternity, Inc., for the purpose of maintaining a chapter house. But, similar to the efforts of other fraternity housing corporations organized around this time, they were not able to accomplish anything of substance. Houses were expensive, and without a large alumni base from which DTD could solicit donations, money was most likely scarce. So, the effort floundered until the fall of 1892, when the gauntlet was thrown down. That semester, the Heth Aleph Res fraternity of the Divinity School opened the first chapter house the school had ever seen, when two members rented rooms in a small house north of campus and set up a boarding plan for the rest of the chapter. This property was soon recognized as Heth Aleph Res's "home," thus ushering in the era of fraternity housing at Tufts College. DTD especially recognized the importance of this action by preparing for an opportunity they hoped would soon come knocking. They did not wait long. By the spring of 1893, Professor William Hooper, a distinguished engineering educator, had moved into his newly built home on Professors Row, thereby vacating his former residence at 12 Conwell Avenue in West Somerville, just a block off campus. For DTD, Professor Hooper's former house was the answer they were looking for, so in March 1893, they rented 12 Conwell Avenue, moved in three members, and began setting up a dining room in the house to feed the chapter.[134]

DTD, though, did more than just move into a house. In a shrewd move (and one not attempted by Heth Aleph Res), they turned the event into a publicity gold mine by holding an open house for faculty, administrators, and undergraduates from the other fraternity chapters a few days after moving in. DTD was showing off itself, pure and simple, but why not? Competition for new members was especially fierce, and through this event, DTD saw a way of distinguishing itself from the rest. President Capen's wife served as a greeter in the receiving line, while the party featured refreshments, music by the campus mandolin and guitar clubs, and a demonstration of the epitome of modern audio technology, the phonograph. All in attendance were duly impressed by the event, especially the editors of *The Tuftonian*, who praised DTD:

> The formal opening of a chapter house by the Delta Tau Delta fraternity, besides being a pleasant occasion for its own members, and those mem-

> bers of the fraternities who attended as delegates, was significant for two reasons. The courtesy shown by Delta Tau Delta to the other fraternities was a most eloquent tribute to the good feeling existing between the different fraternities here; and the fact that one fraternity has a chapter house, must of necessity add stimulus to the efforts of the others to procure houses… Meanwhile, obeisance to Delta Tau Delta.

The prediction espoused by the editors, that the other fraternity chapters would soon follow in DTD's footsteps and open their own homes, was entirely correct.[135]

The house at 12 Conwell Avenue, though DTD's first, would not be its last. For one, it was quite small, since only three men could room there. More importantly, by late spring of 1894, two of DTD's rivals, Theta Delta Chi and Delta Upsilon, had either built a chapter house right on campus or were in the process of doing so, and both of these structures dwarfed 12 Conwell Avenue. The prestige DTD had built up on campus just a year earlier was evaporating quickly, especially since these other two fraternities owned their houses, whereas DTD only rented. The path forward thus became very clear. DTD needed to buy or build a larger house, closer to campus, sooner rather than later. As such, the journey would not go swiftly, but at least it started in the fall of 1894, when the chapter moved into a larger, brand new house at 94 Curtis Street, about a block away from Conwell Avenue. Though not any closer to campus than its current abode, the house at 94 Curtis offered some wonderful modern amenities such as electric lights, furnace heat, a larger dining room, and, most importantly, rooms for six men to live. The men, though, would not be alone in the house. Living alongside them would be their matron, Miss Russell, to make sure they all behaved properly.[136]

DTD's house at 94 Curtis Street, while much better than their first in terms of accommodations, was hardly the best location on campus for a fraternity. So, while the chapter made the most of their home, they also kept looking for a better place. In 1895, an up-and-coming Professor of Classical Philology, Frank Graves, built a house at the corner of Latin Way and Talbot Avenue, nestled between some faculty homes and student dormitories. Professor Graves was a rising star within Tufts College and a major reason the Greek department was so highly regarded at the time. However, just a year after building his home, Professor Graves left Tufts College to become president of the University of Wyoming. For DTD, this departure presented a grand opportunity. His house was newer, larger, and closer to the center of campus than theirs, and represented everything the chapter wanted in a home. So, they went for it. In the end, it took DTD some time to acquire the right to rent the house, but by the fall of 1899, they had moved out of 94 Curtis Street and into Graves House at 18 Latin Way.[137]

Delta Tau Delta members sing on the porch of their house at 18 Latin Way to welcome a new season, March 21, 1918.

After moving, life in the chapter settled down into a familiar routine of rushing new students, holding social events, and competing in intra-fraternity athletics. As with the other fraternities on campus, the outbreak of World War I transformed the chapter, and by their record at least thirty-two active and alumni members entered the service, including a few who joined the Tufts College Ambulance Unit with Herb Miller of Theta Delta Chi, only to haul ammunition for the French army. Of the DTD men in service, it appears only one, Courtney Starkweather, did not survive the war, passing away from influenza (most likely) while stationed at Edgewood Arsenal in Maryland. DTD's house entered the service as well by becoming an Army infirmary during the S.A.T.C. program. Within weeks after the disbandment of the program in late 1918, though, the chapter reoccupied the house and restarted its operations, primarily through the recruitment of new pledges. One of the first activities they held was the ever-popular pledge walk, where "the pledges were loaded in machines and carried, blind-folded, about ten miles into 'no man's land' and dropped penniless and friendless with nothing to guide them home but their good (?) sense of direction." Pledge walks were quite popular in the early 20th century at Tufts, with the administration generally turning a blind eye to their practice. The pledges did make it back to the house that night, but not before grabbing a few street signs and gas lanterns as souvenirs. Mischief, it seems, has long been a part of pledging.[138]

While the undergraduates operated out of 18 Latin Way, the alumni worked behind the scenes to find still better accommodations on campus. Renting was fine, but DTD wanted to own a house, even if it had to build from the ground up. After the reorganization of the chapter following The Great War, the alumni started talking with Tufts about buying a plot of land on campus, where they hoped to build "an elaborate house of the colonial type," but as such this effort went nowhere. There simply wasn't a suitable place to build, nor was there interest on the part of Tufts to sell any land to the fraternity. In 1919, though, opportunity came knocking yet again for DTD. That year, Professor Charles Bray, a long time professor in the engineering department, passed away, and Tufts College took ownership of his house at 98 Professors Row. Built in 1875, the stately Victorian home was right in the heart of campus, and it was surrounded by five other fraternity chapter houses – a perfect place for DTD, if there ever was one. Negotiations with Tufts took about a year, but by early 1921, the two parties reached an agreement. For the grand price of $10,000, DTD became the proud new owner of 98 Professors Row. After decades of searching, they had finally found their home.[139]

Life at 98 Professors Row was good for DTD, with the chapter maintaining a strong presence on campus. About fifteen years after moving in, though, it became apparent to DTD that the old Victorian house was no longer conducive to modern fraternity life. Additionally, Theta Delta Chi's modern Georgian-style brick house just a few hundred feet away, which they had built in 1930, represented the future of fraternity housing, and DTD wanted in. So, during the summer of 1936, the housing corporation took a bold step. They razed the aging Bray house and built a new brick home in its place. As described in the *Tufts Weekly*,

> The first floor contains a beautiful lounge done in knotted pine and yellow. Off the lounge is a card room, a library, and porches on the front and side, to which access is gained by large French doors. Also on the first floor is a large dining room, with a fireplace and window seats. Back of the living room is the kitchen.
>
> Upstairs on the second and third floors are suites for twelve fellows and seven fellows respectively. The basement is divided into a game room, chapter room and furnace room. Baths are on the second and third floors. From twenty-one to twenty-five men will live in the house.

DTD was not the only fraternity to rebuild or renovate their home that summer, as all along Professors Row the old Victorian houses were coming down, and new brick houses were going up. These modern structures were certainly impressive, but ultimately they marked the end of professors living on campus in large number.[140]

DTD's operation out of 98 Professors Row ran relatively smoothly in the years that followed. During World War II, the chapter turned over its house to

Tufts for use as a women's dormitory. The members attempted to keep the fraternity going during the conflict, but with so many men in flux, DTD was forced to cease operations for a time. After the war ended, veterans began returning en masse to restart the fraternity, and by the fall of 1946, the chapter at nearly thirty men strong had regained its house. To honor those men that served, the chapter added a stained glass window to 98 Professors Row, "Dedicated to the 174 Beta Mu Delts who served our country in World War II." Normalcy quickly ensued. However, as society began to change in the years following the war, especially concerning civil rights and the push to end segregation in America, so, too, did Greek life. And while some DTD men were ready to embrace this change, some were not.[141]

Overturning rocks

When the founders of DTD wrote their constitution back in 1858, one item they left out was any restriction on membership, because in reality, they hardly needed one. Social protocol of the day dictated that collegiate men of different religions and races, while they might interact together in the classroom (which would be rare enough), they would not, generally, form close friendships, let alone join the same fraternity. The founders, after all, were white and Protestant, and surely those who joined DTD afterwards would be of this same ilk. It wasn't until 1863 that the first requirement was adopted at the national level, and even then, it was hardly confining – prospective members had to be male, they had to be at least fifteen years old, and they could not be involved in any other secret collegiate society. Of the three, it was the last requirement that was most important to DTD, for in the mid 1800s, it was not uncommon for men of one fraternity (if not all of them) to disaffiliate and join another. Such practice began losing favor at the national level around the time of the Civil War, and by adding this clause, DTD helped stamp out this trend.[142]

As the years went by, the national organization modified those three membership requirements slightly, but in general continued to block outright only a small subset of college students. The bulk of these changes were aimed at tightening and clarifying the prohibition against members of other fraternities from joining DTD, which was still a lingering problem within the national fraternity movement. However, at its 1888 biennial national convention, or Karnea, DTD proposed a radically new membership requirement, which was enacted a year later: all prospective members must be of the Aryan race. For the first time, DTD officially confined membership to white men, though in reality this had been the generally accepted practice for years. As for a reason, it appears the growing ethnic diversity of college campuses across the country was viewed as a threat to many fraternities, not just DTD, so racial clauses began appearing in the constitutions and by-laws of numerous national organizations. For DTD, though, the Aryan clause was hardly the final word on race. At the 1915 Karnea, for example, the fraternity voted to strengthen its racial restrictions by specifically excluding from membership "Black, Malay, Mongolian or Semantic races." Of these expanded restrictions, it was the last that transcended skin color. DTD had long been recognized as a fraternity founded in the Christian faith, but now it was official. No Jews were allowed.[143]

It wasn't until after World War II that DTD began a serious look at the restrictive membership restrictions they'd put in place over the years. At each of the fraternity's Karneas every two years, delegates debated the issue at length and some proposed striking out the racial requirements, only to have the final motions defeated by majority vote. Part of the difficulty was a strong feeling within DTD that those outside the fraternity were unduly trying to influence the debate, which was true on some levels. As national DTD President W. Harold Brenton said during the 1950 Karnea, "The right to change, however, belongs to our Fraternity membership and the decision should be ours and not dictated and influenced by others." So, years continued to roll by without any progress on the issue of restrictive membership clauses, until change finally came at the 1956 Karnea. Following days of discussion and some judicious use of parliamentary procedures, the specific racial and religious exclusions were voted out of the fraternity's constitution and replaced by the following words: "No undergraduate chapter shall enter into any relationship giving any appearance of prospective membership with any person not socially acceptable to all members of the Fraternity." In many ways this language was a compromise, as it left in place unofficial traditions while offering vague official guidelines meant to appease those DTD members, if not whole chapters, that were growing uncomfortable with the membership restrictions. As a policy, the "socially acceptable" clause (as it came to be known) soon proved to be untenable, since in theory each pledge had to receive the support of all 45,000 (or more) members of DTD before being initiated. So, it was no surprise when differing opinions over the meaning of this clause began to appear in DTD chapters across the country.[144]

For the Beta Mu chapter of DTD at Tufts University, "socially acceptable" arrived at their doorstep in the fall of 1961. That semester, a freshman named Steve Karp gained the attention of a number of DTD members. Steve was both a good scholar and a talented athlete, much in line with many in DTD, so soon enough he was being wooed to join the fraternity. However, there was a problem. Steve was Jewish, and while DTD no longer had any official restrictions against Jews, one particular person involved with the fraternity took great offense to this situation. The lone dissenting voice was not from any of the undergraduate members – to their credit, they wanted nothing to do with the restrictions of the past, and they genuinely wanted Steve to join based on his merits. Instead, the dissent came from Joel Reynolds, a 1923 graduate of Tufts

College and alumnus of the Beta Mu chapter of DTD. After graduating, Mr. Reynolds remained an ardent supporter of his fraternity, eventually becoming the national President of DTD as well as the Chairman of the National Interfraternity Conference (now called the North American Interfraternity Conference), the group that oversaw the entire fraternity movement in North America. For decades, he was also the chapter advisor to his beloved Beta Mu. Now, in the fall of 1961, with his chapter about to initiate its first openly Jewish member, Mr. Reynolds said, "no." His DTD was a fraternity of Christian men, of traditions in place for over one hundred years, and he was not going to see that all change overnight, especially within his very own chapter. Unfortunately for Mr. Reynolds, none of the undergraduate members agreed with his opinion. A standoff then ensued, with Mr. Reynolds insisting on conformity, and the undergraduates insisting otherwise. Discussions became arguments, but in the end it was the undergraduates who made the decision, since only they had a vote when it came to the pledging and initiating within the chapter. And when the votes were tallied, the result was clear. The undergraduates wanted Steve in their fraternity. Mr. Reynolds, reluctantly, accepted the vote, but not before leaving the chapter speechless. "I will support you on this… On one condition! That you don't go lookin' under the rocks for any more of 'em!"[145]

Out with the old, in with the new

The members of DTD may have heard these words but they certainly didn't listen to them. Instead, they initiated more Jewish men as time went on, probably to the consternation of Mr. Reynolds, though never again did he challenge the undergraduates on this matter. As such, the evolution of DTD throughout the 1960s was very much in line with the changing attitudes of college students in general, who were pushing aside old traditions en masse. Therefore, by the spring of 1971, a decade of change had made DTD almost unrecognizable from its past. The fraternity had become a fundamentally different organization. Gone were the days of wearing jacket and tie to dinner; now, every day was casual day at the DTD table, when the brothers weren't eating in the new co-ed dining halls. Gone were the filled rooms within the fraternity house; now, most brothers wanted to live in off-campus apartments or better yet, the newly established co-ed dorms, leaving their chapter house under occupied and overburdened, financially. Gone, too, were the regular, productive chapter meetings; with members now dropping out or becoming inactive in large numbers, the business side of the chapter, let alone its heart and soul, were falling by the wayside. Greek life by the early 1970s had become an afterthought on the Tufts campus, and while DTD was not experiencing the worst of it, the chapter was certainly a shell of its former self. And it only seemed to be getting worse each semester. Not all were ready to give up, though, especially Joel Reynolds. He may have had his issues with the chapter in the past, but now with his fraternity on the brink of extinction, he gave one last push to keep the spirit of DTD alive. Over the course of a few semesters, he rallied a core group of men committed to the fraternity, and slowly but surely these undergraduates pulled the chapter back from the brink. While other fraternities on campus such as Phi Sigma Kappa, Alpha Sigma Phi, Alpha Epsilon Pi, Phi Epsilon Pi, and Alpha Tau Omega either closed down or dropped their national affiliation to become local, co-ed groups, DTD did not. Beta Mu chapter kept on.[146]

Still, more changes were coming to DTD, this time involving women. The admission of women as full members was discussed at length during DTD's 1972 Karnea, but it proved to be too radical for the organization, so the change was not adopted. However, in the wake of similar discussions within other national fraternities, an alternative way for women to partake in Greek life began to appear across the country. Known as the "little sisters" program, this approach allowed women to become social members of a fraternity, not privy to the formal rituals and secrets, but with some membership rights and a chance to experience life within a fraternity. DTD, perhaps more than any other chapter at Tufts, embraced this new idea. In the fall of 1972, just a few months after the Karnea where co-ed membership was rejected, the chapter announced its own little sister program on the Tufts campus. For $8 a month, women who joined could eat eight dinners with the brotherhood and attend all social functions. Living in the fraternity house was out of the question – this practice was apparently outlawed by the Tufts administration – but with no rules against women eating in the house, the chapter opened up its meal table to the program. All told, about sixteen women joined the little sister program during the 1972–73 school year, and by most accounts they enjoyed the experience. They helped organize parties, their dues helped the chapter remain financially solvent, and they helped promote DTD as a more inclusive organization, which its members truly wanted to be. However, it appears that after this first year, the chapter abandoned its little sister program, as many of the women graduated, and those who remained on campus decided not to continue. Still, DTD's little sister program is an interesting footnote on how the chapter looked to make a positive impact on campus by embracing co-edification and inclusion. Unfortunately, the chapter would come full circle on this idea twenty years later, and even worse, would start heading radically in the wrong direction.[147]

Falling down

By the late 1970s and early 1980s, when fraternities began making a comeback on the Tufts campus, DTD was well positioned to rise back to the top. The chapter had a stately house, an active alumni group (despite the retirement of Joel Reynolds as advisor in 1976), and a popular reputation on campus. In the fall of 1989, the chapter celebrated its 100th anniversary as part of Homecoming Weekend, with alumni as far back as the class of 1926 returning to the house. Then, in the spring of 1990, the chapter helped overcome a byproduct of the Cold War. One weekend in early March, the Fletcher School of Law and Diplomacy hosted an international conference on arms reduction, and scheduled to lead a panel session was a former diplomat of the Soviet Union, Dr. Igor Kripunov. As a recognized expert in international arms control, Dr. Kripunov's panel discussion was supposed to be a major highlight of the symposium. However, Dr. Kripunov had a problem: he was not allowed to set foot in the Fletcher School. Although the Cold War was essentially over by the spring of 1990, rules within the U.S. State Department still prohibited Soviet diplomats from entering Medford, Massachusetts, where Fletcher School is located. With potential for disaster looming, the group of students organizing the symposium, including a few members of DTD, quickly came up with a solution. The DTD house at 98 Professors Row may only be a few hundred feet from the Fletcher School, but it was a world away from State Department regulations, since it is in the City of Somerville. Therefore, the students arranged for a video satellite link between DTD's living room and the Fletcher School auditorium so Dr. Kripunov could engage his colleagues without violating U.S. law. Although hastily arranged, the panel session went off without a hitch and was seen as a great success of the conference. As an added bonus, Tufts President Jean Mayer also sat in DTD's living room while Dr. Kripunov hosted his panel session, which may have been one of the only times President Mayer was ever in a Tufts fraternity house. Afterwards, the brothers of DTD were able to interact one-on-one with Dr. Kripunov, a fantastic opportunity for those majoring in political science or international relations. In terms of campus prestige, this event was hard to beat. DTD, it seemed, was on top of the campus fraternity world.[148]

But, as the saying goes, what goes up often comes down, and for DTD the slow fall down began just a month later. In April 1990, *The Tufts Daily* published a story detailing the plight of a former member, Otis Damslet, who had come out to his fraternity brothers and the campus at large as being gay. The admission itself was not an issue; what surrounded it was. After confiding to his chapter about his sexual identity, Otis was subject to numerous derogatory comments and jokes about his sexual identity, with many in DTD making no attempt to hide their disdain for his lifestyle, or tone down their homophobia. These comments, though, were not just verbal. They were also written down. Housed in an upstairs bathroom within the DTD house, a room used not just by members but occasionally by guests, was a group journal kept by the members. Private thoughts recorded in a semi-private environment, as it were. After weeks of trying but failing to change the attitudes of his fraternity brothers, Otis decided he'd had enough. In the spring of 1990, he filed harassment charges against DTD with the faculty-led Committee on Student Life (CSL) as a means of effecting real change. To support his claim, he turned over the latest edition of the bathroom journal, which he had taken from the DTD house. Within its pages were numerous homophobic statements, off-color jokes, and derogatory depictions of female students as well as faculty members. It was crass, stupid, and embarrassing, pointless even, but now it was out in the open, especially when a few copies were distributed around campus. Six active members of DTD, in an attempt to control the situation, immediately filed counter charges with the administration against Otis and an associate for stealing private property, to no avail. It was an ugly episode for all involved, but in the end, the CSL did nothing except recommend the fraternity develop a program, "to enable its members to create an environment that does not alienate people on the basis of their sexual orientation." However, the story brought a lot of negative publicity to DTD that semester, mitigated only by the ensuing summer break. It also marked a noted change for the chapter, which twenty and thirty years earlier had been so progressive in welcoming others to membership.[149]

DTD's bathroom journal, though, was more than just an embarrassment for the chapter. It was also a vindication of what many on campus considered to be the negative side, if not the absolute worst, of fraternities. Thus, the journal became the centerpiece of a newly active anti-fraternity movement, one started by a group of faculty and students in the early 1990s looking to expel all fraternities from Tufts campus, or force them to admit women, in order to break down the barriers of exclusion, harassment, and elitism. There were many facets to the anti-fraternity movement, but DTD's bathroom journal was one major piece of hard evidence the coalition used to press their case. Without it, their efforts may very well have floundered. With it, the movement remained in the campus psyche for years, and nearly did bring down the whole Greek system at Tufts. Indeed, in the fall of 1992, after two years of studying the problem, the faculty voted to require all fraternity and sorority chapters at Tufts become fully co-educational or face expulsion; it was only by order of the trustees that the faculty mandate was never enacted. Still, the whole episode left the campus somewhat divided, and it took years for the rift to heal.[150]

The next few years were relatively quiet for the chapter, save for being placed on probation for two years following the publication of a lewd chapter photo in the 1992 edition of the *Jumbo* yearbook. But ten years later, DTD hit rock bottom. By the fall of 2003, the chapter found itself on social probation for the entire school year, meaning they were prohibited from hosting parties or having alcohol in the chapter house. This punishment was a parting gift from DTD's senior class of 2003, who were caught having kegs in their house the week before graduation. Kegs had been banned on campus nearly a decade earlier, and though numerous chapters have been caught in violation of this ordinance over the years, DTD's transgression was part of a pattern of poor choices that needed to be reset, at least in the eyes of the administration. Good behavior during the fall of 2003 led to the chapter's probation being rescinded for the spring 2004 semester. Unfortunately, though, the chapter was not able to handle this newfound freedom. By the end of that spring semester, DTD was once again placed on a yearlong social probation for a number of violations, including "providing alcohol to minors on multiple occasions, having kegs in the house, and committing drinking game violations." Perhaps another year under the condition of reset would help change the now self-destructive culture within DTD.[151]

It did not. One night in late February, 2005, DTD held an event at its house for its pledges, something the chapter had surely done each and every semester for years, as the active membership looked to incorporate the newest men into the fraternity. However, during this event, alcohol was provided to the pledges in clear violation of the chapter's social probation. Then, at one point in the evening, a pledge that had been drinking lay down on a couch and stopped breathing. Apparently, the alcohol in his system mixed with some other medication and caused him to lose consciousness. A few members of DTD happened to find the pledge and get him the medical attention he needed, where he did eventually recover fully from the episode. Still, the seriousness of the situation did not go unnoticed by either the Tufts administration, which opened a formal investigation into the incident, or the national offices of Delta Tau Delta, which immediately suspended Beta Mu's charter while awaiting further details. They didn't have to wait long. A few weeks later, DTD pled guilty to five of the charges levied against them, essentially admitting they had grossly violated the terms of their social probation and been responsible for supplying alcohol to the pledge in question. As for punishment, Tufts announced that DTD would close down immediately, vacate its house for the 2005–06 school year, and then be placed on probation once again for the following school year. It was a harsh punishment for sure, but not without precedent – Zeta Psi had been closed in 2004 following a violation of the school's alcohol policy. Still, not all in DTD could grasp the severity of the situation, including the chapter's president, who seemed more concerned with how the closure would affect DTD's status on campus, rather than how the brotherhood might work to avoid such bad choices in the future.[152]

One organization that did understand the severity of the situation was the national office of Delta Tau Delta. After the Tufts administration announced its punishment, the national organization announced theirs. They were not interested in probationary periods or second chances or even working with the current undergraduate members any longer. Instead, they revoked Beta Mu's charter and put all current members on alumni status. What had been continuously active at Tufts since 1889 was now closed. Delta Tau Delta was no more on the Tufts campus, and would not be again until all of the current members graduated and the national organization could restart the chapter anew. Revoking a charter is the most severe punishment a national organization can impose, one that usually signifies they have lost all confidence in the chapter's current members. As for DTD's house at 98 Professors Row, the building was still there, but it was no longer filled with members of the fraternity. Starting in the fall of 2005, the alumni corporation rented out the rooms of 98 Professors Row to graduate students, since they still had bills to pay and a property to manage. Then, in the fall of 2007, the alumni corporation extended a three-year lease to the Alpha Epsilon Pi (AEPi) fraternity. AEPi had been without a chapter house for a year following a probationary period of their own, but now they occupied one of the largest fraternity houses on Professors Row. For the alumni of DTD, these developments were heartbreaking, but all they could do was wait until the national organization came back to campus and re-colonized the chapter.[153]

Back anew

Beta Mu would not remain dormant for very long. Four years after the fateful event, when all those involved had graduated, the national office of Delta Tau Delta began rebuilding its Tufts chapter, with an emphasis on making the fraternity a positive experience for all involved. In the spring of 2009, the national organization recruited over forty men to form the basis of a chapter colony, and a year later, after much hard work, this group of men were re-chartered as the Beta Mu chapter. The ways of the old had been eradicated. All that was left was to regain occupancy of 98 Professors Row once again. Per the rules of the administration, the chapter had to wait a few years before they could occupy a house, but by the fall of 2011 they had completed this waiting period and moved back in, while AEPi moved back to their former house at 45 Sawyer Avenue. In conjunction with DTD's return to 98 Professors Row, the alumni corporation undertook significant renovations of the property, which had been in dire need of repairs and upgrades for some time. Working from some of the original drawings and architectural plans, the alumni corporation restored the chapter house to its original grandeur from 1936, while adding some modern conveniences such as flat screen televisions and a giant fish tank.[154]

FROM THERE, THE STORY SHOULD HAVE BEEN that life in DTD returned to normal, with the chapter doing all it could to grow its positive influence on campus. But that didn't happen. Instead, everything went awry in an instant. One summer night in 2015, a few DTD brothers living in the house invited some friends over, even though they were expressly forbidden from having guests on the property. Tufts had longed clamped down on fraternities hosting parties over the summer as a means of keeping the greater peace. DTD's small gathering, though, remained relatively quiet and was likely to go unnoticed. However, very late in the evening, and altercation broke out and two of the guests were stabbed (not fatally), allegedly by a DTD member. The details were sketchy and the circumstances very circumspect, but the situation was deadly serious. The Tufts administration responded immediately by issuing a shelter-in-place on campus while the police secured the scene. Luckily, there was no further violence, but there were consequences. The Tufts administration placed the chapter on probation for the upcoming school year, though originally DTD would still be able to occupy its house. However, the City of Somerville took a harder line and revoked DTD's lodging license, thereby closing the fraternity house to residents for the year. Then, in the spring of 2016, Somerville announced the lodging license would not be re-issued until the investigation was over, which would be no earlier than the upcoming fall semester. In the mean time, the DTD housing corporation had taxes to pay and loans to repay, so starting in the fall of 2016, they leased 98 Professors Row to Tufts University for the housing of transfer students. The chapter is currently active and off probation, no doubt looking forward to reoccupying their house, perhaps as early as the next school year. As for the greater future of Beta Mu, though, that will depend if the chapter can put the tumult of the last decade behind them, for good.[155]

THE ENGINEERS FRATERNITY (Local society, 1890 – 1893)

By the end of the Civil War in 1865, many parts of the country that had known battle were in ruins. Buildings, infrastructure, and industry built over decades was destroyed in months by the tools of modern warfare. The southern states, especially Georgia, were hit the hardest, mainly due to the scorched earth policy of General William Tecumseh Sherman. Soon after the last shots of the war were fired, though, the country began the long process of rebuilding. Such efforts required engineers, especially civil engineers, and demand vastly outweighed the supply of educated men to fill these jobs. As a result, many schools expanded or established engineering programs to fill this need. Tufts College was no exception, despite its short history as a classical school with very little emphasis on science and math in its curriculum. Nonetheless, in the 1865–66 school year, Tufts established a three-year program in civil engineering, with the first student enrolling in the fall of 1867. The engineering program grew slowly in terms of students, but fast in terms of scope. In 1869, classes in mechanical engineering were added to the curriculum, followed by a complete electrical engineering course in 1882. By 1890, the engineering program was well established, with students of this school accounting for about 35 percent of the total undergraduates.[156]

Although the engineering students and their liberal arts counterparts pursued noticeably different curriculums, they intermingled on campus much as they do present day. Both groups of students lived in the same dorms, attended daily and weekly chapel exercises together, had some common courses, and joined the same extra-curricular groups including fraternities. However, in 1890 a group of engineers decided to form a new, local organization they called The Engineers Fraternity. As evidenced by its name, The Engineers Fraternity was for engineers only. Very little is known about this group, other than its motto, "Vita sine litteris mors est," which means, "Life without culture is death." Membership in the Engineers Fraternity was quite low throughout its existence, much lower than any of the other Greek-letter fraternities on campus. By the spring of 1892, the Engineers Fraternity could count only eight active members, with four scheduled to graduate that semester. The society presumably disbanded during the 1892–93 school year. Indeed, the demise of the Engineers Fraternity appears to have been hastened by the defection of two members, Edward Byrne and Carl Hathaway, who helped start the Alpha Tau Omega chapter at Tufts in January of 1893. All told, the Engineers Fraternity came and went with little fanfare.[157]

HETH ALEPH RES (Local society / Aleph Chapter, 1891 – 1904?)

Since 1855, almost two dozen fraternities have established or re-established chapters at Tufts. Of these fraternities, Heth Aleph Res has the strongest claim to being the most progressive, most pioneering fraternity ever to exist on campus, even though its last meeting was held over a century ago and all its alumni have left this world. Heth Aleph Res was a fraternity of firsts in both thinking and operation – the first fraternity at Tufts to admit women as equals, the first to occupy a chapter house, the first to establish a chapter boarding plan, the first local to "go national," and the first to practice co-ed living on campus, some eighty years before such arrangements were allowed in dormitories. All be told, Heth Aleph Res is quite the legacy for a bunch of teetotaling ministers-in-training.[158]

Preaching to the choir

For the leaders of the Universalist church in the early 19th century, the chartering of Tufts College was one aspect of a broader educational plan to open a liberal arts college for the training of minds, and a theological school for the training of ministers. Medford, of course, was chosen for the liberal arts college, while Canton, New York, was chosen for the theological school. Canton's remoteness made it an unlikely host, but out of all the municipalities vying for the new religious institution, they pledged the most money towards the effort, so they won out. Of course, with the money came a hitch: the citizens of Canton didn't want just a theological school. They also wanted a larger, non-sectarian university to educate more than just ministers. Out of this demand grew St. Lawrence University, chartered in 1856, with both the College of Letters and Sciences and the Theological School on one campus. The Universalist's tidy plan, it seemed, had been usurped by the highest bidder.[159]

Despite the opening of St. Lawrence University under its larger auspices, Tufts College was content to remain solely a liberal arts institution. That all changed in 1866 following the death of noted trustee and benefactor, Sylvanus Packard. In his will, Mr. Packard left a substantial amount of money to the college specifically to fund a Professorship of Christian Theology. This request posed an immediate problem for the trustees, since the curriculum was decidedly non-sectarian, and they wished to keep it that way. Years of debate over this issue then followed, as the trustees wondered how best to satisfy the constraints of Mr. Packard's gift while still remaining true to their ideals. Eventually they reached a compromise – they would loosen the non-sectarian curriculum and start a divinity school. So, in the fall of 1869, four students and two professors opened the new Tufts Divinity School on the Medford campus and began working out of a single room of Ballou Hall. As the years progressed, the divinity school gained more professors and even more students, including a number who had earned undergraduate degrees at schools such as Buchtel College in Akron, Ohio, and even St. Lawrence University, of all places.[160]

The divinity school as established by the trustees was, in theory, supposed to be independent of the undergraduate college, with its own buildings, dormitories, and professors. Reality told a different story, though, since Mr. Packard's gift was not large enough to fund the construction of a whole separate institution. As a result, divinity and liberal arts students were never truly separated, especially when it came to dormitories and extra-curricular activities. The divinity students did create some organizations just for themselves, including the Zetagathean Society in 1879, which was formed to train its members in the art of public speaking and preaching. This society paralleled the literary Mathetican Society of the undergraduate college, and indeed the two groups maintained a friendly rivalry while both were in existence. Some years after the demise of the Zetagathean Society, divinity students tried to create a similar literary group called the Sawyer Club, but this society was short lived and left no real mark on the college landscape.[161]

These literary societies, though active for a while, failed to satisfy the long-term social needs of divinity students, so some took the next logical step and started a fraternity. In 1889, a first year divinity student named Elmer Felt recruited three of his fellow ministers-in-training, along with three engineering students, and started the Beta Mu chapter of Delta Tau Delta (DTD). For the next few years, DTD attracted other divinity students into its brotherhood, more so than any of the other three undergraduate Greek-letter fraternities in existence at the time. But DTD's near monopoly on new member recruitment from the divinity school would not last forever. Soon, a challenger emerged from within.[162]

Others need not apply

Unlike the liberal arts students at Tufts through the late 1800s, who were mostly young and inexperienced in the world, those in the divinity school were a motely crew. Men barely out of high school studied and preached alongside those who were much older and had already earned their undergraduate degree, or had spent some years working in various trades. All of these men (and it was only men until 1892), though, shared a common bond in their calling to minister. Therefore, in the spring of 1891, some of these students began talking about forming a new fraternity, one solely for themselves, to cement their relationship as friends. Perhaps they were motivated by the start of the Engineers Fraternity a year earlier and felt they should have one all for themselves. Or, perhaps, they felt the other fraternities on campus, while able to offer the benefits of social interaction, could not fully meet their needs as religious men. Regardless, the school year ended that spring without any concrete action. If the divinity students were going to start a fraternity, it appears they would need a push.[163]

That push came just a semester later. The fall of 1891 was a good one for the divinity school, for it welcomed one of the largest classes of first year students in its short history. Among those arriving was Carl Henry, a recent graduate of Buchtel College who moved into West Hall alongside nearly all of his classmates. Carl was also a Phi Delta Theta, having joined the fraternity's Ohio Epsilon chapter while at Buchtel. By virtue of his affiliation with Phi Delta Theta, Carl was ineligible to join any of the other national fraternities represented at Tufts, since all prohibited dual membership by this time. However, he clearly longed for the association he had known in Phi Delta Theta, for early that semester he allied himself with the small but growing group of divinity students looking to start their own fraternity. His experience and leadership as a Phi Delta Theta proved to be just what the group needed to succeed. By late September, they'd begun holding formal meetings and working on a constitution. Then, on October 5, 1891, the local Heth Aleph Res fraternity was officially born, with the following charter members:

Howard Anthony Markley (1893)
Thomas Butler (1895)
Allen Brown (1894)
George Edward Leighton (1894)
Arthur Adolphus Blair (1895)
Alfred James Cardall (1895)
James Dannals Tillinghast (1895)
Carl French Henry

As divinity students, the use of Hebrew letters instead of Greek for their fraternity name must have been a natural choice. It was also groundbreaking – there is evidence Heth Aleph Res was the very first Hebrew letter fraternity in the United States.[164]

Outside of the eight charter members, though, no one else on campus knew of Heth Aleph Res's existence, and with good reason. From 1886 through 1891, the number of fraternities at Tufts had grown from two to five, with members of one additional, Beta Theta Pi, trying in earnest to establish a new chapter on campus. All of these groups competed for members from a relatively small and slowly growing enrollment, so the last thing the existing fraternities wanted was more competition. Therefore, the members of Heth Aleph Res kept a very low profile and operated under the radar of student life, lest they stir up trouble. But with such a small campus, rumors of this new divinity fraternity soon made their way around the grounds, and then into the editorial pages of *The Tuftonian*, the student newspaper of the day. Here, the editors used their voice to disregard and mock this new fraternity, which they hoped would lead to its isolation and eventual abandonment. They even referred to the fraternity as "the non-society society," since no one outside of Heth Aleph Res knew its name.[165]

This uneasiness was probably due in part to Carl. His rumored participation in the new society raised suspicion among the other fraternities that he would morph the group into a chapter of Phi Delta Theta. To the Greek-letter men of Tufts, this was a terrible idea, so they used the loudest voice they had to rail against the group, and that was their editorial control of *The Tuftonian*. However, from the beginning, Heth Aleph Res had no intentions of affiliating with a national Greek letter fraternity. Showing off their playful side, the members of Heth Aleph Res appear to have enjoyed this intrigue, as they made very little effort to quash the negative editorials of *The Tuftonian*. Then, in April of 1892, Heth Aleph Res formally announced their existence to the campus as a brotherhood for divinity students only, which promptly ended most of the gossip and negativity surrounding their organization. But the announcement did not end all speculation, as some were still worried the local fraternity could, eventually, still look to join a national Greek letter organization. These fears were soon laid completely to rest when Heth Aleph Res did something no one expected.[166]

A number of firsts

In the fall of 1892, the members of Heth Aleph Res, and indeed all divinity students, returned to campus to find something they had never seen before at Tufts: three women enrolled in their program, studying alongside them, as equals. Coeducation at Tufts had taken years to bring about, but now it was finally here, with the divinity school welcoming Angie Brooks, Mabel MacCoy, and Eliza Hickok that semester. The significance of this bold step was not lost on the men in Heth Aleph Res. While nearly all Tufts undergraduates railed against the invasion of women into their male Medford sanctuary, the members of Heth Aleph Res did just the opposite. Within a few short weeks after school began, they initiated two of the women, Angie and Mabel, as full members of the fraternity. As for why, history has left only speculation, but perhaps the men wished to embrace the progressive nature of their Universalist church and accept the women as equals, in effect practicing what they would soon be preaching. Regardless, that fall Heth Aleph Res became the very first co-ed fraternity at Tufts College, and one of the first in the country. The editors of *The Tuftonian* praised this development, saying, "We regard this move on the part of the Hebrew letter society with favor, and predict that the ladies will prove a source of social, moral, and intellectual strength to the fraternity." To the established fraternities on campus, this act signified Heth Aleph Res would remain a local society of divinity students, since national Greek-letter organizations generally opposed co-educational membership at the time, and would likely want nothing to do with Heth Aleph Res if they ever sought affiliation. As a result, the fraternities dropped the negative editorials, accepted Heth Aleph Res as an equal on the Tufts campus, and even began interacting socially with the group.[167]

But going co-ed was just the beginning of the firsts for Heth Aleph Res. In November of 1892, just a few weeks after admitting the women, the fraternity took another bold step by establishing a chapter house at 31 George Street, a privately owned house "on the road to Medford" where both Angie and Mabel lived. Here, thirteen members of Heth Aleph Res set up a boarding plan and broke bread together, thus turning the space into a home. Other fraternities at Tufts at the time occupied day rooms at various locations off campus, but these organizations did not live or regularly eat together in these spaces. As a result, 31 George Street in Medford is the first known fraternity house at Tufts, and it would remain Heth Aleph Res's home for two years. Other fraternities quickly saw the benefits of such an operation, for soon they all began opening their own chapter houses on campus, starting with DTD in the spring of 1893 and Theta Delta Chi a semester later.[168]

What do you think you are doing?

The co-ed nature of Heth Aleph Res, while welcomed by the students at Tufts, was apparently too radical an idea for the old men running the school, the trustees. Conservative, Victorian-era morals governing proper interaction between unmarried men and women were still in vogue, and to many of these trustees, the thought of both sexes living and eating together, even if only platonically, must have seemed abhorrent. So, they used their power to put a stop to this progressive experiment. At a meeting in the summer of 1893, the trustees passed a resolution saying, "That the President of the College be instructed to inform several faculties that the maintenance of clubs for the purpose of providing board or lodging for men and women will not be permitted under any circumstance." This act seemed to be aimed clearly at Heth Aleph Res, since they were the only group on campus that included women as equals. As for this edict, the members of Heth Aleph Res simply ignored it. For example, fraternity members James Tillinghast and Mabel MacCoy lived in Heth Aleph Res's chapter house during the 1893–94 school year, in direct violation of this decree. Apparently, though, they suffered no ill consequences over their arrangement, perhaps because James became a married man in 1893 (though not to Mabel – he married Anna Moulton).[169]

A home of their own

Although Heth Aleph Res was the first to open a chapter house on campus in the fall of 1892, it took some of the fraternities less than a year to catch up and then pass them in terms of housing prestige. By the fall of 1893, DTD occupied a larger house closer to campus, and Theta Delta Chi occupied the largest of them all, a six-person home they had constructed right in the heart of campus. Like most of the other fraternities at Tufts, Heth Aleph Res took this development to heart and began working to improve their meager housing situation. And here, they wasted little time. By the end of the 1893–94 school year, the members of the fraternity, with the help of Professor Durkee in the divinity school, formed a housing corporation, Aleph Chapter of Heth Aleph Res, and started negotiating with the trustees for a plot of land to construct their own house. Everything came to fruition over the summer of 1894, when the fraternity built a home at 37 Sawyer Avenue and moved in. Their house was just down the street from Delta Upsilon's new residence, thereby making Sawyer Avenue the first "fraternity row" at Tufts. The Heth Aleph Res house may have been the smallest of the three chapter houses on campus (DTD was still renting off-campus at the time), but it was certainly praised for its appearance, as described in *The Tuftonian*:

> The Heth Aleph Res society has completed its house on Sawyer Avenue. The ground floor contains a reception room, parlor, and dining-apartments; the second floor has sleeping-rooms, while the third contains the private quarters of the fraternity. The house is commodious, and well adapted to the needs of the society.[170]

With a place to call home and a growing membership, Heth Aleph Res soon became very active socially on campus, hosting banquets, card parties (whist being the popular game of choice), and receptions at its chapter house.

Heth Aleph Res members and their two housekeepers (far right) pose at their house, 37 Sawyer Avenue, in 1895. Mrs. Canfield is holding her son, Hubert, likely the only child ever to live in a Tufts fraternity house.

Rest assured, they did not roll out kegs of beer on any occasion – nearly all in Heth Aleph Res were ardent supporters of the temperance movement, if not complete teetotalers. The fraternity often invited members of the other Greek-letter fraternities to their events, and by all accounts Heth Aleph Res was accepted as an equal by these other organizations. But, Heth Aleph Res was no ordinary fraternity, and they did not keep an ordinary fraternity house. For example, in the spring of 1895, the Reverend Harry Canfield (an 1886 graduate of the divinity school), his wife, and their son, Hubert, moved in with the fraternity for a few months. This is probably one of the few instances, if indeed the only one, where a child has lived in a Tufts fraternity house. Rev. Canfield was not a member of Heth Aleph Res, but rather had joined DTD while a student. Apparently, though, there was no room in the DTD inn for the good Reverend and his family. Joining the Canfields in the house that year was a second family, James and Anna Tillinghast, who were both studying in the divinity school.[171]

Even more radical than hosting children, the Heth Aleph Res house also became home to a subset of residents that should not have been living there: unmarried women. Starting in the fall of 1896, and continuing for three more school years, men and at least four women lived alongside one another in the Heth Aleph Res house, in direct violation of the trustees' resolution from 1893. And yet, this information was hardly a secret, since the addresses of all students were published each year in the *Catalogue of Tufts College*. It is hard to fathom how radical a situation this must have been at the time, given the conservative morals of the day. However, there is no evidence anyone in the administration did anything to correct this arrangement or punish the offenders. Perhaps the administrators felt the divinity students, since they were studying to become religious leaders, could handle the situation with dignity. Even more intriguing, though, is whether or not the women who lived in the Heth Aleph Res house during this time were ever initiated into the fraternity. None of these women show up on the scant membership rolls of Heth Aleph Res, but it is easy to imagine they were also a part of the fraternity – they lived in the house, they ate their meals with the fraternity, and they probably participated in the fraternity's social events, at the very least. So, while Angie Brooks and Mabel MacCoy are the only two officially recognized female initiates of Heth Aleph Res, in reality there may have been at least five more: Anna (Moulton) Tillinghast, Tacy Mathew, Lucy Milton, Fannie Austin, and Frances Kimball.[172]

From local to national

While many of the operational aspects of Heth Aleph Res are clouded in mystery, one of the most intriguing is the growth of the fraternity from a local to a national organization. In the 1894 edition of the *Brown and Blue* yearbook (published in the spring of 1893), the members of Heth Aleph Res declared their fraternity was "peaceable in its disposition, purely professional in its nature, local in extent, and modest in its ambitions." As demonstrated in the previous paragraphs, the actions of Heth Aleph Res effectively nullified this last claim, for their ambitions were anything but modest. But that was not the only claim they chose to ignore, for they did not remain local in their extent. The first clue came in 1894, when members started a housing corporation titled "Aleph Chapter of Heth Aleph Res," thus implying the group at Tufts was the founding chapter within a national hierarchy (the Aleph character, being the first in the Hebrew alphabet, is similar to national Greek-letter organizations using "Alpha" to identify their founding chapter). Then, in May of 1897, Heth Aleph Res became a bona-fide national organization when they established their Beth chapter at the Meadville Theological School in Meadville, Pennsylvania. This chapter was likely organized by Henry B. Taylor, a divinity student at Tufts and member of Heth Aleph Res from 1892–94 who transferred to Meadville in the fall of 1895. Very little is known about Meadville's Beth chapter, though it appears to have been active until at least the early 1900s. Additionally, there were likely more chapters of the fraternity established at other theological schools, as a description of the 1902 annual Heth Aleph Res banquet mentions that "delegates from sister chapters were present." All together, this information implies Heth Aleph Res was the first national fraternity to be founded at Tufts College. However, aside from being mentioned in a few newspaper articles, these other chapters left no substantial trace of their operations.[173]

The times, they are a changin'

The future of Heth Aleph Res looked very bright at the end of the 1894–95 school year, with a membership at twenty (similar to the other fraternities on campus) and a lively social calendar. However, as the turn of the century approached, the influx of new students to the divinity school plummeted, and membership in Heth Aleph Res fell off dramatically. Indeed, during the 1898–99 school year, the fraternity members could sense their future as an organization was tenuous at best, especially when it came to maintaining their chapter house. So, before school ended that year, the housing corporation sold 37 Sawyer Avenue back to the Trustees of Tufts College. The following fall found the property a boarding house for women – no more co-educational living, probably to the relief of the trustees. As for the fraternity, it continued to provide a social outlet for divinity students throughout the 1902–03 school year, even initiating seven from the incoming class. However, sometime after the 1903–04 school year, the fraternity appears to have closed down for good at Tufts, and in all likelihood, all of the other chapters, wherever they may have been, also succumbed to dormancy around the same time.[174]

After a brief stint as a women's boarding house, the fraternity's former home at 37 Sawyer Avenue served many purposes in the years ahead, from housing faculty to operating as the women's infirmary. From 1912–16, the house was home to a fraternity once again, when the Tufts chapter of the Commons Club moved in. They did not think too highly of this space at the time (apparently it was not constructed very well), so they moved out as soon as they found a better place to live. In 1955, the house was designated "Bartol House" by Tufts in honor of Mrs. John W. Bartol, and converted into a dormitory for students in the Eliot Pearson school. Present day, Bartol House is used for undergraduate housing and is known the Arts Haus, providing communal, co-educational living for students interested in art. As for the Tufts divinity school, it would last until 1968, one year before its centennial anniversary.[175]

IN THE FINAL ANALYSIS, the Heth Aleph Res fraternity represents a unique aspect of Tufts history, with a list of contributions to campus life few organizations can match, especially since they lasted only thirteen or so years. It is unfortunate so many records of the fraternity have not survived to present day, as there would likely be other stories to tell.[176]

ALPHA TAU OMEGA (Gamma Beta chapter, 1893 – 1974)
ATO of Massachusetts (Local co-ed fraternity, 1974 – present)

In the summer of 1865, nineteen-year old Otis Glazebrook returned home to Richmond, Virginia, to take stock of his previous year. He had been a Confederate soldier, having trained at the Virginia Military Institute (VMI) in Lexington, Virginia, and then baptized under fire in the Battle of New Market. But now the war was over. Otis, upon reflecting on his battlefield experiences, developed a strong conviction that men of both sides should band together and work towards building a lawful and just society. These feelings stemmed from his piety as a devout Christian, for he truly wished to practice the ideals of acceptance and forgiveness with likeminded men. Such a feeling was hardly universal among Confederate war veterans – many felt only bitterness towards their northern countrymen – but Otis was looking forward, not backward. So, during the summer of 1865, he brooded over how best to gather together men who felt the same way.[177]

In the mean time, though, Otis had a school to help rebuild. Towards the end of the Civil War, the Union Army burned the buildings of his beloved VMI to the ground. The school's superintendent, General Francis Smith, was determined to bring the school back to its original form after the hostilities ceased, with the hope of having cadets re-enter in the fall of 1865. Otis worked as the General's aide that summer, and part of his job was processing the incoming correspondence. One day, a letter from a representative of a northern-based Greek-letter fraternity arrived for General Smith, asking for his help in reorganizing its chapters across the South that had been lost to the war. During the conflict, nearly all fraternity chapters at southern colleges, if not also the schools, had closed down. Now, with these institutions rapidly rebuilding and restarting, the national fraternities were interested in bringing back their former chapters. At one point the letter crossed Otis's desk, and when he read it, he immediately knew he'd found the mechanism to bring young men together. He would start his own fraternity.[178]

However, as he engaged in discussions with General Smith about the nature of Greek-letter fraternities, he became slightly disillusioned. Otis liked the concept of fraternal brotherhood, but his religious background rebelled against the idea of basing an organization on the ideals of ancient Greece. Instead, Otis felt Christianity should be at the heart of his fraternity. Within this framework, he then went about creating a constitution, ritual, and symbols for his new fraternity, which he called Alpha Tau Omega (ATO). Here, he kept a vestige of Greek-letter organizations in the name, but the letters served a double purpose, since they had chosen for their Christian significance: the Alpha and the Omega referred to the beginning and the end (or life, and salvation), while the middle letter, Tau, referred to the cross. Then, On September 11, 1865, Otis invited two friends to his Richmond home, and when the three signed the constitution, the Alpha Tau Omega fraternity was born, the first fraternity to be founded after the Civil War.[179]

Aside from the emphasis on Christianity, though, ATO was different from many other Greek-letter fraternities in that it was founded to be a national organization from its very beginning. Before ATO, almost all national fraternities started as local to one school and then expanded to other campuses almost by accident; ATO, though, was primed for expansion from its beginning, in accordance with Otis's idea of joining men across the country into a brotherhood. Here, ATO wasted no time. The fraternity placed a second chapter at Washington College in nearby Lexington, Virginia, just weeks after its founding. Over the next few years, ATO expanded rapidly across the country, though primarily in the southern states. ATO finally reached north in 1881, when it established a chapter at the University of Pennsylvania, and a few years later came to New England via chapters at MIT, the University of Vermont, and Maine State College (now the University of Maine at Orono). It is with Maine's chapter, known as Beta Upsilon, where the story of ATO at Tufts begins.[180]

The apples and the bees

Pearly Wilson, from Solon, Maine, was by all accounts doing well at Maine State College in the early 1890s. He was an athlete, having earned a varsity letter on the baseball team, and he was a fraternity man, having been a founding member of the Beta Upsilon chapter of ATO. He was also a little careless. One night early in the fall semester of 1892, Pearly and a few of his friends developed an insatiable craving for apples. Late night snacking has always been a favorite pastime of college students, but in the late 1800s of rural Maine, there was a distinct lack of options for procuring late night food, other than the great outdoors. So, that is where Pearly and his friends turned – they found a nearby apple orchard and raided the trees for fruit. However, their apple-picking odyssey went horribly awry, as the farmer caught them in the act and chased them away. In their haste to escape, the men knocked over a beehive, where they were all "stung beyond recognition." The administrators of Maine State College were none too pleased with this incident, so in response they quickly expelled the men. Free apples have never cost so much. Pearly and a few others then transferred to Tufts College in time to start classes in the fall of 1892.[181]

As for why Pearly and his group chose to come to Tufts College, one reason may have been George Maguire, a Maine State College alumnus and, along with Pearly, a founding member of the Beta Upsilon chapter of ATO. George was also an enthusiastic supporter of his fraternity and the leader of local Boston ATO alumni. No doubt he realized that if Pearly came to Tufts, the two would have a wonderful opportunity to bring their beloved ATO to the school. So, he and Pearly made it happen. After Pearly enrolled at Tufts, the two recruited a number of undergraduates in the fall of 1892 to form the basis of a chapter, and by the end of the semester, the group had submitted a petition for a charter. This document was approved in part by Otis Glazebrook, who was still actively involved in the national organization. Then, on January 29, 1893, the Massachusetts Gamma Beta chapter of Alpha Tau Omega was officially installed at Tufts College, with ten founding members:

George Edward Strong (1893)
Chesley Metcalf Johnston (1893)
George Gray Homer (1894)
Herbert (Hubert?) Collamore Foss (1894)
Frank George Wren (1894)
Edward Patrick Byrne (1894)
Charles Harrison Page (1895)
Cecil Alonzo Page (1896)
George Francis Maguire (1896)
Eugene Francis Corridan (1896)

Pearly, though active in the chapter, is not considered a founder of the Gamma Beta chapter since he had been previously initiated into the Beta Upsilon chapter. Also, evidence suggests that Herbert and Chesley were involved in the apple orchard incident with Pearly, as they had all been classmates at Maine State College, and they had all transferred to Tufts in the fall of 1892.[182]

The arrival of ATO came as a shock to the Tufts campus, especially the editors of *The Tuftonian*, who wrote, "The matter had been so quietly planned and executed that the news was a complete surprise." At the time, many within the fraternity system were actively campaigning against the formation of other Greek-letter organizations, for they felt Tufts could not support any more. However, it seems that ATO was accepted on campus without much controversy, probably because many of its members were also prominent students. For example, those in ATO comprised nearly half of the football team, "acknowledged to be second only of those of Harvard and Yale," and the baseball team, "equal to those sent out by the majority of colleges." Although intercollegiate athletics was still in its infancy, these two sports in particular were very popular with the students, and the athletes were generally very well known on campus. Meanwhile, others in ATO held highly coveted positions on the staff of *The Tuftonian* and the annual *Brown and Blue* yearbook, which gave them an influence on campus life. All together, ATO was off to a strong start, and quickly recognized as an equal to the other four national fraternities on campus.[183]

Homeward bound

After receiving their charter, the members of ATO then embarked on what they considered the most important task of any fraternity: finding a home. When the chapter was founded, the Heth Aleph Res fraternity had already established the first ever chapter house on campus, and Delta Tau Delta (DTD) was working to open the second. ATO was quick to follow in their footsteps. By the end of that spring semester of 1893, the chapter rented half a duplex on Boston Avenue in the Medford Hillside and set up their home. The duplex was small – only two members lived in the house, and there was not enough space to support a dining room – but it served the men well. In fact, most nights the house was crammed with up to half a dozen members who decided their tiny abode was a better place to sleep than the dormitory. As for meals, the chapter ate together at local boarding houses, often moving from one to another when they could no longer stand the food. The first large-scale student dining hall was still a year away from being established at Tufts, so at the time there was a flourishing business of privately run boarding houses all around campus. The fare at the places, it seems, was not always the most appetizing to the men, but it did give them a chance to eat their meals together. When it came time to initiate the first new group of men that semester, however, the members realized they were missing some important ritual artifacts, including a large cross and column. Rather than buy these items, though, they appropriated some wood from a nearby construction site to build the cross, and rescued a "dismal looking lamp post" for the column. Despite this ethical lapse in judgment, the chapter was now ready to move forward.[184]

Slowing them down slightly was their quest to find the perfect chapter home. They outgrew their tiny duplex after just one year, so they moved into the first floor of a larger, newly built house in the Medford Hillside that was closer to campus. Although the chapter seemed to enjoy this space at first, apparently it had enough shortcomings such that in 1895, they left their house for day rooms in Medford recently vacated by the Theta Delta Chi fraternity. As such, this move marked a step back in accommodations, since the rooms were quite far from campus and could not support the boarding or rooming of any members. Not surprisingly, ATO's stay in Medford proved to be short, just a few months, so once again the chapter was on the move. And again, they chose day rooms over a house, while swapping Somerville for Medford. Over the next few years, the chapter occupied rooms in buildings throughout Davis Square, including Odd Fellows Hall, Columbian Hall, Chapin Hall, and Unity Hall, with changes being necessitated as the membership grew in number. With each passing year, though, the members seemed to bemoan louder their current accommodations, while hoping they would soon occupy a true fraternity house. Near the turn of the 20th century, all of the other fraternities at Tufts were either ensconced in a home on campus or in the process of doing so, as were most other chapters within ATO's national organization. Gamma Beta chapter, on the other hand, was stuck in Davis Square. As the chapter wrote in a letter to its national magazine, the *Alpha Tau Omega Palm*, "Gamma Beta is not satisfied yet and cannot be until it sees itself in a house that it can call its own." They were falling way behind others in terms of housing, and they knew it.[185]

Redemption seemed to arrive at their doorstep in early 1899, when the house owned by the late John D. W. Joy, former President of the Board of Trustees of Tufts College, came up for sale. This house was located at the corner of Curtis Street and Curtis Avenue in Somerville, a perfect location for the chapter. So, they made an offer to buy the property, and with great confidence announced to the campus they'd soon be moving in. This declamation turned out to be premature. Mr. Joy, who was apparently not a fan of fraternities, had a covenant in his will forbidding his estate from renting or selling his house to any such organization. Red faced and embarrassed, ATO could only retreat back to their day rooms and hope.[186]

ATO, though, did not suffer too long, because a few months after this debacle, DTD vacated their chapter house at 94 Curtis Street for a space closer to campus. ATO jumped at the chance to move in, which they accomplished by the fall of 1899. Years of searching and hoping for a chapter home were now finally over. The house at 94 Curtis Street, while not the largest on campus, was big enough so four members could live there and all could eat their meals in the dining room, certainly much better than their day rooms in Davis Square. Once in the new house, ATO established a very active social calendar, including whist parties (which, apparently, were also used as fundraisers for the chapter), smoke talks, and lectures by faculty. However, with the new chapter house came a new problem: drunkenness. Although Victorian-era morals and temperance movements were still quite popular at the turn of the 20th century, they were starting to lose their grip on college students, and the abuse of alcohol, especially, was becoming prevalent. Celebrations after football victories seem to have been the rowdiest parties at the time. ATO did contribute their fair share of inebriants to such gatherings, but as the chapter claimed, they were "a paradise [of self control] in comparison with the Zetes [Zeta Psi] and the Thetes [Theta Delta Chi]." Working to clamp down on such poor behavior was Harry Hersey, a student in the divinity school and Worthy Master, or president, of the chapter circa 1903. He was a little older than the other members of his fraternity, and as a minister-to-be was more sympathetic to the temperance movement. So, he used his influence to rid the chapter of not one but two social evils: alcohol and tobacco. Alas, in this regard he was only half successful. While the members did give up alcohol shortly thereafter, under no circumstances would they give up their tobacco.[187]

One other problem within ATO during this time was the relatively high rate of dropouts within its brotherhood. From the beginning, ATO's membership was primarily comprised of athletes who, unfortunately, were not always the best students. Scholarly achievement was never a top priority within the chapter until 1906, when the brotherhood made a concerted effort to branch out its recruitment and attract more than just the star football or baseball player. This switch had a profound effect on the chapter and helped them focus more on their future, since they were now retaining more of their membership. One long-term project they started around this time was a savings fund for the purchase of a chapter house. Renting 94 Curtis Street was fine, but the chapter knew their future lay in owning a house on campus, the more grand and stately the better. By early 1911, with the housing fund continuing to grow each year, some of the alumni formalized the process by establishing a corporation, the Tufts Alumni Association of Alpha Tau Omega, to oversee the mission. The first chairman of the corporation was Frank Wren, a founding member of the chapter and, at the time, Dean of the College of Letters at Tufts. All ATO needed now was the right house to buy.[188]

As the saying goes, timing is everything, and for ATO, theirs was perfect. Just a few weeks after they established their housing corporation, the school's trustees offered up for sale Professor Amos Emerson Dolbear's house at 134 Professors Row. Professor Dolbear is recognized as having invented the telephone a decade before Alexander Graham Bell, but he never filed a patent application for his device, so he was unable to mount a successful legal challenge against Mr. Bell's invention. The good professor passed away in 1910 after a long and distinguished career in the Physics Department of Tufts College, leaving behind his stately Victorian house on Professors Row. Now it was for sale, and ATO's housing corporation jumped at the chance. The transaction was finalized later that summer, with ATO taking up occupancy in the fall of 1911. A celebration was in order, but so was a chance to brag. The chapter announced their good fortune to their entire national organization with a rousing article and photo in the *Alpha Tau Omega Palm*, thus making up for all the years they had to read about the good housing fortunes of others:

> Massachusetts Gamma Beta's new house at Tufts College is situated at the corner of Curtis Street and Professors Row, near our old house. It faces the old campus and commands a fine view of the Hill. It is the old Dolbear house, built by Prof. Dolbear, late Professor Emeritus of Tufts, and one of the most famous scientific men of the United States.
>
> It contains studies and sleeping rooms for fifteen brothers. On the first floor are the chapter room, library, dining room, kitchen, etc. On the second floor are the studies and a suite of three rooms for the matron, entirely separate from the rest of the house. On the third floor are three "lamb pastures" for the brothers. In the basement is the poolroom. Most of the rooms have hardwood floors, and there are five fireplaces in the house. The house is electric lighted throughout.
>
> The chapter room is 20 feet by 30 feet, and has a large bay window and a stained glass window with a gold A.T.O. on a blue ground. It has a quartered-oak floor and a fireplace. A large closet for our secret work leads off from the room.[189]

The description of the house may have been elegant, but the realities were somewhat different. The heating system was so woefully inefficient the residents were forced to burn coal in their fireplaces for warmth. Those without fireplaces were out of luck and in the cold. Nonetheless, the chapter settled into its new house, and with each arriving school year, continued to grow its membership. By the fall of 1917, ATO stood at nearly thirty active members, the largest it had yet been. Then, of course, life came to a halt.[190]

The war hits home

The catalyst for the sudden change was America's declaration of war on Germany in April of 1917, which upended nearly all of campus life, not just ATO. With each passing month, more men left their college and their fraternity to head to Army bases across the country, if not to the front lines in France. Those that remained on campus worked harder than ever to keep their fraternity going, but theirs was a difficult job. The grand house they worked so hard to buy was slowly turning into a financial nightmare, as the chapter needed at least twenty-five active members each year to pay the bills. Throughout the 1917–18 school year, they managed to exceed this membership need and stay afloat, but as the fall of 1918 approached, they were calling on their alumni, almost desperately, to help send a few good men to ATO, or else they would be crushed by debt. However, just before the school year was to start, the men of ATO heard the news: there would be no school in the fall. Tufts College would become part of the Student Army Training Corps, or S.A.T.C. as it was commonly known, and campus life would be traded for Army life, at least for the men. And here, ATO caught a break. The newly arriving officers of the S.A.T.C., who would oversee the training of the newly impressed soldiers, needed appropriate quarters on campus. Being officers, they could not live in the dormitories with the enlisted men, so after looking around campus, they chose ATO's grand house for their rented billet. In an instant, the chapter's financial problems were solved. ATO had temporarily lost their house to the war effort, but that was much better than losing it permanently to debt.[191]

Then, of course, came a different problem. As the training intensified that fall, the ATO members serving in the S.A.T.C. realized they had lost more than just the use of their house. They had lost their fraternity as well. They were all in the Army now, and the one hour of free time they had each day was meant to take care of personal business such laundry or picking up mail, for example. Under no circumstances were they allowed to meet as a fraternity, for such associations were prohibited by Army regulations. The members of ATO were not so easily dissuaded, and many times they all gave up their free hour so they could secretly meet as a fraternity in Ballou Hall. Here, they talked mainly about the future of their chapter, including which men they had identified as good candidates once the war was over. Optimism was soon running high once again, especially as the progress of the war promised a return to normalcy.[192]

But, as with all war, there was a price to pay, and ATO added their fair share to the ante. William J. Bennett, class of 1914, was the consummate student-athlete, being an accomplished engineering student, a four-year member and captain of the football and baseball teams, a member of the Tower Cross academic honor society, and a brother in Alpha Tau Omega. When the war effort called, he put his engineering skills to use and became a Master Engineer in Headquarters Company, 301st Engineers, 76th Division, American Expeditionary Force. He headed to France in the late summer of 1918, where he and his fellow engineers worked to clear ordinance and open up supply roads, so material could move to the front and wounded could move to the rear. On September 14, Master Engineer Bennett was working with a team of thirteen other soldiers clearing a road, when suddenly there was a huge explosion. No one was certain what, exactly, had happened – it could have been a lone incoming shell, or the unintentional detonation of a supposed dud, or a booby trap – but the ensuing explosion of a nearby ordinance stockpile was massive, and when the dust settled, the outcome was tragic. Master Engineer Bennett lay unconscious by the side of the road, having been hit with two large pieces of shrapnel. He died two weeks later of his wounds in a French hospital. His classmates from 1914 established the William J. Bennett Memorial Scholarship in his honor on the tenth anniversary of their graduation, to recognize the "student who best exemplifies the qualities of true sportsmanship as exhibited by the man whose name it bears." Master Engineer Bennett was one of four gold stars from the chapter, men who left for service but did not return home.[193]

Back to normal?

The arrival of Armistice Day on November 11, 1918, not only marked the beginning of the end of the S.A.T.C. program, it also set the men of ATO into action, as they immediately begin working to rebuild and reinvigorate their chapter. First and foremost was regaining possession of their house, which they accomplished by early January 1919. However, when they opened the front door and peered in, they were horrified. The S.A.T.C. officers had nearly ruined the place. As described by chapter historian Wesley Nichols, "The condition was deplorable; windows were broken, ceilings smashed, floors scratched, furniture stolen, old gifts and treasures also gone." The chapter, though, took everything in stride, and rather than let the situation define them, they worked to correct it. They were rewarded for their efforts with the pledging of ten men just after classes started, one of the largest groups of new members they'd ever had. Soon enough the chapter was growing even more with old brothers returning from war service. From there, life quickly got back to normal for ATO, and

The Alpha Tau Omega basketball team from the 1927–28 intramural season.

their troubles of the past, especially finances, stayed in the past.[194]

Throughout the 1920s and 1930s, ATO continued to rush new members, hold social events, and engage in works of philanthropy. The chapter remained home to numerous athletes, even boasting six team captains one year. Academics were still a struggle at times, but overall members stayed in school and finished their degrees in greater number than they had in the past. However, the physical state of the house was slowly becoming a problem. By the mid-1930s, the chapter realized its grand but aging Victorian-style home was no longer conducive to fraternity life. Additionally, Theta Delta Chi showed all of Tufts the future of fraternity housing when they build their modern brick palace, so it was only a matter of time before the other fraternities wanted the same. For ATO, the call for a new house came to fruition over the summer of 1936, when Professor Dolbear's house was razed and replaced by a brand new brick structure, in the same Georgian-style as the new houses of both Theta Delta Chi and DTD. Indeed, ATO and DTD shared the same architect for their new houses, Tufts graduate Arland Dirlam, who was well known for designing houses of worship across New England. In true fraternal spirit, the interior of the house was set up for communal living, as described in the *Tufts Weekly*:

> The first floor, with woodwork of knotted pine, has a spacious lounge, flanked by a library and card room. On the west of the house is the dining room, with the kitchen in the rear.

On the second floor are eight studies, while the third floor contains a ram's pasture, with beds for eighteen and a bedroom at the rear for three. There is a bath on the third floor.[195]

The new house brought new prestige to ATO, along with an ever-growing membership. Adding to the chapter's allure in 1937 was the appointment of one of their own, George Miller, as Acting President of Tufts College, following the unexpected death of President Cousens. However, the advent of World War II brought drastic change to the chapter, as it did to all fraternities at Tufts. ATO managed to keep its operations going, but by the fall of 1943, the chapter had dwindled to two actives and four pledges. Subsequently, their house became a women's dormitory know as "Dolbear House" for the rest of the war. In the mean time, numerous alumni and actives of Gamma Beta were serving their country on the front lines and at home. One of the biggest war responsibilities lay on the shoulders of Vannevar Bush, class of 1913, who, as Director of the Office of Scientific Research under President Roosevelt, oversaw the Manhattan Project and its development of the atomic bomb.[196]

After the war, the few remaining actives on campus teamed up with returning alumni and restarted their chapter in earnest. As for their house, it took them until the fall of 1946 to reclaim the space and re-hang their fraternity letters on the outside. Luckily, when they moved back in, they found the women had treated the property much better than the S.A.T.C. officers or thirty years prior, so they did not have to spend much time or money repairing and restoring their house. ATO picked up thirty-one pledges that fall, and from there continued in earnest, certainly not without challenges, but overall making a positive impact on campus life. Normalcy, once again. Until, of course, it was upended.[197]

Two different challenges, two different outcomes

The first problem cut to the very heart of ATO as envisioned by Otis Glazebrook in 1865. His was a fraternity for Christian men, and Christian men only. At first, this policy was unwritten, because there was little need for such formality – nearly all heading to college in the mid- to late 1800s were white, Christian men. Over time, though, as the American collegiate system diversified, ATO as a national organization formalized its policy by placing restrictive membership clauses in its constitution. By the mid-1950s, ATO's position was clear: membership was only for white, Christian males. Others need not apply. At the same time, the push for civil rights began exposing the restrictive policies of not just ATO, but other national fraternities including Sigma Nu, which also had an active chapter on campus. Many in the Tufts College community soon added their voices to this debate over discrimination, and by the end of the 1950s, nearly all on campus were calling for ATO and Sigma Nu to remove their restrictive membership practices, or face expulsion.[198]

The situation came to a head in March of 1962, when the Interfraternity Council voted that both ATO and Sigma Nu must remove their discriminatory clauses within months, or else lose their recognition on campus, which would effectively close them down. As a consequence of this and other resolutions, ATO and Sigma Nu were forced to post copies of a signed affidavit around campus disclosing their membership restrictions in no uncertain terms. The postings, which began in January of 1963, were meant to inform the students of the discriminatory practices, so all knew the truth. A modern day scarlet letter, if you will. In the end, both ATO and Sigma Nu at Tufts obtained waivers from their respective national organizations allowing them to ignore the membership restrictions and initiate any man they wished regardless of race, color, or creed. These waivers satisfied the rules and regulations against discrimination as enacted by student and faculty committees, thus ensuring the continued existence of the two chapters at Tufts.[199]

The work to obtain the waiver had taken ATO many years, and while many in the fraternity now thought their biggest issue was behind them, an even greater challenge was looming on the horizon. And once again it was war. During the latter 1960s, the Vietnam conflict divided the campus into various pro- and anti-war factions. A serious debate thus ensued, the likes of which had never encompassed the school so fully. One of the consequences of this debate was a large shift in sentiment away from collegiate traditions of the past. Greek-letter organizations in particular were associated with this old establishment, so almost naturally the younger students began rejecting them en masse. ATO bore a major brunt of this rejection. For example, in the spring of 1967, the chapter stood at eighty-nine active members and pledges, most likely the largest any fraternity had ever yet been at Tufts. Three years later, membership had dwindled to fifteen actives and one pledge, with five seniors set to graduate. And it would only go lower. The bottom had clearly fallen out.[200]

It wasn't just anti-establishment feelings, though, that were contributing to the demise of ATO and the other fraternities. In early 1970, the trustees of Tufts began allowing coeducational dormitories. Soon enough, men and women were living next to each other and eating meals together not just in the dorms, but also in apartments and houses off campus. Confronted with this new liberation, many Tufts men wanted to experience the co-ed way of life rather than the traditional single-sex fraternity system. So, with each passing semester in the early 1970s, membership in ATO continued to drop, as recruitment just could not keep up with those leaving, by graduation or otherwise. The alumni running the housing corporation could read the writing on the wall. With so few members living in the house and paying rent, they were doomed financially. It was only a matter of time.[201]

Still, two alumni in particular, Robert McLaughlin and Bob Jones, refused to give up. They instead began working with the few remaining men in ATO to improve their situation as best they could. They cut back on expenses, eliminated the chapter meal plan, kept on top of rent collection, and recruited just enough men each year to fill rooms in the house so the fraternity could remain viable. Two factors were continuing to work against them, however. The first was the initiation fee. Many of the new men coming into the fraternity balked at the idea of paying $70 (not an insignificant sum of money at the time) to become an official member of ATO, since they were more interested in the house as a living space, not as a fraternity. The second was the national organization itself. Every year the chapter was assessed dues for insurance, as well as to support the headquarters. Many in the chapter felt they got back very little in exchange for these payments. So, as a group they pulled back from ATO. They put away the ritual materials and many of the fraternity's traditions, becoming instead a close-knit living group of men and, on one occasion, a woman – apparently, during the 1972–73 school year, a girlfriend of one member moved into the house, at least for a while. On paper they were still the Gamma Beta chapter of the national Alpha Tau Omega fraternity. In reality, their actions said otherwise.[202]

The nail in the coffin came later that school year. In March of 1973, the famed Boston Garden was home once again to the Eastern Conference Athletic Conference (ECAC) Hockey tournament. Qualifying for the tournament was the team from Cornell University, a powerhouse of ECAC hockey for years. Fans of the team came to Boston from near and far to watch the games and cheer on their favorite players, including a group of ATOs from the Beta Theta chapter at Cornell. Unlike the Gamma Beta at Tufts, though, Beta Theta had maintained a sizeable membership into the 1970s and was considered one of the stronger chapters within the national organization. While in town, the Beta Theta men took advantage of their national affiliation by congregating en masse at 134 Professors Row one night, where they proceeded to throw a party in celebration of their athletic achievement (or, at least, for being such good athletic supporters). Unfortunately, the members of Beta Theta showed very little respect to their Gamma Beta brother or their house, and by the end of the night, had trashed the living room furniture and scrawled "Beta Theta Raiders" on the wall of the library. Their antics were only stopped when one Gamma Beta member returned home late after work and chased them out. In their wake, the Beta Theta Raiders left an estimated $5,000 in damages.[203]

The few remaining members of Gamma Beta, along with their alumni leaders, appealed to the national organization for financial restitution from Beta Theta. Discussions and letters eventually culminated in Gamma Beta sending a representative to ATO's national congress in Atlanta, Georgia, during the summer of 1973 to present their case to the High Council. Unfortunately, it seems the national officers sitting in judgment had little sympathy for the small and non-dues paying Gamma Beta chapter. Instead, they sided with the stronger Beta Theta, swayed by such arguments from the Raiders as, "the furniture and wallpaper [we ruined] was old, anyway, and not worth much." So much for eloquence, or even an apology. In the end, the Beta Theta chapter reimbursed Gamma Beta less than $1,000 for its losses. To those official members of ATO who were still left in the house, and to the alumni running the housing corporation, this was the end. They were done being a chapter of the Alpha Tau Omega national fraternity. As for the future, they had no clear idea, but for now they'd simply take things one semester at a time with a singular, perpetual goal: keep control of the house by filling the beds and paying the bills.[204]

On the flip side, the national organization was also completely fed up with the chapter by this time. For years they worked with Gamma Beta to bring them back into the national fold, to get them to practice the official ritual, to pay their annual dues, to rush new members, and most importantly, have those new members become official brothers of ATO. These efforts had not gone well. So, a few weeks after the Cornell incident in 1973, the national officers put forth a resolution for Gamma Beta. They demanded all men planning to live at 134 Professors Row the next school year (September of 1974) become official, dues paying members of Alpha Tau Omega on or before April 1, 1974, or else they would pull Gamma Beta's charter and throw them all out. The national organization was through having 134 Professors Row act as a boarding house for men not willing to commit to the fraternity.[205]

The national leaders worked with the men through the subsequent fall semester not only to meet the imposed terms, but also to help build a more viable chapter. The undergraduates seemed very receptive to the overall plan, and as part of their progress, they announced to the national office in November of 1973 they would soon initiate all of the men living in the chapter house. The gambit appeared to have worked. At least it seemed that way, until the initiation paperwork from Gamma Beta arrived at the national office. As it turned out, the chapter only officially initiated one man that semester; the rest still refused to pay the initiation fee. A few months later, a member of the national office visited the chapter to assess the situation, and what he found was not encouraging. The chapter had apparently given up. There had been no attempt at rushing new members, no other initiations, no use of the ritual, and the chapter's debt to the national organization had only grown larger. Left with little choice, the national organization followed through with its threat. In the late spring of 1974, after eighty-one years of near continuous existence, they withdrew Gamma Beta's charter. Alpha Tau Omega at Tufts University was no more. The national organization hoped to re-colonize Gamma Beta the following year, as they'd identified a few alumni who were committed to bringing their fraternity back to Tufts anew. Until this effort got off the ground, though, they would simply forget about the people living at 134 Professors Row, for none of them would be involved with the new chapter, anyway.[206]

Normally, when a fraternity loses its charter, it also loses its recognition on campus and is forced to vacate its chapter house. But this was 1974, and the Tufts administration had much bigger problems to worry about, including the rapidly deteriorating financial solvency of the school. Additionally, no students were overseeing the fraternity system at the time, as all peer governance such as the Interfraternity Council had dissolved in the campus unrest of the late 1960s, which left each fraternity to its own devices. Therefore, few outside ATO, if any, even knew Gamma Beta had lost its charter, and those that did probably could not have cared less. In the mean time, Messrs. Jones and McLaughlin remained very supportive of the men still living in the house, and vowed to work with them to define the future of ATO at Tufts, whatever that may be. They surely had some disappointment that eighty-one years of tradition had come to an end, but their interactions with the national organization over the past few years, especially with regards to the Cornell incident, had severely dampened their spirit for Alpha Tau Omega. Instead, they would continue to work towards keeping their house occupied and the finances solvent, while letting the residents, hopefully, decide on a path forward.[207]

Knock, knock, who's there?

In the fall of 1974, a few weeks after school had started, Messrs. Jones and McLaughlin stopped by 134 Professors Row one afternoon to assess the current state of affairs. They were not optimistic. They knew that only about four men were scheduled to move into the house that fall, and the prospects of recruiting others to fill even half the required beds were not good. What they did not know, though, is that the four who returned that fall had come up with a plan to fill, if not save, the house. As for motivation, the four enjoyed living at 134 Professors Row, and the thought of having to move somewhere else was a non-starter. So, when school opened, these four men went around campus and recruited the most attractive woman they could find to move into the house, hoping she would then attract more men. It was an unconventional move, but since the four were no longer bound by the all-male rules of ATO, they could give it a try. It worked. Before long a number of other men and women moved in that fall semester. In one fell swoop, the group was saved from financial ruin. More importantly, those inside also started building a brand new community.[208]

But apparently no one told Messrs. Jones and McLaughlin of this development. So, the two men knocked on the door that day with some trepidation, since they expected they'd soon be shutting everything down. However, they were instead greeted with a surprise. Answering the door was a young woman who introduced herself not only as a resident of the house, but also the treasurer of ATO. What? The two were dumbfounded. Looking around, they soon discovered half a dozen women also living in the house, alongside about an equal number of men. But these women were not just boarders. As the residents told Messrs. Jones and McLaughlin, all of the men and women living at 134 Professors Row were now equal members of a group they were still calling "Alpha Tau Omega." They were not an official chapter within the national organization, but they were a fraternity. Only now, their membership was co-ed.[209]

Before the two alumni could wrap their heads around this development, though, one thought immediately came to their minds: they were going to be hauled off to jail for allowing men and women to live together on campus. Apparently, the two were unaware co-ed living had already been established in the dormitories. A quick inquiry to the trustees assured the two that the living arrangements were acceptable and no one was going to jail. Now, though, the two men had a decision to make. They knew many of the older alumni would be horrified to learn women were living at 134 Professors Row, and these alumni would likely pressure them to shut down the operation so a new, all-male chapter could be reformed. They felt others still might push to sell the house and be done with it all. To their credit, Messrs. Jones and McLaughlin now wanted nothing to do with shutting down or starting over. Instead, they were quick to realize the men and women who lived at 134 Professors Row and called themselves Alpha Tau Omega were an intelligent, enthusiastic, committed group of people who enjoyed each other's company and were willing to work together as a cooperative entity. They were, by definition, a fraternity, even if they no longer used the rituals of the past or looked like any other chapter on campus. So, within short order Messrs. Jones and McLaughlin gave their unbridled support to the new version of ATO, and vowed to back them as they moved forward under their new auspices. It was the fall of 1974, and Tufts University was once again home to a co-ed fraternity on its campus, some eighty-two years after the first one, Heth Aleph Res, blazed this path.[210]

As such, ATO's push to become a local, co-ed organization came at a time when the administration was paying very little attention to the fraternity system as a whole. ATO thus had the freedom it needed to build a viable organization and establish its own traditions. Each year, the chapter recruited both men and women, looking only for enough new members to fill the nineteen beds in the house. Members of the swimming and sailing teams were especially represented in the chapter each year, a trend that continues to this day. In the mean time, as the 1970s progressed, the group generally stayed out of trouble, and when the administration began exerting more control over the Greek system in the early 1980s, ATO was hardly seen as a problem. In fact, ATO was often held up as a shining example of the progressiveness within the Tufts fraternity system. By being co-ed, ATO was a natural counter-punch to the many outsiders who considered the Tufts Greek system to be a bastion of traditional, single-sex organizations. But still, life within ATO was not perfect, for outside forces began bearing down on the group. And they did not seem to be going away.[211]

What's your name, again?

The first to raise their voices were some vocal alumni of Gamma Beta chapter, who continued to be upset their fraternity had not only lost its charter, but had gone co-ed. They wanted back the old Alpha Tau Omega, not necessarily the one exclusively for white, Christian men, but certainly the one that had been active at Tufts and a big part of campus life for decades. Perhaps, too, they wanted Gamma Beta back so their sons and grandsons could also join, thereby starting or continuing a family fraternity legacy. Every year or so, then, some of these men would stop by 134 Professors Row to talk with the residents about giving up the co-ed experiment and returning to normal. Those living in ATO always balked at this idea. They liked the fraternity they had created and were perpetuating. And more importantly, so did Messrs. Jones and McLaughlin, who continued, unequivocally, to support them. After all, the two men still controlled the ownership of the property, and unless someone forced them out, they would let ATO continue as it may.[212]

The second group raising its voice was the national organization of Alpha Tau Omega. After Gamma Beta lost its charter, the national organization essentially forgot about them since their plans for re-colonization did not materialize as hoped. The co-ed chapter that rose out of the ashes of Gamma Beta was also not any of their concern, for the group was now a local organization and not part of their national fraternity in any manner. However, in the mid 1980s, a representative from Alpha Tau Omega's national office made a startling discovery when he ventured through the Tufts campus one afternoon. Not only had the co-ed group at 134 Professors Row kept the words "Alpha Tau Omega" on their door, they also used the fraternity's official crest on their yearly composites, and their members (including the women) wore sweatshirts in public emblazoned with the letters "A T Ω." As such, this practice was hardly a secret on campus. Since becoming co-ed in 1974, ATO at Tufts was constantly referred to as "Alpha Tau Omega" in official campus publications such as the *Pachyderm* student handbook and the annual *Jumbo* yearbook. To the national fraternity, though, this was new information, and it was all illegal, for they owned the trademarks to the name, Greek letters, and symbols of Alpha Tau Omega; ATO at Tufts had no rights to their use. The situation came to a head in the summer of 1988 when the national organization wrote to President Mayer and demanded he take immediate action to end this violation. This situation seemed to catch the administration off guard. With so many other problems surrounding the Tufts fraternity system at the time, a trademark violation seemed almost petty. But it soon involved lawyers and official letters and had to be dealt with, so over the next few months, many within Tufts worked to find a solution.[213]

The process did not go smoothly. The administration notified the chapter of the situation within short order and began working with them to change their name to one that would not be in violation of the trademark. But then it all became more complicated by one simple fact: the corporation that owned 134 Professors Row was officially called "Alpha Tau Omega Associates," a legal and active entity that had been formed in 1937. As a result, the two men running the corporation, Messrs. Jones and McLaughlin, felt they had a right to use the name and letters of Alpha Tau Omega when referring to the house and its occupants – after all, no one had objected to their use when naming the corporation back in 1937, so why now? Being lawyers, they decided rather than acquiesce, they would fight the national organization over the trademark claims. The two men were fiercely proud of what ATO at Tufts had become, and they were darned if they were going to bow to pressure from the organization that had, after all, thrown them out. In the end, the issue dragged on for almost two more decades, all while the co-ed fraternity continued to call itself "Alpha Tau Omega" to anyone who would listen. However, by 2005, the transition was complete. The fraternity had officially changed its name to "ATO of Massachusetts," created a unique crest, and replaced the words "Alpha Tau Omega" on their house with the letters "A T O." They were now, finally, their own named entity.[214]

In addition, by this time ATO of Massachusetts had changed their membership structure. When founded in 1974, the fraternity recruited only enough men and women each year to fill the beds in the house, capping the membership at nineteen. The idea was simple: to be a member, you had to live in the house, for only then could you experience what ATO of Massachusetts was all about. However, as their popularity grew in the early 2000s, they decided to expand their membership by accepting out-of-house members. By the spring of 2013, the chapter was at sixty members. A year later, that number was one hundred and thirteen, the largest any fraternity has ever yet been at Tufts.[215]

SIGMA TAU ALPHA (Local fraternity, 1905 – 1934)
PHI MU DELTA (Nu Iota chapter, 1934 – 1941)

At the start of the 20th century, a Tufts student who wanted to join a fraternity had five options. With enrollment increasing each year, though, many in the community felt these five chapters could no longer support all those interested in Greek life, lest they become too large. The golden age of fraternities at American colleges had just begun, and the growing popularity of these organizations was certainly in play at Tufts. It was only a matter of time, then, until someone organized a sixth. Before 1900, it had been transfer students who started a majority of the Greek-letter fraternities at Tufts. Now, in the dawn of a new century, another transfer student would add to this list.[216]

I hear that train a-comin'

Ernest Hall grew up in the shadows of Tufts College. However, after graduating high school, Ernest decided to look beyond The Hill. He left his hometown in the fall of 1904 and enrolled at Norwich University, an all-male military academy in Norwich, Vermont, one of the oldest schools in the country. Little is known about Ernest's time at Norwich, but three facts are certain. First, he became very intrigued with the vibrant fraternity system on that campus, one that had started before the Civil War and claimed a high percentage of cadets as members. Second, he did not join one. And third, he did not stay at Norwich. After just one year, Ernest returned home and enrolled as a freshman at Tufts College. Then he got to work. Shortly after school started in the fall of 1905, Ernest channeled his interest in fraternities to start his own. His, though, would be a local fraternity unique to the Tufts campus, as opposed to a chapter of a national organization. No doubt his path was influenced by the strong local fraternities he witnessed at Norwich University. Throughout that fall semester, Ernest developed the plans for his new fraternity and sought out others who wanted to build something new. His efforts took a few months, but one night in early December of 1905, Ernest and eight other men trekked down to the Medford Hillside railroad station, in secrecy, to consecrate their new organization. Normally, the station was closed at night, but one in the group was also the night watchman, so he used his key to open the building and give the men the privacy they desired. That night in December, those nine men pledged a bond to one another and formed a brand new fraternity. At their second meeting, they adopted a constitution, which specified the rules and organizational structure of their society. Then, at their third meeting, they decided on a name: Sigma Tau Alpha (STA). The newest Greek-letter fraternity at Tufts, and the first one in the 20th century, had just been created. The founders of STA were:[217]

Harold Leslie Bailey (1909)
Elmer Edward Fickett (1908)
Ernest LeRoy Hall
John Perkins Jackson, Jr. (1908)
Louis Bradford King (1909)
Ernest Howard Merchant (1908)
Francis Joseph Murray (1908)
Henry Cass Whippen (1909)
Joseph Zeller (1908)

After meeting in the railroad station for a few weeks, STA moved to an old boathouse on the Mystic River near Medford Square. Here, the chapter recruited seven additional men from the freshman and sophomore classes, which was quite impressive since almost no one on campus knew of their existence. STA, like many other organizations just starting out, remained sub rosa for a few months, so they could tend to their business without interference. Then, in April 1906, STA was ready. They announced their organization to the campus via the *Tufts Weekly*, and then began the process of gaining official recognition. Just a few years earlier, such recognition would have been moot, since there was little administrative oversight of student groups; fraternities and sororities had essentially governed themselves since the mid 1800s. However, in 1903, the fraternity men created the Interfraternity Council (IFC) to manage the Greek system at Tufts College. The impetus was likely similar actions at other schools, as the golden age of fraternities also ushered in the silver age of fraternity oversight. Some of the IFC's tasks included formalizing the rush process, organizing inter-fraternity athletic competitions, and settling disputes between the chapters and the administration. Additionally, the IFC was in charge of granting official recognition to each chapter. Many national organizations were now demanding recognition of their chapters, as they realized everyone benefitted from a formal relationship between fraternity and college. STA thus became the first fraternity at Tufts to go through this process, which they completed a few years later.[218]

When school resumed in the fall of 1906, STA realized its boathouse on the river was just too far from campus to be an effective meeting place. So, they moved to a private house at 9 University Avenue in the Medford Hillside and set up their first chapter home. Though closer to campus, this house was hardly ideal – they were only able to rent two rooms in the building, no members lived there, and just about all they could do in the space was eat lunch together each day. Despite these limitations, STA continued to grow over the next few years, and within short order one member earned the honor of representing the liberal arts school at commencement, the highest academic praise at the time. By the fall of 1909, the chapter moved to a larger house at 16 Bellevue Street, also in the Medford Hillside, and then in the fall of 1915, the chapter moved again to 163 College Avenue, its largest house yet. That year, STA counted among its membership the captains of the tennis team, the managers of the track and football teams, several varsity baseball players, the senior class historian, the editor-in-chief of the *Tufts Weekly*, and the secretary of the IFC, all positions considered marks of prestige in their day. As a result, by the mid 1910s, STA was a strong force on campus and equal in stature to the other fraternities despite its local status. Newspapers such as the *Boston Globe* and *The New York Times* even reported on many of STA's events, including their Hallowe'en party one year. Such publicity must have been quite flattering to the young organization. It must have also made them feel worthy of something greater.[219]

Can we come in?

A decade after starting as a local organization, those in STA began to think their future lay in affiliating with a national fraternity. As this was a heyday of fraternities in the United States, the national organizations, with their strong peer networks and growing status, appealed far greater to many men than local groups. So almost naturally, by early 1916, those in STA decided they'd like to join a national. They put together a petition outlining the strengths of their local organization, the awards and accolades they'd won, and the resumes they'd accumulated for each member. Included in the petition was a glowing letter of recommendation from the president of Tufts College, Henry Bumpus, himself a fraternity man, who wrote, "I am of the opinion that the 25 or 30 men here at Tufts College, who are members of this organization [Sigma Tau Alpha], would be a credit to any fraternity." As for which fraternity to petition, STA soon decided on Phi Delta Theta, one of the largest and most prestigious of the day. Almost exactly thirty years earlier, Irving Tomlinson of the Tufts Divinity School had tried to start a chapter of Phi Delta Theta on campus, but his efforts were rebuked in part because the organization did not consider Tufts College a worthy host. This time, though, the prospects were much stronger, especially since STA earned the endorsement of the Phi Delta Theta alumni club of Boston, of which Mr. Tomlinson was the president. So, once the documentation was complete in early 1916, STA sent their petition on its way.[220]

Then came the waiting game. At the time, Phi Delta Theta considered petitions at its annual national convention. Unfortunately for STA, there was no Phi Delta Theta convention in 1916, so their document languished until the fraternity did finally meet, in late December 1917. Meanwhile, at least seven other local fraternities had also filed petitions, so when the convention got underway, all were now up for consideration. Two in particular stood out. The petitioners from Washington State College and Oregon Agricultural College, most likely anticipating the competition, set up exhibits in the convention hotel to woo the Phi Delta Theta delegates. Between photographs of their respective campuses, statistical charts showing overall enrollment trends and their academic performance, and good old-fashioned politicking, these two local groups impressed the delegates and easily earned their charters. STA, on the other hand, sent only a couple of members to plead their case in person without any back-up materials, and records indicate the Tufts men failed to make any impression. The trip was a total bust. In the end, Phi Delta Theta granted a record six charters at that convention, with Tufts College excluded.[221]

Curiously enough, STA also petitioned a second national fraternity while they were courting Phi Delta Theta. This was a highly unusual move, as most local groups only petitioned one national at a time so their sincerity could not be viewed as suspect. For this second petition, STA chose a relatively new but

Sigma Tau Alpha members hold their flag in front of their house, 163 College Avenue, November 21, 1916. This house burned down in 1938, just after the chapter moved out.

up-and-coming national fraternity, Sigma Phi Epsilon (SigEp). Sometime in early to mid-1916, they sent a petition to the SigEp's headquarters in Virginia, and then waited while the vetting process took place. Once again, though, STA's timing was far from perfect. From mid-1916 through early 1917, SigEp received no fewer than ten petitions from colleges across the country, including ones from large state schools such as Iowa State University, the University of Illinois, the University of Montana, and Kansas State University. Further muddying the waters was a feeling within SigEp that they were growing too fast as a national organization, so they should slow down their expansion and focus on strengthening the forty-one active chapters they'd already established. For months STA's petition languished as SigEp debated the issue. In the end, SigEp denied the petition, though nearly all others that had applied during that time were eventually granted charters. Apparently Tufts College was just too small in comparison to those large, land grant schools to warrant a charter. But this was 1917, and bigger problems for STA were soon on their way.[222]

WAR!

Life at Tufts College turned upside down when the United States entered the Great War. STA fared no differently than the other fraternities on campus, as their activities ceased all together when Tufts became an Army training base in the fall of 1918. In support of the war effort, two members of STA volunteered for the newest (and extremely hazardous) branch of the armed forces, the Aviation Service. One was Harold Ryan, originally from Charlestown, Massachusetts, who grew up in Brazil and then graduated from Somerville High School. Harold dropped out of Tufts after his junior year to join the U.S. Navy, where he eventually became a seaplane pilot. He spent his time protecting naval convoys while patrolling the waters off the French Coast. One might think his experiences were relatively quiet (being removed from the front lines of the infantry battles), but aviation was hardly a safe enterprise at the time, and indeed he crashed into the ocean on one mission. Harold survived that incident and the war, then returned to Tufts to complete his degree.[223]

A second pilot from STA was Raymond Taylor, a mechanical engineer from the class of 1916. Raymond enlisted into the Aviation Service on April 1, 1917, just five days before the United States officially entered the war. Six months later, he was a commissioned First Lieutenant in France and training to pilot a brand new weapon of war, the two-seater bomber. For months he continued to train, and train, and train, all while waiting to fight. In a letter written a year after he joined the service, Lt. Taylor summed up his feelings about the wait:

> What have we "Great Americans" done in our year of war? I hope to get to the front by the time this letter reaches you, but there seem to be so many side-tracks and the French are quite able to fly their own planes and the British are too darned good flyers to take any chances on greenhorns, – our only hope is to borrow an old bus from somewhere. If you people can fix the heads of those individuals who have held up machine guns, so they can think straight – and fix the spies who help them – you will be doing the Allies the greatest service… it's a shame that many of us have been in training for over a year and we haven't had a look at the Boches [Germans] yet… We want guns, bullets, and planes, and we want them badly.[224]

On July 10, 1918, Lt. Taylor got his wish for action. He made his first combat flight that day as part of the 96th Aero Squadron based in Amanty, France, where he completed his mission and returned successfully, despite acquiring four bullet holes in his French-made Bréguet bomber. He flew a number of combat missions over the next few months and gathered at least thirty-two more bullet holes in his plane, while still returning safely to base each time. He most likely accumulated more bullet holes as the weeks went on, but after acquiring thirty-six, he, along with every other pilot, was ordered to stop marking the damage with little black crosses. At one point he was offered the rank of Captain under the condition that he stop flying combat missions and become an instructor. Lt. Taylor refused. "They need me at the front now more than anywhere else."[225]

Lt. Taylor took off for his last mission on September 16, 1918. That day, he was part of a four-plane serial sent without fighter escort to bomb a heavily defended supply depot near Conflans, France. As they approached Conflans, the four Bréguets bombers noticed twenty-four enemy Fokker and Pfalz fighter planes off in the distance, two types of planes vastly superior in both speed and agility to the slower bombers. Very soon, the German fighters noticed the Americans, and at twenty-four versus four, they must have sensed an easy victory. Lt. Taylor and his group must have also sensed the lopsided situation, but instead of fleeing, they followed their orders and bombed their objectives. Meanwhile, the Germans formed up into three attacking groups: one to cover the rear, one to cut off the American planes so they could not get back to their base, and one to attack. As the slow moving bombers turned and headed for home, the Germans first focused their attention on Lt. Taylor's plane. According to Lt. Charles R. Codman, the only American bomber pilot to survive the attack,

> Their fire [the Germans] was first concentrated upon No. 2 machine (in which was Lieut. Raymond Taylor, pilot, and Lieut. Wm. A. Stuart, observer). I think the pilot was hit by the first burst, as the machine went suddenly out of control, skidded out of the formation, and, according to Lieut. McDowell, my observer, went down in flames…"[226]

Further accounts state that Lt. Taylor was attacked by twelve German planes at once, but before being shot down, he managed to take out at least one fighter. He and his observer, Lt. Stuart, were both killed in action and buried in a field between Mairy-Mainville and Norroy-le-Sec, France, very near the spot where their plane crashed. Lt. Taylor was twenty-three years old. He left behind his wife, whom he had married only a month before heading to France.[227]

Local no more

After the armistice was declared on November 11, 1918, those on the Tufts College campus began the quick transition back to normal college life. Restarting the fraternities, all of which had suspended operations that fall, was seen as a key component of that normalcy. STA was one of the first to reorganize, as they reclaimed their house at 163 College Avenue before January of 1919, and even pledged a few men in the first few weeks of that month. Then, they turned their attention to two pressing matters. The first was opening a brand new chapter house on campus. Beginning in early 1920, the members of STA established a building fund and began asking the Tufts administration for a plot of land on campus so they could build their home. Prospects seemed good that the plan would move forward, but in the end the effort failed. STA would remain at 163 College Avenue for the foreseeable future.[228]

The second matter was affiliation. Soon after returning in 1919, the members of STA decided once again to join a national organization. And once again, they looked to Phi Delta Theta. They prepared a new petition for this effort, most likely augmenting their story with the personal accomplishments of members and alumni during the war. As for recommendations, they secured a second letter from President Bumpus, who once again was happy to endorse the men of STA. "During four years I have been president of Tufts," he wrote, "Sigma Tau Alpha has occupied a prominent place in college affairs, being recognized as the equal of any of the national fraternities. The Sigma Tau Alpha has my hearty approval." But then, it appears the submission stalled yet again. The rest of 1919 and almost all of 1920 passed without a decision by Phi Delta Theta. Towards the end of 1920, STA gained the endorsement of Dean Lee McCollister of the Crane School of Theology, himself a Phi Delta Theta, having joined while an undergraduate at Buchtel College. Then, finally, STA's petition came up for vote at Phi Delta Theta's national convention that year. Once again, though, the competition was fierce, with at least seventeen other local groups looking to enter Phi Delta Theta. When the debates and voting were complete, Phi Delta Theta had only accepted three. Tufts College, once again, was rejected.[229]

After three straight rejections, the men of STA suspended their efforts at national affiliation and instead worked to become the best fraternity they could be at Tufts. Throughout the 1920s and into the early 1930s, they maintained a normal schedule of rushing new members, holding social events, participating in inter-fraternity athletics, and occupying leadership positions within various campus organizations. They remained ensconced at 163 College Avenue, eventually welcoming the Phi Delta, Phi Epsilon Pi, Beta Tau/Beta Kappa, and Sigma Omega Psi fraternities as their neighbors. College Avenue thus became a de facto "Fraternity Row" during this time. In 1930, the chapter celebrated twenty-five years of existence with a grand banquet in Boston. Over one hundred alumni, active members, and pledges attended the event, which also featured a keynote speech by one alumnus, Professor Frederic Weaver of the Engineering department. STA was now the oldest local fraternity at Tufts College, and it appeared they would remain as such.[230]

And so STA did until 1934, when the chapter decided yet again to affiliate with a national organization. This time, they chose a small and relatively new national fraternity, Phi Mu Delta. Born out of a student movement called the National Federation of Commons Club, Phi Mu Delta came into existence in 1918 and then expanded relatively slowly across the country. As for why STA chose Phi Mu Delta, this information has not survived, but the inclusive nature of Phi Mu Delta may have been an attraction. Whereas many national fraternities in the 1930s had membership restrictions based upon race, religion, or creed, Phi Mu Delta did not. Either way, STA sent its petition to Phi Mu Delta and then waited for a response. This time the answer was affirmative. STA was accepted into Phi Mu Delta as the Nu Iota chapter, the nineteenth established by the fraternity. The formal installation occurred on October 21, 1934, with alumni as far back as the class of 1911 being initiated alongside the current undergraduate members.[231]

After becoming Phi Mu Delta, the chapter continued to operate out of its house on College Avenue. Then, in early 1938, they caught a break. After Delta Upsilon moved out of 13 Sawyer Avenue, Phi Mu Delta was offered the chance to move in. Having a home right in the heart of campus was something the fraternity had long desired, so they accepted the offer and occupied the house before school's end that year. As it turned out, this move came not a moment too soon. Late one night during commencement week in June 1938, two men were seen entering the backyard of Phi Mu Delta's old house at 163 College Avenue. A loud explosion ensued, which then set the entire structure on fire. Somerville firemen raced to the scene, but in the end they were unable to save the house. The structure at 163 College Avenue was a complete loss.[232]

Over the next few years, Phi Mu Delta appears to have thrived while operating out of 13 Sawyer Avenue. For example, in the fall of 1939, they secured a pledge class of nineteen men, one of the largest they'd ever had. That year the chapter also counted a number of varsity athletes among its membership, and its social calendar was filled with parties and dances. However, a mere twelve months later, life turned south for the chapter. Phi Mu Delta participated in the fall rush of 1940, but did not appear to secure any new pledges, and in the spring of 1941, they did not submit a chapter photograph for the annual *Jumbo* yearbook. Then, when the students arrived to campus in the fall of 1941, they were greeted with a new sight at 13 Sawyer Avenue. The old Phi Mu Delta House, with its recognizable bright green and white door, had been transformed into a women's dormitory. Phi Mu Delta had vanished from campus without so much as a goodbye. This closure marked the third for fraternities in ten years, so Phi Mu Delta's demise, like that of the other two, was most likely due to the financial stress of the Great Depression.[233]

As for a legacy, STA ushered in the modern fraternity system at Tufts College as the first to be established in the 20th century, and the first to go through the formal recognition process. The chapter also produced a very well respected alumnus. Robert Meserve, from the Class of 1931, served as both President of STA and head of the IFC while an undergraduate, and was initiated into Phi Mu Delta during Nu Iota's installation. After graduating, Robert had a long and distinguished career as a trial lawyer, was president of the American Bar Association from 1972–73, and served as a trustee of Tufts College for twenty-four years. He also earned seven battle stars while serving aboard the aircraft carrier

U.S.S. Langley during World War II. In 1973, he was awarded the Hosea Ballou Medal for his service to the Tufts University community, the highest honor bestowed by the trustees.[234]

COMMONS CLUB (Tufts chapter, 1908 – 1925)
DELTA PHI SIGMA (Local fraternity, 1925 – 1931)
ALPHA KAPPA PI (Tau chapter, 1931 – 1946, merged with Alpha Sigma Phi)
ALPHA SIGMA PHI (Beta Iota chapter, 1946 – 1970, -1973, 1986 – 1992)
KIPPY HOUSE (Local society, 1973 – 1978)

If there ever was an irony among Greek-letter organizations, it was the Commons Club. Born from a desire to bring all men together with democracy and without exclusion, the Commons Club was an appealing alternative for those who did not, or could not, join a fraternity. The organization caught on like wildfire at Tufts, and then became an integral part of the national Commons Club movement. But it did not last, and the group's subsequent evolution is a story unlike any other. No other Tufts fraternity has been associated with as many different national organizations, or been revived as many times, or gained and then lost so much. And if not for two fateful decisions, it might very well still be active today.

What's cooking?

By the latter part of the 19th century, many colleges and universities were adept at housing students on campus, but not at feeding them. The era of large scale, school-wide dining facilities had not yet come into vogue, since many institutions were perfectly content to let others feed their students. Fraternities, which were now building and occupying stately houses, easily filled a portion of this need by opening dining rooms and hiring cooks to provide good, quality food to their members. Additionally, fraternity dining rooms allowed for social interaction on a daily basis, which helped build a strong community. Students not in a fraternity, on the other hand, were often shunted to restaurants or small, privately run boarding houses near campus, facilities that provided little camaraderie or social interaction. They were merely cheap places to eat, with the food not always worth the price.[235]

Wesleyan University in Middletown, Connecticut, at the turn of the 20th century was one such campus living this dichotomy. Wesleyan's strong fraternity system claimed around seventy percent of the men, with each chapter running a dining room in their home. But the Wesleyan fraternities, like many elsewhere, had a reputation for being snobbish, as they tended to exclude anyone who didn't fit their exact mold, especially poorer students who could not afford the financial commitment. As a result, the non-fraternity men were social outcasts in a sense, forced to endure terrible food together in small groups off campus, with little interaction beyond a few close friends. In the spring semester of 1899, a non-fraternity man wrote to the school's newspaper, *The Wesleyan Argus*, bemoaning the situation he and others experienced day after day in the boarding houses. One member of Wesleyan's faculty, Professor Woodrow Wilson (who would become President of the United States in 1912), took this letter to heart and decided to act. Before school let out in June of 1899, he called a meeting of all those interested in starting a college dining club, one that would provide quality meals to the men at an affordable price, backed by a subsidy from Wesleyan. To Professor Wilson's delight, about twenty-five students committed to the plan, so when school started the next fall, they were welcomed into a brand new boarding facility on campus. The dining room was an instant hit with the non-fraternity men, and within short order the group of men expanded into a full-fledged social club. In honor of their original desire to eat around a common table, these men called their organization the Commons Club.[236]

The Wesleyan administration was very supportive of this new club, and soon Professor Frank Nicolson signed on as an advisor. But now that the Commons Club was more than just a dining facility, the members immediately pondered an important question: Whom shall we let in? It was here they made a bold decision. The Commons Club, they decided, would be non-exclusive, and would welcome any student who wanted to join. And while this lack of exclusivity led many at Wesleyan to believe the Commons Club was anti-fraternity (Greek-letter organizations often equate non-exclusivity with anti-fraternity sentiment), it was not. Instead, the Commons Club considered itself "non-fraternity," an alternative to the experience provided by Greek letter organizations. Professor Nicolson drove the non-fraternity sentiment, since he had been educated in Canada at schools with no Greek system, so he knew very little about such organizations. In fact, he was the only faculty member who "found himself among Wesleyan's disorganized minority instead of in a fraternity house." Now, though, the Commons Club was the place on campus he could call home.[237]

With Professor Nicolson's help, the Commons Club developed a constitution outlining its goals, leadership structure, and membership requirements. Democracy was the group's foundation, with each member having a voice from the moment he joined. Pledging and any associated hazing were not part of the Commons Club, as there was not a single test any man had to pass before being admitted. Almost lost in this openness, however, was one exclusionary principle. From the beginning, the Commons Club decided to exclude the fraternity men. This restriction was certainly practical – the fraternities and the Commons Club provided the same functions for their members, so there was no need for a man to join both. And while this was a restriction, it was hardly comparable to the exclusionary membership policies of the fraternities, which discriminated by race, religion, creed, and socio-economic status. As a result, the Commons Club became the most inclusive organization at Wesleyan, even counting a few African-American men as members during its early years, in what was probably one of the first integrated social organizations on any college campus. In addition, the Commons Club as a group firmly supported co-education at Wesleyan, despite the growing chorus of students and faculty to stop admitting women. Loudest of all in their displeasure were the fraternity men, who ostracized the women from their parties and dances. The Commons Club, however, "consistently distinguished themselves as friends of coeducation," and "gave parties to which the Wesleyan women were always invited."[238]

Commons Club goes national

The Wesleyan Commons Club flourished after its founding, with membership claiming nearly twenty percent of the male students by 1908, much larger than any single fraternity on campus. The administration even provided the club with a dormitory to serve as its "chapter" house, thus elevating the group's prestige. More importantly, by this time word of the Wesleyan Commons Club began reaching other college campuses in the Northeast, some of which had similar clubs for their non-fraternity men. Naturally, these various groups became intrigued with each other, so in the winter of 1906–07, the Dartmouth Commons house invited delegates from these clubs to a meeting on its campus. Present for this conference were "common" men from Dartmouth, Wesleyan, and Norwich University, all of whom espoused the same ideals of democracy, inclusion, and openness in their respective organizations. As a result, the delegates combined forces and formed a new organization, the National Federation of Commons Clubs (NFCC), to oversee the individual chapters and, ideally, bring a Commons Club to every college and university across the country. The NFCC got off to a fast start after this meeting by adding chapters from Amherst College, Middlebury College, and Union College. Then, the grand plan went awry. Within two years of the NFCC's founding, the Dartmouth and Amherst chapters became inactive, while the Norwich and Middlebury chapters withdrew to become full-fledged Greek letter fraternities.[239]

Despite these setbacks, the NFCC carried on with its plan to conquer the college world by bringing in more groups, including new organizations at Norwich and Middlebury to replace those that had resigned. The NFCC also began holding a convention every year, where delegates elected new leaders and voted on petitions sent in from clubs wanting to join the national organization. In a somewhat bold (and expensive) step, the NFCC started publishing a national magazine called the *Commons Club Chronicle*, where the various chapters would report on their operations, their history, and their feelings about the non-fraternity movement in general. Conventions and national publications were more the domain of Greek-letter organizations, so many involved with collegiate life began to feel the Commons Club had actually become a de-facto fraternity. However, the NFCC continued to champion their ideal of inclusion, which was radically different from nearly every other fraternal organization. The movement was on a roll. Soon enough, Tufts College crossed its path.[240]

Tufts College and the common man

For the undergraduate men at Tufts in the latter 1800s, it was the Greek-letter fraternities that captured their attention more than any other social organization. Each year, as new men arrived, nearly half of them (if not more) joined one of the active chapters. Participation was far from universal, though, as some did not join a fraternity by choice or by circumstance, and at times there was animosity between those in and those not. But in general the two factions got along reasonably well – Tufts was still a relatively small school, so all on campus were likely familiar, if not friendly with one another. Only when fraternities began occupying chapter houses in the mid 1890s did the divide between the two groups become noticeably apparent. Houses gave the fraternity men a place to live, to eat in comfortable dining rooms, to socialize, and to welcome back alumni. Those not in a fraternity, by contrast, were afforded much less social interaction. So, as early as 1896, the non-fraternity men formed their own social group to counter this situation. At first, they only participated in fraternity competitions such as whist tournaments, which were highly popular in the day. Eventually these men realized they'd be better served through an official association, so they wrote a governing constitution and elected officers. Little is known about the details of this group, but it appears once they became an organized entity, they struggled with cohesion. They never created a name for the group other than "the Non-Fraternity faction," and bickering seems to have been their favorite pastime. For example, one year they won the cash prize in the fraternity whist competition, but in the months following the victory, they argued publicly about how to spend the money. Leaderless and rudderless, the group disintegrated by the fall of 1900.[241]

Nearly a decade later, when Tufts College opened for the fall semester of 1908, the social life of the non-fraternity men had hardly improved. The six active Greek-letter fraternities were still the major hub of campus activity, holding formal dances, smokers, and informal gatherings after hard-fought victories on the football field. But combined, the fraternities counted about forty percent of the Tufts men, leaving a majority on the outside. A similar state of affairs existed for Tufts women, with those in the four sororities having much more social interaction than those not. However, a year earlier some of the non-society women leveled the playing field by starting a social organization called Delphoi that was open to all women. In all likelihood, the non-fraternity men watched the development of Delphoi with interest, because late that fall, they followed suit. On December 18, 1908, a group of students and faculty members met in a room of the Bromfield-Pearson Building for the "formation of a society for the advancement of a better spirit and closer relationship among Tufts men." Called The Union, this society was meant as a social club for students and alumni not affiliated with a fraternity. Although the complete list of founders is unknown, the following were most likely the first members of The Union:[242]

Professor Edward Rockwell
George Burnham (1908)
David Bradford Knowlton (1909)
John Alfred Tuck (1909)
James Earl Douglas (1910)
Frank William Anderson (1911)
Nathan Conant Harris (1912)

Like Delphoi for the women, The Union proved to be an instant hit with the men. Within a few weeks, nearly seventy undergraduates and faculty members had joined or contributed money to The Union, which soon had $1000 to its name. Then as 1908 turned into 1909, those in The Union learned of the NFCC, which happened to be holding their third annual convention in Northfield, Vermont. They quickly sent word to the convention delegates of their society and their desire to join the NFCC. The delegates immediately accepted The Union into the growing organization, though their name officially changed to the Tufts Commons Club. Almost in parallel with this effort, the Tufts Commons Club began sending letters to non-fraternity alumni, informing them of their new organization and asking for financial support. The letter closed by summarizing what the alumni would receive for their money:

> As a member of this Society, its emblem will always assure you of a cordial greeting at Tufts, and a welcome to the spot so dear to us all. May we look for your hearty co-operation with us in this movement, and a pledge to assist the work financially.[243]

While this push to woo non-fraternity alumni was a bold step for the new organization, it was not original. The women of Delphoi had done the same thing a year earlier. However, while Delphoi's plea to alumnae seemed void of any controversy, that of the Commons Club came under harsh scrutiny from the highest level of the Tufts administration. President Hamilton, an alumnus of the Kappa Charge of Theta Delta Chi at Tufts, was an ardent supporter of his fraternity and the Greek system at Tufts College. When word of the Commons Club reached his office, he became very worried this new organization had been formed "to introduce an element of discord into our college life," and for this he would not stand. In an effort to calm the president, a member of the Commons Club, Frank Anderson, wrote an eloquent letter explaining his organization's goal was simply to bring together the non-fraternity men and faculty members into a cohesive group, and to provide non-fraternity alumni a place of welcome when they visit campus. In support of this argument, Frank discussed the "gloomy picture of a graduate wandering aimlessly about the hill after a football game or on Class Day, no one to welcome him and no place where he may feel at home." Frank closed his letter by saying he believed the Commons Club would not compete against the fraternities in anything except "loyalty to our Alma Mater."[244]

President Hamilton responded just a few days later with a noted sigh of relief, even offering his full support to the Commons Club as they worked to become a viable campus organization. As part of that work, the Commons Club secured their first chapter house at 15 Fairmount Street in the Medford hillside during the spring 1909 semester, and then began actively recruiting new members. Here they excelled. By the end of that first year, they had a much larger active membership than any Greek-letter fraternity on campus. To add to their prestige, in February of 1910, the Tufts chapter hosted the 4th annual NFCC convention. By all accounts they impressed the delegates with a full weekend of activities, including a marquee basketball game between Tufts and Syracuse University in Goddard Gymnasium. Based on this success, the Tufts Commons Club hosted the national convention for a second time, in 1913.[245]

The only major upheaval for the Commons Club during its infancy involved the chapter house. After a few years at the Fairmount Street address, the chapter moved to 37 Sawyer Avenue to start the 1912–13 school year, a house originally built in the 1890s for the Heth Aleph Res fraternity. Apparently 37 Sawyer Avenue was not an ideal place to live, for the chapter wanted out almost as soon as they moved in. Indeed, by the summer of 1916, the Commons Club abandoned 37 Sawyer Avenue even though they did not have another place to call home. Over that summer, the men desperately tried to secure a space, including the Knight House at 114 Professors Row, to no avail. Eventually, they found a large house off campus at 890 Broadway Avenue in Somerville, which became their home during the 1916–17 school year and served the chapter well for a while. In the mean time, though, the Commons Club had bigger problems to deal with.[246]

The movement collapses

The NFCC grew quite rapidly in the early 1910s by adding nearly a dozen chapters in just a few years. Helping this growth was the spread of the commons club movement from the Northeast to the Midwest and the West, much to the NFCC's delight, since conquering America was still a major goal. But all was not positive for the NFCC. Although nearly all chapters of the NFCC had originally started to serve the interests of non-fraternity men, many abandoned this principle after a short while and resigned from the NFCC to become full-fledged, Greek-letter fraternities. For example, the second incarnation of the Commons Club at Norwich University resigned after two years to become the local Phi Kappa Delta fraternity, whereas the second incarnation at Middlebury College resigned after five years to become the local Alpha Sigma Phi fraternity. Those two schools in particular, it seems, had a difficult time keeping the spirit of the Commons Club alive.[247]

Besides the resignations, though, the democracy and inclusiveness espoused by the NFCC was also being challenged from within. By the 1910s, many Commons Club chapters had introduced rituals, initiation ceremonies, and initiate pins to their daily life, while others still, especially the newer ones, opted to become exclusive organizations. Some even incorporated Greek-letters into their chapter names – the Commons Club chapter at New Hampshire State College (now the University of New Hampshire), for example, was known as the Delta Kappa Society, while the chapter at Carnegie University was the Delta Sigma Rho Society. These inconsistencies only added to the confusion about what, exactly, the NFCC was aspiring to be: a democratic, all-inclusive organization so championed by the founders at Wesleyan University, or an exclusive fraternity? Unfortunately, the undergraduate volunteers running the NFCC maintained weak oversight over the individual chapters, so the national organization was never able to champion its core principles on a grand scale, or with clear uniformity. Instead, as the NFCC expanded, the individual chapters only seemed to grow further apart.[248]

The Greek-letter fraternities looked at this turmoil in the NFCC with great interest and amusement, for collectively they felt the whole non-fraternity movement was quite ridiculous. After all, in years past they'd witnessed many an organization similar to the NFCC start out with grand, democratic principles, only to abandon those beliefs after some time and become a Greek-letter fraternity. As a result, the national fraternities were not shy about predicting the same fate for the NFCC, which they broadcast to all through their quarterly magazines. This animosity between the Greeks and the NFCC came to a boil on October 13, 1913, when *The New York Times* published a scathing article entitled "Driving the Undergraduate Snob out of College." This commentary, written by an alumnus of the Wesleyan Commons Club, lambasted the national Greek-letter fraternities for their exclusive, snobbish ways, and predicted the NFCC movement, since it was based on democracy and openness, would eventually eclipse all fraternities in terms of prestige. The author called his fellow NFCC members "frat busters," portraying them as heroes, in a sense, since they could see through the guise of the exclusive fraternities and instead be part of a proper, noble college organization. In closing, the author thumbed his nose at the national fraternities by printing some derogatory slogans against them, allegedly used by Commons Club members at Union College and Syracuse University, such as, "the essential thing is purse, not personality in a frat," and "correctly pressed pants take many a freshman into a fraternity; it takes real character and capacity to work to make the Commons Club."[249]

As could be expected, the national fraternities responded immediately to this article, since they knew hundreds of thousands if not millions of *Times* subscribers had read the blasphemy. Many published rebuttal after elegant rebuttal in their national magazines, where they focused on the inconsistencies within the NFCC such as their growing exclusiveness and use of initiation rituals, all in an effort to discredit the organization. Surprisingly, though, a number of rebuttals also appeared from Commons Club members themselves. Many did not agree that they were "frat busters," and they were just as shocked at the harsh words written by one of their own. Indeed, Carl Baldwin, who at the time was the president of both the NFCC and his chapter at Union College, emphatically stated that this article was the sole opinion of one member and it did not, in any way, represent the feelings or attitudes of the NFCC or a large portion of its members. Carl also disavowed any knowledge of the ridiculous slogans attributed to his chapter. He closed his letter by expressing his sincere regret that the article had appeared in print, and hoped all readers understood the true purpose of the NFCC was not anti-fraternity, but non-fraternity.[250]

The rebuttals from Commons Club members helped cool the rhetoric surrounding this article. But problems within the NFCC continued to mount, including the continued confusion over the organization's name. Although the term "Commons Club" was synonymous with the non-fraternity movement in the Northeast, other parts of the country knew "commons club" as just another name for a student dining hall, and nothing more. As pointed out by the Commons Club at the University of Washington, "there seems to be a tradition that a social organization does not possess the strength of a growing and healthy society unless it has a Greek-letter name." The Commons Club moniker was now an albatross around the neck of the NFCC, with chapters outside of the Northeast struggling to recruit because many prospective members just didn't understand what the organization was all about.[251]

The name conundrum first came up for discussion at the NFCC's 1916 convention, but the delegates were unable to reach a resolution, so the debate continued between the individual chapters for months. Then, a year later, in February 1917, the Wesleyan chapter sent a letter to all in the NFCC with a radical solution to the problem. They were convinced the only way to survive as a national organization was to take a new name, one consisting of Greek letters. Under no circumstance were they proposing to abandon their core principles of democracy and inclusiveness, for they were still very proud of the basis of their organization. Instead, as they wrote to the other chapters, they just wanted to change the name. "Let our fraternity be known as Phi Mu Delta, the democratic fraternity."[252]

With their words being reasoned in tone and sound in logic, the authors no doubt felt confident this letter would unite the various chapters and allow them to move forward together, as one. This did not happen. The NFCC chapters that practiced exclusivity in their membership welcomed the proposed change, since they agreed the new name would correctly label their organization for what it was, a fraternity. The other chapters that still admitted all without exclusion, however, felt that adopting a Greek-letter name was nothing short of blasphemous. Rather than drawing the men together, this letter spilt the NFCC into two distinct factions, each seemingly headed in the opposite direction.[253]

The debate over the structure of the national organization continued in chapter correspondence through early 1918. The NFCC struggled to control the conversation, hindered in no small part by the growing shadows of war, which pulled many men away from the cares of such business. Some chapters, rather than waiting for a consensus that might never come, decided to act on their own. First to flee were the groups at Syracuse University and Colby College. Both joined the national Lambda Chi Alpha fraternity soon thereafter. As a result, when the NFCC opened its convention in February of 1918, the spirit of brotherhood was noticeably absent, and the divide between the two factions only wider. The eighteen delegates representing almost half the NFCC chapters tried in earnest to solve the name issue and chart the future direction of their organization, but in the end they could not. The National Federation of Commons Club was no more. Four of the seven chapters at the convention, Union College, New Hampshire State College, the University of Vermont, and Connecticut Agricultural College, resigned from the NFCC to become Phi Mu Delta, a new, national Greek-letter fraternity that practiced selective membership. The other three chapters at the convention, Wesleyan, Tufts, and Massachusetts Agricultural College stayed true to their roots and formed a new national organization called the Commons Club Federation, one that reaffirmed the non-exclusive membership policy.[254]

Unfortunately, eight active chapters of the Commons Club did not sent delegates to the convention, so in the aftermath of the vote, letters were dispatched to these chapters, detailing their options and asking for their choice. In the end, three of these chapters joined the new Commons Club Federation, three others joined Lambda Chi Alpha, and two disaffiliated completely to become local, independent groups. As for the new Commons Club Federation, no one in the organization was talking anymore about conquering the country or displacing the fraternities. The grandeur of the movement was over.[255]

Tufts Commons Club follows the trend

Little is known about the reaction of the Tufts Commons Club to the break-up of the NFCC, though the members must have been disappointed to see the national organization go in different directions. This disappointment, however, became the least of their worries a semester later, when the chapter was forced to disband with the coming of the Army and the S.A.T.C. program to Tufts. It is unknown how many members of the Commons Club served their country in the Great War, but undoubtedly many did. The signing of the armistice brought a quick return to normal college life in the spring of 1919, and with the help of Commons Club members still on campus, the chapter was soon operating out of their old house at 890 Broadway Avenue. But at its core, the Commons Club was changing. Over the next year, the members must have developed serious misgivings about their place within the national organization, for in the spring of 1920, they took a bold act. That semester they tried to leave the federation and join a Greek-letter fraternity. They petitioned the national Theta Chi fraternity for a charter, an organization with exclusive membership and secret rituals that was the polar opposite of the Commons Club. Ultimately this petition was denied and the Tufts Commons Club remained, but the act marked a significant shift away from the original ideals of the organization. After all, only two years earlier the group had passed on becoming an exclusive Greek letter fraternity. Now, it seems, they wanted in.[256]

Meanwhile, the Tufts Commons Club kept looking for a way to move onto campus, paying particular attention to the houses on Professors Row. Prior to 1921, the vast majority of residents on that street were, indeed, professors, all of whom owned their properties. Their houses were elegant, with cupolas, porches, and other features typical of Victorian-style architecture. To the Tufts fraternities, these houses looked to be perfect places to call home, given their presence, their size, and their proximity to campus. But buying or even renting one of these houses was no easy task, as the professors tended to live in their homes for a long time, and in some cases passed them down to their children after they passed on. The year 1921, though, was a banner one for fraternities looking to move. Two houses came up for sale that year, Bray House at 98 Professors Row, and Tousey House at 106 Professors Row, built by Professor William Tousey of the Divinity school in 1875. Delta Tau Delta purchased Bray House, whereas the Tufts Commons Club purchased Tousey House, with the help of a mortgage from the college. The deal took a while to close, but by the late fall of 1922, the Commons Club was comfortably living on Professors Row.[257]

The move to Professors Row by Delta Tau Delta and the Commons Club helped solidify that area of campus as the center of fraternity life at Tufts College. Ironically, though, the Tufts Commons Club had never officially been considered a fraternity, at least not according to the *Ivy Book*, a yearly publication of all things Tufts College started by the sophomore honor society in 1902. Instead, the Commons Club from its inception was listed separate from the fraternities, most likely because of their open admission policy and lack of Greek letters. It did not matter that the Commons Club participated in inter-fraternity athletic competitions, or rushed its new members coincident with the fraternities, or published information in the fraternity section of the *Jumbo* yearbook – the group was not officially a fraternity to the editors of the *Ivy Book*. The move to 106 Professors Row, though, finally changed that designation. In 1922, the Tufts Commons Club was listed as a fraternity for the first time in the *Ivy Book*, complete with a description of the chapter's pledge pin, a circular grey design with a red bulls-eye. As such, the pledge pin and reclassification as a fraternity seem to imply the Commons Club was now an exclusive organization. Times had certainly changed for the organization that was once open to all.[258]

Despite these changes, the chapter was still called the Tufts Commons Club and was still affiliated with the Commons Club Federation, which continued to champion the all-inclusive policy at the national level. As the 1920s progressed, though, the philosophical differences between chapter and national organization became untenable. So, in early January of 1925, the members of the Commons Club resigned from the federation and adopted a brand new name, one that emphasized their status as a fraternity. They became Delta Phi Sigma, the newest local Greek-letter organization on campus. Only, they did not wish to stay local. They wanted to join a national fraternity, the sooner the better. All they needed was someone to take them in.[259]

The quest for affiliation, though, was neither swift nor easy. Although the list of national fraternities that Delta Phi Sigma petitioned or even considered for affiliation is unknown, it is known that for six years, none said "yes." Instead, Delta Phi Sigma remained one of the few local fraternities on campus, relatively strong in terms of membership and campus presence, but local nonetheless. However, in late March of 1931, Delta Phi Sigma petitioned a relatively new national fraternity, Alpha Kappa Pi, for a charter. Affectionately known by its nicknames "Kippie House" or "the Kippies," Alpha Kappa Pi had formed ten years prior on the campus of Newark College of Engineering (now the New Jersey Institute of Technology) and became a national organization in 1926, when they chartered their second chapter at Wagner College on Staten Island. From there, the Kippies expanded in earnest, mostly throughout the eastern portion of the country, but also as far south as North Carolina and as far west as Illinois. So, when the petition from Delta Phi Sigma arrived at their door, Alpha Kappa Pi seized the opportunity. On May 30, 1931, just about a month after filing its petition, Delta Phi Sigma was inducted as the Tau chapter of Alpha Kappa Pi. The Kippies now had seventeen active chapters across the country, making it nearly the same size nationally as Phi Mu Delta, the fraternity that had risen from the ashes of the old NFCC. As for the Commons Club Federation, or what was left of it, no one seemed to be talking about them anymore.[260]

Throughout the 1930s, the Kippies maintained a strong membership and were able to weather the financial hardships of the Depression, helped (at least slightly) when Tufts agreed to lower their mortgage in 1935. But as the decade progressed, they were in danger of being left behind when it came to their house at 106 Professors Row. Although the grand Victorian house conveyed immense presence, it was also very old and outdated. The structure had been constructed over sixty years prior, likely with little thought to lasting quality or upgrades for modern amenities, such as indoor plumbing and electricity. To say the house was non-ideal for a fraternity would therefore be an understatement. Other residents in similarly styled houses on Professors Row such as Delta Tau Delta and Alpha Tau Omega were in the same predicament, but rather than accept the situation, they decided to tear down their old structures and rebuild. In the wake of this construction came two brand new, modern fraternity brick palaces that flanked and dwarfed the outdated Kippie house. So, starting in early 1937, the Kippies sent out an urgent plea to their alumni for donations to help tear down their old house and build a new one, lest they be left behind. With the Depression still on, this was hardly the ideal time to ask for financial support of such a large and expensive project. However, they had no choice. The old house had to go. As it turned out, the alumni responded positively to the call, so in the early summer of 1937, the Kippies razed the old Tousey house and began preparing to build their dream home.[261]

Unfortunately, it seems the chapter was a little too anxious in this effort, for while the money had been raised and the plans had been drawn up, the legal paperwork had not kept pace. This delinquency only came to light following the unexpected death of President Cousens that summer, but it was serious enough to halt construction, leaving the fraternity with little more than a hole in the ground. Weeks went by as the legal matters were all sorted out, and while there was a new structure standing at 106 Professors Row when the students returned in the fall of 1937, it was but a shell of a building, not ready for occupancy. Workmen rushed to complete the house while the other fraternities, in a grand spirit of cooperation, decided to postpone the fall rushing season until the construction was finished. All told the delay was just a couple of weeks, and by the middle of October 1937, the house was finished and all was back to normal.[262]

Over the next few years, the chapter settled into its new home with a steady routine of rushing new members, holding social activities, and participating in athletic competitions. The outbreak of World War II and the subsequent arrival of the Navy V-12 program on campus effectively shut down Alpha Kappa Pi, as it did all other fraternities on campus. The Kippie House at 106 Professors Row was soon taken over by the Tufts administration and used as a student dormitory through the duration of the war. In terms of service, the Kippies had at three gold stars among its membership, including John Scopa. John enrolled at Tufts College in the fall of 1939 and joined Alpha Kappa Pi sometime thereafter, but then dropped out his junior year to enlist in the Army Air Corps. He eventually rose to the rank of sergeant and became a radio operator on a B-17 bomber affectionately named the "Athenian Avenger" by its crew. On March 22, 1944, Sgt. Scopa and the Athenian Avenger were on a mission to bomb industrial targets near Berlin, Germany. Unfortunately, while over Germany, the B-17 took a few direct hits from anti-aircraft fire, broke in two at the tail section, and plummeted to the ground, killing all ten crewmen. The Athenian Avenger was one of twelve B-17s lost that day, out of 660 airplanes assigned to the mission. The other two gold stars for the chapter were Major Robert C. Hawkins and Second Lieutenant Roy H. Baxter, two pilots who were killed in separate airplane crashes.[263]

The end of World War II saw the end of Tufts College as a Navy training base, and within a year after the fighting ended, the school was back to normal operations. During the transition, the Kippies regained occupancy of their house, welcomed back old members (many of whom were veterans), and recruited new men to help rebuild the chapter. But soon after the fall 1946 semester began, the members of the Kippie House awoke one morning to find everything had all changed. Their fraternity, Alpha Kappa Pi, was no more. The national organization had never been very strong, nor had it provided much oversight of its chapters. By the early 1940s they were especially struggling to keep pace, all while membership plummeted and chapters closed. World War II was the final straw for Alpha Kappa Pi. With little hope for the future, the national officers decided they had but one choice if they were to survive in any form, and that was to merge with a stronger fraternity. So, in September 1946, the Kippies joined with the Alpha Sigma Phi fraternity. Founded in 1845 at Yale University as a secret sophomore society, Alpha Sigma Phi had itself undergone a decline and rebirth in the early 1900s before expanding on the national scene. Now, Alpha Sigma Phi was well on its way to becoming one of the larger organizations with chapters across the country, something Alpha Kappa Pi had not accomplished in its lifetime.[264]

The merger, by all accounts, was greeted with enthusiasm in the Tufts chapter, especially since Alpha Sigma Phi was viewed as a strong national fraternity. Prestige was still very important to the men, and the merger had only increased their outlook in this regard. As testament to the enthusiasm, in its first rushing season as Alpha Sigma Phi in the fall of 1946, the chapter recruited thirty-five new members, the largest pledge class of any at Tufts that year. And while the name Alpha Kappa Pi may have disappeared, its legacy remained through its symbols and rituals, which became incorporated into the pledge program of Alpha Sigma Phi. The chapter at Tufts was originally renamed the Massachusetts Tau chapter, but eventually this moniker gave way to Beta Iota, so they would not be confused with the original Tau chapter of Alpha Sigma Phi at Stanford University. Unofficially, though, the fraternity continued to be called Kippie House at Tufts, a nickname that would remain for years given the presence of the letter "Α Κ Π" hewn in the sidewalk near the property. The future certainly looked bright for the chapter, as they were right where they wanted to be – in a beautiful house on Professors Row, with a growing membership, and a strong national organization to back them up. They had certainly come a long way since the days of the Commons Club.[265]

Strange things are afoot at the Kippie House

Throughout the 1950s and 1960s, the Kippies continued to play a prominent role on campus and were generally seen as one of the stronger fraternities. Adding to their reputation was a stance they took on a darker side of fraternity life, hazing. Although practice of demeaning pledges was very much in vogue at this time, a national movement emerged in the 1950s to replace the dreaded "hell week" with "help week." Rather than subjecting pledges to all sorts of mild cruelties as a final test before initiation, fraternities across the country were instead sending pledges out into their local communities to perform needed service. The movement came to Tufts in early 1952, but despite some initial interest, was mostly ignored by the organizations. However, in 1957, the Kippies brought back help week on their own initiative and with much fanfare. Such action was highly welcomed by all in and around Tufts, and other fraternities soon followed in their footsteps. The Kippies, though, did not always stay within the good graces of the administration. Over one weekend in the late spring of 1956, for example, they painted the front of their house completely black (it had been white), presumably for a party. As the front page of the *Tufts Weekly* declared, "The administration did not appreciate this Kippie House painted black," and they demanded the chapter re-paint the house at once.[266]

Towards the end of the 1960s, though, campus turbulence hit the Kippie house hard, as membership began to drop dramatically. The Kippies were hardly alone in this regard, as all fraternities were suffering from the student backlash of anti-war and anti-establishment protests, but they seemed to be suffering much more than their neighbors. By the fall of 1969, the situation had turned desperate. The Kippies could only count fourteen or so active members, when just a few years earlier they had been triple that size. The small membership was not nearly enough to fill the twenty-five beds in the house, so this put enormous financial strain on the chapter and the alumni corporation, which owned the property. During the 1969–70 school year, the Kippies managed to pledge nine men, but still the chapter struggled financially to keep the house running. To combat the situation, they shut down their meal plan and halted most activities, opting to focus solely on inter-fraternity athletics and the occasional social event. What the chapter needed most were men to fill those empty beds in the house. And it was here they made a fateful, if not stupid, decision.[267]

The clichéd joke usually starts, "So a guy walks into a bar..." Only this time, it wasn't a joke. As the story goes, sometime in late 1969, a member of the Kippie house walked into a local bar and started talking with a stranger named Daniel Hodes. The conversation eventually turned to the fraternity and its financial predicament due to the empty beds. By luck, Daniel was new to town and just happened to be looking for a place to live. Of course, he was neither a Tufts student nor a member of the Alpha Sigma Phi fraternity. Instead, he was an enigma, a drifter supposedly from Chattanooga, Tennessee, who claimed to have studied at that state's flagship university. Under normal circumstances, the Alpha Sigma Phi member would probably have finished his beer and the conversation, left the bar, and forever parted ways with Daniel. But circumstances were not normal. His fraternity needed men to live in the house and pay rent, and Daniel was willing to do both. So, the fraternity member acted in what he thought was the best interest of all by offering Daniel a room to let. As a result, Daniel walked out of the bar and into 106 Professors Row as the house's newest tenant – no background check, no references, no paperwork. What could possibly go wrong?[268]

In the beginning, the answer to that question was nothing, for Daniel paid his bills on time and generally kept to himself, giving the fraternity no reason for pause. Unfortunately for the Kippies, though, there was more to their boarder than they knew. Daniel was not just a drifter. He was a promising chemist who had recently learned the art of manufacturing LSD, a hallucinogenic drug popular at the time. Now, he was ready to put his knowledge to use, perhaps even start a drug empire. After moving into the Kippie House, Daniel purchased approximately $3,000 worth of equipment and supplies, set up a laboratory in the attic, and planned to manufacture about $50,000 worth of LSD. Of course, he apparently never mentioned his entrepreneurial plans to the fraternity when he moved in. Instead, he quietly went about the business of building his lab while managing to keep everything a secret. A few days before he was to start the manufacturing process, however, some members of the fraternity discovered the truth. And they wanted absolutely no part of the enterprise. So, they immediately asked Daniel to leave, probably not in the politest of terms. But it wasn't that simple for Daniel, since he'd made quite an investment but hadn't yet made any LSD. He refused to leave, most likely hoping for just a few more days to ply his trade.[269]

The members of Alpha Sigma Phi knew they were in a horrible situation that needed to be corrected immediately. Not only was Daniel operating a criminal enterprise from their house, he was about to start a manufacturing process with highly flammable and reactive chemicals in their wooden attic, hardly the ideal or safest location for such an activity. So, after discovering the lab, someone in the Kippie house made an anonymous call the Somerville police department and explained the situation. The end was not long coming. Within a few hours, elements of the Somerville and Tufts police forces entered the house, arrested Daniel (who admitted to the whole operation), and confiscated his equipment. The arrest was otherwise uneventful, and most on campus probably had no idea what happened until they read about it a few days later in the *Tufts Observer*. For the members of Alpha Sigma Phi, the removal of Daniel and his lab from their house must have come as a big relief. They still had problems, most notably low membership, but at least now they were safe.[270]

Of course, it wasn't that simple, and the headaches for Alpha Sigma Phi as well as the entire Tufts community had only just begun. Upon arrest, Daniel began cooperating with federal and state agencies investigating the drug trade. And here, Daniel had plenty to say, especially about Tufts students heavily involved with illegal narcotics, information he had gathered during the few months he lived on campus. This intelligence was then relayed back to Tufts officials, and they were not pleased. The administration had been concerned with campus drug use for many years, but now there was a sense of urgency since very dangerous drugs such as heroin and LSD were making the rounds. The information provided by Daniel finally pushed campus authorities into action. They had lost control over their students, and they needed to act decisively, the sooner the better, if they were ever to rid their campus of drugs. So, the administration took a radical step, one that had never been executed previously on any other New England college campus. At 1:00 a.m. on the morning on March 28, 1970, just two weeks after Daniel was arrested, state and local police raided a number of dormitories and campus residences, including the Kippie house, looking for specific students and their drugs. Armed with search warrants, master building keys, and the complete blessing of the Tufts administration, the police targeted those thought to be at the heart of the problem. But the events did not go quietly. As word of the raid quickly spread across campus that night, students began gathering near Carmichael Hall, one of the main targets, to protest the actions of the police. Demonstrations soon turned violent as students threw stones at the police officers and smashed the window of a police car. By the end of the night, authorities had regained control of the situation, arrested sixteen people including twelve students, and confiscated large quantities of illegal drugs and drug paraphernalia.[271]

The aftermath of the raid was just as chaotic and frenzied as the raid itself. Dean Alvin Schmidt became the administration's liaison to both the students and the press, and it appears he was completely overwhelmed by circumstance. He tried to be the voice of law and order by playing to common sense, saying Tufts had no choice but to go after those who were bringing illegal drugs and their scourge to campus. But the students were in no mood to be mollified, especially after being confronted by gun-toting police in the middle of the night. Campus protests continued daily, including one where approximately 200 students occupied Ballou Hall for a time. The students were most upset at being sold out by their administration to law enforcement, as they did not appreciate student records being examined by, if not also turned over to, those outside the university. Such actions led students to believe the authorities had an ulterior motive in the raid, and that was to search for dissidents and radicals, especially among the African-American community on campus. The situation turned even more tense about a week later, when police arrested nine additional students based on evidence collected during the initial raid. Protests, teach-ins, and conciliatory meetings between Dean Schmidt and the students helped temper the fury, but bad feelings simmered for weeks until the end of the semester sent most everyone away from campus. In the end, nearly all of those arrested were found guilty of possession or intent to distribute, and sentenced to probation. The Tufts administration, perhaps sensing they could only do more harm than good if they intervened further, decided not to impose additional disciplinary measures on any of those arrested. As for Daniel, his cooperation helped him avoid prison. He was fined $5,000, given a two and a half year suspended sentence, and sent on his way.[272]

FOR ALPHA SIGMA PHI, this whole incident became the nail in their coffin. With mounting financial troubles, low membership, bad publicity from the drug raid, and general student backlash against fraternities in general, those left in the chapter decided to call it quits at the end of that fateful semester. No one on campus seemed surprised by this action. As for 106 Professors Row, the former residents simply packed up and moved out. The house was no longer their problem.

I'll be back

One wet and dreary day in the fall of 1970, the kind that signifies winter is not long coming, a freshman named John Budris found himself walking down Professors Row. The rawness of the afternoon made him wish he had someplace warm and comfortable on campus to call home, instead of his drab dormitory room in the basement of Hill Hall. As he reflected on his situation, he strolled past the old Kippie house, and then paused. The house was hardly a sight to behold. The windows were shuttered, the doors padlocked, and the yard a mess of unkempt weeds. Unlike the stately fraternity houses to either side of it, 106 Professors Row looked like it belonged in the television series *The Addams Family*. But John found the house in its condition to be very intriguing, and he wondered why it was in such bad shape, and why no one lived there. More importantly, he thought if fixed up, it would be a much nicer place to live than his dorm room. So, John returned to Hill Hall and began asking some older students about the house. The stories seemed unbelievable at first – tales of a fraternity in chaos, rampant drug use, even an LSD factory in the attic – but they were mostly true, confirmed a few days later in a conversation with a Tufts administrator. This administrator also mentioned that the house was owned by the alumni of the fraternity, and one of those owners, John Zamparelli, just happened to live nearby campus. So, John took the next logical step, and went to see Mr. Zamparelli.[273]

Meanwhile, the fall of 1970 was anything but a great semester for fraternities on campus. Student sentiment was still decidedly against Greek-letter organizations, and while a number of fraternities were still active, they were not pillars of strength on campus, and many in the Tufts community predicted their total collapse in the near future. In other words, hardly the best time to attempt a restart of Alpha Sigma Phi. But to Mr. Zamparelli, a 1947 graduate of Tufts, World War II veteran, and long time supporter of his fraternity, the arrival of John at his doorstep represented a golden opportunity to bring his chapter back to campus that he was not going to miss. So, he began talking with John about not only re-opening the house, but also restarting Alpha Sigma Phi as well. John knew this would be a daunting challenge as a freshman, since he would be leading the effort from scratch, by himself. But, he was quick to recognize the pay off (a nice house to call home), so he said "yes." Within a few weeks, he found a handful of friends also interested in living at 106 Professors Row, which was a good start. However, when it came to rebuilding the fraternity, the others were not so thrilled. They were mainly interested in living in a nice house. Regardless, John and Mr. Zamparelli decided to move forward with the plan. After all, reoccupying the house was the first part of the journey. The fraternity could come later.[274]

After signing on to the project, John and his small group of friends trekked to 106 Professors Row to examine the interior of the house for the very first time. Armed with a key, they opened the front door and looked around. It was not an encouraging sight. To the group, it was as if time had stopped. Old, half-filled Schlitz beer cans dotted the rooms, being left where they were last put down. Random personal belongings were scattered about, as were piles of trash. And the overly used furniture, arranged for conversations and camaraderie, now spoke in silence of days long past. It appeared as if the former residents just picked up and walked out, leaving most everything else in place. But cleaning up the mess was a straightforward task, so the men got right to work, and by the beginning of the 1971 spring semester, the house was ready for occupancy. All John needed now were a few more tenants to fill the rooms. As the de-facto leader of the group, he became responsible for recruitment, so he turned to others who lived in Hill Hall, along with fellow members of his a cappella singing group, the Beelzebubs. Many heeded the call, and within a few weeks into that spring semester, they had all moved in. The Kippie house at 106 Professors Row was open once again. Now, it just needed to become a fraternity, and the revival would be complete.[275]

Here, though, the journey stalled. While Mr. Zamparelli was very excited about bringing his fraternity back to campus, and while John was willing to work towards this goal, very few of the men living at 106 Professors Row were interested in Alpha Sigma Phi. They were more than content to live in a nice place, maybe host a party or two, but nothing more. As a result, men came and went each semester, and while the house remained filled over time, it never became a cohesive group. It was a lively group for sure, with musicians and athletes and international students all living together, but the turnover did not allow the men to coalesce into a lasting community. The situation grew to bother Mr. Zamparelli, since he was not interested in running a boarding house. He wanted a fraternity. So, he invited Dale Dillon from the Alpha Sigma Phi national office to give the group a pep talk, and get them excited about becoming an active chapter once again. Unfortunately, Mr. Dillon was not the inspiration he needed to be. Many of the men were turned off by his businessman-like appearance, thick Southern accent, and straight-laced nature (remember, this was the early 1970s). Afterwards, only John and three out of the sixteen men living in the house agreed to go forward with restarting the fraternity. It was a small group, but to Mr. Zamparelli, it was at least a start.[276]

The four men spent about a year as a colony, and then on April 26, 1973, they were formally initiated into Alpha Sigma Phi and the charter was returned. The Beta Iota chapter was once again active and operating out of 106 Professors Row. But it was hardly a fraternity, for the group was still not coming together as expected. Recruitment for official members, the lifeblood of any chapter, was turning into an impossible struggle. With each passing semester, the rooms in the house continued to be occupied, but almost none of the residents wanted to join the fraternity. No one was more frustrated than John Budris, who, since moving into the house as a freshman, had done nearly all the work of running the operation. He collected the rent, paid the utility bills, and chased down those who owed money. Now, he was expected to lead the charge of rebuilding a fraternity chapter with men who just were not interested. This was too much. John had done all he could, but he knew it was time to move on. At the start of his senior year, in the fall of 1973, he moved out of the house to an off-campus apartment and pulled away from the fraternity. Not surprisingly, the Beta Iota chapter of Alpha Sigma Phi soon folded. Mr. Zamparelli and the rest of the alumni corporation, though, decided to keep the house open to the boarders. Perhaps, they thought, they could try again with a different group of men in the near future.[277]

Over the next few years, 106 Professors Row remained occupied by about fifteen to eighteen men at any time, but in a subtle shift from the past, most began staying in the house until they graduated. In theory, this situation was a perfect basis on which to build a new fraternity, since long-term residents would naturally form a community that could easily become a brotherhood. In practice, though, the men in the house began morphing into a slightly different, if not unique group. Known collectively once again on campus as the "Kippy House," the residents were not necessarily a fraternity, but they were definitely more than just boarders. They participated in intramural sports, held parties, and were thought of as an exclusive organization, at least by those on the outside, since being allowed to move into the house was seen as a privilege for only a select few. The truth was, the Kippys took on new residents only when a room was vacant, and here it was usually word of mouth between friends that brought a new tenant, not any type of formal recruitment or vote of those who lived there. Indeed, as a group they were all very anti-fraternity and wanted nothing to do with the formalities or rituals associated with Greek-letter organizations. They could live next door to fraternities and compete against them on the athletic field, but they didn't want to be one of them. This sentiment clashed with Mr. Zamparelli, as he wanted to re-establish Alpha Sigma Phi, not continue to run a boarding house filled with men who had no interest in being a fraternity. But the Kippys liked the house and the organization they had made, so they stalled over the years to maintain the status quo, occasionally making some overtures about joining Alpha Sigma Phi, but never taking any serious action. By early 1978, frustration in Mr. Zamparelli and the rest of the alumni corporation had reached a boiling point. They realized the men were never going to restart their fraternity. Therefore, it was time for them to go.[278]

As for who would take their place, the alumni corporation had already solved that problem. Behind the scenes that school year, Mr. Zamparelli had been talking with the newly organized Chi Omega sorority about subletting the house to the women, in place of the men. Chi Omega was currently occupying a house just a few blocks away, at 25 Whitfield Road, but the sorority wanted to be closer to the heart of campus, and 106 Professors Row was viewed as the perfect spot. Additionally, the women promised to take better physical care of the house than the Kippys – many thought it was only a matter of time before the men burned the place to the ground. So, near the end of the 1978 spring semester, the alumni corporation offered a one-year lease with Chi Omega for the upcoming school year, which the sorority enthusiastically signed. The men had been booted to the street by just a few signatures.[279]

To the members of Kippy House, news of their eviction came as a complete surprise, as they were under the impression they'd continue to rent the house indefinitely. To rally sympathy as well as support, they argued to the campus that they had, indeed, worked to make the house a nicer place to live over the years, and would continue to do the same if given the chance. Additionally, the Kippys believed the eviction was patently unfair since it came after the student housing lottery had closed. Thus, the fifteen men who had committed to live

The Kippy House men on the steps of their house at 106 Professors Row in the spring of 1977, a year before they were kicked out. (Courtesy of Digital Collections and Archives, Tufts University)

in the house the following school year were now forced to find off-campus apartments, well after most had been rented. These arguments, however, went nowhere. The alumni corporation had made its decision. As a final response, the Kippys dragged a coffin out of the basement and left it on their front yard to indicate their displeasure to all who walked past. But all hope was not lost for the men. The alumni had only leased the property to Chi Omega for one year, and they indicated there was a good chance that if the men made a serious effort to restart Alpha Sigma Phi during the upcoming school year, they'd get their house back.[280]

This idea never even got off the ground. Without a communal house, and scattered in off-campus apartments, the former Kippys, as could be expected, dissolved as a group the following school year. There would be no concerted effort to restart the fraternity, despite the plans, schemes, and desires of the alumni corporation. The women of Chi Omega, on the other hand, settled into their new house and soon decided they didn't want to leave, for they had found their home. As a result, they looked for a way to stay longer than one year. Soon they uncovered a stark reality, and hit the information jackpot. Between unpaid property taxes, a few outstanding mortgages, and a supposed lack of up-to-date annual reports as required by the Commonwealth of Massachusetts, the Alpha Sigma Phi alumni corporation was a legal and financial mess. This situation was somewhat surprising, for Mr. Zamparelli was a prominent attorney who had run the corporation for many years prior without issue. But the 1970s had not been good to Alpha Sigma Phi. The women of Chi Omega were quick to seize the golden opportunity in front of them, so they worked with the Tufts administration to wrest control of 106 Professors Row. The Alpha Sigma Phi alumni corporation, weakened, demoralized, and in a poor legal position, was unable to hold off the attack. They soon realized they had no choice but to sell their house to Tufts. So, in the spring of 1979, and for a grand total of $30,000 plus assumption of all back taxes and mortgages, the Trustees of Tufts College became the proud new owners of 106 Professors Row. As for the logistics, Tufts agreed to hold the $30,000 due the alumni corporation in the school's endowment, which would be paid out once the fraternity was re-established. The two parties also agreed that while Tufts held the money, the interest it generated would be used support a student scholarship in the name of Alpha Sigma Phi. In the meantime, Chi Omega would get to stay in the house, indefinitely.[281]

Overall, this chain of events marked a low point for the alumni of Alpha Sigma Phi, as they had lost ownership of the house they had built and maintained for nearly fifty years. To make matters worse, it seems that around the time of the sale, the Tufts administration also argued for the legal dissolution of the alumni corporation. This was a curious move, perhaps undertaken so the University would never have to deal with the situation or the alumni corporation ever again, for there seems to be no other motive. However, this new reality forced the alumni corporation into action, for they understood the ramifications. In response, the alumni corporation sued the Trustees of Tufts College, arguing against the dissolution and the "forced" purchase of their house. The end result of the lawsuit was mixed. While the judgment affirmed that the Trustees of Tufts College were indeed the new owners of 106 Professors Row, it also appears to have reaffirmed that the alumni corporation was a viable, legal entity. As a result, the alumni corporation, as they understood the situation, still had $30,000 in the bank (albeit not under their direct control), which they could potentially use to start anew, once Alpha Sigma Phi returned to campus. However, underneath all of the agreements and transactions and lawsuits was another legal nightmare for the alumni corporation just waiting to surface at the worst possible moment. So of course, that's exactly what happened.[282]

Phoenix rising, then falling

As bad as the 1970s was for fraternity life at Tufts, the 1980s was the exact opposite. The decade that brought new wave music and big hair into the mainstream also ushered in not just a resurgence of existing Greek organizations at Tufts, but also two new fraternity chapters, Psi Upsilon and Sigma Phi Epsilon, which were in full operation by the spring of 1985. Later that year, two students,

Chris Koenders and John Keller, looked at the evolving fraternity landscape and decided the time was right to make a mark of their own, before it was too late. The two were seniors, and while seniors do not normally start new organizations given their limited time left on campus, Chris and John felt the call to create a lasting legacy. So, they started a fraternity. As for which, Chris soon had a recommendation from a high school friend, who had joined Alpha Sigma Phi at Cornell. Now all they needed were some undergraduate men to form an interest group, and they could begin the process. They soon found more than a few, but more importantly, they also found an alumnus who could help them in bigger ways. That alumnus, of course, was Mr. Zamparelli, who took an immediate liking to the group and became their advisor.[283]

After months of work, the thirty men became an official colony of Alpha Sigma Phi on May 3, 1986, just days before the school year ended. One of their first tasks, aside from working to regain their charter, was to secure a chapter house. They knew they would need a house in order to compete with the other fraternities for new members, thereby ensuring their long-term viability. However, they knew that reoccupying 106 Professors Row was out of the question, since Chi Omega was well established in the property by 1986, and Alpha Sigma Phi had zero leverage to force them out. So, they instead surveyed the Tufts landscape and took stock of the available housing alternatives. There were none. The rapid growth in the number of fraternities and sororities during the 1980s had vastly outpaced the supply of on-campus houses suitable for Greek-letter organizations. Plans were made to alleviate this situation, but even then, Alpha Sigma Phi was at the back of a long line of organizations wanting a house, so the wait would likely be years, if not longer. As a result, the colony and Mr. Zamparelli (who was still involved with the alumni corporation) decided to bypass the line and solve the housing problem on their own. The alumni corporation would buy the men a house. After all, they had over $30,000 in the Tufts bank, which was more than enough for a down payment.[284]

On the surface, such a plan was hardly controversial. Since first occupying houses at Tufts in the 1890s, and for nearly one hundred years following, fraternities had bought property with their own money and through their own initiative, bypassing the university all together (aside from an occasional mortgage). Indeed, the newly established Sigma Phi Epsilon chapter utilized this approach just a year earlier, when they rented a house in the Medford Hillside in the fall of 1985 with the option to buy. So, the summer after becoming a colony, the members and Mr. Zamparelli began searching for an appropriate space on or near campus. As fate would have it, a house at 80 Powder House Boulevard came up for sale, right across the street from the Latin Way dormitory. Similar to most houses on that street, it was a duplex, capable of legally housing six men without a license, and though it was off campus, it was certainly close enough. So, the Alpha Sigma Phi alumni corporation made an offer. In the meantime, they began what they figured would be the simple process of getting their $30,000 back from Tufts to cover the down payment.[285]

The process was anything but simple, as it involved two major roadblocks. Unbeknownst to those in Alpha Sigma Phi at the time, the Tufts administration was in a very delicate if not tense situation with the city of Medford concerning the future of fraternity housing. The problem had been exacerbated by Sigma Phi Epsilon when, in the spring of 1986, they looked to finalize the purchase of the house they were renting in the Medford Hillside. Their neighbors, not overly thrilled with living next to a fraternity, complained bitterly to the Tufts administration, who solved the problem by moving Sigma Phi Epsilon to an on-campus house the following year. At the same time, Medford residents living near the Alpha Epsilon Pi fraternity house were working to evict that fraternity from their Hillside chapter house. Though numerous Tufts fraternities had called Medford home since the early 1900s, they would all soon be kicked out, forever. True, Alpha Sigma Phi was actually looking to move into Somerville, not Medford, but that city was only slightly more receptive to fraternities than Medford. As a result, the Tufts administration, while supportive of Alpha Sigma Phi in general, did not relish the idea of them moving into an off-campus residential neighborhood, given the current climate. The last thing Tufts needed was a fight with another municipality.[286]

Even if the climate was right for purchasing an off-campus house, though, the Alpha Sigma Phi alumni corporation was getting nowhere in recovering its $30,000 from Tufts. The situation with the money was not as simple as many had believed, so the alumni corporation was unable to secure the funds in a timely manner. Therefore, without the ability to make a down payment, the group had to rescind its offer for the house on Powder House Boulevard, and the situation quietly faded away that fall. In the aftermath, Mr. Zamparelli and other alumni continued working to recover their $30,000 from the university, with the hope of trying again to purchase a house. To Mr. Zamparelli, this all should have been a straightforward matter, as he'd planned for this exact situation. When the alumni corporation under his leadership sold the house to Tufts in 1979, both parties signed a contract stipulating, "the university would retain the principal of $30,000… until the fraternity was reinstated." The fraternity had been reinstated, the reasoning went, so the money should be returned. Tufts balked at the idea, however, for one unbelievable reason: there was no contract. Some eight years after it was supposedly signed, no one – not anyone within the Tufts administration, and not Mr. Zamparelli – could find a copy. It was as if the agreement never existed. Tufts would not be cutting a $30,000 check to Alpha Sigma Phi any time soon.[287]

For the next year and a half, until the fall of 1988, the undergraduate and alumni members of Alpha Sigma Phi tried in vain to recover their money. They requested numerous meeting with and demanded information from President

Jean Mayer and others high up in the administration, but were rebuffed at every turn. Legally, it appears, the Alpha Sigma Phi alumni corporation had no argument to make, given the results of the 1980 lawsuit and the missing contract. Therefore, in late November of 1988, the administration ended the matter by simply stating once again the issue had been resolved in a Massachusetts court many years ago, and there was nothing more the fraternity could do. Both the money and the house at 106 Professor Row were the property of Tufts, and they would remain as such. Alpha Sigma Phi was therefore out of luck. There was no nest egg to help solve their housing problem. Instead, they were on their own, which meant going to the back of the housing line, to wait.[288]

Despite the unwanted distraction surrounding their inability to recover the $30,000, the undergraduate members of Alpha Sigma Phi worked to carve out their niche in the ever-growing Greek system at Tufts. They took an especially vocal stance on alcohol awareness by sponsoring numerous non-alcoholic events for the campus, something the other fraternities did not do with nearly the same amount of enthusiasm. By the spring of 1988, the chapter had grown large enough to petition the Grand Council of Alpha Sigma Phi for their charter. Although the Grand Council was still concerned about their size (the chapter was smaller than the campus average), they were impressed with the group and all they were able to accomplish, so they granted the charter and installed the Beta Iota chapter once again in the fall of 1988. Coincident with the charter was, finally, the return to a chapter house they had wanted for years. That fall, six members of Alpha Sigma Phi moved into a small house at 6-8 Capen Street Extension, a university-owned building administered through the housing office. The men secured the house by the luck of the draw, as their low lottery numbers gave them an early pick of available student housing. It was an unconventional approach, but with Tufts not opening any new chapter houses anytime soon, it was the only move they could make.[289]

Luck can be fleeting, however, and it soon ran out for Alpha Sigma Phi, at least in terms of housing. The following year, the members were not able to secure early picks in the housing lottery, so they were unable to establish a chapter house anywhere on campus in the fall of 1989. Additionally, they ran into their first bit of serious trouble. A semester earlier, the chapter had been charged with violating the university's dry rush policy by serving alcohol to prospective members. Punishment at the time included 100 hours of community service, working with the Inter-Greek Council (IGC) to enhance the dry rush protocol, and holding alcohol awareness events on campus. Now, in the fall of 1989, they were being called to task for not completing all of these requirements. As a result, the Committee on Social Fraternities and Sororities (CFS) placed the chapter under probation, meaning they were severely restricted in terms of the events and activities they could sponsor as a chapter. It appears, though, that there was some miscommunication between the chapter and the CFS regarding the tasks they were required to perform in the wake of the dry rush violations, so Alpha Sigma Phi filed an appeal over their probation. A few weeks into the spring 1990 semester, the appeal was granted and their punishment was reduced to warning status, allowing the fraternity to get back to normal operations. However, the damage had already been done. Recruitment that year had been quite poor, and did not keep pace with those leaving due to graduation. The chapter, it seemed, was heading backwards.[290]

The one bright spot for the chapter during this tumultuous year was its future in terms of housing. Once again some members picked low numbers in the housing lottery, which allowed them to secure the 350s suite in Hillside Apartments as their chapter home the following year. Being in a suite was not as advantageous as being in a house, but it was better than nothing, so the members of Alpha Sigma Phi returned to campus in the fall of 1990 and looked to rebuild their organization. The favorable housing situation, though, could not mask all that was going wrong for the chapter. By this point, they were down to only eleven active members and in serious danger of imploding. They were also failing to meet some of the necessary requirements of a Tufts fraternity, including the attendance of IGC meetings and failure to sign a relationship statement with the University. By the end of the semester, Alpha Sigma Phi was again under the watchful eye of the CFS, who threatened to remove the chapter from campus if they did not improve on a number of deficiencies, most importantly their low membership. They were now down to their last chance. If they failed to recruit a significant number of new men during the spring 1991 rush, they were through.[291]

The members of the chapter rose to the occasion by implementing a spirited and enthusiastic rush program that semester, which they advertised heavily on campus. The plan worked to perfection. At the end of rush week, the chapter had fourteen new pledges, nearly doubling in size to thirty members. From there, they worked to address their problems concerning campus participation, and here they were equally as successful. By April 1991, the chapter was off probation and, more importantly, no one was talking anymore about removing them from campus. Instead, Alpha Sigma Phi was receiving accolades from the CFS for improving so quickly. "They showed signs of real leadership," said the president of the IGC at the time, "and that leadership is getting stronger."[292]

But again, undercurrents of trouble surrounded the chapter. Although they had grown to thirty members that spring, twelve were due to graduate, so they would be in a weak position once again the following school year. Also, they were unable to secure on-campus housing for the 1991–92 school year. They did set up their operations in an unofficial chapter house at 23 Bellevue Street that following year, but being off campus meant they were generally out of view. So, when rush week commenced in the spring of 1992, the chapter once again stepped up recruitment efforts, looking to repeat its success from a year earlier.

This time, though, it would not go as well. There would be no large pledge class, even after the chapter extended its rush past the formal recruitment period. In the aftermath of the poor showing, a serious disagreement developed between the members over the future direction of their chapter. This difference was so strong that it ultimately pulled them apart. On March 11, 1992, the chapter ceased all operations. They returned their ritual materials and charter to the national office of Alpha Sigma Phi, and all active members went on alumni status. Beta Iota chapter of Alpha Sigma Phi was dormant once again.[293]

IN THE END ANALYSIS, the 1980s incarnation of Alpha Sigma Phi could not overcome their situation or setbacks. The inability to secure a permanent chapter house was most likely the largest detriment to their continued success, with the negativity surrounding the probationary periods also weighing the chapter down and limiting their potential for growth. It did not help, too, that the early 1990s brought a major shift in attitudes at Tufts towards Greek life. Many students were now loudly questioning the importance of such organizations, while others worked to remove them completely from campus. This sentiment did not swallow up every organization, but it certainly turned off many who might otherwise have given the Greek system a chance. With fewer men interested, there was bound to be some consolidation, and unfortunately for Alpha Sigma Phi, their chapter bared the brunt of this pull back. One is left only to wonder what would have been, had the alumni corporation kept possession of 106 Professors Row, or recovered the $30,000 from the sale of the house. At the very least, the legacy of Alpha Sigma Phi continues in a scholarship for undergraduate students, established in 1981.[294]

PHI DELTA (Local fraternity, 1913 – 1918, 1919 – 1936, 1948 – 1950)
SIGMA NU (Zeta Eta chapter, 1950 – 2015)

Tucked behind Anderson Hall and Robinson Hall is a third building that is actually the oldest of the triumvirate. Erected in 1893, the Bromfield-Pearson building today looks nearly as impressive as when it was built, and is currently home to the Tufts mathematics department. Over a century ago, though, this building was used for a different purpose. Henry Bromfield Pearson had been an educator nearly all his life, and when he passed away in 1867, he willed part of his family's fortune to establish a preparatory school under the auspices of Tufts College. The trustees eventually utilized this gift to open a new technical school, one to provide preliminary engineering education to those not ready for the full college curriculum. Thus the Bromfield-Pearson Technical School came to be, and in the fall of 1893, the school welcomed its first students, even though the building's interior was not finished and much of the heavy equipment had yet to be installed. Regardless, the school soon became well established in its own right, with its facilities and teachers educating not just the preparatory students, but Tufts engineering undergraduates as well. The story of Phi Delta starts in the fall of 1910, when a twenty-year old from South Boston named Joseph V. Magee enrolled in the Bromfield-Pearson school. Joseph completed the course, and then, a year later, was admitted to Tufts College as an engineering sophomore. He then moved into the East Hall dormitory, where he began making his mark, if not his legacy.[295]

Little is known about Joseph's experiences as an undergraduate, but early in the 1912–13 school year, he decided to start a new fraternity. At the time, nearly sixty percent of the undergraduate men belonged to one of the seven fraternities on campus, a level of participation that has not been equaled in modern times. Despite the near saturation of Greek-letter organizations, though, Joseph felt Tufts could be better served with another one. So, throughout that school year, he gathered eighteen like-minded men, including many of his neighbors in East Hall, and started a local fraternity called Phi Delta. The organization kept quiet for a few months, before finally announcing their presence to the campus in early March of 1913. As reported in the *Boston Globe*, the nineteen founding members of Phi Delta were:

Joseph Vincent Magee (1915)
James Ernest Kindred (1914)
Carl Oscar Carlson (1914)
Joseph Daniel Shiels (1914)
Leon William Peterson (1915)
James Bernard Maguire (1915)
John Arthur Neale (1915)
Maxwell Fish Barnes (1916)
Ralph Loud Armington (1915)
Lester Newton Towne (1916)
Francis Joel Foster (1916)
Henry Edward Halpin (1916)
Chester Thomas Caverly Davis (1916)
William Harrison Proctor (1917)
Dirrell Daniel Sample (1917)
David Ferguson (1917)
John Harold Boss (1917)
Frederick Morrison
Harvey Cedric Yeamans

The eight and newest fraternity quickly found its place amongst the other organizations, especially in the competitive world of interfraternity sports, where the chapter excelled.[296]

Homeward bound

Phi Delta may have been a new organization, but its members were wise enough to know they could not run their fraternity out of an East Hall dorm room when every other chapter on campus had a house. So, in addition to establishing a normal routine of recruitment, social events, and participation in athletics, the members also worked to secure a chapter home, as quickly as possible. And here they were successful, if not nomadic. By the start of the 1913–14 school year, Phi Delta had set up its operations at 22 Bellevue Street, a house in the Medford Hillside. This area just north of campus was fast becoming popular with new fraternities planting their housing roots. Phi Delta's stay at 22 Bellevue would be short lived, however, as a year later they moved a few blocks away to 11 Emery Street. This house served the chapter well for a few years, but by the fall of 1917, Phi Delta had moved again, to 20 Sunset Road in Somerville. Then, the Great War came calling. Throughout that school year and the summer of 1918, it appears every member of Phi Delta left college to support the war effort. As a result, when the Army and the S.A.T.C. program came to campus in the fall of 1918, Phi Delta was no longer active in any form.[297]

The armistice signaled the transition back to normal college life at Tufts. The fraternity men serving in the S.A.T.C. quickly reorganized their chapters and reclaimed their houses on campus. The only fraternity struggling in this regard was Phi Delta, for they had to wait until enough veterans returned to campus before they could restart. As a result, it took the chapter until the late fall of 1919, nearly a year longer than everyone else, to get their operations back to full swing and reopen a new chapter house on University Avenue, in the Medford Hillside. But once again, their housing situation was far from stable, as they moved around quite a bit in the next few years, first to Graves House at 18 Latin Way, and then, by the fall of 1921, back to the Hillside neighborhood at 11 Fairmount Street. Finally, by the fall of 1924, the fraternity's alumni corporation purchased 8 Bellevue Street as the chapter's first permanent home. The roaring twenties were in full swing, and Phi Delta was now positioned, finally, to cement its long-term presence on the Tufts campus.[298]

Life for Phi Delta at 8 Bellevue Street was generally good, as the chapter thrived in membership and contributed positively to campus life. Underneath the lively brotherhood, though, was a serious financial crisis. The members of Phi Delta, it appears, were not always consistent in paying their rent to the alumni corporation, which meant the alumni corporation fell behind on property taxes, utilities, and general house maintenance. The situation muddled along until the fall of 1930, when the undergraduates decided they needed to move. As for a reason, they only had to witness their fraternity neighbors all moving to nicer houses closer to campus. Phi Delta was being left behind, a situation they did not relish. So, that fall they began lobbying the alumni corporation for a new house, arguing they were on the verge of closing down unless they had "a change of scenery." The alumni corporation was hardly a pillar of financial strength, with red ink covering its books on nearly every page, but by early spring of 1931, they decided to support the undergraduates in their request. They bought a house at 167 College Avenue, very close to the Beta Kappa and Sigma Tau Alpha fraternity houses, using what little cash they

Phi Delta members pose on the steps of their house at 11 Fairmount Street, December, 1922. The man with glasses sitting directly behind the banner is likely Joseph Magee, Phi Delta's founder.

had left for the down payment (about $341), and securing a mortgage to cover the rest. As for 8 Bellevue Street, the alumni corporation sold the house to Miss Alice Quinn, although they had to grant her a mortgage in order to complete the transaction. Such an arrangement was common at the time, since formal lending institutions were struggling in the onset of the Depression. However, the sale netted little cash to the alumni corporation, and with bills mounting at an increasing pace, their financial hole was only growing deeper.[299]

Unfortunately for the alumni corporation, one person whose finances were in worse shape than theirs was Miss Quinn. Simply put, with each passing month she failed to pay anything towards her mortgage, and, when asked, offered no plans to rectify the situation. So, by the end of 1931, the alumni corporation foreclosed on Miss Quinn and took back the property. They also doubled-down by purchasing the other half of the duplex, 6 Bellevue Street, again using money they did not have. Now, the alumni were proud owners of three addresses and even more mortgages. To make matters worse, the heating system at 6-8 Bellevue snapped in the winter of 1931, adding yet another major expense to the beleaguered alumni corporation. They were drowning in debt, but somehow managed to keep the bill collectors and tax officials at bay, usually by paying a little now and promising more later. With the Great Depression getting worse with each passing month, Phi Delta was hardly alone in its financial troubles. However, the fraternity's decision to buy and mortgage and pass the buck was not making the situation any easier.[300]

Still, enthusiasm reigned in Phi Delta, and as the 1930s moved on, the chapter set up its operations in 167 College Avenue while working to sell their other house to anyone besides Miss Quinn. In the spring of 1935, Phi Delta was still going strong, especially in terms of interfraternity athletics. But their membership had become quite top heavy, with nearly half of the actives graduating that year. Rush week netted some pledges, but not nearly enough to make up the difference. As a result, when the fall of 1935 arrived, Phi Delta was a shell of its formal self, counting only ten or so active members. They managed to keep their organization together during that fall, even placing well in the interfraternity sports league. However, by the early spring of 1936, Phi Delta was finished. With dwindling membership and mounting financial pressures, especially the multitude of mortgages, those that remained called it quits. Phi Delta then quietly but quickly faded from campus life, in what was an unfortunate trend among a few Tufts fraternities during the Depression.[301]

As for an early legacy of Phi Delta, one need not look further than its founder, Joseph V. Magee. After earning a degree in chemistry, Joseph became a pioneer in the brand new field of aviation, specifically airmail delivery. In the early 1920s, he teamed with Charles Lindberg to establish the first airmail route between the United States and South America. He also headed up a nation-wide project to establish the first system of nighttime flying between the country's airfields, again with Charles Lindberg. At the time, pilots could not fly or land at night, as they relied exclusively on line-of-sight navigation. Joseph helped invent a system of high-powered light beacons that guided pilots along a predetermined route from airfield to airfield across America. While this system was eventually made obsolete by radio communication and then radar, it did have a lasting impact on air transportation. Part of the system Joseph developed included the use of bright lights on the airplane's wingtips as a landing aid. This aviation standard is still in use today.[302]

Phi Delta returns

The Great Depression marked the first time in Tufts history that the number of fraternities on campus shrank considerably over a short period of time. Whereas Tufts could count twelve active fraternities in 1930, a decade later that number had been cut to seven. Of the five that closed down, Phi Delta was the only one never to have affiliated with a national organization. Therefore, when fraternities began making a strong comeback at Tufts after World War II, circumstance implied that Phi Delta would remain closed, since there was no national organization pushing for its re-establishment. However, due to an action by the trustees of Tufts College in the 1930s, Phi Delta would not only re-open, it would be the first of the dormant fraternities to do so.[303]

It all started with a group of a dozen freshmen living in the Fletcher Hall dormitory in the fall of 1947. Throughout their first semester, the men became good friends, certainly a pattern that is repeated each and every year, in each and every dormitory. As the spring semester got underway the following January, the men as a group decided to participate in fraternity rush. They spent a week going from house to house, learning about each chapter, meeting the members, and of course, partaking in numerous parties. Then, they waited for the bids to be handed out, a process that took a couple of weeks while fall grades were processed. Finally, one Sunday night after the bid envelopes were delivered en masse, the men gathered in 42 Fletcher Hall to see where they all ended up. To their dismay, no single fraternity had offered a bid to more than two or three of the men. Disappointment immediately descended upon the group. Many of them wanted to join a fraternity, but they were reluctant to split up their friendships. At some point during the discussion, one of the men put forth a novel solution: they could remain a group by starting their own fraternity. The idea was an instant hit, even if not unanimous – two in the group opted out shortly thereafter. However, those that remained realized this was their chance to create their own experience, one that would outlast their time as undergraduates. As for their immediate goals, they came up with two that same night. First, occupy a chapter house, and second, affiliate with a national fraternity. And of course, they wanted to accomplish both as soon as possible.[304]

The only force potentially standing in the way was the Tufts administration, for the men could not start a new fraternity without their approval. Student life at the time, though certainly not as restrictive as it had been in the past, was still very much under control of the administrators, complete with dress codes, visitation hours for dormitories, and single-sex dining halls. The chain of rules and moral authority was quite clear to every student. At the head of that chain was the college president. So, in a bold move, the men went straight to the top and requested an appointment with President Leonard Carmichael. There were certainly others in the administration that could have been consulted first in this regard, but the men bypassed them all. Perhaps it was bravado mixed with freshmen innocence that led them to ask for this meeting, or perhaps they sensed that President Carmichael, as a Tufts graduate, Theta Delta Chi alumnus, and known supporter of fraternities, would be sympathetic to them and grant permission to continue without delay. Either way, theirs was the correct move. President Carmichael met with the men, heard their plans, and proclaimed to be very much in favor. The new fraternity could go forward.[305]

President Carmichael's support didn't stop there. He soon referred the men to two others who could help them achieve their goals of a house and national affiliation. The first was Dean Nils Wessel, who gave his enthusiastic support to the group, along with a promise: if they paid particular attention to expansion, he remarked, and built the membership up to thirty-five members or so, he would help them secure a chapter house. At the time, veterans were returning to college in ever-increasing number, and this influx put enormous pressure on Tufts to provide them with student housing. The administration, quite simply, was overwhelmed trying to manage the situation. A new fraternity house would help solve this problem, since the overall number of beds would increase, and the chapter (as opposed to the college) could oversee the property. Additionally, Dean Wessel recognized that fraternities were a major force in the social lives of the students due to the popular campus activities they organized, from dances to carnivals to the newly revived Mayoralty contest. He knew Tufts needed more fraternities, and the group of men from Fletcher Hall seemed to him a great addition.[306]

The second reference provided by President Carmichael was Joel Reynolds, a Tufts alumnus and long time advisor to the Delta Tau Delta chapter on campus. On the surface, this referral was somewhat strange, since Mr. Reynolds was very active in Delta Tau Delta and would seemingly have little interest in another group. However, Mr. Reynolds was also quite connected to the national interfraternity scene, and he had contacts (if not close friends) in nearly every national organization. If there was one person who could help the Fletcher men successfully court a national fraternity, it was Mr. Reynolds. Everything, it seemed, was coming together nicely for the group.[307]

At least it was, until one major problem soon came to light. During the Depression, the trustees were all too aware of fraternities getting into financial trouble and closing down. These fraternities were many of the newest to be organized on campus, and when they abruptly closed, they often left behind unpaid mortgages, overdue property taxes, and outstanding utility bills, which by proxy became problems for the college. In response, the trustees passed a resolution during the Depression banning any new fraternities from organizing on campus. They sensed that young organizations were particularly vulnerable to financial ruin, and they wanted to avoid the messiness these groups seemed to bring. Also, they knew that keeping new organizations out would help strengthen the older ones, thus increasing the chances for a continued, viable fraternity system on campus. Now, some ten years after the ban was implemented, Tufts fraternities were no longer in imminent danger of financial collapse, as they were all bursting at the seams with members. But this reality was of little consequence to the trustees. The ban was still in place, leaving the Tufts administration with little choice but to tell the Fletcher men "no," at least for the time being.[308]

Rules, however, are sometimes meant to be re-interpreted when they cannot be ignored. Many within the administration realized the ban on new fraternities was no longer necessary, but they also knew waiting for the trustees to reach this conclusion and rescind the rule could take years. So, the administration proposed an alternative solution. They recommended the Fletcher men restart one of the fraternities that had gone dormant during the Depression. Technically, the argument went, an organization that was revived would not be "new," and therefore would not be violating the ban. But it was certainly against the spirit of the law, and if the trustees wished, they could squelch the whole idea. Despite the risk, the Fletcher men knew this was their only option, so they began researching the dormant organizations. They quickly learned that nearly all of the dormant chapters had been part of a national organization when they went under, so reviving any of these would mean immediately joining a national group. While affiliating with a national fraternity was their goal, the men were not so enthusiastic about selecting from a small subset of organizations, especially ones they knew little about. So, the Fletcher men instead chose to revive the only local fraternity that had gone dormant, Phi Delta.[309]

With this choice, luck was once again on their side. As it turned out, the manager of the Tufts bookstore at the time was none other than Dirrell "Skeets" Sample, a founding member of Phi Delta in 1913. Mr. Sample, after meeting with the Fletcher men, took an immediate liking to the group and pledged his support in the revival of his fraternity. From there, the men worked to get their organization off the ground, even designing a new Phi Delta symbol, badge, and ritual. In this regard, it seems, little of the original Phi Delta documentation had survived. The work continued into the fall 1948 semester, and soon after the start of school, they made everything official. On October 12, 1948, the Phi Delta fraternity was formally revived at Tufts College, the first fraternity ever to come back after such a lapse. Membership was still small, with twelve active members and two pledges on its roster, but all involved knew this was only the beginning. The other fraternity chapters welcomed them with a dance in their honor. By the end of the spring semester in 1949, Phi Delta was a voting member of the Interfraternity Council and was actively participating in many campus activities such as intramural sports and the popular Spring and Winter sings. They hosted social activities out of the Jumbo Lounge in Barnum Hall, and their pledges held a formal in the Jackson gymnasium. Most importantly, Phi Delta grew its membership significantly during the school year, such that they were able to take up Dean Wessel on his promise of a house. True to his word, Dean Wessel told the men that spring to start looking for a home, which Tufts would purchase and rent back to them. The first goal the Fletcher men had laid down a year earlier was about to come to fruition.[310]

The search for a house started right in the heart of campus. Standing at the corner of Professors Row and Packard Avenue is the Fay House, built in the 1874 for Charles Fay, a long serving and well-loved professor. The house was flanked by Zeta Psi on one side and Delta Tau Delta on the other, and had been home to members of the Fay family for nearly eighty years. To the men of Phi Delta, the house was perfectly located, so it became their number one choice. However, the current owner of the house had no intention of leaving or selling. Forced to look elsewhere for a suitable home, the chapter then engaged the services of a realtor. Soon enough they settled on 114 Curtis Street in Somerville. Though not as centrally located at the Fay house, it was very close to Professors Row and offered a great space for the fraternity, though the inside needed quite a bit of renovation. With choice made, Tufts purchased the house in the summer of 1949 and immediately began the remodeling. Members of Phi Delta worked with Tufts Buildings and Grounds that summer to transform the house into a home, complete with common area furnishings from Jordan Marsh, rooming accommodations for twenty, and dining facilities for all. As the start of the fall 1949 semester approached, only the basement was left to finish. So, a number of Phi Delts came to campus a few weeks early to tackle this project. They dug out the dirt basement, poured the concrete, built the bar, and turned the space into their primary party room. When classes began later that September, Phi Delta was ready to go.[311]

The new house was put to good use early that semester as Phi Delta hosted a number of social events. At one of these early parties, a Phi Delta alumnus from the 1930s stopped by the house to reconnect with his old fraternity. He quickly found the basement, where he then spent most of the night hanging out at the bar in the newly finished, but sparsely decorated room. This particular alumnus just happened to be a lumber dealer, and during a festive moment in the party, he offered to donate some knotty-pine paneling to cover the basement walls. Although promises made in the middle of a party are seldom kept, the knotty-pine paneling did show up at the house a short while later, and after its installation, the basement was complete. The gracious lumber dealer, though, apparently never returned to the house to see how the "Ginger Room," as the basement came to be known, turned out.[312]

The biggest challenge in the house that first year turned out to be the dining room. The chapter entrusted the logistics of feeding forty or so men to Al, a chef with an impressive culinary resume they had hired. Unfortunately, Al also had a propensity to get "sauced" before his job was done (or, sometimes, before it was even started), which often left the task of cooking to the undergraduates. Chef Al was soon replaced by Thelma Simmonds, a much more reliable cook who became a presence in the fraternity for many years. With the day-to-day operations of the fraternity settled, the members of Phi Delta then turned their attention to national affiliation. And here, they looked to Joel Reynolds, or "Uncle Joe" as the chapter called him. Nearly every national fraternity was expanding in earnest around this time, so when word hit the street that a local at Tufts was looking to affiliate, many jumped at the chance. Mr. Reynolds helped the men narrow their search, having them focus especially on some of the largest and strongest national organizations. Soon enough, Phi Delta was being courted by a group of very prestigious fraternities. Five made the final round: Pi Kappa Alpha, Sigma Chi, Sigma Nu, Theta Chi, and Sigma Alpha Epsilon. After all the presentations and interviews, there was no clear favorite among the chapter, although Pi Kappa Alpha did itself no favors when it sent a representative who made it very clear who was, and who was not, welcome in his fraternity. Still, the men could not decide. As the end of the semester drew near, and with a desire to reach a consensus before the winter break, the members of Phi Delta gave themselves until their final meeting in December 1949 to choose. That last meeting opened with everyone arranged in small groups based around their first choice for affiliation. Each group gave its pitch, with spirits (and tempers) running high at various points in the meeting. But in the end, the members of Phi Delta made a unanimous choice. It would be Sigma Nu.[313]

Southern heritage, national presence

Sigma Nu is a fraternity born out of the ashes of conflict. When the Civil War ended in 1865, and much of the infrastructure of the South was in ruins, civil engineers were desperately needed to help rebuild the landscape. The Virginia Military Institute (VMI), which had been destroyed during the war but reopened in 1865, was known at the time for its civil engineering program, and soon attracted many veterans of the Confederate Army eager to rebuild. One such veteran entering VMI in the fall of 1866 was James Frank Hopkins from Arkansas. As a first year cadet, James was known as a "rat," a term still used today at the school. And as a rat, he was expected to endure the time-honored tradition of physical punishment and hazing at the hands of the upper classmen. James had tolerated such practices as a soldier since it helped to instill discipline among the troops. Now, though, he had a very hard time rationalizing this behavior at VMI, as the physical punishment he and countless others had to endure seemed counter-productive to what they were trying to accomplish, the rebuilding of their homes. James therefore made a vow to stamp out hazing at VMI. He soon found two others who felt as strongly, Greenfield Quarles from Arkansas, and James McIlvaine Riley from Missouri, and the three spent many nights discussing how to remove hazing from their school. After one particular Bible study session, these three cadets met at a limestone rock on the VMI parade grounds, clasped their hands on a Bible, and proclaimed the birth of a new society based on honor, not hazing. They called their organization "The Legion of Honor" and soon recruited other cadets who shared their values. A new fraternity had just been born. And while they were not the only fraternity at VMI, they kept their name secret for a while, opting instead to use two Greek letters as the public name of their organization: Sigma Nu.[314]

In its first few years of existence, Sigma Nu remained local to VMI, since the founders never intended to extend their fraternity beyond their school.

However, starting in 1871, those who followed in Sigma Nu began placing chapters outside of VMI, including ones at the University of Virginia, the University of Georgia, and the University of Alabama, thus making the fraternity a national organization. However, while the chapter at VMI continued to flourish, most others struggled and closed down within a couple of years. By 1883, only three of Sigma Nu's fourteen established chapters were active – VMI, North Georgia Agricultural College, and Washington & Lee University. The future did not look very bright for Sigma Nu as a national organization, until the fraternity made a number of changes that year which led to a turnaround. First, one member of the North Georgia chapter started a magazine for Sigma Nu members called *The Delta*, which increased communication between the chapters and added to the overall prestige of the fraternity on the national level. Second, a member of the Washington & Lee chapter organized Sigma Nu's first national convention in July of 1884, inviting active members and alumni to meet as a group and conduct important business, such as revising the constitution and the establishing firm procedures for expansion. The convention, called the Grand Chapter, has met every two years since. Following the convention, Sigma Nu began expanding to larger and more prestigious schools all across the country. The fraternity had been exclusively Southern in extent until 1884, when it entered Lehigh University, and then, in the years that followed, spread to all regions of the country including the Northeast. Sigma Nu continued its rapid expansion until slowed by the Depression and World War II. Now, with the war over and fraternities enjoying a spirited comeback across the country, Sigma Nu looked to expand once more.[315]

The members of Phi Delta returned to Tufts in January 1950 and immediately began preparing their petition to Sigma Nu. And with this document, they had to be perfect. Earlier in the 20th century, petitioners often enhanced their written application by personally lobbying members of the fraternity at a national convention to secure the necessary votes. By the 1950s, though, this method had changed, with the petition now standing alone, either to convince the fraternity, or not. Sigma Nu had three approval gates a petition had to pass before acceptance: the governing High Council of national officers, the active chapters within the same geographical division, and then all remaining active chapters across the country. With this in mind, the members of Phi Delta put together a comprehensive twenty-four page petition, complete with historical information on Tufts College and Phi Delta, brief resumes of all active members, recommendations from campus officials, and campus photographs. Jumbo the Elephant, in all his pride and glory, was the centerfold. While the entire petition was certainly impressive, the recommendation from "Uncle Joe" stood out, as he proclaimed "I would enthusiastically vote in favor of a petition of this group if they were on another campus and petitioning for a charter from my own fraternity." By February 1950, the petition was complete and Phi Delta had passed the first two gates. All that was remained was the approval of a super majority of the chapters across the country. So, copies were printed and sent out to these active chapters, about one hundred in total, leaving Phi Delta with nothing to do, except wait.[316]

They did not wait long. Before the end of the 1950 spring semester, the votes from the active chapters had come in, and more than enough were affirmative. Phi Delta had been granted its charter. Now came the details. The chartering process began soon after the final vote, in June 1950, when the members of Phi Delta were pledged to Sigma Nu. Then, a few months later, on October 7, 1950, Phi Delta was installed as the Zeta Eta chapter of Sigma Nu, the 122nd chapter of the fraternity. Thirty-seven undergraduates and nineteen Phi Delta alumni formed the charter group, and together they spent the entire weekend in celebration, from a formal dance in Jackson Gymnasium one night, to a football game and banquet the next. Included in this group of initiates was Skeets Sample, thus linking the old Phi Delta to the new Zeta Eta of Sigma Nu. The second of two goals set out by the founding members had been completed, and not a moment too soon, since many would graduate the following semester.[317]

Issues and obstacles

Once established, Sigma Nu picked up right where Phi Delta left off. Awards and accolades came fast for the chapter that first year, as their candidate was elected Homecoming Queen, they won the Winter Sing competition, they created a winning snow sculpture during the Tufts Winter Carnival, and one of their own, Mal Mooney, was elected Mayor of Tufts College. Membership grew rapidly, too, as within a few semesters, the chapter boasted a brotherhood of nearly sixty men, consistent with the other established fraternities on campus. With interest in Greek life continuing to grow throughout the 1950s, Sigma Nu spent little time as the "new guys" on campus, for within a few years three other fraternities had established or re-established chapters at Tufts. It was certainly a boom time for Tufts fraternities, a situation which has not been repeated since. But even here, amidst all of the optimism and enthusiasm, was a serious problem that threatened to derail Sigma Nu, possibly for good.[318]

The underlying issue was something the men of the chapter had known all along, but could ignore for practical reasons. In 1950, when the Zeta Eta chapter was chartered, Sigma Nu was a fraternity clearly and unequivocally open not to all men, but to some. According to its national constitution at the time, membership was confined to "MEN, free born and of free ancestry, and without Negro blood, and have[ing] the character and bearing of gentlemen." Sigma Nu was not alone in this regard, as numerous national fraternities and sororities had similar restrictions in place (and had so for decades), including many with chapters at Tufts. Such restrictions, though, were generally an afterthought on campus, as a vast majority of students throughout the school's history to the 1950s were white. But the times were changing. Many at Tufts were now questioning these discriminatory practices in Greek-letter organizations and demanding their removal, or else. Similar rallying cries emerged on campuses across the country, as the dawn of student activism began to take hold. A number of national fraternities and sororities responded to this call with change, and by the end of the 1950s, almost all with chapters at Tufts had rescinded their discriminatory membership requirements. All, that is, except two: Sigma Nu and Alpha Tau Omega. Both fraternities were now under a spotlight that was only getting brighter.[319]

Unfortunately, the Tufts chapters of Sigma Nu and Alpha Tau Omega were not in a strong position to affect change. In both national organizations, a majority of chapters, especially the older and more powerful ones in the South, clung to their established traditions. A sizeable minority in each organization openly fought for reform, but until the majority ruled otherwise, there would be no change to their respective membership qualifications. Therefore, the Tufts chapters of Sigma Nu and Alpha Tau Omega could do little except push and wait for the tide to turn. In the interim, however, as other chapters began withdrawing in protest, or were kicked off campus because of their discriminatory clauses, both national organizations established a waiver process to exempt individual chapters from their membership requirements. This process was not without some controversy, but as the early 1960s progressed, it became clear that Sigma Nu and Alpha Tau Omega could only continue at Tufts if they were each granted a waiver. Due to the work of the individual chapters and Joel Reynolds, both Sigma Nu and Alpha Tau Omega at Tufts were granted waivers by the end of 1963, thus allowing them to initiate any man they wanted. These waivers satisfied the official demands of the university, so both could remain on campus. Discrimination within fraternities at Tufts had been beaten. But of course, there were yet other problems on the horizon for Sigma Nu, and these would also prove to be just as formidable.[320]

One problem was their chapter house. Despite the controversy over their membership restrictions, Sigma Nu maintained a relatively large membership, and as the 1960s progressed it became clear to the chapter their house was too small. Here, though, the alumni had a plan. They would tear down 114 Curtis Street and build a brand new, modern fraternity house in its place. Of course, this plan required a lot of money. The estimated cost of the project was $150,000, not including the razing of the existing structure, and while the alumni could finance a portion of this amount, they would need significant help from Tufts to make up the difference. So, in 1965, the alumni association began asking the Tufts administration for a loan to turn their idea into reality. Such a request was not without precedence. A few years earlier, Phi Epsilon Pi had obtained a sizeable loan of $80,000 from the university to renovate their

Sigma Nu members enjoying a cold beverage beside their Jumbo float, which was used to entertain at Tufts football games, circa 1964.

house. So, as the meetings with the Tufts administration got underway, the alumni were optimistic a similar deal could be reached with Sigma Nu.[321]

Optimism soon ran straight into a brick wall. By 1965, the administration could sense a small but growing negative attitude among the students towards the fraternities, and in response they began to worry about the long-term viability of the Greek-letter organizations. Indeed, one fraternity, Tau Epsilon Phi, had recently closed down, the first to do so since the Depression. An investment by Tufts into a new fraternity house now looked very risky. Additionally, the administration worried that if they approved a loan for Sigma Nu, other fraternities such as Theta Chi or Phi Sigma Kappa would soon ask for a similar deal, so they could construct new houses. The prospects of taking on the financial responsibility for all of this building, plus the problem of increasing the number of beds in student housing while enrollment remained flat, weighed heavily on the administration. In the end, they did not approve the loan to Sigma Nu. Not surprisingly, the alumni could not raise the necessary funds on their own, so by the end of 1965, the project to build a new house was quietly abandoned.[322]

As it turns out, the administration had sensed correctly the declining interest in fraternities. Within a few years, the membership of Sigma Nu, which had consistently been 60 or more members since it was founded, began to decline rapidly. Nearly all other fraternities were experiencing similar declines in membership, with a few of them even shutting down completely. Sigma Nu managed to hang on, somehow, but its future did not look bright. By the fall of 1972, the chapter stood at seven men, six being brand new initiates. Those that remained hoped to reorganize and rebuild the chapter in the coming semesters, but two years later the situation had only turned abysmal. When school started in the fall of 1974, Sigma Nu counted just two active members, both seniors. The house at 114 Curtis Street, once been deemed too small, was now essentially empty. The two that remained, however, were not willing to give up, so they tackled the immediate problem of filling the rooms to pay the rent and keep control of the house. And here, they got lucky, for they soon found quite a few men who'd had enough of dormitory life and wanted to live somewhere else. So, in the fall of 1974, about eight men, mostly engineering majors, moved into 114 Curtis Street alongside the two Sigma Nu members. A few of the other struggling fraternities also saw a similar influx of boarders that semester, and these new residents radically changed those organizations by casting aside the old traditions to create a new experience. In Sigma Nu, however, the exact opposite happened. With support and encouragement of local alumni, the men who moved into 114 Curtis Street that fall decided to keep the fraternity going, complete with the rituals and traditions. Sigma Nu would remain an active chapter of a national organization.[323]

Over the next few years, a revitalized Sigma Nu grew to about twenty or so members, which was more than enough to pay the bills and continue in earnest. However, in the fall of 1977, Sigma Nu experienced a slight hiccup when not enough of the men wanted to live in 114 Curtis Street. As a means of keeping the house solvent, the chapter allowed three women to move in that year. The women were not affiliated in any official way with the chapter, though they were included on the fraternity composite that year. The men worried that the national office of Sigma Nu would object to the cohabitation, but in the end this situation never came to light, and after the spring of 1978, the women moved out for good. In the mean time, the chapter caught the wave of renewed fraternity interest in the late 1970s and grew significantly, thereby casting aside any thoughts of dormancy. One major highlight for the chapter came in 1984, when the men won the Gallagher Cup for having the highest grade point average among the 150 active chapters of Sigma Nu. It had been a tumultuous decade for the chapter, but now everything, finally, was looking up.[324]

A "new" old house for Sigma Nu

By 1980, the house at 114 Curtis Street, sometimes embraced while other times maligned, was foremost on the minds of those in Sigma Nu. The structure was now over a century old, and continued maintenance problems coupled with steep rent increases in previous years had put the space in a bad light. The house was also perceived once again as being too small for the growing membership. Unable to revive the effort to build a new house, the alumni began talking with the Tufts administration that year about moving into a larger home. The alumni quickly settled on a first choice, the Hooper Infirmary at 124 Professors Row. Apparently, they were under the impression this house was available, but Tufts quickly put an end to such fancy. The infirmary was not going anywhere. Moving on, the alumni's second choice was a familiar one, and that was the Fay House at 92 Professors Row. By this time, the venerable Fay House had been taken over by Tufts and turned into co-op student housing. There was little interest on the part of Tufts, however, to convert this space into anything else; the administration had much bigger issues to deal with at the time, and worrying about who occupied 92 Professors Row did not warrant their immediate consideration. So, Sigma Nu stayed at 114 Curtis Street and made the best of it. At least they did, until they stopped asking to move.[325]

The surprise came in the early spring of 1985. That semester, the Tufts administration decided to turn over control of 92 Professors Row to the Interfraternity Council (IFC) for use as a chapter house. The motivation for this decision was not hard to see. The number of fraternities at Tufts was once again increasing, but with no available space on campus to call home, these new chapters were starting to secure off campus housing on their own terms, much to the consternation of the administration. Opening another on-campus fraternity house was a simple way of diffusing the often acrimonious relationship between the off-campus fraternities and their neighbors. The Fay House at 92 Professors Row, which was practically surrounded by other fraternities, was an obvious choice for a new chapter house. Therefore, the IFC invited all fraternities and sororities to apply for the right to occupy the Fay House starting in the fall of 1985, with the tenant chosen in coordination with the Tufts administration. Six organizations applied, including the two newest fraternities: Psi Upsilon, Sigma Phi Epsilon, Theta Chi, Kappa Alpha Psi, Sigma Nu, and Alpha Phi, the lone sorority in the mix. Most of this group, aside from Sigma Phi Epsilon and Kappa Alpha Psi, already occupied a chapter house, but the chance to move to the heart of campus was too enticing for the others to ignore. A few weeks later, the IFC had made its choice. They would offer the house to Psi Upsilon first, and if they declined, then to Kappa Alpha Psi, followed by Sigma Nu. The administration, however, saw the situation differently, as they awarded the house to Sigma Nu first, followed by Sigma Phi Epsilon and then Alpha Phi. Despite the noblest of intentions, the process had resulted in a standoff.[326]

The Tufts administration broke the standoff shortly thereafter by cancelling the whole idea, at least temporarily. The conversion of 92 Professors Row into a fraternity house was just one part of a broader housing plan, and when the other pieces fell apart that semester due to legal issues with lodging licenses, the entire project was shelved for a year. In the fall of 1985, though, the problem of off-campus fraternities was once again front-and-center. That semester, Sigma

Phi Epsilon rented its first chapter house at 16 Bellevue Street. Unfortunately, the other residents on the street did not appreciate their new neighbor, so they complained to the Tufts administration early that school year. Now, the university was forced to diffuse the situation. For this, they once again turned to 92 Professors Row, but instead of a process, they simply made a decision. Sigma Nu would move into the Fay House starting in the fall of 1986, and Sigma Phi Epsilon would move into the house Sigma Nu was leaving behind, 114 Curtis Street. It had been thirty-seven years since Phi Delta first attempted to occupy the Fay House. Now, as the fall semester of 1986 drew near, the active and alumni members of Zeta Eta chapter would find out if the house had been worth the wait.[327]

From the outside, the Victorian architecture of the Fay House, though dulled in some places, was still quite impressive, and its appearance along with its location was enough to give the chapter great enthusiasm about their new home. However, it appears no one had closely examined the inside prior to moving day. Opening the front door for the first time therefore revealed an unwanted surprise. The Fay House was an unmitigated mess. True, it was an old house that had been occupied for a long time, but it was clear that maintenance over the years had been woefully lacking, especially during its time as a co-op dormitory. The bathrooms were awash in mold and water damage, the hardwood floors were stained and scratched, the interior walls required more than just a fresh coat of paint, and the main kitchen had but a single four-burner stove, which was woefully inadequate for boarding the chapter. The house was also not very safe. One of the biggest problems was the basement, the largest room in the house and therefore the obvious gathering space for social functions. With an uneven dirt floor, broken support columns, exposed heating system, asbestos-covered pipes, and only one egress, the basement was a disaster waiting to happen. To say the house needed work was an understatement. But real estate is all about location, and in this regard, the house was perfect.[328]

Over the next couple of years the active membership, the alumni, and Tufts Buildings and Grounds worked together to solve the interior problems and transform 92 Professors Row into a bona fide fraternity house. One crucial renovation involved the construction of a second exit out of the basement, so the room could be safely occupied. This renovation was not a priority of the Tufts administration, though, as they were content to seal off the basement and not allow its use. However, the chapter knew it needed this space for a dining room and social area, so on their own they financed the construction of the exit. Supporting this effort with a personal loan was Bruce Victor, who in 1974 had been one of the two active members to rebuild Sigma Nu. By the fall of 1988, a second exit had been carved into the front right corner of the house, and a new industrial kitchen, also financed by the chapter, was in operation. The Fay House had become a home.[329]

Ups and downs

With a new house in the center of campus, Sigma Nu experienced a marked growth in membership during those first few years at 92 Professors Row, eventually climbing to fifty active members by the spring of 1989, the largest the chapter had been since the late 1960s. However, in 1989, almost half of the active membership graduated, and the chapter struggled over the next few semesters to rebuild the membership. Part of the problem was a fast growing negative attitude among the students towards fraternities. The early 1990s saw the first concerted effort in decades to either expel Greek life at Tufts or force the organizations to become co-ed, similar to what happening at other schools such as Colby College, Middlebury College, and Bowdoin College. Sigma Nu, among a few other chapters, took the brunt of this negative attitude. By the fall of 1992, the chapter was down to only thirteen active members including eight seniors, a roster that was below the minimum required to be a fraternity at Tufts University. The chapter knew if they didn't significantly increase their membership that year, they would be de-recognized by the administration and would probably go dormant. However, the chapter was in no way ready to quit on eighty years of tradition, so they got to work. These efforts culminated in February of 1993, when the chapter, in conjunction with representatives from the Sigma Nu national organization and local alumni, pledged twenty-one new candidates to re-colonize the fraternity. More than half of these new members immediately took up leadership positions within the chapter, and by the following semester, operations were back to normal. All thoughts of closing down had been cast aside.[330]

After re-colonization, Sigma Nu continued in earnest. The chapter's fiftieth and sixtieth anniversaries came and went with great fanfare, and by 2010 the chapter was close to fifty active members once again, the largest it had been since the late 1980s. But underneath the growth was a serious problem. The Fay House at 92 Professors Row was not getting any younger, and the yearly maintenance did not keep up with the needs of the structure. As a result, the chapter struggled at times to fill the rooms despite having plenty of members, all due to the house's poor condition. Then, at the end of the 2012 spring semester, disaster. The departing seniors left the house in a deplorable condition after graduating, complete with mountains of trash in bedrooms and the common areas, and damage to walls and doors throughout the structure. The administration, after discovering the mess, eventually decided to expel the chapter from the house, so the remaining members could re-focus on their core values without distraction. A similar situation had occurred with Sigma Phi Epsilon a year earlier, thereby defining a new precedent: trash your house, and you're out. So, in the fall of 2012, those in Sigma Nu returned to campus as an unhoused fraternity, with their former home finally refurbished, but now designated as a dormitory for transfer students. Throughout that year, the members committed themselves to serving out their probation, correcting the errors of their past, and rebuilding the chapter on a strong footing. There was also great optimism that once their probation was over, the chapter would simply return to 92 Professors Row.[331]

Reality, once again, had a different plan. The problem here was Sigma Phi Epsilon, and the situation they had created a year earlier. Their damage to the inside of 114 Curtis Street was so complete that the administration closed the house as a living space, turn in its lodging license, and converted the building into academic offices. Sixty-three years of history as a chapter house were gone in an instant. The administration was seriously considering plans to build another fraternity house as a replacement for 114 Curtis Street, but those plans stalled; neither a suitable location nor the money were available. Now, there was only one extra fraternity house on campus – 92 Professors Row – for the two unhoused chapters on probation. The closing of 114 Curtis Street therefore set up a game of musical houses that someone had to lose. And with Sigma Phi Epsilon a year ahead of Sigma Nu in the rehabilitation process, the loser was obvious. So, much to the consternation of the active and alumni members of Sigma Nu, in the fall of 2013, Sigma Phi Epsilon completed its two-year probation and moved into 92 Professors Row. All hope for Sigma Nu was not lost, however, as Sigma Phi Epsilon was only given a one-year lease, and the administration implied there would be a re-evaluation of fraternity housing assignments before any new lease was issued. It was a long shot, but as Sigma Nu entered its second and final year of probation, a return to 92 Professors Row seemed possible. All that was needed was a second fraternity house to appear on campus, somehow, so both Sigma Nu and Sigma Phi Epsilon could have a home.[332]

Unfortunately, as the fall 2013 semester got underway, the prospects for a second fraternity house looked as bleak as they'd ever been. There just wasn't an obvious choice among the buildings that Tufts owned. Indeed, as the semester started, it seemed to many in the chapter that the administration would simply say "sorry, there is nothing we can do." But, to their credit, they did not. Instead, the administration began working with the members and alumni of Sigma Nu to identify a new space, albeit with some strict boundary conditions: the house had to have an existing lodging license (acquiring a new one was too involved, and without one, the number of residents would be severely limited), it had to be in Somerville (Medford had banned all fraternity houses in 1986), and it could not be a themed house such as the International House or Arts Haus, since replacing any group with a fraternity would be highly unpopular and likely cause a huge uproar on campus. As a result, there were but a few choices, mainly among some small co-op dormitories on the edge of campus. But at least there were choices. For weeks and months the discussions went on between the fraternity and multiple administrative departments, as numerous ideas came and went. Then, as the end of the fall semester drew near, a solution appeared. The dormitory house at 90–94 Curtis Street, a duplex on the edge of campus, would be taken out of the housing lottery and set aside for a fraternity, starting in the fall of 2014. This house was no stranger to Greek organizations, having been the home of Delta Tau Delta and Alpha Tau Omega over a century earlier. Now the only question was, which fraternity would occupy this new space, and which would occupy 92 Professors Row?[333]

This was not an easy question to answer, since both fraternities were in good standing, and given the choice, both opted for 92 Professors Row, which was not surprising due to its location. To break the stalemate, the administration convened a council of undergraduate Greek leaders to consider arguments from both fraternities as to why they should be granted their first housing choice. In late January of 2014, representatives of both fraternities addressed the council, where they outlined their reasons for wanting to occupy 92 Professors Row and discussed their plans for how they would utilize the house. Then, they waited. The verdict came down a day later. For Sigma Nu, it was not the news they wanted to hear. They would be moving to 90–94 Curtis Street, while Sigma Phi Epsilon would stay at 92 Professors Row, at least for another year. As could be expected, the decision was heartbreaking for many in the chapter. But, at least, there were some caveats. For one, the Fay House at 92 Professors Row was not the same space Sigma Nu had known it to be. The basement had been closed permanently in the fall of 2012 per order of the Somerville fire marshal, as indeed the basements of all wooden structures on campus had been summarily placed off limits. Without a basement, over half of the common area space of the house was now unavailable. Also, the Fay House had become very expensive to operate, since the occupants were now responsible for the property tax, which topped $18,000 a year. By contrast, 90–94 Curtis Street had more common area space (even without its basement) and its taxes were significantly less. But most interesting of all, Sigma Nu would not be alone in 90–94 Curtis Street. In a surprise move, the administration paired Sigma Nu in the duplex with the newly formed sorority, Kappa Alpha Theta. Sigma Nu would occupy the slightly larger half, 90–92 Curtis Street, while Kappa Alpha Theta would occupy the other half, 94 Curtis Street. Never before had a Tufts fraternity and a sorority been so closely paired in terms of housing. It was certainly an experiment, but as the end of the 2013–14 school year drew to a close, both chapters were excited about their new house.[334]

Sigma Nu and Kappa Alpha Theta moved into the house in the fall of 2014 and began to make it their home. A ribbon cutting ceremony and house warming party early in the semester welcomed the two chapters back to campus, with Tufts President Anthony Monaco presiding over the ceremony. It had been a long two years without a house for Sigma Nu, but with their probation behind them, the future was once again looking up. Until, of course, it all came crashing down. The problem occurred one night in the spring of 2015, when three pledges, after drinking at the chapter house, ended up in the hospital with high levels of intoxication. This event, coupled with the previous incidents of poor behavior, left the administration with little choice. They closed the chapter, effective immediately. One hundred and two years of fraternity was thus over. The only consolation was an agreement whereby Sigma Nu could look to return anew beginning in the fall of 2019. Until then, the legacy of Joseph V. Magee remains on hold.[335]

PHI EPSILON PI (Omicron chapter, 1916 – 1922, 1925 – 1968, 1969 – 1970)
PHI EPSILON PI CLUB (Local society, 1922 – 1925)
ZETA BETA TAU (Omicron chapter, 1987 – present)

When the trustees of Tufts College opened the doors of College Hall in the fall of 1854, they probably assumed the school would always operate against the backdrop of the Universalist church, with the liberal education of future ministers and teachers its primary (though not exclusive) goal. While it did not take long for the curriculum to evolve into the preparing men and then women for all sorts of endeavors, the religious identity of the students did not evolve as quickly; with few exceptions, those attending Tufts throughout the 19th century were primarily Christian. However, as enrollment expanded in the early 1900s, the school began attracting a more diverse set of students, especially from ethnic neighborhoods around Boston. Soon, the "Universalist" college had a small but enthusiastic group of Jewish undergraduates, men mostly, as the women's enrollment was kept much smaller by design. Schools across the country witnessed a similar trend when Jewish men and women began entering college in ever increasing numbers. When these students arrived on many of these campuses, however, they found almost no one discussing Jewish culture or history, either inside or outside of the classroom. Theirs was an intellectual void just waiting to be filled.[336]

Recognizing the cultural vacuum was one thing; doing something about it was another. Here, almost naturally, the students acted, since the faculty was generally not interested in pursuing such work. One of the first schools to witness action was Harvard University. In 1906, a group of Jewish students started the Harvard Menorah Society, where they would gather regularly to discuss scholarly issues surrounding Judaism. The Menorah Society was almost purely academic in its pursuits, as social interaction was not a priority. After all, dances and banquets had little to do with the formal study of religion. Regardless, the Menorah Society was an instant hit at Harvard. Jewish students at other schools, such as the University of Minnesota and the University of Illinois, started similar societies around the same time, but combined these organizations tended to be islands upon themselves, with almost no contact between them. It was only when Harvard graduates in particular moved on to other schools that the

Menorah Society idea spread en masse to new sets of Jewish students. Before long, campuses across the country had active Menorah Societies based on the Harvard model. Still, these groups remained fairly independent, until they began exchanging correspondence. Then, they made it official. In January of 1913, representatives of twelve Menorah groups trekked to the University of Chicago and created a new national organization called the Intercollegiate Menorah Association (IMA). With a common set of ideals and clear focus, the IMA began to spread in earnest over the collegiate world. Indeed, before the end of its first year, its number of active chapters had nearly doubled.[337]

One of the schools to gain a chapter of the IMA during this time was Tufts College. In the fall of 1913, a group of Tufts Jewish students led by Harry Katz attended a meeting of the Harvard Menorah Society. How the Tufts students learned of this group is not known, but the impact of this meeting is. Harry and company immediately realized the benefits of such an organization, so with the help of the Harvard group, they formed the Menorah Society of Tufts College that fall. A few months later they were officially accepted into the IMA at its national convention. From there, they began working to organize discussions at Tufts on topics such as Jewish history, the Bible, and religion in modern times, both for the members of the society and the campus in general. By all accounts, the Menorah Society led an active life on The Hill for many years, even hosting social events on occasion, despite the IMA's aversion to such activities. However, a larger legacy of the Tufts Menorah Society lies in what came next.[338]

Oh, what a tangled web we weave

It all started in late December of 1915 at the 4th annual IMA convention in Philadelphia, Pennsylvania. Representing the Tufts chapter was its founder, Harry Katz, who took his place among numerous other national delegates for the multi-day event. Also in attendance, however, were a number of men with ulterior motives. These were the fraternity men, representing some of the newest national Greek-letter societies that were either non-sectarian or wholly Jewish in nature. With religious discrimination a tenant of fraternity life in the early 20th century, Jewish men in New York City began creating their own social organizations for camaraderie and mutual support, all while maintaining, if not also emphasizing their Judaism. These fraternities proved to be highly popular, and soon were looking to expand to any school with a significant Jewish population. The IMA convention was therefore the perfect venue to network with students and make their pitch. It did not take long for these men to notice Harry and his school. To the national Jewish fraternities at the time, Tufts College represented the perfect opportunity. There was an active fraternity scene on campus (though none were Jewish in extent), there were plenty of options for a chapter house, and there was a steady enrollment of Jewish men each year.

Prestige among the nascent Jewish fraternity movement was of the utmost importance, and there was no better method of securing prestige than by being the first to a particular campus. The race to woo Harry was on.[339]

First to come courting was Sigma Alpha Mu, a Jewish fraternity founded at the College of the City of New York in 1909 that now boasted ten chapters and wanted to enter Massachusetts. Next was Pi Lambda Phi, a fraternity founded at Yale University in 1895 under non-sectarian principles, although its membership was almost exclusively Jewish at the time. Pi Lambda Phi had nearly gone defunct in the early 1900s, but by 1915 was rapidly rebuilding itself into a prominent national organization. Both of these fraternities lobbied Harry as heavily as they could, even promising financial incentives to join, should he find other men at Tufts willing to partake in the endeavor. Harry took this courting to heart, and soon committed himself to starting a new fraternity. Now he just had to choose. But, a third national fraternity, Phi Epsilon Pi, soon entered into the mix, and they had a secret weapon in Herman Kline, one of the most aggressive traveling secretaries in the business. Herman immediately recognized the opportunity and the challenge at hand, so he got right to work. He wanted to beat Sigma Alpha Mu and Pi Lambda Phi to Tufts by any means necessary.[340]

THEIR FRATERNITY WAS GOING TO BE DIFFERENT. In 1904, seven students at the College of the City of New York (CCNY) looked to bridge the social gap on their campus between Gentile and Jew. Society dictated these groups remain separate, but these seven felt otherwise. So, they started a new fraternity at CCNY called Phi Epsilon Pi (PhiEp), one that welcomed men of all religions. They were not the first to try this approach – Pi Lambda Phi had started under similar auspices nearly ten years earlier – but they were determined to be the best. As a sign of this inclusiveness, the shield of PhiEp, which became a very public symbol of the fraternity, contained a star (albeit with only five points) in reference to Judaism, a cross in reference to Christianity, and a crescent in reference to Islam. Despite the noblest of intentions, however, PhiEp's membership soon became dominated by Jewish students. This reality was almost predictable from the start. When it came to joining fraternities, Gentiles had many options while Jews had few, so they naturally filled those organizations open to them. Nonetheless, PhiEp's official non-sectarian policy played to its favor when it started expanding in 1911. Many campuses would not allow a Jewish fraternity, even if the school had a significant number of Jewish students. A non-sectarian fraternity, on the other hand, was a different story. Indeed, Harry Katz, felt Tufts College would be much more receptive to this type of fraternity. Jews may have been welcomed at Tufts, but it appears many felt they should not be so overt in their religion, at least when it came to a fraternity.[341]

A few days after the convention, Harry began working to building a new Tufts fraternity. He selected fifteen men from the Menorah Society, and together they created a new local organization, Delta Phi Delta. While the meaning and significance of these letters (if any) was not recorded, they would only be temporary at best, for affiliation was close at hand. Helping the men of Delta Phi Delta was Herman Kline himself, who came to Tufts in early 1916. However, Herman's travel budget was quite limited, so when he arrived on campus, he moved into 7 Dean Hall with the president of Delta Phi Delta, Benjamin Golden. From this dormitory room, Herman concentrated on the two goals at hand. The first was to convince the men to forget all about Sigma Alpha Mu and Pi Lambda Phi, and instead go PhiEp. This was easy, since he'd already won over Harry with the non-sectarian aspect of his fraternity, and he had an angle to play with the other men. As it turned out, Herman went to high school with two members of Delta Phi Delta and had known a third since childhood. These personal connections, coupled with a lowering of the initiation fee to $15 a man to match Sigma Alpha Mu and Pi Lambda Phi, soon had those in Delta Phi Delta voting for PhiEp.[342]

Then came the more difficult second goal. Herman now had to convince the national leaders of PhiEp that the men of Tufts were, indeed, worthy of a chapter. After all, the national reputation and prestige of PhiEp were on the line, and just because Delta Phi Delta said "yes" did not mean the national leaders would automatically concur. They had to be thoroughly convinced. So, after the decision by Delta Phi Delta, Herman wrote a letter to Jesse Acker, the national secretary of PhiEp, singing the praises of the Tufts group as a whole and singling out specific men who would make an excellent set of charter members. He vouched for their integrity and spelled out their campus involvement, their innate qualities, and, in some cases, their wealth. No stone was left unturned in his justification for wanting them in the PhiEp national organization. And in the end, he won. On January 7, 1916, twelve Delta Phi Delta men pledged themselves to Phi Epsilon Pi, and shortly thereafter, on January 23, 1916, they were initiated as the charter members of the fraternity's Omicron chapter, the thirteenth to be established by the national organization. These men were:[343]

Benjamin Ira Golden (1918)
William Spunt (1917)
Mendel Waters (1918)
Charles George Kramer (1916)
Bertram Emanuel Green (1918)
Henry Leon Katz (1916)
Max Tennis (1916)
David Segal (1917)
Jesse Moses Aronson (1918)
Hyman William Winer (1919)
Louis Adelson (1917)
Harry London (1919)

Right from the start, the men of Omicron chapter looked to make their mark within PhiEp by hosting a formal banquet for the newly established northern division of their fraternity. With the help of Herman, Omicron scheduled a gala event at the Buckminster Hotel in Boston for February 21, 1916, inviting fraters from all over to celebrate PhiEp's march into New England – by this time, PhiEp had established chapters at the University of Maine, Rhode Island State College, and Brown University. For chaperones, the chapter secured Dean Lee and Mrs. Lizzie McCollester of the Crane Theological School at Tufts, Judge Louis and Mrs. Alice Brandeis (the recently confirmed Supreme Court Justice and eventual namesake of Brandeis University), Mr. and Mrs. Filene of department store fame, and Judge and Mrs. Cohen. They also lined up female companions for the men who would be attending the party stag, a common practice at the time. No expense was spared as they attended to details large and small. All was thus set for a grand event, one that would surely mark the beginning of a fruitful existence for Omicron chapter and the northern division of PhiEp. What could possibly go wrong?[344]

As it turns out, quite a lot went wrong, at least once the party was over. Money was the main issue. Omicron spent way too much, nearly $500 instead of the $300 that had been budgeted. Less than a month into its existence, Omicron was in a huge financial hole as it looked to start its operations and, most importantly, secure a chapter house (the chapter was currently operating out of a room at 98 Bromfield Road, where one of its members lived). The root of this overspending, and indeed a continued source of aggravation for the chapter, was the man who wanted them in the first place, Herman Kline. He had actively encouraged the chapter to overspend for the banquet, telling them they had to host a truly extravagant affair, because "[that] was what the National Committee expected." Tempers flared when the chapter later discovered Herman had an ulterior motive for pushing the expense. Apparently, he was hoping to court one of the attendees for a personal business venture, and he needed the banquet to help make a positive impression. Even before the banquet, though, Herman hurt his standing with the men of Omicron when he embarrassed himself and the fraternity during the installation of chapters at the Rhode Island State College and the University of Maine. The members of Omicron were now completely fed up with Herman. So, a few weeks after the banquet, they wrote a letter to the national organization formally asking for his removal as PhiEp's traveling secretary, even calling him a disgrace to the national organization. As one member of Omicron summed up, "Practically everything he [Herman Kline] uttered, even the most trivial ones, were discovered later to be lies." Soon thereafter Herman resigned from his position, and it appears he never again worked for his fraternity. He did, however, make an attempt at restitution by urging the national organization to loan Omicron chapter the $150 they desperately needed to pay the remaining bills from the banquet.[345]

A rough start gets even rougher

When the members of Omicron returned to campus in the fall of 1916, they retired their animosity towards Herman and instead went to work building their chapter. They started by renting their first bona fide chapter house that fall, at 157 College Avenue in Somerville. A few months later, PhiEp gained full recognition at Tufts College when it was accepted into the Interfraternity Council. This recognition was vitally important, since it meant PhiEp was an equal to the other fraternities. On many other campuses, such recognition was not always granted to Jewish and non-sectarian fraternities, but at Tufts College there was apparently little controversy in this regard. In keeping with the non-sectarian principle of PhiEp, Omicron pledged its first Gentile members in its second year of operation, an act that was viewed favorably by the national organization.[346]

As well as Omicron had been performing on campus, its contribution to the national organization was equally as noteworthy, if not more so. Starting in the fall of 1916, members of the chapter began communicating with local fraternities at the Massachusetts Agricultural College (now the University of Massachusetts – Amherst), Boston University, and Dartmouth College so they could advise the national PhiEp officers of their worthiness as potential chapters. This work was considered vital by the national organization, lest they install a chapter not up to the standards of the fraternity. Omicron also developed its own secret initiation ritual since it was not happy with the "loose-jointed affairs" that typically masqueraded as PhiEp initiations. The national officers appreciated such work and hoped to incorporate major portions of Omicron's ritual as the standard for the entire fraternity. Then, in early 1919, two men of Omicron composed a song for their fraternity, "Phi Epsilon Pi for Aye," which was soon adopted by the national organization. In the mean time, the chapter survived the disruption of The Great War, and in the fall of 1920, moved into a brand new chapter house at 19 University Avenue in the Medford Hillside, a house they came to own. With the Roaring 20's ahead of them, Omicron seemed poised for nothing but continued success.[347]

But, there was a story behind the story, and in the eyes of the national organization, Omicron was falling down. For one, the scholastic record of the chapter had dropped considerably by 1920, with too many members recording too many failures. In addition, the chapter seemed to be pledging and initiating men based heavily on their financial means and not their overall worthiness, a practice frowned upon by the national organization. They did not take these two transgressions lightly. They national organization considered the reputation of its members as sacrosanct, with academic failures and unworthy men seen as a blight that could take down the stature of the entire fraternity. Therefore, at the national convention in December 1920, the Grand Council of Phi Epsilon Pi set up a supervisory committee to oversee Omicron chapter and get them back on solid ground. Leading the committee was a local alumnus of the chapter, Irving Mitchell, who would monitor the actions of the chapter and report back to the Grand Council. However, from the beginning the chapter did not welcome this oversight in the least. Although Omicron was told poor grades were an important reason for instituting the committee, the chapter soon realized the main work of the supervisory committee was to decide who was worthy. Indeed, Irving's first report back to the Grand Council made no mention of scholarship, but did offer a harsh critique of the current pledge class. To the dismay of the chapter, Irving's committee recommended that of the eight current pledges, only one was ready for initiation into Phi Epsilon Pi, with another three possibly ready by the end of the school year. The remaining pledges would be held over until next year for further evaluation, which in all likelihood meant they would drop out entirely.[348]

To the members of Omicron, such oversight went far beyond what they were expecting from the supervisory committee. Omicron wanted to initiate all eight pledges that semester, and indeed needed to for financial reasons. With the purchase of a new house, Omicron was desperate to fill the bedrooms and pay the mortgage, so losing over half of their pledge class would create a huge financial problem. But more importantly, Omicron felt they should be able to choose their members, not some out-of-touch alumni committee acting under the auspices of an even more distant national organization. So Omicron responded by having their pledges skip all required meetings with the supervisory committee. Irving and the others soon realized their work was hopeless in the face of such animosity, so they threw up their hands and walked away, at least for the time being.[349]

The members of the supervisory committee eventually returned, but their work was not getting any easier. From the spring of 1921 until the fall of 1922, Omicron chapter continued its problematic cycle of pledging men not approved by the supervisory committee, having the supervisory committee reject them, and then pleading with the Grand Council for permission to initiate them. The Grand Council refused to intervene, saying they could not override the decisions of supervisory committee. So, with each passing semester, Omicron grew more exasperated, if not desperate. The situation came to a head in December of 1922, when the national committee discovered Omicron had put a man through the initiation ceremony even though he'd previously been depledged by the supervisory committee. Such an act went directly against the fraternity's constitution, and a few chapters of PhiEp had recently been expelled for similar transgressions. The Grand Council had spent two years trying to get Omicron chapter back on the right track, but this unauthorized initiation was the last straw. At the national convention in late December 1922, they brought the matter to the delegates, and after some discussion, they revoked Omicron's charter. What had opened with so much promise nearly seven years earlier was now officially closed down.[350]

Let's try this again?

Usually, the revoking of a charter by a national organization results in the closing of the chapter in question. For Omicron, though, the severance of ties with its national organization had the opposite effect. When classes started up again in September of 1923, the chapter consisted of six men, not the strongest of numbers, but they were now free to run their own affairs. And they could not have been happier. These six immediately reformed themselves into a local fraternity and started anew. As for a name, they kept the old letters on the house and continued to call themselves "Phi Epsilon Pi." This was a somewhat curious move, but it seems many felt their separation from the national organization would be temporary at best, so there was no urgent need to change their name. They did, however, institute a new, secret ritual that was different from the one used by the national organization, though they did keep the same secret handshake or "grip," as it was known to be used by at least five other fraternities, so it wasn't considered much of a secret. Most importantly, Phi Epsilon Pi never lost its recognition with Tufts College or the Interfraternity Council. Both entities had been informed in January of 1923 that Omicron's charter had been revoked, but apparently neither cared. So, "Phi Epsilon Pi" continued on as an active and recognized fraternity at Tufts College. As a first step, the six returning members, with the help of local alumni, recruited twelve new men into the fraternity that fall. The rebuilding of the brotherhood was off to a great start.[351]

It was not long after Phi Epsilon Pi resumed activities in the fall of 1923, though, that the national organization learned what was going on at Tufts, and they were not pleased. In November of 1923, Maurice Jacobs, the executive secretary of PhiEp, wrote a second letter to President Cousens, reminding him that the chapter had been closed back in January, but also telling him that the chapter was still using the fraternity's name and was still initiating members. Mr. Jacobs closed his letter by politely asking President Cousens for assistance, saying, "we hope you can see your way clear to help us prevent the use of our name and ritual illegally." A few weeks later, President Cousens met with Max Tennis, an alumnus and charter member of Omicron, to find out what exactly was going on. Max assured President Cousens that all of the recent initiates knew the chapter was currently a local organization with no ties to the national Phi Epsilon Pi. Additionally, Max told President Cousens the fraternity was allowed to use the letters and name "Phi Epsilon Pi of Tufts College" because that was its original, incorporated name before it affiliated with the national organization in 1916. This second piece of information was a blatant lie. Max was a charter member of Omicron and knew full well the original name his chapter was "Delta Phi Delta." After all, he had signed the pledge document as a member of Delta Phi Delta. However, President Cousens knew nothing of the origins of Omicron chapter, so he took all of the information from Max as fact and simply it passed along to Mr. Jacobs, probably figuring that was the end of the story. Mr. Jacobs, of course, knew the truth, so in a final exchange with President Cousens, he told the real story of the chapter's original name, but agreed to drop the matter since the local organization was using its own ritual, and informing the prospective members they were not joining the national Phi Epsilon Pi organization.[352]

Why Max so blatantly lied to President Cousens is an interesting question. In his letter to Mr. Edward Davis of the national organization, Max offers some insight into his reasoning, by writing, "First of all, let me say that the National has been very unfair to Omicron… I really think that it is nothing more than a grudge of one individual, Frater Jacobs, who had enough influence at the last convention to poison the minds of visiting delegates concerning Omicron." Max continued his letter by saying he cared very much for his chapter, and he hoped the charter would be returned soon, possibly at the next convention in December of 1923. But such action was not to be. As 1923 came to a close, Mr. Jacobs responded point-by-point to the allegations and lies of Max, telling him that his behavior had poisoned the feelings of many in the national organization towards Omicron chapter, and he shouldn't hold his breath for a reinstatement of the chapter anytime soon. So, as 1923 became 1924 and then 1925, the chapter remained a local, going by the name "Phi Epsilon Pi Club."[353]

Omicron returns…

For nearly three years, the Phi Epsilon Pi Club continued as a local organization, successfully initiating new members each year despite the lack of national affiliation. By the spring of 1925, the chapter was twenty members strong, with two juniors the last real initiates of Phi Epsilon Pi. The active members, though, never intended to be a local fraternity for such a long time. They, along with the alumni, wanted to restore Omicron chapter within the national organization, and indeed had made some earlier attempts in this regard, but all were unsuccessful. However, with only two official members now left in the fraternity, the Phi Epsilon Pi Club realized the time to rejoin the fold was now. So, on April 7, 1925, they filed a formal petition with the national organization requesting admission back into the fraternity. Their petition included a glowing recommendation from President Cousens, who especially pointed out the group was interested in "the scholarly work of the College." Failures among the members were now much less than they'd been a few years earlier, thereby negating one of the original criticisms of the chapter. The national organization, as it turned out, was "mighty glad" to receive this request, but given the fast approaching end of the school year, they'd be unable to investigate the Tufts group until the following semester, with a possible vote coming at the convention in December, 1925. This was certainly not the best of news, but it was better than an outright denial.[354]

The members of the local group continued to remain optimistic while they waited, and when school resumed in the fall of 1925, they pushed the national leaders of Phi Epsilon Pi to conduct their evaluation as promised. All reports from the local investigating committee were very positive, including a report from some Omicron alumni who vouched for all the men, saying, "We can enumerate every man and can have their moral, mental, and physical standing as men and as active men in the College; which rates them as the finest body on the Hill." Then it came down to a vote by the delegates at the annual Phi Epsilon Pi national convention in December of 1925. The recommendations, coupled with the lapse in time, seemed to heal all wounds. The delegates overwhelmingly voted in favor of granting Omicron a new charter. Phi Epsilon Pi was officially back at Tufts College.[355]

Well, almost. There was still one problem. While the delegates had voted "yes" for Omicron, the Grand Council of Phi Epsilon Pi wasn't so sure. Ultimately they had the final say, and here, it seems they were not too enthusiastic about the Tufts men. So, the Grand Council put an immediate blackball on the entire Tufts group, until they could interview the men for themselves to determine if they were truly PhiEp material. Such oversight was not uncommon for the time, as many fraternities vetted every single man at the national level before initiation. The interviews began in early 1926, and continued throughout that spring semester. Unfortunately, after all the meetings and interactions, the Grand Council felt that only five of the twenty were worthy enough to be PhiEp men. Fifteen other members were thus cast aside, leaving only one sophomore and four juniors to rebuild the chapter from the ground up the following semester.[356]

Onwards and upwards

Although the loss of three-quarters of the chapter must have been demoralizing to those that remained, as well as financially disastrous, the newest members of Omicron, along with alumni support, began rebuilding their fraternity at Tufts while also mending fences with the national organization. Soon Omicron was holding extravagant formals in Boston at the University Club and Cocoanut Grove (presumably within budget), publishing semi-regular alumni newsletters called *The Omicronian* and *Omichronicle*, and placing first or second in the annual scholarship cup amongst the Tufts fraternities. By the 1930s, when Phi Epsilon Pi was looking to expand across the country, Omicron members played an active part in evaluating potential new colonies of the fraternity, especially one at a familiar place, Massachusetts State College. To the national organization, Omicron was now seen as one of its strongest chapters. All of the problems and challenges from the 1920s seemed to have disappeared.[357]

However, within this era of good feeling came a serious problem for Omicron, and that was the chapter house at 19 University Avenue. By the early 1930s, the undergraduates and the alumni realized the house was inadequate for their needs. It was too old, too hard to maintain, too far from campus, too small to support their growing membership, and too much an unsafe firetrap. Omicron wanted out, the sooner the better. So, starting in late 1931, the members of Omicron began a concerted effort to raise money from their alumni for a new house fund. But with the Depression bearing down, the fundraising soon dissipated, as did the hope for a new house. It wasn't until nearly four years later that the idea surfaced again. And here, it was about opportunity. In early February of 1935, a large house came up for sale at the corner of Curtis Street and Upland Road, right across from "The Rez," the small reservoir on the upper campus. To the chapter this house seemed ideal: it was only twelve years old, it was practically on campus, it had cost $25,000 to build but could probably be purchased for less than half that amount, and it would only require very modest repairs and alterations to make it suitable for them. Unfortunately, the anemic results of their fundraising, coupled with low equity in their current house, meant the chapter could not afford the property on their own without some serious financial help. So, with time running out and nowhere else to go, Omicron turned to their national organization and asked for a loan to cover the difference. The request did not go well. The national organization had been burned by too many bad loans in recent years, and with the poor economic climate bearing down, they decided not to sink any more money into risky real estate. Omicron was forced to pass on the new house, and instead make the best of 19 University Avenue.[358]

A year later, the real estate market for large houses was no better, so the chapter took a different approach. Rather than buy, they would build a brand new house from the ground up. They were hardly alone in this idea. The 1930s saw many fraternities at Tufts tear down their aging Victorian structures and rebuild them into the classical Georgian-style buildings that exist today. Such renovation was a sign of prestige, and Omicron certainly felt the pressure to keep up with the times. In the spring of 1936, the chapter began talking with the college about acquiring land on or near campus for a house, and even drew up architectural plans for their new home. Tufts agreed to the idea and also promised a significant loan to help fund the construction, so long as the fraternity contributed its fair share. Once again, though, Omicron's fundraising stalled from the beginning. The alumni just could not support the project, so the plan was soon shelved. There would be no grand house. In the meantime, 19 University Avenue continued to decline physically, to the point where the members considered it "dilapidated, decrepit, and definitely dangerous to the physical safety of its inhabitants… ceilings are cracking, pipes leak, and walls are crumbling." Additionally, rooms were now going empty each year, as fewer and fewer men wanted to live in the house. The situation was fast becoming untenable.[359]

Over the next two years, Omicron continued talking with Tufts about building a new chapter house, and all the while Tufts kept listening. There was even hope the house would be on Professors Row next to the other new fraternity houses, though a lot on Sawyer Avenue was the more likely location. Omicron just needed to raise $15,000, which Tufts would then match dollar-for-dollar in a loan, and construction could begin. After years of solicitation, though, Omicron's housing fund was a mere $2,000, and the expected proceeds from the sale of 19 University would not make up the difference, since the house was heavily mortgaged. So once again, the chapter put forth a passionate plea to their alumni for funds, this time playing the prestige card. As they wrote in their alumni newsletters, PhiEp was losing the credibility race to the other Jewish fraternity on campus, Sigma Omega Psi (S.O.P.), simply because of their house. Ever since S.O.P. was founded in 1921, PhiEp considered itself the more prestigious Jewish fraternity. Their feeling was hardly alone – many within the national Jewish fraternity system considered S.O.P. an afterthought, since it was never able to establish many chapters or have much of a presence within the Jewish community. Over the years PhiEp routinely used this argument to win the "better" pledges away from S.O.P. However, to a Jewish freshman walking onto the Tufts campus in the late 1930s, S.O.P. looked to be the better fraternity, for it clearly had a nicer house at 151 College Avenue. PhiEp's prestige argument was no longer working, and as a result Omicron chapter, for probably the first time in its history, was falling behind S.O.P., a reality they did not relish. Omicron knew that only a new house would reverse the trend.[360]

Finally, in late December of 1938, Omicron caught a break. Another large house close to campus came up for sale, a duplex at 8 Winthrop Street. This house just happened to be right next door to the one they had considered back in 1935, and it was very similar in size as well as architecture. Even better, 8 Winthrop Street was cheaper, as the Depression had continued to pummel the housing market. With the plan to build having stalled, the members of Omicron realized buying 8 Winthrop Street was probably their best (if not only) chance at a new chapter house. Their housing fund at nearly $1300 was almost enough for the down payment, but the chapter would still need a little more, especially to renovate the duplex into a bona fide fraternity house. So, Omicron turned once again to the national organization. This time, they played the prestige card as well, lamenting how nice S.O.P.'s house was, and how they were losing men simply because of this fact. This time, their plea was answered. The national office of Phi Epsilon Pi agreed to loan the chapter $500, and this amount, along with a sizeable mortgage from Chelsea Savings Bank, allowed Omicron to purchase the property and move in during the fall of 1939. The process had taken nearly a decade, but Omicron chapter of Phi Epsilon Pi was finally home.[361]

War comes to Omicron

Throughout the 1930s, members of PhiEp across the country were very cognizant of the machinations in Europe and the tyranny of Adolph Hitler towards the Jewish people. Although officially non-sectarian, PhiEp committed itself to alleviating the suffering of Jewish men and women in Europe. One such program they championed was the relocation of Jewish university students from the continent to the United States, so they could continue their studies and, more importantly, escape the hostility fast enveloping their lives. Started by the national Phi Sigma Delta fraternity around 1934, this effort was referred to as the "German Jewish Student Refugee" program, and a number of national Jewish fraternities participated as hosts. Beginning in 1936, Omicron chapter began actively working to bring a refugee student to Tufts. Under the auspices of the program, Omicron would take this student into their fraternity house as a boarder with all expenses paid, including tuition. The sponsorship money would come from alumni donations, the national PhiEp organization, and Tufts College itself. While Omicron was very enthusiastic about the program, various setbacks delayed the arrival of a refugee for a few years. However, in the fall of 1940, Omicron finally welcomed into their home Jan J. Rosenbach, a nineteen-year old Jewish teenager from Prague who wanted to study chemistry. Jan's father had been the Chief of Police in Prague, but had died unexpectedly in March of 1939, a day after the Nazis entered the city. A year and a half later, he was safely on the Tufts campus, living in PhiEp's new house as just another Tufts student. Jan was well liked by the chapter and seemed to enjoy his time on campus. In hindsight, Omicron's outreach to Jan likely spared his life.[362]

Despite the situation in Europe and their enthusiasm for the refugee program, the members of Omicron in the late 1930s were actually more aligned with the isolationist movement than the growing chorus for war. For example, in the June 1936 issue of the chapter's newsletter *The Omichronicle*, one undergraduate member wrote an article lambasting what he labeled "the INTERNATIONAL MUNITION MAKERS AND WAR PROFITEERS [emphasis in original]." He actively called for alumni, especially the younger ones, to "join some reputable peace organization and stick by it!" A few months later, Omicron hosted the "world famous Socialist, Norman Thomas," for a dinner and talk at the chapter house. Mr. Thomas was one of the most influential mem-

Phi Epsilon Pi members on the steps of their house at 8 Winthrop Street, 1941. Jan Rosenbach, the refugee, is likely in this photograph.

bers of the Socialist party in America, having run for governor of New York in 1924 and president in 1928, 1932, and 1936. He was also an isolationist, and within a few years he would work with Charles Lindberg and the "America First Committee" to keep the United States out of a European war. According to the men present at the talk, "[Mr. Thomas] lived up to his reputation as being the smartest man in the country and he certainly impressed the boys." This diametric set of feelings, one of sympathy for those caught in Hitler's ambitions, while also one of ardent pacifism, was common among many Americans in the late 1930s.[363]

Everything changed on December 7, 1941. Most of those advocating peace and isolationism the day before now had a much different opinion, including many within Omicron chapter. As a result, life in Omicron immediately shifted away from college and towards war. The chapter kept up its operations as best it could, but starting in July of 1943, the call to service took over. That summer, Tufts became a year-round school in support of the Navy's V-12 training program. Soon enough the campus was inundated with naval officers-in-training, all needing a place to live. The Tufts administration commandeered the PhiEp house at 8 Winthrop Street over the summer of 1943, first making it a dormitory for men in the Fletcher School, then later turning it into a dormitory for civilian men. The loss of their chapter house put a serious damper on Omicron's operations, but the men did their best to continue into the fall of 1943, even holding chapter meetings every other week in Braker Lounge. Numerous Navy men joined Omicron during this period, which helped keep the PhiEp tradition alive. However, with men rotating through the V-12 program rather quickly, and with civilians continuing to leave school to join the war effort, the inevitable could not be stopped. By early 1944, it appears, Omicron was no longer active on campus. PhiEp was certainly not alone in this regard, as nearly every other fraternity chapter at Tufts closed around the same time. Omicron had overcome many obstacles in its nearly thirty years of existence, but it could not overcome this war.[364]

Omicron sent numerous men into service, some into battle, and while almost all returned home, one did not. Omicron's lone gold star was Lieutenant Ralph Sumner Kaye, E1937, who joined the Navy five years after his graduation. In May of 1945, Lt. Kaye was a radar operator on the destroyer U.S.S. Drexler (DD–741), part of a floating fleet of radar stations or "pickets" as they were known, circling the island of Okinawa. On the morning of May 28, 1945, Drexler and another destroyer, the U.S.S. Lowry (DD–770), were on patrol, scanning for incoming Japanese aircraft. As for the weather, "it was a clear day with a calm sea, the type that sailors prefer and kamikazes did not." The Japanese armed forces, desperate to gain any advantage in the battle for Okinawa, sent numerous kamikaze pilots that morning to sink as many radar ships as they could. Soon enough some of these pilots found Drexler and Lowry. American forces managed to shoot down nearly all attacking planes in the first wave, although one kamikaze made it through the barrage and crashed into Drexler's side just above the waterline, causing a power outage and a gasoline fire. Despite the damage, Drexler kept in the battle and shot down at least one more airplane during the next wave of attacks. However, at 7:30 a.m., a second kamikaze crashed into Drexler's superstructure. The resulting explosion of fuel and stored ammunition was immediate and catastrophic. Drexler sank in a mere 49 seconds, taking Lt. Ralph Kaye and 157 other sailors down with her. In honor of his sacrifice, the members of PhiEp established the Ralph S. Kaye Memorial prize in 1947, which is awarded annually to the junior or senior who shows an aptitude for mathematics and participates in extracurricular activities.[365]

The post-war dream

The outbreak of peace following the surrender of Japan was a joy felt by nearly all in the armed forces, for it meant they could go home. Paul Slate was one such veteran eagerly waiting his return to normalcy as the late summer of 1945 wore on. For over two years he'd been in the U.S. Army Air Forces, but now he wanted nothing more than to go back to Tufts College and finish his studies. He got his wish in November 1945, when he was discharged and sent back to civilian life. He immediately set out for the Medford campus. Upon arriving, he found Tufts in full swing, with everything back to normal – classes were in session, men were wearing civilian clothes, sports teams were competing, and the fraternities were coming back to life. Well, almost everything was normal. Paul realized that his fraternity, Omicron chapter of Phi Epsilon Pi, was not among those being revived. He soon figured out why. There were no other undergraduate members of Omicron chapter on campus. Paul had been the first to return.[366]

At this point, he could have waited for other members of Omicron to return before attempting a revival, as some would undoubtedly make their way back to Tufts over the next few months. But Paul was not one to wait. He'd been the Superior (president) of Omicron chapter before the war, and now he could not stand to see his fraternity dormant. He also knew his window of time was limited, since he only had one more year left at Tufts. So, he got right to work. He started by talking to the students around him, to see if any were interested in restarting a fraternity. From the mixture of R.O.T.C. candidates, veterans, and civilians on campus, he soon found a number of Jewish men who were interested in reviving Omicron chapter. This was a great start, but then Paul came to a sober realization: did he even have the authority to do all of this? After all, Omicron chapter of Phi Epsilon Pi was not a functioning entity; Omicron was just him, making promises to men he wasn't sure he could keep. So, a short time into his recruitment efforts, he wrote to the national organization to tell them of his work and his concerns. In the heart of the letter, he openly wondered, "whether or not I am authorized to pledge men and initiate them into Omicron Chapter, Phi Epsilon Pi Fraternity, under the supervision of the alumnae [sic]." He also asked for a swift response, for the competition was heating up. PhiEp's old rival, S.O.P., had not only survived the war, they had emerged a much stronger organization, in part because they had been absorbed by a larger Jewish fraternity, Alpha Epsilon Pi (AEPi). With a limited number of Jewish men on campus in the fall of 1945, and with AEPi wanting to grow their chapter as well, Paul knew he needed to act quickly with the group he had gathered. Otherwise, AEPi just might steal them away.[367]

The response from the national organization was swift in coming, and was overwhelmingly positive. "You don't know how pleased we were to get your letter," wrote David Paul, the Executive Secretary of Phi Epsilon Pi. "We have been waiting patiently for some of you Omicronians to get back to Medford and get the ball rolling." Recognizing the urgency of the situation, David then got right to the point. "Since you are an active member of Omicron chapter, you have every right to constitute yourself the 'chapter' for the purpose of reactivating the chapter, and you are hereby authorized to pledge such men as you may seem fit, subject only to the approval of your alumni group." This was wonderful news to Paul, but it also marked a major change in protocol for PhiEp. Gone was the lengthy evaluation process for each prospective pledge by the national organization, a sacrosanct practice in place from the beginnings of the fraternity. Instead, the decision was now up to Paul and the tacit approval of some local alumni. So, with just a few days left in the fall semester, Paul pledged twelve men, helped in part by the rapid delivery of pledge pins from the national organization. These first pledges were initiated as full members in early January of 1946, and shortly thereafter ten additional men were pledged. By the end of that spring semester, Omicron was up to twenty-four active members, including one more veteran who had returned to campus. PhiEp was back.[368]

Of course, there was one glaring hole in Omicron chapter, and that was the lack of a house. Throughout the 1945-46 school year, the fraternity's former house at 8 Winthrop Street continued to serve as a men's dormitory. That all ended in the late spring of 1946, when Paul and the alumni successfully negotiated its return. However, when they opened the front door that summer to survey the scene, they were aghast, for their tenants had not been kind. The house, to put it bluntly, was trashed. The furnishings they'd left behind in 1943 were nowhere to be found, as the bedrooms were now filled with "Navy double-decker bunks, Navy desks, and makeshift chairs." The house needed some serious renovations, but given the enthusiasm of the new members, this problem was easily solved. They took out an additional mortgage on the property, bought their own materials, repaired what they could, and redecorated where needed. They were helped in part by one of the original founders of Omicron chapter, William Spunt (class of 1917), who donated furniture for the living room. In the end their efforts paid big rewards. When classes resumed in the fall of 1946, the PhiEp house was open once again. Twenty-two men moved in, rush week commenced, and soon Omicron had a roster of fifty-four active members, the largest the chapter had ever been. More importantly, Omicron was fast becoming a positive experience for its members. As a visiting representative from the national organization noted a few semesters later, "The leadership of the chapter is excellent, the morale and discipline good, and the general reputation on campus is fine… We have nothing to worry about with [Omicron] chapter."[369]

There's something happening here

And so it went for PhiEp the next twenty years or so. During this time, Omicron chapter was considered a top fraternity on campus and within the national organization. Their only serious challenger to the scholarship title each year was the other Jewish fraternity on campus, AEPi. These two organizations placed great emphasis on academics, much more so than the others. This was nothing new, for Jewish men (and women) in general had worked hard to overcome prejudice and prove they belonged at college, ever since they started attending in number at the turn of the 20th century. One would think that in the aftermath of World War II, though, attitudes of intolerance towards Jewish men and women would have eased greatly, but they did not. Instead, subtle anti-Semitism remained in play on many campuses including Tufts, which apparently continued to limit the number of Jewish men admitted each year through a quota system. However, with PhiEp and AEPi leading in scholarship, no one could argue their members didn't belong on campus. The constant push for success was a theme emphasized over and over by both PhiEp and AEPi, and this mindset only seemed to make them stronger each year.[370]

As it turned out, PhiEp and AEPi also excelled in other areas besides scholarship. In the early 1950s, the students at Tufts were still almost exclusively white, as they had been for the previous century. Even when non-white students did enroll at Tufts, they did not join the "white" fraternities. Societal practice, coupled with membership restrictions in some of the organizations, tended to keep separate men of different races. In the fall of 1950, Omicron chapter became very outspoken on this issue, as they actively and openly supported the efforts of their fraternity's Upsilon chapter at the University of Connecticut to initiate a negro, to quote the parlance of the day. Omicron's support for this situation was hardly in the mainstream, as the push for racial equality within fraternities was barely in its infancy in the 1950s. But during the following school year, both PhiEp and AEPi tried to break down this barrier at Tufts. Each pledged a black candidate that year in what appears to be the first attempt at racial integration within Tufts fraternities. However, it appears neither candidate made it through the pledging process, so they did not become full, initiated members of their respective fraternities. The desire had been there, but in the end desire was not enough.[371]

A year later brought another chance. In the fall of 1952, a black freshman named Brooks Johnson enrolled at Tufts College where he looked to make his mark, especially in athletics. Hailing from Plymouth, Massachusetts, he had not only been an outstanding high school track athlete, he had also been the first black to lead his class in scholarship, and the first black elected senior class president. His arrival at Tufts was no accident. He'd been heavily recruited based on his accomplishments and to increase the scant racial diversity on campus. Still, that fall he was just one of eight black students on a campus of nearly 3,000 undergraduates. True diversity had a ways to go. He moved into a single room in West Hall, and then like all freshmen, began socializing with his neighbors. Soon enough he became close friends with two men down the hall who just happened to be Jewish. So, when fraternity rush season opened a few weeks into the semester, the trio headed off to the Jewish houses, PhiEp and AEPi, and then to a third fraternity, Delta Upsilon (DU). Although DU was not formally associated with any religion, the chapter's membership had been primarily Christian since its founding. Now, rumors on campus said they were welcoming Jews into their brotherhood, so the men decided to take a look. Of these three fraternities, though, it was PhiEp that impressed Brooks the most. The feeling turned out to be mutual. At the end of rush week, PhiEp offered Brooks a bid to join, and not surprisingly, he accepted.[372]

Of course pledging a fraternity does not always guarantee one full membership, especially when the pledge in question (Brooks) is seen as slightly controversial to the national organization. Upsilon chapter may have already broken the color barrier within PhiEp, but this did not mean everyone within the national organization wished to see the practice expand. As a result, at one point that fall, a group of national officers paid a visit to Omicron, and when it came time to sit down to dinner, they sat right next to Brooks. This was hardly a coincidence. The conversation was pleasant enough, but Brooks soon realized he was being interviewed, the only one in the chapter forced to endure such scrutiny. But, he took the questions in stride, and apparently all went well, for in the end the national officers left him and Omicron chapter alone. A few weeks later everything became official when Brooks was initiated as a full member of Phi Epsilon Pi. This marked the first time a previously all-white fraternity at Tufts had been racially integrated, but Brooks' presence was no mere fluke or publicity stunt. Instead, a few other black men also joined Phi Epsilon Pi in the following years, thus making Omicron the only fraternity on campus to have a racially diverse brotherhood in the 1950s.[373]

Then came the 1960s. From the outside, everything in Omicron chapter seemed to be near perfect. Their membership was always one of the largest on campus, the visitation reports from the national organization were always glowing, and their scholarship was consistently near the top. By 1962, Omicron looked to capitalize on their success by enlarging their chapter house, which once again was proving to be too small. All they needed was money, but here there were no issues. The Tufts administration agreed to loan PhiEp $80,000 for this project, the largest amount they had ever invested in a fraternity. The continued success within PhiEp was certainly a factor in their decision, as evidenced by Dean Alvin Schmidt, who wrote in a letter to Tufts President Nils Wessell, "PhiEp is one of the strongest fraternities on campus, and should be able to maintain its strength unless there's a drop off in interest among the student body with regards to fraternities." A year later, the administration even agreed to increase the loan to $90,000, since construction costs were coming in higher than expected. The Tufts administration was betting heavily on the chapter, but this certainly seemed a safe proposition.[374]

Dean Schmidt's words about declining interest in fraternities, though, soon proved prophetic when the Greek system at Tufts began contracting in the mid-1960s. Omicron managed to buck this trend, for the most part, with membership remaining relatively stable and their operations continuing in earnest. However, there was profound change taking place within the chapter, and it was not all good. Priorities within the brotherhood began to change drastically, especially concerning scholarship. Whereas Omicron had been consistently at the top for decades, by the mid 1960s they were at the bottom. The pursuit of good grades had been replaced by the partaking of greater fun. At no time was this more evident than in February of 1966, when PhiEp threw a party for the ages. With rush week in full swing, and with the weather outside a miserable reminder of winter, PhiEp organized a massive indoor beach party. They trucked eight tons of sand into their main party room and filled a 5,000 gallon swimming pool so their guests could swim indoors. Imitation palm trees, coconuts, and fluorescent lights dotted the rooms, and all were attired in bathing suits, including bikinis for the women. The Argonauts and the Loving Spoonfuls pumped out live dance music, probably to the extreme consternation of the neighbors. By 10:00 p.m., the party was in full swing, with everyone having a great time. Then came disaster. A section of the pool broke apart, and soon enough all 5,000 gallons of water rushed through the rooms, turning the sand and the patrons and the decorations into a sludgy mess. But even this could not stop the fun. The band kept playing, the ladies kept dancing, "and the party went on, wilder than ever." Later, after the mess had been cleaned up (and it had been a colossal mess), a reporter from the *Tufts Weekly* asked Omicron's Superior (president) if it had all been worth it. "Hell, yes," he said, "we want to do it again next year. We have no regrets at all."[375]

The undergraduates may not have had any regrets, but soon enough the alumni did. Since 1916, Omicron's alumni had provided consistent oversight of the chapter, which was one reason for their continued success. Now, the alumni as a group washed their hands of the chapter. They wanted nothing to do, anymore, with the party house that Omicron had become. As the 1960s wore on, Tufts students in general began casting aside the old traditions for a new reality, one that rebelled against authority. It was almost natural, then, that the PhiEp undergraduates and alumni would clash on the fraternity's direction. But in PhiEp, this new order came too hard, too fast, and it did more than drive the alumni away. It also tore the soul out of the undergraduate chapter. Within two years after the infamous beach party, those in PhiEp had essentially given up on fraternity life. The ideals of brotherhood and small group living had been usurped by drinking and drug use. The national organization had little choice but to close down Omicron chapter in the spring of 1968. It had been a heartbreaking turn of events, as Omicron had proved so adept at surviving outside challenges throughout fifty-two years of existence. This time, Omicron could not survive itself.[376]

"We stayed out of trouble"

Despite rescinding Omicron's charter, the national organization wasn't ready to give up on their fabled Tufts chapter. Instead, they wanted to start over. Arriving on campus just one semester later, in the fall of 1968, was Henry Greenstone, the national director of Phi Epsilon Pi, and he had one simple goal. He wanted to find a new group of men to revive Omicron and re-occupy the chapter house, as soon as possible. With interest in fraternities beginning to wane significantly at Tufts, this was hardly the optimal time for a revival, but in many ways Mr. Greenstone had no choice. Phi Epsilon Pi was struggling to stay afloat as a national organization. The general student unrest fast enveloping many campuses had hit PhiEp hard, causing membership to shrink and chapters to close down. Reviving Omicron would certainly provide the national organization with a much needed morale boost (along with much needed income). As a first step, Mr. Greenstone held a recruitment dinner on campus one night, and afterwards, over thirty freshmen signed on to the idea of reviving Omicron. Most in this group did not see themselves as traditional fraternity men, and indeed many had been turned off to the idea after giving other organizations an initial look. But, the idea of building a new chapter and set of traditions from the ground up, and living in a house with a dining room and a cook, was more than enough of an incentive to join. The men got right to work, and by the early spring of 1969, the Phi Epsilon Pi club was in operation and ready for the second part of the challenge, getting back the house.[377]

For nearly a year following the chapter's closure, 8 Winthrop Street had simply been vacant. Therefore, it was of little surprise when the new members of PhiEp opened the door for the first time, and found the interior of the house in a near dilapidated state. Not only was the furniture in terrible shape, but the environmental systems, windows, floors, and kitchen appliances were all in disrepair. What once had been the pride of Phi Epsilon Pi was now a complete mess. Fixing all of this was going to cost a lot of money, but luckily the national organization recognized the chapter needed the house, so they loaned the funds to make it happen. Work commenced over the summer of 1969, and the following fall semester thirty men moved in, which was certainly a great way to begin anew. The chapter was young, the membership was enthusiastic, and the leaders were only looking forward, wondering what they could accomplish. And here, they did some things differently. For one, they petitioned the Dean of Students to allow women to dine in their house. This idea was slightly ahead of its time in the fall of 1969 – neither the dormitories nor the dining halls at Tufts were co-ed (though that would change within a couple of years). The petition was ultimately denied, but the effort at least showed the men thought differently about what fraternity life should be. Secondly, they raised money for the March of Dimes by sponsoring a "walk-a-thon" from the Tufts campus to the Massachusetts State House in Beacon Hill. Philanthropy has always been a hallmark of fraternities, but to organize such a large and successful event as a new organization was a testament to the commitment the men had made to their fraternity. Lastly, they decided to do away with traditional pledging, vowing instead to treat new members as equals and not run any type of "hell week" prior to initiation. Such attitudes and efforts helped dispel the chapter's previous reputation as an out-of-control party house. The payoff came later that fall semester when Omicron regained its national charter. Phi Epsilon Pi was officially back at Tufts University.[378]

However, underneath the enthusiasm and success were significant problems for Omicron, starting with their house. Although PhiEp's alumni corporation had originally purchased the property in 1940, by the middle of the 1960s, they had transferred the title to the national organization. The reason for this transfer is unknown, but it may have been related to the $90,000 loan the chapter had taken from Tufts around that time. The national organization then owned the house for a number of years, until one day when they didn't. In the summer of 1969, while the house was being made ready for occupancy, the national organization sold 8 Winthrop Street to Tufts University. Again the exact reason is unknown, but one can surmise this may have been the easiest, if not the only way to pay for the recent renovations. Regardless, Omicron's chapter house was now in the hands of Tufts University, and it seems the administration wanted a fast return on their investment, for they set the rent higher than any other comparably sized house on campus. Complaints back to the administration over the exorbitant rent went nowhere, leaving the new members of PhiEp to take this situation in stride and budget accordingly, which they did. If all went as planned, they would just about break even financially by the end the year.[379]

What the undergraduates did not count on (or presumably know about) was the deteriorating financial situation of their national organization. Simply put, Phi Epsilon Pi Fraternity, Inc. was running out of cash. This was a huge problem for Omicron, because the chapter was using the national organization as their bank. Direct control over Omicron's coffers, which were now fast filling with room and board payments, was in the hands of an organization that desperately needed money. Malfeasance came quickly. Under the original loan agreement from the spring of 1969, Omicron agreed to pay the national organization for items such as the new furniture over a few years, so they could manage their cash flow for more pressing bills. Unbeknownst to the chapter, though, the national organization reneged on this deal in the early spring of 1970 and withdrew the money from Omicron's account to cover these expenses in full. Additionally, the national organization overpaid the property taxes and insurance for 8 Winthrop Street on Omicron's behalf, and when confronted with the error, did nothing to fix the situation. Now it was Omicron's cash that was drying up, leaving the chapter no choice but to cut back. First on the chopping block were the thousands of dollars in pledge and initiate fees required by the national organization each semester. An act of revenge? Perhaps, but at least it meant the men could keep the lights on and pay their cook.[380]

Aside from finances, the spring semester of 1970 also brought additional challenges to the chapter. Actions on the national stage, such as the shooting at Kent State University and the expansion of the draft lottery, and actions specific to Tufts University, such as the campus-wide drug raid and protests over the war, severely dampened the enthusiasm of those in PhiEp as they looked to recruit new members. With so much chaos and turmoil around them, building up a fraternity seemed much less important. Still, they did not give up, but instead managed to recruit six pledges that spring, which was one of the largest pledge classes on campus. They even planned to close the revenue gap the following year by nearly doubling the dues for each member. Being an active of PhiEp was fast becoming a very expensive endeavor. But, future plans were not enough to stop the present. Omicron, despite the belt tightening, ran out of money later that spring. And when they did, they still owed about $4,000 in rent to the university. So, they let those payments lapse, hoping the administration would understand and give them more time to raise the necessary funds over subsequent semesters. Tufts did not. Once the rent payments stopped, the administration cancelled the fraternity's lease for the following school year. In an instant, PhiEp had been thrown to the street.[381]

And so the 1969–70 school year came to a close, with a large cloud of doubt overshadowing all that PhiEp had accomplished that year. Still, there was work to be done, including the election of a new slate of officers. For this choice, the brotherhood coalesced around two different paths. One faction wanted to close Omicron down in a manner that let the men avoid personal liability for the outstanding debts, which was a fear of many. A second faction wanted to keep trying and not give up. When the votes were counted, this second faction had won the day, but just barely. They would continue on as a fraternity the following year, maybe even set up in a wing of a dormitory, while they worked to pay off their debts and regain control of their chapter house. However, over the summer of 1970, the leadership of Omicron realized they could not overcome the present situation. It was time to shut down. The chapter auctioned off the furniture and appliances to take care of the remaining debt, and then all walked away. There was some talk of possibly re-starting again a year later, in the fall of 1971, but in the end this never happened, and the chapter stayed closed. As a result, PhiEp became one of a few long-standing fraternities to disappear from the Tufts campus in the early 1970s. For those that tried to make the revival a success, though, there were no regrets. As one member of Omicron surmised, "Nobody died in the house while we lived there. We stayed out of trouble. The only thing we ever set fire to was the passions of a very small number of women who tolerated our egos. I learned a lot from that experience, perhaps more than I learned in the Tufts classrooms in terms of organization development, leadership, and basic business."[382]

AS IT TURNED OUT, PhiEp wasn't the only entity to close down during the summer of 1970 – their national organization also came to an untimely end as well. During the 1969–70 school year, with membership in decline and revenue not keeping up with expenses, the national leaders of PhiEp realized they could no longer survive as a collegiate organization. The only option aside from ceasing all activity was to repeat what others in the same position had done, and be acquired by another. Indeed, over the years Phi Epsilon Pi had absorbed two smaller national Jewish fraternities on the brink of extinction, Sigma Lambda Pi in 1932, and Kappa Nu in 1961. Now it was time for Phi Epsilon Pi to lay down its shield and join with someone else. The honor of acquiring them went to Zeta Beta Tau (ZBT), the very first Jewish fraternity to be founded in America. And in this choice, there is no loss of irony. PhiEp often viewed ZBT as its fiercest "enemy" as it expanded across the country, the one fraternity it wanted to best more than others, and this rivalry remained in place up until the end. Now, PhiEp had to put that competition squarely in the past for the sake of survival. The acquisition became official in the fall of 1970, with the new fraternity keeping the name Zeta Beta Tau, while the letters and most of the symbols of Phi Epsilon Pi were retired forever. The alumni of Omicron were automatically added to the rolls of ZBT, though one can imagine this recognition held little significance to those who had disengaged from PhiEp in the late 1960s. In the mean time, the arms of history swallowed up all that was left of Phi Epsilon Pi and Omicron chapter at Tufts.[383]

After the acquisition, ZBT as a national organization managed to survive the turmoil of the 1970s, and even began to expand once again before the end of the decade. An attempt was made to bring ZBT to the Tufts campus in 1977, but this effort never got beyond an informational meeting or two. Then, a revival of Greek life at Tufts in the early 1980s passed the organization on by, as numerous fraternities established new chapters on campus, but not ZBT. Part of the reason was undoubtedly a large disconnect between the old Omicron alumni of PhiEp and the new ZBT. The acquisition had not gone smoothly, and no doubt many enthusiastic Omicron alumni were bitter over the way PhiEp had come to an end. Therefore, if ZBT was ever to return to Tufts, it would have to take a different path, because no one affiliated with the fraternity was leading the charge. Any effort would have to be driven by someone on the outside who wanted in.[384]

While the debate goes on, the fraternity does also

Hugh Bassewitz arrived at Tufts University on a late summer day in August of 1986 ready to begin his college experience. One of the first things he did was sit in a folding chair on the president's lawn, amidst a sea of a thousand other freshmen, for the matriculation ceremony. Undoubtedly all that day were wondering how they would perform academically and what they would do outside of the classroom, given the myriad of activities and organizations at their disposal. Unlike many on that first day, though, Hugh knew without a doubt one thing he wanted to do at Tufts: join a fraternity. He'd grown up hearing about his father's fraternity at the University of Wisconsin, and the stories of community and camaraderie left a very positive impression on him over the years. But, academics were the main priority, so Hugh spent his first semester with his nose in a book, bypassing the fall rush season. He did not pass on spring rush. Jumping into the fray, he had many fraternities to choose from, as up to ten were actively recruiting that spring of 1987. But Hugh was not looking for just any organization. Being Jewish, he wanted to join a historically Jewish fraternity, just as his father had done. The only active fraternity meeting this criterion at the time was Alpha Epsilon Pi (AEPi). So, Hugh spent rush week with AEPi, attending parties and meeting the active members, while also working to stand apart from the crowd in the hopes of securing a bid. Overall, though, the experience turned out to be a disappointment. He just didn't make a strong personal connection with many in AEPi. It was no surprise, then, when a bid to join did not arrive on his doorstep at the end of rush week. However, his brief encounter with AEPi left him committed to the general idea of fraternity, so here he made a fateful decision. Rather than look to join one of the others, he'd bring a new one to campus. As for which one to start, the choice was once again obvious. He'd establish his father's fraternity at Tufts, the one he'd heard so much about while growing up, the one with the oldest legacy as Jewish student organization. That fraternity was Zeta Beta Tau.[385]

In many ways, Hugh could not have picked a better time to start. Interest in fraternities at Tufts was booming by the spring of 1987, and while four other organizations had established new chapters over the past seven years, there certainly seemed to be room for one more. But then came the immediate question: how does one start a chapter of a specific fraternity from the ground up? For Hugh, the process began with a cold call. He phoned the national headquarters of ZBT, introduced himself, and said he wanted to start a new chapter at Tufts. The national organization was immediately receptive to the idea, so they put him in touch with a local expansion consultant and sent along a binder full of materials on how to set up a colony – a do-it-yourself kit, if you will. But first and foremost, the national organization told him, you need additional men to sign onto the idea, the more the better. Hugh took in all of this information and then got right to work. He started by walking down the hallway of his dormitory, Hill Hall, and talking with some of his friends about his idea. In essence he became a door-to-door salesman, peddling a product with no present but plenty of future. It worked. Within a short while, and through word of mouth alone, Hugh had found four interested men, and together they grew the group to twelve and then seventeen. Nearly all were freshmen and sophomores, and though each knew very little about fraternities in general, all were eager to start a new one. The hard work and enthusiasm paid off later that spring semester when the seventeen were officially installed as the Beta Tau colony of ZBT, with the chapter from Boston University responsible for the initiation.[386]

They had little time to rest on their laurels, however, for they had a ways to go before becoming a full-fledged chapter of ZBT. One immediate concern was the need to secure official recognition as a Tufts fraternity. Gone were the days when a fraternity could operate sub rosa, underneath the administration and the general campus populace, while the members worked to establish the chapter. No, the group needed Tufts University to say they were a recognized fraternity, for without such an endorsement, the national organization would not let them continue. The path to recognition seemed straightforward, since it only involved some routine paperwork and a few meetings, tasks certainly within the group's ability. Also, four other fraternities had gone through the process within the past few years, and all had sailed through without controversy or delay. Therefore, ZBT had no reason to expect any sort of hiccup. What they didn't know, unfortunately, was that the rules had just changed.[387]

The process by which any campus organization gains official recognition at Tufts University has morphed many times throughout the school's history, but the end result has always been the same. With recognition, an organization can operate openly on campus, use the name of Tufts University within its literature, and generally go about its business without issue. In the spring of 1987, the recognition of a new fraternity required a "yes" from two entities. The first was the administration. Approval here was more of an informal hurdle, for the administration rarely used its veto power. The second was the judicial board of Tufts Community Union (TCU-J), a subset of the student-run government with constitutional authority to grant formal recognition, or not, to those groups which came asking. At least that had been the way it had worked in years prior, until ZBT came along. By the spring of 1987, oversight of the Tufts Greek system was undergoing an enormous and profound overhaul, with the faculty and students actively working to create a system of government to manage all aspects of the organizations, including disciplinary issues, formal rush procedures, behavioral guidelines, and housing. Such peer oversight had been weak and ineffective since the late 1960s when the original governing system fell apart, and from that time forward, those in the Greek system had only proved they needed someone looking over their shoulder. Thus came along the student-led Inter-Greek Council (IGC) to take on this oversight role. In the spring of 1987, though, the IGC was but a paper tiger, as the council had yet to consolidate its authority or gather any substantive power. One aspect of Greek life the IGC was desperately looking to control was the formal recognition process for fraternities and sororities. However, this process was still the domain of the TCU-J and they were not yet fully on board with the IGC's idea, nor were they comfortable ceding their control. Can you say turf war?[388]

Those in ZBT knew nothing of the inner workings of the IGC or their struggle for power. Instead, they just wanted to be recognized as a Tufts fraternity, so approaching the IGC seemed the obvious starting point. In March of

1987, then, just before the group became a colony, Hugh initiated contact with the IGC to ask about formal recognition. The response was quite positive, with the IGC president saying she was in favor of recognizing them as a fraternity, but she just needed to check with the administration. Hugh decided to be proactive here, so he approached Associate Dean of Students Bruce Reitman and asked for his thoughts. Dean Reitman was also very supportive of the group and its efforts to gain recognition, but he just needed to confirm everything with the IGC president. The runaround, it seems, had officially started, until it abruptly stopped. Within a short while, both Dean Reitman and the IGC president got back to Hugh with some bad news. ZBT could not be recognized as a fraternity at Tufts University, at least not for a while. A few days before Hugh's inquiry, an ad-hoc committee of faculty and IGC members put a moratorium in place barring any new fraternities or sororities from starting on campus, until the details of the IGC were sorted out.[389]

Hugh and the rest of the group were incredulous when told of the news. Here they were, an enthusiastic group of men looking to build something new, only to be told they couldn't because the governing system for fraternities was in the middle of an upgrade. Unwilling to give up so easily, they forged ahead, looking for an angle that could get them around the moratorium. Soon enough they learned of Omicron chapter of Phi Epsilon Pi, which was technically now a part of the ZBT national fraternity even though it was defunct. In other words, Hugh and the rest of the group could argue they were not a new organization at Tufts, but rather an old one looking to return. This logic went nowhere with the IGC. Worse still, the administration and the IGC began encouraging them to cease all activities and dissolve as a group. They did not. Instead, they kept searching for a way around the moratorium.[390]

They soon found a solution. As it turned out, Hugh was friendly with some members of the TCU-J, and when they heard about his struggles for recognition, they encouraged him to apply through their board. After all, they had just recognized Alpha Sigma Phi days before the IGC put their moratorium in place, and they were free to recognize others. Additionally, the moratorium had not come from the TCU-J, and many on the board did not appreciate the intrusion into their authority, especially from a group having trouble getting its act together. So, members of the TCU-J informed ZBT they could gain recognition by submitting some paperwork and awaiting a vote. There would likely be no suspense here, as a majority of TCU-J board members were sympathetic to ZBT's cause and had no issue with them operating on campus. To Hugh and the rest of the colony, this was music to their ears. But, with the 1987 spring semester rapidly coming to a close, time ran out before the process could run its course. ZBT would have to wait until the fall. In the mean time, just before school let out, *The Tufts Daily* announced the arrival of the ZBT colony to the Tufts campus. It was a watershed moment for the men, a positive culmination of their first semester in operation, even if the article mentioned that formal recognition was far from certain.[391]

In hindsight, though, perhaps the article was not the best idea. The problem was the words used to end the text. "ZBT is currently preparing an application to present to TCUJ, to begin recognition." Many on campus probably read this line and thought nothing of it. The members of the IGC, on the other hand, read the line and understood it perfectly, for the colony had just tipped their hand. ZBT was going to try a flanking maneuver on the IGC and the moratorium. Now, it was the IGC's turn to become incredulous, and in their fury they hardened their position. They were not going to let ZBT steamroll their way onto campus. Instead, they used the very next issue of *The Tufts Daily* to stake their position in no uncertain terms. The leaders of the IGC, along with their faculty advisors, published a scathing rebuttal, saying that ZBT was neither a colony nor a fraternity, but rather an informal social group that didn't want to play by the rules. "Zeta Beta Tau has not been recognized by the I.G.C. as a fraternity," the authors concluded, "nor has it been established as a colony; and... there is no way to predict when or whether it might be." These words brought an end to the spring semester of 1987, leaving ZBT the inability to respond, at least in a public forum. But, the situation was now clear. The War of Recognition had begun.[392]

ZBT fired the first salvo when they returned in the fall of 1987 and, as promised, applied for recognition through the TCU-J. The IGC, backed by elements of the Dean of Students office and the leadership of Dean Bobbie Knable, countered with informal appeals to the court of public opinion, urging ZBT to wait until the IGC got their act together. *The Tufts Daily* became a de facto partner of the IGC axis, as their regular coverage of the battle featured smiling pictures of administrators (hooray!) alongside dour-looking photos of Hugh (boo...), who was now the president of the colony. In the mean time, ZBT bolstered their ranks by holding their first open recruitment. Of course, since they weren't yet a recognized fraternity, they were not allowed to use certain language on their advertisements, including the word "rush." To overcome this problem, they turned to an ancient but powerful weapon, the thesaurus, and emblazoned their recruitment posters with the words "hurry," "dash," "bolt," "race," and "speed," along with the catch phrase, "whatever you want to call it, we're doing it." The posters caught the IGC off guard and seemed to shatter their front lines. But, backed by their vast resources, the IGC recovered quickly and forced the removal of all ZBT posters from campus. What looked like an IGC victory, though, soon turned hollow, for ZBT gained a significant number of new pledges that fall, even without their posters. Then, towards the end of October 1987, the combatants noticed a faint noise on the horizon that began to grow louder and louder. It was the TCU-J on final approach, ready to drop the mother of all decisions onto the battlefield. And it was the big one. By a tally of 5-2-1, the TCU-J recognized ZBT as an official organization at Tufts University. Boom.[393]

This decision stunned the IGC and the administration, but it did not take them out of the game, for they were prepared. They immediately appealed ZBT's recognition to the Committee on Student Life (CSL), a faculty and student led group that held authority over the TCU-J. Their appeal was very technical in nature, with the crux of their argument being that fraternities were inherently different from other organizations under jurisdiction of the TCU-J (such as the chess club), so not only did the IGC have the power to recognize them, they also had the power to ban them with their moratorium. While the appeal ran its course, ZBT pulled back from its aggressive stance and pushed for all interested parties to work towards an amicable solution. The IGC wanted none of this, opting instead to let the CSL decide ZBT's fate, which they assumed would be the end of the group. The debate within the CSL lasted a couple of weeks as they gathered information and took statements from both sides. Then came the verdict, and in many ways it was a stunner. The CSL firmly and unequivocally upheld the recognition of ZBT, saying the TCU-J had acted properly and within its power. As for a supporting reason, the CSL ruled the moratorium was invalid because the IGC did not have any authority to enact such a rule. It was a near total defeat for the IGC. The only saving grace was that the CSL realized the issue of fraternity recognition needed to be sorted out, so they would help in the process. To start, they put a new and valid moratorium in place banning the establishment of new fraternities and sororities, until a formal recognition process could be worked out by the various governing entities. In the mean time, ZBT was allowed to move on as a recognized organization. ZBT was not yet, however, a part of the IGC, and given the level of anger within the IGC towards the fraternity, would likely not be invited in anytime soon. So, ZBT kept its thesaurus close at hand, for it still could not use the word "rush" or "fraternity" on any of its advertisements.[394]

The CSL's decision, final and absolute, put an end to the War of Recognition. However, left in the afterglow was a new problem, and that was the deep gulf between ZBT and the IGC. These two groups had fought each other bitterly, but now they had to reconcile, for having ZBT operate long term outside of the IGC would not benefit either group. The journey towards peace began a semester later. First, in April 1988, the faculty established a new Committee on Social Fraternities and Sororities (CFS) that took full control of the fraternity recognition process. This was an important step, for there was no longer any question of authority on this matter. Then, in the fall of 1988, the CFS went into action. That semester they finally and officially recognized ZBT as a colony, giving them the same rights as the other fraternities on campus. In other words, ZBT could now retire its thesaurus from active duty. Colony status would be lifted after one year if they passed a probationary test, which essentially meant they just had to stay out of trouble. Helping ZBT through this new recognition process was none other than the IGC. The passage of time, along with a change in leadership, had completely changed the relationship between the two organizations. Now, in the fall of 1988, ZBT was a welcomed addition to the IGC. "There are no hard feelings with the IGC," said the president of ZBT, Greg Davis. "They have been a great help to us." ZBT was also in the good graces of the administration, too, with no grudges to be found among the Dean of Students office. As a result, ZBT could finally be a fraternity. And here, they succeeded. The colony passed probation with flying colors, and a year later, in the fall of 1989, gained a charter as a full-fledged chapter of ZBT. In a nod to PhiEp's long history at Tufts, the chapter was given the "Omicron" designator, even though ZBT also had an Omicron chapter at Syracuse. Present at the celebration of the charter, and expressing her support for the fraternity, was none other than Dean Bobbie Knable.[395]

Homeward bound

ZBT's evolution from a group of friends to a fully chartered fraternity at Tufts took just over two and a half years. It was a long, sometimes painful journey, but in terms of achieving complete normalcy, ZBT still had a ways to go. What the chapter wanted, and knew they needed for long-term survival, was an official chapter house somewhere on campus. Here, though, loomed an even larger problem that dwarfed their struggle for recognition. Simply put, the options for a chapter house on or close to campus in the late 1980s were almost zero. By the time ZBT started, the town of Medford had banned all fraternity houses from within their borders, and the city of Somerville was close to doing the same – both municipalities were not exactly enamored with fraternities, given the plethora of complaints from neighbors the previous two decades concerning noise, excessive partying, poor behavior, trash, and unkempt lawns. Additionally, the Tufts administration didn't have a surplus of properties on campus it could convert into fraternity houses, and there was certainly no space (or money) to build new facilities. Indeed, the lack of suitable fraternity housing was one reason the IGC and their faculty advisors tried to enact their original moratorium. There was just nowhere to house all of these new organizations.[396]

ZBT was acutely aware of the housing shortage when they started their operations, and were happy to take their place at the back of the line for on-campus housing. In the mean time, ZBT did what numerous other chapters had done over the years, and took the housing matter into their own hands. By the fall of 1988, they had set up their operations in a house on Packard Avenue, about a block south of campus. The house was a duplex, with the first and second floors completely separate, but through some creative construction they built a semi-concealable pass through in an upstairs hallway, thus linking the two spaces. The chapter stayed in this house for a number of years and was quite open about its location, even though the IGC, by this time, did not allow fraternities to occupy unauthorized chapter houses. However, ZBT managed to stay out of trouble while operating off campus, so the IGC and the administration were content to leave them alone. In the mean time, ZBT would wait for an official chapter house to come along.[397]

The amazing Dr. Seuss has described it as "a most useless place, The Waiting Place," and ZBT would get to know this place all too well. But, they had no choice. They were at the back of a line that was not moving with any speed. The early 1990s, finally, saw one new fraternity house open on campus, but this went to another organization ahead of ZBT, thus leaving the fraternity in its various off-campus abodes. Still, ZBT managed to move closer to the front when two other unhoused fraternities, Psi Upsilon and Alpha Sigma Phi, closed down in the early 1990s. By 1994, the list of those waiting for a house had been pared down to three: AEPi, ZBT, and a new sorority, Phi Sigma Sigma. That year also featured another housing opportunity when the house at 126 Packard Avenue, right in the heart of campus, became vacant. Although this was a small house capable of boarding only four people, its location was near perfect. However, in a decision that likely stunned both AEPi and ZBT, the IGC assigned this space to the Phi Sigma Sigma sorority, starting in the fall of 1994. This action was driven to help Phi Sigma Sigma establish itself on campus, as the chapter was struggling to recruit members and needed a larger campus presence. ZBT, on the other hand, was doing just fine without an official house.[398]

The spring of 1995 was a breakthrough moment for both AEPi and ZBT. Both had done extremely well operating out of various off campus locales, but Tufts realized the time had come to bring them back on campus. This change of thought was long in coming, made possible by a sincere cooperation between the students and the administration. When the trustees voted to keep the Greek system at Tufts in 1993, they did so with the stipulation that fraternities in particular be more open to accepting new members. By the spring of 1995, the IGC had amended its rush policies to allow for continuous fraternity recruitment all year round, thus giving those interested more of an opportunity to secure a bid. This change was welcomed and endorsed by the trustees, who then made a commitment to house all recognized fraternities and sororities on campus. As a result, a couple of weeks later, the Tufts administration announced that starting in the fall of 1995, both organizations would be living somewhere on campus. No one could say where the two organizations would be housed, but it would be somewhere, possibly a dorm suite. Then, a month later everything changed. Phi Sigma Sigma announced they would dissolve at the end of the semester and thus vacate their house. In return, ZBT would move into 126 Packard Avenue, while AEPi would move into a larger house about a block away. The wait had taken over eight years, but ZBT was finally home.[399]

ZBT moved in the following fall, and since that time they have continued on campus in earnest. The chapter celebrated a century of legacy at Tufts in the spring of 2016. Part of that legacy is being first Tufts fraternity in modern times to abolish pledging. Back in 1989, the national organization eliminated the pledge period to combat hazing within their chapters. Now, men who accept a bid are initiated as full members within a few days. This program was greeted with much skepticism by other national fraternities when first implemented, but more than a few have since followed this trend. Ironically, when social fraternities first started in the 1800s, and for many decades afterwards, there was no such thing as pledging; men were either accepted as full members right away, or not invited in at all. Finally, in one last coincidental twist of fate, ZBT's current chapter house at 126 Packard Avenue used to be the home of Professor Russell Carpenter, whereas PhiEp's former house at 8 Winthrop Street is now known as Carpenter House, in honor of the beloved professor.[400]

TAU EPSILON PHI (Eta chapter, 1917 – 1931, 1958 – 1963)
TAU PHI (Local fraternity, 1956 – 1958)

In the summer of 1893, just a year after their radical decision to admit women, the trustees of Tufts College made another bold move. That summer they voted to acquire and then transform the failing College of Physicians and Surgeons in Boston into the Tufts College Medical School. The marrying of a medical school to a liberal arts institution was a new concept in higher education, but it soon proved popular as colleges and universities across the country began absorbing professional schools. Tufts College pushed this concept even further in 1899 when the trustees acquired the Boston Dental College, turning it into the Tufts College Dental School. As a result, the turn of the 20th century found the once small Universalist institution acting as a multi-faceted university, with all the different programs of study operating under the singular name of Tufts College. Each school had its own set of administrators in charge of their particulars, but they all reported to the same president, they all listed their students in a singular *Catalogue of Tufts College* each year, and they all sent their student's tuition to the same group of trustees. The relationship between the schools didn't end there, as it was not uncommon for students to start their education in the medical school, for example, and then transfer to the liberal arts school, or vice versa. Additionally, the Medford and Boston campuses shared laboratory facilities at times during the early 20th century, when the medical and dental facilities were not as extensive as many would have liked.[401]

From the student's perspective, though, the marriage between the two campuses in Boston and Medford was hardly a close one. The problem was their physical separation. The exacting curricula within the medical and dental schools left little time for these students to make their way regularly to Medford so they could participate in sports teams or other extra-curricular activities. As a result, the students in Boston were left to create a separate campus life for themselves. In this regard they mimicked their fellow undergraduates, for some of the first organizations they established were Greek-letter fraternities and sororities. Most of these organizations, though, were slightly different than their counterparts in Medford, as they were professional by nature, limiting membership only to medical or dental students. They were social groups, without a doubt, and they incorporated many aspects associated with fraternities such as secret rituals and camaraderie, and a few even maintained chapter houses. However, medical and dental fraternities placed an emphasis first and foremost on helping their members develop into skilled doctors or dentists. It wasn't until the mid 1910s that social fraternities first appeared on the Boston campus, ones that welcomed members from all courses of study. These organizations were perfectly positioned to bridge the Tufts divide between Boston and Medford. The first of these to try was Tau Epsilon Phi.[402]

Knock knock, who's there?

By the early 1900s, Columbia University in New York City had been in existence for nearly one hundred fifty years, and had grown to encompass a few professional schools, including the College of Pharmacy. In the fall of 1910, ten men in this college found themselves fast becoming friends, so they looked for a way to bind their friendship beyond their time as students. They were familiar with the idea of fraternity, as the college had two in operation at the time. However, membership in either was closed to these ten simply because they were all Jewish. Exclusion by religion was quite common in many fraternities during this era, a situation accepted by society as normal for the time. But, these men were not willing to let such exclusion prevent them from growing closer. Instead, they decided to start their own fraternity. After some initial meetings on the subject, they gathered in the pharmacy library one Friday afternoon that fall, pledged a solemn oath to one another, and created Tau Epsilon Phi (TEP). A new fraternity had just been born, joining the ranks of dozens now springing up on campuses all over New York City, for much the same reason as TEP. Some of these new fraternities looked beyond the religious discrimination that led to their founding by declaring themselves non-sectarian and open to all religions. Tau Epsilon Phi, on the other hand, did not. Theirs would be a brotherhood solely for Jewish men.[403]

The founders of TEP, it appears, did not have a strong desire to expand their fraternity beyond Columbia. Instead, it was some early initiates of TEP who realized their fraternity's future lay in branching out to other schools. Leading the call for expansion was an enthusiastic member named Monroe Weil. Beginning just two years after TEP's founding, Monroe established two new chapters at schools within a few miles of Columbia University, thus turning TEP into a national organization. Then, in subsequent years, other members transferred to schools across the state and brought their fraternity with them. By 1915, TEP had grown to six chapters in New York, which was a great start for the young fraternity. In a somewhat uncommon move, however, TEP set up chapters not just at undergraduate institutions such as Cornell University and Fordham University, but also at professional schools such as the New York College of Dentistry and Bellevue Medical College. With professional fraternities becoming very popular at medical and dental schools around this time, many of the social organizations bypassed these institutions all together, opting solely to enter undergraduate colleges. Not TEP, and for a very simple reason: enrollment of Jewish men at medical and dental schools was only increasing each year, which made these schools ripe for a Jewish social fraternity.[404]

Still, expansion within TEP was a delicate issue for a number of years, as the fraternity's leaders struggled to formalize the process and institute an effective national government. While they worked to figure all of this out, they instituted a moratorium against the establishment of any new chapters. Caught up in this edict was a group of Jewish men from Boston University (BU), who had learned of TEP and decided they wanted to bring the fraternity to their school. Their letter of inquiry, unfortunately, arrived shortly after TEP put the moratorium in place, so they were told to wait. Finally, towards the end of 1916, the leaders of TEP enacted a national constitution, which solved the problem of fraternal governance and allowed for further expansion. TEP was now ready to conquer the country. And here, the fraternity wasted no time. As 1917 dawned, just a few weeks after the constitution was ratified, Monroe Weil headed back out on the expansion trail. Boston would be his first stop, and for good reason. He was going to visit that group from BU.[405]

Monroe's destination was a house on Newbury Street, where the BU men lived together. As he approached the house, Monroe must certainly have been excited over the prospects of turning TEP into a true national fraternity, since the BU men could potentially become the first chapter outside of New York. When the door opened, however, his excitement quickly turned to disappointment. The BU group consisted of just a handful of interested students, not nearly large enough to form the nucleus of a new chapter, especially one so far away from the rest of the fraternity. All hope was not lost, though, for there was a surprise waiting for Monroe. Also utilizing the house as their headquarters was a group of Jewish men from the Tufts College medical and dental schools, and they, too, wanted to become a part of TEP. Monroe was so impressed with this group that on January 21, 1917, just a few days after arriving in town, he inducted the fourteen Tufts students into TEP as the fraternity's Eta Chapter, the seventh in the national organization and the first established outside of New York State. Unfortunately, a list of the fourteen founding members has not survived, but it appears the first Chancellor (president) of the chapter was Mark Burke, a second year student in the Tufts Dental School.[406]

A tale of two cities

Little is known about the first few years of the chapter, including its fate or that of its members during the Great War. However, it appears the chapter settled into its own by the 1920s. Eta chapter remained closely associated with their brothers of Theta chapter at BU (they had gained their charter a few months after Eta), sometimes even sharing a fraternity house with them. For the most part, though, Eta chapter members were commuters with little need for on-campus housing, so at times they did away completely with a house. The chapter also remained exclusively the domain of the medical and dental schools, at least until the early 1920s, when members finally began recruiting from the Medford campus. This pursuit of undergraduates did not come about due to a formal outreach to the Medford campus. Rather, some in TEP began recruiting hometown friends who were undergraduates at Tufts College. Soon enough, a few men from The Hill took their place alongside the medical and dental students in Eta chapter, thus representing one of the first instances where students from the two campuses participated in an organization together.[407]

This inclusion of students from Boston and Medford could have grown Eta chapter into a force on both campuses, had the men realized their potential. But, they did not. Instead, once TEP began initiating undergraduates from Medford, a sharp divide developed within the chapter over just what TEP should be. The medical and dental students wanted TEP to act more like a medical fraternity and place greater emphasis on professional development, in lieu of social activities. The undergraduates wanted just the opposite; they were more interested in holding house parties and formal dances, similar to what their fraternal peers were doing on the Medford campus. With the majority of Eta chapter being comprised of medical and dental students, the professional arguments won the day. So, TEP remained based in Boston, operating primarily in the interests of the medical students, with an occasional social activity thrown in for good measure. Undergraduates from Medford were still welcomed in Eta chapter, and a few continued to join nearly every year. However, there was still no concerted effort to attract undergraduates in large numbers. The bridge to Tau Epsilon Phi, it seemed, was quite narrow.[408]

As it turned out, the medical and dental students in TEP chose the wrong path, for they were soon going to need the undergraduates to survive. The problem was the fast evolving student landscape of the medical and dental schools. In the early part of the 20th century, admission to either school was much easier than today. Students with limited qualifications, even those just out of high school, were accepted so long as they satisfied some basic academic requirements that were far below the equivalent of a bachelor's degree. Thus, medical and dental students at the time were relatively young, they were generally new to higher education, and they were more open to joining a social fraternity such as TEP. This demographic changed in the latter half of the 1920s, when the American Medical Association (AMA) began requiring more background work for students who wanted to study medicine or dentistry. In an instant, these students got much older, with almost all coming to Tufts having already earned an undergraduate degree. Once on campus, these men gravitated towards the professional fraternities, and with good reason – these organizations could directly help them in their future careers, whereas a social fraternity such as TEP could not, even though Eta chapter tried to act like a medical fraternity. In many cases, too, these medical and dental students had already joined another social fraternity while an undergraduate, so they were ineligible to join TEP. By the early 1900s, dual membership in social fraternities had been prohibited, whereas membership in both a social and a professional fraternity was considered acceptable, so long as one was not active in both organizations at the same time.[409]

Membership in TEP, after a sharp decrease, seemed to stabilize in the 1920s as the AMA-mandated admission requirements became stronger each year. The future, though, was not bright. TEP was the odd fraternity out at the medical and dental schools, and its members knew it was only a matter of time before their pool of prospective candidates dwindled to almost nothing. By the fall of 1927, the situation had become desperate. The chapter had fourteen men on the roster, but all were in the medical school, and nearly all were scheduled to graduate within two years. So, in a bold decision, the members of TEP abandoned Boston as their headquarters, and looked to Medford. Their hope, quite simply, was to transform TEP from a quasi-medical fraternity to an active social organization on the undergraduate campus, while also having some medical and dental students in the brotherhood. This was a risky move, but it appeared to pay off. The chapter recruited fifteen undergraduates that year, and then with these men, set up their operations in a new chapter house at 11 Fairmount Street, in the Medford Hillside. However, they still had one major problem to overcome. TEP was not a recognized fraternity on the Medford campus, so they could not participate in formal rush, nor could they advertise their existence on campus or hold dance parties in the gymnasium (which were very popular social events of the day). The undergraduate members immediately began rectifying this situation that fall of 1927 by petitioning for the student-run Interfraternity Council (IFC) for full campus recognition and council membership. Unfortunately, this petition fell on deaf ears. The IFC concluded that the Medford campus was already well served by the two other Jewish fraternities in existence, and did not need a third. The petition was denied.[410]

Then, the situation turned even worse. In the wake of the IFC's denial, the Tufts administration announced to the campus that, "no new fraternities, Jewish or non-Jewish, would be recognized in the future." As a result, TEP was doomed to dormancy, for they would never be welcome on the Medford campus. The chapter gave up occupancy of 11 Fairmount Street after just one year, and then, following the graduation in 1931 of nearly all the remaining members, was declared dormant by the national organization.[411]

Welcome back

The overcrowding wasn't supposed to happen, especially not since the massive Carmichael Hall had opened as a men's dormitory the year before. And yet, it did. In the fall of 1955, a larger-than-expected freshman class made its way to campus, and their demand for dormitory rooms quickly overwhelmed the supply. Most found a home, but a sizeable number of students ended up in the Tufts housing department, wondering where they would live. The administration's solution was quick but hardly ideal. The unlucky ones were shunted to rooms in small off-campus houses, somewhat removed from the residential quads and their student communities. One freshman in this predicament was Lewis Smoler. He was assigned to a house on Capen Street, about a block away from campus, along with another classmate. Not surprisingly, the two became fast friends as they stumbled through their first semester together. Then, fraternity rush season came calling. Lewis knew very little about fraternities, but his roommate had his mind set on joining Delta Tau Delta (DTD), so he asked Lewis to tag along for support. Why not, he thought. So, Lewis attended a few of DTD's parties, met some of the members, even talked to a few at length, and soon enough thought this might just be the fraternity for him. However, as rush week neared the end, a DTD member took Lewis aside and gave him the bad news. He would not be receiving a bid to join, because DTD could not give him one. To his surprise, he learned that membership in DTD was restricted to white, Christian males. Lewis satisfied the first criterion, but not the second. He was Jewish, and in the eyes of DTD that was non-negotiable, no matter how much he was interested in the fraternity, or how much the fraternity was interested in him.[412]

This reality caught Lewis somewhat off guard, but he soon learned the full extent of the bitter truth. Nearly all of the chapters on campus had similar bans against Jews. All, that is, except for the Jewish fraternities. But after a week of rushing DTD, Lewis had become greatly interested in the idea of fraternity, so when he finally learned the rules, he turned his attention to the two he was eligible to join: Phi Epsilon Pi (PhiEp) and Alpha Epsilon Pi (AEPi). At the time, PhiEp was heavily represented by athletes, and since Lewis was self-admittedly not one, he instead headed straight over to the AEPi house. His timing, unfortunately, was far from perfect. Not only was rush week coming to a close, but the members of AEPi had already picked their pledge class for the semester, thereby rendering the last few rush events somewhat moot. But there was another, subtler problem. Many in AEPi were not too thrilled about Lewis's earlier interest in DTD, for it meant AEPi was his second choice, and no one in AEPi wanted to be second to anything. However, all hope was not lost, for one AEPi member in particular, Leslie Gelb, took Lewis aside at the end of rush week and encouraged him to try again the following semester. Les, with his powerful presence and radiant charisma, could see something positive in Lewis, and he almost convinced Lewis to take this path. Almost, that is, until Lewis came up with another idea.[413]

It was a matter of perception. During his first few weeks at Tufts, Lewis noticed that his freshmen class was filled with a lot of Jewish men, more so than in years past. He also knew that while many of those men had rushed either PhiEp or AEPi, a significant number had been turned away because the two could not absorb them all. PhiEp and AEPi were bursting at the seams of their chapter houses, as there were only so many chairs they could put around their dining tables, or beds they could cram into their rooms. After reflecting on this situation, Lewis sensed an opportunity. He figured the campus could easily support a third Jewish fraternity, especially if the Jewish enrollment remained strong. Of course, arriving at this realization was easy. The hard part was making it happen. So, Lewis took a leap of faith in himself, and decided to start a new fraternity. How he would do this, he wasn't exactly sure, but he resolved to make it work. The first question to answer was which Jewish fraternity he'd bring to Tufts. Rather than just blindly approach some national organizations, though, he decided to research Tufts history to see what had come before. To his delight he came across Eta chapter of TEP, which had gone dormant some twenty-four years earlier. Even better, he soon met an Eta chapter alumnus, Dr. Isadore Cohen, who then put him in touch with Sidney Suntag of the national TEP organization. Mr. Suntag was an avid supporter of his fraternity, and he was delighted when Lewis came calling to reactivate Eta chapter. However, there was a process to follow, so Mr. Suntag issued his marching orders: gather a group of men, form a local fraternity, gain campus recognition, and then petition TEP for the return of Eta's charter.[414]

Lewis got right to work. By February of 1956, he'd found four others who shared his desire to start new fraternity, and together they formed an interest club called Tau Phi. Despite their use of Greek letters, they were not allowed to call themselves a fraternity, for the Tufts Greek system was highly regulated during the mid 1950s, and only recognized organizations could use this official word. So once again, it all came down to recognition, the same struggle TEP faced back in 1927. This time, though, the odds for Tau Phi were much better since the process was more objective than it had been back then. Tau Phi began their quest for recognition by filing an application with the IFC and the faculty in the fall of 1956. As a result, they were able to recruit new members and get their operations going on their own, independent of the rest of the fraternities on campus. In this area they did quite well, as Tau Phi grew from five to twenty-two members by the spring of 1957. Additionally, the members of Tau Phi began participating in campus activities such as the Mayoralty pageant and intramural sports, two areas considered vital for any group that wished to be a Tufts fraternity. All of these efforts paid off towards the end of that spring semester when Tau Phi gained official recognition as a local fraternity. They still had a ways to go to regain their charter, but in terms of recognition, they'd come further than the earlier incarnation of Eta chapter ever had.[415]

Tau Phi had also come further, in many regards, than Lewis had originally envisioned. Most joining Tau Phi were Jewish, as expected, since the fraternity was one of three courting men of that faith. However, unlike in AEPi (and, to a lesser extent, in PhiEp), religion did not become a major emphasis within the chapter. One reason was Tau Phi's planned affiliation. At the national level, TEP was no longer exclusively Jewish. In 1951, TEP modified its constitution so that the fraternity was now non-sectarian, and had stopped referring to itself as a "Jewish fraternity" in any official capacity. The members of Tau Phi embraced this position by openly declaring themselves non-sectarian and actively recruiting men of different faiths, so they could build a multi-faceted religious identity. But more importantly, the chapter became its own unique entity because those joining were not the traditional fraternity-minded, rah-rah types. Instead they were individuals with strong personalities, many having been rejected by PhiEp and AEPi because they didn't fit the prescribed mold. In retrospect this was not much of a surprise. PhiEp and AEPi, with their large houses, established membership, and extensive alumni advisory networks, represented the typical fraternity experience of the day, so they naturally attracted men who wanted the same. Tau Phi, on the other hand, had none of these traits – no house, no organized alumni oversight, no traditions to uphold – so they tended to attract men who wanted to build something new, from the ground up.[416]

After gaining recognition as a local fraternity, Tau Phi looked to establish a normal existence on campus, beginning in the fall of 1957. That semester they moved into some auxiliary rooms in the basement of West Hall, thus giving the chapter an on-campus presence for the first time. Two other local fraternities, Beta Chi and Theta Delta Theta, had previously used these rooms in their first years of existence, so occupying them was almost a right of passage for Tau Phi. Within this space Tau Phi held meetings, hosted social events, and rushed new members. The chapter also worked to further define their local organization while progressing down the path of affiliation. They designed a unique crest for Tau Phi, made some use of a homegrown ritual for initiation ceremonies, and adopted the pledge pin of TEP as their active member pin. Of these three, the fraternity pin was the most important, since it could then be used to "pin" a sweetheart, a tradition quite popular in the 1950s.[417]

The rooms in West Hall served the chapter well that first year, but those in Tau Phi knew their future lay in occupying a true fraternity house. Otherwise, they'd continue to be the only chapter on campus without one, and this situation would surely hinder future recruitment efforts. The solution to this problem involved one of two choices: wait for the Tufts administration to buy and then rent them a suitable house (as they had done for the previous three new fraternities), or buy one for themselves. They chose the latter. During the 1957–58 school year, the members of Tau Phi began courting their older TEP alumni for funds to purchase a chapter house. These alumni in general were not very involved in Tau Phi's operations, but a number did step up financially. Their contributions, along with promises from the TEP national organization, were large enough for a down payment by the spring of 1958. And sure enough, a large house near campus appeared on the market that spring. With real estate around the Tufts campus at a premium, and large houses for sale being a rarity, the members of Tau Phi knew this was a great opportunity, so they placed an offer on the house. However, just as the deal was coming together, another bidder swooped in and bought the house out from under them. Tau Phi had come close, but in the end they'd have to stay in the basement of West Hall.[418]

Despite this setback, the 1957–58 school year was a rousing success for the chapter. They nearly doubled in size, growing to forty members and pledges by the late spring, still slightly smaller than the other fraternities on campus, but a very good size for such a young organization. Tau Phi also threw its support behind Lin Stiles of Alpha Tau Omega in the spring Mayoralty contest, and sure enough he won, thus giving Tau Phi more credence with the other fraternities. As far as grades were concerned, Tau Phi found itself near the top of all fraternities, a position it would hold for a number of years. Then, on May 14, 1958, two years of hard work from all in the fraternity came to fruition. That night, the members of Tau Phi were officially reinstalled as the Eta chapter of Tau Epsilon Phi. Leading the initiation ceremony for the national organization was Sidney Suntag. TEP was back at Tufts after nearly a twenty seven-year dormancy.[419]

Home sweet home?

With charter in hand, the members of TEP returned to campus in the fall of 1958 ready to tackle the last hurdle to normalcy, and that was securing a chapter home on campus. However, in this regard they would never succeed. At issue was their failed attempt to purchase a house the previous semester, but for a different reason than simply losing out to another bidder. No, the problem here was a grave political miscalculation by TEP. When word reached the IFC president of TEP's attempt to buy a house, he became more than irate. No one in TEP, it seems, had consulted him or the IFC on the matter, and this was a huge mistake. The IFC president read TEP the riot act for ignoring his and the IFC's authority to manage the situation. The ways of the past, where new chapters secured housing on their own, may still have been perfectly legal, but it was no longer acceptable to the IFC and the Tufts administration, two entities that demanded conformity to rules. So, as punishment for this transgression, the IFC president decreed that TEP would never be allowed to occupy a chapter house on campus. Overkill, perhaps, but when one's authority is ignored (and one's ego is bruised), the backlash can be quite severe.[420]

TEP, unfortunately, was in no position to fight this mandate. With stronger alumni support, or closer contacts in the higher echelons of the Tufts administration, they probably could have overridden the IFC and secured a chapter house on campus. But, they did not enjoy this level of influence. Instead, TEP was at the mercy of the IFC and an administration not interested in helping them secure housing. This was in stark contrast to the administration's recent efforts over the past few years, when they specifically bought houses for Phi Delta, Beta Chi, and Phi Sigma Kappa so they could set up their operations on campus. What those three fraternities had, though, were strong alumni backing and good friends near the top of the Tufts administration that could get the job done. TEP only had its undergraduates who were in no position to play the game. Therefore, TEP remained confined to their basement rooms in West Hall until they, and they alone, figured a way out.[421]

The members of TEP took this reality to heart right away by taking action. Shortly after the start of the 1958 fall semester, they began using 98 Electric Avenue, where four members lived, as an unofficial chapter house. TEP still held meetings and events in their basement rooms of West Hall, but 98 Electric Avenue became the preferred locale to socialize formally, for a couple of years. In the mean time, the chapter searched for a house to buy, on or close to campus. The hunt was long and often fruitless, as the real estate market for large houses was extremely tight. Then, over the summer of 1960 came a breakthrough. A three-story duplex at 9 Teele Avenue, about a block away from other fraternity houses including Theta Chi and Theta Delta Chi, came up for sale. Being somewhat removed from the center of campus, the location was not ideal, but in many ways the chapter had no choice. They knew they needed an official house to call home, just like every other fraternity on campus, or else they would continue to suffer as the outsider; three years of operating from the basement of West Hall and the outskirts of Electric Avenue had told them as much. Now, with many in the chapter set to graduate over the next two years, TEP needed lots of younger men if it were to survive, and the best way to attract them, the thinking went, was to have a shiny, new house. So, using alumni donations and a sizeable loan from their national organization, TEP purchased the house over that summer and began renovating the interior to fit the needs of their fraternity. All involved in the purchase, including the national organization (which was bankrolling most of the effort), realized this was a big gamble. But, as stated earlier, they really had no choice.[422]

The move certainly started well, for the fall semester of 1960 began with a big splash for TEP. The opening of their new house garnered some positive press just before the fall rush season, and as a result, TEP recruited ten pledges that term, thereby growing their membership by almost 50%. Additionally, the men hired a cook and set up a dining room, a necessity of fraternity houses at the time, since eating meals together allowed the men to build a stronger community. Normalcy, it seemed, had finally come to TEP after five years of hard work. However, as the school year wore on, those in TEP knew all was not well and good with the present. Their house was proving to be everything they'd hoped for, except affordable. Between boarding costs, utilities, social events, the ever important loan repayments to the national organization, and less than full occupancy of the rooms, the chapter struggled to keep its operations in the black. Then, the bottom fell out. With little money left in the bank, the chapter was forced to fire their cook about a month before school ended.[423]

What TEP needed most were men to fill those empty rooms in their house and those empty seats around their dining table. Here, though, they were somewhat hamstrung. Despite the best of intentions, TEP never developed into a truly non-sectarian fraternity as envisioned by the chapter's early members. Instead, TEP's membership remained primarily Jewish, which meant nearly everyone on campus viewed them as a Jewish fraternity, which meant nearly everyone looking to join was Jewish. Therefore, by the early 1960s, TEP had become the third Jewish fraternity at Tufts. However, TEP was not equal to its rivals in enough key areas. In fraternity scholarship, TEP was strong, as they were often near the top along with PhiEp and AEPi. But, their small brotherhood and isolated house made them seem minor league when compared to PhiEp and AEPi. Firing their cook before the end of the school year didn't improve this image. So, with each successive rush period after that first year in 9 Teele Avenue, Jewish men started passing on TEP, opting instead for PhiEp and AEPi. Then, to make matters worse, Jewish men began looking elsewhere.[424]

The issue was a rapidly changing Tufts fraternity system. By the early 1960s, the other nine fraternities on campus, which for decades had been closed to Jewish men, had abolished their practices of religious and racial discrimination, both at the national and local levels. Now, when it came time for rush week, a Jewish man could honestly consider all twelve fraternities, not just three. TEP just could not compete effectively in such an expanded fraternity landscape. Recruitment, as a result, only continued to plummet each year, while expenses, especially the loan repayments, continued to rise. The downward spiral reached its nadir in the fall of 1963. By this time, the chapter had but a handful of active members, not nearly enough to keep their house open. It was over, for all intents and purposes. The national organization sold off the property just after school started that fall to recover their initial investment, thus scattering the remaining members of TEP about campus. Those left behind made a mild effort to keep their operations going by holding meetings and social events, but soon enough reality swallowed even this activity. Eta chapter of Tau Epsilon Phi was declared dormant once again in the late fall of 1963. Although unbeknownst at the time, TEP's closing marked the start of a general decline in the fraternity system at Tufts, as a number of other organizations on campus would soon succumb to dormancy.[425]

In conclusion, it appears that the second incarnation of TEP suffered most from its inability to establish a chapter house on campus that was appropriately sized for its membership. Their political miscalculation with the IFC was also a contributing factor, as was the inability to garner any real support from prominent Eta chapter alumni, or find friends within the Tufts administration. TEP tried to go it alone, which, though noble, was not the right approach for the time. TEP also suffered some from being characterized as a Jewish fraternity, even though it embraced non-sectarianism early on. As the students became more progressive during this era and broke down well-established religious barriers within fraternities, more non-Jewish men should have been attracted to TEP, as well as PhiEp and AEPi. But, this was not the case. Religious progressiveness in the early 1960s, it seems, only went one way.

A modern-day struggle for Tau Epsilon Phi

All together, Eta chapter of TEP was active at Tufts for about twenty years, initiating nearly two hundred men. This is not the strongest of legacies at Tufts, but the fraternity has certainly fared better at the national level. In the years that followed the closing of its Eta chapter, TEP maintained a reasonable presence across the country, particularly in the eastern part of the United States. In 1999, TEP had forty-two active chapters, which was quite respectable on the national level. Eleven years later, however, the situation was completely different. By 2010, the fraternity had only ten active chapters, and a few of these were looking to close in the near future. To make matters worse, the undergraduates and alumni were embroiled in a major dispute with the leadership of the national organization, mainly around financial issues. The situation came to a head in November of 2010, when a group of alumni filed a lawsuit to remove the leadership, accusing them "of operating the fraternity for their personal gain and driving chapters away by making unreasonable financial demands while providing little or no service." A few months later, as the legal proceedings began to play out and it appeared the alumni would prevail, the leadership responded by declaring Chapter 7 bankruptcy, which, if approved, would dissolve the fraternity in its entirety. TEP had just celebrated its 100th year of existence. Now, it looked as if the fraternity would never see one hundred and one.[426]

TEP undergraduates and alumni from across the country immediately fought back. They challenged the legality of the bankruptcy declaration in court, and within a few months were able to dismiss the bankruptcy filing and remove the current slate of the national leaders from their positions. A new leadership was installed, and as their first order of business they re-activated four chapters, thus bringing the active roll up to fourteen. But more importantly, the new leadership brought much needed enthusiasm and commitment to the fraternity on a national level. TEP is currently looking forward to its next hundred years of existence, as it works to re-establish its legacy, especially on campuses that once held an active chapter. Perhaps that effort will again find Tufts.[427]

BETA TAU (Local fraternity, 1919 – 1925)
BETA KAPPA (Theta chapter, 1925 – 1934)
BETA CHI (Local fraternity, 1954 – 1957)
THETA CHI (Epsilon Theta chapter, 1957 – present)

If ever there was a moment when those running Tufts College had no idea what would happen next, it was January of 1919. The previous semester had seen the college transform almost overnight into an Army base as part of the Student Army Training Corps (S.A.T.C.) program, with soldiers, bugle calls, and strict military discipline the new face of campus life. The armistice, however, brought an end to the S.A.T.C. program much sooner than anyone expected, which left the administration little time to reboot Tufts College as an institute of higher learning. Those in charge were also unable to gauge how many students (and their much-needed tuition money) would come back to campus. This was of no small concern. Tufts College was essentially broke by the end of the war, since the government had yet to reimburse the trustees for using the school as a training facility. In the end, though, everything came together without issue. Men, women, and their tuition money descended upon the campus in great number that January, easily exceeding even the most optimistic of enrollment projections. Included in this student deluge were many ex-S.A.T.C. men who'd gotten their first taste of Tufts College while stationed on The Hill. Having liked what they saw, they decided to stay for an education.[428]

For ten of these men in particular, though, the transition from S.A.T.C. to college was not without regret. Just a few weeks earlier, these ten had been the best of friends, suffering through the misery of Army training while living together in an overcrowded dormitory room. Now, their camaraderie had been broken. They may have all enrolled in the engineering school, and they may have all seen each other frequently around campus, but they were no longer together, especially when classes ended for the day. Some now lived in various dormitories, while others commuted from home, since there were not enough rooms on campus for all who wanted one. This separation, they soon decided, would not do. So, they began looking for a way to join back together and cement their friendship for life. They didn't have to look far. All around campus, Greek life was booming, as the Tufts fraternities restarted their operations and reopened their chapter houses to great fanfare. The ideals of brotherhood and small group living espoused by these organizations captivated these ten veterans. But, rather than join an existing chapter en masse, they opted to start their own, which they figured the campus could easily support given the increased enrollment. They spent months building their organization from the ground up by writing a constitution and secret initiation ritual, designing a shield and pledge pin (a simple blue star), and, most importantly, choosing a name. Finally, in December of 1919, the ten were ready to announce publicly their existence. They were Beta Tau, the newest local fraternity at Tufts College. The ten charter members of Beta Tau, all engineering sophomores of the class of 1922, were:[429]

Henry Francis Bertherman
Walter Lewis Fitzgerald
Alfred Thomas Glynn
Frank Titcomb Lewis
Ernest Linwood Littlefield
Jeremiah Edward Mullins
Everett Hayden Otis
Clifford Benjamin Pool
William Albert Roberts
Maurice Burleigh Tasker

Pushing the envelope

Beta Tau wasted little time getting their affairs in order. Within weeks of their unveiling, they opened a chapter house at 13 Fairmount Street, in the Medford Hillside, and it appears nearly all of the members moved in. Then, they instituted a somewhat radical plan for recruitment. To become a pledge of Beta Tau, one only had to apply; a vote of the active membership was not required. This open policy was similar to that of the Tufts Commons Club, but was remarkably different than every other Greek letter organization on campus, all of which required some vote of the current members before a bid to join could be issued. Beta Tau's inclusive policy proved to be very popular. By early 1922, the active membership of Beta Tau had grown to thirty-four men, making them the largest Greek-letter fraternity on campus that year. Only the Tufts Commons Club, at thirty-five members, was larger. The rapid growth in Beta Tau did have a downside, though, and that was in regards to their chapter house. It had become too small, too fast. So, in the late spring of 1922, the fraternity purchased a larger home at 151 College Avenue, a property also known as the Sheridan Estate. As described in the *Boston Globe*, Beta Tau had upgraded their accommodations quite nicely:

> The fraternity, which was founded in December 1919, has grown so fast that its present quarters on Fairmount St., Medford Hillside, have been outgrown. In its new home, the chapter will have one of the most commodious and handsome of the houses on the hill... The building is of frame construction, three stories high, containing 12 rooms, four on each floor. Several of the rooms have open fireplaces. There is a good basement, which it is planned to convert into a pool-room.[430]

Soon after moving into their new house, the members of Beta Tau decided to bestow honorary membership on one dear to them. Many Greek-letter fraternities throughout their history have welcomed honorary members, usually accomplished adults the chapter wished to recognize, for a variety of reasons. Professors and other school administrators were the most common of honorary members, especially if they helped the fraternity first get organized. In the late fall of 1922, though, Beta Tau, honored someone different. Some of the chapter's members, it appears, were veterans of the famed 26th Infantry Division from the Great War, so they offered an honorary membership to their esteemed commander, Major General Clarence R. Edwards. He gladly accepted the invitation, and as part of Beta Tau's third anniversary celebration, was initiated into the fraternity along side a number of undergraduates.[431]

General Edwards was an interesting choice for honorary membership. He began his career at the U.S. Military Academy at West Point, but rather than excel, he graduated dead last in the class of 1883. Despite this handicap, General Edwards became an Army officer and climbed his way up the promotion ladder by serving in numerous posts, especially overseas in the Philippines and Panama. He thrived in these assignments, and the leadership he displayed soon caught the attention of both military and political leaders, including William Taft, the future president of the United States. Such accolades allowed him to reach the rank of brigadier general by the turn of the century. Then, when the United States declared war on Germany in April 1917, General Edwards organized the 26th Infantry Division, nicknamed the "Yankee Division," from various National Guard units based primarily in Massachusetts, which he then transported in its entirety to France. At the time, moving an Army division across the ocean was no easy task, and General Edwards was the first American officer to accomplish such a feat. He was obviously very good with logistics. The real question was, how would he do in war?[432]

The answer came soon enough. After arriving in France, the 26th saw combat in numerous battlefields such as Chemin des Dames, Chateau Thierry, St. Mihiel, and Marne. By all accounts General Edwards was a very good combat soldier, eventually earning honors that included the Croix de Guerre with palm and the Distinguished Service Cross. More importantly, he was such an inspirational presence to the rank-and-file soldiers of the 26th that they often referred to him as "Daddy." Alas, he could not charm everyone, including his boss and overall commander of the American Expeditionary Forces, General John Pershing. The crux of their failed relationship came after the Second Battle of Marne, when General Pershing relieved General Edwards of his command, mainly because Edwards often "criticized his superior officers within hearing distance of his men..." Such behavior is rarely tolerated in the military regardless of accomplishments or political connections. As a result, General Edwards was sent back to Boston some seventeen days before the war ended, under the guise he was needed to train new divisions to fight. This demotion did not go over well with his men or with politicians in New England. There was nothing they could do, though, except honor the general in as many ways possible. Initiation into Beta Tau was one such honor, coming some ten days after his retirement.[433]

From local to national to history

Beta Tau continued on successfully for a few more years as a local fraternity, until its members decided to pursue national affiliation. Why Beta Tau chose to pursue this path is unknown, for they were certainly holding their own as a local organization. Perhaps they were motivated by the actions of other local fraternities at Tufts who were also looking to join a national organization, and didn't want to get left behind. Prestige, after all, was on the line. As national fraternities grew rapidly in the 1920s, they began to overshadow local organizations, making them less attractive to incoming freshmen. Regardless of reason, Beta Tau began their quest for affiliation sometime around early 1925. They had dozens of national organizations from which to choose, including at least one, Delta Sigma Phi, which had looked to start a chapter at Tufts just a few years earlier. But in the end, Beta Tau chose a small and relatively new national fraternity called Beta Kappa. They submitted their petition in early 1925, complete with a glowing recommendation from President John Cousens. "My judgment is that if Beta Kappa establish a local chapter through the absorption of Beta Tau fraternity," he wrote, "congratulations will be in order from all directions." Congratulations came very soon. On May 4, 1925, Beta Tau became the Theta chapter of Beta Kappa fraternity, marking the first time a local Tufts fraternity had successfully affiliated with a national.[434]

BETA KAPPA IS ONE OF THE UNLIKELIEST OF NATIONAL FRATERNITIES. Its chief founder was D. Paul Rader, a man best known for his legacy as an evangelical Christian minister. Around the turn of the 20th century, though, Paul was a college student on an educational odyssey like no other. He began in the fall of 1897 at the University of Denver, in his hometown. Two years later he transferred to the University of Colorado, where he became an accomplished football player and a boxer. Then, a year later, Paul transferred again, this time

Beta Kappa members on the steps of their house at 151 College Avenue, November 18, 1925.

to Central College in Fayette, Missouri, a school affiliated with his faith, the Methodist Episcopal church. While at Central College, Paul not only played football, he also coached the team. The era of professional coaching staffs in collegiate athletics was still a long way off, so skilled players often assumed such dual roles.[435]

It was at Central College where Paul became a fraternity man. Only it had nothing to do with Beta Kappa. In 1900, Paul joined the Beta Lambda chapter of the Sigma Nu fraternity, a national organization that was rapidly expanding across the country. This was somewhat a controversial move on Paul's part, since Central College expressly forbade students from joining Greek-letter fraternities at the time, lest they be expelled. Alas, the bond of brotherhood and the lure of football were not enough to keep Paul in Missouri. After just one year at Central College, he transferred to Hamline University in St. Paul, Minnesota, a school also associated with his Methodist faith. Once again he joined the football team, and once again he did even more – he became the school's athletic director as well. And while his commitments to athletics and schoolwork must have kept him quite engaged within the Hamline community, he seemed to long for his fraternity, for that year he tried to establish a chapter of Sigma Nu on campus. But here, he ran into a problem. Hamline University, at the time, would not allow any national fraternity on its campus, including Sigma Nu.[436]

With Sigma Nu now out of the question, Paul did the next best thing. He gathered a few of his friends on campus and together they started a new local fraternity called Beta Omicron Sigma Kappa (BOSK). Paul chose the name from the Christian group "Bosk" he had joined in high school, an organization based upon the ideals of congeniality, Christianity, and a morally pure life. Once established, BOSK prospered as a local organization at Hamline, even though the fraternity received no support from the administration and often kept their activities under wraps. But ten years later, BOSK was still going strong, and when they incorporated in 1912 after building a chapter house, they shortened their official name to Beta Kappa. The fraternity remained local to Hamline until 1922, when a second chapter was established at the University of Washington. Over the next three years, the fraternity placed chapters at Nebraska Wesleyan, the University of California at Berkeley, Middlebury College, the University of Cincinnati, Bucknell College, Tufts College, the University of Nevada, and the University of Illinois, thus making it a true national fraternity, and one of the fastest growing at the time.[437]

Beta Kappa's existence at Tufts, unfortunately, would not be so vibrant as first suggested by Beta Tau. One problem was their house at 151 College Avenue. Quite simply, the members felt it was too far from campus, even though it was across the street from the Tufts golf course, and two doors down from another fraternity, Sigma Tau Alpha. Additionally, the house was proving a financial burden to the chapter. By 1927, Beta Kappa was pleading with the Tufts administration to rent a home on campus, as the chapter felt that "[by] leasing a college owned building on the Hill, we can eliminate most of the difficulties we are now experiencing." Unfortunately, the best that Tufts could do was put Beta Kappa at the top of a list, should an on-campus house become available in the future. In the mean time, Beta Kappa would stay at 151 College Avenue, where they continued to struggle financially.[438]

One area where the fraternity did not struggle was its commitment to prohibition, or so it seemed. By 1928, the chapter had enacted a policy whereby any member found guilty of transporting alcohol into the chapter house would be expelled from Beta Kappa. Bringing alcohol into fraternity houses and dormitories was already forbidden by the Tufts administration and the U. S. Government via the 18th amendment, so in adopting this policy, it seems that Beta Kappa wanted to add an additional incentive for members to follow the rules. President Cousens, when told of this new policy, praised the men for their position. However, Beta Kappa's policy appears to have been a ruse, an attempt to keep the administration from snooping around the chapter house. Why? Well, Beta Kappa had a secret. Behind a locked closet in their basement was a homemade still, constructed partially with materials "borrowed" from the Tufts

College chemistry department. Beta Kappa was in the moonshine business. The sour mash whiskey distilled in the closet was likely awful (there was no sign of oak barrels for proper aging), but so long as it was consumed inside the chapter house, no one could be expelled for breaking the transportation rule.[439]

Despite such entrepreneurship, Beta Kappa was unable to improve its situation once the Depression came along. Membership declined steadily in the 1930s, further adding to the financial difficulties of the chapter. By the fall of 1934, after only nine years as a chapter of a national fraternity, Beta Kappa had gone dormant. The Depression was starting to take a major toll on Tufts fraternities, and within a few years of Beta Kappa's closing, a few others would close down as well. In the mean time, the chapter sold their house to a private individual, who then rented it to another Tufts fraternity, Sigma Omega Psi. Then, Beta Tau and Beta Kappa began to fade into Tufts history.[440]

Come Together

The closing of Theta chapter may have ended the fraternity's active life at Tufts, but it did not dampen the Beta Kappa spirit in one particular alumnus, Alfred Grant. A graduate of the class of 1923 and one of the first members of Beta Tau, Alfred was one of only four alumni to be initiated into Beta Kappa when Theta chapter was installed. From there, he maintained a close tie to his new fraternity, and by 1941 had risen to the rank of Grand Arkon of Beta Kappa, the overall leader of the national organization. Once in charge, though, he realized Beta Kappa had some serious problems. The Depression, which had forced many chapters to close, left those that remained ever weaker and more isolated. Unlike most other national fraternities, Beta Kappa never employed a traveling secretary to visit the undergraduate members on a regular basis, so every Beta Kappa chapter was an island unto itself. And with each passing semester, the ocean between each was only growing larger.[441]

Alfred soon realized that for Beta Kappa and its twenty-three active chapters to survive, he'd need to improve drastically the oversight and support of the chapters, so all could weather the continued storm surrounding their fraternity. But, he also knew this would be expensive, and Beta Kappa did not have the money. So, Alfred opted for a different, albeit drastic approach. He would combine Beta Kappa with another organization. Mergers of national fraternities were starting to occur with some frequency by the 1940s, especially among smaller organizations in financial straits. Indeed, Beta Kappa had pondered a merger with another national, Theta Kappa Nu, some ten years earlier, but in the end that merger did not go through. Now, Beta Kappa had no choice. Alfred and the rest of Beta Kappa's national officers sat down with a list of all known national fraternities and looked for a proper suitor. Smaller organizations were eliminated, for they were likely in no better of a situation. Very large fraternities were also eliminated, for even if they were interested (which was doubtful), there would likely be too many conflicts with duplicate chapters on the same campus. Telling two fraternity chapters who had been rivals that they were now "the same" can be difficult to manage, especially if the two didn't happen to like each other. Beta Kappa, therefore, wisely decided to minimize any overlap. This narrowed the list of choices considerably. But, Alfred and the rest of Beta Kappa's leadership soon realized that one fraternity and its fifty-five active chapters stood out above the rest. That fraternity was Theta Chi.[442]

Now Alfred had to sell his idea. In the late summer of 1941, he approached Theta Chi essentially out of the blue and proposed his idea for a merger. Much to his joy, Theta Chi was very receptive to the idea. The two organizations started working together on this goal almost immediately, as there were numerous people to convince and even more details to sort out before the merger could become reality. They finished their work at the national committee level by late 1941, and then they unleashed the proposal on the active members of both fraternities. This was the big test, for if the members objected, the merger would be off. So, over the winter of 1941–42, the active chapters of Beta Kappa and Theta Chi reviewed the proposed merger and voted on whether to accept, or not. Much to the delight of all, there was almost no controversy, and the proposal was accepted "with only a few dissenting votes." The merger became official on April 19, 1942. Beta Kappa, as a fraternity, was no more. In its place was a new, larger Theta Chi, which instantly vaulted from the 16th largest fraternity in the country to the 12th largest, in terms of number of chapters.[443]

This turn of events must have been bittersweet for Alfred. He had certainly saved his fellow Beta Kappa actives and alumni from fraternal oblivion, but at a cost of the symbols, traditions, and lore of the fraternity they all knew. Not surprisingly, more than a few alumni did not approve of the merger, so they severed all contact with Theta Chi. Alfred, on the other hand, whole-heartedly embraced his new fraternity; after all, he'd led the charge. So, shortly after the merger, he became a Theta Chi, and then he set a new goal. He would bring his new fraternity to Tufts College and continue the legacy started by those ten S.A.T.C. veterans in 1919. World War II put a damper on any such plans, and in the immediate years after the war, no effort was made to start a new Theta Chi chapter at Tufts. Then came the 1950s, a boom time for fraternities similar to when Alfred was an undergraduate, some thirty years earlier. Sensing the timing was right, he decided to act. All he needed was someone at Tufts to help champion the effort. Luckily, he knew just the right person.[444]

A better reason, a second chance

Professor Robert Nichols was nothing short of a legend on campus. He was a gifted geologist, an inspiring teacher, and a loyal alumnus to his alma mater, Tufts College. He was also a Beta Kappa. Indeed, it was Alfred who had pinned Robert as a pledge many years prior, and since that time, the two had remained friends. So, in early 1954, Alfred began talking to Professor Nichols about bringing their new fraternity, Theta Chi, to campus. Professor Nichols immediately signed on to the idea, and together the two approached the Tufts administration in May of that year, for they could do nothing without the blessing of the school. Soon enough they were in a room with a few high-level administrators and Joel Reynolds, a Tufts alumnus and member of the Delta Tau Delta fraternity, to discuss the matter. Although not associated with Theta Chi, Mr. Reynolds was very active in the national interfraternity circles and had already helped bring the Sigma Nu fraternity to the Tufts campus just a few years earlier. Now, he was here to help do the same for Theta Chi. The meeting went very well, and by the end Alfred and Professor Nichols had gained permission to begin organizing a new fraternity. Twenty years of dormancy was about to end. All they needed now were some undergraduates willing to start something new.[445]

Professor Nichols knew right where to look. Within days of the meeting, he approached his star geology student, a junior named John Reid, and asked him to sign on to the project. John didn't consider himself a fraternity man, and as a commuter with a part-time job needed to support his tuition, he had little time to devote to activities outside of class. However, John felt indebted to Professor Nichols for setting him up with some wonderful summer jobs in the Arctic and Alaska. So, John said "yes." In the mean time, Dean Clifton Emery, who'd been one of the administrators at the initial meeting, approached a freshman, Warren "Biff" Manhard, and asked him if he was interested in starting a new fraternity. Dean Emery had no connection to Theta Chi, but he had shared a law practice with Biff's father some years earlier, and thought Biff would be a good candidate. Biff was quick to say "yes" as well. Then, another geology student, Tom Rockett, joined the group at the behest of Professor Nichols, and when the three came back to campus in the fall of 1954, they began meeting in Barnum Hall to plan their fraternity. Recruitment was their number one concern. They needed more men if they were to be successful, but they had little to offer except the promise of creating something bigger than any one individual. This simple message, as it turned out, resonated quite well. By the end of that fall semester, the original group of three had grown to nearly a dozen men, with geology students well represented in the mix. The Theta Chi interest group was off to a great start. Then, of course, it all derailed.[446]

The problem was one those in the interest group knew about, but weren't yet in a position to solve. It all came down to who could become a member. Theta Chi, like many national Greek-letter organizations at the time, was a fraternity for Caucasian men, and Caucasian men only. All other races were ineligible for membership. In practical terms, this restriction barred only a handful of men at Tufts from joining the fraternity, since nearly all male students were white. Regardless of this reality, though, not a single member of the interest group supported this rule, and together they vowed to fight against this prejudice once they officially joined Theta Chi. The battle, they figured, could only be fought at the national level, and they could only do this if they were part of the fraternity.[447]

However, there were many in the Tufts community strongly opposed to these restrictive membership policies, and they wanted change, immediately. Jumping to the forefront were the Tufts Student Council and the Interfraternity Council, two student-run groups with the power to set campus policy. They weren't going to wait for the Tufts group to join Theta Chi and then champion this cause, because they weren't going to allow Theta Chi on campus at all. In early January of 1955, just as the spring semester got underway, these two groups passed a resolution disallowing any new Greek-letter organizations from starting on campus if they had restrictive membership policies. The two councils had been discussing and debating the situation for months, so this ban was not a rash decision. But, it seems word of this new policy never made it back to the interest group, and this was a problem – national leaders from Theta Chi were due to arrive on campus in just a few weeks to initiate the men into the fraternity. Luckily, though, the situation never reached this point. As part of the installation process, the president of the interest group, John Reid, approached the Tufts administration in mid January of 1955 seeking formal permission for Theta Chi to establish a chapter on campus. John figured his request would be nothing more than a formality. Much to his surprise, the administration told him "no." Theta Chi was no longer welcome on campus.[448]

The interest group appealed this decision throughout most of that spring 1955 semester, but these appeals went nowhere. To Alfred Grant and Professor Nichols, this turn of events was likely disappointing, especially since they just missed having their fraternity installed by a matter of weeks. However, the undergraduates in the interest group were not as bothered by the setback. After all, their inability to join Theta Chi at present time wasn't their problem, it was Theta Chi's. The men still had each other, and they were quite pleased with the organization they were building. So, with Theta Chi now out of the question (at least for the time being), the group immediately reformed itself as a new local fraternity, one that did not discriminate by race or religion, as proven by their constitution. As for a name, they chose Beta Chi, a hybrid combination of Beta Kappa and Theta Chi that also reflected they remained open to national affiliation, should Theta Chi's membership policy change. Beta Chi easily gained official recognition as a fraternity before the end of that tumultuous spring 1955 semester. It had been an unexpected journey, but when the fall semester of 1955 started, Beta Chi was able to take its place alongside the other Greek-letter organizations on campus and look towards the future.[449]

Home sweet home

Having now sorted out its right to be on campus, Beta Chi turned to its next major challenge, and that was securing a chapter house. Meeting in Barnum Hall as well as member's houses had served them well their first year, but they knew they'd need a stronger campus presence if they were going to continue to attract new men. With real estate at a premium, though, there was simply no place available for Beta Chi when they returned in the fall of 1955. The best the administration could offer were some old, mostly windowless rooms in the basement of the West Hall dormitory. This space was hardly ideal, but with no other realistic option, the chapter moved in. Many a lunchtime and late afternoon then passed with the men of Beta Chi congregating in their basement abode, thus helping to grow a strong sense of camaraderie among the fraternity. Also helping the Beta Chi spirit were numerous social events held in conjunction with other fraternities on campus. Alpha Tau Omega, for instance, often invited the entire Beta Chi chapter to its house for Saturday night parties. In a further demonstration of true cooperation, other fraternities also helped Beta Chi organize their first official rush week, and this recruitment drive ended up being highly lucrative for the young group. All told, the 1955–56 school year was a great success for Beta Chi. Living in a basement, as it turned out, wasn't so bad after all.[450]

But Beta Chi didn't want to stay in the basement. They knew they needed a real house, just like every other established fraternity on campus, if they were going to remain competitive in the future. However, in this regard they were not optimistic. They had no strong alumni base that could either raise money to buy them a house, or lobby the administration to rent them one. They only had themselves, and almost everyone in Beta Chi figured that was not enough. Almost all, that is, except for Albert Simone, who refused to accept such defeatism. Instead, he started asking Tufts to buy a house for Beta Chi and then rent it back to the fraternity, until the chapter could buy it outright. He was relentless in his pursuit, even as everyone else in Beta Chi thought he would never succeed. In the end, though, Albert did. Over the summer of 1956, the Tufts administration bought a duplex at 100 Packard Avenue and converted it into a bona fide fraternity house for Beta Chi. The school even loaned the chapter $6,000 for furniture and interior décor, which was no small amount of money back in the day (the average price of a house was about $12,000). Beta Chi used this capital infusion not only for drapes and couches (the colors of which were expertly coordinated by Biff's mother), but also to build the largest industrial kitchen of any fraternity house on campus. Serving meals was an important part of fraternity life at the time, as the dormitory food was not known for its appeal. Indeed, better food was a major reason many men joined a fraternity.

Beta Chi was therefore well prepared for success at its dining table. With much fanfare, about half of Beta Chi's thirty members moved into the house in the fall of 1956. Then, they all called it home.[451]

The final hurdle

Beta Chi was now almost everything Alfred and Professor Nichols had envisioned. It was a recognized fraternity at Tufts, it had a newly renovated house a block away from the heart of campus, and it had an enthusiastic, fast growing membership. All that remained was national affiliation. Still preventing this was Theta Chi's continued adherence to restrictive membership practices. However, in the background, many in Theta Chi at the national level had been working to correct this situation. The fight began in earnest back in 1952, when the Theta Chi chapter at Dartmouth announced they would no longer adhere to the "Caucasian clause" in the fraternity's constitution. Not surprisingly, the chapter was unceremoniously kicked out of Theta Chi just a few months later. But the revolt within Theta Chi had begun, and soon other chapters were pushing for the membership restrictions to be removed. Some of this was pragmatic – many college campuses (including Tufts, eventually) were beginning to require not just the new ones but all fraternities to drop their membership restrictions, or else face expulsion. However, to say pragmatism was the only, or even driving reason would be false. Many undergraduate members of Theta Chi across the country felt the restrictions were outdated and unwarranted, and they wanted them removed. Finally, in the early summer of 1957, after years of pushing for change, the active chapters of Theta Chi voted to remove the membership restrictions from the constitution. It had been a long and tough fight, but discrimination within the fraternity was finally in the past. Now it was time for Theta Chi to open some doors, and they knew right where to start. Shortly after the vote went through, the Executive Director of Theta Chi, George Chapman, personally wrote to Dean Emery to tell him of the good news.[452]

By this point in time, Beta Chi was three years old and quite established as a local fraternity. Indeed, there was even some talk within Beta Chi about remaining as such. But in the end, those in Beta Chi decided to finish the journey and petition Theta Chi for a charter, which was approved. Just as important, the Tufts administration and all governing groups now welcomed the fraternity with open arms. Therefore, on September 21, 1957, Beta Chi became the Epsilon Theta chapter of Theta Chi at Tufts University. Present at the installation was the one who'd started the effort, Alfred Grant. In addition to seeing his fraternity revived, though, he also made the event a family affair. That night he initiated his son, Ron Grant, into the chapter. Also initiated were fifteen Beta Chi alumni, including the three original members, John Reid, Biff Manhard, and Tom Rockett. Taking his place next to these men was one of Beta Tau's original founders, Frank Lewis, along with some Beta Kappa alumni from the 1920s and 1930s. The legacy was moving forward once again.[453]

Speed bumps

In the years that followed affiliation, Theta Chi continued to build upon its foundation. Membership remained high, at nearly sixty members every year, and participation in the Tufts community remained strong. From social events, to intramural athletics and philanthropy, Theta Chi led a normal fraternity existence for decades. The 1970s saw participation in the chapter drop to about two-dozen men, but this was more than enough to weather the decade of apathy that swallowed up a number of other fraternities on campus. Indeed, there have been just a few bumps in the Theta Chi road over the years. The first serious issue came in the spring of 1998. That semester, the chapter was in a precarious position. Membership had fallen well below fifteen men, the minimum required to remain a recognized fraternity on campus. Rush week that semester was therefore their last hope, for if they didn't recruit at least eight pledges, they would likely lose their house, if not their charter. However, the chapter rallied to the cause and recruited almost double the number they needed. The crisis was averted, and Theta Chi could get back to normal life in "The Barn," a long time nickname for their red house.[454]

A second serious issue happened in the fall of 2013, when a frayed electrical cord sparked a fire in a third floor bedroom. The blaze was easily contained and injuries were happily nonexistent, due to a sprinkler system and a rapid response by the Somerville Fire Department. However, the ensuing water damage forced the chapter to vacate The Barn for a while, just before Homecoming weekend that year. In the end, though, all was repaired and Theta Chi returned to normal. And with each passing year, Theta Chi sets a new record as the longest renter of the same fraternity house at Tufts. They may not own The Barn, but they have certainly made it their home.[455]

PHI BETA DELTA (Xi chapter, 1921 – 1930)

Phi Beta Delta, to put it simply, is an enigma when it comes to Tufts College. The chapter came and went without so much as a whisper, and failed to make any real impact on the landscape of the school. Yet, for a handful of men, this was the fraternity they chose to join over all others. Phi Beta Delta came into existence in 1912 at Columbia University in New York City. At its start, Phi Beta Delta was intended as a non-sectarian fraternity for men of all religions, but quickly became a predominantly Jewish fraternity. The organization expanded quite rapidly after its founding, first to campuses across New York City, then to New England, and finally to the Midwest and West, thus making it truly national in extent. Then, in 1921, Phi Beta Delta came to Tufts. How and why this happened remains a mystery, but sometime in the early spring of that year, six men were initiated as the Xi chapter of Phi Beta Delta, the fraternity's sixteenth overall and third in Massachusetts. Those six founders were:

Samuel Morris Gordon (1922)
Solomon Louis Skvirsky (1921)
Jacob Shapiro (1922)
Benjamin Beale (1924)
Daniel George Cohen (1924)
Monroe David Miller (1924)

Although small in number, these men represented almost the entire of Tufts College in terms of their fields of study – Jacob and Solomon were in the medical school, Monroe was enrolled in the one-year pre-dental program, Benjamin and Daniel were engineering students, and Samuel was a liberal arts student. Rarely has so small a group captured so much of the Tufts educational experience. These six were most likely drawn together through hometown ties, as Samuel and Daniel were both from Roxbury, Massachusetts, and Monroe and Solomon were both from Springfield, Massachusetts.[456]

After its founding, though, Phi Beta Delta never implanted itself firmly on either the Boston (medical school) or Medford (undergraduate) campus. The chapter did not participate in the inter-fraternity sports leagues (which were very popular at the time), nor did it ever occupy a fraternity house. Indeed, the chapter never sought official recognition on the Medford campus, so it was not allowed to participate in formal rush activities. Aside from the composite in 1921, the chapter never included any information in either the undergraduate or medical school yearbooks. But, this does not mean they did nothing. Members of Xi chapter often engaged with their Phi Beta Delta counterparts at the Massachusetts Institute of Technology, which was home to the fraternity's Theta chapter. Also, graduates of Xi chapter were quite active in the fraternity's Boston-based alumni organization. Xi chapter did have one notable alumnus in Dr. Max Tishler from the class of 1928. After receiving his undergraduate degree in chemistry, Dr. Tishler earned a Ph.D. at Harvard University and eventually became a noted research scientist at Merck & Co. It was at Merck where he perfected a number of processes for the mass production of riboflavin and cortisone, two compounds that helped ease the suffering of countless patients. From there, Dr. Tishler led a research group that developed a host of life-altering medicines, including vaccines, streptomycin, and penicillin.[457]

Alas, the world was not long for Phi Beta Delta at Tufts. In 1930, Xi chapter was declared dormant by the national organization, having only initiated about thirty men during its nine-year run. The national organization did not much last longer. In 1941, the entire of Phi Beta Delta was absorbed by Pi Lambda Phi, another fraternity that was founded on non-sectarian principals, yet had evolved into a predominantly Jewish organization. All former Phi Beta Delta initiates became de-facto members of Pi Lambda Phi, while nearly all of the symbols and rituals of Phi Beta Delta were retired, forever. Even though the Tufts chapter was inactive at the time, it was given the designator "Massachusetts Xi" in the Pi Lambda Phi roll of chapters. To date, though, Pi Lambda Phi has never had an active chapter on the Tufts campus.[458]

In all likelihood, Phi Beta Delta was probably one too many Jewish social fraternities for Tufts at the time. With a quota limiting the total number of Jewish undergraduate men, Tufts could not adequately support the four Jewish fraternities trying to establish themselves on the Medford campus in the 1920s. Likewise, on the Boston campus, Phi Beta Delta likely ran into the same problem as Tau Epsilon Phi, in that the older medical and dental students were choosing to join the professional fraternities rather than the social ones. Phi Beta Delta, being small in membership and having no real presence on either campus, was an obvious candidate to fade away.[459]

SIGMA OMEGA PSI (Mu chapter, 1921 – 1941)
ALPHA EPSILON PI (Eta Deuteron chapter, 1941 – 1970, 1976 – 1982, 1983 – 2015)
NICHOLS HOUSE (Local co-ed fraternity, 1976 – 1982)
PI DELTA (Local fraternity, 2015 – 2017)

When it comes to the birth of the Jewish fraternity movement in the early 20th century, the College of the City of New York (CCNY) has a strong case for being the epicenter. Between 1904 and 1910, three national Jewish fraternities started on its campus, and over the next decade, these three all rose to prominence within the Jewish community as they expanded across the country. Then, in 1914, CCNY saw the birth of its fourth national Jewish fraternity, Sigma Omega Psi (SOP), an organization intended exclusively for "any male student of Jewish parentage." SOP, though, was not as ambitious as the others. The fraternity became a national organization quickly enough, as it soon counted six chapters on its roll. All but one of these chapters, however, was confined to New York City, with the sole outlier at Syracuse University in upstate New York. To be considered truly prominent, a fraternity needed to stretch across the country; SOP, by contrast, stretched just a few dozen blocks. As a result, SOP was viewed as a second tier organization to almost all in the Jewish fraternity world.[460]

The founders and early members of SOP seemed to care little for how others saw them. Instead, they were only interested in building their fraternity into a viable organization, and this they did with enthusiasm and success. The eastern half of Massachusetts became fertile ground once the fraternity expanded outside of New York. First, SOP established its Theta chapter at the Worcester

Polytechnic Institute in the spring of 1919, and shortly thereafter, opened Eta chapter at the Lowell Textile Institute and Iota chapter at Boston University. Then, SOP crossed paths with another school near Boston, Tufts College.[461]

Talk about a mistake

In all likelihood, circumstance brought the twelve men together in the fall of 1920. Nearly all were engineering students, commuting to campus each day from nearby towns such as Boston, Revere, and Canton, Massachusetts. As commuters on a residential campus, they were naturally drawn to each other and soon became a group of friends. But, they had more in common. All twelve were Jewish, on a campus that was mostly not. As the school year progressed, the men looked for a way to "make permanent those ties of friendship," and "foster their literary, social, and athletic abilities." What they wanted, they soon realized, was to be a fraternity. At the time, there was one Tufts fraternity open to Jewish men, Phi Epsilon Pi (PhiEp), but this chapter was known for turning away many a good man for lack of a perfect pedigree, if not money. So, these twelve decided to bring a second Jewish fraternity to campus. They certainly had plenty of national organizations to choose from – by 1920, about a dozen Jewish fraternities were actively expanding across New England, and many would have jumped at the chance to enter Tufts College. For reasons unknown, however, these twelve men petitioned SOP, one of the smallest on the national scene. Their petition for a charter was accepted, and on May 19, 1921, the twelve were installed as the fraternity's Mu chapter, the twelfth in the national organization and fifth in Massachusetts. The twelve founders were:[462]

Morris Max Danovitch (1924)	Harry Rodman (1924)
Samuel Freeman (1923)	Nathan Schatz (1922)
Philip Hamburg (1924)	Nathan Sheer (1923)
Harold Horvitz (1922)	Myer Stone
Harry Perlmutter	Myer Tempkin (1923)
Abraham Ponack (1922)	Hymen White (1924)

SOP got off to a strong start when school resumed in the fall of 1921. Recognition by the Tufts Interfraternity Council was fast in coming, which was vitally important since it allowed SOP to operate openly on campus. The men held monthly meetings, usually at Quincy House in Boston, and as the school year progressed, the chapter recruited four new members. Meeting in Boston no doubt allowed the men to interact with their brothers at Boston University (Iota chapter) and Northeastern University (Kappa chapter), and the mutual support afforded to all three must have helped them develop their spirit for

SOP. Ultimately, however, those in Mu chapter wanted an experience similar to the other fraternities at Tufts, and that meant living together in a chapter house on campus. As luck would have it, in the spring of 1922, the Beta Tau fraternity moved out of their chapter house at 13 Fairmount Street, thereby opening up the real estate market. It took Mu chapter a few months to get their finances in order, but with the help of their faculty advisor, Professor Leo Lewis, they made an offer to buy the property in the early fall of 1922. After just two short years on campus, SOP was steps away from owning their first chapter house.[463]

Unfortunately, those steps proved to be too big. As the purchase progressed towards a closing, Professor Lewis requested a face-to-face meeting with President John Cousens to make sure he approved of the transaction. Then, he politely awaited a reply. None came. So, he made a second meeting request, but still no response. In hindsight, Professor Lewis should probably have left well enough alone, and let SOP move forward with the purchase. But, he didn't. Instead, he wrote a formal letter to President Cousens, telling him of the chapter's plans and asking for his opinion on the matter. Now President Cousens was forced to intervene, since a formal letter from a prominent faculty member required a reply. His response, which reached Professor Lewis the very next day, was hardly what SOP had hoped for. Simply put, President Cousens thought the house purchase was a very bad idea. As for reasons, he gave none in his letter, but he did ask the current president of the chapter, Bernard Horowitz, to meet with him as soon as possible for further discussion on the matter.[464]

When a student is summoned by the president of his college, one would assume said student would heed the call immediately. Bernard did not. Instead, he ignored the summons completely. A week later, apparently miffed that no response had come, President Cousens sent a second letter to Bernard, only this one was much more direct. "Please arrange to see me Monday [Oct 11] morning between recitations," President Cousens wrote, in a tone that was decidedly angrier than his first letter. Although the details of this meeting were kept private, the aftermath was unmistakable. SOP would not be moving into 13 Fairmount Street any time soon. The sale was off. All housing hope was not lost, however, as SOP had another option. The Tufts Commons Club had recently vacated their off-campus house at 890 Broadway Avenue in Somerville, and that property was now up for rent. Being much further from campus than 13 Fairmount Street certainly made this house much less attractive, but SOP had no other alternative. So, they moved in during the 1922–23 school year, and did the best they could to make it their home.[465]

Goodbye, Hello?

Operating from 890 Broadway Avenue worked well for the chapter, though it seems they were always striving for a house closer to campus. They got their first chance four years later when they moved to 15 Bellevue Street in the Medford Hillside, just a block away from the house they had tried to purchase on Fairmount Street. Then, in 1929, the chapter moved again, this time to 100 Packard Avenue, right near the heart of campus. Amidst all of this moving, the chapter managed successfully to recruit new members, hold social functions, run a boarding plan, and most importantly, grow a true fraternal spirit. In other words, life within SOP was quite normal during this time. Then came the Great Depression. Like most fraternities on campus, SOP saw its membership contract in the early 1930s, but unlike some of the others, SOP's contraction proved almost fatal. Fewer members led to financial pressures that eventually overwhelmed the chapter. By January 1935, SOP had no choice but to close down their chapter house at 100 Packard Avenue for lack of money. Somehow they managed to retain their pledge class that semester, though rumor had it they were "putting men through [the initiation ceremony] for practically nothing." Those in the chapter hoped to start fresh in the fall of 1935, perhaps even occupy a house again, but everything was stacked against them. There was also serious talk of SOP being de-recognized by the Interfraternity Council and being de-listed from next year's editions of *The Ivy Book* and the student catalogue, actions which likely would have doomed the chapter. SOP was about to disappear off the face of Tufts College without so much as a goodbye.[466]

The national organization, unfortunately, was in no position to help, for they were floundering as well. When Mu chapter lost their house, SOP at the national level only consisted of five or six active chapters (no one seemed completely sure), a far cry from the twenty-six active chapters just a few years earlier. Of those that remained, Mu chapter was considered the strongest, which tells you all you need to know about the state of the national organization. Watching the fall of SOP from the sidelines were the members of Omicron chapter of Phi Epsilon Pi (PhiEp) at Tufts. And they were having a hard time containing their glee. PhiEp had long considered SOP a nuisance at Tufts College, mainly because they felt the school did not have enough Jewish men to support both fraternities. Now they welcomed a reduction in the fraternal playing field, lest they lose even one good man to SOP any longer. As Maurice Jacobs, the executive secretary of PhiEp, wrote to the Tufts chapter, "I am glad to hear, in one sense of the word, of the trouble the S.O.P. fraternity is having, and I sincerely hope they may be eliminated as a competitor [at Tufts] before long."[467]

What PhiEp did not realize, though, was that SOP had absolutely no intention of quitting. Instead, SOP used the rest of the spring and summer of 1935 to get their affairs in order, and then they pulled off the unexpected. When the fall 1935 semester got underway, SOP was not only back in full operation, they were also once again occupying a fraternity house, this time at 151 College Avenue. Formerly the home of the Beta Kappa fraternity, 151 College Avenue became vacant when that chapter folded in 1934, and the new owner of the property was apparently eager to rent it out as a fraternity house. SOP was happy to oblige. Though somewhat off campus, 151 College Avenue was larger than SOP's former house, and it had a nice view overlooking the school's football field and surrounding golf course. The house was also much statelier and impressive than PhiEp's aging structure (much to PhiEp's chagrin), and indeed it helped SOP gain a significant number of new members that semester. Rather than disappear, SOP had made a bold statement. They were not going anywhere, but up.[468]

PhiEp did not take kindly to this turn of events, especially when they realized the truth behind SOP's rapid turnaround. With the Depression in full swing, and money an issue for most who wanted to join a fraternity, SOP came up with a plan that was downright deceitful, but effective. SOP offered to initiate new members for no fee, but then assess them "taxes" once they were official members, to cover the expense. The chapter also apparently offered paid positions to prospective members, such as cook or housekeeper, which then miraculously disappeared once the member was initiated. PhiEp was aghast at such behavior, calling SOP a "third-rate club," among other things. But, PhiEp's complaints fell on deaf ears, as no one else on campus seemed to care. Instead, SOP continued to move along.[469]

One extraordinary highlight for SOP came in the spring of 1937, when the fraternity gained a very special honorary member. Not all Greek-letter organizations grant honorary memberships, but SOP was one that allowed older Jewish men not currently enrolled as an undergraduate to go through the initiation ceremony and become an official member. In May 1937, Benny Goodman and his orchestra were in Boston for a series of performances at the Metropolitan Theater. "The King of Swing" was a giant of the Big Band era, and his performances were the talk of the town for days. Following one particular show, two members of Mu chapter made their way backstage to Mr. Goodman's dressing room, and initiated him into their fraternity. They even used Mr. Goodman's clarinet, rather than the ritualistic scepter, to "tap the neophyte" and complete the ceremony. How and why Mu chapter was able to initiate Mr. Goodman is unknown, but it was certainly a coup for the chapter. Of course, it appears SOP was not the only fraternity to initiate Mr. Goodman – the national Tau Epsilon Phi fraternity also claims him as a member.[470]

Meanwhile, as the 1930s wore on, SOP at the national level struggled to stay afloat. With most of their chapters closed, with war on the horizon, and with no real prospects for growth in the future, the national leaders soon decided their survival lay not in continuing, but in merging with another organization. SOP was hardly alone in its troubles, as a number of other Jewish fraternities (especially smaller ones) were also in dire straits and looking for any way to survive. Therefore, as 1940 got underway, SOP began sending inquiries to other Jewish fraternities about a possible merger. From this work an ideal candidate rose from the mix. This particular fraternity had ideals similar to SOP, and while not considered one of the larger Jewish organizations, it was in much better financial and structural shape than SOP. This fraternity was Alpha Epsilon Pi (AEPi).[471]

Working on the night shift

After working a full eight to ten hour day, heading off to a few hours of classes in pursuit of an undergraduate degree can be quite difficult. Yet for thousands of college students, night school is the only way they can advance their education. Such was the case for Charles Moskowitz in the fall of 1913, when he transferred to New York University's School of Commerce (NYU) as a night student, having previously attended CCNY. After arriving on campus, Charles was recognized as a former CCNY basketball star, and his athletic prowess soon caught the attention of the seven active fraternities in the Commerce school. One fraternity went so far as to give him a bid to join. But, by this time Charles had a group of about six friends on campus that regularly ate dinner together, and he didn't want to leave these men behind. So, he asked the fraternity if his friends could join as well. The answer was "no." The bid was only for him, take it or leave it. Charles had no intention of abandoning his friends, so he passed on the bid, and together they all went back to their mealtime routine.[472]

Dinner for the group each night was a German rathskeller, with franks and sauerkraut the specialty at fifteen cents a plate. A few weeks into the semester, the men were rewarded for their dining loyalty with a private room each night. It was in this room where they started talking about forming their own Greek-letter fraternity. While they certainly desired the close and meaningful friendship offered by such an organization, the logistics of starting one were immediately daunting to the group – after all, they had jobs during the day and classes at night. Free time was not in large supply for any of them, and they knew it would take considerable effort to see their plan to fruition. In addition, the other seven fraternities on campus were quite strong, so they wondered how would their new fraternity fare against these organizations, and if they even stood a chance at survival. But the group of now eleven men felt they had something special together, so they accepted the challenge. As for a name, they became AEPi. As for ideals, they would be a fraternity for Jewish men.[473]

Declaring themselves a fraternity was the easy part, but to be afforded the title in the eyes of NYU and its students, they needed recognition from the campus administration. The process of gaining recognition was straightforward, as it primarily involved asking the dean of the School of Commerce for permission to organize. So, the members of AEPi made their appeal by a formal letter, which they figured should be typed to give the best possible appearance. While typing as a skill is taken for granted these days (given the ubiquity of computers), a hundred years ago such a talent was not widespread, especially among men. However, one of the eleven, David Schafer, did possess the ability, so he typed the letter and submitted it to the dean's office in early October 1913. Then, the men waited. A reply came about a month later, on November 7, 1913, and it was the response they longed to hear: "yes." AEPi was now an official fraternity at NYU.[474]

From the beginning, AEPi set itself up as a national organization. They gave their chapter at NYU the "Alpha" designator in anticipation of an expansion effort, and using the framework of the other national fraternities at NYU, they became an official corporation in 1914. Then, they established their Beta chapter in early 1917 at Cornell University, though the entry of the United States into The Great War nearly ended AEPi – almost every member of both chapters entered military service. But after the war, AEPi regrouped in earnest. Rapid expansion through the 1930s saw AEPi grow to thirty chapters, with outposts scattered across the country, though primarily in the East and Midwest. AEPi's merger with Sigma Omega Psi became official on November 23, 1940, and added three additional chapters to the roll, including the one at Tufts College. More importantly, the merger announced to the fraternity world that AEPi was here to stay.[475]

From obscurity to the head of the class

Back on the Tufts campus, it took just the stroke of a pen in December of 1940 to transform Mu chapter of SOP into the Eta Deuteron chapter of AEPi. For those in the chapter, this change must have been somewhat bittersweet, as they had done reasonably well as SOP, notwithstanding the difficulties of 1935. Now they had to become a different organization with a new legacy, ritual, and direction. To almost all on campus, though, this development probably garnered little attention. Both SOP and AEPi were for Jewish men, so there had been no fundamental shift in the fraternity's mission; the only obvious change was the letters on the outside of the chapter house. To those in PhiEp, however, this change was profound. Whereas just a few years earlier the members of PhiEp were eagerly anticipating SOP's demise, now they faced a revitalized AEPi that was giving them real competition for the best Jewish men, the likes of which they had not seen in the past. AEPi, in the first few semesters after the merger, seemed to gain the upper hand in this regard, as numerous athletes, intellectuals, and campus leaders joined the chapter in large number. These new members helped elevate the fraternity's stature to a level SOP had never achieved. As a result, PhiEp was now talking about AEPi as their equal.[476]

And then came World War II. When the campus mobilized in 1943 to support the war effort, the fraternities answered the call in a unique way. All of their houses were eventually taken over by either the U.S. Navy as part of the V-12 training program, or commandeered by the college for use as dormitory space. All of them, that is, except AEPi's at 151 College Avenue. As the sole renters of an off-campus property (all of the other fraternities owned their houses), AEPi remained open for business; it appears Tufts made no effort to take over or close down private, off-campus residences. The years 1943–46 were certainly lean ones for the chapter, with membership dropping down to just five men at one point. But unlike their rival PhiEp, which ceased operations altogether for a few years, AEPi never closed down and never stopped being a fraternity. This left them in a unique position to regroup quickly once the war ended.[477]

The war, though, did take a personal toll on the chapter. In the fall of 1941, a sophomore from Lynn, Massachusetts named Robert Atlas joined AEPi, and by all accounts he was well liked both in his fraternity (he became the chapter's Master, or president) and on the greater Tufts campus. Outside of AEPi he was a writer, eventually becoming the sports editor of the *Tufts Weekly* and the Tufts correspondent to the *Boston Globe*. He was also well known, in a sense, for calling out Adolf Hitler as a plagiarist, which he did in a letter to *LIFE* Magazine, published in the summer of 1939:

> Sirs:
> I always knew that Hitler was a crook but I thought that it was only in the case of war secrets and military information. But, by saltshakers, if he isn't a literary plagiarist too. LIFE, Aug. 7, had a piece on "How To Kiss," which was taken from the *Völkischer Beobachter.* The almost identical piece appeared in *College Humor* for September, which was out on the newsstands about the middle of June or the first of July.
> ROBERT C. ATLAS, Lynn, Mass.[478]

By saltshakers, indeed! Robert answered the call by joining the Army Air Corps, where he was commissioned as a second lieutenant and eventually assigned as a bomber-navigator on a B-29 Superfortress of the 9th Bombardment Group. The mission of the B-29 was to bomb Japan, pure and simple. In early January 1945, Lt. Atlas returned to campus to visit his fraternity before heading back to his base on Tinian Island in the South Pacific Ocean. A few months later, on the night of May 27–28 1945, Lt. Atlas was part of an eleven aircraft mission dropping mines in the Moji Harbor and Karatsu Bay off the Japanese mainland. Though a nighttime mission, Japanese forces spotted the attack and activated their flak batteries in defense of the harbors. Flak batteries operating at night were not always very effective, and as the mission continued, it appeared all eleven planes would make it through the barrage with only minor damages. However, at one point during the bombing raid, Lt. Atlas's plane was hit by flak, and an instant later began plummeting towards the ground. Other aircrews in the vicinity did not see any parachutes emerge from the stricken

Alpha Epsilon Pi member and 2LT Robert Atlas (standing, second from left) poses with the crew of his B-29 "Thunderin' Loretta" on Tinian Island. All of these men would perish over Japan on May 28, 1945. (Courtesy of Howard E. Mumm)

aircraft. Lt. Atlas and the rest of his eleven-man crew were lost that night. He was Eta Deuteron's only gold star of the war.[479]

When the war ended in August of 1945, Tufts College began the quick transition from a Navy training base to an undergraduate campus. The fraternities led the social transformation, with each organization restarting their operation and then working to get back their chapter house from the administration. AEPi, having never left its house, was well ahead of the field in this regard. As a result, by the early spring of 1946, AEPi was booming, with a mixture of veterans and new students filling the brotherhood. Then, of course, came the unexpected. In February 1946, the owner of 151 College Avenue decided he no longer wanted to rent his house to a fraternity. So, he unceremoniously threw the chapter to the street that month, apparently without warning. It appears AEPi had done nothing egregious to warrant this expulsion, but it did not matter. They were out. This development could not have come at a worse time, since almost all other fraternities were back in to their chapter houses. Now AEPi was on the outside, and this situation looked to severely hamper their future recruiting efforts. As it turned out, any such fears were soon put to rest. Despite being without a house for the next eighteen months, AEPi doubled in membership to over sixty-five men, thus becoming one of the largest fraternities on campus. Adversity, it seems, brought out the best in AEPi. Then, in April 1947, the chapter made an announcement they had wanted to make for almost as long as they had existed: they had purchased a chapter house. Their new abode was 10 Dearborn Road, a multi-story structure just across the street from the Bromfield-Pearson building. The members refurbished their house over the summer of 1947 and then moved in that following fall. As a final touch, they dedicated their chapter room to their gold star member, Lt. Robert Atlas.[480]

With their house now secure, AEPi then continued on a path towards excellence within the Tufts community. Not only did they maintain a strong and larger membership, they routinely led all fraternities in scholastics, and often placed numerous members in the various honor societies such as Tower Cross (Senior class honors), Ivy Society (Junior class honors), Sword and Shield (sophomore class honors), Phi Beta Kappa (liberal arts honor society), and Tau Beta Pi (engineering honor society). AEPi was also heavily represented on sports teams, the *Jumbo* yearbook staff, and the *Tufts Weekly* newspaper editorial board. The only real problem for the fraternity was their house at 10 Dearborn Road. It was proving to be too small for the chapter, since it could only house nineteen of the sixty to eighty members, and its dining room was often crowded beyond capacity. This problem was finally solved in the fall of 1952, when a much larger house at 6–8 Capen Street in the Medford Hillside came up for sale. AEPi immediately recognized the opportunity afforded by this large house, which could house thirty men and board well over twice that number. So, with the help of their national organization, the chapter purchased the building and then looked forward to moving day in the fall of 1953. Most importantly, those in the chapter felt they had finally found a perfect, permanent home, and would never have to move again.[481]

Pushing barriers and paying the price

For nearly the first hundred years at Tufts, the fraternity chapters operating openly on campus were comprised almost exclusively of white men. Part of this was due to the reality of Tufts College/Tufts University up to the 1950s, as nearly all men entering the school were white. Minorities of any type, especially African-Americans, were never present on campus in great number throughout the school's first hundred years. Of course, even if African-Americans had come in large number, they would have been barred from almost all of the fraternities simply because of their race. It wasn't until the years following World War II that undergraduate fraternity members began to challenge this segregation. The movement started at Amherst College in 1948, when the school's Phi Kappa Psi chapter attempted to initiate a black man. Then, the idea reached Tufts. During the 1951–52 school year, both AEPi and PhiEp looked to break the fraternity color barrier for the first time. According to the 1952 edition of the *Jumbo* yearbook, these two organizations each pledged an African-American man that school year. Unfortunately, neither of these men was fully initiated into their respective fraternity, for reasons no longer known. Still, credit is due to both organizations for attempting to be the exception rather than the rule.[482]

A few years later, the undergraduate members of AEPi tried again to break a membership barrier, only this time the hurdle was of a different nature. In the 1950s, many national fraternities also had official restrictions barring membership based on religion. AEPi, as it turned out, did not. From the moment AEPi was founded, its leaders never enacted any official religious requirement for membership, though they did place great emphasis on Judaism in their mission. As a result, many in AEPi felt there was no need for a religious barrier, for they assumed only Jewish men would want to join their fraternity. Unofficially, though, it appears alumni and national officers of AEPi were fully prepared to exert their influence and keep their fraternity wholly Jewish, especially when chapters began to try otherwise. Those at Tufts found this out the hard way. During the 1956–57 school year, for what appears to be the first time in the chapter's history, AEPi offered a bid to a Christian. The chapter's alumni advisor that year, Sumner Berenson of the class of 1939, was also very active within the national AEPi organization (he had recently finished a term as the overall president, or Supreme Master), and he was not pleased with this development. In no uncertain terms, Mr. Berenson told the chapter that the pledging of a Christian would most likely result in the loss of their charter. The undergraduates disregarded this threat and pledged the Christian man anyway. Surprise, surprise, the national organization pulled Eta Deuteron's charter. For a few months, then, the chapter existed in a state of turmoil, operating without a charter while also trying to reach a satisfactory resolution with the national organization. The problem solved itself when the pledge in question dropped out before becoming a full member. With the religious crisis now over, the national office quickly returned Eta Deuteron's charter, and the fraternity continued on as if nothing had happened. All was forgiven.[483]

Additionally, all went back to normal. In the years that followed, those in AEPi retreated from their adversarial positions, and instead became a model chapter. Their membership was consistently one of the largest on campus, their list of honors stretched across pages, and their place within the national organization was securely near the top. Still, the two incidents from the 1950s spoke of a growing awareness within the chapter towards inclusiveness. Such change was also happening in many of the other fraternities on the Tufts campus, but that it was also happening in a historically Jewish fraternity is sometimes lost in the conversation. The seeds of change within AEPi had been planted, and while they did not take hold at first, they were certainly lying in wait. How long would the status quo last?[484]

The house, it is a changin'

The answer came in the fall of 1969. By this time, radical change was coming to dominate nearly every aspect of student life at Tufts. Controversy over the Vietnam War and civil rights, coupled with an influx of illegal drug use, created a growing atmosphere on campus that was definitely anti-establishment and anti-traditional. The fraternities, which just years earlier had been very popular, suffered greatly in this new paradigm. Most were slow to react to these changes, opting to continue as they always had while hoping "normalcy" would soon return. AEPi, on the other hand, caught the wave of this upheaval by soon questioning everything about their organization. After much discussion, the members realized they wanted to be something different, something more than old traditions and tired practices. They wanted to continue as a fraternity, without a doubt, but one that looked and behaved in a new way. So, that fall they voted for change. They would no longer be an exclusive organization of Jewish men. Instead, they would open up their membership in ways not seen before.[485]

Nothing has denied fraternity membership to more men than the blackball, a single "no" vote, often cast in secret, with no chance for appeal. AEPi was one such national organization that utilized the blackball throughout its history to shape its brotherhood. However, in the fall of 1969, AEPi at Tufts voted to eliminate the blackball, opting instead to accept anyone who was interested in the fraternity, Jewish or otherwise. All anyone needed to join was the sponsorship of a single active member, and even this rule was hotly debated within AEPi as being too restrictive. "If two hundred guys want to join AEPi," said Fred Fierst, the chapter president at the time, "then we'll have two hundred guys." But, the chapter didn't stop with the men. In a first, AEPi also considered offering full membership to professors as well as women undergraduates, with the added possibility of having women live in the house. Finally, the chapter relaxed its meal plan requirements. Whereas before all members ate every meal at the chapter house, now they were encouraged to eat some meals in the campus dining halls, and also to invite non-members to their house for meals on occasion. The goal was to increase the interaction between the fraternity and the greater Tufts community. In no small way, the members of AEPi were radically trying to redefine what it meant to be a fraternity. Exclusivity and religious identity and isolation were out; openness and tolerance were in.[486]

Just about the only groups opposed to the new direction were the chapter's alumni and the national organization. To them, the changes were nothing short of blasphemous. After all, AEPi was a Jewish fraternity with a mission to support Jewish men, and for the chapter to turn its back on such core principles was worse than going dormant, at least in their eyes. Many alumni, including Mr. Berenson, tried to intervene and change the mindset within the chapter, but it was too late. The undergraduates had chosen a path, and they were only moving forward. The ways of the past were history.[487]

Throughout the remainder of the 1969–70 school year, as the chapter began implementing many of these changes (though women and professors were apparently never admitted), hopes were high among the brotherhood that their ideas would succeed. However, it was soon apparent the new direction was fraught with unexpected problems. Eating in the dining halls proved to be so popular that by the spring of 1970, the chapter was forced to close their house kitchen for lack of interest as well as funds. Also, the push for open membership did not bring about any great interest in the fraternity. Few at Tufts seemed interested in joining the AEPi experiment, especially as the events of the day overwhelmed many that spring. Between national issues such as the massacre at Kent State and anti-war rallies in Washington, D.C., and local issues such as the drug bust and a general strike, students were being pulled in every direction away from the fraternities. Those remaining in AEPi were not immune to the turmoil. Interest within the chapter began to wane considerably, with more and more members dropping out and becoming inactive. This loss added to the overall financial strain, and as the year came to a close, those remaining in AEPi openly wondered if they'd even be able to occupy the house in the next school year. The answer came soon enough. Buried in debt and apathy, the chapter quietly closed down at the end of the 1970 spring semester after forty-nine years of continuous activity. Everyone moved out, and the owners of the house, the alumni-run Etadee Corporation, leased the property to Tufts for use as a dormitory. AEPi's great experiment had failed miserably. Or so it seemed, at the time.[488]

Brothers and sisters, pump up the volume

The closing of AEPi in the spring of 1970 was by no means an isolated incident within the Greek community at Tufts. Two other fraternities and all three remaining sororities also ceased operations around the same time, leaving many students on campus to predict the rest would soon follow in their wake. The closing of the fraternities was a bigger conundrum for the administration, however, for they were left to deal with the physical houses left behind. Nowhere was this more evident than in AEPi's former house at 6–8 Capen Street. When the administration entered the property in the summer of 1970 to begin transforming it into a dormitory, they discovered a property steeped in disrepair. What had once been a model fraternity house in AEPi's organization was now decrepit. Repair work started that summer, but the state of the structure had hardly improved by the time students moved back in. As described by one of resident that fall, "[there were] large quantities of trash in the hall, rotting electrical wires, dirty toilets, and a lack of light bulbs and shades… Most of the rooms were bare." With no other campus housing options available, though, the students were forced to withstand the Spartan conditions until the administration could finish the necessary repairs. In the meantime, the dormitory was the name "Nichols House," after the long time Professor of Geology and Tufts alumnus from 1926, Robert L. Nichols. The national organization of AEPi, including Mr. Berenson, could only watch from the outskirts and hope for the day when the fraternity could return to their house. But, the early 1970s was not a good time to restart AEPi at Tufts. So Mr. Berenson settled in for the long wait.[489]

Five years it took, until Mr. Berenson decided all had waited long enough. The overall situation with fraternities at Tufts had hardly improved since AEPi closed down, but it hadn't gotten worse, either. So, in the spring of 1975, Mr. Berenson and a few others started working to bring back AEPi. All they needed were a group of men willing to accept the challenge of building a fraternity from the ground up. However, with no substantial contacts among the current undergraduates (all former members of AEPi had long since graduated or moved on), Mr. Berenson took to advertising for the hard sell. "Looking for a few good men," went the flyer, which was soon posted all over campus. Although such outreach is hardly guaranteed to succeed (flyers around campus have a tendency to turn into scrap paper, or be covered by other flyers), in Mr. Berenson's case it worked. Soon enough he had a group of men willing to restart AEPi. But, this group hardly looked like AEPi of the past. Those now interested were a motley crew of rugby players, sailors, swimmers, Deadheads, Jews, and not Jews. If Mr. Berenson was dismayed by the diversity of the men, he did not show it. Instead, he forged ahead with this group as it was, hoping to mold them back into his beloved fraternity.[490]

As a first step, Mr. Berenson officially pledged the men to AEPi that spring, then he started them on the basics of being a fraternity. In addition, he also worked fervently to regain control of the chapter house, which had continued to exist as a dormitory throughout the early 1970s. Here, he was successful, and as the fall of 1975 approached, plans were made for the new incarnation of AEPi to move back in. However, there was a problem – simply put, there were too many rooms and too few members. With taxes to pay, and utilities to pay, and a kitchen to run, the Etadee Corporation needed to fill those rooms or risk financial insolvency. So, the corporation opened the house to boarders not associated with the fraternity. Answering the call were a group of women looking for a place to live. By the fall of 1975, co-ed living on campus was a sanctioned reality in a few of the dormitories, so women and men living together at 6–8 Capen Street was not a controversial issue for the Tufts community. Rules within the national AEPi fraternity, however, prohibited co-habitation in any chapter house, so this situation became an instant headache for the national leaders. To ease the concern, the chapter and alumni corporation argued the presence of women was only temporary, a year at most, until AEPi was large enough to fill all those rooms with official members.[491]

There was only one problem with this argument: the undergraduates in AEPi had no intention of kicking the women out of the house. In fact, the men had no real intention of acting like an official chapter of AEPi at all. They, along with the women living in the house, soon realized they were evolving into a unique community. So, rather than work on growing AEPi into a viable all-male fraternity, the residents morphed into a co-ed organization known on campus as "Nichols House," taking the name from the house's former life as a dormitory. Together the men and women set up leadership positions and held informal recruitment each year, with new members voted in and accepted as equals immediately – no initiation and no hazing. They also established a dining plan that served meals five days a week, with residents acting as the kitchen staff. Nearly all members of Nichols House lived in the home, but the community also welcomed back ex-residents for meals and social events. Ironically, it seemed the vision of AEPi as put forth by the members back in 1969 had finally come to fruition, even though the members of Nichols House knew nothing of this earlier plan.[492]

As the semesters rolled along, the one major concern for those in Nichols House was the national organization of AEPi. Eta Deuteron's charter had been officially returned in May of 1976, and ever since, the national organization assumed a full-fledged chapter was operating out of the house. The members of Nichols House, recognizing the national organization still held considerable power over the group, made an attempt to at least appear as a normal fraternity. The men who joined Nichols House became official members of AEPi, and when the national organization visited each year, these men presented a full slate of officers with correct titles such as Master, Exchequer, and Scribe. These positions, as it turned out, were often decided just before the visitations, and once the national leaders left, control of the house reverted back to the elected Nichols House officers. The women of Nichols House knew to stay away during these visits, lest the national organization become suspicious of their presence. Despite these precautions, it appears that Mr. Berenson knew of this ruse, though surprisingly he chose to ignore it, perhaps hoping everything would eventually right itself. Another concern, though much less minor, was the influx each year of a few students who wanted to join AEPi, the Jewish fraternity of their fathers, many of whom were alumni of the Eta Deuteron chapter. These students were generally appalled at the situation they found in Nichols House, so they usually did not stick around very long.[493]

In the mean time, Nichols House grew into a very popular organization on campus by the early 1980s, especially when it came to social events. Simply put, Nichols House was known for its "work hard, play hard" mentality, and many students, it seemed, wanted in on the play. Parties were held in the basement, a large room painted a rather ugly shade of light brown at the time. This color became the basis for the popular nickname of Nichols House, "KA-KA." Advertising a party at Nichols House became as simple as saying "KA-KA party tonight" in the dining halls and classes, and by 9:00 p.m. the basement would be filled with revelers, often listening to music by the house band, Roadwork, playing sets of Grateful Dead cover tunes all night. On the work side, Nichols House was home to a number of Division III All-American athletes in swimming and sailing, and the members did quite well academically, with no expulsions and a very high overall grade point average.[494]

By 1980, though, it appears the alumni overseeing the fraternity were growing impatient with Nichols House. They wanted a real chapter of AEPi in place. To appease this desire, the residents of Nichols House petitioned the faculty-led Committee on Student Life that fall to recognize AEPi as an official fraternity on campus, a request that was granted. But this turn towards AEPi was an appeasement, not a real change. And, in an apparent dig at the national organization, members of Nichols House began wearing sweatshirts bearing the letters "KA-KA" in the same official blue and gold colors of the fraternity. These sweatshirts were more than a fashion statement. They announced to the world that those in the Nichols House community had no intention of abandoning what they had created, a community that served a particular campus niche quite well for the time. They were idealists, in some ways, but unfortunately, those ideals crashed right into reality.[495]

It happened during the 1981–82 school year. Although Nichols House was strong as ever, two major problems had risen to the top. First, the house at 6–8 Capen Street was again an undeniable mess, certainly not the pristine fraternity house AEPi had known in the past. With every visit, the national organization bemoaned the physical state of the property ever more, and with good reason. A few years earlier, in 1979, the national fraternity granted the Etadee Corporation a mortgage on the house, thus becoming part owner of the property. Now, their investment was deteriorating right in front of them. To the members of Nichols House, the physical state of the house was of no concern, consistent with their laid-back philosophy. Potential members were asked if they could live in a place that wasn't pristine; those looking for cleanliness were shown the door. The decay of the house thus became a self-fulfilling prophecy each semester. Second, the parties and social events were also becoming an issue. Unlike the on-campus fraternity houses, Nichols House was in a neighborhood populated not by college students, but by those with no particular affiliation to (or great affection for) Tufts University. To them, Nichols House was nothing short of a pox on their neighborhood. The loud, late-night parties had turned into a constant source of friction between the residents, the City of Medford, and the administration. Nichols House, it seemed, was now on everyone's radar, and not in a good way.[496]

The school year came to an end with Nichols House still intact, somehow. For the first time, the members published a group photo and write-up in the *Jumbo* yearbook, as if to announce to the campus they were not going anywhere. Curiously, the write-up included the line, "As for the future of Alpha Epsilon Pi – the house is confident that its zenith has not yet been reached." The national organization felt the same way, too, but they were no longer confident the men of Nichols House would even try to approach the zenith. So, in the summer of 1982, and in cooperation with Mr. Berenson and the Etadee Corporation, the national organization threw everybody out. In an instant Nichols House was gone, AEPi was gone, the community was gone. As for reasons, the ones quoted were fairly obvious: the national organization knew women were still living in the house, they knew the men were not using the fraternity's rituals with any regularity, and they knew their expectation of a fraternity was not even close to being met. In addition, they estimated the house needed at least $60,000 to $70,000 of renovations to turn the property back into a respectful fraternity house. The few Nichols House members living there that summer took the brunt of this decision, as they were given very little notice of their eviction, and no chance to appeal. It had all come to an end. But, the pain of losing their home and their community would soon sting even more, once they found out who'd be moving in.[497]

Do you even go to school here?

The closing of AEPi and Nichols House left the Etadee Corporation with a conundrum. Their house was now empty, but they still had bills to pay and maintenance to perform. If they were going to keep control of their house, they would need residents, and soon. Luckily they knew just where to find the perfect ones. Approximately seven miles from Medford is Northeastern University, an urban school in the heart of Boston that is markedly different from Tufts in both size and mission. The two schools have had little in common throughout their histories except for two fraternities: Sigma Omega Psi, which started in 1921 on both campuses, and then Alpha Epsilon Pi. By the fall of 1982, Northeastern's chapter of AEPi was still active, but they, too, were in a conundrum. They needed a new house, since their previous one had been heavily damaged by fire. So, that fall the Etadee Corporation did something unprecedented. They rented their house to AEPi's Northeastern chapter.[498]

The remaining members of Nichols House and their alumni were naturally outraged by this turn of events. Losing their house was bad enough, but to have it turned over to a group that didn't even attend Tufts was inexcusable. One alumnus in particular sent an impassioned plea to the Tufts community a few weeks into the fall semester of 1982, reminding the campus of how AEPi/Nichols House had been an asset to the school, while asking for support as he and other former members tried to bring their organization back. But it was all for naught. The AEPi chapter from Northeastern soon settled into 6–8 Capen Street that semester, the first time a fraternity from another school has set up its operations on the Tufts campus. Ironically, the Northeastern group did not have enough men to fill all the rooms in the house, so they were forced to find boarders from within the Tufts community. Presumably, none of the former members of AEPi/Nichols House were allowed back.[499]

The Northeastern chapter, in addition to occupying Eta Deuteron's old house, also had another mission. They were tasked with helping to start a new, legitimate chapter of AEPi at Tufts from the ground up. No more Nichols House, no more co-ed membership, and no more experimentation with a new fraternal concept. As fate would have it, one of the members of the Northeastern chapter had a good friend at Tufts, a sophomore named Michael Gitten. For a few months, the two talked about restarting AEPi in earnest, and then in the spring of 1983, Michael officially signed on to the project. He started with just a few others that semester, but by the fall of 1983 the group of now eight men were excited about rebuilding AEPi at Tufts and moving back into the chapter house. The national organization felt the same way, so that fall they returned Eta Deuteron's charter to the group, thus making AEPi an active fraternity once again at Tufts. However, the chapter did not yet have enough members to fill all of the rooms in the house. So, 6–8 Capen Street became the simultaneous home of two AEPi chapters, as both the Tufts and Northeastern members lived side-by-side.[500]

This unique housing arrangement proved to be very temporary. By the fall of 1983, interest in fraternities was on the rise once again at Tufts, and AEPi was in a perfect position to tap into such enthusiasm. They were a new chapter offering prospective members, especially those interested in their greater mission of supporting the Jewish community, the chance to rebuild a strong legacy, all while living and working and playing in a stately chapter house. This combination practically sold itself. By the end of the 1983–84 school year, membership in AEPi had grown from eight to about fifty members, which made them one of the largest fraternities at Tufts. The Northeastern chapter therefore moved out after the 1983–84 year. All was finally back to normal for AEPi, and the future looked very bright. So of course, something just had to go wrong.[501]

Helplessly homeless

Throughout the early 1900s, the section known as the Medford Hillside, with streets such as Bellevue Street, Fairmount Street, and University Avenue, could collectively be called a "fraternity neighborhood," given the number of organizations that occupied homes in the area. Newer fraternities in particular settled here during this time, since the houses were affordable and the sizes near perfect for smaller chapters. However, by the 1930s, the Medford Hillside had been all but abandoned by the Greek-letter organizations, with some chapters having moved to larger houses on College Avenue, while others fell victim to the Depression and closed down completely. AEPi became the first to return some twenty years later, when they moved into 6–8 Capen Street in 1953. The houses surrounding AEPi, in the years that followed, became a mixture of co-op dormitories run by Tufts, multi-family units rented privately to Tufts students, and homes rented or owned by residents with no connection to the university. Two of these groups generally got along with AEPi. One did not. As could be guessed, the local residents especially disliked AEPi in their neighborhood, mainly because the chapter house was all too often a beehive of late-night social activity, and the fraternity members were not known for keeping a tidy yard. Every transgression by AEPi over the years, no matter how minor, seemed to hang heavy on the local residents, causing a tension and anger to simmer and grow throughout the neighborhood. It was only a matter of time, then, before a serious confrontation boiled to the surface.[502]

And so it did, in 1982. By this time, many of the local residents felt they had suffered enough through the loud and rambunctious machinations of Nichols House, especially since Tufts had done very little to rein them in. So, when the housing license for 6–8 Capen Street came up for renewal that year, the neighborhood residents, the City of Medford, and Tufts University all agreed to attach some new conditions to the property as a means of bringing peace to the area. The terms were rather straightforward: the chapter house and grounds had to be kept clean, the fraternity had to stay quiet at night, none living on the property could have pets, only thirty residents or less could live in the house, the fraternity was required to have a non-student advisor living in the house, and none of the fraternity members could park in the surrounding neighborhoods. A long list, no doubt, but everyone in AEPi, including both the Northeastern and then the Tufts chapter, looked to abide by these rules.[503]

By all accounts they did, at least for the most part. For example, by the 1985–86 school year, AEPi had abandoned the hosting of large parties at night (probably the number one complaint of their neighbors), opting instead to entertain during the late afternoon and early evening. But still, all did not go gently into the neighborhood. Small transgressions by AEPi continued to add to the collective anger of the local residents, until they finally decided they'd had enough. AEPi, they realized, would never be the perfect neighbor, no matter how many guidelines or rules were enacted. So the local residents, along with the City of Medford, decided to end their AEPi problem once and for all. By Medford law, a house without a lodging license could only hold up to three unrelated residents. Every year, AEPi would apply to renew its housing license so the thirty residents could legally occupy the house, and every year the license was granted. Every year, that is, until the fall of 1986. Under pressure from AEPi's neighbors, the City of Medford said, "No." There would be no lodging license for AEPi. Medford had just invoked the nuclear option, and consequently, fraternity housing at Tufts would never be the same.[504]

This action (as could be expected) immediately set off a flurry of legal activity between the fraternity and the City of Medford, as each tried to support its position in court. Unfortunately for AEPi, the fraternity had little by way of a sound legal argument. A lodging license was a privilege, not a right, and the City of Medford had every authority to grant or deny such a request as they saw fit. As a result, the rulings came quick, and for the fraternity, they were harsh. Medford's decision to pull the license for 6–8 Capen Street was upheld in full, forcing most of the residents to move out of the house, immediately. Six stayed behind, as the fraternity argued the property was technically a two-family duplex, thereby legally allowing two sets of unrelated residents. But even six was too much for the neighbors and for the City of Medford. A month later, Medford deemed 6–8 Capen Street a one family house, thereby forcing three more residents to the street.[505]

With so few residents and no legal recourse, the Etadee Corporation realized the situation was hopeless. The chapter could not maintain the house and pay the bills with only three residents. So, the Etadee Corporation took the only path available, which was to sell the property and move the chapter out for good. In the spring of 1987, and for the price of $240,000, Tufts University became the proud new owner of 6–8 Capen Street. The house was immediately converted into the new academic headquarters of the Boston School of Occupational Therapy (BSOT). This development was somewhat controversial, however, as during that school year, Tufts decided to shutter the undergraduate program within BSOT, citing a decreased enrollment in the course of study. Why, many students wondered, was the BSOT displacing a fraternity, when the BSOT itself was contracting? But there would be no satisfying answer to this question for AEPi, just as there would be no going back. It was 1987, and AEPi was now a fraternity without a house.[506]

There's no place like home

With cash now flooding the coffers of the Etadee Corporation, one would have thought they could just buy a new house for AEPi somewhere close to campus and move on. Unfortunately, it was not that simple. The crux of the problem was not financial, but political. The City of Medford, after denying AEPi a housing license, announced it would no longer issue a lodging license to any fraternity within its borders. Medford, it seems, wanted to ensure none of its residents would ever again have to deal with fraternity problems. At the same time, the City of Somerville was also contemplating a similar statute within its borders. The Somerville residents living near Tufts were just as fed up with fraternities as the residents of Medford Hillside, and they would not have shed a single tear if all the Greek-letter houses were closed down for good. The Tufts Administration, led by President Jean Mayer, worked hard to keep Somerville from invoking its nuclear option, as the school ultimately wanted to keep fraternities and sororities on campus and in their houses. But, the administration also clearly did not want to enflame tensions by having a new fraternity house suddenly appear on the map. For AEPi, that meant their money was no good in either Medford or Somerville. There would be no house purchase. Instead, AEPi had to join three other Greek-letter organizations without an official chapter house in the worst game of all, the waiting game. Waiting, that is, for an existing Greek-letter organization with a house either to close down or move out, for that appeared to be the only viable way a new chapter house would become available. With the rising popularity of both fraternities and sororities at the time, though, such a scenario seemed unlikely. The wait was going to be a long one.[507]

In the mean time, those in AEPi worked to remain a viable fraternity on campus. By the fall of 1987, AEPi set up its operations in an unofficial, off-campus house privately rented by a small group of members. Such an arrangement was technically against the rules of the Tufts Inter-Greek Council (or IGC, of which AEPi belonged), as they had recently barred Greek organizations from occupying unofficial chapter houses. But, since AEPi didn't hang any fraternity letters on the outside of the house or cause any problems for their neighbors, they were left alone. Additionally, AEPi often changed apartments from year-to-year (while other fraternities in a similar situation did not), thus giving them some cover against the IGC's mandate.[508]

Meanwhile, those in the chapter worked to continue their legacy by only looking forward. In the spring of 1988, for example, AEPi organized a lip-sync concert in support of the American Heart Association. Called the "Greek Jam," the event featured song-and-dance acts by nearly all of the active fraternities and sororities in front of a packed house at Cohen Auditorium. This contest soon became an annual event within the Greek community and lasted for over a decade, often raising thousands of dollars in one night for various charities. But aside from the money raised (which was certainly significant and well appreciated), Greek Jam was a success for the enthusiasm it generated. Most organizations wanted to win, and this competitiveness was evident in their preparation. The judges of Greek Jam usually included members of the Tufts faculty and administration, thereby making the event one of the only at the time which brought the Greek community and the administration together in a positive manner. Over the years, AEPi secured major corporate sponsors such as fashion designer Tommy Hilfiger, and the contest even caught the eye of MTV, when their programming was heavily geared towards college students. All told, Greek Jam raised well over $50,000 for various local and national charities before it was discontinued.[509]

Despite all of the positives within the chapter, though, AEPi was continually losing the waiting game. In the fall of 1990, when the Theta Delta Chi fraternity was suspended from campus and forced to vacate its house, it was the Alpha Omicron Pi (AOΠ) sorority that was awarded the space, until Theta Delta Chi came back two years later. In 1992, when Tufts opened up 25 Whitfield Road for Greek housing (the first new house made available for such purpose since 1986), it was AOII that moved in, not AEPi. Two years later, in 1994, a smaller house at 126 Packard Avenue became available, and once again AEPi was passed over in favor of a relatively new sorority, Phi Sigma Sigma. These losses were surely frustrating for the chapter, but there was nothing they could do except wait. Then, just like that, the game suddenly and unexpectedly ended. Phi Sigma Sigma voluntarily closed down at the end of the 1994–95 school year, thereby putting their former house back on the fraternity market. At this point, there were only two active Greek organizations without a house, Zeta Beta Tau (ZBT) and AEPi, both of which had been waiting since 1987. The Tufts administration, to their credit, decided not to choose one over the other, but instead opened up another fraternity space on campus so both chapters could be housed starting in the fall of 1995. For ZBT, their new home was 126 Packard Avenue, whereas for AEPi, their slightly larger home was 45 Sawyer Avenue, a house never before occupied by a fraternity. It had been nearly nine long years since AEPi had been kicked out of 6–8 Capen Street, but their hard work and perseverance had paid off. They had a home once again.[510]

We were just getting settled

When ZBT and AEPi moved into their houses in the fall of 1995, the general thought among the administration was that these residences would be temporary, five years at the most, while they looked to relocate not just the two, but a number of Greek organizations to Professors Row. But, as time went by, both ZBT and AEPi stayed right where they were, as did indeed all other fraternities and sororities on campus – to no great surprise, the plan to house them all in the middle of campus did not come together as expected. In the mean time, AEPi settled into their house and carried on in normal fashion. The first major hiccup came ten years later, in fall of 2005, when the chapter ran into some problems with alcohol abuse and ended up on social probation for the rest of the school year. The terms of this probation were quite clear, as the chapter could not host any official social function, anywhere – not in their chapter house, not in an off-campus apartment, not even in a private establishment such as a bar or restaurant. The chapter complied with these terms for almost the entire year, until they didn't. In April of 2006, AEPi decided to hold a formal dance at a local hotel, in clear violation of their probation. A month later they paid the price. Punishment was left to the faculty-led Committee on Fraternities and Sororities, and what they decided was something AEPi was all too familiar with: the fraternity was officially and indefinitely kicked out of their chapter house. An appeal by the members was unsuccessful, so when the school year started in September 2006, AEPi was once again a fraternity without a house. They were still a recognized, active chapter within their national organization and on the Tufts campus, but they were back to playing the waiting game.[511]

Luckily for AEPi, the waiting game was much different than it had been back in 1987, for now they were the only ones playing. And it just so happened there was an empty fraternity house right in the heart of campus along Professors Row. A couple of years earlier, in 2005, the Beta Mu chapter of Delta Tau Delta (DTD) suffered a near catastrophe when a pledge almost succumbed to alcohol poisoning during a fraternity event. Not only did the fraternity lose their charter in the wake of this event, they were also forced to vacate their house at 98 Professors Row. Afterwards, the DTD alumni corporation (which owned the property) rented out the rooms in their house to graduate students. Then, in the fall of 2007, the DTD alumni corporation leased their house to AEPi, thereby ending the waiting game once again. Decades earlier, SOP members had dreamed of a chapter house on Professors Row. Now the fraternity had finally arrived, even if only for a temporary stay.[512]

Indeed, AEPi spent just four years at 98 Professors Row before the reformed Beta Mu chapter of DTD reclaimed their house in the fall of 2011. AEPi was once again out, but, for the first time in their history, they had not been forgotten. Two years earlier, when it became clear DTD would displace AEPi from their house, the two fraternities worked together to plan for this transition. DTD did not simply want to kick AEPi out, for AEPi had been a model tenant and had proved they deserved a house of their own once again. As a result, AEPi ended up back in a familiar place that fall, 45 Sawyer Avenue, a space it could call its own. The waiting game, it seemed, just might be over forever.[513]

On second thought…

After returning to 45 Sawyer Avenue, AEPi continued to build upon its ninety-four year legacy as a Tufts fraternity, at least to the outside world. A major part of that legacy has been the continued embrace of the Jewish religion. Indeed, AEPi at the national level prides itself on being a fraternity open to all, but dedicated to "develop[ing] leadership for the future of the American Jewish community." At Tufts, however, this mission appears to have lost its appeal in recent years. The members of the chapter instead worked to broaden their identity beyond Judaism by attracting a wider diversity of men into their brotherhood. Unfortunately, this change of direction caused friction within the national organization, which strongly encouraged the chapter to recruit more Jewish men. The divide simmered between the chapter and the national organization until the early spring of 2015, when the members of Eta Deuteron could take no more. Unable to abide by the requests of their national, and unwilling to compromise in the men they wanted in their brotherhood, they took the only route available. They voted unanimously to disaffiliate from AEPi.[514]

This turn of events came as a near complete surprise to the campus, though all were generally supportive of the decision. However, as could be expected, some of the chapter's alumni were upset by this new reality, but the decision was final. The undergraduates spent the rest of that spring semester creating their organization, and then the following fall, announced themselves to the Tufts community. They were Pi Delta, a new local fraternity of members who "strongly believe in diversity of race, ethnicity, religion, sexual orientation, background, and beliefs." Not since 1956 had a Greek-letter organization at Tufts resigned from their national to become a local organization. As a result, the future of Pi Delta is currently an open question.[515]

THETA DELTA THETA (Local society, 1952 – 1957)
PHI SIGMA KAPPA (Iota Tetarton chapter, 1957 – 1976)
25 WHITFIELD (Local co-ed fraternity, 1974 – 1977)

In the fall of 1952, a new group of freshmen arrived on campus, eager (as they always are) to begin their Tufts experience. Many soon realized one of their hardest challenges was not excelling in the classroom, but navigating the dining room. Every day when they headed to the main dining room at Curtis Hall, they were confronted with the same, stressful question: where do I sit? Curtis Hall was often crowded to capacity, so seating was no trivial matter. The older students, of course, knew how to rig the system by reserving tables for their group of friends. The freshmen, by contrast, were often shunted to the outskirts of the room, where they had to sit with strangers, or worse still, alone. For five men in particular, though, this experience soon brought them together. They might not have known each other at the beginning of the school year, but after ending up at the same table for a few meals, they became fast friends. Then, as many freshmen do, these five began socializing together away from Curtis Hall.[516]

As a group, the next collegiate challenge they tackled was fraternity rush season. One of the first events they attended was "Pray For Rain," a glorified hose-and-water-balloon fight between the fraternities and the freshmen. As could be expected, the scene soon turned chaotic, with the fraternities easily gaining the upper hand – years of practice had taught them the tricks of the water battle trade. However, one of the five freshmen, Bruce Gordon, took it upon himself to organize his mob of classmates into a counter attack. To Bruce's surprise, when he called out orders, his fellow students followed his commands, and the fight was back on in earnest. Bruce's leadership caught the attention of Sigma Nu, so the fraternity sent a member out amongst the crowd to ask Bruce for his name and campus address, ostensibly to invite him to upcoming rush events. Here, the Sigma Nu member was successful in meeting Bruce, but then he made a classic mistake. He never followed up with the invitation, as he assumed someone else in his fraternity would handle that detail. As a result, Bruce and his friends never went to any rush parties at Sigma Nu, or any other fraternity, for that matter. This was just as well. The five soon decided their small group offered a shared experience they wanted to continue. They knew they were on to something good, and soon enough, a few others did, too. The group was starting to grow.[517]

When school resumed in the fall of 1953, the social group of now sophomores picked up right where they'd left off. A few of the men lived together in an off-campus apartment at 205 College Avenue, so this house naturally became their social hub. They also used personal contacts to add more friends to their group, thus building a critical mass of both members and ideas. But then, of course, the elephant in the room appeared, and he had a question: "What, exactly, are we trying to do here?" The men began holding regular meetings to discuss the very question of their essence, if not their future. The debate went on for nearly that entire fall semester, but by the end, the members had voted a plan of action. They would work to form an unofficial fraternity at Tufts, one that would cement their friendship into a tangible group. To start the process, they elected their first slate of officers and chose a name, Theta Delta Theta. The five recognized founders, all from the class of 1956, were:[518]

Bruce Gordon
Marty Billings
David Jaroff
Paul Stoddard
Arthur Pollari

As it turned out, the name Theta Delta Theta held no special meaning to anyone in the group. The letters had been chosen at random with no thought to a secret motto, and were meant simply an identifier, though no one outside the group yet knew of this name. Anonymity would not last very long. The members of Theta Delta Theta were waiting for just the right event to announce their existence, one that ideally would capture the attention of the entire campus. Of course, such an event was already on the Tufts calendar. Theta Delta Theta would use the 1954 raucous spring Mayoralty pageant as their coming out party.[519]

Beginning in the spring of 1937, the students of Tufts put on a Mayoralty pageant each year to elect a campus mayor. The event started as an opportunity for those so inclined to hone their political skills, but it quickly became a glorified popularity contest that was a whole lot of fun for everyone. By the 1950s, the Mayoralty pageant had grown to include theatrically elaborate campaigns built around skits, stump speeches, poster parties, and parades, all of which required enormous logistical support. The fraternities and their vast supply of able-bodied workers thus came to dominate the contest, and indeed all serious candidates were backed by one or more Greek-letter organization each year. So, in the spring of 1954, the members of Theta Delta Theta jumped into the fray. They entered one of their founders (and current president) Paul Stoddard as an official candidate. In keeping with the spirit of the contest, Paul took the nom-de-plume of "Darkhorse for Mayor of Tufts University," a name which effectively summed up his chances of winning; Mayoralty did not favor the novice. Nonetheless, by entering this pageant, Theta Delta Theta had made a clear and grand statement. They were no longer an informal social club lurking in the shadows of College Avenue. Instead, they were a new, local fraternity at Tufts.[520]

Paul lost the race as expected, but at least he'd accomplished his mission of introducing Theta Delta Theta to the campus. However, this event had been transformative in a second way that was not as positive. It seems a few within Theta Delta Theta did not agree completely with the plan to become a local fraternity. They wanted Theta Delta Theta to remain an informal social club of friends and nothing more. But after the Mayoralty campaign, there was no turning back. Theta Delta Theta was now a fraternity. Not surprisingly, a few of the group, including one or two who'd already joined another Greek-letter organization, said their goodbyes and dropped out. Theta Delta Theta had just experienced its first rift in membership. Unfortunately, it would not be their last.[521]

The remaining members of Theta Delta Theta returned to campus in the fall of 1954 renewed in their commitment to move forward as a fraternity. Feeling the time was right to make the situation official, they approached the student council and asked for recognition as a Tufts fraternity. Such permission would have allowed them to advertise openly on campus, participate in formal rush, and become a voting member of the Interfraternity Council. Unfortunately, the request was denied. The student council decided Theta Delta Theta was something more than just a social club, but not yet ready to be called a fraternity. Theta Delta Theta may have been sincere in their efforts, but they did not understand fraternity politics, at least not yet. [522]

The aftermath of this vote, however, held little direct consequence for Theta Delta Theta. They could still continue as an organization and recruit new members, they just had to stay outside of the fraternity system. So, throughout the 1954–55 school year, Theta Delta Theta held social events, added more members, and most importantly, worked towards building a stronger case for recognition. As a major step in this regard, the members of Theta Delta Theta teamed with Zeta Psi in the 1955 spring Mayoralty pageant to support their candidate, Captain Questionmark. But, rather than just hand out flyers or help paint posters, Theta Delta Theta organized a number of elaborate publicity stunts to help elect Zeta Psi's Captain. From marching about campus as a squad of Roman soldiers, to holding horse drawn chariot races on the quad, Theta Delta Theta went over the top in their enthusiasm. Such effort did not go unnoticed by the other fraternities, especially when the Captain took home the win. Theta Delta Theta had started playing the political game, and they were winning.[523]

A semester later, in the fall of 1955, Theta Delta Theta returned to campus with twenty or so members, including all five of the group's founders, now in their senior year. Not surprisingly, the future of Theta Delta Theta weighed heavily on everyone's shoulders, especially since their goal had shifted, if ever so slightly. The idea of becoming a local fraternity at Tufts was no longer the singular, unifying quest within Theta Delta Theta. Instead, many in the group, including some of the newest members, felt their future lay in affiliating with a national fraternity. All across the United States, national fraternities were starting to dominate Greek life, helped in no small part by the opening up new chapters in record number. A few well-established local fraternities, including some that had been in existence for over a century, were able to compete successfully for new members in this new environment. But, these locals were the exception. Many within Theta Delta Theta wanted their organization to continue well beyond their undergraduate years, and the best way for this, they argued, was to "go national."[524]

This change of direction opened up a serious and prolonged debate within Theta Delta Theta that fall semester. The group's chapter meetings in Dean Hall soon became contentious, with about one-third wanting to remain local, while the rest felt otherwise. The discussion came to a head on November 1, 1955, when the members took a formal vote on the issue. Local, or national? The decision was not unanimous, but after the votes were tallied, the path was clear. Theta Delta Theta would seek affiliation with a national fraternity. To nine members of Theta Delta Theta strongly opposed to affiliation, including three of its original founders, this vote was too much; they soon resigned in protest, leaving just over a dozen men to carry on. Only two founders from the original Curtis Hall dining group remained, Bruce Gordon and Marty Billings, their commitment to Theta Delta Theta ever strengthened.[525]

Perhaps you'd prefer someone else?

In the aftermath of the vote, Theta Delta Theta took November 1, 1955, as their new "official" founding date, and immediately began working towards national affiliation. First, though, the group needed to secure that vaunted recognition as a local fraternity, for without such recognition, no national would sign on. Fortunately, recognition came swift and easy this time around. The student council eagerly accepted their application in the spring of 1956, without issue, due in no small part to Theta Delta Theta's mastery of fraternity politics over the previous year. Then came affiliation, which began with a few members of Theta Delta Theta making cursory calls to a number of national fraternities.

Soon enough one fraternity stood out above the rest, and that was Tau Kappa Epsilon (TKE). Not only was TKE very interested in expanding to Tufts (the fraternity was well on its way to becoming the largest in the country), but Theta Delta Theta was very impressed with TKE and their policy of non-discrimination. Unlike many other national organizations at the time, TKE was open to all men regardless of race or religion, and all within Theta Delta Theta fully supported this policy. Additionally, TKE's position satisfied the requirements recently enacted by the Tufts administration and the student council, which demanded that any new fraternity at Tufts be free of discriminatory membership practices, no exceptions. All was therefore coming together rather nicely for Theta Delta Theta. To top things off, as that spring semester came to a close, national officers from TKE arrived at Tufts to begin the process of bringing the chapter officially under their fold.[526]

Underneath Theta Delta Theta's effort to go TKE, though, was another political problem that reached all the way to the top of Tufts University. Joel Reynolds, an alumnus of Tufts and an ardent supporter of his fraternity, Delta Tau Delta, was also a Tufts trustee at the time. Additionally, he was very active on the national fraternity scene, as evidenced by his earlier efforts to bring Sigma Nu and Theta Chi to the Tufts campus. He surely watched the rise of Theta Delta Theta with great interest, and most likely felt they would make a wonderful addition to the campus as a chapter in a national fraternity. However, when he heard they wanted to join TKE, his heart sank. Joel Reynolds simply did not like TKE as an organization. Why he felt this way remains a mystery, but reasons were no matter. He had the political means to push Theta Delta Theta away from TKE, so that is what he did. Sometime before the end of the 1955–56 school year, Mr. Reynolds got word to Theta Delta Theta that they should reconsider their choice for affiliation. As for which other national fraternity to pursue, that was up to Theta Delta Theta, but the message was loud and clear: anyone but TKE.[527]

Such a directive came as quite a surprise to the members of Theta Delta Theta. They were strongly in favor of affiliating with TKE, and indeed had even started using the fraternity's pledge materials and part of their ritual, even though they were not yet an official colony. But, Joel Reynolds was not one to cross, especially when those in Theta Delta Theta knew they'd need his help securing a chapter house on campus. As a result, they had no choice but to do as Mr. Reynolds had instructed. But, that didn't mean they had to play fair. Those in Theta Delta Theta knew quite well Tufts would not allow any national fraternity on campus with restrictive membership policies. They also knew Mr. Reynolds could do nothing about this rule, no matter how much he disliked TKE. So, Theta Delta Theta looked to use this rule against him. All they had to do was get TKE to provide a list of fraternities that still practiced discrimination, contact all on the list, tell the Tufts administration they had tried, and then go forward with TKE as planned. A brilliant scheme if ever there was one. Perhaps, though, it was just a little too brilliant.[528]

TKE played the perfect co-conspirator by compiling a list of about half a dozen fraternities that would not be welcome at Tufts. Tasked with calling these organizations on behalf of Theta Delta Theta was a junior named Bill Cummings. One by one he phoned up each fraternity and acted through a rehearsed script, which went something like this: "Hello, is this the Alpha Beta fraternity? Yes, I represent a local organization at Tufts University, and we were wondering if you would be interested in our group for affiliation. First, though, do you have any restrictive membership policies or practices? You do? Oh, that's too bad. Tufts University will not allow you to come to campus. Sorry for the inconvenience." And so it went for Bill as he made his way down the list, all perfectly according to plan. Then he came to Phi Sigma Kappa, a national fraternity founded in Massachusetts. The phone call started as expected, but when Bill got to the question of discrimination, he received an unexpected answer. "No," the Phi Sigma Kappa representative told him, "we no longer practice discrimination in our fraternity." Unbeknownst to TKE, Phi Sigma Kappa had recently opened up the fraternity to men of all races and religions, thus making the organization eligible to enter Tufts. As the conversation progressed, Bill found himself more and more interested in what Phi Sigma Kappa had to say, especially when the fraternity emphatically told him they were committed to diversity among their brotherhood. On the flip side, those in Phi Sigma Kappa became more and more interested in Bill and the story of Theta Delta Theta, to the point where they could no longer contain their enthusiasm. "We would love to come to Tufts!" went the resounding cry from Phi Sigma Kappa.[529]

This conversation left a mighty impression on Bill he could not ignore. So, he went back to Theta Delta Theta and announced there just might be a wrinkle in their affiliation plans. It did not take him long to convince the rest of the chapter that Phi Sigma Kappa merited a closer look. As a first step, Bill arranged for the district director of Phi Sigma Kappa, along with a few members from the MIT chapter, to meet with Theta Delta Theta's leadership over dinner. The presence of MIT undergraduates at such an early meeting was no accident. Phi Sigma Kappa's ability to have undergraduates interact with the Tufts group was a huge plus for the fraternity, and one that TKE could not match, for they did not have an active chapter in the Boston area. Therefore, TKE could only send alumni to talk with Theta Delta Theta, but alumni, unfortunately, have never been completely in touch with the wants or needs of current undergraduates. As a result, Theta Delta Theta's conversations with both fraternities throughout the fall semester of 1956 went in opposite directions, with Phi Sigma Kappa, and not TKE, winning over the hearts and minds of those in Theta Delta Theta. So much for the grand plan to sidestep Mr. Reynolds with tomfoolery. On the contrary, Mr. Reynolds seemed to be getting exactly what he wanted.[530]

In the mean time, the fall of 1956 was shaping up as the best one yet for Theta Delta Theta. That semester the chapter finally had a space to call their own on campus, even if it was only two rooms in the basement of West Hall recently vacated by another local Tufts fraternity, Beta Chi. The chapter got right to work making this space their home by putting a fresh coat of paint on the walls, buying some new furniture, and adding the most luxurious of luxuries, a twenty-one inch DuMont television set, where undoubtedly they spent many an hour watching popular programs such as *Dragnet*, *The Ed Sullivan Show*, and *Alfred Hitchcock Presents*. Also, for the first time since being recognized as an official Tufts fraternity, Theta Delta Theta participated in formal rush, and their efforts brought ten new pledges into the chapter. Membership now stood at almost thirty men, the largest and strongest Theta Delta Theta had yet been. However, as the semester came to a close, all in the chapter realized it was time to decide on affiliation. The debate continued into the new year, and was finally put to a vote on January 14, 1957. In the end, the choice was unanimous. Phi Sigma Kappa.[531]

Home state heroes

When first opened a few years after the Civil War, the Massachusetts Agricultural College (MAC) was a small and humble school, dedicated to instructing its citizens in the ways of agriculture, engineering, and the military. Such curriculum was in sharp contrast to the prestigious liberal arts colleges in the area such as Williams and Amherst, thus giving MAC a reputation as being somewhat of a scholastic experiment. For six men entering their sophomore year in the fall of 1872, this reputation was of no concern, for MAC was exactly where they wanted to be. These six were an eclectic group, teetotalers for certain, but far from being quiet or reserved (two stereotypes often associated with Victorian-era teetotalers), they were all leaders in their class and very good friends. By the spring of 1873, these six men had become impressed with the idea of fraternity, but wholly unimpressed with the two already on the MAC campus. So, they started a new one. As for a name, they chose a cryptic set of three symbols, each roughly in the shape of the letter "T." These symbols stood for the secret motto of the fraternity, but to those on the outside, the inherent mystery soon gave rise to some nicknames, including "the Three T's" and "tea-trade and traffic." As a result, many in the fraternity felt they also needed a recognizable (as well as pronounceable) name for the benefit of the general public. But, this feeling was far from unanimous, so on went the debate for years. Finally, in 1878, the members decreed their fraternity would forever be known as Phi Sigma Kappa.[532]

For the next ten years, Phi Sigma Kappa remained an active local organization on the MAC campus, with no thought of expanding their fraternity to other nearby schools. Then came an opportunity. In the fall of 1887, a Phi Sigma Kappa alumnus from MAC entered the Albany Medical School in upstate New York, and found the campus devoid of fraternity life, if not a social life in general; such was (and still is) the rigors of medical education. So, a semester later, this alumnus started a Phi Sigma Kappa chapter at Albany to enhance the social experience of the students. The fraternity with a strange secret name was now a national organization. From this modest beginning, Phi Sigma Kappa expanded in earnest over the next few decades, mainly in the Northeastern part of the country and even into Canada (though that chapter did not live a long life). By the early 1950s, Phi Sigma Kappa had grown into one of the larger national fraternities, with a true coast-to-coast presence and five active chapters in its home state of Massachusetts. Then, the fraternity received that fateful phone call from Tufts.[533]

Phi Sigma Kappa wasted little time examining Theta Delta Theta as a potential new chapter that spring of 1957. There were meetings, consultations, and visits by Theta Delta Theta to other Phi Sigma Kappa chapters in New England, all aimed at making sure they were right for the fraternity. They were. So, on May 4, 1957, just four short months after their vote, the twenty-eight members of Theta Delta Theta were initiated as the Iota Tetarton chapter of the Phi Sigma Kappa, at a ceremony held in the Cohen Fine Arts Center. Unfortunately, neither Bruce Gordon nor Marty Billings were among this group of initiates, as both had graduated in 1956. However, one person taking a prominent place at the installation banquet was none other than Joel Reynolds, obviously pleased that other fraternity was nowhere to be found.[534]

Mr. Reynolds, though, had more to give the chapter than just a dinnertime speech at the banquet. By the end of that spring semester, Phi Sigma Kappa had solidified plans to move into a bona-fide chapter house at 98 Packard Avenue the following fall, right next door to the Theta Chi fraternity. The location may have been ideal, but the house was not. It was very small, it had no yard, and it needed some serious interior work to accommodate the fraternity. Tufts agreed to loan the chapter $6,000 to renovate the space over the summer, at least until Mr. Reynolds stepped in with a better idea. As luck would have it, a much larger house at 25 Whitfield Road, just a block away, came onto the real estate market in the late spring of 1957. Since this house was much more suited to a fraternity than 98 Packard Avenue, Mr. Reynolds encouraged the Tufts administration to buy the house and rent it back to Phi Sigma Kappa. Tufts agreed to the idea, but left the sale negotiation to an undergraduate member of the chapter, Bill Cummings. Soon enough, Bill had whittled the price down to $25,000, and then Tufts became the proud new owner of 25 Whitfield Road. Most importantly, Phi Sigma Kappa now had a home.[535]

The chapter happily settled into its new quarters in the fall of 1957, and over the next few years began to establish itself firmly on the Tufts campus. The

Phi Sigma Kappa members pose on the steps of their house at 25 Whitfield Road, circa 1961.

late 1950s and early 1960s were halcyon days for fraternities at Tufts, and Phi Sigma Kappa certainly did well during this era, with a strong brotherhood and an active alumni group. But by the late 1960s, the tide of discontent over civil rights and the Vietnam War had enveloped the Tufts campus, and students began to explode in protest. Bearing the brunt of the dissatisfaction were the Greek-letter fraternities. All were soon tagged as an extension of the old "establishment," and seen as too stuck in their conservative and outdated ways, too irrelevant in the modern era. As a result, membership in all Greek organizations fell off dramatically by the early 1970s, even causing a few of the fraternities and all four of the sororities to close down completely. Phi Sigma Kappa managed to hold on during the 1971–72 school year, but its future certainly looked bleak given the small chapter size. Still, those that remained were not ready to give up without a fight. They were confident they could rebuild their chapter in the semesters ahead with some hard work. At least they thought they could, until the cry for help came along.[536]

Burning down the house

Life on the Tufts campus in the summer is considerably more relaxed than during the academic school year, as the student population shrinks to a fraction of its normal size, the campus becomes peacefully quiet, and the vibrant social scene fades into the warm embrace of long, lazy days. For Phi Sigma Kappa, however, the summer of 1972 was anything but tranquil. Under normal circumstances, their house at 25 Whitfield would have been filled with fraternity brothers enjoying their summer together. But, with membership at an all-time low, there just weren't enough men to live in the house, and this situation placed a huge financial stress on the chapter. An obvious solution to the money problem soon appeared to those managing the fraternity's affairs, even if it was slightly unconventional. That summer, to clear the red ink off the books, Phi Sigma Kappa allowed women to move into their house, right alongside the men. Sure enough, a few accepted the invitation, and those in the chapter breathed a little easier. Co-ed living had already been established in a few Tufts dormitories, so such a move was not considered controversial. For Phi Sigma Kappa, however, this arrangement almost led to a tragedy.[537]

It happened in the early morning of July 1, 1972. A loud boom, followed by a blaring fire alarm. Within moments, the residents of 25 Whitfield were all awake and smelling smoke. This was no drill. The house was on fire, and as they ran down to the first floor, they saw flames engulfing the drapes and furniture in the living room. Luckily, all got out of the house unscathed, and the quick response by local fire departments minimized the damage to the structure. But, the emotional damage had been done, for this was no accident. That night, according to the press, the Phi Sigma Kappa fraternity house at Tufts had been firebombed, the first time any fraternity across the country had ever been attacked in such a manner. For the Tufts community, this was hardly an isolated incident, as no fewer than six campus buildings had been firebombed or set ablaze by arsonists in the previous three years, including the Fletcher School, which had a number of offices destroyed, and North Hall, which burned to the ground. Phi Sigma Kappa, it seemed, was in the middle of an arson epidemic, even if no one was exactly sure why the fraternity had been targeted.[538]

The truth, as it came to be known, proved to be somewhat anti-climactic for the conspiracy theorists. Whereas the Fletcher School had been firebombed to protest the school's involvement in "government activities and the [Vietnam] war," and whereas other academic buildings had been targeted for housing elements of the ROTC program, Phi Sigma Kappa's firebombing was not a political statement in any manner. It wasn't even technically a firebombing. Instead, the "attack" was a plea for attention that went awry. On that fateful night, Bill Girolamo, an undergraduate and former member of Phi Sigma Kappa, decided the best way to garner the attention of Kathy, a female resident of 25 Whitfield Road and a woman he had been infatuated with for months (but had spurned all of his advances), was to throw a couple of M-80 firecrackers into the fireplace. How and why Bill though such an act would win the affection he so desired of Kathy is hard to comprehend, but Bill was thought to be conflicted, and indeed had recently been kicked out of the fraternity due to his erratic behavior. The M-80s were just a little too powerful, though, and once detonated they ignited the nearby drapes and furniture. Bill witnessed his mistake, and to his credit, he immediately pulled the fire alarm before running out of the house and into the night.[539]

Over the next few months, life at 25 Whitfield stayed relatively quiet, though not free of anxiety, while the police investigated the fire. Bill was considered a person of interest almost immediately, since his relationship with the fraternity was known to be quite acrimonious, and he'd been heard asking too many questions around campus about firebombs. Still, he remained free until finally surrendering to the police in early September of 1972. Immediately afterwards, the anxiety level in Phi Sigma Kappa dissipated away, which allowed the members to prepare for the upcoming fall rush season, an event they were counting on to rebuild their chapter. But in this regard, their enthusiasm was short lived. Repairs to the house were slow, which made the fire damage hard to ignore; the charred living room certainly gave many a potential rushee great pause. Adding to the dismay was Bill himself, for he was released from custody during the 1972–73 school year and left to go about his merry way. A number of those in Phi Sigma Kappa, fearing Bill might try something else, moved out of the fraternity house that year. As a result, that school year was a disaster for Phi Sigma Kappa. Following graduation in May of 1973, the chapter was down to a mere four members, all rising seniors. What had started with so much promise some sixteen years earlier looked to be headed straight to dormancy.[540]

Let the music play

Even amidst all the negativity, those four who remained were not ready to give up. They returned to campus in the fall of 1973, moved back into their chapter house and got to work rebuilding their fraternity. Their immediate need was filling the empty rooms, so they advertised around campus for men who wanted to move into their spacious house and, hopefully, become part of their small brotherhood. Six sophomores having a miserable experience in the dormitories answered the call, and of these six, four also decided to pledge Phi Sigma Kappa. Such a group was hardly large enough to ease all fears of closing down, but at least the new men gave the fraternity some time to figure out how to rebuild in earnest. These four pledges took the first step in this process when they were initiated into Phi Sigma Kappa in the early spring of 1974, thereby doubling the chapter's size. But, as it turned out, this was as far as the rebuilding effort went. No one else officially joined Phi Sigma Kappa that year, so with graduation looming, the chapter was headed right back to where it had started, clinging to life with only four members.[541]

Faced with this reality, the official members of Phi Sigma Kappa sat down late in the 1974 spring semester to determine their future. The four seniors, having struggled for years to keep their fraternity alive, finally decided they'd had enough. They wanted to close down the chapter for good and use any remaining funds to construct a memorial stone bench on campus. Such a tribute was the proper thing to do, they argued, and would ensure a lasting legacy to all who had come before in Phi Sigma Kappa. The four sophomores, however, had a much different idea. They wanted to use whatever money remained not for a masonic declaration of defeat, but for a renewed commitment to social activities. After all, they lived in a great big house, so why not enjoy the space? The vote was at a stalemate until the sophomores convinced one of the seniors to come to their side. Then, by a five-to-three majority rule, the future of Phi Sigma Kappa was set. The fraternity would go on.[542]

Well, not completely. After the four seniors graduated in 1974, those who remained at 25 Whitfield Road were not stereotypical fraternity men. They, along with their two classmates who'd moved in but hadn't officially joined the fraternity, were self-described "freaks," enthusiastic members of the counterculture, with long hair and radical ideas often at odds with the mainstream. And now that they were in charge, they had absolutely no interest in the traditional Phi Sigma Kappa fraternity experience. Instead, they wanted to build a brand new community at Tufts, one better aligned with their goals and desires. So, when they returned to campus in the fall of 1974, they took down the Phi Sigma Kappa flag, put away the secret fraternity rituals, and renamed their organization "25 Whitfield," although they soon garnered the nickname of "Freak Frat" around campus, for obvious reasons. Officially they were still the Iota Tetarton chapter of Phi Sigma Kappa, for their charter was in place and they were recognized as being active by the national organization. But the relationship with Phi Sigma Kappa was a ruse, kept alive mainly so the group could stay in the house – a dissolution of the chapter, it appears, would have negated the lease agreement and put the residents out on the street.[543]

As for what type of community those in 25 Whitfield wanted to build, the answer was soon obvious. That fall, they embraced the concept of co-educational, cooperative living by inviting both men and women to join their organization. Co-ed living was growing fast on campus, and indeed the ex-members of the Alpha Tau Omega chapter were also in the midst of creating a similar organization in their fraternity house. Soon joining the six in 25 Whitfield at the beginning of the semester were three men and three women, all of whom became full voting members of the cooperative and shared in the responsibility of running the house. Additionally, 25 Whitfield took in a number of dogs as pets, much to the consternation of university administrators, who were not in favor of animals living in fraternity houses at the time. Then, the members of the Freak Frat embarked on their goal of building anything but a typical organization. For example, instead of hosting rowdy keg parties (still very much in vogue on campus), they started a café in the basement of 25 Whitfield, which they named Café Corrina in honor of the folk song "Corrina, Corrina" as well as one of the house dogs. Café Corrina soon became home to a burgeoning campus folk scene, with groups including The Great Next Whatever and Bert and Bart entertaining the masses on many a night.[544]

Indeed, it was with music that the Freak Frat made a significant contribution to campus life, one that is still celebrated today. It all began in the spring of 1975, when the members of 25 Whitfield decided to throw an all-campus party. Such an idea was certainly not new, as the Tufts administration already organized a "Spring Weekend" each year, which featured many different events over the course of a few days such as movie screenings, dance parties, and a concert in front of the bookstore. The party 25 Whitfield had in mind, however, would be a festival of live music with a straightforward implementation: line up a half dozen or so local bands, buy some kegs of beer, set up an outdoor stage on campus, and invite everyone. In addition, the timeframe of this event would be significantly longer. Whereas the events in Spring Weekend were spread out and each lasted no more than one or two hours, 25 Whitfield's party would run continuously for at least eight hours, thus making it an all day extravaganza. As for the name, they decided to call the event "The Fester P. Gazotsky Springtime Orgasm Festival," or "Festers" for short. A strange name, for certain, but one that seemed fitting of the times.[545]

At first, the event seemed simple enough to organize. The members of 25 Whitfield had no trouble finding some open space on campus and bands willing to perform there for free. However, finding the money to hire security personnel and rent sound equipment was proving to be difficult, since potential sponsors such as dormitories or other Tufts students groups were not interested. The idea of selling tickets was soon discounted, for the members wanted the concert to be free. That left one main avenue for revenue: selling beer to thirsty listeners. Those in 25 Whitfield knew that having beer for sale was the key to success, not just financially, but realistically – without such refreshments, the students would most likely have stayed away. However, when they approached local authorities about securing a temporary liquor license, they were told "no." End of discussion. Festers, it now seemed, was headed straight to the scrap heap of good ideas.[546]

Those in 25 Whitfield were not willing to give up so easily. Instead, they employed a trick to skirt the liquor license requirement, one that had been used decades earlier by social clubs to avoid local prohibition laws. To start, the members of 25 Whitfield formed a non-profit organization called Fester Enterprises, with the stated goal of "combat[ing] the chronic ailment of this campus: the lack of parties with live bands and beer." Certainly not the most charitable goal, but at least they were honest. Next, and this was where the scheme came together, they sold shares of the organization at $5 a piece to anyone willing to pay. With the revenue generated from these transactions, 25 Whitfield could then rent the equipment, hire security, and buy the beer, which would then be distributed free at the concert. Free beer, yes, but only to shareholders – all other spectators would have to bring their own. Today, such an arrangement on campus would be outlawed, but in 1975 this was perfectly legal and, somewhat surprisingly, acceptable to the Tufts administration. Once the plan was put in place, all 25 Whitfield needed were students to buy in.[547]

At first, many on campus seemed skeptical of the event, as they wondered just who was this Fester P. Gazotsky character and why he was throwing a party. A letter to the *Tufts Observer* from 25 Whitfield assured the campus the event not a joke, but was instead "a serious attempt by a few students to throw a spring festival on campus for the students." The plea was well received, and soon a number of students owned shares of Fester Enterprises. Finally, on April 26, 1975, Festers went off almost as advertised on the lawn near Ellis Oval. Almost, that is, because those in 25 Whitfield never had any intention of checking for shareholders or even setting up fences. Instead, Festers was an open concert from the very first note, and all who stopped by were able to enjoy free beer, at least until the kegs ran dry. The event was such a success that 25 Whitfield organized a second Festers in the spring of 1976, only this one went for ten hours and was held on the lawn between Lewis Hall (affectionately called "Freefer Hall" at the time) and Tilton Hall. Eventually, and with the help of other campus groups, Festers evolved into the annual end-of-classes party known today on campus as Spring Fling, although the modern-day event features plenty of security, lots of fences, and not a drop of alcohol. Still, the celebration that has brought world famous musicians such as Stevie Ray Vaughn, B. B. King, LL Cool J, and Guster to campus can be traced back to Fester P. Gazotsky and the ingenuity of 25 Whitfield.[548]

LIFE IN 25 WHITFIELD CONTINUED IN EARNEST as the mid-1970s rolled on. Both men and women were welcomed each year as new members, and while none of the men ever joined Phi Sigma Kappa, the fraternal hoax continued. Between 1974 and 1976, officers from the national Phi Sigma Kappa organization made a few visits to 25 Whitfield Road to talk with the members and assess how the chapter was doing. Somehow, the four official members of Phi Sigma Kappa managed to convince these national representatives that they were still operating as an all-male fraternity and still working to grow the chapter, despite the presence of non-members and women in the house. This was a complete and blatant lie by the Tufts group, but again, it allowed them to keep control of the house so they could continue their community. On this front, the Freak Frat soon branched from music to the printed word. In the fall of 1975, the members of 25 Whitfield set up a printing press in their basement and began publishing an alternative literary magazine called *Squid Ink*, which was sold around campus for twenty-five cents. Such an act was reminiscent of fraternity life from a hundred years prior, when Zeta Psi and Theta Delta Chi published the very first literary magazines at Tufts College. Now, it was 25 Whitfield's turn to enlighten the campus with whimsical poetry, enlightened prose, and fanciful artwork. Most importantly, the Freak Frat had finally become a self-sustaining organization, one that seemed primed to continue in earnest. So, almost on cue, trouble just had to come knocking.[549]

One serious problem was the fraternity's lease, which had expired in the summer of 1975. Those in 25 Whitfield knew they needed to remain part of an official organization if they were to keep control of their house in the future. After all, 25 Whitfield Road had been earmarked for and leased to a fraternity, not a random group of residents. But, they also knew they were pushing their luck pretending to be a chapter of Phi Sigma Kappa. Faced with this reality, it appears the members of 25 Whitfield, in cooperation with their alumni, decided to end the ruse. They officially changed their name from "Phi Sigma Kappa" to "25 Whitfield Association" in the spring of 1976, thereby becoming a bona fide Massachusetts corporation as well as a new, local fraternity. With their organization now set, the members of 25 Whitfield then notified the national headquarters of Phi Sigma Kappa they wanted out. The national officers had little recourse but to pull the charter and declare Iota Tetarton as dormant.[550]

Unfortunately, this re-branding effort was soon all for naught. During the summer of 1976, the Tufts administration decided to end its relationship with the Freak Frat. As for a reason, it seems the two sides were unable to agree on the terms of a new lease, though there was probably more to the story than recorded in the press. Regardless, the verdict was clear. The members of 25 Whitfield had but six months, until January of 1977, to vacate their house. That left the fraternity the ensuing fall semester to turn everything around and hopefully secure a new lease. But, it was not to be. The problem was one that has plagued fraternities ever since they started occupying houses: noise. On a Saturday night in the early fall of 1976, those in 25 Whitfield threw a party, as did a number of other cooperative houses on their street, including the German House and the Latin House. For the neighbors, especially those not affiliated with the university, this revelry was too much. Their subsequent complaints to the university were many, including "obscene remarks, a loud song fest, unleashed dogs, trash, blaring music, and a young man who urinated in the neighbors [sic] bushes." And though multiple houses hosted parties that night, it was 25 Whitfield that took the brunt of the blame. The Tufts administration immediately placed the group on social probation, thereby ending the parties for the time being, if not also the chance for a new lease.[551]

As that fall semester went forward, 25 Whitfield successfully appealed their social probation, in part by arguing they had been unfairly singled out for punishment that fateful night. Indeed, they remained in the house for the entire school year, as the Tufts administration probably realized the logistical difficulties they faced trying to fill the house with new residents halfway through the school year. But still, there would be no new lease for 25 Whitfield. Tufts had found another tenant. Throughout the 1976–77 school year, and unbeknownst to 25 Whitfield, the newly formed Chi Omega sorority had been negotiating with the administration about occupying 25 Whitfield Road the following school year. Chi Omega argued that a group of women chartered by a national sorority would be a much better tenant than a co-ed group known as the Freak Frat. The Tufts administration soon agreed wholeheartedly. So, following the end of the 1976–77 school year, one which saw the third annual Festers take place, 25 Whitfield moved out of its house and said goodbye as an organization. The communal and free spirit that was the Freak Frat soon retreated into history.[552]

DESPITE PHI SIGMA KAPPA'S RELATIVELY SHORT TIME ON CAMPUS, the fraternity did turn out more than a few outstanding alumni. One is Bill Cummings of the class of 1958, the same Bill Cummings who pushed for affiliation with Phi Sigma Kappa and negotiated the purchase of 25 Whitfield Road. After graduating, Bill used his house buying experience to help create a very successful commercial real estate company that manages properties along the Route 128 high tech corridor just north of Medford, Massachusetts. Indeed, Bill is a large benefactor of Tufts, having funded a significant portion of the Tufts Cummings School of Veterinary Medicine in Grafton, Massachusetts. Within the past few years, he and his wife, Joyce, have followed in the footsteps of Bill Gates and Warren Buffet by taking the "Giving Pledge" and agreeing to donate ninety percent of their wealth to charity. At present time, their donation is on the order of $1.2 billion dollars.[553]

PSI UPSILON (Zeta Tau chapter, 1981 – 1992)

In the early 1800s, a student looking to attend the largest, most progressive college in America usually looked no further than Union College in Schenectady, New York. Due in no small part to the leadership of Eliphalet Nott, its president, Union College drew the best men from around the country at a time when most other schools only drew from the local area surrounding their campus. Union College back then was a thriving community of a hundred or more students studying not only to be ministers (certainly a common educational path in the early 19th century), but also physicians, lawyers, and businessmen. Outside of the classroom, Union College offered numerous outlets for student expression including literary societies, which first appeared in 1793, and Greek-letter social fraternities, which were first organized in 1825. Of these organizations, it was the three fraternities – Kappa Alpha, Delta Phi, and Sigma Phi – that dominated campus life by the 1830s. Known collectively as the Triad, these three were a powerful political force, especially when it came to academic accolades. If you were not a member of a fraternity in the Triad, you faced an uphill (if not impossible) battle for scholastic honors.[554]

In the fall of 1833, though, a group of five sophomores and two freshmen decided they'd had enough of the Triad and their machinations. The seven were members of the Delphian Institute literary society, but, unlike others in the society, were not in one of the Triad fraternities. As a result, these seven were routinely passed over for honors or leadership positions in Delphian – the fraternity men tended to keep these roles for themselves, a testament of their political power on campus. So, in a form of protest befitting the day, these seven men began meeting on their own, where they recited poetry and discussed essays. Soon enough, conversations quickly centered on forming a brand new secret society, one that could stand on equal footing to the Triad. Then, on November 24, 1833, the seven men wrote and signed the following pledge to each other:

> We, the Undersigned, having a determination to form a secret society, and having had some conversation upon the subject, do now and hereby pledge our sacred honors that we will keep all that has been said and done a most profound secret and that, if we please, at or before the beginning of the next term, we will meet and form a society.[555]

The Psi Upsilon (Psi U) fraternity had just been founded. Still, the men kept their organization a secret from the rest of the campus until June 1834, when they first wore their distinctive diamond badges in public. The members of the Triad were not pleased to see a new fraternity on campus. Intense rivalry between such organizations was the norm for the day, and the Triad collectively vowed to destroy their upstart competitor. To accomplish this feat, they turned to the proven method of humiliation. They would use their collective power to keep qualified members of Psi U from being elected to Phi Beta Kappa, the prestigious honor society. Such exclusion would certainly paint the new fraternity as an inferior organization at Union, while also demonstrating the growing power of the Triad. Word of this exclusion eventually made its way to President Nott's office, and he was anything but amused. He sent a short note to the Triad, threatening to have the faculty appoint Psi U men to Phi Beta Kappa during the next vacation if they did not drop their opposition. The Triad decided to test this threat, and true to his word, President Nott placed a few Psi U men into Phi Beta Kappa. The Triad had miscalculated, and in their error, Psi U instantly became a powerful rival.[556]

Psi Upsilon remained local to Union College until 1837, when a member transferred to New York University (NYU) and organized a second chapter, thereby making the fraternity a national organization. After NYU, Psi U began a period of growth in New England that soon saw the birth of Sigma chapter at Brown University in 1840 and Gamma chapter at Amherst College in 1841. And it is with Sigma and Gamma chapters that the history of Psi U at Tufts begins.[557]

You're not worthy

In the telling and retelling of the history of Tufts College, much is made about the first seven students to enroll in the fall of 1854. However, those seven were not the only men to study at Tufts that school year. In January of 1855, the school welcomed its eighth student, Henry Blanchard, who moved into a freezing cold room on the third floor of College (now Ballou) Hall and began studying under the tutelage of Professor William Drew. Henry survived his first semester, and he returned in the fall of 1855 as a fully matriculated student. Over the next two school years, Henry looked to make his mark on the small campus, which was soon growing in students and opportunities. He watched the first two fraternities arrive on campus, and while it seems he was intrigued by the idea of fraternity, he did not join either of these organizations. Instead, he embarked on a different plan. He wanted to bring a third fraternity to campus.[558]

The genesis of Henry's idea seems to have sprung from the newest professor at Tufts College. In the fall of 1856, Professor Jerome Schneider became an instructor of Modern Languages, after having spent the previous semester at Amherst College. It was at Amherst where Professor Schneider was initiated into the Gamma chapter of Psi U as an honorary member. The practice of admitting honorary members into Psi U, especially among the faculty, was quite common at the time. Now, it seems, Professor Schneider was interested in bringing his fraternity to Tufts through Henry. A first step in this process required Henry to gain the favor of nearby Psi U chapters, so they could advocate for the Tufts group to the national organization. Sometime during the 1856–57 school year, then, Henry made his way to Brown University, to woo the members of Psi U's Sigma chapter. Little is recorded of his effort, except the outcome. Henry was essentially laughed out of the Psi U room. Tufts College, he was told, "was too new [of a school] to be accorded such an honor." So, Henry returned to Tufts empty handed and gave up completely on the idea of fraternity. For Psi U, prestige was sacrosanct, and Tufts just was not worthy, at least for the next one hundred and twenty years.[559]

Of grand plans and stark realities

Most students, when they first arrive at college, often know very little about Greek-letter organizations, unless a parent or older sibling had previously joined such a group. Lowell Thomas was one such freshman in this latter category. When he stepped foot on the Tufts campus in the fall of 1978, he was already familiar with one fraternity in particular, Psi Upsilon. Not only was his father an alumnus of the Zeta chapter at Dartmouth, but his sister was an active member and president of the Iota chapter at Kenyon College. Psi U is one of a few national fraternities that allow co-ed chapters, as its constitution has never contained a clause limiting membership to men. Of course, Lowell could not immediately follow in his family's footsteps since there was no chapter of Psi U at Tufts. Instead, during the fall of 1978, he joined the sailing team and quickly became friends with some sailors who were also members of Delta Tau Delta (DTD). So, when DTD held their rush a few weeks later, Lowell went down to the house, and soon enough was a newly pinned pledge of DTD.[560]

But DTD was not to be for Lowell. Within short order, he realized he did not mesh with most members of the chapter despite a shared connection in sailing, so he dropped out of the fraternity. Retreating back to his dormitory room in Carmichael Hall, he then found himself among a group of friends including Mark McGillivray and Tom Chapin, two freshmen who were interested in fraternity life, but not in those already on campus. Although Lowell's experience in DTD had ended rather quickly, he, too, was still interested in the idea of fraternity, so the group soon embraced the idea of starting a new one. No new national fraternities had come to Tufts since the late 1950s, but with a renewed interest in fraternity life on campus and across the country (helped in no small part by the release of *Animal House* just a few months earlier), the three felt the time was right to expand Greek life. Lowell had the perfect fraternity in mind for this endeavor, which of course was Psi U. The others needed little convincing. They knew Psi U was regarded as a very prestigious organization, with only a select number of chapters at top-level schools, and they also knew the Boston area was home to many prominent Psi U alumni, which certainly offered promise when it came to professional networking. With no downside, Psi U was the clear, and only choice for the group.[561]

Using contacts through Lowell's family, the men gained the backing of the national organization and began building a provincial chapter at the start of the spring 1979 semester. They wasted little time getting to work. Within a few months, they'd grown the chapter to ten men, and, more importantly, gained recognition as a student organization by the Committee on Student Life. Psi U was now officially the newest Tufts fraternity. After reaching this milestone, they decided to emerge from the shadows and announce their existence to the greater community. To accomplish this task, they chose the tried-and-true method of an article in the weekly student newspaper, the *Tufts Observer*. Psi U's announcement, though, contained a surprising and unexpected revelation. Although the current members of Psi U were all men, they intended to admit women and become a co-ed organization within the near future. By this time, ATO of Massachusetts was firmly established as a local co-ed fraternity at Tufts, and Psi U looked to expand on this concept by becoming the first national co-ed organization on campus. When the school year ended a few months later, all in the chapter were excited about what they'd accomplished so far, and were looking forward to what they could become in the future.[562]

Even after the school year ended, the members of Psi U continued to work on building their organization. They knew they needed a chapter house if they were to compete successfully with the other fraternities on campus. So, over the summer of 1979, Mark negotiated the rental of the two-story house at 14 Whitfield Road for use by the chapter. Although somewhat small, the house was relatively close to the other fraternities on Packard Avenue, which gave Psi U the feel, at least, of being an on-campus organization. Additionally, the vacant lot across the street offered the fraternity some open space for outdoor activities, as 14 Whitfield had little in the way of a yard. Unbeknownst to the members at the time, their renting of 14 Whitfield was remarkable in that no other Tufts fraternity since the 1930s had done so without the help or approval of the administration. True, the house was owned and operated by the Tufts-affiliated Walnut Hill real estate corporation, but there is no indication the administration suggested this course of action, or helped the fraternity secure this rental. Such initiative was reminiscent of half a century earlier, when fraternities had to fend for themselves on the housing market. Psi U, by acting on its own, was a case of history repeating itself.[563]

While renting the house was a positive step forward for the chapter, they were forced to take two steps back when school resumed in the fall of 1979. The problem was manpower. Although the chapter's membership roll had grown to ten by the previous May, now some four months later only five remained, as the others, including Lowell Thomas, had dropped out. With rent to pay and rooms to fill, the situation looked to be a complete and utter disaster for the new chapter. Those left in Psi U, however, were not willing to give up so easily. They soon gathered a number of friends and acquaintances to fill the empty rooms, thereby alleviating the financial stress of running their house. And while some of the boarders looked to 14 Whitfield Road as simply a place to live that year, others decided to join the fraternity and help build Psi U into a viable chapter. By all accounts they were successful. When the school year came to a close, Psi U had grown to thirteen members, they'd established a campus presence by hosting parties and sponsoring campus movie screenings, and they'd created an alumni advisory board to help them run their operations and gain a charter from their national organization. Just about the only goal they abandoned was the admission of women into the chapter, mainly due to pressure from certain elements within the national organization. Psi U at Tufts, it seemed, was not destined to become a co-ed organization after all.[564]

The fall of 1980 started off much better for Psi U than the year prior, as their membership stabilized and could now support the financial realities of running a chapter house. But controversy would soon find Psi U, and it was not the sort of attention they wanted, or even expected. In September of 1980, the chapter sponsored a campus-wide screening of the movie *Deep Throat*, a cult classic of the adult film world. While certainly provocative, such a screening was hardly a first. *Deep Throat* had been shown on campus numerous times in prior years by a variety of different organizations, including the Tufts Film Series. These earlier showings had all been received by the Tufts community without noticeable controversy. Now, though, the situation was anything but calm. In the days and weeks that followed the showing of *Deep Throat*, Psi U received many angry letters of protest, mainly from students associated with the Women's Center at Tufts. These women were especially upset with the movie's pornographic content, they felt it should not have been shown on campus, and they blamed Psi U for a complete lack of sensitivity. Other students, including women, disagreed with this opinion and were generally supportive of Psi U's right to sponsor the movie. As the diatribe played out to a stalemate in *The Tufts Daily*, members of the Women's Center escalated the protest by contacting the national office of Psi Upsilon, thus putting the chapter in an awkward if not embarrassing spot as they worked for their charter. Eventually the rhetoric died down, helped in part by an observation that the Women's Center had not protested the screening of *Deep Throat* two years earlier. Still, the whole episode was a public relations setback for the fraternity and, unfortunately, an omen of things to come.[565]

In the mean time, by the spring of 1981, the chapter had put the movie incident behind them and grown their fraternity to twenty-three members. Then, on April 24, 1981, their efforts were rewarded when they were officially installed as the Zeta Tau chapter of Psi Upsilon, only the thirty-sixth chapter ever established in the fraternity's one hundred forty-eight previous years. Zeta Tau was also the first chapter of Psi Upsilon established in the Boston area since 1850, when the Alpha chapter had been placed at Harvard. Those in Zeta Tau were proud of this accomplishment, but knew they had work to do. As they wrote in the fraternity's national magazine, *The Diamond of Psi Upsilon*, "The next few years are critical for this Chapter, if we are to become a stable force on campus and within the Fraternity. We are aware of the challenges we face, and we are eager to meet them."[566]

In the years following its chartering, Psi Upsilon did indeed carve out its own niche on campus, often drawing its members from the baseball, lacrosse, and hockey teams. But to say Psi U was a "jock" fraternity would be incorrect, as the members, similar to the other fraternities at Tufts, had a diverse set of interests. Socially, Psi U became known for their after-hours parties that started at 1:00 a.m. (much to the consternation of their neighbors, at times), and their annual pig roast in the field across the house. However, not all was positive for Psi U, for they continued to push the limits of acceptable behavior. Despite the negative uproar in 1980 surrounding their sponsorship of *Deep Throat*, Psi U decided to try again by screening a different adult movie, *Insatiable*, one Sunday evening in the spring of 1983. Soon after the movie was announced, however, protests erupted from both individual students and the Tufts Women's Center. Only this time, the protesters aligned with the Intercollegiate Women's Coalition, an outside group opposed to pornography and its treatment of women. Together these groups bombarded Tufts president Jean Mayer with angry phone calls demanding the movie be cancelled. The protesters even threatened to demonstrate outside the venue (Cohen Auditorium) should the screening take place, thus forcing Psi U to consider the hiring of police to preserve order. The administration, fearing an escalation of the situation, advised Psi U to cancel the movie outright, which ultimately they did. Such an outcome meant Tufts had come full circle since 1979, when pornography was shown openly and without issue on campus. Now, the idea only brought more unwanted, negative attention on Psi U. And, unfortunately, the worst was yet to happen.[567]

Housing crunch

Meanwhile, after a few years of operating out of 14 Whitfield Road, the members of Psi U began to feel their house was just too small and too limiting, especially when it came to hosting social functions. But, upgrading their accommodations was not a realistic option, as there were no other viable rental properties close to campus, and the Tufts administration didn't exactly care about fraternity housing woes during the early 1980s, so they were of no help. This all changed in the spring of 1985. With Greek life continuing to expand on campus, and with more of these newer organizations looking to take housing matters into their own hands, the administration realized it was losing control of the situation. So, they decided to change the space at 92 Professors Row from a co-op dormitory to a new fraternity house, in order to bring one additional organization onto campus. Originally built for the well-known and well-loved Professor Charles Fay in 1874, the house at 92 Professors Row is one of the few Victorian structures remaining in its near original form. Now, for the first time in its history, 92 Professors Row would be home to a Greek-letter organization. Fraternities and sororities, even those currently housed, were invited to apply for the right to occupy the space beginning the following semester, with the Interfraternity Council (IFC) and the Tufts administration creating a set of criteria to pick the winner. All told, six organizations submitted applications that spring: Psi U, Sigma Nu, Theta Chi, Alpha Phi, Sigma Phi Epsilon, and Kappa Alpha Psi. Then, just before the campus went on spring break, the IFC ranked these organizations against their metric. Psi U, much to their delight, came out on top. It seemed the chapter was finally going to upgrade their accommodations to a larger and more prominent position on campus.[568]

Well, not so fast. The administration, under the guidance of the Dean of Students office, used a different evaluation process than the IFC, and after considering the applicants, they chose Sigma Nu as the rightful new tenant. It seemed Psi U and Sigma Nu were now in a stand-off, with no obvious path to a resolution. But, almost as quickly as these announcements were made to the campus, the situation corrected itself, as the Tufts administration had to cancel the whole idea. The conversion of 92 Professors Row into a fraternity house was part of a broader plan to change the status of a few Tufts-owned properties including 25 Whitfield Road, which was slated to morph from a privately rented house into a dormitory. The legal process of changing and moving all of these housing licenses soon slowed down to a crawl, so by late March of 1985, the administration had no choice but to postpone the entire plan for a year. Meanwhile, both 92 Professors Row and 25 Whitfield Road would remain as they were, much to the disappointment of many in the Greek community.[569]

For Psi U, this hiccup in housing could not have come at a worse time. After years of strained relations with Walnut Hill Properties (the landlord of 14 Whitfield Road), and after the debacle with 92 Professors Row, Psi U was told in the late spring of 1985 that their current lease would not be renewed for the following school year. What seemed so promising in terms of housing just a few weeks earlier had now been completely reversed. Psi U would soon be a fraternity without a home, a position that would put them at a large disadvantage as compared to their peers. To remedy this situation, the members regrouped during the 1985–86 school year and followed the same plan they had used just six years before. On their own initiative, they scoured the neighborhoods around Tufts for a new house to rent, eventually settling on a duplex at 165 College Avenue. This area of Somerville has a storied history in terms of Greek housing at Tufts, as College Avenue had been a second "Fraternity Row" when five different fraternities made it their home during the 1920s and 1930s. The Great Depression, among other factors, forced most of these organizations to close down and give up their houses, and by 1947 the last remaining fraternity left the neighborhood, seemingly for good. Now, almost forty years later, a fraternity flag was coming back to College Avenue.[570]

Heading the wrong way

Psi U settled into their new house and immediately looked to get back to normal operations. But, this was easier said than done. Their house at 165 College Avenue was nestled between many double-and triple-decker structures in a densely populated neighborhood, much more so than on Whitfield Road. As a result, Psi U was now in very close proximity to its neighbors, which was hardly the perfect location for a fraternity house. Additionally, their home was well removed from the center of campus, which put them on the fringes of fraternity life at Tufts, and away from casual interaction with the general student population. Still, the chapter did well, as they recruited new members each year (often using their historical connections to a few sports teams to their advantage), held social events at their house, and were recognized occasionally in *The Tufts Daily* for their philanthropy work. Most importantly, they seemed to have little trouble with the Tufts administration. Being somewhat off campus seemed to be working out quite well for the chapter, after all.[571]

The good situation, unfortunately, did not last. Problems started finding Psi U once again in the spring of 1987, when the student-led Inter-Greek Council (IGC) and the Tufts administration began developing behavioral standards and rules for fraternities and sororities. The push for such oversight was long coming and followed numerous incidents over the years between various fraternities (though not necessarily Psi U), the Tufts administration, and local residents. One core tenet of this new oversight was a rule that fraternities and sororities could only occupy chapter houses officially sanctioned by the administration. Chapters could not simply go out and rent or buy houses for themselves, not anymore. Psi U was one of four fraternities directly affected by this policy, the crux of which said they could no longer use 165 College Avenue as their home.[572]

Thus started a war on semantics that would play out nearly continuously for the next five years between Psi U, the IGC, and the Tufts administration. The problem was the definition of the phrase, "official fraternity house." In reality, 165 College Avenue was rented privately to individuals each school year, and not to a fraternity or their alumni corporation. Most years, all who rented rooms in 165 College Avenue just happened to be members of Psi U, but not always. However, it was an open secret on campus that Psi U considered 165 College Avenue the base of its operations. For example, they often held rush parties and social events at that house, even advertising the address in *The Tufts Daily* for all to see. Psi U was hardly alone in this regard. Zeta Beta Tau, Alpha Epsilon Pi, and Alpha Sigma Phi were also without official chapter houses in the late 1980s, and all three of these fraternities also based their operations in various off-campus properties, sometimes the same house for years. These three also made no secret of their location, as they, too, routinely advertised events and rush parties at their unofficial addresses. However, of the four fraternities playing fast and loose with the new rules, only Psi U felt the wrath of the IGC and the administration with regards to their housing situation, mainly due to unwanted attention.[573]

The first incident happened in late January of 1989. One night that month, a non-Tufts student showed up at 165 College Avenue looking to enter a party being hosted by Psi U. Apparently, Psi U was not his first stop, as he showed up drunk and with a hand stamp, a telltale sign of having been to at least one other social engagement earlier that night. Standing at the door of 165 College Avenue were a number of Psi U members and friends who subsequently denied entry to this individual. He, of course, did not agree with the decision, so a heated discussion ensued, and during the conversation a few punches were thrown, some of which found the individual's jaw in a most unpleasant manner. Such a welcoming convinced the individual to move on for the evening, and the matter appeared closed.[574]

It was not. A few days later, the family of this individual reported the incident to the Tufts Police, which they said had occurred at, "Psi Upsilon, 165 College Avenue." This report triggered an investigation into the incident, but for the victim's family, this was not enough. They also filed a lawsuit against a few of the residents of 165 College Avenue, the national organization of Psi Upsilon, and the Tufts administration over the physical and emotional distress caused by the altercation. Now the chapter had a big problem, for the lawsuit could not be ignored. Additionally, Tufts was forced to take a look at what, exactly, was going on at 165 College Avenue. This part of the investigation fell to the faculty-led Committee on Social Fraternity and Sorority Life (CFS), which soon scrutinized all aspects of the chapter, including their unofficial residence. A semester later, in the fall of 1989, the CFS made their ruling. They determined that Psi U had most likely (but not definitively) maintained an illegal chapter house at 165 College Avenue. The punishment for this, and a few other small transgressions, was to place the fraternity on warning status, meaning any other minor infraction could result in suspension, or even expulsion from campus. In response to this punishment, Psi U filed an appeal with the CFS, claiming 165 College Avenue, while home to many members the past few years, was in no way their official chapter house.[575]

On its surface, the appeal looked to be a non-starter, given the long association between Psi U and that address. However, the chapter had some very strong points in favor of its argument. For one, they had never actually flown the Psi U flag or hung Greek letters on the outside of the house. Second, and more importantly, it seems Psi U was able to point out the double standard in play, given that the three other fraternities without official houses were not facing similar scrutiny over their unofficial, but well-known, residences. In the end, the arguments worked, and the appeal was granted by early February of 1990. Psi U was now off warning status and back in good graces with the administration, at least on paper. So of course, they decided to celebrate with a little sarcasm. A few days after Psi U's appeal was granted, the IGC published a multi-page advertisement in *The Tufts Daily* promoting Greek life on campus, which included submissions from many of the individual organizations. While other fraternities and sororities used this opportunity to highlight positive aspects of their chapter such as recent philanthropic activities or important alumni achievements, Psi U instead submitted the following tongue-in-cheek description of itself:

> Psi Upsilon. The name rings with excellence. The brethren of the Tufts chapter of Psi U excel in every facet of University life. In academics, athletics, social functions, and even personal hygiene, you will find a Psi U brother among the top in all of Tufts.
>
> Many of the brethren's pastimes include chess, horseback riding, croquet, and just meeting an elderly person for tea. And none in Psi U underestimate the pleasure of a good novel.
>
> So, the next time you see a friendly, smiling athlete out for a jog around campus, you can bet your bottom dollar that he's Psi U through and through.[576]

Perhaps the article was written out of spite over the decision by the CFS to place them on warning status, or perhaps it was done purely for fun. Either way, the text stood out in strange contrast to the overall message of the advertisement, and seemed to suggest Psi U was on its own in the Greek community, not afraid to push the limits of expected behavior, and not too concerned about the consequences. The early 1990s were a tumultuous time in Greek-life history at Tufts, with the future of the entire system anything but guaranteed. In fact, many thought the end was most definitely near. And while most other organizations were falling in line with the administration's requests to improve their behavior, Psi U seemed to be balking at the whole thought of conformity.[577]

This bravado caught up to Psi U a semester later. The CFS once again put the fraternity on warning status in the fall of 1990, this time for missing a number of IGC meetings, not filing required paperwork with the administration in a timely manner, and continuing to have members live at 165 College Avenue, thus giving the appearance yet again of maintaining an unofficial chapter house. Then, in the early part of 1991, things went from bad to worse. One night in late February, a group of Psi U members took four pledges to Lexington, Massachusetts, dropped them off, and told them to work together to find their way back to campus. Historically, this event was called a "Pledge Walk," and was a common element of many fraternity programs throughout the early 1900s. The annual event had even been tolerated (but not encouraged) by the Tufts administration back then, provided the participants adhered to some guidelines, such as dropping off the pledges within a fixed distance from campus and ensuring all were back by morning so as not to miss class. The event was discontinued in the 1930s after a number of rules violations and minor accidents – as can be imagined, having college students trample around neighborhoods at 2:00 a.m. looking for a ride back to campus did not always end well.[578]

Unfortunately, just as in some of those earlier Pledge Walks, the four Psi U pledges ran into a bit of trouble that night. While making their way through Lexington, they began gathering street signs, popular souvenirs that have long adorned dormitory rooms and fraternity house basements. Such activity is not exactly quiet by nature, and the ensuing noise in the early morning hours did not go unnoticed by local residents. Soon the four were in custody of the Lexington police department and facing a number of charges, including larceny of personal property, malicious destruction of private property, and rude and disorderly conduct. In addition, Psi Upsilon as a chapter was charged with hazing, since the pledges in question admitted to drinking beer with members before being dropped off. What was supposed to be an exercise in pledge unity had now become another serious legal matter for the fraternity. Over the next few weeks, the incident played out through articles in *The Tufts Daily*, with the details of the evening repeated again and again, thus casting a poor light on Psi U. In the end, the four pledges each received a Level II suspension for their attempts to steal property, and three Psi U members received Level I suspensions for their role in transporting the pledges to Lexington. In addition, the four pledges faced civil penalties including fines and mandatory community service. The fraternity as a whole was ordered to submit for review a comprehensive plan for pledge education, in an effort to make sure a similar incident did not occur in the future. All told, the outcome was much less severe than it could have been (the four pledges were initially suspended from school for a semester), but it certainly cast another bad shadow over the fraternity.[579]

There goes the neighborhood

That shadow was still looming in the fall of 1991 when a number of Psi U members moved back into 165 College Avenue, ready for another year. Then, something else happened. The start of that semester brought new tenants to most other houses on the street, including a group of women at 167 College Avenue, right next door to the unofficial Psi U house. One afternoon in early September, a few members of the fraternity and their friends parked a junk car on the lawn in front of 165 and 167 College Avenue, and then spontaneously adorned the vehicle with spray paint. As for what exactly was painted, well, this was the all-important question. According to the people doing the spray painting, some images were drawn and a few words were scribbled on the car, but nothing was readily discernable, and with so many people participating, everything on the car soon became obscured in layers of paint. However, to the women living next door at 167 College Avenue, the images and words on the car were not only discernable, they were highly offensive and disturbing in their crude vulgarity. These women were not alone in their assessment. As it just so happened, a local Alderman of Somerville, Jack Connolly, drove by the property while the painting was in progress. He, too, was disturbed by the images on the car, so he asked the police to intervene. The authorities responded by ordering the car removed from the lawn and the graffiti painted over, both of which were done within a short time. The incident, it seemed, was over.[580]

Unfortunately for Psi U, the trouble was only beginning. Within a few days, the residents of 167 College Avenue, still upset over what they had seen, filed formal complaints with the Tufts police department and the administration. In addition, Alderman Connolly, who for years had considered the residents of 165 College Avenue a thorn in his neighborhood's side, immediately announced he would investigate the property's landlord and, possibly, bring possible civil action against the residents for hate crime violations. Then, a week later, about fifty students marched in front of 165 College Avenue to protest the incident and the lack of urgency in the investigation, which apparently was not moving fast enough, at least in their opinion. Here, though, the protesters sought to draw attention not just to the spray painting, but to the larger issue of rape and violence towards women. Indeed, by this time, reporters for *The Tufts Daily* were referring to the spray painted artwork not as a crude and vulgar display, but as a depiction and glorification of rape. This new and startling revelation soon captured the attention of other media outlets such as the *Boston Herald*, who then brought the story to a larger audience. The situation had gone viral.[581]

A few days later, the Dean's office announced it would hold hearings to determine if the spray painting violated any obscenity laws. This action immediately triggered a back-and-forth diatribe of opposing voices in *The Tufts Daily*, with many wishing to see Psi U and its members punished severely for such insensitivity towards women, while others steadfastly affirmed those in the fraternity had only exercised their First Amendment rights and therefore deserved no punishment. On a second front, Alderman Connolly brought the full power of local government to bear down on 165 College Avenue and its residents. With his backing, the Somerville Board of Health performed a spot inspection of the property, to determine if it was habitable according to various codes and standards. In addition, Somerville housing inspectors stepped in to see if more than four unrelated individuals living in the same apartment without a proper lodging license, thereby violating a local ordinance. It seemed as if everyone was scrutinizing Psi U and doing all in their power to close down the fraternity.[582]

A few weeks later, the campus learned the results of all those inspections, and for Psi U the news could not have been better. While the Board of Health inspectors found a number of problems with the condition of the 165 College Avenue (Alderman Connolly had called the house "deplorable"), they determined none were large or serious enough to force the eviction of the tenants. Also, the inspectors expressed some confusion as to whether or not 165 College Avenue was a single or multi-family unit. Ultimately they seemed to think the latter was the case, which therefore meant all eight residents could legally remain in the duplex. The slam-dunk against Psi U that Alderman Connelly was hoping for seemed to be a bust.[583]

The good news for Psi U began ebbing about a week later, however, when the administration began its hearings on the spray-painting incident. The panel of judges included two students (one male, one female), two faculty members, and one administrator, who were tasked with determining what exactly had been spray painted on the car, whether or not it was offensive and obscene by Tufts standards, and if so, what punishment would be appropriate for those responsible. With five different people filing complaints (three students, Alderman Connolly, and a Tufts police officer), and nine individuals defending themselves, the hearings lasted a few days while the committee sorted through all of the testimony. Then, on October 24, 1991, they announced their rulings to the campus. Of the nine defendants, six were found guilty of harassment, all of whom were Psi U members and residents of 165 College Avenue, while three others were cleared of all charges. As for punishment, each received a Level I probation for one year, each were required to attend a number of IGC pledge programs (even though all were fully initiated members), and the two of the six were also ordered to perform twenty hours of community service. In addition, the panel decided that the spray-painting on the car, while offensive, did not depict a rape scene as had been suggested, a position the members of Psi U had maintained all along.[584]

It was this last ruling that was probably most surprising to the campus, given the extensive use of the phrase "alleged depiction of rape" by the writers and editors of *The Tufts Daily* in their earlier articles. As it turned out, the female students who originally filed the complaint with the Tufts administration never thought the spray painting depicted a rape scene. Instead, it seems the writers and editors of *The Tufts Daily* had taken some liberties in their initial reporting by creating the phrase on their own. Such a charge was now called false, plain and simple, an incredulous turn of words from a month prior, when nearly every article written perpetuated the now discredited narrative. For the members of Psi U, at least the incident was over, and they were in a position to learn from their mistake and move forward.[585]

But, there was still one more investigation to endure. The administration had focused on the behavior of the participants as individuals, not as members of a fraternity taking part in a chapter-wide event. The task of investigating the fraternity as a whole now fell to the judicial board of the IGC (IGC-J), which would examine Psi U to see if they'd upheld the basic expectations of a Tufts fraternity. Such peer oversight was a consequence of the new relationship between Greek-letter organizations and the Tufts administration that had been forged starting in 1987. In a closed-door meeting, the IGC-J debated a number of charges against Psi U, taking into account the previous work of the administration, as well as statements by the fraternity. Then, the IGC-J rendered its verdict. Psi U as a fraternity was found responsible of one charge, "failure to uphold the general standards of behavior of the [Greek-letter] community." For punishment, the chapter was immediately suspended, unable to recruit new members or participate in any campus event as a fraternity for nearly a year, until August 31, 1992. Following completion of the suspension, Psi U would then be on probation for the ensuing fall semester, and could only give deferred bids during the probationary period. Additionally, the chapter was ordered to update and revise its pledge program, its brotherhood development program, and its by-laws, all as a means of instilling a new behavioral standard within the chapter. The chapter had reached its lowest point, no doubt, but the situation was not completely hopeless. If Psi U could get through the suspension without any further violations or incidents, they would be back as a fully recognized fraternity in January of 1993, ready to rebuild.[586]

I'll be seeing you, in old familiar places

The ruling by the IGC-J marked the end of the various campus-based inquiries and investigations into Psi U, thus leaving the fraternity to serve out its suspension in quiet anonymity. Outside of Tufts, though, there was still Alderman Connolly. He was anything but placated with the punishments levied against Psi U by the administration and the IGC-J, and he was not shy about sharing these feelings with the press. In Alderman Connolly's words, Psi U "got away with murder, [and] the resulting disciplinary action against them was mild." He feared Psi U would continue to operate as a fraternity and use 165 College Avenue as its home, since the Tufts administration admitted to having little control, in general, over its off-campus residents. Additionally, he held no affection for the landlord for 165 College Avenue, whom he thought had never done enough to maintain the residence in a proper condition over the years. All together this was too much for Alderman Connolly. So, he announced there would be a second inspection of 165 College Avenue over the upcoming winter break, to check on the repairs mandated after the first inspection. But the ultimate goal of this inspection, he admitted, was to force the removal of the tenants, thereby ending the relationship between Psi U and the property.[587]

Alderman Connolly's power could only go so far. If the landlord made the repairs and renovations to the house in response to the first inspection, he would have no legal leverage to remove the tenants. And indeed, that is exactly what happened, to Alderman Connolly's dismay. The second inspection revealed much of the repair work had been completed, so the residents of 165 College Avenue could stay. Eviction was no longer an option. Alderman Connolly, though, still had one move left, and that was to take his crusade against Psi U to another, broader audience. He played this move wisely. In early 1992, he worked with *The New York Times* to publish an article about the Psi U chapter at Tufts, talking at length about the spray-painting incident and subsequent punishments imposed on the fraternity, punishments he felt were too lenient. He also made it very clear he wanted the fraternity members out of that house and far away from his neighborhood.[588]

At first, *The New York Times* seemed a strange venue for this story, being so far removed from campus. But Alderman Connolly wasn't interested in reaching the Tufts community. Instead, he wanted to reach the many Psi Upsilon alumni living in and around New York City, as well as the fraternity's national offices in Indianapolis, Indiana, hoping the negative publicity against their fraternity would force them to take action against the Tufts chapter. The reaction from Psi Upsilon was just as Alderman Connolly had hoped. Shortly after the article appeared, the national office decided they'd had enough with their chapter at Tufts. They pulled Zeta Tau's charter, thereby officially closing down the fraternity for good. Now, Alderman Connolly did not have to worry about the fraternity continuing in any form. He had won. It was over.[589]

But then something interesting happened. Although the national office had closed down the chapter, no one from Psi U's headquarters apparently relayed that information in earnest to the Tufts administration. Instead, as the school year continued, the administration viewed Psi U as an official Tufts fraternity, one just quietly serving out its suspension. Since the year passed without any further incident, the administration rescinded the chapter's probation as promised on January 1, 1993, and then announced Psi U was once again a fully recognized fraternity at Tufts. But of course they weren't, for their charter had been pulled a year earlier, and all remaining undergraduates were well aware of this fact. However, these undergraduates went along with the charade, even announcing they would be holding rush that spring semester as they looked to rebuild their chapter. Perhaps they thought that by recruiting new men, they could regain their charter and become an official part of Psi U. Or, perhaps, they thought they could continue the hoax indefinitely, especially since no one in the Tufts administration seemed to question their existence.[590]

As can easily be imagined, the truth could not be kept quiet forever. By the fall of 1993, the national office knew something was amiss at Tufts. After confirming their suspicions, they contacted the administration and told them the charter for their Zeta Tau chapter had been pulled almost two years earlier for "not meeting the standard of the national organization." Such knowledge seemed to catch the Tufts administration by surprise, but they acted swiftly to correct the situation. Without a charter, the administration immediately pulled its recognition of Psi U as an official campus organization. The last remaining members soon graduated, and now it was all truly over.[591]

OR WAS IT? A year and a half later, in the spring of 1995, a group of students came together with the idea of starting a new fraternity on campus. They soon met with Dean Bruce Reitman to discuss the process, and in this meeting they presented a list of national organizations they were considering for affiliation. At the top was Psi Upsilon, seemingly by chance – it appears the group had no knowledge of the earlier incarnation of Psi U at Tufts, nor any interaction with members of the former chapter. Unfortunately for this group, though, time had not completely exonerated their first fraternal choice. Specifically, there was that altercation from January of 1989, which had eventually resulted in lawsuit against a few former Psi U members. After making its way through the civil court system, the lawsuit had been decided in favor of the plaintiff, resulting in monetary damages to be paid by individuals from Psi U. However, by the spring of 1995, none of those damages had been paid, so the lawsuit was back in court to determine who, ultimately, should pay the damages – the individuals, or the Psi Upsilon fraternity as a whole? This was certainly a messy situation, and if Psi U did come back to campus, there was a chance the Tufts chapter, if not the national fraternity, could be held liable. As could be expected, this group of students subsequently dropped Psi U from their list.[592]

SIGMA PHI EPSILON (Massachusetts Zeta chapter, 1985 – 2015)
PI RHO OMEGA (Local chapter, 2015 – present)

Sometimes, it is the path not anticipated that leads to something larger. Take, for example, the journey of Carter Ashton Jenkens. In the fall of 1899, Carter arrived at Rutgers College in New Jersey as a wide-eyed seventeen-year old, ready to begin his studies. Ostensibly he planned to follow in his father's footsteps and become a minister, but for now he was looking to enjoy the collegiate experience. Like many freshmen, he immediately sought out companionship and camaraderie on campus. To his delight he found these traits in the Chi Phi fraternity. He became a full member just a few weeks into his first semester, and then settled into school year surrounded by his fraternity brothers. But, ultimately, Rutgers was not to be for Carter. After just one year on campus, he transferred to Richmond College in Virginia, to begin anew.[593]

Carter's choice of Richmond College was undoubtedly due to its renowned reputation for training ministers in his Baptist faith. What Richmond lacked, though was a chapter of Chi Phi. So, Carter walked onto the campus as an individual, with only the hope of finding good friends like he'd known at Rutgers. Soon enough he befriended Benjamin Gaw, a fellow minister-in-training. Ben was not affiliated with any of the five fraternities on campus, so here Carter sensed an opportunity. As the school year progressed, he began talking to Ben about gathering some other friends and then petitioning Chi Phi for a charter. Then, after one particular discussion, the two men "parted that night pledged to bring to our college the greatest fraternity on earth [Chi Phi]." Once the group numbered six, Carter began making inquiries to the national leaders of Chi Phi through his old chapter at Rutgers about expanding to Richmond. Unfortunately, the response from Chi Phi was "no." The national leaders did not feel that Richmond could support another fraternity, since nearly half of the two hundred students were already affiliated with one of the five chapters on campus. However, one of Carter's fraternity brothers from Rutgers suggested an alternate idea. He encouraged Carter to form a local fraternity at Richmond, so he could at least enjoy the bonds of brotherhood once again.[594]

Such an idea was unexpected, but immediately intriguing to Carter and his group, so they moved forward with the plan to become a new, local Greek-letter fraternity. In this they were successful, as by the fall of 1901, they'd grown to twelve members, despite operating sub rosa. Now it was time to come out of hiding and make it all official. First, though, they needed a Greek name. At Carter's suggestion, they became the Sigma Phi fraternity. Then, they pursued official recognition by the faculty, a necessary step to operate in the open. The process was fairly straightforward in theory, but for Sigma Phi, it soon became complicated. The existing fraternities, worried that more competition on campus would stifle them all, immediately filed counter petitions with the faculty, demanding this new fraternity not be recognized. Theirs was a show of political might, and in the end it forced a response. The faculty called the new fraternity to meet with their committee, in person, to discuss the matter further.[595]

A group of three men including Carter and Ben were chosen to plead their case to the faculty. With heads full of noble ideas and hearts filled with youthful innocence, they entered the faculty chamber ready to fight for their organization. As it turned out, the committee was not necessarily opposed to the group, but they did seem to favor the argument that Richmond already had enough fraternities. Additionally, they wondered if Carter realized there was already another national fraternity called Sigma Phi. This fact caught him off guard, but he soon recovered. "This fraternity," he said, "will be different. It will be based on the love of God and the principle of peace through brotherhood. The number of members will be increased from the undergraduate classes. We will change the name to Sigma Phi Epsilon." In addition, Carter mentioned the ministerial students at Richmond could be an untapped pool of potential members for his fraternity, since the others ignored these men. A short discussion between the faculty and Carter ensued, but in the end, he had gained their permission. Sigma Phi Epsilon (SigEp) was now a recognized local fraternity at Richmond College.[596]

This victory, though, came with an immediate problem. Carter added the Epsilon to the name on a whim, and no one was really sure what the letter might symbolize. So, after the meeting, the group rushed back to Carter's dormitory room to consult their Greek-English dictionary, and luckily they discovered "Epsilon" had a meaning they could embrace. But then came a logistical problem. Anticipating recognition of their fraternity, the men had already ordered their badges from a jeweler, complete with just the letters Σ and Φ. To correct this, they sent off a hurried telegram to the jeweler and asked them to add the Epsilon to the face. The resulting design, a heart shaped badge with a large Σ and Φ atop a skull and crossbones, and a small E squeezed on the bottom, certainly looked awkward, but it sufficed as a temporary fix. Now, it was time to move forward.[597]

And move forward they did. A year after gaining recognition, SigEp realized the fraternity landscape at Richmond was now very crowded, since a sixth national fraternity had restarted a dormant chapter in the fall of 1901. So, they knew it was either expand or wither away, and in this regard SigEp wasted no time. By the fall of 1902, SigEp had opened its second, or Beta chapter at the nearby University College of Medicine in Richmond, thus making the fraternity a national organization. For Carter, SigEp's founder, this reality was bittersweet. Although he wanted his new organization to flourish through expansion, he was already a loyal and lifetime member of Chi Phi, and by the early 1900s, national fraternities excluded their members from joining another national fraternity (though affiliating with a local organization was allowed). So, Carter was forced by honor to break his ties with SigEp, at least on paper, so as to remain a true and loyal member of Chi Phi. However, he was recorded as an honorary member of SigEp, thereby preserving his legacy.[598]

Despite his loyal ties to Chi Phi, Carter must have been proud of his "other" fraternity, for after establishing its Beta chapter, SigEp exploded onto the national scene. By 1903, the number of active chapters had grown to nine and reached from Virginia to Illinois. By 1916, that number was over forty and stretched across the country. SigEp was fast on its way to becoming one of the largest fraternities in North America. Then, they just happened to catch the eye of some men from Tufts College.[599]

You're not worthy

The Tufts men in question were the local fraternity, Sigma Tau Alpha, who as a group had recently embarked on a quest to go national. Why they chose to pursue SigEp is unknown, but one fact is certain: their timing was awful. In the fall of 1916, members and national leaders of SigEp gathered in Richmond, Virginia, for their ninth Grand Chapter Conclave, or national meeting. Among their tasks was an initial review of all the recent petitions from local fraternities looking to join SigEp. This would not be a simple process, for the fraternity was booming – there were no fewer than seven petitions up for initial consideration, and all were from schools much larger (and, therefore, more prestigious) than Tufts College. Then, within months of the convention, three more petitions were added to the fray, with two being from large, land-grant institutions. Tufts College, the small school from Massachusetts, did not stand out in this crowd.[600]

As these petitions poured into the national office, the leaders of SigEp began to take stock of the work ahead. Evaluating petitions was, after all, a serious and time-consuming business, lest they admit an unworthy local organization into their fraternity. However, the national leaders were ill equipped to handle so many applicants in so little time. So, by the spring of 1917, they decided to slow down. As they announced to the collegiate world, "The attention that it is necessary to give to a chapter is of such a character that the growth of the Fraternity must of necessity be somewhat slower in the future." Sigma Tau Alpha at Tufts College ran head first into this perfect storm. Overshadowed by the larger schools, and faced with a fraternity looking to reign in its growth, their petition languished for months, before it was eventually denied. They were certainly not alone, as other local groups were also turned away. But others weren't, including all of the applicants from the large state schools. SigEp, it seemed, had made its choice. Bigger was better, and Tufts was not even close to being big enough. So, the two parted ways, at least for another sixty-eight years.[601]

From one brother to another

What ended the separation was another case of family connection. By the fall of 1983, Greek life at Tufts University was noticeably on the rise. The established fraternities were growing their memberships, and new organizations such as Psi Upsilon and a re-chartered Alpha Epsilon Pi were successfully making their presence known on campus. However, to one group of twelve men in particular that semester, none of the existing fraternity chapters captured their imagination, though they were clearly interested in the idea. So, like many have done before, they decided to form their own. As for which organization to start, that question was easy to answer. One of the leaders of the group, Matt Ahern, just happened to have a brother who was a member of the SigEp chapter at Bentley College. As a result, there really was no other choice for the group. They would pursue SigEp.[602]

The group became an official SigEp colony in the late spring of 1984, and then went to work building their chapter into a viable organization. They started by expanding their membership from twelve to forty-two members during the following school year. Such growth was almost unprecedented, as the colony did not occupy a chapter house on or off campus, so they could not host the large, all-campus parties typical of the fraternity scene at the time. And yet, still they grew into one of the largest chapters at Tufts. As for how, they did so by constantly reminding the campus of their presence. They ate meals together in the dining hall, often wearing bright red sweatshirts emblazoned with the fraternity's letters, and they concentrated on activities that did not require a chapter house, such as hosting all-campus theme parties in dormitories and organizing philanthropy events for the greater community. Their hard work was rewarded in the early spring of 1985, when the chapter's petition to SigEp had been granted. This group of men had succeeded where those in Sigma Tau Alpha had failed so many decades before. Formal installation occurred on March

9, 1985, when the forty-two members of the colony were initiated into Sigma Phi Epsilon as the Massachusetts Zeta chapter.[603]

My kingdom for a house

Despite their strong start, SigEp knew their future required, if not demanded, that they occupy a chapter house. Their initial experience as an unhoused fraternity had obviously gone well, but recruitment is the lifeblood of any fraternity, and SigEp realized theirs would be more difficult going forward without a permanent home on campus. All other fraternities had one, and all would certainly laud that fact over SigEp as they competed for new members. Just as important, though, the members of SigEp recognized the benefits of camaraderie afforded to fraternities that practiced small group living, and they wanted to experience this for themselves. But, while wanting to occupy a house was one thing, moving into one anytime soon was another. After all, the Tufts campus wasn't exactly awash in extra fraternity houses in the 1980s.[604]

SigEp's first housing opportunity came out of nowhere in the spring of 1985, just before they received their charter. That semester, the Tufts administration surprised everyone by announcing a co-op dormitory at 92 Professors Row would be converted into fraternity housing, starting the very next semester. This announcement marked only the second time since 1957 that Tufts had opened a new fraternity house, and the location of the property, right in the heart of campus, could not be beat. SigEp therefore wasted no time submitting their application to the Interfraternity Council (IFC), the student-run group in charge of awarding the house to the rightful fraternity or sorority. As could be expected, SigEp was hardly alone in their quest to move into the new space. Five other organizations also applied to move into 92 Professors Row, including a few that already had chapter houses but wanted to upgrade to a better location. Weeks passed while all six organizations awaited the highly coveted decision. Then, everything fell apart. The morphing of 92 Professors Row into a fraternity house was part of a larger plan to convert a number of buildings into student housing. Unfortunately, the administration ran into unexpected legal roadblocks that spring with the existing leases and lodging licenses for these buildings, and these issues could not be settled as quickly as hoped. So, Tufts was forced to shelve the whole idea for another year.[605]

This turn of events was just as well for SigEp, because they hadn't even come close to winning the IFC vote. Instead, they learned a hard truth. As the newest organization on campus, they were well behind a number of older fraternities either waiting to occupy a house on campus, or wanting to upgrade to someplace better. And, since the Tufts administration was making little effort to accommodate all of these requests, SigEp realized their best chance at securing a house would be to act on their own. Their timing, in this regard, was perfect.

Over the summer of 1985, and just a few months removed from the debacle of 92 Professors Row, a duplex house at 16 Bellevue Street in the Medford Hillside became available for rent. SigEp immediately pounced on the opportunity. Bellevue Street had long been home to Tufts fraternities just starting out in the early 20th century, but none had lived there since the 1930s. Now, some fifty years later, SigEp would re-introduce the neighborhood to Greek life starting in the fall of 1985. Even better, the landlord of the property gave SigEp the option to buy the house outright in the ensuing six to twelve months. The fraternity, it seemed, had just hit the housing jackpot.[606]

The celebration over their good fortune was short lived. After the lease was signed that summer, word soon reached the neighbors that the new tenants would be an organized fraternity chapter. The neighbors instantly worried SigEp would bring loud and obnoxious behavior, too many cars, all night parties, excessive trash, and hoards of people to their doorsteps, especially on the weekends. The Tufts administration, always cognizant of their relationship with the neighbors, openly worried the situation would enflame an already strained relationship with those on Bellevue Street. Being just a few feet off campus, the residents of Bellevue Street had long been familiar with poor student behavior, so the antagonism towards Tufts seemed poised to grow only stronger. SigEp tried to appease the angry factions against them by promising to respect the noise curfew each night, to keep an orderly house and yard, and to have members park their cars anywhere but on the street. The fraternity was certainly saying all the right things, and since neither Tufts nor the neighbors could cancel the lease, all would just have to wait and see if everything worked out as hoped.[607]

As it turned out, though, the neighbors were not the only source of trouble for SigEp. So, too, was the house. When the eight members arrived in the fall ready to move in, they discovered that half of the duplex was still occupied, and the remaining tenant showed no signs of moving out anytime soon. Eight men therefore had to squeeze into one apartment for a few weeks, until the landlord sent the squatter on his way. In the end, this situation was just a nuisance, but it was soon overshadowed by something more serious. SigEp's grand plan involved purchasing the property, converting the space into a single home, and increasing the number of members who could live there. By the laws of the City of Medford, the fraternity needed a lodging house license to make all of this work; otherwise, the structure would have to remain a two-apartment duplex, with each apartment housing only four unrelated individuals. During the negotiations to rent and then purchase the house, the landlord promised SigEp this license would be easy to obtain. However, such a promise was false. The process required many legal hurdles, and even if SigEp successfully navigated them all, there was no guarantee Medford would even grant the license, especially if the neighbors objected (which they were likely to do). As a result, SigEp's grand housing plan for a home in the Bellevue Street neighborhood seemed doomed to failure.[608]

But, that grand plan was all about the future. In the mean time, SigEp needed to make their house successful in the present. To their credit, the fraternity did act as a good neighbor once they moved in that fall of 1985, just as they'd promised. They certainly used their house as intended by hosting a few social events and rush parties, but in general they kept a very low profile on the street, and the entire fall semester passed without serious incident. However, there still was that option for SigEp to buy the property, and this greatly worried the Tufts administration. They simply could not, under any circumstances, allow the sale to go through. While the current school year was going reasonably well, there was no guarantee future years would run so smoothly, and that could only mean headaches for all. Additionally, even without a lodging license, SigEp could still legally house eight men on the property, which was enough to make the space financially viable. So, just as the spring semester of 1986 was about to start, the school made the landlord an offer she couldn't refuse. The trustees bought the house at 16 Bellevue Street right out from under the fraternity, thereby ending SigEp's future in the space. The chapter was allowed to remain in the house for the remainder of the semester, but once school ended, it appeared they would be without a home once again.[609]

However, SigEp would not simply be thrown to the street. Instead, they would win the last open seat in the game of musical houses. In the spring of 1986, the university once again deemed 92 Professors Row a new fraternity house starting the following semester. The administration, in conjunction with the IFC, awarded Sigma Nu the right to move in to the new space. Sigma Nu, in turn, would vacate its current Tufts-owned house at 114 Curtis Street, and in their place SigEp would move in. The house at 114 Curtis Street was hardly bigger than the one 16 Bellevue Street, and the lease came without any option to buy, but for SigEp, the space was exactly what they wanted. They'd finally found a home.[610]

So much for that

Moving into 114 Curtis Street in the fall of 1986 was a major turning point for SigEp, as it marked their emergence from the shadows of fraternity life at Tufts. Now, it was up to the chapter to capitalize on their improved status and build their own, unique identity. They did so immediately. First, they changed the role of their chapter house by eliminating the boarding plan. Although 114 Curtis Street came with an industrial kitchen, and although Sigma Nu had for many years served daily meals to its members out of this house, SigEp decided to forgo this aspect of fraternity life. Perhaps the chapter realized the outdated kitchen required too much overhaul in order to feed the fast growing chapter.

Or, perhaps, they realized a boarding plan would have been too expensive, especially since they had none of the necessary equipment to cook or serve meals, let alone tables and chairs to equip a proper dining room. So, as a group, the members of SigEp continued to eat their meals together in the dining halls. This act, as small as it may seem, proved immensely beneficial.[611]

At the time, though, SigEp's desire to eliminate a boarding plan was in stark contrast to nearly all other Greek-letter organizations with chapter houses, as these groups continued to gather each night in their closed-off dining rooms for a shared meal, something they had done for decades. However, by eating meals amongst the greater Tufts community, SigEp expanded their presence on campus in a manner unlike any other organization. Interactions in the dining hall between those in SigEp and those not essentially became individualized recruiting events, repeated day after day. At no time was this more fruitful than the first few weeks of the fall 1986 semester. Having a new chapter house on campus was one reason for the spike in interest, but so, too, were all of those personal mealtime interactions. By the time their rush week started at the end of September, SigEp had built a sizeable pool of potential new members.[612]

Faced with a very promising rush week that fall of 1986, SigEp made a second change from the norm, the consequence of which is still observed today at Tufts. And was this change immense, for it involved alcohol. Or, as it turned out, a lack thereof. That fall SigEp boldly decided rather than serve drinks to rushees from kegs of cheap beer and bottles of cheaper liquor (the staples of fraternity recruitment since the 1950s, if not earlier), they would not serve alcohol at any point during rush week, period. In previous years, other fraternities at Tufts had held a dry event or two during rush week, usually when the activity involved a sports competition such as pick-up basketball, but the idea never caught on. SigEp, to their credit, committed to the no-alcohol policy throughout their entire rush week. One main reason was certainly pragmatism. Starting in the 1980s, as national fraternities began facing an ever-increasing number of lawsuits over incidents involving alcohol, they looked to de-emphasize the culture of consumption within their chapters. Mandating dry rush was one such path towards this goal, but old fraternity traditions die slowly at best, so many fraternities across the country were loathe to implement the change. The SigEp chapter at Tufts, however, had no strong legacy of over-the-top, alcohol-fueled recruitment parties, so they decided to embrace wholeheartedly the dry rush policy of their national organization. Not all in the chapter agreed with the idea, and many openly wondered if anyone would attend their events, since they would be the only fraternity not serving beer. But, by majority rule, SigEp would go dry and hope for the best.[613]

They needn't have worried. Once rush week got underway, the chapter realized the lack of alcohol at their events had absolutely zero impact in recruitment. Rushees came down to the fraternity in droves each day, and more importantly, stayed throughout the entire event. Soon enough they had more men to choose from than any other fraternity on campus, even though all those other chapters were serving beer. As such, SigEp's experience that semester verified the adage that recruitment is centered on people, and not what is served to those people. As one member of the chapter was quoted as saying that week, "Within five years no one will remember wet rush [where alcohol was served]." It turns out this prophecy was a little too pessimistic. By the fall of 1989, just three years later, wet rush for all fraternities at Tufts University had been abolished completely, per order of the student-run Inter-Greek Council, and certainly SigEp's experience helped bring this mandate sooner rather than later. Even today, alcohol-fueled fraternity recruitment events show no signs of returning.[614]

Throughout the rest of the 1980s and 1990s, SigEp continued in earnest and managed to stay out of trouble, for the most part. The first serious issue arose in the chapter just after the millennium. By the 2000–01 school year, SigEp was having a more difficult time attracting new members. Shifting attitudes among the students and greater scrutiny by the administration caused the entire Greek system to contract slightly, partly in reaction to the unfortunate death of freshman Scott Krueger in an MIT fraternity a few years earlier. No chapter at Tufts was immune to the downturn, but SigEp seemed to take the brunt of this negativity. Each subsequent semester brought fewer and fewer new members, and as their brotherhood contracted, so, too did their hard-earned status on campus. The spring semester of 2002 was the low point, with the chapter gaining only four new pledges, well below their expectations or needs. Their membership was now half of what it had been just three semesters earlier. To make matters worse, during Senior Week 2002, the chapter was caught with a number of beer kegs in its house, a clear violation of university policy – kegs were banned from Tufts fraternity houses a decade earlier. The chapter was immediately fined $300 per keg, which put an even greater strain on their precarious financial situation.[615]

Those who remained in SigEp returned to campus in the fall of 2002 and took stock of their situation. It was not good. Few held any real enthusiasm for the fraternity, anymore, especially among the older members who comprised the bulk of the chapter. There was no money left for social activities, only for the administrative and overhead costs plaguing the chapter. So, in early September 2002, the brotherhood held a meeting to decide their future. After the discussion, they decided to shut down and close Sigma Phi Epsilon at Tufts. "None of us believe that it can be saved," said one senior member of the chapter, a thought echoed by nearly all. But soon afterwards, when they went to the administration with their decision, they hit an unexpected roadblock.[616]

Normally, the administration would not have cared if a fraternity decided to close; many had done so on their own accord in the past. But those closings tended to happen at the end of the school year, when students were moving out and going home. SigEp was in the opposite situation. They were trying to close down at the beginning of the semester, when their chapter house was filling with members who had signed leases for the entire upcoming school year. These members assumed the leases would be valid whether or not SigEp was a recognized fraternity on campus. However, this was not the case. As the Tufts administration understood the situation, if SigEp shut down and was de-recognized by the university, the City of Somerville would likely rescind the lodging license for the house, thereby forcing many of the residents to the street. Also, with dormitories and off-campus apartments essentially full at the start of the school year, there would be no place for the displaced residents to go. Therefore, in an unprecedented move, the administration told SigEp "no." They could not close down, not yet, especially if the residents wanted to stay in the house. Instead they would have to carry on, somehow.[617]

Faced with this reality, the younger members of the chapter took charge. In a complete reverse of sentiment, they decided to rebuild the chapter into a strong entity. They started by electing a new slate of leaders, and then turned to the national office and their alumni for help. The alumni in particular rallied support behind the chapter by raising money and actively advising the undergraduates, especially when it came to recruitment. Within weeks, the chapter went from being on the edge of dissolution to holding rush once again and looking forward to the future. Within a few semesters, the trials and tribulations of 2002 were but a memory, and the chapter was once again growing and thriving on campus.[618]

So much for that, once again

For seniors at Tufts, the week between the end of finals and graduation (called Senior Week, as could easily be guessed) is a celebratory time, filled with galas, barbeques, and candlelight processions around campus. Most years, Senior Week passes without serious incident and simply adds to the collective memories of those graduating. For those in SigEp, though, one Senior Week was a disaster. One night during this special week in May of 2011, the seniors in the chapter decided to hold one last party in their chapter house. However, by this time they were locked out of the space – since none of them had lived in the chapter house during the school year, the Tufts administration had closed the building when the last of the undergraduates moved out a week earlier, per standard policy. But, the seniors wanted in. So, they bypassed the locks, entered their chapter house, and threw a party. A dumb decision, certainly, but nothing compare to what happened next.[619]

Evidently, enjoying some revelry in their chapter house was not enough. No, the SigEp seniors had to leave their mark. And here they did so with aplomb. Before leaving, the seniors proceeded to destroy the inside of their chapter house. They punched holes in walls, ripped out plasterboard, ruined the stairs and interior woodwork, broke doors off hinges, and threw trash all over the house. Then, they left the mess for someone else and went about their way. It did not take long for the landlord of 114 Curtis Street, Bruce Ketchen of Walnut Hill Properties, to discover the horror. It also did not take long for Mr. Ketchen to realize he'd had enough of the fraternity. In a case of swift justice, he immediately threw SigEp out of the house and cancelled the leases of the seven undergraduates scheduled to live there the following school year. "It just wasn't appropriate," he said, "to offer accommodations to an organization that didn't take care of its property."[620]

For the remaining undergraduates in SigEp, the loss of their chapter house could only be described as absolutely stunning. If anything could have killed the morale of the chapter and put it into a death spiral, this was it. But it did not. Instead, the chapter rallied and got to work that fall semester. They convinced the perpetrators to admit to their involvement and, more importantly, agree to pay the damages, which were significant (around $10,000). Then, they began an introspective rehabilitation of their chapter, and worked to redefine what they wanted to be moving forward. They held philanthropy and service events within the greater Tufts community. They recruited new members and vowed never to let such transgressions happen again. Finally, they waited to learn their future with regards to housing.[621]

As the spring semester of 2012 got underway, SigEp seemed confident they'd soon be able to re-occupy the only official chapter house they'd had even known, which had remained empty since they'd been kicked out. But, in an instant, all optimism was lost. In early March 2012, Walnut Hill Properties announced it would convert SigEp's former house into a commercial office, in part to solve a persistent shortage of such space on campus. Therefore, after sixty-one years as a fraternity house, 114 Curtis Street became the Feinstein International Center of the Freidman School of Nutrition Science and Policy. In the mean time, SigEp would remain without an official chapter house despite all their positive efforts to correct the many wrongs. This was hardly the way the chapter had hoped to end the school year, but it was the reality of the situation. There were simply no other houses on campus available for use by a fraternity. That is, until someone else followed in their footsteps.[622]

Welcome to the neighborhood

After the trials and tribulations SigEp experienced throughout the 2011–12 school year, one would think all other fraternities would take extra care of their house, especially during the very next incarnation of Senior Week, lest something similar happen to their chapter. But, you'd be wrong. Instead, at the close of Senior Week in May 2012, the graduating members of Sigma Nu left their chapter house at 92 Professors Row in a dilapidated state. Trash covered most of the floors, empty beer cans littered the basement, and many residents left everything behind in their rooms for someone else to clean up. The physical state of the house had long been a concern for Sigma Nu and the Tufts administration alike (the nearly one hundred-forty year old structure showed its age all too well), but when officials discovered the state of affairs shortly after graduation, they realized the fraternity needed a pause from housing. So, with the precedent set, the Tufts administration cancelled Sigma Nu's lease with 92 Professors Row and send the fraternity to the street. SigEp now had some company.[623]

This action left the administration with an empty house in the middle of campus, and thus a new problem to solve. The school needed the ten beds filled and the rent paid. So, during the summer of 2012, the Tufts administration offered the space to SigEp, starting in the fall. Those in SigEp could hardly believe their good fortune, so they immediately made plans to move in. But, there was a catch. SigEp had to fill the house not with just any ten members, but with ten who were scheduled to live in dormitories for the upcoming school year. As it turned out, Tufts was struggling to find dormitory rooms for a larger-than-expected group of transfer students arriving in the fall. If SigEp could open up ten beds in the dormitories, then two problems would be solved at once. The fraternity was therefore staring at the very definition of a "win-win" situation. All they needed was a few good men to step up.[624]

Unfortunately for SigEp, their efforts to find men willing to occupy 92 Professors Row soon fell flat. A majority of members were upperclassmen who'd already secured choice rooms and suites in the most desirable dormitories. As a result, they were somewhat reluctant to give up these accommodations. Such fears led to just six members willing to trade their dormitory assignment for the fraternity house, while four others agreed to relocate from off-campus apartments. This did not satisfy the school's stated terms, but SigEp hoped it was close enough. It was not. The Tufts administration had no choice but to cancel the plan. The house at 92 Professors Row would not be the new home of SigEp for the 2012–13 school year. Instead, it would be used to house a group of ten transfer students.[625]

This turn of events was yet another huge disappointment for the fraternity, but the members had no one to blame but themselves. However, there was hope on the horizon. The housing of transfer students in 92 Professors Row was only temporary, as the Tufts administration felt the space was much better suited as a fraternity house than a dormitory. And who better to fill that space than SigEp, especially since Sigma Nu was a year behind them in their rehabilitation process. Indeed, a few months into the fall 2012 semester, the administration announced SigEp would move into 92 Professors Row starting the following fall, for a trial year. If everything went well, then the fraternity would likely stay in the space for longer. These terms were hardly ideal (SigEp would have much preferred a long term lease), but this time the fraternity didn't miss out on the opportunity. They moved into their new chapter house in the fall of 2013, and, as could be predicted, made sure everything went reasonably well that year.[626]

As the 2013–14 school year marched on, though, SigEp still worried about its housing future. Their lease was only good for one year, and with Sigma Nu finishing up its probationary period, the members knew they wanted to return to their previous house. But, at least the situation had not devolved into a fight over one space. During that fall semester, Tufts decided to convert a dormitory at 90–94 Curtis Street back into a fraternity house, in anticipation of Sigma Nu's return to housing. With two fraternity houses now available for occupancy, the question simply became which organization would get to live at 92 Professors Row, and which would move to 90–94 Curtis Street. The decision process soon bogged down into a stalemate. As could be expected, both organizations wanted 92 Professors Row as their home, mainly due to the old adage of real estate: location, location, location. When negotiations failed to resolve the standoff, the Inter-Greek Council stepped in to decide. One morning in February of 2014, then, both chapters were summoned by the council to present their case for occupying the house of their choice. After a few hours of deliberation by the council, SigEp got the news they wanted. They were allowed to stay on Professors Row, while Sigma Nu would move to Curtis Street to start anew.[627]

This ruling was unprecedented in many ways, as in the past all other fraternities had summarily retained their chapter houses following a probationary period, even chapters that did not own their space. As a result, one could argue that SigEp had been rewarded for their original transgressions at 114 Curtis Street, for they had traded a smaller house slightly off campus for a larger space right in the heart of Fraternity Row, all at the cost of a two-year probation. But, this was the new reality, and SigEp was now, finally, in control of their housing future. Such stability let them move on to other issues and concerns. And soon, they found a different direction in which to venture.[628]

Keeping the old by starting anew

The news came as a surprise to nearly all in the Tufts community, including SigEp's alumni. In November of 2015, just before the Thanksgiving break, the members of SigEp announced they would leave their national organization and become a new, local fraternity at Tufts, an action they had contemplated for some time. This move was not unprecedented, as a semester before, the Alpha Epsilon Pi fraternity had also resigned from their national organization over differences in membership, thus becoming the local Pi Delta fraternity. SigEp's stated reason for disaffiliating, though, was subtler. "We didn't think that the needs, goals and values that SigEp was about fit what we were about anymore," said one member in summary. An example of this misalignment was instances involving racism in other SigEp chapters across the country, events which put the entire fraternity in a bad light. But, there was another reason. The national organization had long wanted their Tufts chapter to adopt the "Balanced Man program" in lieu of pledging. This program, which is now standard in all SigEp chapters, grants full membership to those who accept a bid to join, thereby eliminating the pledge process. The Tufts chapter had never embraced this change, and indeed faced a deadline to adopt the Balanced Man program by the end of 2015. By disaffiliating, they could continue with their preferred traditional pledging experience.[629]

The following semester, the former SigEp members completed their transformation when they announced their new name to the campus: Pi Rho Omega. As a result, Tufts is now home to three local Greek-letter fraternities, a situation that has not existed on campus in nearly a century. Pi Rho Omega appears to be off to an enthusiastic start, but their history is, as yet, unwritten.[630]

ALPHA PHI DELTA (Delta Sigma chapter, 1996 – 2006)

Throughout the ages, nearly all freshmen heading off to college wonder how they will get along once on campus, who they will meet, and if they will find a true friend or two. Most overcome such obstacles within days after arriving at school, a natural outcome when so many are searching for companionship. However, for those who may be somewhat different than the norm, the path to college contentedness can seem daunting, if not impossible. Consider Syracuse University in upstate New York, in the fall of 1912. That semester, two men of Italian descent, Cesidio A. Guarini and Ferdinand F. DiBartolo, came to campus looking to assimilate into the Syracuse community. In this regard, though, they struggled. Although the school boasted a population of nearly six thousand students, its size bemoaned a lack of diversity, especially when it came to welcoming those who could not trace back their American roots more than a generation. As a result, the ethnicity of Cesidio and Ferdinand, coupled with their incomplete mastery of the English language, pushed many of their classmates away. Worse still, they did not know each other, at least not until the student catalogue was released. Once published, Cesidio thumbed through the pamphlet and looked for other men with Italian-sounding names. Soon enough he found Ferdinand. The two, as could be expected, became friends. Then, more importantly, they decided to create a positive experience for other Italian men who would follow in their footsteps at Syracuse.[631]

Over the next few years, the two expanded their group of friends as more Italian men enrolled in Syracuse University. One of the few social outlets afforded to the men was the Cosmopolitan Club, a loose gathering of students from diverse nationalities who hosted cultural events for the campus, often based around the food and entertainment of the member's ancestral homelands. In early 1913, the group of now seven Italian men, known collectively as Il Circolo Italiano, hosted one such event dedicated to their heritage. The evening was a huge success, and afterwards the men realized their group could be more than just a vehicle for their cultural identity. Over the next few months, this idea germinated into a plan. The men would form a new Greek-letter fraternity, one dedicated to brotherhood and their heritage as Italians. Their efforts culminated on the night of November 5, 1914, when the seven men took an oath to one another and formed the Alpha Phi Delta (APD) Fraternity. The organization established its second chapter at Columbia University just a year later, and from there began a slow but steady growth across the Eastern United States. Then, some eighty years after its founding, APD found its way to Tufts.[632]

Rise and fall

The fall of 1995 brought just over a thousand new freshmen to Tufts, ready to begin their college experience. Among this group was Mark Wasielewski, who arrived on campus and moved into his assigned dormitory, Hill Hall. It was here where Mark soon found a number of friends, and as the weeks went by that first semester, those in the group began talking about joining a fraternity. However, with freshmen ineligible to join fraternities until after they'd completed their first semester, all they could do was talk and plan for the future. Eventually, the conversation switched from which of the chapters on campus they might want to join, to starting one of their own. Not all in the group were on board with this idea, but six including Mark committed to bringing a new fraternity at Tufts. Only, they decided, their fraternity would be somewhat different. They would be a social organization, without a doubt, but also one dedicated to community service in a manner greater the other fraternities on campus.[633]

Word of the group's plans to start a new organization soon spread around the intra-fraternity circles at Tufts. While most chapters were generally indifferent to the idea, the members of the Zeta Beta Tau (ZBT) fraternity were especially intrigued, for their chapter was experiencing a lull in membership at the time and were worried about their continued viability. As a result, representatives of ZBT approached the six men about possibly joining their organization instead of starting a new one. But the group under Mark's direction was steadfast in their plan. They did not want to assimilate with ZBT, or any other national fraternity for that matter, bar one. As it turned out, Mark's brother was an enthusiastic and active member of the Alpha Phi Delta fraternity, having joined the chapter at Villanova University. So, for Mark and then the rest of the group, the choice was clear. They would pursue APD.[634]

The decision to go APD was followed by a few weeks of intense work as the six turned their idea into a reality. They were rewarded for their efforts on

March 3, 1996, when they were initiated as a colony of APD. The founding members of the chapter were:

Michael Chen
Sean DiBartolo
Gabe Guarente
Justin Lee
Douglas Ostrov
Mark Wasielewski

Afterwards, the six spent the rest of the 1996 spring semester working through the various recognition hurdles at Tufts. The administration, in general, was not overly enthusiastic about the arrival of APD, as they worried about finding a suitable chapter house for the fraternity on a campus with few options. But, they were not one to stand in their way. That semester, APD successfully gained recognition as a Tufts fraternity by the Inter-Greek Council, the Interfraternity Council, and even the administration. The newest fraternity was now up and running at Tufts.[635]

The next few years for APD saw the fraternity succeed on almost every level. True to their word, they became heavily involved in philanthropy by participating in Kid's Day, Walk for Hunger, the Dana Farber Marathon Challenge, the JumbOlympics (a Special Olympics fundraiser), and Alpha Epsilon Pi's Greek Jam, one of the more successful and highly competitive charitable events that ran throughout the 1990s. Such efforts won them repeated accolades from the Tufts community. In the fall of 1997, the colony was installed as the Delta Sigma chapter of APD, and within the next few semesters, had grown their membership to over thirty. Everything seemed to be going very well for the young chapter. Everything, that is, except for permanent housing.[636]

From the time APD became a colony, the group had been occupying various unofficial chapter houses off campus, similar in practice to nearly every other new fraternity at Tufts. However, in this regard they had to be careful, for official school policy did not allow a fraternity to occupy an abode in such a manner – the Tufts administration could certainly not stop people from living together off campus, but they could prevent a fraternity from hanging letters on the outside of a house, or flying a flag by the front door. APD, to their credit, kept a low profile off campus, though they did use their unofficial houses for some social events and rush activities. Still, on a campus where every other fraternity had a sanctioned house, APD was at a clear disadvantage, especially in terms of recruitment. They were viewed as the fraternity without a house, and this sentiment alone was soon overshadowing all of their accomplishments.[637]

The chapter's hopes were raised in the fall of 1999 when the Tufts administration announced APD was now eligible for an on-campus residence. However, as the semesters rolled by, the members realized this was an empty promise. Tufts made no real effort to open a new fraternity residence, and while there was talk of moving APD into either the ZBT or Sigma Nu house due to low membership in those organizations at times, no such housing swap occurred. APD thus remained an off campus entity, much to their consternation. Despite such setbacks in housing, though, APD remained strong in its brotherhood, even winning the Outstanding Chapter and Outstanding Community Service award from their national organization in 2000. But what the chapter needed more than anything else was new initiates. By the spring of 2001, membership in the chapter had dropped to just fourteen, with ten slated to graduate a year later. APD was now in crisis mode.[638]

Unfortunately, the lack of an official on-campus house continued to hurt their recruitment efforts throughout the 2001–02 school year, as the chapter did not gain a single new member. The situation looked as if it might improve the following school year, as APD was awarded a suite in the Latin Way dormitory for use as an official chapter home. This space certainly wasn't as large or accommodating as a house on Professors Row, but at least it gave APD an official presence on campus. In the end, though, the suite in Latin Way could not overcome the inevitable. The chapter, which had started to wallow in apathy, was unable to recruit any new members that year or the next. So, when the last initiate graduated in the spring of 2004, APD was effectively dormant. Their charter was officially rescinded two years later, in the spring of 2006.[639]

AUTHOR'S NOTE: While this book was going to print, it was revealed that the Pi Delta fraternity at Tufts would close down at the end of the 2016–17 school year, for reasons not yet publicly disclosed.

THE SOCIAL SORORITIES

4

The rise and fall and rise again of women's societies at Tufts

The undergraduate campus of Tufts University today would be unrecognizable to the men who chartered Tufts College in 1852, and not just due to the multitude of buildings where there was once a clear cut hill, or the densely packed urban landscape where there was once vast farmland. Instead, an even greater shock to the founders of Tufts just might be the presence of women on campus in near equal proportion to, and enjoying the same educational opportunities as, their male counterparts. And don't even mention the side-by-side living arrangements in some of the dormitories. Those distinguished men, after all, had modeled their new school after other prestigious colleges in New England, all of which were exclusively for men. However, Tufts College should not have been like these others. Its financial backing had come from Universalists, members of a protestant faith known for their liberal mindset and progressive attitudes, especially when it came to women and education. Indeed, during the mid- to latter 1800s, the Universalist church founded twenty-two schools including five colleges, and all were co-educational from the start. All, that is, except for Tufts College.[1]

As for why Tufts was only for men at its start, well, there is no reasonable answer. According to one trustee of the college, the Reverend Thomas Whittemore, "the subject of admitting females was never discussed at any meeting of the Trustees we ever attended." So, for lack of a better question, Tufts College started and then remained a bastion of male education through the 1800s. But with each passing year, the exclusion of women from collegiate study fell further by society's wayside, especially as land grant colleges and universities began opening to both sexes across the country. Sensing the winds of change, many in the Tufts community, including alumni and prominent members of the Universalist church, finally began to question the exclusion of women. By the late 1880s, even some in the faculty began pushing for the change, and this was seen as a significant turn of opinion. But the trustees said "no," mainly due to financial constraints. The admission of women, they argued, would require new infrastructure such as a separate dormitory, and Tufts just didn't have the money at the time to support any new buildings.[2]

However, the president of Tufts College during this era, Elmer Capen, was a firm believer in coeducation, and for years he championed the inclusion of women to anyone who would listen. Eventually the trustees heeded his call, though they wanted to start small. In May of 1892, they voted to allow women to study at Tufts in the future – hardly a rousing endorsement of coeducation, but certainly a start. The details of coeducation were left to a committee, though the trustees presumed graduate studies would be the first to open to women, then undergraduate work at a later date. President Capen, though, wanted more. So, when the trustees met again in July of that same year, he made sure the question of full coeducation, without restriction and without delay, was at the top of their agenda. Helping President Capen was the growing popular opinion in this regard, as well as a much-improved financial situation of the college.[3]

The trustee meeting on July 15, 1892, lasted nearly all day, and when the debates and arguments and votes were all over, it was President Capen who emerged to greet members of the press. The first thing they noted was his smile. "Yes," he told reporters of the *Boston Daily Globe*, "all departments of the college are to be thrown open to students without distinction as to sex." Tufts College was now a coeducational institution, some forty years after it was originally chartered.[4]

The task of making coeducation work at Tufts College then fell onto gentlemen who were not exactly enthusiastic about the idea. Nearly every male student greeted this new reality with a giant cry of disbelief, if not pure anguish. They simply did not want the young women anywhere near their beloved male sanctuary, and they were not shy about their feelings when reporters from the *Boston Daily Globe* came asking. One student rationally explained, "I would rather not see the girls on the hill. It doesn't look natural, and we don't feel natural in the classroom with them, either." A second openly worried men could no longer act freely, but now had to watch their manners, for fear of "shocking the girls [with their antics]." A third bemoaned that "couples would go off spooning by themselves," thereby destroying the sacred bonds of friendship between male classmates, bonds that had been forged since the very first days of the college.[5]

Despite the cold shoulder, ten brave women enrolled alongside the men in the fall of 1892, determined to make the most of their educational opportunity. However, when the women set foot on campus, they found Tufts College had not exactly prepared for their experience outside the classroom. There were no clubs for them to join, no female dormitories or dining halls, no athletic teams, no nothing. Well, not quite. There was a small anteroom in the library (now Packard Hall) set aside for their use as a lounge, a humble gesture by the trustees while they worked to build a women's dormitory. There was also something else, at least for the three women enrolled in the Tufts Divinity School. One of that school's organizations, undoubtedly to the surprise of all, decided to welcome the women as equals. The singular group that said "yes" was the all-male Hebrew letter fraternity, Heth Aleph Res.[6]

However, for the remaining six women in the liberal arts college (the seventh apparently dropped out soon after the school year began), all they had was their small anteroom, and hundreds of back-handed whispers from men who resented their very presence. Yet these women did not sit idly by and wonder about their fate, or worry about their supposed role on campus. Instead, they looked to create organizations and activities to enhance their experience at Tufts. And, just as the men had done when they first arrived in the mid 1850s, some of the first organizations they created were secret societies, known as women's fraternities at the time, but now more commonly referred to as sororities. The idea began with one of the first women to enroll at Tufts College, Mabel Bailey, and once two sororities were organized in the fall of 1895, they proved to be very popular with the women for the next sixty years. The tide turned decidedly against the organizations during the late 1960s, however, and by 1972, they had all closed down. But a mere five years later, one sorority re-emerged on campus and ignited a general revival of the system that continues in earnest to this day. This is their story.[7]

ALPHA DELTA SIGMA (Local society, 1895 – 1901)
DELTA SIGMA (Alpha Chapter, 1901 – 1908)
ALPHA OMICRON PI (Delta Chapter, 1908 – 1969, 1986 – present)

In the spring of 1895, as the last "bachelors" of Tufts College were getting ready to graduate (a name the men gave themselves, to identify they had matriculated before women were first admitted), a group of four women led by Grace Fickett started discussing their situation on campus. Women been welcomed at Tufts for the past three years, but the school still offered them few opportunities outside the classroom. In fact, just about all the administration had done was erect Metcalf Hall as a women's dormitory. So, Grace and her friends decided to act where the school would not. They would create the first organization for women at Tufts College, one to celebrate their friendship and enhance their enthusiasm for their beloved alma mater. As for what that organization would be, the group decided to repeat what some of the first men at Tufts had done. They would create a secret society.[8]

The women spent the summer and early fall of 1895 planning their organization in earnest. They wrote a constitution, defined their aims and purpose, developed a secret ritual, and, most importantly, chose a name: Alpha Delta Sigma. When classes resumed in the fall of 1895, these women finalized their plans and even added two freshmen into their group. Then, by the third week of October, they were ready. Together the women pledged an oath to one another, and then they publically announced their existence to the Tufts campus. The six founding members of Alpha Delta Sigma were:[9]

Mary Grace Fickett (1897)
Georgia Louise Hodgdon (1897)
Frances Crocker Gifford (1898)
Martha Lane Root (1898)
Carrie Leeds Worthen (1899)
Kate Elizabeth Cousens (1899)

After the Zeta Psi fraternity started at Tufts, it took a year before their first rival appeared on campus. Alpha Delta Sigma's appeared much sooner. As it turned out, the very same day the campus learned of Alpha Delta Sigma, they also learned of a second women's society, Alpha Kappa Gamma. The race to be the best was now on. But, to say the two societies were overly competitive or cutthroat towards one another would be false. Indeed, for their very first social activity a few weeks later, the women of Alpha Delta Sigma attended a reception hosted by their rival at the home of Professor Knight. From there, Alpha Delta Sigma embarked on a busy social calendar that included hosting whist parties with Delta Upsilon, organizing a campus-wide dance in Metcalf Hall, and holding a reception for Alpha Kappa Gamma, in return for the compliment shown them earlier in the school year. All told, Alpha Delta Sigma's first year was a success, punctuated with the membership growing to twenty by end of the 1895–96 school year.[10]

In Alpha Delta Sigma's second year, though, the women decided to branch out from social activities. That year, one of the newest members, Grace Lane, suggested they add some literary elements to their meetings, such as the reading of essays and holding debates. At the time, many fraternities and sororities across the country devoted significant time to literary discussions, and by all accounts Alpha Delta Sigma's foray into this endeavor was quite popular for many years. But, it was the sorority's annual theatrical production, often held in local halls and churches each spring, which generated the most excitement. These productions started in 1896 and continued until at least 1901, with sorority members and alumnae playing all the parts including the male roles. The exclusion of men, though, didn't always stop at the stage's edge – on at least one occasion, men were not allowed in the audience. These productions were always well liked by the greater Tufts community, and received glowing reviews in the *Boston Globe*. And while the women of Alpha Delta Sigma must certainly have enjoyed their local fame, they didn't want to stop there. Instead, they had bigger plans.[11]

Going mobile

When the six women founded Alpha Delta Sigma, they envisioned their organization as one meant for colleges both near and far. They were certainly not alone in this thought. Numerous women's fraternities all across the United States, having started as local organizations, began expanding rapidly in the late 1890s, with each looking to put their stamp on collegiate life. But, the women of Alpha Delta Sigma were in no hurry. For six years they remained local to Tufts College and simply waited for the right opportunity. One finally came during the fall of 1900, when they learned of a local sorority at Brown University called Delta Sigma. These two societies, which had formed independently at their respective schools around 1895, somehow became acquainted that fall. As luck would have it, the two found much in common, so in early 1901, they merged their operations and formed a new national organization. As for a name, they became "The Secret Order of Delta Sigma," with the Tufts women becoming the Alpha chapter, and the Brown women becoming the Beta chapter. Two years later, Delta Sigma added a third chapter, Gamma, when they absorbed the local sorority Phi Gamma at the University of Maine at Orono. Delta Sigma was thus the first, and so far only national Greek-letter sorority founded at Tufts.[12]

Delta Sigma may have been a small and relatively unknown national organization, but one thing was certain: secrecy was sacrosanct. The sorority refused to publish the names and addresses of the national officers, and refused to announce any information about their annual convention. Such facts were usually public knowledge within the fraternity and sorority world, but for reasons long since forgotten, Delta Sigma chose to be ultra-secretive.[13]

By 1903, news of Delta Sigma had spread to the greater collegiate world, most likely through the distribution of *Baird's Manual of American College Fraternities* and other intercollegiate publications on Greek life. Soon many national organizations were intrigued by Delta Sigma, and a few even made overtures about absorbing all three chapters. The first to come courting was Alpha Omicron Pi, but that organization was "not favorably received," according to accounts of the Tufts women. Then came Kappa Alpha Theta, who nearly succeeded in convincing Delta Sigma to join their organization. But, some in Delta Sigma weren't completely swayed, so as a group they contacted a few more national sororities with the hopes of finding a more suitable partner. In the end, Delta Sigma did not find the perfect fit, so they said "no" to all. They would continue on as they were.[14]

For the next few years, life in Delta Sigma remained fairly normal, with the women holding social events, recruiting new members, performing plays, entertaining the wives of faculty members over tea, and meeting once a year with their sister chapters in a national convention. By this time, the number of sororities at Tufts had grown to three, with the other two also being local organizations. Then came 1907. That year, the local sorority Tau Epsilon Sigma decided to affiliate with a large and growing national organization, Alpha Xi Delta. For the women of Delta Sigma, this move seems to have prompted a serious discussion about their future as a national organization. Delta Sigma had seemingly given up on further expansion at this point – they had not added a single new chapter in over four years, despite a growing interest in sororities across the country. As a result, in 1908, the entirety of Delta Sigma realized their future lay in merging with another, stronger organization. For this, they chose one they had first rejected five years earlier, Alpha Omicron Pi.[15]

A humble start, a national reach

On a snowy day just before Christmas in December of 1896, four women climbed a set of stairs in the Columbia College library and entered a seldom-used storage room. The four were juniors at Barnard College, the women's school affiliated with Columbia University in New York City, and they were on a mission. They wanted to create something that would cement their friendship not just for the rest of their time at Barnard, but forever. So, as they watched the snow flurry past the large Gothic window in the anteroom, the women pledged their loyalty to one another. A week later, they met again in a house near campus, only this time they formally declared themselves a brand new women's fraternity, Alpha Omicron Pi (AOII). From there, AOII become a national organization a year and a half later when they established a second chapter at Sophie Newcomb Memorial College (now Tulane University) in New Orleans, Louisiana. Over the next decade, AOII scattered six additional chapters in all corners of the country, from California to Virginia, Tennessee, Nebraska, and Illinois. Then, in 1908, AOII received a petition to merge with Delta Sigma. Now, they would enter New England.[16]

The formal installation of the three Delta Sigma chapters was a grand, multi-day affair, even drawing one of AOII's original founders to the ceremonies. The Tufts induction was scheduled for the early evening of April 13, 1908, but due to unforeseen travel delays, the installation team realized they would not arrive on campus until after 10:30 p.m. So, they used the state-of-the-art communication system for the day – the telegram – to inform the women, and suggest the ceremony be postponed. Those in Delta Sigma wanted nothing to do with a delay. They wanted in, as soon as possible. Therefore, the women gathered at the off-campus home of an alumna, Mary Ingalls Lambert, and prepared the space for the ceremony. When the officers from AOII finally arrived, they were shocked to find those in Delta Sigma ready to go, even pleading to be initiated then and now. "We were a pretty tired trio," wrote one of the national officers, "but who could have continued to feel fatigued in the face of such honest eagerness as that which greeted us?" The ceremony thus commenced, much to the delight of all.[17]

After joining AOII, life in Delta chapter at Tufts carried on as it had since 1895. The women operated out of the Lambert's home for a number of years, since "the whole house is at our disposal for social functions and general good times." As women's sports were added to the college curriculum, AOII became increasingly proud of their athletes, and many became captain of their respective team. In 1912, when Richardson House opened as a women's dormitory on campus, AOII alumnae sponsored a guest room in the building for use by women visitors, even if they were not members of the sorority. The room, which was adorned in AOII regalia, was dedicated to the memory of five deceased members of the sorority, including two of Alpha Delta Sigma's founders, Georgia Hodgdon and Kate Cousens. Then, of course, came the war.[18]

Out here in the fields

The declaration of war by the United States in the spring of 1917 resonated through the Tufts campus, with many men answering the call to service. For the women of AOII, however, the war was not theirs to fight, but to support. They began in earnest as a chapter in the fall of 1917 by knitting sweaters, hats, and other warm clothing for "our brothers in the [Army] camps, for we are all brothers and sisters now in the common cause." Still, the war seemed a world away the following spring, when those in AOII turned their interests towards the more traditional activities of rushing new members, holding faculty receptions, and throwing bridal showers for recently engaged alumnae. Indeed, in the spring of 1918, three members of AOII were touting their de-facto sorority house in a small, college-owned building, which they used every Wednesday night for dinners with their professors and their wives. Afterwards, all would sit by the fireplace and talk the night away. The war, in many ways, was a reality far removed from The Hill.[19]

Everything changed once school let out for the spring. The women went home, but rather than enjoy a vacation, many became farm hands in place of men who'd gone off to war, or went to work in hospitals. They also knew returning to school in the fall would bring an experience unlike no other. As the chapter wrote in AOII's national magazine, *To Dragma of Alpha Omicron Pi*, "College will indeed be a changed place, and we girls of Alpha Omicron Pi, who *are* going back [emphasis in orignal], must work harder than ever for our college and country." Tufts College was indeed a radically changed place when those in AOII returned in the fall. The campus was now a full-blown military training base. Gone were most of the male students they knew, replaced by hoards of men from New England assigned to Tufts as part of the Student Army Training Corps (S.A.T.C.). The chapter immediately recognized the seriousness

The women of Alpha Omicron Pi on the steps of Eaton Hall, June, 1916.

of the situation, and in conjunction with the other sororities, decided to curtail their operations. Rush week was canceled, as were all formal social activities. Then, the chapter went to work. They raised money to buy Liberty Bonds and War stamps. They held informal, inexpensive receptions for members of the S.A.T.C. and the Naval Unit stationed at Tufts, lest they seem wasteful with their money. They sold posters to support the work of the Young Men's Christian Association (or YMCA, as it is more commonly known), which provided comfort and welfare operations for soldiers. Civic duty, it seems, was first and foremost on the minds of those in AOII.[20]

The service and sacrifice of those in the chapter, though much appreciated, lasted for just over a month. The arrival of the Armistice on November 11, 1918, signaled to all that life would soon return to normal at Tufts College. The remainder of the 1918–19 school year was therefore a transitional one, with the S.A.T.C. disbanding, students and professors slowly returning to campus, and everyone looking for a sense of normalcy. The Tufts sororities reinstituted formal rush in May of 1919, and for AOII, this week of recruitment brought in thirteen new women to the sorority, a very large group for the time. And then, by the fall of 1919, it was as if the disruption of war had never happened. Correspondence from the chapter to the national organization made no mention of the upheaval the previous year – the letters only seemed to be looking forward to the future. AOII was certainly not alone in this regard, as a similar sentiment existed in all other sororities, if not the entire campus. Life at Tufts College had clearly and quickly moved on.[21]

Fading away

In the years and decades that followed World War I, AOII maintained a strong presence on campus and within their national organization. They managed to survive the upheaval of World War II, and were relatively immune from the controversy surrounding restrictive membership clauses in the 1950s, since membership in AOII was open to all regardless of race or creed. Although the chapter never occupied an official house, they continued to occupy various rooms in private residences close to campus, eventually moving to Curtis Hall in the 1950s. In the late 1950s, though, members of AOII did experience life in a chapter house, at least for a night. Starting in 1959, AOII held an annual "Pajama Party" with the Theta Chi fraternity for at least a few years. The party, all details of which had to be pre-approved by the Dean of Women (including the guest list), started with a joint dinner at Theta Chi's house followed by a mixer. However, at 9:30 p.m., the members of Theta Chi vacated their home, leaving AOII alone to sleep in the rooms. Theta Chi rejoined the sorority for breakfast in the morning, thereby ending the excursion. But rest assured, no member of Theta Chi ever snuck back into the house during the night, for the women were always under the watchful eye of two of their mothers, acting as chaperones.[22]

As the 1960s marched on, AOII remained reasonably stable even as a rapidly declining interest in Greek life began to grow among Tufts women. Sure enough, such apathy led the sororities to start closing down in the later 1960s, one after the other. By the 1969–70 school year, it was AOII's turn, as they vanished from campus that year with nary a trace. What had started with some of the first women to enter Tufts some seventy-five years earlier was now over. Just about all that was left was a scholarship in the name of Alpha Omicron Pi, established by the alumnae shortly after Delta chapter was chartered, and awarded each year to an undergraduate "who best represents the combination of very high scholarship and significant participation in social work."[23]

Home, sweet home

AOII remained closed at Tufts for nearly the next two decades, even when sororities returned to campus in the mid 1970s. Of course, this revival of sorority life was hardly robust – of the four organizations that attempted to establish or re-establish a chapter during this era, only two succeeded in earnest, which probably gave great pause to anyone looking to restart AOII. But, by the mid 1980s, the rising popularity of sororities at Tufts was hard to ignore. The two active chapters on campus, Chi Omega and Alpha Phi, had both swelled in membership to a level never before seen at Tufts. Therefore, it wasn't surprising when, during the fall of 1985, a group of about five women began talking about starting a third sorority. These women just all happened to be living together at the time, and thought it would be fun to organize a new group around their friendship.[24]

Of course, starting a new sorority required more than just desire. By 1985, it required adherence to a formal process, one administered by the National Panhellenic Conference (NPC), the organization that oversees twenty-six national women's social fraternities. One of the first steps in this process required the five women to convince the student-run Tufts Panhellenic Council (TPC), which provided oversight to the sororities, that the campus did, indeed, need another one. They had little trouble in this regard. With both Alpha Phi and Chi Omega at over sixty-five members each, those in the TPC were very eager to see a third come to campus, since they could not accept every woman who wanted to join. So, the TPC took the next step by inviting all NPC organizations not currently represented at Tufts to bid for the right to start a new chapter on campus, if so interested. The call went out in early 1986, and a few weeks later, the TPC, along with the group of five women, began interviewing the short list of organizations under serious consideration. Among this group was a sorority that just happened to know the campus quite well, AOII. And as fate would have it, all involved in the decision realized they liked AOII best.[25]

AOII moved quickly to restart Delta chapter. In the ensuing two months, the national officers and the five undergraduates recruited over fifty others to join the group, which was both a testament to the organizational power of AOII, and the strong interest in sorority life. The women then spent the next few semesters working to regain their charter by learning the history of AOII, hosting social and philanthropy events, and getting to know each other. They were rewarded for their hard work in the spring of 1987, when Delta chapter of AOII was officially rechartered. The oldest sorority at Tufts was now back in operation. But, all was not perfect, for AOII still had one major goal left to achieve: they wanted to occupy an official chapter house on campus, something never before achieved in their ninety-plus year history. By then, the other two sororities on campus were safely ensconced in chapter houses, and those in AOII knew they would need a house, too, if they were going to maintain their strong membership in the years ahead. However, they were hardly alone in their desire for a chapter house. Four other fraternities were also searching for accommodations, yet not a single house was available. So, all these organizations could do was get in line, and wait. It looked to be a long one. The Tufts administration wasn't exactly rushing to open any new chapter houses, anytime soon.[26]

For three long years AOII waited while operating out of various classrooms, meeting spaces, and off-campus apartments. Then, in the spring of 1990, an opening appeared. That semester, the Theta Delta Chi fraternity, after a long and bruising battle with the administration, was removed from campus for three years and forced to vacate their chapter house at 123 Packard Avenue.

The alumni owners of the property, who still had to maintain the space and pay taxes, decided to rent their home to another Greek-letter organization while they awaited their fraternity's return. The decision of who would occupy the house went to the student-run Inter-Greek Council (IGC), which had developed a method to award the space based on membership size, years on campus, philanthropy work, and overall disciplinary record. Rising to the top of this rubric was AOII. So, in the fall of 1990, Delta chapter of AOII moved into their first official chapter house at what was now called 125 Packard Avenue. The residence may only have been temporary in nature, but such detail hardly mattered. AOII finally had a home.[27]

As it turned out, AOII's stay at 125 Packard Avenue was indeed temporary, as the Theta Delta Chi fraternity came back to campus a year earlier than expected, and then promptly kicked the sorority out of the house. However, the Tufts administration was reluctant to return AOII to the ranks of the unhoused, especially since they had done well in the space, and had signed a three-year lease. So, the administration moved AOII into another on-campus house at 25 Whitfield Road. Formerly the residence of the Phi Sigma Kappa fraternity and more recently a co-op dormitory, 25 Whitfield Road had not been occupied by a Greek-letter organization for nearly twenty years. Now, for the 1992–93 school year, the house would once again fly a fraternity flag, this one bearing the letters of AOII.[28]

The chapter welcomed these new accommodations, but not without some worry. Their lease for 25 Whitfield Road was only valid for one year, and afterwards, the house would go on the open fraternity market, with an application process to determine which organization would be granted a long-term lease. So, during the 1992–93 school year, AOII was once again in competition for a house, this time with the Alpha Epsilon Pi (AEPi) and Zeta Beta Tau (ZBT) fraternities, both of which were unhoused at the time. AOII need not have worried. The IGC's decision metric was essentially the same as a few years earlier, so to no one's surprise, the sorority came out on top. AOII was allowed to stay at 25 Whitfield Road, this time with a long-term lease.[29]

Ever since the fall of 1992, then, AOII has continued to call 25 Whitfield Road their home. By all accounts, the chapter has thrived in the space, marking both their one-hundredth anniversary as a Tufts sorority in 1995, and their one hundredth anniversary as Delta chapter of AOII in 2008. However, the chapter has experienced some recent turmoil, which may resonate for years to come. In the fall of 2016, a transgendered woman rushed AOII and, much to her delight, was under serious consideration to receive a bid to join. Overseeing rush week was a member of AOII's national staff, and when she learned this woman would likely be extended a bid, she became worried over the potential legal implications. Apparently, this was the first time a transgendered woman had attempted to join AOII, and the national organization was ill prepared for the situation. So, the national officer asked the chapter to pause for a few days while she sought clarification. Unfortunately, what followed next appeared to be quite a bit of miscommunication between the national organization and the undergraduates, the crux being a perceived threat to expel Delta chapter from AOII should the bid be extended. This information (which turned out to be wholly incorrect), coupled with a strong resentment over the situation in the first place, caused many of the undergraduates to lose faith in their governing organization. As a result, shortly after rush week ended, nearly half of the active members dropped out of AOII in protest. So, too, did the transgendered woman, who had indeed been given a bid by the undergraduates (unanimously) after the national organization confirmed she could join the sorority. Those that chose to remain now hope to bring this issue of transgendered membership to light within the greater AOII organization, if not the entire sorority system.[30]

ALPHA KAPPA GAMMA (Local society, 1895 – 1910)
CHI OMEGA (Chi Alpha Chapter, 1910 – 1970, 1977 – present)
COSMOPOLITAN SORORITY (Local society, 1976 – 77)

Mabel Prescott Bailey, by virtue of her place in history, was a very brave woman. She could have made the easy choice and attended a college that was at least receptive to women, if not openly welcoming. Instead, Mabel opted for a challenge, backed securely in her faith as a Universalist. She entered Tufts College in the fall of 1892, just a few weeks after the school decided to admit women, even though it was not going to be easy. After all, the male students and many in Tufts faculty made it very clear they did not want women on their campus. Still, Mabel enrolled alongside three others as the very first women in the freshman class, and then prepared for the worst. "I came [to Tufts] with fear and trembling," she told a reporter for the *Boston Globe* a few months later. "I had an idea they [the men] would snub me or overlook me." She needn't have worried. As it turned out, the harsh treatment never materialized in strength, and a majority of the undergraduate men considerably softened their views towards the co-eds within a month or two.[31]

But those four first-year women were hardly having the typical college experience. None of them lived on campus, as the women's dormitory was but a dream that year. Rather, the women commuted to school each day and returned home each night. Just about the only place the women could gather outside of class was a small room in the library (now Packard hall), set aside for them by the trustees. It was in this room where Mabel and the others studied, ate lunch, and talked about the future. Talking was just about all they could do that first year, as there was not a single sports team, club, or organized campus activity for the women to join. Worse still, the Tufts administration wasn't working to change this situation. Mabel and her classmates eventually realized if they wanted extra-curricular opportunities, they would have to create them. So that's exactly what they did.[32]

And the winner is…

They started in the spring of 1893, or at least they attempted to start. That semester, Mabel put forth the idea of forming a secret society for women. Such organizations were fast appearing on college campuses at the time, especially outside of New England where coeducation had taken hold years earlier. However, Mabel and her classmates soon abandoned this idea, since they thought the four of them were not enough to support a society. But the idea stayed with Mabel as she progressed through Tufts and more women enrolled each year. Then, as a senior in the fall of 1895, she was ready to try again. Feeling there were finally enough women on campus to realize her idea, Mabel gathered a group of friends and began planning a new, secret organization. For weeks they worked together behind closed doors to write their constitution, develop a ritual, and pick a name, Alpha Kappa Gamma. However, just as they were about to announce their presence to the campus, they were usurped by a second group of women who'd had the same idea. This other group, Alpha Delta Sigma, thus became the first women's organization at Tufts. Mabel and the rest of Alpha Kappa Gamma were forced to settle for second place. Nonetheless, Alpha Kappa Gamma came into existence with a grace and flair all their own, and unlike Alpha Delta Sigma, could claim one of the first women to enroll at Tufts as a member. The eight charter members of Alpha Kappa Gamma were:[33]

Mabel Prescott Bailey (1896)
Edith Louise Hodge (1897)
Marion Lenore Flint (1898)
Harriette Johnson Merrill (1898)
Clara Ransom (1898)
Harriette Alice Turner (1898)
Isabella Gertrude Knight (1899)
Ellen Eddy Shaw (1899)

Almost instantly, Alpha Kappa Gamma and Alpha Delta Sigma established a healthy respect for one another as they both looked to make a positive impact on campus life. Combined, the two sororities counted nearly half of all undergraduate women among their membership rolls, so they were certainly positioned well in this regard. Alpha Kappa Gamma took the first step in affecting the social scene when they hosted the first ever reception by a sorority just a few weeks after their unveiling. The venue was Professor Knight's house, a grand Victorian structure in the heart of campus where two of the women boarded, including Professor Knight's daughter Isabella, one of the founding members. Their guests were the women of Alpha Delta Sigma, thus demonstrating the sincere cooperation between these two "rival" organizations as they began their operations. Not surprisingly, Alpha Delta Sigma repaid the favor a few months later by hosting a reception, dance, and whist party for Alpha Kappa Gamma.[34]

In the years that followed, Alpha Kappa Gamma continued to grow their membership, keeping pace in number with both Alpha Delta Sigma and Tau Epsilon Sigma, a third sorority started in 1896. Theirs was an active social calendar each year, complete with parties, receptions, and dances both on and off campus. They also produced theatrical dramas, which were especially popular among Tufts sororities at the time. In February of 1904, for example, the chapter put on a production of *Sweet Lavender*, with the women of Alpha Kappa Gamma playing all the parts including the male roles. But the exclusion of men didn't stop there. As a reporter for the *Boston Globe* wrote in his review, "No man looked on," for men were excluded from the audience. Apparently, though, the production was not solely about entertainment – as one member of Alpha Kappa Gamma wrote on the back of her program, "After seeing this Delta Sigma shakes in her boots. Clement [played by member Winifred Thorpe] is the hero of the evening." The friendly rivalry between the two oldest sororities at Tufts, it seems, turned quite serious when it came to theatrical pursuits.[35]

Alpha Kappa Gamma continued along normally throughout the early 1900s, until actions of the other sororities began to influence its future direction. The issue was extent. In 1901, all three sororities on the Medford campus – Alpha Kappa Gamma, Alpha Delta Sigma, and Tau Epsilon Sigma – were local groups, existing only at Tufts College. Then everything began to change. Alpha Delta Sigma went first, merging that year with a similar organization at Brown University to become part of a new national organization known as Delta Sigma. Tau Epsilon Sigma went next, giving up their local roots in 1907 to affiliate with a fast growing national organization, Alpha Xi Delta. Then, in 1908, Delta Sigma decided to merge with a larger organization, Alpha Omicron Pi. Consolidation among women's fraternities was fast coming into vogue at the time, as women were beginning to show a definitive preference for national organizations over local ones. This trend left Alpha Kappa Gamma, and the newly formed Delphoi Society, as the only local sororities at Tufts. For Alpha Kappa Gamma, the writing on the wall was clear. They knew they had to merge with a large national organization if they were going to thrive amidst their now stronger rivals. For this, they looked westward. Or, at least, mid-westward.[36]

From Arkansas to Boston

In the spring of 1895, just a few months before Mabel and her friends started Alpha Kappa Gamma, four women at the Arkansas Industrial University (now the University of Arkansas at Fayetteville) were contemplating the exact same idea, and for nearly the exact same reasons. Their campus, just like Tufts College, was awash in opportunities for men, including dormitories, athletic teams, and fraternities. But for women, there was almost nothing for them outside the classroom, not even a dormitory. Therefore, these four were left to create something for themselves. As they looked around campus for groups to emulate, they eventually focused on the male fraternities, which were growing rapidly in popularity. So, that spring, the four women formed a club, chose a couple of Greek letters for their name, and called themselves a women's fraternity. Then, however, reality set in. The women really didn't know what they were doing. Their club had no real direction or grand purpose, mainly because they didn't realize those attributes were required of a true fraternal organization.[37]

That could have been the end of the idea, had the four decided to quit. They did not. Instead, they turned to Dr. Charles Richardson for advice. Dr. Richardson was a regent of the university, a national officer in the Kappa Sigma fraternity, and the man responsible for the current growth of fraternity life at Arkansas. Most importantly, he was also a great mentor to the students. So, he met with the women, listened to what they wanted to accomplish, and then pledged to help make their organization a reality. Here, though, he offered more than just moral support. He wrote a constitution and secret ritual for the women, and he also helped them secure a charter from the state, thus giving them a firm legal basis for their organization. Then, on April 5, 1895, the four women and Dr. Richardson came together and formally created the Chi Omega fraternity, the first sorority at Arkansas Industrial University. Dr. Richardson, being a dentist by trade, made the first badge of Chi Omega out of dental gold.[38]

After starting, Chi Omega then did something that the women of Alpha Kappa Gamma at Tufts College never did: they expanded their organization to other campuses. From the very beginning, Chi Omega was conceived as a national organization, no doubt influenced by Dr. Richardson's experience in Kappa Sigma. Chi Omega made this leap in the fall of 1898, when they established a second chapter at Jessamine College in Kentucky, and a third chapter at Hellmuth Women's College in London, Ontario, Canada, thus making the fraternity an international organization. By the turn of the century, Chi Omega had grown to nine active chapters, including a few at large state schools such as the University of Virginia, the University of Tennessee, and the University of Mississippi.[39]

Such expansion over a wide geographical area could easily have created headaches for the nascent organization, but here Chi Omega was well prepared. Regular, formal correspondence between the national officers and the chapters began in 1899 with the publication of the fraternity's magazine, *The Eleusis of Chi Omega*, and with the first biennial convention a year later. Then, by the mid 1900s, Chi Omega had implemented a program of peer supervision, where a national representative visited each chapter on a regular basis. In addition to supervisory work, these national representatives were also tasked with scouting other campuses as potential sites for new chapters. In October of 1908, Chi Omega dispatched their newly elected vice president, Sue Bitting, on such a visit. For the Tufts women of Alpha Kappa Gamma, this trip would be fateful.[40]

First impressions

Sue was certainly on a journey that fall. Her multi-week itinerary included visits to three Chi Omega chapters in succession: Epsilon chapter at Barnard College in New York City, Beta chapter at Colby College in Maine, and then Sigma chapter at Randolph-Macon Women's College in Virginia. While on these various campuses, her job was to interact with and advise undergraduate members, attend initiation ceremonies, spend nights with alumnae in their houses, dine at fancy banquets, and generally immerse herself in all things Chi Omega. Commercial steamships were her main mode of travel, with Boston being one of the waypoints. So, after visiting Colby College, Sue planned to stay in Boston before heading south to Virginia. But this was no mere sightseeing excursion. Sue was going to visit some of the local colleges and meet the undergraduates, in the hopes of finding new sites for chapters of her beloved fraternity. Over the course of three days, she visited Harvard, Wellesley, Boston University, and Tufts College. Of these, only one seemed to impress her: Tufts College. In reflecting on her visit, she wrote, "At Tufts we [she had a traveling companion] were most cordially entertained by some of the students." Although she does not say who these students were, in all likelihood she was talking about the women of Alpha Kappa Gamma.[41]

As it turned out, the feeling was mutual. The women of Alpha Kappa Gamma were so impressed with Sue and her fraternity that within a year or so of the meeting, they petitioned Chi Omega for a charter. Alpha Kappa Gamma's petition, though, would take some time. Chi Omega used their biennial convention to consider petitions from groups looking to join the organization, and unfortunately for the Tufts women, the next convention wasn't until the summer of 1910. So, they could do nothing but wait. In the end, though, it was all worth it, for the petition was accepted.[42]

Chi Omega wasted little time opening their newest chapter. Some two months after the convention, and just a few days before classes were due to begin in the fall of 1910, officers and delegates from Chi Omega made their way to the Tufts campus for the installation. Their destination was Metcalf Hall, which the undergraduate members of Alpha Kappa Gamma had taken over for the event. By the morning of September 17, 1910, all was in place for the ceremony. The installation itself occurred in waves, with seniors and very recent alumnae being initiated first, followed by the remaining undergraduates, and then the older alumnae. Included in this last round of initiations were Isabella Knight and Marion Flint, two of the original founders of Alpha Kappa Gamma, and Edith Bush, a future Dean of Women at Tufts College. Noticeably absent, however, was Mabel Prescott Bailey, even though she was living and working in nearby Brookline, Massachusetts, at the time. Regardless, by the end of the day, Alpha Kappa Gamma was no more, having been replaced by the Chi Alpha chapter of Chi Omega.[43]

Of wars won and battles lost

As the 1910s progressed, Chi Omega continued to provide numerous social and educational opportunities for the Tufts community including dances, tea parties, lectures by professors, dramatic productions, and inter-chapter athletics. Such endeavors, however, began to ebb in late 1917, with the realization that the United States was, indeed, at war. "Perhaps this year more than any other," wrote Marian Peirce, in her correspondence letter to *The Eleusis of Chi Omega*, "our thoughts and actions will be moved by a realization of the sad events which are sobering the world." By the spring of 1918, chapter activities had been effectively subjugated by patriotic ones, with those in Chi Omega joining all women on campus to work with the Red Cross, march in a Liberty Loan parade, and sew a large American flag in honor of the men going off to fight. Some in the chapter even left school that semester to work as farmers, taking the places of the men who'd been drafted to fight. Chapter activities such as meetings and initiations did continue during this time, but in general the women directed their efforts outside the classroom towards the war.[44]

By the fall of 1918, though, life had only grown tougher on campus. As Grace Chilson described in her letter to *The Eleusis of Chi Omega*,

> We have all gone without sugar (forgotten are the former fudge parties), eaten war viands; in short Hooverized our appetites in every conceivable way. We've discarded flimsy wearing apparel for the heavier and warmer garments, in order that fuel might not be needed until later months. Then too, the many nickels and dimes that would persist in urging us toward the favorite drugstore, have been surprised to find themselves spent in the purchasing of Thrift and War Savings Stamps.

The women also spent hours canning and preserving food, even selling the surplus and donating the proceeds to the Red Cross. Some became nurse's aides, and many hoped to travel overseas to help with the wounded, though they were generally encouraged by the War Department to stay in college and help out at home. In short, life had become all about sacrifice on a level none of the women had ever anticipated. Yet, they responded without complaint.[45]

The hardships came to an abrupt halt early in the morning on November 11, 1918. Without warning, chapel bells across Massachusetts began ringing to spread the wonderful news – the war was over! Upon being woken up from sleep, four women of Chi Omega threw on some clothes, ran to the chapel, and added their melody to the cacophony. Then, the party really began. More women emerged from their dormitories, and their screams and shouts soon brought the soldiers out of their barracks. A parade around campus then spontaneously formed, finishing at the campus reservoir, or "Rez," where the group "sang every song we knew." Next, the women and men headed over to a local Y.M.C.A. hall to dance until breakfast called the tired, hungry revelers at dawn. Later that day, professors cancelled classes so the women could march with the soldiers in a victory parade around Medford and Somerville. Finally, all headed off to more dances, which lasted well into the evening. "The day was one long to be remembered," wrote Grace Chilson, "because it was joyous in its declaration of peace and unusual in its celebration."[46]

Both Tufts College and Chi Omega returned to normal in the spring of 1919. Life in the chapter once again became a steady existence of rush, social events, philanthropy, and scholarship. At some point in the 1920s, Chi Omega began renting chapter rooms on or close to campus for meetings and small social events such as tea parties and the occasional chapter dinner. Dances and formals were still held on regular occasion, often in large venues such as Goddard Gymnasium or local hotels. Eventually, Chi Omega began a tradition of selling candied apples at football games, with the proceeds going to charity. By the spring of 1956, Chi Omega, along with all other sororities, moved to chapter rooms in Curtis Hall, a building on the edge of campus that also housed the student center. This move was orchestrated by the administration in an effort to centrally locate all of the sororities, since they still were not in favor of them occupying chapter houses.[47]

Shortly after moving into Curtis Hall, though, Chi Omega experienced their first major internal crisis since starting as a chapter. In the fall of 1955, two African-American women (or "Negro girls" as they were referred to in the *Tufts Weekly*, which was a normal descriptor of the day) enrolled as freshmen. These women were intriguing to those in Chi Omega, but not just because they were the first black female students Tufts had seen in years. Instead, the members were genuinely interested in these women as individuals. Additionally, a national effort to integrate previously all-white fraternities and sororities was starting to take hold, with individual chapters here and there, such as Chi Omega at Tufts, looking to lead the way. The only hiccup was their national organization, since their policies regarding membership were unclear. On one hand, Chi Omega at the time did not have official restrictive membership clauses barring admission based on race. On the other hand, racial diversity among Chi Omega's chapters was essentially non-existent, and there seemed to be little

Chi Omega members pose at the bottom of the hill in front of Ballou Hall, April 6, 1924.

interest within the greater organization to change this fact. The Tufts women, in other words, just might just be running into a headwall of opposition, should they indeed pledge these two women.[48]

As it turned out, the two African-American women joined another sorority, Sigma Kappa, later in the spring of 1956. This left moot the problem of integration within Chi Omega, at least for a few months. After arriving back on campus that following fall, the women of Chi Omega, and indeed all of the Tufts community, were shocked to learn that the national office of Sigma Kappa had revoked the charter of their Tufts chapter, ostensibly for pledging two black women into their previously all-white organization. This action by Sigma Kappa's national organization led to a renewed debate on discrimination among the undergraduate members of Chi Omega, especially when the situation began making headlines across the country. The national Chi Omega organization, sensing the angst within the Tufts chapter, sent a representative to meet with the women and calm them down. This official reassured the women that should they pledge an African-American woman in the future, such action "would create no consternation on this [Tufts University] campus." In other words, if the chapter looked to diversify its membership, the national organization promised there'd be no national media circus, unlike the one currently surrounding Sigma Kappa. This was hardly a rousing endorsement for diversity, but for the undergraduate members of Chi Omega, it was all they would get.[49]

Not surprisingly, the women were quite disappointed with this meeting and the message from their national organization. So, thirteen of the fifty active members, seeing no other alternative, resigned from the chapter in protest that fall of 1956. "The sacrifices of the national affiliation were not commensurate with the benefits," said one of the ex-members when asked for an official explanation. Reading between the lines, though, this statement meant unequivocally that the thirteen wanted nothing to do, anymore, with a discriminatory organization. A reporter for the *Tufts Weekly*, while working to bring this story to the campus, called the national office of Chi Omega for additional comment. The ensuing conversation revealed a harsh reality within Chi Omega that affirmed the actions of these thirteen. "What's dumb on the part of America today is that it can't distinguish between close, intimate groups, and public or semi-public groups," said the Chi Omega official. "Personal friendships are made out of similarities in backgrounds… Negroes are of a different social strata. When you have close interpersonal relations, you invite intermarriage. That's all there is to that." In this official's mind, opening up Chi Omega to women of all races would send America down a cultural death spiral.[50]

Within a few weeks, both the rhetoric and activism surrounding racial inclusion in Chi Omega died down as students turned their attention elsewhere. And while the loss of so many members at once certainly put a strain on operations, the chapter recovered quickly enough. Then, in 1960, the chapter erected a stone bench just outside of Goddard Chapel as part of their 50th anniversary celebration. The bench still sits there today. But as the 1960s marched on, all was not well with the Tufts sororities. In a word, they were becoming unpopular. The social upheavals of the day, coupled with a growing disdain for all things traditional by the younger students, led to a near wholesale rejection of fraternal organizations by women. In 1960, for example, there were five active sororities on campus. Within a decade, four had closed down due to a lack of interest, leaving only Chi Omega. Rush week in the spring of 1970 brought a mere three new members for the chapter, not nearly enough to replace those graduating or choosing to resign. As a result, the few Chi Omegas who returned the following fall could sense the inevitable, so they decided to close down the chapter for good, thereby ending sorority life at Tufts University. Mabel Prescott Bailey's dream of a secret society lasted almost eighty years, but it could not survive the turmoil of the late 1960s.[51]

Disco inferno

After Chi Omega closed down in the fall of 1970, most if not all in the Tufts community probably assumed such organizations were gone forever from campus. Political activism, co-ed living, and a shift towards a more liberal way of thinking were fast becoming the normal way of life at Tufts, while those old, stodgy sororities, with their conservative tendencies, afternoon teas, and chaperoned parties seemed so far removed from the modern campus that few students, if any, actually missed them. The undergraduates had similar feelings of disregard towards the male fraternities on campus, but those groups managed to hang on, barely. Instead, it was the sororities that took the brunt of the progressiveness, for they continued to be seen, in the eyes of so many, as completely useless.[52]

By the mid 1970s, however, a subtle shift in the mindset of the typical student began to take shape. With the Vietnam War fading fast from the headlines (helped in part by the end of the draft in 1973), with the resignation of President Nixon, and with the struggle for civil rights no longer filled with regular violence, college students at Tufts University in particular began to calm down. In addition, students entering Tufts at this time had been too young to appreciate fully those tumultuous events of the late 1960s. The upheaval experienced by the older generation was just not in the younger student's frame of thought, or part of their psyche. Instead, these younger students responded to the present world that was fast filling with arena rock and disco dancing. In short, they were having fun once again. The college counter-culture, which had started as a protest movement, wholeheartedly embraced this new, relaxed way of life, and quickly morphed into the mainstream. Parties replaced protests. Fun replaced angst. Peace, in many ways, had broken out.[53]

During the 1975–76 school year, though, a small group of women at Tufts took a critical look at this new campus lifestyle. They were not particularly enthralled with the counter-culture and its stereotypical liberal/hippie attitude, as they preferred a more conservative approach, especially when it came to balancing school and fun. They were also not as enthusiastic about co-ed living as most students. Although many had fought long and hard for men and women to live side-by-side in Tufts dormitories, the reality of the situation was far from perfect. Some women were less than thrilled to be living next to, and sharing bathrooms with, members of the opposite sex – undergraduate men are not, in general, a particularly neat and tidy group. As a result, these women began looking for an alternative way of campus life, a counter-counter culture askew of the norm. And when they looked, what they especially noticed were the fraternities. These organizations may not have been as popular as they once were, but they all had their own houses, they served meals of better quality than the dining halls, and they all operated as small, close-knit communities, with a general and lasting interest in their members. Such factors were very appealing to these women, much more so than the numerous co-ed living groups rapidly forming on and off campus. So, after much thought and deliberation, the women decided they wanted in. They would form a sorority.[54]

The small group of women knew that success depended on first assembling a critical mass of others. So, in the early spring of 1976, they began recruiting by word of mouth. They started talking to anyone who'd listen – roommates, friends, classmates – and they put up posters around campus, calling for any and all women interested in starting a new sorority. Within weeks, these efforts helped grow the group to a core of twelve women, with more prospects on the horizon. In addition, they began meeting regularly in the 4th floor lounge of Carmichael Hall, where they bonded as friends and worked to make a positive impact on campus. From fielding teams in intramural sports, to running a booth at the annual Kids' Day carnival, to planning social events with the fraternities, the women soon became an active and lively group that semester. As for a name, they called themselves the "Cosmopolitan Sorority." However, this name was only ever meant to be temporary, for the women had no intention of staying local. Instead, they wanted to affiliate with a national organization, the sooner the better.[55]

A few members started the task by researching different national women's fraternities, looking for ones that had ideals, values, and traditions they could embrace. Then, they invited those that seemed most interesting to campus for a round of presentations and interviews with others in the Cosmopolitan Sorority. Afterwards, the women retreated back to their meeting space to discuss the pros and cons of each organization. And while all involved kept an open mind throughout the process, one particular national soon rose to the top, helped by a family connection. A core member of the Cosmopolitan Sorority was related to Maurene Golden, a Tufts alumna from the class of 1959 and ardent member of Chi Omega. Soon enough, Ms. Golden was using her influence to steer the group towards Chi Omega. Backing her were a number of local alumnae who offered the Cosmopolitan Sorority not only additional support, but also the promise of an extensive network of personal and professional connections. The final vote on the matter, as could be expected, was hardly a contest. The Cosmopolitan Sorority decided to pursue affiliation with Chi Omega.[56]

Still, there was more work to be done that spring semester, including further recruitment (which brought the sorority to twenty-six members) and securing official recognition as a student group on campus. Such recognition was vital for the Cosmopolitan Sorority, for without it, affiliation with any national organization would not be possible. So, in March of 1976, the women submitted their application for recognition to the faculty and student led Committee on Student Life (CSL), which had the power to grant, or not, such requests. The CSL considered the matter at a regular meeting soon thereafter, but rather than just rubber stamp the application, they had a plethora of questions for the women, mainly centered on the ideals and goals of the Cosmopolitan Sorority. The women were well prepared for this dialogue. They knew they were already affecting a positive influence on campus, especially in terms of community service, so they had plenty of hard evidence to back up their mission. However, those on the CSL met these responses with a collective frown. Then, they began to openly criticize the women, arguing the aims of their sorority were already satisfied by other existing campus organizations. Some on the committee also railed against the exclusive nature of sorority membership in general, no doubt recalling the earlier discriminatory practices of many Greek-letter organizations in the 1950s and 1960s. The debate went on for some time that night, and for those keeping score, it seemed as if the Cosmopolitan Sorority might lose out.[57]

They did not. Instead, once they were done with their aggressive questioning, those in the CSL realized they were being somewhat unfair to the women. After all, the CSL had officially recognized the eight active fraternities in the past, and they didn't run those organizations through the question gauntlet. So, when all was said and spoken, the CSL granted "conditional approval" to the Cosmopolitan Sorority that semester, which allowed them to move forward, but kept in place "the opportunity [for the CSL] to examine and approve the conditions that would be imposed upon the sorority if it receives the recognition and affiliation [with Chi Omega]." In other words, the CSL wanted to make sure any outdated restrictions on membership were clearly, and firmly, in the past. Regardless, this recognition meant that sororities, after a six year absence, were officially back on campus.[58]

The members of the Cosmopolitan Sorority could hardly revel in their accomplishment, though, for they still had one more major goal to achieve that semester, and that was to secure a chapter house. On the surface, such a goal seemed obvious, since all of the fraternities had homes to call their own. However, the Cosmopolitan Sorority was breaking new ground here, since never in the history of Tufts had a sorority occupied a chapter house on campus. But this was 1976, and the women would not be denied. After all, having a home of their own was a major reason they had started their organization in the first place. So, with the help of Maurene Golden, they worked with the Tufts administration to rent the house at 120 Packard Avenue beginning the next fall. The space was small and had never been used for student housing in its history, but those in the Cosmopolitan Sorority didn't fret such details. Instead, seven women moved in during the fall of 1976, and worked to make it their home. For the first time in its one hundred twenty four years, Tufts University had a sorority house on campus.[59]

Well, we're movin' on up

When those in the Cosmopolitan Sorority gathered for the first time in their new chapter house that fall, they had much to celebrate, for they had accomplished much in a very short amount of time. However, they were far from finished. First up was their planned affiliation with Chi Omega. In early October of 1976, the group became an official colony of Chi Omega, thereby retiring the Cosmopolitan Sorority name. Over the next few weeks, representatives of the Chi Omega national organization began helping the women assimilate into national sorority life, grow the chapter through established practices, and regain their charter. In this regard, though, things did not progress smoothly. The national organization, to the undergraduates, seemed completely out of touch with modern campus life. They were fixated on the ways of the past, and implored the Tufts women to hold ice cream socials, Coca-Cola dance parties, faculty teas, and other outdated events, because that was the way Chi Omega still operated across most of the country. The Tufts women were slightly dumbfounded by this, as the last thing they wanted to do was revert back to the 1950s. They were here to build something new.[60]

Then, to make matters worse, the national organization told the women that alcohol was completely off limits when it came to chapter activities, especially in their house. Beer blasts and cocktail parties were for men's fraternities, not women's fraternities. This rule seemed completely absurd to the women, since the legal drinking age was eighteen at the time, and the consumption of distilled spirits was seen as much less controversial than other recreational substances widely available on campus. However, there was nothing the women could do but accept the situation, since they wanted to join Chi Omega. They were rewarded for all of their hard work just a few months later. On February 13, 1977, the women were officially initiated into Chi Omega, and the Chi Alpha charter was returned to Tufts. This first initiation, though, only involved the original core group of twelve women, in recognition of their role as the primary revivalists of the chapter. Some of these first initiates are:

Jodi Adeson (1979)
Julia Christensen (1978)
Ellen Fitzpatrick (1979)
Christine Johnson (1979)
Laura Lindsey
Patti Litman
Wendy McKinley (1978)
Lisa Romeo (1978)
RuthAnne Silverman
Cynthia Thompson (1978)
Valerie Pagano (1978)

The remaining members became the chapter's first official pledges, and were then fully initiated into Chi Omega later that semester.[61]

With charter in hand, the women next turned their attention to their current accommodations. While the house at 120 Packard Avenue was proving adequate that first year, it was far from ideal. Being located near the Theta Delta Chi and Theta Chi fraternity houses was a nice feature of the property, but it was very small, it could only house a small number, and it could not support a dining room, which the women wanted to establish. So, during the 1976–77 school year, Chi Omega began looking around campus for someplace else to call home. It did not take them long to notice two nice homes right on Professors Row, the social hub of the school due to its concentration of fraternity houses. One of these was 92 Professors Row, an old Victorian structure being used for co-op student housing at the time. This house offered the perfect location for the women, but it wasn't much bigger than 120 Packard Avenue, so it was soon dropped from consideration.[62]

However, a second house on the street appeared much more interesting. Sitting at 106 Professors Row was the old "Kippy" House, so named in the 1930s after the fraternity that built the structure, Alpha Kappa Pi. With its classic Georgian style and prominent position on campus, the Kippy House had all the amenities the women were looking for in a home, including large common areas, lots of bedrooms, and a commercial kitchen with a dining room. However, the Kippy house did have one significant logistical problem. Although the property was no longer home to a recognized fraternity, it was privately owned by the Alpha Sigma Phi alumni corporation, and currently occupied by a group of men fully enjoying the space while supposedly working to revive the fraternity.[63]

Thus, with no available options on Professors Row, the women then looked for another large house somewhere else on campus. They soon found one at 25 Whitfield Road. Originally opened for the Phi Sigma Kappa fraternity in the late 1950s, the house in 1977 was occupied by a local, co-ed fraternity known around campus as the "Freak Frat," so named because the members wholeheartedly embraced the counter-culture. This organization had achieved a modicum of success on campus since its inception a few years earlier, but was in poor standing at the time with the Tufts administration and surrounding neighborhood. The years of excessive noise, all night parties, and other disturbances had taken its toll on too many outside of the Freak Frat, including the landlord, Bruce Ketchen of the Tufts-owned Walnut Hill Properties. As a result, the women of Chi Omega surmised the house was ripe for the taking. All they had to do was convince Mr. Ketchen he'd be better off renting to a bunch of "nice, neat girls" backed by a national organization, instead of the Freak Frat. Helping make the argument was their advisor, Maurene Golden, and soon enough, Mr. Ketchen was in perfect agreement with the idea.[64]

Chi Omega thus left the confines of 120 Packard in the fall of 1977 and moved into 25 Whitfield Road. This new space was certainly more accommodating, as fifteen members were able to live in the house, and its large basement and kitchen allowed the chapter to eat some meals together, thereby fulfilling an original goal of the chapter's founders. Just about the only negative was its location, since it was somewhat removed from the center of campus. To some in Chi Omega, this singular negative greatly outweighed any of the positives afforded by the house. So, a few of the women began working to find someplace better. Rising to the top of the preferred list once again was Kippy House on Professors Row. Of course, nothing about this space had changed in the months since they'd first considered the house – it was still occupied by a group of men in their own community who showed no intention of ever leaving. But by now the women of Chi Omega had amassed considerable political clout (as evidenced in part by their taking of 25 Whitfield Road), and they intended to use it to the fullest extent.[65]

Something for nothing

The house at 106 Professors Row still looked grand from afar, as it had retained much of its luster from when it was built forty years earlier. The view close up, though, told a very different story. Long gone were the days when the house was maintained in earnest by the residents. In its place was nothing short of a disaster waiting to happen. The men of the Kippy House community were known about campus for using their home to excess, with little regard for the consequences. As a result, no one would have been surprised if they ended up burning it down. No one was more disappointed with the situation than John Zamparelli, an alumnus of Alpha Sigma Phi and president of the alumni corporation, which owned the house. Since 1970, Mr. Zamparelli had been managing the property with the hope it would someday host a revival of his fraternity. However, all of his recent efforts in this regard had fallen short, leaving him but a landlord to a group of students he could not control. His patience was wearing very thin.[66]

As fate would have it, one night during the 1977–78 school year, Mr. Zamparelli was walking across campus with Chi Omega's chapter advisor, Maurene Golden. The two were alumni trustees of Tufts and were headed to one of their regular meetings. During their conversation, Mr. Zamparelli lamented to Ms. Golden over the current state of 106 Professors Row, how the residents were destroying the place, and how he didn't know what to do about the situation any more. Ms. Golden instantly recognized the opportunity at hand. She knew Chi Omega had their eyes on this property, so she put forth a simple idea: evict the men and rent the house to Chi Omega, at least temporarily. To Mr. Zamparelli, this was an intriguing proposition. He was certainly looking for any way to motivate the current residents of Kippy House into reactivating his fraternity chapter. A temporary eviction, he surmised, just might push the men to bring back his beloved Alpha Sigma Phi. So, in the spring of 1978, he offered Chi Omega a one-year lease to 106 Professors Row, to start the following fall. Chi Omega, by being in the right place at the right time, had once again obtained a better house.[67]

As could be expected, the current residents of Kippy House were blindsided by this development that spring, and in the weeks that remained before school ended, they desperately tried to keep possession of 106 Professors Row. Their arguments went nowhere. They were just tenants, after all, and the landlord had moved on. Therefore, Chi Omega moved into the house in the fall of 1978, thus fulfilling an original goal of the founders. But all was not perfect with this arrangement. Chi Omega knew their lease was only valid for one year, and they also knew that if the former Kippy House members made a sustained and concerted effort to revive Alpha Sigma Phi, the women would be the ones out on the street next year.[68]

As a result, Chi Omega faced a challenge that ensuing school year of finding a way to stay in 106 Professors Row, for as long as possible. All the sorority needed was someone willing to take up the fight. They found their advocate in Christina Johnson (CJ), one of the original twelve re-founders of Chi Omega. CJ was an engineering student who was used to solving problems. To her, the situation was simply another problem to be solved. So, on her own initiative, she learned all she could about the property and its owners. She made numerous trips into Boston to check the public records of the Alpha Sigma Phi alumni corporation, which had been in existence for over half a century. She also made numerous inquiries to the City of Somerville regarding the payment of property taxes on 106 Professors Row. Her research uncovered two serious problems. One, the alumni corporation hadn't consistently filed the required annual reports in recent years. Second, they were also far behind in paying their property taxes. Suffice to say, the Alpha Sigma Phi alumni corporation by 1978 was a dysfunctional mess, incapable of fulfilling their basic duties. Unfortunately for the corporation, someone outside of their organization now knew this truth.[69]

Armed with this information, CJ and Ms. Golden approached the Tufts administration during the 1978–79 school year to see, ostensibly, if anything could be done to force the hand of the Alpha Sigma Phi alumni corporation and keep the sorority in the house. The administration quickly realized the answer was "yes." They had long been concerned with the state of affairs in the Kippy House since the fraternity left campus in 1970, as the men who'd lived there in the ensuing years had generally been too hard to contain or control. Now, the administration had a solution. In the spring of 1979, they paid the back taxes, assumed the mortgages, and even offered the alumni corporation some consideration towards the principal of the house, which they would hold in escrow for the fraternity. Tufts University had just taken over of 106 Professors Row.[70]

This change of ownership brought an instant sigh of relief among the members of Chi Omega. With the Alpha Sigma Phi fraternity out of the picture, and with a house they now needed to fill with residents, the Tufts administration offered Chi Omega a long-term lease. They accepted, and have called 106 Professors Row their home ever since.[71]

A Bad Decision, A Near Tragedy

Ever since Chi Omega re-established its chapter in 1977, the sorority has maintained a relatively large membership and strong presence on campus. Chi Omega gained their first rival in the fall of 1977, when the Alpha Phi sorority established a new chapter on campus. The two sororities soon found their own niche, so together they helped grow the sorority system into the thriving community of today. Chi Omega has also raised thousands of dollars through various philanthropy events throughout the years, and has continued to provide its members with a social and intellectual outlet. In general, the chapter has done very well with a positive reputation any organization would be proud to hold.[72]

However, Chi Omega has not been perfect, and in one case, a bad decision nearly cost a young man his life. One night in February of 2005, members of the Delta Tau Delta (DTD) fraternity decided to host a pledge activity at their house. They invited a few members of Chi Omega, who were most likely personal friends, to partake in the event. Although the exact nature of what happened (and the level of participation by Chi Omega members) is unclear, what is known is that the event involved underage drinking and, unfortunately, hazing of the DTD pledges. At one point that evening, one of the DTD pledges stopped breathing and had to be resuscitated. The near-death of this individual (who thankfully made a full recovery) resulted in the indefinite closing of DTD and the suspension of Chi Omega for one year, for the sorority admitted to "participating in the hazing of Delta Tau Delta pledges." As part of their suspension, Chi Omega was not allowed to recruit any new members during the ensuing 2005–06 school year.[73]

Chi Omega was able to overcome the suspension without further issues, and in the summer of 2010, the chapter celebrated one hundred years at Tufts University, the second sorority to reach this milestone. Among the guests of honor that weekend were many of twelve re-founding members and their advisor, Maurene Golden. Today, the Chi Alpha chapter of Chi Omega stands at over one hundred fifty members, the largest the chapter has even been in its existence. And of course, they still call 106 Professors Row their home.[74]

TAU EPSILON SIGMA (Local society, 1896 – 1907)
ALPHA XI DELTA (Lambda chapter, 1907 – 1957)
ALETHEA (Local society, 1957 – 1966)

By the fall of 1896, coeducation had been in place at Tufts College for four years, and by all accounts the women had settled in nicely on campus. Not only had Metcalf Hall been erected as their dormitory, but their enrollment in all classes continued to trend upwards, even drawing women from as far away as Montana. Still, there wasn't much for them to do outside of the classroom aside from joining one of the two sororities on campus, Alpha Delta Sigma or Alpha Kappa Gamma, each of which had been active for just under a year. Not surprisingly, many women did join one of these organizations that fall. But not all. Among those not joining were a group of four intrigued by the idea of sorority, just not with the two at Tufts. So, as many have done before, they decided to start a new one. They worked throughout that fall to detail the plans of their new organization, and just as the semester was coming to a close, they reached a milestone. On December 9, 1896, the four women voted to accept the constitution they'd written, thereby committing themselves to the goals, aims, and ideals of their new organization, which they called Tau Epsilon Sigma. The founding members were:[75]

Lucie Marion Gardner (1897)
Fannie Eliza Bradbury (1899)
Grace Willis Carleton (1899)
Helen Loretta Burkett (1900)

For the remainder of the school year, Tau Epsilon Sigma stayed sub rosa, opting not to identify themselves openly on campus. The women used this time instead to create their secret rituals and finalize other aspects of their sorority, while also adding two others to their membership roll. Finally, in June of 1897, they were ready. Their public unveiling occurred through a simple, if not intriguing article in the student newspaper, the *Tufts Weekly*. "A definite report of the formation of a new sorority has reached the Hill this week," wrote the reporter, who was presumably tipped off to the sorority's existence by someone from within. The article concluded with a list of the six members, and no words about the aims of the organization. It appears those in Tau Epsilon Sigma wished to keep secret much of what they were.[76]

Over the next few years, Tau Epsilon Sigma found a place alongside the other two Tufts sororities, and by all accounts achieved an equal stature. Tau Epsilon Sigma hosted numerous social events each year such as a winter dance, tea parties for the women of the college including the wives of professors, and whist parties. The sorority also put on at least one dramatic production, a showing of Richard Sheridan's *The Rivals* during the 1904–05 school year, which generated rave reviews as "one of the best performances of the kind ever given to Tufts women." However, by their own admission, the women were not very successful at philanthropy, as their events did not bring forth the desired results in terms of effort or fundraising. As for academics, Tau Epsilon Sigma became something of a dichotomy – a number of members, especially among the first initiates, achieved numerous scholastic honors, including election to Phi Beta Kappa. In contrast, though, nearly a quarter of those who joined the sorority during its first ten years dropped out of school before earning a diploma.[77]

Hometown heroes

The first major upheaval in Tau Epsilon Sigma came during the 1905–06 school year. Until then, Tau Epsilon Sigma had been content to exist solely as a local organization at Tufts College. This situation was similar to the other two sororities on campus, although one, Alpha Delta Sigma, had recently morphed into a very small national organization of three total chapters. The early 1900s were a time of great consolidation within the women's fraternity movement, with local sororities in particular being absorbed by national organizations looking to grow in rapid fashion. So, it was no surprise that those within Tau Epsilon Sigma were soon discussing affiliation. Most likely initiating the debate was one of Tau Epsilon Sigma's newest members, Beth Nash. She may have only been a freshman, but when it came to understanding national sororities, she likely knew more than anyone else in Tau Epsilon Sigma.[78]

Beth was no stranger to college life. She'd grown up a "faculty brat" on the campus of Lombard College in Galesburg, Illinois, as her father, the Reverend Charles Nash, was the school's president during her formative years. She also had two older sisters, Carrie Ruth and Faith, both of whom earned their undergraduate degrees from Lombard while Beth was in high school. However, in 1905, Reverend Nash resigned his prestigious post to become a lecturer at one of his alma maters, Tufts Divinity School (he also had two degrees from Lombard). Naturally, Beth followed her father to his new school, where she promptly enrolled in the fall of 1905. One of the first things Beth did that year was join Tau Epsilon Sigma. Her decision to join a sorority mirrored that of her sisters, as both Carrie Ruth and Faith had done the same at Lombard. These two, however, had not joined a local organization, but rather the Illinois Beta chapter of the national Pi Beta Phi fraternity. By the early 1900s, Pi Beta Phi was fast growing into one of the more prominent women's fraternities in the country. No doubt Beth talked with her sisters about their fraternal experiences (Faith and Beth lived together in Somerville), and no doubt her sisters began prodding Beth to start a discussion within Tau Epsilon Sigma about affiliation. As for which organization Tau Epsilon Sigma should consider, Pi Beta Phi was likely the natural, if not only choice.[79]

As the 1905–06 school year progressed, those in Tau Epsilon Sigma began a long and earnest discussion about giving up their local roots to affiliate with a national organization. It appears, though, this discussion did not completely go as either Beth or Faith anticipated. By the early spring of 1906, the members of Tau Epsilon Sigma had decided not to pursue Pi Beta Phi. Although no reason was recorded, it is very likely that overtures to Pi Beta Phi from the Tufts women were rebuffed, as Pi Beta Phi had started to curb its expansion into smaller schools, opting instead for larger and more established institutions. But the women of Tau Epsilon Sigma would not be denied. Instead, they soon chose another fast-growing national sorority, one also familiar to Beth, as this group had been active at Lombard while her family lived on campus. This other organization may not have been Tau Epsilon Sigma's first choice, but it would be their last. On Beth's recommendation, they would pursue affiliation with Alpha Xi Delta.[80]

I get by with a little help from my friends

Lombard College (now closed) in Galesburg, Illinois, could easily be considered a sister school to Tufts College. Both were founded by the Universalist church, and both received their charters within a year of each other – Lombard in 1851, Tufts in 1852. But in one particular aspect the two colleges were very different, at least in the beginning. Lombard, by design, was co-educational from its founding, whereas Tufts waited forty years to admit women. Nonetheless, Lombard, like Tufts, attracted a few national Greek organizations early in its history, despite being a small, denominational college. By 1893, the campus was home to two national fraternities for men and one national sorority for women. The lone sorority, Pi Beta Phi, had a reputation among many Lombard women (warranted or not) for only accepting into their chapter those of wealth or considerable social status, instead of more humble qualities such as scholarship and character. A group of ten women in particular felt Pi Beta Phi had it all backwards. So, in the spring of 1893, they formed their own organization to counter this injustice. But, aside from making this decision, they didn't know what to do next. They certainly couldn't ask any in Pi Beta Phi for any help – those women were closely aligned at the time with one of the fraternities on campus, Phi Delta Theta, and the last thing these two groups wanted was an upstart spoiling their operations. Therefore, the group of ten women decided to turn to the other fraternity at Lombard for help and encouragement. That fraternity was the Delta Theta chapter of Sigma Nu.[81]

The women could not have found a better partner. The men of Sigma Nu had long suffered alone in the shadows of Phi Delta Theta and Pi Beta Phi, so when the ten women came asking for help, they responded with all the enthusiasm they could muster. Over the next few weeks, the members of Sigma Nu worked with the women to organize their sorority, write their constitution and ritual, and generally encourage them in their endeavor. Secrecy remained important throughout the process, as the women feared those opposed to their endeavor, including some outside the Greek community (affectionately known as "barbarians," or "barbs"), would work to stamp them out during their organizational phase. By April 17, 1893, the women were ready to announce themselves to the campus. They did so in dramatic fashion. That day, as the students filed into the chapel for regular services, the ten women gathered at the back of the line and waited until all were inside. Then, they each pinned on their emblem, a quill and ribbons in the colors of light and dark blue, and walked in as a group. Immediately the eyes of the entire campus turned towards them. Everyone seemed surprised by the action, but everyone also knew exactly what the gesture meant. The women had just announced the birth of a new sorority at Lombard, Alpha Xi Delta.[82]

Of course, to Phi Delta Theta and Pi Beta Phi, this action was nothing short of blasphemy. They both greeted the new sorority with a mix of disdain and contempt, for the last thing they wanted was serious competition for members on the small campus. Sigma Nu, on the other hand, gave a most cordial welcome to Alpha Xi Delta, thereby cementing a relationship between the two organizations that remains today. Still, as the only local organization on campus, Alpha Xi Delta soon realized their homegrown status put them at a competitive disadvantage when it came to recruitment. Women, similar to men, were beginning to show a strong preference for national organizations over local ones. So, those in Alpha Xi Delta began planning for affiliation with a national sorority, which they thought would be easy. Those thoughts were soon squashed. In the 1890s, many national sororities were beginning to disregard local groups at small, denominational colleges, opting instead to focus solely on larger and more prosperous institutions. The irony here is that many of these national sororities had been founded at small denominational schools, but now they were turning their backs on their roots. Sure enough, the nationals all turned their backs on Alpha Xi Delta.[83]

This rejection ended talks of affiliation in Alpha Xi Delta for a few years, with the members choosing to focus solely on growing their organization at Lombard, which they did with success. But over time, the women of Alpha Xi Delta sensed their sorority was something more than just a local in opposition to Pi Beta Phi at Lombard. They were instead becoming their own established entity, both in thought and practice, and they were proud of what they had made. Out of this revelation, therefore, came a new idea – instead of affiliating with another, Alpha Xi Delta would become its own national organization. The idea simmered within Alpha Xi Delta for a few years, until the chapter finally acted during the 1901–02 school year. They started by seeking the help of a local lawyer they knew well, Mr. J. J. Welsh, who was both an alumnus of Lombard and member of Sigma Nu. Together, Mr. Welsh and the women of Alpha Xi Delta crafted a national constitution and set of by-laws to detail the expansion process. Their work culminated in the summer of 1902 when Alpha Xi Delta established its second chapter, Beta, at Iowa Wesleyan University, thus becoming a national organization. Ironically, Iowa Wesleyan was the same school where Pi Beta Phi established its second chapter, and therefore became a national organization. Alpha Xi Delta didn't stop there. A few months later, in August of 1902, the organization established its third chapter, Gamma, at Mt. Union College in Ohio, and then continued expanding across the Midwest in particular at a rate of approximately two chapters a year. However, in the summer of 1906, a petition arrived at Alpha Xi Delta's doorstep from unchartered territory.[84]

Welcome, now get back to work

The impressive, hand bound document arrived just as the summer of 1906 began. Its thirty pages were filled with campus photos, a brief history of Tufts College and Tau Epsilon Sigma, the complete membership roll including alumnae, a studio photograph of the women in formal attire, and a list of reasons why the women wished to affiliate. While all of this information was quite compelling, one particular entry in this list stood out: "Because of the high esteem in which the Alpha chapter is held by the former president of Lombard College." That president, of course, was Reverend Nash, and his endorsement was no accident. His daughter, after all, was one of the petitioners, and the main reason the Tufts women considered Alpha Xi Delta in the first place. Despite such a strong presentation, though, the national organization could not make an immediate decision. Alpha Xi Delta may have been a young national organization, but its leaders already knew the importance of investigating a local organization in person before accepting them. Therefore, when classes resumed the following fall of 1906, Bertha G. Cleveland, the Editor-in-Chief of the *Alpha Xi Delta* national magazine, came to campus to investigate the petitioners. For three days, Ms. Cleveland met with the active chapter and alumnae of Tau Epsilon Sigma, and observed the general state of sororities at Tufts College. In both areas she was greatly impressed. "The college is a growing and prosperous institution of a class so high," she wrote in her recommendation, "that Alpha Xi Delta would be honored by having a chapter placed there." The petition was accepted.[85]

Installation followed a few months later. On March 8, 1907, members and alumnae of Tau Epsilon Sigma, along with three national officers, gathered at the home of one of the undergraduates for the induction. The ceremony began in the early evening and was elaborate in spectacle, but not particularly fast, given that forty-five women had to go through the initiation ritual. As a result, the hour grew so late that the planned celebratory banquet was cancelled, leaving the women only enough time for a quick supper before retiring for the evening. Nonetheless, there were smiles all around the room that night, for Lambda chapter of Alpha Xi Delta, the eleventh overall in the sorority and first in New England, was now officially in operation. Alas, the women had little time to bask in their newfound national status. The three Alpha Xi Delta officers who'd travelled to Tufts for the installation, after all, had to be entertained for the rest of the weekend. So, the women of Lambda chapter arose early the next day, ready to perform their duties. They started by bringing the officers to their required daily chapel service. Next was an extended tour of the campus and its buildings, followed by lunch and a chapter meeting. Later, they hosted a tea party in honor of their guests, and then they all caravanned into Boston for a night at the theater.[86]

A short while after the installation, however, Lambda chapter ran into two problems. One involved their regular chapter meetings. Standard operating procedure within Alpha Xi Delta called for the women to sing three official sorority songs at each meeting, compositions that celebrated the spirit of their organization. The women, though, didn't know any, as apparently the music had not yet arrived from the national organization. So, when the chapter gathered for one of their first meetings in 1907, the current president of the chapter, Persis Hannah, put one of her poems to some familiar music and created a new song, "The Rose of Alpha Xi," thus giving the women at least one in their repertoire. Her inspiration was the recent and untimely death of her brother, who was also her chief collegiate benefactor. The women of Lambda chapter naturally embraced the song, and then something wonderful happened. Within a few weeks, "The Rose of Alpha Xi" was adopted by the national organization as an official song of Alpha Xi Delta.[87]

Lambda chapter was not so fortunate with their second problem, though, which quickly became embarrassing on a national scale. For some time in the early 1900s, Alpha Xi Delta required all active members to take an annual examination covering the history their organization, the current practices and laws, and the general state of the sorority movement across the country. The idea of the exam, apparently, was to make sure the all of the undergraduates were operating in harmony, and that all were cognizant of Alpha Xi Delta's place among other national organizations. Perhaps to encourage good scholarship, Alpha Xi Delta published the scores of each individual member by name in their quarterly magazine, *Alpha Xi Delta*, which was distributed not just to members and alumnae, but also to other national fraternities and sororities. Such exchanges were the most popular method of communication between national organizations at the time, and in general the magazine's content was meant to impress all who read its words. Therefore, this was not a test anyone in Alpha Xi Delta wanted to fail. So of course, the Tufts women did just that. In the late spring of 1908, Lambda chapter at Tufts College scored at the bottom of all active chapters with a 62.3% average. Many of the sixteen members of Lambda failed the exam outright, and one member, Estella Butterfield, scored a 34% on the exam, the lowest of all active Alpha Xi Delta members across the country. The national organization was especially harsh in their criticism of Lambda's performance, calling their results "inexcusably poor reports for college fraternity women." The following year, though, the national officers had a change of heart. Perhaps sensing the delicate nature of such information, they never again published the names and scores of those failing the test, nor did they level any public scolding of chapters that ranked at the bottom.[88]

War and Lambda

Lambda chapter soon recovered from their poor test-taking ability and settled nicely into a steady routine during the 1910s of rushing new members, holding social functions, singing the correct number of songs at meetings, and participating in social causes, most notably the woman's suffrage movement. Overall, life in Lambda chapter at this time was carefree in many ways, and those in the chapter seemed to be making the most of their collegiate experience. That all changed in an instant when the United States officially entered the Great War in the spring of 1917. American troops may not have been heading to Europe en masse at that point, but the women knew exactly what was on the horizon. "We girls here in the East are so completely overpowered and absorbed by the critical war situation and all that it involves," wrote Grace Sherburne, Lambda chapter correspondent at the time, "that other things for the most part fade into insignificance." That semester, Lambda chapter jumped right into the war effort by working tirelessly to sew fracture pillows and American flags in support of the Red Cross. They also helped create a huge twenty-seven foot American flag to hang on Ballou Hall, part of the patriotic display that overtook the entire campus. The ensuing summer break was anything but, as many of the members continued serving their country, including Grace, who went to work as a stenographer in the office of the United States Marshal. In her position, she helped create the permits that all "enemy aliens" (i.e. German citizens residing in the United States) had to carry with them at all times, for without such papers they could be arrested and sent to jail.[89]

Life under the specter of war only got tougher during the 1917–18 school year. While recruitment activities continued in earnest and chapter membership stayed relatively stable, social activities were almost completely eliminated so the women could do more for the war effort. In this regard they excelled. From making surgical dressings, to gathering books for soldiers to read, to hosting a special dance for a group of U.S. Marines stationed at Charlestown Navy Yard, those in Alpha Xi Delta took seriously their service. They even sponsored a war orphan, a young girl from France whose father had been killed in battle. This opportunity came about through Frances Clement, an alumna of the chapter who spent her war years in New York City helping to run a French relief agency. The women of Lambda chapter took all of this hard work in stride, though, because they felt they were really making a difference. As Grace wrote later that spring in her correspondence letter,

> It is only when we realize how few of the men are left around the Hill, and when our coffee and cereal goes sugarless, that we really seem to come to a realization that this country of ours is actually at war. The only thing for us to do is to go right ahead doing our work, "the duty that lies

nearest" and try to understand that if everyone does his or her duty right must triumph in the end.[90]

But not everything was about sacrifice, because in the summer of 1918, Lambda chapter had a very important ancillary job to do, and that was host Alpha Xi Delta's national convention. This was no trivial matter. By 1918, Alpha Xi Delta's biennial meeting had become a grand multi-day affair, and competition among the chapters to host was fierce, given the prestige within the national organization that came along with the honor. Of course, winning the right to host was the easy part; being the host meant you had to show your sisters in Alpha Xi Delta a thoroughly entertaining time when the business meetings were completed each day, and failure, in this regard, was not an option. Here, the women of Lambda did not disappoint. Their social itinerary over four days in early July of 1918 included a twenty-mile drive along the coast of Marblehead Point, a visit to an amusement park, a tea party, a stunt show complete with circus acts, a trip to historic sights in Lexington and Concord, and a farewell banquet at the Hotel Westminster in Boston. The banquet, though, was hardly a feast, as food production went first and foremost towards the war effort, not fancy parties. Then, for the final event of the convention (aptly timed for the 4th of July), Lambda chapter led the delegates to Camp Devens, so the women could mingle with some of the 40,000 soldiers training for war. The cost for the four-day event, including hotel room and banquet, was $10 per person. In the end, the convention was a rousing success, as evidenced by the letters of praise Lambda chapter received from the delegates.[91]

The war's end on November 11, 1918, came as a surprise to the women of Lambda, as indeed it did to all on the Tufts campus. In the days and weeks that followed, though, it was as if those in the chapter could not forget the war fast enough. Perhaps due the constant strain and sacrifice they'd been under the past eighteen months, they put all of their worry and negativity behind them and moved on, quickly. The women of Alpha Xi Delta were not alone in this new attitude. All around campus there was a renewed spirit for old traditions and rah-rah college enthusiasm, especially when it came to the fraternities and sororities. Lambda chapter couldn't wait to tap into this newfound excitement and rebuild their membership, since recruitment had been on hold the past few months. "To say that everybody is just awfully interested [in Greek life] is putting it mildly," wrote Lambda chapter correspondent Phyllis Jerauld in January of 1919. "It's the kind of thing that makes you thrill inside and begin to realize that you're a *vital* [emphasis in original] one of your fraternity and college." Indeed, within a few weeks into the spring semester of 1919, Lambda chapter had secured one new pledge and planned for many more.[92]

As the years went on, Lambda chapter did indeed grow its membership and maintain an active social presence on the Tufts campus. The chapter survived

The women of Alpha Xi Delta gather for a chapter photo on the steps in front of Eaton Hall, June 9, 1924.

the turmoil of the Great Depression and World War II with no interruption in operation. It wasn't until after the war when life in Lambda went through a seismic shift. Starting in the fall of 1945, students and administrators flocked back to college campuses across the country with one major goal in mind, and that was to bring back a state of normalcy. However, one pre-war aspect of campus life some did not want to revive was the restrictive membership practices of many national fraternities and sororities, policies that were based on race or religion. Such exclusiveness had been quite prevalent for decades and was hardly a secret. Many organizations with such restrictions were usually very open about them, if not also proud of them. Alpha Xi Delta, though, was a little different in this regard. Apparently, Alpha Xi Delta kept their membership restrictions secret from the general public, revealing them only to members after they had been initiated. For nearly a decade after World War II, this revelation did not seem to cause any significant problems for the women who joined Lambda chapter. Then, of course, it did.[93]

We're not gonna take it

Norma Pereira knew almost nothing about sororities when she arrived on campus in the fall of 1953. In fact, she knew very little about college life in general, as she was the first member of her family to pursue higher education. But, once on campus she settled into Tufts College rather easily, and during her second semester, she even got caught up in the excitement of sorority rush. The week-long event featured a festival of parties and skits each night, which allowed Norma to get to know all four sororities and their members, at least on a preliminary level. After all was said and done, though, Norma realized she liked the women of Alpha Xi Delta the best. The feeling was mutual. Lambda chapter offered Norma a bid to join, and a few days later, she was both an official pledge and president of the pledge class. In Norma, Alpha Xi Delta had found a leader.[94]

One of the first issues Norma tackled as pledge class president was membership discrimination. With the national discussion on discrimination within fraternities and sororities starting to capture the attention of the Tufts community, Norma wondered if Alpha Xi Delta had such restrictions. Members of Lambda chapter assured Norma the organization did not, and such declaration was good enough for her. She completed the pledge program, and later that spring was initiated into Lambda chapter as a full member. However, after the initiation, Norma realized that within Alpha Xi Delta's ritual, there was a provision that effectively barred women of color from the sorority. She was horrified to learn this, especially since she'd been told otherwise. But, this clause was part of the secret ritual intended only for full members, so she had no way of knowing about it until she was officially an Alpha Xi Delta.[95]

Norma was not alone in her reaction. Other members were equally as upset to learn the truth, including some of the chapter's Jewish members with relatives who'd suffered in concentration camps during World War II. These members in particular wondered how they could tell their families they were now part of an organization that practiced racial discrimination. Of course, the reality of Tufts College at the time put any talk about discrimination onto the theoretical plane, for there were no women of color on campus. But Norma and others in Lambda chapter were not interested in theory. They recognized this issue of discrimination transcended their own current situation, and they were not willing to simply let it be. Therefore, they realized they had a choice to make: either leave Alpha Xi Delta in protest, or stay and fight for change from within. They chose the latter.[96]

They got their chance to act just a few semesters later. In the fall of 1955, two African-American women enrolled at Tufts as freshmen, the first two black undergraduate women the campus had seen in a few years. This situation naturally brought the discrimination debate front and center within Lambda, and soon enough many in the chapter were calling for action. They wanted the discriminatory membership practice removed from Alpha Xi Delta once and for all, and would not accept anything less. As a start, they contacted their national organization, told them of their concerns and desires, and asked how to proceed. The response was not positive. In no uncertain terms, the national office of Alpha Xi Delta said their attempt would be futile at best. After all, the leaders pointed out, the issue of repealing the membership restrictions had been discussed at four out of the last five national conventions, and even voted on twice with only seventeen percent and then ten percent of chapters in favor of the change. To say Lambda held a minority position within the Alpha Xi Delta organization would thus be an understatement. However, Lambda was offered a path forward. If at least one-third of the active chapters went on record supporting the change in membership requirements, then the issue would be taken up at a future convention.[97]

The women in Lambda were eager to get to work on this issue. In theory they figured their effort would be straightforward, since it mainly involved contacting other chapters for support. But, due to a combination of inexperience (if not naiveté) on the part of the chapter, and apathy (if not obstructionism) on the part of the national organization, the women stumbled. The first setback happened straight away. Once the national organization learned of Lambda chapter's idea to contact others, they told the Tufts women to cease and desist. At the time, the by-laws of Alpha Xi Delta did not allow chapters to communicate officially with one another; only the national organization had that right, ostensibly so they could "prevent the spread of subversive propaganda." Of course, there was no law in Alpha Xi Delta preventing individual members of one chapter contacting those in another, but apparently the national officers failed to articulate this loophole to the women of Lambda.[98]

As could be expected, this reality put a huge damper on the efforts of Lambda chapter. Then, to make matters worse, the national organization began questioning why the women of Lambda were so upset in the first place. As the leaders reminded the chapter members, Alpha Xi Delta's membership restrictions were not some dark secret, but a known fact that had been "definitively available to [the women]... prior to pledging." Essentially, the national organization was telling the women of Lambda, if you were so bothered by these restrictions when you pledged, you should have walked away before being initiated as a full member.[99]

Such attitude did nothing to appease the Tufts women. Instead, they returned to campus in the fall of 1956 with only resentment and anger towards their national organization, if not also a sense of despair towards the situation as a whole. Perhaps feeling the negativity more than anyone in the chapter was Norma, now a senior and chapter president. But then, something happened. Once on campus that fall, the women quickly learned that one of the other sororities at Tufts, Sigma Kappa, had just been kicked out of its national organization, presumably for pledging two black women the previous semester. This action shook the campus to its core, with many outraged by the blatant racial discrimination on display. Enhancing the anger was the viral nature of the story, which reached across the nation in just a few days and caused many eyes to turn towards Tufts. The national leaders of Alpha Xi Delta, knowing of the angst within Lambda, sent a representative to talk with the chapter, calm them down, and hopefully keep them a part of the organization. Norma and the others, though, were in no mood for pacification, especially when the representative tried in vain to explain why Alpha Xi Delta needed to continue its discrimination. "What if you take in a black sorority sister and you have a dance," the representative asked, "and she has a black date, and he asks one of you to dance?"[100]

To Norma, this line of reasoning for continued discrimination within Alpha Xi Delta was beyond absurd, and completely unacceptable. So, when the national representative left campus and she assembled the chapter together for discussion, she knew there was only one option left. In fact, nearly all the women of Lambda felt the same way. Therefore, on September 25, 1956, all of the members of Lambda chapter (sans one) voted to resign from Alpha Xi Delta. They could no longer be a part of a discriminatory organization. To emphasize the point, many sent their initiation badges back to the national organization. In an instant, fifty years of Alpha Xi Delta at Tufts University had come to a close, much to the consternation of the chapter's alumnae, who were blindsided by this decision and did not support the undergraduate's position. They, however, weren't the only ones caught by surprise.[101]

Don't come around here no more

As it turned out, the mass resignation came as a complete shock to the national leadership of Alpha Xi Delta. Indeed, the national officers first heard of the resignation a day after the fact, when a reporter for the *Tufts Weekly* called asking for comment. Gertrude Anderson, the executive secretary of Alpha Xi Delta, was the unfortunate one to pick up the phone that morning. She was forced to listen, dumbfounded, while the Tufts reporter read her the press release announcing Lambda's decision, for she knew nothing of the situation. Instead of a comment, she could only offer an excuse: "You have caught me before my mail." Still, the reporter pushed on. When subsequently asked whether or not Alpha Xi Delta allowed for "the pledging of Negro girls," Gertrude answered, "I think you're getting on to personalities," which seemed to suggest any discrimination within the sorority was a localized phenomenon, not an official policy of the organization. As evidence, Gertrude told the reporter "there is nothing in the [national] charter that would exclude Negro members." Then, Gertrude refused to answer any more questions on the subject, and did all she could to end the phone call as quickly as possible.[102]

Meanwhile, the former members of Lambda chapter were not done with their surprises. United now in their stand against racial discrimination, and wanting to continue as a group, the thirty-five women immediately reformed as a new, local sorority they named "Alethea," a Greek word meaning "truth." The Tufts administration, under the direction of Dean Katharine Jeffers, praised

Alethea holds a "smoking party" in their chapter room on the third floor of Curtis Hall, 1961.

the new sorority and vowed to support the group's efforts at reorganization. Dean Jeffers also helped keep the national media away from the undergraduates, which was no small concern. News of the resignation reached across the country within a few days, with newspapers such as *The New York Times* covering the situation, and Dean Jeffers knew the undergraduates were unprepared for all the attention. Luckily for the women of Alethea, though, the press coverage of their situation paled in comparison with the intense national debate that followed Sigma Kappa's decision to close their chapter at Tufts. As a result, the outside attention on Alethea soon waned elsewhere, leaving the women out of the spotlight and free to build the sorority they wanted.[103]

The undergraduates wasted no time in this regard. They took just a few weeks to create their organization, from detailing their long-term goals, to defining the responsibilities of the officers and procedures for new member intake. This singular document became Alethea's constitution, which was eagerly approved and accepted by the administration in December of 1956. Alethea was now a recognized, official sorority at Tufts. Not surprisingly, the constitution contained no membership restrictions (aside from a minimum grade point average), stating instead that "members shall be selected from duly qualified women students of Jackson College and Tufts School of Engineering regardless of race or religion." As for secret rituals, this aspect of sorority life was not continued, which is not surprising since secrecy had been a root cause of their problems with Alpha Xi Delta. Alethea quickly settled into a normal routine of recruitment, social activities, and philanthropy during that spring semester of

1957. They also took their place in a newly opened chapter room in Curtis Hall, right next door to the other four active sororities.[104]

Despite the rapid progress, not all were happy to see Alethea become so successful, so quickly. The sorority's chief detractors were Lambda chapter alumnae, who were still quite upset the undergraduates withdrew from Alpha Xi Delta without any consultation. In fact, the alumnae tried to meet with the former members that fall semester of 1956 in order to work out a compromise regarding the resignation, but Dean Jeffers quickly rebuffed these efforts. She was quite outspoken in her disdain for racial discrimination, so it seems she did not want the alumnae anywhere near the undergraduates while they worked to build Alethea as an inclusive group. But, Dean Jeffers knew the alumnae had to be appropriately placated for political reasons, so as a compromise she allowed the national vice-president of Alpha Xi Delta, Judge Mary Burt Nash, to come to Tufts and speak with the undergraduates, under one condition: Dean Jeffers had to be present at the meeting. Judge Nash, realizing this was probably the only contact she would be afforded, had no choice but to accept the provision. However, as she later said, having Dean Jeffers in the room made it "not possible to discuss esoteric matters from which the original misunderstandings had stemmed." In other words, it seems Judge Nash could not discuss the discriminatory provisions within the ritual that had started this disagreement in the first place, lest she divulge these secrets to Dean Jeffers. Therefore, the meeting accomplished nothing of substance, Judge Nash left campus nearly as quickly as she'd arrived, and the undergraduate members of Alethea went about their way, unimpeded.[105]

The alumnae, though, were not ready to give up, for they had a plan. First, they convinced the national organization to keep Lambda's charter in place, so that a new group of women could, in theory, revive Alpha Xi Delta without delay. Then, in the spring of 1957, they took their case directly to the Faculty Committee on Student Organizations, effectively bypassing Dean Jeffers. They asked for permission to start recruiting a brand new chapter as soon as possible, especially since there was still one woman left on campus who had not resigned from Lambda chapter. The faculty committee, as expected, was much more sympathetic than Dean Jeffers towards the Lambda alumnae, and even agreed to let them conduct recruitment that semester, after the other sororities finished their formal rush in mid-March. As the saying goes, though, timing is everything, and in this case, the alumnae missed out. Despite a spirited recruitment effort, the alumnae simply could not find enough women interested in reactivating the chapter, most likely because those who wanted to join a sorority had already done so. Additionally, those on campus had likely not forgotten what had happened in Lambda chapter just a semester before.[106]

The failure to revive the chapter, though a setback for the alumnae, was not the end. Rather, they geared up for another effort the very next semester, in the fall of 1957. However, this effort ran into a series of roadblocks. First, they were told they'd have to wait to recruit new members until after formal rush was over for the fall semester, which would be in January of 1958 at the earliest. Then they were told they'd need permission to start recruitment not just from the Faculty Committee on Students Organizations, but also the student-run Panhellenic Council. It was this latter group that was most worrisome, for seated on the council were former members of Lambda chapter who would certainly object to the plan. But, by the middle of January 1958, the administration announced that both groups had given permission, so the alumnae began their efforts. They advertised on campus for prospective new members, and reserved a room on campus for two weeks, which they planned to use for personal interviews. Dean Jeffers even provided the alumnae with a list of those women who might be eligible for membership (pending a required check of grade point average). This time around, recruitment went much better, and the alumnae had found a number of women interested in reviving the chapter. All that was left was the scheduled pledge induction, and Alpha Xi Delta would be back at Tufts.[107]

Well, not exactly. Just as these recruitment efforts were finishing up, the Panhellenic Council made a startling announcement that they had not, indeed, voted in favor of Alpha Xi Delta's return to campus. This caught both the administration and the Lambda alumnae off guard, but worse still, forced the alumnae to suspend their efforts and wait for the Panhellenic Council's approval. They would not enjoy this wait, for it was punctuated with an onslaught of negativity. Soon after the alumnae suspended their efforts, the editors of the *Tufts Weekly* in particular attacked the national Alpha Xi Delta over their continued use of discriminatory membership policies, and made it clear the organization was not welcome on campus. After all, there was still an official Tufts policy in place "not to allow any organization on campus with a discriminatory [membership] clause," and Alpha Xi Delta had not yet, apparently, addressed the issue within their secret ritual. Many students agreed with the editorials, which put the revival of Alpha Xi Delta into serious doubt. A few weeks later, the Panhellenic Council did finally hold a vote, and to no surprise, it wasn't even close. In a 23–0 decision, the council told Alpha Xi Delta "no." Just about the only consolation for the alumnae was a pledge by the Panhellenic Council to revisit the issue again in 1960, since by then all former undergraduate members of Lambda chapter would have left campus.[108]

FOR TWO LONG YEARS, the alumnae of Lambda chapter patiently waited for the Panhellenic Council to keep its word. The alumnae had little recourse otherwise, but luckily their fears of being forgotten did not materialize. What did unfold, though, was not what the alumnae expected. In May of 1960, the Panhellenic Council revisited Alpha Xi Delta's request to return to campus by considering two specific questions, both of which had to be affirmed before the sorority could come back. "Do you favor the re-activation of Alpha Xi Delta?" was the first, while the second was, "Do you think there is enough support for the establishment of a fifth sorority on campus?" Although these two questions may seem to be one and the same, they were separate given the circumstance of the time. Earlier that spring semester, one of the five active sororities, Thalia, had disbanded, thereby leaving only four at Tufts. As a result, there was now a legitimate reason to consider sorority expansion once again at Tufts, and the Lambda alumnae must have been heartened by this situation. But, they must also have been a little worried, since one of the questions was aimed directly at their national organization, and passage was anything but guaranteed.[109]

Further complicating the situation was a change in the rules. The Panhellenic Council, it appears, wasn't comfortable answering these two questions alone. So, they opened up the voting on both questions to all undergraduate members of the four sororities. This reality must certainly have given the Lambda alumnae great pause, as Alethea, being the second largest sorority on campus that semester, would undoubtedly have considerable influence on the decision. And after all the votes were tallied, the Lambda alumnae did indeed face the worst possible outcome. By a total of 119 to 40, the undergraduates voted in support of bringing a fifth sorority to campus. But, by a near similar margin, 138 to 23, they voted against the return of Alpha Xi Delta. The passage of two years had not healed any wounds. Alpha Xi Delta still was not welcome, and would likely not be for more years to come. As a result, the alumnae walked away, and never again tried to bring their organization back to the Tufts campus in the 1960s.[110]

With the controversy surrounding Alpha Xi Delta now fully behind them, the members of Alethea continued on as a local sorority, and in this regard they were quite successful, at least for a time. Membership in Alethea began a steady decline by the mid-1960s, though they were hardly alone. The other sororities at Tufts also faced declining memberships, some more drastically than others. Students by then were beginning to look unfavorably at sororities, especially with other issues such as the civil rights movement and the Vietnam War dominating campus thought. As a result, Alethea was down to a mere twenty members as the spring 1966 rush week approached, less than half the size the chapter had been just a few years earlier. The members knew they'd need to make a strong effort in recruitment if they were to stabilize their membership, let alone reclaim the chapter's glory days. Unfortunately, their hearts just weren't in it any longer. The thought of gearing up for rush and taking in new members and running a pledge program was too much. So, in late February of 1966, Alethea decided to close down. The leadership sent a letter to the Panhellenic Council saying they would not participate in the upcoming rush week, and instead would dissolve immediately. For nearly ten years Alethea had successfully operated at Tufts under the auspices of non-discrimination. But the decade had brought tremendous change to campus, and Alethea was one of many groups (including all other sororities) that did not survive the turmoil of the 1960s.[111]

In conclusion, the organizations Tau Epsilon Sigma, Alpha Xi Delta, and Alethea together spanned nearly seventy years on campus, and certainly helped shape positive experiences for many women at Tufts. But even today, the national organization is hesitant to restart Lambda chapter. In 2012, campus officials offered Alpha Xi Delta the opportunity to participate in sorority expansion at Tufts University. There was certainly no guarantee Alpha Xi Delta would be chosen at the end of the formal selection process, but they were encouraged to apply. They declined, citing concerns over the events from nearly half a century before. The restrictive membership clauses are long gone, but the worry over their history, it seems, is not.[112]

DELPHOI (Local society, 1907 – 1912)
DELTA KAPPA PHI (Local society, 1912 – 1913)
SIGMA KAPPA (Omicron chapter, 1913 – 1956, 1978 – 1981)
THALIA (Local society, 1956 – 1960)

From the time Greek-letter organizations were first founded until well into the 20th century, writers and reporters often referred to members of these organizations as "society" men or women. Inherent in this description was the widely held opinion that a "society" person was of a higher social status than his or her peer, a result of having been accepted by an exclusive organization. Therefore, many were pleased to have this title attached to their name in the press. The same could not be said for the opposite descriptor. When reporters referred to someone as being "non-society," the comment was often viewed as a mild put-down – not necessarily an insult, but a clear reminder that this individual was just that, an individual not associated with any fraternal organization. The use of "society" and "non-society" in the press was especially popular in the early 1900s, when reporters often wrote about the social happenings on college campuses.[113]

This written emphasis of students being society members or not, as could be expected, often created animosity among the latter group. No one likes to be considered second class, especially when barriers to fraternity or sorority membership, such as race, religion, family heritage, and wealth, were often beyond one's immediate control. Still, many non-society men and women came to admire the ideals often espoused by Greek-letter organizations including brotherhood, an enhanced sense of purpose, and a desire to work for something beyond the individual. As a result, non-society undergraduates across the country independently created new organizations that held tight the fraternal tenant of companionship, but removed the inherent elitism by allowing anyone to join.

Such open societies, as they came to be known, burst onto the collegiate scene in the early 1900s, with the most famous (for men) being the National Federation of Commons Clubs. Among women, however, the open-society movement was much more muted, as it was neither as popular nor as well organized as for the men. But, one place where the women at least tried was Tufts College.[114]

All are welcome

In the fall of 1907, seven women at Tufts College found themselves making their way through school as a group of friends. How they came together is a somewhat a mystery – the seven spanned every class from freshman to graduate student, none roomed together, and nearly all had different hometowns. Yet there they were, together. They were also, to quote the parlance of the day, non-society women, for none had joined one of the three sororities active at the time. And yet, all seven were apparently intrigued with the idea of coming together around a common purpose, for that fall semester they began meeting every week in an off-campus home to work towards one simple goal: they wanted to form a new society at Tufts College, one that would bring them closer as friends, while also promoting their enthusiasm and support for their beloved alma mater, Tufts College.[115]

For months the women met, away from the eyes of the campus, to plan their organization in detail. Soon enough they congregated around a fundamental idea. They would be an organization dedicated to aligning the "non-society" women at Tufts College into a cohesive group, with membership open to all. This mantra was a clear departure from the Greek-letter organizations on campus, all of which required a vote on each individual before a bid to join could be extended, so clearly the seven were not fans of exclusion. Consistent with this choice, the women chose not use Greek letters to name their society, but rather the name of a Greek town, Delphoi. The seven women did, however, create an extensive set of secret rituals and symbols, for they recognized that such ceremony could help bring their members closer together. Then, by the spring of 1908, all was ready. The women held an initiation ceremony, and a few days later, on April 30, 1908, they announced Delphoi's existence to the world. The seven founding members were:[116]

Lucy Helen Gage (1899, was a graduate student in 1908)
Beth Boswell (1908)
Isabel Clara Perkins (1908)
Mary Florentia Bogue (1909)
Ethel May Cole (1909)
Annie Morinda Currie (1910)
Ada Bond Seabury (1911)

News of the new organization, which was the first organized open society for women at Tufts, was greeted rather warmly by the campus. As a reporter for the *Tufts Weekly* wrote,

> The Delphoi – This year a new society has quietly found its place and growth in Tufts College. The "non-sorority" girls are organized into Delphoi, which promises to be a power in student life. Its idea is to promote loyalty to Tufts, a democratic spirit and a bond of better good fellowship among its members.

Of course, even open societies have limits on membership, and Delphoi was no different. They soon put two minor requirements into place. First, Delphoi was not open to women who had joined one of the sororities on campus. Such a rule made sense, since Delphoi wanted to be an alternative to the exclusive sororities. Second, Delphoi was not open to any woman with known flaws against her character. This second requirement was common to all national Greek-letter organizations as well, and in the early 20th century, especially, it was often invoked as a cover story to exclude those based on religion, a lack of personal wealth, or less-than-impressive family history. But Delphoi wanted to be an open society, so it is unclear why the founders adopted this second requirement. In fact, they were not at all concerned about the current group of women at Tufts. Soon after the founders of Delphoi announced their existence on campus, they extended an invitation to all of the non-society women on campus without question. In the end, about a dozen women accepted, with only one woman refusing. Delphoi was on its way to becoming a viable campus organization.[117]

The members of Delphoi didn't stop there with their openness. After reaching out to the undergraduates, they next invited all non-society alumnae of Tufts College to join their organization. As for a reason, the founders hoped Delphoi would provide a home for these alumnae when they came back to visit the campus, much as the Greek-letter organizations offered their respective alumni. Although it is unknown how many in total were invited or how many joined, at least one graduate from the Class of 1902 accepted the invitation and she, by all accounts, became a fervent supporter of Delphoi in the years that followed. Then, in an even bolder move, those in Delphoi looked to expand their society to other campuses beyond Tufts. Again, such action was more in line with the way national Greek-letter organizations operated, though almost all waited at least a few years before expanding from their initial chapter. Delphoi, however, was not interested in waiting. Within their first year, they sent letters to other area colleges, looking for enthusiastic women to start a Delphoi chapter and thus grow the open society into a national movement. However, this effort failed to evoke any real enthusiasm from anyone contacted, so they soon gave up the idea. Delphoi would only ever be a local society at Tufts College.[118]

Once Delphoi was operating out in the open, though, the other three sororities on campus quickly viewed the society with some skepticism. These three realized that, aside from the practice of open membership, Delphoi was just like them. After all, Delphoi's stated goals were "to bind its members in a closer loyalty to the college and to each other, to promote the social and intellectual welfare of all, and to give a college home to all its alumnae who returned to visit the 'Hill'." Such goals were identical in spirit to the aims of the other sororities. As a result, these three sororities began insisting that Delphoi join the student-led Panhellenic Association at Tufts, a group which oversaw sorority operations. The sororities argued that joining the association was the only fair way Delphoi could exist at Tufts, since then all would abide by the same rules regarding rushing, pledging, and a requirement that all new pledges be in good academic standing with the college (something the founders of Delphoi had not considered). Soon enough Delphoi agreed. But "fairness" was a relative term. Shortly thereafter, one sorority went so far as to offer a bid to a member of Delphoi, an act of pilfering highly frowned upon in the general fraternity world. This development was met with great consternation in Delphoi, especially since the woman offered the bid was a full-fledged member and not a pledge. This particular woman refused the bid, though, with a statement that soon became Delphoi's motto: "Once a member of Delphoi, always a member."[119]

On second thought...

Over the next few semesters, Delphoi took an equal place among the three sororities as the women settled into a normal routine of holding social events such as dances and teas, and initiating new members from those not chosen by the Greek-letter sororities. The open membership policy seemed to be working very well, and indeed some Tufts men followed in the women's footsteps by creating an open society for those not in a fraternity. But then, during the 1909–10 school year, paranoia appears to have set in. As Tufts College continued to grow its enrollment, some in Delphoi began worrying that those women who could join their organization might not have the same interests and ideals as they did, and accepting them might just hurt the society's greater mission, if not their reputation. Such a thought eventually became so troubling within the organization that during the school year, the members voted to change. Delphoi would no longer be an open society. Instead, a candidate for membership now needed the support of at least three-fourths of the active chapter in order to join. Although the reasons for changing to a closed society were not recorded, it is quite probable this rule was enacted to keep out women of certain races, religions, or ethnicities. Ever since Tufts College had opened in 1854, its students were overwhelmingly white and almost exclusively Christian. But as the college grew in the 1900s so, too, did the diversity of students in terms of their background. Jewish students especially began enrolling in ever-larger numbers, along with foreign students (to a lesser extent) and even a few African-Americans. To the women of Delphoi, such diversity may have been viewed as a real danger to their society, one that could pull them apart rather than bring them closer. So, within three years of their founding, Delphoi had scrapped its utopian idea of openness to become an exclusive sorority on the Tufts campus.[120]

Of course, Delphoi still had its unique name among the women's societies at Tufts, but this, too, would not last. In the spring of 1912, Delphoi completed its transition from open society to Greek-letter sorority by changing their name to Delta Kappa Phi. Although the reasons for this name change are unknown, one may have been to match the status of the other three sororities on campus. By 1912, these three had all affiliated with national Greek-letter organizations, leaving Delphoi as the only local sorority on campus, and the only one with a name not immediately recognizable as a sorority, something that could possibly hurt them when it came to recruitment. But more importantly, it appears that the women of Delphoi were also thinking about giving up their local roots and affiliating with a national organization. In all likelihood, they probably felt their chances for affiliation were better if they used Greek letters for their name. Either way, Delta Kappa Phi was now the successor to Delphoi. All that was left was national affiliation. And for this, they looked north.[121]

Coming to you straight from Maine

In the early summer of 1818, some residents of the town of Waterville, in the soon-to-be new state of Maine, stood at the banks of the Kennebec River and welcomed a small, but special sailboat. On board, and probably looking somewhat haggard after five days at sea, was the Reverend Jeremiah Chaplin, his family, and a handful of college-aged men. No doubt the townspeople were delighted to see the shore party whatever their condition, for it meant the months of planning and hard work had come to fruition. These pioneers had come to open up the recently chartered Maine Literary and Theological Institution at Waterville, a school founded with support of Baptist churches in Maine that would eventually be named Colby College. And in his task, Reverend Chaplin did not fail. He led Colby with aplomb during its early years, allowing the school to evolve from a modest seminary into a premier institution of higher learning, despite its remote location and relatively small number of students, all men. Then in 1871, some fifty years after Reverend Chaplin stepped off the boat, the leaders of Colby took another big step, one almost unprecedented in the northeastern United States at the time, at least for higher education. That year, the school's trustees decided to admit women as students on equal terms with the men. Colby had just become one of the first schools to give up its all-male status in favor of coeducation.[122]

After their decision, though, the trustees must have been scratching their heads in confusion. They had taken a very bold step towards gender equality, yet few women seemed to notice. Indeed, for two years, only one woman enrolled, and that was Mary Caffrey Low, who'd grown up in Waterville. And for Mary, her first two years were very lonely ones. Still she stayed the course, and in the fall of 1873, she was rewarded for her perseverance. That semester four other women from Maine enrolled alongside Mary. As could be expected, this group of five became instant friends. They certainly needed each other, for college officials still had not created anything for them. There were no organized activities for the women on campus, no clubs or athletic teams, no living accommodations, and the women got the sense that neither the male students nor the faculty wanted them around. They, of course, cared little for this attitude. Bound together as outcasts, the women vowed to prove to the men they not only belonged at Colby, they could succeed and flourish in their own right. All they needed was a proper outlet, and since the college wasn't going to help in this regard, they'd do it themselves.[123]

All throughout the 1873–74 school year, then, the women discussed how they might best mark their time on campus. Nothing came of this effort, though, until school let out for the summer and the women had time to reflect upon their year. They quickly realized the two active fraternities, Delta Kappa Epsilon and Zeta Psi, provided the men a very popular social and literary outlet. Not surprisingly, the women soon decided to create their own Greek-letter society, one that would allow them to come together socially and expand their minds through literary pursuits. They spent the remainder of the summer building their organization from the ground up, including a series of secret rites and rituals. In many ways this was all quite remarkable, because the women did this on their own. They had simply observed, reflected, and then created, with no other assistance.[124]

By the time the five women returned to campus in the fall of 1874, they had completed the finer details of their organization and were ready to announce their presence to the campus. But before they took such drastic action, they decided to ask permission from Reverend Henry Robins, the president of Colby College. Such a move was certainly prudent on the part of the women, for college elders held considerable power over all students at the time, and these men would have expected to be consulted on such an important matter. President Robins granted the meeting in early fall, and when the women entered his office, they were certainly full of high expectations and enthusiasm. Then the conversation started, and their hopes seemed lost. The president was not in favor of secret societies in general, and he let the women know this in no uncertain terms. But, he was a fan of justice, and since the men had already established such organizations at Colby, he decided, "that the same toleration must be shown to the ladies as the gentlemen." His formal letter of permission was delivered to the women on November 9, 1874. The five took this as the founding date of their sorority, Sigma Kappa.[125]

From its outset, Sigma Kappa may have been a secret society, but it was not exclusive. As envisioned by the founders, membership in Sigma Kappa was open to all women who enrolled at Colby each year. The sorority would simply issue an invitation to each woman when she arrived on campus, and it was her choice to join, or not. This idea worked reasonably well for nearly two decades, as approximately six women entered Colby each year. As a result, Sigma Kappa was able to stay true to its mission of providing its members the camaraderie and support they needed to succeed. However, by the early 1890s, the situation had changed considerably. Upwards of thirty women were now enrolling in the freshman class each year, and for Sigma Kappa, this was too many. The members realized that if they continued to accept every woman who enrolled, they would become so big that they'd lose the close association they'd worked to achieve, if not also render meaningless their secrets and ideals. But, closing their membership meant erasing twenty years of tradition. A spirited debate thus ensued within the sorority during the fall of 1893, and in the end, the women made the hard choice. Sigma Kappa would become a selective organization, capped at twenty-five members. Instead of inviting all first-year women to join, they'd only admit enough freshmen to replace those who'd graduated.[126]

This change, as could be expected, caused consternation both inside and out of Sigma Kappa. The vote to become exclusive had not been unanimous, and the erasing of twenty years of open membership did not go unnoticed by the campus. What happened next could almost have been predicted. By 1895, a number of women who had been excluded from Sigma Kappa came together and started a second sorority, Beta Phi. Now, for the first time in history, Sigma Kappa had some competition. Worried about losing the prestige battle, those in Sigma Kappa realized they could advance their standing over Beta Phi by becoming a national organization. This idea had actually been considered in the past on numerous occasions, but none of these efforts ever came to fruition. However, in the fall of 1903, Sigma Kappa finally succeeded. That semester, a member of the sorority transferred from Colby to Boston University to finish her studies, and within a few months, she had organized the Delta chapter of Sigma Kappa, thus making the sorority a national organization. From there, Sigma Kappa quickly spread outwards across the country, adding chapters in New York, California, Washington, Illinois, and Rhode Island, to name a few of the states. Then came the inquiry from a small school in Massachusetts.[127]

Welcome, now do better

When the women of Delta Kappa Phi began seriously working towards affiliation in the spring of 1912, they had at least a dozen national organizations from which to choose, and no apparent method of sorting them out. However, word soon came down from not one but two independent sources that the only one they should consider was Sigma Kappa. This recommendation was good enough for Delta Kappa Phi. Soon enough, the mystery ambassadors put the Tufts women in contact with the national officers of Sigma Kappa, and those officers, as it turned out, took an immediate liking to the group. By the early 1910s, though, Sigma Kappa had a formal process by which local organizations were absorbed into their sorority. As a first step, the national officers began corresponding with the women of Delta Kappa Phi (presumably by mail), to explain some of the ideals and customs of Sigma Kappa. These written conversations were billed as a chance to convince the Tufts women they should indeed pursue affiliation with Sigma Kappa, but they also allowed the national officers to make sure the Tufts women fit the Sigma Kappa mold. In total the extended interview went well, and afterwards the undergraduates prepared and then submitted a formal petition for affiliation.[128]

Their timing, in this regard, was perfect. Sigma Kappa's biennial convention just happened to be later that summer of 1912, so the Tufts women would not have to wait very long for an answer. Alongside Delta Kappa Phi's petition at the convention, though, was a second from a local group at the University of Kansas. Such a pairing of petitions usually highlighted just how small Tufts College was on the national landscape, and this realization often resulted in Tufts being cast aside in favor of the larger, and therefore more prestigious school. However, the women of Delta Kappa Phi needn't have worried. The Sigma Kappa delegates looked upon each petition independently, and decided both schools deserved to be home to a new chapter. But, this did not mean a charter was immediately forthcoming. Rather, the affirmative vote allowed the national officers to proceed with a yearlong supervision of Delta Kappa Phi. Should the officers like what they saw during this time, then, and only then, would a charter be granted.[129]

The supervision began in the fall of 1912 when the undergraduates returned to campus. For the next eight months, the officers of Sigma Kappa watched and judged and criticized the women of Delta Kappa Phi, while also teaching them how to be a chapter of a national organization. The officers were in no hurry, for they needed to be sure the Tufts women were truly worthy of a charter. Finally, on April 30, 1913, the undergraduate members of Delta Kappa Phi could sense the light at the end of the supervisory tunnel. That night they were initiated as pledges of Sigma Kappa, with the ceremony occurring at the house of one of the undergraduates. Afterwards, the women continued under supervision for yet another month while the Grand Council of Sigma Kappa met formally to reconsider their petition. Ultimately their vote that spring was "yes." Following this milestone, all alumnae of Delta Kappa Phi were then invited to pledge Sigma Kappa so they, too, could participate in the planned affiliation. A number of alumnae accepted the invitation, including four of the original founders of Delphoi. Then, on May 30, 1913, the thirty-two undergraduate and alumnae pledges were fully initiated into Sigma Kappa, becoming the charter members of Omicron chapter. The initiation ceremony and banquet was held at the Hotel Thorndike in downtown Boston, one of the finest hotels in the city.[130]

After recessing for the summer, the members of Sigma Kappa returned to Tufts in the fall of 1913 ready to begin their operations without any supervision. However, this did not mean they were on their own. Of the four national sororities at Tufts then, Sigma Kappa was the only one to have a sister organization just a few miles away – Delta chapter of Boston University. Therefore, Omicron was expected to interact with Delta on a regular basis, ostensibly to promote the Sigma Kappa spirit in both chapters. Their first formal event came at the end of the fall 1913 semester, when they held a joint initiation and banquet. Such camaraderie, which continued in earnest for decades, helped the young Omicron chapter grow quickly into a viable addition to the national organization. Joining Sigma Kappa, it seems, was working out very well for the Tufts women.[131]

But, the chapter soon learned there was a downside to their situation. Four times a year, the national organization published a magazine called the *Sigma Kappa Triangle*, which covered important events and information that all in the sorority were expected to know. Each chapter was also expected to submit a letter to every issue summarizing their activities over the past few months, and those that did not were publicly scolded for their omission. Most did not repeat their transgression in the following issue. However, even those chapters that did submit a letter on time were not immune from attack. Starting in the mid 1910s, the editors of the *Sigma Kappa Triangle* all too frequently dispensed harsh criticism about the content and form of the letters they received, with words that were embarrassing if not downright insulting at times. To make matters worse, these comments were soon read by many outside the organization, since the magazine was exchanged with most of the other national fraternities and sororities.[132]

Those in Omicron learned all this the hard way, for their chapter letters were proving to be quite inadequate. Cecilia Bullard, for example, was scolded because "the paper was not quite the right size and only one article was sent." One issue later, Karin Sundelof was forced to endure the comment, "Did you read 'What Makes the Editors Take Aspirin'?" while the following year Helen Jackson was reprimanded with, "Newsy but had to be cut," with "newsy" being a euphemism for "boring." At times the chapter did garner some slight praise from the editors with regards to a particular letter (Karin earned "this letter shows marked improvement" after her disastrous first submission), but it must have been a little disconcerting for the corresponding secretary of Omicron chapter with each submission, not knowing if her letter would be criticized harshly or praised tepidly for all in the fraternity and sorority world to read.[133]

The women of Sigma Kappa on the steps of Goddard Chapel, June, 1916.

War and Omicron

Despite suffering some occasional indignities from the editors of the *Sigma Kappa Triangle*, the members of Omicron chapter settled into a normal routine of rush parties, initiations, social functions, and philanthropy events as the 1910s marched on. In this last category, the chapter became an enthusiastic supporter of Sigma Kappa's national effort with the Maine Sea Coast Mission outreach program, an organization dedicated to helping the women and children who live on some of Maine's less prosperous islands. Although by this time the other fraternities and sororities at Tufts were beginning to incorporate social service into their missions, Sigma Kappa was by far the leader in this regard. Then, starting in the spring of 1916, life for the women took a decided turn towards the serious. America had yet to formally enter the Great War, but the women could sense the inevitable. They were not alone in this regard. That spring, local leaders in Boston organized a huge Preparedness Parade with tens of thousands of marchers, both to drum up patriotism and show the world the United States was ready to fight. Due to the rules of the day, the women of Sigma Kappa were not allowed in the parade, so instead they sewed "little brown hats with blue tussles" for the Tufts men to wear while they marched. Additionally, throughout the 1916–17 school year, the women spent every Friday afternoon sewing and cutting surgical dressings. As if these actions weren't enough (the women were full time students, after all), the formal declaration of war in April of 1917 saw them increase their efforts by taking courses in nursing from the Red Cross and, for three hours each week, sewing American flags in Miner Hall, which were then sold in support of the Red Cross.[134]

The unconditional dedication of those in Omicron towards the war effort, as could be expected, began to change chapter life the following school year. Recruitment of new members still continued in earnest throughout 1917–18, but social activities for the most part had been cast aside, since "all interest in mere amusement seemed to vanish." After a fall semester of all work and no fun, though, the women decided they needed a break. They held a formal dance in the spring of 1918, the first such event in over a year, albeit with much trepidation. "We hope we will not seem unpatriotic," wrote Karin in her letter to the *Sigma Kappa Triangle*. "If we do not dance just once in a while we will get stiff and pokey." But such digressions were temporary at best. Participating in Liberty Bond loan drives, knitting sleeping caps for wounded soldiers, and working with the Red Cross constantly reminded the women their country was at war. Over the summer of 1918, many in the chapter continued their service by taking jobs as farm hands, elevator girls, bellhops, and numerous other positions vacated by the men going off to war. The arrival of the Student Army Training Corps (S.A.T.C.) to the Tufts campus in the fall of 1918 brought everything to a fever pitch, especially since the women were expected to obey certain military customs. For example, they had to stand when their professors entered the classroom, and there was even talk of saluting the officers, as all the men were required to do. "Then," as Karin wrote in another chapter letter, "came Peace. Is there one among us who can ever forget that memorable morning of November 11?"[135]

The clamor of celebration began at around 4:00 a.m., when a group of girls on their way to ring the chapel bell woke the Sigma Kappa members living in Richardson House. A spontaneous campus-wide party soon broke out, which had the women marching and singing with the soldiers around "The Rez" for hours. Later that day, the women joined the men of the S.A.T.C. in a victory parade around Somerville. All told, the festivities (which were chaperoned, of course) lasted nearly eighteen hours uninterrupted. But underneath all the happiness was a clear understanding of what had just happened. As Karin wrote,

> This is a wrecked world in which we live. But we are proud to live in it, and glad that Fate destined us for this century. Our hearts and heads and hands were given us for service, and from now on they will be so well occupied with the things worth while [sic] that we cannot have much time left to think of frivolity. We are to make "a world safe for democracy," which means a world filled with intelligent, self-restrained, unselfish individuals, whose brains are good guides to their actions.[136]

Alas, Karin's post-war plea for a new moral compass within her sorority, especially the call to avoid frivolity, seems to have been forgotten within a semester or two. Life at Tufts College began a quick transition back to normalcy in January of 1919, and those in Sigma Kappa were no exception. They settled back into a steady routine of rushing new members, hosting parties, and generally putting the war behind them. But, their commitment to public service did not completely fall away. For example, many in Sigma Kappa became heavily involved with the Intercollegiate Community Service Association, a new organization dedicated to social justice and the helping of those less fortunate. The women embraced the service aspect of their organization with a level of zeal that seemed to rise above those in the other three sororities.[137]

As the years went on, life in Omicron had its minor ups-and-downs, but overall the chapter remained strong at Tufts, even during World War II. However, by the early 1950s, many on campus had taken a profound interest in civil rights, especially when it came to the inherent discrimination in fraternities and sororities. It was believed (and, in some cases, known) that many Greek-letter organizations at the time had informal practices, if not official rules, barring those of certain races or religions from membership. The fraternities, as it turned out, were easy to understand in this regard, for nearly all were open about their restrictive policies. The sororities, on the other hand, were not as forthcoming, preferring instead to keep their membership practices as private. Such caginess caused many to wonder just what these organizations were hiding. As a result, a few women on campus decided to investigate this issue. Soon filling their crosshairs was Sigma Kappa.[138]

The planning stages

To those paying attention, the start of the 1955 fall semester at Tufts was different, indeed. For years the administration had been trying to diversify the racial make-up of its undergraduates, but all too often these efforts went nowhere, and the sea of faces arriving each year stayed white. However, that September two African-American women, Terrie Williams and Eleanor (Ellie) Turpin, enrolled as freshmen, the first women of color the campus had seen in quite some time. Their presence certainly sparked mild curiosity among the students, but in general the two women were welcomed without reservation. But, of course, there was a catch. Normally, all freshmen are paired with at least one other roommate to help with the transition to college. The call for diversity in 1955, however, only went so far – Terrie was placed in a single room within the Richardson House dormitory (Ellie commuted from home). Still, Terrie was not alone, for she was assigned a "big sister" from Richardson House, part of the mentoring program afforded to all first year women. Terrie, as chance would have it, was assigned a junior named Gemma Cifarelli. She could not have been paired with a more able mentor.[139]

Gemma was by all accounts an extraordinary person. She was a history major, a cheerleader, a waitress in Hodgdon Hall's dining room, an active member of the Student Council, a regular on the Dean's list, a friend to all she met, and scheduled to graduate just a few months later due to an overloaded academic calendar. She and Terrie hit it off very well from the start and soon became good friends. As their relationship developed, though, Gemma sensed an opportunity. A year earlier she and her fellow Student Council cohorts had started working to root out discriminatory practices within Greek-letter organizations at Tufts, and while those efforts led to much discussion, they failed to produce significant change. The passage of a year, though, had done little to squash Gemma's interest in exposing the supposed discrimination within sororities. Supposed, that is, because no one was really sure – all talk of sorority discrimination was based heavily on rumors about secret membership clauses and practices that no one outside the system could confirm as fact. Now, Gemma saw a way to discover the truth. She brought her idea to Dean Jeffers, and together the two came up with a plan. Simply put, Gemma would ask Terrie if she'd rush a sorority later that fall to test their membership policies.[140]

Such an approach had never been tried in the past, mainly because very few black women enrolled at Tufts before 1955, and those that had encountered a time when racial exclusion in Greek-letter societies was accepted as the social norm. But this was 1955, life in America was changing, and life at Tufts was changing even faster thanks to a handful of progressive students and leaders. Terrie, though, wasn't so sure about the plan once Gemma told her, mainly because she had no real interest in joining a sorority – she assumed they were all filled with stereotypical pompous, self-centered women, a demographic that did not spark her interest. Instead, Terrie was drawn to the theatre groups on campus, and quickly directed her efforts towards those endeavors. So, as the fall of 1955 came to a close, Terrie passed on sorority rush week, and the clever scheme as hatched by Gemma and Dean Jeffers began to fade into the background.[141]

But then, in an instant, everything changed. On the night of December 11, 1955, Gemma, her date Frederick Hill, and their friend Charles Lund were driving back from a fraternity dance in Boston when their car lost control on Soldier's Field Road and crashed into a tree. All three perished in the hours and days following the accident. The news stunned the Tufts campus, since the three students were well known and well liked. For Terrie the news was especially devastating, as Gemma had been such a positive influence over her during the few months they knew each other. Now, Gemma was gone. After some reflection, Terrie decided one way she could honor Gemma's memory was to go ahead with the plan, and find out the truth about sorority discrimination. So, when the spring rush season of 1956 commenced that April, Terrie signed on to see if any or all of the organizations would exclude her because of her race. Joining her in this escapade was Ellie who, like Terrie, wondered what would happen next.[142]

You shouldn't have done that

Sorority rush that spring of 1956 was certainly unique. For the first time in the history of Tufts, there were two black women amongst dozens of white women looking to join one of four sororities, all of which had only ever had white members. However, those participating in the activities, both the sorority members and the rushees, did not seem to be concerned with making history. They simply went about rush week in the usual manner. Through numerous events such as skits and tea parties, the women of Sigma Kappa especially got to know both Terrie and Ellie, and soon discovered they liked the two for who they were. The feeling turned out to be mutual. So, when the bids went out at the end of rush week, both were offered membership in Sigma Kappa, and both accepted, joining five other white women in the pledge class. Sigma Kappa was thus poised to become the first inter-racial sorority on campus, and one of only a handful across the country. The members of Sigma Kappa, though, were not necessarily interested in this fact – they had not given bids to Terrie and Ellie to make a statement, either on campus or within the national organization. They simply wanted the two as members, and since Sigma Kappa had no official membership restrictions based on race (secret or otherwise), they figured pledging Terrie and Ellie was well within their rights.[143]

The law may have been on their side, but the "spies" were not. During rush week, as was customary, two older alumnae observed the chapter to make sure everything was running smoothly. Such alumni oversight is common even today among fraternity and sorority chapters, so the presence of the two was probably not given a second thought by those in the chapter. However, these alumnae soon learned that both Terrie and Ellie were given bids to join, and apparently they did not approve. They never said anything directly to members of the chapter, but they did pass word to the national organization about the developing situation. The governing council of Sigma Kappa was not pleased. Still, they did not interfere with Omicron's operations at the time, so Terrie, Ellie, and the rest of the group went through the pledge ceremony, thereby beginning their journey to become Sigma Kappas, a journey that would commence in earnest when they returned in the fall.[144]

They would never make it. In late June of 1956, delegates from Sigma Kappa chapters all over the country gathered in Glenwood Springs, California, for the sorority's national convention. Evelyn Harvey went as the representative of Omicron chapter, and while Evelyn probably expected to enjoy the convention in relative anonymity, she was soon under the spotlight. On numerous occasions, Evelyn was approached by national officers and "grilled there about the chapter's reasons for pledging two Negro girls." One can imagine the intimidation she must have felt, but she was not the only one being scrutinized so harshly. As it turned out, the Alpha Zeta chapter at Cornell University had also pledged a black woman in the spring of 1956, and this chapter, too, was being called out for their decision. The convention ended without any action taken against either the Omicron or Alpha Zeta chapters, but clearly the national officers of Sigma Kappa were upset over the situation.[145]

When the convention ended, Evelyn must have felt some relief, possibly even hoping the incident was behind her and Omicron chapter. But Sigma Kappa was not done. Instead, the national leaders used their interim powers after the convention to punish their two renegade chapters. On July 27, 1956, the National Council of Sigma Kappa sent letters to officials at Tufts University, the active members of the Tufts chapter, and the chapter's alumnae stating that, effective immediately, Omicron was no longer a part of Sigma Kappa. A similar letter was also sent to Cornell University and the sorority's Alpha Zeta chapter. The two chapters had been unceremoniously thrown out of the national organization. As for a reason behind the expulsion, the letters were less than vague; the one sent to the president of Omicron chapter did not mention a reason, whereas the one to Dean Jeffers said this action was being taken "for the good of the sorority as a whole." But that line in particular did not fool anyone. Everyone knew both chapters had been expelled because they had the audacity to pledge Negro girls (using the parlance of the day).[146]

If the national leaders of Sigma Kappa hoped this action would remain a private sorority matter, they were sadly mistaken. Instead, the situation went viral. In the days following the expulsion, newspapers around the country picked up the story, often running big, bold headlines such as "Negroes Pledged, Sororities Ousted"; "Sorority Withdraws Charter of Chapter Pledging Negroes"; and "Charter Lost in Color Row." Immediately Dean Jeffers became the sole contact between Tufts and the media. She wanted to shield her students completely from the controversy, as she probably reasoned they were ill equipped to deal with the national attention. As it turned out, though, not everyone in Omicron chapter even knew they had been thrown out. When the story first broke in *The New York Times* on August 2, 1956, Dean Jeffers called Terrie at her home in New York City. Dean Jeffers didn't explain the reason for the call, but she did say everything was fine, and she strongly encouraged Terrie to return to Tufts in the fall and continue to be the fine person she was. Terrie was very confused by this call, as it came completely out of the blue. An hour later, though, a family member handed Terrie the article, and then she knew.[147]

A second member of Omicron who also knew nothing of the expulsion was the chapter president, Audrey Saperstein, who was traveling around Europe that summer. However, the national officers of Sigma Kappa were not aware of Audrey's travels, so they simply sent the expulsion letter to her home address, where it sat, unopened. While traveling abroad, Audrey's only contact with friends and family back home came via the American Express office. So, one day in early August, Audrey walked into one such office in Paris to pick up her mail, and there she found a rather unexpected letter from a friend. Within this letter was a clipping from the *Boston Herald* that detailed the expulsion of Omicron chapter from Sigma Kappa. Her reaction to the news, which she penned in a letter to Dean Jeffers, can best be described as flabbergasted. She knew the chapter was in fine shape both financially and in terms of membership, so they did not meet the usual criteria for expulsion. However, she soon recognized the true reason, even if no one at Sigma Kappa had admitted it outright – during her trip abroad, she'd met a fellow Sigma Kappa from Cornell, and when she learned of that chapter's expulsion as well, she put it all together. In her closing remarks to Dean Jeffers, Audrey wrote, "if the color of their skin is the reason for our suspension by the national council, then we are better off that our affiliation with them is broken."[148]

Over the next few weeks, Dean Jeffers continued to deal with a flood of correspondence regarding the expulsion, and not just from the media. Letters came from students who expressed disgust and amazement at the actions of Sigma Kappa, from alumni who mostly supported the chapter's pledging of Terrie and Ellie (but a few certainly did not), and from another national organization, the newly formed Delta Pi sorority, offering their help and support to the former members of Omicron chapter. Other Tufts alumni from across the country, no doubt shocked at reading about their school on the front page, sent in press clippings from dozens of newspapers, lest Dean Jeffers hadn't heard the news. In her responses to many of these inquiries, Dean Jeffers made it clear she supported the actions of Omicron chapter to pledge Terrie and Ellie, and thought the chapter's expulsion from Sigma Kappa was a cowardly act of an outdated mindset. However, it was in the correspondence with one alumna where Dean Jeffers forcibly fought for her students. In one of her responses to this particular alumna, Dean Jeffers wrote:

> It seems to me especially important that young men and women of college age should have an opportunity to mingle in a group as variable as possible. The two young negro women who were in our freshman class last year made a real contribution to their classmates. I hope we shall always have foreign students, negro students, Jewish students, and those of oriental background mixed in with those who are regarded as "long-time American" here at Jackson College.[149]

The alumna's subsequent response, though cordial, was filled with further anecdotes about why the races should not mingle, and how integration was slowly ruining the United States from within. Apparently, Dean Jeffers was in no mood to continue the conversation. She offered no further reply.[150]

All of those articles about the expulsion, as they continued to be reprinted across the country, soon captured the attention of not just Tufts University, but other schools as well. Within months, administrators at the University of Michigan and the University of Minnesota, for example, were actively calling for an end to discrimination in fraternities and sororities on their campuses, using the expulsion of Sigma Kappa at Tufts and Cornell as the rallying cry. One local sorority at Penn State, which had submitted a petition to join Sigma Kappa, withdrew their application in response. The Massachusetts House of Representatives even entered the debate, eventually issuing a report in December of 1956 that called for all social organizations at the University of Massachusetts to end their discriminatory membership practices by 1958, with the hope that other colleges and universities in the state would follow suit. The effort to remove discrimination within fraternities and sororities had now taken off across the country, and while it would take another decade to remove, finally, all of these restrictions, a big push had come, in part, because Gemma Cifarelli and Dean Jeffers had a plan.[151]

What about us?

Hidden, for the most part, from this turmoil of letters, articles, and official governmental resolutions were the former members of Omicron chapter. Dean Jeffers, by being the sole intermediary to the outside world, deliberately insulated the women from the media circus so they could simply be college students. And this they did as a group, one that included Terrie and Ellie. To a member they all wanted to continue as a social organization (they were not going to let Sigma Kappa break them up), so during those first few weeks of the fall 1956 semester, they reformed as a new, local sorority called Thalia, named after a Greek muse of comedy and poetry. Their first act was to write their constitution and declare their criteria for membership. In no uncertain terms, Thalia was a sorority open to women of any race or creed. The Tufts administration quickly recognized the new organization, and the other sororities immediately brought Thalia into the Panhellenic Council, thus preventing any prolonged disconnect with the Tufts community. In many ways, at least to those outside the organization, all that had really changed was their name. But Thalia, of course, was different now, for it was the first Tufts sorority to break down the racial barrier.[152]

Once the logistics of reorganization were complete, it did not take those in Thalia very long to settle into a normal routine. The sorority maintained a strong membership, took in new pledges with each successive rush, and kept an active social calendar, often hosting parties with their "brother" fraternity, Alpha Tau Omega. More importantly, many women on campus were now openly asking the other sororities during rush week about their restrictive membership practices, as they generally did not want to join an organization that discriminated. Such was the immediate impact of Thalia. Additionally, Thalia implemented one other change to sorority life, though this change was strictly internal. The women did away with the secret rituals and ceremonies that were a mainstay of Sigma Kappa, since that aspect of sorority life was no longer appealing to them. All told, Thalia was affecting a positive influence on campus.[153]

However, as the semesters passed on by, the initial enthusiasm inside Thalia began to wear off, and in its place came a growing sense of uneasiness among the women about what they were trying to accomplish as an organization. They were, in many ways, adrift. Part of this angst was likely due to Thalia's isolation from the media. While Dean Jeffers had worked very hard to keep the women out of the national limelight so they could go on with their normal lives (and in this regard she did a remarkable job), a downside to this approach was that the members of Thalia, as time went on, were not fully aware of their place in history. Those in the sorority simply did not know about the multitude of letters supporting their action to pledge Terrie and Ellie, nor were they fully cognizant of the dialogue on discriminatory practices their expulsion from Sigma Kappa had started on other campuses. All of this correspondence, information, and energy was instead absorbed by Dean Jeffers, and she appears to have kept everything to herself. This growing disconnect left Thalia as a group to find its own path without knowledge of its national impact, or reminders of its greater purpose. And with each successive semester, that path was getting harder to find.[154]

Compounding this situation was the reality of another sorority on campus, Alethea. Started the very same semester as Thalia by former members of the Alpha Xi Delta chapter, Alethea, too, was born out of protest against restrictive membership practices. Unlike Thalia, however, Alethea received lots of attention and praise for their progressive stance on membership, mainly because they had not been thrown out of Alpha Xi Delta, but had resigned on their own accord. This courageous act put Alethea in the headlines of the *Tufts Weekly* every few months as they battled Alpha Xi Delta's desperate attempts to return to campus. The various articles and editorials describing the conflict were quick to remind the campus of Alethea's history, which most certainly kept the sorority in a positive light. Thalia, on the other hand, received essentially zero press coverage about their mission. Instead, within a few semesters after Thalia had started, many began to forget the events that led to their founding, or that Sigma Kappa had been their precursor. Thalia was thus confined to being known simply as a local sorority at Tufts, one that came about for reasons no one talked about, anymore.[155]

Then came the start of the spring semester of 1960. The persistent uneasiness within Thalia, which had only grown with each successive semester, finally reached a tipping point. Rush season was fast approaching once again, and rather than looking forward to the events, the women could only see dread. They just did not have the energy needed to attract new members, especially when the other four sororities were still very enthusiastic and looking forward to their future. Adding to this negative feeling in Thalia was the remote location of their chapter room in Curtis Hall, a building on the outskirts of campus that also housed the student center (known as the "Kursaal" at the time). Though hundreds of undergraduates walked through the Kursaal every day, almost none walked past Thalia's room, since it was three stories up. Instead, this isolated hideaway remained simply a place for the women to meet once a week, or host rush events once a semester. The chapter room did not otherwise bring the members of Thalia together, and it certainly never became their home. It was in this space, then, that the women gathered on the night of January 4, 1960, to talk about their future. The discussion was both earnest and reflective, if not ultimately a statement of truth. The women realized they were not the vibrant social, academic, and philanthropic organization they had set out to be some three-and-a-half years earlier. Instead, they were done. They took a vote that night to make it official, and in the end the vote was unanimous. Thalia as an organization would disband immediately. What had started with so much promise was now over.[156]

Thalia notified the campus a few days later of its decision via a letter to the *Tufts Weekly*. The women were very forthright with their reasons for disbanding, an extremely rare admission by a group closing down – all other Greek-letter organizations that left Tufts prior to 1960 had simply disappeared without any fanfare or explanation. The administration under Dean Marguerite Wynne-Roberts was disappointed in this outcome, as she in particular had long viewed Thalia as a positive influence on campus. But Dean Wynne-Roberts understood the reasons for disbanding, so she and the rest of Tufts let Thalia begin its fade into history without much protest. As it turned out, the closing of Thalia was a precursor into the future. Within ten years, all four of the remaining sororities at Tufts would also close down, as the women collectively decided they wanted to turn their attention elsewhere.[157]

Controversy, what controversy?

One outcome from the demise of all sororities at Tufts in 1970 was that the campus community, as a whole, lost a connection to this history. Therefore, when sororities did finally come back to Tufts in 1976, no one likely knew of the controversy surrounding Sigma Kappa's earlier expulsion from campus. After all, that had happened some twenty years prior, and even the current Tufts administration was two generations removed from the incident. The only ones who could have passed down the story of Sigma Kappa were the undergraduates, through word and voice. The six-year absence of sorority life, however, effectively nullified this conversation. So it was with absolutely no controversy that Omicron chapter looked to return to campus in the spring of 1978. Tufts, by this time, was home to three other sororities, as women once again were embracing Greek life. Spearheading the effort were a number of local Sigma Kappa alumnae living in the Boston area (though nearly all were from chapters other than Omicron) and a small group of about half a dozen undergraduates, all commuting students. These women were hoping Sigma Kappa would be the social outlet they were missing, if not a way to connect with the greater Tufts community on a deeper level. In May of 1978, these undergraduate women were initiated into Sigma Kappa, thereby officially marking the revival of Omicron chapter. As these newest members then left campus for summer break, they were excited about their future, and looked forward to rebuilding a strong organization.[158]

And for the next couple of years, they at least tried. Starting in the fall of 1978, they settled into a normal routine of holding regular chapter meetings, engaging in philanthropy events, and hosting social functions including some with their sister chapters at Boston University and the University of Massachusetts at Amherst. But in many ways, these accomplishments were a façade. The women struggled with cohesiveness, since they could not secure a regular, private space on campus for meetings. Instead, they often ended up gathering at one of their houses off campus, which in many ways defeated their goal of interacting more with the school community. Not surprisingly, this isolation then caused the chapter to struggle in new member recruitment. They simply could not grow their organization to a sustainable level. In reality, the four active sororities were twice as many Tufts could support at the time, since women were not flocking back to Greek life in the expected number. Sigma Kappa, being the smallest and least known on campus, suffered the most in this regard. Therefore, with as little fanfare as when it opened, Omicron chapter closed down once again in the spring of 1981, when, it seems, all of its re-founding members graduated.[159]

Since 1981, Sigma Kappa has not attempted a third restart of Omicron chapter at Tufts. More importantly, the national leaders still have yet to offer a rational, truthful explanation as to why Omicron chapter was expelled in the first place some sixty years ago. One of the only public comments about Omicron came in 2006, when the national president of Sigma Kappa was quoted as saying, "the sorority [Sigma Kappa] has been unable to confirm why our Omicron chapter at Tufts University was closed in 1956."[160]

PHI SIGMA SIGMA (Beta Chapter, 1918 – 1922, -1977, 1990 – 1995)

When historians talk about the birthplace of fraternities in America, they often mention Union College in New York state and Miami University in Ohio, as these two schools have each seen the establishment of six national organizations, including some of the oldest in the country. Often overlooked or at least understated in these discussion is the importance of New York City to the national fraternity movement. Colleges in Manhattan saw the birth of dozens of national fraternities and sororities from the mid 1800s up through the early 1900s, organizations that have since expanded to every corner of the country, if not beyond – certainly no small historical achievement. One such school in this category was the Normal College of the City of New York (NCCNY), now known as Hunter College. Founded by Thomas Hunter in 1870, NCCNY was opened specifically to train schoolteachers at the elementary level. As a result, NCCNY began as a school for women only (since traditionally only they taught children), and remained as such even when the curriculum expanded some thirty years later to include a Bachelor of Arts course.[161]

Ethel Gordon and her younger sister, Lillian, were two such women studying at NCCNY in the early 1910s. In addition to providing the women a number of educational opportunities, the campus afforded a full slate of extracurricular activities such as academic clubs, athletic teams, theater troupes, and student government. Additionally, NCCNY was home to a dozen or so local and national sororities that claimed nearly half of the undergraduates as members. So, it was no surprise that in the fall of 1913, Ethel and Lillian became interested in Greek life and decided to rush one sorority in particular. Unfortunately, they soon rushed straight into a brick wall. Before they could even be considered for membership, this particular sorority sent the two away, simply because they were Jewish. This exclusion, it seems, came as a shock to the two women, for NCCNY had long prided itself on the religious diversity of its students, something the Gordon sisters admired. Yet, as they had found out so harshly, the sororities did not share such enthusiasm for inclusion.[162]

Following their disastrous rush week experience, Ethel and Lillian retreated back to their circle of friends at their collective lunch table, where the conversation quickly turned to the religious segregation within the sororities. They soon hit upon a stark realization. The religious unanimity within each sorority at NCCNY meant that the women, despite being the best of friends, could not collectively join any one of the organizations, since they were of different faiths. So strong were their feelings against this injustice that they decided to act. Theirs was a special friendship, one that transcended religious barriers, and since no sorority would let them all join, they'd start their own. As for a name, they chose Phi Sigma Omega, and as for principles, they were decidedly and proudly non-sectarian, open to women of all religious backgrounds, the first such sorority ever founded in this regard. Unfortunately, the group soon learned another organization in New York City had already claimed their Greek moniker, so they were forced to make a slight change. Then, on November 26, 1913, the ten women became known officially as the Phi Sigma Sigma sorority. Non-sectarianism had been given a fresh, new voice at NCCNY. It was only a matter of time before the sorority expanded into a national organization. And for this, they looked to Tufts College.[163]

Here today, gone tomorrow

Actually, expansion came about by circumstance, rather than a concerted effort. In the fall of 1914, a freshman named Belle Heyman arrived on the campus of NCCNY, and one of the first things she did was join Phi Sigma Sigma. Belle, however, was not the only member of her family to join a Greek-letter organization. A few years later in the fall of 1917, her fraternal twin, Morris, enrolled at Tufts College to study electrical engineering, and one of the first things he did was join the Omicron chapter of Phi Epsilon Pi, a national organization that was rapidly spreading across the eastern half of the country. Morris, it appears, soon regaled Belle with exotic tales of life in a national organization, so almost naturally she became intrigued with the idea. In early 1918, then, she returned to NCCNY and started a conversation within Phi Sigma Sigma about expansion, which was well received. As for where to expand, that choice became very clear – they would turn to Tufts College. So, with Morris's help, they began contacting "qualified girls, similarly minded" at Tufts that semester, and soon enough they'd identified five women to spearhead the expansion effort. These five were initiated into Phi Sigma Sigma on April 12, 1918, thereby becoming the sorority's Beta chapter, in what was the beginning of a marked expansion across the country. The five founders of Beta chapter were:[164]

Miriam Goldshine (1919)
Rose Bolonsky (1921)
Sara Gelfand (1921)
Bertha Vivian Hershman (1921)
Dora Margolis (1921)

As for personal connections between the women, Rose and Sara were roommates that school year, while Bertha and Dora appear to have been hometown neighbors from Chelsea, Massachusetts. Additionally, all five women were most likely Jewish. While Phi Sigma Sigma had been founded on non-sectarian principles, the sorority was quickly morphing into a predominantly Jewish organization. Such was the reality of many non-sectarian fraternities and sororities founded in the early 1900s. Religious inclusion in Greek-letter organizations, while progressive in theory, proved very hard to maintain at the time.[165]

A few months after their installation, a few from Beta chapter attended the inaugural national conference of Phi Sigma Sigma, which could now claim three chapters including Gamma at New York University. However, despite their initial enthusiasm for Phi Sigma Sigma, those in Beta chapter were never able to establish their sorority at Tufts College. There is no record Phi Sigma Sigma ever participated in any organized campus or Panhellenic event such as rush or scholarship, nor is there any evidence the sorority was even recognized as an official student organization. Indeed, it is highly likely Beta chapter never initiated any other members besides the five founders. By the start of the 1919 school year, only Rose and Dora remained at Tufts College, as Miriam had graduated, Sara had transferred to Radcliffe College, and Bertha had transferred to Wellesley College. With little fanfare and with little choice, the national organization declared Beta chapter dormant in 1922. Phi Sigma Sigma, for all intents, therefore vanished from the Tufts campus without making any impact or leaving any legacy.[166]

The five women of Beta chapter, though they were not able to sustain their sorority, did maintain a sincere affection for Phi Sigma Sigma in the years following their graduation. In 1926, for example, all five submitted information about their lives for publication in the sorority's national magazine, *The Sphinx*. Miriam Goldshine, after graduating Tufts, eventually found her way to the University of California at Los Angeles, where she helped organized the sorority's Zeta chapter in 1921. She was also a guest of honor when the chapter held its 20th anniversary in 1941. Finally, even as late as 1944, some alumnae of Beta chapter were actively involved in Phi Sigma Sigma's Boston alumnae chapter. Phi Sigma Sigma, it seems, made quite a large impression on the five women from Tufts College despite its short existence.[167]

Let's try this again

The closing of Beta chapter so soon after its founding, though certainly disappointing to many in Phi Sigma Sigma, did little to stop the sorority's growth as a national organization. But with each passing decade, Beta chapter remained dormant even though Boston was home to an active alumnae chapter. National leaders explored the possibility of restarting Beta chapter in 1959, but by then there were already five active sororities at Tufts, and the administration felt the campus could not realistically support another. So, Phi Sigma Sigma looked elsewhere for two more decades, until Tufts University came back onto its radar screen. The year was 1977, and in terms of sorority life at Tufts, the situation was only getting better. Not only had the national Chi Omega and Alpha Phi sororities managed to establish chapters, but one, Chi Omega, even occupied an on-campus chapter house. The national leaders, it appears, rightly sensed that sororities at Tufts were on the rise once again, so they decided to revive Beta chapter. They began their efforts in the spring of 1977 with the help of local alumnae, and soon enough built a colony around a core group of undergraduates. By all accounts this colony got off to an enthusiastic start that semester, even participating in the annual Kid's Day festivities on campus. The following fall, the chapter held a series of rush activities and began holding social events, including a wine-and-cake party for all fraternity and sorority chapter presidents, as a way of introducing themselves to the entire community. However, it seems all this work was for naught. The chapter was unable to recruit enough new members to sustain their operations, and appears to have folded just a semester or two later. The women of Tufts University, it seems, were just not ready to support more than two sororities.[168]

ONCE AGAIN BETA CHAPTER OF PHI SIGMA SIGMA was confined to dormancy after just a brief existence. Meanwhile, the sorority system at Tufts coalesced around Chi Omega and Alpha Phi for a number of years, before finally expanding once again. Indeed, it wasn't until 1986 that a third sorority, Alpha Omicron Pi, joined the other two in earnest. From there, interest in sororities grew so much that demand began to exceed the "ideal" chapter size. Predominant wisdom at the time said sorority membership should be less than seventy-five women per chapter, but all three sororities had eclipsed this number and were thus turning away women who otherwise wanted to join. Therefore, in the early spring of 1990, the student-run Panhellenic Council, which governed the sorority system at Tufts, knew the time was right to bring on a fourth organization. Unlike fraternities, though, sorority expansion is governed by a formal process that is administered through a national umbrella organization of twenty-six women's fraternities. The Panhellenic Council took the first step in this process by contacting each of the twenty-six organizations not currently on campus, to see which would be interested in starting a new chapter at Tufts. Fourteen responded favorably, which was then whittled down to four serious contenders. Making this cut was none other than Phi Sigma Sigma.[169]

While the national organizations jockeyed behind the scene for the right to start a new chapter, the Panhellenic Council also worked the campus end of the problem by organizing an interest group of women as the basis for the new sorority. By March of 1990, approximately twenty-five women had joined the project. Then came the round of interviews between the Panhellenic Council, the faculty-led Committee on Fraternities and Sororities, the women of the interest group, and the four national finalists. The goal was to find the best match, especially between the undergraduate interest group and the sorority. The process took a number of months, but in the fall of 1990, a winner was announced, and it was Phi Sigma Sigma. Beta chapter would once again be coming back to Tufts.[170]

Those in the interest group wasted no time getting organized that semester. Helping was a representative from the national organization, who worked with the women over an entire school year on how to be a chapter of Phi Sigma Sigma. They started that fall by holding formal rush activities (which were limited to sophomores and juniors), organizing social and philanthropy events, and electing officers. Campus recognition came just a few weeks later, and by the time the 1990–91 school year ended, the colony stood at a respectable thirty-seven members. Overall this was a very good start, even if the chapter was only half the size of the other three sororities. Nonetheless, the women returned to the campus the following fall ready to grow their organization and expand their presence on campus. Then, on November 2, 1991, the women were fully initiated into Phi Sigma Sigma, thereby regaining their charter. It had taken some seventy-three years, but Beta chapter was, for the first time in its history, officially an active and recognized sorority at Tufts University.[171]

Despite the positive first year, though, all did not stay well within Beta chapter as the semesters moved forward. In key areas of philanthropy, social activities, scholarship, and affecting an overall positive impact on campus, Phi Sigma Sigma did very well and without complaint. The problem was membership. By this time, formal sorority rush was governed by a number of rules such as pre-registration, a requirement to visit all chapters at least once during recruitment week, and a maximum number of pledges in any one chapter. These procedures were designed to give each organization a fair chance, which, over the long run, would theoretically equalize the size of each chapter and thus ensure the success of the entire sorority system. However, Phi Sigma Sigma consistently found themselves with the smallest pledge class each and every semester, and this unfortunate result kept their overall membership at about half the other three chapters. The women of Beta chapter made numerous efforts to overcome this discrepancy by holding informal, open rush events throughout the year when other chapters were not recruiting, but these efforts, ultimately, did not close the gap. It was as if the women couldn't break away from their reputation as a small group, no matter what they did. Upon reflection, they felt they knew exactly why.[172]

The tipping point came as rush week approached in the spring of 1994. Rather than being excited for recruitment, the women were once again dreading the effort. The main culprit, they'd come to believe, was their housing situation, or lack thereof. Phi Sigma Sigma was the only sorority at the time that did not occupy an on-campus house, mainly because the Tufts administration had no appropriate space to allocate to them, at least not yet. Those in Phi Sigma Sigma felt this situation put them at a distinct and unfair advantage when it came to rush week. The other three sororities could show off their nice, impressive homes during events, whereas Phi Sigma Sigma was forced to set up in classrooms and common lounge areas, hardly the most inspiring of venues. Therefore, the chapter decided to even the playing field, as it were. Through the Panhellenic Council, they proposed that all sororities be required to use campus-wide facilities for rush week, thereby allowing the community to practice the unity they so often preached. This idea, though, went absolutely nowhere. The other sororities just were not interested in giving up their homes during rush week.[173]

Faced with such lack of support from the other organizations, Phi Sigma Sigma felt they had no choice but double down. They pulled out of formal rush that semester, opting instead to recruit new members on their own schedule and their own terms. Then, they publically lambasted the other sororities. In a Letter to the Editor of *The Tufts Daily*, two members of Phi Sigma Sigma, who were also on the Panhellenic council, expressed their disdain for the rush process in no uncertain terms. "The Tufts Panhellenic continues to structure rush so that the other sororities benefit from their large sisterhoods, their houses, and their general privilege," they wrote, "all at the expense of Phi Sigma Sigma." These and other words in the letter certainly marked a turn towards poorer relations among the sororities which, until then, had been quite cordial. But, if the women had hoped their diatribe would spark a change, they were mistaken. The other sororities essentially shrugged off the complaints and moved on. To make matter worse, Phi Sigma Sigma's informal rush week did not go as hoped, with their efforts once again yielding but a small pledge class.[174]

However, all was not completely wasted, for the Panhellenic Council did make one positive change that semester which looked to benefit Phi Sigma Sigma more than the others. In the aftermath of that 1994 spring rush, the council modified their rules to assure a bid to any woman who participated in either fall or spring rush, beginning the following fall. This system of guaranteeing a bid to all who rushed had recently been enacted due to a mandate from the trustees of Tufts College, but it had only applied to spring rush since that was when first year women (who made up the bulk of rushees) were allowed to participate in recruitment. In theory, expansion of assured bidding to include the fall semester would generate a more even distribution of pledges among the four sororities, since women would be now rushing the Panhellenic system throughout the entire year. Of course, this rule had hardly worked as designed so far, at least as far as Phi Sigma Sigma was concerned. But overall, this change did give some hope to the women and their continued future as an organization.[175]

Soon adding to the optimism was something even better. In the fall of 1994, Beta chapter finally took its place among the other organizations as a sorority with a bona fide chapter house. For many years, the small but distinguished Victorian house at 126 Packard Avenue, which was owned by Tufts, had been the residence of a professor. The house was practically surrounded by other fraternity and co-op student houses, so when the professor vacated the property, the alumni of Beta chapter began negotiating with the Tufts administration for the right of occupancy. Their efforts came to fruition that fall when Phi Sigma Sigma was awarded the space as their new home. In many ways this was a huge coup for the sorority. Two fraternities, Zeta Beta Tau and Alpha Epsilon Pi, had been waiting much longer for their own space on campus, yet Phi Sigma Sigma had been granted the right to move in. So, when the women walked through the doors of their new home for the first time, they felt ready to affect a major turnaround in Beta chapter, and not a moment too soon. Membership stood at just thirteen members. By way of comparison, the other three sororities were each about four times larger. But, if all went well, Beta chapter would narrow this gap considerably over the coming year.[176]

All, unfortunately, did not go well. Despite high hopes, the new rushing rules and the move to 126 Packard Avenue did not provide the spark Beta chapter needed to increase their membership. Fall rush was a disaster, and formal rush in the spring of 1995 was only slightly better, with the chapter gaining just two new pledges, not nearly enough to remain viable. With little to show despite an all-out recruitment effort, with dues now higher than the other sororities in order to support its chapter house, and with its national organization very concerned about their size, Beta chapter could only submit to the inevitable that spring. In a joint decision of the undergraduate active members and the national organization, Beta chapter of Phi Sigma Sigma disbanded at the end of that school year, and its charter was returned once again to the national organization. All members were put on alumnae status for the remainder of their time at Tufts. As for their house at 126 Packard Avenue, it was subsequently leased to the Zeta Beta Tau fraternity the following fall.[177]

UPON ANALYSIS, it appears that despite the initial enthusiasm surrounding Beta chapter's re-founding in 1990, the campus was not ready to support four sororities. Part of this reason may simply have been bad timing – although the Greek system had been growing steadily throughout the late 1980s, by the early 1990s both the fraternities and sororities were under an enhanced scrutiny from students, faculty, and Tufts administrators. The inquisitorial spotlights shone down in many places, with the largest highlighting the inherent exclusivity within the organizations. Many on campus led a huge effort to force fraternities and sororities to adopt open membership, or else be expelled from campus. This effort seemed to dampen the enthusiasm for Greek-letter organizations among students while it played out over a number of semesters, and though the conflict effectively ended in 1993 without affecting major changes, the affair did leave behind an undercurrent of negative feeling about the general Greek system. Such sentiment most likely hurt Phi Sigma Sigma as they looked to attract enough new members when they were needed the most.[178]

But, there may have been another reason why Phi Sigma Sigma struggled with membership, especially towards the end. By the spring of 1993, it was well known on campus that the chapter had an openly gay member. While in theory this situation should not have made any difference, it seems that the Tufts community, in general, was not ready to accept this as normal at the time. Throughout history, nearly every fraternity and sorority chapter has had gay members, but the vast majority of these individuals (at least through the early 1990s) tended to keep their sexual identity private, if not hidden. For one member of Beta chapter to come out publicly as a lesbian was therefore extremely courageous, and by all accounts this member was supported fully by the rest of her chapter. But, homophobia is a powerful force, and at the time such progressiveness in Phi Sigma Sigma was likely beyond the comfort zone of many. And while there is no direct proof that women stayed away from the chapter over this issue, it is entirely plausible that some who may have otherwise joined Phi Sigma Sigma chose to go elsewhere, simply because one member was openly gay.[179]

DELTA ZETA (Delta Iota chapter, 1956 – 1970)
DELTA ZETA DELTA (Local society, circa 1988)

By 1913, a mere twenty-one years after women were first admitted to Tufts College, four national sororities had firmly established chapters on campus. And for the next forty-three years, those four had the campus all to themselves, as no other sorority was able to sustain a chapter at Tufts, despite a general increase in women's enrollment as those years progressed. Phi Sigma Sigma came close in this regard when they tried to establish their Beta Chapter in 1918, but this group would only ever gain five total members before disappearing without a trace in 1922. Instead, it was the Delta Zeta sorority, born at Miami University in Oxford, Ohio, that would break the drought and finally give Tufts its fifth active sorority.

Down by the river

Miami University, named for the river that flows through a nearby valley, can trace its origins back to 1792, when none other than President George Washington signed the bill that led to its spiritual founding. The actual building of the university took some time, but by 1824, the university was up and running as a true entity, with its first class graduating two years later. Fraternities arrived at Miami University in 1833, when Alpha Delta Phi established a chapter on campus, in what was the beginning of a nationalization movement among these organizations. From there, fraternities began to flourish at Miami University, and indeed some of the oldest and largest of today got their start on campus. As for sororities, well, there were none, at least not during the 19th century. From its founding, Miami University was a school for men only, certainly not uncommon in the day. This status changed in the 1870s when women were allowed to attend on equal terms as the men, at least on paper. In truth, the trustees and many school administrators (all men) were very much opposed to women in the classroom. The male students generally felt the same way, so amidst all that negativity, very few women ever enrolled at Miami University before 1900. Indeed, it wasn't until the dawn of the 20th century that the first three women graduated from Miami University, out of a total class of sixteen students.[180]

A mere two years later, though, co-education at Miami started in earnest. The forces behind this change were twofold. First, the state of Ohio authorized the establishment of a normal college as part of the university in the spring of 1902. Since normal colleges trained teachers, and since the profession was almost exclusively the domain of young women, this act meant women would be arriving in force the following fall. Second, and equally important, Miami University had just installed the Reverend Guy Potter Benton as its new president, and he was a strong proponent of coeducation. "The girls are coming," he proudly announced in September of 1902, hoping that perhaps fifty would come to his campus. To his surprise and delight, seventy-eight women arrived on the school's doorsteps and immediately descended upon the nearby town of Oxford, towing their bags and looking for rooms.[181]

When those women stepped on the campus that fall, though, the lack of adequate housing wasn't the only issue they faced. They also ran straight into a problem common to many schools (including Tufts College) which switched from all-male to coeducational overnight – there was nothing whatsoever for them to do outside of the classroom. But among the newly arrived co-eds were a group of six women who weren't content to wait for opportunity to come to them. Instead, they looked around campus for ideas, and what they noticed most of all were the five active fraternities. In these organizations they saw companionship and social camaraderie, two attributes solely lacking among the women due to the scattered nature of their living arrangements. Therefore, they decided to start a fraternity for women. Of course, they had little idea what to do next, so they turned for help to President Benton, the man who so eagerly welcomed them to campus in the first place. President Benton was himself a member of the Phi Delta Theta fraternity, one of a few founded at Miami University (though he had joined at a different school), and after meeting with the six women, he gave them his support and encouragement. The group's efforts came to fruition just a few weeks later. On October 24, 1902, the Delta Zeta sorority was incorporated, marking the first women's organization on the campus of Miami University. Six years later, Delta Zeta became a national organization when they opened their second chapter, Beta, at Cornell University in upstate New York. From there, Delta Zeta grew rapidly across the country, especially after merging with two smaller national sororities in the 1940s. A decade later, Delta Zeta was still growing through mergers, but also through expansion into new schools. One was Tufts University.[182]

The best of times, the worst of times

The letter came out of the blue. One day in early spring of 1954, Dean Katharine Jeffers sorted through her mail and found an inquiry from the national office of the Delta Zeta sorority. Simply put, they wanted permission to come to campus and talk with undergraduates about possibly starting a new sorority. Why Delta Zeta chose Tufts that spring is a mystery, but the logic behind it is not. Fraternities and sororities were growing by leaps and bounds across the country, as the post-World War II normalcy had brought renewed interest in old traditions. Delta Zeta, it appears, was aggressively using this enthusiasm to establish new chapters in regions where it had never been, such as Massachusetts, and at schools with a strong Greek system, such as Tufts. Unfortunately for Delta Zeta, though, Dean Jeffers had no intent of granting permission. In a quick but terse response penned the very same day, she told the national officers that Tufts College didn't need another sorority at the time.[183]

A year and a half later, though, the situation had changed considerably. By the fall of 1955, the other four sororities, due to a renewed wave of popularity, were in danger of becoming too large for the school's liking. The Tufts administration therefore looked to solve this problem by inviting a fifth sorority to campus. And here, they had the perfect candidate: Delta Zeta. Of course, there was a catch. The push for civil rights was growing rapidly on college campuses at the time, and this movement put Greek-letter organizations in the crosshairs due to their policies of exclusion based on race, religion, and creed. At Tufts, the trustees responded to this effort in 1955 by prohibiting a fraternity or sorority from starting a new chapter on campus if they practiced official membership discrimination. Before going any further, then, Delta Zeta was asked to comment on their membership policy. The response came in October of 1955, and it was unequivocal. Delta Zeta had no discriminatory clauses in its constitution based on race or religion.[184]

Such a declaration was all that was needed to move forward. A few months later, a representative from the national organization came onto campus to interview prospective members. After nine days of meetings, twenty-eight women representing all except the senior class had been chosen as the charter members for the new colony. They were initiated as pledges a few days later, and then on May 12, 1956, the now twenty-five (three apparently dropped out) were fully initiated into Delta Zeta, thus marking the birth of the Delta Iota chapter. It had taken forty-three years, but Tufts finally had a viable fifth sorority on campus. The charter members of Delta Zeta were:

Carol Tillinghast	Ann M. Polcari
Janet Smith	Joan Westwood
Paula Rivituso	Paula E. Gross
Patricia Bourque	Deborah Williams
Betty MacEnteggart	Claire Garabedian
Hinda Greyser	Mary R. Urbanawicz

Nancy Green	Carol Perry
Gloria Vincz	Janet De Luca
Elaine Smith	Carolyn E. Conley
Sheila McDermott	Carol J. Schneider
Irene Kemp	Sondra M. Symczak
Jolyne Fournier	Janet Davenport

Heather Campbell

After gaining their charter, Delta Zeta moved into a chapter room in Curtis Hall, similar to the accommodations provided to the other sororities on campus.[185]

No sooner had the Delta Zeta been founded, though, than turmoil erupted within the Tufts sorority system. When school started up again in the early fall of 1956, two of five sororities on campus unexpectedly made national headlines for being in the middle of the growing civil rights movement. One sorority, Sigma Kappa, had their charter pulled without warning for pledging two African-American women earlier that spring, even though their organization had no official restriction against race. The women of Sigma Kappa immediately reformed as a local sorority called Thalia. A second sorority, Alpha Xi Delta, saw nearly all of their members resign in protest early that fall over a secret clause in their ritual barring minorities from membership. The women who resigned from Alpha Xi Delta also reorganized as a local sorority, which they named Alethea. In general, the Tufts community supported the stand against membership restrictions as taken by these two groups. But for those new members of Delta Zeta, the events must have been a little disconcerting as they looked to start operations on a campus in so much turmoil.[186]

Soon, though, the conversations involving Sigma Kappa and Alpha Xi Delta settled down on campus, thanks in large part to Dean Jeffers acting as the information filter between Tufts and the outside world. As a result, Delta Zeta was able to settle into the normal routines of rush events, pledging, social gatherings, and philanthropy work each school year. The chapter grew quickly in stature during its first few years of operations, becoming relatively equal to the other sororities. It was in intramural sports, though, where Delta Zeta excelled, as the chapter retired the basketball and volleyball trophies for winning so many championships. However, outside of Delta Zeta, all was not well. As the 1950s neared its end, the popularity of sororities at Tufts began to wane. One reason was most likely the continuing discussion of membership discrimination still within some Greek-letter organizations, including the Alpha Xi Delta sorority, which was attempting a return to campus. This publicity tended to put all sororities in a negative light and undoubtedly drove some potential members

Delta Zeta rush party, likely in their chapter room in Curtis Hall, circa 1956.

away. Indeed, in the spring of 1960, the local Thalia chapter disbanded due to declining interest. Over the next few years, the remaining four sororities managed to stay afloat, but all saw their membership levels gradually decrease, a trend also fueled by the general unrest on college campuses over larger issues such as the Vietnam War. The second organization to succumb to low membership was the local Alethea chapter, which disbanded in February of 1966, just before sorority rush week was due to start. This caused all eyes turned on Delta Zeta, now the smallest of the remaining three sororities with just thirteen active members. Everyone wondered, were they next?[187]

The answer was soon obvious. Spring rush of 1966 was a complete disaster for Delta Zeta. The sorority gained but one pledge, nowhere near the number they needed to sustain their future. Morale sank to a new low, and the women began to lose interest in working together as an organization. A semester later, in the fall of 1966, the chapter could count but two active members. Delta Zeta was, for all intents and purposes, finished. But these two women, along with the national organization and the Panhellenic Council at Tufts, were not ready to give up. Instead, the Panhellenic Council organized a special rush in the late fall of 1966 just for Delta Zeta, hoping to gather a new group of enthusiastic women to continue the chapter. This rush was much more successful than the previous one, and by early December of 1966, Delta Zeta had re-colonized with fourteen new pledges, all freshmen, with Anne Marie Jones and Gail Scott (the only remaining actives) staying on as advisors to the group.[188]

This new group of women tried in earnest to grow Delta Zeta into a viable organization following their installation as full chapter in the spring of 1967, but the circumstances of college life at the time were too much to overcome. Interest in sororities continued to decline rapidly in the latter 1960s, with Delta Zeta absorbing the brunt of this indifference. During the year and a half after re-colonization, the chapter never had more than a dozen or so active members at any given time, with the majority scheduled to graduate in two years. Then, after the spring of 1968, it appears the women had given up and walked away. Not surprisingly, the national organization declared its Delta Iota chapter dormant after the 1970 graduation. The two remaining sororities, Alpha Omicron Pi and Chi Omega, soon followed Delta Zeta along this path, such that by the fall of 1970, sorority life had come to an end at Tufts University.[189]

What do you think you're doing?

Delta Zeta's fourteen-year existence on campus, though brief, certainly experienced the gamut of emotions, from enthusiastic acceptance in the beginning, to utter rejection at the end. The return of sorority life to Tufts in the mid 1970s, though, did not seem to revive any nostalgic feelings within the alumnae of Delta Iota chapter or the national organization, for a restart was never attempted in the years that followed. It wasn't until the fall of 1988 that Delta Zeta was even mentioned again in conjunction with the Tufts campus. Sometime that semester, a group of fifteen or so women took a look at the three active sororities on campus and decided none were a good fit. But, since they were very interested in sorority life, they decided to start their own. And when it came to which sorority they wanted to start, in this regard they were united – it would be Delta Zeta. The women were drawn to Delta Zeta not because of any past history with Tufts, but rather due to the organization's reputation as one of the largest sororities in the country. So, they came together as a group under the name Delta Zeta Delta (DZD) and registered as a student club. Then, they began working to gain recognition as a sorority on campus, a process they started that fall. On the surface this task seemed straightforward, if not trivial.[190]

The process was actually quite complicated. The entire Greek system at Tufts, at least from an oversight perspective, was in flux when DZD started in the fall of 1988. Various entities were vying for the authority to grant official recognition to Greek-letter organizations, including the faculty-led Committee on Social Fraternities and Sororities (CFS), and, for sororities, the student-run Tufts Panhellenic Council. DZD had unfortunately jumped right into the middle of this power struggle, one that seemingly would take some time to resolve, which meant the women would have to wait for official recognition. Though disappointed with this situation, DZD continued on as a group while biding their time until recognition was possible. However, one of the first steps they took was backwards. Over the course of a few nights that fall, the women stole composites and other memorabilia from a few fraternity houses as a prank. While they hoped to gain some positive attention for DZD from this event, they instead gained some unwanted notoriety, since their prank coincided with an attempted theft of President Jean Mayer's license plate and physical damage to the Zeta Psi house. DZD quickly apologized for their prank and were also absolved of any responsibility for the other incidents. But not everyone within the Greek community was pleased – while most of the affected fraternities took the temporary thefts in stride, some condemned the idea and wished instead the women had chosen a more positive outlet for expression, such as organizing a charity event.[191]

From there, DZD stayed out of the spotlight and grew their organization to twenty or so members that year. However, as the school year went on, they became increasingly frustrated at the slow progress of the Tufts Panhellenic Council and the CFS to sort out the recognition process. So, with no end to the waiting game in sight, the women took matters in their own hands. They approached Associate Dean of Students Bruce Reitman and asked for his help in gaining recognition as a chapter of Delta Zeta. Dean Reitman was quite supportive of the women and their goal of recognition, so he encouraged them to forge ahead. After this meeting, it appears the women of DZD then contacted the national Delta Zeta organization to get the recognition process moving forward. This turned out to be a fatal mistake.[192]

The phone call came out of the blue. Dean Reitman picked up, and on the other end was a woman with a thick Southern accent who had but one question: "Dean Reitman, what do you think you're doing?" The woman asking was the head of the National Panhellenic Conference (NPC), an oversight and advocacy group for twenty-six social sororities that included Delta Zeta. As she explained over the phone, the NPC (and thus Delta Zeta by proxy) had a clear and unambiguous process that governed sorority expansion, and neither DZD nor the Tufts administration was following the rules. Therefore, she demanded that Dean Reitman tell the women to halt their efforts to affiliate with Delta Zeta and instead abide by the NPC expansion process, one that in theory would take at least another semester or two to play out. This realization seemed to surprise both DZD and Dean Reitman. The undergraduates were operating under the assumption that starting a new chapter of a national sorority was under their control, when in reality the Tufts Panhellenic Council held considerable power in this regard. As a first step in the NPC process, the Tufts Panhellenic Council had to vote in favor of bringing a new sorority to campus, something they were reluctant to do while the whole authority over recognition was unsettled. So, DZD was left with no choice but to wait some more.[193]

This delay, it appears, was too much for the members of DZD. For two semesters they'd worked and tried to build their organization, even going so far as to manufacture and wear initiate pins of their own design. Now, though, it was abundantly clear they were not going to become a chapter of Delta Zeta any time soon. Therefore, by the start of the fall semester in 1989, it appears the group had disbanded, with the women going their separate ways. DZD was now but a mere afterthought, relegated to the back pages of Tufts history. Frustration over the inability to control their own destiny was their ultimate downfall, aided in no small part by the uncertainty in the sorority recognition process that played out during the 1988–89 school year. Of course, had the women waited just a little longer, they may have been successful. In the late fall of 1989, the recognition problem had been sorted out, and the Tufts Panhellenic Council had even voted to establish a fourth sorority on campus, the key event that then triggered the official NPC expansion process.[194]

On a larger scale, the unsuccessful plight of DZD highlights the modern-day difference between fraternity and sorority expansion. Had DZD been a group of men wishing to affiliate with a national organization, they most likely could have done so on their own volition, for the national oversight group for fraternities, the North American Interfraternity Conference, has no set rules for the expansion process. Instead, that decision is left to each organization. Such policy led to the independent establishment of four fraternities at Tufts during the 1980s, and in all four cases the men were able to affiliate with the organization of their choosing. The NPC, by contrast, treats expansion as a system-wide issue for their member sororities, one that should be managed to ensure all have an equal opportunity to grow.[195]

ALPHA PHI (Zeta Theta chapter, 1977 – present)

From the time women were first admitted into Tufts College in 1892 until the last sorority went dormant in the fall of 1970, six different national women's fraternities had established chapters on campus. Some of these chapters lasted but a few years, others nearly eighty, but among them all were groups of dedicated alumnae who wanted to see their organization back on campus, someday. Chi Omega, in the spring of 1976, became the first of these dormant organizations to re-emerge at Tufts, and their rebirth brought such a renewed interest in sorority life that soon thereafter, three additional sororities appeared, including revivals of Sigma Kappa and Phi Sigma Sigma. As it turned out, these three additional sororities were two too many for the time. Neither Sigma Kappa nor Phi Sigma Sigma became viable organizations despite promising starts. Instead, the one that did survive had no earlier association with the Tufts campus. That organization was Alpha Phi.[196]

A straightforward answer to a simple question

In September of 1871, forty-one students and five professors gathered in a chapel in Syracuse, New York, to inaugurate the newly opened university bearing the city's name. The journey to that point had taken nearly two years, with the original plan being the relocation of Genesee College from the nearby town of Lima. The townspeople of Lima objected to the transfer, however, so Syracuse was left to build their own school, which they did with aplomb. Still, when those men and women first gathered in the chapel that fall to begin their studies, there was little to bring them together as a community – there was no physical campus beyond some rented space in the downtown area, and the first permanent building, though under construction, would not open for another two years. All Syracuse University had that September were some pieces pried from Genesee College – its library, a few of its best professors, and a secret society for men, the local fraternity Upsilon Kappa. Within a few months, though, Syracuse University caught the attention of one of the largest fraternities in the United States at the time, Delta Kappa Epsilon, and soon enough their newest chapter was up and running on campus.[197]

Among those who took note of the two fraternities at Syracuse were students Martha Foote, Clara Sittser, and Kate Hogoboom. As women, they were not eligible for membership in either organization. But, they were clearly intrigued by the operations of the fraternities, for one day in September of 1872, one of them asked, "Girls, why can't we have a society as well as the men?" It was a simple question born from curiosity, and while the three women soon answered with a rousing "we can!" their next step was anything but clear. Simply put, they knew almost nothing about the operations of fraternities. There were only a handful of such organizations for women in existence at the time, but all were located at schools far away, so they were likely unknown to the Syracuse group. As a result, these three were on their own, armed with nothing more than a determination to succeed.[198]

It was all they would need. A few days after posing the question, the three invited all undergraduate women at Syracuse, about ninety in total, to gather in Clara and Kate's rented room. A sizeable number answered, thus filling the tiny bedroom. Clara opened a box of homemade treats to sweeten the conversation, and once the food was gone, the three spoke of their true intention, to form a new secret society "similar to the men's." Not all were up for the idea, especially when a few of the girl's parents voiced their objections to the presumed expense for such an operation, both in terms of money and time away from studies. However, a few days later, seven of the invitees decided to join Clara, Kate, and Martha in their endeavor. They gathered at a local home, pledged their loyalty to one another as sisters, and then sat down to a home cooked, celebratory banquet. The Alpha Phi fraternity for women had just been born.[199]

From there, Alpha Phi prospered at Syracuse, and soon welcomed a rival sorority, Gamma Phi Beta, just two years later. Alpha Phi remained a local organization until the opportunity to go national came along in 1881. That spring, a group of young women at Northwestern University in Evanston, Illinois, looked to start the first sorority on a campus, no doubt inspired by the popularity of the fraternities at the school. Wishing to put some serious thought into their selection of a name, the group approached Dean of Women Jane Bancroft, and asked to borrow a Greek dictionary as a guide. Dean Bancroft, as it turned out, was an alumna of Syracuse and proud member of Alpha Phi. The students would not need her dictionary. Instead, by the end of that spring semester, she had convinced them to abandon their plans for their own organization, and become the Beta, or second chapter of Alpha Phi. From there, Alpha Phi embarked on a steady expansion across the country, including its Eta chapter at Boston University in 1883. However, after coming to Boston, Alpha Phi never looked to expand into nearby schools such as Tufts College. In 1903, the small national sorority Delta Sigma, which had a chapter at Tufts College, considered merging with Alpha Phi, but in the end the group decided to merge with Alpha Omicron Pi. All told, it would take nearly one hundred years before Alpha Phi considered starting another chapter in the Boston area.[200]

When Irish eyes are smiling

The mid-1970s was, in many respects, a chaotic dichotomy at Tufts University. The school was stumbling in its efforts to find a new president and its financial situation was precarious at best, but the drinking age was eighteen and the students, through their newfound free spirits, looked to change campus life for the better. Among the new ideas they embraced during this era was special interest housing. Here, students came together in co-op living groups organized around an ethnic theme (mostly) such as the German House, the French House, and the Latin-American House. One such group joining the mix was the Irish-American Society. In theory, this group was formed to allow Irish-Americans at Tufts a chance to live together and experience the culture of their ancestral homeland. In reality, though, the Irish-American Society had other ideas. To start, they convinced the Tufts administration to given them two adjoining suites in Wren Hall as their home, one for women and one for men. Then, they built an ornate bar between the two suites, approved and paid for by the administration, for the simple goal of having fun. The inevitable "Happy Hour" parties came next, and by all accounts, these get-togethers helped make the Irish-American Society a household name on campus.[201]

Among those living in the Irish-American co-op during the 1976-77 school year was sophomore Lori Reed. As the weeks passed, she and her society mates became close friends. Then, at some point that year, Lori approached the other women with an idea of starting a new sorority at Tufts. Sororities had only recently come back on campus with the arrival of Chi Omega a year earlier, but Lori wasn't interested in joining that chapter. Instead, she wanted to bring a new organization to campus, one she knew very well, even if her classmates did not. That sorority was Alpha Phi, the same one her older sister had joined at Florida State University. Soon enough Lori had gathered seven other like-minded women, and in late spring of 1977, they were pledged to Alpha Phi at a ceremony in the Colonial Inn, right in the heart of historic Concord, Massachusetts. The newest sorority at Tufts was off and running.[202]

Off and running that is, straight into a crowded field. By the fall of 1977, a third sorority, Phi Sigma Sigma, had also started operations at Tufts, and a fourth, Sigma Kappa, would soon follow. All of these organizations were chasing a renewed interest in sorority life at Tufts, an interest they all, unfortunately, seemed to over-estimate. It soon became obvious there just weren't enough sorority-minded women to support the four organizations, despite the initial enthusiasm. As a result, two of the four closed down within a few years. But not Alpha Phi. The chapter was able to rise above the fray, most likely because its members had a slight edge in recruitment. Alpha Phi drew many from the Boston School of Occupational Therapy and child study programs, two courses of study not significantly represented in the other sororities – Chi Omega, for example, tended to be the choice for engineering students at the time, while Sigma Kappa drew from a small band of commuters. Of course, exceptions abounded to these generalizations, but at the very least, it appears those in Alpha Phi relied heavily on personal connections from the classroom to grow their membership, which they used to great success.[203]

The members of Alpha Phi spent the 1977–78 school year bringing their organization to the campus. Philanthropy became a centerpiece of their activities, as did social events with a number of other Greek organizations at a time when such interaction was not popular. But it was the close friendships that developed among the founders and first members that became a strong suit of Alpha Phi, and this naturally drew others looking for a similar experience. Still, the one thing missing from the chapter was a house to call their own. Since forming they'd been meeting in various dormitory or suite rooms, but after a while the desire for a chapter house became strong. In this regard, though, Alpha Phi was not poised for success, for the administration showed no interest in finding a space for the sorority. Yes, Tufts had offered enormous help to Chi Omega in their quest for a house, but they were backed by the strong political clout of their alumnae network. Alpha Phi, on the other hand, had yet to graduate a single member. However, all hope was not lost. They soon realized there was a path, albeit unorthodox, for the chapter to obtain a home, and that was through the student housing lottery. So, in the spring of 1978, a number of rising seniors in Alpha Phi entered the lottery and hoped for low numbers, ones that would allow them to choose among a few Tufts-owned houses on, or very close to campus. In this regard, they won. With a favorable position in the lottery, six women secured the house at 128 Curtis Street and designated it the Alpha Phi house, at least for the upcoming school year. It may not have been permanent, but it was a start.[204]

The women moved into 128 Curtis Street the fall of 1978, and then turned their attention to another matter, which was formal initiation into Alpha Phi. This they accomplished on November 11, 1978, when thirty-three women were initiated into Alpha Phi, becoming the Zeta Theta chapter. The charter members were:

Ruth Cogan	Fay Minda Foster
Laurie Gallagher	Lori Reed
Ellen Sullivan	Sally Utzinger
Kirsten Webster	Jill Blumenthal
Beverly Brine	Pamela Cook
Darshana Doshi	Catherine Jones
Deborah Leonard	Stephanie May
Beth Miller	Mary Money
Sheri O'Boyle	Julia Witmer
Martha Griffith	Philomena Hastings
Deborah Narkun	Suzanne Paquin
Janett Selby	Ilene Siegal
Katelyn Quynn	Georgia Serevetas
Sandra Weinberger	Ruth Gold
Joan Tierney	Karen Sullivan
Nancy Squitieri	Sheila Buckley

Nancy Shalowitz

Pinning the initiate badge onto Lori was her older sister, Gayla (Reed) Brown.[205]

A house to call home

Following the installation, the members of Alpha Phi settled into their new home and continued moving forward. However, the uncertainty over their housing situation loomed large, since there was no guarantee they'd be so lucky each year in the housing lottery. As it turned out, though, their luck held just fine. The chapter was able to remain at 128 Curtis Street for the following two school years, which helped the women solidify their presence on campus and grow their membership. Then came the housing bombshell in the spring of 1981. The Tufts administration had just finished constructing its new Latin Way dormitory and was working to obtain the required housing license from the city of Somerville. This license did not come cheap. As part of the agreement between the school and the city, Tufts had to close a number of its smaller, off-campus residential houses before the license would be granted. Included on the closure list was Alpha Phi's house at 128 Curtis Street. This was a disappointment to many in Alpha Phi, but the administration, to its credit, appeased the situation by assigning the sorority a suite of rooms in the Latin Way dormitory. This decision was somewhat controversial, as not all within the administration approved (they were worried about establishing a new precedent, should the situation arise again), but in the end, Alpha Phi moved into the 360s section of Latin Way in the fall of 1981. This marked the first time a Greek-Letter organization at Tufts had ever called a dormitory suite their official home.[206]

Any controversy over this move would be short lived, however, as Alpha Phi's stay in the Latin Way dormitory would be very brief. Throughout the 1981–82 school year, members of the sorority worked with the Tufts administration to find a space they could truly call a home. Sure enough, that year the house at 14 Sawyer Avenue became available. Built nearly eighty years earlier for Professor Charles Wade, 14 Sawyer Avenue then served as a women's dormitory from time-to-time after the professor moved on from Tufts. The structure was small by chapter house standards, as only nine women could live there, and the common areas were hardly large enough to support the growing membership. But, this was the best the administration could do, so in the fall of 1982, Alpha Phi moved into 14 Sawyer Avenue and made the space their home.[207]

The move has worked out well. Since 1982, Alpha Phi has enjoyed a strong presence on campus operating out of their home, and has a record of accomplishment that any organization would envy. The only serious glitches for the chapter came in the spring of 2003 and then 2008, when they were suspended for a time due to hazing and alcohol violations. In both cases, though, Alpha Phi was able to make amends for the transgressions, keep control of their chapter house, and redirect their energy to more positive goals. A mainstay of the chapter the past few years is its philanthropy, specifically the annual "Bid Your Heart Out" auction in support of women's health issues. Since starting this event in the spring of 2010, Alpha Phi has raised tens of thousands of dollars for charity, making it one of the largest student-run, Greek-led fundraisers on campus.[208]

KAPPA ALPHA THETA (Eta Psi chapter, 2013 – present)

Among the dozens of Greek-letter organizations that have ever come to Tufts, Kappa Alpha Theta is one of a select few that took an enormous amount of time between almost starting a chapter and actually doing so – one hundred and ten years. The story begins in 1903, when the women of the Delta Sigma sorority at Tufts College considered a bold move. While they were already part of a national organization (along with the coveted Alpha chapter designation), their sorority's overall reach was quite limited, with only three active chapters. National women's fraternities were exploding onto the college scene at the turn of the 20th century, but rather than establish more chapters, it seems the women of Delta Sigma felt a brighter future lay in merging with a larger organization, one that would conceivably bring them a stronger community, if not a higher stature among their peers. The national Alpha Omicron Pi came calling first that year, but the organization was rejected by the women of Delta Sigma. Instead, it appeared they would accept an offer to merge with Kappa Alpha Theta, one of the largest women's fraternities of its day.[209]

Go fly a kite

Bettie Locke of Greencastle, Indiana, had only one realistic choice for continuing her education beyond the secondary level, and that was Indiana Asbury College (now DePauw University), a small liberal arts school founded by the Methodist church in 1837. Not only was the school located in the town she'd called home for the past seven years, it was also where her father was a well liked and respected mathematics professor. Standing in the way of her education, though, was one significant problem: Indiana Asbury was only for men. As fate would have it, though, the trustees of Indiana Asbury finally allowed women to enroll starting in the fall of 1867, the very semester Bettie was ready for college. So, Bettie began her studies that fall, where she was joined by three other women as the first at Indiana Asbury. However, while the four were allowed on campus, they were hardly welcomed. So strong was the negative feeling among some men that as soon as the semester started, they began petitioning college authorities to kick the women out for good. Such action only fueled the women's collective determination to show everyone at Indiana Asbury they could succeed "[not] just for ourselves – but for all the girls who would follow." Naturally, then, the four women formed a special bond of friendship that year, one that helped them navigate the sea of hostility.[210]

For two years they continued on as friends and students, while the men continued to resent, in varying degrees, their presence on campus. But then, something happened. During the fall of 1869, Bettie noticed a few of the women on campus had started wearing fraternity pins on their blouses, for all to see. These women were not official members, but rather wore the pins to show their support for that particular men's organization, usually at the request of a friend or classmate. Seeing women sport fraternity pins soon gave Bettie an idea. She would start a fraternity just for them. Bettie was no stranger to fraternities, as her father was a Beta Theta Pi, and her brother was a Phi Gamma Delta. So, Bettie approached her father with the idea, and he immediately signed on in support. Next, Bettie confided her plans to a student she knew well, Alice Allen, one of the "original four" women at Indiana Asbury. Alice agreed, and the two spent the rest of the fall of 1869 meeting regularly and working on the details of their organization, including the constitution and ritual. They also gave strong consideration to the other twelve women on campus, to see if any should be invited into their organization. Eventually they chose two, and on the night of January 27, 1870, Bettie led the group through the initiation ritual. The Kappa Alpha Theta fraternity for women had just been born.[211]

Of course, no one on the outside knew of this event, for the women kept their organization secret in the weeks that followed, while they planned for their public unveiling. And for this, they would use their newly minted fraternity pins. Around the time of the initiation, Bettie contracted a jeweler in New York City to design and manufacture the badge based on a simple request. She wanted "something near enough to the Phi Gamma Delta badge… and yet slenderized." For two long months the women of Kappa Alpha Theta waited, until finally the package arrived from the jeweler. On March 14, 1870, the now five women of Kappa Alpha Theta walked into chapel services as they always had, only this time wearing their new badges for all of the campus to see. The fraternity men of Indiana Asbury noticed first, and their reaction was probably not what the women expected. In a word, they laughed. The men openly ridiculed the badge, saying it looked like a kite and, like the organization it represented, would soon flutter away in the wind. The women, however, were undeterred. They were going to build Kappa Alpha Theta into a viable organization. As for the remark about the kite, soon enough it became an endearing symbol of Kappa Alpha Theta.[212]

The women wasted little time growing their organization from a local at Indiana Asbury to a bona fide national organization. By the middle of May 1870, Kappa Alpha Theta had established a second chapter at Indiana University with the help of Bettie's father. From there, Kappa Alpha Theta continued to place chapters in the Midwest, before reaching the rest of the country. Then, in 1897, Kappa Alpha Theta entered Brown University in Providence, Rhode Island, joining the year-old Delta Sigma sorority on that campus. It is most likely through this relationship that Kappa Alpha Theta, in 1903, approached the national leaders of Delta Sigma and looked to bring the smaller sorority into their fold, including their chapter at Tufts College. Soon enough, a fair number of women in Delta Sigma were in favor of the merger. But then for reasons lost to history, the women decided to investigate a few other national sororities, perhaps to improve their bargaining position with Kappa Alpha Theta, or perhaps to find a group that had a larger presence in New England (most of Kappa Alpha Theta's chapters were in the Midwest and western part of the country at the time). Either way, the planned merger was eventually abandoned. Kappa Alpha Theta would not be coming to Tufts College anytime soon.[213]

Welcome back, and pleased to meet you

For the next one hundred ten years, Kappa Alpha Theta continued to expand all over the country. Starting in 1943, the organization came to Massachusetts, with the opening of chapters at the University of Massachusetts at Amherst, MIT, and Harvard University. Then, in the fall of 2012, an opportunity appeared once again to expand in the commonwealth. For a number of years, the Tufts administration was concerned about the growing popularity of the three sororities on campus, which had pushed membership in each to record high (if not also unwieldy) numbers. An obvious remedy was to start at least one more sorority, an idea that was supported by the existing organizations. But sorority expansion requires more than just desire. Per the rules of the National PanHellenic Conference (NPC), the governing body that oversees twenty-six collegiate women's fraternities, Tufts started the process that fall by inviting all NPC organizations not currently on campus to apply for the right to start a chapter. Of the ten that responded, four made it to the final round the following semester: Gamma Phi Beta, Kappa Alpha Theta, Kappa Kappa Gamma, and Alpha Gamma Delta. They were each invited to give presentations to a student-run extension committee of women representing the three sororities as well as other groups on campus. For Kappa Alpha Theta, this was the first time they had considered Tufts University since 1903. Perhaps it was all worth the wait, for after the presentations, the extension committee took a vote, and the winner was Kappa Alpha Theta.[214]

The organization wasted little time. In the fall of 2013, two consultants from Kappa Alpha Theta came to campus with the task of starting the new chapter. To do so, they primarily used personal salesmanship. Soon after classes began, they set up a table in the Campus Center and simply started talking about Kappa Alpha Theta to any woman who passed on by. They also held informational meetings on campus, where they encouraged interested women to sign up for a personal interview. Those passing the interview and meeting certain scholastic requirements such as a minimum grade point average were then invited to join the colony. Not all were chosen, but by the end of September, Kappa Alpha Theta had found seventy-seven women to form the basis of the new chapter, and for the next six weeks the women worked to earn their charter. They were rewarded for their efforts on November 2, 2013, when all seventy-seven were initiated as the Eta Psi chapter of Kappa Alpha Theta. Tufts was now home to four active sororities for the first time in over twenty years.[215]

The following semester, the women of Kappa Alpha Theta used the enthusiasm to gain upwards of thirty new pledges, thus pushing the total size of their chapter over one hundred members. Kappa Alpha Theta was therefore the first organization to reach over one hundred members in such a short amount of time. Then, in a stroke of good luck, the Tufts administration announced that Kappa Alpha Theta would occupy a chapter house the very next semester, just one year after starting on campus. Under normal circumstances, new Greek-letter organizations are required to wait at least three years after forming before moving into a university-sanctioned chapter house. However, for Kappa Alpha Theta, opportunity trumped rules. The Tufts administration decided to convert a co-op dormitory at 90–94 Curtis Street into fraternity housing starting in the fall of 2014. The house was a duplex, and while the Sigma Nu fraternity would move into one side of the structure, Kappa Alpha Theta would move into the other. This marked the first time a fraternity and sorority have shared a chapter house, even though there is no direct interior access between the two sides of the house. The two organizations celebrated with a house warming and ribbon-cutting ceremony just after school got underway that fall, with President Anthony Monaco wielding the ceremonial scissors.[216]

Since then, Kappa Alpha Theta has settled into the Tufts community quite nicely. The chapter's signature philanthropy event is a four-hour dance party known as "Thetathon" which, over the first two years, has raised more than $16,000 in support of the Court Appointed Special Advocates, an organization that works with children as they go through the foster or court system. As for the enduring legacy of Kappa Alpha Theta, that is still an open question. However, the chapter appears to be off to a very strong start.[217]

THE CULTURAL ORGANIZATIONS 5

Black, Latino, and multicultural fraternities and sororities

Walking around the campus of Tufts University today are students from many different cultures and countries. Such diversity, though, is somewhat atypical when considering the overall history of the school. For the first one hundred plus years after its founding, Tufts College and then Tufts University was a school with a predominantly white, Christian, American student population. Students of different races, religions, and nationalities were few and far between, and when they did enroll, they were often without a strong support network. Instead, they had to contend with prejudices and bigotry both on and off campus, which, though typical for the time, must have made their life difficult in many ways. Jewish students were one exception to this general rule, as they came to Tufts in large enough number to create and sustain various religious and social groups for themselves, which undoubtedly helped improve their overall collegiate experience. Other minorities, however, such as African-Americans, Asians, and Hispanics were not as fortunate. Combined they represented but a tiny percentage of the student population well into the 1970s, if not later. They arrived in small groups at best in those earlier years, and while they were accepted into the classrooms, the athletic teams, and the dormitories, they faced barriers when it came to membership in social organizations, especially the fraternities and sororities.[1]

This lack of campus diversity up through the latter 20th century was not unique to Tufts, as many American colleges and universities at that time were similarly homogenous. But unlike many other schools across the country, Tufts was not an isolated bastion of education. The large number of schools in and around Boston offered the relatively small number of minority students at each an opportunity to join together for support and companionship. So that is just what they did. In the early 20th century, it was the African-American students at Tufts who would enjoy this camaraderie first, helped by the birth of eight Black Greek-letter organizations (BGLOs) across the country, four for men and four for women. While none of these eight were founded in Boston, five expanded to the area quite early in their history, and it did not take long for them to bring Tufts students into their fold. Later in the 20th century, Hispanics and Asians would come together in much the same manner, fueled by the rapid growth of multicultural and ethnic Greek-letter organizations. And once again, a number of Tufts students have found their way to these organizations over the years. In a few cases, Tufts students were among the founding members of the chapter.[2]

Historically, though, many in the Tufts community have known very little about the BGLO and multicultural organizations, mainly because these groups have yet to occupy a chapter house on campus. These particular fraternities and sororities can also go many years without initiating a Tufts undergraduate, thus making their presence very understated over time. Nonetheless, for the students who do join these organizations, their experiences are just as important and meaningful as those who join the social Greek-letter organizations. Here are their stories.[3]

ALPHA PHI ALPHA (Sigma chapter, est. 1915; Rho Nu chapter, est. 1989)

Noted Tufts historian Professor Russell Miller, in his seminal work *Light on the Hill – Volume II*, wrote that the first Black Greek-letter organization (BGLO) came to Tufts in 1975, with the formation of the Theta Iota chapter of Kappa Alpha Psi. As it turns out, Professor Miller was incorrect in both the year and the organization. Instead, the year was 1915, and the fraternity was Alpha Phi Alpha. That fall seven young men, all recent college graduates and members of Alpha Phi Alpha from a few different chapters, came to Boston to pursue graduate studies at Boston University and Harvard University. As can be expected, these men looked to each other for mutual support, and recognizing the opportunity at hand, they petitioned Alpha Phi Alpha for the right to establish a new chapter in Boston. For quite some time the national organization had wanted to start a chapter in the area, so the petition was quickly accepted. Thus, on November 28, 1915, Sigma chapter of Alpha Phi Alpha came into being, the seventeenth in the fast growing national organization. Then, just one semester later, the fraternity came to Tufts. In the spring of 1916, Sigma chapter initiated David M. Scott, a fourth-year student in the Tufts Medical School, as part of its first group of new initiates. David thus holds a place in history as the first African-American at Tufts to join a fraternity.[4]

From its beginning, Sigma chapter looked to fill a number of roles for its members, from a social outlet and peer support network, to a vehicle for social change. The chapter staged mock trials, as many members were studying law at Boston University, and these events gave those aspiring lawyers a chance to hone their litigation skills while also discussing relevant issues of the day. Additionally, many within the chapter became outspoken against segregation and helped support a burgeoning movement in Boston. Community involvement was a mainstay of Alpha Phi Alpha from the beginning, a commitment that still stands today. Then came The Great War. America's entry into the conflict effectively shut down Sigma chapter in the fall of 1918, as all members either enlisted or became part of the Student Army Training Corps program on their respective campus. But the men of Sigma chapter certainly had a much different service experience than their white classmates. Not only were they segregated because of their race, they were also relegated primarily to support roles such as servants, drivers, cooks, and medical staff, since prevailing military wisdom at the time said African-American men were generally unfit for front line duty. Still, by all accounts, the men of Alpha Phi Alpha served with enthusiasm, and did all they could to help win the war.[5]

Following the armistice, men from Sigma chapter began streaming back to their respective locales and immediately began working to restart their fraternity, which they accomplished in earnest by the early spring of 1919. Next, the men quickly focused on another goal, that of occupying a chapter house. Such a move, the men knew, would bring them prestige both within Alpha Phi Alpha and the general fraternity movement, for chapter houses were fast becoming the rule across the country. Indeed, national fraternity magazines at the time including Alpha Phi Alpha's *The Sphinx* were filled with pictures of smiling men standing on the steps of their grand houses, for all to admire. Unfortunately, in this quest the men of Sigma soon hit a roadblock. While they were all united in their desire for a house, they simply could not decide where. By the early 1920s, over half of Sigma chapter's fifty or so active members attended Harvard University, while the other half were enrolled at other area schools including Tufts, MIT, and Boston University. Naturally, the Harvard contingent wanted the chapter house close to Cambridge, whereas the other half saw central Boston as a better location. The debate went on for a couple of years, but in the end the men were unable to bridge the real estate gap. So, in the fall of 1921, those in Sigma decided to take a radically different path. They split in two, with the members from Harvard becoming a new chapter, Alpha Eta of Alpha Phi Alpha, while the rest remained in Sigma. By all accounts the separation was amicable, and the two chapters did enjoy very close relations for a number of years.[6]

The now Harvard-less members of Sigma wasted no time following the split to establish their long sought chapter house. Just a semester later, in the spring of 1922, they set up their operations in a brownstone at 558 Massachusetts Avenue in Boston. This structure, though, was no ordinary row house. Built by retired Army captain William Rice Carnes in 1858, the house soon became a stop on the Underground Railroad, with Captain Carnes taking in numerous slaves on their journey to freedom. Then, in 1920, the mansion was sold to the League of Women for Community Service, an organization started by women during the Great War to support black soldiers stationed in the Boston area. Now, in 1922, the women opened their house to the men of Sigma chapter, letting them use a number of rooms for their fraternal activities. One of the first things the men did after moving in was elect a new slate of officers for the upcoming year. Installed as chapter president was William Brown, a dentist and former football star at Tufts College. In William, the men of Sigma had elected a man whose strength went beyond the physical.[7]

WILLIAM WAS BY ALL ACCOUNTS A GIFTED ATHLETE, and this, unfortunately, made him a target on the playing field. In the fall of 1916, he was the starting left tackle for the Tufts football team, even though he'd already earned his dentistry degree (he was doing post graduate work at the time). Starting at left guard was his friend and fellow dentistry student, Edward Morrison. Together these two were the only men of color on an otherwise all-white Tufts team. And while it appears their race was not an issue for the Tufts team or its coach, Dr. Charles Whelan, it was an issue for some of their opponents. One weekend in October that year, the Tufts team travelled to Princeton University for a regularly scheduled game. However, when they arrived at the stadium, the players and fans took one look at the Tufts men and promptly announced they did not want William or Edward anywhere on the field because they were black. Coach Whelan would have nothing of this. A heated argument ensued, but in the end, Tufts was allowed to play both men. Of course, the men on the Princeton team were not happy with this situation, so they went after both William and Edward with the goal of knocking them out of the game, by any means necessary. Edward was hurt so significantly that he "went into convulsions between the halves." As a result, all of Princeton's rage during the second half was directed solely towards William. He was forced to withstand every piece of "filthy and vile language" his opponents threw at him, and these insults got so bad he was forced to complain to the referees. In the end, though, both the words and the game ceased, with Princeton a three-to-zero victor on what was described as a fluke kick.[8]

Just two weeks later, both William and Edward were with the team once again, only this time they were headed to the biggest game Tufts has ever played. The opponent was Indiana University, and the location was Washington Park, a 35,000-seat arena in downtown Indianapolis, by far the largest venue ever to host a Tufts team. However, when the men arrived at the hotel the night before the game, there was a problem. The hotel manager refused to give rooms to William and Edward, again because they were black. Upon hearing this, Coach Whelan became enraged. He demanded, in no uncertain terms, that accommodations for the two men be made, or else "[the entire team] would go back to dear old Massachusetts without playing." The hotel manager soon acquiesced, even setting aside a separate room in the hotel so the team could eat its meals together. The next day, both William and Edward hit the gridiron where, it appears, the screaming fans and the Indiana players were only interested in football, not the race of the players. Both men played the entire game (as they normally did), and when the clock ran down to zero, Tufts had pulled out a twelve-to-ten win over the Hoosiers. And while the treatment of William and Edward both on and off the field was hardly out of the ordinary for the time, the incidents must have been disconcerting for the two men.[9]

THROUGHOUT THE 1920S, Sigma chapter continued to initiate men from the Tufts medical and dental schools in Boston as well as the undergraduate campus in Medford. Among these men were a few standouts in their time, including athletes Claude Randolph Taylor and Ernie Martin. The chapter also played an important role in the local community through the "Go To High School, Go To College" program, a movement for young black men championed by the national Alpha Phi Alpha organization. Despite the strong brotherhood, though, all was not well within Sigma chapter. They were forced to give up their home at 558 Massachusetts Avenue in the early 1930s due to dwindling membership. Then, just a couple of years later, the Alpha Eta chapter at Harvard dissolved, as there just weren't enough African-Americans at the school to support the chapter. Harvard men were therefore eligible once again to join Sigma chapter. Even this change, however, could not keep Sigma afloat. By early 1934, Sigma chapter was also declared inactive by the national organization, in what was a growing trend across the country, due in no small part to upheaval of The Great Depression.[10]

As fate would have it, Sigma's dormancy would be very brief. By December of 1935, the chapter was back in operation, with a renewed focus on recruitment. To that end, Sigma chapter began initiating members from numerous schools far outside the Boston area, including Rhode Island State College (now the University of Rhode Island) and Bates College in Lewiston, Maine. Although having members spread over at least three states did not allow for regular contact between the men, the chapter did have a number of formal gatherings for all such as an annual celebration of the Yale–Harvard football game, often a social highlight of the school year. The advent of World War II did not appear to shut down the chapter, as Sigma continued to pledge and initiate men, albeit in smaller numbers than years prior. Two of the initiates from Tufts during this time were brothers Milton and Vincent Conliffe, both biochemistry majors who went on to medical school after graduating in 1943. Milton, using a bit of foresight, penned a detailed description of Sigma's contribution to the war effort in the fraternity's national magazine, *The Sphinx*. In his article, among various promotions and honors earned by Sigma members in the service, he noted that, "Brother Bernard Robinson [of Sigma chapter]… became the first Negro in New England history to be appointed to a commission in the Navy." Milton and others in Sigma chapter also wrote numerous letters to President Roosevelt and other prominent military leaders calling for not only the independence of India from Britain, but also the integration of all armed forces. Social action continued to be a key aspect of the fraternity's activities, even in wartime.[11]

In the spring of 1952, Sigma chapter welcomed into its fold a graduate student studying systematic theology at Boston University. This particular gentleman had initially pledged Alpha Phi Alpha while an undergraduate at Morehouse College, but he'd graduated before becoming a full member, a process referred to as "crossing the sands." Therefore, when he came to Boston, he joined seven other men in a pledge line of Sigma chapter that spring. He eventually did cross the sands later that year, and though no one at the time could have known his exact future, many sensed his promise as a leader. Within short order, this particular member grew to become the most recognized name in the struggle for civil rights. He was the Reverend Dr. Martin Luther King, Jr., by far the most famous member of Sigma chapter to date. Although it is unknown if any Tufts men were active in Sigma chapter at the same time as Martin, his legacy is undeniable and is still a sense of great pride for all members of the fraternity.[12]

Throughout the 1950s and 1960s, members of Sigma chapter operated much as they had in the past, holding banquets, attending conventions at the national and regional level, and working towards the betterment of their community, especially their fraternity's signature program, "Go To High School, Go To College." Ending segregation in schools was a major effort of the national fraternity during this time, and Sigma chapter was often in the middle of this debate. But by the mid 1970s, interest in Alpha Phi Alpha among men in Boston had dwindled, and by 1976, Sigma chapter was essentially dormant, having gone a year or so without reporting on its activities. Participation in all fraternities across the country was generally falling off at this time, as undergraduates were souring on organized Greek life. However, amidst this turmoil, the national offices of Alpha Phi Alpha sensed an opportunity for growth, this time on the campus of Tufts University. In the spring of 1977, Alpha Phi Alpha pledged and then initiated seven undergraduates from Tufts University, known collectively as "Seven Pharaohs of Faith," and planned for these men to form the basis of a new chapter on the Medford campus. However, after some reflection, the national organization felt their long-term prospects at Tufts were not as good as first imagined, so the abandoned the idea and instead placed the seven men into Sigma chapter, which helped re-vitalize the group.[13]

Men from Tufts would continue to join Sigma chapter throughout the 1970s and 1980s, helping the chapter fulfill its mission of social action, especially with regards to young people. As one member of Sigma chapter wrote, "Young people are the future leaders of this world; for this reason the Brothers [of Sigma chapter] will be venturing into high schools. Our objective will be to express upon the minds of our young brothers and sisters the importance of an education. If we don't help our own, who will?" With renewed enthusiasm, Sigma chapter continued to grow, helped in part by its frequent interactions with two alumni chapters in the area, Epsilon Gamma Lambda and Nu Xi Lambda. This growth soon caught the attention of the national organization, which decided the time was right for a second undergraduate chapter in the Boston area, something not tried since the Alpha Eta chapter at Harvard back in the 1920s. Therefore, on September 26, 1989, the Rho Nu chapter of Alpha Phi Alpha came into existence, with its mission of serving three area schools: Harvard University, Massachusetts Institute of Technology, and Tufts University. Among the eight charter members of Rho Nu chapter was Ethan Che Cole of Tufts.[14]

Since then, both Rho Nu and Sigma chapters continue to operate in the Boston area, and the two frequently hold joint events around both community service and social activities. One area where both chapters have been quite successful is in the area step competitions. For a number of years, the combined team of Rho Nu and Sigma dominated events such as the New England Step Fest and the Northeastern Step Fest.[15]

OMEGA PSI PHI (Gamma chapter, 1916 – 1995, 2007 – present)

In the fall of 1909, three young freshmen – Edgar Love, Oscar Cooper, and Frank Coleman – arrived on the campus of Howard University in Washington, D.C., ready to start their college career. As first-year students are apt to do, these three fast became friends, and as a group it did not take them long to notice the one fraternity on campus, Beta chapter of Alpha Phi Alpha. The three looked upon Alpha Phi Alpha with some interest, but over time they began to feel those in the fraternity were too concerned with superficial qualifiers such as money and social status, so they decided it was not for them. However, they were intrigued by the idea of fraternity, and this interest led them to start their own. The effort took a few semesters to complete, but on November 17, 1911, they were ready. That Friday night, the three gathered with Professor Ernest Everett Just in his office, and taking the initials of their motto "Friendship is essential to the soul" for their name, the four established the Omega Psi Phi fraternity.[16]

Then, of course, the real work began. They had to write their constitution, recruit additional members, and most importantly, gain the approval of the administration. The first two steps were relatively easy, as within a month they had recruited eleven additional members and adopted their constitution, one that defined a mechanism for expansion beyond the Howard campus. But every time they asked for a meeting with the faculty over recognition, they were rebuffed. Two administrators in particular, Dean Kelly Miller and Dean George Cook, did all they could to discourage the group, telling them instead to join Alpha Phi Alpha since the chapter was already established on campus. These two deans, in some sense, had an ulterior motive in this request – they were both members of Alpha Phi Alpha, and probably felt the men would be a good addition to their fraternity. Still, the undergraduates said "no," they wanted to start their own. And still the Deans said they could not.[17]

With the standoff showing no sign of abating, the members of Omega Psi Phi decided to act decisively, if not recklessly. They printed up flyers and cards identifying themselves by name as members of Omega Psi Phi, and then posted these documents on trees around campus for all to see. Out of the shadows they came, a public declaration signifying there was no going back. It did not take long for word of this new fraternity and their stunt to reach the administration. Not surprisingly, the elders of the school were not happy. At chapel that very same day, the president of Howard University, Reverend Wilbur Thirkield chastised the fraternity in front of the students, demanding they meet with him immediately after the service, where many thought he would suspend if not expel the men. But the members of Omega Psi Phi were not worried, for they were all good students, and did not think they would be punished so harshly. As it turned out, they were correct. President Thirkield ordered the men to remove their posters (which they did), and then told them he would grant a hearing with the faculty council, so they could plead their case for recognition.[18]

A few months later, the members of Omega Psi Phi finally found themselves in front of the faculty council, with Dean Miller taking the lead for the administration. And once again Dean Miller voiced his opposition to the establishment of a new fraternity at Howard, especially one that looked to become a national organization. As justification, he remarked there was quite a bit of opposition to fraternities on many college campuses, with schools now feeling such organizations hindered rather than enhanced campus life. But then came the opportunity. "How do we know that this fraternity [Omega Psi Phi] will continue to be the kind of fraternity that you men represent here? You are gentlemen." The compliment was not lost on the men, and in their response they said they hoped to lead by example, keeping in place the high standards they set upon themselves. The faculty, being swayed by the arguments, soon gave their consent for recognition, but with one condition: Omega Psi Phi would have to remain local to Howard University. There would be no expansion to other schools, at least not yet.[19]

For over two years, the members of Omega Psi Phi abided by this condition and worked solely to establish themselves at Howard University. However, the members kept in place their constitutional provisions for expansion, as they anticipated the restriction would eventually be lifted. They did not have to wait long. By early 1914, the faculty had indeed rescinded their condition, so Omega Psi Phi worked quickly to establish its second chapter, Beta, at another historically black school, Lincoln University in Pennsylvania. Then, for its third chapter, Omega Psi Phi looked not to one specific college campus, but to a region. In the fall of 1916, three members from Alpha chapter at Howard and two from Beta chapter at Lincoln converged on Boston, ready to pursue their graduate studies. Among this group of five was Edgar Love, one of the original founders of the fraternity, now studying at the School of Theology at Boston

University. His presence especially brought the men together and helped them formalize plans to establish a chapter in Boston. As in many young national fraternities, the power to grant additional charters did not reside with a centralized committee, but rather with the "mother" chapter, in this case the Alpha at Howard University. Therefore, the men wrote to Alpha chapter concerning their desire for a charter, and after a few rounds of letters, their request was approved. On December 13, 1916, Gamma chapter of Omega Psi Phi was officially established as a regional chapter, open to college men in the greater Boston area.[20]

The chapter got off to a quick and energetic start. Recruitment brought in seven new initiates by the end of that first school year, and even more the following year. Enthusiasm in Gamma was running high, helped in no small part by regular chapter meetings, initiations, and social events such as smokers and banquets. Then, just as quickly, life changed. The Great War was the main culprit, as all throughout 1918, men began answering the call to service in ever-greater number, thus leaving Gamma more and more shorthanded. Those who remained found it increasingly difficult to maintain their fraternal spirit let alone regular contact, a consequence of having members spread over a wide geographical area. To those watching, it appeared Gamma might fold completely. However, due to the efforts of one member in particular, R. George Robinson, Gamma found new life following the armistice. In early 1919, George began sending letters, telegraphs, and even making personal visits to any Omega Psi Phi man he could find, asking him to come to Boston for both school and fraternity. He also went out and secured the one thing he thought Gamma needed the most, and that was a chapter house in the heart of Boston, even though he did not have the men, yet, to fill it. He was "all in" as the saying goes, doing everything he could to set up Gamma for success. And it worked. By the fall of 1919, a number of Omega men had made their way to Harvard, Boston University, and MIT, and they soon rebuilt Gamma with a number of new initiates before 1919 was through. Without a doubt, the chapter house helped tremendously in this regard.[21]

From there, Gamma was able to turn its attention away from merely surviving towards being a positive force for its members. Social events including banquets, dances, and smokers were quite commonplace as the 1920s progressed, but so, too, was the chapter's commitment to helping African-Americans in the local community. Again, the chapter house played a large part in this effort, as the members used their space to host lectures on "Negro History and Literature" in conjunction with the national fraternity's outreach effort. Then, it seems, Gamma chapter turned its eyes towards Tufts College. Clarence Albert Hays holds the distinction of being the first active member of Gamma chapter from Tufts College. Originally initiated into the fraternity's Alpha chapter while an undergraduate at Howard University, Clarence moved to Boston in the early

Installation of officers, Gamma Chapter, Omega Psi Phi Fraternity, January 22, 1927. (Courtesy of Christopher Bennett)

1920s to study medicine, where he affiliated with Gamma chapter. Other Tufts students from the 1920s in Gamma chapter include Henry Joseph Jeffress of the class of 1925. In addition to holding the position Basileus (chapter president) for at least one semester, Henry competed on the track team, worked for the *Tufts Weekly*, participated on the debate team, and even helped run the Student Union. By the spring of 1926, another Tufts student, Cuthbert Phillibert, had also joined Gamma chapter, where he eventually rose to the position of Vice-Basileus. All told, about eleven Tufts men joined Gamma chapter in the 1920s, with many going on to earn medical or dental degrees.[22]

As part of its community outreach in its earlier years, Gamma chapter often recognized outstanding achievement within the local African-American communities in and around Boston. Such was the case in the spring of 1937, when the chapter honored the athletic achievements of Edward "Eddie" Dugger, a senior at Medford High School who showed great promise as a multi-sport athlete. Little did they know the success he would realize. Eddie enrolled at Tufts College the following fall, where he quickly became one of the best-known and best-liked students of his era. On the track team he knew no equal, earning a number of National Collegiate and IC4A (Intercollegiate Association of Amateur Athletes of America) championships in the hurdles. Had it not been for World War II, he may have very well made the Olympic team in the high hurdles, where he certainly would have been a medal contender. Eddie, though, was more than just a great athlete. Academically, he was at the top of his electrical engineering class, earning membership into the prestigious Sword and

Shield and Tower Cross honor societies. As a senior he also won the Bennett Memorial Scholarship in recognition as the best student-athlete at Tufts College. On top of all this, he also found the time not only to join the fraternity that had honored him in high school, but also to become Basileus of Gamma chapter during his senior year. Eddie then graduated Tufts College in 1941 and went on to a long career as an aeronautical engineer at Wright Patterson Air Force Base in Dayton, Ohio, one of the first African-Americans to work in such a field. All told, Edward Dugger personified the four principles of Omega Psi Phi: manhood, scholarship, perseverance, and uplift.[23]

World War Two put a damper on the chapter's activities, but by the fall of 1947, Gamma was up to thirty-five members and ten pledges, including a few men from Tufts College. With renewed enthusiasm, the members of Gamma also set out to re-establish a chapter house in Boston, as they had been without one for a number of years. It appears this effort fell short, however, as Gamma chapter was never able to re-establish a permanent chapter house in Boston despite years of effort. Instead, those in the chapter concentrated on other aspects of fraternal life. Gamma organized numerous civic and social events, especially in conjunction with the Delta Sigma Theta sorority, hosted the annual Grand Conclave for the national organization on occasion, continued to recruit men from local area schools, and participated in local step contests once these events became popular in the 1980s. As such, these activities continued in earnest up through the early 1990s, when a number of Tufts men not only joined Gamma chapter, but also made the Medford campus a second hub of Omega Psi Phi activity. MacPhie Pub and Capen House became host to Gamma chapter social events, and the Tufts members all lived together in an apartment at 245 Boston Avenue, thereby creating a pseudo-chapter house. Life in Gamma chapter seemed to be moving in the right direction.[24]

Until, unfortunately, it did not. By 1995, Gamma chapter was at a crossroads. Membership had fallen off dramatically, such that recruiting, let alone even getting the word out that Gamma chapter existed, became extremely difficult. One by one, it seemed, the various campuses around Boston were left without any active members due to graduation. And as for new members, it seemed students no longer wanted to join Omega Psi Phi. Part of the reason was certainly the negative press the national organization was receiving regarding hazing in some of its chapters (though not Gamma). These unfortunate incidents were fast turning into lawsuits, thereby driving many away on principle. But another, more serious problem was also in play, and that was a general apathy for the BGLO experience by African-American students. Whereas decades earlier their fathers, uncles, and grandfathers had come to Boston and joined Omega Psi Phi to form connections to their community, the men arriving at college in the late 1990s and beyond showed a lack of zeal in following in these footsteps. Opportunities for black students had grown over time such that they didn't necessarily need the fraternity as their relatives once had. As a result, in 1996, the national office of Omega Psi Phi declared Gamma chapter officially dormant, thereby ending nearly eighty years of brotherhood, at least temporarily.[25]

Efforts to revive the chapter took some time, but after about fifteen years of dormancy, local members of Omega Psi Phi were finally able to coalesce as a group and restart Gamma chapter in earnest. Currently, the chapter is small, consisting mainly of men from Harvard and MIT. To date it appears no one from Tufts has joined Gamma chapter since its reactivation. However, the Tufts administration, through the office of Fraternity and Sorority Affairs, is actively looking to have Omega Psi Phi establish a presence on the Tufts campus once again. With any luck, Tufts undergraduate men will help Gamma chapter celebrate its 100th anniversary in 2016.[26]

DELTA SIGMA THETA (Iota chapter, est. 1921; Xi Tau chapter, est. 1980)

In the antebellum days of Greek-letter fraternities, when they were relatively young and malleable, it was not uncommon for members of one organization to resign en masse and either join another, or start their own. The reasons for defection were usually based on ideological grounds, such as a protest against a perceived wrong, or a statement that as a group they could be better. For example, in 1855, six members of the Delta Kappa Epsilon chapter at Miami University in Ohio were asked to support a fellow brother who was seeking a campus leadership position. These six felt their candidate was woefully unqualified for the job, so rather than support him (as they were expected to do, without question), they resigned in protest and went on to organize the Sigma Chi fraternity, one of the largest in the country today. Such drastic practices within fraternities had generally stopped by the end of the 19th century as the national organizations became more established, especially in their governance over individual chapters. But in the early 20th century, history would repeat itself within the newly established black Greek-letter community.[27]

It was the fall of 1912, and the students returning to Howard University stepped onto a campus awash in change. The school had a new president and a new library, a new hospital was under construction, and a new music conservatory was finally moving forward after years of planning. Among the students, there was also renewed enthusiasm for intellectual pursuit as the school worked to broaden its curriculum, especially in the field of education. Outside of the classroom, Washington, D.C., was the scene of fervent political happenings, with the women's suffrage movement gaining in popularity and a presidential election that looked to unseat the incumbent, President William Howard Taft. All told, it was a veritable cauldron of activity that could not help but inspire those looking for something more.[28]

The enthusiasm and energy was certainly not lost on the twenty-two active members of the local Alpha Kappa Alpha (AKA) sorority at Howard, founded just four years earlier. As the members of the sorority took stock of their organization that fall, they felt they were falling behind their original mission. To them, their organization had become more of a local social club than a Greek-letter sorority, as it had yet to incorporate, devise a plan for expansion to other schools (something the younger members felt was vitally important), or even set up a procedure to keep in touch with the chapter's alumnae. Also, many of the newer members felt their name, Alpha Kappa Alpha, was chosen not because of any significant symbolism, but rather as a derivative of the first fraternity at Howard University, Alpha Phi Alpha. So, the women in particular decided to make a change. Within short order, they proposed expanding the activities of the sorority to include social action and political activism. They proposed changing the rituals and symbols of the sorority, ostensibly to refocus the members on a new set of core values. Finally, they proposed changing the sorority's name to Delta Sigma Theta, an action meant to signify their new direction. The women were helped in their efforts by quite a few outside the organization, including two of the founders of the Omega Psi Phi fraternity. Not surprisingly, some of the new proposed symbols and colors were similar to those used by Omega Psi Phi.[29]

With all of the changes ready, the twenty-two women of AKA called a formal meeting to adopt the provisions of the re-organization. Since all in the chapter were for the changes, they did not expect any dissent. However, also present at the meeting was an alumna and past president of the chapter, Nellie Quander, and to put it bluntly, she was "horrified" at what was taking place. So, she let the chapter know her opposition to the plans in no uncertain terms. Then, before leaving the meeting in angered haste, Nellie gave them a deadline to drop their idea and "return to the fold." But the twenty-two women were not swayed. They let the deadline come and go without action, which could only mean one thing: these twenty-two were no longer members of AKA, but rather a brand new organization called Delta Sigma Theta. Then, before the Christmas holiday of 1912, they submitted their application to the administration seeking the right to incorporate, and on January 13, 1913, it was granted, thus marking the official start of the sorority. In a stroke of irony, however, they were not the first sorority at Howard to incorporate. Rather, the alumnae of AKA, knowing full well the plans of Delta Sigma Theta, also sought the right to incorporate, and indeed they were granted a charter by the administration a mere twenty minutes before their rival.[30]

Still, the women of Delta Sigma Theta faced the same problem at Howard as the Omega Psi Phi fraternity – the faculty would not allow them to expand to other schools, despite their desire to do so. But this proved to be just a minor obstacle, and in early 1914, Delta Sigma Theta established their second chap-

Delta Sigma Theta member Mae Tyson Wright (third from right) on the steps of Eaton Hall with some classmates, November, 1923. She was likely the first woman of color to join a Greek-letter organization at Tufts.

ter, Beta, at Wilberforce University, a historically black school in Ohio. Other chapters soon followed, especially in Ohio and New York, and then the sorority turned to New England. On December 29, 1921, Iota chapter of Delta Sigma Theta was chartered as a citywide organization in Boston for students at area schools including Boston University, Northeastern, Boston College, Radcliffe, Wellesley, Tufts, and even schools farther away such as Mount Holyoke and Smith College. Iota chapter, though, wasn't just for undergraduates, but rather was a mixed chapter, open to graduate members of Delta Sigma Theta as well.[31]

Iota chapter's first member from Tufts College was most likely Mae Tyson Wright. Mae entered Tufts College in the fall of 1923 as a young sixteen-year old from Baltimore, Maryland, but her age was not much of a barrier, for all she did at Tufts was excel. She moved into Richardson Hall, became a history major, and even joined the basketball and tennis teams. By all accounts, she also fit in well with her schoolmates, but undoubtedly life must have been difficult for her as the only woman of color on campus. Ostensibly for this reason, at some point during her undergraduate days, she joined Iota chapter of Delta Sigma Theta. One of the activities she undoubtedly helped plan with her sorority was a new musical variety show called "Jabberwock," which hit the stage for the first time in 1925. This show eventually became a yearly event that raised money in support of educational scholarships in the Boston area as well as other public service projects. The program was a major success each year, and was eventually adopted by the national organization as their annual signature event.[32]

Mae graduated from Tufts in 1927 with a degree in history (cum laude) and was also elected to Phi Beta Kappa. Afterwards, she went on to a forty-one year career as a teacher of English and Latin in the Baltimore School system. Her sorority, though, was never far from her mind. She became quite active in the Baltimore Alumnae chapter for many years, and was also the national president of Delta Sigma Theta from 1944 through 1947. Mae Wright, therefore, joins but a handful of Tufts alumni who've gone on to preside over their respective national organization for a time.[33]

Iota chapter continued to initiate women from Tufts up until 1980, when a second chapter for undergraduates was established in the area. Known as the Xi Tau chapter, their charter covers the campuses of Babson College, Bentley University, Brandeis University, Harvard University, Lesley University, MIT, Wellesley College, and Tufts University. Both Iota and Xi Tau chapters are still active today in the Boston area, and indeed as recently as 2015, Xi Tau chapter had one undergraduate woman from Tufts on its active membership roll.[34]

ALPHA KAPPA ALPHA (Epsilon chapter, est. 1924)

Sometimes, it's the relationship between teacher and student that can lead to something more than just the transfer of knowledge. In the fall of 1904, Ethel Hedgeman, a bright student from St. Louis, Missouri, headed east to start her college career at Howard University. Health problems interrupted her studies early on, but she was eventually able to recover and return to school where she excelled both in and out of the classroom. At some point during her education, Ethel's course of study led her to Professor Ethel Robinson of the English department. Professor Robinson was not much older than her students, as she had only recently graduated from Brown University, but she had the spark that inspired. Ethel in particular took to this enthusiasm whole-heartedly. Professor Robinson thus became her mentor, and while their discussions must certainly have centered on the study of English, there also spoke frequently on sorority life. Neither was intimately familiar with such organizations, but Professor Robinson knew about sorority life in general, having witnessed two in action while at Brown University. Apparently Professor Robinson liked what she'd seen of sororities, for soon enough she was encouraging Ethel to start her own. And soon enough, Ethel was.[35]

Ethel worked on her plans in earnest during the summer of 1907, and when she returned to campus in the fall, she was ready to act. All she needed were some other women to join her. Here, Ethel faced a formidable challenge, for she was breaking new ground. In 1907, there were no sororities for African-American women anywhere in the country, so she was selling a concept rather than a known entity, and this must have been difficult on some levels. However, by focusing on her ultimate goal of creating an organization based on mutual support and encouragement of its members, she found eight other women in the junior and senior classes interested in making the journey with her. As it turned out, another group at Howard University was making a similar journey. That very semester, the year-old Alpha Phi Alpha fraternity from Cornell University was courting a group of men at Howard to become the organization's second, or Beta chapter. Among those joining in this endeavor was George Lyle, who was both a classmate and good friend of Ethel. Such connection helped Ethel and the rest of the women as they worked to start their organization. Then, on January 15, 1908, the group of nine women officially declared their intention to form a sorority, which they named Alpha Kappa Alpha (AKA). They still had quite a bit of work to do, from writing a constitution to defining their symbols, but within a few weeks they had accomplished this and, most importantly, obtained recognition from the faculty as an official organization at Howard University. The first sorority for women of color had just been born.[36]

At the core of AKA, though, were some serious issues that would play out over the next few years. For one, the sorority was missing some key elements found in nearly all Greek-letter organizations. In the beginning there was no ritual, creed, or oath of membership. The group, though recognized as a student organization at Howard, was not incorporated and had no means for defining expansion. There was also little in the way of exclusivity, as the only criteria for membership was the completion of at least three semesters of school and a cumulative grade point average of C+ or better. Nearly all of the women at Howard joined AKA once eligible, and while the group as a whole did fill a social need, the organization seemed adrift in its mission, especially after the original founders graduated. The situation came to a head in the fall of 1912, when all of the active undergraduate members decided to morph AKA into a different, if not wholly new organization. The women were interested not only incorporating the sorority as a legal entity ready for expansion, but also in changing the name and symbols. Many felt "Alpha Kappa Alpha" was too similar in name to the Alpha Phi Alpha fraternity, so they wanted a new identity. By 1913, this transformation was complete, as the women had formed a brand new sorority called Delta Sigma Theta. To those on the campus of Howard University, it seemed as if AKA would be no more.[37]

But of course, the end was not to be. Although the undergraduate members had all resigned, the alumnae of AKA were not as ready to give up their sorority. Instead, under the guidance of one alumna in particular, Nellie Quander, AKA not only reformed, but also incorporated, a move that would allow them to expand to other campuses and become a national organization. As fate would have it, AKA's petition to the faculty for a charter as a corporation was approved about twenty minutes before Delta Sigma Theta's petition, thus making Alpha Kappa Alpha the first chartered sorority at Howard University. Recognition of both groups did not immediately give them the right to expand beyond Howard, but within a few years both had established chapters at various colleges and universities. For AKA, that expansion first went west, to the universities of Chicago, Illinois, Kansas, and California-Berkeley, among other schools.[38]

Then, AKA came to Boston. On May 3, 1924, the sorority established its Epsilon chapter with seven charter members. With the founders studying at different schools, Epsilon became a citywide organization and included all surrounding institutions, even those not in Massachusetts. Indeed, Epsilon chapter's second round of initiates came from schools including Emerson College, Portia Law School (now the New England School of Law), Simmons College, and Rhode Island College of Education. From its beginning, Epsilon chapter was quite active socially, as the women hosted beach trips in the summer, dances in the fall, card parties in the spring, and tea parties near the end of each school year. Epsilon also hosted community events such as "Negro History Day," and worked with the newly established AKA graduate chapter, Psi Omega, to raise scholarship money for area students. As for Tufts College, Epsilon's first initiate appears to have been Mary Crutchfield, a student in the pre-dental program who joined the chapter circa 1927. After completing the one-year preparatory program, Mary matriculated to the Tufts Dental School and eventually became the second African-American woman to graduate from the program. As it turned out, the first African-American woman to graduate from the dental school, Dr. Jessie Garnett, also became a member of AKA, albeit a few years after Mary, and through the Psi Omega graduate chapter. Nonetheless, such is the early legacy of Alpha Kappa Alpha in Boston, with both women enjoying successful and pioneering careers as dentists in the Boston area.[39]

As the 1930s progressed, Epsilon continued to maintain a regular social calendar, often times planning joint events with Psi Omega chapter as well as other BGLOs in the Boston area. Their mission of community service appears to have been a secondary concern, though they did award annual scholarships and utilized some of their social events to raise money for various community causes. By 1933, the chapter had established a regular meeting place at 464 Massachusetts Avenue in Boston, home to the Women's Service Club of Boston, an organization dedicated to servicing the African-American community. This row house became the headquarters of Epsilon for many years, though it is unclear if any members lived in this house or just utilized space for meetings and events. In 1939, the chapter was honored to host AKA's twenty-second annual national convention, or Boule as it is called within the organization. Epsilon chapter also hosted a regional conference a few years later. It wasn't until after World War II started, though, until those in Epsilon began to focus more on service and less on social activities. For example, both Epsilon and Psi Omega chapters, as a group, began lobbying the Massachusetts state government in 1945 to establish a Fair Employment Practices Committee, a cause they worked on for a couple of years. The two chapters also took up other causes such as education, youth initiatives, and cross-cultural programs, where they put on a series of lectures with leaders of ethnic communities to examine their roles as minorities in post-war America. Social events were still held with regularity, but when it came to describing their activities via the sorority's national magazine, *The Ivy Leaf*, Epsilon chapter had clearly changed their message.[40]

Still, Epsilon chapter had little presence on the campus of Tufts College and then Tufts University during its first fifty years or so. One major reason was certainly the dearth of African-American women at Tufts during this time. Prior to World War II, for example, only four black women graduated from Tufts College, a number that only rose by twenty more in the twenty years after the war. But something else kept women away from AKA post conflict. In the late 1950s and early 1960s, some African-American women who enrolled at Tufts and wanted to join a sorority turned not to AKA or any other historically black organization based in Boston, but instead to the two local (and predominantly white) sororities on the Medford campus, Thalia and Alethea. A similar phenomenon was also happening within the previously all-white fraternities on campus, as a number of black males began joining some of those organizations, most notably Phi Epsilon Pi. This new reality where both white and black students could, indeed, coexist within a fraternal organization was certainly due to the burgeoning civil rights movement, and at Tufts, many embraced this change. Epsilon chapter continued on during this time, but it appears it was no longer a destination for the few African-American women enrolled at Tufts.[41]

Then, of course, came 1970, which saw the shut down of all sororities on the Tufts campus. These organizations eventually returned six years later, but at least for African-American women, who were now coming to Tufts in larger number, they were no longer appealing. Instead, these women turned once again towards the historically black sororities and their city-wide chapters in Boston. The reasons for this shift were many, but the strongest was family. These women had mothers and fathers who'd joined historically BGLOs when they were undergraduates, and these parents were now encouraging their daughters to do the same. At no time did this manifest more at Tufts than in the spring of 1981. That semester, seven African-American women on the Medford campus pledged Epsilon chapter. Known collectively as "Ivy Divine," many of the seven originally came to AKA because of connections to family and friends, though they were also drawn to Epsilon's record of public service that had continued unabated for decades. But not all was work, for they also managed to have fun through regular social activities, hosted either on the Tufts campus, or at the other campuses represented in the chapter such as Northeastern and Harvard. Collectively the seven Tufts women were initiated into Alpha Kappa Alpha in May of 1981. Then, they did something no BGLO had ever done before at Tufts. They placed a composite photograph in the 1981 edition of the *Jumbo* yearbook. A small act, but significant nonetheless, for it showed AKA was part of the Tufts community. A year later, Epsilon chapter counted fifteen Tufts women on its active roll, and once again placed a composite photograph in the yearbook, right alongside the other Greek-letter organizations.[42]

From there, membership in Epsilon chapter by Tufts women has waxed and waned over the years. However, when Tufts women have been active in the chapter, they tend to make history. In 1990, for example, Epsilon chapter (which included some Tufts women) teamed up with the Delta chapter of Alpha Omicron Pi on the Medford campus to promote recycling. This event was likely the very first time where a traditionally black and a traditionally white sorority at Tufts came together for a service project. As of 2016, there is currently one undergraduate member from Tufts in Epsilon chapter, though AKA in general is still very active in the Boston area.[43]

KAPPA ALPHA PSI (Chi chapter, est. 1924; Theta Iota chapter, 1975 – 2010)

Indiana University, in the early 1900s, was not exactly a school that welcomed African-American men to its campus with open arms. They may have been allowed to enroll, but once on campus they were summarily ostracized by the white students and ignored by the administration. They were also subject to discriminatory rules that were normal for the day, but harsh nonetheless. For example, African-American men could not live in the dormitories with the white students, nor could they participate in any contact sport such as football. Just about all the men could do outside of the classroom, in terms of an organized activity, was join the track and field team. However, there was one place on campus where black men were not only tolerated but welcomed, and that was in the various fraternity houses. Of course, these men were not welcomed as members or equals by any stretch of the imagination – they were, after all, barred from membership due to their race through the written and unwritten rules of each fraternity. Instead, the men entered the various fraternity houses each day as waiters, hired to serve meals to the all-white chapters.[44]

In the fall of 1910, a group of ten African-American men enrolled at Indiana University where, like many who had come before them, they were expected to fail as students. However, these men were interested in succeeding, not failing, and during the first few weeks they realized that if they came together as a group to support and encourage one another, they could prevail. To accomplish this, they simply looked inside the various fraternity houses where they worked. Each day they witnessed groups of men coming together in camaraderie and mutual support, something they as a group desperately sought. Almost naturally, then, the men decided to start their own fraternity. As for a name, they would be Alpha Omega, at least until a more meaningful moniker could be chosen. Then, on January 5, 1911, the ten men declared the official start of their organization, and by the end of the semester had settled on a new name, Kappa Alpha Nu. These three Greek letters were probably chosen in deference to an earlier organization for African-American men at Indiana University called Alpha Kappa Nu, which had a brief existence some eight years prior. But Kappa Alpha Nu was a completely new organization. In terms of its mission, the fraternity was committed to upholding Christian ideals while also encouraging achievement among its members. Incorporation came a few months later, and as a statement against the racism and prejudice the men knew on a daily basis, the men did not establish any official membership restrictions based on race, creed, or nationality.[45]

Kappa Alpha Nu's public unveiling came a few months later. In May of 1911, the chapter held their first "house party," a three-day social event which drew not only other black students at Indiana, but also members of the African-American community from nearby states, including a number of prospective students. Overall the event was a great success and provided the young fraternity with their first publicity in the school's newspaper, *The Indiana Daily Student*. Such parties became an annual tradition, as the event continued to draw attendees from neighboring communities and beyond. Most importantly, these parties offered hope to African-American men who wanted to attend Indiana University, hope that they would not be alone once they came to campus. And so they did come, in small groups at first, but enough to keep Kappa Alpha Nu active. In 1913, the fraternity became a national organization when they established their Beta chapter at the University of Illinois in Urbana-Champaign, and their Gamma chapter at the University of Iowa a year later. However, it was during 1914 when some members of the Alpha chapter at Indiana ran into a slight problem with the fraternity's name, one that could not be ignored.

"He certainly presents a pretty picture skimming those hurdles," said one white Indiana University student to another while watching Frank Summers, a member of Kappa Alpha Nu, compete on the outdoor track. "He is good fraternity material."

"He is a member of Kappa Alpha Nig," replied another student.

Unbeknownst to the two white students, other members of Kappa Alpha Nu were within earshot, including Elder W. Diggs, one of the founders of the fraternity. "The Fraternity is Kappa Alpha Nu," Elder replied to the two men, making it clear he would not have his fraternity mocked.[46]

But the Summers incident, as it came to be known, caused the members of the fraternity to reflect upon their name during their national meeting later that year. After much discussion, they decided to drop the last letter of their name in favor of another Greek letter. Then, on April 15, 1915, the change became official. The name of the fraternity was now Kappa Alpha Psi.[47]

Over the next nine years, Kappa Alpha Psi expanded at a steady pace across the Midwest, entering both historically black schools such as Wilberforce University and predominantly white schools such as the University of Chicago. World War I put a damper on Kappa Alpha Psi's activities, but following the war the fraternity re-doubled their efforts to establish new chapters. Much of this growth was due to members moving about the country, where they set up both graduate and undergraduate chapters. Such was the case in 1921 when two Kappa Alpha Psi men came to Boston to further their education. For the next three years they dreamed of starting a chapter in Boston, but were unable to gather enough of the right men until early 1924, when they had recruited five others. They petitioned the national organization for a charter on February 15, 1924, and after a mere 10-hour wait, their petition was accepted. Chi chapter of Kappa Alpha Psi was now officially open in Boston as a citywide fraternity serving a number of area campuses. Among the charter members of Chi chapter was J. Logan Jenkins, a former student at Tufts College who had spent the previous school year in the Pre-Medical/Pre-Dental program.[48]

After gaining their charter, Chi chapter immediately worked on forming its first pledge line. One of the first men they found was Clifford Crawford, a sophomore pursuing a Bachelor of Science degree on the Medford campus of Tufts College, and he was initiated before school ended for the year. Then, in the spring of 1925, Chi chapter organized its second pledge line, which included a young man not currently studying at Tufts College, but would soon do so. He would also become, in many regards, the most famous member of the chapter to date. His name was Jester Hairston, and his educational odyssey was something else.[49]

JESTIE HAIRSTON WAS THE GRANDSON OF A SLAVE, born in North Carolina but raised near Pittsburgh, Pennsylvania, where many in his family worked the steel mills. Jestie, though, seemed destined for a different life, even from an early age. As a student in the first grade, his antics resulted in laughter so often that he earned the nickname "Jester" from his teacher, a name he soon took for his own, years before he understood its true meaning. In the fall of 1920, Jester headed to Massachusetts Agricultural College (or MAC, now The University of Massachusetts at Amherst) with fifty dollars to his name, ready to study landscape architecture. He jumped right in to college life, even becoming the quarterback of freshman football team and singing with various choral groups including the glee club. However, his money ran out after just one year, so he worked on the docks of Boston until he could earn enough to support a second year at MAC. It was during this time in Boston when Jester joined Chi chapter of Kappa Alpha Psi. He remained a dock worker for a number of years, and then in the fall of 1926, he returned to MAC for his sophomore year. And while he gave up playing football, he did join the glee club once again.[50]

Of course money was still an issue for Jester, so after returning to campus he also became a freelance singer-for-hire in local churches. It was through these weekend gigs where he befriended Anna Laura Kidder, a local teacher and musician who often accompanied him on the piano. Immediately recognizing his talent as a performer, she encouraged him to give up his study of landscape architecture and instead pursue music at a first rate school in Boston. Money, or lack thereof, was still a major concern for Jester, and he didn't think he could afford such a change in school. Money, however, was not a major concern for

Kappa Alpha Psi member Jester Hairston (far right) poses with his singing group The Shenley Four, February 10, 1929.

Ms. Kidder. She offered to pay for his schooling, so long as he pursued music. It was an offer Jester could not refuse. So, he applied to Tufts College, which was well known for its music program under Professor Leo Lewis, and waited for word back. He felt so confident he'd be accepted that he even dropped out of MAC. Of course, this turned out to be a mistake. "The junior class is closed," said the letter from Tufts. Jester's application had been denied.[51]

Embarrassed and now rudderless, Jester decided to forgo a return to MAC and instead head off to work once again, this time for a shipping company that transported goods between Boston and New York City. During one of his trips between the two cities, he met Claude Randolph Taylor, an African-American man about his age who just happened to be a graduate of Tufts. Claude was not surprised to hear of Jester's rejection, for he'd heard numerous stories within the African-American community of Tufts only accepting black men for a compelling reason, such as prowess on the athletic field (which had been Claude's gift). So, he encouraged Jester to try again by making a personal appeal to Professor Lewis. "Write a letter," Claude said, "and lay it on thick." Jester did just that.

> Dear Professor Lewis – For years I have been reading every article in the press about the wonderful work you are doing with young people at Tufts College. It would mean a great deal to me if I could meet with you so that I could write to my mother in Pennsylvania and tell her I had at last seen the great Professor Lewis and heard about his wonderful work in person.[52]

It worked. Professor Lewis granted Jester an interview during the summer of 1927. One day, then, Jester arrived at Professor Lewis's house on campus, greeted the professor on his porch, and simply started to sing. He was accepted on the spot. Jester enrolled the following fall and spent the next two years at Tufts, where he excelled in the classroom and on the stage. He graduated cum laude in the spring 1929, and then went on to a long and storied career as a singer, song arranger, and actor. He is best known for his work as Leroy and Henry Van Porter in *Amos and Andy*, and as Deacon Rolly Forbes in the television show *Amen*.[53]

AS THE YEARS MOVED FORWARD, Chi chapter gained a steady number of initiates on a regular basis, including some men from Tufts every now and again. The chapter competed in athletic competitions against other fraternities and local clubs, sponsored lectures by influential leaders as part of their national "Guide Right" youth development program for high school and college students, and held social events with other area BGLOs. By the mid-1970s, though, Chi chapter had reached a crossroads with their mission. That year, a group of nine MIT students looked to bring a new chapter of Kappa Alpha Psi to their campus, one that could more readily serve the black community in Cambridge and beyond. As a result, on October 11, 1975, Theta Iota chapter of Kappa Alpha Psi was chartered at MIT, and then expanded to include other area schools such as Tufts, Harvard, and the University of Massachusetts at Amherst.[54]

Theta Iota chapter initiated a number of Tufts men in the years after its founding, especially in the early 1980s. Indeed, it was in the spring of 1985 when the chapter, at twenty-five members strong including five from Tufts, attempted something no BGLO has ever done, and that was occupy a chapter house on the Medford campus. Early that semester, the Tufts administration announced the former Fay house at 92 Professors Row would be made available for occupancy by a Greek-letter organization the next school year. All interested fraternities and sororities on campus were invited to apply for the right to call this house their home. Theta Iota chapter of Kappa Alpha Psi was one of six organizations to apply, all of which were then evaluated by student-run Interfraternity Council against a set criteria, including number of years in existence, community involvement, and reason for wanting the space. When the evaluations were completed, Kappa Alpha Psi was ranked second behind Psi Upsilon. This was not the ideal position, obviously, but there was still a chance they'd be awarded the house. Then, a few weeks later, the Tufts administration unexpectedly cancelled the whole plan, saying they needed another year to sort out some of the finer details such as a lodging license. This delay, coupled with the graduation of a few of the Tufts members, led Theta Iota to abandon their plan for a chapter house on campus.[55]

Theta Iota continued in earnest for a number of years, but by 2010 the chapter was declared inactive, with students from Tufts eligible to join Chi chapter once again.[56]

ZETA PHI BETA (Theta Alpha chapter, est. 1933)
PHI BETA SIGMA (Beta Alpha chapter, est. 1935)

Among the world of Greek-letter organizations, a few sororities share a special bond with a particular fraternity, forged at the time the sorority was first established. For example, in 1893, members of the Sigma Nu fraternity at Lombard College were instrumental in helping the women of Alpha Xi Delta organize their sorority. These two organizations are thus forever linked though this connection, as are the Phi Delta Theta fraternity and Delta Gamma sorority, and the Kappa Sigma fraternity and Chi Omega sorority, for similar reasons. But aside from a historical curiosity (and an honorary member or two), these three pairs of organizations do not share any official connection. They are each their own, with unique aims and goals. Such is not the case between the Phi Beta Sigma Fraternity, Inc., and the Zeta Phi Beta Sorority, Inc. Their bond goes deeper than just the help some Phi Beta Sigma members gave to the founders of Zeta Phi Beta. Instead, these two organizations are officially joined to each other through their constitutions, the very documents that are the heart and soul of Greek-letter organizations. Dedicated to supporting each other in their respective missions, Phi Beta Sigma and Zeta Phi Beta are the only Greek-letter entities to date that have such a close and official relationship. They are, in essence, two halves of a whole.[57]

Of the two organizations, it was Phi Beta Sigma that came first. During the summer of 1910, a recent high school graduate named A. Langston Taylor found himself working in Memphis, Tennessee. In a few short months he would head east to Howard University, in Washington, D.C., to begin his collegiate studies. But for the time being, he was a working man. One "dull summer day," as Langston described, he walked into the Bumper Beale Grocery Store on his way home, looking to catch up on the latest news. Such was the way one learned the important gossip a century ago, when communication was much more personal, if not simpler. As luck would have it, Langston just happened to meet an alumnus of Howard inside the store that day. The two struck up a conversation, with the alumnus sharing all sorts of information about his beloved alma mater. One topic in particular, though, really caught Langston's attention. "He dwelt at length on the activities of Greek letter fraternities," Langston recalled. "His talk gave me an idea." That day, and in that store, Langston decided he would start a new fraternity at Howard University.[58]

Langston arrived on campus later in the fall of 1910 ready to put his idea into action. But while he had the drive and desire to create his new fraternity, he had no realistic idea of how to proceed. For that, Langston decided to watch, learn, and take his time. His efforts took three years, but in the fall of 1913, he was finally ready. All he needed were others to join his cause. He first approached a former roommate, Leonard Moore, where he confided in his plans to start a new fraternity. Leonard signed on, and together the two men invited a mutual friend, Charles Brown, to join their group. The three then spent the rest of the semester formalizing their plans while also gathering nine other men as their initial members. Then, on January 9, 1914, the group of twelve met at a local YMCA, and after some discussion, voted to become the Phi Beta Sigma Fraternity. Langston's vision, over three years in the making, had finally been realized. Recognition by the faculty of Howard University came a few months later, and in 1915, the fraternity had established its second, or Beta chapter, at Wiley College in Marshall, Texas, thus turning Phi Beta Sigma a national organization. From there, the fraternity began making plans for rapid expansion elsewhere in the East and the South. A few months later, however, representatives of the Kappa Alpha Psi fraternity approached the leaders of Phi Beta Sigma with an offer to merge the two young organizations, since they were operating primarily in different parts of the country. Discussion inside Phi Beta Sigma lasted about a week, but then the offer was refused. Phi Beta Sigma would remain its own growing force within the black Greek community.[59]

World War I put a damper on Phi Beta Sigma's operations, but the fraternity recovered very quickly after the conflict and began expanding once again. Then, in 1919, the fraternity had another idea. At Phi Beta Sigma's national meeting that year, delegates voted to help expand the reach of black sororities. They were motivated in part by the changes taking place in American society, from the rise of anti-immigration feelings, to the call for Prohibition, to the push for women's suffrage. The situation was ripe, they felt, for another organization that could give more young black women a chance to grow and thrive. So, the fraternity appointed Langston and a new initiate, Charles Taylor, to investigate the idea. The two men quickly coalesced around the idea of creating a sister organization to Phi Beta Sigma, one that shared a similar set of goals and idealism, but just for women. All they needed were some women willing to join the effort. Luckily, Charles knew the perfect candidate: Arizona Leedonia Cleaver, a fellow classmate at Howard University. "She had character and gifts," Charles described of her. "She had a beautiful spirit and intellectual effectiveness. She had appeal in her personality and in her words." All he needed for the plan to succeed, he knew, was for her to join on.[60]

She did. Arizona got right to work, and soon found fourteen other women willing to build a brand new organization. Langston and Charles then worked with these women during the fall of 1919 to help plan their sorority and write their constitution, which they based on Phi Beta Sigma's governing document. The work took a few months, but on January 16, 1920, the group of fifteen came together as the Zeta Phi Beta sorority at Howard University. Then, in the years that followed, both Phi Beta Sigma and Zeta Phi Beta saw rapid growth in chapters and membership. As for Boston, the two came to the area in the 1930s. Zeta Phi Beta was first, establishing its Theta Alpha chapter as a city-wide organization in 1933. Phi Beta Sigma came two years later, establishing its Beta Alpha chapter in 1935, also as a city-wide organization.[61]

In terms of a presence on the Tufts campus, though, it appears that both Phi Beta Sigma and Zeta Phi Beta have had a very limited reach since their establishment in the early 1930s. It is unclear when either organization gained its first initiate from Tufts, but both have had students from the Medford campus on their active rolls, especially in the late 1990s. Phi Beta Sigma first appears in print in 1992, when the fraternity co-sponsored a lecture on campus with Dr. Betty Shabazz, the widow of civil rights leader Malcolm X. In 1997, though, Phi Beta Sigma made history at Tufts. One night that fall, Beta Alpha chapter co-sponsored a campus-wide, alcohol-free "Men In Black" themed dance with the Zeta Psi fraternity in the MacPhie/Dewick Dining Hall. Although historically black fraternities have operated at Tufts since 1916, and historically white fraternities since 1855, this dance was one of the first instances where the two groups came together for a formal social activity.[62]

SIGMA GAMMA RHO (Kappa Nu chapter, est. 1984)

When people hear of the Ku Klux Klan, nearly all think of the infamous society of hatred associated with its name. But at its beginning, the Ku Klux Klan was something much less ominous. Started by a group of Confederate veterans from Tennessee following the Civil War, the Ku Klux Klan was intended to be a secret social club, based heavily on a defunct college fraternity called Kuklos Adelphon. The group then morphed into a racially tinged terrorist organization, before fading into relative obscurity the 1880s. It wasn't until three decades later when the Klan was reborn into its modern embodiment of intolerance. One place where the Ku Klux Klan grew especially strong during this time was the state of Indiana. By the early 1920s, the Indiana Klan stood at nearly 300,000 members, nearly one-third of all white males in the state, thus giving rise to the nickname "Klandiana." The Klan's presence and influence were not hard to miss, especially on the campus of Butler College (now Butler University) in the state's largest city of Indianapolis. At least one trustee of the school was an ardent supporter of the Klan, and the area around the campus was so Klan friendly that its leader, known as the Grand Dragon, moved into a house right next door to the college by the mid 1920s.[63]

Such was the atmosphere at Butler surrounding seven African-American women studying to become teachers. Butler College had been open to black students since its founding seventy years earlier, but to say these students were overly welcomed throughout that time would be false. So, in November of 1922, and in the face of such outward prejudice and bigotry, these seven women came together to form the Sigma Gamma Rho sorority. Originally intended as a professional organization for African-American women studying education, Sigma Gamma Rho offered its members a level of support and encouragement not afforded anywhere else on the Butler campus, and not surprisingly, the organization thrived from the start. Then, it became even stronger. By 1925, the sorority had expanded their mission to include activism and service to the greater African-American community. The sorority also opened up membership to all majors, not just teachers. Then, in 1929, the group changed again, this time into a national, incorporated collegiate sorority, and declared their chapter at Butler as the Alpha of Sigma Gamma Rho. National expansion then began in earnest, and by 1940, the sorority could be found in thirteen states with sixteen undergraduate and four alumnae chapters.[64]

As for the Boston area, Sigma Gamma Rho would arrive many years later, when they established their Kappa Nu chapter at Northeastern University in the spring of 1984. Although originally intended solely for Northeastern students, Kappa Nu officially became a citywide chapter in 1998, thus opening membership to women of many area schools including Tufts University. However, based on information published in a few editions of the *Jumbo* yearbook, it appears only a small number of women from Tufts have joined Kappa Nu chapter since its expansion, and none in the last decade.[65]

LAMBDA UPSILON LAMBDA (La Unidad Latina, Nu chapter, est. 1994)

With over 4,000 active members in 60 fraternity and sorority chapters, Cornell University in Ithaca, New York, has one of the largest Greek-letter communities in the country, one that started shortly after the school opened in 1868. The community is also very diverse, as it includes many traditional social fraternities and sororities, along with historically black, Latino/a, Asian-American, and multicultural organizations. But this has not always been the case. During the summer of 1981, for example, a group of Latino students began talking about the idea of joining a fraternity. At the time, Latino men at Cornell had only two choices if they wanted to pursue this idea: they could either join a historically white organization, or a historically black organization. Such reality was not very appealing to this particular group of men, though the idea of fraternity was. As a result, they began discussing the avenues available to celebrate brotherhood and camaraderie within their Latino heritage, while also inspiring them to be better men. There were some organizations on campus at the time dedicated to serving the Latino community, but these men felt they needed something stronger. So, as the summer of 1981 went on, the men talked more about starting the perfect embodiment of their idea, a Latino fraternity.[66]

At the time, there were only a handful of Latino-centered fraternities scattered around the country, and no sustained communication between them.

Thus, the group at Cornell was essentially alone in their pursuit. They started by first forming an official club at Cornell, which they called La Unidad Latina. Under the auspices of this club, the men then gathered a core group of about thirty members through the fall of 1981, and together they looked to support each other, especially scholastically. Indeed, one of the main activities of the club was going to the library en masse to study. But during this time they also began transforming their club into a full-fledged fraternity. Their work in this regard was not without its challenges, and by the spring semester of 1982, only thirteen of the original thirty remained. The men who stayed, though, were up to the challenge. On February 19, 1982, the thirteen took their oath and became brothers, or Hermanos, in the La Unidad Latina, Lambda Upsilon Lambda Fraternity, Inc. (LUL). They were the fourth Latino fraternity to be organized in the United States since 1931, and the first to start on the campus of an Ivy League school.[67]

Four years later, LUL became a national organization when they opened their Beta chapter at the State University of New York at Binghamton. From there, LUL expanded to numerous schools in New York, New Jersey, Connecticut, and Rhode Island. Then, LUL came to Boston. In 1993, two Hermanos from different chapters, including one studying at the Fletcher School of Law and Diplomacy at Tufts, kept crossing paths around Boston as they searched for community. Together they found a group of like-minded Latino men studying at Harvard University, and sensing an opportunity, worked with these men to bring a chapter of LUL to the Boston area. By 1994, they had succeeded with the chartering of Nu chapter to serve the campuses of Harvard, Tufts, MIT, and Boston College.[68]

Nu chapter first came to Tufts University during or just before the 1997–98 school year. Similar to most of the citywide BGLO and multicultural chapters, LUL does not generally practice outward and open recruitment via a traditional a rush week. Instead, Nu chapter has held informational sessions on local campuses every so often to let the Latino community know of their existence. Then, they let the men come and engage them. Otherwise, Nu chapter has been very active within the Latino community in the Boston areas as well as the hometowns of the members. A signature effort of the chapter has been getting young Latinos to strive towards higher education. The members of Nu chapter recognize their fraternity should represent a pillar of success in their community, so they take their mission to heart and make it the focus of the chapter. As a result, service events have far outnumbered social events in the history of Nu chapter.[69]

Although Nu chapter currently has no Tufts undergraduate on the membership roll, numerous Jumbo alumni are still quite active in the organization. In total, approximately ten men from Tufts have joined Nu chapter since its founding.[70]

ALPHA RHO LAMBDA (Alianza de Raices Latinas, Beta chapter, est. 1996)

Since the founding of Phi Beta Kappa in 1776, all-male fraternities have been established in far greater number than all-female sororities, in all categories except one. The lone exception is the culturally based, all-female Latina sororities, which currently outnumber their all-male Latino counterparts by nearly two to one. During the 1990s in particular, Latina sororities exploded onto the national scene, with sixteen new organizations coming into existence compared to only two Latino fraternities. One of these sororities was Alpha Rho Lambda, Inc., otherwise known as Alianza de Raices Latinas. Founded on March 22, 1993, by ten Latina women at Yale University, Alpha Rho Lambda became their vehicle for sisterhood and service to the Latino community in and around New Haven, Connecticut. The sorority remained local to Yale for just over two years, until a second group came calling from a very familiar location.[71]

The fall of 1995 was particularly trying for six undergraduate Latina women at Tufts. They had come together as friends, but they longed for something more. Ideally, they were looking for an organization that would support them and their heritage on a campus with relatively few Hispanics. At first they turned to existing Tufts organizations such as the Latino Center, but soon felt these groups could not meet their needs as a small cadre of women. So, they began looking outside for a new organization they could bring to campus, one that could bring them closer as friends while also allowing them to express their culture as Latinas. The women also viewed service to their community and a dedication to scholarship as vitally important, so they wanted their new organization to focus on these issues and transcend normal campus boundaries. Their search eventually led to the local Alpha Rho Lambda sorority at Yale, a group that matched their ideals perfectly. The women became a colony of the sorority the following spring, and then on May 4, 1996, the six were formally installed as the Beta chapter of Alpha Rho Lambda, thus making the sorority a national organization. The six founders of Beta chapter were:[72]

Vivian Baez-Montero (1997)
Allison Koplik (1997)
Maritza Tavarez (1999)
Maribel Lara (1999)
Erika Suarez (1999)
Wendy Vargas (1998)

The women of Beta chapter wasted little time in growing their organization. The next semester, in the fall of 1996, they began actively seeking potential new members at both Tufts and other Boston-area campuses, as they envisioned

Beta chapter becoming citywide in extent. Recruitment on the Medford campus was especially challenging, though, since they were competing against the established sororities with chapter houses, large membership rolls, and years of history. However, the members of Alpha Rho Lambda had something unique they could offer Latina women in particular, and that was a feeling of "home." In this regard they succeeded, as they were able to recruit a number of new initiates from Tufts each year. But similar to other citywide fraternities and sororities operating in the Boston area, Beta chapter soon became a mixture of women from area schools including Boston College, MIT, Simmons, Boston University, and Northeastern.[73]

In terms of service to the Hispanic community, Beta chapter took on this mission from the start. One signature event they started at Tufts was the Latino Culture Show, a multi-faceted gathering that featured dance, music, and food. The event proved to be very popular on campus and is still celebrated today, though the Association of Latin American Students now hosts the event, rather than the sorority. In addition, Beta chapter also sponsored a scholarship that gave book money to a first-year Latina student at Tufts. Unfortunately, Beta chapter has not initiated a Tufts woman since the spring of 2003, and indeed by 2009, the chapter as a whole appears to have gone dormant. All told, about fifteen of the thirty total initiates of Beta chapter were from Tufts.[74]

LAMBDA PI CHI (Nu chapter, est. 1999)

The Latinas Promoviendo Comunidad/Lambda Pi Chi sorority, Inc., holds the distinction of being the first Latina sorority founded at an Ivy-league school. Started in 1988 by five women at Cornell University, Lambda Pi Chi was intended to "transcend their collegiate experience and consolidate their strength as responsible leaders of the community." The organization remained local to Cornell for two years, until the establishment of their Beta chapter at Columbia University. From there, Lambda Pi Chi expanded mainly in the Northeast, but also to Duke University in North Carolina and George Mason University in Virginia. Then, Lambda Pi Chi came to Boston. Four women from Harvard and Northeastern University accepted the challenge of building a new sorority dedicated to supporting the Latino culture. Their efforts came to fruition in the fall of 1999, when the four became the founding members of Nu chapter.[75]

Lambda Pi Chi first came to Tufts University some fourteen years later. In the fall of 2013, four Tufts women – Lesly Ruelas, Kendra Baldazo, Yareliz Diaz, and Soerny Cruz – reactivated Nu chapter in the Boston area. Since then, Nu chapter has been a force in the Latino community, especially on the Medford campus. From sponsoring lectures on Afro-Latino roots of Caribbean Music, to bringing noted Latina authors to campus, to collecting needed personal items for the Somerville Homeless Coalition, the women of Nu chapter have taken their service mission to heart. Additionally, Nu chapter has partnered with the other social sororities on campus for a number of these projects. Such efforts are bridging the gap between the multicultural and traditional Greek-letter groups. In the spring of 2016, Lambda Pi Chi initiated five new Hermanas from Tufts into Nu chapter, thereby continuing the legacy.[76]

DELTA LAMBDA PHI (Alpha Chi Chapter, est. 2001, re-est. 2011)

One long-standing criticism of fraternities and sororities is they generally exclude members who are openly gay. This situation has nothing to do with the restrictive membership clauses, official practices, or so-called "gentlemen's agreements" that were quite common until the latter half of the 20th century. Rather, the exclusion of gays is generally an unwritten rule few talk about. The problem over the years has been the reaction to openly gay members by those within the larger Greek-letter community. Ostracism of the gay member if not the entire chapter is common, but the negativity doesn't stop there. Vandalism of chapter houses and violence against their gay members is also a very real occurrence. So great is the fear that some chapters have publically expelled members who are just suspected of being gay, lest they be labeled a "gay" fraternity or sorority as a whole.[77]

The irony in all this is that throughout history, numerous (if not most) Greek-letter organizations across the country have had gay members. However, few in the particular chapter are ever cognizant of this fact at the time, for gay members often hide their sexuality during their undergraduate years. This complex if not contradictory situation has led to a general feeling of animosity between the gay and Greek communities over the years, one that makes it seem as if the two might never come together. About thirty years ago, however, some in the gay community felt they could finally bridge this gap. Driven by a desire to form bonds with other men based on the same ideals as many fraternities – friendship, loyalty, service – a group of young gay men in Washington, D.C., felt the best way to achieve this goal was to form a Greek-letter fraternity. By the fall of 1987, these twenty-four men had formed the Alpha chapter of Delta Lambda Phi fraternity (DLP), one of the first fraternities for "men of all races, colors, creeds, irrespective of sexual orientation." The fraternity grew fast, as within a year it had become a national organization with sixteen active chapters and four more in the colony stage. Somewhat surprisingly, the loudest voices against the group came from the gay community, which was not very supportive of the fraternity given that history of animosity. But as a movement DLP soon proved popular and helped spark the formation of over a dozen national fraternities and sororities for gays and lesbians.[78]

DLP's initial expansion throughout the 1990s focused on larger state schools in the Midwest and West regions of the country. New England was noticeably without a chapter until 1998, when an opportunity came knocking. One day during the school year 1997–98, Paul Mercurio, a student at Boston University (BU), had a conversation about fraternities with his dormitory peer advisor (resident assistant, or RA). As a bisexual male, Paul felt uncomfortable rushing the established fraternities at BU, but was clearly interested in the general idea of a fraternity. His RA proceeded to tell him about DLP and their mission. With his interest piqued, Paul then scoured the nascent internet for information on the group. His research only furthered his interest, and soon he was looking to start a colony of DLP in Boston. Here, though, he had a slight problem, as his interest group was just him. To form a colony he needed others, so to find them he turned to the often despised, but sometimes effective tool known as spam email. He sent an email blast in the summer of 1998 to all he knew in the Boston area, and then simply waited for a response.[79]

Meanwhile, on the campus of Tufts University, a student named Jason Fox was following in a path similar to Paul's – he, too, was interested in fraternity life at Tufts, but didn't think he'd be accepted for who he was as a gay man. However, while attending a seminar about the relations between the gay community and fraternities, Jason heard about DLP. So, a few months later, when Paul's email blast made its way to his inbox, he enthusiastically jumped on board. By the fall of 1998, the group was up to eight men, and in October of that year they became an official colony of DLP. Nearly three years later, in 2001, the colony was installed as the Alpha Chi chapter of Delta Lambda Phi. For the most part, the group based its operations on the BU campus, as most of its members were students at BU. Members from other area schools such as MIT and the New England Conservatory were also on the chapter's rolls, but aside from Jason, there were no others from the Tufts campus. The chapter continued its operations for a few years, but struggled to attract enough new members, especially after the founders of the chapter graduated and moved away. Such a loss of enthusiasm is an unfortunate but common occurrence in new chapters, and represents one of the biggest challenges faced by young organizations. The situation culminated in 2007 when the chapter was officially closed due to low membership. However, in 2011, an alumnus of BU and former member of DLP revived the chapter when he returned to his alma mater for graduate studies. The chapter is now currently active, though it has not yet re-established a presence on the Tufts campus.[80]

SIGMA LAMBDA UPSILON (Senoritas Latinas Unidas, Chi Chapter, est. 2001)

Of the approximately three-dozen national Latino fraternities and sororities currently in existence, about a third were founded on various campuses in the state of New York. Among these various schools, it is the State University of New York (SUNY) system that is especially well represented. Such was the case on December 1, 1987 on the campus of SUNY-Binghamton, when four women created Sigma Lambda Upsilon/Senoritas Latinas Unidas Sorority, Inc., to offer their Latina classmates a sense of sisterhood and mutual support. In addition, the founders saw their organization as a champion of scholarship, academic achievement, and service to the greater Latino community. The sorority remained local to Binghamton until 1989, when they placed their second, or Beta chapter in Buffalo, New York, to serve three area campuses, thus becoming a national organization. From there, Sigma Lambda Upsilon expanded further, primarily throughout New York state and the Northeast. Then, after establishing a chapter on the campus of the University of Massachusetts at Amherst, the sorority had the opportunity to expand into Boston.[81]

The effort began during the 2000–01 school year, when two undergraduate women at Boston University (BU) felt their school needed a campus organization dedicated to serving the Latina community in both mind and spirit. Their search for such a group eventually led them to Sigma Lambda Upsilon. So, the women established contact with the sorority, and soon joined a pledge line of Delta chapter at Brown University. Then, on April 27, 2001, they were initiated into Sigma Lambda Upsilon, and this event simultaneously marked the establishment of Chi chapter in Boston, the sorority's newest citywide group. A year later, Chi chapter came to Tufts when they formed their next pledge line, with Wilnelia Rivera as the sole pledge. As it turned out, Wilnelia was the last undergraduate initiate in Chi chapter during that era. Then, after she and the two members from BU graduated, Chi chapter effectively shut down.[82]

As is the case with many historically black and Latino Greek-letter organizations today, outward and open recruitment is not a normal part of their operations, especially for ones based in Boston. With no physical house to support, these organizations are not concerned about the quantity of people they attract, but rather the quality. And if they can't find the right people they are looking for, then so be it – they are willing to wait for the right people to come find them, even if this journey takes years, and even if the chapter goes dormant in the mean time. Contributing to the success of this approach is a genuine commitment of many members to remain active past graduation, wherever they establish a residence. Such involvement at the national level allows for a quick revival of dormant chapters, should an opportunity then arrive. Such was the case with Chi chapter. In the fall of 2006, a student named Vanessa Salazar enrolled at Tufts where, like most new students, she looked to find her niche. As a Latina woman on campus with few others, she was naturally drawn to the Latino Center for support and camaraderie. But still, she wanted something more, something deeper that could provide her with a sense of belonging. From a friend, she eventually learned about the Sigma Lambda Upsilon sorority and its mission to serve and support the Latino community. She was especially excited about the sorority's commitment to literacy, a cause near to her heart. So, she sought out contact with an alumna of Chi chapter, asking for more information about the organization. This first contact soon led to more meetings with Boston-area alumnae of Sigma Lambda Upsilon, and as Vanessa reflected on this group of women, she felt they were all quite inspiring, if not special.[83]

As fate would have it, in the fall of 2008, five other women in the Boston area were also looking to join the sorority, including Vanessa's friend from Tufts who had first mentioned the idea to her. Together the group of six formed a pledge line, and under the supervision of local alumnae, worked towards initiation and the re-activation of Chi chapter. They accomplished this in due time and then, as a chapter, turned their efforts towards community service. During the 2009–10 school year, for example, members of Chi chapter organized a health fair at BU, put together a movie night at MIT, worked with City Year to paint a school, held a "Bowling for Haiti" event in support of earthquake relief, and helped record textbooks for blind and dyslexic students. In recognition of their outstanding achievement in philanthropy, Chi received the "2010 Mt. Olympus" award from Tufts University as the Greek chapter of the year, which was quite an accomplishment considering their relatively small size. To date, Chi chapter is the only non-traditional fraternity or sorority to receive this award at Tufts, which has been given annually since 2002.[84]

Chi chapter was further honored in December 2010 when Sigma Lambda Upsilon held its national convention under the auspices of the chapter. But while Chi chapter was reaching all of these milestones, they failed to attract any new members after the fall of 2008. As a result, by the spring of 2010, all undergraduate members of Chi chapter had once again graduated, relegating the organization to dormancy for a second time. Still, with many Hermanas in the Boston area, the promise of revival remains strong.[85]

DELTA PSI SIGMA (Boston chapter, est. 2002)

Delta Psi Sigma represents the newest of multicultural Greek-letter organizations to come to Tufts University. Founded in New York City in 2001 and dedicated to encouraging diversity in cultures while demonstrating a dedication to service, Delta Psi Sigma is predominantly (though not exclusively) Asian and Asian-American in membership. The organization became national in extent when they established their city-wide Beta chapter in Boston on December 7, 2002. Although none of the founding members were from Tufts University, many of the initiates in the years that followed were from the Medford campus. In total, approximately sixteen women from Tufts have been initiated into Delta Psi Sigma. Overall, the organization has remained quite small, with only three chapters organized to date, serving communities in New York City, Boston, and New Jersey.[86]

OMEGA PHI BETA (Pi chapter, est. 2002)

As discussed earlier in this chapter, when it comes to the establishment of Latina sororities, campuses in the state of New York have been fertile ground, especially when these organizations exploded onto the national scene in the 1980s and 1990s. Such was the case at the State University of New York at Albany when, in the spring of 1989, seventeen women of mixed ethnic background (though mostly Latina) formed the first Latina-based organization at their school, which they called Omega Phi Beta. They were drawn together in their hope of empowering women to become leaders, both on campus and in their communities. Soon thereafter, Omega Phi Beta became a national organization when they expanded to a number of other schools in New York State. Indeed, thirteen of the first sixteen chapters established were in New York, and even today their home state is well represented on the chapter list.[87]

Omega Phi Beta's first foray outside of New York saw the establishment of chapters much farther south, in Virginia and North Carolina. Then, the sorority looked closer to home in Massachusetts. Only here, the journey was long. The effort began in the spring of 1997, when Epsilon chapter of Omega Phi Beta at Long Island University/C. W. Post oversaw the start of a new colony at Boston University (BU). Two women at BU signed on to the project, and the colony seemed to be off to a good start. However, these two women were both second semester seniors, so their impending graduation put the continued future of the colony in question. Indeed, both women were initiated as full members but they were unable to gain a charter, ostensibly because they left the area following their time at BU. As a result, the Boston colony, as it was known, remained just an idea for a few more years, until the spring of 2001, when the sorority recruited one undergraduate woman at BU to lead the effort. And this time, everything went as planned. A year later, in the spring of 2002, Omega Phi Beta officially chartered its Pi chapter at Boston University.[88]

Once established, though, Pi chapter struggled to recruit women from BU, gaining only two more members in the spring of 2003. In recognition of this dilemma, the national organization changed Pi chapter into a citywide group that year, giving the members the ability to recruit from campuses in and around Boston. This change finally allowed Omega Phi Beta to become a viable organization, and from 2005 through 2007 the chapter added thirteen new members to their roll. Included in this group were two women from Tufts, Vanessa Rojo and Jennifer Reyes, who pledged during the spring of 2006. With their involvement in Pi chapter, Omega Phi Beta gained recognition that year as an official sorority on the Medford campus. Additionally, Pi chapter also earned "Chapter of the Year" in 2006 from their national organization. The following school year was especially productive, as the members of Pi chapter raised thousands of dollars for charity and sponsored a program on domestic violence at Tufts University. However, after initiating two more Boston-area women in the spring of 2007, it appears that Pi chapter did not gain any additional new members, so the chapter went dormant after all remaining actives had graduated.[89]

FOUR FOR A HUNDRED

6

Four stories of Greek life at Tufts, spanning nearly a century

Greek life at Tufts University has certainly evolved over the years, with individuals acting through their respective organizations being a primary force of change. However, this personal accounting of history is not the complete story, since the various fraternity and sorority chapters have never existed as islands unto themselves. They are now, and have always been, intimately intertwined with each other as well as the entire Tufts community, with mutual interaction a daily occurrence. And it is in the prolonged interaction where an interesting history can be found. Sometimes the relationship has been mutually supportive to all, while other times it has decidedly not. Either way, examples are plentiful, but this history seems best represented by four particular stories, chosen for two main reasons. First, each goes beyond one single entity by speaking of shared struggles searching for their own version of success. Second, these four span a significant portion of the 20th century with little overlap in years. As a result, they give us an intimate look at the evolution of the Greek community, if not Tufts University itself. Between unspeakable religious quotas, unimaginable undergraduate chaos, unequivocal membership clauses, and unflappable equality demands, the campus of Tufts University has seen plenty of disruption at the hands of the Greek community, and visa-versa. That both are still standing means little; that both have changed means everything.

ALPHA EPSILON PHI
THIS QUOTA'S FOR YOU

Professor Russell Miller, in his seminal history of Tufts College, *Light On The Hill*, discusses at length the school's sixth president, John Albert Cousens. When reading this history, it is easy to gain an appreciation for the man and his work. President Cousens came into the position despite the misgivings of some powerful trustees, who thought he was not up to the task since he was neither an ordained Universalist minister nor a well-known educator in college circles. However, once given the chance, he devoted his life to the betterment of his alma mater, and it seems everyone, from the trustees on down to the students, was dutifully impressed with his leadership throughout his tenure. But, there is more to the story. John Albert Cousens had a dark side of intolerance. Simply put, he didn't particularly care for Jews, at least when it came to their presence on the Tufts campus. Of course, in the early 20th century, such prejudice and bigotry against Jews in general was a common, if not an accepted part of American society. Many bastions of higher education in the Northeast – Harvard University, Trinity College (Hartford, Connecticut), Temple University, and even Tufts College, for example – embraced such a mindset, as they limited Jewish students through admission quotas, if not outright discrimination. They all got away with such practices because they never officially admitted to anything. Well, almost never. For President Cousens, that all changed in 1922, when he was reluctantly forced to acknowledge the words he wanted no one to hear.[1]

The situation had started a few months earlier. During the fall of 1921, a small group of Jewish women led by Louise Adelberg realized they'd reached a crossroads. For many years prior, the enrollment of Jewish women at Tufts College had been very low, and those on campus, including Louise and her friends, had struggled to create a lasting support network. Academically, they were accepted by their Gentile peers, as religion does not appear to have been a barrier in the classroom. Outside, though, was a different story. The issue was sorority membership. Many national organizations, including some with chapters at Tufts College, simply would not allow Jewish women as members. Others would, but only under certain conditions, and only so long as the total number of Jews remained low, if not hidden. At the time, sororities dominated the social lives of Tufts women (there being few other outlets), so the exclusion of Louise and her friends was no small matter. The women were socially isolated from their classmates, and while they had each other, they longed for the camaraderie and closeness they saw within the sororities. So, they decided to act. To ease the injustice, they would start their own sorority, one specifically open to Jewish women. As for which, they knew the perfect organization.[2]

The sorority was Alpha Epsilon Phi. Founded in 1909 by seven Jewish women at Barnard College in New York City, Alpha Epsilon Phi was originally intended as a non-sectarian organization. However, the sorority soon became almost wholly Jewish in membership when they expanded beyond the walls of Barnard College, much like nearly every national non-sectarian fraternity and sorority founded around this time – with so few social options for Jewish students, it was only natural they gravitated to, and then dominated, those open to them. By the time Louise and her friends went looking for a sorority, Alpha Epsilon Phi had grown into a strong Jewish organization with seventeen chapters spread across the country. So, in early 1922, Louise sent a petition to Alpha Epsilon Phi asking for a charter. The national organization was thrilled upon receipt of this document, and immediately began making plans to process the request. After all, Louise and her friends would have to be interviewed by Alpha

Epsilon Phi alumnae to see if indeed they were worthy of a charter. But first, there was one small, tiny hurdle. The national office needed the full permission of the Tufts College administration before they'd begin the investigation, for they wanted to be sure they were welcome on campus.[3]

The handwritten letter from Dorothy Grant, Field Secretary of Alpha Epsilon Phi, arrived in President Cousen's mailbox just after Valentine's Day, 1922. Her request to establish a new chapter at Tufts was straightforward if not boilerplate, with the text espousing the idealism and high standards within the sorority, lest there be any question otherwise. Then came the all-important question. "Should our investigation prove the group to measure up to our standards," Ms. Grant wrote, "we wish to know whether our establishment of a chapter at Jackson College would meet with your approval." Conspicuously absent from the letter was any mention of the religious characteristic of Alpha Epsilon Phi. Perhaps Ms. Grant knew better, opting to take the silent approach – if you don't say anything about religion, I won't either. Or, perhaps, she thought President Cousens knew nothing about Alpha Epsilon Phi, and would think it was a Greek-letter sorority just like any other. Either way, the ruse didn't work.[4]

President Cousens had been anticipating this letter. He knew all about Louise's desire to bring Alpha Epsilon Phi to campus, as apparently Louise had already discussed the idea with Dean of Women Caroline Davies, and Dean Davies was kind enough to bring the matter to the president's attention. He waited a few days before replying. "I regret to be obliged to tell you," he wrote back to Ms. Grant, "that I am emphatically opposed to granting the petition for a new sorority in Jackson [College]." As for a reason, he mentioned the existence of four other sororities on campus, which counted a vast majority of the hundred seventy-five women among their combined membership, thereby implying Tufts didn't need or want a fifth sorority. He closed by saying, "I hope, therefore, that it may be made quite plain to the young women... petitioning for a charter that there is no possibility that their wishes may be realized." Of course, this was not all that President Cousens had to say in his reply. One sentence in particular stands out rather ominously, as it would soon come into play. "I understand that membership in Alpha Epsilon Phi is mainly confined to Jewish girls, but this has nothing to do with my decision in the present case."[5]

This rejection must have been extremely disappointing to Louise and her friends. Even worse, it appears the national leaders of Alpha Epsilon Phi did not challenge President Cousens on any front, opting instead to let the matter drop. But then something interesting happened. During that very same spring of 1922, Harvard University faced a crisis regarding student enrollment. Simply put, too many wanted in. The school's admission department was drowning in applications, and worse still they lacked an effective method of deciding who should be accepted, and who should not. Within short order the crisis reached the office of Harvard's president, A. Lawrence Lowell. Luckily, he had an idea for a solution, even if it was a little radical. In a private meeting, he and his fellow administrators discussed setting an admission quota on one specific group of applicants. Over the past few years, students from this particular group had nearly doubled, which was one of the reasons Harvard was now bursting at the seams. The group in question was the Jews. President Lowell held no affection for members of this religion, so in many ways his proposal was personal. He would limit their number to no more than ten percent of the total student enrollment. Of course, this was only a proposal, and would only work if the school found a way to implement such a plan without explicitly using the words "Jewish" and "quota," for that was verboten. In the mean time, all he had to do was keep everything a secret while the details were worked out.[6]

He would never finish those details. Contrary to President Lowell's desire, the minutes of that fateful meeting did not stay private. His idea of a Jewish quota at Harvard was soon leaked to the public, and then the outrage began. "Discrimination Against Jews Suspected in New Harvard Policy on Admission," and "Harvard Stirred By Talk of Limitation," went the headlines in *The New York Times* and the *Boston Globe*, respectively. Soon enough President Lowell and his administrators were backtracking on their words, saying they were misconstrued and that no one at the school ever intended to single out Jews in such a manner. No one was fooled. The incident became known as the "Harvard Affair" and fueled a general discussion on the discrimination of Jews in higher education for months. Tufts College was even dragged into the conversation when a reporter asked the school to clarify its position on the admission of Jewish men and women. According to a college representative, scholarship was the official, if not only basis for admission into Tufts. "We have no other consideration here [for admission]," said the unnamed Tufts official, who clearly wanted to put some distance between his school and the mess at Harvard.[7]

To the leaders of Alpha Epsilon Phi, it appears the Harvard Affair and its surrounding dialogue caused them to reconsider the plight of Louise and her friends. As a result, during the summer of 1922, Alice Greene, the national president of Alpha Epsilon Phi, came to campus and met with President Cousens to discuss once again the idea of placing a chapter at Tufts. She followed up this meeting with a letter reiterating the poor plight of Jewish girls at the college when it came to social inclusion. "Jewish girls are not eligible to [join] existing sororities at Jackson [College]," she wrote, "and for that reason feel themselves a thing apart from all others... I ask you to consider whether it is fair to make the life of the Jewish girl so isolated and to send her forth from college embittered." To Mrs. Greene, the only solution to this injustice would be to allow Louise and her friends to start a Jewish sorority on campus. Helping her case was an admission President Cousens made during their face-to-face discussion. As it turned out, his real main argument for rejecting Alpha Epsilon Phi had little to do with the current state of sororities on campus. Instead, as he told Mrs. Greene, he didn't want Alpha Epsilon Phi on campus because of what the organization would undoubtedly attract. And that, of course, was more Jewish women.[8]

The issue in play for President Cousens was the size of Jackson College. Although limited by charter to no more than two hundred women at the time, the school had never reached that level of enrollment. President Cousens reasoned to Mrs. Greene that if he allowed Alpha Epsilon Phi to campus, then undoubtedly more Jewish women would want to come to Tufts, and since the school had the space, they would be admitted so long as they were academically qualified. This nightmare scenario of a rapid and unstoppable influx of Jewish women, it appears, scared him more than anything. Mrs. Greene tried to assuage his fear by saying that in her experience, the establishment of Alpha Epsilon Phi on other campuses did not lead to a surge in enrollment of Jewish women, and she predicted the Tufts chapter would never be more than ten to twelve girls maximum, hardly "obnoxiously large" as President Cousens was predicting. Such line of reasoning worked. After these discussions, President Cousens was still personally opposed to the sorority, but he stated in his response to Mrs. Greene that "your letter [requesting to establish Alpha Epsilon Phi] will be referred to the Dean of Jackson and to the two women teachers on the Jackson faculty, so you may be assured the question will receive most careful consideration and analysis." In other words, President Cousens was punting on the whole situation. He'd let someone else make the decision.[9]

Mrs. Greene was probably elated by this statement, as she'd spoken with Dean Davies a few months earlier and knew neither she nor the faculty were in opposition to the sorority. As the fall semester of 1922 went on without word from Dean Davies, though, Mrs. Greene must have sensed something was wrong, presumably at the hands of President Cousens. So, On November 18, 1922, she wrote directly to Dean Davies, pleading with her to do what she could to overcome the personal objections of President Cousens as quickly as possible and allow the sorority to organize before some of the women graduated in the spring. But Dean Davies couldn't resolve the situation in favor of Alpha Epsilon Phi because she had a problem as well, and that, too, was President Cousens. Apparently, during the fall of 1922, President Cousens reverted back to his original stance of being in complete opposition to the sorority. But still, he wanted to stay out of the matter, and instead have Dean Davies put an end to the issue post haste. Dean Davies, despite being in favor of the sorority, did as instructed and crafted the rejection letter. However, when she gave it to President Cousens to review, the letter came back with some of the text removed. Dean Davies was stunned. After all, she'd only restated his position. In her original response, she wrote:

> I find, however, that thinking the matter over since then he [President Cousens] is quite convinced that not only is it inexpedient for us with

our small student body to add another chapter but that we cannot run the risk of an inundation which would undoubtedly follow the establishment of such an attraction for Jewish girls. Whether the chapter included all the Jewish girls in college or not, many would be drawn by the hope of being bidden to join. With our limitation to two hundred students, a number we have never reached, he [President Cousens] feels that the quota of Jewish girls should not be increased.[10]

President Cousens, in a moment of clarity it seems, knew he couldn't allow such words in print, especially with "Jewish" and "quota" so prominent, so he struck them out. However, without those words, Dean Davies knew she had a very weak argument against Alpha Epsilon Phi, which meant Mrs. Greene would undoubtedly keep pushing the issue. Dean Davies, now caught in the middle, was left with little choice. In her frustration, she wrote a letter to President Cousens, essentially saying he'd made a huge mess of this whole situation, and if he doesn't want the sorority, he'll have to tell Alpha Epsilon Phi himself, because neither she nor the faculty were opposed to its formation.[11]

A week later, President Cousens finally put an end to his indecision. In a letter to Mrs. Greene, he flatly and firmly denied permission for Alpha Epsilon Phi to organize a chapter at Jackson College. He also left no room for compromise. After some customary pleasantries, including an opening of "My dear Mrs. Greene," and an excuse for his tardy reply, he got right to the point:

> The tentative petition, therefore, for the establishment of a chapter of the sorority in which you are interested is denied. Our discussion [between Cousens, Dean Davies, Professor Bush, and Miss Tousy] divided itself into the consideration of two questions. First, the general question of the desirability of more sororities in Jackson College, and second, when the unanimous decision was reached as stated above, consideration was given to the question as to whether the interests of the group of Jewish girls in the College was adequately and justly taken care of in a situation affected by the decision. Our conclusion, from consideration of this question, is that the interests of the Jewish girls do not demand the establishment of a chapter of Alpha Epsilon Phi.
>
> We found that two of the four sororities already established in Jackson there has been no legislation [sic], either locally or nationally, which prevents the admission of Jewish girls, and further, that several Jewish young women have been initiated into these sororities. In the case of one of the two remaining sororities, there seems to be some sort of barrier to Jewish women, the nature of which is not clear to us. In the other case there is a religious barrier which would prevent the entrance of an Orthodox Jewess but which does not prevent the entrance of a Jewess because of race.

From these facts it appears that Jewish girls in Jackson College do not lack the opportunities for sorority life... As I think I suggested in our very frank and agreeable conversation last summer, it may be that Tufts College will have, at some time, a problem if and when boys and girls from Jewish families apply for entrance here in such numbers as to throw out of balance the homogeneity of the student community. We do not face such a problem at the present time. The boys and girls of Jewish origin who come to us are welcome and find places among us agreeable to themselves and their associates.

We were so frank in our talk together that I am sure you will believe Tufts College will never adopt any subterfuge in connection with the problem if and when it comes, and that in this particular case you will understand our position is based upon the reasons stated and no others. Very cordially yours, President.[12]

President Cousens had crafted this response very carefully. He avoided the word "quota" and instead talked about the "balance of homogeneity of the student community," as if diversity was something Tufts College needed to avoid for as long as possible. He didn't want problems; he wanted Jews to assimilate, if not also keep quiet. He also mentioned Louise and her friends were welcome in half of the sororities, thereby insinuating they should have looked to these organizations rather than separate themselves from their peers. In other words, he turned the whole situation around by suggesting the women were partially responsible for part of the "injustice" they felt so strongly. Mrs. Greene, to her credit, realized she'd reached the end. She did not craft a response, at least not one that was recorded in any fashion. Instead, Alpha Epsilon Phi turned away from Tufts College and towards the establishment of chapters elsewhere in the country, which they did with great success.[13]

In summary, the whole incident speaks of a Tufts administration under the unwavering control of a president determined to keep the number of Jewish students at a minimum. Professor Miller has called President Cousens a "strong opponent of ethnic separatism on campus," and indeed offered that as the reason he disallowed Alpha Epsilon Phi on campus. Such a statement, though, seems inaccurate given his own words. Anti-Semitic is probably more appropriate. The irony, of course, is that by 1922, four of the thirteen fraternities with members on the Medford campus – Tau Epsilon Phi, Phi Beta Delta, Phi Epsilon Pi, and Sigma Omega Psi – were comprised mainly if not solely of Jewish men. Indeed, both Phi Beta Delta and Sigma Omega Psi had only been established at Tufts in 1921, which President Cousens must surely have known about. In the case of Jewish fraternities and their possible attraction to men, though, President Cousens did not have the same worry. The admission of Jewish men was already controlled, since more men in total applied to Tufts each year than were spaces available. Therefore, President Cousens could justifiably turn away Jewish men without raising any eyebrows. But, since he could not do the same for Jewish women, he made sure there was little to nothing of welcome for them on the Tufts campus.[14]

SIXTY YEARS LATER, another Tufts president faced a similar situation. It is how he reacted, though, that completes the story. In the spring of 1984, representatives of the national Sigma Chi fraternity sent a letter to President Jean Mayer asking permission to come to campus and possibly establish a new chapter. At the time, President Mayer wasn't sure he wanted another fraternity at Tufts, especially one that was asking about a chapter house – student housing was a continued concern for the administration at the time, and extra fraternity houses in particular were nonexistent. However, what bothered President Mayer more were some aspects of Sigma Chi as an organization. As he wrote in a memo to Dean of Students Bobbie Knable, "I do not see any nonwhite faces in the materials they sent me." He also wrote he did not think the women on campus would be pleased with the fraternity's selection of a "Sweetheart of Sigma Chi" every year. Clearly, President Mayer was not impressed with Sigma Chi, and no one would have blamed him if he told the organization "no," just as President Cousens had done to Alpha Epsilon Phi.[15]

He did nothing of the kind. Instead, his response to Sigma Chi simply stated the fraternity only needed to gather seven interested students to begin the process of becoming an official Tufts organization, and his permission for such action was not necessary. He did warn that housing would not be available any time soon, so if Sigma Chi wanted a fraternity house they would have to find one themselves "near but outside the limits of campus." As for his personal objections, President Mayer did not let them interfere with an issue he felt belonged to the students. If they wanted Sigma Chi to come to the Tufts campus, he would not stand in their way.[16]

In the end, he never had to think about the issue again. A semester later, Sigma Chi wrote back thanking President Mayer for his response, and hoped that Tufts would consider the fraternity for expansion in the future. To date, Tufts has not. Of course, Sigma Chi didn't help their cause at the time by addressing their letters to "Ms. Mayer," a mistake that showed the fraternity knew very little about Tufts University or its esteemed president.[17]

THE SPRING MAYORALTY CAMPAIGN
HERE COMES CHAOS

Jack Crockett of Lewiston, Maine, was an unlikely Tufts student. He began his college career in the fall of 1932 at his hometown school, Bates College, and by all accounts he thrived there. When he wasn't in the classroom, he was either competing on the athletic field (he ran both track and cross country) or promoting independent athletic events such as tennis tournaments and cross-country races. Outside of athletics, though, Jack also turned his attention to politics, especially when it came to the election each spring of a campus mayor. The week long event at Bates, which allowed amateur politicians a chance to practice their skills, focused on personal appearances and stump speeches by each candidate – retail politics at its finest. However, these campaigns were hardly serious in nature. The candidates often espoused all sorts of ridiculous promises to win votes, such as "No more chapel," "Two A. M. curfews," and "Vacation every other week," silly statements that garnered enthusiasm but hardly advanced society forward. The winner as chosen solely by the students was not expected to make any serious attempt at implementing his platforms, since the elected mayor generally held no real power; the process more than the outcome was most important to those involved. Nonetheless, the mayor's contest was very popular at Bates and other New England campuses such as the University of Maine and the University of New Hampshire. Then, it found Tufts College.[18]

The path to Tufts, though, was due to an unfortunate turn in Jack's life. During his junior year, he contracted polio and took a year off from school. Rather than return to Bates in the fall of 1936 for his senior year, though, he transferred to Tufts College to complete his education. Transferring as a senior is never an easy transition for any student, but Jack took his focus and his drive, which in the past had been directed towards athletics, and instead directed them towards student life on his new campus. His efforts culminated in the spring of 1937 when, with only two months left before graduation, he decided to have one last bit of fun. He would bring the mayor's contest to Tufts.[19]

His call to the campus came via a well-crafted and high-spirited letter to the editor of the *Tufts Weekly* in the middle of April. "Ladies and gentlemen," he began, "I suggest to you the idea of a college mayoralty campaign–this very spring right here on our campus." The idea met with instant approval, for despite the lateness of the plea, five candidates signed up for the three-day contest. Of course, none of the five really knew what they were doing, but under Jack's guidance they, and the rest of the campus, jumped right into the spirit of the event. Opening night of the campaign featured ten-minute stump speeches by each candidate under the portico of Ballou Hall. During their allotted time, the five made all sorts of ridiculous promises such as "six-day weekends" and "women permitted in men's dorms at all hours." Some used music to liven the crowd, others handed out cheap cigars. All used humor, and all instantly fell in love with the contest. After a second round of speeches (complete with some muckraking) and a tallying of the votes, Tufts College had its first mayor, Don Simonds. Even the pessimistic editors of the *Tufts Weekly*, who were originally skeptical of the event, gave Jack's contest glowing reviews. And just like that, an annual tradition had been born.[20]

The Mayoralty campaign, as it came to be known, then hit the campus each spring in much the same manner as the first. But not two years later came controversy. In the spring of 1939, a young woman named Betty Lou Troup decided to enter the contest. With her easily identifiable red hair and the backing of her Chi Omega sorority sisters, Betty was a formidable candidate right from the start. "She is one of the most finished politicians in the district," wrote a reporter in the *Tufts Weekly*. "She knows all the tricks." To the Tufts administration, however, she was a threat. The Dean of Women, Edith Bush, issued a "cease and desist" order to Betty, forcing her to relinquish her candidacy. No explanation was given, but apparently the thought of a woman competing against men in a popularity contest was too much for Dean Bush. So, Betty did as she was told, order was restored, and the contest proceeded on as if nothing had happened. Betty's sorority sisters wrote a press release explaining the reasons for her untimely exit, but the truth, apparently, was too much for the Tufts administration, so the document was buried and not released to the public. The message here was loud and clear. The students may have run the Mayoralty campaign, but the administration was firmly in control. At least it was, until the war.[21]

The contest in the spring of 1941 was the last for a while, as World War II enveloped Tufts College and put an end to most traditions, at least temporarily. However, in the spring of 1947, the students not only revived the Mayoralty campaign, they brought it back with a new level of excitement. Publicity for the upcoming contest became so intense that *LIFE* magazine sent a photographer to campus to see what the noise was all about. The magazine was not disappointed. Three of the four candidates that year adopted over-the-top themes for their candidacy, with personas such as Geronimo, the Native American chief with a retinue of squaws and a campaign promise "to give back Tufts to the Indians"; General Joe McCarthy, a Confederate rebel who vowed to lynch the faculty; and Sheriff Ed Meehan, a singing cowboy who cooked food on campus over open campfires at night. The fourth entrant, Ted Vogel, ran under his own name as the "common man's candidate," and what he lacked in flair he made up for in an unrealizable promise, that of a five hundred dollar monthly stipend for all veterans on campus (they were currently receiving $90 a month). The adoption of dramatic personas among the candidates was nothing new, as others had taken part in such fun before the war. This year, though, it all seemed different. This was something livelier.[22]

The increased intensity of the campaign, though welcomed by students and photographers alike, eventually took a dark turn before it was over. On the day before the vote, two candidates went missing. In one case, the joke was easily seen. General McCarthy was said to be "missing and presumed dead" by his followers, so they organized a funeral procession and marched a casket around campus, complete with scores of mourners dressed in black. At the end of the parade, General McCarthy emerged from this coffin very much alive, and very much to the delight of the crowd. In the second case, though, some eyebrows were raised. Geronimo, unbeknownst to all, physically kidnapped Sheriff Meehan and locked him away in an undisclosed location. His goal was to influence the election if not steal a victory by preventing Sheriff Meehan from appearing at some last minute rallies. However, Geronimo had miscalculated. The students in charge of running the election were not amused with this stunt, for a forced kidnapping had clearly crossed the line. They ordered Geronimo to release the good sheriff. He did, and Sheriff Meehan went on to victory.[23]

The shenanigans of 1947, both good and bad, marked a decided turn of events in the Mayoralty campaign. No longer were stump speeches and ridiculous promises the required tools for victory. Now, publicity stunts became a requisite part of any serious campaign, the more outrageous the better. Still, it wasn't as if the overall contest had changed. Winning the Mayoralty campaign meant little beyond the ceremonial top hat and the right to cut in line at the dining hall, not exactly riches anyone dreamed about. Yet clearly the desire to win had taken hold. Helping fuel this desire was the fun factor. Everyone seemed to be having a good time while the campaign was in progress, and with the addition of the elaborate stunts, everyone's enjoyment level seemed only to have increased. But with the growing scope of the contest came a real need for manpower. As candidates planned bigger campaigns with even bigger stunts, they needed a large team of supporters to help turn these ideas into reality. So, they turned to campus organizations with large blocs of members that could be easily conscripted into action. At the top of the list were the fraternity and sorority chapters. Once asked, these groups jumped in with both feet and never looked back. Yes, the Mayoralty campaign was still about campus politics, but it was no longer about the individual. Now it was about winning. And the Greek-letter organizations, it appeared, were willing to do whatever it took to come out on top.[24]

Nowhere was this more evident than in the publicity stunts, which pushed the limits of the acceptable. The spring campaign of 1953 was a prime example. Two contestants entered the fray that year: "Buccaneer Bob" Meehan (the younger brother of Sheriff Meehan) who ran as a marauding pirate, and Jack "Lucky Pierre" Murdock who ran as a French revolutionary. With numerous, high-energy supporters drawn from the fraternities and sororities in particular, each campaign went overboard in their efforts to win votes. Buccaneer Bob paraded slave girls in chains around campus and held mock naval battles. He and his marauders also raided the Boston Public Garden and captured the Swan Boats, much to the surprise of the park manager, who knew nothing of the invasion, but surrendered quite quickly. The pirates then paddled around the pond distributing fake gold tickets to bewildered adults and screaming children. Not to be outdone, "Lucky Pierre" Murdock stormed Paige Hall under a volley of flour and tomatoes, looking to capture Marie Antoinette and King Louis

Mayoral candidate Nero being paraded around campus by his supporting staff, spring, 1956. (Courtesy of Robert Hayden)

XVI. Lucky Pierre and his crew also set up a mock guillotine on the campus of Harvard University and "beheaded" a few peasants who would not submit to his rule. Outrageous? Yes. Appropriate? That was a more difficult question to answer.[25]

To anyone watching the Mayoralty campaign from the outside, it was clear the event was ballooning out of control. Yet, the administration did nothing to reign it in. Just a decade earlier they shut down the prospect of a single woman entering the race, lest the chaos ensue. Now, the administration seemed okay with turning a blind eye to the event, which was surprising since they controlled a majority of student life through rules and regulations. This lack of oversight left the outrageousness to grow, unabated. By the spring of 1957, the event had become a multi-week affair, with each candidate backed by a sizeable committee including a campaign manager, a treasurer, a skit coordinator, and a host of others. Supporting fraternities held "poster parties" during this time for their candidate, and at these parties any student could come by the house, help build the floats and campaign materials, and drink beer. Lots of beer. In fact, the fraternities needed these students, for it was in the sale of beer and hard alcohol to these folks where the money was raised to support their elaborate campaigns. At the time, the drinking age in Massachusetts was twenty-one and the sale of alcohol required a license, but these two laws hardly proved an impediment for the fraternities. Instead, the fraternities raised enormous amounts of money, well into the thousands of dollars, and looked to spend it all on the extravaganza. Mayoralty had hit the big time.[26]

Then came the spring of 1958. As the inevitable approached, many (but not all) fraternities took an introspective look at the Mayoralty contest and came to a stunning conclusion: it just wasn't worth it. The campaigns, they realized, were too long, too costly, and required too much work. Many also questioned why they went through such trouble when winning meant so little. Being the Mayor of Tufts was so much the afterthought as compared to the campaign. So, a number of organizations decided to sit this one out, including Alpha Tau Omega (ATO). Helping in this decision was the early entry of one candidate in particular. Well before the Mayoralty season began, the Alpha Epsilon Pi (AEPi) fraternity got off to an enthusiastic start in support of one of their own, Mike Leven. In the eyes of many, Mike was the ideal candidate – well known on campus, a respected athlete, and a member of the theater group Pen, Paint, and Pretzels (3Ps). As for a theme, he would become "Diamond Mike," a flamboyant riverboat gambler patterned after the new hit television show, *Maverick*. To anyone paying attention, it looked as if the contest was over before it had even begun.[27]

What evolved next brought out the best, and the worst, of the student community. Although ATO had definitely decided to stay away from the contest this year, one night a group of brothers including Linford (Lin) Stiles were enjoying a beer at the Jumbo Café when the topic of Mayoralty came up. The more they talked, the more they realized they didn't like being on the sidelines. They also didn't like the idea of Diamond Mike's ascent to victory, since no serious challenger had yet to enter the race. After all, they reasoned, AEPi as a group had mostly stayed out of the Mayoralty contest until the previous year, and now they were poised to win it all, with a well-liked candidate who had a flair for presentation. So, in a brash move that night they decided to sponsor one of their own, Lin, for Mayor. But they also decided they weren't entering just for the thrill of competition. ATO wanted to win. The magic of Mayoralty had returned.[28]

At this point, however, the race between the two candidates hardly seemed fair. AEPi had been working on the campaign for months and had already lined up major support from other organizations. They were also well ahead in fundraising and enthusiasm. The campus knew Diamond Mike was serious about the campaign, and the overall feeling regarding his candidacy was quite positive, especially since he promised to do things as Mayor throughout the school year, such as organize a Mardi Gras weekend and lead half time shows at the football games. In essence, the contest was AEPi's to win. ATO, on the other hand, jumped in on a whim after drinking some beers in a bar. They had no other organized support, no finances in place, and almost no real chance at closing the gap. But the very next day, ATO began working in earnest to gather support for their candidate, Lin "Huckleberry Finn" Stiles. Soon they had two fraternities and two sororities on their team, all eager to work. Soon they were hosting poster parties and raising money through beer sales. Soon they were parading Huckleberry Finn around campus, surrounded at times by a Dixieland jazz band and twenty-five jalopies they'd bought from a junkyard and turned into floats. The race, if not the chaos, was most definitely on.[29]

The signature event for each candidate that year was the skit, a thirty to sixty minute show meant to be the signature moment of the campaign. On the night before the vote, Huck Finn took the stage in Cousens Gym first with his rendition of *Manners and the Man*. The skit was received well, but what really helped Lin was the overt support of a number of previous mayors. These winners from years past were still very well known on campus, and when they showed up in support of Lin, people noticed. Then came Diamond Mike. His production of *Showboat* was, unlike Lin's, a full-blown affair featuring dancers, musicians, actors, and lots of pizzazz, helped in no small part by members of the 3Ps. The large cast entertained a packed house for over an hour, and in a word, the audience loved it. After all was said and done, Diamond Mike's extravaganza had firmly planted Huckleberry Finn as the underdog.[30]

Then came the voting, where almost everyone expected Diamond Mike to win. But in a shocking turn of events he did not. Lin "Huckleberry Finn" Stiles came out on top, in what was supposedly a very close vote. Both candidates were summarily stunned by the news, though for Lin the shock soon turned into an all-out party back at the ATO house. As mayor, he would now enjoy a host of perquisites including the right to go into any of the women's dorms to eat dinner and the right to park anywhere on campus via a special license plate. Lin was also now welcome to dinner at any of the fraternity houses, was now an honorary member of the student council, and was now responsible for overseeing the morale of the students. Lin Stiles had become, by definition, the big man on campus.[31]

Mike Leven, on the other hand, was not, despite all of the hard work so many had put into the campaign. He retreated after the vote to a very quiet AEPi house, where all he and his fraternity brothers could do was wonder why they had lost. In retrospect, there were two main reasons. The first was the campaign itself. Many students came to see the idea of "Diamond Mike" as being too glitzy, too over-the-top, and too polished. Gambling in the late 1950s was hardly viewed as a noble activity, with places like Las Vegas having a less-than-honorable reputation, and some students questioned the use of such a campaign theme. Sure, in the past the students had no problem supporting a confederate general, a marauding pirate, a circus entertainer, even the Roman emperor, Nero. But now, in 1958, they were a little more critical of their mayoral candidate personas, and Mike paid the price for this new scrutiny.[32]

It was the second reason, though, that easily trumped the first, for it reared its ugly head in two ways. The issue in play was discrimination. Although the civil rights movement was well underway by the late 1950s, and Tufts was generally a progressive campus that enthusiastically supported this movement, some old feelings and prejudices still lingered below the surface of acceptance. For starters, AEPi was a Jewish fraternity on an overwhelmingly Christian campus, so some anti-Semitism probably hindered support for Mike. But even this was likely not enough to derail his path to victory. Instead, one specific incident may have been the biggest problem of them all. A week before the vote (and with the campaign in full swing), Mike was finishing up rehearsal with the 3Ps theater group when his friend, Terrie Williams, asked if he'd like to go to the Louis Armstrong concert that night. "Satchmo" Armstrong, who was very popular at the time, was playing what promised to be a hot gig in Cousens Gym, so Mike accepted the invitation and the two began walking across campus to the concert. They arrived to find the gym packed with students, nearly half the campus by some accounts, with anticipation and excitement running high. The pair were some of the last to arrive, and when they walked in, the spotlights immediately turned on them, as if to say, "Here comes the next Mayor of Tufts, everyone!" However, what the audience saw in that spotlight was Diamond Mike Leven escorting Terrie Williams, an African-American woman, on an apparent date.[33]

On the surface this should not have been an issue. During the 1950s, many students at Tufts had worked diligently to end racial discrimination, especially within fraternities and sororities. Indeed, in 1956, Terrie was accepted as a pledge of a previously all-white sorority, Sigma Kappa, and when that group lost its charter over this event, all in the chapter reformed as a new local sorority, Thalia. Also in 1956, all but one in Alpha Xi Delta at Tufts (which was entirely white) resigned in protest over that sorority's restrictive membership clause over race. The three local fraternities founded at Tufts during the 1950s (Beta Chi, Tau Phi, and Theta Delta Theta), were all openly against racial discrimination based on race, a fact they made known to anyone who'd listen. But despite these strong feelings of acceptance and equality, the thought of an inter-racial couple at Tufts University was too much for some students, even though Mike and Terrie were not, technically, a couple. In all likelihood, Diamond Mike lost more than a few votes that night, especially among the women of Jackson College, for simply going to a concert with a friend.[34]

THE MAYORALTY CAMPAIGN OF 1958, as it turned out, marked the beginning of its end. By this time the administration under President Nils Wessell had finally soured on the chaos that Mayoralty had become. The excessive partying, the selling of alcohol, the skits and parades that interrupted campus life and annoyed the professors, the lack of a perceived educational benefit, everything about Mayoralty went against President Wessell's vision of Tufts University as a highly prestigious, world-class educational institution. In addition, the lack of interest among the mayors to do anything positive for the campus once they won further deteriorated the contest in the eyes of the administration. So, early in the spring of 1959, the administration put an end to the madness. They cancelled Mayoralty. The students, at first, were generally upset by this announcement, and they threatened riots and panty raids all semester long in protest. But these were just words. As the editors of the *Tufts Weekly* reflected on the cancellation later that spring, they realized, "This university is better off without Mayoralty." For one, the editors noted, student attendance at baseball games was up, and they opined that other events such as student-run musicals and plays were filling the void in a more positive manner than those poster parties ever could. Many students and alumni certainly missed Mayoralty, but their voices were drowned out by those in charge. Twenty-one years of tradition had finally succumbed to the weight of its own creation.[35]

There were some attempts in later years at a revival of Mayoralty, but all fell short. The first came in the spring of 1960. That semester, a few students put the question of revival directly to all through a campus-wide poll. Although the results showed a majority of the students and fraternities were in favor of bringing back Mayoralty, only a small minority said they would support the contest financially, and only one fraternity showed interest in putting forth a candidate. Without the overwhelming backing of the fraternities, the organizers knew the pageant would not succeed, so they cancelled the event once again. A few years later came a second attempt. In the spring of 1966, some student organizers again decided to revive the Mayoralty contest as part of a larger spring weekend near the end of the semester. Traditional campus activities were fast being cast aside as students turned their attention to more pressing matters such as civil rights and the Vietnam War, so a revival of Mayoralty was seen as a way of capturing some of the fading school spirit. By then, of course, it had been eight years since the last contest, and none of the current students had ever witnessed a Mayoralty campaign. Still, three candidates gave it a try: Denis "The Golden Batman" Golden, Robert "Flugie" Flug, and Don "Fabulous Floyd" Lange. The campaign, which lasted a mere three days from start to finish, was nowhere as elaborate as before, but it did prove somewhat successful, as it returned again in the spring of 1967. That year, five candidates entered the fray including Al "Haile Selassie" Sugarman, who took the persona of the popular King of Ethiopia for his campaign and espoused such crazy ideas as "love and peace." Despite being the only non-fraternity candidate in the contest, Al captured the title, much to the surprise of all. In many ways, Al's victory showed just how much the influence of fraternities on campus had waned in just ten years.[36]

A year later, though, Mayoralty was nowhere to be found. It probably did not help matters that Al graduated shortly after being elected, so he was not

Tufts Mayor Haille [sic] "Hi You" Selassie directs traffic and hands out cigars, spring, 1967. (Courtesy of Thomas Hart)

on campus during the 1967–68 school year to promote the job or the contest. Additionally, 1968 was a big year for college protests, and the administration was probably leery of having large groups of students come together for any organized purpose, including Mayoralty, for fear of what might happen. With not a word, then, Mayoralty was relegated to the pages of history. And it might have stayed there, except for one last blast from the past. In the fall of 1984, the Tufts administration organized a "Carnival of Mayors" as part of the homecoming weekend, where they invited many previous candidates to compete once again for the title. None other than "Diamond Mike" Leven showed up to join the festivities. He pulled out his old riverboat gambler costume from 1958, campaigned for a single day just like the rest of the contestants, and this time, he took home the title of Mayor of Tufts. But the process failed to capture the attention of the students and the contest was not revived the following spring. In its place, the Tufts administration instituted a new celebration called "Tuftonia's Day" to celebrate the spirit of the school and its history, complete with a carnival and fireworks for the students. This event, while still celebrated today, has never been as large or encompassing as the Mayoralty campaigns of old. Nor has it ever been as chaotic.[37]

In conclusion, Mayoralty was unlike any other community-wide activity ever to set foot on the Tufts campus. It started for simple, if not noble reasons, but then quickly became a victim of its own success. The publicity afforded to the contest by *LIFE* and *LOOK* magazines came just at the right time to push Mayoralty into the realm of the ridiculous, helped in no small part by the enthusiasm and support of the Greek-letter organizations. Without such influence, Mayoralty would certainly not have grown to be so big or popular. The administration, meanwhile, let it be and watched from the sidelines for over twenty years with only the faintest hint of concern. That they finally took control before someone got hurt was certainly proactive on their part. That no one had in the past was just plain lucky.

THE END OF THE WORLD AS WE KNOW IT, PART I
CLAUSES, CLAUSES, CLAUSES

Ever since the Kappa chapter of Zeta Psi was organized in the fall of 1855, Greek-letter organizations have existed continuously on the Tufts campus. They have managed to survive numerous wars, political upheavals, student apathy, and, at times, their own poor decisions. But their existence has not always been greeted with enthusiasm by the entire Tufts community, nor has their continued future always been certain. This state of affairs is certainly not unique to Tufts, as fraternities and sororities across the country have been under scrutiny since Phi Beta Kappa was first organized in 1776, with loud choruses calling for their end at various times in history. Some of these shouts have indeed come from Tufts, and therein lies a story.

Looking back, the one person who could have stopped the entire fraternity movement at Tufts before it even started, with little controversy or backlash, was its first president, Hosea Ballou 2d. With the faculty holding near ultimate power over the students in 1855, and President Ballou the head of the faculty, he could easily have said "no" when Benjamin Hathaway gathered a group of Tufts men and formed Kappa chapter of Zeta Psi. But President Ballou did nothing to stop Zeta Psi that year, nor did he do anything to stop Augustus Scott a year later when he started Kappa charge of Theta Delta Chi. As for why President Ballou allowed the fraternities to exist, one reason may be that he was comfortable with secret organizations – he was, indeed, a long time member of the Ancient Free and Accepted Masons, a secret society hundreds of years old. Or, perhaps, he was just too concerned with other pressing matters associated with running a brand-new institution. Either way, he probably did not anticipate the positive impact fraternities would have as they shaped student life at Tufts College for decades. Nor could he have predicted the issues the organizations would face a century later.[38]

The turning point was World War II. When the conflict ended in the late summer of 1945, and men in particular began streaming back to Tufts College as bona fide civilian undergraduates, one of their first actions was to reclaim and restart their fraternities, actions repeated on numerous campuses across the country. But quite a bit had changed in the psyche of America over the course of the war, and soon many involved in higher education were looking at Greek-letter organizations in a whole new light. What now bothered the educational community was the hypocrisy of fraternity life. During the war, men of all religions and races fought together to free the world from the tyranny of dictators and fascists, only to return to campus and find tyranny alive and well in restrictive membership practices that prevented this diverse cadre of men from joining the same fraternity. Exclusions based on race and religion, so prevalent in Greek-letter organizations at the time, and so tolerated for decades, were now under intense scrutiny by a new anti-fraternity movement. Only this one was much more powerful and determined than any in the past. One of the first confrontations occurred in January 1946, when Amherst College worked to re-start their fraternities, some of which had been founded in the antebellum days one hundred years prior. In a bold step, the administration said they would only allow the fraternities to re-activate if each individual chapter dropped their restrictive membership practices or, if not allowed by their national organization, sever their national ties and restart as a local fraternity without said restrictions. The demands of Amherst College were soon copied by Williams College and the University of Washington. Change, it seemed, was coming fast.[39]

Still, these demands were mainly words from college administrators, and while they came with deadlines and ultimatums, they were slow to force a real difference. What the words needed was a challenge. That finally came in 1948, when the Phi Kappa Psi chapter at Amherst College pledged an African-American student, Thomas Gibbs. Ironically, Phi Kappa Psi as a national organization had no official membership restriction based on race, but when the situation came to light at the fraternity's national convention that summer, the Amherst chapter was told to drop Thomas from membership. The chapter steadfastly refused. Later that fall, when the chapter made plans to initiate Thomas as a full member of Phi Kappa Psi, the national organization revoked their charter, claiming "unfraternal conduct" by the Amherst group. The Rubicon had been crossed, for Phi Kappa Psi had just validated the argument against fraternities that Amherst administrators were trying to make. Now, Amherst officials could claim to the world, "See? We told you they needed reform!"[40]

The Amherst chapter did reorganize as a local organization called Phi Alpha Psi, with Thomas a full member, and soon the story went national. In response to this incident other schools, including the University of Michigan, Wayne State University, and The University of Chicago, began taking a hard look at their respective fraternity systems and ultimately adopted resolutions similar to what Amherst had decreed – reform, or get out. At Tufts College, however, the Amherst incident went seemingly unnoticed, with the campus remaining quiet on the issue of discrimination, probably because no chapter of Phi Kappa Psi had ever existed at Tufts. Quiet, that is, until the fall of 1950 when another incident of discrimination did finally resonate on campus. It all began earlier in the year, when the Upsilon chapter of Phi Epsilon Pi (PhiEp) at the University of Connecticut pledged Al Rogers, an African-American student. Among his impressive accomplishments, Al was president of his freshman class and a member of the varsity football team. But, in the eyes of the PhiEp national organization, he was unwanted, simply because of his race. The irony in this position cannot be understated, since PhiEp was founded as a non-sectarian fraternity in protest of restrictive membership practices. Yet here they were, not practicing what they preached.[41]

PhiEp's Omicron chapter at Tufts first heard about this injustice during their national convention in the summer of 1950. At one point a motion came to the floor to blackball Al, thus denying Upsilon chapter the right to initiate him. The motion passed, though with a sizeable dissent including the Tufts chapter. Not content to accept this outcome, the members of Omicron continued to fight for Al in the months following the convention. They spearheaded the effort to overturn the blackball by contacting other PhiEp chapters across the country, gathering a larger bloc in favor of initiating Al, and pressing the national organization for another vote, which ultimately was successful. Still, few on the Tufts campus knew about this incident until articles appeared in the *Tufts Weekly* that fall praising the members of Omicron chapter for their efforts to overturn the blackball. Fraternity discrimination, for the first time, was now on the front page at Tufts.[42]

Later that fall, the entire Tufts community began an introspective look at the fraternity system, specifically with regards to discrimination. The chief provocateur was the editor of the *Tufts Weekly*, Richard Goodwin, who published his first editorial on the subject entitled, "An Ideal Thwarted." Here, he laid out the problem of fraternity discrimination in the straightest of terms. "Jews only are admitted to two fraternities. Christians only admitted to the others. Negroes and Orientals are not admitted to any fraternity… How can we expect to train men to overcome the virulent venom of intolerance and hatred that exists in our land, if we do not show them within the university… that Jew and Gentile, Negro and White can live side by side in an atmosphere of mutual respect and liking?" As for a solution to the problem, Richard proposed bringing to Tufts College what had been put in place at Amherst and other schools, namely that any fraternity with restrictive membership practices should either remove them, resign their national affiliation, or be expelled from campus. Though short on details (Richard's proposal was more passion than blueprint), his was a real start of the conversation, for he forced the fraternities to begin defending themselves in public. The Alpha Tau Omega (ATO) chapter at Tufts was the first to respond in print, admitting that as a member of a predominantly southern fraternity, they "naturally excluded negroes." However, the chapter did say they were working within the confines of their organization to change the membership rules, but only by remaining a part of the national could they ever hope to effect such change. Going local, in other words, was not a part of their thinking, not yet. ATO ended their response by saying, "Until discrimination is officially outlawed, we are doing our best, don't you think, Mr. Goodwin?"[43]

He did not. Instead, starting in the spring of 1951, Richard began publishing more editorials on the subject of fraternity discrimination, which grew to forums and open meetings on campus for discussion of the issue at length. Two factions soon developed, one that sided with the fraternities as they looked to fight discrimination within their national organizations (which, undoubtedly, would take time), and a second that wanted the chapters to drop their national affiliation now, and reform as local groups without membership restrictions. The editorial staff of the *Tufts Weekly* was clearly on the side of disaffiliation, and they kept the issue in the forefront of campus life through the power of the press. In the fall of 1951, for example, they published information about each fraternity chapter including the specifics of their discriminatory clauses, quite possibly the first time the campus had seen these policies stated in black and white. Three fraternities in particular stood out as discriminatory: Delta Tau Delta, ATO, and Sigma Nu, all of which were founded at southern schools, all of which had restrictions at the national level that barred certain races and creeds. Richard kept up the pressure, urging freshmen in particular who joined a fraternity to work harder for change.[44]

But such work was not fast, and inevitably the push for reform from outside the fraternity system slowed as new editors took over the *Tufts Weekly* and shifted focus to other campus issues. Discrimination next came to the forefront in the fall of 1954, when the Tufts Student Council asked the Interfraternity Council (IFC), the student-run oversight group of all campus fraternities, to investigate the discriminatory practices of its chapters. The Panhellenic Council (PHC), a similar oversight group for the sororities, was likewise asked to investigate discrimination within its chapters. By early spring of 1955, the IFC had completed its investigation and passed four resolutions, all aimed at requiring every chapter on campus to support actively the removal of official and unofficial restrictive membership practices within their organization. In addition, the IFC passed a fifth resolution such that "no fraternity be considered for addition to our college community if it had a written discriminatory clause in its constitution, by-laws or ritual." The PHC endorsed similar resolutions for the sororities a short while later. The message, it seemed, appeared to be one of compromise. Those organizations currently on campus could still adhere to their national policies of discrimination so long as they actively worked to change the system, but any newcomer to campus had to be free and clear right from the start.[45]

The first affected by these resolutions were a group of men who, in the spring of 1955, looked to join the national organization of Theta Chi. Their request was rejected by the IFC, however, since at the time Theta Chi's constitution contained a discriminatory membership clause. They reformed as a local fraternity called Beta Chi with no such restrictions, so they were allowed to stay on campus. Then, at the start of the fall semester in 1956, the issue of discrimination blew up the campus, metaphorically. Students returned that semester to a shocking discovery. Over the summer, the national organization of Sigma Kappa had revoked the charter of their Omicron chapter at Tufts, because Omicron had the audacity to pledge two African-American women. Actually, officials from Sigma Kappa never stated this as the reason for pulling the charter, but it was all too obvious, especially since they had also revoked the charter of their Cornell chapter since they, too, had pledged an African-American woman. Those of Omicron chapter, in a sign of solidarity, quickly reformed as a local sorority called Thalia without any membership restrictions. A few weeks later, in response to this event, almost the entire of Lambda chapter of Alpha Xi Delta at Tufts resigned in protest over their sorority's secret membership restriction, and then reformed as a local group called Alethea without restrictions. The wheels had come off the wagon, as the saying goes, once again placing the issue of discrimination in fraternities and sororities on center stage within the *Tufts Weekly*. Carrying the discussion forward were two editors in particular, and this time they would elevate the situation higher than had ever been done in the past.[46]

Tom Baer and Neil Peck made a good team. Though a couple of years apart in age (Tom was class of 1957, Neil class of 1959), they had gone to high school together and were fraternity brothers in PhiEp. They would also both become editors of the *Tufts Weekly*, where they took up the issue of discrimination with zeal. Tom stepped up first in the fall of 1956. The incident with Sigma Kappa galvanized him and his staff into action, resulting in numerous editorials that discussed and researched the problem of discrimination. His first, entitled "A modest proposal," appeared the same day the Sigma Kappa expulsion was announced to the campus, and here Tom laid out an argument for the complete abolishment of sororities at Tufts, the first time such a thought had been voiced so strongly. He argued that all sororities were too worried about finding the "right girls" as members, so everyone at Tufts would be better off if they simply faded away. Then, a few weeks later, Tom criticized the administration for not forcing an edict on the fraternities and sororities to end discrimination, similar to what had been done at other schools such as Amherst and Dartmouth. Going further, he also faulted the trustees of Tufts College for their lack of action on this issue, and even sent a formal letter to them asking for further explanation of their position and their silence. Tom had elevated the debate to the highest level possible within the administration. Unfortunately, those at the top weren't in the mood to talk.[47]

Responding for the trustees was Joel Reynolds. As a long time member of Delta Tau Delta (he had joined the chapter at Tufts while an undergraduate),

Mr. Reynolds was an unabashed supporter of fraternities and sororities, especially when it came to their membership practices. He was in no way willing to force Greek-letter organizations to change, nor did he think anyone else should, either, especially some pesky editor of the *Tufts Weekly*. Through back channels, he even threatened to have the administration censor the paper's editorial board, lest they keep agitating the campus on this subject. Luckily these threats against the students never materialized. But, neither did the trustees do anything substantive with regards to discrimination, presumably because of Mr. Reynolds's influence. Still, Tom's efforts were not completely in vain, as once again the *Tufts Weekly* began publishing the membership restrictions as practiced by each fraternity chapter before rush week. At the very least, the students knew such practices were still going on.[48]

A few years later, in the spring of 1959, Neil Peck took over as editor of the *Tufts Weekly*. The issue of discrimination was still being discussed, occasionally, in the paper, but it was certainly not receiving the attention it had years earlier. Such was the consequence of an ever-changing campus. At some point during that school year, however, Neil started talking with his roommate in PhiEp, Peter Livingston, about fraternity discrimination and how it was still present at Tufts. The two agreed something should be done to address this problem once again, so Peter suggested Neil use his power of the press. He did. In early February of 1959, Neil published his first editorial on discrimination in the *Tufts Weekly*, the first the campus had seen in two years. Simply entitled "Clauses – Anti American," Neil's words, short and succinct, came to light just as rush week was about to end. He encouraged the freshmen to "open their eyes and their minds wide and examine carefully such things as... a 'restrictive clause'," which he personally decried as being inherently "anti-American." But that was about it. And if he had stopped there, it may have well been ignored.[49]

However, neither Neil nor Peter, who helped write the editorials, was content to stop. Instead, they worked to escalate the discussion. Editorials then appeared nearly every week that semester, all titled "Clauses – II", "Clauses – III", etc., and with each sentence, the call for reform within the fraternity system grew louder. Then, Neil aimed his criticism directly at the trustees for allowing such discrimination to continue at Tufts. While addressing the Tufts Student Council on the issue at hand, he described the trustees as "30 old soldiers sitting in the Coolidge room," and called them "cowardly" for their inaction. Fighting words if there ever were any, aimed at men (and, as it turned out, three women) accustomed to complete respect. As for action, Neil proposed the Tufts Student Council send a letter to the trustees, calling on them to address the issue of discrimination outright, to take a stand in favor of its removal from campus, and to speak loud and clear about its injustice. The council did, via a unanimous vote. As for a response? None. Silence. The trustees would not take the bait. So, Neil called them out. "Gentlemen, your silence is as serious a violation of the ideals and intellectual freedom and moral equality as are the discriminatory practices themselves." This, for the trustees and other prominent alumni, was finally too much. Now they felt forced to respond, and they were none too happy.[50]

The two responses came a couple of weeks later, one from Dean Emeritus George S. Miller, former Acting President of Tufts, and a second from Robert Meserve, a prominent trustee of Tufts College. Both men, as could be expected, were not in favor of any action against fraternity discrimination, preferring instead to have the students handle the issue. They were, however, quite belittling of Neil and the *Tufts Weekly*. "In my opinion," wrote Dean Miller, "a letter addressed to the Board of Trustees by a body that shows as little respect for them... does not deserve an answer." As for Mr. Meserve, he wrote, "The proper channel for communication with the trustees is through the Office of the President of the University and, if I may suggest, in tones somewhat more suitable for adult discussion than the vituperative ones employed in this 'editorial.' " In closing, Mr. Meserve also stated, "As an old Navy hand, I rather resent the reported references... to the 'thirty old soldiers.' " It seemed the dialogue had become very personal.[51]

Neil's editorial response came just a few days later, and rather than backing off the discussion, he kept up the attack. He belittled Mr. Meserve's arrogant tone with biting sarcasm, saying in his apology for breaking protocol that he had "innocently assumed... the Board of Trustees would be approachable via the United States mail." Then, he noted Mr. Meserve's personal opinion that fraternities should have the freedom to choose their own members was not all that far from the one he was espousing in his editorials, but the problem was some did not have such freedom due to restrictive clauses, and he needed the administration's help to affect change at the national level. Along this line, Neil ended with a proposal that the university should give all fraternity chapters until 1963 to remove their restrictive membership clauses, or else drop their affiliation and become a local organization. Believe it or not, the trustees actually agreed with this proposal in spirit when they met a few weeks later. They issued a statement firmly saying they were against the restrictive membership practices, both official and unofficial, but they would not set a deadline, nor would they force any action. Instead, they encouraged the fraternities themselves to work to remove these clauses through the means and systems of their national organizations. Neil managed one last editorial that semester, where he was glad to see the trustees disapproved of discriminatory clauses, but called their hands off approach as "extremely unrealistic." Then, that was it. Neil graduated, new editors came on board the *Tufts Weekly* the following year, and the public discourse on fraternity discrimination went silent once again.[52]

In hindsight, it seems the editorial trio of Goodwin, Baer, and Peck, though passionate in their stance, were unable to produce the change they wanted in part because a large majority of the campus did not rise up with them in action. Tufts University was not exactly a model of diversity in the 1950s, as the campus looked much as it always had, with its students primarily Christian and overwhelmingly white. A supposed quota kept the total of Jewish students to no more than 10%, while other minorities were represented in much smaller proportions (though not by quotas), so the practical impact of the restrictive clauses was quite limited. The trustees must have sensed this general apathy among the students, as they knew the fraternities with restrictive membership clauses were still able to recruit new members, every year, while few dropped out over injustices the *Tufts Weekly* editors talked so much about. Therefore, the trustees seemed content to stay on the sidelines and watch. At least they were, until the fuss got too big to ignore.[53]

That fuss would take a few years to boil over, but meanwhile, the issue of fraternity discrimination came back to the forefront on its own in the fall of 1961. That semester, IFC president Stan Lewis and Dean Myra Herrick, were tasked with investigating the status of discriminatory practices within the Greek-letter organizations at Tufts. The impetus for this study is unclear, but it appears to have been instituted by some of the trustees for the benefit of the entire board. Stan and Dean Herrick personally asked each chapter president to list the type of restriction (Gentiles, Jews, Negroes, Orientals [sic]) and the source (constitutional or "gentleman's agreement") in their organization, should one or more exist. The responses were startling. Six of the twelve fraternities and one of the five sororities had at least one restriction in place, even though four of these organizations had previously stated "no restrictions" on numerous occasions. But before the trustees could process this information, the survey results were leaked to the campus. And then the floodgates opened, bringing fraternity discrimination front and center once again. Taking charge of the debate this time was the editor of the *Tufts Weekly*, Peter Bloch. Editorials under his direction appeared almost immediately after the leak, calling yet again for chapters to either remove their membership restrictions, or resign from their national.[54]

Helping fuel this issue was the continued apathy of the national fraternities and sororities with regards to addressing, let alone correcting the problem. Not two weeks after Peter's first editorial was printed, the National Interfraternity Conference (NIC), an oversight body for the entire social fraternity system in the United States, held its annual convention in Boston. The Chairman of the NIC at this time was none other than Tufts trustee Joel Reynolds, and while the delegates discussed the issue of restrictive membership practices at length, their resolution was hardly surprising: let the restrictive practices stay. As one delegate so eloquently stated, "Fraternities are private associations of men seeking out other men who are congenial and as such must resist those who would reshape them from whatever motives." The NIC had dug in its heels, vowing in a sense never to surrender to the calls for equality coming from schools such as

Tufts University. Such obstinance caused some to act on their own accord that year, including the Alpha Tau Omega (ATO) chapters at Stanford University and Bowdoin College, both of which resigned over their national's continued practice of only allowing Christians into membership. By breaking from its respective national organization, each chapter nullified such practices and was able to recruit any man they wanted. But no such actions occurred at Tufts, at least not yet.[55]

Meanwhile, Peter, through his position as editor, continued to push for change from within. He strongly advocated that those chapters with restrictive membership policies follow in the footsteps of others and resign, as soon as possible, from their national organizations, so that "Tufts students [would be] given the complete freedom to pick their own associates." Peter's repeated charge each week finally brought forth a response from the fraternities just as the fall semester of 1961 came to a close. Stan responded emphatically to Peter and the *Tufts Weekly* for the "sensational articles" about fraternity discrimination. Stan was incensed at Peter and his call for immediate change, both for the impossibility of this request and the implication that the IFC and the fraternities at Tufts were not working on the problem. They were, and had been since before Peter had started writing his editorials. "The editor is more interested in exploiting the issue for its sensational purposes," Stan was quoted as saying, "than he is in recognizing the efforts of the various house residents, the administration, and myself to remedy the situation peacefully and with the exclusion of malice and slander." In the past, such a verbal spat between an editor of the *Tufts Weekly* and the IFC president would likely have been downplayed, if not ignored, by many on campus, just as the editorials of Goodwin, Baer, and Peck had often fared. Not this time. Now, student voices from numerous corners began rising up in opposition to the fraternities, and they all sounded angrier than ever before.[56]

The editors of the *Tufts Weekly* kept up their fight when classes resumed the following spring. On their own initiative, they asked each fraternity chapter to comment again on their restrictive membership practices or lack thereof, and these responses were then published for all to see just before rush week began (the sororities were not asked to participate). Though just a few weeks removed from the work of Stan and Dean Herrick on the same subject, the results were quite peculiar. Some fraternities now claimed they did not discriminate in any form, while others simply refused to answer the question. Perhaps as a result of this confusion, the Tufts Student Council passed a resolution asking the IFC and the PHC to report "on the problem of clauses and practice of discrimination in fraternities and sororities, and the action which fraternities and sororities propose to take individually and collectively." This marked the first time the Tufts Student Council had demanded such information from the organizations, and many wondered if Stan as head of the IFC would even honor this request, given his outspoken disdain for Peter and the *Weekly*. However, just over a week later, the response came in. Discriminatory practices, identified by the faculty as existing in seven chapters just four months earlier, were now only in three: ATO, Sigma Nu, and, coming in at a complete surprise, Chi Omega. For the two mentioned fraternities, the restrictions were as they had always been known. For Chi Omega, however, this was the first time the sorority had ever publically admitted to a "mutually-acceptable agreement" within their national organization, an informal policy that effectively barred African-American women from membership.[57]

This unexpected revelation about Chi Omega sent Peter and others at the *Tufts Weekly* into action. They organized on-campus discussion forums and even instituted calls for "Negro members of Jackson College to… rush Chi Omega." The object of such cries, quite clearly, was to force the Tufts chapter to test their national organization. Additionally, Peter called on the IFC to take substantive action to end the continued discrimination within ATO and Sigma Nu. While nearly all on campus supported this effort (including active members of the three organizations under scrutiny), many were starting to dislike Peter's heavy handedness. Subtlety and tact were just not part of his approach. But he didn't care about any critique of his method, opting instead to push for change as hard as he could. His efforts soon came to fruition. By the middle of the semester, the IFC made good on its promise and passed a resolution giving ATO and Sigma Nu until January 1, 1963, to "free themselves of their respective national discriminatory membership practices… [or face] immediate revocation of the privileges to operate as a fraternal organization at this University." This was the first resolution of its kind passed by the IFC, and in many ways it was monumental. Stan, who initiated this motion, was even praised for this action in the *Tufts Weekly*, the first such praise offered to him in print. Then came word about Chi Omega. A few weeks earlier, it was reported, the chapter amended its own by-laws to state that female students of any race, creed, or religion were now eligible for membership. When asked about this change, the national office of Chi Omega offered no opposition. In other words, Chi Omega was now free to choose their members based on merit without fear of repercussion.[58]

As it turned out, though, the IFC resolution was more than just a public stance by the fraternities at Tufts against discrimination. It was a calculated attempt by Stan to bring about real action. He and others in the IFC knew that those in ATO and Sigma Nu were in a tough spot, since a vast majority of them did not agree with the membership restrictions. However, in 1962, both of these national organizations had established well over one fifty hundred chapters, and getting the required majority to agree on a wholesale change of their discriminatory practices, ones that had been in place for nearly a century, was not going to happen quickly. Still, there was a solution for ATO and Sigma Nu at Tufts, at least in the short term. They could obtain a waiver from their nationals allowing them to ignore the restrictive membership practices. Such waivers were starting to be granted to individual chapters across the country, but they were not easy to obtain without a compelling reason. Now, due to Stan's efforts, both the ATO and Sigma Nu chapters at Tufts had a compelling reason, since there was an official deadline less than a year away, one with severe consequences should they fail to end their restrictive membership practices. Of course, what few undergraduates appreciated at the time were the other players in the game, and these players were not about to be dictated to by a bunch of pesky, upstart students or the faculty (who also supported the deadline). These players, of course, were the trustees, and leading them from behind the curtain was Joel Reynolds.[59]

WHEN IT CAME TO INFLUENCING GREEK LIFE AT TUFTS, Joel Reynolds held considerable power. Not only was he an ardent supporter and past national president of his own fraternity, Delta Tau Delta, he was also plugged in to most other national organizations given his long ties to the NIC. And when it came to matters of fraternity on the board of trustees, he was their go-to man. So, while Peter, Stan, and the faculty were working to remove discrimination from the Tufts campus, Mr. Reynolds was not only watching, he was also undermining their efforts, to a degree. Driving Mr. Reynolds was his complete and total disdain for the setting of any deadlines to remove restrictive membership clauses. He did not feel anyone had the right to tell long standing national organizations how to act. Therefore, as the debate unfolded on the Tufts campus in the spring of 1962, Mr. Reynolds kept national officers of both the ATO and Sigma Nu fraternities abreast of the situation. He sent them press clippings from the *Tufts Weekly*, sometimes with smarmy comments about the student authors. He sent them letters, both in his official capacity as head of the NIC, and as a private citizen. Most importantly, he asked them a very specific question regarding their discriminatory clauses: "As I have previously advised you both, what do <u>you</u> want done for <u>your</u> best interests. Do you prefer that the College set a deadline and then have your Chapters petition [for a waiver] or would you prefer to let things ride without a deadline?"[60]

Both organizations were adamant in their opinion. "We, too, hate deadlines," wrote Richard Fletcher, the Executive Secretary of Sigma Nu Fraternity, "and view with concern the afterwards of them." Stewart Daniels, the Executive Secretary of the Alpha Tau Omega Fraternity, agreed completely. Therefore, when the trustees of Tufts emerged from their meeting in the fall of 1962, their subsequent plan for action looked nothing like the motion passed a semester earlier by the student-run IFC. Instead, the trustees only agreed to part of the resolution passed by the faculty, that those fraternities and sororities with restrictive practices in place (which still only applied to ATO and Sigma Nu) simply had to report their restrictions once a year to the Committee on Student

Organizations, and this report would then be posted on campus before each rush season for all to read. No deadlines to remove clauses, no threat of punishment should they stay, nothing of that sort. ATO and Sigma Nu just had to inform the campus they practiced discrimination. As for a reason, the trustees under the influence of Mr. Reynolds were still clinging to the "right of freedom of association," a sacred tenent that fraternities and sororities should be allowed to choose their own members as they each (at their national level) saw fit. The trustees were just not going to demand that ATO and Sigma Nu change their restrictive clauses. Of course, the trustees hoped the two fraternities would indeed remove their clauses of their own volition, but as such this was the choice and responsibility of the fraternities, not of the trustees.[61]

If Joel Reynolds thought this trustee mandate would calm down the situation, he was sadly mistaken. Many within the Tufts community were outraged the trustees had taken such a weak stance on discrimination, and they vowed to keep up the fight. The trustees, though, didn't much care. They had made their ruling and moved on to other issues. With such a stark disconnect between the students and the trustees, then, it was only a matter of time before the situation hit the boiling point. Indeed, it took less than a year. In early October of 1963, the national officers of ATO received a letter from Robert Alger, the Worthy Scribe (secretary) of its Tufts chapter, and he was worried. That semester, an organization calling itself the Tufts Civil Rights Group had appeared on campus, and as one of their first acts, they were planning to picket in front of ATO and Sigma Nu during next semester's rush week as a means of discouraging students from joining the two fraternities. Robert and the rest of his ATO brothers realized such a protest would "cripple our Rush Week program so severely that, coupled with the damage done last year, the house may not be able to continue on campus for more than two years for financial reasons." As a result, they needed help. For years, the chapter had worked to remove the restrictive membership clauses at their fraternity's biennial convention, but such efforts had always come up short. Now, they could no longer wait for a wholesale change at the national level. They needed a waiver from their fraternity's national policy of discrimination. With it, they could nullify the protest and get back to normal. Without it, they were done.[62]

The response from ATO's national headquarters to the conundrum was generally positive, though the national leaders let it be known the waiver process was more involved than just a simple request. There was a formal protocol that had to be followed, and as such would take some time before an official waiver could be granted. However, ATO and Sigma Nu at Tufts had even less time than they thought. Soon after Robert wrote his letter, the Tufts Civil Rights Group decided to accelerate its timeline for protest. Now, the group was making plans to picket the campus in just a few weeks, during Homecoming weekend. To help in this effort, the group began posting flyers all over campus, asking for students to take action. "Are you willing to allow this moral injustice to remain on our campus?" the flyer went. "Help us blot out this disgrace. Work for action – NOW!" Many responded to the call, which then led many within the administration to worry about the chaos that might unfold. Picketing, after all, was not something normally done at Tufts. The organizers of the demonstration went to great lengths to ensure the event would be peaceful and polite, even going so far as to instill a dress code. But the protest would also be direct and to the point. The organizers wanted nothing less than to force the trustees, at their next meeting, to set a deadline for ending discrimination within the fraternities at Tufts. And this time, they seemed poised to win.[63]

Mr. Reynolds watched all of this unfold before him. He dutifully reported the situation to national officers of Alpha Tau Omega and Sigma Nu and offered thoughts on how to proceed, just as he always had. But his anger was clearly growing. He was increasingly incensed by the planned protest, especially when he learned other fraternity men, including a member of his own Delta Tau Delta chapter were planning to join the picket line. Mr. Reynolds was also upset that outside forces, specifically the National Association for the Advancement of Colored People and the Congress of Racial Equality, seemed to be coordinating the work of the Tufts Civil Rights Group. He would have liked nothing more than to fight such radicalization and protect the fraternity system he so loved from outsiders. But, quite a bit had changed in just one year, and after what must have been some soul-searching introspection, he finally saw the writing on the wall. He knew both ATO and Sigma Nu were going to need those waivers or else they would not survive at Tufts. The national leaders of both organizations agreed – in fact, they'd come to the same conclusion weeks earlier – and they let Mr. Reynolds know that if their chapters applied, a waiver would almost certainly be granted. The fight to protect the traditional way had just been lost. Still, Mr. Reynolds had one trick up his sleeve. He refused to allow any official deadline for a waiver to be obtained by the ATO and Sigma Nu chapters. "I hate capitulation under such circumstance," he wrote in a memo to a number of national fraternity leaders, "but waivers, if they could be granted, without the administration, through the trustees, setting a deadline, would eliminate any action [against the Tufts chapters] and I feel would solve the problem."[64]

The end came shortly thereafter not with a bang, but with a huge sigh of relief. Mr. Reynolds got word to the Tufts administration that both chapters would soon be granted waivers, and the administration then got word to the protesters, who agreed at the last minute to call off their protest. Of course, there was some chicanery here, as apparently the Tufts Civil Rights Group was told the trustees would impose a deadline, when indeed that was never the plan. But in the end such detail did not matter. A few weeks after Homecoming, the campus learned that the "fraternity discriminatory clauses [within ATO and

Sigma Nu] would be 'promptly eliminated'." Then, a month later, the news so many had wanted to hear. "Waivers End Fraternity Discrimination," went the title, in big, bold letters across the front page of the *Tufts Weekly*. Both ATO and Sigma Nu had been granted waivers, thus allowing them to pledge and initiate any man at Tufts University regardless of religion, race, or creed. Fraternity discrimination was, finally, dead.[65]

The collective effort to get to this point had taken about thirteen years in total, having started in the aftermath of World War II and carried forward by a host of undergraduates. Now, the entire Tufts community could move forward. But before moving on, Mr. Reynolds just had to have the last word. As he pointed out in a letter to a number of national fraternities just before the waivers were granted, their approval would not likely impact the membership of either ATO or Sigma Nu. "I do not believe that anything would change in the... chapters as they now exist. Enrollment of undergraduates currently ineligible [for membership in ATO and Sigma Nu] is so small as to be considered insignificant. I believe there were none in last year's entering class and it probably wouldn't total three or four currently enrolled." His prediction may have been true for a few more years, but overall he has been very wrong.[66]

IN HINDSIGHT, IT IS CLEAR MANY IN THE TUFTS COMMUNITY had no idea the role Joel Reynolds played to shape and influence the debate on fraternity discrimination just as it heated up in the early 1960s. He worked tirelessly to preserve a fraternity system he had come to love, even though the times were casting out its worst aspect more quickly than anyone could have imagined. Had he not been involved, the students would likely have prevailed in their quest to set a deadline, meaning both ATO and Sigma Nu would probably have emerged in a different form, if they survived at all. But he was involved, for better or worse. And so onwards went the fraternity and sorority system at Tufts University, sans editorials and the posting of membership restrictions. But the ride was not always gentle for the Greeks, and within thirty years, an even larger test of their resolve would play out on campus.[67]

THE END OF THE WORLD AS WE KNOW IT, PART II
HERE COMES THE CO-EDS?

The Tufts fraternity system, for all intents and purposes, died a quick and painless death in the early 1970s. Never before in the history of the school had the students so actively and forcefully pushed out the old traditions to make way for a new campus reality, one that radically de-emphasized Greek life, especially in terms of leadership. Chapters that just a few years earlier had dozens of enthusiastic members were now closing down completely or reforming as local groups, including all of the sororities and nearly a third of the fraternities.

More importantly, the student-led Interfraternity and Panhellenic councils as governing bodies dissolved, thereby removing nearly all peer oversight of what remained of the Greek community. This system of checks and balances had helped mold the Greek community into a positive force on campus for nearly a century, but now it was gone. All that was left were the individual fraternity chapters to survive or not, to grow or not, to move in the right direction, or not. The choice was theirs to do as they pleased. Meanwhile, Tufts President Burton Hallowell could only watch this downfall, for he had bigger problems to solve. Massive upheaval such as protests over the Vietnam War and the construction of the Lewis Hall had caught his administration completely off guard and totally unprepared to keep the peace. The resulting multi-year struggle to return life to normal consumed nearly all President Hallowell's resources, leaving his administration to adopt a radical, if not simple way to deal with the fraternities. This policy would eventually become known as "benign neglect."[68]

As could be expected, such lack of oversight allowed the fraternities to change their operations from historical norms. One aspect that saw great upheaval was recruitment. Ever since the early 1900s, fraternity recruitment had been an organized affair, with chapters abiding by the same rules such as behavioral standards, rigid timelines, and minimum thresholds for membership based on class year and grade point average. Now, those rules were gone, leaving each chapter to create their own system for recruitment, and these systems were as varied as the organizations. This reality did not tend to promote the Greek community as a whole, nor did it always ensure that higher ideals such as good scholarship were emphasized within each organization. But more importantly, also now gone were the rules and regulations regarding alcohol in chapter houses, though this had less to do with student turmoil and more with the lowering of the drinking age to eighteen. After this change, beer and liquor became ubiquitous with fraternity life and turned chapter house basements into popular destinations for keg-fueled parties, open to all. Problems soon began arising in this new era, from disciplinary infractions to property damage to a sense the whole Greek system, or what remained of it, was out of control. True, the rest of the campus was hardly a collection of teetotalers in the 1970s, but the fraternities seemed to be pushing the envelope when it came to risky behavior. It was only a matter of time before someone was forced to reign them in.[69]

That someone was Jean Mayer. When installed as the tenth president of Tufts University in 1976, Jean Mayer faced a myriad of problems, not the least of which was the financial solvency of the school. That the fraternity system was able to continue operating with "benign neglect" well into the late 1970s was due in no small part to this state of affairs – President Mayer, like President Hallowell before him, had much bigger issues to worry about. However, by the early 1980s, many of the major problems had been stabilized, leaving President Mayer and his administration more time to concentrate on secondary issues.

Nearing the top of that list were the fraternities. The incident reports over the years had become too numerous to ignore, with noted infractions including fraternity members nearly rioting with Somerville police officers, pledges hurling racial insults at groups of students, chapters showing pornography during rush events, and underage students engaging in rampant drinking despite a rise in the legal drinking age. Systemic problems within fraternities were not unique to Tufts, and indeed more than a few schools, especially in New England, responded with the nuclear option. Colby College, Amherst College, American International College, and a few others got so fed up with the state of affairs that they threw their Greek-letter organizations off campus, rather than work through the problems. President Mayer didn't want to take such an extreme route just yet, but he knew he had to do something before a serious tragedy occurred.[70]

Then came the letter. In the spring of 1984, President Mayer received a formal letter from a confidant and trustee of the university, Thomas O'Brien. In his letter, Mr. O'Brien suggested that Tufts would be better served by phasing out the fraternity system and converting the houses into dorms, study areas, or recreational centers. He even offered his help in examining this idea and then ultimately presenting it to the other trustees. In many ways, this letter showed how far the fraternity system had fallen, since Mr. O'Brien had been an enthusiastic member of Delta Tau Delta while a Tufts undergraduate in the late 1950s. Also, Mr. O'Brien was the current alumni advisor for the chapter, a position usually held by one with great dedication to his fraternity. Yet here he was calling not just for the end of his fraternity on campus, but for the end of the entire system, because in his opinion all had lost their way and become a detriment to student life. President Mayer and his advisors wondered what to make of this letter, as they had not asked Mr. O'Brien for advice on this topic, and they knew other trustees might not react kindly to this idea. So, after a few days President Mayer sent a cordial response, saying the problems with fraternities at Tufts were not too bad aside from a few isolated incidents, and the new Campus Center should offer the community exactly the type of space Mr. O'Brien wanted to see on campus. President Mayer ended his letter with a general comment about the fraternity system – "If it ain't broke, don't fix it."[71]

But it was broken and President Mayer knew it. A few days after President Mayer's response to Mr. O'Brien (perhaps coincidentally, but perhaps not), the dean of the College of Arts and Sciences, Frank Colcord, sent a memo to the other deans on campus about the idea of forming an ad-hoc faculty committee to study the fraternity system. The questions the committee would be considering were far reaching, both in scope and effect, and were potentially transformative. "Do we support new ones on campus? Do we wish to exert greater control over the real estate? Do we wish to assist groups buying or renting houses? Do we set aside specific areas on campus for fraternities and sororities?" For the first time in decades, the administration wanted to take a long, hard, serious look at the fraternity system, and while they were not considering its removal from campus as was immediately wondered, they were most certainly looking to affect a positive change. Still, they recognized this as a very serious and complex issue, so they were not looking to act in haste. This would take some time.[72]

This work proceeded far from the eyes of the students until it was finally revealed to the campus in January of 1987, through an article in *The Tufts Daily*. By then, fraternities and sororities were in the midst of a popular upswing, growing in both the number of chapters and individual membership. Student oversight of the system had been restored, somewhat, by the formation of the Inter-Greek Council (IGC) years earlier, but in general the IGC held little power to mold the individual chapters. Now, Dean Colcord with his ad-hoc faculty committee was ready to examine Greek life and create new rules and regulations to help govern the system as a whole. His goal was to make Greek life safer for all, both in terms of the overall experience afforded to the members and the physical state of the properties, some of which needed major repairs and safety upgrades. The IGC, though, was not exactly willing to sit idly by, so they vowed to work with the ad-hoc committee to create the new policies, especially ones that looked to curtail social activities. President Mayer was firmly behind this combined effort, saying quite frankly that, "if fraternities do not discipline themselves, they will disappear at Tufts." The burden to make substantial change was certainly greater for the IGC, because they knew if they did not, the faculty would gladly do it for them.[73]

As a first step, the IGC recognized they needed a new constitution to define clearly a set of rules and regulations governing the Tufts Greek system as a whole. Led by their president and Delta Upsilon member Andy Rockett, the IGC intended to use this new constitution to assert their authority over the fraternities and sororities, with real power to create the rules and enforce them. But starting from scratch was neither a quick nor a smooth process. This would take some time. Additionally, the IGC's overt grab for power was not exactly welcomed by other oversight groups such as the faculty-led Committee on Student Life or the student-led Tufts Community Union Judiciary, both of which held, and wanted to keep, considerable power over the fraternities and sororities. The devil was surely in the details, but to Andy's credit he navigated the political minefield before him and turned the IGC into an organization with real authority. He also started the IGC working on much needed reforms within the individual chapters, including the setting of behavioral standards, the re-establishment of an alcohol-free rush period, and the exclusion of first-semester students from the recruitment process. Rush week had long been a particular concern for President Mayer and his administration, since the week long series of alcohol-fueled parties at the beginning of the school year had all too often been marred by poor behavior. Now, it looked as if such problems might actually go away.[74]

Not to be outdone, the faculty also asserted its authority over the process by forming the Committee on Social Fraternities and Sororities (CFS). In essence, the CFS became the formal extension of Dean Colcord's earlier ad-hoc committee, whose official work came to an end with the publication of its findings and recommendations. But, in a change from the old, the new CFS included not just faculty but students, including the president of the IGC, as voting members. By the end of spring term 1988, the CFS had developed its constitution and looked to implement many of the new policies being considered by the IGC. Everything was actually coming together, which was no small feat given the general mistrust that existed between the fraternities and the administration at the time.[75]

Significant change came in the fall of 1988 when, for the first time since the 1960s, fraternities held a uniform rush week and, for the first time since even longer, all recruitment events were dry. The Greek community as a whole was not completely enamored of this new system, with many grumbling about less rushees in total than years prior since now each rushee had to divide his time between the different chapters. But change was here to stay, and the students quickly adapted to the new system. Another substantial change involved a new set of acceptable behavioral practices the CFS had developed, which the fraternities and sororities were expected to sign by the end of September, 1988, or lose their recognition. This document relied heavily on the findings and recommendations of the Dean Colcord's earlier ad-hoc faculty committee and included new regulations such as minimum levels of liability insurance for each organization and standards related to the upkeep of chapter property. Most fraternities signed the document straight away, but a few held out, citing the need for legal opinions from their alumni or national organizations. These excuses, though, belied another reason a few didn't want to sign – the agreement would classify their privately-owned properties as "University housing," subject to the same rules and regulations as dormitories such as a ban on firearms, for example. These particular fraternities felt the administration had no right to impose such regulations on private property, so they stalled. President Mayer, though, was in no mood for holdouts. Sign the document or get lost, he said, in no uncertain terms. Eventually, all did sign that semester. Following this effort, the CFS moved on to its next phase of oversight, and that was a two-year evaluation of the fraternity system and its efforts within to remove offensive and poor behavior. While this work garnered little attention by the students at the time, it would soon be the start of something quite controversial.[76]

Meanwhile, more changes came via the student-run IGC. Under President Mayer's direction, the IGC formulated new policies to reduce the amount of alcohol consumption by students in fraternity houses. He was no longer going to tolerate the modus operandi of the fraternities, which was to buy a bunch of beer kegs, charge students an admission fee at the door, and pack them into their basement for a party. So, the IGC got to work and created a series of mandates including the need for fraternities to register their parties in advance, hire a policeman, adhere to a 2:00 a.m. curfew, provide food and non-alcoholic beverages, and stop charging an admission fee. Of course, many of these policies were already in effect within some fraternity chapters due to their liability insurance policies. These particular fraternities all belonged to the Fraternity Insurance Purchasing Group (FIPG), a coalition of national organizations formed in 1987 that was committed to reducing the ever-escalating cost of liability insurance by reducing the risk. Enforcement of these policies by the national organizations, though, was somewhat lacking, as they did not have the resources for such close oversight of their chapters, especially during this transitionary time. In a sense, the new rules were too easy for the individual chapters to ignore, so the status quo of keg parties had remained. But now, the IGC and campus officials had the necessary authority for enforcement. Change did take some time, but a few years later the signs were obvious. Beginning in the spring of 1990, for example, the IGC began enforcing the ban on beer kegs in fraternities that belonged to the FIPG, a rule that affected half of the chapters on campus. Within a few years, this policy became universal, and the era of large-scale fraternity keg parties at Tufts was over, likely forever.[77]

While the IGC was hard at work out in the open, the CFS went behind closed doors to examine how well the fraternity and sorority chapters were adhering to the new IGC policies. The CFS wanted to investigate the academic performance, disciplinary status, and finances of each chapter, ostensibly to make sure the chapters were doing exactly as they'd said. The CFS then planned to present their findings to the entire faculty in the spring of 1990 so action could be taken, if necessary. The undergraduates in the IGC were generally not too worried about this report, as both they and administration officials presumed any such action would be limited in scope, possibly removing one or two poorly performing chapters, but otherwise leaving the system in place. However, the CFS was not the only entity now looking closely at the fraternities and sororities. For the first time in decades, a viable anti-fraternity movement was starting to grow on campus. Those in this camp may have been new to the game, but they soon coalesced around a clear goal. They wanted to see wholesale change in the Greek system.[78]

First, though, came the report. By early April 1990, the CFS had finished its work and was ready to present to the faculty. Word on the street said that overall, the CFS was pleased with the improvements the Greek system had made over the past two years, especially in resolving disciplinary issues among certain chapters, and in having all of the chapters sign the new relationship statement. In summary, the CFS felt the organizations had earned the right to remain on campus. Eagerly waiting the report, however, was the identifiable leader of the anti-fraternity movement, Wally Pansing. Wally was a member of the Tufts Community Union senate and passionate in his opinion that the school's Greek system in its current form was inherently flawed, because it was only "perpetuating and encouraging homophobia, sexism, and racism." Not surprisingly, Wally was highly critical of this report, which he felt was biased in favor of the fraternities, and he was dismayed the CFS left the Greek system to continue on the path of its own definition. So, he took to *The Tufts Daily* to push his opinions. And in this he was very clear. He wanted "either a co-ed Greek system or no Greek system at all."[79]

This rallying cry to admit women into fraternities, a process that would become widely referred to as "coedification," was new at Tufts, but not so new on other campuses. Two New England schools, Middlebury College and Bowdoin College, had recently required their fraternities to become co-ed, or face expulsion from campus. The process as it played out was certainly not without issues, but to Wally and the anti-fraternity movement, coedification was the savior that could banish all of the current problems. Only by allowing women into fraternities, Wally and others preached, could the organizations overcome their "inherently violent and sexist" behavioral patterns of the past. This opinion was not held universally on campus, as evidenced by the ensuing passionate, back-and-forth debate in the editorial pages of *The Tufts Daily*. However, while the debate played on, the anti-fraternity voice under Wally only grew louder. More were starting to listen.[80]

Indeed, while this conversation played out amongst the students, some members of the faculty began to think they, too, should enter the debate and look closer at the Greek system. The report of the CFS, after all, was just a report, and though the faculty planned to discuss the details at an upcoming meeting, they were only being asked by the CFS to accept the findings or not – there was no call for big changes to the system. Yet, that is precisely what some professors now wanted, if not demanded. But, just as with the students, there were others on the faculty who felt just as strongly the Greek system should be left alone, for it was none of their business. Thus, the stage was set for confrontation when the faculty met on May 7, 1990, and came to the agenda item regarding the CFS report. Professor Daniel Mulholland started by firing the opening shot. He immediately proposed a motion "that the faculty takes note of the [CFS] report and moves on to other business." In other words, thank you for this study, now let's leave this issue behind and get to the real work of the faculty. Almost immediately, the opposition came forward. Led by Professor Stephen Bailey, the discussion soon devolved into a full-blown assault on the Tufts Greek system. Professor Bailey, who was decidedly in the anti-fraternity camp, had clearly done his homework, as he made point after point against the continued existence of the Greek system, backing up his opinions with anecdotal and statistical evidence. Eventually, the rounds of discussion resulted in an idea by Professor Bailey. He wanted to form a new ad-hoc committee of the faculty to answer a fundamental question: Should fraternities and sororities be allowed to continue their existence at Tufts? A majority of the faculty, after more debate, agreed with Professor Bailey. They passed a motion to "study and report (no later than December 3, 1990) on whether or not sororities and fraternities at Tufts should continue to exist." As for the original report by the CFS, it no longer really mattered. The faculty wanted real action and here, it seemed, there was little doubt. Many wanted nothing less than the end of the Greek system at Tufts, some one hundred thirty-five years after it had started.[81]

With Professor Bailey as its co-chair, the ad-hoc committee then went to work. However, it did not take the group very long to realize the issues surrounding the Greek system they wanted to study, such as alcohol abuse, racism, sexism, and homophobia, were not simple. They were going to need much more time to understand the problem, let alone propose a course of action to the faculty. So, one of the first actions taken by the committee was to throw out the self-imposed deadline of December 1990, and not set another in its place. Then came the gathering of information, from published literature, to inputs from students within both the pro- and anti-fraternity movements, to the opinions of other campus oversight groups such as the Tufts Community Union Senate and the Committee on Student Life. On paper this all seemed rather straightforward, but in reality it was overwhelming. The scientific literature published on Greek life was not as extensive as hoped, and the conclusions were hard to generalize to life at Tufts. In addition, the committee spent an enormous amount of time developing a survey to gauge the opinions of students about certain aspects of Greek life, but in the end this, too, proved to be somewhat inconclusive. For example, the survey showed that where students lived on campus (dormitory, off-campus apartment, or fraternity/sorority house) greatly affected their responses. Somewhat surprisingly, the survey also showed there was a lot of alcohol abuse in dormitories, something the committee had not considered at the beginning of its effort. Still, the committee worked to reach a conclusion and, most importantly, develop a sound resolution on the future of Greek life at Tufts.[82]

All told, the process took just over two years, much longer than any had predicted. Indeed, the committee that started this effort was not entirely the same that finished the work. But in the end they produced a thirty-one-page report with a six-page addendum, and this package was presented to the faculty at their meeting on May 11, 1992. Within the pages of the report, the members of the committee discussed the approaches they took in examining the fraternity system, the problems they encountered within their research, the assumptions they had to make, the conclusions they reached, and finally, their single recommendation. By unanimous vote, the committee recommended that all of the fraternities and sororities abandon their practice of exclusivity and open their memberships to any student at Tufts who wishes to join, regardless of "race, religion, gender, sexual orientation, and cultural or ethnic affiliation." The organizations could stay, they said, but they now had to play by the same rules as the other groups on campus, the very same position Wally Pansing had articulated a few years earlier. If someone wanted in, they were in until they, and they alone, decided otherwise. No more single-sex memberships, no more blackballing of potential members, no more system of privilege, all in the name of democracy and diversity. As for a start date, the committee proposed the beginning of the next academic year, in the fall of 1993. As to the logistics of how to make this work, there were none. Just do it, the recommendation said.[83]

Well, not so fast. The faculty was not expected to vote on the recommendation at the meeting, as they needed time to digest the report before making a decision. With the school year just about over and summer break set to begin, they would have plenty of time to review and reflect before a vote in the fall of 1992, when school was back in session. But, this timeframe came with a price, for surely the students would learn of the recommendation before the vote, and surely they would react. Indeed, the report was released to the students about a month before the scheduled faculty vote, and almost immediately *The Tufts Daily* was bombarded with rebuttals in opposition. Many students both inside the Greek community and out were up in arms, blasting the report as biased and claiming the members of the ad-hoc committee were hardly open-minded on the subject. The student presidents of the IGC and the Tufts Community Union (TCU) were especially critical in their remarks, forcing Professor Bailey to address a number of perceived shortcomings of the study, such as the very small number of students who participated in the survey, and the lack of a wider comparison between Greek and non-Greek students. His explanations, though, only added fuel to the debate fire.[84]

Then, there were more delays with the report, with the faculty holding off on its vote until the end of November. The students used the intervening period to influence the conversation as best they could. The *Tufts Daily* ran a student opinion poll about the Greek community, which came back overwhelmingly in favor of the current system and against coedification. The TCU Senate, after a long debate, voted in favor of supporting the fraternities and sororities in their current form, while a separate group of students gathered over fourteen hundred signatures from across the undergraduate spectrum in support of the current system. The students, it seemed, had spoken quite loudly against forced coedification. Would the faculty hear?[85]

In the end, they would not. Rather, the faculty voted overwhelmingly in favor of Professor Bailey's report (64 to 27, with 5 abstentions), which henceforth required the Greek system at Tufts to coedify by the start of the 1993–94 school year. The meeting itself was quite contentious, with points and counter-points made by faculty and students alike. In one of the more aggressive confrontations, Professor Zella Luria broke decorum and started ranting about her own views of fraternities, claiming the Greek system as a whole treated women, especially freshmen, as "meat." Professor Luria had made other unsubstantiated and exaggerated claims in the past, but her arguments were persuasive and her influence on the debate was undeniable. One of the more interesting comments on the opposing side came from Professor Frank Colcord, an original member of the ad-hoc committee who had quit halfway through, who opined "it was clear from the beginning that the committee was interested in destroying the system, not reforming it." His views, though, were decidedly in the minority. For Professor Bailey, the passage of the recommendation by such a strong majority was gratifying, as it meant many of his peers had accepted and supported the path he championed. But even Professor Bailey knew the passage of the recommendation was not the rule of law. It was only a recommendation, one to be given to the trustees, who could then accept or reject on their own accord, and on their own timetable. While the faculty could advise, only the trustees could enact. Would the trustees hear the faculty?[86]

In the end, they would not. After the vote, the faculty recommendation made its way up the chain of command within the administration, as required, until finally landing on the trustee's door before its first meeting of 1993. The trustees, though, had a multitude of issues to discuss at this time, so they announced they would not be voting on the faculty recommendation any time soon. But this announcement was somewhat misleading, for the trustees, while recognizing the Greek system had problems, were not all that enthusiastic about the faculty's research or conclusions. Instead, the trustees announced they would create their own ad-hoc committee to investigate the Greek system at Tufts. The trustees felt strongly the faculty recommendation represented but one side of the debate, and they wanted to hear from more. So, six trustees signed on to the ad-hoc committee and as a group began their work, away from the campus limelight. As a result, the diatribe on campus between the pro- and anti-fraternity factions soon calmed down that semester, with students moving on to other issues and concerns. Then, when school resumed in the fall of 1993, the fraternities and sororities started up their operations as they always had, with no group switching to co-ed membership. The deadline imposed by the faculty recommendation a year earlier had been breached, without protest.[87]

The trustees finally spoke on the issue in November of 1993. Their ad-hoc committee had spent months investigating the strengths and weaknesses of Greek system while considering four possible options: eliminate it completely, require coedification (as the faculty wanted), modify the current system in a few limited ways, or leave everything alone. Their choice, ultimately, was the third one on this list. They recognized that problems did exist within the Greek community, such as alcohol abuse, disciplinary infractions, a lack of advisors, and a lack of social alternatives to fraternity parties, so they created a series of nine recommendations to address these issues. In general, these ideas were not controversial, and they generated little reaction from the campus. However, the trustees saved a tenth recommendation for what they saw as the biggest problem with fraternities, and that was their practice of membership selectivity. They were decidedly against fraternities having the power to reject potential members. A few years earlier, the sororities at Tufts had adopted a new policy where all rushees were guaranteed a bid to join at least one organization, and the trustees felt this policy had resulted in positive change within those organizations. They now wanted to see the same system of guaranteed membership for the fraternities. The organizations could remain single-sex, but they could no longer exclude – they now had to accept any qualified rushee who wanted to join, where qualified referred to objective criteria such as a minimum GPA, a clean disciplinary record, and having been on campus for at least one semester prior. As for a deadline, the trustees gave the Greek system until September 1995 to act on all ten recommendations. As for Professor Bailey and his committee's recommendation to coedify the system, that was all now just a footnote in history.[88]

Undergraduate members of the Greek community responded positively to the actions by the trustees, which is hardly surprising since their system was left intact. Once again, though, the devil was in the details of how to implement that one recommendation regarding guaranteed membership in fraternities. The IFC, to their credit, immediately got to work creating a new rush system that complied with the trustees' request, which they planned to implement in the spring 1994, the very next semester. But within short order the IFC ran into a serious problem. The national fraternities represented at Tufts were not interested in an open membership system. They all felt strongly that the members of their respective chapters, and those members alone, had the right to determine who was in and who was out. The national organizations would simply not accede to this new policy. So, the IFC tabled their new rush system while they worked to find a compromise the national organizations could accept. The effort took a year, but by the spring of 1995, the IFC had come up with an idea. Formal rush would be held as in the past without the guarantee of a bid, but immediately following this process there would be an informal rush period, where those who did not get a bid could rush another chapter. A bid to join was still not guaranteed for those participating in the informal process, but this new policy at least gave all interested rushees two chances to secure membership in a fraternity. The national organizations represented on campus approved of this policy, which was consistent with their evolving approach to recruitment as a year-long process. More importantly, the trustees approved this plan, which meant their job of reforming the Greek system was essentially finished. The students paid little attention to this detail, with no real cries of disapproval.[89]

The same could not be said for the faculty members of the CFS. Lost in the years of debate and actions by the trustees was the CFS, which was still overseeing the operations of the Greek system but had consistently been left out of the decision making process. Instead, the CFS had been shunted to an impossible spot. Ever since the trustees passed their ten recommendations in 1993, the CFS was forced to support this position, for the trustees were their bosses. However, the position of the trustees was in sharp contrast to the will of CFS's faculty peers, who had voted overwhelmingly for coedification of the Greek organizations. Now, to make matters worse, the trustees were even retreating on their one substantial recommendation of guaranteed bids, something generally in favor with the faculty. This was too much for the CFS to bear. Throwing up his hands in disgust was the chair of the CFS, Professor Mulholland, who back in 1990 had argued against faculty intervention in the Greek system in the first place. He called out the machinations of the trustees, the IFC, and the national organizations for implementing such a retreat, and then he took the only action left – he disbanded the CFS. If the Greek system and the trustees weren't interested in talking with the CFS, then the CFS wasn't interested in overseeing the system. Someone else would have to take up the thankless job. The natural choice was the larger faculty-led Committee on Student Life (CSL), but even they wanted no part of the discussion. At their last meeting in the spring of 1995, the CSL voted to end their involvement in all matters related to fraternities and sororities. The faculty as a whole had called "uncle." They would let the Greek system remain.[90]

ALL TOLD, THE FACULTY HAD WAGED A SEVEN-YEAR BATTLE to affect radical change within the fraternities and sororities, and in the end very little of their vision had been realized. The organizations were still single-sex by choice, they were still selective, and they were still on campus. But the scrutiny they started has not ended. Since 1995, there have been numerous calls for significant change to the Greek system, including its complete removal from campus. Such efforts are followed almost immediately by predictable rebuttals from those in support of the organizations. This work is mostly carried out by different generations of students each time, as every five or six years the Greek system is placed under the microscope for weeks if not months, until other campus issues become more important. Taken on a small scale, it would be easy to conclude all of these conversations in opposition to the Greek system have not had much impact – problems still remain, solutions often seem fleeting, and the two sides of the debate seem no closer together. But to say their efforts have completely failed would be a complete mistake. In the late 1980s the faculty, more than any group, pushed the dialogue regarding acceptable and unacceptable behavior within fraternities and sororities just when it was needed the most, and their calls for change certainly led to the development of an IGC with real power to make and enforce rules. The re-establishment of formal rush, campus-wide standards regarding chapter house safety, and continued peer oversight are but three legacies of this effort, and they are likely to remain in place for a long time. Other positive changes pushed by these conversations have taken much longer to come to fruition, but that they have taken place is testament to those who fought for them so passionately, including Professor Bailey and Wally Pansing. For example, in the fall of 2010, many fraternity and sorority chapters openly displayed the rainbow flag on the sides of their houses, in support of the lesbian, gay, bisexual, and transgendered (LGBT) community at Tufts, while others looked to start conversations about how to bring the Greek and LGBT communities together. Twenty years earlier, such support was nonexistent. One can only hope the debate will continue in the years ahead, for it does often lead to positive change, even if it takes longer than anyone could imagine.[91]

7 FINAL THOUGHTS

On the current state, and future of, Greek life at Tufts

The history of Greek life at Tufts since 1855 can be viewed as a journey of change on time scales both short and long. Indeed, in the six and a half years it took to write this book, the Greek system experienced a number of upheavals that could eventually rival some of the more tumultuous decades in terms of historical impact. Two fraternities, upset at the actions and attitudes of their national organizations, broke their historic ties and successfully reformed as local organizations, the first time this has occurred at Tufts since 1956. One new sorority came to campus and secured a chapter house after just one year of existence. Approximately one quarter of all undergraduates now participate in Greek life, a higher percentage than those in varsity athletics, and some chapters now number well over one hundred members for the first time in their history. New procedures implemented by the students and the administration have led to enhanced oversight of fraternity social functions, as all work to reduce alcohol abuse on campus. Money raised by fraternity and sorority philanthropy projects each year now routinely reaches into the thousands of dollars, and only seems to be growing. To any looking at such accomplishments, it appears all is well with Greek life at Tufts.[1]

But of course it is not. During this last school year alone, evidence of hazing and sexual misconduct in a number of fraternities has surfaced, resulting in investigations if not ultimately suspensions of more than a few chapters. The members of Delta Tau Delta are still not allowed to occupy their chapter house because of a stabbing incident on their property nearly two years prior. Nearly half of the active membership of Alpha Omicron Pi (AOΠ) resigned in the fall of 2016 when their national organization stumbled on the issue of transgender membership. This event made national news, the first time a Tufts sorority has been in the national spotlight since the 1950s. In the wake of these and other issues, fraternity and sorority recruitment for the spring of 2017 has been suspended – spring is normally the season when most join a fraternity and sorority, so the loss of new members could have a profound effect in many organizations going forward. Some on campus, including members of fraternities and sororities, are even calling for the complete disbandment of the entire Greek system at

Tufts, lest any more problems continue. To any looking at such transgressions, it appears all is for naught with Greek life at Tufts.[2]

And it may very well be. Tufts president Anthony Monaco, in response to this negativity, recently organized a committee of alumni, administrators, students, and local community leaders to study Greek life and make recommendations about its future, should there be a future at all. Such deep introspection is hardly unique in the history of Tufts, and seems to arrive every generation or so; the previous hard look at the Greek system came in the early 1990s. Should this latest state of affairs result in the continuance in the Greek system, surely the next generation of students will ask more questions of fraternities and sororities, when their time comes. All this, of course, will be left for someone else to write and discuss.[3]

In the mean time, the potential for positive if not transformative change in Greek life appears to be underway. For example, the remaining active members of AOII are now advocating for major changes within their national organization, and this effort could be as important as the push to end discriminatory practices back in the 1950s. The fraternities have vowed to spend this coming semester rethinking their approach to new member education, inclusion, acceptance, and respect for others. The outcome of this effort could be a new definition of what it means to be a fraternity at Tufts.[4]

In closing, I hope that whatever the future of fraternities and sororities may be on campus, it will be a future driven by the students. Such is their responsibility, shared in part with those who have come before, to those who will come after.

NOTES

ABBREVIATIONS

AJHS–PhiEp	Phi Epsilon Pi Records, 1912–1969, I–76, American Jewish Historical Society archives, New York, NY
ATO–A	Alpha Tau Omega Fraternity archives, University of Illinois, Urbana–Champaign, IL
CofTC	*Catalogue of the Officers and Students of Tufts College*
B&B	*Brown and Blue Yearbook of Tufts College*
BG	*Boston Globe*
JUMBO	*Jumbo Yearbook of Tufts College and Tufts University*
LOTH–1	*Light on the Hill, Volume 1*
LOTH–2	*Light on the Hill, Volume 2*
NYT	*New York Times*
TD	*The Tufts Daily*
TO	*Tufts Observer*
TT	*Today Tufts*
TW	*Tufts Weekly*
UA	Tufts University Archives, Medford, MA
UA–I	University Archives, University of Illinois, Urbana–Champaign, IL
UA–NC	University Archives, University of North Carolina, Chapel Hill, NC

INTRODUCTION

1. The question asked to Charles Tufts, I would guess, is surely one of lore, but it has been reported and repeated in so many historical publications that it could be considered a "fact" at this point. See, for example, Brooks and Usher, *History of the Town of Medford*, 309; and Ballou, *Hosea Ballou*, 257, both of which include the quoted answer. For a description of the views from Walnut Tree Hill (which is also referred to as Walnut Hill), see Brooks, *History of the Town of Medford*, 10–11. For the second quotation, see Ballou, 255. On the Universalists and the reasons behind their desire to start schools of higher education, see Eddy, *Universalism in America*, chapter VI.

2. A very good description of the process by which Tufts College came to be founded on Walnut Tree Hill is given by Miller, *LOTH–1*, chapters 1–3. Of note is that other towns such as Brattleboro, Vermont; Worcester, Massachusetts; and Springfield, Massachusetts, were also in contention early on in the debate. Hosea Ballou 2d, who would eventually become the first president of Tufts College, was the sole vote against Walnut Tree Hill when the trustees finally decided on a site in 1851. Among his reasons, he thought the smaller town of Franklin would offer students much less distractions than the big city of Boston. He also feared the school would be forever in the shadow of Harvard University if located on Walnut Tree Hill.

3. Ballou Hall was officially named as such by a vote of the trustees on July 12, 1892. See Office of the Board of Trustees records, 1848–2013, Executive Committee, 1854–2000, Meeting minutes 1854–1962, UA003.002 Box 112, Folder 6 (Executive committee minutes, vol. 5, 1889–1896: July 12, 1892). Before then, the structure was known as College Hall or College Building. On the laying of the cornerstone and description of events, see Ballou, 278; and Miller, 3–4. Quotation from *Tufts Collegian* 1, no. 3 (November 1874): 23.

4. On the real estate transactions of Charles Tufts, see Miller, chapter 3. Quotation from "Reminiscences of College Days," *The Tuftonian* 15, (May 4, 1889): 199–205.

5. Tufts College was never a religious school per se, as a particular religious affiliation was never an official requirement for admission. However, there is some evidence that in the early to mid 1900s, Jewish student enrollment was limited by practice if not decree, as will be discussed in the stories of Phi Epsilon Pi, Tau Epsilon Phi, and Alpha Epsilon Phi.

6. I don't mean to diminish in any way these earlier works of Tufts history, as they represent a wonderful achievement in research, and they tell a great story as well. However, throughout my years of studying military history, I have always been much more interested in the privates on the front line than the generals in the back room. I have carried that attitude to this history.

CHAPTER 1

1. The degree granting colleges in operation as of July 4, 1776, using their modern-day monikers and in the order of their founding, were: Harvard University, the College of William and Mary, Yale University, Princeton University, the University of Pennsylvania, Columbia University, Brown University, Rutgers University, and Dart-

mouth College. College life in colonial America is discussed in numerous sources, including Sheldon, *Student Life and Customs*, 81–142; and Axtell, *The School Upon a Hill*, 234–244. Also, Zubatsky, *The History of American Colleges* give a fantastic overview on and bibliography of the subject. The rigidity of instruction and rules governing student behavior carried well into the start of Tufts College, though the practice of physical punishment appears not to have been used.

2. Many works have been published on literary societies and their history. For some examples, see Sheldon, 125–142; Syrett, *The Company He Keeps,* 16–17; and Lombardi, "Phi Beta Kappa," 8. Linonia at Yale is also referred to as the "Linonian Society" in many works.

3. On the history of F.H.C., see Lombardi, 8; Bement, *The Story of Zeta Psi,* 13, 16–17; and "The Flat Hat Club," *William and Mary College Quarterly Historical Magazine* 25, no. 3 (1917), 161–164. On the use of secrecy, see also Syrett, 25.

4. Ibid. President Jefferson, when asked later in his life about his membership in F.H.C., remarked, "the F.H.C. society, confined to the number of six students only, of which I was a member, but it had no useful object." I have not come across a reference that spells out the meaning behind the letters "P.D.A." Thus, the secret may still be intact!

5. On the founding and early operations of Phi Beta Kappa, there are numerous sources including Lombardi, 8–9; Copeland, *Men and Days in Phi Beta Kappa,* 19–25; Voorhees, *The History of Phi Beta* Kappa, 1–17; Hadzsits, *Handbook of the University of Pennsylvania Chapter of Phi Beta Kappa,* 6–9; and Taylor, "Original Records of the Phi Beta Kappa Society," 213–261.

6. Ibid. Ritual text quoted from Taylor, 216. Over the years, secrecy in Phi Beta Kappa would become a delicate and detracting issue, but in the beginning it was a major aspect of the organization.

7. The best source for the detailed operations of Phi Beta Kappa at this time is Tyler, 213–240. On the establishment of other chapters, see Voorhees, 12, 15, 21; Palmer, "The First Greek Letter Society," 190–191; and Tyler, 230–231, 233–236. The only two charters not granted to nearby towns were ones for Harvard (Epsilon) and Yale (Zeta). On the connection to freemasonry, see Voorhees, 11–12. It is in these pages where Mr. Voorhees identifies Samuel Hardy as the member responsible for the motion to investigate expansion, but the transcription in Tyler of the meeting on May 4, 1779, does not state the name of the member who first proposed the idea. However, in a later meeting on July 10, 1779, Mr. Hardy is entrusted to organize Beta chapter, so one can assume expansion was probably his idea in the first place.

8. On Elisha Parmele, see Voorhees, 20–23; Tyler, 230–231; and Palmer, 191–192. It appears Mr. Parmele was not a student at W&M, but rather a tutor who worked nearby and was known to members of the fraternity. By 1779, Phi Beta Kappa had allowed the initiation of non–students into its fraternity. On the closing of W&M and Phi Beta Kappa, see Voorhees, 16–17; and Hadzsits, 9–10. In Tyler, 240, the situation is summarized by the entry, "1781. On Saturday, the 6th of January, a meeting of Phi Beta Kappa was called for the Purpose of Securing the Papers of the Society during the Confusion of the Times, & the present Dissolution which threatens the University." According to Lombardi, 10, Phi Beta Kappa would not return to W&M until 1851, when history repeated itself and the school, along with Phi Beta Kappa, eventually closed once more, this time due to the Civil War. Then, in 1893, Phi Beta Kappa returned in

earnest to the campus of its founding.

9. For a discussion on the naming convention, see Palmer, 194. There is some confusion as to when, exactly, the designators of "Epsilon" and "Zeta" were dropped for the chapters at Harvard and Yale. The original records in Tyler, 233–234, clearly refer to Epsilon and Zeta when talking about the chapters at Harvard and Yale, but then on page 242, there is a reprint of the charter for Harvard, dated December 4, 1779, which uses the designator "Alpha of Massachusetts Bay." However, I tend to think the explanation offered by Palmer, which I used to write my text, is more plausible. The chapters in existence in 1825 were Yale, Harvard, Dartmouth College, Union College, and Bowdoin College. As a side note, the two schemes used by Phi Beta Kappa for naming other chapters are by far the most popular among national Greek–letter fraternities today, which use either successive letters in the Greek alphabet, or a combination of the state name and a successive Greek letter.

10. On the backlash against secret organizations, see Armstrong, *Sermons and Addresses on Secret Societies,* 3–48; and Davis, *Fear,* 82–84. On the Morgan Affair and its aftermath, see Sibley, *The Story of Freemasonry,* 41–51. Mr. Morgan's body was recovered a couple of years later.

11. On Avery Allyn, which apparently was a pseudonym, see Oscar Vorhees, "Phi Beta Kappa Under the Searchlight," *The Phi Beta Kappa Key* 4, no. 9 (October 1921), 506–507; and Morgan, *Phi Beta Kappa: Alpha of Wisconsin Catalogue*, 16–19. On secrecy within Phi Beta Kappa and its abolishment, see Lord, *History of Dartmouth College*, 540–547.

12. Boyd, "The Original Kappa Alpha," 355–361. Leroy Boyd was a member of the Kappa Alpha Order fraternity, which is not related to Kuklos Adelphon except for the coincidental use of the same Greek letters, K A. However, Mr. Boyd became obsessed with this earlier organization, and spent decades researching its story, lest it be lost forever. I can commiserate with his effort!

13. Ibid. On the stealing of fraternity secrets, see Van Bokkelen, *A Record of the Members of the Kappa Alpha Fraternity*, 87–88; and Clarence F. Birdseye, "How the College Abandoned its Home Functions," *The American College* 1, no. 4 (January 1910): 289–90. The stealing of fraternity secrets by rival groups was eventually frowned upon within the national organizations, as discussed in William Levere, *The History of the Sigma Alpha Epsilon Fraternity* (Chicago, IL: The Lakeside Press, 1911), 276–279.

14. Boyd, 355–361.

15. Ibid. Kuklos Adelphon may have disappeared from college life in 1866, but it was reborn elsewhere. That same year, six veterans of the Confederate Army met in Tennessee to form a new, secret social club, not for any noble pursuit, but rather to have fun. They based their organization on the name and ritual of Kuklos Adelphon, so apparently one or more of those men had been a member of the fraternity. However, they did change the name of their organization ever so slightly, calling themselves the Ku Klux Klan. For more information, see Michael Newton, *The Ku Klux Klan in Mississippi: A History* (Jefferson, NC: McFarland & Company, 2010), 3; Chester L. Quarles, *The Ku Klux Klan and Related American Racialist and Antisemitic Organizations: A History and Analysis* (Jefferson, NC: McFarland & Company, 1999), 32; and Christopher Long, "KU KLUX KLAN," *Handbook of Texas Online* (http://www.tshaonline.org/handbook/online/articles/vek02), accessed February 26, 2014. Published by the Texas State Historical Association.

16. Sheldon, 144; and Bagg, *Four Years at Yale*, 235–236, which includes the quotation. On the use of secrecy within Chi Delta Theta, see Cutting, *Student Life at Amherst College*, 49. On the percentage of students elected into Phi Beta Kappa at Yale in this era, see Voorhees, *The History of Phi Beta Kappa*, 56.

17. Cutting, 49–51. Phi Beta Kappa established a chapter at Amherst in 1853, when it was operating as an honor society and not as a secret fraternity.

18. On the closing of Chi Delta Theta, see Cutting, 50–51; and Bagg, 236. On the evolution of Chi Delta Theta at Yale, see Loomis Havemeyer, *Yale's Extracurricular and Social Organizations*, http://www.library.yale.edu/mssa/YHO/ExtracurricularandSocialOrganizations.pdf (accessed March 1, 2014).

19. Van Bokkelen, 7–10; and excerpts from Tarleton, *The Spirit of Kappa Alpha*, https://www.ka.org/public2.asp (accessed March 1, 2014). Some historians have argued that the oldest national social fraternity is actually Chi Phi, since its first chapter was established at Princeton in 1824. However, this organization lived for just one year before expiring, and was only rediscovered in 1854 when a book of the "Chi Phi Society" was found on campus bearing the constitution, ritual, and other papers. Included was a list of members, but unfortunately the names were all given in code, and to my knowledge no one has ever been able to determine definitively the identities of all these men. As fate would have it, this book and papers were destroyed by fire in 1858. For more information, see "1824," *The Chi Phi Quarterly* 5, no. 2 (April 1880): 73–78. Today, Chi Phi Fraternity claims its existence from December 24, 1824, with Robert Baird as the recognized founder. See http://www.chiphi.org/history (accessed August 13, 2016). Regardless, I tend to agree with most other historians who recognize Kappa Alpha at Union College as the first Greek-letter social fraternity, since it has been continuously active since 1825. Chi Phi does hold a solid place in the history of national fraternities, though, as it was the first to establish a chapter outside of the United States. On June 1, 1867, Chi Phi chartered its Theta chapter at the University of Edinburgh, Scotland, to serve a group of thirteen members studying abroad. Alas, Theta chapter remained active for only three years before surrendering its charter. See *The Chi Phi Register*, (New York: unknown publisher, 1908), 350–351.

20. Van Bokkelen, 7–10; and excerpts from Tarleton.

21. Randolph, "Greek Letter Societies in American Colleges," 70–77; and Maxwell, *Greek Letter Men of the Pacific Coast and Rocky Mountain States*, 15, 24–28, 158–175. The first Kappa Alpha (Kuklos Adelphon), though founded in 1812, did not establish a second chapter until 1842, according to Boyd, 350. The six national fraternities founded at Union are: Kappa Alpha, Sigma Phi, Delta Phi, Psi Upsilon, Chi Psi, and Theta Delta Chi. The six national organizations founded at Miami of Ohio are: Beta Theta Pi, Phi Delta Theta, Sigma Chi, Delta Zeta (sorority), Phi Kappa Tau, and Delta Sigma Epsilon (sorority). The debate as to which school is really the "mother of fraternities" will likely go on forever, since both schools have been heavily influential in the national development of the Greek–letter fraternity system.

22. On Lucy Pattie (also spelled "Patty" in some references), see Levere, *A Paragraph History of Sigma Alpha Epsilon*, 28; "A Woman Brother," *The Alpha Tau Omega Palm* 34, no. 3 (September 1914): 351; and Nancilee D. V. Gasiel, "The Romantic Story of Lucy Pattie," from the archives of the Sigma Alpha Epsilon fraternity, http://saerecord.net/2012/05/archivesfeaturestory/ (accessed March 1, 2014). On women in Beta Theta Pi, see "Hellenic," *The Scroll of Phi Delta Theta* 37, no. 4 (March 1913): 413.

One noted exception to the exclusion of women is the Psi Upsilon Fraternity. Their original constitution made no mention of gender in their requirement for membership, and the fraternity has never changed this position. As a result, Psi Upsilon is one of just a few national fraternities established before 1900 that has co-ed chapters.

23. Becque, *Coeducation and the History of Women's Fraternities*, 1, 11–13. On the history of Mount Holyoke College, see "A Detailed History," Mount Holyoke College, https://www.mtholyoke.edu/about/history/detailed (accessed March 2, 2014). The use of the descriptor sorority versus women's fraternity is primarily one of convenience. However, many sororities, both local and national, do not use this word in their official name, opting for the term fraternity instead. I will endeavor to use the word sorority when referring to women's fraternities in general, but will use the word fraternity when it is part of the organization's official name.

24. Butler, *Historical Record of Macon and Central Georgia*, 81, 297–299; and Jones, "Education in Georgia," 90–99, which includes the quotation. Slavery accounted for nearly half of Macon's population at that time, though there were some "Free negroes" living near the area, as discussed in Butler, 100. The college's name change had occurred in 1843, according to Jones, 97.

25. "Wesleyan in 1851," 19–22, which includes the first quotation. On Masonic activities in the town, see Butler, 81, 92, 177, 314. The Masonic temple seemed to be nearly as important a building as the church in Macon, so I am assuming many men from the area were active Masons. On the founding of Adelphean, see MacDonald, *History of Alpha Delta Pi*, chapter 1, which includes the second and third quotations from page 3. According to the website of the Alpha Delta Pi national fraternity, to which Adelphean evolved, the six recognized founders of the organization were Eugenia Tucker Fitzgerald, Ella Pierce Turner, Octavia Andrew Rush, Mary Evans Glass, Sophronia Woodruff Dews, and Elizabeth Williams Mitchell. However, numerous other sources state Adelphean had sixteen founders, with a different list of six women being recognized as the main force behind the organization. I will leave it for others to rectify this discrepancy!

26. On the founding of Philomathean Society, see "A History of Phi Mu Fraternity," *The Aglaia of Phi Mu* 11, no. 2 (January 1917): 68–69. By the early 1900s, the Philomathean Society had evolved into a full–fledged Greek–letter organization called Phi Mu, while the Adelphean Society had morphed similarly into Alpha Delta Phi and then finally Alpha Delta Pi. According to the website of the national Alpha Delta Pi fraternity, Wesleyan Female College abolished sororities in 1913, though by then both Phi Mu and Alpha Delta Pi had established a few other chapters elsewhere. On Chi Theta Delta, see "The First Sorosis," *The Shield* 13, no. 2 (June 1897): 151–154. Chi Theta Delta was most likely the first women's organization to use Greek letters, but it has been overlooked in history since it lived but a short existence on just one campus. On societies at Elmira College, see Meltzer, *The Beginnings of Elmira College*, 111–118; and Barber, *Elmira College*, 169–172. As at Wesleyan, the two societies at Elmira eventually evolved into Greek-letter organizations, with Callisophia becoming Kappa Sigma (no relation to the male Kappa Sigma fraternity) and Philomathea becoming Phi Mu (no relation to the Phi Mu of Wesleyan Female College). However, these two sororities never expanded beyond Elmira College and both disbanded in 1911.

27. On correspondence between schools, see Meltzer, 138. The two organizations founded at Wesleyan Female College, Phi Mu and Alpha Delta Pi, did eventually be-

come national organizations, but well after other sororities had done so.

28. Becque, 13–17. On the founding of Monmouth, see Davenport, *Monmouth College*, 13–20. On the founding of male fraternities at Monmouth, see Baird (1st ed. 1879), 40, 43, 177; and Clarke-Helmick, *The History of Pi Beta Phi Fraternity*, 19. Other national fraternities also started operations at Monmouth within a few years, including Phi Gamma Delta, Phi Delta Theta, and Phi Kappa Psi. On the founding of I. C. Sorosis, see Clarke-Helmick, 19–22, which includes the quotation; Becque, 19–21; and Davenport, 93.

29. Clarke-Helmick, 31–36; Becque, 21; and Davenport, 94. By 1888, I. C. Sororsis had established eleven total chapters in Illinois, Iowa, Kansas, Colorado, Michigan, and Indiana.

30. For a summary of the names and founding years of the national women's fraternities, see Levere, *Leading Greeks*, 10. As presented in Baird (1st ed. 1879), 5–6, forty-one of the forty-five listed "General Fraternities" for men and all seven of the "Ladies Societies" used Greek letters in their public name, thus demonstrating the popularity of the approach. Interestingly, I. C. Sorosis is not listed anywhere as an organization in this first edition of Baird's manual, perhaps because Latin–sounding names were more associated with open literary societies and not selective fraternities. On the transformation to Greek letters within I. C. Sorosis, see "I. C.–Pi Beta Phi," *The Arrow* 3, no. 1 (December 1886): 26–28, which includes the quotation; "Chapter correspondence–Illinois Delta," *The Arrow* 4, no. 4 (September 1888): 175–176; and "The Convention," *The Arrow of Pi Beta Phi* 5, no. 1 (December 1888): 6–7. On the previously secret motto, see Becque, 19. The Kappa Alpha Theta Fraternity, founded in 1870 at what is now called DePauw University, was the first national women's fraternity to use Greek letters from its inception. As a result, Kappa Alpha Theta makes the claim of being the first national women's Greek–letter fraternity ever established in America. However, I agree with others who cite Pi Beta Phi as being first on the national scene.

31. Turk, *Bound By A Mighty Vow*, 165; and Mary Whitford, "A Retrospect," *The Crescent of Gamma Phi Beta* 4, no. 4 (November 1904): 144–145. On the displeasure over the word sorority, see "That Word 'Fraternity'," *The Arrow of Pi Beta Phi* 37, no. 2 (December 1920): 278. Frank Smalley first mentioned the word "sorority" to the women of Gamma Phi Beta in 1882, just after they had established their second chapter at the University of Michigan. As it turned out, Professor Smalley's sister, Honta, eventually joined the Michigan chapter of Gamma Phi Beta and, as an alumna, became the Grand President of the sorority. For reference, see the history of Gamma Phi Beta as published by the national organization on their website, http://gammaphibetahistory.org/decades/ (accessed February 23, 2016). As could be expected, Gamma Phi Beta as an organization is quite proud of the word invented by Professor Smalley, and uses it in its official name. However, their use of the word sorority is certainly in the minority among women's fraternities.

32. Sauna, *Going Greek*, 25–46; Shapiro, *The Untapped Potential of Jewish Greek Life*, 12–16; and Syrett, 168–169.

33. "Pi Lambda Phi History," Pi Lambda Phi Fraternity, http://www.pilambdaphi.org/site/c.plKXL7MPIqG/b.3609919/k.A021/Pi_Lam_History.htm (accessed March 12, 2014), which contains the quotation.

34. Ibid. Pi Lambda Phi as an organization remained wholly dormant until 1908 when students at Columbia University began its revival.

35. Weil, *The First Twenty-Five Years*, 13–27; and Shapiro, 16. Quotation of Isaiah 1:27 is from the Revised Standard Version, 2 ed., 1952. On the growth of ZBT during the early 20th century, see Baird (9th ed. 1920), 393–396. According to the website of the Zeta Beta Tau national fraternity, membership was constitutionally limited to Jewish men until this restriction was lifted in 1954.

36. Fran Becque, "Iota Alpha Pi, Founded in March 1903, is the Only NPC Group to Disband," http://www.franbecque.com/2013/03/18/iota-alpha-pi-founded-in-march-1903-is-the-only-npc-group-to-disband/ (accessed March 15, 2014); and Rebekah Kohut, "Jewish Women's Organization in the United States," *The American Jewish Yearbook 5692* 33 (Sept. 12, 1931–Sept. 30, 1932): 197–198.

37. Sanua, *Going Greek*, 47–50, 61–68, 78–79. Some non-sectarian fraternities, though, did not always embrace their religious diversity. Phi Epsilon Pi often looked solely for Jewish men to start a new chapter, as they considered ZBT and Sigma Alpha Mu, two wholly Jewish organizations, their chief competitors. For emphasis on recruiting only Jewish members to start a new chapter, see letter from Herman Kline to Jesse [Acker], undated but surrounding contents place it in early January, 1916, AJHS–PhiEp, Box 31, Folder 5 (Omicron–Tufts College). However, as discussed in Sanua, 63, one of the founding members of the Xi chapter of Phi Epsilon Pi at Georgia Tech University (established in 1916) was a Roman Catholic, since officials at Georgia Tech would not allow a wholly Jewish fraternity to organize at the time. On the transformation of Delta Sigma Phi, see Sanua, 78. Also, Baird (6th ed. 1905), 125, states Delta Sigma Phi was founded "upon a non-sectarian basis, that is providing for the admission of Christians and Jews." However, in Baird (9th ed. 1920), 166, the description of the fraternity had changed to "It is a sectarian fraternity," and in Baird (10th ed. 1923), 144, "Membership is confined to men of the Caucasian race, whose 'ideals and beliefs are those of modern Christian civilization'." Delta Sigma Phi, it appears, was the only fraternity to start as non-sectarian but then switch to exclude Jewish men. Today, membership in Delta Sigma Phi is open to men of all races and creeds, a policy that has been in place since 1959.

38. Sanua, *Going Greek*, 75–78, 100–107, 152–154, 156–164. On the transformation of fraternities in the 1950s and 1960s, see Toll, *Alpha Epsilon Pi*, 19–30. The mission statements of Alpha Epsilon Pi and Alpha Epsilon Phi are taken from their respective national websites, http://www.aepi.org/about-aepi/mission-statement/ and http://www.aephi.org/aephi_story/aephi_today (both accessed March 12, 2014). Other historically Jewish organizations, including ZBT, Sigma Alpha Mu, Delta Phi Epsilon, and Sigma Delta Tau do not have similar wording in their mission statements.

39. Torbenson and Parks, *Brothers and Sisters*, 57–59; Kimbrough, *Black Greek 101*, 22–23; Syrett, 168, 172–173; Brown et. al., *African American Fraternities and Sororities*, 59–63; and Poindexter, "Some Student Experiences," 335–338.

40. Kimbrough, 22–23; Crump, *The Story of Kappa Alpha Psi*, 2; and "Greek News and Clippings," *Delta Kappa Epsilon Quarterly* 22, no. 1 (February 1904): 68, which stated the membership was ten men. According to Crump, nine founders of Alpha Kappa Nu were: James Silvester Knight, Howard Thompson, Edgar Burnett Keemer, Charles Frederick Williamson, John Alfred Hodge, Thomas Henry Reynolds, Mr. Hill, Robert Alpheus Roberts, and Gordon Singleton Merrill. With the exact founding date of Alpha Kappa Nu apparently still hiding in history, I am assuming it was during the fall of 1903 for two reasons. First, the February 1904 announcement in the *Delta Kap-*

pa Epsilon Quarterly was the earliest printed record I could find that mentioned the new fraternity. Second, the 1902–03 edition of the *Indiana University Catalogue*, which was printed in May 1903, only lists four named members of Alpha Kappa Nu as matriculated students, while the 1903–04 edition, which was printed in May 1904, lists all as matriculated except Howard Thompson.

41. Ibid. The announcement in the *Delta Kappa Epsilon Quarterly*, which incorrectly called the fraternity "Alpha Kappa Mu," was cited from an earlier edition of *The Record of Sigma Alpha Epsilon*, but I was unable to locate this original publication, as the 1903 edition of *The Record of Sigma Alpha Epsilon* has not been digitized for research. However, this announcement was repeated word for word in numerous other national fraternity journals, such as "Greek News," *The Crescent of Gamma Phi Beta* 4, no. 1 (June 1904): 134, only with the information being credited from an unnamed Chicago newspaper. Despite also being unable to find this newspaper article, I have chosen to refer to the unnamed Chicago newspaper as the source of the original announcement, as it seems the most plausible. One of the most stinging commentaries of Alpha Kappa Nu came from "Greek Notes and Clippings," *The Kappa Alpha Journal* 21, no. 4 (March 1904): 465, which referred to the new fraternity as "Kappa Omicron Omicron Nu." The *Kappa Alpha Journal* is the national magazine of the Kappa Alpha Order, a fraternity founded at Washington and Lee University in Lexington, VA in 1865. Kappa Alpha Order was an unabashedly Southern fraternity in the early 1900s, and like many fraternities founded in the south, was not known for its racial sensitivity at the time. Today, Kappa Alpha Order welcomes men of all races and creeds into membership. For one of the only known photographs of Alpha Kappa Nu members, see Crump, 2. At least two members of Alpha Kappa Nu did go on to graduate–Thomas Henry Reynolds, class of 1906, and Charles Frederick Williamson, class of 1907. See *The Arbutus* (1906 ed.), 60; and *The Arbutus* (1907 ed.), 69. Both of these men listed their affiliation with Alpha Kappa Nu in their respective yearbooks.

42. Wesley, *History of Sigma Pi Phi*, 22–34, which includes the quotation; and Kimbrough, 23–29.

43. Ibid.

44. McGinnis, *A History and Interpretation of Wilberforce University*, 171–173; and Kimbrough, 29–30. One of the only known photographs of the Beta Kappa Sigma Fraternity at Wilberforce is available through the National Afro–American Museum and Cultural Center, http://www.ohiomemory.org/cdm/compoundobject/collection/p15005coll34/id/660/rec/17 (accessed August 20, 2016). There is evidence to suggest other black fraternities also existed around this time, such as Pi Gamma Omicron at the Ohio State University, but, like Alpha Kappa Nu, these organizations lived a short life and did not have a significant impact on the development of the black fraternal movement.

45. Marcus Walter, "Historian: Early black students were 'part and apart' at CU," *Cornell Chronicle*, October 23, 2009; Charles Wesley, "The Alpha Chronicle of 50 Years," *The Sphinx* 42, no. 3 (August 1956): 4–9, 59; "The History and Purpose of Alpha Phi Alpha," *The Sphinx* 3, no. 2 (April 1917): 6–8; Kimbrough, 32–33; Ross, *The Divine Nine*, 5–7; and Henry Callis, "Notes on the Founding of Alpha," *The Sphinx* 38, no. 1 (February 1952): 8–11, back cover.

46. Ibid. On Mr. Poindexter's reluctance to form an exclusive fraternity, see Poindexter, 335–338.

47. Ibid. On the expansion of Alpha Phi Alpha, see Baird (10th ed. 1923), 609. I am basing the claim of Alpha Phi Alpha being the largest Greek letter fraternity in the world from the information on the website http://www.greekrank.com/rankings/size/ (accessed March 16, 2014). For the list of countries where Alpha Phi Alpha is active, see the fraternity's national website, http://www.alpha-phi-alpha.com/index.php (accessed March 16, 2014).

48. Kimbrough, 30–36; and Ross.

49. Torbenson and Parks, 83–85.

50. Ibid. On the description of the Chinese fraternity, see Charles P. Boone, chapter correspondence for California Beta, University of California, Berkeley, in *The Record of Sigma Alpha Epsilon* 21, no. 4 (December 1901): 357–358. On the move to exclude non–whites from most national fraternities, see Syrett, 172.

51. "Turning 100," *The Trinity Reporter* 40, no. 2 (Winter 2010); Chen Ping Lin, "The Fraternity Movement Among Chinese Students," *The Delta Upsilon Quarterly* 37, no. 8 (June 1919): 215; and P. T. Chen, "Chinese Fraternities in America," in *American University Men in China*, American University Club of Shanghai (Shanghai: Comacrib Press, 1936), 153–160. The initials of the fraternity, F. F., led to its nickname, "Flip Flap."

52. On the formation of Rho Psi, see P. T. Chen, 162–164; Chen Ping Lin, 215; and James A. Banks, ed., *Encyclopedia of Diversity in Education* (Thousand Oaks, CA: SAGE Publications, 2012), 929–930. Chen Ping Lin, a Chinese national, joined the Delta Upsilon fraternity while studying at the University of Rochester from 1916–18, and he was the first from his nation to graduate from that school. As a foreign national, his membership in Delta Upsilon was certainly an anomaly at the time, though by all accounts he was a well-respected member of the fraternity. He was also strongly in favor of fraternities embracing international students, a trend that is now, nearly a hundred years later, coming to fruition within the traditionally white fraternities. On the greater movement involving Asian and Asian-American Greek-letter organizations, see Torbenson and Parks, 85–100.

53. Torbenson and Parks, 104–111; *The Transit* (1900 ed.), 77, 91; Baird (10th ed. 1923), 675–677; *Blue and Gold* (1922 ed.), 600; *Blue and Gold* (1923 ed.), 492; "A Sigma–Iota Chapter: International Student Society Enters Syracuse University," *The Syracuse Herald*, October 3, 1913; and "Phi Lambda Alpha and Sigma Iota To Unite," *The Tech*, January 8, 1932.

54. Torbenson and Parks, 109–117, 128–129; and Kimbrough, 177–184. On the use of "Latino/a" as a designator, see Torbenson and Parks, 130. Information about the number of active chapters and colonies from the Phi Iota Theta national website, http://www.phiota.info/?page=Chapters_Colonies (accessed on March 21, 2014).

55. The sheer number of new national Greek-letter organizations that have been established over the past thirty years is quite staggering. On organizations geared towards Native Americans, see Torbenson and Parks, 133–156. On general multicultural organizations, see Torbenson and Parks, 157–183. On organizations geared towards gays, lesbians, bisexuals, and transgendered persons, see Torbenson and Parks, 184–209. On the establishment of religious–based fraternities and sororities other than those for Jewish men and women, see Torbenson and Parks, 220–236. There is already some evidence of these various national organizations consolidating or closing down entirely, but such changes are beyond the scope of this work.

56. Some schools, such as the University of Alabama, have struggled not only with integrating their Greek-letter organizations, but even just having the different groups coexist with one another. In 1986, for example, the historically black sorority Alpha Kappa Alpha moved to a chapter house on Sorority Row, the first time a black organization had done so. They were promptly greeted with a burning cross on their lawn. For a discussion of this incident, see Steve Curwood, "Reports of Racism on Campus Rising, Observers Say; Several Incidents Occurred At New England Colleges," *BG*, December 21, 1986.

CHAPTER 2

1. Start, *History of Tufts College*, 23–24, 33–34, 45; and Miller, *LOTH–1*, section 3.2. For the list of courses available that first school year, see *CofTC* (1854–55 ed.), which was reprinted in Start, 354–357. Although the catalogue lists the course of study for all four classes (freshman through senior), I am assuming the seven who started in the fall of 1854 followed the freshman course of study that first semester. One of the three professors, William A. Drew, lived in College Hall with the seven men that first year. He was also the first professor to quit Tufts College just a couple of years later–coincidence, or not?

2. Start, 24; and Miller, *LOTH–1*, section 11.3. On the ages of the first enrolled students, see Start, 115, 252. Although Start does not provide the birthdate for all students, it appears many of them were in their early twenties when they started their college careers. On the founding date and room location, see Mathetican Society Records 1854–1962, UA 079.001 Box 1, Folder 3 (Secretary's Record Book, 1854–1863).

3. Mathetican Society Records; and Hill, "History of Debating in Tufts College," 203. Note that Hill lists Heman Dearborn as a founder of the society, but this is not possible since Heman did not enroll at Tufts College until the fall of 1855. Since the early meetings of the Mathetican Society all happened in dormitory rooms, either after class or on weekends, I am assuming the faculty were not involved in any way with the creation of the organization. Of these seven founders, five would become some of the first graduates of Tufts College, and I have indicated their graduation year in parentheses. Edward Sampson is listed in Start, 302, as a non-graduate from the class of 1857. Very little is known about Nathaniel Faunce, although he does appear regularly in the minutes of the Mathetican Society throughout the 1854–55 school year (he was the group's first treasurer). After the spring of 1855, though, it appears Nathaniel left Tufts College, never to return. The first use of the name "Mathetican" in the minutes of the society appeared on October 18, 1855, the first anniversary of the organization.

4. Mathetican Society Records, which includes the first quotation; and Hill, 203–205, which includes the second quotation. On the Know Nothing Society, see George F. Hoar, *Autobiography of Seventy Years: Volume I* (New York, NY: Charles Scribner and Sons, 1905), 188–191; Albert W. Macy, *Curious Bits of History* (New York, NY: The Cosmopolitan Press, 1912), 23–24; and Humphrey J. Desmond, *The Know-Nothing Party: A Sketch* (Washington, DC: The New Century Press, 1904). The Know Nothing Society did practice secrecy on some levels, which is somewhat unique for a political party. Its name supposedly came about as the answer its members were to repeat when asked about their organization: "I know nothing about it."

5. Mathetican Society Records; and Hill, 203–205, which includes the quotation. On the building of the first dormitory (now known as Packard Hall), see Tolles, *Architecture & Academe*, 132–134. The location of the Mathetican Society within College Hall is placed by a few sources, including UA Edwin B. Rollins Papers 1860–1976, Notebooks, 1940–1955, MS054.001 Box 1, Folder 1 (The Earlier Buildings of Tufts College 1940–1955). Start, 24, mentions in his book that two rooms in College Hall were specifically designed for literary societies when the building was constructed. However, these rooms were used as living quarters that first year, since the Mathetican Society records clearly indicate the men operated out of individual dormitory rooms. In all likelihood, the Mathetican Society was given its room in College Hall only after the student boarders moved out.

6. Hill, 204; and UA Edwin B. Rollins Papers 1860–1976, Notebooks, 1940–1955, MS054.001 Box 2, Folder 5 (Reminiscences 1940–1955). According to the *CofTC* (1857–58 ed.), the freshman and sophomore classes each numbered twelve men, so we can assume the membership in the Walnut Hill Fraternity at its start was probably no more than twelve to fifteen men in total. Unfortunately, it appears the Walnut Hill Fraternity kept scant records of its operations. According to Hill, 204, the first president of the society was Lorin L. Dame. The merger of the Walnut Hill Fraternity with the Mathetican is discussed briefly in the Mathetican Secretary's Record Book dated June 5 and June 9, 1857, but the entries are hard to understand, and it may have been that the two societies only agreed to work together to plan the first commencement exercises, rather than combine. However, according to Mathetican Society Records 1854–1962, UA 079.001 Box 2, Folder 7 (Treasurer's Book, 1855–1873), the Walnut Hill Fraternity transferred $18 to the Mathetican on July 11, 1858, which I assume as the official end to the Walnut Hill Fraternity.

7. Hill, 206–207, which includes the quotation; and UA Edwin B. Rollins Papers 1860–1976, Notebooks, 1940–1955, MS054.001 Box 2, Folder 5 (Reminiscences 1940–1955). On the founding of the Divinity school, see Miller, *LOTH–1*, 111–123. The founding date for the Zetagathean Society, September 18, 1871, is listed in *The Tuftonian* 1, no. 8 (December 1871). While archival records on the Zetagathean are scant, copies of the anniversary programs from 1874, 1877–81, and 1883 are housed in Crane Theological School Records 1855–1987, Subject Files, 1855–1973, UA 008.001 Box 9, Folder 6 (Zetagathean Society 1889). I do find it somewhat preposterous the Zetagathean Society not only argued against religious freedom, but won. In 1890, some divinity students created the Sawyer Club as the successor to the Zetagathean Society, but as such these efforts essentially went nowhere, and the Sawyer Club disbanded soon thereafter.

8. Hill, 205–206. The rise of the two fraternities, Zeta Psi and Theta Delta Chi, is discussed at length in chapter 3 of this work. The terms "society" and "non-society" when referring to men or women were commonly used until the early twentieth century to distinguish between those in a fraternity or sorority, and those not. I will use these descriptors when appropriate for the time period under discussion.

9. Hill, 207–209; and Miller, *LOTH–1*, 302. On the use of the name "Mathetican" by the group wishing to become a chapter of Delta Upsilon, see "The Delta Upsilon Movement at Tufts College," *The Delta Upsilon Quarterly* 5, no. 2 (January 1887): 89–90. "Mathetican" was misspelled as "Mathelican" in the article.

10. The thoughts here are essentially my opinions on the demise of the Mathetican.

However, as we shall see in the story of the Commons Club in Chapter 3, and the Delphoi Society in Chapter 4, open membership in a broad-reaching group can be difficult, if not impossible, to maintain over the long run.

11. Miller, *LOTH–1*, 62–63; and "The Kappa Semi-Centennial," 265–266. This article in *The Shield* is a reprint of a number of speeches given on the fiftieth anniversary of the founding of the Kappa Charge of Theta Delta Chi, and as such it contains many inconsistencies with regards to names. For example, the head of the boarding room in Packard Hall is identified as both Mr. Tower and Mr. Talbot in the article, but I have assumed Mr. Tower is correct, whereas "Talbot" was probably a slip of the tongue. Newton Talbot, a local businessman, became a trustee of Tufts College ten years after the founding of the Order of the Coffee Pot, and by the late 1800s, a street on campus had been named in his honor. Therefore, his name would have been well known to alumni. But, he had nothing to do with the founding of the Order, nor was he ever a dormitory cook. On the price of board in 1858, see the *CofTC* (1857–58 ed.), 16. Various on-line inflation calculators show $2 in 1857 is worth just over $50 in 2014. Espressos Pizza and Hee Kar Lau were two favorites of mine for late-night food while an undergraduate at Tufts in the late 1980s, so I couldn't resist mentioning them by name. According to Tolles, 132–33, the building now known as Packard Hall was first called Building A, then West Hall, Middle Hall, and finally Packard Hall, in 1910. I have chosen to refer to this building exclusively as Packard Hall to avoid confusion, since there is another dormitory on campus known as West Hall.

12. "The Kappa Semi-Centennial," 265–266; and Miller, *LOTH–1*, 384. The membership roll for the Order of the Coffee Pot was first published in *The Tuftonian* 1, no. 1 (November 1864), and from this article it appears the organizers of the club may have been Oscar Sawyer, George Hathaway, and William Johnson. Also listed as members were Benjamin Hathaway, a founding member of the Zeta Psi chapter at Tufts, and Elmer Capen, a founding member of the Theta Delta Chi charge at Tufts.

13. Miller, *LOTH–1*, 384. The logo for the Order of the Round Table was printed in many editions of *The Tuftonian* including vol. 1, no. 7 (November 1870). The membership roll for the Order of the Round Table was also first published in *The Tuftonian* 1, no. 1 (November 1864), and by examining various editions of the *CofTC*, I was able to determine the class years of the members. Also, by crosschecking these names in the *Zeta Psi Semi-Centennial Biographical Catalogue* and Griffing, *Sixth Catalogue of Theta Delta Chi*, I was able to determine which men were in each fraternity. The translation of the Latin motto was provided by Barbara Vitale.

14. The ending date for the Order of the Coffee Pot is based upon information from *The Tuftonian* 1, no. 5 (November 1868), which lists only two seniors as active members, and *The Tuftonian* 1, no. 6 (November 1869), which does not list any undergraduates as current members. The ending date for the Order of the Round Table is based upon information from *The Tuftonian* 1, no. 7 (November 1870), which listed three active members, and *The Tuftonian*, December 1871, which stated the organization was no longer active. Publication of *The Tuftonian* was not as well organized between 1870 and 1878 as it had been, with the use of edition and issues numbers notably lacking in the text. On the efforts of President Carmichael to obtain the fob, see the various letters in Activities and Organizations records, 1875–2013, UA 024.001 Box 6, Folder 8 (Order of the Coffee Pot 1866–1950). On the attempted revival of the Order of the Coffee Pot, see "Coffee Pot Society Formed to Perk Up School Spirit," *TW*, October 4, 1951.

According to this article, the Order was active for a little while as a secret society, with two members each from the sophomore, junior, and senior classes. The idea behind this revival was to promote school spirit, but it appears the Order did not capture the attention of the students, and was not mentioned again in print.

15. *The Tuftonian* 1, no. 1 (November 1864). Again, by crosschecking the names of the members as listed in this publication with *Zeta Psi Semi-Centennial* and Griffing, I was able to determine that all of the undergraduate members of Epsilon Pi Kappa Chi were also in either Zeta Psi or Theta Delta Chi. In Miller, 386, the author refers to the organization as "Epsilon of Pi Kappa Chi," implying it was perhaps the Epsilon chapter of a larger Pi Kappa Chi organization. However, I believe this is in error, as the listing in *The Tuftonian* does not use the word "of" in the group's name. Also, there is no evidence of a national organization called Pi Kappa Chi in existence at the time.

16. *The Tuftonian* 1, no. 1 (November 1864); and *The Tuftonian* 1, no. 2 (November 1865). Again, crosschecking the membership rolls showed that some were also in Zeta Psi or Theta Delta Chi.

17. *The Tuftonian* 1, no. 2 (November 1865). In this edition, organizations listed in the "Secret Societies" section include Zeta Psi, Theta Delta Chi, Order of the Coffee Pot, Order of the Round Table, Old Gimlet Fraternity, and The Pentagon, whereas the "Public Societies" section lists only the Mathetican.

18. *The Tuftonian* 1, no. 7 (November 1870); and *The Tuftonian*, December 1871. Interestingly, both Start, 46, and Miller, *LOTH–1*, 384, claim this organization was called "So Fa." However, the group's logo as published in *The Tuftonian* only has the initials "S. F." and does not identify what these letters mean. Perhaps Start and Miller came across other documentation within the Tufts archives that explained these initials or used these words. However, I was unable to find any such documentation.

19. *The Tuftonian* (1873–74 ed.).

20. *B&B* (1879 ed.); and *The Tuftonian* 5, no. 8 (May 1879).

21. Miller, *LOTH–1*, 385–86.

22. Sheldon, *Student Life and Customs*, 97–102; and Syrett, *The Company He Keeps*, 18–19. A complete look at inter-class hazing is beyond the scope of this work, and these sources are but two of many. On the hazing practices at Tufts and its "death" in 1882, see Start, 34, 64–65.

23. Start, 65; "Greek Letter Gossip," *The Delta Upsilon Quarterly* 4, no. 2 (January 1888): 125, which includes the first quotation; and *B&B* (1888 ed.), 44–45, which includes the second quotation. The cryptic names of the members as listed in *B&B* included N. E. Verwas, N. E. Verwillbe, I. S. Entwas, and A. L. Lofus.

24. Start, 65; *The Tuftonian* 22, no. 7 (May–June 1896): 229; and *The Tuftonian* 23, no. 1 (October 1896): 20.

25. On the requirement for daily chapel, see *CofTC* (1897–98 ed.), 130. Chapel rushes were common on many campuses throughout the 1800s and early 1900s, though as class sizes became bigger, colleges began cracking down on the event due to the fear of grave injury. It did not help, too, that many administrators resented sanctuaries being used in such an inappropriate manner. For example, see Conrad V. O'Malley, "The Clarkson Monitor," *Clarkson Bulletin* 5, no. 4 (October 1908): 163; "Cane Rush," *The Lafayette* 30, no. 1 (September 25, 1903): 5; and "The Proposed Resolutions," *The Hamilton Literary Monthly* 25, no. 6 (February 1891): 216. Other types of rushes remained popular, however, including the "cane rush," where freshmen

attempted to carry canes around campus and other class members looked to steal them. On the crackdown of President Capen, see "No More Hazing at Tufts," *Boston Evening Transcript*, October 5, 1898. On the dwindling popularity of Rho Kappa Tau in the aftermath of this decree, see "Rho Kappa Tau," *TW*, October 4, 1899, which is the last reference I have found to this group. Despite the crackdown on chapel rushes and the demise of Rho Kappa Tau, inter-class hazing of some form at Tufts continued well into the 1960s, until a greater social upheaval ended many of the traditions at Tufts.

26. On the founding and activities of Tower Cross, Ivy Society (originally called Ivy Leaf), and Sword and Shield, see their entries in *Concise Encyclopedia of Tufts History*, http://hdl.handle.net/10427/14829 (accessed August 21, 2016). On the Full Moon Club, see *B&B* (1904 ed.), 142, which includes the first quotation. On the description of the activities of the Full Moon Club, see Nichols, *History of Gamma Beta Tufts*, 7, which includes the second quotation. Of the twelve members in the club, two were also in Theta Delta Chi, three were in Delta Tau Delta, two were in Zeta Psi, one was in Delta Upsilon, and four were in Alpha Tau Omega.

CHAPTER 3

1. I can almost hear the groans from the alumni and active members of both Zeta Psi and Theta Delta Chi for combining their histories into one section, while every other organization has its own. However, their stories overlap so much, more than any other two organizations at Tufts, that they can only be told together. The six college presidents as referred to in the text are as follows: From Theta Delta Chi, Reverend Elmer Hewitt Capen (Tufts College, 1875–1905); Reverend Frederick W. Hamilton (Tufts College acting President 1905–1906, President 1906–1912); William Leslie Hooper (Tufts College, acting president 1912–1914); Samuel P. Capen (University of Buffalo, 1922–1950); and Leonard Carmichael (Tufts College, 1938–1952). From Zeta Psi, Almon Gunnison (St. Lawrence University, 1899–1914).

2. McElroy, *The Jubilee of the Zeta Psi Fraternity of North America*, 44–49, which includes the quotations; Bement, *The Story of Zeta Psi*, 26–28; Zeta Psi, *Semicentennial Biographical Catalogue*, 17–18; and Maxwell, *Greek Letter Men of Boston*, 295–96. On the three fraternities active at NYU in 1847, see also Baird (1st ed. 1879), 178.

3. Ibid. Concerning the legacy of Mr. Dayton, I ran into considerable confusion about his whereabouts during the 1846–47 school year. Numerous (but not all) sources, including Bement, 28, and Birchfield, *Zeta Psi Fraternity of North America Double Diamond Jubilee 1847–1997*, 46, state that Mr. Dayton was a student at NYU when he joined up with Mr. Sommers. However, after corresponding with an archivist at NYU, I was told there is no record of Mr. Dayton ever enrolling at the school, whereas Messrs. Sommers and Skillman are listed as sophomores in the *Catalogue of the Officers and Students of the University of the City of New York* (1846–47 ed.), 14. Still, Mr. Dayton's signature is clearly visible on the pledge form the three men signed on June 1, 1847, as shown in Bement, 48–49, so he must have been in New York City when the fraternity was officially founded. The ages of the men on June 1, 1847 are based on the birthdays as provided in Bement, 27, 33, 35, although in the case of Mr. Dayton, only his birth year (1827) is mentioned.

4. Again, there is considerable confusion over the path Mr. Dayton took to UNC.

A few sources, including Birchfield, 46; Bement, 29, 33–34; and Zeta Psi, 17–18, claim that Mr. Dayton enrolled at UNC and completed his freshman year (supposedly 1846–1847) before passing away. However, the archivists at UNC were unable to find any record of Mr. Dayton ever enrolling at the school. Therefore, it appears that Mr. Dayton was never an enrolled student at either NYU or UNC. One certainty seems to be the date of Mr. Dayton's death, August 17, 1847, as reported in Bement, 32. UNC would eventually gain the Upsilon chapter of Zeta Psi in 1858. On the expansion of Zeta Psi, see Baird (1st ed. 1879), 125–127.

5. Although rankings of various colleges and universities over time are always subjective, many historians have remarked on the prestige enjoyed by Union College under the leadership of Rev. Nott, who served as president from 1804–1866. For example, see *Union College, 1795–1895: A Record of the Commemoration June Twenty–First to Twenty–Seventh, 1895* (New York: The DeVinne Press, 1897), 37–60. On the enrollment of Union in comparison to other schools, see *Union College*, 56. On the founding of Theta Delta Chi, see Griffing, *Sixth Catalogue of Theta Delta Chi*, 33; and "History," from the website of the national Theta Delta Chi fraternity, http://thetadeltachi.net/index.php?option=com_content&view=article&id=123&Itemid=531 (accessed April 5, 2014). The five national fraternities started at Union College and active in 1848 were: Kappa Alpha (1825), Sigma Phi (1827), Delta Phi (1827), Psi Upsilon (1833) and Chi Psi (1841). The sixth organization active at the time was Delta Upsilon, whose chapter dated back to 1838. With regards to the founding date of Theta Delta Chi, the national organization refers to that first meeting in May of 1847 as the official start of the fraternity. However, it appears the men did not formalize their organization until June 5, 1848, as discussed in Griffing, 33; "History of Theta Delta Chi, 1848–98," *The Scroll* 23, no. 6 (June 1899): 620–621; and Baird (1st ed. 1879), 120–121.

6. Baird (1st ed. 1879), 121; and Griffing, 38.

7. Bement, 324–325. The Reverend Hosea Ballou 2d reluctantly accepted the presidency of Tufts College only after the first choice of the trustees, Thomas Jefferson Sawyer, demanded too much money in salary. Rev. Ballou worried he was too old for the job, and he feared financial ruin should the college fail. See Miller, *LOTH–1*, 50–51. On the travels of Rev. Ballou, see Ballou, *Hosea Ballou*, 175–189. He returned to the Tufts campus on November 18, 1854, about a month after classes had started.

8. Zeta Psi, *Catalogue of the Zeta Psi Fraternity*, 43; Zeta Psi, *Semicentennial Catalogue*, 22, 403; and Start, *History of Tufts College*, 207. Unfortunately, the relationship between Morse and Flagg of Harvard, and Hathaway of Tufts has been lost to history. Of the founders, John C. Redman and John F. Wood are listed in Start, 303, as non-graduates from the class of 1859.

9. Bement, 325–326, which includes the quotation. Although the resolutions against Kappa chapter were passed just a few days before the initiation of the Tufts men, I assume word did not reach Rho chapter until after Kappa chapter had been established by initiation. The four resolutions as passed seem to indicate the grand officers only had a problem with the procedure used to establish Kappa chapter, as opposed to any negative bias against Tufts or its students, for they clearly told the Harvard men to keep pursuing the effort. One can easily imagine that the grand officers, by calling for a vote amid such uncertainty, felt they would win handily and tamp down any further dissent.

10. Bement, 326–327, which includes the quotation. Bement's description of the

various motions at the convention is somewhat confusing, so I have done my best to interpret how everything played out.

11. Ibid. It is unclear to me when, exactly, a vote affirming the Tufts petition was taken, but based on the information in Bement, I assume it was later in that convention of July 1856. Regardless, Zeta Psi Fraternity recognizes October 22, 1855, as the official start of its Kappa chapter.

12. Zeta Psi, *Semicentennial Catalogue*, 405; Start, 207; and Bement, 328, which includes the quotation. Fraternity houses were not yet in vogue in the 1850s, as fraternity chapters instead operated out of rooms or meeting halls they rented off campus. See Syrett, *The Company He Keeps*, 30. There is some confusion on the dates and locations of Zeta Psi's early chapter rooms. Concerning the first room, Bement claims the chapter rented the space from Angel "at the end of the first year," whereas the *Semicentennial Catalogue* states the chapter used a dormitory room for the first year and then moved to a room off campus on December 10, 1856. Start confirms this latter version as well, though he does not give an exact date as to when the chapter moved off campus. Therefore, I tend to believe the date as presented in the *Semicentennial Catalogue*, but the story as presented in Bement and Start. Concerning the second room, the *Semicentennial Catalogue* claims this was in Usher's Block (which is in West Medford), but does not give a specific date when the chapter moved there. However, both Bement and Start say the second room was on Main St. in Medford, a few miles away from Usher's Block. Also, Bement and Start discuss the subsequent fire, and Bement even quotes recollections from members who were active at the time. Therefore, I tend to believe Bement and Start in this case. Zeta Psi did end up in Usher's Block of West Medford, where it maintained chapter rooms for over thirty years, but I believe this residency started after the Civil War, as will be discussed later in this section.

13. *CofTC* (1857–58 ed.), 5; "The Kappa Semi-Centennial," 265; and Marvin, *A History of Kappa Charge*, 2.

14. "The Kappa Semi-Centennial," 265. I am assuming Augustus would have preferred to stay at Brown, given the way he reminisced about his freshman year during this speech.

15. "The Kappa Semi-Centennial," 266–267; and Start, 212. On the date of the charter, see Griffing, 137, although the founding year is listed as 1854 and not 1856, which I believe a printing error.

16. "The Kappa Semi-Centennial," 266–267, which includes the quotation; and Marvin, 2. The list of charter members is from Griffing, 137, where I have also indicated the graduation years for some of the men. According to Start, 302, Oscar Sawyer was a non-graduate from the class of 1860. Horatio McIntire does not show up in the directory of either graduates or non-graduates in Start, so I assume he did not graduate, either. Apparently, he was only a student for the 1856–57 school year.

17. "The Kappa Semi-Centennial," 267; Marvin, 2; and Holmes, *Memorial History of Theta Delta Chi*, 110. According to Augustus's recollection, the firehouse was "on the side of the street just off from Main Street, this side of Medford Square."

18. "The Kappa Semi-Centennial," 270; Holmes, *Memorial History of Theta Delta Chi*, 110; and Marvin, 3, which includes the quotation. The writing and subsequent reading of poetry at national conventions was quite popular with fraternities at the time, as literary activities were still a major part of their operations.

19. W. N. Freeman, "The Little Old Fraternity of Our Daddies," *The Shield* 37, no.

1 (October 1920): 94–96; and Holmes, 100, which includes the quotation. According to Griffing, 19, the 12th convention was held on Troy, NY from June 9–10, 1859, and was subsequently covered by the press in "Theta Delta Chi," *New York Saturday Press*, June 11, 1859, 2; The convention of 1859 marked a turning point in the governance of Theta Delta Chi, as the fraternity abandoned the rule of Alpha Charge and organized a Grand Lodge to oversee national issues.

20. I am basing the claim of Tufts students supporting the Union from an article in *The Tuftonian* 1, no. 1 (November, 1864): 4, which lists the names of forty students from the classes of 1858–68 who enlisted in Union regiments from Massachusetts, New Hampshire, Vermont, New York, Maine, and Kentucky. No student was listed as joining a Confederate regiment – Kentucky sent many men to fight for Confederacy, but the Union also organized regiments from that state later in the war, as will be discussed shortly. Also, I arrived at the 30% figure by counting the total number of alumni from 1858–68 (one hundred twenty-four in all) as listed in Start, 253–262. I did not include non-graduates in this percentage.

21. "Alumni Notes–1863," *The Tufts College Graduate* 5, (April 1907–January 1908): 44; "Col. Horatio Bisbee–Death Occurred, Yesterday at His Summer Home In Dixfield," *The Lewiston Daily Sun*, March 24, 1916; "Bisbee, Horatio," *Concise Encyclopedia of Tufts History*, http://hdl.handle.net/10427/14829 (accessed April 8, 2014); "Bisbee, Horatio, Jr.," *A Biographical Congressional Directory: 1774–1903*, (Washington, D.C.: Government Printing Office, 1903), 393–394; "Letter from 9th Maine Regiment," *Lewiston [Maine] Daily Evening Journal*, October 12, 1861, 2; and Charles Francis, "Canton's Horatio Bisbee," http://bisbeefamily.com/histories/bisbee/horatio_4239/h4239.pdf (accessed April 8, 2014). As can be expected, there is some contradictory information about Horatio Bisbee in these sources. For one, *Concise Encyclopedia* claims Bisbee rose to the rank of Brigadier General, but this appears to be false given that his obituary only mentions the rank of Colonel. Also, the *Biographical Directory* states Bisbee lasted only three months in the 5th Massachusetts Regiment, whereas Frank J. Bisbee says it was five months. Horatio Bisbee never returned to Tufts after dropping out in 1861, but he was eventually awarded his A.B. and A.M. degrees with the class of 1863 in honor of his service. Finally, I have used the common convention of referencing Civil War infantry regiments simply by their number and state – see *Record of the Federal Dead Buried from Libby, Belle Isle, Danville & Camp Lawton Prisons and at City Point, and in the Field before Petersburg and Richmond* (Philadelphia, PA: U. S. Christian Commission, 1866).

22. "Tufts College Record," in *The Universalist Register, Containing the Statistics of the Denomination for 1866* (Boston, MA: New England Universalist Publishing House, 1866), 68–69; Zeta Psi, *Semi-Centennial Catalogue*, 407–413; Thomas Laurens Smith, *History of the Town of Windham* (Portland, ME: Hoyt & Fogg, 1873), 54–55; *Minutes of the General Convention of Universalists in the United States, 1865* (Philadelphia, PA: John Alexander Printer, 1865), 51–52; and Start, 208. There is considerable conflicting information in these sources. Concerning Lt. Lowell, Smith does not mention his capture by the Confederacy, claiming instead he died on the battlefield, but *Minutes of the General Convention*, Zeta Psi, and Start do mention his capture, so I defer to these three sources. Concerning Lt. Walton, "Tufts College Record" claims he died in Louisiana in 1864, but this is not possible since the Battle of Cedar Creek was fought in Virginia, 1864, as correctly mentioned in Zeta Psi and Start.

23. Gardner, *History of Calhoun County Michigan*, 553; *Collections and Researches Made by the Michigan Pioneer and Historical Society–Volume 28*, (Lansing, MI: Robert Smith Printing Co., 1900), 30; Zeta Psi, *Semi-Centennial Catalogue*, 412; and "Obituary Notes," *NYT*, December 19, 1896. There is some confusion over the exact dates of Lt. Loud's service with the 1st Michigan Cavalry as listed in these named sources, so I am not exactly sure when he left Michigan to head back to Massachusetts. On the dates of Lt. Loud's commissions as a Union officer in the 5th Massachusetts Colored Cavalry, see *Public Documents of Massachusetts*, 982. According to this source, the 5th Massachusetts Colored Cavalry was organized between January 9, 1864, and May 5, 1864. Colored units, which consisted of black soldiers, black NCOs, and white officers, were somewhat experimental at the time, for reasons that seem rather silly today – the generals and leaders of the armed forces, who were all white, wondered if blacks could fight as well as their white counterparts. To test the theory, they organized colored units. The 5th Massachusetts Colored Cavalry was one of three to come out of Massachusetts, with the other two being the 54th and the 55th regiments.

24. Conn, *History of the New Hampshire Surgeons in the War of Rebellion*, 302–303; Major W. H. Hodgkins, ed., *Military Record of the Sons of Dartmouth in the Union Army and Navy, 1861–1865* (Boston, MA: Trustees of Dartmouth College, 1908), 118; While units organized at the state level were common in the Civil War, there were also other units organized at the federal level, such as the 5th U. S. Colored Cavalry (U. S. C. C.), which was wholly separate from the 5th Massachusetts Colored Cavalry. On the organization of the 5th U. S. C. C., see *The War of the Rebellion: A Compilation of the Official Records of the Union and Confederate Armies: Series 1, Vol. 49, Part 1* (Washington, D.C.: Government Printing Office, 1897), 895; "City Intelligence," *Sacramento [CA] Daily Union,* May 13, 1865; and "James B. Brisbin," in *Encyclopedia of Contemporary Biography of Pennsylvania: Vol. 3* (New York, NY: Atlantic Publishing & Engraving Co., 1898), 125–126.

25. On the men who went to war, see Marvin, 3. "Winsor Brown French," *The Shield* 6, no. 1 (April 1890), 15–17. On General Bidwell and the Battle of Cedar Creek, see David J. Eicher, 752. The Battle of Cedar Creek, by coincidence, was where Lt. Henry Walton, Zeta Psi, was killed.

26. On the dates of Capt. Lewis's commissions and confirmation of his death, see *Public Documents of Massachusetts*, 916–917; and Start, 258. On the assault at Petersburg, VA, see Eicher, 720–723. On the quotation from Capt. Lewis, see *B&B* (1894 ed.), 73.

27. Start, 208; Bement, 328–329; *B&B* (1894 ed.), 67; Zeta Psi, *Catalogue of the Zeta Psi*, 43–45; and Zeta Psi, *Semicentennial Catalogue*, 404, 408–414. These latter two sources list the initiation dates of each member, and show that none were initiated between October 1861, and September 1864. The group of nine men, it appears, originally came together with the hopes of securing a charter from the Chi Phi national fraternity. However, their efforts were not successful, so they decided to join Zeta Psi instead.

28. The claim of Kappa Charge graduating men throughout the Civil War is supported by Griffing, 137–138, which shows at least one member in each graduating class. On the activities of Kappa Charge during the war, see Marvin, 3–4. On the relations between Zeta Psi and Theta Delta Chi during the early 1860s, see Bement, 329. On the publication of *The Tuftonian*, see Martin, 4; Zeta Psi, *Semi-Centennial Catalogue*, 404;

Bement, 330–331; and Elias B. Armstrong, "History of Journalism at Tufts College," *The Tuftonian* 30, no. 8 (May, 1905): 310–314. According to Marvin, 3, Kappa Charge did publish a weekly called *Literary Paper* starting in 1863, but it is unclear if this was meant just for the Charge, or the Tufts College campus as a whole, so I am considering *The Tuftonian* as the first campus publication. Also it appears no copies of *Literary Paper* have survived to the present day.

29. Armstrong, 310–314; Marvin, 4–5; Bement, 331–332; Miller, *LOTH–1*, 417–420; and Activities and Organizations records, 1875–2013, UA 024.001 Box 16, Folder 9 (Theta Delta Chi 1857–1971), which contains copies of *The Budget*. As discussed in Armstrong, 311, the use of the word *Collegian* was eventually abandoned because too many other schools used it in the titles of their publications, thereby creating confusion among the college publishing world. Concerning the colors of brown and blue for Tufts, these only became official in 1960 following a vote of the trustees. The fraternities did not have as much control over the content of the *Brown and Blue* yearbook, since its publication was eventually taken over by the junior class.

30. Hosea M. Knowlton, "Beginning of Baseball in Tufts College," *The Tuftonian* 27, no. 7 (April, 1902): 169–173; and Charles C. Stroud, "History of Baseball at Tufts," *The Tuftonian* 28, no. 8 (May 1903): 273–275.

31. Ibid. On the election of Henry Cory as first captain, see Knowlton, "Reminiscences of College Days," 199–205. By crosschecking the student's names in the *CofTC* (1864–1865 ed.) and "Athletic Rosters of Tufts University–Baseball, 1864," http://hdl.handle.net/10427/14797 (accessed April 12, 2014) against Zeta Psi, *Catalogue of the Zeta Psi Fraternity*, 43–45, and *Theta Delta Chi*, 59–62, I was able to determine the percentage of fraternity men on the baseball teams. For quotation, see Stroud, 273–274.

32. *The Tuftonian* 1, no. 1 (November 1864): 2; Bement, 330; Start, 47–48; "Athletic Rosters of Tufts University–Rowing/Crew, 1864–1871," http://hdl.handle.net/10427/14797 (accessed April 12, 2014); and Knowlton, 199–205. Start mentions the boats were only four-oared, but *The Tuftonian* and the Athletic Rosters mention the boats had six oars. By crosschecking the names on the athletic rosters with Zeta Psi, *Catalogue of the Zeta Psi Fraternity*, 43–45, and Griffing, 137–140, I was able to determine that the Undine Boat Club was made up almost exclusively of Zeta Psi members. Concerning the "Theta Boat Club," I also found references that stated the club's name was "Theta Kappa Boat Club," but I settled on the former since it is more prevalent. Finally, based on the article in *The Tuftonian*, it appears the motivation for starting the boat clubs was not necessarily athletic competition. As written in this article, "The members of these clubs [Theta and Undine] have manifested considerable interest in boating, but it is a matter of grave doubt whether it has been through a desire for exercise simply, or to attract the attention of the 'fair damsels' of Medford. The popular opinion, however, inclines towards the latter."

33. Bement, 330.

34. Marvin, 6; "Kappa–Tufts College," *The Shield* 4, no. 1 (February 1888): 36; and Holmes, 181, 206, 215, 249. Information regarding Kappa's help in re-starting the Charge at MIT was provided by Adam McCready, a former President of the Grand Lodge of Theta Delta Chi.

35. Holmes, 110–114; Start, 53–76; Rudolf Tombo, "In Memoriam," *The Shield* 21, no. 2 (June, 1905): 166–196; and Linus C. Coggan, "A History of Tufts College: Chapter 4 – President Capen's Administration," *The Tuftonian* 30, no. 8 (May, 1905):

276–279. On the influence President Capen had over the active Charge, see Marvin, 4–5, and "The Greek Press," *The Phi Gamma Delta* 27, no. 6 (April 1905): 565–566. On the list of Theta Delta Chi alumni who became presidents of Tufts College, see Note 1. As mentioned in *The Tuftonian* article, Elmer Capen was actually the second choice for president in 1875. The first choice, Hon. Israel Washburn, Jr., was a former U. S. Congressman, Governor of Maine, and a trustee of Tufts College. He also helped found the national Republican Party in 1854 when the Whig Party broke apart. However, being the president of a small college was not something he wanted. He declined the job as soon as he was elected.

36. Marvin, 5; Holmes, 110–114, 223–224; National fraternities still publish semi-annual journals, but they are much different in scope and form than the publications from the late 1800s, when each fraternity was really trying to outdo all others. One of the more interesting sections in each journal was the "Greek Gossip" section, where the fraternity publishing the journal would comment on various articles in other journals. These comments are often filled with a dry, sardonic humor meant to embarrass, if not belittle other organizations. Interfraternity rivalry played out well in these journals, there being no other medium of mass communication available at the time.

37. Bement, 332–333. It was not uncommon in the late 1800s for national fraternities to remove chapters from schools they no longer felt worthy. Part of this was due to a changing attitude about what it meant to be a Greek-letter organization – fraternities were starting to rent and build houses, and those chapters that were unable to afford such expenditure were often the first to be culled. Reputation was everything; chapters that could not keep up were soon left behind. See Syrett, 82–94, 161–165.

38. Bement, 334–335, which includes the quotation. I do find it amusing that Mr. Pierson was able to get away with his scheme. Apparently no one else in the leadership of Zeta Psi checked on what he sent out to the chapters.

39. Z. Kent Graham, "History of Alpha Epsilon of Chi Psi," *The Michigan Alumnus* 3, no. 20 (October–November 1896): 21–30; Andrew Robert Warner, ed., *The Sixth Decennial Catalogue of the Chi Psi Fraternity* (Auburn, NY: Chi Psi Fraternity, 1902), 249–252; and "The First Fraternity House in America," *The Purple and Gold* 16, no. 3 (April, 1899): 215–218. There is some confusion as to the year the lodge was built, as most sources say 1846, but Graham says the year was 1845. For this discrepancy, I have deferred to the majority of sources, especially since Warner lists David James as a member of the Class of 1849, which means he would most likely not have been a student in the spring of 1845. This lodge was obviously quite different than the modern-day fraternity house, as no member ever roomed or boarded there. Nonetheless, it was the first house to be occupied solely by a college fraternity. To honor their place in history, chapters of the Chi Psi fraternity still refer to their houses as "lodges."

40. On the evolution from meeting room to fraternity house, see Syrett, 30. This is by no means an exhaustive look at the trend, but details are beyond the scope of this work, even though I find the architecture of those early fraternity houses quite fascinating. On the work of the housing committee and formation of the corporation, see Activities and Organizations records, 1875–2013, UA024.001 Box 16, Folder 10 (Theta Delta Chi 1881–1967); and Marvin, 5–7.

41. Board of Trustees records, 1848–2013, Executive Committee, 1854–2000, Meeting minutes 1854–1962, UA003.002 Box 112, Folder 6 (Executive committee minutes, vol. 5, 1889–1896: June 20, 1892). On the occupancy of fraternity houses by

Heth Aleph Res and Delta Tau Delta, see their sections later in this chapter.

42. Board of Trustees records, 1848–2013, Full Board, 1851–2012, Meeting Minutes 1851–1955, UA003.001 Box 106, Folder 1 (Full Board Minutes vol. 3, 1887–1895: May 8, 1893, and July 24, 1893); Activities and Organizations records, 1875–2013, UA024.001 Box 16, Folder 10 (Theta Delta Chi 1881–1967); *Tuftonian* (June 26, 1893); and Marvin, 7–8, which includes the quotation. Though Goddard Chapel and the original Theta Delta Chi house shared the same architect, the two structures could not be more different. Goddard Chapel, made of stone, looks as if a hurricane could not move it. The original Theta Delta Chi house, made of wood, looked as if a gentle breeze could topple it over. In today's money, the cost of Theta Delta Chi's land and house is approximately $180,000, according to various on-line inflation calculators. Such money would not go very far towards housing in either Medford or Somerville today.

43. Bement, 333–335; Zeta Psi, *Semi-Centennial Catalogue*, 405; Walter H. Belcher, "Organization of the Corporation," *The Mystic Chain* 1, no. 1 (December 15, 1939): 3; Walter H. Belcher, "History of the Fraternity," *The Mystic Chain* 1, no. 2 (January 19, 1940); and Walter H. Belcher, "History of the Corporation," *The Mystic Chain* 1, no. 3 (March 15, 1940): 5. *The Mystic Chain* was a short-lived alumni newsletter for Kappa chapter of Zeta Psi. These three copies are housed in UA, Russell Carpenter Papers 1833–2012, Personal Papers, 1938–1969, MS041.004 Box 10, Folder 13 (Zeta Psi). On Zeta Psi's refusal of the lot on the newly constructed Sawyer Avenue, see Board of Trustees records, 1848–2013, Executive Committee, 1854–2000, Meeting minutes 1854–1962, UA003.002 Box 112, Folder 6 (Executive committee minutes, vol. 5, 1889–1896: June 21, 1893). No reason is given for the refusal, just a note by the trustees that they were turned down by Zeta Psi. I can assume they must have offered the land to the fraternity at an earlier point in time, but I could not find the record within the minutes. In 1895, the trustees did agree to entertain offers from Zeta Psi once again for the purchase of other plots of land on campus, but apparently none were to be had. In fact, the sale to Delta Upsilon in 1894 was the last time the trustees sold a lot of campus land to a fraternity.

44. On Professor Shipman's life, see Start, 116–118. On the building of 80 Professors Row, see UA Edwin B. Rollins Papers, 1300[sic]–1976, Notebooks, 1940–1955, MS054.001 Box 2, Folder 1 (Campus Homes, Part 1(a) 1940–1955); *The Mystic Chain*, no. 2; and Office of Alumni Relations records, 1850–2014, Oral histories, 1977–, UA011.003.004.00001 (Dr. Nichols 1977-0-04: 11 min., 19 sec.). On Alfred Shipman's departure from Tufts in 1895, see Zeta Psi, *Semi-Centennial Catalogue*, 438. On the conversation with Professor Lewis, see *The Mystic Chain*, no. 2.

45. Bement 335; and *The Mystic Chain*, no. 2 and no. 3. The first reference I could find to Zeta Psi occupying the house at 80 Professors Row was "Five Candidates Taken In," *BG*, October 9, 1898, which mentions a reception at the fraternity house on Professors Row. While undoubtedly this event was likely reported in the *Tufts Weekly*, there are currently no copies of the newspaper before 1900 that are available for research – the issues in the Tufts archives are too fragile, if not damaged completely. As such, I missed out on purchasing near pristine copies of the *Tufts Weekly* from 1895 through 1899 on eBay by a mere two weeks. They sold for a grand total of $5.00.

46. "The Kappa Semi-Centennial," 260–284, which includes both quotations. Unfortunately, I could find no record of Zeta Psi's fiftieth anniversary celebration, though

I imagine there was one.

47. On the number of men who dropped out to enlist, see "From Harvard Alone 1500 Students Are In Some Form of War Service," *BG*, May 27, 1917. On the percentage of men, the *CofTC* (1916–1917 ed.), 266, lists a total of four hundred thirty-three men in the School of Liberal Arts and the Engineering School that year. On participation of Tufts men in the Naval Coast Defense Reserve, see "Naval Coast Defense Reserve," *TW*, March 14, 1917. On the formation of the Tufts Ambulance Corps, see "Volunteer Ambulance Corps," *TW*, May 2, 1917; "Tufts and the War," *TW*, May 2, 1917; "Ambulance Unit Increasing," *TW*, May 9, 1917; "Ambulance Unit To Sail," *TW*, May 23, 1917; and "From Harvard Alone 1500 Students Are In Some Form of War Service." On the journey to France, see "Brown and Blue to France," *TW*, May 30, 1917; "College Sendoff for Tufts Ambulance Unit," *BG*, May 30, 1917; and "Harvard Unit Sails Today," *The Crimson [Harvard]*, June 2, 1917. These articles mention the names of many men who helped organize the ambulance unit, including Professor Hooper, who was instrumental in raising the money needed to purchase the ambulance and supplies. However, the articles "From Harvard Alone 1500 Students Are In Some Form of War Service," and "Brown and Blue to France," both mention that Herbert Miller was the student most responsible for gathering up his classmates to join the unit, so I have chosen to single him out in the text. Not all who joined the Ambulance Corps did so because they had some strong desire to fight – many joined for humanitarian reasons. For a complete list of the men who joined the unit and sailed to France, see "Brown and Blue to France." Eighteen of the twenty-two men in the unit were Tufts students, while the remaining four were local residents from Belmont and Everett.

48. James William Davenport Seymour, ed., *History of the American Field Service in France: "Friends of France" 1914–1917, Told by its Members, Volume III* (Boston, MA: Houghton Mifflin Company, 1920), 7–21; "From Trench And Camp–With Our Unit," *TW*, December 12, 1917; "Moriarty Anxious To Return To Front," *BG*, December 13, 1917; "Roslindale Boy Tells Of War With French Army," *BG*, December 13, 1917; and "Tufts Men Back From France," *TW*, January 9, 1918. I find it interesting that it took over six months for word to reach campus that the Tufts Ambulance Unit had changed to TM 184. As it turned out, the *Tufts Weekly* printed a photo of the unit on October 10, 1917, but made no mention its mission had changed. However, a number of students did write personal letters to Tufts College President Bumpus during the summer of 1917, where they detailed the transportation work they were doing, along with the hazards they faced every day. These letters, apparently, were not made public to the campus. For copies of the letters, see UA Melville S. Munro Papers, 1858–1959, Tufts and the War, 1914–1919, MS036.007 Box 44, Folder 1 (Ambulance Corps 1918). Part of the reason the Ambulance Corps units were allowed to change their mission is that the United States officially entered the war on April 6, 1917, thus making Americans eligible for combat duty.

49. Ibid. On the return of Herbert Miller, see "Tufts Men Back From France," *TW*, January 9, 1918; and Marvin, 10–12, which includes the quotation. The campus honored Herb Miller by electing him the Chapel Orator for commencement exercises in June, 1918. See "H. L. Miller Elected Tufts Chapel Orator," *BG*, March 23, 1918.

50. Marvin, 11–12; Bement, 336–337; Miller, *LOTH–1*, 482–485; and various articles in *TW*, October 25, 1918. The latter two sources talk about the transition of the campus to the S.A.T.C. program. The opening of the college was delayed a few weeks

that fall due to the flu epidemic, which killed a number of Tufts students stationed at various Army bases across the country.

51. Marvin, 12; Bement, 336–337; Miller, *LOTH–1*, 484–488; "Charge Letters–Kappa, Tufts College," *The Shield* 35, no 2. (December 1918): 102–103. The term "gold star" implies the service man or woman has given his or her life to the cause. The family of the slain soldier will then hang from their house a red and white banner with a gold star in the middle, signifying the sacrifice. This tradition started in 1918, and has been carried on ever since. For the list of Tufts men who died in the service, see "Tufts Men Who Died In Service," in Office of the President Records, 1828–2007, Hermon Carey Bumpus, administrative records and related papers, 1913–1919, UA001.006 Box 1, Folder 6 (World War 1 1917–1919). Of the twenty-one gold stars, approximately twelve died of influenza or other disease, far from the front lines. Some of the more compelling stories of fraternity men who earned a gold star are told in their respective sections later in this chapter.

52. Marvin, 10–11; *The Mystic Chain*, no. 1–3.

53. *The Mystic Chain*, no. 3, which includes the quotation. The first serious attempt by the trustees to invoke this clause would come in 2004, as will be seen later in this section.

54. *The Mystic Chain*, no. 3, which includes the quotation.

55. Marvin, 12; and correspondence between Clarence "Pop" Houston and President Cousens, June 1928, in Activities and Organizations records, 1875–2013, UA024.001 Box 16, Folder 10 (Theta Delta Chi 1881–1967).

56. Marvin, 13; Activities and Organizations records, 1875–2013, UA024.001 Box 16, Folder 10 (Theta Delta Chi 1881–1967); "Old Frat House Razed To Ground," *TW*, May 21, 1930; and "Thete House Receives Enthusiastic Comment," *TW*, September 24, 1930. The architecture firm of Andrew, Jones, Biscoe, and Whitmore designed the house. This firm also designed Cousens Gymnasium in 1931, and Gifford House (the president's residence) in 1938, using the same Georgian style. As the editors of the *Tufts Weekly* remarked in the article from September 24, 1930, "The present structure not only represents the best that could be done with the money on hand but it is also the corner stone upon which the other fraternities may build for better accommodations, better social contacts, and a more beautiful Tufts."

57. On Zeta Psi's plans for a new house, see letter from "Scoop" Wilson to "Bud" (Russell Carpenter), February 10, 1930, in UA, Russell Carpenter Papers 1833–2012, Personal Papers, 1938–1969, MS041.004 Box 10, Folder 14 (Zeta Psi, correspondence). On Theta Delta Chi's boom after building its new house, see Marvin, 13–15. The push to be seen as the "best" cannot be understated here, as fraternities have always competed against one another for prestige, both at the local and national levels. Housing accommodations is one area that tends to play heavily in this competition.

58. "Three Fraternity Houses Remodelled [sic]," *TW*, September 24, 1936. The five fraternity houses remodeled or rebuilt during the 1930s all stand today in roughly the same form. The only drawback to this construction was the razing of those old Victorian houses with their attractive, and irreplaceable, architecture.

59. Miller, *LOTH–1*, 634–643; "Army Reserve Faces Immediate Call," *TW*, January 23, 1943; "Tufts Faculty Votes Trimester Year; New Calendar Puts Tufts on a Year-Round Plan Like Navy," *TW*, March 25, 1943; "Can This Light Be Dimmed Out?" *TW*, April 15, 1943; and "1000 Navy Men Begin training At Tufts," and "College

Buildings Undergo Changes," *TW*, July 10, 1943. As pointed out in Miller, *LOTH–1*, 640, the student population jumped from 700 to over 1,200 in a matter of months as the V-12 program kicked into high gear. Absorbing all of these men proved to be a logistical challenge, the likes of which have not been seen since.

60. Miller, *LOTH–1*, 640; Marvin, 16–17; "Active Chapters Plan Limited Fraternity Life," *TW*, July 29, 1943; "Fraternity News," *TW*, September 9, 1943; "Zetes Plan Gala New Year's Party," *TW*, December 23, 1943; and "Fraternities Less Hit by War At Tufts Than on Other College Campuses," *TW*, January 27, 1944. Also, information about training injuries suffered by Navy men comes from private conversations with Ms. Nancy Potter, an undergraduate on campus from 1943–46. She lived in the Zeta Psi house while a student, and often saw the ambulances bringing the injured men to 123 Packard Avenue. The Navy had constructed an obstacle course for physical training, and this regimen was the cause of most injuries.

61. On the disbandment of the V-12 program, see Miller, *LOTH–1*, 643–659. On the restarting of fraternity operations, see "The Fraternity Supplement," *TW*, May 9, 1946; "Alpha Sigma Phi Grabs Rush Honors With 35 Pledges," *TW*, November 7, 1946; and Marvin, 17, which also lists the seven gold stars from Theta Delta Chi. Unfortunately, records of Zeta Psi members who joined the service are rather incomplete, so I was unable to determine if the chapter also lost members to the war. Given that nearly every other fraternity on campus had at least one gold star, though, I can imagine Zeta Psi did as well.

62. I do not mean to gloss over the operations of the two fraternities up to the 1970s, but in terms of major turning points, there simply were none. Both continued to initiate men, hold social functions, place members in positions of leadership around campus, and stay out of trouble, for the most part. And while it appears both did have some restrictive membership practices in place at the national level in the 1950s and 1960s, neither was engulfed in the issue that affected other chapters during this time. From a historical point-of-view, then, their operations were quite normal, if not a little boring.

63. For the attitude of Theta Delta Chi in 1970, see "Fraternity Profile," *TO*, March 13, 1970, which includes the first quotation. On the operations of Kappa Charge during the 1970s, see "A Letter From The Graduate Corporation," *Kappa Kourier*, November 1979, housed in the Theta Delta Chi Fraternity Archives, Boston, MA, which includes the second quotation. Also of interest is the description, or lack thereof, offered by Theta Delta Chi in the 1975–76 and 1976–77 editions of *The Ivy Book*, an all-campus guide to student life at Tufts. While the other fraternities wrote some form of description about their respective organization, Theta Delta Chi did not, opting instead to simply list its address. Lastly, the release of the movie *Animal House* in 1978 played no small part in the revival of Theta Delta Chi and other fraternity chapters on campus, as discussed in Joseph C. Goodman, "A Greek Revival," *Tufts Criterion* 11, no. 2 (December 1978): 27.

64. "Theta Delta Chi Disciplined by Student Activities Office," *TD*, November 14, 1980.

65. On the incident of March 1981, see "Campus Police Break Up Unscheduled Theta Delta Chi Fraternity Party," *TD*, March 17, 1981 [printing error lists date on publication as March 16]; and "Report Examines Past Incidents Involving Theta Delta Chi, Psi U," *TD*, November 18, 1992. On the other mentioned incidents, see "Fra-

ternity Criticized for Safety Violations," *TD*, April 21, 1982; "Letter To The Editor–Combat Pornography," *TD*, October 7, 1983; "Police Beat," *TD*, October 4, 1985; "Knable Calls on Greeks To 'Define Values'," *TD*, March 26, 1987, which includes the quotation by President Mayer; "CSL To Hear Alcohol Poisoning Cases," *TD*, September 30, 1987; "Police Respond to Weekend Fights," *TD*, February 9, 1988; and "Letter To The Editor–123 Restoration," *TD*, September 6, 1988. By 1980, "123" had become a common nickname for Theta Delta Chi, given its address. While other fraternities certainly had issues of public safety and problems with the Tufts administration during the 1980s, Theta Delta Chi by far had the most.

66. I am basing this information mostly on my own personal observations while an undergraduate at Tufts (1985–89). It seemed to me the students rarely if ever referred to the fraternity as "Theta Delta Chi," opting instead for "123." The quotation on the t-shirt was the opening lyric of the song "Rock and Roll Fantasy" by Bad Company. As a fan of Bad Company, I clearly remember seeing members wearing this t-shirt on numerous occasions and thinking it was pretty clever, while also somewhat accurate. Also, I knew quite a few members of 123 through other associations including sports teams, academics, and dormitory housing. During each pledging season, I never saw any prospective member wear a pledge pin, but I did see them wear that orange hat and trench coat around campus during hell week, as they were required to wear the outfit everywhere, even to class.

67. The efforts of the administration to affect greater control over the Greek–letter organizations are detailed in Chapter 6. On the legal agreement between the Trustees of Tufts College and the Kappa Charge of the Theta Delta Chi Fraternity, see "Option and Restriction Agreement," Massachusetts Land Records, Middlesex South Registry, Book 19259, Page 54, dated August 10, 1988. As for how this agreement came to be signed when it did, I have been unable to determine the specifics, but I have seen similar agreements with other housing corporations around this time, so this was not unique. I suspect these agreements were put in place following the expulsion of all fraternities from the City of Medford. The City of Somerville was also considering a similar expulsion, so these agreements may have been a way to stave off such drastic change, by giving the Tufts administration greater power to control the fraternities that owned their houses. The termination of this agreement requires the death of three named individuals plus twenty-one years.

68. On the placing of Theta Delta Chi on warning status, see Anna George, "CFS Warns Greeks After Heath Report," *TD*, November 9, 1989. On the philanthropy efforts of Theta Delta Chi, see "ASCE Completes Healy Playground," *TD*, October 16, 1989; "Letters To The Editor–Pine Street Inn thanks Theta Delta Chi," *TD*, December 7, 1989; "1-2-3 digs in for school, then feeds homeless," *The Greek Gazette* 3, no. 1 (February 8, 1990), as published in *The Tufts Daily*. On the violation of dry rush, see "Theta Delta Chi Found in Violation of Dry Rush," *TD*, March 2, 1990. The policy of dry rush was put in place starting in the spring semester of 1989, and has been in effect ever since.

69. "Theta Delta Chi Recognition Suspended by IGC Judiciary," *TD*, March 5, 1990, which includes quotation; and "Theta Delta Chi International Suspends Fraternity," *TD*, March 6, 1990.

70. "Theta Delta Chi Plans to Appeal," *TD*, March 8, 1990; "123 To Appeal to CSL," *TD*, March 28, 1990; and "CSL Upholds Theta Delta Chi Suspension," *TD*,

April 4, 1990, which includes the quotation. The open-ended invitation for Theta Delta Chi to return after three years is somewhat standard for fraternities facing suspension, as after three years all current members would have graduated, thus leaving the fraternity a clean slate from which to rebuild its organization. Some schools, such as Lehigh University, even impose up to a ten-year waiting period after suspension.

71. Letter from Warren Carley to Sol Gittleman, April 6, 1990, and letter from Sol Gittleman to Warren Carley, April 9, 1990, which includes the quotation, in Office of the President Records 1828–2007, Jean Mayer, administrative records and related papers, 1976–92, Subject Files, UA001.013 Box 10, Folder 22 (Fraternities and Sororities 1989–1992). Provost Gittleman copied his response to President Mayer, and included a note saying that he'd been contacted by three former trustees (Warren Carley, Robert Meserve, and William McMahon), but had "told them all the same message – 'stay out of this'."

72. "AOPi Gets 123 House," *TD*, September 12, 1990.

73. Various letters and memos to and from President Mayer and Provost Gittleman, in Office of the President Records 1828–2007, Jean Mayer, administrative records and related papers, 1976–92, Subject Files, UA001.013 Box 10, Folder 22 (Fraternities and Sororities 1989–1992). Quotation from memo from Sol Gittleman to David Hendrich, Theta Delta Chi alumnus.

74. "Theta Delta Chi Sues University," *TD*, September 11, 1991.

75. Correspondence from 1991, and memo from Mary Lee Jacobs to President Mayer, Sol Gittleman, and Steven Manos, dated January 21, 1992, in Office of the President Records 1828–2007, Jean Mayer, administrative records and related papers, 1976–92, Subject Files, UA001.013 Box 10, Folder 22 (Fraternities and Sororities 1989–1992); and "Tufts, Theta Delta Chi Settle Lawsuit," *TD*, February 11, 1992.

76. "Theta Delta Chi Sees Settlement As Victory; Members Saw Tufts' Case As Weak," *TD*, February 13, 1992; and letter from Joel Rose to Dean Reitman, February 13, 1992, in Office of the President Records 1828–2007, Jean Mayer, administrative records and related papers, 1976–92, Subject Files, UA001.013 Box 10, Folder 22 (Fraternities and Sororities 1989–1992). I have chosen to abbreviate the name of the undergraduate in question, since his role in causing the suspension back in 1990 was not mentioned publicly in *The Tufts Daily* article. Instead, he was named in the referenced letter.

77. "University Repudiates Fraternity's Remarks," *TD*, February 14, 1992; and "University Dissolves Settlement With Theta Delta Chi Fraternity," *TD*, February 21, 1992.

78. "Tufts Announces New Settlement," *TD*, February 26, 1992; "Tufts, Theta Delta Chi Release New Settlement," February 27, 1992; and "Theta Delta Chi Pledges Announced," *TD*, March 26, 1992.

79. On the tenure of Robert Meserve and his participation in the hiring of Jean Mayer, see Miller, *LOTH–2*, 391–392. On the correspondence between Mr. Meserve and President Mayer, see letters from February 1992, in Office of the President Records 1828–2007, Jean Mayer, administrative records and related papers, 1976–92, Subject Files, UA001.013 Box 10, Folder 22 (Fraternities and Sororities 1989–1992). Quotation from letter dated February 17, 1992. On the removal of President Mayer and subsequent passing, see "Jean Mayer, 72, Nutritionist Who Led Tufts, Dies," *NYT*, January 2, 1993; and Gittleman, *An Entrepreneurial University*, chapter 4. Reading these letters

of correspondence was remarkable in many ways, as the letters started friendly enough, but quickly devolved into sniping and bickering.

80. On the reorganization in 2003, see "Several Fraternities Returning To Full Function In Spring; Probations, Renovations To End Next Semester," *TD*, December 5, 2003. On the one hundred fiftieth anniversary celebration, see "Kappa Celebrates 150 Years At Tufts University," *Kappa Kourier* 150, no. 1 (Summer 2006): 1–2, housed in the Theta Delta Chi Fraternity Archives, Boston, MA.

81. On the racial incident involving Zeta Psi and the Asian House, see "Letters to the Editor; Accept Our Apologies," *TD*, March 19, 1982; "Students, Faculty Discuss Implications of Frat Incident," *TD*, March 26, 1982; "CSL Gives Fraternity Ultimatum in Racial Incident," *TD*, April 16, 1982; and "CSL Alters Ruling; Mayer Upset With Fraternity," *TD*, April 21, 1982. As a result of this incident, which involved some pledges yelling slurs at the Asian House residents, Zeta Psi faced a number of sanctions from the faculty-led Committee on Student Life (CSL), including the loss of a pledge class for the entire school year. This sanction was rescinded a few days later, however, as the fraternity argues the inability to recruit new members during the 1982–83 school year would put the chapter in jeopardy of closing down, since a large portion of the brotherhood was due to graduate by 1983. Also, Zeta Psi as a fraternity apologized in earnest for the incident, which no doubt helped in reducing the punishment. On the firearms violation, see "Zeta Psi Fire Damage Estimated at $20,000," *TD*, October 5, 1987; "Student to Take Legal Action Following Housing Expulsion," *TD*, November 13, 1987; and "Court Upholds Housing Expulsion," *TD*, December 1, 1987. While the incident involving the storage of firearms in Zeta Psi did not lead to any sanctions against the fraternity, it was a catalyst for greater oversight of the entire Greek system by the administration, as is discussed in Chapter 6. Finally, I do not mean to gloss over both of these incidents, as they were quite serious at the time and represented some of the worst aspects of fraternity life. However, from a historical perspective, both incidents were quickly resolved and had no lasting negative impact on Zeta Psi.

82. On the history of music, see Hersey, *History of Music at Tufts College*, 15–24. On the new music building, see "Future of Zeta Psi House Being Negotiated," *TD*, October 7, 1999; and "Proposal To Build New Music Facility Leads To Controversy," *TD*, February 23, 2000. Although the article in October appears to be the first article in *The Tufts Daily* discussing at length the new music center, references to the upcoming construction were made a semester earlier, in the spring of 1999. For example, see "Majors Week Events–Music Meeting," *TD*, March 1, 1999, which advertised a meeting to "share exciting news about the new music building."

83. "Future of Zeta Psi House Being Negotiated," and "Proposal To Build New Music Facility Leads To Controversy." I do find it interesting the Zeta Psi alumni corporation tried to argue the covenant from 1918 was no longer valid just because so much time has passed. The provision as written into the deed had no expiration date.

84. "New Music Facility Initiative Lacks Funding," *TD*, April 1, 2001; and "Spring 2002 Deadline Set For New Music Building," *TD*, September 1, 2001. By the fall of 2002, the Zeta Psi housing corporation has agreed to a purchase price of $1.5 million, which was the fair market value at the time. More importantly, though, they insisted Tufts build them a new house before razing their old one.

85. "Location of Music Building Causes Musical Chairs," *TD*, October 3, 2002; "Musical Chairs," *TD*, October 3, 2002; "Save Ballou's House," *TD*, October 17, 2002,

which includes the quotation.

86. "City Objects to Dorm's Construction," *TD*, May 18, 2003; and "No Music Building Groundbreaking In Near Future," *TD*, April 7, 2004. In addition to the problems with the SHPC, the administration was struggling to raise enough money to build the music center. Costs kept going up, but donations did not keep pace. However, it appears the issues with the SHPC stalled the project in 2003 and 2004 more so than the lack of donations.

87. "Medford, Somerville To Receive $1.25 Million Each From Tufts," *TD*, September 9, 2004; "Master Plan Rises From Agreements With Cities," *TD*, October 5, 2004; and "Timetable, Location Reset For Construction of New Music Building," *TD*, December 6, 2004. It appears the efforts to construct the new dormitory and music building came at a time of strained relations between Tufts and the cities of Medford and Somerville. However, the payments in lieu of taxes to the two cities alluded to in the first mentioned article seemed to help ease the tension.

88. "Zeta Psi Pledge In Hospital," *TD*, February 24, 2003; "Zeta Psi Closed Temporarily," *TD*, February 26, 2003; "Zeta Psi Faces Six Allegations," *TD*, April 14, 2003; and "Zeta Psi Shutdown Follows Summer of Miscommunication," *TD*, September 4, 2003.

89. "Zeta Psi Shutdown Follows Summer of Miscommunication," and "Zeta Psi House Closed For School Year," *TD*, September 2, 2003.

90. Ibid. On the problems with other fraternities and sororities, see "Delta Upsilon Closed Temporarily," *TD*, March 10, 2003; "Three Strikes and You May Be Out," *TD*, March 25, 2003; "Liberal Alcohol Policies Can Prevent Alcohol Abuse, Students Say," *TD*, March 27, 2003; and "Greeks In A Rush To Get Back On Their Feet," *TD*, February 23, 2004;

91. On the issue involved Delta Tau Delta and Chi Omega, see "Greek System is Under Fire for Multiple Violations," *TD*, May 22, 2005; and their respective sections later in this chapter (Delta Tau Delta) and Chapter 4 (Chi Omega). On the supposed violation of the alcohol policy by Zeta Psi, see "Police Find Keg in Zeta Psi," *TD*, April 14, 2005. On the lack of punishment, see "AEPi Suspended for Fall Semester," *TD*, September 5, 2006. While the case against Zeta Psi seemed to be air tight, there must have been some uncertainty regarding the presence of a keg in the house, as the fraternity was clearly off probation in the fall of 2005, as discussed in "Detlef Schrempf!," *TD*, October 18, 2005.

92. "The Kappa Semi-Centennial," 275, which includes the quotation.

93. Delta Upsilon, *One Hundred Years*, 7–9; Craig S. Sowell, *Revealing the Non-Secrets: The History and Founding of Delta Upsilon Fraternity* (Createspace, 2009), 31–34; "Historical Sketch of Williams Chapter," in *The Delta Upsilon Quinquennial Catalogue*, ed. William Sheafe Chase (Delta Upsilon Fraternity, 1884), 130–134; and "History of K. A. at Williams College," in *A Record of the Members of the Kappa Alpha Fraternity*, 87–88.

94. Delta Upsilon, 8–20; "Historical Sketch of Williams Chapter," 130–139; and "History of the Fraternity," http://www.deltau.org/nosecrets/history/historyofthefraternity (accessed April 21, 2014).

95. Fairbanks, 89–92; Delta Upsilon, *One Hundred Years*, 144–145; and "History of the Young Chapters," in *Delta Upsilon Quinquennial Catalogue* (Delta Upsilon Fraternity, 1891), xxii–xxiv. The statistic of one-third being fraternity men is based on

the list of approximately 102 enrolled students in the *CofTC* (1877–78 ed.) versus the named 39 members of Zeta Psi and Theta Delta Chi in the *B&B* (1879 ed.), which was actually published in 1878 (yearbooks were originally numbered by the graduation year of the junior class). Unfortunately, there was no yearbook published again until 1888, but I assume the percentage of fraternity men did not change significantly throughout the 1880s, until Delta Upsilon received its charter in 1886. On Mr. Tomlinson's background and membership in Phi Delta Theta, see Start, 296. Interestingly enough, Mr. Tomlinson is never mentioned by name in his dealing with the men who became the Tufts chapter of Delta Upsilon, but instead is only referred to as "Mr. T." However, I am confident that Mr. T. is indeed Irving Tomlinson, because the references do mention Phi Delta Theta, and Mr. Tomlinson was the only active student at the time with the byline of Phi Delta Theta and a last initial of "T."

96. Ibid. Although how Wilson and the other men came to know about the existence of Delta Upsilon has been seemingly lost to history, we do know that back in 1883 another group at Tufts was also interested in pursuing a charter with Delta Upsilon, but that attempt went nowhere. It may have been that Wilson and some in his group knew of this earlier attempt, possibly even some of the men involved. This theory is backed by Delta Upsilon, *One Hundred Years*, 144, but here the facts are limited and the inferences many, so I chose not to discuss in the text.

97. Ibid. While the men took the name of the Mathetican Society, it appears they made no concerted effort to restart the waning literary society with its principle of open membership. Instead, it seems they just liked the name.

98. Ibid., with quotation from Delta Upsilon, *One Hundred Years*, 145. For a list of the charter members, see Melvin Gilbert Dodge, ed., *The Delta Upsilon Decennial Catalogue* (Delta Upsilon Fraternity, 1902), 843–845.

99. On the reaction of Zeta Psi and Theta Delta Chi, see *The Tuftonian* 13, no. 3 (November 5, 1886), which includes the first quotation; "History of the Young Chapters," xxiv; and "Letters From Chapters," *The Delta Upsilon Quarterly* 5, no. 2 (January 1887): 111. On campus accolades, see "Letters From Chapters," January 1887, 111; "Chapter News–Tufts College," *The Delta Upsilon Quarterly* 5, no. 3 (April 1887): 215–216; and "Letters From Chapters," *The Delta Upsilon Quarterly* 5, no. 4 (July 1887): 256–257, which includes the second quotation. On the formation of the musical groups, see "Chapter Correspondence–Tufts College," *The Delta Upsilon Quarterly* 10, no. 1 (November 1891): 66–67; and "Chapter Correspondence–Tufts College," *The Delta Upsilon Quarterly* 10, no. 3 (May 1892): 252.

100. Fairbanks, 89. At the time, Phi Delta Theta was considered one of the most prominent fraternities in America, and with that feeling came quite an attitude. To be shown such disrespect from a non-member at a small Northeastern college must really have upset the national officers.

101. On the initial response, see "Editorial," *The Scroll of Phi Delta Theta* 11, no. 10 (June 1887): 401–402, which includes the first quotation. On the subsequent response, see "Editorial," *The Scroll of Phi Delta Theta* 13, no. 6 (March 1889): 261, which includes the second quotation.

102. Wilson L. Fairbanks, "The Tufts Chapter and Phi Delta Theta," *The Delta Upsilon Quarterly* 7, no. 3 (May 1889): 214–216, which includes the quotation.

103. "Editorial," 402, which includes the quotation; and Fairbanks, "The Tufts Chapter and Phi Delta Theta," 214–216.

104. On Irving Tomlinson, see A. I. Spartan, ed., *Fifty Years of Buchtel: 1870–1920* (Akron, OH: Buchtel College Alumni Assoc., 1922), 145. On Mr. Fairbanks, see "Wilson Fairbanks, Noted Editor, Dies," *NYT*, February 17, 1953.

105. On the early location of Delta Upsilon's chapter room, see "Letters From Chapters," January 1887, 111, which includes the quotation; and "Chapter Correspondence–Tufts College," November 1891, 66. In 1888, it appears the chapter relocated temporarily to West Medford when a new landlord took over their building, but within a year they were back in their original rooms in Davis Square. See "Chapter Correspondence – Tufts College," *The Delta Upsilon Quarterly* 7, no. 3 (May 1889): 254. On the activities and parties, see "Letters From Chapters," July 1887, 256–257; "Letters from Chapters," *The Delta Upsilon Quarterly* 6, no. 2 (January 1888): 105–106; "Chapter Correspondence–Tufts College," November 1891, 66–67; "Chapter Correspondence–Tufts College," May 1892, 252; and "Chapter Correspondence–Tufts College," *The Delta Upsilon Quarterly* 10, no. 4 (August 1892): 348–349. The discussion of American novels is noted on many occasions in these references, so I can assume such literature was not a normal part of their collegiate curriculum. The spelling bee as mentioned in the May 1892 correspondence is certainly different, as I have not come across any other fraternity chapter engaging in a similar activity.

106. The evolution of the chapter house is a fascinating part of fraternity history, and is discussed briefly in the section on Zeta Psi and Theta Delta Chi as related to Tufts. Within the national Delta Upsilon organization, "house envy" is evident by the early 1880s, as chapters routinely described the accommodations of their rivals, and bigger always meant better. For example, see "Letters From Chapters–Williams Chapter," *The Delta Upsilon Quarterly* 2, no. 4 (November 1884): 169–171; and "The Fraternity Houses at Hamilton College," *The Delta Upsilon Quarterly* 8, no. 2 (February 1890): 172–177. Also, early editions of Baird's *American College Fraternities* made special mention of the houses owned by fraternities, along with an estimated value of the property, as Mr. Baird realized the prestige of an organization was often tied to its home. On the efforts of the Tufts chapter to secure a house, see UA, W. G. Brooks Papers, 1890–1995, Delta Upsilon Materials, 1915–, MS092.002 Box 1, Folder 2 (Delta Upsilon Founding Documents 1890–1920). I am basing the claim that it was the undergraduates, and not the alumni, who were involved in setting up the corporation and conducting the negotiations due to documentation in this folder. For example, G. M. Winslow is identified as negotiating with Somerville for the building permit. According to Dodge, 848, Guy Monroe Winslow was an undergraduate member of the chapter in 1894. On the sources of the mortgage, see Activities and Organizations records, 1875–2013, UA024.001 Box 2, Folder 16 (Delta Upsilon 1894–1952). I'm sure Charles Tufts rolled over in his grave when the college sold of a parcel of land he donated for a mere $1.

107. "Local News," *The Tuftonian* 21, no. 1 (October 5, 1894): 13, which includes the quotation. The construction of the Heth Aleph Res fraternity house is discussed later in this chapter.

108. On the depression of 1893, see Walter W. Price, *We Have Recovered Before! A Comparison of the Present Depressions with the Major Depressions of the Past Century: 1837, 1857, 1873, 1893* (New York: Harper & Brothers, 1933), chapter IX; and W. Jett Lauck, *The Cause of the Panic of 1893* (Boston, MA: Houghton, Mifflin and Company, 1907). Information concerning Delta Upsilon and their issues with 13 Sawyer Avenue is scattered among the archives. I have therefore tried to piece together the chain of

events as best I could from the following sources: Minutes from November 27, 1894; February 26, 1895; and March 31, 1896, in Office of the Board of Trustees records, 1848–2013, Executive Committee, 1854–2000, UA 003.002 Box 112, Folder 6 (Executive Committee minutes, volume 5 1889–1896); various letters from November 15, 1894, through July 26, 1896, in Activities and Organizations records, 1875–2013, UA 024.001 Box 2, Folder 16 (Delta Upsilon 1894–1952); and Massachusetts Land Records, Middlesex South Registry, Book 12920, Page 489, which states the deed for 13 Sawyer Avenue was conveyed to the Trustees of Tufts College on April 25, 1896. On Albert Metcalf, see Start, 62, 66–67.

109. Minutes from May 26, 1896; June 29, 1896; and July 28, 1896, in Office of the Board of Trustees records, 1848–2013, Executive Committee, 1854–2000, UA 003.002 Box 112, Folder 6 (Executive Committee minutes, volume 5 1889–1896). In these minutes, the trustees refer to written arguments as submitted by Delta Upsilon on the matter, which may have shed some light on why they reversed course regarding the women's dormitory, but I was unable to find these documents in the archives. At the very least, it seems there was an informal agreement to rent the house back to the fraternity after the sale, and perhaps this was initially overlooked by the trustees, until further clarification was provided.

110. On the convention, see "The LXII Annual Convention," *The Delta Upsilon Quarterly* 15, no. 1 (December 1896): 11–17; and "Chapter News and College Items," *The Delta Upsilon Quarterly* 15, no. 1 (December 1896): 94–95, which includes a photograph of the chapter house in all its glory. On the yearly rental and the inability to secure a long term lease, see various letters from 1896 through 1925 in Activities and Organizations records, 1875–2013, UA 024.001 Box 2, Folder 16 (Delta Upsilon 1894–1952); various editions of the Tufts Chapter Corporation Report through 1908 in UA, W. G. Brooks Papers, 1890–1995, Delta Upsilon Materials, 1915–, MS092.002 Box 1, Folder 2 (Delta Upsilon Founding Documents 1890–1920); letters from the trustees to Tufts Chapter Corporation, April 19, 1901, and February 20, 1902, in UA, W. G. Brooks Papers, MS092.002 Box 1, Folder 4 (Delta Upsilon – Correspondence 1890–1920); and Delta Upsilon Records–Unprocessed–2011.076, UA217 Box 1. Even in 1908, rent was still listed at $560 a year, and by 1925, it appears to have been reduced to $400 a year. A bargain!

111. On the solicitation of the alumni and their responses, see various letters in UA, W. G. Brooks Papers, 1890–1995, Delta Upsilon Materials, 1915–, MS092.002 Box 1, Folder 3 (Delta Upsilon Treasurer's Documents 1890–1920); and records in Delta Upsilon Records–Unprocessed–2011.076, UA217 Box 1. This box of unprocessed records was recently donated by an alumnus of the fraternity and contains numerous chapter materials from 1894 to 1923. Many of the letters in this collection (from alumni who were unable to afford the dues) were quite apologetic in tone, but at least one was dismissive in a forceful way. Apparently this particular alumnus did not have a good experience as an undergraduate in Delta Upsilon, and let it be known in no uncertain terms. Professor Bray did eventually sell his house to the Delta Tau Delta fraternity, about ten years later.

112. On the anniversary party, see "Tufts Celebrates Its 25th Anniversary," *The Delta Upsilon Quarterly* 30, no. 2 (March 1912), 56–57. In reading through the numerous fraternity journals from different national organizations, I get the sense that these anniversary banquets were not just about celebrating the past, but also a statement on the

present. Inter-fraternity competition for prestige was at its height in the early 1900s, and holding a banquet at a fancy hotel in a big city was one way of demonstrating superiority. On the death of Frank Melcher, see "Obituaries – Frank Otis Melcher, Tufts, '87," *The Delta Upsilon Quarterly* 30, no. 2 (March 1912), 78–79. Anniversary celebrations within fraternities are still popular today, they just aren't as widely advertised or reported to the public as they were a century ago.

113. On the transformation of Tufts College under the S.A.T.C., see Miller, *LOTH–1*, 482–485; and *TW*, October 25, 1918, which also discusses the commandeering of 13 Sawyer Avenue for a women's dormitory. All fraternities were essentially shut down during the S.A.T.C. program, though informal chapter meetings away from the eyes of the authorities did take place. On the status of Delta Upsilon when school opened in the fall of 1918, see "Chapter and Alumni Notes – Tufts," *The Delta Upsilon Quarterly* 37, no. 2 (March 1919): 174–175.

114. On the claim of every member being involved in the war effort, see "Chapter and Alumni Notes–Tufts," *The Delta Upsilon Quarterly* 37, no. 2 (March 1919): 174–175. As stated in this article, after graduation in the summer of 1918, Delta Upsilon had sixteen men on its active roll. Thirteen of these men entered military service (including the six in the S.A.T.C. program), while the remaining three went to work for the U. S. Government in direct support of the war effort. For a brief synopsis of the three named men who died in service, see "Tufts Men Who Died In Service." On the odyssey of Mr. Briggs, see "Obituaries–Albert J. Briggs," *The Delta Upsilon Quarterly* 37, no. 2 (March 1919): 141, which includes the quotation. On the history of Camp Dick, see "Turned Out 25,000 Fliers," *NYT*, December 9, 1918. Concerning the fate of Mr. Stiles, see "Annual Report to Alumni for 1919," as contained in Activities and Organizations records, 1875–2013, UA 024.001 Box 2, Folder 16 (Delta Upsilon 1894–1952); and "The Roll of Honor–Tufts," *The Delta Upsilon Quarterly* 37, no. 2 (March 1919): v. This "Roll of Honor" incorrectly lists Maynard F. Lydiard, class of 1919, as a casualty. Mr. Lydiard was not the only Delta Upsilon member from across the country to be mistaken for dead, and in the next issue of the *Quarterly*, the editors were forced to apologize for their grave errors. Concerning the fate of Lt. Henry, see "The Roll of Honor–Tufts," *The Delta Upsilon Quarterly* 37, no. 3 (June 1919): v; and "Brunonians Far And Near–David E. Henry," *Brown Alumni Monthly* 19, no. 9 (April 1919): 196, which contains an obituary and portrait. Lt. Henry started his education at Tufts College where he joined Delta Upsilon, but then transferred to Brown University and graduated in 1914. The 76th Infantry Division was comprised mainly of draftees from New England. It was the first division in World War I organized around draftees, instead of National Guard units or volunteers.

115. On the closing of the S.A.T.C. program, see Miller, *LOTH–1*, 483–485, which also talks about the uncertainty in future enrollment; and "S.A.T.C. Will Leave Hill," *TW*, December 4, 1918. On Delta Upsilon regaining the house in the beginning of 1919, see "Annual Report to Alumni for 1919." I am assuming the desire by the college administration to return to normal operations weighed heavily on the decision to rent 13 Sawyer Avenue to the fraternity, because it seemed everyone felt the S.A.T.C. program, though necessary for the war effort, had been so disruptive to campus life. Also, in reading through various articles in the *Tufts Weekly* around this time, I got the sense the campus especially missed the activities of the fraternities during the war, and wanted them back as soon as possible.

116. "Chapter and Alumni Notes–Tufts," *The Delta Upsilon Quarterly* 37, no. 2 (March 1919): 174–175; "Chapter and Alumni News–Tufts," *The Delta Upsilon Quarterly* 37, no. 3 (June 1919): 265–266; and "Frats Make Debut," *TW*, January 8, 1919. By early January 1919, I suspect the administration soon regretted renting the house at 13 Sawyer Avenue to Delta Upsilon, as the number of women coming campus actually exceeded all expectations. In fact, it was the largest enrollment of women to date, and there were not enough dormitory rooms to house them. So, the administration commandeered the home of ex-President Bumpus on Professors Row as a new women's dormitory, which it remained for decades. Known as Capen House, the property had been home to a few presidents of Tufts College, but following the resignation of President Bumpus in late 1918, it would never again be home to an administrator.

117. Notes dated June 15, 1925, in Activities and Organizations records, 1875–2013, UA 024.001 Box 2, Folder 16 (Delta Upsilon 1894–1952).

118. "A New House for Tufts Chapter of DU On Its Golden Jubilee," dated May 1936, in Activities and Organizations records, 1875–2013, UA 024.001 Box 2, Folder 17 (Delta Upsilon 1914–1936). Although Delta Upsilon rented 13 Sawyer Ave., they were also responsible for routine repairs and maintenance, and based on documents in the aforementioned archive, it seems they were barely able to keep up with the immediate concerns (a broken window, malfunctioning heater, burst water pipe, etc.). Preventive maintenance was seemingly never a priority, though in many ways one cannot blame Delta Upsilon. They really had no incentive to invest in the long-term needs of the house, since they were only given a lease one year at a time. On the renovations of other fraternity houses, see "Three Fraternity Houses Remodeled," *TW*, September 24, 1936.

119. On the newsletter, see "A New House for Tufts Chapter of DU On Its Golden Jubilee." On the history of 114 Professors Row, see UA Edwin B. Rollins Papers, 1300[sic]–1976, Notebooks, 1940–1955, MS054.001 Box 2, Folder 2 (Campus Homes, Part 1(b) 1940–1955). On the acquisition of 114 Professors Row, see letters dated April 1937, in Activities and Organizations records, 1875–2013, UA 024.001 Box 2, Folder 16 (Delta Upsilon 1894–1952); and "Construction Necessitated by Purchase of Knight House By Delta Upsilon," *TW*, April 8, 1937. I have been unable to discern why, exactly, the trustees decided to sell Knight House to Delta Upsilon, as articles in the *Tufts Weekly* and records in the Tufts archives shed no light on the decision or its rationale. Immediately after selling the house, though, the trustees announced they would expand one of the women's dormitories, Metcalf Hall, to make up for the loss of Knight House. As it turned out, the sale of Knight House to Delta Upsilon in 1937 was the last time to date the Tufts administration sold any of its property to a fraternity.

120. "Campus Improved by Exclusive Construction," *TW*, September 23, 1937; "D.U., A.K.Pi Latest Additions to Revamped Row; New Fraternity Houses Add Much to Appearance," *TW*, January 6, 1938, which includes the quotation. It is somewhat surprising that six of the fraternities at Tufts in the 1930s, including Delta Upsilon, were able to rebuild or renovate their houses in the midst of the Great Depression. Phi Mu Delta's time at 13 Sawyer Avenue would be short and sweet, as discussed later in this chapter. By the fall of 1941, Phi Mu Delta had folded, and the house was then, finally, turned into a women's dormitory known as Davies House, named after Dean Caroline Davies, the first dean of Jackson College for Women. In 1972, Davies House was converted once again, this time into co-educational special interest housing known

as the International House, or I-House, to provide students a chance to live together in an international community. The I-House is still operating out of 13 Sawyer Avenue today.

121. On the operations of Delta Upsilon on the late 1930s, see "Delta Upsilon," *Jumbo* (1939 ed.), 124. Concerning the establishment of the V-12 program, see "Tufts Faculty Votes trimester Year." On the takeover of 114 Professors Row by the Navy, see "College Buildings Undergo Changes." On the activities of Delta Upsilon during the war, see "Active Chapters Plan Limited Fraternity Life"; and "Tufts Mailbag–War Time Fraternities," *TW*, October 15, 1943. For a broad overview of life at Tufts during World War II, see Miller, *LOTH–1*, chapter 15. On the V-12 program, see "Navy V-12 Program, 1942–1945," *Concise Encyclopedia of Tufts History*, http://hdl.handle.net/10427/14829 (accessed May 7, 2014).

122. The USS LCT–30 was part of the flotilla delivering men and equipment right to the beaches of Normandy, France, on June 6, 1944. "LCT" stands for "Landing Craft, Tank," as its main purpose was to bring tanks ashore, but it was also used to bring troops in much larger number than the smaller "Higgins boats," which brought the first wave of men to the beach. For information on Ensign Taylor and the USS LCT–30, see http://www.wfirg.com/mia_cases_pending/anderson_john_e (accessed May 7, 2014). There is also a small obituary for Ensign Taylor in *The Delta Upsilon Quarterly* 64, no. 4 (October 1946): 293. Undoubtedly, the Tufts chapter of Delta Upsilon had other gold stars among its membership from World War II, but Ensign Taylor was the only one I came across in my research.

123. On the revival of fraternities following World War II, see "The Fraternity Supplement"; "Alpha Sigma Phi Grabs Rush Honors With 35 Pledges"; and "Fraternity Supplement – Delta Upsilon," *TW*, October 9, 1947. On Delta Upsilon's non-restrictive membership policies, see "DU Always Open to All Men," http://www.deltau.org/nosecrets/history/challengesandeducation (accessed May 10, 2014). As testament to this policy, one of the founding members of the Tufts Chapter of Delta Upsilon was Clemente Valdes, a Mexican national. Mr. Valdes may indeed be the first non-white member of a fraternity at Tufts. On the death of Wilson Fairbanks, see "Wilson Fairbanks, Noted Editor, Dies," *NYT*, February 17, 1953.

124. On controversies within the brotherhood surrounding the ROTC program, see "Chapter News Letters–Tufts," *Delta Upsilon Quarterly* 87, no. 3 (July 1969): 154. On membership reduction and subsequent rebuilding, see "Chapter Activities Review–Tufts," *The Delta Upsilon Quarterly* 90, no. 1 (January 1972): 29; and "Good News About Fraternities," *TO*, October 27, 1972, 12. On the incident in 1971, see "Women's Equality Group Protests Frat Strip Show," and "The Incident at the Delta Upsilon House," *TO*, November 12, 1971. My conclusions about why Delta Upsilon in particular did not suffer to the same extent as nearly all of the other fraternities is based in part on discussions with chapter alumni from the 1970s. Also, it seems that while many on campus were not in favor of joining a fraternity, they certainly were in favor of attending DU's parties, which featured free beer and live music. Concerning the dissatisfaction with secret rites and rituals, I am basing this claim on interviews with alumni from Phi Sigma Kappa and Alpha Tau Omega who graduated during the early to mid 1970s. Many of these alumni told me the secrecy within a particular organization turned off a lot of potential members. In response, these two fraternities in particular put away their ritual books and ignored that aspect all together.

125. On the state of the DU chapter during the 1970s, see the chapter letters in *The Delta Upsilon Quarterly* from 1973–78. On the connection to *Animal House*, and for a description of the alleged pledge activities in Delta Upsilon, see "A Greek Revival." For the problems with Chi Omega and subsequent punishment, see "CSL Suspends DU's Activities," *TD*, April 24, 1985. Other probationary periods are described in articles such as "Delta Upsilon Closed Temporarily," *TD*, March 10, 2003; and "Delta Upsilon Set To Move Off Probation," *TD*, September 19, 2012. In the fall of 2013, members of Delta Upsilon could be seen around campus wearing t-shirts that read "On probation since 1886," which was likely a reference to their past troubles. No doubt Wilson Fairbanks and the other founders of the chapter would be upset with such glorification of mediocrity.

126. On the problems in 2010, see "Tearing It Down," *TD*, May 3, 2010, which includes the quotation. On the closing of the house in 2011, see "DU House Renovation Nears Completion," *TD*, September 14, 2011.

127. On the five schools founded by Universalists, see "Colleges, Theological Schools and Academies," *The Universalist Register* 73, (1908): 100–109. Tufts College and Buchtel College seemed especially well connected in the late 1800s and early 1900s. In 1900, for example, Buchtel bestowed an honorary Doctor of Laws degree on Tufts President Elmer Capen, Tufts Professor E. A. Dolbear gave the commencement address at Buchtel, and Tufts College donated eighty-six volumes to Buchtel's library, the largest donation of any kind that year, as described in *Catalogue of Buchtel College and Preparatory School, 1898–1899 and 1899–1900* (Akron, OH: Akron Printing Company, 1900), 86, 88, 90. There were also a number of Tufts graduates who went on to academic positions at Buchtel, including Professor Charles Bates, who became Chair of the Latin and Greek departments in 1882, and Professor Charles Knight, who began his long career as a science teacher in 1875. In 1907, Buchtel College dropped its affiliation with the Universalist church to become a non-denominational school, then renamed itself the University of Akron in 1913.

128. D. Duane Cummins, *Bethany College: A Liberal Arts Odyssey* (Atlanta, GA: Chalice Press, 2014), 64; and "History," from the website of Delta Tau Delta national fraternity, http://www.delts.org/history/ (accessed May 14, 2014). According to Cummins, 334, the Neotrophian Literary Society was founded on November 5, 1841, some four days after the first one hundred and two students arrived to begin their education. A second, the American Literary Society, was founded five days afterwards. With regards to the circumstances surrounding the founding of Delta Tau Delta (DTD), I encountered much confusion in print. Some sources, including articles in early editions of the fraternity's national magazine, *The Crescent*, mention an opposition to the machinations of the Phi Kappa Psi fraternity at Bethany as the reason for DTD's founding. However, the Phi Kappa Psi chapter at Bethany, as best as I can discern, was chartered a few months after DTD came into being. As such, it appears the early records of DTD did not survive the Civil War. There is even confusion over the number of founders, with some sources such as Baird (1st ed. 1879) claiming only four. In the end, I deferred to the history as told by the national organization, and expanded upon by Cummins.

129. On the early establishment of DTD chapters and troubles at the national level, see Baird (1st ed. 1879), 61–66; and Baird (5th ed. 1898), 104–114. On the establishment of the Arch Chapter, see also Start, 222–223. On the merger with Rainbow Fraternity, see "Two Secret Societies United – Delta Tau Delta and the Rainbow Society

Join Hands," *NYT*, March 28, 1885. The legend of the intrepid DTD men traversing the winter storm is repeated on a number of DTD chapter websites, including http://wiudelts.com/fast-facts/history/ (accessed May 15, 2014). However, aside from the article in *The New York Times* (which was written just months after the merger between W. W. W. and DTD, and therefore fixes the date), I am not completely comfortable with the sources used for this section. The various Baird's manuals, for example, are notorious for having wrong dates, incomplete information, and gross errors. Nonetheless, I am confident the general idea here is correct, even if some of the dates may not be.

130. On the student residences, see *CofTC* (1888–89 ed.), 10–13, 38–39. At the time, there were about one hundred twenty men enrolled across all programs at Tufts College, so I assume most everyone on campus knew each other. In 1888, both the engineering and divinity courses were three-year programs, so all six founding members of DTD were in their first year of school when they established the chapter. On the establishment of chapters at Tufts College and Boston University, as well as the controversy surrounding Northeast expansion, see "Our Recently Organized Chapters," *The Rainbow of Delta Tau Delta* 13, no. 1 (October 1889): 15–18.

131. "Greek Letter Gossip," *The Delta Upsilon Quarterly* 7, no. 3 (May 1889): 224.

132. On the announcement of DTD to the Tufts community, see *The Tuftonian* 15 (May 20, 1889), which includes the quotation. Editorials against secret societies in *The Tuftonian* had been published in earnest as recently as 1885, so I am assuming there was still some strong anti-fraternity sentiment on campus in 1888 and 1889. However, the late 1880s and early 1890s were one of the boom times for new chapters on the Tufts campus, as the number of fraternities rose from two to seven. On the early life of the chapter, see "Beta Mu–Tufts," *The Rainbow of Delta Tau Delta* 13, no. 1 (October 1889): 50–51; "Beta Mu–Tufts College," *The Rainbow of Delta Tau Delta* 13, no. 2 (January 1890): 57; and "Beta Mu–Tufts College," *The Rainbow of Delta Tau Delta* 14, no. 1 (October 1890): 51–52. In the late 1800s, the sports teams were often referred to by the number of regular players, such as the "foot ball eleven" and the "base ball nine," though more were on the roster than just the minimum.

133. On the departure of Elmer Felt, see "Beta Mu–Tufts College," *The Rainbow of Delta Tau Delta* 14, no. 1 (October 1890): 51–52. On the incident involving Delta Upsilon, see "Beta Mu–Tufts College," *Rainbow of Delta Tau Delta* 13, no. 2 (January 1890): 57, which includes the quotation.

134. On the formation of the corporation, see Activities and Organizations records, 1875–2013, UA 024.001 Box 2, Folder 15 (Delta Tau Delta 1921–46). The exact founding date for the corporation was February 17, 1890, and the first meeting was held on March 7, 1890 in Elmer Felt's room (#2) of West Hall. On the opening of the chapter house at 12 Conwell Avenue, see "Beta Mu–Tufts College," *The Rainbow of Delta Tau Delta* 16, no. 3 (May 1893): 172–173; and *The Tuftonian* 19 (March 20 and April 5, 1893). Professor Hooper built his house at 124 Professors Row in 1892, where, according to the *Concise Encyclopedia of Tufts History*, he resided until his death in 1918. Today, Hooper House is the site of the campus infirmary, though the original structure is long gone. For an example of the importance the national organization placed on occupying chapter homes, see "Our History for the Past Two Years," *The Rainbow of Delta Tau Delta* 18, no. 4 (June 1895): 253.

135. "Beta Mu–Tufts College," *The Rainbow of Delta Tau Delta* 16, no. 3 (May 1893): 172–173, which includes the quotation; and *The Tuftonian* 19, April 5, 1893. In

the spring of 1893, the four other undergraduate fraternity chapters on campus were Zeta Psi, Theta Delta Chi, Delta Upsilon, and the newly organized Alpha Tau Omega. All would soon follow in DTD's path of establishing bona fide chapter houses on or close to campus. The demonstration of the phonograph is especially interesting from a historical perspective, as the article in *The Rainbow* seems to imply this technology was not widely available.

136. On the move to 94 Curtis St., see "Tufts College," *BG*, June 11, 1894; "Beta Mu–Tufts College," *The Rainbow of Delta Tau Delta* 17, no. 4 (June 1894): 129–130; and "Local News," *The Tuftonian* 2, no. 1 (October 5, 1894): 13. Heth Aleph Res and DTD may have started the era of chapter houses, but Theta Delta Chi and Delta Upsilon took it to a whole new level when they constructed their houses in 1893 and 1894, respectively. Concerning the house number on Curtis St., these early sources do not list the exact address, as they refer instead to its location as the intersection of Curtis St. and Raymond Ave. I did come across a later article in the *Boston Globe* that identifies the chapter house specifically at 92 Curtis St. However, in Start, 70–71, there is a photograph of this house, and this structure today is known as 94 Curtis St. Also, the chapter refers to the address as 94 Curtis St. in a letter from 1899 as published in *The Rainbow of Delta Tau Delta*. Therefore, I have chosen to refer to this house as 94 Curtis St. to avoid ambiguity. As for the fate of Miss Russell, she is mentioned but once in *The Tuftonian* and never again, so it is unclear how long she lived in the house, or what influence she had over the chapter. If I had to guess, I would say her stay at 94 Curtis St. was probably brief.

137. On Professor Graves, see Start, 141–142; and "Boston Man Chosen," *BG*, June 15, 1896. In 1896, the University of Wyoming had a grand total of 100 students, according to their website, http://www.uwyo.edu/president/past-presidents/frank-graves.html (accessed May 21, 2014), which was about 20% smaller than Tufts College. President Graves, who was all of 27 when he left for Laramie, was the youngest university president at the time. On the date that DTD occupied 18 Latin Way, see "Stray News Items," *TW*, October 4, 1899; and UA Edwin B. Rollins Papers, 1300[sic]–1976, Notebooks, 1940–1955, MS054.001 Box 2, Folder 3 (Campus Homes, Part II 1940–1955). Interestingly, Professor Graves' address in the *CofTC* (1895–96 ed.), 17, is listed as "Cor. ______ and Talbot," as it appears the road did not have an official name just yet. By 1899, it appears the road had been named "Latin Way," though some sources such as the *Boston Globe* give the name as "Appian Way."

138. On the chapter's involvement in World War 1, see "In Their Country's Service–Beta Mu–Tufts College," *Rainbow of Delta Tau Delta* 41, no. 2 (January 1918), 160–161; and "Chapter Eternal–Beta Mu–Courtney Nash Starkweather," *The Rainbow of Delta Tau Delta* 42, no. 2 (January 1919), 193. I am assuming Courtney died of influenza or pneumonia, as those diseases caused the majority of deaths in Army camps – see "Health Conditions at Army Camps Within The United States As Reported to the Surgeon General for Week Ending Nov. 15," *The Official U.S. Bulletin* 2, no. 471 (November 23, 1918): 17–18, 35. On the restarting of operations after the war, see "Beta Mu–Tufts College," *The Rainbow of Delta Tau Delta* 42, no. 3 (March 1919), 290–291, which includes the quotation; and "Beta Mu – Tufts College," *The Rainbow of Delta Tau Delta* 42, no. 4 (June 1919), 477–479. On the rules of pledge walks and their controversy, see correspondence between President Cousens and fraternity members from 1932–33 in Activities and Organizations records, 1875–2013, UA 024.001

Box 4, Folder 10 (Interfraternity Council 1932–1968). I find it interesting the men bragged about stealing in their national magazine, especially since chapter letters from this era were all about maintaining prestige within the organization. Letters were normally filled with self-praise about good grades, efficient fraternity operations, successful social events, and prominence on sports teams, not petty thievery.

139. "Tufts Fraternity Has Acquired New Home," *BG*, January 27, 1921, which includes quotation; "Delta Purchase Home on Professors Row," *TW*, February 9, 1921; UA Edwin B. Rollins Papers, 1300[sic]–1976, Notebooks, 1940–1955, MS054.001 Box 2, Folder 2 (Campus Homes, Part 1(b) 1940–1955); and "Beta Mu–Tufts College," *The Rainbow of Delta Tau Delta* 44, no. 3 (March 1921), 366–367. In this letter to *The Rainbow*, the chapter promised to publish an extensive article describing its new chapter home in a later edition of the magazine. Unfortunately, the chapter never got around to publishing this story, which would have been an interesting look at a house that no longer stands. On the purchase price of $10,000, see letter dated January 15, 1921 in Activities and Organizations records, 1875–2013, UA 024.001 Box 2, Folder 15 (Delta Tau Delta 1921–1946). On Professor Bray, see Start, 123–124; and "Bray Memorial Laboratory of Mechanical Engineering, 1947," *Concise Encyclopedia of Tufts History*, http://hdl.handle.net/10427/14829 (accessed May 24, 2014). By 1921, it appears Tufts had long abandoned the idea of selling land to a fraternity, as the last such sale went through in 1894. Instead, starting in the early 1900s, Tufts switched to selling fraternities the houses of deceased professors, but even this practice would stop in 1938.

140. "Three Fraternity Houses Remodelled [sic]," *TW*, September 24, 1936, which includes quotation.

141. On the fate of DTD's house during the war, see "College Buildings Undergo Changes," *TW*, July 10, 1943. On the problems of keeping the fraternity in operation, see "Beta Mu–Tufts," *The Rainbow of Delta Tau Delta* 66, no. 3 (August 1943): 244; "The Delt Alumni Chapters," *The Rainbow of Delta Tau Delta* 67, no. 2 (May 1944): 77; and "Beta Mu–Tufts," *The Rainbow of Delta Tau Delta* 68, no. 1 (November 1944): 30. On the restarting of DTD after the war ended, see "Beta Mu–Tufts," *The Rainbow of Delta Tau Delta* 69, no. 1 (November 1945): 30–31; "Beta Mu–Tufts," *The Rainbow of Delta Tau Delta* 69, no. 3 (May 1946): 125; and "Living In Shelter," *The Rainbow of Delta Tau Delta* 70, no. 1 (November 1946): 39, which mentions the chapter had just reoccupied its house. On the building of the window, see "Beta Mu – Tufts," *The Rainbow of Delta Tau* Delta 70, no. 2 (February 1947): 9, which includes the quotation. All told, the Beta Mu chapter of DTD saw approximately 27% of all its initiates serve in the war effort. Of those that served, two did not return. One was Captain Charles Edward White, who was captured by Japanese forces on the island of Corregidor in 1942, but was then killed in 1944 when his POW ship, while en route to Tokyo, was mistakenly torpedoed by U.S. naval forces. For more information on Captain Charles White, see "Charles E. White–Cullum No. 11376–September 7, 1944," http://apps.westpointaog.org/Memorials/Article/11376/ (accessed September 9, 2014). The other was Lt. Robert C. Mountford, who was killed in action on November 28, 1944, while fighting with the 26th Infantry Division near the Saar River in Germany.

142. Hartford, *Sing to the Royal Purple*, 199–200. For a broader look at membership restrictions in the pre- and post-antebellum eras, see Syrett.

143. Hartford, 201–203, which includes the quotation. There are a multitude of sources available that discuss the growing religious and racial exclusions of fraterni-

ties near the turn of the 20th century, including Syrett, Sanua, Ross, and Kimbrough. Concerning the religious aspect of DTD, nearly all national Greek-letter fraternities founded before the early 20th century were influenced by various Protestant religions, and these influences often showed up in their secret rituals, for example.

144. Hartford, 203–206, which includes the quotations. There were other reasons behind the passing of the "socially acceptable" clause in 1956 besides the changing attitudes of the younger members in particular. By then, college administrators were beginning to demand that the restrictive membership policies of fraternities and sororities be removed for good, or else they would expel their specific chapters from campus. Such outside pressure from college officials was quickly growing in strength across the country, and numerous national organizations in addition to DTD made similar changes to their constitutions and by-laws in order to comply with the mandate. For a larger discussion on this topic as it relates to Tufts University, see chapter 6. On the conflicts over membership practices that erupted within DTD chapters across the country during this timc, scc Hartford, 207–212.

145. "When the Frat Recruited a Jew: Reliving a Painful Past," *NYT*, May 17, 2005; and Karp, *Fraternity*, which includes the quotation from page 65. Note that while the quotation is from dialogue in a theatrical play about the incident as written by Mr. Karp, others within DTD at the time recall Joel Reynolds uttering a similar, if not the exact phrase. Concerning the leadership positions held by Joel Reynolds, see "First NIC President," *The Rattle of Theta Chi* 50, no. 2 (Winter 1962): 3; and "Tufts–Beta Mu," *The Rainbow of Delta Tau Delta* 94, no. 4 (Summer 1971), 44. Concerning the overwhelming support of the chapter for the initiation of Mr. Karp, DTD at the time required a unanimous vote of the chapter for initiation, and since he was initiated, I am assuming there was no dissent. Also, as discussed in Hartford, 206, there was a mechanism for the national Arch chapter to enforce the "socially acceptable" clause within the chapter, but it appears Mr. Reynolds nor anyone else brought the Tufts incident to the attention of the national organization. Finally, it appears Steve Karp was not the first Jewish member of Beta Mu chapter of DTD, but he was the first to be openly recognized as such. The earlier Jewish members had kept quiet about their religion to all but a few within the chapter (and they certainly didn't tell Joel Reynolds).

146. On the transformation of DTD during the 1960s to its state in the spring of 1971, see letter from Joel W. Reynolds to Jack L. Anson, February 28, 1971, in Activities and Organizations records, 1875–2013, UA 024.001 Box 4, Folder 4 (Fraternities 1956–1971). This letter is a fascinating glimpse into the state of fraternity affairs on campus at the time, at least as seen through the eyes of Mr. Reynolds. He really thought the whole system was about to go under, and lamented he could not do more to bring back the fraternities and sororities of old. On the efforts of the chapter to stabilize itself, see "Tufts–Beta Mu," *The Rainbow of Delta Tau Delta* 94, no. 4 (Summer 1971), 44; "Tufts–Beta Mu," *The Rainbow of Delta Tau Delta* 95, no. 2 (Winter 1971): 35; and "Tufts–Beta Mu," *The Rainbow of Delta Tau Delta* 96, no. 2 (Winter 1972): 35; For the demise or transformation of the mentioned organizations, see their particular sections within this chapter.

147. On the proceedings of the 1972 Karnea, see Hartford, 212–213. One other national fraternity which almost went co-ed was Phi Sigma Kappa, as discussed later in the chapter. On the implementation of DTD's little sister program, see "Good News About Fraternities," *TO*, October 27, 1972; and DTD press release, May 18, 1973,

in Activities and Organizations records, 1875–2013, UA 024.001 Box 2, Folder 15 (Delta Tau Delta 1921–1946). For more information on the little sister movement on campuses throughout the country, which became especially popular in the 1980s but were then phased out, see, for example, "Little Sisters a Part of the Family," *The Cavalier Daily,* October 15, 1985; "Little Sister Programs Fading From Campus Fraternity Life," *Times Daily [Northwest Alabama]*, October 24, 1989; and "Campus Life: California; Fraternities Phase Out 'Little Sister' Groups," *NYT*, September 17, 1989. Additional information on DTD's little sister program was provided through interviews with Gael (McTammany) Casner and John Kubisch.

148. On the retirement of Joel Reynolds, see "Tufts–Beta Mu," *The Rainbow of Delta Tau Delta* 99, no. 3 (Spring 1976): 37. On the 100th anniversary celebration see "Tufts–Beta Mu," *The Rainbow of Delta Tau Delta* 113, no. 2 (Winter 1989). Concerning the hosting of Dr. Kripunov, see "Emergency Hosts," *The Rainbow of Delta Tau Delta* 113, no. 3 (Spring 1990): 8–9; and "Soviet Envoy Speaks on Reducing Militarization," *TD*, March 5, 1990. The ban on Soviet diplomats from entering Medford appears to have been part of a tit-for-tat response to the Soviet Union's ban on American diplomats entering certain areas within their country. This all seems rather silly today, but the Cold War was unlike any war that never progressed to armed combat. As for President Mayer, he was not known for being overly chummy with the students, so I am assuming this incident was one of the few times during his tenure, quite possibly the only time, that he ever set foot inside a fraternity house. I know he certainly did not ever walk into the Sigma Nu house while I was a member (1986–1989), despite living a stone's throw away.

149. "CSL Finds DTD Not Guilty of Harrassment [sic] But Insensitive About Sexual Preference," *TD*, April 18, 1990, which includes the quotation; and "University Declines to Act Upon A Complaint Filed by DTD Members," *TD*, April 27, 1990. As for the bathroom journal in question, I have never seen a copy, as none reside in the official Tufts University archives. However, Otis did allow the staff of *The Tufts Daily* to look through the journal, and its contents were summarized in the first mentioned article.

150. The anti-fraternity movement of the 1990s is discussed in detail in chapter 6.

151. Concerning DTD's probation, see "Fraternity Placed on Two Year Probation," *TD*, February 4, 1993. As a matter of interest, the 1992 edition of the *Jumbo* yearbook is missing from the stacks of the Tisch Library on the Tufts campus. However, a copy of the yearbook is housed in the official Tufts archives, so I was able to see the photo. Nowadays, embarrassing photos are all too commonplace due to the rise of digital social media. On DTD's transgressions in 2003 and 2004, see "DTD Dry Through May '05," *TD*, May 3, 2004, which includes the quotation; and "University Administration Maliciously Targets Delta Tau Delta Again," *TD*, May 3, 2004.

152. "DTD Undergoes Inquiry After Pledge Hospitalized," *TD*, March 30, 2005; and "DTD Closed for a Year; On Probation Until 2007," *TD*, April 12, 2005. The latter article contains quotes from the DTD chapter president that suggest to me he really didn't understand the severity of the situation, that someone nearly died in his house. Yes, he apologized for the "bad experience for the young gentleman," but the apology came after he lamented DTD's loss of status as the number one fraternity on campus. One would expect more compassion and introspect from a true leader.

153. On the revocation of the charter and subsequent rental of the property to graduate students, see "DTD Houses Grad Students," *TD*, September 6, 2005. On the

occupancy of 98 Professors Row by Alpha Epsilon Pi (AEPi), the earliest reference I could find was "Police Briefs–If None of You Broke the Window, What Are You Arguing About?" *TD*, March 28, 2008, which specifically mentions AEPi as residing at that address. Therefore, I assume AEPi first moved in during the fall of 2007.

154. On the re-colonization, see "DTD Attracts Over 40 Recruits as it Creates A New Image," *TD*, March 2, 2009. On regaining the Beta Mu charter, see "DTD Officially Recognized as Fraternity On Campus," *TD*, May 23, 2010. On the return to 98 Professors Row and the house renovations, see "DTD To Move Into AEPi House," *TD*, September 30, 2010; "DTD Returns to 98 Professors Row," *TD*, September 6, 2011; and "Home Sweet Home," *TD*, November 18, 2011. All told, the alumni corporation spent over $400,000 to renovate the chapter house.

155. "DTD Brothers Navigate Probation Amid Ongoing Criminal Investigation," *TD*, September 25, 2015; "DTD to Face Another Year Without Its Fraternity House," *TD*, May 22, 2016; and "DTD House Leased to Tufts, Used for Transfer Student Housing," *TD*, September 6, 2016. In the aftermath of the stabbing, rumors began circulating as to its cause, but to date very few official details have been released to the public. Therefore I chose not to mention the rumors, and leave the truth for a future edition. The alleged suspect has not been identified publicly at the time of this writing.

156. For a more detailed look at the rise in Civil Engineering programs after the Civil War, see the section on Phi Delta / Sigma Nu later in this chapter. On the establishment of the Engineering program at Tufts, see *CofTC* (1865–66 ed.), 17–19; *CofTC* (1867–68 ed.), 7, which lists the first Civil Engineering student, Frederic Howard White; and Start, 43–44, 54. On the percentage of engineering students in 1890, see *CofTC* (1890–91 ed.), 10–13. I have ignored the Special Students as listed on Page 14 from this calculation, since their course of study was unclear.

157. Concerning the founding date of The Engineers Fraternity, see *B&B* (1892 ed.). For the fraternity's motto, see "Greek Letter Gossip," *The Delta Upsilon Quarterly* 10, no. 2 (February 1892): 120. Concerning the low membership within The Engineers Fraternity, see *B&B* (1892 and 1893 ed.), which published the membership rolls for all fraternities. I am assuming the Engineers Fraternity met its demise during the 1892–93 school year since it is not represented in the 1894 edition of the *Brown and Blue*, published in the spring of 1893 (the edition was named for the junior class, which published the book). Concerning Edward Byrne and Carl Hathaway, see the section on Alpha Tau Omega later in this chapter.

158. The story of Heth Aleph Res surprised me greatly, because I knew nothing of the fraternity when I started this project, and yet its influence on modern-day Greek life at Tufts is undeniable. Professor Russell Miller, when he was putting together his seminal work entitled *Light on the Hill* in the early 1950s, was probably the last researcher who could have contacted former members of Heth Aleph Res to hear their story. However, his research focused on the larger picture and not necessarily the individual student. It also appears he did not undertake interviews of alumni as part of his effort. As for the culture within Heth Aleph Res, many members were very active in the national temperance and prohibition movements.

159. The founding of St. Lawrence University is beyond the scope of this work, but a good source of material is Gates Curtis, ed., *Our County and its People: A Memorial Record of St. Lawrence County New York* (Syracuse, NY: D. Mason and Company, 1894), 446–458; and *Sixty Years of Saint Lawrence* (Canton, NY: St. Lawrence University,

1916), 7–16. According to the latter source, Canton beat out eleven other municipalities in New York for the right to host the theological school.

160. Miller, *LOTH–1*, 112–113. On the curriculum in place around the time Mr. Packard bequeathed his money to Tufts, see *CofTC* (1865–66 ed.), 12–19, and *CofTC* (1866–67 ed.), 12–18.

161. Miller, *LOTH–1*, 112–117. On the formation of the Zetagathean Society and the Sawyer Club, see Chapter 2.

162. On the formation of the Beta Mu chapter of DTD, see its section earlier in this chapter. In Start, 297–299 and 317–320, the alumni and non-graduates of the divinity school are listed along with their fraternity affiliation. These listings show that DTD was the preferred choice of divinity students, although at least two joined Theta Delta Chi.

163. On the diverse ages of the divinity students versus the younger undergraduates, see Start, 253–320, which lists the alumni and non-graduates by class year, and includes their birth dates (when known). On the Engineers Fraternity, see their section earlier in this chapter. On the attempts to start a fraternity in the spring of 1891, see *B&B* (1894 ed.), 92–94.

164. Concerning Carl's affiliation with Phi Delta Theta, see *Annual Circle Letters of the Seventy Active Chapters of the Phi Delta Theta Fraternity* 20, (1906): 305–306, which lists him as an 1891 graduate of Buchtel. On the large enrollment of the first year (Junior) class, see *CofTC* (1891–92 ed.), 80–81, which lists fourteen students; the previous year listed but five – see *CofTC* (1890–91 ed.), 41. On the early history of Heth Aleph Res and the identification of its charter members, see *B&B* (1894 ed.), 92–94. As it turned out, Carl Henry did not graduate from the Tufts Divinity School, according to Start, 320. He did, however, become a Universalist minister, and in 1924, Tufts awarded him an honorary Doctor of Divinity degree. On the claim to Heth Aleph Res being the first Hebrew-letter fraternity, see "First Hebrew Letter Fraternity," *Boston Evening Transcript*, November 19, 1900. This article was a response to an earlier publication, "Hebrew Letter Fraternity," *The St. Louis Republic*, November 16, 1900, which claimed the first Hebrew-letter fraternity had been organized at Kentucky University in 1900. Hebrew-letter fraternities are somewhat rare, with most collegiate fraternal organizations choosing Greek letters for identification. Some, though, combined Greek and Hebrew letters in their name, such as the national organization Beta Samach. Finally, a number of Heth Aleph Res members over the years were also members of national Greek letter fraternities, including Henry B. Taylor (Beta Theta Pi) and William Taylor (Phi Gamma Delta).

165. On the disdain for the formation of any new fraternities, and the mocking of the supposed "non-society society," see various editorials in *The Tuftonian*, November 5, 1891; December 20, 1891; and February 20, 1892. On the failed efforts of some Beta Theta Pi members studying at Tufts to establish a chapter of their fraternity, see "Impressions of the 54th Convention," *Beta Theta Pi* 21, no. 2 (November 1893): 7, 73, 142. This effort appears to have started around 1890 (though the exact date is unclear), and was independent of the one to start Heth Aleph Res.

166. On the intrigue surrounding Carl Henry, and Heth Aleph Res's enjoyment of the situation, see *B&B* (1894 ed.), 92–94. On the announcement of the fraternity's existence to the campus, see "Theologicana Section," *The Tuftonian*, April 5, 1892. A few weeks later, on April 20, 1892, an editorial appeared in *The Tuftonian* praising the

existence of Heth Aleph Res since it added to the overall experience of Tufts, while also discouraging them from seeking affiliation with a national Greek letter fraternity. The fear, still, was that if Heth Aleph Res went national, it would compete against the other four fraternities for members, and all would suffer.

167. On the identification of the three women who enrolled in the divinity school that fall, see *CofTC* (1892–93 ed.), 94. Also, Start, 66, mentions that three women enrolled in the Divinity School in the fall of 1892, though they are not named. On the identification of Angie Brooks and Mabel MacCoy as members of Heth Aleph Res, see *B&B* (1894 ed.), 92. Unfortunately, a group photo was not included in the *Brown and Blue* yearbook, and indeed I have been unable to find any photo of Heth Aleph Res that shows the men and women alongside one another. Although determining when the first co-ed fraternity appeared in America is beyond the scope of my research, there is some discussion on this topic in Note 22, Chapter 1. In general, though, it seems many national fraternities frowned upon the idea of co-ed membership. For example, see "Greek Press," *The Kappa Alpha Journal* 7, no. 5 (February 1890): 19, where the editors affirm their belief that, "a 'co-ed' fraternity is wrong; or, if not wrong, would certainly be embarrassing. The majority of boys have sufficient sisters already." On the reaction of the campus to the initiation of Angie Brooks, and Mabel MacCoy, see "Theologicana Section," *The Tuftonian*, October 20, 1892, which includes the quote.

168. On the claim of 31 George St. being the first Tufts fraternity house, my reasoning is as follows. This address is listed as the residence of Angie Brooks and Mabel MacCoy in *CofTC* (1892–93 ed.), 94. In an article from the November 20, 1892, edition of *The Tuftonian*, which includes the quotation, the author describes a boarding plan that had just been put in operation at this address. While the author does not mention the boarding plan as being specifically for Heth Aleph Res, he does list all of the names belonging to the plan, and all except for "Price" were members of the fraternity, according to *B&B* (1894 ed.), 92. However, there is no student with a last name of "Price" in the 1892–93 edition of the *CofTC*, so I assume this was a misprint – the author may have meant George Rice, who, I must admit, is not listed as a member of Heth Aleph Res in the few membership rolls I have found (though none of these lists are specific to the fall of 1892). However, later articles in *The Tuftonian* from November 20, 1893, and January 20, 1894, specifically mention 31 George St. as the fraternity's chapter house, and the 1893–94 edition of the *CofTC* lists two members of Heth Aleph Res, James Tillinghast and Mabel MacCoy, as residing in the house. Therefore, I claim that 31 George St. was indeed the fraternity's chapter house beginning in the fall of 1892, thus making it the first at Tufts, even if it was not recognized as such by the general campus until a year later. Unfortunately, I have been unable to determine where, exactly, 31 George St. was located back in the fall of 1892, as maps from that era are not complete. Today, there is no building with the number 31 on George St. On the occupation of chapter houses by Delta Tau Delta and Theta Delta Chi, see their sections earlier in this chapter.

169. On the passing of the resolution banning co-ed lodging and boarding clubs, see Office of the Board of Trustees records, 1848–2013, Executive Committee, 1854–2000, Meeting minutes 1854–1962, UA003.002 Box 112, Folder 6 (Executive committee minutes, vol. 5, 1889–1896: June 24, 1893). On the occupancy of Heth Aleph Res's chapter house by James Tillinghast and Mabel MacCoy during the 1893–94 school year, see *CofTC* (1893–94 ed.), 98–99. As shown in this catalogue, enrollment in the divinity school was still heavily tilted towards men, so the banning of women from join-

ing Heth Aleph Res had little practical impact on the fraternity's operations. However, as we will see later in this section, women were still a part of the fraternity as the years went on. For more information on Anna (Moulton) Tillinghast and her marriage to James in 1893, see http://www.cbp.gov/about/history/did-you-know/anna-tillinghast (accessed June 26, 2014).

170. On the formation of the Aleph Chapter of Heth Aleph Res corporation, see *Abstract of the Certificates of Corporations Organized Under the General Laws of Massachusetts Together With the Annual Returns Required by Chapter 106 of the Public Statues During the Year 1894* (Boston, MA: Wright & Potter Printing, 1895), 13. Concerning the negotiations to buy the land and the subsequent build of the chapter house, see *The Tuftonian*, June 5, 1894; and "Tufts College," *BG*, June 11, 1894. For the quotation, see "Divinity School," *The Tuftonian*, October 5, 1894. To help build the house, the trustees agreed to give the corporation a mortgage, as discussed in Board of Trustees records, 1848–2013, Full Board, 1851–2012, Meeting Minutes 1851–1955, UA003.001 Box 106, Folder 1 (Full Board Minutes vol. 3, 1887–1895: June 11, 1894).

171. On the activities of Heth Aleph Res in the year after occupying their new house, see "Divinity School," *Tuftonian,* November 20, 1894; "Divinity School," *Tuftonian*, February 5, 1895; "Divinity School," *Tuftonian*, February 20, 1895, which includes the information on Rev. Canfield living in the chapter house; "Divinity School," *Tuftonian*, May 20, 1895; and "Divinity Students' Banquet," *BG*, December 11, 1895. On Rev. Canfield's membership in DTD, see Start, 295–296. On the residency of the Tillinghasts within the Heth Aleph Res house, see *CofTC* (1894–95 ed.), 112–113.

172. I am still somewhat in disbelief that the Tufts administration allowed unmarried men and women to live together, openly, on campus, in the late 1800s, especially when they expressly forbade it. Perhaps they just had bigger problems to deal with – the United States was in a Depression during the mid 1890s, and Tufts was certainly feeling the financial pressure. On the living arrangements, see *CofTC* (1896–97 ed.), 30; *CofTC* (1897–98 ed.), 30–31; and *CofTC* (1898–99 ed.), 224, which shows the women living alongside men such as Edson Reifsnider and Charles Petty. Finally, it appears that of the seven women who were known or likely members of Heth Aleph Res, all but Angie Brooks became ordained ministers in the Universalist church. Indeed, Mabel MacCoy was the first woman to be ordained in Massachusetts as a minister, which coincided with her calling to the First Universalist Church in Mansfield, MA, in 1895. For more information, see "Women Preacher: Mrs. MacCoy Installed at Mansfield," *BG*, March 14, 1895. However, according to Start, 323, Mabel MacCoy did not, in fact, graduate from Tufts College, though she did complete two years of study.

173. For the first quotation, see *B&B* (1894 ed.), 94. On the existence of a second chapter of Heth Aleph Res at Meadville, see "Divinity School Notes," *TW*, May 5, 1897, which mentions the chapter was recently formed; "Divinity School Notes," *TW*, May 26, 1897; and "First Hebrew Letter Fraternity," *Boston Evening Transcript*, November 19, 1900. Although my claim that Henry B. Taylor was responsible for the second chapter at Meadville is somewhat speculative, I have come to this conclusion based on his biography as published by Marquis, *The Book of Minnesotans*, 505, which is the most direct link I have found between the Tufts divinity school, Heth Aleph Res, and the Meadville Theological School. During my research I contacted a librarian at the Meadville Theological School, but he was unable to find any records of Heth Aleph Res within the school's archives. The Meadville Theological School, though it still retains

its original name, has long since relocated from its original home in Pennsylvania to Chicago, so the lack of any records relating to Heth Aleph Res is not surprising. On the possible existence of even more chapters, see "Tufts College," *Boston Evening Transcript*, February 21, 1902, which includes the second quotation. As mentioned in the text, the wording of this particular article implies there were more than two chapters of Heth Aleph Res. Along this line, in Marquis, *The Book of Detroiters,* 444, I did come across a reference to a Heth Aleph Yodh fraternity that possibly operated out of the McCormick Theological Seminary, Chicago, IL, in the early 1900s. This fraternity may have been a chapter of Heth Aleph Res, but aside from this one entry in a who's-who book, I can find no other information about this organization.

174. On the chapter size at the end of the 1894–95 school years, see *B&B* (1896 ed.). On the sale of 37 Sawyer Avenue to the trustees, see Entry 21 in Massachusetts Land Records, Middlesex South Registry, Book 12920, Page 489. For operations of Heth Aleph Res into the early 1900s, see various articles in the *Tufts Weekly* from May 1, 1901; May 15, 1901; February 27, 1902; November 13, 1902; and November 20, 1902. Also, see *B&B* (1899 ed.), and *B&B* (1904 ed.), where the latter lists the names of seven first year students who had just joined the fraternity. Indeed, by crosschecking this membership roll with the *CofTC* (1902–03 ed.), 265, it appears all divinity students were members of Heth Aleph Res at the time. Concerning the dwindling enrollment in the divinity school at the turn of the century, see various editions of the *CofTC.* For example, the 1899–1900, 1901–02, and 1902–03 editions list about fifteen to sixteen students in the divinity school each year, less than half of what enrollment had been just five years earlier, and those numbers continued to slide as the years progressed. In addition, the decline of the divinity school is discussed in "Crane Theological School, 1869–1968," *Concise Encyclopedia of Tufts History*, http://hdl.handle.net/10427/14829 (accessed June 28, 2014).

175. On the transformation of 37 Sawyer Avenue, see "Bartol House, 1894," *Concise Encyclopedia of Tufts History*, http://hdl.handle.net/10427/14829 (accessed June 30, 2014). On the Commons Club, see their section later in this chapter. On the closing of the divinity school in 1968, see Miller, *LOTH–2*, 54–73.

176. Concerning any meaning behind the letters "Heth Aleph Res," I asked the opinion of a number of Rabbis across the country, with no clear consensus. In all likelihood, the three letters were an abbreviation for the fraternity's secret motto, which is still secret. I suspect someone out there, somewhere, has more information on Heth Aleph Res, which would be fascinating to examine.

177. "The Official Story of our Founding," http://www.ato.org/AlphaTauOmega/atohistory/foundingstory.aspx (accessed July 2, 2014). The Battle of New Market, Virginia, on May 15, 1864, featured a battalion of soldiers from VMI including Otis Glazebrook, who were entering the conflict for the first time. Although outnumbered, the Confederates won the battle, in part because of the efforts of the VMI men.

178. Ibid; Reno, *The Manual of the Alpha Tau Omega Fraternity*, 1–7; and Maxwell, *Greek Letter Men of the Pacific Coast and Rocky Mountain States*, 585–587.

179. "The Official Story of our Founding"; Reno, 7–14; and Maxwell, *Greek Letter Men of the Pacific Coast and Rocky Mountain States*, 585. The three founders of Alpha Tau Omega were Otis Allen Glazebrook, Alfred Marshall, and Erskine Mayo Ross. All three had been cadets at VMI before the Civil War and were veterans of the Confederate army. Of the three, Otis and Alfred returned to VMI in the fall of 1865 to continue

their education. Erskine, who had graduated in the spring of 1864, left for Los Angeles, California shortly after his initiation. The emphasis on Christianity within Alpha Tau Omega would prove to be problematic nearly one hundred years later.

180. On the establishment of ATO as a national fraternity from its founding, see Reno, 10–11. On the establishment of the other mentioned chapters, see Reno, 14–15, 31, 37, and 38. The Zeta Psi fraternity, as discussed earlier in this chapter, was one other founded with a national role in mind.

181. On the athletic record of Pearly Wilson, see "Baseball," http://umaine.edu/mclub/files/2011/07/10-Baseball.pdf (accessed July 7, 2014). Note his first name is spelled "Perley" in this record. The story of the apples and the bees comes from Nichols, *History of Gamma Beta Tufts*, 3, which includes the quotation. However, this record is very vague on the timing of the incident. Since apple season in New England is typically late summer, I am assuming the raid took place in early September for the following reason. According to the *Catalogue of the Maine State College of Agriculture and Mechanic Arts* (1892–93 ed.), 80, Maine State College began classes on August 29, 1892. Tufts College, according to the *CofTC* (1892–93 ed.), 4, opened for classes a few weeks later, on September 22. Therefore, it is plausible that Pearly and friends started the semester at Maine State College, raided the orchard, got expelled, and then transferred to Tufts College. The only caveat to this reasoning is the article "Maine Beta Upsilon–Maine State College, Orono," *Alpha Tau Omega Palm* 12, no. 4 (August 1892): 204–206, which mentions that Pearly had left school before the end of the spring semester, 1892. I don't see how Pearly and friends could have gone apple picking in the early summer of 1892, since the apples would not have been in season. Perhaps Pearly's withdrawal from school that spring term was for a different reason, and the orchard raid did indeed take place in the late summer of 1892, when he returned to Maine State College to continue with his studies. At the very least, there was some reason why Pearly transferred to Tufts in the fall of 1892, so the story as presented by Nichols ultimately seems quite plausible, even if not completely verifiable. On the enrollment of Pearly at Tufts in the fall of 1892, see *CofTC* (1892–93 ed.), 18. On Pearly's involvement in the founding of Beta Upsilon chapter, see "Maine Beta Upsilon–Maine State College, Orono," *Alpha Tau Omega Palm* 11, no. 2 (April 1891): 32–33.

182. Nichols, 3–4; *Tuftonian*, February 4, 1893; and "Massachusetts Gamma Beta, Tufts College, College Hill," *Alpha Tau Omega Palm* 13, (June 1893): 224–226, which also lists Carl Hathaway as an early (though not founding) member. The article in *The Tuftonian* excludes George Strong from the list of charter members, but he is named by the other two sources, so I believe he was a charter member. Matt DeWolf, a national officer of the Alpha Tau Omega fraternity, provided the reasoning for Pearly's exclusion as a founding father. On the claim that Herbert Foss and Chesley Johnston were part of the group expelled from Maine State College, see *Annual Report of the Maine State College for the Year 1893: Part I*, (1894): 67, which lists the two men as non-graduates and gives their address in 1893 as being College Hill, Massachusetts. One of the founding members of the chapter, Frank Wren, became one of its most prominent, at least in Tufts history. After graduating in 1894, Mr. Wren became a mathematics professor at Tufts and eventually a Dean of the College of Letters in 1907, even though he was the youngest member of the faculty at the time. He also served as an officer in the national offices of Alpha Tau Omega in the early 1900s, and helped start the Gamma Sigma chapter of Alpha Tau Omega at Worcester Polytechnic Institute, which is still active

today. Both the dormitory Wren Hall and the Wren Faculty Dining Room are named in his honor. Finally, concerning Mr. Foss, I have seen his first name spelled both as "Herbert" and "Hubert" in these references, so I am unsure as to the correct spelling.

183. *The Tuftonian*, February 4, 1893, which includes the first quotation. On the controversy over the establishment of another fraternity, see the discussion within Heth Aleph Res earlier in this chapter. On the prominent positions held by ATOs and the fraternity's early reputation on campus, see "Massachusetts Gamma Beta, Tufts College, College Hill," *Alpha Tau Omega Palm* 13, (June 1893): 224–226, which includes the second and third quotations; and "Mass. Gamma Beta, Tufts College, Medford," *Alpha Tau Omega Palm* 14, no. 1 (February 1894): 53–54.

184. Nichols, 4–5, which includes the quotation; and "Massachusetts Gamma Beta, Tufts College, College Hill," *Alpha Tau Omega Palm* 13, (June 1893): 224–226. On the establishment of the Commons dining hall (now known as Curtis Hall) in 1893, see Start, 62–63; and "Curtis Hall, 1893," *Concise Encyclopedia of Tufts History*, http://hdl.handle.net/10427/14829 (accessed July 6, 2014). In the earliest years of Tufts College, there were small-scale dining halls run out of the dormitories, but as the college's enrollment grew after the Civil War, the administration turned over the feeding of its students primarily to private enterprise, until the Commons Hall was established.

185. The housing odyssey for ATO, unfortunately, is not documented with the greatest of detail, so I have done my best to piece together the journey. On the move to the new house in the Medford Hillside, then to the rooms vacated by Theta Delta Chi, and finally to Davis Square in Somerville, see Nichols, 6. Here, Nichols mentions the chapter rented rooms in the Odd Fellows Hall, but gives no date for when this occurred. On ATO's occupancy of Columbian Hall in West Somerville (a building which, unfortunately, I have not been able to find under that name), see "Tufts College Notes," *BG*, October 15, 1896. On a change in occupancy during the 1896–97 school year to the Chapin Building, see "Mass. Gamma Beta, Tufts College," *Alpha Tau Omega Palm* 17, no. 2 (February 1897): 230; and "Clippings–A Reporter's Mistake," *Alpha Tau Omega Palm* 17, no. 4 (July 1897): 246. On the move from Chapin Building to Unity Hall, see "Mass. Gamma Beta, Tufts College," *Alpha Tau Omega Palm* 19, no. 1 (November 1898): 66; and "Mass. Gamma Beta, Tufts College," *Alpha Tau Omega Palm* 19, no. 2 (March 1899): 202. On the lamentations over a lack of a chapter house, see "Mass. Gamma Beta, Tufts College," *Alpha Tau Omega Palm* in the following issues: vol. 16, no. 2 (March 1896): 124; vol. 17, no.1 (November 1896): 74; vol. 17, no. 2 (February 1897): 230; vol. 18, no. 4 (July 1898): 282; vol. 19, no. 1 (November 1898): 66, which includes the quotation; and vol. 19, no. 2 (March 1899): 202. Chapter letters within ATO's national magazine at this time were generally written to emphasize, almost continually, how the men were not just doing well, but exceeding in many facets of college life. A chapter's greatest fear, it seemed, was to be deemed below average (or worse) in the eyes of their peers. For the members of Gamma Beta chapter at Tufts, I got the sense they felt their lack of a chapter house was lowering their prestige within the national organization, so they looked to offset this demerit by announcing over and over again, "hey, we're working on it." For more about how the need for prestige was so prevalent in the fraternity system around the turn of the 20th century, see Syrett, chapters 3 and 4.

186. On the announcement of the supposed purchase by ATO, see "Stray News Items," *TW*, February 2, 1899. On the redaction, see "Stray News Items," *TW*, February 15, 1899. No reason was given as to why Mr. Joy was so opposed to a fraternity

owning his property.

187. On DTD's vacating of its house at 94 Curtis St., see "Stray News Items," *TW*, October 4, 1899. On ATO's subsequent occupancy of 94 Curtis St., see "Alpha Tau Omega Initiates," *TW*, October 18, 1899, which is the earliest reference I have found concerning their residence on Curtis St. The campus map as printed in *CofTC* (1900–01 ed.) confirms this address as 94 Curtis St. On the social activities hosted by the chapter, see "Fraternity Gathering at Tufts," *BG*, February 15, 1900; and "Mass. Gamma Beta," *Alpha Tau Omega Palm* 21, no. 2 (March 1901): 180–181. On the chapter's issues with alcohol and tobacco, see Nichols, 7–8, which includes the quotation. It is unclear how long the chapter remained alcohol free, but I would suspect only until Harry graduated in the spring of 1903.

188. On the effort to diversify the brotherhood, see Nichols, 9–10. A membership roster from 1908, as printed on a letter to alumni and housed in ATO–A, Series 41/95/1, Box 144 (Tufts), shows the chapter was still heavily stocked with athletes, but only a few of them were varsity letter winners, while the rest were involved more in class and inter-fraternity competition. Complementing the athletes was one member who had been chosen as the "Tree Orator" for the 1908 graduation, which, believe it or not, was a highly prestigious honor at the time. His job was to wax poetic about the trees being planted on campus as part of the graduation exercise. On the establishment of the corporation, see Nichols, 10–11, which lists the corporation's founding date as April 25, 1911. Also see Somerville Alderman Minutes, May 11, 1911, http://www.somervillema.gov/sites/default/files/1911_0.pdf (accessed October 1, 2016). On the career of Dean Frank Wren, see "Frank George Wren," *Alpha Tau Omega Palm* 27, no. 2 (June 1907): 161. The push to buy a grand house on campus was motivated in part, I assume, by the near constant stream of articles within the *Alpha Tau Omega Palm* detailing the mansions owned by various ATO chapters across the country. The stately house was an undeniable mark of success within the national fraternity, and I am sure the members of Gamma Beta read these articles and viewed these photos with a certain amount of lodging envy.

189. On the purchase of the house and its description, see Nichols, 12; and "The New Chapter House of Massachusetts Gamma Beta," *Alpha Tau Omega Palm* 31, no. 4 (December 1911): 381–382, which includes the quotation. On Professor Dolbear, see "Dolbear, Amos Emerson, 1837–1910," *Concise Encyclopedia of Tufts History*, http://hdl.handle.net/10427/14829 (accessed July 8, 2014).

190. On the problems with the heating system, see Nichols, 12. On the membership in 1917, see *The Alumnus* 4, no. 7 (November 15, 1917): 1, in ATO–A, Series 41/95/1, Box 144 (Tufts), Publications, 1908–68, 1986.

191. On the financial and membership struggles of the chapter, see Nichols, 14–15; *The Alumnus* 4, no. 6 (June 15, 1917): 1–2; *The Alumnus* 4, no. 7 (November 15, 1917): 2–6; and *The Alumnus* 5, no. 1 (June 7, 1918): 1–4, all in ATO–A, Series 41/95/1, Box 144 (Tufts), Publications, 1908–68, 1986. On the transformation from college to S.A.T.C., see various articles in *TW*, October 25, 1918. On the occupancy of the house by the S.A.T.C. officers, see "Gamma Beta: Tufts College," *Alpha Tau Omega Palm* 39, no. 1 (March 1919): 143–144. Although Tufts College became an Army base for the men in the fall of 1918, women were still enrolled as regular students in Jackson College.

192. Nichols, 15–16.

193. On William J. Bennett, see "Bennett, William Joseph, 1894–1917," and "Bennett Memorial Scholarship," which includes the quotation, in *Concise Encyclopedia of Tufts History*, http://hdl.handle.net/10427/14829 (accessed July 16, 2014); "Medford," *BG*, March 22, 1924; Richard B. Coolidge, "William J. Bennett Memorial," *The Medford Historical Register* 27, no. 3 (September 1924): 58–61; and *The Three Hundred and First Engineers: A History, 1917–1919* (Boston, MA: Houghton Mifflin Company, 1920): 104–105, 309. As discussed in Nichols, 17, there were a total of seventy-six Tufts ATO active undergraduate and alumni members who entered the service. The three other gold stars for the chapter, according to "Tufts Men Who Died In Service," were Cpl. Windom Alpheus Allen '16, who died of pneumonia in a military hospital months after the war ended; 2nd Lt. Paul Thomas Kearney '15, who was killed in action in the Argonne while leading his machine gun platoon; and Lt. George Edward Richardson '97, who died of pneumonia while serving on board the U.S.S. Huron. These men are identified as being members of Alpha Tau Omega in "Honor Roll of Tufts Men Who Served Our Country in the Great War" in Office of the President Records, 1828–2007, Hermon Carey Bumpus, administrative records and related papers, 1913–1919, UA001.006 Box 1, Folder 6 (World War 1 1917–1919); and "16th Gold Star," *TW*, February 5, 1919.

194. Nichols, 15–17, which includes the quotation. On pages 19 and 20 of his history (which he wrote in 1922), Nichols makes an interesting comment about the state of the men who enrolled at Tufts College after the war. Essentially, Nichols felt many men were suffering from psychological trauma at the time, and as a result were not saving and spending their money as wisely as they had in the past. Now, they were more reckless and careless than they've ever been. As a result, the chapter struggled financially when the house reopened after the war, but nowhere near as much as before the war, when they didn't have enough men to fill the rooms and pay the bills. Nowadays, the situation is called post-traumatic stress disorder, but back in 1919, many didn't know what to make of it.

195. On ATO's athletic prowess, see "Gamma Beta, Tufts," *The Palm of Alpha Tau Omega* 55, no. 3 (May 1935): 299. On ATO's house renovation, see "Three Fraternity Houses Remodelled [sic]," *TW*, September 24, 1936, which includes the quotation. On Arland Dirlam's reputation, see "Plan New Advent Church Building," *Portsmouth [NH] Herald*, May 16, 1940, 16. Arland Dirlam was Tufts class of 1926, and designed a number of buildings on the Tufts campus including the War Memorial Library attached to Eaton Hall. The presence of a "ram's pasture" did not mean the house was home to a petting zoo. The term refers to a large bedroom for unmarried men, usually in the attic. Although the tearing down of the original Victorian structures on Professors Row in the 1930s was apparently not questioned by anyone, Tufts College did lose a piece of its history with all of those renovations.

196. On the appointment of George Miller as Acting President of Tufts College, see "ATO President and Assistant President at Tufts College," *The Palm of Alpha Tau Omega* 57, no. 5 (December 1937): 411. On the state of 134 Professors Row during the war as well as the struggle to maintain membership, see "Jackson Gains Two New Houses, ATO and Kippy," *TW*, November 18, 1943; and "The Fraternity Supplement–Alpha Tau Omega," *TW*, May 9, 1946. The work of Vannevar Bush during World War II is covered by many sources. For one, see "ATO... and the Atomic Bomb," *The Palm of Alpha Tau Omega* 65, no. 3 (September 1945): 4–6. Vannevar Bush's name, though, it

not as well known today as others involved in the Manhattan Project such as Robert Oppenheimer and Richard Feynman.

197. On the return of the chapter after the end of World War II, see "Alpha Sigma Grabs Rush Honors With 35 Pledges," *TW*, November 7, 1946; and "What's new Among Chapters and Alumni–Tufts," *The Palm of Alpha Tau Omega* 66, no. 4 (December 1946): 46. Although the list of gold stars from Gamma Beta chapter of ATO is probably incomplete, I have been able to identify four men who gave their lives in service: Ens. Gerald Bennett, Lt. W. H. Ringer, Lt. E. E. Backman, and Cpl. Walter Mann. For information on these men, see "Gold Stars of Alpha Tau Omega," *The Palm of Alpha Tau Omega* 66, no. 1 (March 1946): 20, 32; and *The Palm of Alpha Tau Omega* 67, no. 2 (June 1947): 17, 19.

198. The issue of restrictive membership practices in Alpha Tau Omega at the national level is complex and well beyond the scope of this work. For some general information, see Alpha Tau Omega's history as posted on their website, http://www.ato.org (accessed October 1, 2016). This topic is also discussed on a national scale by Syrett, 248–261. For more information about how the push to remove the restrictions played out at Tufts, see chapter 6. For a specific reference that mentions ATO's membership restrictions in the mid 1950s, see "Paper Views Frat Clauses," *The Cornell Daily Sun*, October 22, 1956.

199. The issue of removing restrictive membership practices within fraternities at Tufts is discussed and referenced in greater detail in chapter 6.

200. The turmoil on the Tufts campus in the 1960s and early 1970s is beyond the scope of this work. For more detailed information, see Miller, *LOTH–2*, chapters 15, 16, and 21. Concerning ATO's chapter size, see the 1967 composite as published in the *Jumbo* (1968 ed.). Having looked through all of the yearbooks and viewed countless fraternity composites, it is my strong opinion that the ATO chapter in 1967 was the largest any chapter had ever yet been at Tufts. On the membership size of ATO in 1970, see the visitation report from Hugh L. Rice, April 21–22, 1970, as housed in ATO–A, Series 41/95/1, Box 144 (Tufts), Visitation File, 1967–74.

201. On the arrival of co-ed living at Tufts, see "Co-educational Dorms Approved; Parent Permission Required," *TO*, March 16, 1970, which mentions that the first co-ed dorms would open in the fall of 1970. On the rejection of fraternity living in favor of co-ed arrangements, see visitation report from Hugh Rice, April 21–22, 1970.

202. The material for the rest of this section is based primarily on alumni interviews with numerous alumni of Alpha Tau Omega and ATO of Massachusetts, including Robert McLaughlin (January 26, 2012, and May 10, 2012), George Haug (January 18, 2012, and January 20, 2012), Bill Mintz (January 19, 2012), Jack Obadia (February 15, 2012, and February 17, 2012), and Amy Friedlander (January 26, 2012). While the details these alumni provided were not always consistent, the overall message was. I have supplemented this oral history with chapter visitation reports and correspondence as housed in the ATO–A archives. According to Mr. McLaughlin, the Tufts administration put great pressure on the alumni corporation in the early 1970s to sell 134 Professors Row to the university, so they could then lease the house back to the fraternity. The alumni corporation wanted no part of this plan, as they were skeptical the Tufts administration would honor its commitment to house the fraternity indefinitely. Therefore, keeping the house financially viable was the utmost concern, lest they lose control of the property.

203. On Cornell's participation in the ECAC tournament, see "Year-By-Year Results," http://cornellbigred.com/documents/2010/5/11/Results.pdf?id=2960 (accessed August 1, 2014), which lists the 1973 ECAC tournament as being played in Boston, MA on March 9 and 10. Additionally, Cornell played at the Boston Garden the following week as part of the NCAA tournament, so in theory the incident with the Beta Theta chapter could have happened during the NCAA tournament and not the ECAC tournament, but one alumnus I spoke with regarding the incident specifically mentioned it was the ECAC weekend. Numerous other alumni described the Cornell incident and provided estimates of the monetary damages.

204. Again, the information here is based primarily on the alumni interviews referenced in Note 202, including the supposed remark as uttered by the Beta Theta chapter in their defense. The incident with Cornell is first mentioned in a letter from Arthur Mayo to Mr. Richard Gunn, Director of Chapter Services for Alpha Tau Omega, March 22, 1973, ATO–A, Series 41/95/1, Box 144 (Tufts), Visitation File, 1967–74, and here the author mentions the alumni were particularly upset over the whole incident, for the Cornell chapter refused to take responsibility for their actions at the time. Unfortunately, the ATO–A archives for Tufts contain almost no other information with regards to this incident. The payment from Beta Theta appears to have been made nearly a year later, based on the letter from Rick Gunn to Worthy Master [of Gamma Beta chapter] George Haug, March 28, 1974, ATO–A, Series 41/95/1, Box 144 (Tufts), Correspondence, 1970–75. In this letter, Mr. Gunn recommends George send an acknowledgement to the Beta Theta chapter for receipt of the money. Apparently, the two chapters were still not on speaking terms.

205. The resolution was first discussed in letters from Arthur Mayo to Richard Gunn dated March 22, 1973, and March 28, 1973. The proposal was accepted by Mr. Gunn a few weeks later, according to a letter from Arthur Mayo to Mr. Richard Gunn, April 13, 1973, ATO–A, Series 41/95/1, Box 144 (Tufts), Visitation File, 1967–74. Concerning the ritual, by this time it appears that the members of Gamma Beta changed the wording of the Alpha Tau Omega ritual to be more accommodating to their Jewish members, and the national office was quite displeased to learn of this development.

206. On the announcement of the resolution to the chapter, see letter from Arthur Mayo to Mr. Richard Gunn, April 13, 1973. On the chapter's willingness to work towards making Gamma Beta a viable part of Alpha Tau Omega, see visitation report from Andy Arnold, Chapter Service Consultant, October 22–24, 1973, ATO–A, Series 41/95/1, Box 144 (Tufts), Visitation File, 1967–74. On the chapter's plan to initiate all men living in the house, see letter from Andy Arnold to George Haug, November 12, 1973, ATO–A, Series 41/95/1, Box 144 (Tufts), Correspondence, 1970–75. In this letter, Mr. Arnold was pleased to hear the chapter would soon be initiating everyone, and he asked George to provide the specific date when this would all happen. On the subsequent initiation of one man, see letter from Jane Meyer to George Haugh [sic], November 12, 1973, ATO–A, Series 41/95/1, Box 144 (Tufts), Correspondence, 1970–75. Apparently, Mr. Arnold was not aware Ms. Meyer had already processed the initiation paperwork for Gamma Beta, which had only been filed for one man. On the failure of Gamma Beta to realign itself with the national organization, and of the hope for re-colonization in the next year, see the visitation report from Andy Arnold, March 20–22, 1974, ATO–A, Series 41/95/1, Box 144 (Tufts), Visitation File, 1967–74. On the revocation of the charter, see the High Council Meeting Minutes from May 4, 1974,

and August 16 and 21, 1974, as housed in ATO–A, Series 41/90/1, Box 1. Note that many within the ATO of Massachusetts community claim the fraternity gave up its charter in order to admit women as equals. This is incorrect. Women were only admitted as members after Gamma Beta's charter had been revoked.

207. On the poor financial state and other pressing problems of Tufts University in the early to mid 1970s, see Gittleman, chapter 2. On the fragile state of the fraternity system at Tufts in the early 1970s, see letter from Joel W. Reynolds to Jack L. Anson, February 28, 1971, in Activities and Organizations records, 1875–2013, UA 024.001 Box 4, Folder 4 (Fraternities 1956–1971). Concerning the low morale of the chapter and the alumni following the Cornell incident, see visitation report from Dave Buckingham, Chapter Services Consultant, April 12–13, 1973, ATO–A, Series 41/95/1, Box 144 (Tufts), Visitation File, 1967–74.

208. One of the four men involved in the process of recruiting the first women was Jack Obadia, the president of the chapter at the time.

209. On the evolution of ATO to a co-ed fraternity and the support by the alumni corporation, see "ATO: A Different Sort of Fraternity," *TO*, October 24, 1975. This article mentions the chapter severed its ties to the national organization in 1972. However, as mentioend above in Note 206, this is incorrect, as the official separation did not occur until the charter was pulled in 1974.

210. The support by Robert McLaughlin and Bob Jones for the co-ed group cannot be understated. They could have easily quashed the new fraternity that fall, but they did not, opting instead to give the group a chance.

211. On the issues and problems within the Tufts Greek community in the 1980s, see chapter 6.

212. Even as recent as 2010, Mr. McLaughlin was receiving correspondence from alumni urging him to close down 134 Professors Row, as many see the fraternity as nothing more than a co-ed boarding house. Mr. McLaughlin, though, is still unwavering in his support of ATO of Massachusetts.

213. The use of the words "Alpha Tau Omega" and associated symbols of the national fraternity by ATO of Massachusetts was widespread in official campus literature as mentioned in the text. Additionally, when I was a student in the late 1980s, I can recall seeing the words "Alpha Tau Omega" on the door of the fraternity house, Alpha Tau Omega's official crest on the composites, and the Greek letters "ATΩ" on sweatshirts of members both male and female. On the discovery of the trademark violation and efforts to reach a quick solution, see letters from Mark Thorsby, Executive Director of Alpha Tau Omega to President Jean Mayer, June 22, 1988; Cathy Harder-Bernier to Michael Zinn, President of ATO of Massachusetts, August 29, 1988; Marcia Kelly, Tufts Student Activities Director, to Michael Zinn, November 30, 1988; and Marcia Kelly to Mary Lee Jacobs, December 1, 1988, as housed in the Office of the President Records 1828–2007, Jean Mayer, administrative records and related papers, 1976–92, Subject Files, UA001.013 Box 10, Folder 21 (Fraternities 1983–1988). Also see letters from Bruce Reitman to Mark Thorsby, January 23, 1989; Mark Thorsby to Fraternal Composite Service, May 3, 1989; and Mark Thorsby to Robert Jones, May 4, 1989, as housed in the Office of the President Records 1828–2007, Jean Mayer, administrative records and related papers, 1976–92, Subject Files, UA001.013 Box 10, Folder 22 (Fraternities and Sororities 1989–1992).

214. Concerning Alpha Tau Omega Associates, Incorporated, see Massachusetts

corporation records, http://corp.sec.state.ma.us/CorpWeb/CorpSearch/CorpSummary.aspx?FEIN=046188591&SEARCH_TYPE=1 (accessed August 1, 2014). This corporation, it appears, was not the original housing corporation discussed previously in Note 188. The original corporation must have gone defunct at some point before 1937, and was then revived with a different name. I have assumed the use of the name "ATO of Massachusetts" and new crest became official in 2005, as this was the first year the information was printed in the *Jumbo* yearbook, whereas "Alpha Tau Omega" had been used exclusively in years prior. This name and crest may have been in use prior to 2005, but certainly not in the *Jumbo* or any other campus publications I could find. Still, even today there is evidence the group continues to use the name "Alpha Tau Omega" in reference to their fraternity. For example, I recently came across a photo from 2013 as posted on the chapter's website that shows men and women wearing sweatshirts emblazoned with the letters "A T W." See blog entry "ATO Students Prepare for Another Finals Week," December 9, 2013, http://sites.tufts.edu/atoofmassachusetts/ (accessed August 1, 2014).

215. On the capping of members to nineteen each year, see for example "Alpha Tau Omega," *TD*, March 6, 1981. I know this practice was still in place throughout the late 1980s when I was an undergraduate at Tufts. Unfortunately I have not been able to determine exactly when ATO of Massachusetts expanded its membership beyond nineteen, but I assume it was sometime in the 2000s, certainly before 2010, as emails from alumni state the chapter was over fifty members that year. The membership figures for ATO of Massachusetts in 2013 was estimated from a composite photograph displayed on their website, while that of 2014 was provided by Su McGlone, Director of Fraternity and Sorority Affairs at Tufts University. To the best of my knowledge, no fraternity chapter has even been larger, though currently all four sorority chapters at Tufts exceed this membership total.

216. The cyclical nature of the popularity of fraternities throughout history is beyond the scope of this work, but certainly the late 1800s and early 1900s featured an explosion of new organizations across the country, the likes of which have not been repeated. For more information, see Syrett, Chapter 4. On the feeling that Tufts needed more fraternities, see "Phi Mu Delta Enters Tufts," 7. The three Tufts fraternities founded by transfer students prior to 1900 were Theta Delta Chi (Augustus Scott, from Brown University), Delta Tau Delta (Elmer Felt, from Buchtel College), and Alpha Tau Omega (Pearly Wilson, from Maine State College).

217. "Phi Mu Delta Enters Tufts," 7–9; and "Sigma Tau Alpha," *TW*, April 26, 1906. Concerning Ernest's time at Norwich University, see *Catalogue of Norwich University* (1904–05 ed.), 46. On the active fraternity system at Norwich in the early 20th century, see Ellis, *Norwich University Vol. III*, 671. In this roster of cadets, Ernest Hall is listed as a non-graduate from the class of 1908, and without a fraternity affiliation. Nearly 90% of his classmates are listed as belonging to one of three fraternities: Theta Chi (founded at Norwich in 1856 and had only just established its second chapter in 1903), Alpha Sigma Pi (a local started in 1857), and Sigma Phi Epsilon (founded as the local Delta Kappa Psi in the spring of 1905 when Ernest was a freshman, but then affiliated with Sigma Phi Epsilon in 1908). Ernest, it appears, was not the best of students, which is probably the reason he left Norwich after one year. He is listed as a freshman in both *CofTC* (1905–06 ed.), 303, and *CofTC* (1906–07 ed.), 300. Also, it appears he never graduated from Tufts. Therefore, I left off his class designation. Finally, con-

cerning Ernest's hometown, the *Catalogue of Norwich University* lists Medford (without a street address), while both *CofTC* (1905–06 ed.) and *CofTC* (1906-07 ed.) list Dow Street in West Somerville, which is about two blocks from the campus.

218. "Phi Mu Delta Enters Tufts," 7–9; and "Sigma Tau Alpha," *TW*, April 26, 1906. Concerning the establishment of the Interfraternity Council and efforts to oversee the fraternity system in the early 1900s, see "Tower Cross, 1987–1970," *Concise Encyclopedia of Tufts History*, http://hdl.handle.net/10427/14829 (accessed August 8, 2014). According to the article in the *Phi Mu Delta Triangle*, it took three years for STA to gain full campus recognition, though details of the process were not discussed. Having recognition be a requirement for a charter on the national level is beyond the scope of this work, but by the early 1900s, many national organizations realized that chapters operating without faculty and campus approval rarely survived more than a few years. As a result, many fraternities only established chapters at schools where they were openly welcome. Today, unrecognized chapters are extremely rare, but they do still exist.

219. "Phi Mu Delta Enters Tufts," 7–9. Sigma Tau Alpha's housing odyssey is derived from the campus maps as printed in various editions of the *Catalogue of Tufts College*. Additionally, Doane, *Here and There at Tufts*, 113, shows a picture of the first Sigma Tau Alpha house at 9 University Avenue (which still exists today), while the article in the *Phi Mu Delta Triangle* shows the house at 163 College Avenue. On the Hallowe'en party, see "Tufts Sophomores Win," *NYT*, November 3, 1912. On coverage of the fraternity's activities in the *Boston Globe*, see for example, "Sigma Tau Alpha House Party," *BG*, April 9, 1915.

220. The evolution of the national fraternity system in the United States during the early 1900s is beyond the scope of this work, but more information is available in Syrett, Chapter 4. Concerning the petition of STA to Phi Delta Theta, I have again made assumptions as to its contents, as the original document has not survived to this day. However, in the early 1900s, it was very common for petitions to contain the information I have described. On the recommendation and subsequent quotation, see letter from President Bumpus to H. C. Davis, Alpha Province, Phi Delta Theta, dated February 1, 1916, in Activities and Organizations records, 1875–2013, UA 024.001 Box 13, Folder 12 (Sigma Tau Alpha 1916–1937). President Bumpus joined the Delta Phi national fraternity while an undergraduate at Brown University. On the endorsement of the Boston alumni, see "Alumni Clubs–Boston, Massachusetts," *The Scroll of Phi Delta Theta* 41, no. 5 (May 1917): 645. While not certain, I suspect Irving Tomlinson had to be the one who recommended the idea to STA of affiliating with Phi Delta Theta. For more efforts on his earlier attempt to start a chapter at Tufts, see the section on Delta Upsilon.

221. On the convention of 1917–18, see "Convention Aftermath," *The Scroll of Phi Delta Theta* 42, no. 4 (March 1918): 263–265. The author of this article mentions that he met the men from Tufts, but says nothing of the encounter, while instead waxing poetically about other petitioning groups. The six schools gaining charters at the convention were: Swarthmore College, Colgate University, the University of Oklahoma, the University of Pittsburg, Washington State College (now Washington State University), and Oregon Agricultural College (now Oregon State University). Aside from STA, it appears a petitioning group from the University of Denver was also turned down at this convention.

222. On Sigma Tau Alpha's petition to Sigma Phi Epsilon, see "The Richmond

Conclave," *The Sigma Phi Epsilon Journal* 14, no. 2 (December 25, 1916): 154–155; "Hellenic," *The Shield of Phi Kappa Psi* 37, no. 3 (February 1917): 168; and "Sigma Phi Epsilon Expansion," *The Sigma Phi Epsilon Journal* 14, no. 4 (May 10, 1917): 474. In this third referenced article, the author states the petition from "Sigma Tau – Tufts College" had been circulated for review to the other chapters, which was often the final step before a charter was approved. Then, the trail went cold, but certainly a charter was never issued. I contacted the national office of Sigma Phi Epsilon to obtain a copy of this petition, but unfortunately their records only went back as far as 1917. Of the ten petitions submitted around that time, the only other to be rejected besides Tufts was the University of Chattanooga. Although I do not know the exact dates that STA's petitions were submitted to either Phi Delta Theta or Sigma Phi Epsilon, I am confident that both petitions were submitted in early to mid-1916, so there must have been some overlap, since the process of granting a petition was hardly quick. STA's decision to petition two national fraternities may have ultimately been the cause for both denials. After all, with national prestige on the line, no organization would be eager to accept another's reject. On Sigma Phi Epsilon's rapid rise as a national fraternity, see Baird (9th ed. 1920), 361–363.

223. The transition of Tufts to an Army training base as part of the Student Army Training Corps, or S.A.T.C., is covered in more detail earlier within this chapter, especially the section on Zeta Psi / Theta Delta Chi. On Harold Ryan, see Ticknor, *New England Aviators*, 424–425. Undoubtedly, there were other STA active and alumni members who participated in the war effort, but I was only able to identify the two pilots. Indeed, according to "Sigma Tau Alpha At Tufts To Publish Book," *BG*, December 9, 1919, the chapter had multiple gold stars, but the names of these other soldiers were not mentioned.

224. Ticknor, 146, which includes the quotation from a letter written on May 9, 1918. Unfortunately, the recipient of the letter is not identified.

225. Ticknor, 146–148, which includes the quotation.

226. Ticknor, 148, which includes the quotation; "Memorial Service for Lieut Taylor Sunday," *BG*, April 5, 1919; and "Arlington Memorial for Lieut Taylor," *BG*, April 7, 1919. The crew that survived, led by Lt. Codman, was flying the newest Bréguet bomber out of the four, which was faster than its predecessors and the only one with an armored gas tank that could not explode. The Fokker and Pfalz aircraft were considered two of the best fighter planes at the time, so in many ways it is remarkable that even one American bomber made it back to safety.

227. Ibid.

228. On the restarting of Sigma Tau Alpha in late 1918, see "Tufts Traditions Revival," *TW*, December 4, 1918; and "Frats Make Debut," *TW*, January 8, 1919, which mentions STA had already made plans for its upcoming pledge dance two days hence. On Sigma Tau Alpha's work to secure a new chapter house, see "Tufts Sigma Tau Alpha Asks Chapter House Site," *BG*, June 3, 1920.

229. On the recommendation, see letter from President Bumpus to Phi Delta Theta, May 20, 1919, as housed in Activities and Organizations records, 1875–2013, UA 024.001 Box 13, Folder 12 (Sigma Tau Alpha 1916–1937), which includes the quotation. On the endorsement of Dean McCollister, see "Sigma Tau Alpha Gives Banquet to Initiates," *TW*, December 15, 1920, which also mentions STA had submitted its petition. On the consideration of the petition and its subsequent rejection at the 1920

convention, see "Editorials–New Chapters," *The Scroll of Phi Delta Theta* 45, no. 3 (February 1921): 313, 323–324. The 35th convention was held at the end of December, 1920. On page 313 of this article, the author mentions there were twenty-one petitioners that year, while on page 323 he mentions there were only eighteen in total, so I am unsure as to the exact total. Either way, Tufts College probably struggled to stand out in this crowd, just as it had struggled back in 1917. The schools gaining new chapters were The University of Montana, Kansas State Agricultural College, and Colorado State College. Clearly, Phi Delta Theta preferred large, land-grant institutions at this time.

230. Between 1916 and 1938, four other fraternities beside STA made their home on College Avenue: Phi Delta (167 College Ave.), Phi Epsilon Pi (157 College Ave.), Beta Tau/Beta Kappa (151 College Ave.), and Sigma Omega Psi (151 College Ave.), according to information in various editions of the *Catalogue of Tufts College*. For more information, see their relevant sections later in this chapter. On Sigma Tau Alpha's twenty-fifth anniversary, see "Tufts College Fraternity Is Quarter Century Old," *BG*, December 14, 1930.

231. "Phi Mu Delta Enters Tufts," 6–7. The history of Phi Mu Delta as a national organization is covered in more detail in the next section pertaining to the Tufts Commons Club.

232. On the move to 13 Sawyer Avenue, see "Tufts Phi Mu Delts Move Into Former Delta Upsilon Home," *TW*, February 10, 1938. On the fire at their old chapter house, see "Old Phi Mu Delta House Totally Destroyed by Fire Commencement Weekend," *TW*, June 14, 1938. It is unknown if the arsonists were ever caught. The structure at 163 College Avenue was eventually rebuilt in a different architectural form.

233. On the successes of Phi Mu Delta, see for example *Jumbo* (1939 ed.), 128. On the status of the chapter during the 1939–40 school year, see *Jumbo* (1940 ed.), 143. On the participation of Phi Mu Delta in the fall 1940 rush, see "Rush Week Rolls On for Frosh, Fraternities," *TW*, October 3, 1940. On the lack of success, see "Delts, A. K. Pi's Take Rushing Honors," *TW*, October 10, 1940. Here, Phi Mu Delta is not listed as gaining any pledges for the year. On the transformation of 13 Sawyer Avenue, see "Davies House is New Dormitory," *TW*, September 26, 1941.

234. "Meserve, Robert W., 1909–95," *Concise Encyclopedia of Tufts History*, http://hdl.handle.net/10427/14829 (accessed August 10, 2014). According to "Phi Mu Delta Enters Tufts," 6, Robert Meserve was initiated into Phi Mu Delta.

235. The evolution of college housing and dining is beyond the scope of this work. See for example Syrett, 162–165. On the poor quality of food as served in private boarding clubs, see for example, "The Commons Club," 260–261, and Nichols, 4–5. The early years of Tufts College featured small dining rooms in the basement of Packard Hall and then East Hall, but a full scale dining facility, Curtis Hall, was not established until 1893. See Miller, *LOTH–1*, 286–287.

236. "The Commons Club," 260–261; and Mike Raymond, "Commons Clubs' Influence on the Fraternity," *Cross and Crescent* 93, no. 7 (July 2006): 8–9. The percentage of Wesleyan men in fraternities is taken from data in the first referenced article, which mentions that through the year 1910, Wesleyan had graduated 2,726 men, and all but 716 of them had joined a fraternity. When the Commons Club was established, the price of meals was set at a mere $2.25 per week, which is equivalent to $63 today when adjusted for inflation. Finally, Woodrow Wilson was a member of the Phi Kappa Psi fraternity.

237. "The Commons Club," 261; and "Driving the Undergraduate Snob out of College," *NYT*, October 19, 1913, which includes the quotation.

238. Ibid. On the practice of democracy and inclusion, see also "A Sketch of the Commons Club," *The Rainbow of Delta Tau Delta* 45, no. 2 (January 1922): 346–348. On the acceptance of African-American men in the Wesleyan Commons Club, see David B. Potts, *Wesleyan University, 1831–1910: Collegiate Enterprise in New England* (Hanover, NH: Wesleyan University Press, 1992), 209–210. According to Mr. Potts, there were eight African-American students at Wesleyan between 1902 and 1911, and a number of them joined the Commons Club. Such was the case on at least one other campus. For example, Aaron Lawson MacGhee, as a young African-American man, was a founding member of the Colby Commons Club while a student at Colby College in Waterville, Maine. Although Aaron's journey is beyond the scope of this work, more information can be found in Nora M. Nercessian, *Against All Odds: The Legacy of Students of African Decent at Harvard Medical School Before Affirmative Action, 1850–1968* (Boston, MA: Harvard Medical School, 2004), 117–118. On the support for co-education by the Wesleyan Commons Club, see Louise Wilby Knight, *The "Quails": The History of Wesleyan University's First Period of Coeducation, 1872–1912* (honors thesis, Wesleyan University, May 1972), 107–108, 119, which includes the quotations. Of course, the Wesleyan Commons Club did exclude one other group of people, the women. However, this exclusion came straight from the Wesleyan administration, since the school forbade women and men from eating or living together on campus.

239. On the activities of the Wesleyan Commons Club after its founding, see "The Commons Club," 261. According to this article, membership in the Commons Club in 1914 was sixty-seven men, while the overall number of men at Wesleyan in 1910 was estimated at three hundred, according to Burton R. Clark, "The Wesleyan Story: The Importance of Moral Capital," in *Academic Transformation: Seventeen Institutions Under Pressure*, ed. David Riesman and Verne A. Stadtman (New York: McGraw–Hill, 1973), 367–369. On the formation of the National Federation of Commons Clubs, its mission, and its rocky start, see Ellis, *Norwich University Vol. I*, 499–500. On the withdrawal of the mentioned chapters, see also "A Sketch of the Commons Club," 346. Unfortunately, the referenced sources do not present a consistent history of the NFCC, so I am not convinced I understand which schools and chapters were involved at the beginning, which came later, and which dropped out. At the very least, we know there was much turmoil in the early days of the NFCC. The group from Middlebury became the founding chapter of the Kappa Delta Rho national fraternity, whereas the group from Norwich became the local Delta Kappa Psi fraternity, and then later, a chapter of the national Sigma Phi Epsilon fraternity.

240. On the organization of a new Commons Club chapter at Norwich, see Ellis, *Norwich University Vol. I*, 499–500. On the new organization at Middlebury, see Baird (8th ed. 1915), 621. Ironically, both of these chapters resigned from the NFCC within a few years to become full-fledged Greek letter fraternities. On the establishment of the *Commons Club Chronicle*, see "Driving the Undergraduate Snob out of College." On the national conventions of the NFCC, see "A Non–Fraternity Federation," *The Outlook* 88, no. 6 (February 8, 1908): 332; and "A Sketch of the Commons Club," 348–349.

241. The percentage of men involved in the Tufts fraternity system in the late 1800s is estimated from membership lists in various editions of the *Jumbo* yearbook, as well as

the register of students in various editions of the *CofTC*. On the formation of a non-fraternity group in 1896, see "Local Briefs," *TW*, November 24, 1896. On the development of a constitution and by-laws, see "Local Briefs," *TW*, December 15, 1896; "Local Briefs," *TW*, December 22, 1896; and "Non–Fraternity Constitution," *The Tuftonian* 23, no. 4 (January 1897): 93. On internal problems within the group, see "Non Fraternity," *TW*, December 15, 1897; "Tufts College Publishers," *BG*, May 12, 1898; and "Non Fraternity Election," *TW*, June 1, 1898. The last article I could find mentioning any information about the non-fraternity group was "Tufts Non-Fraternity Faction," *BG*, May 5, 1900, so I assume the group disbanded shortly thereafter.

242. The percentage of men involved in the Tufts fraternity system in 1908 is estimated from information in the 1904 edition of the *Jumbo* yearbook (the only one produced between 1899 and 1917), and the 1908 edition of the *CofTC*. For information on Delphoi, see the section in chapter 4. Note that while Delphoi was formed in 1907, it was not announced to the campus until the spring of 1908. On the formation of The Union, see "Non-Fraternity Club," *TW*, December 21, 1908, which lists the men named as founders; and letter to "Dear Sir" dated December 30, 1908, in Activities and Organizations records, 1875–2013, UA 024.001 Box 2, Folder 10 (Commons Club 1908–1968). Note that Nathan Conant Harris is mentioned as a member of the Commons Club in the referenced letter, but not the referenced *Tufts Weekly* article. Instead, the *Tufts Weekly* identified G. H. Harris as a member, but I could not find a listing for this person in the *CofTC* (1908–09 ed.). Additionally, Nathan Conant Harris is listed as living in the Delta Upsilon house in the *CofTC* (1910–11 ed.), 325, so it seems he eventually dropped out of the Commons Club to join the Delta Upsilon fraternity.

243. Ibid. On the addition of the Tufts chapter to the NFCC, see Ellis, *Norwich University Vol. I*, 499–500. For quotation, see letter to "Dear Sir."

244. Letter from F. W. Anderson to President Hamilton dated January 17, 1909, which includes the second and third quotations; and letter from President Hamilton to F. W. Anderson dated January 17, 1909, which includes the first quotation, in the Activities and Organizations records, 1875–2013, UA 024.001 Box 2, Folder 10 (Commons Club 1908–1968).

245. Ibid. On the opening of a chapter house, see "The Commons Club," *TW*, April 5, 1909. While this article only mentions the house as being on Fairmount St., the campus map as printed in *CofTC* (1909–10 ed.) lists the specific address as 15 Fairmount St. On the hosting of the 4th annual NFCC convention, see "Tufts Will Entertain Commons Clubs," *BG*, February 20, 1910; "Travis, New President," *BG*, February 27, 1910; and "Commons Club Convention," *TW*, March 3, 1910. On the hosting of the convention in 1913, see "Driving the Undergraduate Snob Out Of College."

246. The housing odyssey for the Commons Club is detailed in the campus maps as printed in the relevant editions of the *CofTC*. On the dissatisfaction with 37 Sawyer Avenue, the inquiry into renting 114 Professors Row, and the subsequent response, see letters between the Commons Club and President Cousens dated July 11 through August 1, 1916, in the Activities and Organizations records, 1875–2013, UA 024.001 Box 2, Folder 10 (Commons Club 1908–1968). For information on Heth Aleph Res, see its section earlier in this chapter.

247. For a partial list of the chapters of the NFCC across the country, see "A Sketch of the Commons Club," 346. This list, though probably incomplete, is the most comprehensive I've been able to find. On the resignation of the second Norwich chapter of

the Commons Club, see Ellis, *Norwich University Vol. I*, 499–500. On the resignation of the second Middlebury chapter, see Baird (8th ed. 1915), 621.

248. "A Sketch of the Commons Club," 348–352.

249. On the feelings of national organizations towards those who wanted to see fraternities removed from campus, see for example "Antics of the 'Antis'," *The Phi Gamma Delta* 36, no. 4 (April 1914): 655–657. On the predicted demise of the Commons Club movement, see also "Anti-Fraternity Organizations," *To Dragma of Alpha Omicron Pi* 9, no. 3 (May 1914): 265–266. On the animosity towards Greek-letter organizations from the NFCC, see "Driving the Undergraduate Snob Out Of College," which includes the quotations. Although the article in *The New York Times* does not list the author, his identity was revealed as Harry W. Laidler in "National Federation of Commons Clubs," *Union Alumni Monthly* 3, no. 1 (November 1913): 64. Apparently, Harry was not aware of, or chose to ignore, the turmoil within the NFCC when he predicted the Commons Club would soon eclipse the fraternities in terms of prestige. Harry eventually became a prominent leader of the Socialist political movement in America.

250. For some examples of the response to *The New York Times* article, see "The Frat Busting Frat," *The Signet* 5, no. 3 (December 1913): 112–114; "The Frat Busting Frat," *The Alpha Tau Omega Palm* 34, no. 3 (September 1914): 351–354; and "Concerning 'The Commons Club'," *The Angelos of Kappa Delta* 10, no. 4 (September 1914): 333–334. On articles and letters from Commons Club members lambasting *The New York Times* article, see "National Federation of Commons Clubs"; and "Why the Commons Club," *To Dragma of Alpha Omicron Pi* 9, no. 3 (May 1914): 264.

251. "A Sketch of the Commons Club," 348–350, which includes the quotation.

252. Ibid, which includes the quotation.

253. Ibid.

254. "A Sketch of the Commons Club," 350–351. Wesleyan's vote was somewhat surprising, since they were the ones who originally brought up the idea of changing their name to Phi Mu Delta. However, it appears they were turned off by the exclusiveness that was to be part of Phi Mu Delta fraternity.

255. Ibid. Of the chapters not present at the convention, Hobart, Allegheny, and St. Lawrence opted to join the Commons Club Federation, while West Virginia University and Carnegie Institute of Technology disaffiliated completely to become their own local groups. The chapters at the University of Washington, Wabash, and Western Reserve resigned soon after the convention, and then petitioned Lambda Chi Alpha for charters. All of these petitions were granted before the end of that school year.

256. The transition of the Tufts campus under the S.A.T.C. program is covered in earlier sections within this chapter. On the return of the Commons Club in the spring of 1919, see "Tufts Traditions Revival," *TW*, December 4, 1918; "Frats Make Debut," *TW*, January 8, 1919; and "Commons Club Active," *TW*, January 15, 1919, which mentions the chapter was back in its house on Broadway Ave. Unfortunately, I have not come across any record that details the service and sacrifices of Tufts Commons Club members in the Great War, but I have to assume the chapter sent numerous men to fight. On the petition to Theta Chi, see letter of recommendation from Acting President Cousens to F. W. Ladue, National Secretary of Theta Chi, dated February 26, 1920, as housed in Activities and Organizations records, 1875–2013, UA 024.001 Box 16, Folder 11 (Theta Chi 1920–1970). Although this correspondence is considered part of Theta Chi history, it is more pertinent to the Commons Club, as Theta Chi

did not enter Tufts University until 1957. Unfortunately, this recommendation is the only information about the petition that survived, so I am at a loss as to how or why the Commons Club picked Theta Chi for affiliation. As for the inclusive nature of the Tufts Commons Club, it is unknown if the chapter still held to this belief in the early 1920s. I would suspect, though, that the chapter did utilize some elements of a fraternity such as ritual by this time. For example, the crest of the Commons Club, as printed in the *Jumbo* (1922 ed.), 133, shows a number of symbols whose meaning is not readily apparent, and indeed some of these symbols, such as the clasped hands, appear in the crests of secret fraternities.

257. The story of the original houses on Professors Row and how they came to be built, though fascinating, is unfortunately beyond the scope of this work. I have been unable to determine the exact date that the Commons Club bought 106 Professors Row, but I assume it was sometime in late 1921 or early 1922. In the archival collection on the buildings of Tufts, UA Edwin B. Rollins Papers, 1300[sic]–1976, Notebooks, 1940–1955, MS054.001 Box 2, Folder 2 (Campus Homes, Part 1(b) 1940–1955), Edwin Rollins states the chapter bought the house at 106 Professors Row in 1921. However, the Commons Club was still residing at 890 Broadway as late as November 1921, according to "Tufts 'Frats' Hosts Parties And Dances," *BG*, November 6, 1921. Therefore, I suspect the Rollins information may be incorrect. Indeed, it is not until the 1922–23 school year that the address of the Commons Club is listed as 106 Professors Row in both the *Ivy Book* and the *CofTC*. On Delta Tau Delta's purchase of the Bray house, see their section earlier in this chapter.

258. For information on the Ivy Society and its publication of the *Ivy Book*, see "Ivy Society, 1901–1970," and "Ivy Book, 1902–1971," *Concise Encyclopedia of Tufts History*, http://hdl.handle.net/10427/14829 (accessed August 27, 2014). For copies of the *Ivy Book*, see UA Ivy Society Publications 1895–1977, The Ivy Book 1902–1974, UP 016.002 Boxes 1 and 2. For a description of the pledge pin, see the *Ivy Book* (1922–23 ed.).

259. On the transformation to Delta Phi Sigma, see "Commons Club Now Delta Phi Sigma Fraternity," *TW*, January 14, 1925. This article mentions that nearly all alumni of the Commons Club were in full support of this change. On the desire of Delta Phi Sigma to affiliate with a national fraternity, see Activities and Organizations records, 1875–2013, UA 024.001 Box 1, Folder 10 (Alpha Kappa Pi 1906–1939). Since records of the national Commons Club Federation are virtually non-existent, I am assuming the chapter resigned from the organization to become the Delta Phi Sigma fraternity, for there would have been no compelling reason to stay. As such, the Wesleyan chapter followed in the footsteps of Delta Phi Sigma by resigning from the Federation in 1928 to become a chapter of the national Sigma Chi fraternity. Finally, one reason for choosing the name Delta Phi Sigma may have been interest from the national Delta Sigma Phi fraternity, who were actively looking to place a chapter at Tufts in early 1920. See letter from R. P. Ashley of Delta Sigma Phi to President Cousens dated January 7, 1920, in Activities and Organizations records, 1875–2013, UA 024.001 Box 4, Folder 4 (Fraternities 1956–1971). However, this connection is purely speculative and based solely on the similarities of the two names, since I was unable to find any direct proof. Also, there is a five-year gap between correspondence from Delta Sigma Phi and the name change of the Commons Club, so this link between the two groups is less than compelling.

260. On the petition to Alpha Kappa Pi, see letter from President Cousens to Alpha Kappa Pi dated March 23, 1931, in Activities and Organizations records, 1875–2013, UA 024.001 Box 1, Folder 10 (Alpha Kappa Pi 1906–1939). Although the exact date the petition was sent to Alpha Kappa Pi is not noted, I am assuming it was filed around the time President Cousens wrote his letter of recommendation. A write-up of the chapter in the 1934 edition of the *Jumbo* yearbook mentions the petition was filed on April 27, 1931, but this article has so many other errors with regards to important dates that I find it unreliable. On the history of Alpha Kappa Pi, see Baird (14th ed. 1940), 71–72. On the installation of Tau chapter, see "Delta Phi Sigma to Become Alpha Kappa Pi," *TW*, May 27, 1931, which mentions the upcoming ceremony will take place on May 30. On the number of chapters of Phi Mu Delta established by 1931, see the fraternity's website, http://phimudelta.publishpath.com/chapters-colonies (accessed August 31, 2014).

261. On the reduction of the mortgage, see letter from Professor E. Rollins to President Cousens dated April 17, 1935, in Activities and Organizations records, 1875–2013, UA 024.001 Box 2, Folder 10 (Commons Club 1908–1968). On the construction of new houses by Delta Tau Delta and Alpha Tau Omega, see their relevant sections in this chapter. On the call to Commons Club, Delta Phi Sigma, and Alpha Kappa Pi alumni to find the construction of a new house, see letter from Bob Lybeck to President Cousens dated April 5, 1937, in Activities and Organizations records, 1875–2013, UA 024.001 Box 1, Folder 10 (Alpha Kappa Pi 1906–1939). On the date of the house razing, see Melville S. Munro, Alpha Kappa Pi House Ground Breaking, June 12, 1937, Tufts University, Digital Collections and Archives, Medford, MA. http://hdl.handle.net/10427/11610 (accessed August 31, 2014).

262. "Campus Improved by Exclusive Construction," *TW*, September 23, 1937; "The Inter-Fraternity Council Delays Rushing Until Oct. 4," *TW*, September 23, 1937; and "D. U., A. K. Pi Latest Additions to Revamped Row; New Fraternity Houses Add Much to Appearance," *TW*, January 6, 1938.

263. The impact of the outbreak of World War II and the subsequent taking over of the college by the Navy V-12 program is discussed in earlier sections of this chapter. On the commandeering of the house at 106 Professors Row, see "College Buildings Undergo Change," *TW*, July 10, 1943. This article lumps Alpha Kappa Pi into the statement, "other fraternity houses will be used chiefly as dormitories for civilian men students." Certainly, within a few weeks of this article, Alpha Kappa Pi had moved out of its house and was using Alpha Tau Omega's space for meetings, according to "Active Chapters Plan Limited Fraternity Life," *TW*, July 29, 1943. On the war record of Sgt. John Scopa and the Athenian Avenger, this material is primarily culled from websites dedicated to the history of the 8th Air Force, 333rd Bomber Squadron, 94th Heave Bomber Group in World War II. See, for example, http://www.8thafhs.com/get_mia_aircraft.php?acgroup_id=7&mission_date=1944-03-22, (accessed September 1, 2014). Apparently, the plane crashed right in the center of Berlin. On the death of 2LT Roy H. Baxter, see "Brothers In The Service–Our Gold Stars," *The Alpha of Alpha Kappa Pi* 17, no. 2 (February 1943): 60; and Rodney G. Cardell, *Wings Around Us: Wartime Memories of Aviation in Northern Australia* (Brisbane, Australia: Amphion Press, 1992), 51. On April 21, 1942, 2LT Baxter was the co-pilot of a B-28 Marauder that crashed during take off from a base in Australia, while heading out on a combat mission. On the death of Major Robert C. Hawkins, see "Alpha Kappa Pi News–Killed In Accident,"

The Alpha of Alpha Kappa Pi 19, no. 1 (December 1944): 6–7. Major Hawkins was a Marine Corps pilot who had seen extensive combat in the battle for Guadalcanal. He crashed and was killed in August 1944 while on a training exercise in North Carolina.

264. On the restarting of Alpha Kappa Pi after the war, see "The Fraternity Supplement–Alpha Kappa Pi," *TW*, May 9, 1946; and "Calling All Tau Men!" *The Alpha of Alpha Kappa Pi* 20, no. 4 (September 1946): 89. On the merger with Alpha Sigma Phi, see "Alpha Kappa Pi–Convention Resolutions," *The Tomahawk* 42, no. 4 (November 1946): 86, 88; and "A. K. Pi Merges; Will Take New Name of A. S. Phi," *TW*, October 3, 1946. The merger occurred on September 7, 1946. On the general history of Alpha Sigma Phi, see the fraternity's national website.

265. On the enthusiasm over the merger, see "A. K. Pi Merges; Will Take New Name of A. S. Phi"; and "The Tufts Weekly Fraternity Supplement–Alpha Sigma Phi," *TW*, October 9, 1947. The chapter name "Massachusetts Iota" is mentioned in the first referenced article. It is unknown when the chapter's name was changed to Beta Iota, but I would imagine it was shortly after the merger. On the absorption of Alpha Kappa Pi into Alpha Sigma Phi, see Robson, *Baird's Manual of American College Fraternities*, 776–777. I will continue to refer to the chapter as The Kippies for the time being, as the *Tufts Weekly* and many Tufts alumni from the 1950s and 1960s used this descriptor exclusively when referring to the chapter.

266. Help Week as a national movement was started in 1949 by the Alpha Tau Omega chapter at Indiana University, according to various sources including "The Good They Do Now," *The Rattle of Theta Chi* 39, no. 3 (April 1952): 23; and "ATO's Build Walk During Help Week," *American University Eagle* 34, no. 25 (March 23, 1960): 4. The first mention of Help Week at Tufts came towards the end of 1951, when the editors of the *Tufts Weekly* hoped the fraternities would soon embrace this concept. They did not, except for the Alpha Tau Omega chapter, which made a modest effort that semester. See "Editorial," *TW*, December 6, 1951; "Will Frats Raise Hell or Help?" *TW*, January 10, 1952; and "Empty Classrooms, Stunts Mark Hell Week Madness," *TW*, February 21, 1952. On Alpha Sigma Phi's revival of Help Week, see "28 Tufts Pledges To Aid Civic Center," *BG*, February 5, 1957; and "Kippie Pledges Aid Medford In Beneficial 'Hell Week'," *TW*, February 15, 1957. A year later, Help Week was still going strong at Tufts, according to "Students 'Help Week' Projects," *BG*, April 13, 1958, which included participation by the Theta Chi and Theta Delta Chi chapters. On the painting of the Kippie House, see the front page (there was no article, just some photos), *TW*, May 12, 1956, which includes the quotation.

267. On the state of the chapter during the 1969–70 school year, including the membership size, see "Fraternity Profile," *TO*, March 13, 1970. As for the number of beds in the house, see information printed in the Alpha Kappa Pi section of the *Jumbo* (1939 ed.), 118.

268. "Visitor at Tufts is Suspected of LSD 'Factory'," *BG*, March 12, 1970; and "Youth Arraigned on Drug Charges After Arrest Wednesday At Tufts," *TO*, March 13, 1970. The member of Alpha Sigma Phi who met Daniel in the bar is not identified in this article, nor is he named in any other source I could find.

269. Ibid.

270. Ibid. As a fan of the television series *Breaking Bad*, I found this story of Daniel Hodes to be particularly fascinating. Based on some cursory research into the manufacturing process for LSD, I cannot imagine the laboratory he set up in the attic was even

remotely safe. The chemicals needed to synthesize the hallucinogen are extremely dangerous and require proper ventilating equipment, or else death is a distinct possibility.

271. "Tufts University, Police Cooperate On Drug Raid at Medford Campus," *BG*, March 28, 1970; "16 Persons Arraigned After Tufts Drug Raid," *BG*, March 29, 1970; and "Bust Supplement," *TO*, April 3, 1970. In this last referenced article, Dean Alvin Schmidt mentions that the arrival of Daniel Hodes at Tufts was no accident, as he'd been recruited by some former and current Tufts students to manufacture LSD in the Alpha Sigma Phi house. This may indeed be plausible, but so is the story of meeting the Alpha Sigma Phi member in the bar, since this is what Daniel told the police after his arrest, according to "Youth Arraigned on Drug Charges After Arrest Wednesday At Tufts."

272. On events that happened in response to the raid, see "Bust Supplement"; "200 Enter Building to Protest Tufts Drug Raid," *BG*, March 31, 1970; "Tufts Students, Deans Meet," *BG*, April 1, 1970; "Tufts Student Panel Won't Act On Arrests," *BG*, April 2, 1970; and "Drug Teach-In At Tufts," *BG*, April 6, 1970. On the arrest of nine additional students, see "2d Drug Raid on Tufts Student," *BG*, April 4, 1970; and "8 More Tufts Students Charged," *BG*, April 7, 1970. On the aftermath of the raid including the guilty verdicts, see "The Drug Bust, 1970," *Concise Encyclopedia of Tufts History*, http://hdl.handle.net/10427/14829 (accessed September 4, 2014). On the fate of Daniel, see "Hillel Daniel Hodes Fined, Given Suspended Sentence," *TO*, April 3, 1970. After this incident. Daniel went on to earn a Ph.D. in Organic Chemistry from Boston College in 1976. But, he found the drug business hard to quit. In 1984, he was arrested for attempting to manufacture Fentanyl, a narcotic considered incredibly more potent than heroin, in quantities with a street value of nearly $750 million. He had also allegedly manufactured and sold crystal methamphetamine to undercover officers. For more information, see "Navy Lab Chemist Held in Drug Case," *The Washington Post*, September 11, 1986; and "Chemist Sentenced in D.C. Drug Case," *The Washington Post*, November 28, 1986.

273. The bulk of the information in the next few paragraphs is derived mainly from interviews with John Budris (February 23, 2013) and William Gehling (February 25, 2013, and February 28, 2013). Mr. Gehling, who recently retired as the Athletic Director at Tufts University, was one of the first to sign on with John and re-open 106 Professors Row as a boarding house.

274. On the student sentiment towards fraternities in the fall of 1970, see "Rush Week Next Week," *TO*, November 6, 1970. In this article, the author implores students to be open minded and stop by a fraternity house to give them a chance. For a short biography of Mr. Zamparelli, see "John F. Zamparelli–Biography," http://dca.lib.tufts.edu/features/nrotc3/9.html (accessed September 15, 2014). Unfortunately, Mr. Zamparelli passed away before I was able to contact him about this history.

275. See Note 273 above.

276. Ibid.

277. Ibid. Robert W. Kutz, the past Grand Historian of the Alpha Sigma Phi Fraternity, confirmed the installation date.

278. Information about the Kippy House in the following paragraphs was derived mainly from interviews with two former members, Leo Roche (January 18, 2012) and Gregory Matthews (February 16, 2012). Additionally, I am now using a different spelling for "Kippy" in the text, as this is how the group was referenced on campus at the time. On the relationship between the alumni corporation and the Kippy residents, see

"Kippy Loses House," *TO*, April 21, 1978.

279. On the behind-the-scenes dealings of the alumni corporation with Chi Omega, see the sorority's section in Chapter 4. For the announcement of the lease to the campus, see "Kippy Loses House."

280. See Note 278. On the reaction to the eviction of Kippy House members, see "Kippy Loses House," and "Letter to the Editor–Kippy House Should Stay Frat," *TO*, April 21, 1978. This letter in support was co-authored by two men who were not members of Kippy House.

281. Now for the difficult part of this section, and that is sorting out the chain of events that led to Tufts University purchasing 106 Professors Row from the Alpha Sigma Phi alumni corporation. I am still not convinced I know the entire story, or have all of the details perfectly correct, but I have done the best with the information I was able to gather. I first learned of the investigation into the alumni corporation during an interview with Christina Rush (May 7, 2011), an undergraduate member of Chi Omega during the 1978–79 school year. From what I understand, she was primarily responsible for uncovering the legal problems surrounding the Alpha Sigma Phi alumni corporation and bringing it to the attention of Tufts University. She was helped in part by Chi Omega's alumnae advisor, Ms. Maurene Golden. More information on this topic can be found in Chi Omega's section of Chapter 4. Concerning the problems with unpaid taxes, see Massachusetts Land Records, Middlesex South Registry, Book 13982, Page 452, which mentions the City of Somerville took the house on August 8, 1973 for non-payment of property taxes back in 1971; and Massachusetts Land Records, Middlesex South Registry, Book 13949, Page 550, which mentions that taxes were still outstanding in July of 1978. Finally, for a summary of the events surrounding the house sale, including the subsequent deposit of the $30,000 into the Tufts endowment, see "Alpha Sigma Phi Seeks $30,000 From Tufts," *TD*, March 31, 1987.

282. "Alpha Sigma Phi Seeks $30,000 From Tufts," and Massachusetts Land Records, Middlesex South Registry, Book 13982, Page 454, which discusses the conveyance of the deed to the Trustees of Tufts College as the conclusion of the lawsuit. Concerning the legal status of the alumni corporation at this time, see Letter from the Secretary of the Commonwealth, Massachusetts Land Records, Middlesex South Registry, Book 13982, Page 453. This letter clearly states that the alumni corporation, known officially as Tufts Alpha Sigma Phi Associates, Inc., "still has a legal existence." Therefore, I am assuming that Tufts was unable to have the alumni corporation declared defunct. On the future use of the proceeds from the sale, it seems in 1981 there may have been a plan to simply donate the money to Tufts, but Mr. Zamparelli was so upset with the way he'd been treated by the administration that he threatened to do something else with the money. See letter from John Zamparelli to C. Russell deBurlo dated February 8, 1981, in Office of the President Records 1828–2007, Jean Mayer, administrative records and related papers, 1976–92, Subject Files, UA001.013 Box 10, Folder 23 (Fraternities and sororities 1976–1982).

283. Robert W. Kutz, the past Grand Historian of the Alpha Sigma Phi Fraternity, provided the information concerning the efforts of Chris and John to restart the chapter at Tufts. Also see "New Fraternity Formed At Tufts," *TD*, April 16, 1986.

284. Ibid. On the shortage of suitable housing for fraternities and sororities, see "Greek Seek More Houses," *TD*, October 20, 1986.

285. As will be discussed in later sections within this chapter, it was quite normal

for fraternity chapters to secure their own housing from the 1890s through the 1970s, and they often ended up in off-campus neighborhoods, especially the Medford Hillside. That all changed in the 1980s, when those same neighborhoods were no longer receptive to the idea. On the attempted purchase of a house by Sigma Phi Epsilon, see their section later in this chapter. In the end, this sale fell through, but in its aftermath Sigma Phi Epsilon was offered the rental of an on-campus house, bypassing at least one other organization, Psi Upsilon, that was technically ahead of them in the housing line. On the efforts of Alpha Sigma Phi to purchase the house on Powder House Boulevard, see "Fraternity Seeks To Recover Funds For House Purchase," *TD*, October 31, 1986. Being a duplex was important, as Somerville laws restrict the number of unrelated residents in a single house or apartment without a lodging license (which can be very difficult to obtain).

286. On the issues of Sigma Phi Epsilon and Alpha Epsilon Pi regarding their chapter houses in the Medford Hillside, see their respective sections later in this chapter.

287. "Alpha Sigma Phi Seeks $30,000 From Tufts." The situation described here, of a contract supposedly signed but now missing, is mind-boggling to me, since Mr. Zamparelli was a very successful lawyer, and keeping track of legal documents over the long term was a normal part of his job.

288. On the efforts of alumni to recover what they felt was their money, see various memos and letters as housed in Office of the President Records 1828–2007, Jean Mayer, administrative records and related papers, 1976–92, Subject Files, UA001.013 Box 10, Folder 21 (Fraternities 1983–1988). Within this folder is a copy of "Phoenix Risen" from the fall of 1988, a newsletter published by the undergraduate members of the Alpha Sigma Phi colony that detailed the situation for the alumni, and was the catalyst for the bombardment of correspondence directed at Tufts. Many responded to this newsletter by writing directly to President Jean Mayer. On the ending of the diatribe, see letter from Steve Manos to Walter Brent dated November 29, 1988, in the above referenced archive. This letter discusses the lawsuit from 1980 and how in the wake of the judgment, "… the house was ordered sold [to Tufts] and the proceeds disposed of [by Tufts]." As a result, it appears that Tufts acquired 106 Professors Row without paying out a single dollar to the folks who built it.

289. On Alpha Sigma Phi's activities leading up to their charter, and their securing of 6–8 Capen St. Extension as a chapter house, see "Phoenix Risen." According to Robert W. Kutz, the past Grand Historian of the Alpha Sigma Phi Fraternity, Beta Iota's charter was returned on September 17, 1988.

290. On Alpha Sigma Phi's suspension, see "CFS Warns Greeks After Health Report," *TD*, November 9, 1989. On Alpha Sigma Phi's appeal, see "Greek Chapters To Appeal," *TD*, November 13, 1989; and "CFS Approves IGC's Appeal For Changes to Greek Health Report," *TD*, February 5, 1990.

291. On Alpha Sigma Phi's occupancy of the 350s Hillside Apartments, see "Graduate Student Killed In Accident," *TD*, December 3, 1990. This article describes a very unfortunate event that resulted in the death of an Alpha Sigma Phi alumnus, Brian Kane, who had come back to visit his old chapter. The 350s suit was on the third floor, and apparently Mr. Kane fell over the railing outside the suite to the bottom of the stairwell, sustaining a traumatic injury. Further investigation revealed the incident was not caused by intoxication or drugs. Instead, it was just a horrible, tragic accident, as reported in "Kane Investigation Officially Closed," *TD*, January 10, 1991. On the sub-

sequent return to probation, see "CFS Imposes Three Warnings and Two Probations on Greek Chapters," *TD*, November 15, 1990.

292. "Alpha Sigma Phi Off Probation," *TD*, April 2, 1991, which includes the quotation.

293. On Alpha Sigma Phi's use of 23 Bellevue St. as their unofficial chapter house, see "Fraternity Rush," *TD*, January 17, 29, and 30, 1992. On the subsequent informal rush see their advertisement, *TD*, February 25, 1992. On the dissolution of the chapter, see "Alpha Sigma Phi Disbands," *TD*, February 27, 1992. Further information about the disbanding of Beta Iota chapter was provided by Robert W. Kutz, the past Grand Historian of the Alpha Sigma Phi Fraternity; also see letter from Jeffrey Owens, Director of Alpha Sigma Phi, to Dean Bobby Knable dated March 16, 1992, in Office of the President Records 1828–2007, Jean Mayer, administrative records and related papers, 1976–92, Subject Files, UA001.013 Box 10, Folder 22 (Fraternities and Sororities 1989–1992).

294. The shift in sentiment towards Greek life in the 1990s is discussed further in Chapter 6. On the existence of the Alpha Sigma Phi scholarship fund, see http://uss.tufts.edu/stuServ/bulletin/Archived%202005_2006/scholarships.html (accessed September 17, 2014).

295. On the establishment of the Bromfield-Pearson School, see *LOTH–1*, 289–298; Start, 62; and Doane, *Here and There at Tufts*, 84. At its inception, the school offered either a one-year preparatory course, or a two-year complete course that was the equivalent of an Associates Degree today. Enrollment in the school was typically on the order of a dozen or so students each year, though many regular Tufts engineering students took courses in the school as part of their study. On the matriculation of Joseph V. Magee, see *CofTC* (1910–11 ed.), 332; and *CofTC* (1911–12 ed.), 316.

296. The figure of 60% of undergraduates belonging to fraternities is an estimate based on the Register of Students in the *CofTC* (1912–13 ed.), 315–324, which shows many of the men as living in fraternity houses. On the founding of Phi Delta and the list of charter members, see "New Tufts Fraternity," *BG*, March 12, 1913. Later sources, such as "Fraternity Directory," *TW*, March 25, 1914, state that Phi Delta was founded in 1912, but the article in the *Boston Globe* was the first printed record I could find regarding the fraternity. Unfortunately, the *Tufts Weekly* was not published during the 1912–13 school year, so there is no student-centric archive to examine for confirmation of the fraternity's start date. Concerning the founding members and their residences, see *CofTC* (1912–13 ed.), 315–324. Of the nineteen founders, ten lived in East Hall that year. Concerning the founder Frederick Morrison, I could not find his name listed in any editions of the *CofTC*. There is an "Arthur Winchester Morrison" listed, but this could be an entirely different person. Concerning founder Harvey Cedric Yeamans, he is listed in the *CofTC* (1912–13 ed.), 318, as a freshman, but he is not listed ever again as a Tufts student. With regards to the founders listed as graduating in 1917, it appears many had to repeat a year of college, thus embarking on the five-year plan. On the prowess of Phi Delta with regards to inter-fraternity athletics, see for example "Tufts InterFraternity Games," *BG*, May 16, 1914.

297. The housing odyssey for Phi Delta is unfortunately not completely clear, as the documentation is spotty in places, if not downright contradictory. In the campus maps as printed in *CofTC* (1909–10 through 1914–15 eds.), the Sigma Tau Alpha fraternity is listed as being at 16 Bellevue St. However, in the *Ivy Book* (1913–14 ed.), Sigma Tau

Alpha is listed as being at 22 Bellevue St., while Phi Delta is listed at 16 Bellevue St. Meanwhile, the campus map of *CofTC* (1913–14 ed.) does not list Phi Delta's address. Since the *Ivy Book* and *CofTC* were often printed at different times of the year, I believe that Phi Delta did indeed occupy a chapter house during the 1913–14 school year, but that it was actually they who were at 22 Bellevue St., while Sigma Tau Alpha remained at 16 Bellevue St., consistent with the campus maps. Starting with the campus map in *CofTC* (1914–15 ed.), and continuing for three years, Phi Delta is listed at 11 Emery St., consistent with relevant editions of the *Ivy Book*. Indeed, a group photograph from 1916 also seems to verify this address. On the move to 20 Sunset Road, see campus map in *CofTC* (1917–18 ed.) and *Ivy Book* (1917–18 ed.), both of which are consistent. On the wholesale enlistment of Phi Delta members and the suspension of the fraternity by the fall of 1918, see "Phi Delta At Tufts To Open New Chapter House," *BG*, November 28, 1919; "Phi Delta Fraternity Is Restored At Tufts," *BG*, January 23, 1920. The S.A.T.C. program and transition of Tufts during the fall of 1918 is discussed earlier in this chapter.

298. On the restarting of Phi Delta after the war, see "Frats Make Debut," *TW*, January 8, 1919, which mentions Phi Delta was having trouble getting organized; "Phi Delta To Start Again in its New Home," *TW*, November 26, 1919; "Phi Delta At Tufts To Open New Chapter House"; "Phi Delta To Open At Tufts Tomorrow," *BG*, January 1, 1920; and "Phi Delta Fraternity Is Restored At Tufts." As for Phi Delta's housing after the war, the situation is again murky in spots. Although the campus map of *CofTC* (1919–20 ed.) says Phi Delta was at 20 Sunset Road, this is clearly a misprint as the articles from the fall of 1919 state the chapter was not yet in a house. The first mention of a house for Phi Delta is the *Boston Globe* article from January 1, 1920, which gives the address as University Avenue, though it does not identify a house number. The next identification of a chapter house comes though the article "Phi Delta Holds Open House Saturday," *TW*, May 25, 1921, which mentions the chapter was now in Graves House at 18 Latin Way. This house is confirmed by a photograph in *The Elephas*, 22. Then, in the campus map as printed the following year in *CofTC* (1921–22 ed.), Phi Delta is listed at 11 Fairmount St., where it remains for the next three years. Finally, according to the campus map as printed in *CofTC* (1924–25 ed.), Phi Delta is listed at 8 Bellevue St., where they remain until 1931. Unfortunately, the 1925–26 and 1926–27 editions of the *Ivy Book* still list Fairmount St. as Phi Delta's location, but I tend to believe the campus maps instead for these years.

299. On the housing trials and tribulations of Phi Delta, see "Alumni Secretaries Report 1931–32," Phi Delta and Sigma Nu Fraternity records, 1930–1975, UA194.001 Box 1, Folder 1 (Phi Delta 1930–1932), which includes the quotation. This report, written by Phi Delta alumnus Donald B. Willard (a feature writer for the *Boston Globe* at the time), utilizes a lighthearted style that is somewhat tongue-in-cheek in places, making it difficult to ascertain certain facts, especially concerning the exact number of mortgages taken out by the alumni corporation, or how they were able to keep the debt collectors at bay for so long. Nonetheless, I feel the overall information in this report is correct, and that I have explained the chain of events as best I can, given the documentation.

300. Ibid.

301. On the membership of the chapter in 1935, see *Jumbo*, (1935 ed.), 159, which lists a total of eighteen undergraduates including ten seniors. On the demise of Phi Del-

ta, see *Ivy Book* (1935–36 ed.), which lists Phi Delta as an active fraternity; "Final Freshman Rushing Results Announced By 8 Fraternities," *TW*, October 10, 1935, which does not list Phi Delta as having gained any pledges; and "The Omichronicle–February 1936," AJHS–PhiEp, Box 31, Folder 5 (Omicron–Tufts College), which states "[Phi Epsilon Pi] just missed out on winning the president's JUMBO TROPHY by having a rating only a few points behind the Phi Delta Fraternity, a local with a very small membership which has now gone off hill and dissolved." Finally, the fraternities at Tufts that went inactive during the depression were Beta Kappa, Tau Epsilon Phi, Phi Delta, Phi Mu Delta, and Phi Beta Delta.

302. Part of the fun of this research has been learning the ancillary stories of Tufts alumni, including that of Joseph Magee. Unfortunately, his story, though well worthy of its own treatment, is clearly outside the bounds of this work. On Joseph's work in establishing an airmail route to Latin America, see Dr. Wesley Phillips Newton, "The Role of the Army Air Arm in Latin America, 1922–1931," *Air University Review* 18, no. 6 (September–October 1967), 76–90; and "Air Mail Line to Panama Next," *The New York Sun*, January 3, 1929. On Joseph's work with nighttime flying, see Glenn L. Martin, "Night Flying Made Practical Through Artificial Light," *U.S. Air Services* 8, no. 8 (August 1923): 25–28; M. L. Patterson, "Night Flying Progress," *U.S. Air Services* 8, no. 11 (November 1923): 30–31; C. Moran, "The Gay White Way of the Air Mail," *U.S. Air Services* 9, no. 2 (February 1924): 34–38, which includes a photo of Mr. Magee; and "New Radio For Air-Mail Route Over Continent," *The Daily News [Huntingdon, PA]*, November 2, 1929.

303. In 1930, the twelve active fraternities included Tau Epsilon Phi and Phi Beta Delta, two national organizations that were not officially recognized on the Medford campus, though both had undergraduates in their membership. Therefore, I consider these two relevant to this time period. The chapters that closed during the Depression were Beta Kappa, Phi Beta Delta, Tau Epsilon Phi, Phi Delta, and Phi Mu Delta. Before the Depression, the only other fraternities at Tufts to close down were the Engineers Fraternity in 1893, and Heth Aleph Res, circa 1904.

304. The bulk of the information about the formation of Phi Delta comes from Ted Snowe, an alumnus who was involved in the organization from the beginning. Indeed, it was Mr. Snowe who lived in 42 Fletcher Hall as a freshman and hosted the bid night meeting. Mr. Snowe wrote his history of the founding back in 1990 to mark the 40th anniversary of Sigma Nu at Tufts, and he was kind enough to give me a complete copy some twenty years later. While personal histories written decades after the fact are not always the most reliable, I have endeavored to confirm dates and facts with other timely sources, such as the *Tufts Weekly*. Additionally, Mr. Snowe's account when originally written was reviewed by numerous other alumni involved in the revival of Phi Delta, so it represents a collective memory of the early history. The text I have written over the next few paragraphs is paraphrased from this account.

305. Ibid. While I do not explicitly delve into the evolution of campus rules at Tufts over the years in this work, suffice to say that in the late 1940s, there were rules covering most aspects of student life outside of the classroom. Therefore, seeking permission to do or start something new was considered the norm.

306. Ibid. Dean Wessel would succeed Leonard Carmichael as President of Tufts College in 1953.

307. Ibid. Mr. Joel Reynolds is certainly a controversial figure in the history of fra-

ternities at Tufts, as discussed in other sections and chapters of this work. However, to all of the Phi Delta and Sigma Nu alumni who knew him, he was one of their biggest supporters, and none had anything negative to say about him.

308. Ibid. Unfortunately, I was not able to find documentation of the edict in the records of the trustees of Tufts College, because the records are only in paper form, they are not indexed, and I do not know the year that the ban was put in place. However, the ban is mentioned in "Phi Delta Fraternity Revived; Hopes To Affiliate With National," *TW*, January 20, 1949.

309. Ibid.

310. Ibid. On the revival date, see "Phi Delta Fraternity Revived; Hopes To Affiliate With National." On the acceptance of Phi Delta into the Interfraternity Council and subsequent dance, see "IFC To Sponsor Reception For Phi Delta," *TW*, January 27, 1949.

311. Ibid. On the history of Fay House and 114 Curtis St. (also known as Harmon House), see UA Edwin B. Rollins Papers, 1300[sic]–1976, Notebooks, 1940–1955, MS054.001 Box 2, Folder 2 (Campus Homes, Part 1(b) 1940–1955). Interestingly enough, Dirrell Sample was living at 92 Professors Row at the time Phi Delta wished to occupy the space. On the activities of the chapter during this time, see *Jumbo* (1949 ed.). The fraternity composite in this yearbook shows just the original fourteen members.

312. Ibid. "Ginger Room" was the name given by the Phi Delts to their basement.

313. Ibid. Thelma Simmonds would go on to cook for the men of Phi Delta and Sigma Nu for the next twenty or so years. On the national fraternities under consideration, Kappa Delta Rho was also in the mix early on since one of the Phi Delts, Bill Wright, had a family connection to the organization. However, Kappa Delta Rho was dropped early on due to its small size at the national level. According to recollections of those who met with the various organizations, the gentleman from Pi Kappa Alpha lived in infamy, as he was proud to announce that his fraternity had only ever initiated white men. This apparently turned off many in Phi Delta. Of course, at the time the other four fraternities on this list also had restrictive membership policies in place, but apparently these restrictions were not used as selling points to the men of Phi Delta. Concerning how Sigma Nu in particular entered the mix, there is a letter within the Sigma Nu archives in Lexington, Virginia, from an unnamed national officer to the members of the high council (undated, but circumstance suggests the fall of 1950), which describes how the petition from Phi Delta came to be. While somewhat tangential to the story, it is worth mentioning here. The process started when Joel Reynolds attended the installation of a Delta Tau Delta chapter at the University of Delaware and met some members of the Sigma Nu national organization, who were guests at the banquet. Mr. Reynold's enthusiasm for Tufts and the Phi Delta men was very clear to the Sigma Nu officials, so they eventually sent a representative to meet Phi Delta and talk with the men, around the same time other organizations came courting. But even here, Sigma Nu officials did not want to be seen as too pushy or forceful. He really wanted them to reach their own conclusion among the fraternities under consideration. He did, however, send along some pertinent information, including the latest edition of *The Delta* and a copy of a recently filed petition from Norwich University. Apparently this information, along with Sigma Nu's description in the latest edition of *Baird's Manual of American College Fraternities*, helped convince Phi Delta.

314. On the destruction of VMI and its reopening after the Civil War, see *Register of the Officers and Cadets of the Virginia Military Institute* (1869 ed.), 3–5; and Jennings C. Wise, *The Military History of the Virginia Military Institute* (Lynchburg, VA: 1915), 352–419. On the founding of Sigma Nu, see Scott, *The Story of Sigma Nu*, chapters 1–4. The other two fraternities in operation at VMI when Sigma Nu formed were Alpha Tau Omega and Kappa Sigma Kappa.

315. On the growth of Sigma Nu as a national organization through the 1800s, see Scott, chapters 5 through 23.

316. Petition of Phi Delta Fraternity to Sigma Nu Fraternity, February 1950, Sigma Nu Fraternity archives, Lexington, VA, which includes the quotation.

317. "Phi Delta Goes National; Joins Sigma Nu Body," *TW*, September 28, 1950; "New Sigma Nu House Installed," *TW*, October 12, 1950; and "Installation of Zeta Eta Chapter," *The Delta of Sigma Nu*, (March 1951): 1–3. According to Robert McCully, Grand Historian of Sigma Nu, Dirrell Sample was initiated as Zeta Eta #38, thus making him the first initiate among the old Phi Delta alumni.

318. On the awards and accolades, see "Sigma Nu's Lovely Alice Fitzpatrick Wins Queen Title At IFC Formal," *TW*, November 30, 1950; and "Students Choose Mooney in Raucous, Riotous Race," *TW*, May 17, 1951. On the number of active members in Sigma Nu and other fraternities in 1957, see Petition of Theta Delta Theta to Phi Sigma Kappa in Activities and Organizations records, 1875–2013, UA 024.001 Box 2, Folder 12 (Theta Delta Theta 1958). The three national fraternities establishing chapters at Tufts after Sigma Nu were Theta Chi, Phi Sigma Kappa, and Tau Epsilon Phi, as discussed later in this chapter.

319. The issue of restrictive membership clauses is discussed in Chapter 6. On Sigma Nu's policy in 1950, see "Statement of the College Relations Committee of the Sigma Nu Fraternity, A National Society of College Men," Phi Delta and Sigma Nu Fraternity records, 1930–1975, UA194.001 Box 1, Folder 2 (Sigma Nu 1950–1975), which includes the quotation. Also, while many of the other fraternities at Tufts had rescinded their official membership clauses by 1960, many still followed a set of unwritten practices, particularly when it came to restricting Jewish men. According to Robert McCully, Grand Historian of Sigma Nu Fraternity, Sigma Nu's membership restrictions were removed completely in 1968.

320. Ibid. On the granting of a waiver to Alpha Tau Omega and Sigma Nu, see "Waivers End Fraternity Discrimination," *TW*, December 13, 1963. In Sigma Nu, the controversy over the membership restrictions resulted in a number of chapters across the country closing down, including Stanford University, the University of Connecticut, and Brown University. Numerous other chapters did obtain a waiver, including the University of Michigan, as discussed in "Waiver Given to Sigma Nu At Michigan," *The Cornell Daily Sun*, April 23, 1962.

321. On the attempt of Sigma Nu to obtain a loan from Tufts University, and the estimated costs of building a new chapter house, see various letters dated January 12, 1965, to April 23, 1965, in Activities and Organizations records, 1875–2013, UA 024.001 Box 4, Folder 4 (Fraternities 1956–1971). On the loan to Phi Epsilon Pi, see letter from Tufts Finance Committee dated October 8, 1962, in Activities and Organizations records, 1875–2013, UA 024.001 Box 10, Folder 4 (Phi Epsilon Pi 1920–1969).

322. On the closing of Tau Epsilon Phi, see their section later in this chapter. On

the reluctance to loan the money in support of Sigma Nu, see letter from Vice President L. Mead to Zeta Eta alumni corporation president Harry Wilcott dated January 12, 1965, in Activities and Organizations records, 1875–2013, UA 024.001 Box 4, Folder 4 (Fraternities 1956–1971).

323. On the state of the chapter in the fall of 1972, see "Good News About Fraternities," *TO*, October 27, 1972. The information about the state of the chapter in the fall of 1974 is derived from interviews with a number of men who moved into 114 Curtis St. and rebuilt the fraternity, including Dr. Robert Stern (February 2, 2012), John Harrington (June 25, 2012), and Dr. Daniel Walter (June 28, 2012). The decision of these men to continue Sigma Nu as a traditional fraternity, rather than make a new community as was happening in Phi Sigma Kappa and Alpha Tau Omega, was certainly not a sure bet, as a majority of students were still very much opposed to fraternities.

324. The information concerning women in the chapter house was provided by Dr. Robert Stern, who lived alongside the women during the 1977–78 school year. In fact, Dr. Stern eventually married one of them! On Zeta Eta's winning of the Gallagher Cup, see "Sigma Nu Wins Prestigious Gallaher [sic] Cup," *TO*, August 31, 1984.

325. On the state of 114 Curtis St. in 1979, see letter from Daniel Walter to President Jean Mayer dated October 29, 1979, and on the effort to move to Hooper Infirmary and then the Fay House, see correspondence between Harry Wilcott and President Jean Mayer dated April 11, 1980, to August 2, 1982, in Office of the President Records 1828–2007, Jean Mayer, administrative records and related papers, 1976–92, Subject Files, UA001.013 Box 10, Folder 23 (Fraternities and sororities 1976–1982). The global issues surrounding Tufts University in the late 1970s and early 1980s is discussed in Gittleman, chapters 2 and 3.

326. On the status of 92 Professors Row, see "House Available For Fraternity," *TO*, February 22, 1985; "IDC Announces Housing Changes," *TD*, February 28, 1985; "Administration To Decide Professors Row Fate," *TD*, March 6, 1985; and "Psi U Prez [sic] Protests 92 Decision," *TD*, April 2, 1985, which mentions the result of the voting. The choice of Kappa Alpha Psi marks the closest that a historically black fraternity has come to occupying a chapter house on the Tufts campus. The housing odyssey of Psi Upsilon is discussed in detail in their section later in the chapter.

327. On the shelving of the plan in 1985, see "Administration Changes Status of 92 Professors Row," *TD*, March 29, 1985. On Sigma Phi Epsilon's occupancy of 16 Bellevue St., see their section later in this chapter. On the subsequent assignment of new chapters houses in the spring of 1986, see "Sigma Nu To Get 92 Professors Row," *TD*, March 7, 1986; and "HTANA Sees Decline In Community Relations," *TO*, March 7, 1986. Of course, not all residents of Professors Row were happy that Sigma Nu was moving in. Following the announcement in the spring of 1986, Delta Tau Delta threw a "There Goes The Neighborhood" party, as relations between the two chapters were anything but cordial at the time.

328. The state of 92 Professors Row when Sigma Nu moved in is based mainly on my own personal recollections. I was active in the chapter when we first occupied 92 Professors Row, and I can still recall the poor shape of the house that first year until improvements were made. At the time, we took the situation in stride, because we were all excited to be closer to the heart of campus. However, in hindsight I find it amazing that Tufts turned over the house in its near dilapidated condition to the chapter, especially with the multitude of problems in the basement, a room they knew we would use for

social events. The asbestos was finally removed the fall of my senior year, 1988. We also utilized the attic space for meetings and initiations, but this room was no safer than the basement since it, too, had only one exit. The attic was sealed off completely in the mid 1990s, and the basement was sealed off in 2012.

329. Renovations of 92 Professors Row are again based on my personal recollections, as I was active at the time the second egress was constructed and the new kitchen installed. Many of the active members carved their initials and pin numbers into the freshly poured concrete of the basement exit, which are still visible today.

330. The push to expel fraternities and sororities from Tufts over the years is discussed in detail in chapter 6. The removal of the Greek systems at Colby, Middlebury, and Bowdoin in the 1980s and 1990s are stories unto themselves, but space does not permit a proper discussion. On the re-colonization of Sigma Nu, see "Recolonization is a Success for Sigma Nu," *TD*, March 18, 1993; and "ZH Chapter Recolonizes–21 New Members," *Sigma Nu News* 3, no. 1 (Winter 1993): 1.

331. On the removal of Sigma Nu from 92 Professors Row, see "SigEp to Remain Homeless," *TD*, September 4, 2012; and "Sigma Nu House Becomes Transfer Student Residence," *TW*, September 10, 2012. On Sigma Phi Epsilon's housing problems, see their section later in this chapter. The push to make 92 Professors Row a dormitory for transfer students was one of necessity, since more decided to enroll at Tufts that year than were expected, and all of the other dormitories were full. But, administration officials told me the house was never intended to remain a dormitory beyond the 2012–13 school year.

332. Much of the information from this section comes from meetings with university officials between the fall of 2012 and the spring of 2014, including Dean Bruce Reitman and Su McGlone, Director of Fraternity and Sorority Affairs. As President of Zeta Eta Alumni of Sigma Nu, Inc., and as the chapter advisor for the undergraduates, I was engaged in many discussions with these officials following the expulsion of Sigma Nu from 92 Professors Row. Both Dean Reitman and Ms. McGlone expressed regret that the landlord of 114 Curtis St., Walnut Hill Properties (the real estate arm of Tufts University), turned in the housing license with no plans to open an another fraternity house from their inventory. Had the license not been turned in, I was told that Sigma Phi Epsilon would simply have gone back to 114 Curtis St., and Sigma Nu would have returned to 92 Professors Row, once their probationary periods were over. Apparently, a plan to build a new fraternity house had been in the making for a few years, and the closing of 114 Curtis St. brought new life to the project. But it was only a dream, for the space chosen on Sawyer Avenue was not ideal, and there was no money to tear down the existing structure or build a proper fraternity house in its place. On the awarding of 92 Professors Row to Sigma Phi Epsilon, see "SigEp to Move Into House on Pro Row," *TD*, November 27, 2012; and "SigEp Settles Into New House on Pro Row," *TD*, September 9, 2013.

333. Again, much of the information in this section comes from personal recollections of meetings with university officials. Credit goes to Dean Reitman and Vice President of Operations Linda Snyder for their efforts to find a house for Sigma Nu, when they could have easily said "no." Credit also goes to Yolanda King, Director of Residence Life, who agreed to transfer 90–94 Curtis St. from her jurisdiction so it could be occupied by a fraternity. Notably absent from any meetings or discussions on fraternity housing was Sigma Phi Epsilon. After all, they were now in a house, so they

apparently had no desire to contribute to the solution.

334. Information about the council is based on my correspondence with Ms. McGlone and the members of Sigma Nu during this time, as I was heavily involved in the process (though I did not attend the council meeting). Information about the closing of basements in wooden houses and the assumption of property taxes was provided by Dean Bruce Reitman and Ms. McGlone. On the decision regarding the occupancy of 90–94 Curtis St., see "SigNu, Theta to Receive Building on Curtis Street," *TD*, March 4, 2014. For information on Kappa Alpha Theta, see their section in Chapter 4. The pairing of Sigma Nu and Kappa Alpha Theta came as a complete surprise, since technically the sorority was not eligible for housing for two more years, but it did solve the problem of filling the entire house with residents. Sigma Nu, in anticipation of returning to 92 Professors Row, had only lined up eleven members to move into the chapter house, but 90–94 Curtis St. had nineteen total beds that needed to be filled.

335. On the opening of the chapter house, see "Theta and SigNu Move Into New House on Curtis Street," *TD*, September 22, 2014. On the disbandment of Sigma Nu, see "Chinese House Moves to Curtis Following Sigma Nu Suspension," *TD*, September 8, 2015. Writing about the untimely demise of my own chapter has been the most difficult part of this effort.

336. The early religious identity of Tufts College is discussed in detail in Miller, *LOTH–1*, 377–381. According to Start, 81, the Tufts Divinity School gained its first Jewish professor, Bernard Maimon, in 1879. Alas, Professor Maimon lasted but one year at the college. On the rise in Jewish enrollment at schools across the country, see Sanua, *Going Greek*, 40–44. On the lack of cultural programs in colleges and universities related to Judaism, see *The Menorah Movement*, 1–4.

337. On the formation of the Harvard Menorah Society and similar organizations, see *The Menorah Movement*, 1, 5–7. On the formation of the IMA and its early expansion, see *The Menorah Movement*, 7–14. In many ways the IMA was similar to a national Greek-letter fraternity. The association held a national convention each year, where one of its tasks was to approve or reject petitions from new chapters of the Menorah Society. Starting in 1915, the IMA also published a semi-annual magazine called *The Menorah Journal*, which included articles about contemporary Jewish issues, essays from renowned Jewish scholars, and activity reports from the various chapters. However, the IMA was unlike a fraternity in two main areas. First, the organization was not social in nature, but academic. Chapters of the Menorah Society were actively discouraged from holding regular social functions such as parties and dances, as those activities had very little to do with studying Judaism, at least in the eyes of the IMA. Second, membership in each chapter of the Menorah Society was open to all associated with the particular college or university – students, faculty, administrators, and women as well as men. Such a practice of allowing a wide group of members, especially both men and women, was unheard of at the time in the national fraternity system. Indeed, one did not even have to be Jewish to be a member of the Menorah Society; while the main purpose of the group was the study of Jewish culture and history, the organization was officially non-sectarian.

338. On the formation of the Menorah Society of Tufts College, see *The Menorah Movement*, 140; and "Menorah Society," *TW*, November 12, 1913. Harry Katz identified himself as the founder of the Menorah Society in a letter published in *Omichronicle* 1, no. 2b (February 1936): 2, in AJHS–PhiEp, Box 31, Folder 5 (Omicron–Tufts

College). On the acceptance of the Tufts chapter in to the IMA, see *The Menorah Movement*, 159–161. On the activities of the Menorah Society, see "Menorah Society," *TW*, November 4, 1914; "Tufts College," *The Menorah Journal* 1, no. 5 (December 1915): 329; "Tufts College," *The Menorah Journal* 2, no. 2 (April 1916): 127; "Menorah Prize Competitions," *The Menorah Journal* 2, no. 4 (October 1916): 323; and "Tufts College," *The Menorah Journal* 3, no. 1 (February 1917): 59. Although social activities were highly discouraged in the Menorah Society, the Tufts group did hold a few banquets as discussed in the aforementioned articles. Despite great enthusiasm at its start, the Menorah movement and the IMA were not long for this world. By the late 1920s, the organization began to wane at both Tufts and the national level. Student apathy, combined with the rise competeing organizations such as Hillel, led to the eventual demise of the IMA. For more information, see Alfred Jospe, *Jewish Students and Student Services at American Universities*, (Washington, D.C.: B'nai B'rith Hillel Foundations, 1963), 18–22.

339. On the attendance of Mr. Katz at the 1915 convention and the wooing by various fraternities, see his letter in *Omichronicle* 1, no. 2b (February 1936): 2. On the formation of Jewish fraternities in general, see chapter 1. The push to be "the best" among the Jewish fraternities is discussed at length in Sanua, chapters 1 and 2.

340. On the specific fraternities that courted Mr. Katz, see letter from Herman Kline to Jesse [Acker], undated but context places it in early January 1916, in AJHS–PhiEp, Box 31, Folder 5 (Omicron–Tufts College). In this letter, Mr. Kline gives a passionate account of how he wants nothing more than for PhiEp to be the first at Tufts. On the founding of Pi Lambda Phi and Sigma Alpha Mu, see Baird (10th ed. 1923), 292–293, 312–314.

341. On the founding of Phi Epsilon Pi and its issues with non-sectarianism, see Sanua, 61–68. On the reluctance of college officials to welcome a Jewish fraternity, see Sanua, chapter 5. On Harry's affinity for a non-sectarian fraternity, see his letter in *Omichronicle* 1, no. 2b (February 1936): 2. Despite its early emphasis on non-sectarianism, PhiEp would never achieve religious equality among its members. Faced with this reality, the national organization in 1923 began to de-emphasize its non-sectarianism by removing the cross and crescent from its shield. As years went on, the organization further emphasized Jewish culture and identity within its operations, thus solidifying its reputation as a Jewish fraternity. Officially, though, Phi Epsilon Pi always remained non-sectarian. The fear on many campuses was that the establishment of Jewish fraternities would lead to increasing enrollment of Jewish men at the school. Jews in many ways were seen as second-class citizens, and many at the time felt they did not deserve the same chances when it came to higher education. Unfortunately, this discrimination was all too real at Tufts College in the early 1920s, though it was more of an issue with Jewish women.

342. Letter from Herman Kline to Jesse [Acker], undated but context places it in early January 1916, in AJHS–PhiEp, Box 31, Folder 5 (Omicron–Tufts College). In this letter, Mr. Kline incorrectly refers to the local group as Phi Delta Phi. Apparently the name of the local fraternity was not of great concern!

343. Ibid; letter from Delta Phi Delta members to Phi Epsilon Pi dated January 7, 1916, in AJHS–PhiEp, Box 31, Folder 5 (Omicron–Tufts College); and "Phi Epsilon Pi Fraternity," *TW*, January 26, 1916. There is some confusion over the actual number of Omicron charter members. The article "Omicron To Entertain," *TW*, February 16,

1916, does not include Harry Katz and Bertram Green among the list of charter members. However, I have chosen to include these two men as founders of the chapter, since they were signers of the original pledge document and initiates of PhiEp.

344. Letter from Herman Kline to Jesse Acker dated January 18, 1916; letter from Benjamin Golden, Omicron, to Elmer Harris, Grand Superior of Phi Epsilon Pi, undated but context places it as early February 1916; and letter from unknown to Mendel Waters, Omicron, dated February 9, 1916, in AJHS–PhiEp, Box 31, Folder 5 (Omicron–Tufts College); "Omicron To Entertain," *TW*, February 16, 1916; and "Tufts Chapter Host," *TW*, February 21, 1916.

345. Letter from Mendel Waters, Omicron, to Jesse Acker dated March 7, 1916, which includes both quotations; and letter from Herman Kline to Jesse Acker, May 23, 1916, in AJHS–PhiEp, Box 31, Folder 5 (Omicron–Tufts College). Unfortunately there is no mention in these letters of the specific actions by Herman at the other chapter installations that caused Omicron so much embarrassment. The $500 price tag for the party comes out to about $10,500 in today's money, when adjusted for inflation. That must have been some party.

346. On the address of the chapter for the 1916–17 school year, see campus map, *CofTC*, (1916–17 ed.). On recognition by the Interfraternity Council, see *TW*, February 13, 1918; and letter from Alex Horenstein, Omicron, to Jesse Acker dated February 22, 1918, in AJHS–PhiEp, Box 31, Folder 5 (Omicron–Tufts College). The problems faced by Jewish fraternities seeking IFC recognition at other campuses are discussed in, 189–191. On the initiation of the first Gentiles into Omicron chapter, see letter from Alex Horenstein to "Dear Fraters" dated December 15, 1917, in AJHS–PhiEp, Box 31, Folder 5 (Omicron–Tufts College). Unfortunately, Alex does not identify the Gentiles by name. Regardless, this letter is the first documented instance of religious integration within a Tufts fraternity chapter.

347. On the investigation by Omicron for potential PhiEp chapters at area schools: for Massachusetts Agriculture College (MAC), see letter from William Spunt, Omicron, to Jesse Acker, undated but context places it during the 1916–17 school year; for Dartmouth College see letter from Jesse Aronson and Max Tennis, Omicron, to Jesse Acker dated November 10, 1917; and letter from Max Tennis to Jesse Acker, November 26, 1917; for Boston University (BU), see letter from Jesse Aronson and Max Tennis to Jesse Acker dated October 23, 1917; letter from Max Tennis and others to Jesse Acker dated November 26, 1917; and letter from Alex Horenstein to Jesse Acker, March 5, 1918, in AJHS–PhiEp, Box 31, Folder 5 (Omicron–Tufts College). The content of these letters, along with the responses by Jesse Acker, indicate all took the evaluation process very seriously. In the end, PhiEp declined to enter MAC or BU at the time (with Omicron's poor opinion of the BU men a major reason for the refusal at that school), but it did place its Alpha Alpha chapter at Dartmouth in 1920. On the development of an improved ritual, see letter from Alex Horenstein to Jesse Acker dated October 17, 1917, in AJHS–PhiEp, Box 31, Folder 5 (Omicron–Tufts College). On the composition of "Phi Epsilon Pi for Aye," see correspondence between Alex Horenstein and Jesse Acker dated March 27, 1919, through April 20, 1919, in AJHS–PhiEp, Box 31, Folder 5 (Omicron–Tufts College). On the occupancy of 19 University Avenue by PhiEp starting in the fall of 1920, see *CofTC*, (1920–21 ed.), 258; and *Omichronicle* 2, no. 1 (undated but context places it November 1920), in AJHS–PhiEp, Box 31, Folder 5 (Omicron–Tufts College). Unfortunately, I have been unable to discover any

significant information relating to Omicron members who served in the Great War, other than two men who were drafted in late 1917, William Spunt (class of 1917) and George Lubinsky (class of 1919). It appears both men survived the war.

348. Letter from Jimmy Welansky, Omicron chapter Superior, to Frater [Oberdorfer], Grand Superior of Phi Epsilon Pi dated January 2, 1921; letter from E. G. Zacharias to Jimmy Welansky, undated but context places it shortly after January 2, 1921; letter from Irving Mitchell, Chairman Omicron Supervisory Committee, to Frater [Oberdorfer] dated January 26, 1921; and letter from Grand Superior Oberdorfer to Max Tennis dated February 25, 1921, all in AJHS–PhiEp, Box 31, Folder 5 (Omicron–Tufts College). These letters offer wonderful insight into the extent of control exerted by the national organization over Omicron chapter, and they also detail the subsequent frustration of Omicron members who felt they were being treated like children. Grand Superior Oberdorfer was a polarizing figure within Phi Epsilon Pi, as he was responsible for throwing out a number of chapters he deemed unworthy, including Rhode Island State College, New York University, and Carnegie Tech. For further information, see Sanua, 161–164.

349. Letter from Irving Mitchell, Chairman Omicron Supervisory Committee, to Frater [Oberdorfer] dated January 26, 1921.

350. On the general frustration felt by Omicron, see letter from Grand Superior Oberdorfer to Omicron chapter Superior chapter dated April 23, 1921; letter from Charlie Smith, Omicron chapter Superior, to Maurice Jacobs, Executive Secretary of Phi Epsilon Pi dated March 3, 1922; and letter from Maurice Jacobs to Charlie [Smith] dated March 9, 1922, in AJHS–PhiEp, Box 31, Folder 5 (Omicron–Tufts College). On the issue surrounding the unauthorized initiation and expulsion of other chapter for such an offense, see letter from Saul Ravitch, Omicron chapter Superior, to Maurice Jacobs, undated but context places it fall 1922; and letter from Maurice Jacobs to Saul Ravitch, December 11, 1922, AJHS–PhiEp, Box 31, Folder 5 (Omicron–Tufts College). On the revocation of Omicron's charter, see letter from Maurice Jacobs to The [Tufts College] President and the Tufts College Interfraternity Conference dated January 10, 1923, in AJHS–PhiEp, Box 31, Folder 5 (Omicron–Tufts College). The official reason given in this letter for the revocation was "a violation of the national constitution."

351. On the operations of Phi Epsilon Pi in the fall of 1923, see letter from Max Tennis to Edward Davis dated December 3, 1923, in AJHS–PhiEp, Box 31, Folder 5 (Omicron–Tufts College). On the notification of charter revocation, see letter from Maurice Jacobs to The [Tufts College] President and the Tufts College Interfraternity Conference dated January 10, 1923, in AJHS–PhiEp, Box 31, Folder 5 (Omicron–Tufts College). Despite this letter, Phi Epsilon Pi remained a recognized fraternity at Tufts, as it was listed each year in *The Ivy Book* throughout this era. Unfortunately, there is little discussion in the AJHS–PhiEp archives as to why the Tufts men kept the name "Phi Epsilon Pi" after they lost their charter, so the reason I stated is a guess.

352. On the second notification, see letter from Maurice Jacobs to President Cousens dated November 16, 1923, which includes the quotation. On the meeting between Max Tennis and President Cousens, see letter from President Cousens to Maurice Jacobs dated December 3, 1923. On the response, see letter from Maurice Jacobs to President Cousens dated December 8, 1923. Copies of these particular letters are housed in AJHS–PhiEp, Box 31, Folder 5 (Omicron–Tufts College) as well as Activities and

Organizations records, 1875–2013, UA 024.001 Box 10, Folder 4 (Phi Epsilon Pi 1920–1969).

353. On the animosity between Max and Mr. Jacobs, see letter from Max Tennis to Edward Davis dated December 3, 1923, which includes the quotation; and letter from Maurice Jacobs to Max Tennis dated December 9, 1923, in AJHS–PhiEp, Box 31, Folder 5 (Omicron–Tufts College). Mr. Jacobs ended his letter with "You have my sincerest good wishes for success in your chosen profession. With the best of good wishes to you and the rest of the fraters, although I imagine very few of them care to receive these greetings, I am, Fraternally yours, Maurice Jacobs." The pen is, at times, so much mightier than the sword. On the use of the name "Phi Epsilon Pi Club," see *Jumbo* (1925 ed.). One can assume they added "Club" to their name to prevent further problems with the national organization.

354. On the attempts to bring the Tufts group back into the national organization prior to 1925, see letter from Maurice Jacobs to Max Tennis, December 9, 1923; and Committee Report of Investigation of Phi Epsilon Pi Fraternity at Tufts College, March 1924, in AJHS–PhiEp, Box 31, Folder 5 (Omicron–Tufts College). On the attempt in 1925, see letter from President Cousens to Mr. J. Lavenstein, Secretary of Phi Epsilon Pi, dated March 13, 1925, which includes the first quotation; Petition of Phi Epsilon Pi Club to Phi Epsilon Pi Fraternity, April 7, 1925; letter from D. J. Benoliel, Chairman of Extension Committee, to H. M. Sesen, Omicron secretary, dated May 1, 1925, which includes the second quotation; letter from H. M. Sesen to D. J. Benoliel dated May 16, 1925; letter from D. J. Benoliel to H. M. Sesen dated May 20, 1925; and letter from D. J. Benoliel to H. M. Sesen dated June 10, 1925, in AJHS–PhiEp, Box 31, Folder 5 (Omicron–Tufts College).

355. Letter from H. M. Sesen to Mr. Benoliel dated October 6, 1925; letter from D. J. Benoliel to H. M. Sesen dated October 10, 1925; letter from William Spunt to Edward Davis dated October 19, 1925, which includes the quotation; and letter from Emanuel Wirkman to Edward Davis dated May 20, 1926, which mentions the delegates had voted to restore Omicron's charter, in AJHS–PhiEp, Box 31, Folder 5 (Omicron–Tufts College). Edward Davis was the Grand Superior of Phi Epsilon Pi at the time, according to the letter dated May 20, 1926.

356. Letter from Emanuel Wirkman to Edward Davis, May 20, 1926, AJHS–PhiEp, Box 31, Folder 5 (Omicron–Tufts College). Mr. Wirkman, who apparently was not a Tufts alumnus, was part of the investigative committee formed after the Grand Council had put the blackball in place, and he was the one who recommended only five out of the twenty. This letter appears to have been the penultimate action with regards to Omicron chapter, as the closing text makes it clear the decision now rested solely in the hands of Grand Superior Davis. He must have said "yes," for the chapter resumed normal operations in the fall of 1926, albeit with only five members. On the practice of national intervention in choosing new members and the use of the blackball, see Sanua, 152–164.

357. Throughout the rest of the 1920s and into the 1930s, Omicron chapter held a number of formal events, and copies of invitations to these events are housed in AJHS–PhiEp, Box 31, Folder 5 (Omicron–Tufts College). The Cocoanut Grove became infamous in November 1942, when a fire killed nearly 500 patrons. On the evaluation of other chapters, see correspondence between Maurice Jacobs and Joseph Sonneborn of Omicron chapter from March 1, 1932, through May 16, 1932, in AJHS–PhiEp, Box

31, Folder 5 (Omicron–Tufts College). On the evaluation of the group from Massachusetts State College, see letter from Harry Hymanson to Maurice Jacobs dated November 22, 1932, in AJHS–PhiEp, Box 31, Folder 5 (Omicron–Tufts College). Once again, the Tufts group did not think too highly of the Massachusetts men. However, in his reply, Maurice Jacobs urged the members of Omicron to give the Mass. State College men a break, especially now that the school was branching out to fields other than agriculture. In the end, it appears UMASS-Amherst never did gain a chapter of Phi Epsilon Pi.

358. On the start of the fundraising effort, see "Superior's Message," *The Omicronian* 1, no. 1 (November 28, 1931): 1, in AJHS–PhiEp, Box 31, Folder 5 (Omicron–Tufts College). The "Rez" was a reservoir situated in what is now the common space between Houston, Carmichael, and Miller dormitories. For more information see "Reservoir, 1865–1944," *Concise Encyclopedia of Tufts History*, http://hdl.handle.net/10427/14829 (accessed October 21, 2014). On the effort in 1935 to purchase the house at 176 Curtis St., see letter from Harold Slate, Superior of Omicron, to Maurice Jacobs dated January 31, 1935; letter from Maurice Jacobs to Harold Slate dated February 2, 1935; and letter from Harold Slate to Maurice Jacobs dated February 12, 1935, in AJHS–PhiEp, Box 31, Folder 6 (Omicron–Tufts College). After this last letter, there is no more talk of buying the house at 176 Curtis St. in any future correspondence or newsletters, so I assume the matter died out.

359. On the push to build a new house, see "Omicron Lays Plans for a New House To Be Erected in 3-Yrs," *Omichronicle* 1, no. 3 (May–June 1936): 4, 12, in AJHS–PhiEp, Box 31, Folder 6 (Omicron–Tufts College). I am assuming the project was shelved because the idea of a new house is not mentioned again in chapter newsletters until the fall of 1938. On the description of the physical problems with and lack of boarders in 19 University Avenue over the years, see letter from Ralph Rittenburg, Superior of Omicron, to Mr. Pascal Greenberg dated March 6, 1939, which includes the quotation, in AJHS–PhiEp, Box 31, Folder 6 (Omicron–Tufts College).

360. Letter to "Dear Brother," undated but context places it in 1937 or 1938; "Omicron Has A Goal," *Omichronicle* 3, no. 1 (September–December 1938): 5–6, which contains a drawing of the proposed house; and "Omicron's Objective," *Omichronicle* 3, no. 2 (December 1938–March 1939): 6, in AJHS–PhiEp, Box 31, Folder 6 (Omicron–Tufts College). Sigma Omega Psi's description as a second-tier Jewish fraternity is based heavily upon the words written by PhiEp members in their correspondence with their national organization and their alumni newsletters, so this is a somewhat jaded view. However, even at its height, S.O.P. was not a powerhouse fraternity, for it only ever established twenty chapters , with most in New York and Massachusetts. Also, its history was not well preserved, so there is little information to refute PhiEp's description. More information about S.O.P. can be found in its section later in this chapter.

361. Letter from New House Committee to "Fellow Alumnus" dated December 29, 1938; letter from Ralph Rittenburg to Mr. Pascal Greenberg, March 6, 1939; and letter from Maurice Gurin, Executive Secretary, to Members of the Grand Council dated October 20, 1940, in AJHS–PhiEp, Box 31, Folder 6 (Omicron–Tufts College). Originally, Omicron asked for a loan of $1300, but the national organization would only give them $500. The total price paid for the house was $9,250, with all but $1,000 being mortgaged. On the occupancy of the house starting in 1939–40, see *Jumbo* (1940 ed.), 141.

362. On the German Jewish Student Refugee program, see Sanua, 236. This is a

fascinating topic, but is unfortunately beyond the scope of this work. On Omicron's effort to host a refugee, see letter from Maurice Jacobs to Maurice Crevoshay, Secretary of Omicron, dated July 21, 1936, which mentions a refugee will be coming to Tufts soon (this apparently did not happen); "The Case of the Jew," *Omichronicle* 1, no. 3 (May–June 1936): 2, 9; letter from Maurice Crevoshay to "Dear Frater" dated July 28, 1936, which asks alumni for money to sponsor the refugee, as Tufts College would fund about half of the required amount; letter from Irving Rosen, Superior of Omicron, to Maurice Jacobs dated December 14, 1936, which mentions Omicron would like to wait until September 1937 before hosting a refugee (again, it appears this did not happen); "German Refugee," *Omichronicle* 1 [misprint on document, should be 2], no. 1 (September–December 1936): 5; and "Omicron Planning For Arrival of German Refugee," *Omichronicle* 3, no. 2 (December 1938–March 1939): 10, in AJHS–PhiEp, Box 31, Folder 6 (Omicron–Tufts College). On the arrival of Jan Rosenbach at Tufts College and his subsequent experience, see telegram from Maurice Gurin to Mr. Stuart Stern, Recording Secretary of Omicron, dated September 18, 1940; letter from Stuart L. Stern to Maurice Gurin dated October 2, 1940; letter from Maurice Gurin to Members of the Grand Council dated October 20, 1940, which gives the details of Jan Rosenbach's life and his family's situation; and letter from Maurice Gurin to Dr. Nils Wessel, Dean of Men at Tufts College, dated October 21, 1940, in AJHS–PhiEp, Box 31, Folder 6 (Omicron–Tufts College). Jan did become a pledge of PhiEp in the fall of 1940, but it is unclear if he was ever initiated fully into the fraternity. On the Nazi occupation of Prague, see William L. Shirer, *The Rise and Fall of the Third Reich* (New York: Touchstone, 1959), 428–454. Finally, the odyssey of Jan Rosenbach is a story unto itself, as his journey to Tufts College and Omicron chapter was by no means a straight line. Indeed, without the offer to attend Tufts, Jan may well have been deported from Ellis Island back to his homeland, where he faced a grim future. For more information, see Case No. 1576, American Friends Service Committee (A.F.S.C.) Refugee Assistance Case Files, Accession Number 2002.296, United States Holocaust Memorial Museum archives. Within this file is documentation regarding the elder Rosenbach's premature death on March 16, 1939.

363. On the pacifism within the Omicron, see "Do You Know That Your Name Has Been Set Down On A Death-List?" *Omichronicle* 1, no. 3 (May–June 1936): 5, in AJHS–PhiEp, Box 31, Folder 6 (Omicron–Tufts College), which includes the first two quotations. On the lecture by Norman Thomas, see "Norman Thomas Visits Omicron; Famous Socialist Impressive," *Omichronicle* 1 [misprint on document, should be 2], no. 1 (September–December 1936): 7, in AJHS–PhiEp, Box 31, Folder 6 (Omicron–Tufts College), which includes the next two quotations. On the journey of Norman Thomas, see Harry Fleischman, *Norman Thomas; A Biography: 1884–1968, With a New Chapter The Final Years* (New York: W. W. Norton, 1967). Norman Thomas would go on to run for President of the United States three more times, in 1940, 1944, and 1948. The America First Committee, as its name suggests, was an anti-war, anti-intervention movement that was widely popular from its founding in 1940 until the bombing of Pearl Harbor on December 7, 1941.

364. On the switch to a full year calendar, see "Tufts Faculty Votes Trimester Year," *TW*, March 25, 1943. This article mentions the switch was intended to match the needs of the U.S. Navy, so Tufts could host the V–12 program. For more information on the V–12 program, see "Navy V–12 Program, 1942–1945," *Concise Encyclopedia*

of Tufts History, http://hdl.handle.net/10427/14829 (accessed October 28, 2014). On the commandeering of 8 Winthrop St. for use as a Fletcher dormitory, see "College Buildings Undergo Changes," *TW*, July 10, 1943. On the operations of Phi Epsilon Pi during the all of 1943, see "Active Chapters Plan Limited Fraternity Life," *TW*, July 29, 1943; "Fraternity News–Phi Eps Elect," *TW*, September 9, 1943; and "War-Time Fraternities," *TW*, October 15, 1943. On the change of 8 Winthrop St. to a civilian men's dormitory, see "Phi Ep House Made Men's Dormitory," *TW*, July 13, 1944. My assertion the chapter shut down in early 1944 is a guess, as it was around this time the chapter was no longer mentioned in the *Tufts Weekly*.

365. On the sacrifice of Lt. Ralph Kaye, see Robin L. Rielly, *Kamikazes, Corsairs, and Picket Ships: Okinawa 1945* (Havertown, PA: Casemate, 2010), 285–286, which includes the quotation; Charles D. Brown and Robert L. Anteau, *Historical Review: U.S.S. Drexler DD–741* (privately published, 2002), http://wgordon.web.wesleyan.edu/kamikaze/books/ships/drexler/index.htm (accessed October 28, 2014); and "Drexler," http://navylog.navymemorial.org/drexler (accessed October 28, 2014), which includes Lt. Kaye in the Lost At Sea Log. On the establishment of the Ralph S. Kaye prize, see "Kaye Mathematics Scholarship Established by Phi Epsilon Pi," *TW*, February 20, 1948. This article also mentions Lt. Kaye was the chapter's only gold star of World War II.

366. Letter from Paul Slate to Frater Miller dated December 1, 1945; and "Phi Ep In The Past," *The Omichronicle* 1, no. 1 (April 1947): 3, in AJHS–PhiEp, Box 31, Folder 6 (Omicron–Tufts College). On the return of normal operations at Tufts College following the end of World War II, see Miller, *LOTH–1*, 643–659.

367. Letter from Paul Slate to Frater Miller dated December 1, 1945, which includes the quotation, in AJHS–PhiEp, Box 31, Folder 6 (Omicron–Tufts College). On the absorption of Sigma Omega Psi by Alpha Epsilon Pi, see the pertinent section later in this chapter.

368. Letter from David Paul, Executive Secretary of Phi Epsilon Pi, to Paul Slate dated December 4, 1945, which includes the quotations; "Phi Ep In The Past," *The Omichronicle* 1, no. 1 (April 1947): 3; and telegram to Paul Slate dated December 6, 1945, in AJHS–PhiEp, Box 31, Folder 6 (Omicron–Tufts College). The easing of membership requirements was most likely a combination of changing attitudes within the national fraternity, a desire to get chapters going again as quickly as possible, and a realization that such oversight at the national level was no longer practical, especially as the fraternity grew in chapters and members.

369. On the efforts to regain control of the chapter house, see letter from Paul Slate to Frater Miller dated December 1, 1945; "Phi Ep In The Past," *The Omichronicle* 1, no. 1 (April 1947): 3; and "Phi Ep In The Future," *The Omichronicle* 1, no. 1 (April 1947): 4, which includes the first quotation, in AJHS–PhiEp, Box 31, Folder 6 (Omicron–Tufts College). Also see "Phi Epsilon Pi," *TW*, May 9, 1946. On the observation by the national organization, see letter from Paul Spiwak, Executive Secretary, to Members of the Grand Council, dated December 9, 1948, which includes the second quotation, in AJHS–PhiEp, Box 31, Folder 6 (Omicron–Tufts College).

370. On the success in scholarship within Phi Epsilon Pi and Alpha Epsilon Pi, see the yearly grade reports from this era as housed in Activities and Organizations records, 1875–2013, UA 024.001 Box 4, Folder 4 (Fraternities 1956–1971). Also see Visitation Report for Omicron chapter dated April 14–16, 1951; letter from Richard Kelly, Assistant Dean, to Paul Spiwak dated November 19, 1951; and Visitation Report

for Omicron chapter dated January 15–16, 1954, in AJHS–PhiEp, Box 31, Folder 6 (Omicron–Tufts College). The drive for scholarship by Jewish students in general, and fraternity men in particular, is outside the scope of this work, but is discussed by others including Sanua and Syrett. Concerning a Jewish quota system at Tufts College, it appears one was in place in the 1920s. In his annual report to the trustees in 1929, President John Cousens writes, "This is on the assumption that the Trustees continue to believe that the setting of a quota for Jewish students is wise." See Board of Trustees records, 1848–2013, Full Board, 1851–2012, Meeting Minutes 1851–1955, UA003.001 Box 110, Folder 5 (Full Board Minutes Volume 10 1926–1930: October 31, 1929). Additionally, there are some curious statements in the Phi Epsilon Pi archives that suggest the quota system was still active some decades later. For example, in the Visitation Report for Omicron Chapter dated February 7–8, 1952, in AJHS–PhiEp, Box 31, Folder 6 (Omicron–Tufts College), the author writes, "Tufts is one of the few all-male schools in the New England area [women were technically in Jackson College] to continue a flat 10% quota on Jewish students, thus 250 of the 2,500 students are Jewish." Rather than being appalled by this fact, the author of the report (who is not identified) then says, "I believe that this has been a force for good as the men are carefully screened before admission and, consequently, are excellent scholars and highly personable young men." Other documents within the AJHS–PhiEp archives from this era consistently list the number of Jewish men at Tufts as being approximately 10% of the total number of students.

371. On Omicron's support of the Upsilon chapter at the University of Connecticut, see "Phi Eps Back UCONN Group On Bias Issue," *TW*, October 12, 1950; and "Phi EP Admits Rogers, Negro, To Membership," *TW*, January 11, 1951. Al Rogers was the first black to be initiated into Phi Epsilon Pi, when he became a full member of Upsilon chapter at the University of Connecticut. On the first black pledge for AEPi at Tufts College, see *Jumbo* (1952 ed.), which shows Reginald Alleyne in the chapter photo and some candid photographs. However, according to James Fleischer of the national Alpha Epsilon Pi fraternity, Reginald was never initiated as a full member of the fraternity. Indeed, he is not pictured in later editions of the *Jumbo* yearbook as being associated with Alpha Epsilon Pi. On the first black pledge for PhiEp at Tufts College, see *Jumbo* (1952 ed.), which shows Robert Jones in the chapter photo. Robert is also listed as a pledge on the membership roster of Omicron Chapter dated October 25, 1951, in AJHS–PhiEp, Box 31, Folder 6 (Omicron–Tufts College). However, Robert does not appear on any subsequent membership rosters, nor is he pictured in later editions of the *Jumbo* yearbook as being associated with Phi Epsilon Pi.

372. The material for the next two paragraphs is based heavily on interviews with Brooks Johnson (March 18, 2013, and March 20, 2013). On the pledging of Brooks, see "169 Pledges Announced by 9 Fraternities," *TW*, November 6, 1952. Also see Semi-Annual Membership Report, November 1952; and Visitation Report, November 16–18, 1952, in AJHS–PhiEp, Box 31, Folder 6 (Omicron–Tufts College). Concerning Delta Upsilon, the fraternity has never had any official membership restrictions based on race, color, or creed throughout its history, according to its national website.

373. On Brooks' initiation into Phi Epsilon Pi, see Semi-Annual Membership Report, October 28, 1953, in AJHS–PhiEp, Box 31, Folder 6 (Omicron–Tufts College). On further integration of the chapter, see Visitation Report, January 15–16, 1954, in AJHS–PhiEp, Box 31, Folder 6 (Omicron–Tufts College); and Phi Epsilon Pi compos-

ite photos in *Jumbo* (1955, 1956, and 1957 eds.).

374. Letter from Alvin Schmidt to President Nils Wessell dated June 6, 1962, which includes the quotation; memo from Tufts Finance Committee dated October 8, 1962, approving the $80,000 loan; and letter from Phi Epsilon Pi to Tufts Finance Committee dated August 7, 1963, requesting an increase to $90,000 (which was eventually approved), all in Activities and Organizations records, 1875–2013, UA 024.001 Box 10, Folder 4 (Phi Epsilon Pi 1920–1969).

375. On the decline of Omicron chapter in the latter 1960s, see "Phi Epsilon Pi Reopens; Frosh Seek Frat Status," *TO*, March 7, 1969; and letter from Joel Reynolds to Jack L. Anson, Executive Director of the National Interfraternity Conference, February 28, 1971, in Activities and Organizations records, 1875–2013, UA 024.001 Box 4, Folder 4 (Fraternities 1956–1971). On the epic beach party, see "Spring Floods at Phi Ep," *TW,* February 11, 1966, which includes the two quotations. Rumor had it that the band playing at this gig was the world-renowned Lovin' Spoonful, which, if true, would have made this party even more amazing than it must have been. I have been unable to confirm this fact, however, so I listed the band name as it appeared in the *Tufts Weekly* article.

376. "Phi Epsilon Pi Reopens; Frosh Seek Frat Status"; and letter from Joel Reynolds to Jack L. Anson, February 28, 1971.

377. "Phi Epsilon Pi Reopens; Frosh Seek Frat Status"; and interviews with Phi Epsilon Pi alumni involved in the revival, including Chet Webster (June 17, 2011) and Dennis Burnham (June 20, 2011). Concerning the decline of Phi Epsilon Pi at the national level during the mid 1960s, one additional reason is that the fraternity had lost its niche. With most national fraternities having given up their discriminatory membership policies by this time, Jewish men were now free to join any fraternity they wished. Many did just that, leaving the historically Jewish fraternities behind. Ideally this newfound religious migration within fraternities should have been reciprocal, but non-Jewish men were not attracted to Phi Epsilon Pi or other historically Jewish organizations in nearly the same number.

378. On the state of 8 Winthrop Street and subsequent renovations, see "Phi Epsilon Pi Reopens; Frosh Seek Frat Status"; and interviews with Phi Epsilon Pi alumni Chet Webster and Dennis Burnham. Concerning the number of men involved in the revival of Omicron, I have not been able to determine an exact figure, as the number varies depending on the source. However, the average quoted number is about 30 men. On the efforts of Phi Epsilon Pi to run their fraternity differently, see "March of Dimes Drive Set," *TO*, October 3, 1969; "Fraternity Profile," *TO*, March 13, 1970; and "Commentary–R. Rosenberg–Once Again," *TO*, March 27, 1970. Co-ed dormitories first came to Tufts at the start of the 1970–71 school year, according to "Co-educational Dorms Approved," *TO*, March 6, 1970. Co-ed dining halls arrived around this same time as well. I am unsure exactly when Omicron's charter was returned, but the article "Phi Epsilon Pi Reopens; Frosh Seek Frat Status" mentions the national organization planned to return the charter in the fall of 1969.

379. On the transfer of 8 Winthrop Street from Phi Epsilon Pi Fraternity, Inc. to the Trustees of Tufts College on July 10, 1969, see Massachusetts Land Records, Middlesex South Registry, Book 11717, Page 289. This deed mentions Phi Epsilon Pi Fraternity, Inc. became the owner of the property on December 4, 1964, as recorded in Massachusetts Land Records, Middlesex South Registry, Book 10853, Page 378. How-

ever, the deed on Page 378 is unrelated to this transaction, so it appears this reference is in error. On the details of the rent increase, see press release from Tufts University News Bureau, unsigned and undated, but context places it after the spring of 1970, in Activities and Organizations records, 1875–2013, UA 024.001 Box 4, Folder 4 (Fraternities 1956–1971).

380. Press release as referenced above. Also, I am basing the information in the next three paragraphs on personal interviews with Phi Epsilon Pi alumni who were active at the time, including Dennis Burnham and Chet Webster. Concerning the precarious financial situation of Phi Epsilon Pi Fraternity, Inc., some of what I have written is projection on my part, as I have found little documented evidence on this topic. The AJHS–PhiEp archives, for example, are only complete to 1957. However, in 1970, Phi Epsilon Pi Fraternity merged with the national Zeta Beta Tau Fraternity. This merger is discussed in detail in "ZBT, Phi Epsilon Pi to Merge As Fraternities Unite Nationally," *The Cornell Daily Sun*, February 2, 1970, and here, the author writes a main reason for the merger was, "the fraternity [Phi Epsilon Pi] has sought financial help from ZBT." Therefore, I feel confident that Phi Epsilon Pi was indeed in dire straits financially by the end of the 1960s. Otherwise, I cannot understand why they would sell 8 Winthrop Street or misappropriate Omicron's money as they did.

381. Ibid.

382. Ibid, with quotation from a Phi Epsilon Pi alumnus. The fraternities that closed down at Tufts during the early 1970s were Phi Epsilon Pi, Alpha Epsilon Pi, Phi Sigma Kappa, and Alpha Tau Omega, though the latter two reformed as co-ed, local fraternities.

383. Sanua, *Here's to Our Fraternity*, 251, 255–257, 269–271, 297.

384. On the troubles concerning the acquisition, and examples of alumni unease over the process, see Sanua, *Here's To Our Fraternity*, 269–271. On the effort to start a ZBT chapter at Tufts in 1977, see advertisements in *TT*, October 12, 1977; and *TO*, October 28, 1977. The claim that the older Omicron alumni were not all that interested in restarting as ZBT at Tufts is based on interviews with those who did establish ZBT at Tufts in 1987. These men mentioned that no Omicron alumni played any part in their effort.

385. Interview with Hugh Bassewitz (February 23, 2012). Alpha Epsilon Pi, although it has officially been open to men of all religions for decades, still retains a strong emphasis on its Jewish heritage. Indeed, as they proclaim on their national website, "Alpha Epsilon Pi is a Jewish fraternity." Zeta Beta Tau, which has been officially non-sectarian since 1954, also looks to "preserve and cultivate its relationships within the Jewish community," according to the mission statement on its national website. In the spring of 1987, there were ten active fraternities on campus. However, rush week was not standardized at the time, so it is possible that not all ten were recruiting at the time; I can't remember, and there is no record in *The Tufts Daily*.

386. The information for the next few paragraphs was gathered through interviews with many ZBT alumni, including Hugh Bassewitz (February 23, 2012), David Lickstein (February 13, 2012), Eric Shapiro (June 2, 2012), and Corey Ackerman (March 7, 2012). Hugh, David, and Corey were three of the original four members of the colony. As it turned out, at least one other man recruited by the original four had a close relative in ZBT. Personal connections to a specific fraternity are always helpful, especially when a new chapter is starting out and has yet to make a name for itself on campus.

387. Ibid. Before ZBT came to Tufts, nearly every other fraternity chapter operated in secret for a semester or two, until they got their act together and were ready to announce their existence to the general public. But, with liability becoming a huge issue for national fraternities in the 1980s, operating in secret could no longer be tolerated. The other four fraternities that had been recently recognized at Tufts were: Psi Upsilon, Alpha Epsilon Pi, Sigma Phi Epsilon, and Alpha Sigma Phi.

388. A detailed explanation of student and faculty government is beyond the scope of this work (and would probably be rather boring, to be quite honest). Therefore, I have attempted to keep the alphabet soup of agency acronyms to an absolute minimum. Prior to the 1960s, both the Interfraternity Council and the PanHellenic Council (for sororities) ran tight ships when it came to overseeing their respective organizations, especially regarding social activities, recruitment, and discipline. However, this system fell apart amidst the campus turmoil of the late 1960s. Various attempts to restart these two oversight organizations in the 1970s generally went nowhere. The evolution of the IGC as an effective organization is discussed further in Chapter 6. The IGC mentioned in this paragraph was first organized in November of 1986, according to the article, "For Ballou, Greeks: Same Goal, Different Path," *TD*, February 11, 1988. The inability of the IGC to wield power is described and referenced in detail throughout the next few paragraphs.

389. Interview with Hugh Bassewitz (February 23, 2012); and "Greek Recognition in Flux," *TD*, September 18, 1987. On the establishment of the moratorium, see "Z.B.T. Not A Colony," *TD*, April 27, 1987.

390. Interviews with numerous ZBT alumni including Hugh Bassewitz, David Lickstein, and Eric Shapiro. Back in 1948, the Phi Delta fraternity successfully used the argument of being an old fraternity looking to return, to sidestep a similar moratorium enacted by the trustees.

391. Interview with Hugh Bassewitz (February 23, 2012). On the recognition of Alpha Sigma Phi by the TCU-J just prior to the moratorium, see "Greek Recognition in Flux," *TD*, September 18, 1987. On the announcement of the colony, see "New Fraternity Colonized," *TD*, April 24, 1987.

392. "New Fraternity Colonized," *TD*, April 24, 1987, which contains the first quotation. On the response by the IGC, see "Z.B.T. Not A Colony," *TD*, April 27, 1987, which includes the second quotation.

393. The War of Recognition, as I have called it, played out publicly through articles and letters in *The Tufts Daily*. As an undergraduate student at the time, I can remember reading these articles and rooting for ZBT, for they were certainly the David to the administrative Goliath. Also, I personally knew many in ZBT and I wanted to see them succeed. On the attempts by the IGC and the administration to discredit ZBT, see "Greek Recognition in Flux," *TD*, September 18, 1987; "IGC To Vote on Moratorium," *TD*, September 25, 1987; "IGC Upholds Moratorium," *TD*, October 1, 1987; "Judiciary Cannot Recognize ZBT," *TD*, October 20, 1987; and "Greek Council Asserts Recognition Authority," *TD*, October 22, 1987. On ZBT's deployment of the thesaurus, see their rush advertisement, *TD*, September 21, 1987, which include the quotations. On the granting of recognition to ZBT, see "Judiciary Recognizes ZBT," *TD*, October 23, 1987. The personal photos accompanying these articles are somewhat humorous, with Deans Knable and Reitman sporting big smiles, while Hugh displays only a big frown. I am probably overstating the role of *The Tufts Daily* in the debate, but

to this day, many ZBT alumni involved in the process are still bitter over the way they were portrayed in various articles, as they felt their side of the story was not adequately covered.

394. On the appeal of the IGC to the CSL, see "CSL Tables Recognition Appeal," *TD*, November 4, 1987. While some of the technical arguments in the appeal are discussed in this article, a more thorough list is given in "Judiciary Cannot Recognize ZBT," *TD*, October 20, 1987. On ZBT's attempt to mitigate the situation by calling for dialogue, see "A Call for Cooperation," *TD*, October 26, 1987. On the IGC's response, see "Denying Power," *TD*, October 27, 1987. On the decision by the CSL and subsequent moratorium, see "CSL Upholds ZBT Recognition," *TD*, November 12, 1987. As evidenced in these articles, the IGC president in particular was greatly upset with ZBT and their actions, for she felt they were undermining everything the IGC was trying to accomplish. However, aside from denying ZBT the use of certain words, the IGC wasn't exactly accomplishing much at the time. They still didn't even have a constitution in place.

395. On the creation of the CFS and subsequent full recognition of ZBT, see "ZBT Gains recognition," *TD*, November 15, 1988, which includes the quotation. On the granting of the charter, see "ZBT Receives National Charter," *TD*, November 2, 1989. Although some of the original colony members had graduated by this point, all were able to make it back to campus for the installation ceremony.

396. The ban on fraternity houses in Medford is discussed in detail later in this chapter, in the section on Alpha Epsilon Pi. On the lack of housing as a reason for the original IGC moratorium, see "Z.B.T. Not A Colony," *TD*, April 27, 1987; and "Greek recognition in Flux," *TD*, September 18, 1987.

397. On the publication of ZBT's address, see for example "Fraternity Rush–Coming Events," *TD*, September 19, 1989, which lists 22–24 Packard Avenue as the fraternity's address. The ban on the occupation of unofficial chapter houses was put into effect in 1988 when the IGC developed its constitution and became a governing organization with some authority. These efforts are discussed in more detail in chapter 6.

398. Dr. Seuss, *Oh the Places You'll Go* (New York: Random House, 1990), which includes the quotation. In 1992, the Tufts administration opened 25 Whitfield Road as a chapter house for the Alpha Omicron Pi sorority (it had been privately rented since the late 1970s). More information on this can be found in their section within chapter 4. On the occupancy of 126 Packard Avenue by Phi Sigma Sigma, see their section in chapter 4.

399. On the decision to finally house AEPi and ZBT, see "ZBT and AEPi Will Move Into On-Campus Houses by Next Fall," *TD*, February 22, 1995. On the dissolution of Phi Sigma Sigma and subsequent housing assignments for ZBT and AEPi, see "Phi Sigma Sigma Will Be Dissolved This Year," *TD*, March 28, 1995. On the housing of AEPi, see their section later in this chapter.

400. On the abolishment of pledging, see "ZBT's No-Pledging Policy First In Nation," *TD*, September 11, 1989. For an overview of pledging within national fraternities, see Syrett, 152–154, 246–247. Some other national fraternities that have abolished pledging include Lambda Chi Alpha, Alpha Gamma Rho, Sigma Phi Epsilon, and Sigma Alpha Epsilon, which just recently enacted this policy in 2014. Professor Carpenter is listed as residing at 126 Packard Avenue in various correspondence from the 1950s as housed in UA, Russell Carpenter Papers 1833–2012, Personal Papers, 1938–1969,

MS041.004 Box 10, Folder 13 (Zeta Psi). On the legacy of Carpenter House at 8 Winthrop St., see "Carpenter House, 1940," *Concise Encyclopedia of Tufts History*, http://hdl.handle.net/10427/14829 (accessed November 30, 2014).

401. Miller, *LOTH–1*, 208–240. The medical and dental schools also, on occasion, included their information alongside the undergraduates in the annual *Jumbo* yearbook until 1924, when they began independently publishing their own, *The Caduceus*.

402. The evolution of medical and dental fraternities and sororities at Tufts is a fascinating topic unto itself, but unfortunately a proper treatment of the subject is beyond the scope of this work. However, they are worth a quick mention. According to Baird (6st ed. 1905), 365–66, 407, 560, the medical fraternity Alpha Kappa Kappa (for male medical students) was the first to arrive at Tufts in 1893, followed by Alpha Delta (for female medical students) in 1894, and Psi Omega (for male dental students) in 1895. Nearly three decades later, the roster of medical and dental fraternities had grown to eleven, according to Baird (10th ed. 1923), 823. As discussed in chapter 5 under the section for Alpha Phi Alpha, there were some dental students who played for the Tufts football team in the mid 1910s, but in general there was almost no coordinated interaction between the professional students in Boston and the undergraduates in Medford at this time.

403. On the early history of Tau Epsilon Phi, see the website of the national organization, http://www.tep.org/the-story-of-tep (accessed December 7, 2014). The date of the fateful meeting was October 19, 1910. For more information on the Jewish fraternity movement in New York City, see Sanua, *Going Greek*, chapters 1–3.

404. Ibid. On the expansion of Tau Epsilon Phi, see also Baird (10th ed. 1923), 354–356. This was the first time Tau Epsilon Phi was mentioned in *Baird's Manual of American College Fraternity* (they were not listed in the 1915 or 1920 editions).

405. Ibid; and Suntag, *The History of Tau Epsilon Phi*, 40–41.

406. Suntag, 40–41; and *CofTC* (1917–18 ed.), 254, which lists both a Mark Manuel Burke from Providence, RI, and Marcus Francis Burke from Clinton, MA as second year dental students. In his book, Suntag clearly spells the first name as "Mark," but he also says this gentleman was from Boston, not Providence. Therefore, it seems there is a chance the first Chancellor may indeed have been Marcus Burke. Inquiries to the Tau Epsilon Phi national organization on the subject of Eta's founding were not returned. As it turned out, the group from BU was inducted into Tau Epsilon Phi as its Theta chapter a few months later.

407. Suntag, 40–41. On the earliest record of undergraduates in Eta chapter, see the list of Tau Epsilon Phi members in *The Caduceus* (1924 ed.), which states there were two undergraduates along with 29 medical and dental students in the chapter that year. On the intermingling of students from the two campuses, I did not perform an in-depth study of this phenomenon, so I am not sure what was the first organization to bridge the campus gap. As mentioned earlier in these notes, I know there were at least a few professional students who played on Tufts College varsity sports teams around this same time, so this was certainly another avenue that brought the students together, albeit on a very limited basis. On the operations of Eta chapter during its first few years, see, for example, "Tau Epsilon Phi 'Frat' Has Luncheon and Dance," *BG*, May 2, 1919, which mentions a new house for the Tufts, BU, and Harvard chapters of TEP had just opened at 234 Newbury Street in Boston; and "Tau Epsilon Phi Holds Its Annual Smoker," *BG*, March 5, 1921.

408. Ibid.

409. Ibid. On the evolution of admission requirements for the medical and dental schools, see Miller, *LOTH–1*, section 8.3. Dual membership in social fraternities has been frowned upon since the mid 1800s, as discussed in Syrett, 46–50, and "University Societies," *The University Magazine* 10, no. 1 (March 1894): 216. The practice was eventually banned by each national organization starting in the late 19th and early 20th century. For example, see "The Fraternity Hyphenate," *The Phi Gamma Delta* 39, no. 3 (December 1916): 224–225; "Acacia Definitely Abolishes Dual Membership," *Banta's Greek Exchange* 9, no. 3 (July 1921): 149; and "Concerning Transfers Of Membership," *The Omegan* 10, no. 1 (March 1933): 9–10. On the acceptance of membership in both a social and a professional fraternity, see "The Fraternity Hyphenate."

410. Ibid. On the decline of membership within Eta chapter, see the 1924–27 editions of *The Caduceus*, all of which contain information about the fraternity, including the names of all chapter members and their courses of study. In summary: 1924, 31 total members, with 2 undergraduates; 1925, 19 total members, with 2 undergraduates; 1926, 19 total members, with 3 undergraduates; 1927, 19 total members, 0 undergraduates. On the move of Eta chapter to 11 Fairmount St., see *The Caduceus* (1928 ed.), which lists 31 total members, including 15 new undergraduates and one new medical student. Five of these undergraduates are also listed as living at 11 Fairmount St., in *CofTC* (1927–28 ed.), 265–277. On TEP's pursuit of recognition on the Medford campus, see "Jewish Fraternity Now Has 16 Active Chapters," *BG*, April 30, 1929. Although this article clearly states it was the undergraduate-run IFC that decided not to allow any more Jewish fraternities on campus, I strongly suspect members of the Tufts administration influenced this decision, especially President John Cousens. Back in 1922, he had openly stated that he did not want more Jewish fraternities and sororities on campus, for he feared they'd attract Jews in larger number to Tufts. This incident is discussed further in chapter 6 under the section for Alpha Epsilon Phi.

411. Suntag, 40–41. On the moratorium barring any new fraternities from the Medford campus, see "Jewish Fraternity Now Has 16 Active Chapters," *BG*, April 30, 1929, which includes the quotation. I am assuming TEP gave up its chapter house based on information in the *CofTC* (1928–29 ed.), which does not list any student living at 11 Fairmount St. Instead, all of the known members of TEP are listed as residing in different dormitories that year. Suntag, in his history of the chapter, mentions a few men joined Eta chapter after that first school year in Medford (1927–28), but he does not say if these were undergraduates or medical/dental students. Finally, the closing of TEP marked the beginning of a downturn in fraternities at Tufts College, mainly due to the Great Depression. By 1935, three other chapters had joined TEP in dormancy.

412. The information for the next few paragraphs was gathered through interviews with many Tau Phi and TEP alumni including Lewis Smoler (September 19, 2011, and November 23, 2011), Musawwir Spiegel (September 9, 2011), and Earle Yaffa (February 7, 2011, and February 21, 2011). As it turned out, Delta Tau Delta did announce their membership restrictions to the campus at the start of rush week via an article on the *Tufts Weekly*. However, it appears Lewis did not see this article. See "Fraternity Season Opens," *TW*, October 21, 1955. On the restrictive membership practices within Delta Tau Delta, see their section earlier in this chapter.

413. Ibid. Although I stand by the second sentence of this paragraph as written, I feel I must clarify its meaning. Of the eight non-Jewish fraternities on campus in the

fall of 1955, only three had official clauses barring Jewish men: DTD, Sigma Nu, and Alpha Tau Omega. The remaining fraternities – Zeta Psi, Theta Delta Chi, Delta Upsilon, Alpha Sigma Phi, and Beta Chi – did not have official restrictions against Jews, but from what I understand, they also didn't exactly roll out the red carpet for them. Instead, men who were openly Jewish and wanted to join a Tufts fraternity in 1955 (or earlier, for that matter) were expected to make their way to either Phi Epsilon Pi or Alpha Epsilon Pi. There were undoubtedly a few Jewish men scattered about these other eight fraternities at the time, but chances are, they were not very overt about their religion. Finally, I mentioned Leslie Gelb in this section, as he eventually went on to become an advisor to two U.S. presidents, an esteemed writer for *The New York Times*, and president of the Council on Foreign Affairs.

414. Ibid. Concerning the Tau Epsilon Phi alumnus who helped re-organize his fraternity, Lewis Smoler remembered his name as Dr. Isadore Cohen. However, Eta chapter membership lists in the 1924 through 1928 editions of *The Caduceus* (which are not complete, by any means), did not mention this exact name. Rather, Dr. Julian Cohen and Dr. Isadore Coriat are listed as a fraternity members of the faculty. Unfortunately, the national offices of Tau Epsilon Phi did not respond to my request for information regarding early members of Eta chapter, which could have helped sort out this confusion. Therefore, I decided to report the name as remembered by Lewis.

415. On the early activities of Tau Phi, including its application to the IFC and the faculty, see "Beta Chi Brothers Moving Into Packard Avenue House," *TW*, September 21, 1956. On Tau Phi becoming a recognized local fraternity, see "Tau Phi Attains Local Standing," *TW*, May 3, 1957. Also see Suntag, 40, although this particular history contains a number of factual errors concerning dates.

416. On Tau Epsilon Phi's change to its constitution so it was no longer a Jewish fraternity, see Suntag, 199. This change was fortuitous, because by the mid 1950s, the Tufts administration would not allow any new fraternity on campus that had official, restrictive membership policies. Those on campus with such practices were allowed to remain in operation, for now, but no new ones could start. Therefore, had Lewis instead courted a fraternity still bound to the Jewish faith, his efforts would have failed out of the gate.

417. On the occupying of rooms in West Hall, see *Jumbo* (1958 ed.). Information about the crest, ritual, and active pin of Tau Phi was provided by Tau Phi alumni who were active at the time, including Lewis Smoler, Musawwir Spiegel, and Earle Yaffa. However, it does not appear that the use of ritual and secrecy were a major component of Tau Phi's operations.

418. Interview with Lewis Smoler (September 19, 2011). The failure to buy the house was a minor issue at the time, but it would soon become a major headache for the chapter, as will be discussed in later paragraphs.

419. "I.F.C. Admits Tau Phi," *TW*, March 26, 1958; and "TEP Reactivated On Hill; Twelfth National Here," *TW*, May 16, 1948. On the scholastic accomplishments of Tau Phi and Tau Epsilon Phi, see various grade reports in Activities and Organizations records, 1875–2013, UA 024.001 Box 4, Folder 4 (Fraternities 1956–1971).

420. Interview with Lewis Smoler (September 19, 2011).

421. Although this is somewhat speculative, I believe TEP never got an on-chapter campus house because the chapter never gained the favor of Joel Reynolds, the long-time DTD alumni advisor and promoter extraordinaire of the fraternity system in

general. If he had supported TEP (as he had the other three fraternities mentioned), I have no doubt the IFC president's ban would have been rendered moot, and the administration would have found a house on campus for the fraternity. But, apparently, Mr. Reynolds never had any desire to work with TEP. As for why, I can only assume he did not like the men, or the Tau Epsilon Phi national fraternity, or both.

422. On the use of 98 Electric Avenue as an unofficial chapter house, see Tau Epsilon Phi's section in *Jumbo* (1959 ed.), 206–207; and *Jumbo* (1960 ed.). I also spoke with some TEP alumni who lived at 98 Electric Avenue, including Musawwir Spiegel. On the purchase of 9 Teele Avenue, see Suntag, 41; and "T E P Purchases Fraternity House," *TW*, October 14, 1960.

423. Suntag, 41; and "T E P Purchases Fraternity House." Details about the firing of the cook during the spring of 1961 were provided in interviews with alumni who lived in the house that first year, including Earle Yaffa.

424. On the scholastic success of TEP, see the fraternity grade reports from this era as housed in Activities and Organizations records, 1875–2013, UA 024.001 Box 4, Folder 4 (Fraternities 1956–1971). On the recruitment struggles, see Suntag, 41.

425. As discussed in the earlier section on Delta Tau Delta, the early 1960s marked the first time an openly Jewish man joined a non-Jewish fraternity at Tufts. This event seemed to open the doors for other Jewish men to follow. On the selling of the chapter house and closing down of TEP, see Suntag, 41; and "TEP National To Sell Local House; Brotherhood Continues Activity Here," *TW*, September 20, 1963. Suntag claims the chapter was down to five active members when the house was sold, whereas the article in the *Tufts Weekly* says there were still sixteen active members. Of course, Suntag also has the year of the house sale listed as 1964, not 1963. Therefore, I suspect the number of active members in the fall of 1963 is probably closer to sixteen than five. Either way, this was too few to fill the twenty beds in the house.

426. On the total number of Eta chapter initiates, see Suntag, 41. On the chapter roll of Tau Epsilon Phi, see their national website, http://www.tep.org/chapters/chapter-roll (accessed December 21, 2014). All together, Tau Epsilon Phi has chartered around 140 chapters, though it never had more than about 50 active at any one time. On the initial lawsuit by the alumni, see "Tau Epsilon Phi, Founded 100 years Ago at Columbia, Is Convulsed By a Lawsuit," *NYT*, November 21, 2010, which includes the quotation. On the filing of Chapter 7 bankruptcy, see "A Fraternity's Fight Could Lead to Its End," *NYT*, January 28, 2011; and "Amid Controversy, TEP National Organization Files For Bankruptcy," *The Cornell Daily Sun*, January 23, 2011.

427. "Settlement End Bitter Infighting at a Fraternity," *NYT*, July 22, 2011. The settlement is described at http://www.graberfirm.com/wp-content/uploads/2011/07/SETTLEMENT-AGREEMENT-FINAL1.pdf (accessed December 21, 2014).

428. The arrival of the S.A.T.C. to the Tufts Campus is described in earlier sections within this chapter, as well as Miller, *LOTH–1*, 480–487. Adding to the overall dismay of the Tufts administration was the sudden resignation of the president, Hermon Bumpus, which took effect in early 1919.

429. "Beta Tau, Newest Local, Joins Hill Fraternities," *TW*, December 10, 1919; "New Fraternity Being Organized at Tufts," *BG*, December 11, 1919; and "Beta Kappa" in *Jumbo* (1934 ed.). On the resurgence of fraternities at Tufts in early 1919, see "Frats Make Debut," *TW*, January 8, 1919. Note many of their initials of the ten charter members were reported incorrectly in the *Boston Globe* article. Therefore, I have ratio-

nalized the names based upon the roll of students in *CofTC* (1919–20 ed.), 261–264. Here, all ten are listed as sophomores in the engineering school. In the fall of 1919, Alfred and Frank lived in 23 East Hall, Jeremiah and William lived in 2 West Hall, and Maurice and Everett lived in 34 East Hall. The remaining members were commuters.

430. On the occupation of the chapter house, see "New Fraternity Being Organized at Tufts"; and *CofTC* (1920–21 ed.), 258–281. Also, a photograph of the structure appears in Beta Tau's section of *The Elephas*, 25, and this house is clearly 13 Fairmount Street. It is unknown how long Beta Tau kept its policy of open membership in place, but in all likelihood the practice ended for good once Beta Tau affiliated with the national Beta Kappa fraternity, as Beta Kappa was known to have restrictive membership policies. See "It Might Have Been Beta Kappa Nu," *Cross & Crescent* 94, no. 6 (June 2008): 7–9. The sizes of the fraternity chapters and the Tufts Commons Club have been estimated from their respective group photographs in the *Jumbo* (1922 ed.). On the move to 151 College Avenue, see "Beta Tau Fraternity, Tufts College, Buys New Quarters," *BG*, March 23, 1922, which includes the quotation.

431. The issue of honorary membership into a fraternity or sorority is beyond the scope of this work, but suffice to say the practice is not as widespread now as it used to be in the early 20th century. On the initiation of General Edwards, see "Maj Gen Edwards Joins Beta Tau Of Tufts," *BG*, December 12, 1922. Unfortunately, I have not been able to determine a direct link between any one member of Beta Tau and the 26th Infantry Division or General Edwards, but I assume there must have been one. It appears that General Edwards was the only honorary initiate of Beta Tau.

432. Although the story of General Edwards is somewhat askew to this work, I decided to include it because I found it so interesting. Much of the information on General Edwards comes from Michael Shay, *Revered Commander, Maligned General: The Life of Clarence Ransom Edwards, 1859–1931* (Columbia, MO: University of Missouri Press, 2011); and the biographical sketch in the collection guide summary, Clarence Ransom Edwards papers, Massachusetts Historical Society, http://www.masshist.org/collection-guides/view/fa0323 (accessed December 29, 2014).

433. Ibid. For the quotation, see the biographical sketch, Clarence Ransom Edwards papers, Massachusetts Historical Society. On the backlash over the demotion of General Edwards just before the end of the war, see "General Edwards' Friends Want Inquiry," *NYT*, December 9, 1918.

434. By 1925, at least two other local fraternities at Tufts, Sigma Tau Alpha and the Tufts Commons Club, had sought affiliation with large national fraternities, but both were unsuccessful despite numerous attempts. I suspect these failures may have been one reason why Beta Tau avoided courting the larger ones. On Delta Sigma Phi's attempt to place a chapter at Tufts, see letter from R. P. Ashley of Delta Sigma Phi to President Cousens dated January 7, 1920, in Activities and Organizations records, 1875–2013, UA 024.001 Box 4, Folder 4 (Fraternities 1956–1971). On Beta Tau's petition to Beta Kappa, see letter from President Cousens dated March 9, 1925, in Activities and Organizations records, 1875–2013, UA 024.001 Box 2, Folder 2 (Beta Kappa 1925–1928), which includes the quotation. On the installation of Theta chapter, see "Theta Chapter" *Beta Kappa Journal* 2, (1925): 19–20. Note that while Beta Tau was the first local fraternity at Tufts to gain national affiliation, four local sororities at Tufts had already accomplished this feat decades earlier.

435. On the educational odyssey of D. Paul Rader, see his biography in the collec-

tion guide for Ephemera of Daniel Paul Rader, Collection 38, Billy Graham Center Archives, http://www2.wheaton.edu/bgc/archives/GUIDES/038.htm#3 (accessed December 30, 2014). On the history of Central College, see http://www.centralmethodist.edu/about/history.php (accessed December 29, 2014). Central College is now known as Central Methodist University.

436. On the history of Beta Lambda chapter of Sigma Nu at Central College, see Scott, 328–329. The prohibition against joining a fraternity is also listed in *Catalogue of Central College, Fayette, MO* (1899–1900 ed.), 71–72. Bob McCully, the Grand Historian of Sigma Nu, confirmed D. Paul Rader's initiation into Sigma Nu as the 44th member of Beta Lambda chapter. On D. Paul Rader's transfer to Hamline University where he was both a student and faculty member, see *Catalogue of Hamline University* (1901–02 ed.), 7, 12.

437. On the founding of Beta Kappa, see "Beta Kappa Fraternity, 1901–1942," *The Rattle of Theta Chi* 31, no. 2 (December 1942): 20–22. D. Paul Rader, as it turned out, never graduated from Hamline University. He instead became a Congregational minister in 1904, only to resign his faith a few years later. In 1912, though, he experienced an epiphany of faith on a business trip to New York City. From there, Rev. Rader became a world-renown evangelical preacher, and he was one of the first to use mass media such as radio to reach his audience. He passed away in 1938.

438. On Beta Kappa's unhappiness with 151 College Avenue, see correspondence between Beta Kappa alumni and President Cousens dated October 12, 1927, and October 18, 1927, in Activities and Organizations records, 1875–2013, UA 024.001 Box 2, Folder 2 (Beta Kappa 1925–1928), which contains the quotation.

439. On Beta Kappa's pledge to uphold the ban on liquor transportation, and President Cousen's subsequent approval, see correspondence between Edward Wright, Beta Kappa scribe, and President Cousens, dated May 20, 1928, to May 22, 1928, in Activities and Organizations records, 1875–2013, UA 024.001 Box 2, Folder 2 (Beta Kappa 1925–1928). On the hidden still, see "A. E. Pi's Find Old Still; Reconstruction Planned," *TW*, February 20, 1941.

440. The decline in Beta Kappa's membership is documented in composite photographs the chapter submitted to various editions of the *Jumbo* yearbook. For example, the *Jumbo* (1931 ed.) shows 35 members in the chapter. By the spring of 1934, which was the last time Beta Kappa made an appearance in the *Jumbo*, the chapter was down to 14 members. The exact date of Beta Kappa's demise was apparently not recorded (such events rarely are), but they did not report any pledges, according to "Pledges Announced By Fraternities," *TW*, October 11, 1934, so I am assuming this is roughly when they shut down. According to the campus maps as published in *CofTC*, the Sigma Omega Psi fraternity moved into 151 College Avenue starting in the fall of 1935.

441. "Beta Kappa Fraternity Joins Theta Chi," *The Rattle of Theta Chi* 30, no. 5 (April–May 1942): 3–4; "Beta Kappa Fraternity, 1901–1942," *The Rattle of Theta Chi* 31, no. 2 (December 1942): 20–22; and "Merger of Beta Kappa with Theta Chi Fraternity Six Decades Past," *The Rattle of Theta Chi* 82, no. 1 (Spring 2002): 28–29. This last referenced article is mostly a reprint of excerpts from 1942 about the merger, as published in both *The Rattle of Theta Chi* and the *Beta Kappa Journal*.

442. Ibid. On the mergers of other national organizations, see for example, "Beta Kappa Fraternity, 1901–1942." This article also discusses some of the smaller national fraternities that had closed down completely in the wake of the Depression. On the

proposed merger between Beta Kappa and Theta Kappa Nu, see "It Might Have Been Beta Kappa Nu."

443. Ibid. For quotation, see "Beta Kappa Fraternity Joins Theta Chi." Theta Chi was founded in 1856 at Norwich University in Vermont by Arthur Chase and Frederick Norton Freeman. Like Beta Kappa, Theta Chi remained local to its home campus for decades. In 1902, Theta Chi established a second chapter at MIT. The fraternity then began expanding in earnest around 1907, as it added three or four new chapters a year until the Depression slowed its growth. Its merger with Beta Kappa was the second largest in history, to that point in time.

444. On the reluctance of some Beta Kappa alumni to join Theta Chi, see Alfred Grant's excerpt in "Merger of Beta Kappa with Theta Chi Fraternity Six Decades Past." Also, the chapter of Beta Kappa at the Georgia Institute of Technology opted not to join Theta Chi after the merger. Instead, they resigned from Beta Kappa, formed a new local organization called Alpha Gamma, and joined the national Lambda Chi Alpha fraternity as its Beta–Kappa Zeta chapter in the fall of 1942. From what I understand, none of the symbols, rituals, or secrets of Beta Kappa were preserved in the merger with Theta Chi.

445. For a biography of Professor Nichols, see "Nichols, Robert L., 1904–1995," *Concise Encyclopedia of Tufts History*, http://hdl.handle.net/10427/14829 (accessed January 6, 2015). On the formation of the colony and its early history, see "IFC Bans A Local Theta Chi Chapter," *TW*, May 13, 1955. Also, information in this and the following paragraphs was gathered through interviews of Theta Chi alumni, including John Reid (May 28, 2011, and February 25, 2013), Warren "Biff" Manhard (May 26; May 27; June 24; and June 28, 2011), Tom Rockett (May 28, 2011), Ed Farley (October 16, 2011), and Ron Grant (June 18, 2011, and August 7, 2011). The story of Alfred Grant pinning Robert Nichols as a pledge was provided by his son, Ronald Grant. As testament to the influence of Professor Nichols, both John Reid and Tom Rockett would go on to careers as geology professors.

446. "IFC Bans A Local Theta Chi Chapter." I do find it interesting that Dean Emery helped in recruitment. I can think of no other instance where such a high level Tufts administrator was involved in the initial organization of a fraternity.

447. I was fortunate to speak with Theta Chi alumni who were so forthright and open about this issue, as their side of the story was not, in my opinion, adequately reflected in Miller, *LOTH–2*, 210. Every alumnus I spoke with affirmed his disdain for the restrictive membership policy of Theta Chi, and they were eager to take up the fight once they were an official part of the fraternity.

448. "Council, I.F.C. Reject Theta Chi Constitution," *TW*, April 22, 1955; and "IFC Bans A Local Theta Chi Chapter." The story of the fight against restrictive membership clauses in fraternities at Tufts is covered in more detail in Chapter 6.

449. "IFC Bans A Local Theta Chi Chapter."

450. On Beta Chi's move to rooms in West Hall, see "Guest Speakers and Parties Highlight Rushing Programs," *TW*, October 28, 1955. Information about Beta Chi's activities during the school year was provided by numerous alumni who were active in the chapter at the time.

451. Details of Albert Simone's efforts to secure the house were provided by other Beta Chi alumni. On the renovation and then occupancy of 100 Packard Avenue, see "Beta Chi Brothers Moving Into Packard Ave. House," *TW*, September 21, 1956. Al-

though it appears Tufts was open to selling the house to the fraternity at the time, this sale never happened, and I suspect it never will. The era when fraternities could buy houses on campus is long gone.

452. The incident involving the Alpha Theta chapter of Theta Chi made national news at the time, as the awareness over civil rights began to grow in the country. See "Dartmouth Society Drops Bias Clause," *NYT*, April 26, 1952; "Dartmouth Theta Chi Votes To Ignore Nat'l Bias Clause," *The Cornell Daily Sun*, May 1, 1952; "Dartmouth Frat Removes 'Caucasian Clause'," *Jet* 2, no. 2 (May 8, 1952): 21; "Charter Is Revoked," *NYT*, July 28, 1952; and "Dartmouth Frat Bucks Bias, Ousted," *Jet* 2, no. 15 (August 7, 1952): 31. A few years later, undergraduates in the Theta Chi chapter at Lafayette took up the issue, and their efforts led to the repeal of the clause in 1957. On the announcement to Tufts that Theta Chi had removed its restrictive membership clause, see correspondence between George Chapman, Executive Director of Theta Chi, and Dean Emery between June 3, 1957 and June 5, 1957, in Activities and Organizations records, 1875–2013, UA 024.001 Box 4, Folder 4 (Fraternities 1956–1971).

453. "Theta Chi Becomes 11th National Fraternity On Hill," *TW*, September 27, 1957; and "Tufts Home of 121st Unit," *The Rattle of Theta Chi* 46, no. 1 (Fall 1957): 9–10. In hindsight, I wish someone had sat down with Mr. Lewis on the night of the installation to hear his story of how Beta Tau came to be.

454. On the operations of Theta Chi in the 1970s and 1980s, see "Good News About Fraternities," *TO*, October 27, 1972; "IFC Corner," *TD*, October 14, 1982; and "IFC Corner–Theta Chi," *TD*, October 24, 1983. On the membership issues in 1998, see "Spring Rush Ends With Much Success," *TD*, February 11, 1998.

455. "Theta Chi Experiences House Fire," *TD*, October 10, 2013.

456. On the founding of Phi Beta Delta and chapter roll, see Baird (10th ed. 1923), 220–222. According to Andy Gilbert of the national Pi Lambda Phi fraternity, the Xi chapter of Phi Beta Delta was organized sometime in 1921. However, the exact date is no longer known since the early records of Phi Beta Delta have been lost. On the founding members of Xi chapter, see *The Elephas*, 26. Here, I am assuming all six men pictured in the fraternity composite were the founders of the chapter. For the graduation years and hometowns of the six men, see *CofTC* (1920–21 ed.), 260, 277, 291, 295, 297. Note that in *The Elephas*, Samuel Gordon is listed as a 1920 graduate of Tufts College. However, this is not completely correct, since he was only given a War Certificate in 1920, which was "Granted to Tufts men who do not hold the Tufts degree and who served in the forces of the United States during the Great War," according to *CofTC* (1920–21 ed.), 252.Samuel did eventually graduate Tufts College in the spring of 1922, according to *CofTC* (1922–23 ed.), 250, 254 and *Jumbo* (1922 ed.), 36. Therefore, I have chosen to signify Samuel as being from the class of 1922.

457. For mention of Phi Beta Delta at Tufts College, see "Theta Chapter – Tufts College, Massachusetts," *Beta Kappa Journal* 2, (1925): 20; "Miss Yankelewitz and Jacob Shapiro Married," *BG*, June 22, 1925; "Phi Beta Delta Conference Ends," *BG*, February 24, 1929; and "Jewish Fraternity Now Has 16 Active Chapters," *BG*, April 30, 1929, which mentions Xi chapter had less than ten members and did not occupy a chapter house. On the alumni activities, see "Dr. Seplow to Marry Daisy Derfner Today," *BG*, March 5, 1933, which mentions Dr. Seplow was still quite active in Phi Beta Delta affairs, and a number of his fraternity brothers would be attending the wedding. There are also references to the Boston alumni group of Phi Beta Delta in old editions

of the fraternity's national magazine, *The Tripod*, but unfortunately I only have access to a small portion of these journals through Google Books, so I cannot examine the contents in full or provide a complete journal reference. On a biography of Max Tishler, see *Chemical & Engineering News* 86, no. 14 (April 7, 2008), http://pubs.acs.org/cen/priestley/recipients/1970tishler.html (accessed January 12, 2015). Dr. Tishler is listed as a member of the Massachusetts Xi chapter, Pi Lambda Phi fraternity, on the organization's website, http://www.pilambdaphi.org/site/c.plKXL7MPIqG/b.8066301/ (accessed January 12, 2015). However, Dr. Tishler was initiated into the Xi chapter of Phi Beta Delta sometime between 1924 and 1928, which were the years he was listed as a student in the *CofTC.*

458. On the total number of initiates, see Baird (11th ed. 1927), 137, which has the number at twenty-eight, and Baird (14th ed. 1940), 150, which has the number at thirty. Baird's manuals, however, are notoriously inaccurate when it comes to information of this sort. The closing date of 1930 for Xi chapter is listed in Baird (14th ed. 1940), 150, and was confirmed by Andy Gilbert of the national Pi Lambda Phi fraternity. On the merger of the two organizations, see "Pi Lambda Phi and Phi Beta Delta Will Merge," *Lewiston Daily Sun*, December 23, 1940. According to Andy Gilbert of the national Pi Lambda Phi fraternity, the official closing date of the merger was February 1, 1941. After the merger, it appears a star from the Phi Beta Delta badge was added to Pi Lambda Phi's badge, to signify the former's history.

459. As discussed in Note 370 for the Phi Epsilon Pi section of this chapter, it appears Tufts did have an official Jewish quota for undergraduates at Tufts College around the time Phi Beta Delta was active. For further information, also see the section on Alpha Epsilon Phi in chapter 6. The four Jewish fraternities at Tufts College during the 1920s were Phi Epsilon Pi, Sigma Omega Psi, Tau Epsilon Phi, and Phi Beta Delta. Tau Epsilon Phi, as it turned out, went dormant shortly after Phi Beta Delta.

460. My claims of prominence within the Jewish fraternity movement, or lack thereof, are opinions and thus are open for debate. However, my reasoning is as follows. The three national fraternities founded at CCNY prior to Sigma Omega Psi were Phi Epsilon Pi (1904), Sigma Alpha Mu (1909), and Tau Delta Phi (1910). Each of these three, within ten to fifteen years of starting, had expanded to schools across the country, and certainly by the 1950s they were well known and well respected organizations within the Jewish collegiate community. For chapter rolls of each, see Sanua, Appendix A. Sigma Omega Psi, on the other hand, did not have nearly as large a reach. On Sigma Omega Psi's chapter roll within its first decade, see *The Pickout* (1920 ed.), 112–113; and *The Pickout* (1925 ed.), 122–123. Additionally, Sigma Omega Psi made very little effort to promote itself in *Baird's Manual of American College Fraternities*, as demonstrated in Baird (10th ed. 1923), 678. This lack of a proper listing one hundred years ago would be equivalent (in my opinion) of not having a website today. In other words, inexcusable. Finally, on Sigma Omega Psi's membership qualification, see *Handbook of Temple University* (1936 ed.), 68, which includes the quotation.

461. On SOP's establishment of its Theta chapter, see "Institute Notes," *The Journal of the Worcester Polytechnic Institute* 22, no. 4 (July 1919): 374, which lists the founding date as May 3, 1919. On SOP's establishment of its Eta chapter, see *The Pickout* (1920 ed.), 113, which gives the founding date as January 23, 1920. On SOP's establishment of its Iota chapter, see *Syllabus* (1925 ed.), 169, which lists the founding year as 1919 (no day or month, however). For some reason, SOP did not assign chapter names in

alphabetical order based on their founding – by convention, "Eta" should have been established before "Theta" and "Iota," yet it was the last of the three. Perhaps, and this is just pure speculation, chapter names were assigned when a petition was first filed, and not when the actual charter was issued. Finally, the Lowell Textile Institute today is known as the University of Massachusetts at Lowell.

462. On the founders of Mu chapter and its early history, see the Sigma Omega Psi section of *Jumbo* (1934 ed.), which includes the quotations, and *Jumbo* (1939 ed.), 130. On the hometowns, majors, and class years of ten of the twelve founding members, see *CofTC* (1920–21 ed.), 273–280. Note that neither Harry Perlmutter nor Myer Stone is listed as a student in the *CofTC* (1920–21 ed.). There is a Samuel M. Perlmutter listed as a first year pre-medical student in *CofTC* (1920–21 ed.), 289, but I am not sure if this is the same person. Regardless, I decided to list the founders as reported in *Jumbo* (1939 ed.), 130. On the founding date of Mu chapter, see "Leery Lines," *TW*, June 8, 1921.

463. On the early meetings of Mu chapter, see "Tufts Sigma Omega Psi Meets," *BG*, March 29, 1922. On the interaction of Mu chapter with its other chapters in Massachusetts, see "Sigma Omega Psi Holds Pledge Dance," *TW*, January 11, 1922; and "Annual Informal Dance of SOP," *TW*, March 1, 1922. Professor Lewis was an interesting choice as a faculty advisor for SOP, since he was a member of a different fraternity, Zeta Psi. See "Lewis, Leo Rich, 1865–1945," *Concise Encyclopedia of Tufts History*, http://hdl.handle.net/10427/14829 (accessed January 22, 2015). On the number of pledges gained by SOP during the 1921–22 school year, see the membership roll in *Jumbo* (1922 ed.), 131. Finally, I am unsure exactly when SOP was recognized by the Tufts Interfraternity Council, but I assume it was early on in the chapter's existence, otherwise their activities would likely not have been reported in the *Tufts Weekly*. SOP was certainly recognized before 1929, according to "Jewish Fraternity Now Has 16 Active Chapter," *BG*, April 30, 1929. Recognition was vitally important for survival, as was discussed earlier in this chapter in the sections on Tau Epsilon Phi and Phi Beta Delta.

464. Letter from Professor Lewis to President Cousens dated October 4, 1922; letter from President Cousens to Professor Lewis dated October 5, 1922; and letter from President Cousens to Bernard Horowitz dated October 5, 1922, in Activities and Organizations records, 1875–2013, UA024.001 Box 13, Folder 10 (Sigma Omega Psi 1922). Why Professor Lewis made such an effort to secure the advice of President Cousens is an interesting question, of which there is no hint of an answer in the documentation that has survived to this day.

465. Letter from President Cousens to Bernard Horowitz, October 11, 1922, which includes the quotation, in Activities and Organizations records, 1875–2013, UA024.001 Box 13, Folder 10 (Sigma Omega Psi 1922). Why President Cousens was against the purchase is not known, though I suspect he was not in complete favor of having a second Jewish fraternity on campus. For more information on this idea, see the section on Alpha Epsilon Phi in chapter 6. There is some confusion as to when, exactly, SOP moved into 890 Broadway Ave. In the campus map of *CofTC* (1922–23 ed.), SOP is shown to be at this address, but in the *Ivy Book* (1922–23 ed.), SOP is not listed as residing in any chapter house. These two publications were known to be issued at different times during the school year, and the *Ivy Book* was also known to re-print the previous year's information on occasion. Therefore, I have deferred to the campus map in the *CofTC*, since, during the 1920s, this map seems to have been updated every year.

466. On the move of SOP to 15 Bellevue St., see campus map in *CofTC* (1926–27 ed.). On SOP's move to 100 Packard Ave., see campus map in *CofTC* (1929–30 ed.). As discussed earlier in this chapter in the section on Theta Chi, 100 Packard Avenue was a duplex at the time SOP occupied the house. On SOP's struggles in the spring of 1935, see letter from Harold Slate, Omicron chapter of Phi Epsilon Pi, to Maurice Jacobs, Executive Secretary of Phi Epsilon Pi dated January 31, 1935; letter from Maurice Jacobs to Harold Slate dated February 2, 1935; letter from Harold Slate to Maurice Jacobs dated February 12, 1935; and letter from Sumner Daniel Charm, Quarterly representative of Omicron Chapter, to the Phi Epsilon Pi Quarterly, May, 1935, which includes the quotation, in AJHS–PhiEp, Box 31, Folder 5 (Omicron–Tufts College).

467. Ibid, with quotation from letter dated February 2, 1935. On the demise of Sigma Omega Psi as a national organization during the Depression, see Toll, *Alpha Epsilon Pi*, 166. This reference states that only four chapters of SOP were active in the mid- to late-1930s, but other references such as the letters in the AJHS–PhiEp archives mention this number was six.

468. On SOP's occupancy of 151 College Ave., see campus map in *CofTC* (1935–36 ed.).

469. *Omichronicle* 1, no. 3 (May–June 1936): 6–7, 9, as housed in AJHS–PhiEp, Box 31, Folder 5 (Omicron–Tufts College), which includes the quotations. According to this article, SOP was also renting out its house as a party space to other organizations on occasion. So, it seems that money was still a problem in SOP, but this time around they managed to stay afloat.

470. I find this story to be one of the most fascinating I've come across, given the stature of Benny Goodman at the time. How the members of Sigma Omega Psi managed to make such a personal connection with Mr. Goodman is a mystery, but at least the outcome was recorded. On Benny Goodman's initiation, see "Goodman Initiated Into Tufts Sigma Omega Psi," *BG*, May 22, 1937, which includes the quotation. Mu chapter members Harold Zimmon and Michael Rossman were responsible for the induction ceremony. On Benny Goodman's concerts in Boston, see "Benny Goodman To Make Debut In Boston At Met," *BG*, May 17, 1937; and "King of Swing Sees It As Boon To Young," *BG*, May 24, 1937. As mentioned in the text, the national Tau Epsilon Phi fraternity claims Benny Goodman as a member of their fraternity, as discussed in "Tau Epsilon Phi, Founded 100 Years Ago At Columbia, Is Convulsed by a Lawsuit," *NYT*, November 21, 2010. Since Mr. Goodman did not attend an undergraduate college, he was most likely an honorary member of Tau Epsilon Phi as well.

471. Toll, 166; and "Sigma Omega Psi Combines With Alpha Epsilon Pi To Form Strong New Chapter," *TW*, November 29, 1940. Although all Sigma Omega Psi alumni were automatically added to the rolls of Alpha Epsilon Pi after the merger, it does not appear that Benny Goodman has ever been acknowledged as being a member of Alpha Epsilon Pi.

472. Toll, 40–41.

473. Toll, 41–42. On the membership restrictions, see Toll, 50. The founders of AEPi did not include any formal restrictions on a religious requirement for membership in their original constitution, but their emphasis on Judaism was abundantly clear, as they felt their fraternity should act as a vehicle to improve the greater Jewish community.

474. Toll, 42–48.

475. On the establishment of Beta chapter, see Toll, 50–52. On the chapter roll of

AEPi through the 1930s, see Sanua, *Going Greek*, 304–305. On the merger of SOP and AEPi, see Toll, 166; and "Sigma Omega Psi Combines With Alpha Epsilon Pi To Form Strong New Chapter."

476. Mu chapter's transformation to Eta Deuteron chapter of AEPi was announced to the campus in the *Tufts Weekly* on February 6, 1941. This article mentioned the actual installation ceremony had been held a couple of months earlier, on December 18, 1940. On AEPi's recruitment following the merger, see Toll, 630–631. The turnaround in PhiEp's attitude from what it had been towards SOP, is based primarily on a lack of criticism of AEPi within PhiEp's alumni newsletters and official correspondence with their national organization. Also, in the years that followed (especially the 1950s), PhiEp and AEPi developed a very healthy competitive relationship, as the two constantly battled one another for top campus honors, more so than any other fraternity on campus.

477. On the commandeering of the other chapter houses during the war, see their sections earlier in this chapter. On AEPi's operations during the war, see Toll, 630–631. Some of the other fraternities remained active throughout the war, but only AEPi continuously occupied a chapter house between 1943 and 1946.

478. On the initiation of Robert Atlas into AEPi and his activities while a student at Tufts College, see Toll, 630. On his letter to *LIFE*, see "Hitler on Kissing," *LIFE* 7, no. 9 (August 28, 1939): 2.

479. The story of Robert Atlas is one that played out for numerous Tufts students during the war. It is a story of profound change, from carefree college student to serious soldier. On Robert's visit to his chapter, see "AEPi Elects; Bob Atlas Visits," *TW*, January 18, 1945. On Robert's sacrifice, see Lawrence S. Smith, ed., *History of the 9th Bombardment Group (VH) 1st, 5th, and 99*th *Squadrons as a B–29 Superfortress Unit In World War II: In Training at McCook AAF, Nebraska and In Combat as a Unit of the 313th Bombardment Wing on Tinian Island in the Marianas under the XXI Bomber Command of the 20th Air Force* (Princeton, NJ: The 9th Bomb Group Association, 1995), 104, 121, 197; and "AEPi Dedicates Room to Bob Atlas, Alumnus Killed In War," *TW*, December 9, 1948. The *Tufts Weekly* article incorrectly states that Lt. Atlas was killed over the island of Okinawa.

480. On AEPi's resurgence after the war, see Toll, 631. On AEPi's loss of 151 College Ave., see press release from Alpha Epsilon Pi, Eta Deuteron Chapter, dated April 29 (no year, but context places it in 1946), and *Eta Deuta Data*, May 12, 1951, in Activities and Organizations records, 1875–2013, UA 024.001 Box 1, Folder 7 (Alpha Epsilon Pi 1922–1967). On AEPi's purchase and occupancy of 10 Dearborn Road, see Toll, 631; and "Fraternity Supplement – Alpha Epsilon Pi," *TW*, October 9, 1947, which mentions the chapter moved in that fall. On the dedication of the chapter room, see "AEPi Dedicates Room to Bob Atlas, Alumnus Killed In War."

481. AEPi's accomplishments during the late 1940s and early 1950s are detailed in full by Toll, 631–633. On the purchase of 6–8 Capen St., see Toll, 633; and "Alpha Epsilon Pi To Buy New House Near Rez," *TW*, November 20, 1952; and "New AEPi House Has Many Modern Features," *TW*, January 14, 1954.

482. While it appears that no African-American men joined the historically white fraternities at Tufts prior to 1952, a number of Latino men did join some of the chapters as far back as 1886 – for example, one of the founding members of the Tufts Delta Upsilon chapter was a Mexican national, and in the early 1900s, the Sigma Tau Alpha

chapter had a Brazilian national among the brotherhood. On the incident at Amherst College, see Syrett, *The Company He Keeps*, 248–249. In the end, the national leaders of Phi Kappa Psi would not allow the initiation of the black man in question, Thomas Gibbs, so the chapter disaffiliated with the national and became the local Phi Alpha Psi fraternity. As an interesting aside, just this year (2014), Amherst College has officially banned Greek organizations from its campus, some 178 years after they were first founded on campus. The pledging of the two African-American men is also discussed earlier in this chapter, within the Phi Epsilon Pi section. Such a bold move, it seems, did not cause any type of racial upheaval or controversy on campus. However, in the composite photo sections for both the Alpha Omicron Pi and Chi Omega sororities in *Jumbo* (1952 ed.), women can be seen in blackface, presumably for a skit or party. The barrier may have been broken, but the stereotypes were still alive and well.

483. Information about the pledging of a Christian and loss of the charter came from interviews with Eta Deuteron alumni from this era, including Michael Leven (May 4, 2012). Unfortunately, I was unable to confirm this incident with the national headquarters of Alpha Epsilon Pi. Throughout this work I have shied away from relying solely on alumni histories for information, but in this case I decided to make an exception, for an incident such as this is not soon forgotten.

484. On the accomplishments of Eta Deuteron during this era, see Toll, 633–635. The issue of racial inclusion is also discussed in chapter 4 under the sections for Sigma Kappa and Alpha Xi Delta.

485. On the general state of the campus in the late 1960s, see Miller, *LOTH–2*, 216–217. On the vote to change AEPi's mission at Tufts, see "AEPi Considers Major Changes," *TO*, September 19, 1969.

486. The blackball, named after the color of the marble ball one would drop (often in secret) into the box to deny membership, has been around since the very beginning of Greek-letter organizations, though not all use this system. Some organizations require a super-majority of yea votes in order to issue a bid to a candidate, or fully initiate a member, while others allow for a single negative vote so long as it is made openly in front of the rest of the chapter. The use of the blackball is discussed in more detail earlier in this chapter, in the section on Phi Epsilon Pi. For the details of AEPi's plans, see "AEPi Considers Major Changes," which includes the quotation; and "AEPi Plans Advance," *TO*, October 3, 1969. As written in Toll, 635, about the changes within the chapter, "the winds of student unrest were sweeping across American educational institutions, and nowhere did they find more fertile ground than at Tufts, a traditionally liberal institution."

487. The reaction of the alumni and national organization is based upon interviews with AEPi alumni who were active at the time, including the chapter president, Fred Fierst (July 24, 2012).

488. On the problems faced by AEPi as the 1969–70 school year went on, see "Fraternity Profile," *TO*, March 13, 1970. On the impact of social upheaval on campus during this time, see Miller, *LOTH–2*, 276. On the leasing of AEPi's house to the university, see Toll, 635.

489. On the administration's issues with AEPi's house and its physical transformation into a dormitory, see "T. U. Housing Hurting," *TO*, September 18, 1970, which includes the quotation. In this article, the author mentions that the Tufts administration purchased the house, but I can find no evidence in the Registry of Deeds for South

Middlesex County, Massachusetts that the house was sold at this time. Additionally, Toll, 635, says the house was leased and not sold to Tufts. Professor Nichols is the same as discussed in the section on Beta Tau earlier in this chapter.

490. The re-formation of AEPi is, unfortunately, based almost solely on hearsay, as I was unable to find much documented evidence on the revival. Therefore, I am relying on interviews with AEPi/Nichols House alumni from the mid- to late 1970s for this information, including Lowell Thomas (February 1, 2012, and February 5, 2012), Tom Fantini (May 5, 2012), Miles Rubin (June 27, 2012), and Sarah Shrewsbury (March 28, 2012). According to Toll, 635, Mr. Berenson was an officer in the national organization at the time he led the revival, and was assisted by a few others, including Larry Bernstein, an alumnus of the chapter.

491. Ibid. The actual timeframe for the revival and re-occupancy of the house is not all that clear given a lack of complete documentation, but I have assumed the fraternity was re-organized in the spring of 1975 and then back in its house a semester later for two reasons. First, Toll, 635, mentions this year in specific. Second, the article "ATO: A Different Sort of Fraternity," *TO*, October 24, 1975, mentions that AEPi was once again in operation at 6–8 Capen Street, albeit as a co-ed organization. As mentioned in the article, "Women live in Alpha Epsilon Pi but aren't full fledged members of the fraternity." Therefore, the timeframe I have described seems very plausible.

492. The information for this and the next few paragraphs is derived from interviews with AEPi/Nichols House alumni including Lowell Thomas, Tom Fantini, Miles Rubin, and Sarah Shrewsbury. On the continuation of Nichols House as a co-ed organization, see for example the recruitment advertisement, *TO*, February 18, 1977, 10.

493. Ibid. On the return of Eta Deuteron's charter, see Toll, 635. On the initiation of the men living in Nichols House into AEPi, see Toll, 636, which, of course, makes no mention of the women. That Mr. Berenson chose to ignore the co-ed situation existing in his fraternity house is extremely interesting, but will unfortunately remain a mystery. Various alumni told me that he was a furniture dealer in the Boston area, so perhaps his business, along with his duties as a national officer in Alpha Epsilon Pi, left him little time to worry about his old chapter. He did, though, sell furniture to Nichols House on a regular basis, since the members were the epitome of the saying, "this is why we can't have nice things."

494. Ibid. Nichols House member Paul Dickey won the Everett Morris Memorial Trophy in 1981 as the "Best Intercollegiate Sailor," while Jim Lilley and John Montesi earned All-American honors in swimming in 1982.

495. Ibid. On the attempt to appease the national organization, see "CSL Approves Alpha Epsilon Phi [sic]," *TD*, September 24, 1980. In this article, the author mistakenly refers to the fraternity as "Alpha Epsilon Phi," which is actually a historically Jewish sorority.

496. On the mortgage given to the alumni-run Etadee Corporation by the national organization in 1979, see Massachusetts Land Records, Middlesex South Registry, Book 13792, Page 657. The poor relation between Nichols House and their neighbors is discussed later in this section, when AEPi was established once again in 1983.

497. Nichols House composite photo, *Jumbo* (1982 ed.), 116, which includes the quotation. On the end of Nichols House and Eta Deuteron chapter, see "Nichols House Site of New Alpha Epsilon Pi," *TD*, September 9, 1982.

498. Kappa chapter of Sigma Omega Psi at Northeastern College was established

just a few months before Mu chapter at Tufts, according to "Sigma Omega Psi at Northeastern," *BG*, March 14, 1921. On the renting of 6–8 Capen Street to the Northeastern chapter, see "Nichols House Site of New Alpha Epsilon Pi."

499. On the reaction of the alumni, see "AEP Absence Arouses Alumnus," *TO*, September 10, 1982. Part of the reason many of the men of Nichols House were upset is they'd paid their required dues to the national AEPi organization, but were receiving no support from them on this matter. Indeed, since the national Alpha Epsilon Pi fraternity was a part owner of 6–8 Capen Street, they likely knew of and approved the expulsion of Nichols House. On the need for boarders, see "Nichols House Site of New Alpha Epsilon Pi"; and "A E Pi Fraternity Revived, House on Capen," *TD*, September 29, 1983. According to the latter article, the Northeastern chapter only had a dozen men living in the house that first year, which was less than half the capacity.

500. On the mission of the Northeastern chapter and its success, see "Nichols House Site of New Alpha Epsilon Pi"; and "A E Pi Fraternity Revived, House on Capen." On the number of men who revived Eta Deuteron chapter, see "IFC Corner–AEPi," *TD*, October 24, 1983.

501. The growth of fraternities at Tufts in the late 1970s and early 1980s is discussed in detail is chapter 6. Information about Eta Deuteron's growth during the 1983–84 school year was based upon interviews with AEPi members active at the time, including Michael Gitten (February 1, 2012).

502. The fraternities that called the Medford Hillside home at one point in the early 1900s were Sigma Tau Alpha, Phi Delta, Phi Epsilon Pi, Beta Tau, Sigma Omega Psi/Alpha Epsilon Pi, and Tau Epsilon Phi, as discussed in their sections within this chapter. The relationship between the local residents of Medford and Somerville and the Tufts community is a long and complicated one, certainly beyond the scope of this work. But, suffice to say, the presence of fraternity houses in the Medford Hillside was fraught with conflict almost from the beginning. The houses were just too close together, and the social calendars of the fraternities were often diametrically opposed to the needs of their neighbors.

503. On the restrictions imposed onto AEPi, see "Prudhomme, Fraternities React to AEPi Dilemma," *TD*, September 9, 1986. For quiet hours, AEPi had to shut off the noise by 11:00 p.m. on weeknights and 12:30 a.m. on weekends. As mentioned in this article, neighborhood complaints against AEPi started in the 1970s.

504. AEPi's holding of parties in the late afternoon and early evening is based on my personal recollection, as I went to a few of them as a freshman. On the initial denial of the housing license, see "Judge Postpones Action in AEPi Case; Senate Calls on Admin To Support Fraternity," *TD*, September 16, 1986.

505. The dispute between AEPi and the City of Medford made headline news in *The Tufts Daily* on a regular basis that fall. See "Judge Postpones Action in AEPi Case"; "Judge Backs City Council on AEPi Dispute," *TD*, October 6, 1986; and "City Manager Deems AEPi a One Family House," *TD*, November 19, 1986. For discussion on the tension between AEPi and their neighbors, see "AEPi Neighbors File Complaints With Tufts," *TD*, November 21, 1986; and "Davids Responds to Neighbor Complaints," *TD*, November 24, 1986.

506. On the sale of the house and its future use, see "Tufts To Buy AEPi House," *TD*, January 16, 1987; "6–8 Capen To House BSOT," *TD*, January 22, 1987; and "Certificate of Vote," Massachusetts Land Records, Middlesex South Registry, Book

17877, Page 535–536, dated February 17, 1987, which lists the sale price. On the controversy surrounding the BSOT program, see "Semester In Review," *TD*, December 8, 1986; and "Semester In Review," *TD*, April 27, 1987.

507. The information in this paragraph was based primarily on interviews with a number of Tufts administrators, including Dean of Students Bruce Reitman (October 31, 2012; and November 16, 2012) and Professor Sol Gittleman (October 17, 2012), who, at the time of AEPi's house sale, was serving directly under President Jean Mayer as Provost. From these conversations, it was clear that Somerville came very close to following in Medford's footsteps. For more discussion on this issue, see the section on Alpha Sigma Phi earlier in this chapter.

508. On AEPi's move to a new space, see "Alpha Epsilon Pi–RUSH, Fall 1987," *TD*, October 5, 1987. The address of AEPi is given as 46 Winthrop Street in this ad, so it's not as if the members tried to hide their location. I also personally remember seeing AEPi composite photos hanging inside this house. The growth of the IGC and its subsequent ban on unofficial chapter houses is discussed in the section on Psi Upsilon later in this chapter. The other two fraternities occupying unofficial chapter houses at this time were Psi Upsilon and Zeta Beta Tau.

509. On the success of the Greek jam over the years, see "Greeks Jam for Heart Association," *TD*, March 7, 1988; "Greeks Jam for a Worthy Cause," *TD*, March 6, 1989; "Greek Jam A Success," *TD*, March 15, 1990; "Greek Jam One of the Best Yet," *TD*, March 11, 1992; "AEPi Greek Jam Raises $3500," *TD*, April 12, 1993, which mentions the interest of MTV; "Letter to the Editor–Theta Chi Mars Otherwise Successful Greek Jam," *TD*, March 17, 1999, which mentions the sponsorship of Tommy Hilfiger and 54 other organizations; and "We Hope You Like Greek Jammin' Too," *TD*, April 1, 2002. After 2002, it appears that the IGC took over Greek Jam from AEPi and held the event during the annual Spring Fling Weekend for a few years, before retiring the event. AEPi was certainly not the only fraternity to organize such a large, annual philanthropy event at the time, as many other chapters did as well (Sigma Nu, for example held an annual Dance Marathon/Super Dance for over a decade in the 1980s and 1990s). However, I chose specifically to mention AEPi's event because of the manner in which it brought the students together while also engaging the Tufts administration. This was a time of great angst and mistrust between the Greek organization and the faculty, as is discussed in chapter 6, but AEPi's Greek Jam was one of the few events to bridge the divide. As an aside, I participated in the first Greek Jam in 1988, and I was duly impressed with the organization of the event. Too many fraternity philanthropy events were hackneyed affairs; AEPi's was not. Finally, in the late 1980s and early 1990s, MTV made a concerted effort to attract college-aged viewers with programs such as "Remote Control," a Jeopardy-type game show and "Spring Break," which featured major concerts in exotic locations such as Florida, Mexico, and Jamaica.

510. On the housing of AOII and Phi Sigma Sigma, see their sections in chapter 4. On the awarding of chapter houses to ZBT and AEPi, see "ZBT and AEPi Will Move Into On-Campus Houses By Next Fall," *TD*, February 22, 1995; and "Phi Sigma Sigma Will Be Dissolved This Year," *TD*, March 28, 1995. Before AEPi moved into 45 Sawyer Avenue, the house had been a Tufts dormitory for many years, assigned through the general housing lottery. The decision by the administration to offer on-campus housing to both ZBT and AEPi, finally, appears to have been motivated by new student-driven policies regarding fraternity recruitment. Under the direction of the IGC,

the fraternities by early 1995 had formulated a plan to allow for multiple rounds of recruitment each school year as a means of giving more men a chance to join. This satisfied a key requirement the trustees of Tufts College had put forth a couple of years earlier, thereby allowing for them to open up more on-campus housing. See "Board of Trustees Approves Policy for Second Fraternity Rush Period," *TD*, February 23, 1995. This situation is discussed in more detail in chapter 6.

511. On the plan to relocate many of the Greek-letter organizations to the center of campus, see "Phi Sigma Sigma Will Be Dissolved This Year." According to discussions I had with numerous Tufts administrators on this plan, a lack of money is the main reason why this vision of centralized Greek housing has not yet come to fruition. The plans have been there, but not the cash. On AEPi's suspension from housing, see "AEPi Suspended for Fall Semester," *TD*, September 5, 2006.

512. On the trials and tribulations of DTD, see their section earlier in this chapter. On AEPi's occupation of 98 Professors Row starting in 2007, see "Police Briefs–If None Of You Broke The Window, What Are You Arguing About," *TD*, March 28, 2008, which specifically mentions the chapter address as 98 Professors Row; and "Home, Sweet Home," *TD*, November 18, 2011, which mentions AEPi had been occupying the house since the fall of 2007. On Sigma Omega Psi's desire to live on Professors Row, see *Jumbo* (1939 ed.), 130.

513. "DTD Returns to 98 Pro Row," *TD*, September 6, 2011.

514. "Alpha Epsilon Pi Disaffiliates From National Organization," *TD*, January 30, 2015; and "A Message to the Tufts Community from the Former Members of Alpha Epsilon Pi Fraternity," *TD*, January 30, 2015. For the quotation, see AEPi's mission statement on its national website, http://www.aepi.org/about-aepi/mission-statement/ (accessed November 3, 2016).

515. "Letter to AEPi National Organization, Former Brothers of AEPi at Tufts University," *TD*, February 9, 2015; and "Former AEPi Brothers Adjust to New Status as Local Fraternity Pi Delta," *TD*, October 2, 2015, which includes the quotation.

516. Much of the information in following paragraphs about the origins of Theta Delta Theta came from interviews of alumni involved in the group, including Bruce Gordon (September 3, 2011; September 7, 2011; and October 6, 2011). Also see "The Unique Origin of Theta Delta Theta," *The Signet of Phi Sigma Kappa* 49, no. 4 (November 1957): 195–196; and the petition of Theta Delta Theta to Phi Sigma Kappa, Activities and Organizations records, 1875–2013, UA 024.001 Box 16, Folder 12 (Theta Delta Theta 1958). I'm sure most, if not all alumni have vivid memories of walking into a dining hall for the first time and wondering just where they would sit. On the history of Curtis Hall, see "Curtis Hall, 1893," *Concise Encyclopedia of Tufts History*, http://hdl.handle.net/10427/14829 (accessed February 21, 2015).

517. Interview with Bruce Gordon. From what I have come across in issues of the *Tufts Weekly*, "Pray For Rain" was a popular activity throughout the 1950s, and alumni from the 1970s have also mentioned this event occurred with some regularity.

518. "The Unique Origin of Theta Delta Theta," and Petition of Theta Delta Theta to Phi Sigma Kappa. Note that the petition does not list Marty Billings as a founder of Theta Delta Theta. However, I have decided to include Marty Billings as a founder of Theta Delta Theta for two reasons. First, Marty was recognized as a founder by Bruce Gordon, who was also Marty's freshman roommate. Second, the petition was written after the original founders had graduated, so it is entirely plausible that Marty's name

was simply left off the "official" list of founders by accident.

519. Ibid.

520. Ibid. The history of the Mayoralty pageant is discussed in more detail in chapter 6. Paul's campaign as the Darkhorse for Mayor failed to be taken seriously by reporters for the *Tufts Weekly*, as evidence by the lack of coverage within the newspaper. However, his entrance was more of a publicity stunt than a real campaign.

521. Ibid.

522. Ibid.

523. Ibid. I cannot imagine the current Tufts administration allowing a horse-drawn chariot race around the academic quad!

524. Ibid. In the 1800s and early 1900s, local and national fraternity chapters often existed side-by-side on many campuses, including Tufts College. After World War II, however, national fraternities fast became the preferred choice for many. At some schools, particularly in New England, the prolonged existence of local fraternities throughout the entire 20th century was not uncommon, and a few are still active today, including Kappa Kappa Kappa at Dartmouth College (founded in 1842) and Lambda Iota at the University of Vermont (founded in 1836, and currently scheduled to return to campus in 2020). As an example of the national fraternity surge during the 1950s, consider the case of the Sigma Nu fraternity. During the thirteen-year period between 1930 and 1943, Sigma Nu opened only seven new chapters, mainly due to the constraints of the Depression and World War II. By contrast, over the thirteen-year period from 1947 to 1960, Sigma Nu opened up twenty-nine new chapters and re-chartered a number of others.

525. Ibid. Additional details of the debate within Theta Delta Theta were also provided through interviews with alumni, including Bruce Gordon and Bill Cummings (October 12, 2011; and October 17, 2011). The chapter size is estimated from the composite photograph of Theta Delta Theta in *Jumbo* (1956 ed.), 145, which was probably taken just a few weeks after the vote.

526. On the official founding date and campus recognition of Theta Delta Theta, see Petition of Theta Delta Theta to Phi Sigma Kappa. Information on Theta Delta Theta's courting of TKE (pronounced "teek") was provided by a number of alumni active at the time, including Bruce Gordon and Bill Cummings. Also see "Beta Chi Brothers Moving Into Packard Avenue House," *TW*, September 21, 1956, which mentions Theta Delta Theta "are interested in the national Tau Kappa Epsilon." The issue of discriminatory membership practices in fraternities is discussed further in chapter 6. On the lack of discrimination within Theta Delta Theta, see "11 Fraternities Disclose Vital Facts and Figures To Freshman Rushees," *TW*, November 30, 1956. On the banning of fraternities that still had these restrictions, see Miller, *LOTH–2*, 210. On the visit with the national officers of TKE, see "National Pres. To Visit TDT On April 17," *TW*, April 13, 1956. According to this article, local TKE alumni teaching at both Tufts and Harvard were responsible for working with Theta Delta Theta on a consistent basis. However, these men apparently made little by way of impression, for no alumnus of Theta Delta Theta could remember their names.

527. So yes, Joel Reynolds appears yet again. I learned of his involvement in Theta Delta Theta, and his dislike of TKE, though alumni interviews. Dislike, though, may be too mild of a descriptor regarding his feelings for TKE – "hated" seems closer to the truth, according to what I was told. Also, it seems Mr. Reynolds never spoke to Theta

Delta Theta directly regarding TKE, but by proxy through Tufts administration officials.

528. Information regarding the deception was provided through interviews of alumni, including Bill Cummings.

529. The conversation quoted here is purely hypothetical and is only intended to represent how the plan worked in practice. Phi Sigma Kappa removed all membership restrictions based on race and religion in the summer of 1956, according to Frank Prentice Rand, *All the Phi Sigs–A History* (Phi Sigma Kappa Fraternity, 1993).

530. Information regarding the gravitation towards Phi Sigma Kappa and away from TKE was provided through interviews of alumni, including Bill Cummings.

531. "The Unique Origin of Theta Delta Theta," and Petition of Theta Delta Theta to Phi Sigma Kappa. On the move into the rooms in West Hall, also see "Beta Chi Brothers Moving Into Packard Ave. House." I am assuming those three television shows were among programs watched on the brand new set, given that they were among the most popular of the time. See for example, Harry Castleman and Walter J. Podrazik, *The TV Schedule Book: Four Decades of Network Programming from Sign-on to Sign-off* (New York: McGraw Hill, 1984), 79–85. Finally, some alumni of Theta Delta Theta mentioned another reason the decided against TKE was the fraternity required a significant amount of money from any group looking to join its national organization. Theta Delta Theta, it seems, did not have enough money to cover this fee. However, not every member of Theta Delta Theta I interviewed recalled money being an issue with TKE.

532. Frank Prentice Rand, *Phi Sigma Kappa: A History, 1873–1923* (The Council of Phi Sigma Kappa, 1923), 11–49; and Baird (1st ed. 1879), 135. The six founder of Phi Sigma Kappa were Jabez William Clay, Joseph Franklin Barrett, Henry Hague, Xenos Young Clark, Frederick George Campbell, and William Penn Brooks. The other two fraternities in operation at the time of Phi Sigma Kappa's founding were D. G. K., which eventually became a chapter of the national Kappa Sigma, and Q. T. V., which eventually became a small national organization before reverting once again to a local. See Baird (6th ed. 1905), 173, 409–410.

533. Rand, *Phi Sigma Kappa*, 53–62. Phi Sigma Kappa is one of a few relatively large national fraternities founded within the borders of Massachusetts, including Delta Upsilon, Lambda Chi Alpha, and Delta Delta Delta. On Phi Sigma Kappa's growth into the 1950s, see http://en.wikipedia.org/wiki/List_of_Phi_Sigma_Kappa_chapters (accessed March 9, 2015).

534. "Theta Delta Theta," *Jumbo* (1957 ed.); "The Birth of Iota Tetarton," *The Signet of Phi Sigma Kappa* 49, no. 4 (November 1957): 193, 194, 196; and "Phi Sigma Kappa Becomes National Fraternity On Hill," *TW*, May 10, 1957. Apparently, the *Jumbo* yearbook was printed before the installation of Phi Sigma Kappa. I am certainly using a bit of conjecture concerning the happiness of Mr. Reynolds over the installation of Phi Sigma Kappa, but I cannot imagine he would have even attended the banquet had Theta Delta Theta gone TKE!

535. Phi Sigma Kappa's planned occupancy of 98 Packard Avenue is mentioned in Petition of Theta Delta Theta to Phi Sigma Kappa. The turn of events leading to their occupancy of 25 Whitfield Road was provided in an alumni interview with Bill Cummings. On the involvement of Mr. Joel Reynolds in this acquisition, see "The Birth of Iota Tetarton."

536. The rise of the fraternity system at Tufts in the 1950s, and its subsequent decline in the 1960s, is discussed in Miller, *LOTH–2*, 208–217. On the struggles within

Phi Sigma Kappa in the late 1960s and early 1970s, see "Iota Tetarton–Tufts University," *The Signet of Phi Sigma Kappa* 78, no. 3 (Winter 1968): 31; "Iota Tetarton–Tufts University," *The Signet of Phi Sigma Kappa* 62, no. 4 (Fall 1970): 32; "Images of Us," *The Signet of Phi Sigma Kappa* 63, no. 3 (Summer 1971): 15; and "Iota Tetarton–Tufts University," *The Signet of Phi Sigma Kappa* 64, no. 2 (Spring 1972): 21. Apparently, the editors of *The Signet* made a mistake in terms of the volume numbers, for I cannot imagine why Volume 78 was published in 1968, while Volume 64 was published four years later in 1972. Therefore, I reported the edition numbers as printed on the mastheads. Within almost every issue of *The Signet* from this era are numerous articles detailing and lamenting the general decline of fraternities across the nation.

537. Information about Phi Sigma Kappa's struggles during the summer of 1972 was provided through an interview with Steve Trinward (August 29, 2012), an alumni advisor of the chapter at the time. Co-ed dormitories first arrived at Tufts University in the fall of 1970, according to "Co-educational Dorms Approved; Parental Permission Required," *TO*, March 6, 1970. As it turned out, Phi Sigma Kappa as a national fraternity nearly became a co-ed organization in 1970, according to Steve Trinward, "My Very First Libertarian National Convention," in *Why Liberty–Personal Journeys Toward Peace and Freedom*, ed. Marc Guttman (Cobden Press, 2010), 267–272; and "Summary of Convention and Grand Council Actions," *The Signet of Phi Sigma Kappa* 62, no. 4 (Fall 1970), 4.

538. "Fire Damages Tufts Dormitory," *BG*, July 2, 1972; and "Student Arrested For Firebombing," *TO*, September 15, 1972. Concerning the other two mentioned fires, see "Fletcher School at Tufts Firebombed," *BG*, March 22, 1971; and "Fire on Tufts Campus Rules Arson," *BG*, February 18, 1972.

539. On the rash of arsons at Tufts, see Miller, *LOTH–2*, 290–294; and "Fletcher School at Tufts Firebombed," which includes the quotation. On the incident at 25 Whitfield Road, see "Student Arrested For Firebombing." This article publicly identifies William F. Girolamo as the suspect, though it does not discuss the motive behind his actions. Rather, I learned of the reasons behind Bill's actions through interviews with alumni who were on campus that summer.

540. On Phi Sigma Kappa's struggles during the 1972–73 school year, see "Good News About Fraternities," *TO*, October 27, 1972. Additional information was provided by Steve Trinward. The legal saga of Bill following his arrest is not well documented, but numerous Phi Sigma Kappa alumni have told me he was eventually released from custody, and then made his way back to the area (he had grown up in Waltham, Massachusetts). Bill did go on to graduate from Tufts University in 1978, according to records within the Tufts Alumni Directory.

541. "Extra Effort–How Did Your Chapter Fare?" *The Signet of Phi Sigma Kappa* 66, no. 2 (Spring 1974), 16, which lists the number of pledges and total initiates for the school year; and interviews with alumni of the chapter, including Tony Bove (October 9, 2010; October 30, 2010; and November 7, 2010), who was one of the four sophomores to be initiated into the fraternity that spring of 1974. Tony checked many of the details we discussed with other members of the fraternity who wish to remain anonymous.

542. Interviews with Tony Bove.

543. Ibid. The need for the ruse in order to keep the lease is a little speculative on my part, but it does seem highly plausible. The Tufts administration, through its

Walnut Hill properties division, leased the property at 25 Whitfield Road to Phi Sigma Kappa, Inc., the alumni housing corporation formed in 1957 for the purpose of maintaining a chapter house. For information on this corporation, see Minutes of the Regular Meeting of the Board of Aldermen, City Hall, Somerville, September 12, 1957, page 320, and November 26, 1957, page 431. Phi Sigma Kappa, Inc., then rented rooms to individual members of the fraternity. Based on this arrangement, it seems that if the fraternity lost its charter, the lease would be in jeopardy.

544. Ibid.

545. "Fester Manifesto," *TO*, April 11, 1975; and advertisement for THE FESTER P. GAZOTSKY SPRINGTIME ORGASM FESTIVAL, *TO*, April 11, 1975. On the existing Spring Weekend as put on by the Tufts administration that semester, see an advertisement in *TO*, May 2, 1975.

546. Information on the logistics surrounding the first Festers was provided through interviews with Tony Bove.

547. "Fester Manifesto," which includes the quotation; and "Fester is no Jester," *TO*, April 18, 1975. According to Douglas Hodgkin, *Lewiston Politics in the Gilded Age, 1863–1900* (Portland, Maine: self published, 2015), 33, this "corporation scheme" was used in the latter part of the 19th century in Maine, for example, to skirt that state's prohibition laws. In 1975, the drinking age in Massachusetts was 18, which I can assume is the main reason the Tufts administration allowed the event to go on as planned. Indeed, Tufts routinely sponsored keg parties on the academic quad to welcome new students to campus in the mid 1970s. According to Tony Bove, the only real concern Tufts had with Festers was security. Tony assured the administration this detail had been considered in depth, when in reality there was no plan to provide security.

548. "Fester is no Jester," which includes the quotation. This letter states the event would take place on the lawn next to 25 Whitfield Road, but many remember the concert occurring near Ellis Oval, before moving to Hodgdon Hall later in the day to finish. For information on the second Festers, see "II Annual Spring Fester," *TO*, April 30, 1976. The odyssey from Festers to Spring Fling is worth noting in detail. In the spring of 1977, 25 Whitfield planned to hold its 3rd annual Festers in much the same way it had the two previous years. By then the concert had grown considerably in popularity, so a conglomerate of student groups including the Inter Dormitory Council, the Leonard Carmichael Society, the Arts Commission, and a few individual dorms looked to hold a similar all-day music festival on the last day of classes, not necessarily to compete with Festers, but to provide another opportunity to party. In early April of 1977, though, the Tufts radio station, WMFO, was heavily damaged when a fire broke out in Curtis Hall. The blaze nearly wiped out the station's entire collection of music, which was almost exclusively in the form of vinyl records. In response to this unfortunate event, the two groups planning their separate spring concerts decided to join forces, hold one big festival, and donate the profits to WMFO for its rebuilding. The new event was simply called "The Festival," and it worked on the same principle as the original Festers: students who bought "contribution tickets" to the concert were entitled to free beer and punch throughout the day, according to "Fester Slated to Rise Again," *TO*, April 15, 1977; and "Fester Funds go to MFO," *TO*, April 29, 1977. The Festival was also held on the fields near Ellis Oval, according Kevin Lowther, one of the organizers of the concert. As it turned out, the 1977 concert was the last one involving the group from 25 Whitfield, since they disbanded at the end of that school year when

they lost possession of their house. In the spring of 1978, other groups kept the tradition alive by holding separate all-day concerts. The Interfraternity Council started the season by holding its 1st Annual Spring Festival on April 22, 1978 (see ad in *TT*, April 21, 1978). Next, A group of uphill dorms along with AppleJam, an organization of Tufts musicians, held a seven-hour "Spring Celebration Festival" on the academic quad a week later (see ad in *TO*, April 28, 1978). Finally, on May 4, 1978, the "Spring 78 Last Day Festival" was held (see ads in *TO*, April 28, 1978; and *TT*, April 26, 1978). All of these events featured free beer alongside live music, and all ran for six or more hours. However, in one marked difference from years past, the Student Activities Office at Tufts helped organize and run the concerts that year. The involvement of the university was most likely prompted by the popularity of the concerts, as well as growing concerns over security. In the spring of 1979, AppleJam held their "Third Annual Rites of Spring All-Day Festival," and featured bands such as The Mystic Valley Mountaineers, Foreplay, Fine Lines, and Roadwork (see ad in *TO*, April 20, 1979). For the first time, this concert was held not on the academic quad or near Ellis Oval, but rather on the lawn right behind the president's house. In 1980, the student-run TCU Senate found itself with a surplus of money, so they decided to step in and sponsor the big end-of-the-spring semester celebration. They called the event "Spring Fling," and the party featured many different activities over the weekend including an extended all-day concert, once again on the lawn behind President Mayer's house. And ever since 1980, there's been a Spring Fling concert on the President's lawn at the end of April as organized by the university. But, as mentioned in the main text, the days of free beer are long gone. On the bands that have played at Spring Fling, see "Spring Fling, 1980," *Concise Encyclopedia of Tufts History*, http://hdl.handle.net/10427/14829 (accessed March 17, 2015). Unfortunately, this article makes absolutely no mention of the yearly concerts that came before it, and seems to imply that Spring Fling came from nowhere.

549. One element of the ruse utilized by 25 Whitfield was to publish their information in campus guides under the name "Phi Sigma Kappa." See, for example, *The Ivy* Book (1975–76 ed.), 72. Additionally, the group submitted cursory information about the chapter to Phi Sigma Kappa's national magazine, *The Signet of Phi Sigma Kappa*, which seemed to suggest the chapter was gaining new, official members each year. On 25 Whitfield's literary efforts, see UA Short-Run Student Publications, 1901–2012, UP215.001, Box 1, Folder 5 (Squid Ink 1975); and "Year of the Fester (Want-Ad Blues)," *Jumbo* (1976 ed.), 9–32.

550. On the name change, see document filed with Massachusetts on April 13, 1976, which officially changed the name of the alumni corporation (and hence the chapter) from "Phi Sigma Kappa, Inc." to "25 Whitfield Association, Inc." See http://corp.sec.state.ma.us/CorpWeb/CorpSearch/CorpSearchRedirector.aspx?Action=PDF&Path=CORP_DRIVE1/2014/0314/000556345/0059/201477902420_1.pdf (accessed March 21, 2015). On the pulling of the charter by the national organization, see "Late News – Tufts Bit the Dust," *The Signet of Phi Sigma Kappa* 68, no. 4 (Fall 1976): 10. On the expiration of the lease in 1975, see "Frat Fests Stopped," *TO*, October 8, 1976.

551. On the struggles with renewing the lease, see "Frat Fests Stopped." On 25 Whitfield's planned eviction in January of 1977, see "Letter to the Editor," *TO*, September 17, 1976. On 25 Whitfield's run-in with the neighbors and the Tufts administration, see "Parties Banned," *TO*, September 24, 1976, which includes the quotation;

"Observations – Letters to the Editor," *TO*, October 1, 1976; "Frat Fests Stopped"; and "Winant on Whitfield," *TO*, October 8, 1976. By the fall of 1976, Whitfield Road had become home to a number of cooperative theme houses, which were co-ed dormitories organized around a common purpose. Two examples include the German House and the Latin House, both of which also hosted parties on the Saturday night in question (September 18, 1976).

552. On the successful appeal by 25 Whitfield, see "CSL Removes Party Ban," *TO*, October 22, 1976. No doubt 25 Whitfield's appeal was helped by letters of support from a few of their neighbors, which were published in the *Tufts Observer*. The loss of 25 Whitfield Road to Chi Omega is covered in more detail in their section of chapter 4.

553. On the charity of Bill Cummings including the Giving Pledge, see the website of his foundation, http://www.cummingsfoundation.org (accessed March 19, 2015).

554. For information regarding the courses of study at Union during the early 19th century, see *A General Catalogue of the Officers, Graduates, and Students of Union College from 1795 to 1854* (Schenectady, NY: Union College, 1854), 11–50. On the formation of the literary societies, see *Historical Sketch of Union College* (Washington, D.C.: Government Printing Office, 1876), 41–42. On the formation of the Greek-letter fraternities, see chapter 1.

555. Leo Weldon Wertheimer, ed., *The Twelfth General Catalogue of the Psi Upsilon Fraternity* (New York, NY: Psi Upsilon Fraternity, 1917), xvi–xxiii; Earl D. Babst, *Occasions in Psi Upsilon* (New York, NY: 1933), 75–78; and *Annals of Psi Upsilon 1833–1941* (New York, NY: Executive Council of Psi Upsilon, 1941), 56–63, which includes the quotation.

556. Ibid.

557. *Annals of Psi Upsilon*, 69–117; and *The Twelfth General Catalogue*, xviii–xix.

558. Henry Blanchard, "In The Days of President Ballou," *The Tufts College Graduate* 1, no. 3 (October 1903): 1–4. The opening of Tufts College is discussed in chapter 2.

559. Ibid, which includes the quotation. The link between Henry Blanchard and Psi Upsilon is somewhat speculative on my part, but I feel it is a reasonable explanation. Someone planted the idea of joining Psi Upsilon into Henry Blanchard, and the most obvious candidate is his professor, for no one else on campus was associated with the fraternity. At the time, Psi Upsilon also had an active chapter at Harvard University, but Henry makes no mention of Harvard in his article. On Professor Schneider's affiliation with Psi Upsilon, see *Catalogue of the Psi Upsilon Fraternity* (Executive Council of Psi Upsilon, 1879), 135; and Start, 113–114. Unfortunately, Henry does not identify any other men who were involved in his efforts to secure a charter from Psi Upsilon.

560. Information on the genesis of Psi Upsilon at Tufts was provided in an interview with Lowell Thomas (February 5, 2012). Lowell had quite the fraternal odyssey while a student at Tufts. After dropping out of both DTD and Psi Upsilon, he then joined Nichols House / AEPi, where he lived for a while. He also spent one semester living in the Theta Delta Chi fraternity house, though he was not officially associated with the fraternity.

561. Interviews with alumni involved in the starting of Psi U, including Lowell Thomas and Mark McGillivray (April 11, 2011). Also see "New Fraternity Organized," *TO*, March 2, 1979. Before Psi Upsilon, the last new national fraternity to come to campus was Phi Sigma Kappa, in 1957. The release of the movie *Animal House* is often cited as a catalyst for renewed interest in fraternities in the late 1970s, even though most

national organizations disavow the depiction of fraternity life in the movie.

562. "New Fraternity Organized." After this article appeared, it seems that a local Psi U alumnus, who was helping to organize the Tufts group, told the members he was very much against the idea of a co-ed chapter, so he began lobbying heavily for the group to drop the idea, which they soon did.

563. Information on the securing of 14 Whitfield was provided by Mark McGillivray, who was involved in leasing the house from Walnut Hill. Although owned by Tufts, Walnut Hill is a real estate corporation independent of the academic administrators of the university. Mark mentioned he had wanted to rent the larger house at 25 Whitfield Road for Psi U, but was denied by Walnut Hill, as they had already leased the property to a number of students. The renting of houses by fraternities up through the 1930s is discussed in earlier sections in this chapter.

564. Information about that first year in 14 Whitfield Road was provided by a number of Psi U alumni, including Mark McGillivray. See also "Provisional Chapter–Tufts University," *The Diamond of Psi Upsilon* 66, no. 4 (Summer 1980): 19. Alumni from this era do not recall any serious attempts to follow through on the idea of a co-ed chapter.

565. On the earlier showing of *Deep Throat*, see "The One and Only Deep Throat," *TO*, April 30, 1976; and "Film Series Goes Down With 'Deep Throat'," *TO*, April 27, 1979. Also, other alumni have mentioned the movie had been shown on campus at other times in the late 1970s, again without any controversy. On the negative reaction to Psi U's screening by the Women's Center, see "Movie Irks Women's Center," *TD*, September 18, 1980; and "Women's Center Protest," *TD*, September 23, 1980. On the support shown by students, see "Protest Letter Upsets Student," *TD*, September 23, 1980, which was written by a female who was against censorship; and "Another 'Throat' Letter," *TD*, September 25, 1980, which pointed out the Women's Center had not protested when the movie was shown two years earlier.

566. "Zeta Tau–1981," *The Diamond of Psi Upsilon* 67, no. 1 (Autumn 1981): 20, which includes the quotation. The Alpha chapter of Psi Upsilon was active at Harvard University from 1850 through 1873, according to the fraternity's national website. Unfortunately, a complete list of the charter members was not provided in this referenced article, and inquiries to the national Psi Upsilon organization regarding the list were not returned.

567. On the activities of Psi Upsilon in the early 1980s, see "Psi Upsilon," *Jumbo* (1982 ed.), 101; "IFC Corner," *TD*, October 15, 1982; and "IFPC Corner," *TD*, October 21, 1983. Additional information about chapter life was provided through alumni interviews, including Tom Snarsky (April 9, 2013). On the troubles over the planned screening of *Insatiable*, see "Pressure Forces Psi U to Cancel X-Rated Movie," *TD*, March 18, 1983. The Intercollegiate Women's Coalition was quite successful in the early 1980s in dissuading local universities from showing pornography on campus. For example, see "Forum on Pornography Held," *The Tech*, February 7, 1984, which describes the group's crusade on the MIT campus.

568. On the announcement that 92 Professors Row would be converted into Greek housing, see "House Available for Fraternity," *TO*, February 22, 1985; and "IDC Announces Housing Changes," *TD*, February 28, 1985. Apparently, the student-run Tufts Community Union Senate was not happy about this change, as they were not consulted on the manner. In response, they voted to keep 92 Professors Row in the general hous-

ing lottery, according to "Senate Addresses Eaton, Snack Bar Closing; Votes 12–11 to keep 92 Prof Row," *TD*, March 5, 1985. This vote was apparently non-binding, since the administration went ahead with the conversion plans. Professor Fay's house, which was built in 1874, remained in his family after his death in 1931, though it was converted into a duplex shortly thereafter. From 1931 forward, the property housed numerous campus administrators including President Carmichael for a time. By the early 1980s, the property had been purchased by Tufts and converted into student housing. For more information, see "History of Homes on Professors Row," *TD*, April 28, 1989; and UA Edwin B. Rollins Papers, 1300[sic]–1976, Notebooks, 1940–1955, MS054.001 Box 2, Folder 2 (Campus Homes, Part 1(b) 1940–1955). On the organizations that applied to move into 92 Professors Row, see "Administration to Decide Professors Row Fate," *TD*, March 6, 1985. On the decision to award the house to Psi U, see "Frat Loses House; Co-op Turns To Singles," *TO*, March 29, 1985; and "Psi U Prez [sic] Protests 92 Decision," *TD*, April 2, 1985.

569. On the decision to award the house to Sigma Nu, see "Psi U Prez [sic] Protests 92 Decision." On the postponement of the plan due to the issues over housing licenses, see "Frat Loses House; Co-op Turns To Singles," and "Administration Changes Status of 92 Professors Row," *TD*, March 29, 1985.

570. Psi U's loss of 14 Whitfield Road after the spring semester of 1985 was confirmed through interviews of number of alumni who were active at the time, including Dan Walsh (April 12, 2013). Apparently, over the years Psi U's relationship with Walnut Hill had deteriorated, especially after the members made unauthorized alterations to the interior of the house, including the construction of a bar in the basement. The decision not to renew the lease was also influenced by an embarrassing incident involving some of the Psi U members living at 14 Whitfield Road for the 1984–85 school year. However, I was unable to determine the nature of this incident. Regardless, when school resumed in the fall of 1985, Psi U was no longer at 14 Whitfield. On Psi U's subsequent occupancy of 165 College Avenue, see an advertisement for a rush party, *TD*, October 30, 1986. This advertisement is the first reference to 165 College Avenue I came across in print. Additionally, in the fall of 1986, I was a sophomore at Tufts, and I distinctly recall 165 College Avenue as being associated with Psi U. It does appear that some members of Psi U occupied half of the duplex at 155 College Avenue for the 1985–86 school year, but then moved to 165 College Avenue the following year, where they occupied the entire structure. However, I did not find any printed reference to 155 College Avenue as it related to Psi U.

571. The idea of Psi U being on the fringes of campus life is based heavily on circumstance, as most students did not generally walk past 165 College Avenue on a daily basis. On recognition of Psi U for philanthropy work, see for example, "Thank You to Psi-U," *TD*, January 20, 1987.

572. The improved oversight of the Greek system at Tufts is discussed in detail in chapter 6. The three other unhoused organizations were Alpha Sigma Phi, Alpha Epsilon Pi, and Zeta Beta Tau. The Alpha Omicron Pi sorority was also unhoused at the time, but they had made no effort to secure an off-campus chapter house.

573. Numerous Psi U alumni, who were active in the chapter in the late 1980s, have mentioned that while nearly all of the tenants of 165 College Avenue over the years were members of Psi Upsilon, some were not affiliated with the fraternity. In March of 1985, a number of Zeta Tau graduates started the "Psi Upsilon Alumni Association of

Boston, Inc.," for the purposes of helping to maintain a chapter house. However, it does not appear this corporation continued in its mission, as there are no filings on record with Massachusetts after the initial Articles of Organization, dated March 15, 1985.

574. "Police Log–January 31," *TD*, February 8, 1989.

575. On the police report, see "Police Log–January 31," which includes the quotation. The lawsuit would play out for a number of years, as discussed later in this section. On the investigation by the CFS, see "CFS Warns Greeks After Health Report," *TD*, November 9, 1989.

576. On Psi U's appeal, see "CFS Warns Greeks After Health Report," and "Greek Chapters to Appeal," *TD*, November 13, 1989. On the removal of warning status for Psi U, see "CFS Approves IGC's Appeal For Changes to Greek Health Report," *TD*, February 5, 1990. On Psi U's published self-description, see "Psi U Means 'Excellence'," *TD*, February 8, 1990, which includes the quotation.

577. Psi U's article appeared in a section of *The Tufts Daily* called "The Greek Gazette," and every other organization submitted a positive statement about what they bring to the Tufts campus and the greater community. Psi U's article clearly seemed satirical in this context.

578. On Psi U's return to warning status, see "CFS Imposes Three Warnings and Two probations on Greek Chapters," *TD*, November 15, 1990. On Psi U's troubles with their Pledge Walk, see "Psi Upsilon Charged With Hazing, Distributing Alcohol to Minors," *TD*, March 5, 1991. As mentioned in the text, pledge walks were a common part of fraternity life in the early 20th century. For example, see various letters on the topic between 1922 and 1933 in Activities and Organizations records, 1875–2013, UA 024.001 Box 4, Folder 10 (Interfraternity Council 1932–1968); and "A Vice-Superior Walks With The Pledges," *The Alumni Bulletin* 1, no. 1 (November 1933): 10–12, in AJHS–PhiEp, Box 31, Folder 5 (Omicron–Tufts College).

579. "Psi Upsilon Charged With Hazing, Distributing Alcohol to Minors"; "Former Psi Upsilon Pledges Face At Least One Semester Suspension," *TD*, March 11, 1991; "Court Places Former Pledges on Probation," *TD*, March 26, 1991; "Administration is Using Pledges as Pawns," *TD*, March 28, 1991; "Former Pledges Put On Probation," *TD*, April 3, 1991; and "Psi U Brothers Placed On Probation," *TD*, April 11, 1991. According to these articles, Level II suspension meant that one more infraction and the student in question would be kicked out of Tufts for one full semester. Additionally, a Level II suspension is noted on the student's transcript. A Level I suspension was more of a general warning, and no record was entered on the student's transcript.

580. "Rape Protest Held at Psi Upsilon," *TD*, September 23, 1991; "Alleged Depiction Accounts Conflict," *TD*, September 24, 1991; "Somerville Considering Civil Action After Incident," *TD*, September 24, 1991; and "Senate Votes on ARA, Outreach; Angry Division on Response to Alleged Rape Depiction," *TD*, September 24, 1991. In today's modern age, with digital cameras as ubiquitous as any piece of clothing, it can be hard to remember a time when film-based cameras were almost a rarity. In this case, a photograph of the car's artwork would have made all the difference, but, alas, it appears none was ever successfully taken.

581. Ibid. The article "Rape Protest Held at Psi Upsilon" contains the first reference to the spray-painting as allegedly being a "depiction of rape." However, this description was not corroborated by independent witnesses who had seen the artwork, according to "Witnesses Do Not Feel Grafitti [sic] Depicted Rape," *TD*, September 26, 1991. In-

stead, this phrase appears to have been created by the author of the article, and was then repeated in nearly every report to follow. On the subsequent coverage by the *Boston Herald*, see "Reitman Discusses Alleged Depiction," *TD*, September 26, 1991.

582. On the decision to hold hearings, see "Reitman Discusses Alleged Depiction." On the resulting opinions about the situation, see "Witnesses Do Not Feel Grafitti [sic] Depicted Rape"; "Offensive Pranks," *TD*, September 26, 1991; "First Amendment Rights Are Examined In Obscenity Case," *TD*, September 27, 1991; and "Point of Protest Missed," *TD*, September 27, 1991. On the spot inspection of 165 College Avenue, see "Somerville to Inspect Psi Upsilon House for Building Code Violations," *TD*, September 30, 1991.

583. "Inspection Report May Be Released," *TD*, October 11, 1991, which includes the quotation. Although the report had not been released when this article was printed, the housing inspectors divulged much of its contents to the reporter from *The Tufts Daily*.

584. "Hearing on Alleged Rape Scene Set," *TD*, October 7, 1991; "CFS Examines Status Relationship Between Greek System, University," *TD*, October 17, 1991; "Depiction Hearing to Continue," *TD*, October 21, 1991; "Six Students Found Guilty of Harassment; Panel Finds Car Not Depicting 'Rape'," *TD*, October 24, 1991; and "Details of Depiction Case Released," *TD*, October 29, 1991. Unfortunately for Psi U, the hearings were not the fraternity's only troubles to make campus headlines. See "Psi Upsilon Brother Charged with DUI; Car Accident Leaves Three Injured," *TD*, October 7, 1991. The title of the article speaks for itself.

585. On the confusion over the use of "alleged depiction of rape," see "Six Students Found Guilty of Harassment," which states "there was 'no suggestion by the complaining parties that the much-publicized rumors that the painting depicted a rape scene were true.' "

586. "IGCJ Panel Suspends Psi Upsilon Fraternity," *TD*, November 8, 1991, which includes the quotation. Psi U was found "not responsible" on three other charges, ranging from harassment to "failing to discourage sexual misconduct [and] failure to properly instill the values, ideals, and responsibilities of the fraternity." The creation of the IGC is discussed further in chapter 6.

587. "Somerville Hopes to Dislodge Psi Upsilon," *TD*, December 5, 1991; and "Campus Life: Tufts; A Fraternity, Disciplined Twice, Faces New Threat," *NYT*, January 5, 1992, which includes the quotation. The landlord of 165 College Avenue, Frank Fodera, owned upwards of twenty or thirty other duplexes around campus at the time.

588. On the aftermath of the inspection, see "City Pressures Psi U Landlord," *TD*, January 27, 1992. On bringing the story to a wider audience, see "Campus Life: Tufts; A Fraternity, Disciplined Twice, Faces New Threat."

589. On the pulling of Zeta Tau's charter in February of 1992, see "Psi Upsilon's Charter Now Officially Pulled," *TD*, November 3, 1993.

590. "Psi U is Off Probation." *TD*, February 10, 1993.

591. "Psi Upsilon's Charter Now Officially Pulled," which includes the quotation.

592. "Students May Look to Begin a New Fraternity," *TD*, April 27, 1995. On issues relating to the lawsuit, see also "Psi Upsilon's Charter Now Officially Pulled." According to this article, the damages were set at $35,000, and though I have not confirmed this, I suspect none of this money has yet been collected. The group of students, in the end, did not start a new fraternity as planned.

593. McKee et. al., *Sigma Phi Epsilon*, 9; and "How It Happened," *The Sigma Phi Epsilon Journal* 10, no. 3 (March 1, 1913): 241. On the enrollment of Carter Jenkens at Rutgers College, see *Catalogue of the Officers and Alumni of Rutgers College* (Trenton, NJ: Rutgers College, 1916), 217.

594. McKee et. al., 9–15; and "How It Happened," 241–242, which includes the quotation. On the fraternities active at Richmond College in 1900, see Baird (5th ed. 1898), 386; and Baird (6th ed. 1905), 555.

595. McKee et. al., 10–17; and "How It Happened," 241–242. Note there is some confusion as to how large the chapter was when it applied for faculty recognition. McKee et. al. says there were twelve members, while "How It Happened," which was written by Carter Jenkens, says there were twenty members. In this case, I deferred to McKee et. al., since this is the official history as published by the fraternity.

596. McKee et. al., 16–17, which includes the quotation; "How It Happened," 242; and "The Story of Our Expansion," *The Sigma Phi Epsilon Journal* 10, no. 3 (March 1, 1913): 246–247, which mentions the recruitment of ministerial students. There is evidence that other fraternities at Richmond did indeed have ministerial students on their membership rolls, thus negating part of the SigEp's argument for going forward. See for example, "Omicron–Richmond College," *The Shield and Diamond* 11, no. 2 (December 1901), 82–83, which discusses a ministerial student in the Pi Kappa Alpha chapter.

597. Ibid. I do find it interesting that Carter Jenkens had never heard of the Sigma Phi fraternity, especially since it had been in existence as a national organization for nearly seventy-five years. A photo of the badge with the hastily added Epsilon is shown in McKee et. al., 17.

598. McKee et. al., 18–19; "Our First Sub-Chapter," *The Sigma Phi Epsilon Journal* 10, no. 3 (March 1, 1913): 242–243; "The Story of Our Expansion," 246–248; and "How It Happened," 242. The idea of dual affiliation in national fraternities fell out of favor in the late 1800s. Apparently, though, Chi Phi did not have an issue with Carter's honorary membership in SigEp.

599. On the rapid growth of SigEp in the early 1900s, see "The Story of Our Expansion," 248–250. Today, Sigma Phi Epsilon is one of the largest fraternities in the country, with approximately 240 active chapters.

600. "The Richmond Conclave," *The Sigma Phi Epsilon Journal* 14, no. 2 (December 25, 1916): 154–157. For more information on Sigma Tau Alpha and their petition, see their section earlier in this chapter.

601. "Sigma Phi Epsilon Expansion," *The Sigma Phi Epsilon Journal* 14, no. 4 (May 10, 1917): 474, which includes the quotation. Note that this article incorrectly lists the local fraternity at Tufts as "Sigma Tau." Unfortunately, the national office of Sigma Phi Epsilon no longer has a copy of the petition from Sigma Tau Alpha, as apparently they disposed of all petitions filed prior to 1917.

602. "New Fraternity, Sigma Phi Epsilon, Growing Fast," *TD*, February 9, 1984; and interviews with SigEp alumni involved in the early years of the chapter, including Ken Languedoc (March 26, 2011).

603. Ibid, and "Already A Leader at Tufts: Chartered with 42 Members," *The Sigma Phi Epsilon Journal* 82, no. 3 (May 1985): 6. SigEp's ability to grow so much during its start-up phase without a house was no small feat. Indeed, they were the first fraternity to succeed in such a manner since the 1950s. A list of the charter members was not provided in the referenced article.

604. The desire to occupy a house has been one of the basic goals of almost all fraternity chapters at Tufts since they first moved into houses at the end of the 19th century. SigEp was certainly no different in this regard, as evidenced by the paths they took after starting on campus. However, by the 1980s, there just weren't many options available for new fraternity houses, aside from small, wooden-framed structures in the streets and neighborhoods close to campus. But even then, many of these houses were not desirable since they were surrounded by residents not affiliated with Tufts.

605. "Administration to Decide Professors Row Fate," *TD*, March 6, 1985; "Administration Changes Status of 92 Professors Row," *TD*, March 29, 1985; and "Frat Loses House; Co-op Turns To Singles," *TO*, March 29, 1985. Also see the relevant discussions in the sections of Sigma Nu and Psi Upsilon earlier in this chapter. In the fall of 1957, Tufts opened up the house at 25 Whitfield for use by a fraternity. The administration did not open another chapter house until the fall of 1976, when it converted 120 Packard Avenue into Chi Omega's sorority house for one year. Next came the house at 14 Sawyer Avenue, which was opened up for the Alpha Phi sorority in the fall of 1982.

606. On the results of the vote by the IFC, see "Psi U Prez [sic] Protests 92 Decision." On SigEp's acquisition of 16 Bellevue Street, see "Fraternity Finds a Home," *TO*, August 30, 1985, which incorrectly stated that twenty-two members will be living in the house that fall; "Fraternity Defends House Purchase," *TD*, September 17, 1985; and "Fraternity Defended," *TO*, September 20, 1985. By coincidence, the Sigma Tau Alpha fraternity occupied this same house in the early 1910s.

607. "Fraternity Finds a Home"; "Fraternity Defends House Purchase"; and "Fraternity Defended."

608. Letter from Dean Bruce Reitman to Chuck White, Director of Sigma Phi Epsilon national fraternity, dated September 23, 1985, in Office of the President Records 1828–2007, Jean Mayer, administrative records and related papers, 1976–92, Subject Files, UA001.013 Box 10, Folder 21 (Fraternities 1983–1988). As it turned out, the City of Medford banned all fraternity houses from within its borders just a year later, in the fall of 1986, so the housing license really was doomed from the start.

609. As a freshman at Tufts in the fall of 1985, I can attest that the SigEp house was hardly a destination for those interested in the social fraternity scene at the time, as many students didn't know where it was. After all, the house lacked any type of outside identifier and it was not on a street one had to walk down in order to get to class or a dining hall. On their use of the house for rush events, see advertisements in *TD*, October 21, 1985; and *TD*, February 3, 1986. On the purchase of 16 Bellevue Street by the Trustees of Tufts College, see "Quitclaim Deed," Massachusetts Land Records, Middlesex South Registry, Book 16720, Page 1, dated January 17, 1986. The former owner of the house, Ms. Kathleen Spinosa, had only bought the property less than a year earlier, according to "Quitclaim Deed," Massachusetts Land Records, Middlesex South Registry, Book 16186, Page 256, dated May 29, 1985. In selling the house to Tufts, Ms. Spinosa made a profit of $52,000, nearly 22% of the sale price.

610. "HTANA Sees Decline in Community Relations," *TO*, March 7, 1986; and "Sigma Nu to Get 92 Professors Row," *TD*, March 7, 1986. Also see the relevant discussion in the section on Sigma Nu earlier in this chapter.

611. SigEp's decision not to institute a boarding plan is based on my own personal recollections, as well as interviews with SigEp alumni active at the time, including Ken Languedoc. I recall speaking with SigEp members that fall about why they decided not

to serve meals out of their house, and while there was no single definitive reason, the practicality of setting up a boarding plan was the main theme. Also, the small size of the dining room would not have allowed the entire chapter to fit in one sitting. Sigma Nu, by contrast, had a smaller chapter, so feeding all at one time was not an issue.

612. When SigEp moved into 114 Curtis Street that fall, there were seven other fraternity chapters with on campus houses, and all of these other organizations ran some form of boarding plan, from a simple five dinners per week to a full twenty-one meals per week. That SigEp did not was certainly an anomaly. However, by eating their meals together in the same dining hall each night, SigEp effectively invited the campus into their dining room. Other fraternities also ate some meals together in the dining halls – for example, during this time Alpha Epsilon Pi always ate lunch together in Carmichael dining hall. But SigEp took the practice to a new level, and was a major reason they did so well recruiting new members, at least in my opinion.

613. "SigEp Holds Dry Rush," *TD*, September 25, 1986; "Pass Me a Cold One," *TD*, October 3, 1986; and "Massachusetts–Tufts," *The Sigma Phi Epsilon Journal* 84, no. 1 (February 1987): 14. According to these articles, SigEp had upwards of fifty rushees each night, and they ended up with a pledge class of twenty-two, which was the largest of any fraternity that fall. By contrast, my fraternity that fall held recruitment events with themes such as International Beer, Pizza, and Foosball Night; Around The World cocktails; BBQ and Brews; and, to cap off the week, a toga party. We probably had no more than twenty-five to thirty rushees each night, and ended up pledging fourteen. This was still a very good result as it grew our chapter size by 50%, but that fall, it was clear to all in the Greek system that SigEp had won the recruitment game.

614. Ibid, with the quotation from "SigEp Holds Dry Rush." On the establishment of dry rush for all fraternities during the 1988-89 school year, see "Tufts' Greek System Enters an Era of Reform and Progress," *TD*, Commencement Issue, 1989. This mandate marked the first time since Prohibition that alcohol had not been part of fraternity recruitment at Tufts.

615. "SigEp to Remain on Campus, For Now," *TD*, September 26, 2002. This article mentions the struggles of the entire Greek system during this time, with only 11% of students being members of the various organizations, down from 18% just a few years earlier. On the unfortunate death of Scott Krueger, see "A Drinking Death Rattles Elite M.I.T.; Latest Fraternity Party Case Underscores Nationwide Problem," *NYT*, October 1, 1997. This incident understandably put all Greek organizations under enhanced scrutiny for years. Additionally for SigEp, there was also an unfortunate incident in 2000, when the chapter's president was taken to Somerville District Court to answer charges of providing alcohol to minors. The court eventually decided on continuance for SigEp's president. However, the publicity surrounding this case undoubtedly led many to shy away from SigEp that subsequent school year. See "Administration Charges Tufts Fraternity President with Serving Alcohol to Minors," *TD*, September 1, 2000; "Fraternity Leaders Plead Case in Somerville Court Hearing," *TD*, September 1, 2000; and "Fraternity President Attends Court Hearing," *TD*, September 1, 2000.

616. "SigEp To Remain on Campus, For Now," which includes the quotation.

617. Ibid. Details of this incident were also provided through interviews of Tufts University officials, including Dean Bruce Reitman (October 31, 2012; and November 16, 2012). Finally, the owners of the property, Tufts-affiliated Walnut Hill properties, would also have lost significant rental income had the lodging license been revoked.

618. Ibid; and "Greeks in Rush to Get Back on Their Feet," *TD*, February 23, 2004.

619. On the actions by the SigEp seniors, see "SigEp Loses House in Wake of Senior Week Damages," *TD*, September 8, 2011.

620. "SigEp Loses House in Wake of Senior Week Damages," which includes the quotation. This article mentions that someone had taken pictures of the damages, and these photos were described as shocking by those in SigEp who saw them. Therefore, my descriptions of the damages are assumptions based on this wording as well as conversations I had with Tufts administrators about the damages, including Dean Bruce Reitman and Su McGlone, Director of Fraternity and Sorority Affairs. I did not, however, see any of these aforementioned photos.

621. Ibid; and "SigEp Remains Active Despite Challenges of Homelessness," *TD*, November 15, 2011.

622. "Former SigEp House to Become FIC Office," *TD*, March 6, 2012. The Feinstein International Center (FIC) had been located in a commercial building on Boston Avenue, but was kicked out that year to make room for more laboratories for the biology department.

623. "SigEp To Remain Houseless," *TD*, September 4, 2012; and "Sigma Nu House Becomes Transfer Student Residence," *TD*, September 10, 2012. Unlike the situation at 114 Curtis Street a year earlier, this time the administration took photos of the interior of 92 Professors Row when they discovered the mess. I was able to view those photos a few months later when I became an alumni advisor to the chapter. The house was certainly a mess, but as described further in the section on Sigma Nu in this chapter, maintenance and upkeep of 92 Professors Row had lagged over the years, with the tenants bearing some responsibility, but the landlord bearing some as well.

624. Ibid.

625. "SigEp To Remain Houseless."

626. "SigEp To Move into House on Pro Row," *TD*, November 27, 2012; and "SigEp Settles into New House on ProRow," *TD*, September 9, 2013. Ironically, the photo in *The Tufts Daily* accompanying the first mentioned article shows 92 Professors Row halfway through its renovations, and it is clear that maintenance of the exterior of the structure had long been neglected by the landlord.

627. As chapter advisor to Sigma Nu during the 2013–14 school year, I was very much aware of the process by which 92 Professors Row and 90–92 Curtis Street were assigned to the two fraternities via the Inter-Greek Council. It was unfortunate that, at the time, the process dragged out so long, for it did create some animosity between the two organizations, at least from my perspective. For more information on this decision process, see the appropriate paragraphs in the section on Sigma Nu earlier in this chapter.

628. To quote a Tufts University official, "It was never our intention to reward SigEp [following their expulsion from 114 Curtis Street] with the house at 92 Professors Row." And yet that is exactly what they did.

629. "Tufts' Sigma Phi Epsilon Chapter Disaffiliates from National Organization," *TD*, November 19, 2015. It appears the chapter's alumni were never consulted on the plan to disaffiliate. On the Balanced Man program, see information on the fraternity's website, http://www.sigep.org/about/what-we-do/BMP.html (accessed November 12, 2016). Information about the resistance in the Tufts chapter to the Balanced Man program was provided by Su McGlone, Director of Fraternity and Sorority Affairs at Tufts,

and by members of SigEp's national staff through a blog post, https://www.facebook.com/SigEpBlogFans/posts/10153391626298897 (accessed November 12, 2016). On the emergence of Pi Delta, see the section on Sigma Omega Psi/Alpha Epsilon Pi earlier in this chapter.

630. "Former SigEp Brothers Establish Pi Rho Omega as Independent Fraternity," *TD*, January 25, 2016.

631. "Fifteen Years Ago," *The Magazine of Alpha Phi Delta*, 1, no. 1 (December 1929): 3–9, 29; *The History of Alpha Phi Delta Fraternity*, unknown author and publisher, http://issuu.com/apdcentraloffice/docs/original_history_of_alpha_phi_delta_12ab7126f5f305/1?e=4671410/9944659 (accessed May 31, 2015); and the official Alpha Phi Delta history as posted on the national fraternity's website, http://www.apd.org/the-beginning.html (accessed May 31, 2015). Unfortunately, these three sources are not consistent in terms of how Cesidio and Ferdinand met, or when they first arrived at Syracuse University. Therefore, I have attempted to rationalize the information as best I can.

632. Ibid. According to "Fifteen Year Ago," the positive review of Il Circolo Italiano's cultural event was published in *The Daily Orange [Syracuse University]* on February 9, 1914. Alpha Phi Delta would remain true to its Italian roots until 1965, when the fraternity officially opened membership to all men. For more information, see "Italian Heritage–The Transition," *The Kleos* 71, no. 3 (Spring 2000): 12.

633. Interview with Mark Wasielewski (February 19, 2011); and "Six Freshmen Form New Fraternity," *TD*, April 25, 1996. According to Mark, there were originally twelve or thirteen men interested in starting a new fraternity, but as the work progressed, a number dropped out, leaving just a core group of six.

634. Ibid.

635. Ibid. The initiation of the colony took place in the house of a local Alpha Phi Delta alumnus, according to the chapter's history as posted on its website, http://ase.tufts.edu/apd (accessed May 31, 2015).

636. On the philanthropy and service activities of the chapter, see "Fraternity Hoping To Create Escort Service," *TD*, November 18, 1996; "Alpha Phi Delta Volunteers in Community," *TD*, December 2, 1997; "Tufts Newest Fraternity is Making Itself Known," *TD*, December 4, 1997; "Letters to the Editor–Theta Chi Mars Otherwise Successful Greek Jam," *TD*, March 17, 1999; and "IGC Update–APD," *TD*, April 20, 1999. On the installation of the colony as the Delta Sigma chapter in the fall of 1997, see "Tufts Newest Fraternity is Making Itself Known."

637. Information on the housing woes of APD was provided in an interview with Mark Wasielewski. Alpha Phi Delta first occupied a house at 13 Emery Street, then moved to 211 College Avenue by the fall of 1998, according to various rush week advertisements as published in *The Tufts Daily*.

638. On the announcement of a chapter house, see "Future of Zeta Psi House Being Negotiated–Alpha Phi Delta To Get House," *TD*, October 7, 1999. Information about APD's possible occupancy of either ZBT or Sigma Nu's house was provided in an interview with Mark Wasielewski. On the accomplishments of the chapter in the early 2000s, see "Tufts University," *The Kleos* 71, no. 3 (Spring 2000): 5; "Convention Issue," *The Kleos* 72, no. 1 (Fall 2000): front cover; "Tufts University," *The Kleos* 73, no. 1 (Fall 2001): 5; and "We Hope You Like Greek Jammin' Too," *TD*, April 1, 2002. On the membership roll of APD in the spring of 2001, see the chapter's website, http://ase.

tufts.edu/apd (accessed May 31, 2015).

639. Although membership records for Alpha Phi Delta are scant, it appears the fraternity did gain a few pledges after the spring of 2001, but was unable to initiate any of them as full members. See "Administration Calls For Improvement To Greek System," *TD*, November 14, 2002; and "Why Greeks Are In Demise," *TD*, March 2, 2006. The chapter's website, http://ase.tufts.edu/apd (accessed May 31, 2015), lists the initiates through the Iota pledge class (spring of 2001). On the move to the suite in Latin Way, see "Interest Group to Petition for Fourth Tufts Sorority," *TD*, October 16, 2002. Finally, in Alpha Phi Delta's section of *Jumbo* (2003 ed.), the chapter mentions there had been no further pledge classes beyond Iota, and admits "[they had] been through some trying times in recent years," which I assume is in reference to poor recruitment. On the official closing of the Delta Sigma chapter, see "National Council," *The Kleos* 77, no. 3 (Summer 2006): 12.

CHAPTER 4

1. On the preponderance of all-male colleges and universities in 1850's New England, see Start, *History of Tufts College*, 65. Some of the most prestigious schools in New England, such as Williams, Amherst, Bowdoin, Harvard, Colby, Wesleyan, Trinity, Yale, Brown, and Middlebury were exclusively for men. On the founding of Tufts College by the Universalists, see Miller, *LOTH–1*, 163–165; and Miller, *LOTH–2*, 92–94. On the opening of other schools by the Universalists in the 1800s, see Ann Lee Bressler, *The Universalist Movement in America: 1770–1880* (New York, NY: Oxford University Press, 2001), 91.

2. On the quote by Reverend Thomas Whittemore, see Miller, *LOTH–2*, 92. On the push to make Tufts a coeducational school, see, for example, Mary Caroline Crawford, *The College Girl of America* (Boston, MA: L. C. Page & Company, 1905), 285–286; and "Jackson College Celebrates Its Second Anniversary as a Separate Institution for Women," *NYT*, May 5, 1912. The evolution of Jackson College as an entity within Tufts is beyond the scope of this work, but is discussed in great detail in Miller, *LOTH–1*, 163–198; and Miller, *LOTH–2*, 109–113. On the rejection of coeducation by the trustees, see "Coeducation at Tufts," *BG*, May 11, 1892; and "Admits Women: Tufts College Throws Its Doors Wide Open," *BG*, July 16, 1892.

3. On the series of incremental steps, see "Coeducation at Tufts"; and "Tufts To Admit Women," *BG*, May 18, 1892. On President Capen's strong desire to implement coeducation, see "Admits Women: Tufts College Throws Its Doors Wide Open."

4. "Admits Women: Tufts College Throws Its Doors Wide Open," which includes the quotation.

5. On the anguish of the male students, see " 'Co-eds' at Tufts: Why Some of the Fellows Do Not Like Them," *BG*, May 21, 1893, which includes the quotations; and "College Annuals," *The Rainbow of Delta Tau Delta* 16, no. 4 (July 1893): 212–213. This latter reference includes a copy of a poem to be included in the upcoming edition of the *Brown and Blue* yearbook, presumably written by a male student: "Oh, keep the girls far away, friends, Send them to places at will; Don't let them come here to stay, friends, Here at fair Tufts on the Hill." The article in the *Boston Globe*, however, does seem to indicate that men's feelings towards their female classmates had started to ebb

significantly by the end of that first year.

6. On the opening of the anteroom in the library for the women, see Board of Trustees records, 1848–2013, Full Board, 1851–2012, Meeting Minutes 1851–1955, UA003.001 Box 106, Folder 1 (Full Board Minutes vol. 3, 1887–1895: October 10, 1892). On the decision of Heth Aleph Res to admit women, see the fraternity's section in Chapter 3.

7. According to "Co-eds at Tufts: Why Some of the Fellows Do Not Like Them," there were "10 [women enrolled] during the early part of the school year, but one dropped out." The nine pioneering women as recorded that fall of 1892, according to the *CofTC* (1892–93 ed.), 15, 17, 19, 94, were: Henrietta Noble Brown, Mabel Prescott Bailey, Ethel Munroe Hayes, Blanche Harwood Hill, Gertrude Holbrooke Meacom, and Laurie Frazeur in the Classical and Philosophical Courses; and Angie Maye Brooks, Eliza Mary Hickok, and Mabel Lilla MacCoy in the Tufts Divinity School.

8. On the founding of Alpha Delta Sigma, see Start, 231–232; "History of Delta Chapter," *To Dragma of Alpha Omicron Pi* 6, no. 1 (November 1910): 8–9; and Alpha Omicron Pi Fraternity, *History of Delta Chapter*, 1. On the construction of Metcalf Hall, see Start, 66. Note that in 1895, the term "sorority" was not in general use at Tufts College. Instead, "society" was the preferred term when referring to a social organization of students, especially women, at least for a few years. It seems Grace Fickett's full name was Mary Grace Fickett, according to Start, 232, and *CofTC* (1894–95 ed.), 23. However, it appears she did not go by "Mary," according to the other listed sources.

9. Ibid. On the announcement of Alpha Delta Sigma to the Tufts Campus, see "Alpha Delta Sigma," *TW*, November 5, 1895. On the names of the six founding members, see "History of Delta Chapter," 8. On the use of secrecy within the society, see *History of Delta Chapter*, 1.

10. On the formation of Alpha Kappa Gamma, see "Alpha Kappa Gamma," *TW*, November 5, 1895. This society is also discussed in more detail in the next section of this chapter. On Alpha Delta Sigma's social activities throughout their first school year, see "Student Life," *The Tuftonian* 22, no. 7 (May–June 1896): 227–228; and "Alpha Delta Sigma Entertains," *TW*, March 24, 1896. Professor Knight lived in a grand Victorian-style house at 114 Professors Row. This structure was eventually purchased by the Delta Upsilon fraternity and then razed to allow the construction of the brick structure that still stands today.

11. On the literary exercises of fraternities across the country in the late 1800s, see Syrett, *The Company He Keeps*, 28–29, 59, 149. At Tufts, both the Zeta Psi and Delta Upsilon chapters were known to emphasize the literary element within their brotherhoods at this time. On Alpha Delta Sigma's inclusion of a literary element to their society, see "History of Delta Chapter," 1. On Alpha Delta Sigma's theatrical productions, see "Alpha Delta Sigma Entertains," *TW*, March 24, 1896; "Alpha Delta Sigma Presents its Annual Play," *TW*, March 12, 1898; "It's A Theory of Mine," *BG*, March 10, 1899; "Audience of Women Only – Dramatic Evening by Alpha Delta Sigma Sorority of Tufts College," *BG*, March 31, 1900; and "Tufts Girls Give A Play," *BG*, April 19, 1901. Some of the plays performed by Alpha Delta Sigma included *It's A Theory of Mine*, written by a member of the sorority, Katherine Louise Stubbins; *She Stoops To Conquer*, by Oliver Goldsmith; and *Cricket On The Hearth*, by Charles Dickens.

12. "History of Delta Chapter," 8; and *History of Delta Chapter*, 1–2. Delta Sigma at Brown University had formed in 1896, just a year after Alpha Delta Sigma at Tufts.

Unfortunately, how the Brown chapter and the Tufts chapter managed to learn about each other is unknown, but in all likelihood they first learned of each other through *Baird's Manual of American College Fraternities*. For example, Baird (5th ed. 1898), 293, 298, lists information about Alpha Delta Sigma and Delta Sigma. On the merger of the Tufts and Brown chapters to form Delta Sigma, see "Now Delta Sigma," *TW*, January 5, 1901. Given the publication date of this article, it is very plausible the two chapters began talking about a merger the previous fall. However, there is no record of when their first meeting took place, or how long they were in discussions about the merger. On the absorption of Phi Gamma from the University of Maine, see "Gamma of Delta Sigma and Gamma of Alpha Omicron Pi," *To Dragma of Alpha Omicron Pi* 5, no. 2 (February 1910): 66–67.

13. On the ultra-secrecy surrounding Delta Sigma, see Martin, *The Sorority Handbook*, 77–78. I found it interesting that the women of Delta Sigma were so obsessed with secrecy. Indeed, I have not come across any other instance of a fraternity or sorority keeping its national officers and place of convention from the public.

14. *History of Delta Chapter*, 2–3, which includes the quotation. Again, my assertion that other organizations learned of Delta Sigma through *Baird's Manual of American College Fraternities*, though very plausible, is entirely speculation. On Delta Sigma's entry, for example, see Baird (6th ed. 1905), 314.

15. On the operations of Delta Sigma, see for example, "Delta Sigma Sorority," *BG*, January 19, 1902; *History of Delta Chapter*, 3; "Alpha Chapter Dance," *BG*, January 22, 1904; "Delta Sigma Play," *TW*, March 10, 1904; and "Delta Sigma Convention," *TW*, November 9, 1905. On the absorption of Tau Epsilon Sigma by Alpha Xi Delta, see the appropriate section later in this chapter. On the absorption of Delta Sigma by Alpha Omicron Pi, see "History of Delta Chapter," 9; *History of Delta Chapter*, 4–5; and "New National Sorority," *TW*, April 16, 1908.

16. On the founding of Alpha Omicron Pi, see the national fraternity's website, http://www.alphaomicronpi.org/our-beginning (accessed June 12, 2015). Unfortunately, any correspondence between Delta Sigma and AOII regarding the merger has not survived to this day.

17. "History of Delta Chapter"; "Join the Alpha Omicron Pi," *BG*, April 15, 1908; and "The Installation of Delta Chapter," *To Dragma of Alpha Omicron Pi* 4, no. 2 (February 1909): 111–112, which includes the quotation. Mary Lambert lived at the home of her parents, 16 Dearborn Road, just across from the Bromfield-Pearson building, according to the campus map in *CofTC* (1907–08 ed.). Her father was a professor in the biology department at the time. The national officers who performed the installation ceremony were Mrs. Helen St. Clair Mullen (one of the original founders of AOII), Elizabeth Toms, and Helen Hoy-Greeley. The trio also initiated a number of Alpha Delta Sigma and Delta Sigma alumnae into AOII the following day, April 14, 1908. Afterwards, the national officers travelled to the University of Maine to initiate the Gamma chapter of Delta Sigma into AOII.

18. On life in Delta chapter in the early 1910s, see for example, "Delta, Tufts College," *To Dragma of Alpha Omicron Pi* 4, no. 1 (November 1908): 130–131, which includes the quotation; and "Delta, Tufts College," *To Dragma of Alpha Omicron Pi* 8, no. 1 (November 1912): 140. On the opening of the AOII room in Richardson House dormitory, see "Delta, Tufts College," *To Dragma of Alpha Omicron Pi* 8, no. 3 (May 1913): 213; and "A History of Boston Alumnae Chapter," *To Dragma of Alpha Omicron*

Pi 9, no. 2 (February 1914): 141–144.

19. "Delta – Jackson College," *To Dragma of Alpha Omicron Pi* 13, no. 2 (February 1918): 144, which includes the quotation; and "Delta – Jackson College," *To Dragma of Alpha Omicron Pi* 13, no. 3 (May 1918): 258–259. Unfortunately, this latter article does not mention where, exactly, this cooperative house was located on campus. The *CofTC* (1917–18 ed.), 218–221, lists three such possibilities, known as Alpha, Gamma, and Richardson houses. All housed women both in AOII and not that school year. Therefore, wherever the AOII women lived, they were not the exclusive residents, so this was not a bona fide sorority house. Finally, there is no evidence that AOII continued such a close living arrangement after the 1917–18 school year.

20. "Delta–Jackson College," *To Dragma of Alpha Omicron Pi* 14, no. 1 (November 1918): 48, which includes the quotation; "Delta–Jackson College," *To Dragma of Alpha Omicron Pi* 14, no. 2 (February 1919): 134–135. The opening of Tufts College that fall was delayed approximately three weeks, to the beginning of October, in order to halt the spread of influenza. For more information on the S.A.T.C. program, see chapter 3.

21. "Delta–Jackson College," *To Dragma of Alpha Omicron Pi* 15, no. 1 (November 1919): 53–54; and "Delta–Jackson College," *To Dragma of Alpha Omicron Pi* 15, no. 2 (February 1920): 147–148. Note this latter reference is from an edition of *To Dragma* that is incorrectly marked as Volume 16. The lack of any reference to the war effort or upheaval in the chapter letters shows, I believe, how quickly people wish to put such grave conflicts behind them.

22. The activities of AOII post-World War I are quite normal, with no serious issues or upheavals; hence, there is little to discuss from a historical perspective. The issue of racial discrimination in sororities is discussed further in the sections on Sigma Kappa and Alpha Xi Delta later in this chapter. Although I have not been able to determine if AOII ever had restrictive membership clauses or practices, they certainly did not by the 1950s, when such practices came under intense scrutiny at Tufts. See Chapter 6 for more information. On the occupancy of chapter rooms by the sorority, see, for example, *Jumbo* (1940 ed.), 151; "Alpha Pi, Sigma Sororities Present Facts on Chapter," *TW*, November 14, 1946; and "Sorority Supplement– Alpha Omicron Pi," *TW*, November 13, 1947; and "Sorority Open House," *TW*, April 18, 1956, which talks about the recent opening of sorority rooms in Curtis Hall. On the pajama parties with Theta Chi, see correspondence and notes from 1959 and 1961 in Activities and Organizations records, 1875–2013, UA 024.001 Box 1 Folder 6 (Alpha Omicron Pi 1912–1968).

23. Unfortunately, I could not determine the exact date of closure for Delta chapter of Alpha Omicron Pi. It appears that by the fall of 1970, no sorority remained in active operation at Tufts, so I am assuming AOII shut down by the spring of 1970 at the latest. Just two years earlier, during the 1967–68 school year, the chapter had thirty-five active members listed on what was the last published roster. See Activities and Organizations records, 1875–2013, UA 024.001 Box 1, Folder 6 (Alpha Omicron Pi 1912–1968). On the establishment of the Alpha Omicron Pi scholarship, see *CofTC* (1909–10 ed.), 207; and https://ase.tufts.edu/epcshd/documents/undergradAwardDescriptions.pdf (accessed November 15, 2016), which includes the quotation. This scholarship is still awarded today.

24. Information about the initial interest in forming a new sorority was provided through interviews of alumni involved in the effort, including Meredith Kaplan Stoma (February 22, 2012). On the efforts to restart sorority life in the 1970s, see the sections

for Chi Omega and Alpha Phi later in this chapter.

25. Information about the National Panhellenic Conference, and their criteria for starting new chapters of organizations under their umbrella, can be found on their website, https://www.npcwomen.org (accessed June 20, 2015). On the process as it played out at Tufts, see "New Sorority Invited to Tufts," *TD*, February 4, 1986; and "Alpha Omicron Pi Accepts Invitation," *TD*, February 6, 1986.

26. On the establishment of the colony, see "Join the Reactivation of Tufts' Oldest Sorority," *TD*, February 27, 1986; and "Alpha Omicron Pi Congratulates Our New Colony Members," *TD*, April 1, 1986. On the reinstallation of Delta chapter and the problems with Greek housing, see "The Role of Sororities," *TD*, February 19, 1987; and "AOPi Installed as Chapter," *TD*, April 16, 1987. The other organizations without an on campus house were Psi Upsilon, Alpha Epsilon Pi, Alpha Sigma Phi, and Zeta Beta Tau. For more information on the housing shortage, see the sections of these fraternities in Chapter 3.

27. On the trials and tribulations of Theta Delta Chi, see the appropriate section in chapter 3. On the awarding of 125 Packard Avenue to the sorority, see "AOPi Gets 123 House," *TD*, September 12, 1990. The address was changed to 125 Packard Avenue when the sorority moved in, since the previous address was also the nickname of Theta Delta Chi, "123."

28. "Tufts, Theta Delta Chi Release New Settlement," *TD*, February 27, 1992; "Sorority to Remain In House," *TD*, April 15, 1993. On the original opening of 25 Whitfield as a fraternity house in 1957, see the section for Phi Sigma Kappa in chapter 3. The house was also home to the Chi Omega sorority for one year, 1977–78.

29. "Sorority To Remain In House." According to this article, AOII amassed 45.95 points in the decision rubric, Alpha Epsilon Pi had 42.675, and Zeta Beta Tau had 35.13. AOII benefitted from an increase of points due to the "gender equity mandate," since far fewer women by percentage lived in a chapter house.

30. On the one hundredth anniversary celebration for Delta chapter, see "Delta," *To Dragma of Alpha Omicron Pi* 72, no. 3 (Summer 2008): 56. On the division within Delta chapter, see "Half of AOII Sisters Drop to Protest National Organization," *TD*, November 4, 2016; "AOII: Sisters Still," *TD*, November 7, 2016; and "A Letter from AOII: An Official Response to our Recent Chapter Division," *TD*, November 15, 2016. This incident, no doubt, could turn out to be a very positive turning point for AOII and Delta chapter. Unfortunately, I will have to leave the details to future historians.

31. The push for coeducation was discussed earlier in this chapter. On Mabel Prescott Bailey's journey to Tufts, see "Co-eds at Tufts: Why Some of the Fellows Do Not Like Them," which includes the quotation. This article does not mention Mabel Bailey by name, but I strongly believe Mabel was quoted in the article as I wrote in the text. The reporter describes his source for the quotes as a young woman with glasses. The four youngest women to enter Tufts that fall were Mabel Bailey, Ethel Munroe Hayes, Blanche Harwood Hill, and Gertrude Holbrooke Meacom, according to *CofTC* (1892–93 ed.), 17. The latter three appear in an 1896 photograph without glasses – see http://hdl.handle.net/10427/47893 (accessed June 22, 2015). Therefore, this leaves Mabel Bailey as the likely interviewee. Indeed, Mabel is shown wearing glasses in a later photograph within the Radcliffe College Archives. See http://via.lib.harvard.edu/via/deliver/deepcontentItem?recordId=olvgroup11707%2CRAD.ARCH%3A1135680 (accessed June 22, 2015).

32. On the location of the hometowns for the four women, see *CofTC* (1892–93 ed.), 17. The women's dormitory in question was Metcalf Hall, which was completed by the start of the 1893–94 school year, according to "Metcalf Hall, 1893," *Concise Encyclopedia of Tufts History*, http://hdl.handle.net/10427/14829 (accessed June 22, 2015). On the library room set aside by the trustees for the women, see note 6 earlier in this chapter.

33. On the founding of Alpha Kappa Gamma, see Start, 233–234. On the announcement of the new sorority to the campus, see "Alpha Kappa Gamma," *TW*, November 5, 1895.

34. My estimate of half the women undergraduates belonging to a sorority was determined by comparing membership rosters as published in Start, 232–233, which lists twenty-four total names, against the student directory as published in *CofTC* (1895–96 ed.), 23–29, which lists approximately fifty-one undergraduate women. On the hosting of the first reception, see "Student Life," *The Tuftonian* 22, no. 7 (May–June 1896): 227–228.

35. On the events and activities of Alpha Kappa Gamma in the late 1890s and early 1900s, see, for example, "Given The Secrets," *BG*, October 17, 1899; "Many Initiated," *BG*, October 21, 1902; "Gave Dancing Party; Guests of Alpha Kappa Gamma of Tufts Enjoyed Themselves," *BG*, October 29, 1902; "Alpha Kappa Gamma Dance," *BG*, March 7, 1903; "Nine Join Sorories [sic]," *BG*, October 10, 1903; "Alpha Kappa Gamma Dance," *BG*, March 12, 1904; "Musical at Tufts College," *BG*, January 27, 1906; and "Reception To Graduates," *BG*, June 13, 1909. On the production of *Sweet Lavender*, see "No Man Looked On," *BG*, February 27, 1904. The production was held in Social Hall of Somerville, which was attached to the First Universalist Church. On the hand-written comment, see the program for *Sweet Lavender* in Activities and Organizations records, 1875–2013, UA 024.001 Box 1, Folder 8 (Alpha Kappa Gamma 1904–1910).

36. The consolidation and mergers within the national women's fraternity movement is beyond the scope of this work, but suffice to say this practice mirrored the consolidation seen in men's fraternities around the same time as well. A good discussion of the appeal of national fraternities over local ones can be found in Syrett, *The Company He Keeps,* 83, 105–118, 211, 213. On the national aspirations of Alpha Delta Sigma and Tau Epsilon Sigma, and the birth of the Delphoi Society, see their respective sections in this chapter.

37. On the opposing conditions for women and men at Arkansas Industrial University in the spring of 1895, see *Twenty-Second Catalogue of the Arkansas Industrial University* (1894–95 ed.), 31–34. Here, parents of young ladies were warned to be "well satisfied as to her discretion, or else should place her under the control of the family with whom she boards." On the founding of the group by the four women, see Hugh and Thomas, *History of the University of Arkansas*, 340. The four women were: Jobelle Holcombe, Jean Vincenheller, Ina May Boles, and Alice Simonds. The fraternities at Arkansas in 1895 were Kappa Sigma, Sigma Alpha Epsilon, and Kappa Alpha, according to Baird (6th ed. 1905), 527.

38. Hugh and Thomas, 340; and the history of Chi Omega as published by on the national organization's website, http://www.chiomega.com/aboutus/historyofchiomega (accessed June 28, 2015). Dr. Richardson, along with the four women mentioned in the previous notes, are considered the five founders of the Chi Omega fraternity. Note

that Chi Omega does not use the word "sorority" to describe its organization in an official sense. Chi Omega is not the only women's fraternity to have a man as an official member. George Banta, a member of the Phi Delta Theta men's fraternity, was also an initiated member of the Delta Gamma women's fraternity, in recognition of his help in expanding that organization around the Midwest.

39. On the establishment of Chi chapter at Jessamine College and Phi chapter at Hellmuth Women's College, see "Editorial," *The Eleusis of Chi Omega* 6, no. 1 (February 1904): 38–39; and "Editorial," *The Eleusis of Chi Omega* 6, no. 4 (November 1904): 336–337. There is also, supposedly, an in-depth article on these two chapters in the first edition of *The Eleusis of Chi Omega*. Unfortunately, this edition has not yet been made available for research in digital form. Chi Omega's foray into international space did not last very long, as Phi chapter at Hellmuth Women's College closed after just one year of operation, due to a mass exodus of students and subsequent closing of the school. See "The Business Side of the Convention," *The Eleusis of Chi Omega* 2, no. 2 (October 1900): 90–91. To date, this is the only chapter outside of the United States ever established by Chi Omega. On the chapter roll in 1900, see "Chapter Correspondents," *The Eleusis of Chi Omega* 2, no. 1 (June 1900): 2.

40. Chi Omega's establishment of a fraternity publication and biennial convention so early in its history is most likely a major reason why the organization flourished in the early 20th century, and soon grew to be one of the largest women's fraternities in the country. No doubt Dr. Richardson, through his experiences with Kappa Sigma, helped establish these two important aspects of the fraternity. Indeed, he contributed many articles to early editions of *The Eleusis of Chi Omega*, on topics specific to Chi Omega along with the general history and growth of women's fraternities. On the visitation of Sue Bitting, see "The Visits of the S.T.B.," *The Eleusis of Chi Omega* 11, no. 1 (February 1909): 12–18.

41. "The Visits of the S.T.B.," which includes the quotation. Sue's travelling companion was a fellow Chi Omega alumna who apparently was not on any official duty with the fraternity, but there to keep her company. As mentioned in the text, Sue does not identify the women who impressed her at Tufts College, but I have to believe it was Alpha Kappa Gamma, since they did ultimately petition for a charter.

42. I am uncertain as to when, exactly, the women of Alpha Kappa Gamma submitted their petition to Chi Omega, but I have a strong suspicion it was sometime in early 1909, given that Eleanor Duncan Shannon, an officer in Chi Omega, talks about a visit to Tufts College that year. See "The Installation of Chi Alpha," *The Eleusis of Chi Omega* 12, no. 4 (November 1910): 408–413. On the positive reaction of other chapters to the news that Alpha Kappa Gamma's petition had been accepted, see ""Epsilon–Barnard College," *The Eleusis of Chi Omega* 12, no. 3 (August 1910): 346–347; and "Alpha–University of Washington," *The Eleusis of Chi Omega* 12, no. 3 (August 1910): 351–352.

43. "The Installation of Chi Omega"; "Chi Omega Initiation," *BG*, September 19, 1910; and "A.K.G. Joins National Sorority," *TW*, October 4, 1910. I do find it intriguing that Mabel Prescott Bailey chose not to be initiated into Chi Omega, despite living so close to campus. Concerning Edith Bush, she apparently hid her association with Chi Omega in later years as Dean of Women (1925–1952). I've spoke with numerous alumni from that era who recalled Dean Bush as someone who disliked sororities in general. All were generally shocked when I told them she was an initiate of Chi Omega.

44. On the chapters activities in the 1910s, see for example, "Chi Alpha – Jackson College," *The Eleusis of Chi Omega* 12, no. 4 (November 1910): 476–477; "Jackson Sorority Girls Entertain," *BG*, February 28, 1912; "Chi Alpha–Tufts College," *The Eleusis of Chi Omega* 14, no. 2 (May 1912): 183–184; "Jackson College Sorority Dance," *BG*, December 6, 1914; and "Chi Omega Banquet," *BG*, April 6, 1915. Although all women were technically enrolled in Jackson College at this time, the school existed mostly in name only, for they were not wholly segregated from the men of Tufts College. On the transition into war, see "Chi Alpha–Tufts College," *The Eleusis of Chi Omega* 20, no. 1 (February 1918): 95–96, which includes the quotation; "Chi Alpha–Jackson College," *The Eleusis of Chi Omega* 20, no. 2 (May 1918): 214–215; and "Chi Alpha–Jackson College," *The Eleusis of Chi Omega* 20, no. 3 (September 1918): 347–349.

45. "Chi Alpha–Jackson College," *The Eleusis of Chi Omega* 20, no. 4 (November 1918): 506–507, which includes the quotation. I get the sense that college students today would not be so ready to sacrifice as their compatriots did over a hundred years ago in the event of war. But, perhaps this is testament to the lack of a modern global conflict on the scale of the Great War.

46. "Chi Alpha–Jackson College," *The Eleusis of Chi Omega* 21, no. 1 (February 1919): 76–77, which includes the quotations. One reason the women were first to rise on the morning of November 11th was that the men on campus, being soldiers in a military outfit, were generally not allowed to leave their barracks at night without permission. Apparently, the officers made an exception once they realized the situation.

47. On the return to normal operations within Chi Omega following the war, see for example, "Chi Alpha–Jackson College," *The Eleusis of Chi Omega* 22, no. 1 (February 1920): 82; and "Chi Alpha (Jackson), *The Eleusis f Chi Omega* 22, no. 1 (February 1920): 112–114. On the use of chapter rooms by Alpha Kappa Gamma and then Chi Omega, the earliest reference I could find was from the fall of 1899, which mentions Alpha Kappa Gamma had rooms on Curtis Street that semester. See "Given The Secrets," *BG*, October 17, 1899. However, I did not encounter another reference to chapter rooms until the spring of 1921. See "Chi Alpha–Jackson College," *The Eleusis of Chi Omega* 23, no. 2 (May 1921): 174–175. Of course, this reference is somewhat unclear, as it could have been talking about member's individual dormitory rooms in Metcalf Hall. A definite reference to chapter rooms can be found in "Chi Alpha Chapter," *Jumbo* (1940 ed.), 155, but even here the location of the rooms is not specified. Finally, in "Sorority Supplement," *TW*, November 13, 1947, the location of the Chi Omega chapter rooms is identified as 47 Curtis Avenue, but it is unclear how long the chapter had been operating out of this location. On the move to rooms in Curtis Hall, see "Sorority Open House," *TW*, April 18, 1956. The administration's position on sorority housing seems to have been rooted in longstanding practice, rather than an outright edict from the trustees or other campus officials. The first reference I found directly discussing sorority housing was a "Urge Sorority Houses for Jackson Students," *TW*, January 21, 1920; and "Letter to the editor–Sorority Houses," *TW*, January 28, 1920. Furthermore, Acting President George Miller offered this response when asked about the opening of sorority houses: "The suggestion… of housing sororities [sic] girls has received consideration in the past but has never seemed feasible… also, the students don't seem to be asking for this." See letter from Miller to Mrs. H. W. Roberts dated May 12, 1938, in Activities and Organizations records, 1875–2013, UA 024.001 Box 13, Folder 15 (Sororities 1923–1950). It wasn't until the mid 1960s, when the system was starting a

drastic decline, that students began actively pushing to establish sorority houses.

48. "Sorority Troubles Continue; Thirteen Chi Omegas Quit," *TW*, October 19, 1956. The racial diversification of fraternities and sororities on a national level after World War II, or at least the attempt at such diversification, is beyond the scope of this work. However, for some background information, see Syrett, 248–260. Concerning Chi Omega's membership restrictions, the national organization may not have had official membership restrictions, but they certainly used pressure to keep their chapters from breaking the color barrier. For example, see Katie Daigle, "Prejudicial Preferences–The Discriminatory Selection Practices of Colby's Greek Letter Societies," Digital and Special Collections, Colby College, http://www.colby.edu/specialcollections/wp-content/uploads/sites/114/2014/09/Fraternity-and-Sorority-Presentation-Website-Final.pdf (accessed July 7, 2015); and Katie Daigle, "Online Narrative to Prejudicial Practices," Digital and Special Collections, Colby College, http://www.colby.edu/specialcollections/wp-content/uploads/sites/114/2014/09/Online-Descriptions.pdf (accessed July 7, 2015).

49. "Sorority Troubles Continue; Thirteen Chi Omegas Quit," which includes the quotation. On the pledging of the two women by Sigma Kappa, and the subsequent fallout, see that organizations section later in this chapter.

50. Ibid. The Chi Omega official in question, Mary Love Collins, often cited communist infiltrators as the ones behind the push to diversify fraternity and sorority membership across the country. She was not alone in her thinking on this topic.

51. I do not in any way wish to make light of the "return to normal" following the events of that fateful fall. However, as I discuss later in the section on Sigma Kappa, the Tufts Administration, under the direction of Dean Katharine Jeffers, worked hard to keep its students out of the national discussion on fraternity discrimination that fall of 1956. As a result, Tufts students turned their attention to other issues, especially since the campus was anything but racially diverse at the time. The students, however, would eventually return to this cause in earnest, as documented in chapter 6. Information about the closing of Chi Omega in the fall of 1970 was provided through interviews with Chi Omega alumnae active at the time, including Pam (Mosny) Veasy (September 24, 2012) and Susan (Mosny) Steed (October 1, 2012).

52. The general mindset of students at Tufts towards Greek-letter fraternities during the 1970s is based on interviews with Tufts administrators on campus at the time, including Dean Bruce Reitman (October 31, 2012; and November 16, 2012), Professor Sol Gittleman (October 17, 2012), and undergraduates who lived through the decade. Also, numerous articles were written later in the 1970s that reflected on this time when Greek life was hugely out-of-favor at Tufts. See, for example, "Frats Prepare for Rush," *TO*, October 21, 1977; "Fraternities '78: All's Forgiven," *BG*, September 17, 1978; "A Greek Revival," *Tufts Criterion* 11, no. 2 (December 1978): 27; and "Greek System at Tufts: Alive and Well," *TD*, September 30, 1980.

53. Again, interviews with numerous Tufts alumni from the 1970s are the main inspiration for this paragraph. As such, these first two paragraphs are not intended to be an in-depth look at student life in the 1970s, but rather a short segue into the topic at hand.

54. Interviews with a number of re–founding and first members of Chi Omega including Lisa (Romeo) Thompson (February 19, 2011; and February 21, 2011), Christina (Johnson) Rush (May 3, 2011; and May 6, 2011), and a few others who wish to

remain anonymous.

55. Ibid. Also see "Sororities Returning to TU Hill," *TO*, April 9, 1976, which discusses the activities of the Cosmopolitan Sorority that semester.

56. Interviews with Thompson, Rush, and Maurene Golden (June 20, 2011). According to the article "Sororities Returning to TU Hill," two other national organizations under consideration were Alpha Omicron Pi and Alpha Xi Delta. Both of these sororities had a long and storied history at Tufts. For more information, see their respective sections in this chapter.

57. "CSL Approves Sorority Culture House, Polo Club," *TO*, March 26, 1976.

58. Ibid, which includes the quotation. I found no evidence the CSL ever went back and revisited its conditional approval for the Cosmopolitan Sorority, even when the group did affiliate with Chi Omega.

59. On the awarding of 120 Packard Avenue to the Cosmopolitan Sorority, see "Sororities Returning to TU Hill," and "Sorority Establishes Itself," *TO*, October 8, 1976.

60. "Sorority Establishes Itself." Information about the demands of the Chi Omega national was provided through interviews with a number of alumnae involved in the effort, including Lisa (Romeo) Thompson, Christina (Johnson) Rush, and a few others who wish to remain anonymous. As it turned out, the women did, indeed, follow the advice of their national organization on occasion when it came to 1950s-inspired rush parties. See, for example, "Sundaes Night at Chi Omega," *TT*, September 26, 1977; and rush advertisement, *TT*, February 3, 1978, which featured a pizza night, a movie night, and an ice cream social.

61. Ibid. The prohibition on alcohol in Chi Omega, and indeed nearly every other national woman's fraternity, is still in place today. On the re-chartering of Chi Alpha, see "Tufts University – Chi Alpha," *The Eleusis of Chi Omega* 79, no. 2 (Summer 1977): 261. Note that this article also lists Teresa Walsh as a charter member. However, the other charter members listed in the text recall Teresa as one of the first pledges and not a charter member. Additionally, Teresa is not present on the 1977 Chi Omega composite, which was dedicated to the twelve re-founding members. One additional charter member asked to remain anonymous.

62. Information on the pursuit of a second chapter house was provided through alumna interviews of a few Chi Omegas who were heavily involved in the process, including Lisa (Romeo) Thompson, Christina (Johnson) Rush, and Maurene Golden.

63. Ibid.

64. Ibid. The takeover of 25 Whitfield was confirmed in an interview with Bruce Ketchen (June 15, 2012). For further information on the Freak Frat and their expulsion from 25 Whitfield Road, see the section on Phi Sigma Kappa in chapter 3.

65. Ibid.

66. "Kippy Loses House," *TO*, April 21, 1978. For more information on the state of affairs of the Kippy House residents, see the section on Alpha Sigma Phi in chapter 3.

67. Information on the meeting was provided through an interview with Maurene Golden.

68. "Kippy Loses House." On the reaction of the residents to this news, see "Kippy House Should Stay Frat," *TW*, April 28, 1978.

69. Interview with Christina (Johnson) Rush. Although in general I do not like to rely solely on personal testimony for history, the information presented by Ms. Rush

was very consistent with how the situation eventually played out. I doubt the Tufts administration was very aware of the poor state of affairs in the Alpha Sigma Phi alumni corporation before Ms. Rush brought this to their attention. Although many of these records are now available on line, back in the 1970s, they were buried in filing cabinets of various city and state governing agencies, and if someone wanted the information, they had to go looking for it. Ms. Rush, I believe, was the one who went looking.

70. Ibid. Also see "Alpha Sigma Phi Seeks $30,000 From Tufts," *TD*, March 31, 1987. Again, more information about this taking of the house, and the aftermath for Alpha Sigma Phi, can be found in chapter 3.

71. Ibid.

72. For information on Alpha Phi, see their section later in this chapter. Just about the only evidence I could find that showed Chi Omega in a negative light was the article "Gals Veto Houses," *TO*, December 8, 1978. However, this article also talks about how Chi Omega was helping to revive the sorority system at Tufts, as evidenced by the large number of women who were participating in rush events that fall.

73. "DTD Undergoes Inquiry After Pledge Hospitalized," *TD*, March 30, 2005; "Greek System Under Fire for Multiple Violations," *TD*, May 22, 2005; and "DTD Houses Grad Students," *TD*, September 6, 2005, which includes the quotation.

74. On the 100th anniversary celebration, see "Chi Alpha Chapter Celebrates 100 Years at Tufts University," *The Eleusis of Chi Omega*, (Summer 2010): 26–29. According to the Office of Fraternity and Sorority Affairs at Tufts University, Chi Omega had 154 active members and pledges in the spring of 2014.

75. Coeducation at Tufts would actually go through somewhat of a painful growing process over the years, as many within the Tufts community continued to think the admission of women was a bad idea. For more information see Miller, *LOTH–1*, chapter 6. On the founding of Tau Epsilon Sigma, see "New Sorority Reveals Itself," *TW*, June 9, 1897; and Petition to Alpha Xi Delta from Tau Epsilon Sigma, June 23, 1906, as housed in the Alpha Xi Delta Fraternity Archives, Indianapolis, Indiana. On the graduation years for the four women, see *CofTC* (1896–97 ed.), 23–26.

76. "New Sorority Reveals Itself," which includes the quotation; and Petition to Alpha Xi Delta from Tau Epsilon Sigma. The *Tufts Weekly* began publication in 1895.

77. On the activities of Tau Epsilon Sigma, see for example, "Given The Secrets," *BG*, October 17, 1899; "Essentially A Woman's Day," *BG*, March 23, 1900; "Tufts Girls Drank Tea," *BG*, May 10, 1901; "Tufts Initiates," *BG*, November 1, 1902; and "Tufts Sorority Dance," *BG*, February 13, 1903. On the production of *The Rivals* and the failed attempt at philanthropy work, see "The Installation of Lambda Chapter," *Alpha Xi Delta* 4, no. 3 (May 1907): 111–113, which includes the quotation. The mention of philanthropy work during the early days of Tau Epsilon Sigma is one of the first references to such activities in a Tufts fraternity or sorority that I've found. On the scholastic achievements of those in Tau Epsilon Sigma, see Petition to Alpha Xi Delta from Tau Epsilon Sigma. Of course, the petition does not mention why these women dropped out, but one explanation could be that many of these women married while still an undergraduate, and thus left school to start their new life. Most of the Tau Epsilon Sigma women who did graduate went to work as teachers.

78. The story of how Tau Epsilon Sigma came to affiliate with the Alpha Xi Delta fraternity as presented in the next few paragraphs is, I must admit, based not on direct evidence, but on reasonable speculation using indirect information from a number of

reliable sources, as detailed below. On the enrollment of Beth Nash as a freshman in the fall of 1905, see *CofTC* (1905–06 ed.), 304.

79. On the tenure of Reverend Charles Nash at Lombard College, see *Catalogue of Lombard College* (Galesburg, Illinois: Mail Printing Company, 1904), 15; and Carl Sandburg, *Ever The Winds of Chance* (Urbana, IL: University of Illinois Press, 1983), 59–60. On the arrival of Reverend Nash at Tufts College, see *CofTC* (1905–06 ed.), 36. On the membership of Carrie Ruth Nash and Faith Nash in Pi Beta Phi, see "Illinois Beta–Lombard University," *The Arrow of Pi Beta Phi* 19, no. 2 (January 1903): 123–124, where Carrie Ruth is described as "a most loyal Pi Phi"; and "Illinois Beta–Lombard College," *The Arrow of Pi Beta Phi* 19, no. 4 (July 1903): 256. According to Fran Becque, the national historian and archivist for Pi Beta Phi, Faith Nash is listed in the 1907 fraternity directory as living at 220 School Street, Winter Hill Station, which is in Somerville, Massachusetts. This address is the same as listed for Beth Nash in *CofTC* (1905–06 ed.), 304. Therefore, it is highly plausible, if not definitive, that Faith and Beth Nash were living in the same house when Beth was a freshman at Tufts College. Consequently, it is plausible to assume they talked about their collegiate experiences, especially when it came to sorority membership. On Beth Nash's membership in Tau Epsilon Sigma, see Petition to Alpha Xi Delta from Tau Epsilon Sigma, where she is definitively listed as a full member and not a pledge, and "Fraternity Directory," *TW*, February 1, 1906. Finally, I could not find any information linking any other member of Tau Epsilon Sigma to a national sorority.

80. Again, while I do not have direct evidence that Tau Epsilon Sigma sought affiliation with Pi Beta Phi, it is entirely plausible, in my opinion, given Beth Nash's family connection to the fraternity through her two older sisters. However, according to Fran Becque, any inquiry to Pi Beta Phi from Tufts College was likely doomed from the start. In the early 1900s, Pi Beta Phi had become quite particular when it came to expansion. The fraternity judged every school under consideration against a series of minimum standards in areas such as number of students, total endowment, and faculty qualifications. Those schools not meeting these standards were not considered, no matter how qualified the individual women may have been. As a result, between 1905 and 1909, Pi Beta Phi only entered the following very select group of universities: Stanford University (1905), Iowa State University (1906), the University of Minnesota (1906), the University of Washington (1907), Washington State University (1907), the University of Toronto (1908), and the University of Arkansas (1909). That Pi Beta Phi passed on Tufts College at the time seems hardly a surprise. Additionally, Faith Nash was clearly interested in helping her sister's organization affiliate with a national, as evidenced by the testimonial she wrote in the Petition to Alpha Xi Delta from Tau Epsilon Sigma – "For four years I knew and loved the Alpha [Xi Delta] girls at Lombard. I think I have a good idea of what a chapter in this Fraternity should be. From my short acquaintance with the Tau Epsilon Sigma girls at Tufts I have found them to be girls of high character, noble ambitions, cordial, courteous, and womanly; in short all, I am sure, that Alpha Xi Delta girls should be." I find it difficult to believe Faith would have written such a testimonial if Tau Epsilon Sigma had not first tried to affiliate with Pi Beta Phi. On Beth's recommendation to pursue Alpha Xi Delta, see "Lambda," *Alpha Xi Delta* 5, no. 1 (November 1907): 42, which mentions "We greatly miss Ruth [this is a typo, should have said Beth], as it was she who first interested us in Alpha Xi Delta thro [sic] her friends at Lombard."

81. On Lombard College, see for example, Richard Eddy, *The Universalist Register: Giving Statistics of the Universalist Church, And Other Denominational Information, etc., for 1896* (Boston, MA: Universalist Publishing House, 1896), 87–90. On the Greek organizations at Lombard in the 1890s, see "A Retrospect," *Alpha Xi Delta* 1, no. 1 (February 1904): 3–4; and Baird (5th ed. 1898), 379. Of course, the criticism of Pi Beta Phi being only for those wealthy enough was written by Alpha Xi Delta, hardly an independent observation!

82. "A Retrospect," 3–5; "Our Beginning," *Alpha Xi Delta*, 10, no. 1 (March 1913): 22–23; and Scott, *The Story of Sigma Nu*, 295. The term "barbarians" or "barbs" was commonly used at the time by those in a fraternity or sorority to describe those not affiliated with such an organization. It was not a term of endearment. The founding members of Alpha Xi Delta were: Cora Josephine Bollinger, Alice Helen Bartlett, Bertha Alice Cook, Lucy W. Gilmer, Almira L. Cheney, Francis Elizabeth Cheney, Lewie Strong, Hattie McCullom, Eliza M. Curtis, and Maude Foster.

83. "A Retrospect," 5, 10; and "The National Movement," *Alpha Xi Delta*, 10, no. 1 (March 1913): 23–25. It appears Alpha Xi Delta never made it to the petition stage with any national organization, but was rather turned away upon first inquiry.

84. "A Retrospect," 9–13; and "The National Movement," 24–29. On Pi Beta Phi's establishment of its Beta chapter at Iowa Wesleyan in 1868, see Clark-Helmick, *History of Pi Beta Phi*, 31–33. At the time, Pi Beta Phi was known by its original name, I. C. Sorosis.

85. Petition to Alpha Xi Delta from Tau Epsilon Sigma, which includes the quotations. The petition is dated June 23, 1906, but the latter pages contain letters of recommendation written in the early fall, including the one written by Ms. Cleveland. These letters, I assume, were added to the petition before the final vote on acceptance was taken by the national organization.

86. "The Installation of Lambda Chapter," and Helen Willis Lynn, *History of Alpha Xi Delta Fraternity, 1893–1923* (Menasha, WI: The Collegiate Press), 67. The installation took place at the home of Ethel Fuller in Everett, Massachusetts. On the daily chapel requirement in 1907, see *CofTC* (1906–07 ed.), 185. Finally, in October of 1913, Alpha Xi Delta officially dropped the "sorority" moniker in favor of fraternity, according to "Some Actions Taken By The Seventh Convention," *Alpha Xi Delta* 10, no. 4 (December 1913): 276.

87. "Persis Hannah Brown Recalls Originating 'Rose of Alpha Xi'," *The Quill of Alpha Xi Delta* 58, no. 2 (1961): 76–78; and "The Rose of Alpha Xi," *Alpha Xi Delta* 4, no. 3 (May 1907): 114. After graduating from Tufts College, Persis Hannah became a very well known writer and editor of the *Boston Herald* and the *Boston Traveler*, a remarkable achievement given that women were not well represented in journalism at the time. However, you won't find many of her columns under her own name – she published under the pseudonyms Phoebe Dwight and Ruth Cameron.

88. "Examination Grades," *Alpha Xi Delta* 5, no. 4 (August 1908): 244–245, which includes the quotation. By this time, there were thirteen active chapters in Alpha Xi Delta, with Lambda being one of the largest. Ethel Fuller, who hosted the installation in her house, scored the highest of the chapter with a 75.5%. I find it interesting that Alpha Xi Delta chose to publish this information that summer of 1908, for the results that year were not particularly flattering to the organization as a whole. In general, fraternity and sorority quarterly magazines throughout the early 1900s were filled mainly

with all that was going right within each organization, and almost nothing about what was going wrong.

89. On life in Lambda chapter in the early 1910s, see for example, "Lambda – Jackson College," *Alpha Xi Delta* 11, no. 3 (September 1914): 327–329; and "Lambda – Jackson College," *Alpha Xi Delta* 12, no. 4 (December 1915): 458–460, which mentions Lambda chapter alumna Ruth Sibley Haskell was president of the College Suffrage Association. The Haskell Hall dormitory is named in honor of her and her husband. On the dramatic shift in activities and thought within Lambda chapter following the declaration of war, see "Lambda–Jackson College," *Alpha Xi Delta* 14, no. 2 (June 1917): 174, which includes the quotation. Fracture pillows, as their name implies, were meant to aid in the healing of bone fractures. See G. S. Mulliner, *How To Make Surgical Dressings* (New York, NY: British War Relief Association, 1917), 15. On the summer work of Lambda members, see "Lambda–Jackson College," *Alpha Xi Delta* 14, no. 3 (September 1917): 284–285. On the treatment of German nationals, see "Gregory Defines Alien Regulations," *NYT*, February 2, 1918. The monitoring of "enemy aliens" was allowed under the Alien Enemies Act of 1798, which was also used during World War II to inter Japanese in camps.

90. "Lambda–Jackson College," *Alpha Xi Delta* 14, no. 4 (December 1917): 379–380; "Lambda–Tufts College," *Alpha Xi Delta* 15, no. 1 (March 1918): 107–108; "War Work of the Chapters–Lambda," *Alpha Xi Delta* 15, no. 2 (June 1918); 159–160; "War Work–Lambda," *Alpha Xi Delta* 15, no. 2 (June 1918); 184; and "Lambda – Jackson College," *Alpha Xi Delta* 15, no. 2 (June 1918): 226–227, which includes the quotation. On Frances Clement's role in the French relief agency, Le Paquet du Soldat, see Ida Clyde Clarke, *American Women and the World War* (New York, NY: D. Appleton and Company, 1918), 464.

91. On Lambda's successful hosting of the Alpha Xi Delta convention, see "Lambda As Hostess," *Alpha Xi Delta* 15, no 3 (September 1918): 290–291; and "Convention Impressions," *Alpha Xi Delta* 15, no 3 (September 1918): 294–299. The $10 price tag for the convention attendee translates to about $160 in today's value, which is still a great bargain. The conserving of food and other consumer items was known as "Hooverizing" at the time, in reference to Herbert Hoover's directive as head of the United States Food Administration.

92. In looking through Lambda's chapter letters as published in the *Alpha Xi Delta* quarterly magazine, I was struck by how quickly the narrative changed once the war ended. The letters between 1917 and 1918 were filled with dread, foreboding, maybe even a sense of helplessness. Then, in an instant, that negativity was gone, and the war was rarely mentioned ever again. On Lambda's resumption of activities after the armistice, see "Lambda – Jackson College," *Alpha Xi Delta* 15, no. 4 (January 1919): 444–445, which includes the quotation; and "Lambda – Jackson College," *Alpha Xi Delta* 16, no. 1 (March 1919): 81–82.

93. The change in attitude towards discrimination in fraternity and sorority membership practices after World War II is well documented by others, including Syrett, *The Company He Keeps*, 248–261. The efforts by those at Tufts University to remove membership restrictions are discussed in chapter 6. The secret Alpha Xi Delta membership restriction, which apparently barred women of color from the organization, was discussed by Phil Primack, "Joining the Good Fight," *Tufts Magazine* (Spring 2006), http://www.tufts.edu/alumni/magazine/spring2006/features/feature1sidebar.html (ac-

cessed August 8, 2015).

94. Interview with Norma (Pereira) Atkinson (April 2, 2012).

95. Interview with Norma (Pereira) Atkinson; and Primack, "Joining the Good Fight."

96. Ibid.

97. The arrival of the two black women in the fall of 1955, and their subsequent impact on sorority life at Tufts, is discussed later in the chapter in the section on Sigma Kappa. On the efforts of Lambda chapter to work for change, see "Report of Alpha Xi Delta," undated but context places it circa April 1958, as housed in Activities and Organizations records, 1875–2013, UA 024.001 Box 1, Folder 13 (Alpha Xi Delta 1941–1960). This document, while offering a thorough synopsis of the events that transpired between Lambda chapter and the national organization during this time, does not adequately document the dates of meetings and correspondence. Therefore, I am unsure of exactly when all of this transpired, though it obviously happened before Lambda chapter resigned from Alpha Xi Delta in September of 1956.

98. "Report on Alpha Xi Delta," which includes the quotation. This report, which was written by a few alumnae of the chapter, is heavily weighted in opinion towards the national organization, and essentially dismisses the behavior of those in Lambda chapter as youthful ignorance, while rationalizing every action taken by the national leaders. Change of the magnitude being attempted by Lambda chapter never comes easy or without fervent dissent.

99. "Report on Alpha Xi Delta," which includes the quotation. Norma (Pereira) Atkinson vehemently denies she knew of the membership restriction before she joined Alpha Xi Delta, and would never have joined had she known.

100. On the situation with Sigma Kappa, see the appropriate section later in this chapter. On the meeting between Lambda chapter and the national officer, see "Report on Alpha Xi Delta"; and Primack, "Joining the Good Fight," which includes the quotation.

101. Primack, "Joining the Good Fight"; "Report on Alpha Xi Delta"; "Tufts Sorority Quits National Group Over Bias," *BG*, September 27, 1956; "Sorority Cancels Ties," *NYT*, September 27, 1956; "Alpha Xi Delta Withdraws from National Group," *TW*, September 28, 1956; and Tufts University press release dated Wednesday, September 26, 1956, in Activities and Organizations records, 1875–2013, UA 024.001 Box 1, Folder 13 (Alpha Xi Delta 1941–1960).

102. "Alpha Xi Delta Withdraws from National Group," which includes the quotations.

103. "Alpha Xi Delta Withdraws from National Group"; "Tufts Sorority Quits National Group over Bias"; and "Sorority Cancels Ties." On the national coverage of Sigma Kappa's situation, see the appropriate section later in this chapter. Of the two stories, Sigma Kappa's dominated on a national level.

104. On the constitution of Alethea and its acceptance on December 5, 1956, see documents in Activities and Organizations records, 1875–2013, UA 024.001 Box 1, Folder 4 (Alethea 1956–1965). Information on the lack of secret rituals within Alethea was provided through interviews with Alethea alumnae, including Norma (Pereira) Atkinson and Jane (Kraft) Haymon (September 25, 2011). Apparently, in later years, Alethea did make use of a simple ritual for new members, but an elaborate use of secrecy was never part of the organization.

105. On the efforts of the alumnae, see "Report on Alpha Xi Delta," which includes the quotation. On Dean Jeffers and her position on racial discrimination, see Miller, *LOTH–2*, 211–212.

106. "Report on Alpha Xi Delta"; and "One Alpha Xi Too Little Delta," *TW*, March 22, 1957. In many ways, it is amazing the alumnae thought they could succeed with their efforts in the spring of 1957, given that so many former members of Lambda chapter were still on campus.

107. "Report on Alpha Xi Delta"; and "Alpha Xi Delta Plans Return," *TW*, February 14, 1958.

108. On the reaction and embarrassment of the alumnae, see "Report on Alpha Xi Delta." On the student uproar following Alpha Xi Delta's announcement of a planned return to campus, see "No, Not Again," *TW*, February 14, 1958; and "Council Opposes Return," *TW*, February 28, 1958, which includes the quotation. I do find it interesting that the administration allowed Alpha Xi Delta to go ahead without verifying the Panhellenic Council had, indeed, voted in favor of this action. It may have been that the administration felt the Panhellenic Council would simply go along with whatever the faculty committee decided. After all the 1950s was the age of conformity. How dare the undergraduates usurp the decision of the faculty!

109. "Pan-Hellenic Council To Vote on Alpha Xi Delta," *TW*, May 13, 1960; and "PanHell Council Votes Down AXD," *TW*, May 20, 1960, which includes the quotations. On the disbanding of Thalia, see the appropriate section later in this chapter.

110. "PanHell Council Votes Down AXD." As could be expected, every single member of Alethea voted to deny Alpha Xi Delta the right to return to campus. On the reluctance of the alumnae and the national office of Alpha Xi Delta to attempt recolonization in the near future, see letter from Dean Herrick to Judge Nash dated May 13, 1960, and letter from Judge Nash to Dean Herrick dated July 13, 1960, in Activities and Organizations records, 1875–2013, UA 024.001 Box 1, Folder 4 (Alethea 1956–1965). According to these letters, it appears Dean Herrick was in favor of bringing back Alpha Xi Delta, while Judge Nash thought the "attitude of the other groups on the Jackson campus" didn't support recolonization any time soon.

111. On the dwindling membership within Alethea, see membership lists from 1962 through 1966 in Activities and Organizations records, 1875–2013, UA 024.001 Box 1, Folder 4 (Alethea 1956–1965). On the closing of Alethea, see "Alethea Decides to Dissolve Itself," *TW*, February 25, 1966.

112. Information about the reluctance of Alpha Xi Delta to participate in sorority expansion in 2012 was provided by Su McGlone, Director of Fraternity and Sorority Affairs at Tufts University.

113. The use of "society" and "non-society" is based on my observation after reading hundreds of newspaper articles from the late 19th and early 20th century on Greek life. Nowadays, newspapers only cover fraternity or sorority parties when they go horribly wrong.

114. The open society movement as related to the National Federation of Commons Clubs is covered in the section on the Tufts Commons Club in chapter 3.

115. "History of Delta Kappa Phi," *Sigma Kappa Triangle* 7, no. 4 (September 1913): 315–318; and Kinne, *History of Sigma Kappa Sorority 1874–1924*, 77–81. On the hometowns and campus addresses of the founders of Delphoi, see *CofTC* (1907–08 ed.), 296–308.

116. Ibid. Interestingly enough, three of the women would graduate or leave Tufts College just a few weeks after this official announcement.

117. On the announcement, see "The Delphoi," *TW*, April 30, 1908, which includes the quotation. On the membership requirements, see "History of Delta Kappa Phi"; and Kinne, 78. On the reluctance of one non-society woman to join Delphoi, see Kinne, 78. The use of the "good character" clause to exclude potential members in the early 20th century is discussed in various sources such as Syrett, chapter 4; and Sauna, *Going Greek*, chapters 2 and 3.

118. "History of Delta Kappa Phi"; and "Kinne, 78–79. On the initiation of alumnae into Delphoi, see, for example, John William Leonard, ed., *Woman's Who's Who of America 1914–1915* (New York, NY: The American Commonwealth Company, 1914), 263, which lists Mary Parker Dunning from the Tufts class of 1902 as an initiated member of Delta Kappa Phi, the successor of Delphoi in name. Ms. Dunning would eventually be initiated into the Omicron chapter of Sigma Kappa alongside her Delta Kappa Phi sisters. The effort to turn Delphoi into a national organization was quite ambitious for such a young organization. Unfortunately, copies of the letter sent to various colleges have not been located to date. These would be fascinating to read, should a copy turn up someday.

119. "History of Delta Kappa Phi," which contains the first quotation; and Kinne, 78–79, which includes the second quotation. The practice of poaching members from one Greek-letter organization to another was widely frowned upon within the national fraternity world by the early 1900s, and indeed many national organizations disallowed the initiation of those who'd already joined another. Delphoi, as a local society, was viewed a little differently in this regard, but the attempt in this case seems a little underhanded, given that the other sororities at Tufts wanted to bring Delphoi into their fold as an equal. But, at least the action gave rise to a great motto!

120. The open society movement for men is discussed in the section on the Tufts Commons Club in chapter 3. The exact timing of when Delphoi abandoned open membership is not documented very well, but it appears to have occurred during the suggested time frame based on information in the *Ivy Book*. For example, the 1909–10 edition of the *Ivy Book*, which was most likely published later in the fall semester of that school year, contained a description of Delphoi in the section on student clubs, and not in the section for sororities. However, a year later in the 1910–11 edition, Delphoi is definitively listed as a sorority at Tufts. This change in classification makes me believe Delphoi's transformation to an exclusive organization occurred sometime during the latter portion of the 1909–10 school year. The transformation is also discussed in "History of Delta Kappa Phi" and Kinne, 78–79, but these sources do not give a date. However, something clearly spooked the women of Delphoi around this time with regards to the new women entering Tufts. As described identically in the two aforementioned sources, "… there was a constant danger of members being taken into an open society like Delphoi who were not of the type for which Delphoi had stood, *then* [original italics] the society closed its doors to any who were not desired by at least three fourths of the members." I believe it is entirely plausible that an influx (real or presumed) of Jewish, Catholic, foreign, or African-American women was the catalyst for change.

121. "History of Delta Kappa Phi"; and Kinne, 78–79. Again, these sources do not pinpoint exactly when the change in name occurred. However, the first reference to Delta Kappa Phi occurs in the 1912–13 edition of the *Ivy Book*, which suggests the

name change came about in the spring of 1912. Also, Kinne, 79, mentions that Delta Kappa Phi filed its petition with Sigma Kappa over the summer of 1912, which means the name must have been in use by then. On the national affiliation of the other three sororities (Alpha Omicron Pi, Chi Omega, and Alpha Xi Delta), see their respective sections earlier in this chapter.

122. The story of the founding of Colby, though somewhat tangent to this work, is interesting enough in its own right, for it harkens back to a time when travel was not easy. Today, one can travel from Boston to Waterville, Maine in about three hours by car. Not so in the early 1800s. Five days it took, and even that depended on favorable winds to power the various sailboats. On the founding of Colby, see Henry S. Burrage, *History of the Baptists in Maine* (Portland, Maine: Marks Printing House, 1904), 172–173; Edwin Carey Whittemore, *Colby College, 1820–1925: An Account of its Beginnings, Progress, and Service* (Waterville, Maine: Trustees of Colby College, 1927), 19–22, which includes a transcript of Mrs. Chaplin's diary; Earl H. Smith, *Mayflower Hill: A History of Colby College* (Lebanon, NH: University Press of New England, 2006), 5–13; Edward W. Hall, *History of Higher Education in Maine* (Washington, D.C.: Government Printing Office, 1903), 103–104; and Edwin Carey Whittemore, ed., *Centennial History of Waterville, Kennebec County, Maine* (Waterville, ME: Executive Committee of the Centennial Celebration, 1902), 295–298. On the transformation to coeducation, see Hall, *History of Higher Education*, 114–117.

123. On the enrollment of women at Colby College, see *Catalogue of the Officers and Students of Colby University (CofCU)* (1871–72 ed.), 10; *CofCU* (1872–73 ed.), 9; and *CofCU* (1873–74 ed.), 6, 8; On the women's actions, see Kinne, 17–21.

124. Kinne, 17–23. On the two active fraternities at the time, see Baird (1st ed. 1879), 166. According to Baird (1st ed. 1879), 69, the Delta Upsilon chapter was not active at Colby in 1873.

125. Kinne, 19–24, which includes the quotation. The founding date is quoted from the national website of Sigma Kappa, https://www.sigmakappa.org/Milestones/ (accessed September 7, 2015).

126. The transformation from an open to an exclusive organization is detailed in Kinne, 29–34. I find it interesting how the history of Delphoi at Tufts parallels the transformation of Sigma Kappa, albeit over a much reduced time scale. Open organizations just do not have a strong record of surviving over the long term.

127. Expansion within Sigma Kappa was first talked about back in 1875, when the sorority was but one year old. On the eventual expansion of Sigma Kappa, see Kinne, 209–215; and "The Installation of Beta Chapter," *The Eleusis of Chi Omega* 9, no. 1 (February 1907): 9–14. On the location of Sigma Kappa chapters prior to 1912, see Baird (7th ed. 1912), 519.

128. How Delta Kappa Phi came to Sigma Kappa was unfortunately not documented very well, and the two sources who initiated the conversation between the organizations were never identified by name, at least in the materials I could find. See "History of Delta Kappa Phi"; and Kinne, 79–80. I suspect that Grace Ada Small, a national officer for Sigma Kappa, had something to do with all this, as she was living about a mile from campus in Somerville at the time. As for the Sigma Kappa mold, the sorority was known to make use of Christian ideals within its organization, so I suspect the national officers wanted to confirm the religious affiliation of those in Delta Kappa Phi. Sigma Kappa also had a problem admitting women of color, as is discussed later in this section.

129. "History of Delta Kappa Phi"; and Kinne, 79–80, 240. In the early 1900s especially, petitions from various local organizations at Tufts to national fraternities and sororities were routinely denied because of the size of the school. For example, see the sections on Sigma Tau Alpha and Sigma Phi Epsilon in chapter 3, and Alpha Xi Delta earlier in this chapter.

130. Ibid. The yearlong supervisory period of Delta Kappa Phi by national officers, though very common today, was not as widespread within fraternities and sororities at the time. Charters were usually granted or not based upon the petition alone. The founders of Delphoi who were subsequently initiated into Sigma Kappa were Helen Gage, Beth Boswell, Isabel Perkins, and Ada Seabury.

131. Interaction between Omicron and Delta chapters was most likely mandated by the national organization, as there was great emphasis at the time on national identity. As the organization grew in the years ahead, though, such closeness between members and chapters became harder to maintain. On the interaction between Omicron and Delta, see, for example "Sigma Kappa Fraternity," *BG*, December 21, 1913; "Omicron – Jackson College," *Sigma Kappa Triangle* 8, no. 2 (March 1914): 307; "Sigma Kappa Sorority Initiation and Banquet," *BG*, March 3, 1918; "Sigma Kappa Sorority Initiation," *BG*, March 6, 1921; "Honor Sigma Kappa Grand President," *BG*, April 23, 1924; "B.U. and Tufts Students at Sigma Kappa Sorority," *BG*, February 13, 1927; and "Sigma Kappa Sorority Entertains at College," *BG*, November 9, 1930.

132. The practice of open criticism within the pages of the *Sigma Kappa Triangle* appears to have started soon after Omicron received its charter. See "A Word to the Wise," *Sigma Kappa Triangle* 8, no. 1 (December 1913): 136–137. I do find it interesting that the editors were so open in their critique, given that their magazine was exchanged with other national organizations. Admitting even the smallest of flaws in these publications was rare, for they were intended in many ways to project strength, not weakness.

133. On the shortcomings of Omicron's corresponding secretaries, see "Omicron–Jackson College," *Sigma Kappa Triangle* 12, no. 2 (March 1918): 211–213; "Omicron–Jackson College," *Sigma Kappa Triangle* 12, no. 3 (June 1918): 348–349; and "Omicron–Tufts College," *Sigma Kappa Triangle* 13, no. 4 (September 1919): 441–442. On Karin's redemption, see "Omicron–Tufts College," *Sigma Kappa Triangle* 13, no. 2 (March 1919): 166–167. Criticism of chapter letters continued well into the 1920s.

134. Sigma Kappa at the national level began a relationship with the Maine Sea Coast Mission in the early 1900s, and that relationship still exists today, according to information on their national website. Having read through numerous fraternity and sorority journals from this era, it is my contention that philanthropy and service were at best a nascent aspect of most organizations before World War 1, both at the local and national levels. Sigma Kappa was a noted exception. On the war work within Omicron, see "Our Active Chapters and the Red Cross – Omicron," *Sigma Kappa Triangle* 11, no. 4 (September 1917): 407, which includes the quotation; and "Omicron–Jackson College," *Sigma Kappa Triangle* 11, no. 4 (September 1917): 464–465. On the Preparedness Parade, see for example, "All Plans Completed For Tomorrow's Parade," *BG*, May 26, 1916. Although the article from the *Sigma Kappa Triangle* mentions the women were not allowed to march in the parade, the article from the *Boston Globe* does state that around 200 of the 45,000 marchers were women. I suspect, then, that the prohibition was put in place by the Tufts administration.

135. On the curtailing of social activities, see "Omicron – Jackson College," *Sigma*

Kappa Triangle 11, no. 4 (September 1917): 464–465, which contains the first quotation. On the formal dance, see "Omicron–Jackson College," *Sigma Kappa Triangle* 12, no. 3 (June 1918): 348–349, which includes the second quotation. On the war work of the women, see "Omicron–Jackson College," *Sigma Kappa Triangle* 12, no. 2 (March 1918): 211–212; and "Omicron–Jackson College," *Sigma Kappa Triangle* 12, no. 4 (September 1918): 464–465. The arrival of the S.A.T.C. is discussed in greater detail within chapter 3. On the end of the war, see "Omicron–Tufts College," *Sigma Kappa Triangle* 13, no. 2 (March 1919): 166–167, which includes the third quotation.

136. "Omicron–Tufts College," *Sigma Kappa Triangle* 13, no. 2 (March 1919): 166–167, which includes the quotation. "The Rez" refers to the former reservoir on campus, which occupied the area now bordered by Houston, Carmichael, and Miller dormitories. The astute reader will no doubt realize that the end of World War I as experienced by the Tufts campus is covered in differing detail within each section of the four active sororities – Alpha Omicron Pi, Chi Omega, Alpha Xi Delta, and Sigma Kappa. This was intentional. As I researched each organization, I found it curious how the various corresponding secretaries recorded the events of that day. While they all told the same general story, the writers were each affected in a unique way by the events of November 11. Therefore, I decided to add some of this flavor to my text.

137. On the return to normalcy, see "Omicron–Tufts College," *Sigma Kappa Triangle* 13, no. 3 (June 1919): 251–252. On Omicron's work with the Intercollegiate Community Service Association (I.C.S.A.), see "Omicron–Tufts College," *Sigma Kappa Triangle* 13, no. 4 (September 1919): 441–442. While this article mentions that numerous Tufts women besides those in Sigma Kappa participated in the organization, I did not come across any mention of the I.C.S.A. within chapter letters of the other three sororities active at the time. Also, many in Omicron participated in the I.C.S.A. for years, as evidenced by, "Omicron – Tufts College," *Sigma Kappa Triangle* 15, no. 4 (September 1921): 562–563. Therefore, it appears that the commitment to service by those in Sigma Kappa was above the norm for the day (at least in terms of Greek–letter organizations), which certainly deserves mention. On the I.C.S.A. and its mission, see *Intercollegiate Community Service Quarterly* 2, no. 4 (July 1917): 2–3.

138. The efforts of those in the Tufts community to change the discriminatory membership practices of fraternities and sororities are discussed in detail in chapter 6.

139. Phil Primack, "Opening Doors," *Tufts Magazine* (Spring 2006), http://www.tufts.edu/alumni/magazine/spring2006/features/feature1.html (accessed September 19, 2015); and interview with Terri (Williams) Schachter (May 28, 2012; May 29, 2012; and August 27, 2012). Ellie Turpin did eventually move onto campus later that fall, but she, too was housed in a single room.

140. On Gemma's accomplishments and activities, see "Gemma Cifarelli Was Active Campus Citizen," *TW*, December 15, 1955. On Gemma's involvement in fighting discrimination within Greek-letter organizations, see "Viewing The Council," *TW*, November 18, 1954. On Gemma and Dean Jeffers working to construct the plan, see Primack, "Opening Doors." According to Ms. Schachter, her relationship with Gemma was genuine and went way beyond any plan to test sorority discrimination. The two were friends, first and foremost. Finally, it appears Dean Jeffers did not have any specific sorority in mind when she and Gemma concocted the plan, as she thought they all practiced discrimination when it came to choosing new members.

141. Primack, "Opening Doors"; and interviews with Terri (Williams) Schachter.

142. "Popular Students' Deaths Sadden Tufts Campus," *BG*, December 12, 1955; "Gemma Cifarelli Was Active Campus Citizen"; and "Charles Lund Was An Engineer, Sigma Nu," *TW*, December 15, 1955. The third victim was Frederick Hill, who succumbed to his injuries a few days after the accident. On the decision to go forward with the plan, see Primack, "Opening Doors"; and interview with Terri (Williams) Schachter.

143. The contention that sorority rush in the spring of 1956 was not all that contentious for the participants is based upon Primack, "Opening Doors"; and interviews of numerous alumnae who were on campus that semester, including Terri (Williams) Schachter and Audrey (Saperstein) Shapiro (May 1, 2012), who was Omicron chapter's president at the time. On the claim that Omicron chapter may have been one of the first inter-racial sororities in America, see "Negroes Pledged, Sororities Ousted," *NYT*, August 2, 1956. It appears that in 1956, Sigma Kappa did not have any official restrictions on membership based on race, but instead relied upon other, informal techniques such as alumnae oversight to keep out certain groups of women. At Tufts, this had not ever been an issue since so few women of color had enrolled prior to 1955, and none had looked to join Sigma Kappa. On the seven women who pledged that spring, see "Notices–Sigma Kappa," *TW*, April 28, 1956.

144. Information on the appearance of the two older alumnae at the rush events was provided in an interview with Audrey (Saperstein) Shapiro. Although not proven definitively, I find it highly plausible these two alumnae were the ones who alerted the national officers of Sigma Kappa about Omicron chapter's intent to pledge two black women, since they would certainly have known whom to contact within the organization.

145. On the trials and tribulations of Evelyn Harvey as well as Alpha Zeta chapter at Cornell, see "Negroes Pledged, Sororities Ousted," which includes the quotation. Evelyn was also asked, to a lesser extent, about Omicron's past financial and scholarship deficiencies, but these issues had been resolved by the time of the convention so they were no longer a problem for the chapter. See letter from Dean Katharine Jeffers to Dean E. G. Williamson dated September 5, 1956, in Activities and Organizations records, 1875–2013, UA 024.001 Box 13, Folder 9 (Sigma Kappa 1935–1956).

146. Letter from the National Council of Sigma Kappa to Audrey Saperstein, and letter from the National Council of Sigma Kappa to Dean Katharine Jeffers, both dated July 27, 1956, in Activities and Organizations records, 1875–2013, UA 024.001 Box 13, Folder 9 (Sigma Kappa 1935–1956). Note that the letter to Dean Jeffers contains the quotation, whereas the letter to Audrey Saperstein lists no reason for Omicron's ouster. On the ousting of Alpha Zeta chapter at Cornell, see "Negroes Pledged, Sorority Ousted."

147. On the headlines across the country, see for example, "Sorority Withdraws Charter of Chapter Pledging Negroes," *The Ocala [Florida] Star-Banner*, August 2, 1956; and "Charter Lost in Color Row," *The Spokesman-Review [Spokane, Washington]*, August 3, 1956. This story was repeated in dozens of newspapers over the next few days. Information about Dean Jeffers' call to Terri was provided in an interview with Terri (Williams) Schachter. According to Ms. Schachter, Dean Jeffers delivered the news to Ellie and her parents in person, since Ellie lived in Cambridge, Massachusetts, at the time.

148. Interview with Audrey (Saperstein) Shapiro. Also see letters from Audrey Saperstein to Dean Jeffers dated August 6 and August 7, 1956, in Activities and Organi-

zations records, 1875–2013, UA 024.001 Box 13, Folder 9 (Sigma Kappa 1935–1956). Quotation is from letter dated August 6, 1956.

149. The letters and correspondence are all housed in Activities and Organizations records, 1875–2013, UA 024.001 Box 13, Folder 9 (Sigma Kappa 1935–1956). One of the letters of support for the chapter came from Karin (Sundelhof) Asbrand, who was the corresponding secretary of Omicron back in the late 1910s and was quoted earlier in this section. On the inquiry from Delta Pi sorority, see letter from Carol Lustig to Dean Jeffers dated August 8, 1956. No doubt the Delta Pi sorority was hoping to take the ex-Omicron chapter under its wing. On the quotation, see letter from Katharine R. Jeffers to Mrs. Ronald A. Rhodes dated August 6, 1956.

150. Letter from Mary Sears Rhodes to Dean Jeffers, August 13, 1956. This letter, along with her initial letter from August 2, 1956, offer a look inside the mindset of someone who held what was probably a common opinion at the time regarding integration. Mrs. Rhodes was a graduate of the Class of 1924 and a member of Alpha Omicron Pi.

151. The national reaction to the expulsion of Omicron chapter was quite amazing on many levels, since Tufts wasn't well known outside of New England at the time. However, it appears the expulsion was one of those events that came along just as many wanted to take action regarding racial and religious discrimination within fraternities and sororities. Omicron's ouster, it seems, was the spark needed to start those actions, probably because it was such a blatant case of racism. On the interest from the University of Minnesota, see correspondence between E. G. Williamson, Dean of Students at the University of Minnesota, and Dean Katharine Jeffers, between August 24, 1956, and September 5, 1956, in Activities and Organizations records, 1875–2013, UA 024.001 Box 13, Folder 9 (Sigma Kappa 1935–1956). On the interest from the University of Michigan, see telegram to Dean Jeffers dated September 29, 1958, in Activities and Organizations records, 1875–2013, UA 024.001 Box 13, Folder 9 (Sigma Kappa 1935–1956); and "Michigan Student Group Acts Against Sorority Bias Clause," *The Minnesota Daily*, December 7, 1956. On the change of heart by the local sorority at Penn State, see "Trion Drops Petition To Go National," *The Daily Collegian*, March 27, 1957. On the efforts of those in the Massachusetts state government, see "Fraternities Differ on How To Fight Bias," *BG*, September 21, 1956; "Bias of Some Campus Groups Shocks Conte," *BG*, October 5, 1956; "Legislators Rap Fraternity Bias In UMass Talks," *BG*, October 19, 1956; and copies of Massachusetts House Resolution #3285 dated August 10, 1956, and Report #2977 dated December 1956, in Activities and Organizations records, 1875–2013, UA 024.001 Box 13, Folder 9 (Sigma Kappa 1935–1956).

152. On the founding of Thalia, see "Sigma Kappa Local Sorority," *TW*, November 2, 1956. A copy of Thalia's constitution is housed in Sigma Kappa Sorority records, 1907–1956, UA 205 Box 1, Folder 14; and Activities and Organizations records, 1875–2013, UA 024.001 Box 7, Folder 4 (Pan Hellenic: hearing 1957–1960). The specific membership requirement as written was "Any student of Jackson College for Women or any woman student of Tufts College of Engineering shall be eligible for membership, regardless of race, religion, or nationality, so long as this girl meets with the voting requirements of the sorority." This requirement appears to have been a three-fourths majority of all active members.

153. Information about Thalia's activities in its first few semesters was provided

through interviews of alumnae including Terri (Williams) Schachter and Audrey (Shapiro) Saperstein. All active sororities were set up in chapter rooms in Curtis Hall in the spring of 1956, with Sigma Kappa/Thalia's being one of the larger ones, according to the letter from Dean Herrick to Dr. Leonard Mead, Provost, January 26, 1960, in Activities and Organizations records, 1875–2013, UA 024.001 Box 4, Folder 1 (Delta Zeta 1954–1968). By the 1959–60 school year, it appears those in Thalia had started making use of a secret initiation ritual, according to Barbara (Haroian) Solakian, the president of the chapter that year.

154. Information about the growing discontent within Thalia was provided through an interview with Barbara (Haroian) Solakian (August 24, 2011). The "media wall" as constructed by Dean Jeffers was quite remarkable, for it lasted nearly fifty years. None of the alumnae of Thalia and Sigma Kappa that I spoke with ever saw any of the letters or press clippings. In fact, they first learned about all of this documentation when I brought up the subject in our interviews.

155. For information on Alethea, see the previous section in this chapter. The lack of discussion about Thalia as a contributing factor in its demise is mostly a conjecture on my part, since I obviously do not have documentation to back up this claim. However, I did find it very interesting that so little was written about Thalia in the *Tufts Weekly* after December of 1956. On the contrary, every few months there was an article about the national Alpha Xi Delta trying to come back to campus, and this set off a firestorm of criticism in the editorial section. Institutional memory can be quite fleeting, especially since students come and go every semester. Therefore, I find it highly plausible that by 1958, most on campus probably did not know there was ever a Sigma Kappa chapter at Tufts, or why it had gone away.

156. Interview with Barbara (Haroian) Solakian; and "Thalia Disbands; Denotes Failure To Achieve Aims," *TW*, January 8, 1960.

157. Ibid. Dean Wynne-Roberts was promoted following the untimely death of Dean Katharine Jeffers (she, unfortunately, committed suicide in May of 1959).

158. Although not often discussed, the passing down of traditions through conversation from one undergraduate to the next happens on just about every college campus. I've certainly witnessed this during my research, as many current undergraduates have asked me questions about their own organizations that often started, "Over the years we've heard…" and "There's been a long-standing rumor that…" Hardly scientific, I admit, but it does help explain how Sigma Kappa was able to come back to campus in 1978 without anyone protesting – no one remembered what had happened, because no one had talked about them in years. On the re-founding of Omicron chapter, see "Sigmas… Here and There," *Sigma Kappa Triangle* 72, no. 3 (Fall 1978): 35; "Awards," *Sigma Kappa Triangle* 72, no. 2 (Fall 1978): 8; "Massachusetts," *Sigma Kappa Triangle* 72, no. 2 (Fall 1978): 23; and "Tufts," *Sigma Kappa Triangle* 72, no. 3 (Winter 1978): 30. Although I cannot prove definitively, I suspect Omicron chapter came about due to a family connection. Within these articles, the first president of Omicron chapter was listed as Franca Barsanti, while one of the alumna advisors was listed as Sandra Barsanti. I would not be surprised if these two women were related. However, I was unable to contact either to confirm any relationship. The other sororities in operation in 1978 where Chi Omega, Alpha Phi, and Phi Sigma Sigma.

159. On the operations of Omicron chapter, see "Tufts," *Sigma Kappa Triangle* 72, no. 3 (Winter 1978): 30; "Massachusetts," *Sigma Kappa Triangle* 72, no. 4 (Spring

1979): 38; "More On Greek Life," *Tufts Criterion* 11, no. 4 (May 1979): 3; and "Massachusetts," *Sigma Kappa Triangle* 74, no. 4 (Spring 1981): 36. Additional information was provided through an interview with Cindy Vide (October 1, 2015), an alumna of the chapter who was active from 1978 to 1981. On the closing of Omicron chapter, see "Massachusetts," *Sigma Kappa Triangle* 75, no. 2 (Fall 1981): 14, which no longer lists any contact information for the chapter. Therefore, I've taken this to indicate the chapter was effectively closed by the fall of 1981. In terms of recruitment, it appears Omicron did enjoy some success. According to "Conventions Top Winners," *Sigma Kappa Triangle* 74, no. 2 (Fall 1980): 7, Omicron chapter won an award that year for achieving its recruitment goal. However, it appears this was too little, too late.

160. Primack, "Opening Doors," which includes the quotation. Within this article, Sigma Kappa's national president also stated that "Sigma Kappa both welcomes and appreciates women of all races, creeds, national origins, and prohibits discrimination in its constitution."

161. The lack of recognition for New York City as a birthplace of national fraternities and sororities is certainly my opinion, as a general and thorough discussion of this topic is well beyond the scope of this work. Additionally, there are plenty of other locales within the United States where a number of national Greek-letter organizations came into existence, such as rural Virginia and northern California, so the issue is much more complex than presented in the text. On the founding of the Normal College of the City of New York, see *Commemorating The Diamond Jubilee of Hunter College of the City of New York* (New York, NY: Hunter College, 1945).

162. On the state of campus affairs at NCCNY in the early 1910s, see *Wistarion* (1911 ed.) and *Wistarion* (1912 ed.). The percentage of women in sororities was estimated based upon information provided for members of the senior class. On the rejection of Ethel and Lillian, see "Our Fraternity's Founding Explored," *The Sphinx* 58, (Winter 1984): 4–5.

163. "Our Fraternity's Founding Explored." Additional information on the founding, including the date, can be found on Phi Sigma Sigma's national website, http://www.phisigmasigma.org/aboutus/heritage/history (accessed September 30, 2015). Note that by 1913, a number of fraternities in New York City had been founded on non-sectarian principles, including Delta Sigma Phi and Phi Epsilon Pi. However, these organizations were probably unknown to the women of NCCNY since there were no male undergraduates on campus. Also, as Phi Sigma Sigma would soon discover, starting out as non-sectarian was much easier than staying that way. The sorority became predominantly Jewish within a few years.

164. On the connection between Belle Heyman and Tufts College, see "In Memoriam," *The Sphinx* 41, no. 4 (Fall 1963): 12. On Morris Heyman as a student at Tufts College and a member of Phi Epsilon Pi, see *CofTC* (1917–18 ed.), 226. On the establishment of Beta chapter, see "Silver Threads Among the Gold… And Blue!" *The Sphinx* 13, no. 4 (November 1938): 5–6, which includes the quotation. On the founding members of Beta chapter, see letter from Mrs. Albert Bloom, Grand Archon of Phi Sigma Sigma, to Dean Herrick dated January 19, 1960, in Activities and Organizations records, 1875–2013, UA 024.001 Box 6, Folder 10 (Pan Hellenic 1920–1959).

165. On the local addresses of the women, see *CofTC* (1917–18 ed.), 218, 220. The morphing of non-sectarian fraternities and sororities into predominantly Jewish organizations is discussed in detail in other sources, such as Sanua, *Going Greek*, and Syrett.

166. The inability of the five to establish Phi Sigma Sigma is not much of a surprise, given that life at Tufts College was upended just a semester later with the arrival of the S.A.T.C. program. A thorough search of sorority and Panhellenic records within the Tufts University archives failed to find any mention of Phi Sigma Sigma during the years the chapter was supposedly active. Indeed, the only record I did find was correspondence between Dean Jeffers and Ann Reiter, Director of Expansion for Phi Sigma Sigma, between March 18, 1959, and January 26, 1960, in Activities and Organizations records, 1875–2013, UA 024.001 Box 6, Folder 10 (Pan Hellenic 1920–1959). In one response, Dean Jeffers writes, "Your letter came as a complete surprise because I was never aware that there had been a chapter of Phi Sigma Sigma at Jackson College." Dean Jeffers even went on to ask if Phi Sigma Sigma was a social or professional society. On the total number of initiates in Beta Chapter, see Baird (13th ed. 1935), 366. On the continued enrollment at Tufts for Rose Bolonsky and Dora Margolis, see *CofTC* (1919–20 ed.), 255. On the transfer of Sara Gelfand to Harvard, see *Harvard University Catalogue* (1921–22 ed.), 280. On the transfer of Bertha Hershman to Wellesley College, see *The Wellesley Legenda* (1921 ed.), 122.

167. On the continued interest in Phi Sigma Sigma from the founders of Beta chapter, see "Beta Chapter," *The Sphinx* (1926): 23; and "Boston Tea Party Held at the Miles Standish," *The Sphinx* 19, no. 4 (November 1944): 20. On the efforts of Miriam Goldshine to establish Zeta chapter at UCLA, see "In Memoriam–Miriam Goldshine Waters, Beta '19," *The Sphinx* 17, no. 3 (May 1942): 15.

168. On the inquiry of Phi Sigma Sigma in 1959, see correspondence between Dean Jeffers and Ann Reiter, Director of Expansion for Phi Sigma Sigma, between March 18, 1959, and January 26, 1960, in Activities and Organizations records, 1875–2013, UA 024.001 Box 6, Folder 10 (Pan Hellenic 1920–1959). On the establishment of Chi Omega and Alpha Phi in the mid 1970s, see their sections within this chapter. On the re-establishment of Beta chapter and their activities, see rush advertisement, *TT*, September 27, 1977; "Frats Prepare for Rush," *TO*, October 21, 1977; and "Undergraduate Happenings," *The Sphinx* (December 1977): 10. The last mention I could find regarding Phi Sigma Sigma was "Gals Veto Houses," *TO*, December 1, 1978, as this article lists the total number of sororities at three. While two of these sororities were most definitely Chi Omega and Alpha Phi, the third was likely Sigma Kappa, as that chapter had just been reactivated the previous semester. Therefore, it appears Phi Sigma Sigma closed down before the fall of 1978.

169. On the efforts to bring a fourth sorority to campus, see "New Sorority May Form," *TD*, February 26, 1990; and "New Sorority Could Be At Tufts By September," *TD*, March 15, 1990. On the suggested limit of seventy-five members per sorority chapter, see "Phi Sigma Sigma Group Forms On Tufts Campus," *TD*, October 3, 1990. This upper limit of chapter size was attributed to the National Greek Council, which does not appear to be a real organization. Instead, I suspect the report meant to say the National Panhellenic Conference (NPC), which is the governing body for twenty-six social sororities. Indeed, it is the NPC that put the expansion rules in place.

170. Ibid.

171. "Phi Sigma Sigma Group Forms on Tufts Campus"; "New Sorority Gains Recognition," *TD*, November 14, 1990; and "Beta–Tufts University," *The Sphinx* 71, (Spring 1992): 23. My contention that this incarnation of Beta chapter was the first to be both active and recognized at Tufts is based on the inability of Beta chapter to

gain campus recognition back in 1918 (the chapter operated with no knowledge of, or support from, the administration and the student-run Panhellenic Council), and the inability of Beta chapter to regain its charter in 1977–78 timeframe.

172. On the successes of Phi Sigma Sigma, see, for example, "Phi Sigma Sigma Blasts Off to an Exciting Year," *TD*, February 24, 1992; "Phi Sig Volunteers the Town Red," *TD*, April 27, 1992; "Beta–Tufts University," *The Sphinx* 71, (Spring 1992): 23; "Phi Sigma Sigma Continues To Grow," *TD*, October 2, 1992; "Phi Sigma Sigma Has Busy Fall," *TD*, November 20, 1992; and "Greek Organizations Reevaluated By CFS," *TD*, November 8, 1993, which mentions the chapter faced a challenge in attracting new members. Information about the struggles within the chapter was provided through interviews with Beta chapter alumnae, including Gayle Pitman (March 29, 2013) and Kristina Brunelle (July 25, 2013).

173. "Rush System Does Not Do Justice For All," *TD*, March 16, 1994, which includes the quotation. Information about Phi Sigma Sigma's proposal to equalize the rush venues was provided through interviews with Beta chapter alumnae including Gayle Pitman. All sororities are created equal, except those that are more equal than others.

174. Ibid. In hindsight, I suspect that pulling out of formal rush did more harm than good for Phi Sigma Sigma, as it only isolated them from the rest of the community. On Phi Sigma Sigma's recruitment efforts, see advertisements in *The Tufts Daily*, February 14–16, 1994. Formal sorority rush had already been concluded by this time.

175. "Panhellenic Council Established More Open Policies for Fall Rush," *TD*, Commencement, 1994. Sorting through the changes in sorority rush policies during the late 1980s and early 1990s has been difficult at best, since the changes were not well documented at the time of their implementation. Thus, I will try my best. Prior to 1987, sororities held recruitment activities independent of one another, much as fraternities operated. However, according to "New Sorority Rush System Introduced," *TD*, November 9, 1987, that year a number of new policies were implemented, including a requirement for all rushees to sign up ahead of time, to visit each sorority at least twice during recruitment week, and, at the end, to list the sororities they wished to join by order of preference. Bids were then assigned based on these preferences, assuming there was a match and that the particular sorority had not exceeded its quota. By 1993, this procedure had evolved into a system known as "generally assured bidding," whereas all women who went through rush week and met the scholastic requirements were assured a bid to join at least one of the sororities (though not necessarily their top choice). This policy had been implemented to comply with a mandate from the trustees of Tufts College, who wanted to make the Greek system more accessible to new members – see "Members of Greek System React to the Board of Trustees' Report," *TD*, November 11, 1993. Additionally, this issue is discussed in more detail within chapter 6. The policy of generally assured bidding is one reason why today, in 2016, the four active sororities each number around one hundred members. At some schools with similar practices, such as the University of Arizona, average sorority membership size is now past two hundred.

176. Unfortunately, the awarding of 126 Packard Avenue to Phi Sigma Sigma was not documented in *The Tufts Daily*, but starting in the fall of 1994, the sorority began listing 126 Packard Avenue as its address. Information on how the chapter acquired the space was provided through interviews with Beta chapter alumnae, including Kristina

Brunelle. The housing struggles of Zeta Beta Tau and Alpha Epsilon Pi are discussed in detail in their relevant sections within chapter 3. One reason why Phi Sigma Sigma beat out the two fraternities for the new house was probably a desire on the part of the Tufts administration to achieve equity in terms of Greek housing, since percentage-wise, more fraternity members lived in chapter houses than sorority members.

177. "Phi Sigma Sigma Will Be Dissolved This Year," *TD*, March 28, 1995.

178. This is all certainly my opinion, but having spoken to numerous alumni who were active in Greek-letter organizations during the early 1990s, I feel confident in making this claim. The issue of forcing fraternities and sororities to open their membership is discussed in detail in chapter 6.

179. On Phi Sigma Sigma having an openly gay member, see "Discussion Concerning Greek Life at Tufts Shift to Television Show," *TD*, February 17, 1993. Otherwise, the rest of this paragraph is essentially my own opinion, supported in part through interviews with Beta chapter alumnae. For the record, I am not opposed in any manner to gay, bisexual, or transgender members within a fraternity or sorority. I was active in two chapters of Sigma Nu (Tufts and the University of Arizona), and in both there was more than one member who, after graduation, subsequently came out as gay. These men are still my fraternity brothers, and they are still my friends; they will always be as such. However, I do remember the general feelings of Tufts students regarding openly gay classmates when I was an undergraduate in the late 1980s, and it was not a good one. Homophobia was alive and well at the time, for reasons that make no sense to me now. But, I do feel there has been a positive change in attitude over the years. For example, a couple of years ago, I walked past the Delta Upsilon house on the Tufts campus and noticed a rainbow flag hanging from one of the windows in support of gay rights. No Tufts fraternity would have flown that flag in the 1980s. To do so would have been the kiss of death when it came to recruitment.

180. Havighurst, *The Miami Years*, 12–16, 134, 151–152, 167; and *Recensio* (Oxford, OH: Junior Class of Miami University, 1905), 29. On the establishment of Alpha Delta Phi at Miami University, see the fraternity's national website, http://www.alphadeltaphi.org/AboutUs/Chapters/tabid/59/agentType/View/ChapterID/23/Default.aspx (accessed October 11, 2015). Miami University to date has seen the founding of six national fraternities and sororities, including three before the Civil War: Beta Theta Pi (1839), Phi Delta Theta (1848), and Sigma Chi (1855). As a result, many refer to Miami University as the "Mother of Fraternities," especially since these three are some of the largest in existence today. Of course, by 1847, Union College in Schenectady, New York had also seen the birth of six national fraternities, including the first three modern-day organizations. Thus, Union College also has a strong claim to the title "Mother of Fraternities." The debate over which is the true mother will likely last an eternity. Note that Miami University was closed to all students from 1873 to 1888.

181. Havighurst, 173–175, which includes the quotation.

182. On the founding of Delta Zeta, see Havighurst, 100; and information as posted on the national organization's website, http://www.deltazeta.org/about-us/history/ (accessed December 3, 2016). On Delta Zeta's expansion as a national organization, see Baird (8th ed. 1915), 427–428. On the number of active fraternities at Miami in 1902, see Baird (6th ed. 1905), 547.

183. Letter from Violet S. Whitfield to Miss Nellie Reynolds, Registrar of Tufts, dated Mach 8, 1954; and letter from Dean Katharine Jeffers to Mrs. Robert H. Whit-

field dated March 12, 1954, in Activities and Organizations records, 1875–2013, UA 024.001 Box 4, Folder 1 (Delta Zeta 1954–1968).

184. On the reasons for Delta Zeta's founding at Tufts, see "Delta Zeta Sorority Installed," *TW*, May 16, 1956; and interview with Paula (Rivituso) Itaya (November 11, 2012). The issue of membership discrimination and the action of the trustees in 1955 is discussed further in chapter 6. On Delta Zeta's declaration, see letter from Ida Fleming to Assistant Dean Marguerite Wynne-Roberts dated October 19, 1955, in Activities and Organizations records, 1875–2013, UA 024.001 Box 4, Folder 1 (Delta Zeta 1954–1968). Note that in this letter. Ms. Fleming did admit that Delta Zeta's ritual contained a line from the New Testament, "which Jewish girls are made aware of before being initiated." Also note that in *LOTH–2*, 210, Miller argues that the rule of the trustees apparently did not apply to sororities, since Delta Zeta was supposedly known to have "an 'understanding' rather than a constitutional provision" that "excluded Negroes." However, in this I believe Professor Miller is incorrect, as the information within the Tufts University archives does not support his conclusion that new sororities were exempt from the rule of the trustees. Based on my research, it seems that this "understanding" within Delta Zeta (if one even existed) was not known at the time the sorority was approved as a campus organization. Indeed, one of the charter members of Delta Zeta told me during an interview that she knew of no discriminatory policies within the sorority, official or otherwise, and had there been one, she would never have joined (her parents were of a mixed background). Instead, it appears this information first came to light in the fall of 1961, when the Tufts administration asked each organization to comment on its membership policies. The president of Delta Zeta answered "yes" with regards to a "Gentleman's agreement" that was in place at the national level to restrict Negroes. But then, a few months later, the chapter president revised this statement by saying, "Delta Zeta has no codified policy on discrimination," which was interpreted to mean that "D[elta] Z[eta] will consider each applicant as an individual." See "Student View To Be Published Soon," *TW*, February 23, 1962. Quite frankly, in light of this conflicting information, I don't know what to believe when it comes to any Gentleman's agreement or not within Delta Zeta. But at the very least, I believe that if there was any inkling of systematic discrimination within Delta Zeta in 1955, the organization would never have been allowed on campus.

185. "Girls Pledged in Delta Zeta; New Sorority On Hill," *TW*, March 30, 1956; "Delta Zeta Sorority Installed"; and "A First For Bay State," *The Lamp of Delta Zeta* 46, no. 1 (Autumn 1956): 30–31.

186. The controversies surrounding Sigma Kappa and Alpha Xi Delta are discussed in their relevant sections earlier in this chapter. I can't help but imagine, though, that the national Delta Zeta organization was somewhat spooked by everything that happened at Tufts during the fall of 1956.

187. On the activities of Delta Zeta after its founding, see letter from Pamela Spence, historian of Delta Zeta, to Professors Miller, dated May 30, 1964, in Activities and Organizations records, 1875–2013, UA 024.001 Box 4, Folder 1 (Delta Zeta 1954–1968). The demise of Thalia and Alethea is discussed in earlier sections within this chapter. On the size of Delta Zeta, see membership rosters from 1959 through 1968, as contained in Activities and Organizations records, 1875–2013, UA 024.001 Box 4, Folder 1 (Delta Zeta 1954–1968). According to these rosters, Delta Zeta stood at sixty-three members and pledges in the spring of 1960. Six years later, that number was reduced to fifteen,

with two studying abroad.

188. On the demise of Delta Zeta between the spring of 1966 and the fall of 1966, and its subsequent re-colonization, see membership lists within Activities and Organizations records, 1875–2013, UA 024.001 Box 4, Folder 1 (Delta Zeta 1954–1968); and "Delta Zeta Sorority Finished Early Rush," *TW*, December 16, 1966. The date of the re-colonization is unknown, as this article only mentions "the pledging took place last week."

189. On the installation of Delta Zeta, see "Delta Zeta," *Jumbo* (1968 ed.), 255. On the dwindling size of Delta Zeta, see membership lists from 1966 through 1968 in Activities and Organizations records, 1875–2013, UA 024.001 Box 4, Folder 1 (Delta Zeta 1954–1968); and Activities and Organizations records, 1875–2013, UA 024.001 Box 7, Folder 3 (Pan Hellenic Council 1962–1968). Within this latter source is a note, dated March 14, 1968, that expresses worry over the general lack of interest among women for sorority life. On the demise of Alpha Omicron Pi and Chi Omega, see their respective sections earlier in this chapter.

190. "DZD Apologizes for Thefts," *TD*, November 29, 1988. Registering as a student club at Tufts is not the same as gaining official recognition as a fraternity or sorority chapter. The recognition process is much more involved.

191. "DZD Apologizes for Thefts"; "CFS To Consider Limits on Greeks," *TD*, November 15, 1988; and "Clarification," *TD*, December 2, 1988.

192. Information on DZD's attempt at recognition was provided through an interview with Dean of Students Bruce Reitman (October 31, 2012; and November 16, 2012).

193. Ibid. The quote in this paragraph is a paraphrase based on Dean Reitman's recollection of his interaction with the NPC official. Although in general I have avoided relying solely on personal interviews, in this case I made an exception since Dean Reitman's recollection of this incident was very fresh in his mind; I do not doubt the authenticity of the conversation. As for how the NPC found out about DZD's plans, the most plausible explanation in my opinion is the one offered in the text, that members of DZD, after meeting with Dean Reitman, called Delta Zeta to get the process started, and then Delta Zeta spilled the beans to the NPC. However, I do not have definitive proof of this chain of events, as I was unable to speak with any of the former members of DZD. The NPC expansion process has been discussed in more detail earlier in this chapter, specifically in the sections on Alpha Omicron Pi and Phi Sigma Sigma. Suffice to say, the path DZD was trying to take in its quest to become a chapter of Delta Zeta was (and still is) allowed under NPC rules, provided the Tufts Panhellenic Council gave its blessing first. Since this approval was never forthcoming, there was no way the national organization of Delta Zeta would get involved with DZD. For the official rules regarding expansion in NPC organizations, see http://www.npcwomen.org/resources/pdf/unanimous%20agreements.pdf (accessed October 24, 2015).

194. Ibid. On the demise of DZD, see "Search For New Sorority Underway," *TD*, November 30, 1989. The search for a new sorority eventually culminated in the reestablishment of Phi Sigma Sigma at Tufts.

195. The four fraternities established at Tufts during the 1980s were, in order of founding: Psi Upsilon, Sigma Phi Epsilon, Alpha Sigma Phi, and Zeta Beta Tau. All of these chapters were established from the ground up by undergraduates.

196. The revival of Chi Omega, Sigma Kappa, and Phi Sigma Sigma is discussed in

their respective sections earlier in this chapter.

197. Frank Smalley, ed., *The Golden Jubilee of Syracuse University, 1870–1920* (Geneva, NY: W. F. Humphrey, 1920?), 7–11; and information from the website of Syracuse University, http://archives.syr.edu/history/founding_su.html and http://archives.syr.edu/collections/org_non_su/sua_gnc.htm (accessed October 27, 2015). Genesee College, it appears, was also coeducational for many years prior to its eventual closing in 1875. On the transfer of Upsilon Kappa from Genesee College to Syracuse University, see Baird (1st ed. 1879), 105. Upsilon Kappa, in 1875, became the Pi chapter of the national Psi Upsilon fraternity and is still active today at Syracuse, as is Delta Kappa Epsilon's Phi Gamma chapter.

198. *The History of Alpha Phi International Fraternity, 1872–1930* (New York, NY: The Century Co., 1931): xix–xx, 132–133, which includes the quotation. According to Baird (1st ed. 1879), 143–147, there were three active national Greek-letter sororities in 1872: Delta Gamma, Kappa Alpha Theta, and Kappa Kappa Gamma, but these organizations were relatively small and confined to the Midwest. A third national sorority, I. C. Sorosis (now Pi Beta Phi) was also active and similarly scattered about the Midwest (apparently Mr. Baird was not familiar with this organization when he complied his book). Elmira College, some ninety miles south of Syracuse, was home to two local sororities at the time, but it appears unlikely the women of Syracuse knew of these organizations given the distance between the two campuses.

199. *The History of Alpha Phi International Fraternity*, 132, which includes the quotation.

200. On the founding of Gamma Phi Beta, see Baird (1st ed. 1879), 145. On the founding of Beta chapter at Northwestern and the number of fraternities on campus at the time, see *The History of Alpha Phi International Fraternity*, xxiii–xiv, 149–151; and information on the website of Beta chapter, http://www.northwesternalphaphi.com/#!history/cyp0 (accessed October 28, 2015). The existence of five fraternities at Northwestern is confirmed by Baird (1st ed. 1879), 178. On the near merger of Delta Sigma with Alpha Phi, see the section on Alpha Omicron Pi earlier in this chapter. On the founding date of Eta chapter at Boston University, see *The History of Alpha Phi International Fraternity*, 190–191.

201. On the state of Tufts University in the 1970s, see Miller, *LOTH–2*, chapters 21–22; and Gittleman, *An Entrepreneurial University*, chapter 2. On the growth ethnic societies, see "Ethnic Societies Flourish on Tufts Campus," *TO*, November 21, 1976. According to this article, there were fifteen ethnic societies at the time, though not all had living spaces to call their own.

202. "Zeta Theta Installed at Tufts University," *The Alpha Phi Quarterly* 91, no. 2 (Spring 1979): 56–57. Additional information was provided through interviews of charter members including Nancy Shalowitz (October 9, 2012), Ellen (Sullivan) Gaudiano (January 21, 2013), and Sheri (O'Boyle) Montgomery (August 15, 2011).

203. Ibid. Each organization undoubtedly had members from a wide variety of backgrounds and major courses of study, but in talking with the founders of both Chi Omega and Alpha Phi, it was clear that engineers played an important role in the former, while Child Study and BSOT students played an important role in the latter.

204. On Alpha Phi's activities during the 1977–78 school year, see "Alpha Phi Was Forgotten," *TO*, November 18, 1977. On the chapter's occupancy of 128 Curtis Street, see "Zeta Theta Installed at Tufts University." Additional information was provided

through an interview with Sheri (O'Boyle) Montgomery, who was one of the residents of the chapter house that first year.

205. "Zeta Theta Installed at Tufts University."

206. "CSL Conditionally Grants Sorority Campus Housing," *TD*, February 11, 1981; and "Six Houses Close to Students," *TO*, March 6, 1981. Although these articles do not give a reason why the city of Somerville required the closings as a condition for the new housing license, one reason was probably to keep the net increase in dormitory beds at a minimum. I suspect Somerville feared the new dormitory would result in a marked increase in students coming to campus, which would put a strain on the city's resources as well. Managing growth has long been a concern for the school and the surrounding communities.

207. Unfortunately, Alpha Phi's move to 14 Sawyer Avenue was not reported in either *The Tufts Daily* or the *Tufts Observer*. However, an advertisement for Alpha Phi's "End of Summer Party," *TD*, September 20, 1982, clearly lists the address of the new chapter house. Professor Wade taught Greek and literature, and the first mention of his house shows up in *CofTC* (1906–07 ed.), 29, 42. For more information on 14 Sawyer Avenue, see UA Edwin B. Rollins Papers, 1300[sic]–1976, Notebooks, 1940–1955, MS054.001 Box 2, Folder 3 (Campus Homes, Part II 1940–1955). Finally, when I was researching Chi Omega, I had the pleasure of interviewing Maurene Golden, and alumna of the chapter and major force behind the sorority's return in 1976. She mentioned helping Alpha Phi acquire their chapter house at 14 Sawyer Avenue.

208. On the transgressions of Alpha Phi, see "Alpha Phi Sorority Temporarily Shut Down," *TD*, March 3, 2003; "University Reaches Agreement with Fraternities, Sororities," *TD*, April 25, 2003; and "Alpha Phi Suspended for Hazing, Alcohol Violations," *TD*, March 13, 2008. On Alpha Phi's recovery, see "After Suspension, Alpha Phi Enjoys High Rush Turnout," *TD*, October 7, 2009. Alpha Phi's "Bid Your Heart Out" charity event began in 2010, according to "Alpha Phi Hosts Charity Auction Soiree," *TD*, October 21, 2011. On the latest success, see "Alpha Phi Raises $15,000 Through Bid Your Heart Out Fundraiser," *TD*, March 2, 2015. Since 2013, the total amount raised is over $41,000.

209. Information about Delta Sigma's near affiliation with Kappa Alpha Theta can be found in the section on Alpha Omicron Pi earlier in this chapter.

210. Sweet, *Indiana Asbury–DePauw University*, 198–199; Turk, *Bound By A Mighty Vow*, 16–18, which includes the quotation; and Becque, *Coeducation and the History of Women's Fraternities*, 34. The negative reception afforded the women at Asbury was similar to the one the women at Tufts received when they were first allowed to enroll, in the fall of 1892.

211. Sweet, 198–199; Turk, 18–19; and Becque, 34–35. I am continually amazed at the spirit of the women who started their fraternal organizations during this era, as they were surrounded by so much negativity from their male classmates. Finally, of the four women who first enrolled at Indiana Asbury, three joined Kappa Alpha Theta, while the fourth became a founding member of the I. C. Sororis chapter (later Pi Beta Phi) on campus.

212. Sweet, 199; Turk, 19–20; and Becque, 35, which includes the quotation. I am unsure as to when, exactly, Bettie first sought out the services of the New York jeweler, as no exact date is given in any of these three sources. However, the solicitation appears to have happened around the end of 1869 or the beginning of 1870. Oh, you men of

Indiana Asbury! Did you really think laughing would derail the plans of such strong and independent women?

213. Becque, 36; and Baird (6th ed. 1905), 316–322. The rejection of Kappa Alpha Theta by the women of Delta Sigma is also discussed further in the earlier section on Alpha Omicron Pi within this chapter.

214. Information about Kappa Alpha Theta's expansion into Massachusetts is taken from the organizations national website, https://www.kappaalphatheta.org/collegians/aboutourchapters/chapter_listing.cfm?from=HomeHeaderLink (accessed November 14, 2015). On the NPC expansion process at Tufts during the 2012–13 school year, see "Kappa Alpha Theta to Join Greek Community," *TD*, April 4, 2013.

215. "Kappa Alpha Theta to Join Greek Community," *TD*, August 28, 2013; and "Kappa Alpha Theta Welcomes 77 New Members," *TD*, September 23, 2013. Information about the chartering date for Eta Psi chapter was taken from Kappa Alpha Theta's national website, https://www.kappaalphatheta.org/collegians/aboutourchapters/find-achapter/chapter_detail.cfm?chapterId=2108 (accessed November 14, 2015).

216. "SigNu, Theta to Receive Building on Curtis Street," *TD*, March 4, 2014; and "Theta and SigNu Move Into New House on Curtis Street," *TD*, September 22, 2014. Information on the size to Kappa Alpha Theta at the end of the 2013–14 school year was provided by Su McGlone, the Director of Fraternity and Sorority Affairs at Tufts University. As to why Kappa Alpha Theta was able to occupy a chapter house well before conventional rules allowed, I do believe convenience played a large part. Opportunities to open a new fraternity or sorority chapter house on the Tufts campus are few and far between these days, and the house at 90–94 Curtis Street was well suited to hold two organizations given its layout as a duplex.

217. "Theta Hosts First Large–Scale Thetathon Fundraiser," *TD*, October 28, 2014; and "Theta Hosts Second Annual Thetathon to Raise Money for CASA," *TD*, October 5, 2015. To raise over $16,000 in just two years is very impressive.

CHAPTER 5

1. This text is meant to be an overall introduction to the topic of minority representation on the Tufts campus, and not an exhaustive treatise on the subject For more information, see Miller, *LOTH–2*, Chapter 12; and Gerald Gill, "Another Light on the Hill: Black Undergraduates and Tufts," *Tufts Online Magazine* (spring 2002), http://www.tufts.edu/alumni/magazine/spring2002/blackundergrads.html (accessed November 14, 2015). Although Tufts did not keep records of the ethnicity of its students throughout most of its history, other entities did. For example, see "Many Students Registered At Tufts College," *The Afro-American*, November 6, 1926, which listed thirty African-American men and women as being enrolled at Tufts in the fall of 1926; and "The American Negro In College, 1932–33," *The Crisis* 40, no. 8 (August 1933), 181, which listed three as being enrolled that year. This latter periodical, *The Crisis*, published statistics of black enrollment at Tufts and other schools over many years. Racial barriers to membership in social fraternities and sororities at Tufts eventually came down, starting in the 1950s. For more information, see chapters 3, 4, and 6.

2. The topics and ideas presented in this paragraph are described in detail within this chapter.

3. It is only within the last thirty years or so that the Tufts community has been regularly (and, sometimes, irregularly) reminded of the presence of BGLOs and multicultural organizations on campus. See, for example, "Many Benefits to Predominantly Black Greek Organizations," *TD*, March 16, 1988; "Greeks Plan Interracial Unity Jam," *TD*, February 20, 1992; "These Greek Organizations Aren't Just for Partying," *TD*, March 13, 2006; "Tufts Groups Entertain Local Children," *TD*, April 14, 2008; "Despite No Tufts Houses, Students in Ethnic Greek Organizations Find Community Rich in Tradition," *TD*, March 18, 2010; "Fraternity and Sorority Affairs Looks to Revive Dormant Multicultural Greek Organizations," *TD*, October 18, 2012; and "Multicultural Greek Council Established on Campus," *TD*, April 18, 2014. Prior to 1988, there is essentially nothing written about these organizations in the student newspapers.

4. Professor Miller, in his first book on Tufts history, *Light on the Hill*, makes almost no mention of people of color at Tufts. It wasn't until he published his second volume in 1986 that he considered the plight of students who were not white. Therefore, it is not surprising he knew nothing about the BGLOs which been active in the Boston area since 1916. On his mention of Kappa Alpha Psi, see Miller, *LOTH–2*, 217. On the founding of Sigma chapter, see "Sigma–Harvard University," *The Sphinx* 2, no. 1 (February 1916): 11; and chapter history, http://17th-house.com/Chapter_History/ (accessed November 15, 2015). On the initiation of David Scott, see "Sigma–Harvard University," *The Sphinx* 2, no. 2 (April 1916): 15.

5. On the activities of Sigma chapter, see, for example, "Sigma–Harvard University," *The Sphinx* 2, no. 2 (April 1916): 15–16; "Sigma Chapter–Boston Mass.," *The Sphinx* 2, no. 4 (December 1916): 20–21; and "Sigma Chapter," *The Sphinx* 3, no. 2 (April 1917): 27. On the involvement of Sigma in the war effort, see "Sigma Chapter," *The Sphinx* 4, no. 1 (April 1918): 17; and "Sigma Chapter," *The Sphinx* 4, no. 2 (December 1918): 13–14. On the general topic of segregation in the Army at the time, see for example, Chad Williams, "African Americans and World War I," http://exhibitions.nypl.org/africanaage/essay-world-war-i.html (accessed November 15, 2015). Also, according to http://schuylkillcountymilitaryhistory.blogspot.com/2010/04/schuylkill-county-african-americans-in.html (accessed November 15, 2015), a number of African-American men saw front-line combat while serving under French command.

6. On the restarting of Sigma chapter in 1919, see "Sigma Chapter," *The Sphinx* 4, no. 2 (December 1918): 13–14. On the struggle over the chapter house decision and the formation of the Alpha Eta chapter, see "Sigma and Alpha Eta," *The Sphinx* 8, no. 1 (February 1922): 15–16. I have to imagine the Tufts men in the chapter probably wanted the house in Cambridge as well, but no mention is made in this article of their preference.

7. On the establishment of the chapter house, see "Sigma Chapter," *The Sphinx* 8, no. 3. (April 1922): 13. On the history of 558 Massachusetts Avenue, see Mary Melvin Petronella, ed., *Victorian Boston Today* (Boston, MA: Northeastern University Press, 2004), 30; and Nancy C. Curtis, *Black Heritage Sites: An African American Odyssey and Finder's Guide* (Edwards Brothers, Inc., 1996), 302. It is unclear how many rooms Sigma chapter had use of in this house, or whether or not members also lived in the home. However, in various articles within *The Sphinx*, Sigma members refer to this space as their chapter home. Finally, the men of Sigma chapter had a working relationship with the League of Women for Community Service for a couple of years prior to moving in, as discussed in "Sigma Chapter," *The Sphinx* 6, no. 2 (May 1920): 26. On the election

of William Brown, see "Sigma Chapter–Boston," *The Sphinx* 8, no. 4 (May 1922): 7–8.

8. Although the story of William Brown and Edward Morrison is somewhat peripheral to this section, I felt it was an important piece of history that was worth retelling. On the status of William and Edward in the fall of 1916, see *CofTC* (1916–17 ed.), 257, 265. On the incident at Princeton, see "Morrison and Brown Play Against Princeton," *The Chicago Defender*, October 21, 1916; and "Princeton May Bar Tufts From Games," *The Chicago Defender*, October 28, 1916, which includes both quotations. This latter article mentions that since Brown and Morrison were eligible to play for a few more seasons, Princeton wanted to drop Tufts from its regular schedule. Indeed, when Princeton's schedule was announced a few months later, Tufts College was not on the list. See "Princeton Announces 1917 Football Schedule," *The Deseret News [Salt Lake City, Utah]*, February 13, 1917.

9. The Tufts versus Indiana football game is one of the more interesting aspects of Tufts history I've stumbled upon, for this game was clearly an anomaly for both schools, and I have been unable to determine how or why the contest was scheduled in the first place. On the problem at the hotel, see "Tufts Defeats Indiana 12–10," *The Chicago Defender*, November 4, 1916, which includes the quotation. On the game itself, see "Morrison to Play Against Indiana," *The Chicago Defender*, October 14, 1916; "Tufts Ready For Battle," *Logansport [Indiana] Pharos Tribune*, October 28, 1916; "Tufts Squad Ready for Game With I.U.," *Fort Wayne [Indiana] Sentinel*, October 28, 1916; "Let's Fight 'Em, Indiana!" *The Indiana Daily Student*, October 28, 1916; "Indiana Vs. Tufts," *The Chicago Defender*, October 28, 1916; "Tufts Winner Over Indiana, 12 to 10," *BG*, October 28, 1916; "Indiana Holds Tufts 12 to 10," *The Indiana Daily Student*, October 30, 1916; and "Tufts Defeats Hoosiers," *TW*, November 1, 1916. The articles from Indiana newspapers were definitely skewed in the opinion that Indiana had won a moral victory for keeping the game so close. Incidentally, the only article which mentions the incident at the hotel is the one from November 4, 1916, in *The Chicago Defender*. The other articles make no mention of this incident, or that Tufts had an integrated team at the time. Finally, this game was one of the first football contests to feature the use of a huddle before the snap, at least according to "Delt Spotlight–Instant Replay," *The Rainbow of Delta Tau Delta* 94, no. 1 (Fall 1970): 36.

10. On the involvement of Jay Ernest "Ernie" Martin in Sigma chapter, see "Sigma Chapter–Boston, Mass.," *The Sphinx* 9, no. 4 (October 1923), 15–16. On Ernie's prowess on the football field, see "Ernie C. Martins of Bluefield Observe Silver Anniversary," *The Sphinx* 36, no. 2 (Spring–Summer 1950): 19. On the initiation of Claude Randolph Taylor, see "Sigma Chapter, Boston," *The Sphinx* 11, no. 1 (February 1925): 32. On Claude's prowess in football, basketball, and track, see "Taylor Is Best Tufts Athlete," *The Afro American*, April 9, 1927. On the community service of Sigma chapter, see for example, "The 'Go-To-High-School, Go-To-College' Movement," *The Sphinx* 10, no. 2 (April 1924): 18. On the closing of Alpha Eta chapter at Harvard, see *The Sphinx* 18, no. 2 (May 1932): inside front cover. On the closing of Sigma chapter, see *The Sphinx* 20, no. 1 (March 1934): inside front cover. Note that Sigma chapter has not occupied a fraternity house since giving up their rooms in 1930.

11. On the revival of Sigma chapter, see *The Sphinx* 21, no. 1 (December 1935): inside front cover, which lists the chapter as being active once again. On the branching out to initiate men from Rhode Island State College and Bates College, see "Sigma Chapter–Boston Massachusetts," *The Sphinx* 23, no. 2 (May 1937): 33; and "Sigma

Chapter–Boston Massachusetts," *The Sphinx* 23, no. 4 (December 1937): 25, which also talks about the annual banquet held in honor of the Harvard-Yale football game. According to this latter article, Sigma chapter had three members from Rhode Island State College and six from Bates. On the involvement of Milton and Vincent Conliffe in Alpha Phi Alpha, see "Sigma Chapter–Boston Massachusetts," *The Sphinx* 29, no. 4 (December 1942): 33–34, which includes the quotation; and "Students at Tufts Say Entrance not Difficult," *The Afro American*, October 23, 1943. On Bernard Robinson being the first commissioned Naval officer, see for example Stephen Howarth, *To Shining Sea: A History of the United States Navy, 1775–1998* (Norman, OK: University of Oklahoma Press, 1999), 414.

12. On the pledging and initiation of Rev. Dr. Martin Luther King, see "Sigma Reports to Alpha," *The Sphinx* 42, no. 2 (May 1956): 40; and "The Birth of A New Age," *The Sphinx* 55, no. 3 (October 1968): 8. This latter issue of *The Sphinx* was dedicated to the legacy and memory of Dr. King. Finally, I refer to Dr. King as "Martin" in the last sentence, as it appears that is how his peers knew him while studying at Boston University (BU), including Nancy Potter, a Tufts alumna who interacted with Dr. King on a number of occasions one summer at BU.

13. On the plethora of activities of Sigma chapter during the 1950s and 1960s, see for example, "Sigma Reports to Alpha," *The Sphinx* 42, no. 2 (May 1956): 40; "Fraternity Aids N.A.A.C.P. in Schools Row," *BG*, August 20, 1963; and "School Imbalance To Go–Peabody," *BG*, August 21, 1963. On the inactivity of Sigma chapter in 1976, see chapter listing, *The Sphinx* 62, no. 3 (October 1976): 75. On the pledging and initiation of seven men from Tufts in 1977, see "History of Alpha Phi Alpha–Sigma Chapter, Boston," http://17th-house.com/site/?page_id=33 (accessed October 19, 2012). Additional information was provided through an interview with Namsoo Dunbar (September 12, 2013), one of the "Seven Pharaohs of Faith."

14. On the activities of Sigma chapter in the 1980s, see for example, "Boston University," *The Sphinx* 66, no. 4 (Winter 1980): 29, which includes the quotation; "Boston University," *The Sphinx* 68, no. 4 (Winter 1982): 39; "Massachusetts," *The Sphinx* 70, no. 2 (Summer 1984): 43–44; "Massachusetts," *The Sphinx* 70, no. 3 (Fall 1984): 42; "Metro Boston," *The Sphinx* 71, no. 1 (Spring 1985): 36–37; "Metro Boston," *The Sphinx* 71, no. 4 (Winter 1985): 23; "Metropolitan Boston," *The Sphinx* 72, no. 2 (Summer 1986): 22–23; and "Massachusetts," *The Sphinx* 74, no. 1 (Spring 1988): 35. On the founding of Rho Nu chapter, see http://onecaalphas.com/rho-nu (accessed November 20, 2015).

15. On the collaboration between Sigma and Rho Nu chapters and their activities, see "Sigma–Boston, MA," *The Sphinx* 80, no. 3 (Fall 1995): 60; "Sigma, Boston Metro," *The Sphinx* 87, no. 2 (Summer 2002): 38, which also discusses Rho Nu's success at the New England Step Fest; and "Epsilon Gamma Lambda, Sigma, Rho Nu, Xi Lambda, and Mu Theta Lambda," *The Sphinx* 88, no. 2 (Summer 2003): 35.

16. The bulk of the information on the history of Omega Psi Phi is drawn from Ross, *The Divine Nine*, 74–78; and an undated oral history of the fraternity entitled "The History of Omega Psi Phi," as recited by Bishop Edgar Amos Love. See https://s3.amazonaws.com/ClubExpressClubFiles/957295/documents/Bishop_Loves_Omega_Address.pdf?AWSAccessKeyId=AKIAIB6I23VLJX7E-4J7Q&Expires=1448223554&response-content-disposition=inline%3B%20file-name%3DBishop_Loves_Omega_Address.pdf&Signature=rHP7u3j9%2BubThiuw-

gHZ6BcBfph0%3D (accessed November 22, 2015). Also see Baird (10th ed. 1923), 214–215.

17. Ibid.

18. Ibid. Of note is that President Thirkield was white. For more on President Thirkfield's time at Howard, see Walter Dyson, *Howard University, The Capstone of Negro Education, A History: 1867–1940* (Washington, D.C.: The Graduate School of Howard University, 1941), 10, 64, 65, 70, 113, 358, 391–393, 409, 418, 420.

19. Love, "The History of Omega Psi Phi," which includes the quotation; and Ross, 74–78.

20. On the establishment of Beta chapter, see "Beta Chapter" *The Oracle* (June 1919): 11; and information as posted on the national fraternity's website, http://thepearlofomega.org/historyofthepearl (accessed November 29, 2015). On the founding of Gamma chapter, see "Gamma Chapter," *The Oracle* (June 1919): 12–13; and "Gamma Chapter–Boston, Mass.–Historical Sketch," *The Oracle* (1921): 11–12. Note that early editions of *The Oracle* did not list volume numbers, only publication year and occasionally the month. Gamma chapter, when it was opened, accepted men as far north as Bates College and as far south as Yale University.

21. "Gamma Chapter," *The Oracle* (June 1919): 12–13; and "Gamma Chapter–Boston, Mass.–Historical Sketch," *The Oracle* (1921): 11–12. Unfortunately, the address of Gamma's first chapter house was not listed in the latter article. However, by 1921, Gamma chapter was ensconced in a row house at 19 Braddock Park in downtown Boston. In the fall of 1922, the chapter moved to 22 Claremont Park in Boston, where they remained until 1931. This appears to be the last chapter house occupied by Gamma chapter to date. The importance of chapter houses among BGLOs at this time cannot be understated, as many campuses (such as Harvard University) did not provide housing for their black students.

22. Ibid. On activities of Gamma chapter as the early 1920s progressed, see "Survey of Gamma Chapter During 1921–22," *The Oracle* 1, no. 3 (September 20, 1922): 20–23. The names of Tufts men on the initiate roll of Gamma chapter has been painstakingly researched by Tufts graduate and Omega Psi Phi member David Carl, as he prepares for Gamma chapter's 100th anniversary. On Clarence Hays, see *CofTC* (1919–20 ed.), 285; and *CofTC* (1920–21 ed.), 295. On Henry Jeffress and his accomplishments at Tufts College, see Gill, "Another Light on the Hill." On the involvement of Henry Jeffress in Omega Psi Phi, see "Gamma Chapter, Boston, Mass.," *The Oracle* 3, no. 1 (March 1925): 23; and "Gamma Rays," *The Oracle* 4, no. 3 (November 1925): 102. On the involvement of Cuthbert Phillibert in Gamma chapter, see "Gamma–Boston, Mass.," *The Oracle* 9, no. 1 (April 1930): 5. Other initiates from this era include Rudolph U. Lanclos, Paul Lincoln Jones, Cyril Fitzgerald Atkins, Malvin J. Proctor, Samuel Leon McCoy, Jr., George Sheehy, Robert Morris James, and Edwin Hugh Conyers.

23. On the awarding of an achievement medal to Edward Dugger, see "First District Activities," *The Oracle* 16, no. 3 (September 1937): 20. On the athletic achievements of Edward Dugger, see Edwin Bancroft Henderson, *The Negro in Sports* (Washington, D.C.: The Associated Publishers, 1949), 90, 92, 406, 410, 413–415, 417; and "Eddie Dugger Elected Tufts track Captain," *The Afro American*, March 23, 1940. On the scholastic achievements of Edward Dugger, see "Dugger, Edward Jr., 1919–75," *Concise Encyclopedia of Tufts History*, http://hdl.handle.net/10427/14829 (accessed November 29, 2015). On Edward Dugger's involvement in Gamma chapter, see "Chapter

Caravan," *The Oracle* 20, no. 1 (March 1941): 21, 33; and Joseph Mason Andrew Cox, *Great Black Men of Masonry* (Lincoln, NE: Blue Diamond Press, 1982), 132.

24. Information concerning Gamma's activities during the war is not readily available, as I was unable to locate any editions of *The Oracle* between 1941 and 1945. However, in the June 1945 edition of *The Oracle*, Edward Dugger and Reginald Pearman are still listed as Gamma chapter officers, just as they were in 1941. By this time, Mr. Dugger in particular was known to have relocated to Dayton, Ohio. Therefore, it seems entirely plausible that Gamma chapter was effectively dormant during the war. This conclusion is supported by the article "Gamma Chapter," *The Oracle* 37, no. 3 (September 1947): 10, which mentions the chapter was reorganized on October 1, 1946. On the activities of Gamma chapter through 1969, see "New England 'Q's' In District Meet," *The Oracle* 39, no. 1 (March 1949): 10; "Gamma Brothers Plan Frat House," *The Oracle* 39, no. 1 (March 1949): 21; "Boston Chapter to Press for '50 Grand Conclave," *The Oracle* 39, no. 4 (December 1949): 5, 8; "Omega Psi Phi Members Found of Nearly Every Campus," *BG*, April 23, 1950; "Boston Quettes Honor the New Grand Basileus," *The Oracle* 95 [this is likely a misprint in the document], no. 4 (December 1955): 5; "Sailing With Gamma in '67–'68," *The Oracle* 58, no. 3 (Fall Edition 1968): 5–6; and "Growing Gamma," *The Oracle* 58, no. 3 (Fall Edition 1969): 18. Information about Gamma chapter's activities in the 1980s and 1990s was provided through interviews with Christopher Bennett (September 16, 2013) and Dr. Harry Lightfoot (September 24, 2013), who were both active members at the time.

25. Information on the struggles within Gamma chapter and its eventual closing was provided through an interview with Dr. Harry Lightfoot and Christopher Bennett. For a more in-depth discussion of the problem surrounding hazing in Omega Psi Phi as well as other BGLOs, see Kimbrough, *Black Greek 101*, 112–119. Also see, for example, "Fraternity Hazing–The Nightmare of Omega Psi Phi unfolds at the University of Florida," *The Evening Independent [St. Petersburg, Florida]*, May 22, 1979; "Fraternity Members in Hazing Must Perform Volunteer Service," *The Baltimore [Maryland] Sun*, June 29, 1994; "Greek Tragedy," *Washington [D.C.] City Paper*, June 18, 1999.

26. Information about the reactivation of Gamma chapter was provided through interviews with Dr. Harry Lightfoot and Christopher Bennett. Also see "Re-Activation of Gamma Chapter," *The Oracle* 81, no. 23 (Winter 2011): 22.

27. On the founding of Sigma Chi, see Baird (5th ed. 1898), 219–221. Mass defections also plagued the Kuklos Adelphon fraternity, as discussed earlier in chapter 1. Other defections are discussed in Baird (1st ed. 1879), 129–130.

28. Giddings, *In Search of Sisterhood*, 46–48; and Ross, *The Divine Nine*, 237. President Taft, as it turned out, went on to suffer the worst defeat to date of an incumbent president, as he won only 8 out of 531 possible electoral votes.

29. Giddings, 48–50; and Ross, 237.

30. Giddings, 50–52, which includes the quotations; and Ross, 219–223, 237.

31. On the establishment of Beta chapter at Wilberforce University, see Giddings, 69–70. On the establishment of Iota chapter in Boston, see Giddings, 87; and the history as posted on the chapter's website, https://iotachapterdeltas.com/chapter-history/ (accessed December 2, 2015). The list of charter members on this website does not appear to include any women from Tufts College. Iota stayed a mixed chapter until 1945, when a separate Boston-area alumnae chapter was established.

32. On the educational career of Mae Tyson Wright, see Cynthia Earl Kerman and

Richard Eldridge, *The Lives of Jean Toomer: A Hunger for Wholeness* (Baton Rouge, LA: Louisiana State University Press, 1987), 12–13; Gill, "Another Light on the Hill"; and "Many Students Registered at Tufts College," *The Afro American*, November 6, 1926, which lists Mae Wright as the only black female on campus. On the living accommodations of Mae Wright while a student at Tufts, see the 1923–24 through 1926–27 editions of *CofTC*. On the Jabberwock event, see Giddings, *In Search of Sisterhood*, 110.

33. On the educational success of Mae Wright, see "Phi Beta Kappa," *The Afro American*, November 19, 1927. On Mae Wright's career as well as her continued service to Delta Sigma Theta, see "Mae Peck-Williams, Retired Teacher," *The Baltimore Sun*, April 12, 1995. Other Tufts alumni who have led their respective organizations include Joel Reynolds (Delta Tau Delta) and Harry Wilcott (Sigma Nu).

34. On the formation of Xi Tau chapter, see history as posted on the chapter's LinkedIn page, https://www.linkedin.com/groups/2661860/profile (accessed December 3, 2015). Unfortunately, information about the specific involvement of Tufts women in Iota and Xi Tau chapters is quite scant. However, Delta Sigma Theta is mentioned as being active at Tufts in a number of *Jumbo* yearbooks, including the 1987, 1991, 1992, 1995, 1997, 1998, 2007, and 2008 editions. Information on Xi Tau having a Tufts member through 2015 was provided through an interview with Su McGlone, the Director of Fraternity and Sorority Affairs at Tufts University (September 18, 2012).

35. Ross, 187–188, 201–202; Giddings, 43–44; Parks, *Black Greek-Letter Organizations in the Twenty-First Century*, 41–43; and Carroll L. L. Miller and Anne S. Pruitt–Logan, *Faithful to the Task At Hand: the Life of Lucy Diggs Slowe* (Albany, NY: State University of New York Press, 2012), 32–33. Note that half of these sources also mention a second professor, Elizabeth Appa Cook, as helping to encourage Ethel Hedgeman in her drive to create a new sorority. However, since not every source mentioned Professor Cook, I decided only to mention her in these notes. The two sororities active at Brown University while Ethel Robinson was an undergraduate were Delta Sigma and Kappa Alpha Theta, according to Baird (6th ed. 1905), 317–318, 530.

36. Ibid. Ethel Hedgeman would go on to marry George Lyle. Beta chapter of Alpha Phi Alpha was founded at Howard University on December 20, 1907, according to the chapter's website, www.betachapter.org/home/#!/page_more (accessed December 8, 2015).

37. On the early struggles within Alpha Kappa Alpha, see Giddings, 44–45. On the spilt in 1912, see the section on Delta Sigma Theta earlier in this chapter.

38. On the incorporation of Alpha Kappa Alpha, see Ross, 219–223; and Giddings, 44. On the expansion of Alpha Kappa Alpha, see information as published on the organization's national website, http://www.aka1908.com/home (accessed December 8, 2015).

39. On the founding of Epsilon chapter, see "Epsilon–Boston, Mass.," *The Alpha Kappa Alpha Ivy Leaf* 4, no. 1 (1925): 18–19. I was unable to definitively determine where the seven founders went to school, though none appeared to have been students at Tufts College. Also, one of the chapter's founders is listed in a later article within the *Ivy Leaf* as having graduated from Smith College. On the early activities of Epsilon chapter, see "Epsilon, Boston, Mass.," *The Alpha Kappa Alpha Ivy Leaf* 5, no. 1 (1926): 26–27; "Epsilon Chapter, Boston, Massachusetts," *The Alpha Kappa Alpha Ivy Leaf* 6, no. 1 (1927): 17–18, which lists Mary Crutchfield as an active member of the chapter; "Psi Omega Chapter," *The Ivy Leaf* 8, no. 1 (March 1930): 9; "Epsilon Chapter–Boston,"

The Ivy Leaf 8, no. 1 (March 1930): 8; and "Epsilon Chapter," *The Ivy Leaf* 8, no. 3 (September 1930): 6. On the legacy of Dr. Mary (Crutchfield) Thompson, see "Dr. Mary Thompson, 83, Founded Dental Clinic, Worked With Poor," *BG*, March 20, 1985; and "Dr. Mary Thompson; Memorial Service Sunday," *BG*, November 18, 1985. On the legacy of Dr. Jesse Garnett, see "Party to Aid Black Colleges," *BG*, February 22, 1976; and "Jesse Garnett, Boston's First Black Woman Dentist," *BG*, September 6, 1976.

40. On the activities of Epsilon chapter in the 1930s, see for example, "Epsilon Chapter," *The Ivy leaf* 9, no. 1 (March 1931): 10–11; "Epsilon," *The Ivy leaf* 15, no. 4 (1937): 36; and "Epsilon," *The Ivy Leaf* 17, no. 4 (1939): 28. On the establishment of a meeting place at 464 Massachusetts Avenue in Boston, see "Epsilon Chapter," *The Ivy leaf* 11, no. 1 (March 1933): 13. On the Women's Service Club of Boston, see for example, Hope J. Shannon, *Legendary Locals of Boston's South End Massachusetts* (Charleston, SC: Arcadia Publishing, 2014), 63. The organization is still active at the same address today. On the hosting of national and regional conferences for Alpha Kappa Alpha, see "Greetings from the Twenty-Second Annual Boule," *Ivy Leaf* 18, no. 1 (March 1940): 6–7; and "Twelfth Annual North Atlantic Regional Conference," *Ivy Leaf* 20, no. 1 (March 1942): 19. The transition from reporting on social activities to service initiatives is most likely a reflection of the times. The push for civil rights took a big leap forward following World War II, as many began questioning the "normal" practice of discrimination within America and started working in earnest for change. This shift in mindset is reflected in the articles submitted by Epsilon chapter to the *Ivy Leaf*. See, for example, the contrast between "Psi Omega and Epsilon Chapters," *Ivy Leaf* 18, no. 1 (March 1940): 15, which uses the whole letter to talk about a recent tea party; and "Epsilon and Psi Omega Chapters," *Ivy Leaf* 22, no. 2 (June 1944): 9, which talks about the chapter's educational outreach during Negro History Week, including a speech given to elementary school children entitled "Brown America–Past and Present." On the lobbying of the Massachusetts state government, see "Epsilon Chapter," *Ivy Leaf* 23, no. 2 (June 1945): 10; and "Psi Omega and Epsilon Chapters," *Ivy Leaf* 24, no. 1 (March 1946): 15. On the efforts of Epsilon in other social causes, see "Psi Omega and Epsilon Celebrate Together," *Ivy Leaf* 25, no. 1 (March 1947): 6. Finally, it appears that the official title of Alpha Kappa Alpha's magazine changed over time, from *Alpha Kappa Alpha Ivy Leaf*, to *The Ivy Leaf*, to finally just *Ivy Leaf*. These changes are reflected in the references above.

41. My assertion that almost no Tufts women joined Epsilon chapter in its first fifty years is based on a lack of information about Tufts in any of the chapter's articles within the *Ivy Leaf*. Instead, most of the members tended to be from Boston University, Northeastern, Harvard, and Wellesley. It is likely there were other Tufts women in Epsilon chapter prior to 1981 besides Mary Crutchfield, but I just wasn't able to find anything about these women. On the statistics regarding enrollment of black women at Tufts, see Gill, *Another Light on the Hill*. On the integration of Thalia and Alethea, see the appropriate sections earlier in the chapter. On the integration of Phi Epsilon Pi, see their section in chapter 3. Finally, the continuance of Epsilon chapter was demonstrated through their semi-regular submissions of chapter letters to the *Ivy Leaf*.

42. On the closing of sororities on the Medford campus, see the section on Chi Omega earlier in this chapter. Information about the "Ivy Divine" pledge line was provided through interviews with Robin Scott-Hawkins (November 2, 2013, and November 4, 20133) and Saundria Grey (November 2, 2013), both of whom were part of the

seven. Robin Scott-Hawkins was drawn to the chapter in part by a woman she'd known in high school who also joined Epsilon chapter, whereas Saundria Grey counted both her mother and some aunts as members of Alpha Kappa Alpha. On Epsilon chapter's activities at Tufts, see for example, "Notices," *TD*, February 27, 1981; and "Sororities," *TD*, February 24, 1982. On Alpha Kappa Alpha's entries into the *Jumbo* yearbook, see *Jumbo* (1981 ed.), 155; and *Jumbo* (1982 ed.), 105.

43. On Epsilon chapter's event with Alpha Omicron Pi, see "Epsilon Does Their Part to Preserve Mother Earth," *The Ivy Leaf* 68, no. 1 (Spring 1991): 32, which mentions the event took place the previous November. Unfortunately, this event was not covered in *The Tufts Daily*. After 1982, Alpha Kappa Alpha is listed as a sorority in the *Jumbo* yearbook for years 1986, 1987, 1992, 1995, 1996 (five women shown in the photo), 1997, 1998, 2007, and 2008. Note that not every edition of the yearbook since 1982 has contained information about fraternities and sororities, so there are likely other years that Tufts women were active in Epsilon chapter.

44. Parks, 116–117; Crump, *The Story of Kappa Alpha Psi*, 1–4; and Ross, 46–48.

45. Ibid. The ten founders of Kappa Alpha Nu are: Elder Watson Diggs, Byron Kenneth Armstrong, Guy Levis Grant, Ezra D. Alexander, Edward G. Irvin, Paul W. Caine, Marcus Peter Blakemore, John Milton Lee, George Edmonds, and Henry T. Asher. Parks, 116, mentions that two of the founders, Diggs and Armstrong, started their collegiate career at Howard University, where they became familiar with the Alpha Phi Alpha fraternity on campus, and that this probably influenced the founding of their organization.

46. Crump, 10–25, which includes the quotations. On the establishment of Beta chapter, see also "Kappa Alpha Nu," *Alumni Quarterly of the University of Illinois* 7, no. 1 (January 1913): 131; "A Colored One At last," *The Kappa Alpha Journal* 31, no. 1 (October 1913): 142; and "Beta Chapter, Kappa Alpha Nu Fraternity Organized," *Phi Chi Quarterly* 10, no. 4 (November 1913): 321.

47. Crump, 24–29.

48. On the early expansion of Kappa Alpha Psi, see Baird (9th ed. 1920), 213–214. On the activities of Kappa Alpha Psi during World War I, see Crump, 36–41. On the establishment of Chi chapter, see Crump, 66–67. J. Logan Jenkins is listed as a Pre-Medical/Pre-Dental student in the *CofTC* (1922–23 ed.), 292. This appears to be the first and last listing of J. Logan Jenkins in a Tufts College student catalogue.

49. On the establishment of the first pledge line in the spring of 1924, see Crump, 67; and information as posted on the chapter's website, http://chi1924.com/lineage.html (accessed April 17, 2013). On the enrollment of Clifford Alfred Crawford when he pledged Chi chapter, see *CofTC* (1924–25 ed.), 262. Unfortunately, there is scant information available on Clifford Crawford and his time at Tufts College.

50. Wiencek, *The Hairstons,* 220–222; "Hairston, Jester, 1901–2000," *Concise Encyclopedia of Tufts History*, http://hdl.handle.net/10427/14829 (accessed December 14, 2015); "Tufts University Information on Jester Hairston," http://www.choralnet.org/view/151236 (accessed December 14, 2015); and "Alumnus Jester Hairston Dies at 98; Actor-Composer Helped Preserve Negro Spirituals," http://www.umass.edu/chronicle/archives/00/01-28/Hairston18.html (accessed December 14, 2015). The educational odyssey of Jester Hairston, though documented in these sources, is somewhat inconsistent, especially when it comes to the time he spent between his first year at MAC and Tufts College. Therefore, the timeline presented in the text is based more on original

sources such as yearbook entries and newspaper articles than these secondary sources. On Jester's initial enrollment at MAC, see *The Index* (1922 ed.), 116, which lists him as a freshman during the 1920–21 school year. In the very next edition of the yearbook, *The Index* (1923 ed.), 103, Jester is listed as an "Ex-1924" student, meaning he had dropped out. On Jester Hairston's joining of Chi chapter of Kappa Alpha Psi, see information as posted on the chapter's website, http://chi1924.com/lineage.html (accessed April 17, 2013). On Jester's return to MAC, see *The Index* (1928 ed.), 97, which lists him as a second year student for the 1926–27 school year. On Jester's participation in the Glee Club, see *The Index* (1928 ed.), 185–186; and "The Men's Musical Clubs," *The Massachusetts Agricultural College Alumni Bulletin*, May 25, 1927.

51. Ibid. For the quotation, see Wiencek, 221.

52. Ibid. For the quotations, see Wiencek, 221. Jester Hairston later admitted his letter was a lie – he knew almost nothing about the work of Professor Lewis when he applied to Tufts. On Claude Taylor's legacy as a Tufts athlete, see "Taylor is Best Tufts Athlete," *The Afro American*, April 9, 1927.

53. Ibid. On Jester's enrollment at Tufts College, see *CofTC* (1927–28 ed.), 267; *CofTC* (1928–29 ed.), 265; and "Freshman Football Squad of 49 Reports for Tufts," *BG*, September 23, 1927. This article mentions Jester reported for the first practice that fall, but it is unclear if he ever played for the team.

54. On the activities of Chi chapter of Kappa Alpha Psi throughout the years, see for example, "Sacred Hearts' Finish Stirs at Boy's Club Match," *BG*, May 9, 1926, which discusses a loss on the basketball court by Chi chapter to the Boys' Club of Boston; "Washington Negro Judge Speaks at Meeting Here," *BG*, May 17, 1936, a meeting organized by Chi chapter; "College Stars' Game to Benefit Freedom House," *BG*, March 27, 1949, which discusses Kappa Alpha Psi's upcoming intramural basketball game against Alpha Phi Alpha; "Plan Panhellenic Dance," *BG*, February 18, 1962, which lists Mat Whitehead from Tufts as the president of Chi chapter; and "Judge to Address Kappa Alpha Psi," *BG*, June 23, 1963, which was sponsored under the "Guide Right" program. On the founding of Theta Iota chapter, see William H. Tibbs, IV, *History of the Northeastern Province, Kappa Alpha Psi Fraternity, Inc., 1930–2008*, 127, http://www.kapsinep.com/index.php/the-province/province-history (accessed December 15, 2015).

55. On the attempt by Kappa Alpha Psi to occupy a chapter house at Tufts, see "House Available for Fraternity," *TO*, February 22, 1985; "Administration to Decide Professors Row Fate," *TD*, March 6, 1985; "Administration Changes Status of 92 Professors Row," *TD*, March 29, 1985; and "Psi U Prez [sic] Protests 92 Decision," *TD*, April 2, 1985. On the size of Kappa Alpha Psi in the spring of 1985, see "Campus Greeks," *TD*, April 5, 1985. In the end, the house at 92 Professors Row was awarded to the Sigma Nu fraternity in the fall of 1986.

56. On the continued involvement of Tufts men in Theta Iota, see "Black Fraternities and Sororities," *The Harvard Crimson*, May 4, 1988; and editions of the *Jumbo* yearbook from the years 1986, 1987, 1991, 1992, 1995, 1997, and 1998. Note that not every edition of the *Jumbo* yearbook contains information on Greek-letter organizations, so there are probably other years when Theta Iota had active members from the Tufts campus. On the closing of Theta Iota chapter, see "KAPsi, RCA Cooperate on Hazing Incident," *The Tech*, December 6, 1994. On Chi chapter being open once again to men from Tufts, see "The Mighty Chi Chapter: An Introduction," *The Diamond*

Newsletter [Northeastern Province of Kappa Alpha Psi], (Fall 2010): 10.

57. The stories of the founding of Alpha Xi Delta and Chi Omega, complete with the help they received from their partner fraternity, are discussed earlier in this chapter in the appropriate sections. On the relationship between Delta Gamma and Phi Delta Theta, see "History of Delta Gamma," *The Anchora of Delta Gamma* 31, no. 2 (January 1, 1915): 126–132.

58. Ross, 102–103; and Parks, 95–96, 100–101, which includes the quotations.

59. Parks, 95–98.

60. Parks, 106–109, which includes the quotation.

61. Ross, 266–271; and Parks, 107–109. On the establishment of Theta Alpha chapter of Zeta Phi Beta, see *Northeastern National Pan-Hellenic Council: Divine 9 at a Glance*, https://issuu.com/nucampusactivities/docs/d9_at_a_glance (accessed December 13, 2016), page 9. On the establishment of Beta Alpha chapter of Phi Beta Sigma, see information as posted on the chapter's website, http://www.ba1935.com/chapter-history/ (accessed December 16, 2015).

62. On the presence of Phi Beta Sigma and Zeta Phi Beta on the Tufts campus, see editions of the *Jumbo* yearbook for the years 1992, 1995, 1996, 1997, and 1998. On the lecture sponsorship by Phi Beta Sigma, see advertisement, *TD*, February 24, 1992, 6. On the joint Phi Beta Sigma-Zeta Psi party, see "Can We Have Integrated Parties… Without Alcohol?" *TD*, October 14, 1997. Sadly, it appears this event was a flop, the reasons of which are discussed in the article. In 1992, the Sigma Phi Epsilon fraternity also teamed up with a number of BGLOs for a "Unity Jam" dance to raise money for the Ronald Blackburn Scholarship Fund. See "Greeks Plan Interracial Unity Jam," *TD*, February 20, 1992.

63. For information on the founding of the Ku Klux Klan, see Note 15 for chapter 1. On the development of the Ku Klux Klan in Indiana, see Ross, 298; and Parks, 125–126.

64. Ross, 298; and Parks, 125–127.

65. On the establishment of Kappa Nu chapter, see information as posted on the chapter's website, http://www.sgrhoboston.org/sgrho-in-boston.html (accessed December 17, 2015). On Kappa Nu's presence at Tufts University, see various editions of the *Jumbo* yearbook including 1995, 1997, and 1998. Kappa Nu's website also lists the various pledge intake lines from each year, but a quick search of the names did not turn up any graduates of Tufts University.

66. On the history and current status of the Greek system at Cornell, see information on the school's website, http://dos.cornell.edu/fraternity-sorority-life (accessed December 17, 2015). On the history of La Unidad Latina, see Torbenson and Parks, *Brothers and Sisters*, 111–112; and information as posted on the fraternity's national website, http://www.launidadlatina.org/about-lul/history/story (accessed December 17, 2015).

67. Ibid.

68. On the expansion of La Unidad Latina, see information as posted on the fraternity's national website, http://www.launidadlatina.org/membership/chapters/undergraduate-chapters (accessed December 17, 2015).

69. On the presence of Lambda Upsilon Lambda at Tufts in 1998, see *Jumbo* (1998 ed.). Information about the history of Nu chapter in relation to Tufts University was provided through an interview with Glenn Garcia (April 17, 2013), who was active in

the chapter as an undergraduate and as an alumnus. Also see *Jumbo* (1998 ed.).

70. Information about the total number of Tufts men to join Nu chapter was provided through an interview with Glenn Garcia.

71. On the dates of establishment for national collegiate fraternities and sororities, see Torbenson and Parks, 277–285. On the founding of Alpha Rho Lambda, see Torbenson and Parks, 114, 129, 284; and the history of Alpha Rho Lambda as published on the organizations website, http://alpharholambda.net/aboutus/history (accessed April 18, 2013).

72. Information about the founding of Beta chapter comes from the national organization's website, http://alpharholambda.net/chapters/beta (accessed April 18, 2013). Additional information was provided through an interview with Valerie M. Avila (October 25, 2013; and October 31, 2013), an alumna of the chapter.

73. On the pledge lines of Beta chapter between 1996 and 2006, see information as published on their website, http://www.oocities.org/aplbeta/hermanas.html (accessed December 19, 2015). Also see *Jumbo* (1998 ed.); and *Jumbo* (2001 ed.).

74. Information about the activities of Beta chapter was provided through an interview with Valeria M. Avila. Also see "Benefits of Going Greek," *Lakeland [Florida] Ledger*, March 13, 2000. On the sponsorship of Latino Culture night by the Tufts Latino Center, see for example http://ase.tufts.edu/latinocenter/newsEvents/archives/2013spring.asp (accessed December 19, 2015).

75. On the founding of Lambda Pi Chi, see Torbenson and Parks, 117–118, which includes the quotation; and information as posted on the national organization's website, http://www.lambdapichi.org/?page=history (accessed December 21, 2015). On the founding of Nu chapter, see http://www.lambdapichi.org/Default.asp?nu_chapter (accessed December 21, 2015).

76. On the reactivation of Nu chapter by Tufts women and their subsequent activities, see http://www.lambdapichi.org/news/150739/Welcome-to-Our-Fall-2013-Hermanas.htm (accessed December 13, 2016); "Growth of Greek Life at Tufts," *TD*, March 4, 2014; "Visiting The Hill This Week," *TD*, September 30, 2014; "Visiting the Hill This Week," *TD*, October 27, 2014; and "Tufts Seniors Organize Drive to Collect Feminine Hygiene Products," *TD*, April 15, 2015. On the state of Nu chapter in 2016, see https://www.facebook.com/tuftsgreeks/ (accessed December 13, 2016).

77. The relationship between the gay community and Greek-letter organizations is very complex and well beyond the scope of this work. See for example Syrett, *The Company He Keeps*, which examines this issue in depth. On some recent examples of animosity if not hatred directed at gays in Greek-letter organizations, see "Vandals Mar Smoot Marks, LCA House with Anti-Gay Graffiti," *The Tech*, May 5, 1998; "Vandalism at ATO Investigated," *The Emory Wheel [Emory University]*, March 28, 2006; "U-M Fraternity Damaged by Vandals," http://blog.mlive.com/annarbornews/2007/05/um_fraternity_damaged_by_vanda.html (accessed December 19, 2015); and "Gays and Greeks," *The Towerlight [Towson University]*, October 31, 2011.

78. On the founding of Delta Lambda Phi, see Torbenson and Parks, 184–188, which includes the quotation; and information as published on the fraternity's national website, http://dlp.org/about/history/ (accessed December 19, 2015).

79. "DLP – Not Just Another Fraternity on Professor's Row," *TD*, February 25, 2000.

80. Ibid. On the re-founding of Alpha Chi chapter, see "A Fraternity Comes Back

To Life," *BU Today*, December 1, 2011.

81. On the general establishment of Latino fraternities and sororities since 1975, see Torbenson and Parks, 282–285. On the founding of Sigma Lambda Upsilon, see the history as published on the organization's website, http://sigmalambdaupsilon.org/Hermandad#History (accessed December 20, 2015).

82. On the founding of Chi chapter, see information as posted on the organization's website, http://sigmalambdaupsilon.org/index.php?option=com_content&view=article&id=162&Itemid=176 (accessed November, 2013). Information about Wilnelia Rivera's involvement in Chi chapter was provided through an interview with Vanessa Salazar (November 14, 2013).

83. Interview with Vanessa Salazar.

84. Ibid; and "Despite No Tufts Houses, Students in Ethnic Greek Organizations Find Community Rich in Tradition," *TD*, March 18, 2010.

85. Ibid.

86. On the founding and history of Delta Psi Sigma, see information as posted on the organizations website, http://deltapsisigmainc.org (accessed December 20, 2015). Note that an earlier version of this website, accessed in November of 2013, listed the roster of the Boston chapter by year and school. According to this earlier website, Tufts women joined Delta Psi Sigma in 2003, 2004, 2006, 2008, and 2009. Others may have joined since 2009, but information is incomplete in this regard.

87. On the general establishment of Latino fraternities and sororities in the 1908s and 1990s, see Torbenson and Parks, 282–285. On the establishment of Omega Phi Beta, see information as published on the national organization's website, http://www.omegaphibeta.org/?page=Herstory (accessed December 21, 2015).

88. On the founding of Pi chapter, see information as published on the national organization's website, https://girasol.wordpress.com/about/ (accessed December 21, 2015).

89. Ibid. On the various pledge lines in Pi chapter, see the listing on the national organization's website, https://girasol.wordpress.com/sister-profiles/ (accessed December 21, 2015). On the activities and awards of Pi chapter, see information on the national organization's website, https://girasol.wordpress.com/accomplishments/ (accessed December 21, 2015); and "Tufts Groups Entertain Local Children," *TD*, April 14, 2008. On the sponsorship of a lecture on domestic violence by Pi chapter, see https://girasol.wordpress.com/upcoming-events/ (accessed December 21, 2015). On the dormancy of Pi chapter, see "Fraternity and Sorority Affairs Looks To Revive Dormant Multicultural Organizations," *TD*, October 18, 2012.

CHAPTER 6

1. On President John Albert Cousens and his tenure at Tufts College, see Miller, *LOTH–1*, chapter 13. I realize that my statement regarding President Cousens and his feelings on Jewish students may be seen as inflammatory if not blasphemous, but this is my conclusion based upon his words and actions while corresponding with the Alpha Epsilon Phi sorority between the spring and fall of 1922. On the Jewish enrollment in American college and universities at the time, see "Survey of Jews in 17 Colleges in 1919 Gave Harvard Fewest," *BG*, July 2, 1922. This article mentions that when one

hundred six institutions were considered, average Jewish enrollment was 9.7%. Tufts College, at the time, was double the national average. On the existence of a Jewish quota at Tufts College in the 1920s, see Note 370 in chapter 3.

2. Exclusion of Jewish women from national sororities is discussed in detail in Sanua, *Going Greek*, chapters 1–3. One of the only extra-curricular outlets for Jewish students at Tufts College was the Menorah Society, which is discussed in further detail in the Phi Epsilon Pi section of Chapter 3. Indeed, during the 1921–22 school year, Louise Adelberg was the secretary of the Menorah Society, according to *Jumbo* (1922 ed.), 194. However, the Menorah Society was more of an intellectual organization than a social one.

3. On the history of Alpha Epsilon Phi, see the information as published on the sorority's national website, https://www.aephi.org/aephi_story/history (accessed December 25, 2015). Unfortunately, it appears the original petition has not survived to this day. For reference to this petition, see letter from Dorothy Grant, Field Secretary, to President Cousens dated February 14, 1922, in Activities and Organizations records, 1875–2013, UA 024.001 Box 1, Folder 14 (Alpha Epsilon Phi 1922).

4. Letter from Dorothy Grant, Field Secretary, to President Cousens dated February 14, 1922, in Activities and Organizations records, 1875–2013, UA 024.001 Box 1, Folder 14 (Alpha Epsilon Phi 1922), which includes the quotation.

5. Letter from President Cousens to Dorothy Grant dated February 20, 1922, in Activities and Organizations records, 1875–2013, UA 024.001 Box 1, Folder 14 (Alpha Epsilon Phi 1922), which includes the quotations. The statement about the Jewish nature of Alpha Epsilon Phi seems curiously out of place in this letter, but its meaning becomes clearer as the correspondence continues. In 1922, women were technically enrolled in the all-female Jackson College, which was essentially a wholly owned subsidiary of Tufts College. I have avoided discussing this topic, as the separation between Jackson College and Tufts College is not relevant to this history.

6. The attempt by President Lowell of Harvard to institute a Jewish quota, though a fascinating story in its own right, is well beyond the scope of this work. For a summary of the debacle and the anti-Semitism of President Lowell, see for example Sanua, *Going Greek*, 121–123.

7. "Discrimination Against Jews Suspected in New Harvard Policy on Admission," *NYT*, June 2, 1922; and "Harvard Stirred By Talk of Limitation," *BG*, June 2, 1922. On the policies of Tufts College concerning Jewish students, see "Proposed Inquiry on Harvard Ban," *NYT*, June 3, 1922, which includes the quotation. Articles on the Harvard Affair appeared regularly in *The New York Times* and the *Boston Globe* throughout the rest of 1922 and into 1923. A very good summary from the perspective of Jewish students can be found in "The Affair At Harvard," *The Menorah Journal* 8, no. 5 (October 1922): 263–276.

8. Letter from Mrs. S. Alice Borchard Greene, National President of Alpha Epsilon Phi, to President John F. Cousens dated July 28, 1922, in Activities and Organizations records, 1875–2013, UA 024.001 Box 1, Folder 14 (Alpha Epsilon Phi 1922), which includes the quotation. Although notes of the earlier conversation between the two were not recorded, Mrs. Greene refers to this conversation extensively in her letter.

9. Letter from Mrs. S. Alice Borchard Greene, National President of Alpha Epsilon Phi, to President John F. Cousens dated July 28, 1922, in Activities and Organizations records, 1875–2013, UA 024.001 Box 1, Folder 14 (Alpha Epsilon Phi 1922),

which includes the first quotation. Letter from President Cousens to Mrs. S. Greene dated August 3, 1922, in Office of the President Records, 1828–2007, John Albert Cousens, administrative records and related papers, 1920–1937, UA001.007 Box 2, Folder 2 (Correspondence 1922–1925), which includes the second quotation.

10. Letter from Mrs. S. Alice Borchard Greene to Mrs. Caroline S. Davies dated November 18, 1922, in Activities and Organizations records, 1875–2013, UA 024.001 Box 1, Folder 14 (Alpha Epsilon Phi 1922); and letter from Caroline S. Davies to President John A. Cousens dated November 22, 1922, in Activities and Organizations records, 1875–2013, UA 024.001 Box 1, Folder 14 (Alpha Epsilon Phi 1922), which includes the quotation. This letter from Dean Davies to President Cousens is one of the few instances where I have seen an official reference to a Jewish quota at Tufts College. That Dean Davies reiterated the offending text is fortunate from a historical perspective, as her original draft letter to Mrs. Greene has not survived.

11. Letter from Caroline S. Davies to President John A. Cousens dated November 22, 1922, in Activities and Organizations records, 1875–2013, UA 024.001 Box 1, Folder 14 (Alpha Epsilon Phi 1922). In this letter, Dean Davies makes it clear both she and the faculty were in favor of Alpha Epsilon Phi establishing a chapter at Tufts. She had even crafted a response for President Cousens to that effect.

12. Letter from President Cousens to Mrs. S. Greene dated November 29, 1922, in Activities and Organizations records, 1875–2013, UA 024.001 Box 1, Folder 14 (Alpha Epsilon Phi 1922), which includes the quotation.

13. Ibid, which includes the quotation. The insistence of President Cousens that two of the Tufts sororities allowed Jewish members, though technically true, was quite misleading. He must have known that Jewish women would never be accepted en masse in these sororities, especially if their names were easily identifiable as Jewish. That one or two Jewish women did join was the exception rather than the rule.

14. On the quotation, see Miller, *LOTH–2*, 208. Calling President Cousens an anti-Semite may be harsh if not unfair since I have not studied his history in great detail, but in my opinion it is accurate based on the words he wrote, and those he did not allow Dean Davies to write. On the operations of the four mentioned fraternities, see their sections in chapter 3.

15. Letter from William Bringham, Sigma Chi national organization, to Ms. Mayer dated February 23, 1984, and letter from President Mayer to Dean Bobbie Knable dated March 22, 1984, which includes the quotations, both in Office of the President Records 1828–2007, Jean Mayer, administrative records and related papers, 1976–92, Subject Files, UA001.013 Box 10, Folder 21 (Fraternities 1983–1988).

16. Memo from Dean Knable to President Mayer dated March 29, 1984, and letter from President Mayer to William Bringham dated April 10, 1984, which includes the quotation, both in Office of the President Records 1828–2007, Jean Mayer, administrative records and related papers, 1976–92, Subject Files, UA001.013 Box 10, Folder 21 (Fraternities 1983–1988).

17. Letter from Sigma Chi national office to Ms. Mayer dated September 10, 1984, in Office of the President Records 1828–2007, Jean Mayer, administrative records and related papers, 1976–92, Subject Files, UA001.013 Box 10, Folder 21 (Fraternities 1983–1988). You would have thought Sigma Chi would have confirmed the sex of President Mayer before writing, seeing as they were the ones who initiated the conversation. Talk about not doing your homework!

18. On Jack Crockett's time at Bates College, see "Obituary–John C. Crockett," *The Lewiston Sun-Journal*, December 6, 2001. On his efforts organizing athletic competitions, see "Virginia Straus Wins Lewiston Indies Girl's Tennis Tournament," *The Lewiston Daily Sun*, September 21, 1933; and "Lewiston Indies Hold Second Annual Marathon July 28," *The Lewiston Daily Sun*, July 9, 1934. On the existence of mayor's contests at the University of New Hampshire and the University of Maine, see "Tufts College Has Campaign For Mayor," *The Lewiston Daily Sun*, May 24, 1937. On the silly campaign platforms, see "Realism in Campus Politics," *TW*, April 15, 1937, which includes the quotations.

19. "Obituary–John C. Crockett."

20. On the call to campus for a mayor's contest, see "Realism in Campus Politics," which includes the first quotation. On the response by the campus, see "Four Candidates to Start Lively Campaign in Effort to Win Coveted Election in First Campus Mayoralty Here in May," *TW*, April 29, 1937; "Five Candidates Throw Hats in Ring in Tufts Mayoralty Contest," *TW*, May 6, 1937; and "Candidates for Mayor Vision Coming Utopias," *TW*, May 13, 1937, which include the quotations on campaign promises. On the victory of Don Simonds, see "Donald Simonds Elected First Mayor of Tufts," *TW*, May 20, 1937. Over 800 students voted their choice for mayor, the largest turnout ever seen for a campus election.

21. On the entrance of Betty Lou Troup into the Mayoralty contest, see "Mayoralty Contest Begins Next Week," *TW*, May 11, 1939, which includes the quotation. On the exit of Betty Lou Troup from the contest, see press release "Attractive Co–ed Withdraws from College Mayoralty Contest" dated May 17, 1939, in UA Memory Books, 1849–1996, MS075.001 Box 73, Folder 1 (Chi Alpha Chapter of Chi Omega Scrapbook 1938–1945). Given that this press release was inside the scrapbook, I assume it was written by members of the Chi Omega chapter with the intent of having it published in the *Tufts Weekly*. It was not. Instead, the very next day, the *Tufts Weekly* featured an article about the mayoral candidates, and Betty's name was nowhere to be found. See "Candidates For Mayor To Open Campaign Tonight at Barnum," *TW*, May 18, 1939. Censorship at the hands of someone (likely Dean Bush), it appears, was alive and well in 1939. Eventually women did enter the Mayoralty campaign, and one, Audrey "Annie Oakley" Hallberg, won in the spring of 1955. On Audrey's victory, see *Jumbo* (1956 ed.), 138.

22. "Campus Campaign: Confederates, Cowboys, Indians Elect a Mayor of Tufts College," *LIFE*, June 16, 1947, 119–122, which includes the quotation. As evidenced by the choice of characters, political correctness was not in vogue at the time. For perspective, tuition at Tufts College was about $500 a year, so candidate Vogel's promise was way over the top.

23. Ibid. No doubt the stunts were influenced by the presence of the *LIFE* photographers, as all were probably looking to get their picture in the magazine, where it would then be seen by tens of millions of readers. Not to be outdone, *LOOK* magazine covered the 1948 Mayoralty contest, but unfortunately I have been unable to find this publication in print.

24. The spoils of victory evolved over time, though the Mayoralty contest never featured winnings worth any significant value. Essentially, the Mayor was the big man on campus the following year, not a horrible thing to be at all. See "Mayor Enjoys Privileges," *TW*, March 14, 1958. Fraternities and the sororities as groups were active

in the contest from its earliest days, but by the 1950s, they had clearly taken over. A non-fraternity man had little to no chance of winning (Audrey Hallberg, the winner in 1955, was a member of the Alpha Omicron Pi sorority). On the influence of Greek-letter organizations, see for example, "The Class of 1952," *TD*, April 1, 2002.

25. "Tufts Buccaneers–Er Electioneers–Take Boston Fleet," *BG*, May 7, 1953; and "Mayoralty Began in 1937," *TW*, April 22, 1954. Other stunts that occurred in contests around this same time included live animal parades through campus, candidates jumping from the roofs of buildings, the holding of a "slave auction" for dates to a dance, simulated sex between two students in public, and homemade catapults that launched all sorts of projectiles across campus. See *Jumbo* (1954 ed.), 162–165.

26. On the poster partiers, see "Mayoralty Began in 1937"; "Mayor Enjoys Privileges"; and "Work Parties This Week Begin Mayoralty Season," *TW*, April 11, 1958. While technically the Mayoralty contest lasted just one week, the unofficial preparation for a campaign required many more weeks beforehand. Information about the selling of beer and alcohol to support Mayoralty was provided through an interview with Linford Stiles (April 30, 2012), the winner of the 1958 contest. In his estimate, his fraternity, Alpha Tau Omega, spent upwards of $20,000 on his campaign, so the number quoted in the text is probably too low. That the fraternities were able to get away with selling alcohol speaks to their collective power in the 1950s. The Tufts administration must have known, for example, what was going on in the fraternity houses during Mayoralty week. And yet they did nothing.

27. Information about the 1958 campaign was provided through interviews of the two contestants, Mike "Diamond Mike" Leven (May 4 and May 7, 2012) and Lin "Huckleberry Finn" Stiles. On the candidacy of Mike Leven and Lin Stiles, see "Mississippi Mood to Reign During Mayoralty," *TW*, March 19, 1958.

28. Ibid.

29. Ibid. Also see "Work Parties This Week Begin Mayoralty Season." The last line of this article issues a challenge to the students, saying, "It's up to each of you to make this year's the wildest campaign yet."

30. Programs for "Manners and the Man" and "Showboat" in Activities and Organizations records, 1857–1999, UA 024.001 Box 6, Folder 1 (Mayoralty campaign 1939–1956). Additional information on the performances was provided through interviews of Lin Stiles, Mike Leven, and Terri (Williams) Schachter (May 28, 2012).

31. Interview with Lin Stiles. The coronation of Lin Stiles as mayor was confirmed in a photo in the *Tufts Weekly* dated May 14, 1958.

32. Interviews with Mike Leven and Lin Stiles.

33. Interviews with Mike Leven and Terri (Williams) Schachter. On the performance of Louis Armstrong in Cousens gym, see "Ivy Weekend Offers Sing, 'Satchmo,' Dance, Concert," *TW*, April 30, 1958.

34. Ibid. Also see "Mike Leven's Retiring, But One Would Never Call Him Shy," *Franchise Times*, March 2007. Even Dean Katharine Jeffers, who so championed the integration of the sororities at Tufts, drew the line with interracial couples. In a response she penned to a Tufts alumna regarding her support of Sigma Kappa's effort at integration, she wrote, "This does not mean that I am an advocate of inter-racial marriages." See letter from Katharine R. Jeffers to Mrs. Ronald A. Rhodes dated August 6, 1956, in Activities and Organizations records, 1857–1999, UA 024.001 Box 13, Folder 9 (Sigma Kappa 1935–1956). Such sentiment was probably commonplace on campus.

35. "Council Hears Negative Mayoralty Sentiment," *TW*, March 20, 1959; "Mayoralty," *TW*, April 8, 1959; and "Spring Silence," *TW*, May 8, 1959, which includes the quotation. That spring, there was indeed some instances of rioting and "panty raids" in the girls dormitories, but these events were unrelated to the canceling of Mayoralty, as others have suggested. Indeed, the incidents of 1959 were the second year in a row, and encouraging the men in the panty raids were none other than their fellow female students. However, since these acts occurred in the spring, they were lumped into the chaos of Mayoralty, at least in the eyes of the administration. See "Tufts Students Riot; Invade Women's Dorm and Ignite Dempster Dumpsters," *TW*, April 10, 1959.

36. On the attempted revival in 1960 and results of the questionnaire, see "Students Asked to Express opinions on Mayoralty Issue at Registration," *TW*, January 21, 1960; "Students Express Mixed Sentiments at Mayoralty Poll," *TW*, February 12, 1960; and "Council Mayoralty Report Indicates No Present Action," *TW*, March 4, 1960. On the revival in 1966, see "Ivy Weekend Will Revive Mayoralty Contest," *TW*, April 29, 1966. The Ivy Weekend was a large springtime celebration that encompassed a number of activities such as a soapbox derby race, a Spring Sing competition, and a student-run carnival on the quad. I was unable to determine who won the contest in 1966, as the results were apparently not reported in the *Tufts Weekly*. On the 1967 contest, see "It's Piano Smashing Time at Tufts," *BG*, April 30, 1967. Additional information was provided through an interview with Al Sugarman (May 23, 2012). On his win, see "Ivy Weekend Results," *TW*, May 12, 1967.

37. "Mayoralty Campaigns," undated and no author; and "Tufts Mayoralty Campaigns," undated and no author, in Activities and Organizations records, 1857–1999, UA 024.001 Box 6, Folder 1 (Mayoralty campaign 1939–1956). Additional information was provided through interviews with Al Sugarman and Mike Leven. On the history of Tuftonia's Day, see "Tuftonia's Day, 1985," *Concise Encyclopedia of Tufts History*, http://hdl.handle.net/10427/14829 (accessed January 2, 2016).

38. On Hosea Ballou 2d's membership in the Masons, see M. W. Charles Carroll Hutchinson and R. W. Sereno D. Nickerson, *Proceedings of the Most Worshipful Grand Lodge of Ancient Free and Accepted Masons of the Commonwealth of Massachusetts* (Boston, MA: Rockwell and Churchill, 1897), 410–411. On Hosea Ballou 2d's general acceptance of fraternities, see "The Kappa Semi-Centennial," *The Shield* 22, no. 4 (December 1906): 275. The continued acceptance of fraternities at Tufts College, especially during the late 1800s and early 1900s, was not universally repeated on other campuses. Instead, there was quite a large anti-fraternity sentiment across much of the country. See, for example, various articles in *Banta's Greek Exchange* 1, no. 1 (December 1912) and no. 3 (July 1913).

39. The anti-fraternity sentiment at Tufts College, which had existed at times in previous decades, came back to life during World War II, though the sentiment produced little action. See "Fraternities are Needed," *TW*, December 23, 1943; and "Prexy Upholds Fraternities as Anti-Greek Fight Grows," *TW*, April 12, 1945. On the efforts to address fraternity discrimination at Amherst, Williams, and the University of Washington, see Wurgaft, *Jews at Williams*, 96–97.

40. The Thomas Gibbs incident, as it came to be known, made headlines across the country. See, for example, "Victory at Amherst," *NYT*, November 15, 1948; "PKP Council Upholds Act of President," *Columbia Spectator*, November 30, 1948; "Hail to Phi Alpha Psi," *The Milwaukee Journal*, May 30, 1949; and Alfred McClung Lee,

Fraternities Without Brotherhood: A Study of Prejudice on the American Campus (Boston, MA: The Beacon Press, 1955), 28–32.

41. Ibid. On the issue of Al Rogers at The University of Connecticut, see "Phi Eps Back UCONN Group On Bias Issue," *TW*, October 12, 1950.

42. "Phi Eps Back UCONN Group On Bias Issue"; "Referendum Denied Phi Eps; Issue Pending," *TW*, November 9, 1950; "Phi Ep Admits Rogers, Negro, To Membership," *TW*, January 11, 1951. Just a few years later, Omicron chapter of Phi Epsilon Pi initiated a few African-American men, thus becoming the first inter-racial chapter at Tufts.

43. "An Ideal Thwarted," *TW*, October 26, 1950, which includes the first quotation; and "ATO President Writes Editor In Defense of Fraternity System," *TW*, November 16, 1950, which includes the second and third quotation. With regards to the quoted statement, at the time racial discrimination was, in fact, legal in the United States.

44. On the ensuing campus discussion, see "Democracy Can Work–II," *TW*, March 8, 1951; "Liberal Union Sponsors Open Fraternity Forum," *TW*, March 22, 1951; and "Fraternity Bias Forum Attracts Large Turnout," *TW*, April 26, 1951. On the publishing of the discrimination policies within certain fraternities, see "Fraternity Statistics," *TW*, October 18, 1951; and "To Freshmen–A Challenge," *TW*, October 18, 1951. Other New England schools were starting to react to the situation as well. See, for example, "D.U. At Bowdoin Leaves National on Bias Question," *TW*, October 18, 1951. This article states that within the Tufts chapter of Delta Upsilon, "a non-sectarian policy has continuously been followed by the fraternity at Tufts."

45. That the issue of discrimination faded for a while speaks of a general problem with campus activism, and that is graduation coupled with a prolonged summer break can often derail the call for change. Students return each fall awash in new ideas, and they don't always pick up the fights of the past. On the return of fraternity discrimination to the forefront, see "Anti-Discrimination Trend is Evident in N.E. Colleges" and "Fraternity Statistics," *TW*, October 15, 1954; and "Con On Fraternity" and "Place of Fraternity," *TW*, October 21, 1954. On the efforts of the Tufts Student Council, the IFC, and the PHC, see "Viewing The Council," *TW*, November 18, 1954; "I.F.C. Opposes Discrimination," *TW*, February 25, 1955, which includes the quotation; and "Prejudice is Opposed By Panhell," *TW*, March 4, 1955.

46. On the rejection of Theta Chi, see "Council, I.F.C. Reject Theta Chi Constitution," *TW*, April 22, 1955. Two years later, Theta Chi was allowed on campus after the national organization revised its membership policy. For more information, see the section on Theta Chi in chapter 3. For information about Sigma Kappa and Alpha Xi Delta, see the appropriate sections in chapter 4.

47. On the initial editorial, see "A Modest Proposal," *TW*, September 21, 1956, which includes the quotation. On the call for action by the trustees, see "For a Vigorous Policy," *TW*, October 19, 1956. Back in 1942, there was nearly the abolition of sororities on campus, but this was more a reaction to the disruption of college life caused by the war. See "Stand On Your Own Two Feet, Jackson," *TW*, October 8, 1942.

48. Information about the response of Joel Reynolds was provided through an interview with Tom Baer (November 8, 2012). According to Mr. Baer, Mr. Reynolds sent a PhiEp alumnus to talk with Tom and get him to stop raising such a ruckus. Tom did nothing of the kind. On the publication of membership restrictions within each fraternity, see "11 Fraternities Disclose Vital Facts and Figures to Freshman Rushees,"

TW, November 30, 1956; and "Twelve Houses Release Vital Statistics," *TW*, September 27, 1957.

49. "Clauses–Anti-American," *TW*, February 6, 1959, which includes the quotation. The editorial was a mere seven sentences long, the shortest the campus would see that spring on the subject. Additional information about the involvement of Peter Livingston was provided through an interview with Neil Peck (November 2, 2012).

50. "Clauses–II," *TW*, February 11, 1959; "Clauses–III," *TW*, February 18, 1959; "Council Will Request Statement on Clauses From Trustees; Passes Peck-Crowley Motion Unanimously," *TW*, February 27, 1959, which includes the first quotation about the old soldiers; "Clauses–IV: An Open Letter to the Board of Trustees," *TW*, February 27, 1959, which includes the second quotation.

51. "Letters to the Editor," *TW*, March 11, 1959, which include the quotations. In reading these letters, I do get the sense these two men were more bothered by the lack of respect shown to them by the students than the issue at hand. Priorities, I suppose.

52. "Clauses VI–A Reply and a Proposal," *TW*, March 13, 1959, which includes the first quotation; "Trustees Send Reply to Student Council Letter," *TW*, April 24, 1959; and "Clauses–VII," *TW*, April 24, 1959, which includes the second quotation. The next time any mention of fraternity discrimination appears in the *Tufts Weekly* was months later, and even then it was via reprint of an article, not an original reporting, See "War On Fraternities," *TW*, December 11, 1959.

53. I do not mean to belittle in any way the efforts of Goodwin, Baer, and Peck, nor do I wish to defend in any manner the presence of discriminatory clauses in fraternities at Tufts. Instead, this paragraph is simply my opinion of why greater change did not come forth in the late 1950s. On the supposed quota of Jewish students, see the discussion in the section on Phi Epsilon Pi in chapter 3. On the easing of membership restrictions within national fraternities, see for example the section on Beta Chi/Theta Chi and Phi Sigma Kappa in chapter 3.

54. On the survey and its aftermath, see Miller, *LOTH–2*, 213. The results of the survey were part of a larger report to the trustees that has not survived to this day. However, I did come across a single, loose sheet of paper containing the summary of the restrictive membership practices within each organization. See "Fraternity and Sorority Membership Policies And Practices," dated November 15, 1961, in Activities and Organizations records, 1857–1999, UA 024.001 Box 4 (the paper was not filed in any particular folder, but was instead loose within this box). This survey lists constitutional restrictions as existing in Delta Tau Delta, Alpha Tau Omega, and Sigma Nu, and "gentleman's agreements" as existing in Alpha Epsilon Pi, Theta Chi, Zeta Psi, and Delta Zeta. To be honest, I am very skeptical of this survey, as the results do not make sense based on other information I have gathered. For example, by the fall of 1961, Delta Tau Delta had eliminated its constitutional restrictions to membership, and indeed pledged a Jewish man that semester. True, Delta Tau Delta's alumni advisor (and Tufts trustee) Joel Reynolds was not in favor of admitting Jewish men at the time, but there was no official rule against this within the fraternity (see the section on Delta Tau Delta in chapter 3). Additionally, the founders of Theta Chi at Tufts were vehemently against membership restrictions, and if any "gentleman's agreements" had been in place at the time, I am convinced they never would have pursued affiliation (see the section on Theta Chi in chapter 3). Therefore, I suspect that IFC president Stan Lewis and Dean Herrick may have asked the wrong question when compiling their results. Additional-

ly, though Delta Zeta was called out on this survey as having restrictive policies, they cleared up the confusion later. See " 'Student View' To Be Published Soon; Council Hears of 'Tuftonian' Problems," *TW*, February 23, 1962. On the subsequent reaction of Peter Bloch, see "Fraternity Discrimination I," *TW*, November 16, 1961; and "Fraternity Discrimination II," *TW*, December 1, 1961.

55. On the National Interfraternity Conference in Boston, see "Firm Stand Urged for Fraternities," *NYT*, December 2, 1961, which includes the quotation; and "Right to Select Fraternity Brothers Defended at NIC," *TW*, December 6, 1961. On the tenure of Joel Reynolds as head of the NIC, see "Saturday Session," *National Interfraternity Conference Yearbook* (1961): 10; and "Leadership at 53rd Annual Meeting Held in Boston," *The Rattle of Theta Chi* 49, no. 2 (1962): 3, 12. On the resignation of the Stanford chapter of Alpha Tau Omega, see "Check on Integration Acts Involving Greek Societies," *Lawrence [Kansas] Journal-World*, February 18, 1964, which mentions the split happened in 1961. On the resignation of the Bowdoin chapter of Alpha Tau Omega, see "Because of Clause Bowdoin Fraternity Severs Nat. Bonds," *TW*, January 12, 1962. Alpha Tau Omega was not the only national fraternity to see chapters withdraw in protest during the late 1950s and early 1960s. In fact, nearly all of the largest fraternities and sororities lost chapters in this manner – Phi Delta Theta, Sigma Nu, Lambda Chi Alpha, Delta Tau Delta, Gamma Phi Beta, Delta Gamma, the list goes on.

56. On Peter Bloch's continued push for change, see "Fraternity Discrimination III," *TW*, December 6, 1961, which includes the first quotation; "Frets and Regrets," *TW*, December 6, 1961; and "Fraternity Discrimination IV," *TW*, December 14, 1961. On the response by Stanley Lewis, see "I.F.C. Prexy Attacks 'Weekly' for "Sensational" Editorials," *TW*, December 14, 1961, which includes the second quotation. On the growing response to the issue from within the general Tufts community, see Letters to the Editor, *TW*, December 14, 1961. These letters marked a significant shift in student opinion on the matter.

57. On the initial survey of fraternity chapters by the *Tufts Weekly*, see "Frats Answer 'Weekly' Questionnaire; Several Balk on Discriminatory Query," *TW*, February 5, 1962. In this survey, only one fraternity, Sigma Nu, admitted to having a discriminatory clause. Alpha Tau Omega, which was known to have a clause in place at the time, refused to answer the question. Also refusing were Delta Tau Delta, Delta Upsilon, Phi Sigma Kappa, and Theta Delta Chi. I suspect animosity between the fraternities and the *Tufts Weekly* was a major reason why these organizations chose not to respond. On the response of the Tufts Student Council, see "Fraternity Discrimination–A New Turn," *TW*, February 9, 1962; and "Council Asks IFC for Clause Report," *TW*, February 9, 1962, which includes the quotation. On the response of Stanley Lewis, see "Lewis Discusses Clauses; Speaks of IFC Progress," *TW*, February 15, 1962. As mentioned in the text, this marked the first time Chi Omega at Tufts was quoted as having a restrictive membership policy. For more information on Chi Omega, see the relevant section in Chapter 4.

58. On the reaction of the campus to learning of a "mutually acceptable agreement" in Chi Omega, see "Go Chi O," *TW*, February 15, 1962, which includes the first quotation. On the calls for action by Peter Bloch and the *Tufts Weekly*, see "Bloch Notes Discrimination Progress; Accuses Tufts of Tolerating Clauses," *TW*, February 23, 1962; and "Damn Discrimination," *TW*, February 23, 1962. On some pushback to Peter Bloch's methods, see "Blast Bloch," *TW*, February 23, 1962. On the resolutions

demanding ATO and Sigma Nu end discrimination by January 1, 1963, see "IFC Takes Action Against Discriminatory Practices," *TW*, March 9, 1962, which includes the second quotation; "I.F.C. Resolution," *TW*, March 9, 1962, which offers praise to Stanley Lewis; and "Council Approves I.F.C. Action; WTCR and NSA Considered," *TW*, March 16, 1962, which also discusses the efforts of Chi Omega to ignore their "mutually acceptable agreement."

59. Stanley Lewis did mention the idea of a waiver for both ATO and Sigma Nu when he announced the deadline to the campus. This was the first time such an idea was presented in public. On the support of the faculty, see "Fraternity, Sorority Practices Attacked in Faculty Proposal," *TW*, March 30, 1962; and "Council Back Faculty Plan to End Frat. Discrimination," *TW*, May 11, 1962. One difference in the faculty motion was the date for compliance, as they voted to give ATO and Sigma Nu until September 1, 1963, to remove their restrictive membership clauses.

60. All records of correspondence between Joel Reynolds and the national office of the Alpha Tau Omega fraternity are contained in ATO–A, Series 41/90/10, Box 2 (Tufts, 1961–65). Also contained in this archive are letters of response from national officers of the Sigma Nu fraternity. On the question of whether ATO and Sigma Nu were in favor of a deadline, see letter from Joel W. Reynolds to Stewart Daniels [Alpha Tau Omega] and Richard Fletcher [Sigma Nu] dated October 5, 1962, in ATO–A, Series 41/90/10, Box 2 (Tufts, 1961–65), which includes the quotation.

61. On the response of Sigma Nu, see letter from Richard Fletcher, Executive Secretary, to Joel Reynolds dated October 10, 1962, in ATO–A, Series 41/90/10, Box 2 (Tufts, 1961–65), which includes the first quotation. On the response from Alpha Tau Omega, see letter from Stewart Daniels to Joel Reynolds dated October 26, 1962, in ATO–A, Series 41/90/10, Box 2 (Tufts, 1961–65). On the influence of Joel Reynolds with regards to squashing the deadline, see letter from Joel Reynolds to Stewart Daniels and Richard Fletcher dated October 22, 1962, in ATO–A, Series 41/90/10, Box 2 (Tufts, 1961–65), where he states unequivocally, "NO DEADLINE WILL BE RECOMMENDED." On the outcome of the trustees' meeting, see "Trustees Renege on Discrimination Resolution; Maintain 'Right of Freedom of Association'," *TW*, November 2, 1962; and "Discrimination Continues," *TW*, November 2, 1962. A copy of the report stating the specific restrictions of ATO and Sigma Nu, dated January 22, 1963, is contained in ATO–A, Series 41/90/10, Box 2 (Tufts, 1961–65). For Alpha Tau Omega, the restriction was, "Only white male Christians are eligible." For Sigma Nu, "To be initiated an individual must be a man, free born and of free ancestry, having the character and bearing of a gentleman."

62. On the response of the campus to the wishy-washy resolution of the trustees, see "Attack Trustees' Discrimination Position," *TW*, November 7, 1962; "Which Side Are You On?" *TW*, November 9, 1962; "IFC On Discrimination," *TW*, November 16, 1962; Letters To The Editor "Free Association" and "Tufts Shamed," *TW*, November 16, 1962; "To The Editor–Discrimination," *TW*, November 28, 1962; "To The Board of Trustees–Policy On Discrimination," *TW*, November 30, 1962; and Letters To The Editor "Fix Up" and "The Mix Up," *TW*, January 5, 1963. I chose not to focus on this conversation within the text, however, as the real action was going on behind the scenes with Mr. Reynolds. The students were making a lot of noise, but Mr. Reynolds was not listening. On the cause for alarm within ATO, see letter from Robert Alger, Worthy Scribe, to Stewart D. Daniels dated October 4, 1963, in ATO–A, Series 41/90/10,

Box 2 (Tufts, 1961–65), which includes the quotation. On the efforts of the Tufts ATO chapter to combat discrimination at the national level, see "From The Editors' Desk–ATO Defends Its Position," *TW*, December 7, 1962. In this article, the members note that, "At the biannual [sic] congress, Gamma Beta [chapter of ATO at Tufts] has consistently supported modification of the restrictive part of its constitution," and, as they saw the situation, "such modification will occur in the near future." Indeed, Alpha Tau Omega would drop its discriminatory membership restrictions once and for all in 1966, according to information on the fraternity's national website, http://www.ato.org/AlphaTauOmega/atohistory/HistoryTheATOStory.aspx (accessed January 11, 2016).

63. On the response of Alpha Tau Omega to the request for a waiver, see letter from Stewart Daniels to Robert Alger dated October 21, 1963, in ATO–A, Series 41/90/10, Box 2 (Tufts, 1961–65). On the information session for the picketers, see advertisement dated October 14, 1963, in ATO–A, Series 41/90/10, Box 2 (Tufts, 1961–65), which includes the quotation. On the rules as set forth by the organizers of the protest, see "Picketing Rules and Wednesday Meeting Schedule," no date but context puts in in mid October, 1963, in ATO–A, Series 41/90/10, Box 2 (Tufts, 1961–65). The list of rules is quite extensive, if not also very explicit: "NO signing [sic, probably meant singing], talking, reference to fraternities, drinking either before or during, violence or disorderly conduct, food or littering. DRESS: coats and ties for the boys, no slacks or shorts for the girls, show incredible school spirit at the [football] game."

64. On the mindset of Joel Reynolds, see his correspondence with Stewart Daniels and Richard Fletcher between October 11, 1963, and November 1, 1963, in ATO–A, Series 41/90/10, Box 2 (Tufts, 1961–65). Mixed with this correspondence are copies of articles from the *Tufts Weekly*. Also, on a poster advertising a meeting to plan the picketing, Joel Reynolds added a handwritten note for Stewart Daniels – "The 'hand' of the 'pro' shows! NAACP and CORE are in on it!" For the quotation, see letter from Joel Reynolds to Stewart Daniels and Richard Fletcher dated October 25, 1963, in ATO–A, Series 41/90/10, Box 2 (Tufts, 1961–65). By this time, both ATO and Sigma Nu at the national level were feeling a lot of heat from numerous chapters across the country, some wanting waivers, some resigning outright, many in general turmoil. So, it is no surprise they came to their conclusion about the fate of their Tufts chapters much earlier than Joel Reynolds. See for example, "Racial Bias Continues In Nat'l.: Stanford Sigma Nu Withdraws," *TW*, February 4, 1963.

65. On the cancellation of the picketing, see "Picketing Off Sat. If Action Expected," *TW*, October 25, 1963; and letter from Joel Reynolds to Stewart Daniels and Richard Fletcher dated October 30, 1963, in ATO–A, Series 41/90/10, Box 2 (Tufts, 1961–65). In this letter, Mr. Reynolds writes, "It took a lot of fast footwork on Friday, the 25th, and some real pressure on the lawyer that the Civil Rights group have engaged to get the proposed picketing called off." No word on what the pressure might have been. On the granting of the waiver for both ATO and Sigma Nu at Tufts, see correspondence between Joel Reynolds, Stewart Daniels, and Richard Fletcher between October 25, 1963, and December 20, 1963, in ATO–A, Series 41/90/10, Box 2 (Tufts, 1961–65). Also see "'Prompt Elimination' Of Clauses Anticipated," *TW*, November 6, 1963, which includes the quotation; and "Waivers End Fraternity Discrimination," *TW*, December 13, 1963. This article made a curious reference to the outside influence of Joel Reynolds by stating, "Since, as a general rule, many fraternity nationals do not grant waivers to clauses unless school officials apply pressure to involved houses, it is

believed by some that the Tufts Trustees probably took some action to achieve this end." Truer words were never spoken.

66. On the quotation, see letter from Joel Reynolds to Stewart Daniels and Richard Fletcher dated October 25, 1963, in ATO–A, Series 41/90/10, Box 2 (Tufts, 1961–65).

67. As mentioned elsewhere in this work, Joel Reynolds is a complex historical figure, and I know there is more to his story than I've managed to discuss within my work. To many of the alumni I interviewed, including the founders of my own fraternity at Tufts, he was "Uncle Joel," a helpful advisor who wanted nothing but success for all in the Greek system. To others, he was "a storm trooper Nazi," who disliked (if not hated) Jews, blacks, and anyone who tried to mess with tradition.

68. The turbulence of Tufts during the early 1970s is a fascinating story unto itself, one that is unfortunately beyond the scope of this work. For more information, see Miller, *LOTH–2*, chapters 15, 16, and 21. Further information was provided through an interview with Professor Sol Gittleman (October 17, 2013), who was witness to the changing times. On the use of the term "benign neglect" to describe the fraternity system, see "Administration To Examine Greek System," *TD*, January 22, 1987. Professor Gittleman also mentioned this term during our interview.

69. The rules and regulations regarding fraternity recruitment were published annually in the *Ivy Book* publication until 1970–71 edition. See UA Ivy Society Publications, 1895–1977, UP016.002, Boxes 1–3 (The Ivy Book, 1902–1974). On the lowering of the drinking age in Massachusetts, see "Bar Door To Swing Open for 18-Year-Olds," *BG*, February 25, 1973; and "18-year-olds Ring In Legal Drinking Era," *BG*, March 1, 1973. On the general state of fraternities as the 1970s progressed, see "Frats Prepare For Rush," *TO*, October 21, 1977; "Decline In Traditions Attributed To Changing Values," *TO*, November 18, 1977; and "A Greek Revival," *Tufts Criterion* 11, no. 2 (December 1978): 27. Of course, fraternities were not the only place to find keg parties. Indeed, in the fall of 1976, the Tufts administration sponsored a keg party on the quad in front of Carmichael Hall to welcome all the new freshmen. See *TO*, March 14, 2011, 16. Something tells me the school will never do that again.

70. On the ascendency of President Jean Mayer and the issues he faced in 1976, see Gittleman, *The Entrepreneurial University*, chapters 1–3. On the problems facing the Greek system at Tufts in the early 1980s, see various letters to President Jean Mayer dated between January 3, 1980, and April 26, 1982, in Office of the President Records 1828–2007, Jean Mayer, administrative records and related papers, 1976–92, Subject Files, UA001.013 Box 10, Folder 23 (Fraternities and sororities 1976–1982). Also see a summary entitled "Partial History of Fraternities At Tufts University Since 1981," contained in Office of the Dean of Students Records, 1966–1999, UA038.002, Box 2, Folder 36 (Fraternities, ad-hoc committee on fraternities and sororities 1986–1992). On the raising of the drinking age to twenty in 1979, see "Here's The New Massachusetts Drinking-age Law at a Glance," *BG*, April 15, 1979. On the raising of the drinking age to twenty-one in 1985, see "Youth and Drinking; Legal Age In State Rises To 21 Today," *BG*, June 1, 1985. One of President Mayer's biggest fears was the death of a student on campus due to alcohol or drugs.

71. Letter from Thomas O'Brien, Financial Vice President of Harvard University, to President Jean Mayer dated April 16, 1984; memo from Joseph Lambert to President Jean Mayer dated April 18, 1984; and letter from President Jean Mayer to Thomas O'Brien dated April 25, 1984, all in Office of the President Records 1828–2007, Jean

Mayer, administrative records and related papers, 1976–92, Subject Files, UA001.013 Box 10, Folder 21 (Fraternities 1983–1988). The quotation is from the last named letter. Additional information was provided through an interview with Thomas O'Brien (January 22, 2014).

72. Memo from Dean Frank Colcord to other Deans of Tufts University dated May 11, 1984, in Office of the President Records 1828–2007, Jean Mayer, administrative records and related papers, 1976–92, Subject Files, UA001.013 Box 10, Folder 21 (Fraternities 1983–1988), which includes the quotation.

73. "Administration To Examine Greek System," *TD*, January 22, 1987. As a sophomore at the time of this article's release, I can remember the fear that spread through my own chapter as we worried just what the administration had in mind. At the time, the faculty-led Committee on Student Life was responsible for disciplining fraternities, with the IGC having almost no input. See "Knable Calls on Greeks To 'Define Values'," *TD*, March 26, 1987. On the efforts of the IGC to affect real change, see "Formation of Greek Guidelines Underway," *TD*, October 29, 1987. On President Mayer's views, see "Mayer Warns Greeks," *TD*, October 30, 1987, which includes the quotation.

74. On the development of the IGC constitution and policies, see "Rockett To Propose New Constitution for IGC," *TD*, January 22, 1988; "AdHoc Committee Sees Progress on Greek Guidelines," *TD*, February 25, 1988; "The Future of Fraternities At Tufts," *TD*, Commencement Issue, 1988; and "Tufts' Greek System Enters an Era of Reform and Progress," *TD*, Commencement Issue, 1989. Having witnessed a number of rush weeks in the mid to late 1980s, I can attest to the over-abundance of alcohol that was routinely made available to the rushees.

75. On the formation of the CFS, see "A&S Approves Greek Committee, Passes Budget Resolution," *TD*, April 12, 1988. The faculty meeting where the CFS was created was quite contentious, with opinions (if not tempers) flaring on both sides of the issue. For the student's reaction to this meeting and the formation of the CFS, see "Defending The Greek System," *TD*, April 14, 1988. On the conclusion of Dean Colcord's ad-hoc committee and the publication of its final report, see "Rockett Sees Relations Improving with Administration," *TD*, September 23, 1988. This article mentions the report was delivered to President Mayer on March 30, 1988.

76. On the implementation of new rush policies, see "New Rush Policies Affect Attendance," *TD*, September 28, 1988. On the relationship statement and the implied threat from President Mayer, see "Some Greeks Delay Signing Statement," *TD*, October 4, 1988. The fraternities holding out at the time were Zeta Psi, Theta Delta Chi, and Alpha Epsilon Pi. They all eventually did sign the agreement, though *The Tufts Daily* did not report this milestone. One of the reasons this agreement came about was an incident involving Zeta Psi in 1987, where a resident was found to be storing firearms in the chapter house. See "Zeta Psi Fire Damage Estimated at $20,000," *TD*, October 5, 1987; and "Student to Take Legal Action Following Housing Expulsion," *TD*, November 13, 1987. The discovery of firearms unnerved the administration, as they realized they were not in a strong legal position to ban weapons in privately owned fraternity houses. The relationship agreement helped solve this conundrum.

77. On the changes being put in place by the IGC, see "Greek Committee Amends Relationship Statement," *TD*, October 26, 1988; "IGC Seeks Campus Leadership Role," *TD*, November 28, 1988; "IGC Seeks Faculty Advisors," *TD*, December 8, 1988; and "Tufts' Greek System Enters an Era of Reform and Progress," *TD*, Commencement is-

sue, 1989. Also see "A Review of the Social Policy Over the Past Decade," *TD*, February 26, 1990. On the Fraternity Insurance Purchasing Group and the subsequent banning of kegs in fraternity houses, see "National Policies Banning Kegs to Affect Six Tufts Fraternities," *TD*, February 28, 1990; "IGC Forms Ad Hoc Group on Keg Ban," *TD*, March 1, 1990; "Four Fraternities to Implement Keg Ban," *TD*, April 17, 1990; "IGC Seeks Keg Party Alternative," *TD*, September 19, 1990; "Greeks Will Challenge BYOB Rule," *TD*, September 24, 1990; and "University Considers Amending Alcohol and Social Events Policy," *TD*, November 22, 1993. I was unable to determine exactly when kegs were finally banned from all fraternity houses, but administrators have told me the ban took effect sometime in the mid 1990s.

78. "CFS Study Evaluates Status of Greek System," *TD*, October 13, 1989. At various times throughout the history of Tufts College and Tufts University, there have been groups of students who have come together in opposition of fraternities. However, these groups were never able to sustain any real momentum or force any real change. That streak came to an end in the early 1990s. On the genesis of the anti-fraternity movement, see "Fraternities Should Be Co-ed," *TD*, January 24, 1989; and "Election Special–David Wally Pansing," *TD*, April 10, 1989.

79. "CFS To Report To A&S Faculty on the State of the Tufts Greek System," *TD*, April 6, 1990. On the response to this report by Wally Pansing, see "Either A Co-ed Greek System or No Greek System At All," *TD*, April 9, 1990, which includes the quotations.

80. On the evolution of the Greek systems at Middlebury and Bowdoin, see for example, "Frat Row: At Middlebury College, Sexism Puts Traditional Greek houses On The Ropes," *Los Angeles Times,* February 9, 1990; "Campus Life; The Idea of Coeducational Fraternities Is Catching On in the Northeast," *NYT*, April 8, 1990; and "CAMPUS LIFE: Bowdoin, Fraternity Members Give Female Members Equal Standing," *NYT*, September 29, 1991. On some of the problems with forcing chapters to go co-ed at Bowdoin, see "Bowdoin Fraternity Accused," *The Lewiston Sun-Journal,* December 22, 1991. On the quotation, see "Fraternities Should Be Co-ed." This quote is not attributed to Wally Pansing, but it effectively sums up the opinion of those who were against the fraternities. On the backlash, see Letters to the Editor, *TD*, April 18, 1990, which includes "Greek should stop excluding women"; "Tufts Greeks not as bad as others"; "Sororities can provide bonds"; and "Greek system instills values." Also see Letters to the Editor, *TD*, April 20, 1990, which includes "Those pesky Greeks"; "Greek system already co-ed"; "A case for abolishing single sex clubs…"; "… and a case against"; "Women are included"; and "All are responsible for isolated incidents." This is just a subset of the letters received around this time.

81. "Faculty Members Discuss the Greek System," *TD*, April 30, 1990; and *Report of Committee on Social Fraternity and Sorority Life*, Arts and Sciences Faculty Meeting, May 7, 1990, in Secretary of the Faculty for Arts, Sciences and Engineering Records, 1854–2013–05–16, Faculty meeting minutes, UA037.001 Box 67, Folder 15 (Faculty Arts and Sciences 1989–1990), which includes the quotations. Additional information was provided through an interview with Professor Stephen Bailey (September 14, 2012).

82. "Committee Begins Look at Tufts' Greek System," *TD*, October 25, 1990; "Committee to Begin Greek Evaluation," *TD*, February 6, 1991; and "Greek Committee Set To Distribute Survey Soon," *TD*, March 28, 1991. Additional information was provided through an interview with Professor Stephen Bailey.

83. *Report of the Ad Hoc Committee on Fraternities and Sororities to the Faculty of Arts and Sciences of Tufts University*, Arts and Sciences Faculty Meeting, May 11, 1992, in Secretary of the Faculty for Arts, Sciences and Engineering Records, 1854–2013–05–16, Faculty meeting minutes, UA037.001 Box 68, Folder 7 (Liberal Arts and Jackson Faculty meetings 1992–1993). The quotation is from a summary of the report as contained in the same location. Additional information was provided through an interview with Professor Stephen Bailey.

84. "Students Critical of Greek System Report," *TD*, September 21, 1992; and "Committee Chair Responds to Critical Remarks About Report," *TD*, September 25, 1992.

85. "Vote on Greek System Comes After Over Five Years of Debates, Report," and "Students to be Barred from Nov. 23 Meeting," *TD*, November 11, 1992; "Poll Shows Most Tufts Students Support Form of Greek System," *TD*, November 19, 1992; "TCU Senate Passes Resolution Supporting Greek System, 19-6," and "Petition Circulates, Supporting Tufts' Greek Life Existence," *TD*, November 23, 1992; and "Coedification Only Avoids The Problems," *TD*, November 23, 1992.

86. Minutes of the Arts and Sciences Faculty Meeting, November 23, 1992, in Secretary of the Faculty for Arts, Sciences and Engineering Records, 1854–2013–05–16, Faculty meeting minutes, UA037.001 Box 68, Folder 10 (Arts and Sciences faculty meetings 1992–1993); "Faculty Supports Revamping Greek System," *TD*, November 24, 1992, which includes both quotations; and "Letters to the Editor–Viewpoint Was Unfair," *TD*, December 4, 1992. On Professor Luria's earlier complaints against the Tufts Greek system, see for example "A&S Approve Greek Committee, Passes Budget Resolution," *TD*, April 12, 1988; and "Letters to the Editor–The Right to Oversee," *TD*, April 29, 1988. Additional information was provided through an interview with Professor Stephen Bailey.

87. "Trustees to Discuss Fraternities, Sororities," *TD*, February 24, 1993; "Trustees Set budget, Tuition for 1993–94," *TD*, March 1, 1993; and "DiBaggio Addressed TCU Senate Sunday," *TD*, March 2, 1993. Additional information was provided through an interview with Professor Sol Gittleman. The six trustees named to the committee were Dr. William W. Sellers, William S. Cummings, Sheila A. McDermott, Inez Smith Reid, Gordon S. Wood, and John Baronian. Trustee Thomas O'Brien, who had called for the end of fraternities some nine years prior, was no longer on the board by this time.

88. "Board of Trustees Has Weekend Agenda Set," *TD*, November 4, 1993; "Trustees Offer Recommendations for Improving the Greek System," *TD*, November 9, 1993; and Minutes of the Arts and Sciences Faculty Meeting dated December 6, 1993, and Recommendations dated December 6, 1994 [sic, should be 1993] in Secretary of the Faculty for Arts, Sciences and Engineering Records, 1854–2013–05–16, Faculty meeting minutes, UA037.001 Box 68, Folder 18 (Arts and Sciences faculty meetings, 1993–94 (2 of 2)). I do not wish to make light of Professor Bailey's work, as he and his committee put a great deal of time and effort into their report, and ultimately I do think this report helped improve the Greek system. However, even he admitted the trustees would likely never act on the suggestion to coedify the Greek system. On the changes to the sorority rush system, see "Panhellenic Council Establishes More Open Policies for Fall Rush," *TD*, Commencement 1994.

89. On the response of the students to the trustees report, see "Members of Greek System React to the Board of Trustees' Report," *TD*, November 11, 1993. On the effort

by the IFC to establish an open rush policy, see "IFC Votes to Change Rush Policy," *TD*, December 3, 1993. On the problems encountered by the IFC, see Committee on Social Fraternity and Sorority Life Annual Report, 1993–1994 dated May 6, 1994, in Secretary of the Faculty for Arts, Sciences and Engineering Records, 1854–2013–05–16, Faculty meeting minutes, UA037.001 Box 68, Folder 11 (Arts and Sciences faculty meetings, 1993–94 (1 of 2)). On the subsequent policy of establishing formal and informal rush periods, see "Board of Trustees Approves Policy for Second Fraternity Rush Period," *TD*, February 23, 1995.

90. On the frustrations of the CFS, see "CFS Member Shows Article's Inaccuracies," *TD*, February 25, 1995; "Faculty Debates CFS Proposal to Disband," *TD*, March 13, 1995; and "Motion to Disband CFS Passed at Faculty Meeting After Much Debate," *TD*, April 11, 1995. On the reluctance of the CSL to get involved, see "CSL Will Sever Ties to Greek Organizations," *TD*, Commencement 1995. Faculty oversight of the Greek system would be restored in 2002, according to "CFS Proposes Office of Greek Life," *TD*, April 1, 2002.

91. The ideas in this paragraph are essentially my opinions based on the overall story. On the continued scrutiny of the Greek system, see for example, "A Greek Tragedy," *The Primary Source*, April 8, 1999; "Proponents of Greek Life 'Pledge' That Stereotypes are Misguided," *TD*, April 1, 2002; "Poll: Students Apathetic Towards Greek System," *TD*, April 1, 2002; "Administration Calls for Improvement of Greek System," *TD*, November 14, 2002; "Frat Attack," *The Primary Source*, April 21, 2005; "Tufts Greek System Under Fire for Multiple Violations," *TD*, Commencement 2005; "Bacow Supports the Greek System, and Greeks Agree," *TD*, October 13, 2006; "Quit Your Belly-Aching and Do Something!" *TD*, October 17, 2006; "Suspensions. Disunity. Community Service? It's All Greek to Tufts," *TO*, September 25, 2007; "Pro: Long Live the Greeks," and "Con: It's All Greek To Me," *TD*, November 8, 2012. On the support for the LGBT community by the fraternities and sororities, see "Senator Reaches Out to Greeks on LGBT Concerns," *TD*, November 8, 2010. My statement regarding the nonexistent support for LGBT concerns some twenty years prior is based on my own experience as an undergraduate and active member of Sigma Nu from 1986 through 1989. No attempt was made back then to engage the LGBT community in any form of discussion or outreach.

CHAPTER 7

1. On the relative size of Greek life at Tufts and the efforts of fraternities to improve alcohol awareness, see "With Rapid Growth, Tufts Greek Life Continues to Address Issues," *TD*, March 4, 2016.

2. On the instances of hazing and sexual misconduct, see "Abolish Fraternities," *TO*, November 7, 2016; and "Fraternity Activities Suspended at Tufts After Hazing Reports," *BG*, December 6, 2016. On the issue with Delta Tau Delta, see "DTD House Leased to Tufts, Used for Transfer Student Housing," *TD*, September 6, 2016. On the situation with AOII, see "Half of AOII Sisters Drop to Protest International Organization," *TD*, November 4, 2016. Within days of this publication, the story would go national. See, for example, "Delayed Approval to a Transgendered Woman Prompts Half a Sorority Chapter to Quit," *The Kansas City Star*, November 11, 2016; and "Tufts

University AOII Runs Into Issue with National Policy," *Spartan Daily [San Jose State University],* November 16, 2016. On the suspension of recruitment, see "Fraternity, Panhellenic Sorority Spring Recruitment Suspended," *TD*, December 1, 2016. On the call to end Greek life at Tufts, see "Former Sorority Sisters Urge Eradication of Greek Life at Tufts," *BG*, December 19, 2016.

3. On the establishment of a committee to look into Greek life, see "Tufts President Appoints Panel to Look Into Greek Life," *BG*, December 22, 2016; and "Monaco Announces Committee to Assess Greek Life, Undergraduate Climate," *TD*, January 19, 2017.

4. On the efforts of AOII members to affect change at the national level, see "Current, Former AOII Sisters Work to Make Changes as Greek Life Evolves," *TD*, December 5, 2016. On the efforts within Tufts fraternities to change their behavior, see for example "A Message from the Brothers of Delta Tau Delta," *TD*, November 10, 2016.

BIBLIOGRAPHY

Manuscript and Archive Collections

Ann Arbor, Michigan
    Hathi Trust Digital Library
Boston, Massachusetts
    Theta Delta Chi Fraternity archives
Brentwood, Tennessee
    Alpha Omicron Pi Fraternity archives
Chapel Hill, North Carolina
    University of North Carolina archives
Indianapolis, Indiana
    Alpha Xi Delta Fraternity archives
    Delta Tau Delta Fraternity archives
    Delta Upsilon Fraternity archives
    Theta Chi Fraternity archives
Lexington, Virginia
    Sigma Nu Fraternity archives
Medford, Massachusetts
    Tufts University archives
        Activities and Organizations records, 1857–2013
        Office of the Board of Trustees records, 1848–2013
        Crane Theological School records, 1855–1987
        Edwin B. Rollins papers, 1300[sic]–1976
        Ivy Society publications, 1895–1977
        Mathetican Society records, 1854–1962
        Melville S. Munro papers, 1858–1959
        Office of the President records, 1828–2007
        Phi Delta and Sigma Nu Fraternity records, 1930–1975
        Russell Carpenter papers, 1833–2012
        Secretary of the Faculty for Arts, Sciences, and Engineering records, 1854–2013–05–16
        William G. Brooks papers, 1890–1995
New York, New York
    American Jewish Historical Society archives
    Associated Press archives
    New York University archives
Oxford, Ohio
    Phi Delta Theta Fraternity archives

San Francisco, California
Internet Archive
Urbana-Champaign, Illinois
Alpha Tau Omega Fraternity archives
University of Illinois archives
Washington, D.C.
United States Holocaust Memorial Museum archives
Wheaton, Illinois
Billy Graham Center archives

Newspapers, Magazines, and Other Periodicals

The Adelphean of Alpha Delta Phi
The Afro-American
The Aglaia of Phi Mu
The Alpha of Alpha Kappa Pi
The Alpha Phi Quarterly
Alpha Xi Delta / The Quill of Alpha Xi Delta
Alpha Tau Omega Palm / The Palm of Alpha Tau Omega
American Jewish Archives
The American Jewish Yearbook
The Anchora of Delta Gamma
The Arbutus [Indiana University]
The Arrow / The Arrow of Pi Beta Phi
The Baltimore [Maryland] Sun
Banta's Greek Exchange
The Beta Kappa Journal
Blue and Gold [University of California at Berkeley]
Boston Globe
Brown and Blue [Tufts College]
The Caduceus [Tufts College Medical School]
Catalogue of the Officers and Students of the University of the City of New York
Catalogue of Officers and Students of Tufts College
The Cavalier Daily [University of Virginia]
The Chicago Defender
The Cornell Daily Sun
The Crescent of Gamma Phi Beta
The Crisis
Cross & Crescent [Lambda Chi Alpha]
Delta Kappa Epsilon Quarterly
The Delta of Sigma Nu
The Delta Upsilon Quarterly
The Diamond of Psi Upsilon
The Elephas [Tufts College yearbook of 1921]
The Eleusis of Chi Omega
Hamilton Literary Monthly

Handbook of Texas Online
Indiana University Catalogue
The Index [The University of Massachusetts at Amherst]
The Ivy Book [Tufts College]
The Ivy Leaf [Alpha Kappa Alpha]
Jet
The Jumbo [Tufts University]
The Kappa Alpha Journal
The Key Reporter [Phi Beta Kappa]
The Kleos [Alpha Phi Delta]
The Lamp of Delta Zeta
The Lewiston (Maine) Daily Sun
The Lewiston (Maine) Sun Journal
LIFE
The Massachusetts Agricultural College Alumni Bulletin
The Menorah Journal
The Menorah Monthly
The Michigan Alumnus
The New York Times
The Omegan [Theta Upsilon Omega]
The Oracle [Omega Psi Phi]
Phi Epsilon Pi Quarterly
The Phi Gamma Delta
The Phi Mu Delta Triangle
Pickout [Lowell Textile School]
The Purple and Gold [Chi Psi]
The Rainbow of Delta Tau Delta
The Rattle of Theta Chi
The Record of Sigma Alpha Epsilon
The Scroll [Phi Delta Theta]
The Shield [Theta Delta Chi]
The Shield and Diamond [Pi Kappa Alpha]
The Shield of Phi Kappa Psi
Sigma Phi Epsilon Journal
Sigma Kappa Triangle
The Signet [Phi Sigma Kappa]
The Sphinx [Phi Sigma Sigma]
The Sphinx [Alpha Phi Alpha]
The Syllabus Yearbook [Boston University School of Management]
The Syracuse (New York) Herald
The Tech [Massachusetts Institute of Technology]
Technique [Massachusetts Institute of Technology]
Today Tufts
To Dragma of Alpha Omicron Pi
The Tomahawk [Alpha Sigma Phi]
The Transit [Rensselaer Polytechnic Institute]
The Triangle [Phi Mu Delta]

The Tuftonian
The Tufts College Graduate
Tufts Criterion
The Tufts Daily
Tufts Magazine
The Tufts Observer
Tufts Pachyderm
The Tufts Weekly
The Universalist Register
The University Magazine
The Voice of the Negro
The Wellesley Legenda
William and Mary College Quarterly Historical Magazine
Wistarion [Normal College of the City of New York]

Books, Articles, and Pamphlets

Alpha Omicron Pi Fraternity. *History of Delta Chapter, Alpha Omicron Pi 1896–1914.* Brentwood, TN: published by Alpha Omicron Pi Fraternity, unknown date.

Armstrong, L., D. Dow, W. P. McNary, R. T. Cross, J. Williams, J. Sarver, J. Blanchard, H. H. George, J. G. Carson, M. S. Drury, R. Armstrong, and A. L. Post. *Sermons and Addresses on Secret Societies.* Chicago, IL: Ezra A. Cook, Publisher, 1882.

Axtell, James. *The School Upon a Hill: Education and Society in Colonial New England.* New Haven, CT: Yale University Press, 1974.

Bagg, Lyman Hotchkiss. *Four Years At Yale.* New Haven, CT: Charles C. Chatfield & Co., 1871.

Baird, William Raimond. *American College Fraternities: A Descriptive Analysis of the Society System in the Colleges of the United States, with a Detailed Account of Each Fraternity.* Philadelphia, PA: J. B. Lippincott & Co., 1879.

________. *American College Fraternities: A Descriptive Analysis of the Society System in the Colleges of the United States, with a Detailed Account of Each Fraternity.* 5th ed. New York, NY: William Raimond Baird, 1898.

________. *American College Fraternities: A Descriptive Analysis of the Fraternity System in the Colleges of the United States, with a Detailed Account of Each Fraternity.* 6th ed. New York, NY: The Alcolm Company, 1905.

________. *American College Fraternities: A Descriptive Analysis of the Fraternity System in the Colleges of the United States, with a Detailed Account of Each Fraternity.* 8th ed. New York, NY: The College Fraternity Publishing Company, 1915.

Ballou, Hosea Starr. *Hosea Ballou, 2d, D.D., First President of Tufts College: His Origin, Life, and Letters.* Boston, MA: E. P. Guild & Company, 1896.

Barber, Charles W. *Elmira College: The First Hundred Years.* New York, NY: McGraw–Hill Book Company, 1955.

Becque, Frances DeSimone. *Coeducation and the History of Women's Fraternities 1867–1902.* Dissertation, Southern Illinois University Carbondale. Ann Arbor, MI: UMI, 2002. (Publication number 3065337).

Bement, Howard and Douglas Bement. *The Story of Zeta Psi: An Informal Chronicle of Eighty–Four Years.* New York, NY: Zeta Psi Fraternity, 1932.
Birchfield, John R. *Zeta Psi Fraternity of North America Double Diamond Jubilee 1847–1997.* Paducah, KY: Turner Publishing Company, 1997.
Boyd, Leroy Stafford. "The Original Kappa Alpha." *Banta's Greek Exchange* 7, no. 4 (September 1919): 355–361.
Brooks, Charles. *History of the Town of Medford, Middlesex County, Massachusetts, From its First Settlement, in 1630, to the Present Time, 1855.* Boston, MA: James M. Usher, Publisher, 1855.
Brooks, Charles and James M. Usher. *History of the Town of Medford, Middlesex County, Massachusetts, From its First Settlement, in 1630, to the Present Time, 1855; Revised, Enlarged, and Brought Down to 1885.* Boston, MA: Rand, Avery, & Co., 1886.
Brown, James T., ed. *American College Fraternities: A Descriptive Analysis of the Society System in the Colleges of the United States, with a Detailed Account of Each Fraternity.* 9th ed. New York, NY: James T. Brown Publishing, 1920.
_________. *American College Fraternities: A Descriptive Analysis of the Society System in the Colleges of the United States, with a Detailed Account of Each Fraternity.* 10th ed. New York, NY: James T. Brown Publishing, 1923.
Brown, Tamara L., Gregory S. Parks, and Clarenda Philips, ed. *African American Fraternities and Sororities: The Legacy and Vision.* Lexington, KY: The University Press of Kentucky, 2010.
Butler, John C. *Historical Record of Macon and Central Georgia, Containing Many Interesting and Valuable Reminiscences Connected with the Whole State Including Numerous Incidents and Facts Never Before Published and of Great Historic Value.* Macon, GA: J. W. Burke & Co., 1879.
Clark-Helmick, Elizabeth Allen. *The History of Pi Beta Phi Fraternity.* Fort Sheridan, IL: Pi Beta Phi Fraternity, 1915.
"The Commons Club." *To Dragma of Alpha Omicron Pi* 9, no. 3 (May 1914): 258–266.
Copeland, Arthur. *Men and Days in Phi Beta Kappa.* Newark, NY: The Du Bois Press, 1907.
Conn, Granville P. *History of the New Hampshire Surgeons in the War of Rebellion.* Concord, NH: New Hampshire Association of Military Surgeons, 1906.
Crump, William L. *The Story of Kappa Alpha Psi: A History of the Beginning and Development of a College Greek Letter Organization 1911–1983.* 3rd ed. Philadelphia, PA: Kappa Alpha Psi Fraternity, 1983.
Cutting, George Rugg. *Student Life at Amherst College: Its Organizations, Their Membership and History.* Amherst, MA: Hatch & Williams, 1871.
Davenport, F. Garvin. *Monmouth College: The First Hundred Years, 1853–1953.* Cedar Rapids, IA: The Torch Press, 1953.
Davis, David B. *Fear: Images of Un–American Subversion from the Revolutionary to the Present.* Ithaca, NY: Cornell University Press, 1971.
Delta Upsilon Fraternity. *Delta Upsilon: One Hundred Years, 1834–1934.* Camden, NJ: The Delta Upsilon Fraternity, 1934.
Doane, Lewis, ed. *Here and There at Tufts.* Medford, MA: Tufts College, 1907.
Eddy, Richard. *Universalism in America: A History, Vol. II, 1801–1886.* Boston: Universalist Publishing House, 1886.

Eicher, David J. *The Longest Night: A Military History of the Civil War.* New York, NY: Simon and Schuster, 2001.

Ellis, William Arba, ed. *Norwich University 1891–1911: Her History, Her Graduates, Her Roll of Honor, Volume I.* Montpelier, VT: The Capital City Press, 1911.

________. *Norwich University 1891–1911; Her History, Her Graduates, Her Roll of Honor, Volume III.* Montpelier, VT: The Capital City Press, 1911.

Fairbanks, Wilson L. "The Delta Upsilon Movement at Tufts College." *The Delta Upsilon Quarterly* 5, no. 2 (January 1887): 89–92.

Gardner, Washington. *History of Calhoun County Michigan: A Narrative Account of its Historical Progress, its People, and its Principal Interests–Volume 1.* Chicago, IL: The Lewis Publishing Company, 1913.

Giddings, Paula. *In Search of Sisterhood: Delta Sigma Theta and the Challenge of the Black Sorority Movement.* New York, NY: Morrow, 1988.

Gill, Gerald. "Another Light on the Hill: Black Undergraduates and Tufts." *Tufts Magazine* 9, no. 3 (Spring 2002).

Gittleman, Sol. *An Entrepreneurial University: The Transformation of Tufts, 1976–2002.* Medford, MA: Tufts University Press, 2004.

Griffing, Edward Stetson, ed. *Sixth Catalogue of Theta Delta Chi.* New York, NY: Theta Delta Chi, 1911.

Hadzsits, George Depue, ed. *Hand Book of the University of Pennsylvania Chapter of Phi Beta Kappa, Delta of Pennsylvania.* Unknown publisher, 1919.

Hartford, Robert L. *Sing to the Royal Purple: 120 Years of Delta Tau Delta.* Indianapolis, IN: Delta Tau Delta Fraternity, 1978.

Havighurst, Walter. *The Miami Years 1809–1959.* New York, NY: G. P. Putnam and Sons, 1958.

Hersey, Harry Adams. *A History of Music In Tufts College, 1856–1943.* Medford, MA: The Trustees of Tufts College, 1947.

Hill, Robert William. "History of Debating in Tufts College." *The Tuftonian* 28, no. 6 (March 1903): 203–214.

Holmes, Clay W., ed. *Memorial History of Theta Delta Chi Fraternity: With an Account of the Semi-Centennial Convention and Banquet.* Elmira, NY: Clay W. Holmes, 1898.

Jones, Charles Edgeworth. "Education in Georgia." *Bureau of Education–Circular of Information,* no. 5 (1889), 90–101.

"The Kappa Semi-Centennial." *The Shield* 22, no. 4 (December 1906): 260–284.

Karp, Steve. *Fraternity.* Woodstock, IL: Dramatic Publishing, 2006.

Kimbrough, Walter M. *Black Greek 101: The Culture, Customs and Challenges of Black Fraternities and Sororities.* Madison, NJ: Fairleigh Dickinson University Press, 2003.

Kinne, Emma Elizabeth. *The History of Sigma Kappa Sorority, 1874–1924.* Menasha, WI: George Banta Publishing Co., 1924.

Knowlton, Hosea M. "Reminiscences of College Days." *The Tuftonian* 15, (May 4, 1889): 199–205.

Levere, William C. *A Paragraph History of Sigma Alpha Epsilon from the Founding of the Fraternity to the Present Years.* Evanston, IL: unknown publisher, 1916.

________, ed. *Leading Greeks: An Encyclopedia of the Workers in the American College Fraternities and Sororities.* Evanston, IL: unknown publisher, 1915.

Lombardi, Michael. "Phi Beta Kappa." *The Key Reporter* 77, no. 2 (September 2012): 8–11.

Lord, John King. *A History of Dartmouth College, 1815–1909.* Concord, NH: The Rumford Press, 1913.

Lynn, Helen Willis. *History of Alpha Xi Delta, 1893–1923.* Menasha, WI: George Banta Publishing Co., 1923.

MacDonald, Jessica North, ed. *History of Alpha Delta Pi.* Ames, IA: The Powers Press, 1930.

Marquis, Albert Nelson, ed. *The Book of Detroiters: A Biographical Dictionary of Leading Living Men of the City of Detroit.* Chicago, IL: A. N. Marquis & Co., 1914.

________. *The Book of Minnesotans: A Biographical Dictionary of Leading Living Men of the State of Minnesota.* Chicago, IL: A. N. Marquis & Co., 1907.

Martin, Ida Shaw. *The Sorority Handbook.* Boston, MA: Ida Shaw Martin, Publisher, 1907.

Marvin, Nathan L. *A History of the Kappa Charge–Theta Delta Chi at Tufts University, 1856–1956.* Unknown publisher, 1957.

Maxwell, Will J. *Greek Letter Men of Boston.* New York, NY: The College Book Company, 1900.

________. *Greek Letter Men of the Pacific Coast and Rocky Mountain States.* New York, NY: The College Book Company, 1903.

McElroy, William H., ed. *The Jubilee of the Zeta Psi Fraternity of North America, 1847–1897.* New York, NY: Edward H. Litchfield, 1903.

McGinnis, Frederick A. *A History and an Interpretation of Wilberforce University.* Wilberforce, OH: unknown publisher, 1941.

McKee, Shane, Carey Heckman, and Gay-Lyn Carpenter, ed. *Sigma Phi Epsilon: The Lifetime Responsibility of Brotherhood.* Sigma Phi Epsilon Fraternity, 2011.

Meltzer, Gilbert. *The Beginnings of Elmira College, 1851–1868.* Elmira, NY: The Commercial Press, 1941.

The Menorah Movement: History, Purposes, Activities. Ann Arbor, MI: Intercollegiate Menorah Association, 1914.

Miller, Russell E. *Light on the Hill: A History of Tufts College 1852–1952.* Boston, MA: Beacon Press, 1966.

________. *Light on the Hill, Volume II: A History of Tufts University Since 1952.* Cambridge, MA: Mass Market Books, 1986.

Morgan, Bayard Quincy, ed. *Phi Beta Kappa: Alpha of Wisconsin Catalogue.* Madison, WI: The University of Wisconsin, 1917.

Nichols, Wesley. *History of Gamma Beta Tufts, June 1922.* Unpublished. Alpha Tau Omega Chapter Files, Series No. 41/95/1, Box 144 (Tufts), Alpha Tau Omega Archives Holdings, University of Illinois at Urbana-Champaign.

Parks, Gregory S., ed. *Black Greek-letter Organizations in the Twenty-First Century: Our Fight Has Just Begun.* Lexington, KY: The University of Kentucky Press, 2008.

Palmer, Walter B. "The First Greek Letter Society." *The Scroll of Phi Delta Theta* 13, no. 5 (February 1889): 185–195.

"Phi Mu Delta Enters Tufts." *The Phi Mu Delta Triangle* 15, no. 4 (November 1934): 6–10.

Poindexter, Charles C. "Some Student Experiences." *Voice of the Negro* 3, no. 5 (May 1906): 335–338

Public Documents of Massachusetts Being The Annual Reports of Various Public Officers and Institutions for the Year 1864: Vol. 2, No. 7. Boston, MA: Wright & Potter, 1865.

Randolph, Eugene H. L. "Greek Letter Societies in American Colleges." *New England Magazine* 17, (September 1897–February 1898): 70–82.

Reno, Claude T. *The Manual of the Alpha Tau Omega Fraternity.* Champaign, IL: Alpha Tau Omega Fraternity, 1929.

Reynolds, John Hugh and David Yancey Thomas. *History of the University of Arkansas.* Fayetteville, AR: University of Arkansas, 1910.

Robson, John, ed. *Baird's Manual of American College Fraternities.* 19th ed. Menasha, WI: Baird's Manual Foundation, 1977.

Ross, Lawrence C., Jr. *The Divine Nine: The History of African American Fraternities and Sororities.* New York, NY: Kensington Publishing Co., 2000.

Sanua, Marianne R. *Going Greek: Jewish College Fraternities in the United States, 1895–1945.* Detroit, MI: Wayne State University Press, 2003.

________. *Here's to Our Fraternity: One Hundred Years of Zeta Beta Tau, 1898–1998.* Hanover, NH: University Press of New England, 1998.

Sauer, Anne, Jessica Branco, John Bennett, and Zachary Crowley, ed. *Concise Encyclopedia of Tufts History.* Medford: Tufts University, Digital Collections and Archives, 2000. http://hdl.handle.net/10427/14829 (Accessed March 30, 2014).

Scott, John C. *The Story of Sigma Nu: A Narrative History of the Fraternity, 1869–1926.* Indianapolis, IN: Sigma Nu Fraternity, 1927.

Shapiro, Rebecca. *The Untapped Potential of Jewish Greek Life.* Master's Thesis, Brandeis University, 2011. http://hdl.handle.net/10192/24429

Sheldon, Henry D. *Student Life and Customs.* New York, NY: D. Appleton and Co., 1901.

Sibley, William G. *The Story of Freemasonry.* Gallipolis, OH: The Lion's Paw Club, 1913.

"A Sketch of the Commons Club." *The Rainbow of Delta Tau Delta* 45, no. 2 (January 1922): 346–352.

Start, Alaric Bertrand, ed. *History of Tufts College, 1854–1896.* Medford, MA: Tufts College, 1896.

Suntag, Sidney S. *The History of Tau Epsilon Phi: 75 Years of Friendship, 1910–1985.* Atlanta, GA: The TEP Foundation, 1986.

Sweet, William Warren. *Indiana Asbury–DePauw University: 1837–1937.* New York, NY: The Abingdon Press, 1937.

Syrett, Nicholas L. *The Company He Keeps: A History of White College Fraternities.* Chapel Hill, NC: The University of North Carolina Press, 2009.

Taylor, Lyon G. "Original Records of the Phi Beta Kappa Society." *William and Mary College Quarterly Historical Magazine* 4, no. 2 (April 1896): 213–261.

Theta Delta Chi, Issued in the Fifth Month of the Twentieth Year of the Fraternity. New York, NY: Theta Delta Chi fraternity, 1867.

Ticknor, Caroline, ed. *New England Aviators 1914–1918; Their Portraits and Records, Volume 1.* Boston, MA: Houghton Mifflin Company, 1919.

Toll, George S. *Alpha Epsilon Pi: The First Sixty–Five Years, 1913–1978.* New York, NY: Alpha Epsilon Pi Foundation, 1980.

Tolles, Bryant F. Jr., *Architecture & Academe: College Buildings in New England Before 1860.* Lebanon, NH: University Press of New England, 2011.

Torbenson, Craig L. and Gregory S. Parks, ed. *Brothers and Sisters: Diversity in College Fraternities and Sororities.* Madison, NJ: Fairleigh Dickinson University Press, 2009.

Turk, Diana B. *Bound By A Mighty Vow: Sisterhood and Women's Fraternities, 1870–1920.* New York, NY: New York University Press, 2004.

Van Bokkelen, L. M., Talcott M. Banks, James G. McLoughlin, and Henry Allen Tenney. *A Record of the Members of the Kappa Alpha Fraternity and a City and Town Directory 1825–1892.* New York, NY: A. H. Kellogg, 1892.

Voorhees, Oscar M. *The History of Phi Beta Kappa.* New York, NY: Crown Publishers, 1945.

Weil, Clarence K., ed. *Zeta Beta Tau: The First Twenty–Five Years.* New York, NY: Zeta Beta Tau Fraternity, 1923.

Wesley, Charles H. *History of Sigma Pi Phi: First of the Negro-American Greek-Letter Fraternities.* Washington, DC: The Association for the Study of Negro Life and History, Inc.: 1954.

"Wesleyan in 1851." *The Adelphean of Alpha Delta Phi* 1, no. 1 (March 1907): 19–22.

Wiencek, Henry. *The Hairstons: An American Family in Black and White.* New York, NY: St. Martin's Press, 2000.

Wurgaft, Benjamin Aldes. *Jews at Williams: Inclusion, Exclusion, and Class at a New England Liberal Arts College.* Williamstown, MA: Williams College Press, 2013.

Zeta Psi Fraternity. *Catalogue of the Zeta Psi Fraternity.* New York, NY: Zeta Psi, 1867.

________. *Semicentennial Biographical Catalogue of the Zeta Psi Fraternity.* New York, NY: Zeta Psi, 1900.

Zubatsky, David S. *The History of American Colleges and Their Libraries in the Seventeenth and Eighteenth Centuries: A Bibliographical Essay.* Champaign–Urbana, IL: University of Illinois Graduate School of Library Science, US ISSN 0073–5310, 1979.

INDEX

Fraternity & sorority chapter houses

General subject index